3

THIRD
EDITION

Educational Psychology

Developing Learners

Jeanne Ellis Ormrod

University of Northern Colorado
University of New Hampshire

MERRILL
an imprint of Prentice Hall
Upper Saddle River, New Jersey   Columbus, Ohio

Library of Congress Cataloging-in-Publication Data
Ormrod, Jeanne Ellis.
    Educational psychology : developing learners / Jeanne Ellis
Ormrod.—3rd ed.
        p.   cm.
    Includes bibliographical references and index.
    ISBN 0-13-013648-4
    1. Educational psychology. 2. Teaching. 3. Learning.
    4. Classroom management. I. Title.
    LB1051.066 2000
    370.15—dc21   99-29741
                                                          CIP

Executive Editor: Kevin M. Davis
Developmental Editor: Linda Ashe Montgomery
Production Editor: Julie Peters
Design Coordinator: Diane Lorenzo
Text and Cover Designer: Ceri Fitzgerald
Production Manager: Laura Messerly
Editorial Assistant: Holly Jennings
Photo Research: Nancy Ritz
Director of Marketing: Kevin Flanagan
Marketing Manager: Meghan Shepherd
Marketing Coordinator: Krista Groshong

This book was set in Garamond by Carlisle Communications, Inc. and was printed and bound by
R. R. Donnelley & Sons Company. The cover was printed by Phoenix Color Corp.

©2000, 1998, 1995 by Prentice-Hall, Inc.
Pearson Education
Upper Saddle River, New Jersey 07458

Photo Credits: Robert Brenner/Photo Edit, p. 346; Susan Burger Photography, pp. 13, 31, 48, 86, 91, 107,
140, 148, 156, 175, 203, 241, 254, 271, 286, 303, 401, 408, 422, 479, 490, 508, 553, 564, 601, 621, 635, 640;
Paul Conklin, pp. 64, 493; Elizabeth Crews, pp. 325, 376, 380, 470, 516, 556, 566; Scott Cunningham/
Merrill, pp. 2, 5, 18, 81, 90, 94, 126, 135, 144, 199, 224, 259, 283, 363, 409, 436, 486, 502, 525, 541, 583,
596, 608, 647, 654, 661, 677, 681; Mary Kate Denny/Photo Edit, p. 442, 444; Laura Dwight Photography,
pp. 218, 394, 587; Jeff Greenberg/Photo Edit, p. 27; Larry Hamill/Merrill, p. 277, 616; Will Hart/Photo Edit,
p. 166, 577, 599; Richard Hutchings/Photo Edit, p. 74; Richard Hutchings/Photo Researchers, p. 118;
Bonnie Kamin/Photo Edit, 62; KS Studios/Merrill, p. 450; Anthony Magnacca/Merrill, p. 17, 174, 350, 356;
J. Nourok/Photo Edit, p. 342; Alan Oddie/Photo Edit, p. 56; PhotoDisc, Inc., p. 208; Elena Rooraid/Photo
Edit, p. 461; Barbara Schwartz/Merrill, p. 227; James L. Shaffer, pp. 193, 549; Elliot Smith/International
Stock, p. 181; Tom Watson/Merrill, p. 11, 320, 418; Timothy White/Superstock, p. 447; David Young-Wolff/
Photo Edit, pp. 24, 39, 256, 264, 296, 371, 434, 484, 519, 569, 632.

Printed in the United States of America

10 9 8 7 6 5 4 3

ISBN: 0-13-013648-4

Prentice-Hall International (UK) Limited, *London*
Prentice-Hall of Australia Pty. Limited, *Sydney*
Prentice-Hall of Canada, Inc., *Toronto*
Prentice-Hall Hispanoamericana, S. A., *Mexico*
Prentice-Hall of India Private Limited, *New Delhi*
Prentice-Hall of Japan, Inc., *Tokyo*
Prentice-Hall (Singapore) Pte. Ltd., *Singapore*
Editora Prentice-Hall do Brasil, Ltda., *Rio de Janeiro*

Preface

Soon after I wrote the first edition of *Educational Psychology,* I had the good fortune to return to a middle school classroom teaching geography to two sections of sixth, seventh, and eighth graders. On my first day back in a K-12 setting, I was quickly reminded of how exciting and energizing the process of teaching growing children can be. This experience confirmed once again what I have always known—that the principles of educational psychology have clear relevance to the decisions a classroom teacher must make on an ongoing basis. How children and adolescents learn and think, how they change as they grow and develop, why they do the things they do, how they are often very different from one another—our understanding of all these things has innumerable implications for classroom practice and, ultimately, for the lives of the next generation.

I have been teaching educational psychology since 1974, and I have loved every minute of it. Because I want the field of educational psychology to captivate you the way it has captivated me, I have tried to make the book interesting, meaningful, and thought-provoking as well as informative. I have a definite philosophy about how future teachers can best learn and apply educational psychology—a philosophy that has guided me as I have written all three editions of this book. More specifically, I believe that you can construct a more accurate and useful understanding of the principles of educational psychology when you:

www.prenhall.com/
ormrod

- Focus on core principles of the discipline
- Relate the principles to your own learning and behavior
- Mentally "process" the principles in an effective manner
- Consider numerous classroom applications of the principles

As I will show you in a moment, I have incorporated numerous features into the book that will encourage you to do all of these things. I hope that you will learn a great deal from what educational psychology has to offer, not only about the students you will be teaching but also about yourself—a human being who continues to learn and develop even now.

Features of the Book

Focusing on Core Principles

Rather than superficially explore every aspect of educational psychology, I have chosen to offer in-depth treatment of the fundamental concepts and principles that have broad applicability to classroom practice. If I myself couldn't imagine how a concept or principle could be of use to a teacher, I left it out. I have highlighted many of the key principles in the *Principles/Assumptions* tables that appear throughout the book.

▲ FOCUSING ON PRINCIPLES

Throughout the text, principles and
core concepts are identified,
discussed in depth, and then
summarized for you in
Principles/Assumptions tables.
Each table includes educational
implications and concrete examples.

Relating Principles to Your Own Learning and Behavior

A central goal of this text is to help you discover more about yourself as a thinker and
learner. If you can understand how you *yourself* learn, you will be in a better position
to understand how your students learn and, as a result, to help them learn more effectively. Throughout the book, I've provided many exercises to help you discover important points firsthand and thereby construct a more complete, meaningful understanding of psychological principles of learning, development, motivation, and behavior.
Appearing as *Experiencing Firsthand* features, these exercises are in some ways similar
to the "hands-on" activities that can help students learn in elementary and secondary
classrooms. But because I ask you to use your mind rather than your hands, you might
more accurately think of them as "head-on" experiences.

▢ EXPERIENCING FIRSTHAND

Numerous exercises embedded in
the text allow you to experience
firsthand some of the concepts and
principles we examine. The
understanding you gain from these
experiences will enable you not only
to see more vividly how psychology
principles operate, but also to use
these principles more effectively in
your own classroom teaching.

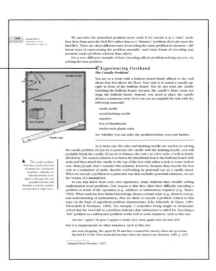

"Processing" Principles Effectively

Research tells us that many students, including many at the college level, use relatively ineffective strategies for reading, studying, and learning. But research also tells us that students *can acquire* effective strategies and that when they begin to use such strategies, they find themselves successfully learning and remembering what they read and hear.

One important principle of learning is that people learn and remember new information more effectively when they relate it to what they already know—a process called *meaningful learning.* I will ask you to reflect on your own knowledge and experiences at the beginning of each chapter and in *Thinking About What You Know* features at various other spots throughout the book. In addition, some of the margin notes designated with a ▨ symbol will ask you to consider personal experiences or to recall ideas discussed in previous chapters.

Another effective strategy is *organization*—making connections among the various pieces of information that you're learning; the *Compare/Contrast* tables that appear throughout the book will help you organize some of the key ideas in each chapter. Still another learning strategy is *elaboration*—expanding on information as you study it, drawing inferences, thinking of new examples, making predictions, and so on. Many of the ▨ questions in the margin will encourage you to elaborate on concepts and principles as I describe them. The ▲ notes in the margin can help you with both organization and elaboration: They may show you how you can connect the material you are reading with ideas presented in later chapters, or they may provide additional, "elaborative" information about those ideas.

Taking Principles Into the Classroom

Throughout the text, I consistently apply psychological concepts and principles to classroom practice. Some of these applications are summarized and illustrated in *Into the Classroom* features and *Students in Inclusive Settings* tables; many others are highlighted with a 🍎 in the margin. Furthermore, the ▨ questions will sometimes ask you to consider possible applications in your own specific circumstances as a teacher.

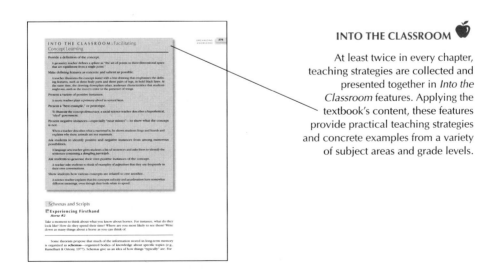

INTO THE CLASSROOM 🍎

At least twice in every chapter, teaching strategies are collected and presented together in *Into the Classroom* features. Applying the textbook's content, these features provide practical teaching strategies and concrete examples from a variety of subject areas and grade levels.

🍎 DIVERSITY AND INCLUSION

Each chapter contains a section that examines pertinent issues of diversity and exceptionality. In addition, practical and applied teaching strategies are described in tables that can help you work with *Students in Inclusive Settings*.

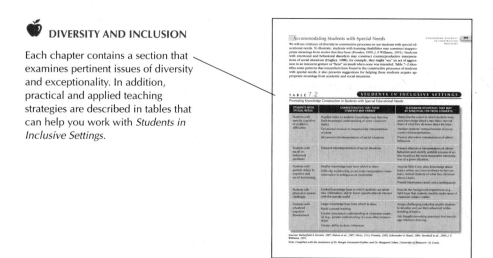

In addition, every chapter begins and ends with *case studies*. The case study at the beginning of each chapter presents an example of one or more students dealing with a particular classroom learning task. As we proceed through the chapter, we will continually relate our discussion back to this case, helping you connect chapter content to a classroom context. The case study at the end of each chapter focuses on teachers and teaching; it will help you apply ideas you have encountered in the chapter and make instructional decisions based on what you have learned.

🍎 CASE STUDIES

Each chapter opens with a case that is referred to throughout the chapter, helping you tie psychological principles to the authentic context of the classroom. Chapters also end with *case studies* that give you an opportunity to apply what you have learned to teaching decisions.

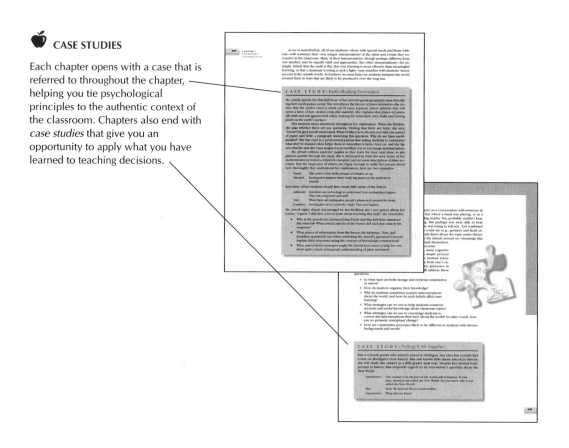

Changes in the Third Edition

Although most of the content in the second edition remains in the third, I have made several changes to reflect current trends in educational psychology and educational practice. Among the most significant changes to this revision are: the addition of three new chapters, including Learning in the Content Areas, Promoting Learning Through Student Interactions, and Students with Special Educational Needs; new and expanded topics; and a reorganization of Part 3.

New Chapter on "Learning in the Content Areas"

Chapter 9 applies principles of cognitive psychology to learning reading, writing, mathematics, science, and social studies. Four general themes—constructive processes, the influence of prior knowledge, metacognition, and developmental differences—and many content-specific teaching strategies appear throughout the chapter.

New Chapter on "Promoting Learning Through Student Interactions"

Discussion of instructional strategies has been expanded to two chapters, and Chapter 14 is now devoted exclusively to describing interactive approaches to instruction including: communities of learners, class discussions, reciprocal teaching, cooperative learning, and peer tutoring.

New Chapter on "Students with Special Educational Needs"

Chapter 5 describes recent trends in special education and presents numerous strategies for teachers who work in inclusive classrooms. (The "Students in Inclusive Settings" tables that appeared in each chapter of the second edition remain in the third edition as well.)

New and Expanded Topics

The third edition includes new sections on contemporary applications of Vygotsky's ideas; theoretical perspectives on language development; heredity, environment, and group differences in intelligence; how procedural knowledge is learned; critical thinking; setting events; behavioral momentum; positive behavioral support; self-regulated learning; lesson plans; direct instruction; and working effectively with parents. Discussions of other topics have, of course, been updated in keeping with recent developments in theory and research.

Reorganization of Part 3

Topics related to planning for instruction—identifying instructional goals, conducting task analyses, and developing lesson plans—now appear at the beginning of Chapter 13 ("Choosing Instructional Strategies") and pave the way for the discussion of instructional strategies. Chapter 15 is now devoted entirely to the topic of "Creating and Maintaining a Productive Classroom Environment."

Supplementary Materials

Numerous supplements to the textbook are available to enhance your learning and development as a teacher.

Student Study Guide. The *Student Study Guide* provides many support mechanisms to help you learn and study more effectively. These include focus questions to consider as you read the text, a chapter glossary, application exercises to give you practice in applying concepts and principles of educational psychology to classroom settings, answers to selected margin notes, sample test questions, and several supplementary readings.

Simulations in Educational Psychology and Research (**Compact Disk**). A compact disk accompanies the third edition of the textbook. This CD contains four activities that resemble actual research studies in educational psychology: "The Pendulum Experiment" (to be used with either Chapter 2 or Chapter 9); "Assessing Moral Reasoning" (to be used with Chapter 3); "Bartlett's Ghosts" (to be used with Chapter 7); and "Intuitive Physics" (to be used with Chapter 7, 8, or 9). As you use the CD, you will find yourself "participating" in the activities in much the same way that students in the original research studies did; the CD will ask you to respond to various situations and then give you feedback about your responses. The CD will also help you connect the activity with educational practice.

SIMULATION EXERCISES

CD-ROM icons in the text margins indicate places where one of the simulation exercises on the CD *Simulations in Educational Psychology and Research* is relevant to chapter content. Through these simulation exercises, you will be able to explore learning experiences related to Piaget's developmental stages, misconceptions and conceptual change, schemas and the construction of meaning, and Kohlberg's stages of moral development.

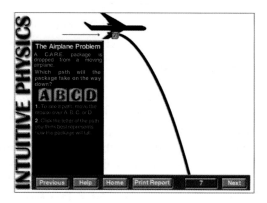

Companion Website. You can find the Website for *Educational Psychology: Developing Learners* at **www.prenhall.com/ormrod.** For each chapter of the book, the Website presents Key Questions that identify the chapter's central issues, a chapter glossary, key terms linked to Internet destinations, and a quick self-test (multiple-choice and essay questions that let you self-assess what you've learned). The Website also provides Syllabus Manager™, which your instructor may use to post and occasionally update the course syllabus, as well as an interactive "Message Board" through which you and your classmates can engage in discussions about chapter content.

Videotapes **and** ***MultiMedia Guide.*** Videos are a highly effective means of visually demonstrating concepts and principles in educational psychology. The eight videotapes that accompany this textbook portray a wide variety of teachers, students, and classrooms in action. Six videos present numerous case studies in many content domains and at a variety of grades levels. Two additional videos are: "A Private Universe" (which examines learner misconceptions in science) and Constance Kamii's "Double-Column Addition: A Teacher Uses Piaget's Theory" (which depicts a constructivist approach to teaching mathematics). Opportunities to react to these videos in class discussions will further enhance your ability to think analytically and identify good teaching practices. Your instructor will have a *MultiMedia Guide* to help guide and enrich your interpretation and understanding of what you see in the videos.

Instructor's Manual. Available to your instructor are suggestions for learning activities, additional "head-on" exercises, supplementary lectures, case study analyses, discussion topics, group activities, and additional media resources. These have been carefully selected to provide opportunities to support, enrich, and expand on what you read in the textbook.

Transparencies. The transparencies that your instructor may use in class will include tables and classroom exercises similar to those found in your textbook. These transparencies are designed to help you understand, organize, and remember the concepts and principles you are studying.

PowerPoint Slides and Supplementary Lectures and Activities. Your instructor may use a CD-ROM that includes PowerPoint versions of the transparencies, supplementary lectures, and activities that appear in the *Instructor's Manual.*

Test Bank. Many instructors use the test questions that accompany this textbook. Some items (lower-level questions) will simply ask you to identify or explain concepts and principles you have learned. But many others (higher-level questions) will ask you to apply those same concepts and principles to specific classroom situations—that is, to actual student behaviors and teaching strategies. The lower-level questions assess your basic knowledge of educational psychology. But ultimately, it is the higher-level questions that will assess your ability to use principles of educational psychology in your own teaching practice.

Acknowledgments

Although I am listed as the sole author of this textbook, I have been fortunate to have had a great deal of assistance in writing it. First and foremost, I must thank my editor, Kevin Davis, whose ideas, insights, and clear commitment to the field of educational psychology have provided much of the driving force behind my writing and productivity. Kevin is a task master, make no mistake about it, and he always insists that I stretch my talents to the limit. Yet he also provides the guidance (scaffolding) I need to achieve things that initially seem so impossible. After spending countless hours working with Kevin, I can say that he is not only my editor but also my friend.

I am equally indebted to Linda Montgomery, developmental editor for the third edition, whose extensive experience as both an elementary school teacher and an editor have greatly enriched the quality of this edition. Linda's creativity, commitment to excellence, and ongoing support have always been there for me when I've needed them most. I must thank Linda Peterson as well; as developmental editor for both the first and second editions, she helped define much of the pedagogy of the book. Her continuing insistence on *application, application, application!* kept my focus on the things that future teachers really need to know.

Others at Merrill/Prentice Hall have also contributed in important ways. Copy editor Sue Snyder has gone through my manuscript with a fine-toothed comb and teased out many little places where the text wasn't quite right. Photography editor Nancy Ritz has located many photographs that have given life to the words on the page. And Julie Peters, as production editor for all three editions, has flawlessly coordinated and overseen the entire process of transforming a manuscript into a book—an incredibly complicated task that, in my mind, should far exceed any normal human being's working memory capacity.

In addition, many colleagues across the country have given the book a balance of perspectives that no single author could possibly do on her own. Drs. Margie Garanzini-Daiber and Peggy Cohen provided some of the ideas for the *Students in Inclusive Settings* tables. Dr. Ann Turnball offered many helpful suggestions for enhancing my discussions of students with special needs. Many other individuals have strengthened the final product considerably by reviewing one or more versions of the book.

Reviewers for the first and second editions were Margaret D. Anderson, SUNY—Cortland; Timothy A. Bender, Southwest Missouri State University; Stephen L. Benton, Kansas State University; Kathryn J. Biacindo, California State University—Fresno; Barbara Bishop, Eastern New Mexico University; Karen L. Block, University of Pittsburgh; Robert Braswell, Winthrop College; Randy L. Brown, University of Central Oklahoma; Kay S. Bull, Oklahoma State University; Margaret W. Cohen, University of Missouri—St. Louis; Roberta Corrigan, University of Wisconsin—Milwaukee; Richard D. Craig, Towson State University; José Cruz, Jr., The Ohio State University; Peggy Dettmer, Kansas State University; Joan Dixon, Gonzaga University; Leland K. Doebler, University of Montevallo; Joanne B. Engel, Oregon State University; Kathy Farber, Bowling Green State University; William R. Fisk, Clemson University; Roberta J. Garza, Pan American University—Brownsville; Cheryl Greenberg, University of North Carolina—Greensboro; Richard Hamilton, University of Houston; Arthur Hernandez, University of Texas—San Antonio; Frederick C. Howe, Buffalo State College; Dinah Jackson, University of Northern Colorado; Janina M. Jolley, Clarion University of Pennsylvania; Caroline Kaczala, Cleveland State University; CarolAnne M. Kardash, University of Missouri—Columbia; Nancy F. Knapp, University of Georgia; Mary Lou Koran, University of Florida; Randy Lennon, University of Northern Colorado; Pamela Manners, Troy State University; Hermine H. Marshall, San Francisco State University; Teresa McDevitt, University of Northern Colorado; Sharon McNeely, Northeastern Illinois University; Michael Meloth, University of Colorado—Boulder; Janet Moursund, University of Oregon; Gary A. Negin, California State University; Judy Pierce, Western Kentucky University; James R. Pullen, Central Missouri State University; Gary F. Render, University of Wyoming; Robert S. Ristow, Western Illinois University; Gregg Schraw, University of Nebraska—Lincoln; Dale H. Schunk, Purdue University; Mark Seng, University of Texas; Johnna Shapiro, University of California—Davis; Harry L. Steger, Boise State University; Julianne C. Turner, University of Notre Dame; Alice A. Walker, SUNY—Cortland; Mary Wellman, Rhode Island College; and Jane A. Wolfle, Bowling Green State University.

Coming on board for the third edition were these reviewers: Joyce Alexander, Indiana University; J. C. Barton, Tennessee Technical University; Phyllis Blumenfeld, University of Michigan; M. Arthur Garmon, Western Michigan University; Arthur Hernandez, University of Texas, San Antonio; Mary Lou Koran, University of Florida; Victoria Fleming, Miami University of Ohio; Jennifer Mistretta Hampston, Youngstown State University; Pamela Manners, Troy State University; Bruce P. Mortenson, Louisiana State University; Joe Olmi, The University of Southern Mississippi; Helen Osana, University of Missouri, Columbia; Gregory Schraw, University of Nebraska, Lincoln; Dale H. Schunk, Purdue University; Bruce Torff, Hofstra University; Ann Turnbull, University of Kansas; Glenn E. Snelbecker, Temple University (ancillary material to text); and Karen Zabrucky, Georgia State University.

Last but certainly not least, I must thank my husband and children, who have been ever so patient as I have spent countless hours either buried in my books and journals or else glued to my computer. Without their continuing support and patience, this book would never have seen the light of day.

J. E. O.

Brief Contents

Contents

PART 2

Understanding How Students Learn

CHAPTER 6

Learning and Cognitive Processes 218

CHAPTER 7

Knowledge Construction 264

CHAPTER 8

Higher-Level Thinking Skills.....................296

CHAPTER 9

Learning in the Content Areas 342

CHAPTER 10

Behaviorist Views of Learning......394

CHAPTER 11

Social Cognitive Views of Learning......434

CHAPTER 15

Creating and Maintaining a Productive Classroom Environment 596

CHAPTER 16

Assessing Student Learning........................632

1

Educational Psychology and Teacher Decision Making

At some point in your life, you have undoubtedly tried to teach something to someone else. Perhaps you have had some teaching experience in the public schools. Perhaps you have given an oral presentation in one of your college classes or have helped a friend learn how to use a computer. Perhaps you have taught a small child how to tie shoelaces or ride a bicycle.

Reflect for a moment on the kinds of teaching experiences you've had. What strategies did you use in your attempts to help others learn? For instance, did you provide verbal explanations, demonstrate certain actions, ask your "students" to practice what you taught them, or give them feedback about their performance? And what assumptions about human learning influenced the way that you chose to teach? For instance, did you assume that your students could learn from a verbal explanation, or did you believe that demonstrating an action would be more effective? Did you think that "practice makes perfect"? Did you think that feedback was essential for learning and motivation?

Helping students learn is what our job as teachers is all about. To help them learn, we find ourselves taking on a variety of roles in the classroom, including subject matter experts, tutors, consultants, motivators, behavior managers, confidantes, and evaluators. But above all, we are *decision makers*: We must continually choose among many possible strategies for helping students learn, develop, and achieve. In fact, some researchers (C. M. Clark & Peterson, 1986) have estimated that teachers must make a nontrivial instructional decision approximately once every two minutes! Yet wise educational decisions are not made in a vacuum; they are based on a genuine understanding of how students learn and develop and on solid data about which classroom techniques are effective and which are not.

My purpose in writing this book is to show you how educational psychology can help you in your all-important role as educational decision maker. Together we will explore various theoretical perspectives and research findings on how students develop throughout the elementary and secondary school years, how they differ from one another in ways that affect their classroom performance, how they learn most effectively, what things motivate them, and how their learning and achievement can best be measured and evaluated. In the process, we will identify principles of human learning, development, and behavior that can help us make informed decisions in the classroom.

In this first chapter, we will get a taste of what educational psychology is all about, sampling research findings in child development, learning, instruction, and classroom assessment practices. We will also address these questions:

- How much can common sense guide us as we try to help our students learn successfully?
- What kinds of conclusions about learning and development can we draw from psychological and educational research studies?
- How can principles and theories of learning and development assist us as we make decisions about how best to help students learn and achieve?
- How can we continue to improve as teachers throughout our professional teaching careers?

The chapter closes with an overview of the book and several strategies for studying and learning educational psychology effectively.

CASE STUDY: More Than Meets the Eye

Rosa is a personable, outgoing twelve-year-old. Born in South America, she has lived in this country for only three years, but she seems to have adjusted well to her new home. She now converses in English with only the slightest hint of an accent. She has made many friends and has an active after-school social life. She has blossomed into a talented athlete, seemingly a natural in almost any sport she tries, and is becoming especially proficient in volleyball and basketball. She also does well in art class and in the school choir, although she sometimes has trouble learning the lyrics.

But after three years in her new homeland, Rosa is still having difficulty in language arts, social studies, science, and mathematics. She often seems distracted in class and sometimes has trouble answering even the simplest questions her teachers ask her. Her test scores are inconsistent—sometimes quite high, but more frequently near the bottom of the class.

Rosa's teachers see occasional indicators that she is a bright and talented girl. For example, she is a skillful "peacemaker," frequently stepping in to help resolve interpersonal conflicts among her classmates. Her short stories, although often filled with grammatical and spelling errors, are imaginative and well developed. And of course there are the occasional high test scores. Rosa's teachers are convinced that Rosa is capable of achieving at a much higher level, but they are puzzled about just how to help her be more successful in her classroom activities.

- What are some possible explanations for Rosa's poor academic performance? Could the source of difficulty lie in her limited experience with English? in her cultural background? in her motivation? in her study skills? in the ways her knowledge is assessed? or perhaps in some combination of these things?

OOPS—A Pretest

You probably have several hypotheses about why Rosa might be having difficulty. You've been a student for many years now, and in the process you've certainly learned a great deal about how students learn and develop and about how teachers can best help them achieve. But exactly how much *do* you know? To help you find out, I've developed a short pretest, *Ormrod's Own Psychological Survey* (OOPS).

Experiencing Firsthand
Ormrod's Own Psychological Survey (OOPS)

Decide whether each of the following statements is *true* or *false*.

1. Most children five years of age and older are natural learners; they know the best way to learn something without having to be taught how to learn it.   T   F

2. When we compare boys and girls, we find that both groups are, on average, very similar in their mathematical and verbal aptitudes.   T   F

3. The best way to learn and remember a new fact is to repeat it over and over again.   T   F

As teachers, we will continually be making decisions about how best to help students learn, develop, and achieve.

4. Although students initially have many misconceptions about the world, they quickly revise their thinking once their teacher presents information that contradicts what they believe.   T   F

5. Students often misjudge how much they know about a topic.   T   F

6. Taking notes during a lecture usually interferes with students' learning more than it helps.   T   F

7. When we ask children to tutor their classmates in mathematics, we help only the students being tutored; the students doing the tutoring gain very little from the interaction.   T   F

8. When a teacher rewards one student for appropriate behavior, the behavior of other students may also improve.   T   F

9. Anxiety sometimes helps students learn and perform more successfully in the classroom.   T   F

10. The ways in which teachers assess their students' learning influence what and how the students actually learn.   T   F

Answer Key for the OOPS

Now let's see how well you did on the OOPS. The answers, along with an explanation for each one, are as follows:

1. *Most children five years of age and older are natural learners; they know the best way to learn something without having to be taught how to learn it.*

FALSE—Many students of all ages are relatively naive about how they can best learn something, and they often use inefficient strategies when they study. For example, most

How often do you elaborate when you read your textbooks?

Can you recall times when your own teachers may have treated boys and girls differently because of an erroneous belief about gender differences?

elementary students and a substantial number of high school students don't **elaborate** on classroom material; they don't analyze, interpret, or otherwise add their own ideas to the things they need to learn (Pressley, 1982; Schommer, 1994a; Siegler, 1991). (To illustrate, many students are likely to take the information presented in a history textbook strictly at face value; they rarely take time to consider why historical figures made the decisions they did or how some events may have led inevitably to others.) Yet elaboration is one of the most effective ways of learning new information—students learn information more quickly and remember it better. We will look at developmental trends in elaboration as we discuss cognitive development in Chapter 2. We'll also explore the very important role that elaboration plays in long-term memory as we discuss cognitive processes in Chapter 6.

2. *When we compare boys and girls, we find that both groups are, on average, very similar in their mathematical and verbal aptitudes.*

TRUE—Despite commonly held beliefs to the contrary, boys and girls tend to be similar in their ability to perform both mathematical and verbal academic tasks (Eisenberg, Martin, & Fabes, 1996; Hyde & Linn, 1988; Jacklin, 1989; M. C. Linn & Hyde, 1989). Any differences in the average performance of boys and girls in these areas are usually too small for teachers to worry about. We will explore gender differences—and similarities as well—in Chapter 4.

3. *The best way to learn and remember a new fact is to repeat it over and over again.*

FALSE—Although repeating information is better than doing nothing at all with it, repetition is a relatively ineffective way to learn. Students learn information more easily and remember it longer when they connect it with the things they already know and when they elaborate on it (Brainerd & Reyna, 1992; Bransford, Franks, Vye, & Sherwood, 1989; Mayer, 1996). Chapter 6 looks in greater depth at how to promote students' long-term memory for school subject matter.

4. *Although students initially have many misconceptions about the world, they quickly revise their thinking once their teacher presents information that contradicts what they believe.*

FALSE—As you will discover in Chapter 7, students typically have many misconceptions about the world (e.g., they may believe that rivers always run south rather than north or that the earth is round only in the sense that a pancake is round). They often hold strongly to these misconceptions even in the face of contradictory evidence or instruction (Chinn & Brewer, 1993; Shuell, 1996; Winer & Cottrell, 1996). As teachers, one of our biggest challenges is to help students discard their erroneous beliefs in favor of more accurate and useful perspectives; some strategies for promoting such *conceptual change* appear in Chapter 7.

5. *Students often misjudge how much they know about a topic.*

TRUE—Contrary to popular opinion, students are usually *not* the best judges of what they do and do not know. For example, many students think that if they've spent a long time studying a textbook chapter, they must know its content very well. Yet if they have spent most of their study time inefficiently (perhaps by "reading" without paying attention to the meaning or by mindlessly copying definitions), they may know far less than they think they do (L. Baker, 1989; Schommer, 1994a). We will consider this *illusion of knowing* further in our discussion of study strategies in Chapter 8.

6. *Taking notes during a lecture usually interferes with students' learning more than it helps.*

FALSE—Generally speaking, students who take notes learn more material from a lecture than students who don't take notes (Hale, 1983; Kiewra, 1989). Note taking appears to facilitate learning in at least two ways: it helps students put, or *store,* information into memory more effectively, and it allows them to review that information at a later time (Di Vesta & Gray, 1972). Chapter 8 presents research concerning the effectiveness of various study strategies.

7. *When we ask children to tutor their classmates in mathematics, we help only the students being tutored; the students doing the tutoring gain very little from the interaction.*

FALSE—When students teach one another mathematics, the tutors often benefit as much as the students being tutored (L. Fuchs, Fuchs, & Karns, 1995; L. Fuchs et al., 1996; Inglis & Biemiller, 1997). For instance, in one research study, fourth graders who were doing relatively poorly in math served as arithmetic tutors for first and second graders; the tutors themselves showed a substantial improvement in arithmetic problem-solving skills (Inglis & Biemiller, 1997). We will look at the effects of peer tutoring in Chapters 9 and 14.

8. *When a teacher rewards one student for appropriate behavior, the behavior of other students may also improve.*

TRUE—When teachers reward one student for behaving in a particular way, other students who have observed that student being rewarded sometimes begin to behave in a similar way (Bandura, 1977, 1986). We will identify numerous roles that observation plays in learning as we explore social cognitive theory in Chapter 11.

9. *Anxiety sometimes helps students learn and perform more successfully in the classroom.*

TRUE—Many people think that anxiety is always a "bad" thing. Yet for some classroom tasks, and especially for relatively easy tasks, a moderate level of anxiety actually *improves* students' learning and performance (Kirkland, 1971; Shipman & Shipman, 1985). We will consider the effects of anxiety on learning and performance in more detail when we discuss motivation in Chapter 12.

10. *The ways in which teachers assess their students' learning influence what and how the students actually learn.*

TRUE—What and how students learn is, in part, a function of how they expect their learning to be assessed (N. Frederiksen, 1984b; J. R. Frederiksen & Collins, 1989; Poole, 1994). For example, students typically spend more time studying the things they think will be on a test than the things they think the test won't cover. And they are more likely to organize and integrate class material as they study if they expect assessment activities to require such organization and integration. Chapter 16 describes the effects of classroom assessment practices on learning.

How many of the OOPS items did you answer correctly? Did some of the false items seem convincing enough that you marked them true? Did some of the true items contradict certain beliefs that you had? If either of these was the case, you are hardly alone. College students often agree with statements that seem obvious but are, in fact, completely wrong (Gage, 1991; Lennon, Ormrod, Burger, & Warren, 1990). And many students in teacher education classes reject research findings when those findings appear to contradict their own personal experiences (Borko & Putnam, 1996; Holt-Reynolds, 1992).

Keep an open mind as ▲ you read this book. When you encounter ideas that at first seem incorrect, try to think of personal experiences and observations that support those ideas.

Drawing Conclusions from Psychological and Educational Research

It's easy to be persuaded by "common sense" and become convinced that what seems "logical" must be reality. Yet common sense and logic do not always tell us the true story about how people actually learn and develop, nor do they always give us accurate information about how best to help students succeed in the classroom. Educational psychologists believe that knowledge about teaching and learning should come from a more objective source of information—that is, from psychological and educational research.

Most of the ideas presented in this book are based either directly or indirectly on the results of research studies. Let's take a look at three major types of research—descriptive, correlational, and experimental—and at the kinds of conclusions that we can draw from each one.

Descriptive Studies

A **descriptive study** does exactly what its name implies—it *describes* a situation. Descriptive studies might give us information about the characteristics of students, teachers, or schools; they might also provide information about the frequency with which certain events or behaviors occur. Descriptive studies allow us to draw conclusions about the way things are—the current state of affairs. The left column of Table 1–1 lists some examples of questions we could answer with descriptive studies.

Correlational Studies

A **correlational study** explores relationships among different things. For instance, it might tell us about the extent to which two human characteristics are associated with one another, or it might give us information about the degree to which certain human behaviors occur in conjunction with certain environmental conditions. In general, correlational studies enable us to draw conclusions about **correlation**—that is, about the extent to which two variables are interrelated.

TABLE 1.1   **COMPARE/CONTRAST**

Questions We Might Answer with Descriptive, Correlational, and Experimental Studies

DESCRIPTIVE STUDIES	CORRELATIONAL STUDIES	EXPERIMENTAL STUDIES
What percentage of high school students can think abstractly?	Are older students more capable of abstract thought than younger students?	Can abstract thinking skills be improved through specially designed educational programs?
What kinds of aggressive behaviors do we see in our schools, and with what frequencies do we see them?	Are students more likely to be aggressive at school if their parents are physically violent at home?	Which method is most effective in reducing aggressive behavior—reinforcing appropriate behavior, punishing aggressive behavior, or a combination of both?
To what extent are gender stereotypes evident in books commonly used to teach reading in the early elementary grades?	Are better readers also better spellers?	Which reading program produces greater gains in reading comprehension—RIF or RAF?
How well have our nation's students performed on a recent standardized achievement test?	Do students who get the highest scores on multiple-choice tests also get the highest scores on essays dealing with the same material?	Does the use of multiple-choice vs. essay tests in the classroom encourage students to study in different ways and therefore affect what students learn?

The middle column of Table 1–1 lists some examples of questions we might answer with correlational studies. Notice how each of these questions asks about a relationship between two variables—between age and abstract thought, between student aggression and parental violence, between reading and spelling, or between multiple-choice test and essay performance.

Correlations between two variables allow us to make *predictions* about one variable if we know the status of the other. For example, if we find that older students are more capable of abstract thought than younger students, we can predict that tenth graders will benefit more from an abstract discussion of democratic government than fourth graders. If we find a correlation between multiple-choice test and essay scores, we can predict that those students who have done well on essays in a biology class will probably also do well on a national test covering the same topics in a multiple-choice format.

▲ Correlations are often described numerically with a statistic known as a *correlation coefficient.* Correlation coefficients are described in Appendix B.

Experimental Studies

Descriptive and correlational studies describe things as they exist naturally in the environment. In contrast, an **experimental study,** or **experiment,** is a study in which the researcher somehow changes, or *manipulates,* one or more aspects of the environment (often called *independent variables*) and then measures the effects of such changes on something else. In educational research, the "something else" being affected (often called the *dependent variable*) is usually some aspect of student behavior—perhaps an increase in achievement test scores, skill in executing a complex physical movement, persistence in trying to solve difficult mathematics problems, or ability to interact appropriately with classmates. When carefully designed, experimental studies enable us to draw conclusions about *causation*—about *why* behaviors occur.

The right column of Table 1–1 lists examples of questions that might be answered through experimental studies. Notice how each question addresses a cause-effect relationship—the effect of educational programs on abstract thinking, the effect of reinforcement and punishment on aggressive behavior, the effect of a reading program on the development of reading comprehension, or the effect of test questions on students' learning.

As you can see from the examples in the table, the difference between correlational and experimental research is an important one: Whereas correlational studies let us draw conclusions about relationships, only experimental studies enable us to draw conclusions about cause and effect. The following section describes how one phenomenon in particular—visual-spatial thinking—has been studied with both correlational and experimental research studies and looks at the conclusions we can draw from each type of study.

Can you think of other questions that each type of research might address?

An Example: Research on Visual-Spatial Thinking

Visual-spatial thinking is the ability to imagine and mentally manipulate two- and three-dimensional figures in one's mind. The exercise that follows provides three examples.

Experiencing Firsthand
Three Examples of Visual-Spatial Thinking

1. The figure on the left is a flag. Which one or more of the three figures on the right represent(s) the *same* side of the flag? Which one or more of them represent(s) the *flip* side?

Model   a   b   c

2. When the figure on the left is folded along the dotted lines, it becomes a three-dimensional object. Which one or more of the four figures on the right represent(s) how this object might appear from different perspectives?

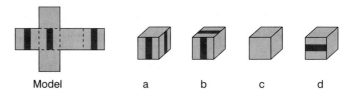

Model   a   b   c   d

3. When the object on the left is rotated in three-dimensional space, it can look like one or more of the objects on the right. Which one(s)?

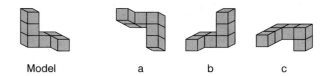

Model   a   b   c

Answer key: (1) Flags *a* and *b* are the flip side; flag *c* is the same side. (2) Depending on the perspective, the object might look like either *a* or *d*. (3) The object can be rotated to look like either *a* or *c*.

Visual-spatial thinking appears to be related to mathematics achievement, although the nature of this relationship is not totally clear (Fennema & Sherman, 1977; Friedman, 1995; Threadgill-Sowder, 1985). Many correlational studies have found a relationship between gender and visual-spatial thinking: On the average, boys have slightly better visual-spatial thinking skills than girls (N. S. Anderson, 1987; Halpern, 1992; Law, Pellegrino, & Hunt, 1993). But such studies do not tell us why this difference occurs. Are males genetically more capable of visual-spatial thought? Do parents encourage their sons to think in "visual-spatial" ways more frequently than they encourage their daughters? Do the typical childhood experiences of boys promote greater development of visual-spatial thinking ability? Unfortunately, correlational studies, although they demonstrate that a relationship exists, do not tell us *why* it exists; they don't tell us whether genetics, parental encouragement, childhood experiences, or perhaps something else is the cause of the difference we see.

An experimental study by Sprafkin, Serbin, Denier, and Connor (1983) identifies one probable cause of the gender difference in visual-spatial thinking. These researchers hypothesized that typical "male" toys (e.g., wooden blocks, Legos, trucks) provide greater opportunities for children to explore visual-spatial relationships than do typical "female" toys (e.g., dolls, board games). To test their hypothesis, they randomly selected half of the boys and girls enrolled in a preschool to be members of an experimental group, or **treatment group,** leaving the remaining children as an untrained **control group.** Children in both groups took a test of visual-spatial thinking, revealing that the treatment and control groups were equal (on the average) in visual-spatial ability. Dur-

Do you think that you have good visual-spatial skills? If so, how did you develop them?

---

[1]The three exercises on pp. 9–10 are modeled after Thurstone & Jeffrey (1956); Bennett, Seashore, & Wesman (1982); and Shepard & Metzler (1971), respectively.

ing the next six weeks, the experimental group participated in twelve sessions involving instruction and structured play opportunities with blocks, building toys, puzzles, dominoes, and various other materials requiring visual-spatial thought. At the end of the six-week period, these specially trained children obtained higher average scores on a test of visual-spatial thinking than the untrained, control group children.

From this study with preschool children, we can draw a conclusion about a cause-effect relationship: We can say that structured exposure to certain types of toys promotes increased visual-spatial thinking ability. Other characteristics of the two groups of children were the same; for example, both groups began with equivalent visual-spatial thinking ability, and all the children attended the same preschool. Furthermore, because the children were randomly assigned to the training and nontraining conditions, we can assume that both groups were approximately the same (on the average) in terms of such other factors as general intelligence, prior exposure to different types of toys, and home environment. Because the researchers eliminated other possible explanations for the differences they observed in the two groups of preschoolers, they could reasonably draw a conclusion about a cause-effect relationship: Increased exposure to certain types of toys fosters the development of visual-spatial thinking skills.

Early exposure to certain types of toys encourages greater visual-spatial thinking ability for both boys and girls.

Here the researchers ▲ separated the possible variables affecting visual-spatial thinking and kept all but one of them constant. Chapters 2 and 9 describe this process of *separating and controlling variables*.

Drawing Conclusions from Research: A Cautionary Note

To draw conclusions about causal relationships, we must eliminate other possible explanations for the outcomes we observe. As an example, imagine that the Hometown School District wants to find out which of two reading programs—*Reading Is Fantastic* (RIF) and *Reading as a Foundation* (RAF)—leads to better reading in third grade. The district asks each of its third-grade teachers to choose one of these two reading programs and use it throughout a particular school year. The district then compares the end-of-year achievement test scores of students in the RIF and RAF classrooms and finds that RIF students obtained significantly higher reading comprehension scores than RAF students. We might quickly jump to the conclusion that RIF promotes better reading comprehension than RAF—in other words, that a cause-effect relationship exists between instructional method and reading comprehension. But is this really so?

The fact is, the district hasn't eliminated all other possible explanations for the difference in students' reading comprehension scores. Remember, the third-grade teachers selected which instructional program they used. Why did some teachers choose RIF and others choose RAF? Were the teachers who chose RIF different in some way from the teachers who chose RAF? Had RIF teachers taken more graduate courses in reading instruction, did they have higher expectations for their students, or did they devote more class time to reading instruction? If the RIF and RAF teachers were different from each other in any of these ways (or in some other way we might not happen to think of), then the district hasn't eliminated an alternative explanation: the possibility that the RIF teachers and RAF teachers were somehow different from one another. A better way to study the causal influence of reading program on reading comprehension would be to randomly assign teachers to each program, thereby making the two groups of teachers roughly equivalent in areas such as amount of education, expectations for students, and class time devoted to reading instruction.

Draw conclusions about cause-effect relationships only when you have an experimental study—one in which other factors possibly having an effect on behavior have been controlled.

As a general word of caution, be careful that you don't jump to unwarranted conclusions about what actually causes changes in student behavior. Scrutinize descriptions of research carefully, always with a particular question in mind: *Have the researchers ruled out other possible explanations for their results?* Only when the answer to this question is an undeniable *yes* should you draw a conclusion about a cause-effect relationship.

Experimental studies that *do* support causal relationships help researchers develop *principles* and *theories* of human behavior and educational practice. Principles and theories will help us make informed decisions about how best to facilitate our students' learning and achievement.

Deriving Principles and Theories

When similar research studies yield similar results time after time, educational psychologists derive **principles** identifying the factors that influence students' learning, development, and behavior. Consider these two principles as examples:

- *Taking notes during a lecture leads to better recall of the information presented than does listening to the lecture without taking notes.*
- *When one person's behavior is followed by reinforcement, other people who observe that behavior being reinforced often show an increase in the same behavior.*

Each principle describes how one thing—taking notes, or observing another person's reinforcement—causes or influences something else—better memory for information, or higher frequency of a particular behavior.

Because principles are usually derived from multiple research studies, rather than from just a single study, they can be generalized to a wide variety of situations and to many different types of people. And when principles describe cause-effect relationships, they enable us to facilitate students' classroom performance by manipulating the factors that affect learning, development, and behavior.

Yet educational psychologists go a step further: They develop **theories** to explain why these principles are true. Theories describe possible underlying, unobservable mechanisms that regulate human learning, development, and behavior. They typically incorporate many principles and encompass a multitude of interrelationships. To illustrate, let's consider a possible theoretical explanation for each of the two principles just presented:

Principle:
Taking notes during a lecture leads to better recall of the information presented than does listening to the lecture without taking notes.

Possible theoretical explanation:
Information is better remembered when it is mentally processed—that is, when people think about it and do something (mentally) with it. Taking notes is one way of processing information. At a minimum, note takers must mentally "translate" the spoken word into the written word. Most note takers also interpret and summarize the information they hear.

Principle:
When one person's behavior is followed by reinforcement, other people who observe that behavior being reinforced often show an increase in the same behavior.

Possible theoretical explanation:
People show an increase in a particular behavior when they form an expectation that they will receive reinforcement for the behavior. When they see someone else being reinforced for behaving in a particular way, they are likely to expect that they themselves will be reinforced for behaving similarly.

Notice how each of the two theoretical explanations proposes an internal mechanism—*mental processing* in the first case and an *expectation* in the second—to explain human performance.

In general, principles describe the *whats* of human behavior—they describe what things happen under what conditions—whereas theories describe *why* those things happen. Table 1–2 presents several examples of principles, possible theoretical explanations for these principles, and implications for classroom practice.

As we examine numerous principles and theories related to student learning and classroom practice, keep in mind that these principles and theories are not necessarily set in stone; they simply represent our current "best guesses" about why students learn and behave as they do. As future research yields new information, our conceptions of human learning, development, and behavior will

We can best improve our educational practices when we identify the specific factors that affect students' learning, development, and behavior.

TABLE 1.2

Examples of Principles, Theories, and Their Implications for Teaching Practice

PRINCIPLE	POSSIBLE THEORETICAL EXPLANATION	EDUCATIONAL IMPLICATION
Taking notes during a lecture leads to better recall of the information presented than does listening without taking notes.	People remember information better when they mentally process it in some way.	Suggest that students do something with the information they hear in a lecture—for example, take notes, put definitions in their own words, or think of applications.
Students remember information better when they are instructed to form mental images of it.	Visual imagery is one effective method by which people can store information in memory.	When reading a story to students, encourage them to imagine the characters and situations.
Students perform more poorly on difficult tasks when they are highly anxious.	Excessive levels of anxiety interfere with one's ability to pay attention and mentally process information.	When assigning a challenging task, give students plenty of time to complete it. Don't weigh the importance of any single task too heavily in overall evaluations of students' performance.
When one person's behavior is followed by reinforcement, other people who observe that behavior being reinforced often show an increase in the same behavior.	People show an increase in behavior for which they expect to receive reinforcement.	To promote appropriate social skills (e.g., sharing or working cooperatively), reinforce such behaviors often.
Older students are more likely than younger students to obey rules in situations where there are no rewards for obedience and no punishment for disobedience.	Moral development is characterized by a series of stages in which people gradually internalize society's rules and conventions.	Encourage adherence to school rules in ways appropriate for students' developmental levels. Young children may need rewards (e.g., praise) for following rules; rewards are less important for older students.

continue to evolve into more complete and accurate explanations. Yet, incomplete as current principles and theories in educational psychology may be, they provide numerous ideas and insights about how best to help our students achieve academic and social success.

Using Principles and Theories to Make Classroom Decisions

THINKING ABOUT WHAT YOU KNOW

Picture yourself standing in front of thirty students. You are trying to teach them something; perhaps you are describing the difference between nouns and pronouns, or explaining how an automobile engine works, or encouraging them to project their voices as they rehearse a medley from *Phantom of the Opera.* Those thirty students are staring back at you with blank faces, and you're certain that they haven't learned a thing.

- Why aren't your students learning? What are some possible reasons related to your students' age level? What are some possible reasons why your students may not *want* to learn whatever it is you are trying to teach them? What are some possible reasons why even the most capable and motivated students may be unable to learn the material?

There are many possible explanations as to why your students aren't learning. Perhaps they don't have enough previous experience with the topic at hand to understand what you are saying to them. Perhaps they are having trouble comprehending something in the abstract manner you have explained it. Perhaps they are distracted by some other event in the classroom and so aren't really paying attention to the lesson. Or perhaps they aren't motivated; they just don't want to learn whatever it is you are trying to teach them.

So what do you do now? Let's consider several principles and theories that might relate to your students' difficulty in learning and then identify possible teaching strategies to be derived from each one:

- *New learning builds on things students have previously learned.* Perhaps your students don't have the background knowledge to understand the material you are presenting. If you think this might be the case, then find out what your students do and don't know about the topic and build instruction on the things they *do* know. (The idea that new learning builds on previous learning underlies many theories of learning but is a particularly prominent feature of cognitive psychology, described in Chapters 6 and 7.)

- *Children's ability to think about abstract ideas emerges later than their ability to think about concrete objects.* Perhaps your students have not yet developed the capacity for abstract thinking. If you think this might be so, then you might make the lesson less abstract—for example, by providing concrete examples or by having students practice the behaviors you want them to learn. (Piaget's theory of cognitive development, described in Chapter 2, proposes that abstract thought emerges in adolescence, in the last of four stages of cognitive development.)

- *Attention is essential for learning to take place.* Perhaps your students were not paying attention. If you think they were not, then you might eliminate any obvious sources of distraction so that students can concentrate on the lesson. (Attention plays an important role in both cognitive psychology and social cognitive theory, as we will discover in Chapters 6 and 11.)

- *Behaviors increase when they are followed by pleasant consequences (i.e., by reinforcers).* Perhaps your students are not improving their performance because there is no desirable consequence for doing so. If so, then you might tell them that

Which of these italicized statements propose an internal mechanism to explain human performance? In other words, which ones are theories rather than principles?

they will have ten minutes of "free time" after they master the lesson. (Reinforcers play a particularly important role in behaviorism, described in Chapter 10.)

- *Learning increases when learners have a reason for wanting to learn the information or skill being taught.* Perhaps your students don't see the relevance of the lesson for their own lives. If so, then you might explain to students how the information or skills you are teaching will be useful to them, either now or in the future. (We will examine the importance of relevance in our discussion of motivation in Chapter 12.)

How can we most effectively help students achieve success in the classroom? There is no easy answer to this question—no recipe for effective teaching. As teachers, we must continually choose from a multitude of possible instructional strategies and approaches, and the choices we make should be based on a solid understanding of basic principles and theories of how human beings learn and develop. Fortunately, our decision making will inevitably become easier as we gain more experience in the classroom.

Developing as a Teacher

As a beginning teacher, you may initially find your role a bit overwhelming. After all, you may have twenty-five to thirty-five students in your classroom at any one time, and they are all likely to have different backgrounds, ability levels, and needs. In such a situation, your role as decision maker will be a challenging one indeed. So in the first few weeks or months, you may need to rely heavily on the standard lessons that curriculum development specialists provide (Berliner, 1988). But as time goes on, you will eventually be able to make decisions about routine situations and problems quickly and efficiently, giving you the time and energy you need to think creatively and flexibly about how best to teach your students (Borko & Putnam, 1996; Sternberg, 1996a).

The chapters that follow describe many ways you can help your students learn and develop. But it is equally important that *you* learn and develop as well, especially in your role as a teacher. Here are several strategies for doing so:

- *Continue to take courses in teacher education.* Additional coursework in teaching is one surefire way of keeping up to date on the latest theoretical perspectives and research results related to classroom practice. In general, teacher education definitely *does* enhance teaching effectiveness (Darling-Hammond, 1995).

Continue taking coursework related to effective teaching practices.

- *Learn as much as you can about the subject matter you teach.* When we look at effective teachers—for example, those who are flexible in their approaches to instruction, help their students develop a thorough understanding of classroom subject matter, and convey obvious enthusiasm for whatever they are teaching—we typically find teachers who know their subject matter extremely well (Borko & Putnam, 1996; Brophy, 1991; Cochran & Jones, 1998; Phillip, Flores, Sowder, & Schappelle, 1994).

Continue to read and learn about the subject matter you teach.

- *Learn as much as you can about specific strategies for teaching your particular subject matter.* In addition to knowing general teaching strategies, it is also helpful to develop strategies specific to the topic you are teaching; a repertoire of such strategies is known as **pedagogical content knowledge.** Effective teachers typically have a large number of strategies specific to teaching various topics and skills (Borko & Putnam, 1996; Brophy, 1991; Cochran & Jones, 1998; Shulman, 1986). Furthermore, they can usually anticipate—and so can also address—the difficulties students will have, and the kinds of errors they will make, in the process of mastering a skill or body of knowledge (Borko & Putnam, 1996; D. C. Smith & Neale, 1991). Some teachers keep journals or other records of the strategies they develop and use in particular situations; they then draw on some of the same strategies again when similar situations arise (Berliner, 1988).

Acquire strategies specific to teaching your subject matter.

- *Believe that you* can *become an effective teacher.* In Chapter 11, we will find that students who believe that they are capable of performing a particular task—

Believe that you *can* be effective.

INTO THE CLASSROOM: Becoming a More Effective Teacher

Use some of the standard lessons that curriculum development specialists provide, especially in your first few weeks or months in the classroom.

> A history teacher consults the teaching manual that accompanies her class textbook for ideas about how to make history come alive for her students.

As you gain confidence as a teacher, begin to adapt standard lessons and develop your own lessons.

> When a high school mathematics teacher begins using a new geometry textbook, he peruses the teacher's manual that accompanies the book. He notices that the manual's lesson plans focus almost exclusively on meaningless memorization of geometric concepts and principles. Rather than use these lessons, he develops his own classroom activities—ones that will encourage his students to apply geometry to real-life situations.

Keep a journal of the instructional strategies you use and their relative effectiveness.

> As a way of winding down at bedtime, a new teacher reflects back on his day in the classroom. He picks up the notebook and pen on his bedside table and jots down notes about the strategies that did and did not work well in class that day.

Seek the advice and suggestions of your more experienced colleagues.

> A fourth-grade teacher is teaching her students long division, but after a week they still don't understand what they are supposed to do. Over the weekend, she telephones two of her fellow teachers for ideas about how she might approach the topic differently.

Continue your education, both formally and informally.

> A middle school science teacher takes advantage of a tour package to Costa Rica designed specifically for teachers. There she will study the plants, animals, and ecology of the rain forest.

Remember that teaching, like any other complex skill, takes time and practice to master.

> A teacher continues to try new instructional techniques that he sees described in professional journals. As he does so, he adds to his repertoire of effective teaching strategies and becomes increasingly able to adjust his methods to the diverse population of students he has in his classroom.

students who have high *self-efficacy*—are more likely to perform that task successfully. You, too, must have high self-efficacy—you must believe that you can be a good teacher—to overcome occasional setbacks and ultimately be effective in the classroom (Ashton, 1985). Students who achieve at the highest levels are most likely to be those whose teachers have confidence in what they themselves can do for their students (Ashton, 1985).

Teaching, like any other complex skill, takes time and practice to master. And you, like any other learner, will inevitably make a few mistakes, especially at the beginning. But you *will* improve over time. If you base classroom decisions on documented principles and sound educational practice, you *can* make a difference in the lives of your students.

Looking Ahead to the Following Chapters

As teachers, we are decision makers. And we are most likely to make wise decisions when, in the process, we consider questions such as these:

- What characteristics do our students bring to the classroom?
- What do we know about how students learn?
- How can we convert our knowledge about development, diversity, and learning into effective teaching practice?

Let's look briefly at how each part of the book addresses these questions. As we do so, let's also identify places where we might find possible strategies for helping Rosa, the student in our opening case study.

- *What characteristics do our students bring to the classroom?* Part 1 of the book, "Understanding Student Development and Diversity," focuses on how our students are likely to be different from one another. Chapters 2 and 3 look at developmental changes in thinking, language, personality, social skills, and morality as students progress through the elementary and secondary school years. Chapters 4 and 5 describe common sources of diversity among students at the same grade, including intelligence, creativity, ethnicity, gender, socioeconomic background, and exceptionalities. For instance, when you read about Rosa, you may have wondered how her language and ethnic background influence her classroom performance. We'll identify strategies for addressing linguistic and ethnic differences in Chapters 2 and 4, respectively.

- *What do we know about how students learn?* Like many students, Rosa learns in some areas of the curriculum more successfully than in others. Part 2 of the book, "Understanding How Students Learn," explores the nature of human learning, thinking, behavior, and motivation. Chapters 6 through 8 focus on the mental processes involved in learning; Chapter 9 shows how such processes may be somewhat different in reading, writing, mathematics, science, and social studies. Chapters 10 and 11 explain how students' behaviors are influenced by environmental events, especially in the early years, and how students can become increasingly self-regulating over time. Chapter 12 describes a variety of motives that are likely to affect students' classroom performance.

When reading about Rosa, you may have noticed that many of her strengths—her ability to interact with other people, her skill in volleyball and basketball, and her ability to perform in the school choir—are things she can learn through watching and modeling the behaviors of others; such *modeling* is a topic we will consider in Chapter 11. And Rosa's *need for affiliation*—her desire for friendly relationships with others—will be a topic in Chapter 12.

- *How can we convert our knowledge about development, diversity, and learning into effective teaching practice?* Part 3, "Understanding Instructional Processes," applies principles of student development, diversity, and learning to classroom practice. Chapters 13 and 14 identify instructional strategies that are suitable for different situations and different students; for instance, when you read Chapter 14, you will discover that Rosa would probably learn quite effectively through cooperative learning activities. Chapter 15 presents strategies for maintaining a productive learning environment—one in which students are

As teachers, we should develop a wide variety of strategies for teaching our subject matter.

As teachers, we will be far more effective if we adapt instruction to the diverse backgrounds and needs of our students.

actively engaged in achieving instructional objectives for much of the school day. Chapter 16 describes principles of effective classroom assessment; at that point, we will identify several issues to consider when we see low test scores in students such as Rosa.

☐ What specific topics do you hope this book will cover? In what chapters are you most likely to find them?

Figure 1–1 provides a graphic overview of the book, with examples of questions that each chapter addresses. Take a moment to think about specific topics you hope the book will cover and identify the chapters in which you are most likely to find them.

The Big Picture: Common Themes Throughout the Book

Chapters 2 through 16 present many implications that psychological principles and theories have for classroom decision making. Throughout the book, certain themes underlying effective educational practice pop up over and over again. Some particularly prominent ones are these:

- *Interaction.* To learn and develop, students need numerous opportunities to interact both with their physical environments and with other people.
- *Cognitive processes.* How effectively students learn and achieve is a function of how they mentally think about—that is, how they *process*—information. Students need ample time to think about classroom subject matter and develop appropriate responses to tasks and questions.
- *Relevance.* Students must discover how new information and skills are related both to the things they already know and to their own personal lives and needs.
- *Classroom climate.* Students learn more effectively in a supportive classroom atmosphere—one in which they believe that they are valued as human beings, and one in which they feel comfortable taking academic risks.

UNDERSTANDING STUDENT DEVELOPMENT AND DIVERSITY

- What characteristics do our students bring to the classroom?

Chapter 2. Cognitive and Linguistic Development
- How does logical thinking change with age?
- How do students' learning processes change over time?
- How do students' language skills develop during the elementary and secondary school years?

Chapter 3. Personal, Social, and Moral Development
- What can we do to promote students' self-esteem?
- What roles do students' classmates play in development?
- How do we help students develop a "conscience" about right and wrong?

Chapter 4. Individual and Group Differences
- What are intelligence and creativity?
- How do students' cultural backgrounds influence their classroom performance?
- How are boys and girls similar and different?

Chapter 5. Students with Special Educational Needs
- Why are students with disabilities often educated in regular classrooms?
- In what ways are students with special needs different from their peers?
- What instructional strategies are effective for students with special needs?

UNDERSTANDING HOW STUDENTS LEARN

- What do we know about how students learn?

Chapter 6. Learning and Cognitive Processes
- What is learning?
- Why do students sometimes forget what they've learned?
- How can we help students remember things more effectively?

Chapter 7. Knowledge Construction
- Why do different students often learn different things even though they all participate in the same lesson?
- What misconceptions are students likely to have about classroom topics?
- How can we correct students' misconceptions?

Chapter 8. Higher-Level Thinking Skills
- How can we teach new concepts?
- How can we help students apply the things they learn to real-world situations?
- How can we help students learn to study effectively?

Chapter 9. Learning in the Content Areas
- How can we help students read and write more effectively?
- How can we help students solve math and science problems more successfully?
- What developmental differences are we likely to see in reading, writing, mathematics, science, and social studies?

Chapter 10. Behaviorist Views of Learning
- What role does reinforcement play in learning?
- In what situations is reinforcement counterproductive?
- How can we encourage productive classroom behaviors?

Chapter 11. Social Cognitive Views of Learning
- What can students learn from watching others?
- How can we enhance students' self-confidence about performing classroom tasks?
- How can we help students regulate their own behavior?

Chapter 12. Motivating Students to Learn
- How can we foster intrinsic motivation to learn?
- How does anxiety affect learning and behavior?
- Why do some students have trouble accepting responsibility for their own actions?

UNDERSTANDING INSTRUCTIONAL PROCESSES

- How can we convert our knowledge about development, diversity, and learning into effective teaching practice?

Chapter 13. Choosing Instructional Strategies
- How can we develop useful classroom objectives?
- How can we make our classroom lectures and explanations more effective?
- In what situations might it be valuable to let students discover important ideas by themselves?

Chapter 14. Promoting Learning Through Student Interactions
- How do class discussions promote students' learning?
- What strategies can we use to help students work cooperatively with one another?
- Why do students who tutor their classmates often benefit from the tutoring process?

Chapter 15. Creating and Maintaining a Productive Classroom Environment
- How can we get the school year off to a good start?
- How can we keep discipline problems to a minimum?
- How can we collaborate with parents to maximize students' classroom performance?

Chapter 16. Assessing Student Learning
- How do classroom assessment practices affect students' learning?
- When is it inappropriate to assess student achievement with paper-pencil tests?
- How do we know when the results of our assessments are accurate?

FIGURE 1.1
Overview of the book: Examples of questions we will address in each chapter

■ *Challenge.* Students are most likely to learn and develop when they encounter challenging tasks—those at which they can succeed only with effort and persistence and those that require them to use newly learned knowledge and procedures. Students should find that they can ultimately be successful at classroom tasks most of the time; however, they must also learn to deal with and benefit from the occasional failures they are likely to encounter along the way.

■ *Expectations.* Students achieve at higher levels when their teachers' expectations for their performance are challenging yet attainable. Students exhibit more appropriate and productive classroom behaviors when teachers' expectations for their performance are communicated clearly and concretely.

■ *Diversity.* Students will bring a wide variety of backgrounds, abilities, perspectives, and needs to any classroom. As a result, some students may benefit more from one instructional strategy, whereas others may benefit more from a very different approach.

Which of these themes have you encountered in other courses in education or psychology?

The table in Appendix A presents some examples of where each theme appears throughout the book. The last theme—diversity—appears in every chapter. Let's look at this theme more closely.

Considering Student Diversity

THINKING ABOUT WHAT YOU KNOW

In what ways are you different from other students? What exceptional strengths do you have? What difficulties do you have in comparison with your classmates? What things might your instructor do to accommodate your strengths and weaknesses?

All students are unique individuals who bring different strengths and weaknesses to the classroom. In many cases, we will be able to accommodate our students' unique needs within the context of general classroom practices and activities. Yet some students have characteristics that require specially adapted instructional materials or practices. Now, more than ever before, many of these **students with special needs** are in general education classrooms—a practice called **inclusion.** Chapter 5 describes characteristics that students with exceptionalities are likely to have.

Each of the following chapters includes a section on accommodating the student diversity we are likely to find in any classroom. Each chapter also includes a "Students in Inclusive Settings" table that provides instructional strategies for students within five general categories of special needs. These categories are described and illustrated in Table 1–3. Keep in mind, however, that categorizing students with special needs in *any* way is a controversial issue (more about this in Chapter 5). Ultimately, we must remember that all of our students, including those with special needs, can benefit from having instruction tailored to their unique characteristics.

As a teacher, you must ultimately make your own decisions about how best to teach each and every one of your students. Your instructional decisions will be affected not only by the characteristics that your students bring to the classroom but also by your objectives, your resources, and your own personality. Every teacher is likely to develop a unique approach to teaching. As long as your own approach is based on solid research findings about how children and adolescents learn and develop, your students will undoubtedly come out ahead.

TABLE 1.3

Categories of Students with Special Educational Needs

GENERAL CATEGORY	DESCRIPTION	SPECIFIC CATEGORY(IES) INCLUDED	EXAMPLE
Students with specific cognitive or academic difficulties	These students exhibit an uneven pattern of academic performance; they may have unusual difficulty with certain kinds of tasks yet perform quite successfully on other tasks.	Learning disabilities Attention-deficit hyperactivity disorder Speech and communication disorders	James has exceptional difficulty learning to read but seems to grasp ideas in science and mathematics quite easily.
Students with specific social or behavioral problems	These students exhibit social, emotional, or behavioral difficulties serious enough to interfere significantly with their academic performance.	Emotional and behavioral disorders Autism	Amy has frequent aggressive outbursts during which she hits or kicks whomever happens to be near her. She rarely interacts with either her teacher or her classmates in a socially acceptable manner.
Students with general delays in cognitive and social functioning	These students exhibit low achievement in virtually all academic areas, and they have social skills typical of much younger children.	Mental retardation	Although Margaret is thirteen years old, her academic skills are similar to those of a seven-year-old, and she often blurts out whatever is on her mind without considering how other people might react to her comments.
Students with physical and sensory challenges	These students have disabilities caused by medically detectable physiological conditions.	Physical and health impairments Visual impairments Hearing loss Severe and multiple disabilities	After sustaining a brain injury in a car accident, Jonathan tires easily, and he has trouble remembering some of the things that he studies in class.
Students with advanced cognitive development	These students have unusually high ability in one or more areas.	Giftedness	Mike shows exceptional skill and creativity in writing; for instance, he has won several district and statewide writing contests.

Studying Educational Psychology More Effectively

As you read the book, you will gain insights about how you can help your students more effectively learn the things you want to teach them. At the same time, I hope you will also gain insights about how *you yourself* can learn course material. But rather than wait until we get to our discussion of learning in Part 2, let's look briefly at three general principles of effective learning—three principles that you can apply as you read and study this book:

• *Students learn more effectively when they relate new information to the things they already know.* Try to connect the ideas you read in the book with things you are already familiar with—for example, with your own past experiences, with your previous course work, with things you have observed in the schools, or with your general knowledge about the world. The "Thinking About What You Know" features in each chapter should give you some ideas about how to apply this strategy.

• *Students learn more effectively when they elaborate on new information.* As noted earlier, elaboration is a process of adding one's own ideas to new information. In most situations, elaboration enables us to learn information with greater understanding, remember it better, and apply it more readily at times when we need it. So try to think *beyond* the information you read. Generate new examples of concepts and principles. Draw inferences from factual statements. Identify educational applications of various principles and theories.

• *Students learn more effectively when they periodically check to make sure they have learned.* There are times when even the best of us don't concentrate on what we're reading—when we are actually thinking about something else as our eyes go down the page. So stop once in a while (perhaps once every two or three pages) to make sure you have really learned and understood the things you've been reading. Try to summarize the material. Ask yourself questions about it. Make sure everything makes logical sense to you. Don't become a victim of that *illusion of knowing* I mentioned earlier.

How frequently do you apply these principles when you study?

Perhaps you are a student who has been following these principles for years. But in case you are someone for whom such learning strategies are relatively new, I've provided margin notes (designated by a ▣ to help you learn and study throughout the book. These notes will give you some suggestions for how you might think about the material you read. With practice, the strategies I recommend will eventually become second nature to you as you read and study in all your classes.

Furthermore, the case studies in each chapter can help you relate many of the principles to concrete classroom situations. The case study at the beginning of each chapter presents an example of one or more students dealing with classroom learning tasks. As we proceed through the chapter, we will continually relate our discussion back to this case, helping you relate chapter content to a classroom context. The case study at the end of each chapter focuses on teachers and teaching. Here I will ask you questions about the case that will help you apply the principles you have learned in the chapter. Let's see if you can apply what you've learned in this chapter to a case entitled "More Harm Than Good?"

CASE STUDY: More Harm Than Good?

Mr. Gualtieri, a high school mathematics teacher, begins his class one Monday with an important announcement. "I've just obtained some new instructional software programs for the school's computer laboratory. These programs will give you practice in solving mathematical word problems. I strongly encourage you to stay after school once or twice a week to get extra practice on the computer whenever you're having trouble with the homework assignments I give you."

Mr. Gualtieri is firmly convinced that the new instructional software will help his students perform better in mathematics. To test his hypothesis, he keeps a record of which students report to the computer lab after school and which students do not. He then looks at how well the two groups of students perform on his next classroom test. Much to his surprise, he discovers that, on the average, the students who have stayed after school to use the computer software have gotten *lower* scores than those who did not stay after school. "How can this be?" he puzzles. "Is the computer software actually doing more harm than good?"

- Is the computer software somehow making mathematics *more* difficult for students? Or is there another explanation for the students' lower scores?

- Which kind of study has Mr. Gualtieri conducted—descriptive, correlational, or experimental?

- Is it possible that the two groups of students (those who used the computer lab and those who did not) were different in some way that might affect their performance on Mr. Gualtieri's math test?

- Did Mr. Gualtieri make a good or a bad decision in advising his students to use the computer software? Is there any way to answer this question from the information he has obtained?

Summing Up

Importance of Research for Teachers

Many people hold misconceptions about how students learn and develop and about how teachers can most effectively promote students' classroom success. The most accurate information about learning, development, and classroom practice comes from research findings. Different types of research studies—descriptive, correlational, or experimental—answer different questions about education, but all can help us in our classroom decision making.

Principles, Theories, and Decision Making

When research studies yield similar results time after time, educational psychologists derive principles and theories that describe and explain people's learning, development, and behavior. Our job as teachers is to translate these principles and theories into classroom practice. To illustrate, if research consistently tells us that "students learn more effectively when they relate new ideas to their existing knowledge," then we can facilitate our students' learning by helping them connect new material to what they have previously learned or experienced.

Developing as a Teacher

We don't yet have all the answers about how best to help children learn and develop, so we must continue to keep ourselves current about research results, theoretical developments, and educational innovations. As a beginning teacher, you may initially find your classroom a bit overwhelming, but with experience and continuing education, you can eventually become an expert in the teaching profession.

Overview of the Book

In Parts 1 and 2 of the book, we will examine the diverse characteristics that students bring to the classroom and the nature of human learning and motivation. In Part 3, we will draw on principles from Parts 1 and 2 as we consider effective classroom practice.

Reading About and Studying Educational Psychology

As we examine the ways that people think and learn, we will discover how people learn most effectively. You can use this information not only to help your students be successful in the classroom but also to help *yourself* learn successfully. For instance, you should relate new information to what you already know, elaborate on that information, and occasionally stop to test yourself on the content you've studied.

Common Themes

Seven themes underlie many of the recommendations that appear throughout the book: interaction, cognitive processes, relevance, classroom climate, challenge, expectations, and diversity. Diversity is the most prominent theme, appearing in every chapter of the book.

KEY CONCEPTS

elaboration (p. 6)
descriptive study (p. 8)
correlational study (p. 8)
correlation (p. 8)
experimental study (p. 9)

visual-spatial thinking (p. 9)
treatment group (p. 10)
control group (p. 10)
principles (p. 12)

theories (p. 12)
pedagogical content knowledge (p. 15)
students with special needs (p. 20)
inclusion (p. 20)

Cognitive and Linguistic Development

W hat differences have you noticed in the nature of instruction at various grade levels? For instance, what things do first-grade teachers, sixth-grade teachers, and high school teachers do differently as they teach classroom subject matter? How are the topics and skills they teach different at each of these grade levels? How are their expectations for student behavior different?

Such issues are the focus of Part 1 of the book, "Understanding Student Development and Diversity." Chapters 2 and 3 describe how students change and develop as they grow older, looking at cognitive and linguistic development (Chapter 2) and personal, social, and moral development (Chapter 3). Chapters 4 and 5 describe the diversity we are likely to see at any single grade level, considering both how students typically differ with respect to intelligence, ethnic background, gender, and so on (Chapter 4) and how some students require adapted classroom environments or instruction and special educational services to accommodate physical and mental exceptionalities (Chapter 5). Once you have finished Part 1, you will have learned a wide variety of strategies for adapting instruction to the developmental levels and individual characteristics of the students you are likely to have in your classroom.

As we look at cognitive and linguistic development in this chapter, we will address several questions:

- What general principles characterize human development?
- What principles and theories can guide our efforts not only to adapt instruction to students' cognitive abilities but also to promote their cognitive development?
- How do students' language abilities change with age, and what implications do such changes have for classroom practice?
- How might our students differ from one another in terms of their cognitive and linguistic development, and how can we accommodate their differences?

CASE STUDY: Economic Activities

The students in Mr. Sand's advanced high school geography course are struggling with their reading assignments, and they readily share their frustration with their teacher.

"The textbook is really *hard*. I can't understand it at all!" Lucy whines.

"Same here!" Mike shouts out. "I'm really trying, Mr. Sand, but most of the time I have no idea what I'm reading." Many other students nod their heads in agreement.

"Okay," Mr. Sand responds. "Let's see if we can figure out why you might be having trouble. Look at the section called 'Economic Activity' on page 55, which was part of last night's reading."

The class peruses this excerpt from the book:

Economic activities are those in which human beings engage to acquire food and satisfy other wants. They are the most basic of all activities and are found wherever there are people. Economic activity is divided into four sections. *Primary activity* involves the direct harvesting of the earth's resources. Fishing off the coast of Peru, pumping oil from wells in Libya, extracting iron ore from mines in Minnesota, harvesting trees for lumber in Chile, and growing wheat in China are all examples of primary production. The commodities that result from those activities acquire value from the effort required in production and from consumer demand.

The processing of commodities is classified as a *secondary activity*. In this sector items are increased in value by having their forms changed to enhance their usefulness. Thus, a primary commodity such as cotton might be processed into fabric, and that fabric might be cut and assembled as apparel. Textile manufacturing and apparel manufacturing are both secondary activities.

An economic activity in which a service is performed is classified as a *tertiary activity*. Wholesaling and retailing are tertiary activities by which primary and secondary projects are made available to consumers. Other tertiary activities include governmental, banking, educational, medical, and legal services, as well as journalism and the arts.

The service economy of the technologically most developed countries has become so large and complex that a fourth sector of *quarternary activity* is sometimes included. Institutions and corporations that provide information are in the quarternary sector. (Clawson & Fisher, 1998, p. 55)

"Tell me the kinds of problems you had when you read the passage," Mr. Sand suggests. "Then maybe I can help you understand it better."

The students eagerly describe their difficulties.

"I never heard of some of these words. What's *tertiary* mean? What's *quarternary*?"

"Yeah. And what are *commodities*?"

"There's too much to learn. Do you expect us to memorize *all* of this stuff?"

"Okay, okay, I see your point," Mr. Sand responds. "I guess this stuff can be pretty abstract. No, I *don't* want you to memorize it all. What's most important is that you get the main idea, which in this case is that different levels of economic activity build on one another. Here, let me show you what I mean. We start out with primary activities, which involve direct use of natural resources." Mr. Sand writes "Primary activity—using natural resources" on the chalkboard. "Who can give me some examples of natural resources we use right here in Pennsylvania?"

"Coal," Sam suggests.

"Milk," Kristen adds.

"And vegetables," Nikki says.

"Excellent examples!" Mr. Sand exclaims. "Now in secondary activities, people change those items into other things that can be used." Mr. Sand writes "Secondary activity—changing natural resources into other products" on the board. "Let's identify some possible examples for this one. . . ."

- Why are the students having trouble reading their textbook? What characteristics of the text seem to be interfering with their understanding?

- What strategies does Mr. Sand use to help the students understand the passage about economic activities?

Basic Principles of Human Development

The college-level textbook Mr. Sand has chosen for his advanced geography class is very difficult for his high school students. As Mr. Sand points out, the book's content is quite abstract—it is almost completely removed from the concrete, everyday world that his students encounter on a regular basis. The book also uses words—*tertiary, quarternary, commodities,* and so on—that are not part of the students' existing vocabularies. Mr. Sand's choice of textbooks may not be developmentally inappropriate, either cognitively or linguistically, for the students in his class. But Mr. Sand does do a couple of things that probably *are* appropriate for his students' developmental levels. For one thing, he describes what his students need to do as they read and think about chapter content; in particular, he tells them to find the main ideas in what they are reading. Second, he shows them two things they can do to help them as they study: write down key concepts and generate new examples.

As we study various theories of cognitive and linguistic development in the pages ahead, we will gain additional insights about the case. But before we look at specific developmental theories, let's consider several principles that seem to hold true regardless of the aspect of development that we're talking about. Here are four important ones to keep in mind as you read Chapters 2 and 3:

• *Development proceeds in a somewhat orderly and predictable pattern.* Human development is often characterized by **developmental milestones** that occur in a predictable sequence. For example, children typically learn to walk only after they have already learned to sit up and crawl. They learn the stereotypical behaviors of males and females—for example, that men are more likely to become doctors and women are more likely to become nurses—only after they have learned to distinguish between men and women. They begin to think logically about abstract ideas only after they have learned to think logically about concrete objects and observable events. To some extent, then, we see **universals** in development: We see similar patterns in how children change over time regardless of the specific environment in which they are raised.

• *Different children develop at different rates.* Descriptive research in child and adolescent development tells us the average ages at which various developmental milestones are reached. For example, the average child can hop several times on one foot at age three, starts using repetition as a way of learning information at age seven, and begins puberty at age ten or eleven (for girls) or twelve (for boys) (Berk, 1997; Kail, 1990; G. R. Levin, 1983). But not all children reach developmental milestones at the "average" age; some reach them earlier, some later.

Determining the approximate ages at which children can perform certain behaviors and think in certain ways allows us to form general expectations about the capabilities of children at a particular age level and to design our educational curriculum and instructional strategies around these expectations. At the same time, we should never jump to conclusions about what any individual student can and cannot do on the basis of age alone.

• *Periods of relatively rapid growth (spurts) may appear between periods of slower growth (plateaus).* Development does not always proceed at a constant rate. For example, during the early elementary school years, children gain an average of two or three inches in height per year; during their adolescent growth spurt, they may grow as much as five inches per year (Berk, 1997; A. C. Harris, 1986). Toddlers may speak with a limited vocabulary and one-word "sentences" for several months, yet sometime around their second birthday a virtual explosion in language development occurs, with vocabulary expanding rapidly and sentences becoming longer and longer within just a few weeks.

At what age did you first walk? speak your first word? say your first sentence? Do you know when such milestones in your life occurred?

Descriptive research of child development tells us the *average* age at which various developmental milestones are reached. But we must remember that individual children develop at different rates.

Some theories of how students develop describe **stages** that reflect this pattern of uneven growth and change. We will encounter several stage theories in this and the following chapter.

• *Virtually every aspect of development is affected by both heredity and environment.* Any aspect of development is affected either directly or indirectly by a child's genetic makeup. Not all inherited characteristics appear at birth; heredity continues to control a child's growth through the process of **maturation**—an unfolding of genetically controlled changes as the child develops. For example, motor skills such as walking, running, and jumping develop primarily as a result of neurological development, increased strength, and increased muscular control—changes that are largely determined by heredity.

Yet the environment plays an equally critical role in most aspects of development. For example, although children's heights and body builds are primarily inherited characteristics, the nutritional value of the food they eat also makes a difference. The success experiences that children have affect the development of their self-esteem and motivation. And the families and cultures in which children are raised have a significant impact on the cognitive abilities, moral values, and social skills the children acquire.

Heredity and environment typically work together to promote development in ways that we can ultimately never disentangle. In some situations, heredity predetermines a **sensitive period**—an age range during which a growing child can be especially influenced by environmental conditions. For instance, as we will discover later in the chapter, some theorists have found evidence that children learn a language more easily when they are exposed to it in their early years rather than in adolescence or adulthood. Others speculate about a possible sensitive period in cognitive development, as we shall see now.

> This question of *nature vs. nurture* continues to be a source of controversy among developmental theorists. To what extent do *you* believe that various human characteristics are influenced by heredity and environment?

Role of the Brain in Development

Most psychologists believe that the synapses (interconnections) between neurons (brain cells) provide the primary means through which people learn and remember (Byrnes & Fox, 1998). The great majority of synapses form within the first ten years of life; in fact, people have more synapses at age 10 than at any other time (Bruer, 1997). Synapses that are used frequently remain intact; those that are not used at all eventually disappear (Bruer, 1997). Some educators have proposed that such findings point to a sensitive period in cognitive development during the preschool and elementary years, and they urge us to maximize children's educational experiences during this time period.

Yet many others question the relevance of current neurological research for educational practice (Brown & Bjorklund, 1998; Bruer, 1997; Byrnes & Fox, 1998; Mayer, 1998; Stanovich, 1998). They point out that new synapses continue to develop throughout life as a result of experience (O'Boyle & Gill, 1998). They remind us, too, that people often learn a great deal during adolescence and adulthood, including information and skills in areas they have never previously studied (Brown & Bjorklund, 1998; Fischer & Rose, 1996). And they point out that, to date, we have no evidence to indicate that sensitive periods exist for traditional academic subjects such as reading, writing, or mathematics (Bruer, 1997; Geary, 1998).

It is imperative that we remain optimistic about the cognitive abilities that students can develop *throughout* the elementary and secondary grade levels (Brown & Bjorklund, 1998; Bruer, 1997; Byrnes & Fox, 1998). The experiences we provide for our students *will* make a difference in their lives. Yet we should also remember that such experiences can facilitate change only when students' maturational level also allows such change to occur. The importance of both environment and maturation has been incorporated into a number of developmental theories. Jean Piaget's theory of cognitive development is a case in point.

Piaget's Theory of Cognitive Development

Experiencing Firsthand
Beads, Beings, and Basketballs

Take a moment to solve these three problems:

1. Here are ten wooden beads. Eight are brown and two are white.

   Are there more brown beads or more wooden beads?

2. If all children are human beings,
   And if all human beings are living creatures,
   Then must all children be living creatures?

3. If all children are basketballs,
   And if all basketballs are jellybeans,
   Then must all children be jellybeans?

You undoubtedly found the first problem ridiculously easy; there are, of course, more wooden beads than brown beads. You may have found the second problem a little more difficult but were probably able to conclude fairly quickly that, yes, all children must be living creatures. The third problem is a bit tricky: It follows the same line of reasoning as the second but its conclusion—yes, all children must be jellybeans—contradicts what is true in reality.

In the early 1920s, the Swiss biologist Jean Piaget began studying children's responses to problems similar to these. He found, for instance, that four-year-olds often have difficulty with the "beads" problem—they are likely to say that there are more *brown* beads than wooden beads—but that seven-year-olds almost always answer the question correctly. He found, too, that ten-year-olds have an easier time with logical problems that involve real-world phenomena (e.g., the "human beings" problem) than with problems that involve hypothetical and contrary-to-fact ideas (e.g., the "basketballs" problem); only adolescents can effectively deal with the latter kinds of problems.

Piaget was particularly curious about the origins of knowledge, a branch of philosophy known as *epistemology*. To discover where knowledge comes from and the forms that it takes as it develops, Piaget and his colleagues conducted a series of studies that provide many unique insights about how children think and learn about the world around them (e.g., Inhelder & Piaget, 1958; Piaget, 1928, 1952, 1959, 1970, 1980). Let's explore basic assumptions underlying Piaget's theory and look at the four stages of logical thinking that he proposed.

Have you encountered Piaget's theory in other courses? What do you already know about his theory?

Piaget's Basic Assumptions

Piaget introduced a number of ideas and concepts to describe and explain the changes in logical thinking that he observed in children and adolescents:

• *Children are active and motivated learners.* Piaget believed that children are not just passive receivers of environmental stimulation; instead, they are naturally curious about their world and actively seek out information to help them understand and make sense of it. They continually experiment with the objects they encounter, manipulating things and observing the effects of their actions. For example, when my son

Capitalize on students' natural curiosity.

Alex was a child, he was always fiddling with and manipulating *something.* Some of his "experiments"—such as setting up and maintaining a terrarium in which two lizards could survive and grow—made his mother proud. Others—such as sitting on a kitchen barstool and seeing how far he could lean back on two legs without falling over—drove me absolutely crazy.

• *Children construct knowledge from their experiences.* Children's knowledge is not limited to a collection of isolated pieces of information. Instead, children use the information they accumulate to construct an overall view of how the world operates. For example, through his experiences with lizards and a terrarium, Alex developed an understanding of how aspects of the environment such as food, water, and climate interact to sustain life. Through his experiences on the kitchen barstool, he learned a basic principle of physics: the law of gravity. Because Piaget proposed that children construct their own body of knowledge from their experiences, his theory is sometimes called a **constructivist** theory.

In Piaget's terminology, the things that children learn and can do are organized as **schemes**—groups of similar thoughts or actions. To illustrate, an infant may have a scheme for putting things in her mouth, a scheme that she uses in dealing with a variety of objects, including her thumb, her toys, and her blanket. A seven-year-old may have a scheme for identifying snakes, one that includes their long, thin bodies, their lack of legs, and their slithery nature. A thirteen-year-old may have a scheme for what constitutes *fashion,* allowing her to classify her peers as being either "totally radical" or "complete dorks."

Over time, children's schemes are modified with experience and become increasingly better integrated with one another. For instance, children begin to recognize the hierarchical interrelationships of some schemes—the fact that cats and dogs are all animals, for instance. This progressively more organized body of knowledge allows children to think in increasingly sophisticated and logical ways.

• *Children learn through the two complementary processes of assimilation and accommodation.* Although children's schemes change over time, the processes by which children develop them remain the same. Piaget proposed that learning and cognitive development occur as the result of two complementary processes—assimilation and accommodation. **Assimilation** is a process of dealing with an object or event in a way that is consistent with an existing scheme. For example, the infant may assimilate a new teddy bear into her putting-things-in-the-mouth scheme. The seven-year-old may quickly identify a new slithery object in the backyard as another snake. The thirteen-year-old may readily label a new classmate as being either radical or dorkish.

But sometimes children cannot easily interpret a new object or event in terms of their existing schemes. In these situations, one of two forms of **accommodation** will occur: They will either modify an existing scheme to account for the new object or event or form an entirely new scheme to deal with it. For example, the infant may have to open her mouth wider than usual to accommodate a teddy bear's fat paw. The thirteen-year-old may have to revise her existing scheme of fashion according to changes in what's hot and what's not. The seven-year-old may find a long, thin, slithery thing that can't possibly be a snake because it has four legs. After some research, the child develops a new scheme—*salamander*—for this creature.

Assimilation and accommodation typically work hand in hand as children develop their knowledge and understanding of the world. Children interpret each new event within the context of their existing knowledge (assimilation) but at the same time may modify their knowledge as a result of the new event (accommodation). Accommodation rarely happens without assimilation: Our students can only benefit from (accommodate to) new experiences when they can relate those experiences to their current knowledge and beliefs.

Provide experiences to help students construct an increasingly more accurate and complete understanding of the world.

Help students assimilate new material into existing schemes by tying it to things they have already learned.

Encourage accommodation by providing information that students cannot totally assimilate into existing schemes.

• *Interaction with one's physical and social environments is essential for cognitive development.* New experiences are essential for learning and cognitive development to occur. For this reason, Piaget stressed the importance of allowing children to interact with their physical environment. By manipulating the environment—for example, by playing with sand and water, measuring things, practicing with footballs and basketballs, or experimenting in a science lab—children can develop an understanding of cause-effect relationships, the nature of physical characteristics such as weight and volume, and so on.

Social interaction is equally critical for cognitive development. Through interaction with other people, children begin to realize that different individuals see things differently and that their own view of the world is not necessarily a completely accurate or logical one. To illustrate, a preschool child may have difficulty seeing the world from anyone's perspective but his own. Through social interactions, both pleasant (e.g., a conversation) and unpleasant (e.g., an argument), he begins to realize that his own perspective is a unique one not shared by others. Similarly, an elementary school child may recognize the logical inconsistencies in what she says and does only after someone else points them out. And through discussions with classmates or adults about social and political issues, a high school student may modify some initially abstract and idealistic notions about how the world *should* be to reflect the constraints that the real world imposes.

• *The process of equilibration promotes progression toward increasingly more complex levels of thought.* According to Piaget, children are sometimes in a state of **equilibrium**—they can comfortably explain new events in terms of existing schemes. But this equilibrium doesn't continue indefinitely. As children grow, they often encounter events they cannot adequately explain in terms of their current understanding of the world. Such inexplicable events create **disequilibrium,** a sort of mental discomfort. Only through replacing, reorganizing, or better integrating their schemes (in other words, through accommodation) do children become able to understand and

Provide hands-on experiences with physical objects. Allow and encourage students to explore and manipulate things.

Provide opportunities for children to discuss and exchange ideas and perspectives.

Students benefit from exploring and manipulating physical objects.

explain those previously puzzling events. The movement from equilibrium to disequilibrium and back to equilibrium again is known as **equilibration.** Equilibration and children's need to achieve equilibrium promote the development of more complex levels of thought and knowledge.

To illustrate the process of equilibration, let's return to the "beads" problem I gave you earlier. Imagine that we show the ten wooden beads (eight brown and two white) to four-year-old Abby and ask her, "Are there more brown beads or more wooden beads?" Abby tells us that there are more brown beads and seems quite comfortable with this response; in other words, she is in equilibrium. So we ask her to count the brown beads (she counts eight of them) and then to count the wooden beads (she counts ten). "So then, Abby," we say, "there are *eight* brown beads and *ten* wooden beads. Are there more brown beads or more wooden beads?" If Abby can recognize the inconsistency in her reasoning—that eight cannot possibly be more than ten—she will experience disequilibrium. At this point, she may reorganize her thinking to accommodate the idea that some beads are simultaneously both brown and wooden and so should be included in both categories at the same time.

• *Cognitive development can proceed only after certain genetically controlled neurological changes occur.* According to Piaget, cognitive development depends to some degree on maturation of the brain. Piaget believed that, because of their neurological immaturity, elementary school children cannot think as adults do, no matter what parents or teachers might do to encourage adultlike thinking. Preschoolers are even less neurologically mature and so are further limited in their cognitive abilities. Piaget proposed that major physiological changes take place when children are about two years old, again when they are six or seven, and again around puberty, and that these changes allow the development of increasingly more complex thought. We should note that psychologists disagree about the extent to which such neurological changes actually occur (H. Epstein, 1978; R. W. Marsh, 1985; Rosser, 1994).

Provide information and experiences that contradict students' existing beliefs.

Piaget's Stages of Cognitive Development

A major feature of Piaget's theory is his description of four stages of logical reasoning capabilities:

1. Sensorimotor stage (birth until 2 years)
2. Preoperational stage (2 years until 6 or 7 years)
3. Concrete operations stage (6 or 7 years until 11 or 12 years)
4. Formal operations stage (11 or 12 years through adulthood)

These stages are briefly summarized in Figure 2–1. Each stage has its own unique characteristics and capabilities, and each builds upon the accomplishments of former stages, so children must progress through the four stages in the same invariant sequence.

For reasons described later, many psychologists question whether cognitive development is as stagelike as Piaget proposed. Nevertheless, Piaget's stages do provide insights into the nature of children's thinking at different age levels, and so it is helpful to examine the characteristics associated with each one. Note that the ages associated with each stage are *averages*; some children may reach a stage at a slightly younger age than average, and others may reach it at an older age. Also, some children may be *transitional* from one stage to the next and so may display characteristics of two adjacent stages during the same time period.

Sensorimotor Stage (birth until 2 years)

Imagine that we show a colorful stuffed clown to six-month-old Karen. Karen reaches for it in much the same way that she reaches for her teddy bear and her stacking blocks; in other words, she has a reaching-and-grasping scheme with which she assimilates this new object. Karen then drops the clown and watches it fall to the floor, applying her letting-go and visually-following-a-moving-object schemes in the process. Now imagine that we put Karen's clown inside a box so that she can no longer see it. Karen seems to forget the clown and turns to play with something else, acting as if she cannot think about a clown that she cannot actually see.

Piaget proposed that children in the **sensorimotor stage** develop schemes based primarily on behaviors and perceptions. They are not yet capable of *mental* schemes that enable them to think about objects beyond their immediate view, partly because they have few if any words they can use to represent mentally the things they cannot see.

Nevertheless, important cognitive capabilities emerge during the sensorimotor stage, especially as children begin to experiment with their environments in a trial-and-error fashion. For example, during the latter part of the stage, children develop **object permanence,** the realization that objects continue to exist even when they are removed from view. And after repeatedly observing that certain actions lead to certain consequences, they begin to develop an understanding of *cause-effect relationships.* Such ideas as object permanence and cause-and-effect are basic building blocks on which later cognitive development depends.

Preoperational Stage (2 years until 6 or 7 years)

Children who show preoperational thought can form schemes that are relatively independent of immediate perceptions and behaviors. For example, as Karen reaches the **preoperational stage,** she will be able to think about a clown without having one directly in front of her. This ability to represent external objects and events in one's head **(symbolic thinking)** marks the beginning of true thought as Piaget defined it.

Language skills virtually explode during the early part of the preoperational stage. The words in children's rapidly increasing vocabularies provide labels for newly developed schemes and serve as symbols that enable them to think about objects and events even when such things are not directly in sight. Language also provides the basis for a new form of social interaction—verbal communication. Children can now express their thoughts and receive information from other people in a way that was previously not possible.

At the same time, preoperational thinking has some definite weaknesses, especially as we compare it with concrete operational thinking (see Table 2–1). For example, children in this stage exhibit **preoperational egocentrism,** an inability to view situations from another person's perspective. They may have trouble understanding why they must share school supplies with a classmate or why they must be careful not to hurt someone else's feelings. They may play games together without ever checking to be sure they are all playing according to the same rules. They may also exhibit **egocentric speech,** saying things without really considering the perspective of the listener; for example, they may leave out critical details of a story, giving a fragmented version that their listener cannot possibly understand.

Preoperational thinking is also illogical (at least from an adult's point of view), especially during the preschool years. For instance, you may recall Abby's insistence that there were more brown beads than wooden beads in a collection of ten wooden beads

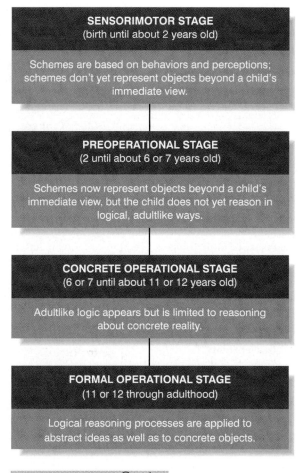

SENSORIMOTOR STAGE
(birth until about 2 years old)

Schemes are based on behaviors and perceptions; schemes don't yet represent objects beyond a child's immediate view.

PREOPERATIONAL STAGE
(2 until about 6 or 7 years old)

Schemes now represent objects beyond a child's immediate view, but the child does not yet reason in logical, adultlike ways.

CONCRETE OPERATIONAL STAGE
(6 or 7 until about 11 or 12 years old)

Adultlike logic appears but is limited to reasoning about concrete reality.

FORMAL OPERATIONAL STAGE
(11 or 12 through adulthood)

Logical reasoning processes are applied to abstract ideas as well as to concrete objects.

FIGURE 2.1
Piaget's stages of cognitive development

To help young students shed their preoperational egocentrism, ask them to present their perspectives to one another and to you, and express your confusion when they do not explain themselves clearly.

TABLE 2.1

Preoperational Versus Concrete Operational Thought

PREOPERATIONAL THOUGHT	CONCRETE OPERATIONAL THOUGHT
Preoperational Egocentrism Students do not see things from someone else's perspective; they think their own perspective is the only one possible. *Example:* A student tells a story without considering what prior knowledge the listener is likely to have.	**Differentiation of One's Own Perspective from the Perspectives of Others** Students recognize that others see things differently than they do; they realize that their own perspective may be incorrect. *Example:* A student asks for validation of his own thoughts (e.g., "Did I get that right?").
Lack of Conservation Students believe that amount changes when a substance is reshaped or rearranged, even though nothing has been added or taken away. *Example:* A student asserts that two rows of five pennies similarly spaced have equal amounts; but when one row is spread out so that it is longer than the other, she says that it has more pennies.	**Conservation** Students recognize that amount stays the same if nothing has been added or taken away, even if the substance is reshaped or rearranged. *Example:* A student asserts that two rows of five pennies are the same number of pennies regardless of their spacing.
Irreversibility Students don't recognize that certain processes can be undone, or reversed. *Example:* A student doesn't realize that a row of five pennies made longer can be shortened back to its original length; the student also treats addition and subtraction as two unrelated processes.	**Reversibility** Students understand that certain processes can be reversed. *Example:* A student moves the five pennies in the longer row close together again to demonstrate that both rows have the same amount; she also recognizes that subtraction is the reverse of addition.
Inability to Reason About Transformations Students focus on static situations; they have difficulty thinking about change processes. *Example:* A student refuses to believe that a caterpillar can turn into a butterfly, instead insisting that the caterpillar crawls away and the butterfly comes to replace it (K. R. Harris, 1986).	**Ability to Reason About Transformations** Students can reason about change and its effects. *Example:* A student understands that metamorphosis is the process whereby a caterpillar becomes a butterfly.
Single Classification Students are able to classify objects in only one way at any given point in time. *Example:* A student denies that a mother can also be a doctor.	**Multiple Classification** Students recognize that objects may belong to several categories simultaneously. *Example:* A student acknowledges that a mother can also be a doctor, a jogger, and a spouse.
Transductive Reasoning Students reason by combining unrelated facts; for instance, they infer a cause-effect relationship simply because the events occur close together in time and space. *Example:* A student believes that clouds make the moon grow.	**Deductive Reasoning** Students can draw a logical inference from two or more pieces of information. *Example:* A student deduces that if all children are human beings and if all human beings are living things, then all children must be living things.

(her error reflects single classification, described in Table 2–1). Here is another example of what we might see:

> We show five-year-old Nathan the three glasses in Figure 2–2. Glasses A and B are identical in size and shape and contain an equal amount of water. We ask Nathan whether the two glasses of water contain the same amount, and he replies confidently that they do. We then pour the water from Glass B into Glass C. We ask him whether the two glasses of water (A and C) have the same amount. Nathan replies, "No, that glass [pointing to Glass A] has more because it's taller."

Nathan's response illustrates lack of **conservation:** He does not realize that because no water has been added or taken away, the amount of water in the two glasses must be equivalent. Young children such as Nathan often confuse changes in appearance with changes in amount.

As children approach the later part of the preoperational stage, perhaps at around four or five years of age, they show early signs of being logical. For example, they sometimes draw correct conclusions about conservation problems (e.g., the water glasses) or multiple classification problems (e.g., the wooden beads). They cannot yet explain *why* their conclusions are correct, however; they base their conclusions on hunches and intuition, rather than on any conscious awareness of underlying logical principles. When children move into the concrete operations stage, they become increasingly able both to make logical inferences and to explain the reasoning behind their conclusions.

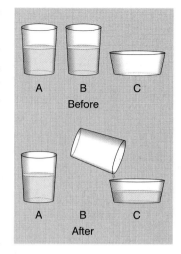

F I G U R E 2.2
Conservation of liquid: Do Glasses A and C contain the same amount of water?

Concrete Operations Stage (6 or 7 years until 11 or 12 years)

Piaget proposed that children's thought processes gradually become organized and integrated with one another into larger systems of mental processes. These systems, which Piaget called **operations,** allow children to pull their thoughts together in ways that make sense and, therefore, to think logically. Such integrated and coordinated thought emerges at the beginning of the **concrete operations stage.**

Concrete operational thought differs from preoperational thought in a number of ways (see Table 2–1). For example, students now realize that their own thoughts and feelings are not necessarily shared by others and may reflect personal opinions rather than reality. As a result, they know that they can sometimes be wrong and begin to seek out external validation for their ideas.

Students in the concrete operations stage are capable of many forms of logical thought. For one thing, they show conservation: They readily understand that amount stays the same, despite changes in shape or arrangement, if nothing is added or taken away. They also exhibit **multiple classification:** They can readily classify objects into two or more categories simultaneously. And they demonstrate **deductive reasoning:** They can draw logical inferences from the facts they are given.

Children continue to develop their newly acquired logical thinking capabilities during the elementary school years. For instance, they become capable of dealing with increasingly more complex conservation tasks. Some forms of conservation, such as conservation of liquid and conservation of number (illustrated by the "pennies" problem in Table 2–1), appear at six or seven years of age, but other forms may not appear until several years later. Consider the task involving conservation of weight in Figure 2–3. Using a balance scale, an adult shows a child that two balls of clay have the same weight. One ball is removed from the scale and smashed into a pancake shape. Does the pancake weigh the same as the unsmashed ball, or do the two pieces of clay weigh different amounts? Children typically do not achieve conservation of weight—that is, they do not realize that the flattened pancake weighs the same as the round ball it was earlier—until sometime around age nine to twelve (Sund, 1976).

Although students displaying concrete operational thought show many signs of logical thinking, their cognitive development is not yet complete (see Table 2–2). For one

Begin to explore hierarchical relationships in the early elementary grades. For example, examine the various levels of classification that biologists use to describe plant and animal life.

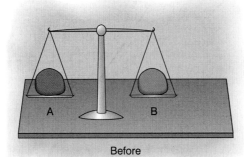
Before

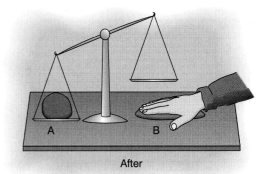
After

FIGURE 2.3

Conservation of weight: Ball A and Ball B initially weigh the same amount. When Ball B is flattened into a pancake shape, how does its weight now compare with that of Ball A?

TABLE 2.2

COMPARE/CONTRAST

Concrete Operational Versus Formal Operational Thought

CONCRETE OPERATIONAL THOUGHT	FORMAL OPERATIONAL THOUGHT
Dependence on Concrete Reality Students can reason logically about concrete objects they can observe; they are unable to reason about abstract, hypothetical, or contrary-to-fact ideas. *Example:* A student has difficulty with the concept of negative numbers, wondering how something can possibly be less than zero.	**Ability to Reason About Abstract, Hypothetical, and Contrary-to-Fact Ideas** Students can reason about things that are not tied directly to concrete, observable reality. *Example:* A student understands negative numbers and is able to use them effectively in mathematical procedures.
Inability to Formulate and Test Multiple Hypotheses When seeking an explanation for a scientific phenomenon, students identify and test only one hypothesis. *Example:* When asked what makes a pendulum swing faster or more slowly, a student says that the weight of the pendulum is the determining factor.	**Formulation and Testing of Multiple Hypotheses** Students seeking an explanation for a scientific phenomenon formulate and test several hypotheses about possible cause-effect relationships. *Example:* When asked what makes a pendulum swing faster or more slowly, a student says that weight, length, and strength of the initial push are all possible explanations.
Inability to Separate and Control Variables When attempting to confirm or disconfirm a particular hypothesis about cause-effect relationships, students test (and thereby confound) more than one variable simultaneously. *Example:* In testing possible factors influencing the oscillation rate of a pendulum, a student adds more weight to the pendulum while at the same time also shortening the length of the pendulum.	**Separation and Control of Variables** When attempting to confirm or disconfirm a particular hypothesis, students test one variable at a time while holding all other variables constant. *Example:* In testing factors that influence the rate of oscillation, a student tests the effect of weight while keeping length and strength of push constant; the student then tests the effect of length while keeping weight and push constant.
Lack of Proportional Reasoning Students do not understand the nature of proportions. *Example:* A student does not understand the relationship between fractions and decimals.	**Proportional Reasoning** Students understand proportions and can use them effectively in mathematical problem solving. *Example:* A student works easily with proportions, fractions, decimals, and ratios.

thing, they have trouble understanding and reasoning about abstract and contrary-to-fact ideas. They also have difficulty handling problems that require them to consider many hypotheses or variables simultaneously.

Formal Operations Stage (11 or 12 years through adulthood)

Consider the following situation:

> Julie and Joséfa are working together on an assignment on World War II for their high school history class. Julie is puzzled as she reads the assignment:
>
> *Given what you know about the strengths and weaknesses of the Allied Forces and the Axis countries in 1941, how might the war have ended if the Japanese had not bombed Pearl Harbor?*
>
> "I don't get it," Julie says.
>
> "What don't you get?" Joséfa asks her.
>
> "I don't understand what we're supposed to do."
>
> "Well, we're supposed to speculate on what would have happened if Pearl Harbor hadn't been bombed. For example, maybe the United States wouldn't have joined the Allied Forces. Maybe the Axis powers would have won the war. Maybe all of Europe would be Fascist right now."
>
> Julie just shakes her head. "I still don't understand this assignment. After all, the Japanese *did* bomb Pearl Harbor. And because of that action, the United States joined the Allied Forces. How can we pretend these things didn't happen?"

Julie's thinking is concrete operational: She is unable to speculate about what might have happened if the Japanese had not bombed Pearl Harbor, when in fact the Japanese *did* bomb Pearl Harbor. Yet Joséfa has no difficulty with the same task. Like Joséfa, students who display the **formal operations stage** can think about concepts that have little or no basis in concrete reality—concepts that are abstract, hypothetical, or contrary-to-fact. Furthermore, they recognize that what is logically valid is different from what is true in the real world; for example, if all children are basketballs, and if all basketballs are jellybeans, then all children must be jellybeans, even though children really *aren't* jellybeans. Several abilities essential for sophisticated scientific and mathematical reasoning—formulating and testing multiple hypotheses, separating and controlling variables, and proportional reasoning—also emerge in formal operations (see Table 2–2).

Let's consider how students' capabilities in mathematics are likely to improve once formal operational thinking develops. Abstract problems, such as mathematical word problems, should become easier to solve. Students should become capable of understanding such concepts as *negative number, pi* (π), and *infinity*; for instance, they should now comprehend how temperature can be below zero and how two parallel lines will never touch even if they go on forever. And because they can now use proportions in their reasoning, they can study and understand fractions, ratios, and decimals, and they can use such proportions to solve problems.

Try the following exercise as an illustration of proportional reasoning.

During the elementary years, focus on concrete objects and events. At the secondary level, increase discussion of abstract concepts and hypothetical ideas but avoid strictly abstract methods of presenting information (e.g., entirely verbal lectures) until students show signs of abstract reasoning.

Experiencing Firsthand
Thinking About Proportions

Mr. Little and Mr. Big are two men from the planet Xeron. People on Xeron don't use centimeters or inches to measure things; instead, they use a unit of measurement called a "greenie." Mr. Little is **4** greenies tall. Mr. Big is **7** greenies tall.

One day, the two men travel to the planet Phylus. Phylus has a different unit of measurement—the "reddie." Mr. Little is **10** reddies tall. Figure out how tall Mr. Big is in reddies. (Adapted from Ormrod & Carter, 1985).

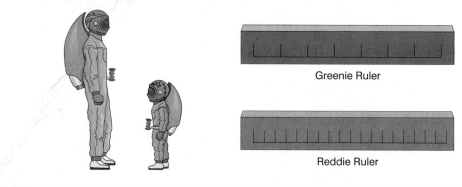

Greenie Ruler

Reddie Ruler

The proportions of the two men's heights in greenies and in reddies should be the same. If we think of Mr. Big's height as *x,* then:

$$\frac{4 \text{ greenies (Mr. Little)}}{7 \text{ greenies (Mr. Big)}} = \frac{10 \text{ reddies (Mr. Little)}}{x \text{ reddies (Mr. Big)}}$$

Solving for x, we find that Mr. Big is 17½ reddies tall.

Because proportional reasoning typically does not appear until students are eleven or twelve at the earliest (Schliemann & Carraher, 1993; Tourniaire & Pulos, 1985), extensive work with fractions in elementary school may be premature. For example, my daughter Tina began working with complicated fraction problems, such as adding and subtracting fractions with different denominators, in the fourth grade. She learned the correct procedures for adding and subtracting fractions, but she had absolutely no understanding of what she was doing; in a sense, she was just going through the motions. Before proportional reasoning emerges, students may not be cognitively ready to comprehend the reasons underlying the procedures they learn for dealing with fractions and decimals.

Scientific reasoning is also likely to improve once students are capable of formal operational thought. Three formal operational abilities—reasoning logically about hypothetical ideas, formulating and testing hypotheses, and separating and controlling variables—together allow formal operations individuals to use a *scientific method,* in which several possible explanations for an observed phenomenon are proposed and tested in a systematic manner. As an example, consider the pendulum problem in the exercise that follows.

Experiencing Firsthand
Pendulum Problem

An object suspended by a rope or string—a pendulum—swings indefinitely at a constant rate (a playground swing and the pendulum of a grandfather clock are two everyday examples). Some pendulums swing back and forth rather slowly, whereas others swing more quickly. What characteristics of a pendulum determine how fast it swings? Write down at least three hypotheses as to what variable or variables might affect a pendulum's rate of swing (i.e., oscillation rate).

Now gather several small, heavy objects (an eraser, a bolt, and a fishing sinker are three possibilities) and a piece of string. Tie one of the objects to one end of the string and set your pendulum in motion. Conduct one or more experiments to test each of your hypotheses.

What can you conclude? What variable or variables affect the rate with which a pendulum swings?

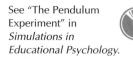

Hold off on problems involving fractions, ratios, and decimals until students show some capability for proportional reasoning.

See "The Pendulum Experiment" in *Simulations in Educational Psychology.*

As adolescents become increasingly able to reason about abstract, hypothetical, and contrary-to-fact ideas, they also become increasingly idealistic about how the world should be.

What hypotheses did you generate? Four possible variables you might have considered are the weight of the object at the bottom, the length of the string, the force with which the pendulum is pushed, and the height from which the object is first dropped; you may have formed additional hypotheses as well.

Did you then test each hypothesis in a systematic fashion? A student capable of formal operational thinking *separates and controls variables,* testing one at a time while holding all others constant. For example, if you were testing the hypothesis that weight makes a difference, you might have tried objects of different weights while keeping constant the length of the string, the force with which you pushed each object, and the height from which you dropped it. Similarly, if you hypothesized that the length of the string was a critical factor, you might have varied the length of the string while continuing to use the same object and starting the pendulum in motion in the same manner. If you carefully separated and controlled each variable, then you would have come to the correct conclusion: Only length affects a pendulum's oscillation rate.

Because individuals capable of formal operational reasoning can deal with hypothetical and contrary-to-fact ideas, they can envision how the world might be different from—and possibly better than—the way it actually is. As a result, they may exhibit some idealism about social, political, ethical, or religious issues. Many secondary school students begin to show concern about world problems and to devote energy to worthy causes such as the environment or world hunger; we should note, however, that their devotion is usually evident more in their talk than in their actions (Elkind, 1984).

Idealistic adolescents often present recommendations for change that seem logical but that may not be practical in today's world. For example, they may argue that racism would disappear overnight if people would only just begin to love one another, or that a nation should eliminate its armed forces and weapons as a way of moving toward world peace. Piaget suggested that adolescent idealism reflects **formal operational egocentrism**—in this case, an inability to separate abstract logical thinking from practical considerations and the unpredictability of human behavior. Only through experience do adolescents eventually begin to temper their optimism with some realism about what is possible in a given time frame and with limited resources.

Recall our earlier discussion of the importance of separating and controlling variables in experimental research (Chapter 1).

Encourage adolescents to discuss "ideal" situations, but point out instances when their ideals are unrealistic.

In your own words, can you summarize the characteristics of each of Piaget's four stages?

Current Perspectives on Piaget's Theory

Piaget's theory has sparked a great deal of research about children's cognitive development. In general, this research supports Piaget's proposed *sequence* in which different abilities emerge (Flavell, 1996; Siegler & Richards, 1982). For example, the ability to reason about abstract ideas emerges only after children are already capable of reasoning about concrete objects and events. And the order in which various conservation tasks are mastered is much as Piaget proposed. Researchers are beginning to question the *ages* at which various abilities actually appear, however. They are also finding that students' logical reasoning capabilities may vary considerably, depending on their previous knowledge and experiences related to the topic at hand.

Capabilities of Preschool Children

Preschool children are apparently more competent than Piaget's description of the preoperational stage would indicate. Children as young as three or four years old are not completely egocentric. In many situations, preschoolers *can* take another individual's perspective; for example, they can often identify such emotions as sadness or anger in others (Lennon, Eisenberg, & Carroll, 1983; Newcombe & Huttenlocher, 1992). Children at this age can also draw logical deductions; for instance, they frequently make inferences when they listen to stories (Donaldson, 1978; Gelman & Baillargeon, 1983). Children as young as four sometimes show conservation; for example, they are more likely to answer a conservation problem correctly if the transformation occurs out of sight so that they are not misled by appearances (Donaldson, 1978; Rosser, 1994; Siegel & Hodkin, 1982). And many supposedly preoperational children can correctly solve multiple classification problems if words are used to draw attention to the entire group; for example, many four- and five-year-olds realize that, in a *forest* of eight pine trees and two oak trees, there must of course be more trees than pine trees (Gelman & Baillargeon, 1983; Resnick, 1989; Rosser, 1994).

🍎 Expect some aspects of concrete operational thought in preschool children.

Capabilities of Elementary School Children

Piaget may also have underestimated the capabilities of elementary school students. For example, many elementary students occasionally show evidence of abstract and hypothetical thought (S. Carey, 1985b; Metz, 1995). Consider this hypothetical (and therefore formal operational) situation:

> All of Joan's friends are going to the museum today.
> Pat is a friend of Joan.

Children as young as nine can correctly deduce that "Pat is going to the museum today" even though the situation involves people they don't know and so has no basis in their own concrete reality (Roberge, 1970). Also, some older elementary school children are able to separate and control variables, especially when they are given hints about the importance of controlling all variables except the one they are testing (Danner & Day, 1977; Metz, 1995).

🍎 Begin to present tasks requiring formal operational thought in the later elementary years.

Capabilities of Adolescents

Consider again our opening case study in which Mr. Sand's high school geography students had trouble understanding an abstract college textbook. Formal operational thought processes probably appear later and more gradually than Piaget originally proposed. High school and college students often have difficulty with tasks involving formal operational thinking (Karplus, Pulos, & Stage, 1983; Pascarella & Terenzini, 1991; Siegler & Richards, 1982). Furthermore, students may demonstrate formal operational thought in one content domain while thinking more concretely in another. Evidence of formal operations typically emerges in the physical sciences earlier than in such subjects

🍎 Throughout the high school years, continue relating abstract and hypothetical ideas to concrete objects and observable events.

FIGURE 2.4

What are some possible reasons that Herb is catching more fish than the others?
Based on Pulos & Linn, 1981.

as history and geography; students often have difficulty thinking about abstract and hypothetical ideas in history and geography until well into the high school years (Lovell, 1979; Tamburrini, 1982).

Effects of Prior Knowledge and Experience

It is becoming increasingly apparent that the ability to think logically depends greatly on a student's knowledge and background experiences. Preschoolers are less likely to exhibit transductive reasoning—for example, saying that clouds make the moon "grow"—when they have accurate information about cause-effect relationships (S. Carey, 1985a). Four-year-olds begin to show conservation after having experience with conservation tasks, especially if they can actively manipulate the materials in question and discuss their reasoning with someone who already exhibits conservation (Field, 1987; Mayer, 1992). Ten-year-olds can learn to solve logical problems involving hypothetical ideas if they are taught relevant problem-solving strategies (Lee, 1985). Junior high and high school students, and adults as well, often apply formal operational thought to topics about which they have a great deal of knowledge and yet think concretely about topics with which they are unfamiliar (Girotto & Light, 1993; M. C. Linn, Clement, Pulos, & Sullivan, 1989; Schliemann & Carraher, 1993). In the opening case study, Mr. Sand's students probably had had little if any prior experience studying economics and so, quite understandably, had trouble making sense of *primary, secondary, tertiary,* and *quarternary activities*—all very abstract concepts indeed.

As an illustration of how knowledge affects formal operational thinking, consider the fishing pond in Figure 2–4. In a study by Pulos and Linn (1981), thirteen-year-old students were shown a similar picture and told, "These four children go fishing every week, and one child, Herb, always catches the most fish. The other children wonder

Make sure students
have sufficient knowledge
about a topic to think
logically about it.

why." If you look at the picture, it is obvious that Herb differs from the other children in several ways, including the kind of bait he uses, the length of his fishing rod, and his position by the pond. Students who were avid fishermen more effectively separated and controlled variables for this situation than they did for the pendulum problem described earlier, whereas the reverse was true for nonfishermen (Pulos & Linn, 1981).

Piaget Reconsidered

Can cognitive development truly be characterized as a series of stages? Some contemporary theorists have proposed stage theories that may more adequately account for current findings about children's logical thinking (Case, 1992; Fischer & Bidell, 1991; Fischer & Farrar, 1987). But many others now believe that cognitive development can better be described in terms of gradual *trends* than in terms of specific, discrete stages; they also believe that the nature of cognitive development may be somewhat specific to different contexts and content areas (Flavell et al., 1993; Rosser, 1994; Siegler & Ellis, 1996). Later in the chapter, when we consider information processing theory, we will identify several general developmental trends in children's ability to think and learn in the classroom.

Yet many of Piaget's basic assumptions—for instance, his beliefs that children construct their own understandings of the world, that they must relate new experiences to what they already know, and that they can most effectively learn when they interact with their physical and social environments—are ideas that have stood the test of time. And the many tasks that Piaget developed to study children's reasoning abilities (tasks dealing with conservation, classification, separation and control of variables, etc.) can give us valuable insights about the "logic" that our students use when they think about their world.

In the 1920s and 1930s, while Piaget was working in Switzerland, Russian psychologist Lev Vygotsky was also conducting research to describe and explain children's cognitive development. Vygotsky's theory is quite different from Piaget's, and yet it, too, gives us many valuable insights about how children's thinking skills develop over time.

INTO THE CLASSROOM: Applying Piaget's Theory

Provide hands-on experiences with physical objects, especially when working with elementary school students. Allow and encourage students to explore and manipulate things.

> A kindergarten teacher and his students work with small objects (e.g., blocks, buttons, pennies) to explore such basic elements of arithmetic as conservation of number and the reversibility of addition and subtraction.

Ask students to explain their reasoning, and challenge illogical explanations.

> When learning about pendulums, students in a ninth-grade science class experiment with three variables (weight, length, and height from which the pendulum is first dropped) to see which variables determine the rate at which a pendulum swings. When a student asserts that weight affects oscillation rate, his teacher points out that he has simultaneously varied both weight and length in his experiment.

When students show signs of egocentric thought, express confusion or explain that others think differently.

> A first grader asks, "What's this?" about an object that is out of the teacher's view. The teacher responds, "What's *what*? I can't see the object you're looking at."

Be sure students have certain capabilities for mathematical and scientific reasoning (e.g., conservation of number, reversibility, proportional reasoning, separation and control of variables) before requiring them to perform tasks that depend on these capabilities.

In a unit on fractions in a seventh-grade math class, students express confusion about why ⅔, ⁴⁄₆, and ⁸⁄₁₂ are all equivalent. Before beginning a lesson about how to add and subtract fractions with different denominators—processes that require an understanding of such equivalencies—their teacher uses concrete objects (e.g., sliced pizza pies, plastic rods that can be broken into small segments) to help students understand how two different fractions can be equal.

Relate abstract and hypothetical ideas to concrete objects and observable events.

An eighth-grade science teacher illustrates the idea that heavy and light objects fall at the same speed by having students drop objects of various weights from a second-story window.

Vygotsky's Theory of Cognitive Development

Vygotsky conducted numerous studies of children's thinking from the 1920s until his premature death from tuberculosis in 1934. Western psychologists did not fully appreciate the value and usefulness of his work until several decades later, when his major writings were translated into English (e.g., Vygotsky, 1962, 1978, 1987, 1997). Although Vygotsky never had the chance to develop his theory fully, his ideas are clearly evident in our views of learning and instruction today.

Vygotsky's Basic Assumptions

As you should recall, Piaget proposed that, through assimilation and accommodation, children develop increasingly more advanced and integrated schemes over time. In Piaget's view, cognitive development is largely an individual enterprise; growing children, it seems, do most of the mental work themselves.

In contrast, Vygotsky believed that the adults in a society foster children's cognitive development in an intentional and somewhat systematic manner. They continually engage children in meaningful and challenging activities and help them perform those activities successfully. Because Vygotsky emphasized the importance of society and culture for promoting cognitive growth, his theory is sometimes referred to as the **sociocultural perspective.** We can summarize this perspective in terms of several major assumptions:

- *Complex mental processes begin as social activities; as children develop, they gradually internalize these processes and begin to use them independently.* Vygotsky believed that many thinking processes have their roots in social interactions. Children first talk about objects and events with adults and other knowledgeable individuals; in the process, they discover how the people around them think about those objects and events. As an example, consider our opening case study, "Economic Activities." When Mr. Sand discovers that his students are having difficulty understanding their geography text, he engages the class in a discussion of how new concepts relate to things they already know—a strategy that should help the students read difficult text more effectively in the future. (Unfortunately, he does so fairly late in the game, after his students have experienced considerable frustration with the assignment.)

Show students how you think as you deal with academic tasks.

In Vygotsky's view, dialogue with others is an essential condition for promoting cognitive development. Gradually, children incorporate the ways that adults and others talk about and interpret the world into their own ways of thinking. The process through which social activities evolve into internal mental activities is called **internalization.**

Not all mental processes emerge through children's interactions with adults, however; some also develop as they interact with their peers. As an example, children frequently argue with one another about a variety of matters—how best to carry out an activity, what games to play, who did what to whom, and so on. According to Vygotsky, childhood arguments help children discover that there are often several points of view about the same situation. Eventually, children can, in essence, internalize the "arguing" process, developing the ability to look at a situation from several different angles *on their own.*

• *Thought and language initially develop independently of each other; the two become interdependent when children are about two years old.* For us as adults, thought and language are closely interconnected. We often think in terms of the specific words that our language provides; for example, when we think about household pets, our thoughts contain words such as *dog* and *cat.* In addition, we usually express our thoughts when we converse with others; as we sometimes like to put it, we "speak our minds."

But Vygotsky proposed that thought and language are separate functions for infants and young toddlers. In these early years, thinking occurs independently of language, and when language appears, it is first used primarily as a means of communication rather than as a mechanism of thought. But sometime around age two, thought and language become intertwined: Children begin to express their thoughts when they speak, and they begin to think in terms of words.

When thought and language merge, we begin to see **self-talk**[1] (whereby children talk to themselves out loud) and eventually **inner speech** (whereby children "talk" to themselves mentally rather than orally). Remember Piaget's observation that young children often say things without taking into account the listener's perspective. Vygotsky proposed that such egocentric speech is better understood as "talking to oneself," rather than as talking to someone else. He pointed out that people are more likely to talk to themselves when they are performing difficult or frustrating tasks. Talking aloud seems to help guide and direct them as they attempt to perform such tasks.

According to Vygotsky, both self-talk and inner speech have a similar purpose: By talking to themselves, children learn to guide and direct their own behaviors through difficult tasks and complex maneuvers in much the same way that adults have previously guided them (also see Berk, 1994; Schimmoeller, 1998). Self-talk and inner speech, then, are examples of the internalization process: Children gradually internalize the directions that they have initially received from those around them, so that they are eventually giving *themselves* directions.

Encourage students to talk themselves through new and difficult tasks.

THINKING ABOUT WHAT YOU KNOW

Can you think of times when you talk to yourself? For example, have you found it easier to perform a difficult task by talking your way through it—perhaps when you were first learning to use a computer, trying to perform a complicated dance step, or beginning to drive a car with a clutch and a stick shift?

• *Through both informal conversations and formal schooling, adults convey to children the ways in which their culture interprets the world.* Let's return again to Mr.

---

[1]This is sometimes called *private speech.*

Sand's classroom. The economics textbook passage describes four kinds of economic activities: primary, secondary, tertiary, and quarternary. By presenting these four concepts, it shows the students how geographers conceptualize and categorize (i.e., how they think about) economic activities. More generally, adults share with children the *language* of their culture, including the specific concepts and terminology used in various academic disciplines (Vygotsky, 1962). Although Vygotsky, like Piaget, saw value in allowing children to make some discoveries themselves, he also saw value in having adults describe the discoveries of previous generations (Karpov & Haywood, 1998).

• *Children can perform more challenging tasks when assisted by more advanced and competent individuals.* Vygotsky distinguished between two kinds of abilities that children are likely to have at any particular point in their development. A child's **actual developmental level** is the extent to which he or she can perform tasks independently, without help from anyone else. A child's **level of potential development** is the extent to which he or she can perform tasks with the assistance of a more competent individual.

Children can typically do more difficult things in collaboration with adults than they can do on their own. For example, children just learning to hit a baseball are often more successful when adults guide their swing. Children can play more difficult piano pieces when adults help them locate some of the notes on the keyboard. And notice how a student who cannot independently solve division problems with remainders begins to learn the correct procedure through an interaction with her teacher:

The teacher writes the division problem $6\overline{)44}$ on the board.

Teacher: 44 divided by 6. What number times 6 is close to 44?

Child: 6.

Teacher: *(Writes 6.)* What's 6 times 6?

Child: 36.

Teacher: *(Erasing the 6)* 36. Can you think of one that's any closer?

Child: 8.

Teacher: What's 6 times 8?

Child: 64 . . . 48.

Teacher: 48. Too big. Can you think of something . . .

Child: 6 times 7 is 42. (adapted from Pettito, 1985, p. 251)

• *Challenging tasks promote maximum cognitive growth.* The range of tasks that children cannot yet perform independently, but *can* perform with the help and guidance of others, is known as the **zone of proximal development (ZPD)**. A child's zone of proximal development includes learning and problem-solving abilities that are just beginning to develop within that child—abilities that are in an immature, "embryonic" form. Naturally, any child's ZPD will change over time; as some tasks are mastered, other, more complex ones will appear to provide new challenges.

Vygotsky proposed that children learn very little from performing tasks they can already do independently. Instead, they develop primarily by attempting tasks they can accomplish only in collaboration with a more competent individual—that is, when they attempt tasks within their zone of proximal development. In a nutshell, it is the challenges in life—not the easy successes—that promote cognitive development.

As teachers, then, we should assign some tasks that our students can perform successfully only with help from others. In some cases, such assistance must come from more skilled individuals, such as adults or older students. In other situations, however, students of equal ability can work together on difficult assignments, thereby jointly accomplishing tasks that none of them might be able to accomplish on their own. To some extent, students with different zones of proximal development may need

Show students how various academic disciplines conceptualize the world.

Have students collaborate with adults or other students when they work on particularly challenging assignments.

different tasks and assignments—a strong case for providing as much individualized instruction as possible.

Contemporary Applications of Vygotsky's Ideas

In the past two decades, learning theorists and educators alike have made considerable use of Vygotsky's ideas. For one thing, they describe the value of teaching students how to give themselves instructions (i.e., how to self-talk) as they complete challenging tasks; we will consider such *self-instructions* in Chapter 11. They also encourage us to use *guided participation, scaffolding, apprenticeships,* and *peer interaction* in promoting cognitive development. Let's look briefly at each of these strategies.

Guided Participation

THINKING ABOUT WHAT YOU KNOW

When you were a young child, did you sometimes help your mother, father, or an older sibling bake things in the kitchen? Did the "cook" let you pour, measure, and mix ingredients when you were old enough to do so? Did the cook also give you some guidance as you performed these tasks?

Older family members often allow young children to perform household tasks—cooking, cleaning, painting, and so on—while providing guidance about how to do these tasks appropriately. Teachers, too, often introduce students to adult tasks within a structured and supportive context. For instance, they might ask students to conduct laboratory experiments, write letters to members of Congress, or search the Internet for specific information, while always providing the support the students need to accomplish such tasks successfully.

> Engage students in realistic adult tasks, giving them the guidance they need to be successful.

When we give our students the assistance they need as they perform adultlike activities, we are engaging them in **guided participation** in the world of adults (Radziszewska & Rogoff, 1991; Rogoff, 1990, 1991). As we guide them, we should also use some of the language that adults frequently use in such contexts; for example, when students conduct scientific experiments, we should use words such as *hypothesis, evidence,* and *theory* as we help them evaluate their procedures and results (Perkins, 1992).

Scaffolding

Theorists and educators have given considerable thought to the kinds of assistance that can help students complete challenging assignments. The term **scaffolding** is often used here: Adults and other more competent individuals provide some form of guidance or structure that enables students to perform tasks that are in their zone of proximal development. To understand this concept, let's first think about how scaffolding is used in the construction of a new building. The *scaffold* is an external structure that provides support for the workers (a place where they can stand) until the building itself is strong enough to support them. As the building gains stability, the scaffold becomes less necessary and is gradually removed.

> What task have you recently performed that was in your zone of proximal development? Who scaffolded your efforts so that you could successfully complete it?

In much the same way, an adult guiding a child through a new task may provide an initial scaffold to support the child's early efforts. In the teacher-child dialogue about division presented earlier, the teacher provides clues about how to proceed (e.g., search for the multiple of 6 closest to but still less than 44). Similarly, a beginning piano book might help a student locate different musical notes (see Figure 2–5). As teachers, we can provide a variety of support mechanisms to help students master tasks within their zone of proximal development; here are some examples:

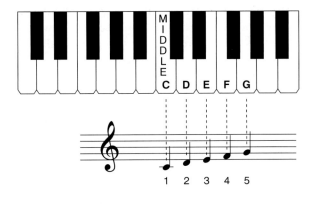

Brother John

FIGURE 2.5
When children first begin piano lessons, they often have considerable scaffolding to help them remember which fingers go where.

- Work with students to develop a plan for dealing with a new task.
- Demonstrate the proper performance of the task in a way that students can easily imitate.
- Divide a complex task into several smaller, simpler tasks.
- Provide structure or guidelines regarding how the task should be accomplished.
- Ask questions that get students thinking in appropriate ways about the task.
- Keep students' attention focused on the relevant aspects of the task.
- Keep students motivated to complete the task.
- Remind students what their goal is in performing the task (e.g., what a problem solution should look like).
- Give frequent feedback about how students are progressing.

As students develop increasing competence, we can gradually withdraw these support mechanisms, eventually allowing students to perform the task independently. In a manner of speaking, when we remove such scaffolding, we allow and encourage students to stand on their own two feet.

Apprenticeships

In an **apprenticeship,** a learner works intensively with an expert to accomplish complex tasks that he or she could never do independently. The expert provides considerable structure and guidance throughout the process, gradually removing scaffolding and giving the learner more responsibility as competence increases (Rogoff, 1990, 1991). Many cultures use apprenticeships as a way of gradually introducing children to the practices of the adult community, including such skills as weaving, tailoring, or midwifery (Lave & Wenger, 1991; Rogoff, 1990). We also see apprenticeships frequently in music instruction—for instance, in teaching a student how to play a musical instrument (Elliott, 1995).

Provide the scaffolding students need to perform challenging tasks successfully; gradually withdraw it as they become more skilled.

Occasionally perform difficult tasks in partnership with students.

Teacher scaffolding helps students perform tasks that will maximally promote cognitive development.

Through an apprenticeship, a student often learns not only how to perform a task but also how to *think about* a task; such a situation is sometimes called a **cognitive apprenticeship** (J. S. Brown, Collins, & Duguid, 1989; John-Steiner, 1997; Rogoff, 1990). For instance, a student and a teacher might work together to accomplish a challenging task or solve a difficult problem (perhaps conducting a complex science experiment, solving a "brainteaser" mathematical problem, or translating a difficult passage from German to English). In the process of talking about various aspects of the task or problem, the student and the teacher together analyze the situation and develop the best approach to take, and the teacher models effective ways of thinking about and mentally processing the situation.

Although apprenticeships can differ widely from one context to another, they typically have some or all of these features (A. Collins, Brown, & Newman, 1989):

- *Modeling.* The teacher carries out the task, thinking aloud about the process at the same time, while the student observes and listens.
- *Coaching.* As the student performs the task, the teacher gives frequent suggestions, hints, and feedback.
- *Scaffolding.* The teacher provides various forms of support for the student, perhaps by simplifying the task, breaking it down into smaller and more manageable components, or providing less complicated equipment.
- *Increasing complexity and diversity of tasks.* As the student gains greater proficiency, the teacher presents more complex, challenging, and varied tasks to complete.
- *Articulation.* The student explains what he or she is doing and why, allowing the teacher to examine the student's knowledge, reasoning, and problem-solving strategies.
- *Reflection.* The teacher asks the student to compare his or her performance with that of experts, or perhaps with an ideal model of how the task should be done.
- *Exploration.* The teacher encourages the student to frame questions and problems on his or her own and, in doing so, to expand and refine acquired skills.

Apprenticeships are clearly labor intensive; as such, their use in the classroom is not always practical or logistically feasible (e.g., De Corte, Greer, & Verschaffel, 1996). At the same time, we can certainly use elements of an apprenticeship model to help our students develop more complex skills. For example, we might use prompts like these to help students think about writing tasks in the same ways that expert writers do (Scardamalia & Bereiter, 1985):

Encourage the thought processes that experts use when they engage in a complex task.

- "My purpose . . . "
- "My main point . . . "
- "An example of this . . . "
- "The reason I think so . . . "
- "To liven this up, I'll . . . "
- "I'm not being very clear about what I just said, so . . . "
- "I'm getting off the topic, so . . . "
- "This isn't very convincing because . . . "
- "I can tie this together by . . . "

Such prompts provide the same sort of scaffolding that an expert writer might provide, and they help students develop more sophisticated writing strategies (Scardamalia & Bereiter, 1985).

Apprenticeships frequently take place in natural settings——for example, in a studio, workshop, or place of employment—and involve real-life tasks. Many theorists believe that such *authentic activities* are an essential part of effective instruction. We'll look at authentic activities more closely in Chapters 7 and 13.

Peer Interaction

As noted earlier, students can often accomplish more difficult tasks when they work together rather than alone; in such situations, students are essentially providing scaffolding for one another's efforts. In recent years, researchers and practitioners alike have become increasingly convinced that interactive approaches to instruction, in which students work collaboratively rather than in isolation, can be highly effective in promoting both cognitive development and classroom achievement. Chapter 14 focuses on the value of peer interaction in classroom learning.

INTO THE CLASSROOM: Applying Vygotsky's Theory

Encourage students to talk themselves through difficult tasks.

As his students work on complex mathematical equations such as this one,

$$x = \frac{2\,(4 \times 9)^2}{6} + 3$$

a junior high school mathematics teacher gives students a mnemonic ("*P*lease *e*xcuse *my dear Aunt Sally*") to help them remember the order in which various operations should be performed (*p*arentheses, *e*xponents, *m*ultiplication, *d*ivision, *a*ddition, *s*ubtraction).

Demonstrate and encourage adultlike ways of thinking about situations.

A high school chemistry teacher places two equal-size inflated balloons into two beakers of water, one heated to 25°C, and the other heated to 50°C. The students all agree that the balloon placed in the warmer water expands more. "Now *how much more* did the 50-degree balloon expand?" the teacher asks. "Let's use Charles's Law to figure it out."

Present some tasks that students can perform successfully only with assistance.

A fifth-grade teacher assigns students their first research paper, knowing that he will have to give them a great deal of guidance as they work on it.

Provide sufficient support (scaffolding) to enable students to perform challenging tasks successfully; gradually withdraw the support as they become more proficient.

An elementary physical education teacher begins a lesson on tumbling by demonstrating front and back somersaults in slow motion and physically guiding her students through the correct movements. As the students become more skillful, she stands back from the mat and gives verbal feedback about how to improve.

Have students work in small groups to accomplish complex tasks.

A middle school art teacher asks his students to work in groups of four or five to design large murals that depict various ecosystems—rain forest, desert, grassland, tundra, and so on—and the species of plants and animals that live in each one. The groups then paint their murals on the walls in the school corridors.

Vygotsky described general mechanisms (internalization, self-talk, and so on) through which children might gradually acquire adultlike ways of thinking about the world. More recently, many other theorists have tried to characterize how children think as they grow older. But unlike Piaget, who focused on the development of various logical thinking skills, these theorists study the mental processes that influence children's thinking and learning in general. We turn to this perspective, called information processing theory, now.

An Information Processing View of Cognitive Development

THINKING ABOUT WHAT YOU KNOW

Considering your own observations of children, do you think children become better at paying attention as they grow older? Do you think older children remember more than younger children, or vice versa? In what ways do high school students learn and study differently from elementary students?

Such questions reflect the approach of information processing theory, an approach to cognitive development that has evolved primarily within the last three decades. Information processing theory is actually a collection of theories that emphasize the development of **cognitive processes**—changes in the ways that children acquire, think about, remember, and mentally change information as they grow older.

Information processing theorists reject Piaget's notion of discrete developmental stages. Instead, they believe that children's cognitive processes and abilities develop through more steady and gradual *trends*; for example, they propose that children learn faster, remember more, and handle increasingly complex tasks as they grow. They have found trends in at least four areas: attention, learning strategies, knowledge base, and metacognition.

Attention

Two trends in cognitive development relate to children's attention and its impact on learning:

• *Children become less distractible as they grow older.* Young children's attention often moves quickly from one thing to another, and it is easily drawn to objects and events unrelated to the task at hand. But as children grow older, they become better able to focus their attention on a particular task and keep it there, and they are less distracted by irrelevant occurrences (Higgins & Turnure, 1984; Lane & Pearson, 1982; Ruff & Lawson, 1990). For example, in one experiment (Higgins & Turnure, 1984), children at several grade levels were given a difficult learning task. Some children worked on the task in a quiet room, others worked in a room with a little background noise, and still others worked with a great deal of background noise. Preschool and second-grade children learned most quickly under the quiet conditions and most slowly under the very noisy conditions. But the sixth graders were able to learn just as easily in the noisy room as in the quiet room. Apparently, the older children could ignore the noise, whereas the younger children could not.

• *Children's learning becomes increasingly a function of what they actually intend to learn.* Complete the following exercise before you read further.

Keep unnecessary distractions to a minimum, especially for young children.

▣ Experiencing Firsthand
Six Cards

Look at the following six cards. Try to remember the *colors* of the cards and the order in which each color appears. Study them for about 30 seconds and then cover them with your hand.

Now that you have covered the six cards, answer these questions:

- In which spot is the yellow card? the green card? the purple card? the blue card?
- Where is the cake? the flowers? the guitar? the pair of scissors?

(modeled after a task used by Maccoby & Hagen, 1965)

How accurately did you remember the colors of the cards? How accurately did you remember the objects pictured on the cards? If you are like most adults, you had better success remembering what you intended to learn (the colors) than what you did *not* intend to learn (the objects).

Perhaps because of their distractibility, younger children often remember many things unrelated to what they are supposed to be doing or learning (Hagen & Stanovich, 1977). For example, when students in grades 1 through 7 were asked to perform a series of tasks similar to the one just described, older students remembered the background colors more accurately than younger students. Yet the older students were no better than the younger ones at remembering the objects pictured on the cards; in fact, the oldest group in the study remembered the *fewest* number of objects (Maccoby & Hagen, 1965). Older children, then, are better at learning and remembering the things they *intend* to learn; they are not necessarily better at learning irrelevant information.

Tell your students what is most important for them to learn.

Learning Strategies

Preschoolers often recognize the need to remember something but seem to have little idea of how to go about learning it, apart from looking or pointing at it (Kail, 1990; Wellman, 1988). As children grow older, however, they develop a number of **learning strategies**—specific methods of learning information—that help them learn. Here are four commonly observed trends in the development of learning strategies:

- *Rehearsal increases during the elementary school years.* What do you do if you need to remember a telephone number for a few minutes? Do you repeat it to yourself over and over again as a way of keeping it in your memory until you dial it? This process of **rehearsal** is rare in kindergarten children but increases in frequency and effectiveness throughout the elementary school years (Bjorklund & Coyle, 1995; Gathercole & Hitch, 1993; Kail, 1990).

Model rehearsal for elementary students.

- *Organization improves throughout elementary and secondary grades.* Before you read further, try the following short learning exercise.

▪ Experiencing Firsthand
Mental Maneuver

Read the twelve words below *one time only*. Then cover up the page and write the words down in the order that they come to mind.

daisy	apple	dandelion
hammer	pear	wrench
tulip	pliers	peach
banana	rose	saw

In what order did you remember the words? Did you recall them in their original order, or did you rearrange them somehow? If you are like most people, you grouped the words into three categories—flowers, tools, and fruit—and remembered one category at a time. In other words, you imposed **organization** on the information.

Research consistently shows that organized information is learned more easily and remembered more completely than unorganized information (see Chapter 6). As children grow older, they more frequently organize the information they receive. This tendency to organize begins in early childhood and continues to develop well into the high school years (Bjorklund, Schneider, Cassel, & Ashley, 1994; DeLoache & Todd, 1988; Plumert, 1994).

• *Elaboration emerges around puberty and increases throughout adolescence.* If I tell you that I lived in Colorado for many years, you will probably conclude that I also lived in or near the Rocky Mountains. You might also infer that perhaps I did a lot of skiing, hiking, or camping. In this situation, you are learning more than the information I actually gave you; you are also learning some information that you yourself are supplying. This process of using what you already know to expand on new information is called **elaboration.** In our "Economic Activities" case study, Mr. Sand encourages his students to elaborate by generating their own examples of economic concepts.

Elaboration clearly helps students learn and remember classroom material more effectively than they would otherwise (see Chapter 6). Yet as a learning strategy, it appears relatively late in child development (usually around puberty) and gradually increases throughout the teenage years (Flavell et al., 1993; W. Schneider & Pressley, 1989). Even in high school, however, it is primarily high-ability students who use their existing knowledge to help themselves learn new information. Lower-ability high school students are much less likely to use elaboration strategies as an aid to learning (Pressley, 1982).

Earlier, we encountered the process of *construction* in our discussion of Piaget's basic assumptions. Both organization and elaboration are constructive in nature: You take new information, structure it or add to it based on what you already know, and so construct an understanding that is uniquely your own.

• *Learning strategies become increasingly efficient and effective.* When children first acquire new learning strategies, they use them infrequently and often ineffectively. But with time and practice, they become increasingly more adept at applying their strategies quickly, efficiently, and successfully as they tackle challenging classroom learning tasks (Flavell et al., 1993; Siegler, 1991).

Knowledge Base

Children's knowledge of specific topics and of the world in general—their **knowledge base**—changes in at least two ways as they develop:

• *The amount of knowledge that children have increases over time.* There is no question that children acquire more and more information as they grow older. This increasing knowledge base is one reason why adults and older children learn new things

Show students how they can organize new material.

Encourage students to elaborate on new material—to expand on it using information they already know.

We will look at rehearsal, organization, and elaboration more closely in Chapter 6.

more easily: They have more existing knowledge to help them understand and elaborate on new events (Flavell et al., 1993; Halford, 1989; Kail, 1990). Consider the case of an Inuit (Eskimo) man named Tor as an example.

Experiencing Firsthand
Tor of the Targa

Tor, a young man of the Targa tribe, was out hunting in the ancient hunting territory of his people. He had been away from his village for many days. The weather was bad and he had not yet managed to locate his prey. Because of the extreme temperature he knew he must soon return but it was a matter of honor among his people to track and kill the prey single-handed. Only when this was achieved could a boy be considered a man. Those who failed were made to eat and keep company with the old men and the women until they could accomplish this task.

Suddenly, in the distance, Tor could make out the outline of a possible prey. It was alone and not too much bigger than Tor, who could take him single-handed. But as he drew nearer, a hunter from a neighboring tribe came into view, also stalking the prey. The intruder was older than Tor and had around his neck evidence of his past success at the hunt. "Yes," thought Tor, "he is truly a man." Tor was undecided. Should he challenge the intruder or return home empty handed? To return would mean bitter defeat. The other young men of the tribe would laugh at his failure. He decided to creep up on the intruder and wait his chance. (A. L. Brown, Smiley, Day, Townsend, & Lawton, 1977, p. 1460)

- On what kind of terrain was Tor hunting?
- What was the weather like?
- What kind of prey might Tor have been stalking?

You probably used your knowledge about Inuits (Eskimos) to speculate that Tor was hunting polar bears or seals on snow and ice, possibly in freezing temperatures or a bad blizzard. But notice that the story itself didn't tell you any of these things; you had to *infer* them. Like you, older children often know a great deal about how Inuit people live and can use that information to help them understand and remember (to elaborate on) this very ambiguous story about Tor. Younger children are less likely to make connections between a new situation and what they already know (A. L. Brown et al., 1977).

The more information children already have, the more easily they can remember new information. In cases where children have more information than adults, then children are often the more effective learners (Chi, 1978; Rabinowitz & Glaser, 1985). For example, when my son Alex and I used to read books about lizards together, Alex always remembered more than I did, because he was a self-proclaimed "lizard expert," and I myself knew very little about reptiles of any sort.

- *Children's knowledge base becomes increasingly integrated.* Remember, older children are more likely to organize information as they learn it. They are also more likely to make connections between new information and the things they already know. Not surprisingly, then, children's knowledge becomes increasingly better integrated as they grow older. The knowledge base of older children includes many associations and interrelationships among concepts and ideas (Bjorklund, 1987; Flavell et al., 1993). In contrast, the knowledge base of younger children includes many separate, isolated facts. This difference may be one reason why older children can think more logically and draw inferences more readily: Their information is better integrated and interconnected.

Metacognition

As an adult with many years of formal education behind you, you have probably learned a great deal about how you think and learn. For example, you may have learned that you

Might you see better performance in "low ability" students if you encourage them to work with a topic they know a lot about?

Show students how concepts and ideas are related to one another.

cannot absorb everything in a textbook the first time you read it, or that you remember information better when you elaborate on it, rather than when you simply repeat it over and over in a meaningless fashion.

The term **metacognition** refers both to the knowledge that people have about their own cognitive processes and to their intentional use of certain cognitive processes to facilitate learning and memory. As children develop, their metacognitive knowledge and skills improve in several ways:

• *Children become increasingly aware of the limitations of their memories.* Young children tend to be overly optimistic about how much they can remember. As they grow older and encounter many new learning tasks, they begin to discover that their memories are not perfect—that they can't remember everything they see or hear.

Let's consider an experiment with elementary school children (Flavell, Friedrichs, & Hoyt, 1970) as an example. Children in four age-groups (ranging from preschool to fourth grade) were shown strips of paper with pictures of one to ten objects. The children were asked to predict how many of the objects they could remember over a short period of time. The average predictions of each age-group and the average number of objects they actually *did* remember were as follows:

Age-Group	Predicted Number	Actual Number
Preschool	7.2	3.5
Kindergarten	8.0	3.6
Grade 2	6.0	4.4
Grade 4	6.1	5.5

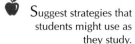
Give practice in memory tasks so that students begin to get a sense of how much they can reasonably learn and remember within a certain time period.

Notice how all four age-groups predicted that they would remember more objects than they actually could. But the older children were more realistic about the limitations of their memories than the younger ones. The kindergartners predicted they would remember eight objects, but they actually remembered fewer than four!

• *Children become more knowledgeable about effective learning strategies.* As mentioned earlier, children show greater use of such learning strategies as rehearsal, organization, and elaboration as they grow older. With experience, they also become increasingly aware of which strategies are effective in different situations (Lovett & Flavell, 1990; Short, Schatschneider, & Friebert, 1993; Wellman, 1985). For example, consider the simple idea that, when you don't learn something the first time you try, you need to study it again. This is a strategy that eight-year-olds use, but six-year-olds do not (Masur, McIntyre, & Flavell, 1973). In a similar way, tenth graders are more aware than eighth graders of the advantages of using elaboration to learn new information (Waters, 1982). Even so, many students of all ages (college students included) seem relatively uninformed about which learning strategies work most effectively in different situations (e.g., Knight, 1988; Ormrod & Jenkins, 1989; Waters, 1982).

Learning strategies make such a difference in students' classroom achievement that we shouldn't leave the development of these strategies to chance. As we ask our students to study and learn classroom subject matter, we should also give them suggestions regarding *how* they might study and learn it. Such an approach is consistent not only with information processing theory, but also with Vygotsky's proposal that adults can better promote children's cognitive development by talking about the ways that they themselves think about challenging tasks. Chapter 8 explores the nature of metacognitive knowledge and skills in more detail and provides suggestions for promoting students' metacognitive development.

Suggest strategies that students might use as they study.

• *Children become increasingly able to identify the things they do and do not know.* Young children (e.g., those in the early elementary grades) often think they know or understand something before they actually do. As a result, they don't study classroom material as much as they should, and they often don't ask questions when

INTO THE CLASSROOM: Applying Information Processing Theory

Minimize distractions, especially when working with young children.

As her class begins a writing assignment, a first-grade teacher asks her students to put all objects except pencil and paper inside their desks.

Model effective learning and study strategies and encourage students to use such strategies themselves.

A chemistry teacher tells her students, "Learning the symbols for all the elements is going to take some time. Some, like H for hydrogen and O for oxygen, are easy. But others, like K for potassium and Na for sodium, are more challenging. Let's take five new symbols each day and develop a strategy to help ourselves remember each one."

Base instruction on what students already know.

A music teacher introduces a new topic by saying, "We already know the scale in C major. Today we're going to study the scale in C minor and see how it is both similar to and different from C major."

Provide opportunities for students to test their learning efforts—to find out what they do and don't know.

A social studies teacher has his students read a textbook chapter at home and then gives them a nongraded quiz to help them identify parts of the chapter that they may need to read again.

they receive incomplete or confusing information (Markman, 1977; McDevitt, Spivey, Sheehan, Lennon, & Story, 1990).

Even high school and college students sometimes have difficulty assessing their own knowledge accurately. For example, they often think they can spell words they actually cannot spell (P. A. Adams & Adams, 1960; Ormrod & Wagner, 1987). And they often overestimate how well they will perform on an exam (Horgan, 1990). My own students occasionally come to my office expressing frustration about doing poorly on an exam. "I knew the material so well!" they tell me. But when we sit down and begin to talk about the exam material, it usually becomes clear that in fact they have only a very vague understanding of some ideas and an incorrect understanding of others.

As teachers, we must keep in mind that children of all ages (younger ones especially) are often less efficient learners than adults. A variety of factors that affect children's ability to learn—factors such as attention, intention to learn, prior knowledge, and the awareness and use of effective learning strategies—develop gradually throughout the school years. We cannot expect that our students will always learn as quickly as we do, or even in the same way that we do.

Give students opportunities to test themselves to find out what they do and do not know.

Comparing Piaget, Vygotsky, and Information Processing Theory

At first glance, the three views of cognitive development described in this chapter seem very different from one another. Piaget's theory portrays cognitive development as a sequence of relatively discrete stages, each with its own set of abilities and limitations. In contrast, information processing theorists describe cognitive development in terms of gradual changes in cognitive processes and metacognitive awareness. And Vygotsky's approach focuses more on the social conditions that facilitate cognitive development than on changes in children's thinking per se.

Despite such differences, several common themes run through at least two of the theories, and sometimes through all three. From these themes, we can formulate several general principles of cognitive development. These principles are as follows (also see Table 2–3):

• *Children actively construct their knowledge.* All three perspectives portray children not as passive receptacles for incoming information, but as active, constructive processors of that information. Piaget described cognitive development as a process of constructing one's own understanding of the world. Vygotsky believed that children actively talk themselves through difficult tasks and that children and adults often work collaboratively to develop a viable approach to a difficult task. And information processing theorists have proposed that children use such constructive learning processes as organization and elaboration to help them learn and remember classroom subject matter.

• *Social interaction is essential for cognitive development.* Social interaction is a key element in both Vygotsky's and Piaget's theories. Vygotsky stressed the importance of dialogue between children and adults as a way of helping children acquire more mature ways of thinking about and interpreting objects and events. And both Piaget and Vygotsky pointed out that when children disagree and argue with one another, they gain an appreciation for the fact that there are often multiple perspectives with regard to any single situation.

• *Cognitive development involves relating new information to prior knowledge.* Piaget proposed that children adapt to their world through the two processes of assimilation and accommodation, both of which involve relating new experiences to previously learned information. Information processing theorists stress the importance of prior knowledge as well: The more children already know about the world, the greater is their ability to understand, elaborate on, and remember new information.

Through arguments and conflicts with one another, children eventually learn that a single situation can be seen through multiple perspectives.

• *Children often think in different ways at different ages.* Changes in children's thinking processes are elements of both Piaget's theory and information processing theory. Piaget portrayed these changes in terms of four qualitatively different stages of thought and reasoning capabilities. Information processing theorists have instead proposed that young children lack many of the learning strategies (e.g., organization, elaboration) and metacognitive sophistication (e.g., knowing *when* they know something) that adolescents possess. Either way, we must remember that children often think and learn quite differently than adults do.

• *Children's knowledge and cognitive processes become increasingly better organized and integrated.* Both Piaget and information processing theorists characterize children's knowledge and cognitive processes as becoming increasingly better organized and integrated over time. When children move from Piaget's preoperational stage to concrete operations, they become better able to combine two ideas together to help them make logical decisions. Likewise, information processing theorists emphasize the importance of organizing information and have observed that as children grow, they are more apt to organize information.

General Principles of Cognitive Development

PRINCIPLE	EDUCATIONAL IMPLICATION	EXAMPLE
Children actively construct their knowledge.	Give students many opportunities to experiment with new objects and experience new events.	Have students view a wide variety of objects (e.g., tiny insects, leaves, bacteria from a local stream, pieces of their own hair) under a microscope.
Social interaction is essential for cognitive development.	Give students opportunities to share their ideas, perspectives, and beliefs.	Ask students to describe how their families celebrate holidays. Students can discover that people celebrate holidays differently, and that even for religious holidays, traditions are not necessarily set in stone.
Cognitive development involves relating new information to prior knowledge.	Ensure that students have prior knowledge and experiences to which they can relate new material. Use their background knowledge to help them understand new ideas.	When describing the representative nature of a democratic government, show students how the federal legislature is similar to the student government system at their own school.
Children often think in different ways at different ages.	Ask students to describe how they are thinking about classroom subject matter and to explain the logic they are using when drawing conclusions.	Ask high school students what they do and how they think when they study for tests. If some of them depend primarily on rehearsal to learn classroom material, teach them how they might also organize and elaborate on the ideas they are studying.
Children's knowledge and cognitive processes become increasingly better organized and integrated.	Help students discover relationships among concepts and ideas.	To introduce the hierarchical nature of the animal kingdom, draw a chart on the chalkboard showing how dogs, cats, and horses are all mammals and how mammals, birds, and fish are all vertebrates.
A child's readiness for a particular task determines the extent to which the task promotes cognitive development.	Remember that some students may not yet be capable of understanding certain ideas or accomplishing certain tasks. Gear classroom tasks and assignments to students' developmental levels.	When introducing the concept π (*pi*) to middle school students, try describing it simply as being "approximately 3.14." Middle schoolers may not yet be ready to understand that *pi* is a number we can never specify with total precision—that it is a decimal that essentially goes on forever.
Cognitive development and linguistic development are closely intertwined.	Simultaneously help students develop both the thinking processes and the language associated with a given subject area.	When first teaching students about persuasive writing, describe the importance of having an *introduction*, several *supporting arguments*, and a *conclusion*. Then provide some suggestions for writing each of these components of a persuasive essay.

• *A child's readiness for a particular task determines the extent to which the task promotes cognitive development.* In all three theories, children's readiness for different tasks determines the extent to which those tasks promote learning and cognitive development. Piaget argued that children can benefit from certain experiences only when they begin to make the transition into a stage that allows them to deal with and conceptualize those experiences appropriately (e.g., they benefit from hearing abstract ideas only as they begin to make the transition into formal operations). Vygotsky characterized readiness in terms of the zone of proximal development: Children benefit from tasks that they can perform only with the assistance of a more skilled individual. From an information processing perspective, students can learn from new experiences only when they have sufficient prior knowledge with which to interpret those experiences.

• *Cognitive development and linguistic development are closely intertwined.* All three theoretical perspectives acknowledge that the development of cognitive abilities and the development of language are interdependent. Cognitive development is obviously critical for the development of language: Children can only talk and write about things that they can first *think* about. Yet language is equally critical for children's cognitive development: It facilitates their interaction with others, provides symbols and concepts through which they can mentally represent and interpret their world, helps them make associations among various pieces of information, and enables them to internalize the thinking processes and problem-solving strategies that adults verbalize.

Linguistic Development

THINKING ABOUT WHAT YOU KNOW

What kinds of knowledge and skills related to language are essential for effective communication with others? To what extent do we need a large vocabulary on which to draw? What kinds of rules must we follow to combine words into meaningful sentences? What must we know about how to produce the various sounds of speech? And what courtesies must we show others when we converse with them?

Using human language is a complex endeavor. Indeed, we must have a working knowledge of thousands of words, and we must be able to put these words together to communicate with one another. We must be able to articulate such vowel sounds as "ay" and "ee" and such consonants and consonant blends as "buh," "duh," and "struh." And to be truly effective communicators, we must follow certain social conventions as we speak; for instance, we should respond to someone else's greeting (e.g., "How are you?") with a greeting of our own (e.g., "Fine, thanks, and how about you?"), and we should let a person with whom we are conversing finish a sentence before we speak.

At the present time, there is probably no single theory that gives us a great deal of guidance about how we can most effectively promote students' language development in the classroom. Yet as teachers, we need to know what linguistic knowledge and skills students of different ages are likely to have so that we can have realistic expectations for their performance. In the pages that follow, we will briefly examine theoretical perspectives on language development and then look more closely at how various aspects of language are likely to change over time. We will also consider research findings related to second-language learning and bilingualism.

Theoretical Perspectives on Language Development

Many theorists believe that human beings are born with a predisposition to learn language—that, to some degree, our knowledge of language is "built in" (Cairns, 1996; N. Chomsky, 1972; Crain, 1993; Karmiloff-Smith, 1993; Lenneberg, 1967). Although we almost certainly are not born knowing any *particular* language, we nevertheless inherit some constraints regarding the form that our language must take. Theorists describe several sources of evidence to support such a contention. First, all languages seem to share certain traits, such as similar rules for forming negatives and asking questions (N. Chomsky, 1965). Second, all members of a particular society acquire what is more or less the *same* language, despite widely differing early childhood experiences and a general lack of systematic instruction regarding appropriate language use (Crain, 1993; Cromer, 1993). And third, there may be *sensitive periods* in some aspects of language development: To some extent, children benefit more from exposure to a particular language when they are young. For instance, children have an easier time mastering a language's various verb tenses and learning how to pronounce words flawlessly when they are immersed in the language within the first five to ten years of life (Bialystok, 1994; Bruer, 1997; Newport, 1993).

But environment, too, must obviously play a role in language development. Children can learn a language only if the people around them converse in that language. It may be that children acquire language, at least in part, because it enables them to accomplish certain goals—perhaps to influence another person's behavior, obtain a desired object, and so on (Bates & MacWhinney, 1987; Budwig, 1995). Yet it is clear that children do not directly "absorb" the language spoken around them; instead, they use what they hear to *construct* their own understanding of the language, including knowledge about what words mean, rules governing how words can be combined into meaningful sentences, and so on (Cairns, 1996; Cromer, 1993; Karmiloff-Smith, 1993).

Trends in Language Development

Children begin using recognizable words sometime around their first birthday and are putting these words together by their second birthday. During their preschool years, they become capable of forming increasingly longer and more complex sentences. By the time they begin school, at five or six years of age, they use language that seems adult-like in many respects. Yet students' language capabilities continue to develop and mature throughout the school years. Numerous changes occur in both **receptive language**—students' ability to understand what they hear and read—and **expressive language**—their ability to communicate effectively through speaking and writing. Let's examine several aspects of linguistic development—vocabulary, syntax, listening comprehension, oral communication, and metalinguistic awareness—and their implications for us as teachers. We will postpone our discussion of reading and writing development until Chapter 9.

Development of Vocabulary

One obvious change in students' language during the school years is the increase in their vocabulary. It has been estimated that the average first grader knows the meanings of 8,000 to 14,000 words, whereas the average high school graduate knows the meanings of at least 80,000 words (S. Carey, 1978; Nippold, 1988). Children learn some words through direct vocabulary instruction at school, but they probably learn many more by inferring meaning from the context in which the words are heard or read (Nippold, 1988; Owens, 1996; Pinker, 1987).

Students' knowledge of word meanings, or **semantics,** is not always an all-or-none thing. In many cases, their early understanding of a word's meaning is somewhat vague

Can you think of
words whose meanings are
still unclear to you?

and "fuzzy"; they have a general idea of what the word means but define it imprecisely and sometimes use it incorrectly. Through repeated encounters with words in different contexts and through direct feedback when they use words incorrectly, students continue to refine their understandings of what different words mean.

One common error that students make in their understanding of words is **undergeneralization:** The meanings they attach to some words are too restricted, leaving out some situations to which those words apply. For example, I once asked my son Jeff, then six years old, to tell me what an *animal* is. He gave me this definition:

> It has a head, tail, feet, paws, eyes, noses, ears, lots of hair.

Like Jeff, young elementary school children often restrict their meaning of *animal* primarily to mammals, such as dogs and horses, and insist that fish, birds, and insects are *not* animals (Saltz, 1971).

Another frequent error is **overgeneralization:** Word meanings are too broad, and so words are applied to situations in which they're not appropriate. For example, when I asked Jeff to give me some examples of *insects,* he included black widow spiders in his list. Jeff overgeneralized: All insects have six legs, so eight-legged spiders do not qualify.

Sometimes even common words have subtleties that children don't master until the upper elementary grades or later. For example, nine-year-old children sometimes confuse situations in which they should use the articles *a* and *the* (Reich, 1986). Children in the upper elementary and junior high grades have trouble with many connectives—words such as *but, although, yet, however,* and *unless* (Nippold, 1988; Owens, 1996). As an illustration, do the following exercise.

Experiencing Firsthand
Using Connectives

In each of the following pairs of sentences, identify the one that makes more sense:

> Jimmie went to school, but he felt sick.
> Jimmie went to school, but he felt fine.

> The meal was good, although the pie was bad.
> The meal was good, although the pie was good.

Even twelve-year-olds have trouble identifying the correct sentence in pairs like these, reflecting only a vague understanding of the connectives *but* and *although* (E. W. Katz & Brent, 1968). (The first sentence is the correct one in both cases.)

Words such as *but* and *although* may be particularly difficult for elementary school children because their meanings are fairly abstract. If we consider Piaget's proposal that abstract thought doesn't emerge until early adolescence, then we realize that students may not fully understand abstract words until the junior high or high school years. Young children in particular are apt to define words (even fairly abstract ones) in terms of the obvious, concrete aspects of their world (Anglin, 1977; Ausubel, Novak, & Hanesian, 1978). For example, when Jeff was four, he defined *summer* as the time of year when school is out and it's hot outside; by the time he was twelve, he knew that adults define summer in terms of the earth's tilt relative to the sun—a much more abstract notion.

To some extent, we must obviously tailor our lessons and reading materials to our students' vocabulary, yet we must not restrict instruction only to words that our students already know. One way to promote students' semantic development is to teach vocabulary words and definitions directly, for instance, by having students define new vocabulary in their own words and use this vocabulary in a variety of contexts. We should also correct any misconceptions (e.g., under- or overgeneralizations) that reveal themselves in stu-

Consider students'
existing word knowledge
when choosing
instructional materials, but
teach new words on an
ongoing basis.

dents' speech. And we must encourage our students to *read, read, read:* Avid readers learn many more new words than do students who read infrequently (R. C. Anderson, Wilson, & Fielding, 1988). Chapter 7 presents additional ways of teaching word meanings.

Development of Syntax

Experiencing Firsthand
Four Sentences

Which of the following sentences are grammatically correct?

The flowers in the garden have grown up straight and tall.

I in garden the pick weeds nasty dare don't.

Why they not does they homework when suppose?

Why aren't you doing your homework?

You undoubtedly recognized that the first and last sentences are grammatically correct and that the two middle ones are not. But *how* were you able to tell the difference? Can you describe the specific grammatical rules you used to make your decisions? The rules that we use to put words together into grammatically correct sentences—rules of **syntax**—are incredibly complex, and to a great extent we aren't consciously aware of the nature of these rules (N. Chomsky, 1972; N. C. Ellis, 1994).

By the time children begin school, they have already acquired many syntactic rules; nevertheless, their knowledge of correct syntax continues to develop throughout the elementary years (Owens, 1996; Reich, 1986). For instance, children in the early elementary grades often make an error known as **overregularization:** They apply syntactical rules in situations in which such rules don't apply (Cazden, 1968; Marcus, 1996; Siegler, 1994). To illustrate, young children might add *-ed* to indicate past tense or *-s* to indicate plural when such suffixes are inappropriate (e.g., "I *goed* to the store," "I have two feet*s*"). This overregularization gradually disappears as children learn the words they should actually use (e.g., past tenses of irregular verbs) in such situations (Marcus, 1996).

We see further evidence of incomplete syntactic development in children's responses to the complex sentences they hear. For example, children in one study (C. S. Chomsky, 1969) were shown a doll with a blindfold over its eyes and asked, "Is this doll easy to see or hard to see?" Children as old as eight had trouble interpreting the question. The following conversation with six-year-old Lisa provides an illustration:

Teach exceptions to general rules regarding past tense and pluralization.

Experimenter:	Is this doll easy to see or hard to see?
Lisa:	Hard to see.
Experimenter:	Will you make her easy to see?
Lisa:	If I can get this untied.
Experimenter:	Will you explain why she was hard to see?
Lisa:	(To doll) Because you had a blindfold over your eyes.
Experimenter:	And what did you do?
Lisa:	I took it off. (C. S. Chomsky, 1969, p. 30)

Young children may also have difficulty interpreting passive sentences (e.g., "The boy is pushed by the girl") and those that contain two or more clauses ("The dog stands on the horse that the giraffe jumps over") (Karmiloff-Smith, 1979; Owens, 1996; Sheldon, 1974).

Students' knowledge of syntax and grammar continues to develop even at the secondary level (e.g., Perera, 1986). At this point, most syntactical development probably

Remember that students in the primary grades often have difficulty comprehending sentences with passive verbs or multiple clauses.

🍎 Continue instruction
and practice in grammar
throughout high school.

occurs as the result of formal language instruction, especially courses in language arts, English composition, and foreign language. Therefore, we should continue instruction and practice in grammar and composition throughout the high school years. Our students are more likely to improve their speech and writing when they have ample opportunities to express their ideas orally and on paper and when they receive direct feedback about ambiguities and grammatical errors in their speech and writing.

Development of Listening Comprehension

Our students' ability to comprehend what they hear will obviously be influenced by their knowledge of vocabulary and syntax. But other factors contribute to students' listening comprehension as well. For instance, it appears that children's conceptions of what listening comprehension *is* change throughout the elementary school years. Children in the early elementary grades believe they are good listeners if they simply sit quietly without interrupting the teacher. Older children (e.g., eleven-year-olds) are more likely to recognize that good listening also requires an *understanding* of what is being said (McDevitt et al., 1990). Elementary school children also differ in their beliefs about what to do when they don't understand something the teacher says. Many children, younger ones especially, apparently believe that it is inappropriate to ask for clarification, perhaps

🍎 Encourage students to
ask questions when
they don't understand what
they are being told.

because they have previously been discouraged from asking questions at school or at home (McDevitt, 1990; McDevitt et al., 1990). For example, children growing up in certain cultures, including those in many Asian and Mexican American communities, may believe that initiating a conversation with an adult is disrespectful (Delgado-Gaitan, 1994; C. A. Grant & Gomez, 1996; Trawick-Smith, 1997).

Furthermore, young children's comprehension of what they hear is influenced by the context in which they hear it. Using various nonverbal contextual clues, they recognize that what is said in a situation is sometimes different from what is actually meant. For example, they may interpret a statement such as "Goodness, this class is noisy today!" to mean "Be quiet" (Flavell, 1985). They may also realize that by asking "Who's jacket is this lying on the floor?" their teacher is actually requesting the jacket's owner to pick it up and put it where it belongs. But unfortunately, younger children are sometimes *too* dependent on the context for determining the meaning

Children in the early elementary grades believe that good listening simply means sitting quietly without interrupting.

of language, to the point where they don't listen carefully enough to understand a spoken message accurately. They may "hear" what they *think* we mean, based on their beliefs about our intentions, rather than hearing what we really do mean (Donaldson, 1978). It is important, then, not only to ask students whether they understand what they hear but also to check for that understanding by asking them to rephrase a message in their own words.

🍎 Occasionally check
students' understanding of
what you've said to them.

As children get older, they become less dependent on context to understand what others say to them. They also become increasingly able to look beyond the literal meanings of spoken messages (Owens, 1996). Children in the early elementary grades take the words they hear at face value; for instance, when we describe someone as being "tied up" or "hitting the roof," they are likely to take us literally. And they have little success drawing generalizations from such proverbs as "Look before you leap" or "Don't put the cart before the horse." Students' ability to interpret proverbs in a generalized, abstract fashion continues to develop even in the high school years (Owens, 1996).

🍎 Minimize use of
figurative speech in the
early years.

Development of Oral Communication Skills

To speak effectively, children must know how to pronounce words correctly. During the preschool and early elementary years, many children have difficulty pronouncing some sounds in the English language; for instance, they may struggle with *r, th, dr, sl,* and *str* (Owens, 1996). Most students have mastered the sounds of English by age eight or nine; if pronunciation difficulties continue after that time, we may want to consult with the school's speech pathologist about possible remediation strategies.

To communicate their ideas effectively, children also need to consider the characteristics (e.g., age, prior knowledge, perspective) of the person receiving their message. As noted earlier, young children sometimes say things without really considering the listener's perspective (Piaget called this egocentric speech). Even four-year-olds adapt their speech somewhat to the age of their listeners, however; for example, they use simpler language with two-year-olds than they do with their peers (McDevitt & Ford, 1987; Shatz & Gelman, 1973). Yet throughout elementary school, children have some difficulty taking other characteristics of their listeners into account; for example, they don't always consider what prior information their listeners are likely to have (Glucksberg & Krauss, 1967; McDevitt & Ford, 1987). As teachers, we must let our students know exactly when we don't understand them. For instance, we can ask them to explain who or what they are talking about when they refer to people or things with which we are unfamiliar, and we can express our confusion when they describe events and ideas ambiguously.

In addition, children must learn **pragmatics,** the social conventions regarding appropriate verbal interactions with others. Pragmatics include not only rules of etiquette—taking turns speaking when conversing with others, saying goodbye when leaving, and so on—but also strategies for beginning and ending conversations, changing the subject, telling stories, and arguing effectively. Children continue to refine their knowledge of pragmatics throughout the elementary grades (Owens, 1996); my own observation has been that this process continues into the middle and high school years as well. When students haven't mastered certain social conventions—for instance, when they interrupt frequently or change the subject without warning—others may find their behavior irritating or strange; a lack of pragmatic skills, then, can seriously interfere with students' relationships with their peers. It is important to observe students' pragmatic skills as they interact both with us and with their classmates and to give students guided practice in any skills that they may be lacking.

Development of Metalinguistic Awareness

Throughout the school years, students exhibit a tendency to "play" with language—a tendency reflected in rhymes, chants, jokes, puns, and so forth (Christie & Johnsen, 1983; Owens, 1996). Such word play is almost certainly beneficial; for instance, rhymes help students discover the relationships between sounds and letters, and jokes and puns may help students come to realize that words and phrases often have more than one meaning (L. Bradley & Bryant, 1991; Cazden, 1976). In the latter case, we enhance students' **metalinguistic awareness**—their ability to think about the nature of language itself.

Relatively speaking, metalinguistic awareness seems to emerge fairly late in the game. During the elementary years, students gradually become capable of determining when sentences are grammatically acceptable and when they are not (Bowey, 1986). As they move into the upper elementary and middle school grades, they begin to analyze speech in terms of its component parts (nouns, verbs, adjectives, etc.); such growth is almost certainly due, at least in part, to the formal instruction they receive about parts of speech. High school students enhance their metalinguistic awareness still further as they consider the figurative nature of words—the nonliteral meanings of proverbs, the symbolism in poems and literature, and so on. Studying a second language also promotes metalinguistic awareness, as we shall see now.

Remember that some pronunciation difficulties are normal in the early elementary years.

Give students lots of practice speaking in class and let them know when you don't understand what they have said.

Teach the social conventions of language so that students can interact more effectively with others.

Encourage word play.

Provide instruction regarding the nature of language itself.

Students can develop effective communication skills only when they have opportunities to practice those skills.

Learning a Second Language

As the adult workplace becomes increasingly international in scope, the need is greater than ever for children to learn one or more languages in addition to their native tongue. As noted earlier, there may be a sensitive period for learning language, thus making exposure to a language in the first few years of life ideal. Yet research evidence regarding the best time to learn a *second* language is mixed and often tainted by serious methodological problems (Bialystok, 1994; Hakuta & McLaughlin, 1996; Long, 1995; Newport, 1993). In general, early instruction in a second language is important for mastering correct pronunciations, especially if the language is very different from a student's native tongue (Bialystok, 1994). But to some degree, children and adolescents can develop fluency in a second language regardless of when they begin instruction.

Although there may be no hard-and-fast sensitive period for learning a second language, beginning second-language instruction in the early years has definite advantages. For one thing, it appears that learning a second language facilitates achievement in such other academic areas as reading, vocabulary, and grammar (Diaz, 1983; Reich, 1986). Instruction in a foreign language also sensitizes young children to the international and multicultural nature of the world. Students who learn a second language during the elementary school years express more positive attitudes toward people who speak that language and are more likely to enroll in foreign language classes in high school (Reich, 1986).

Teach a second
language at any
grade level.

Bilingualism

A *bilingual* student speaks two languages fluently. Some bilingual children have been raised in families in which two languages are spoken regularly. Others have lived for a time in a community where one language is spoken and then moved to a community where a different language is spoken. Still others live in a bilingual society—for example, in Canada (where both English and French are spoken), Wales (where both English and Welsh are spoken), and certain ethnic communities in the United States (where a language such as Spanish or Chinese is spoken along with English).

Research reveals some advantages to being bilingual. For example, bilingual children, when they are truly fluent in both languages, tend to perform better on tasks requiring complex cognitive functioning (e.g., on intelligence tests or on tasks requiring creativity). They also appear to have greater metalinguistic awareness—a better understanding of the nature of language itself (Diaz & Klingler, 1991; Garcia, 1994; C. E. Moran & Hakuta, 1995).

Promoting bilingualism. In some situations, learning a second language is essential; this is the case for non-English-speaking students whose families intend to become long-term or permanent residents of an English-speaking country. In other situations, learning a second language, though not essential, is highly desirable; this is the case for English-speaking students who may wish eventually to study or work in societies where a different language is spoken. Bilingualism has social benefits as well: In classrooms in which different students speak only one of two different languages (perhaps some speaking only English and others speaking only Spanish), increased fluency in the second language facilitates interaction among classmates (A. Doyle, 1982).

How can we help children become fluent in a second language? Unfortunately, research on this topic is often correlational rather than experimental, making it difficult to draw firm conclusions about cause-effect relationships (Lam, 1992; Willig, 1985). Considering the limited research results that we have, it appears that the best approach to teaching a second language depends on the situation. For English-speaking students learning a second language while still living in their native country, total **immersion** in the second language—hearing and speaking it almost exclusively within the classroom—appears to be an effective method. Total immersion helps students become proficient in a second language relatively quickly, and any adverse effects of such immersion on students' achievement in other areas of the curriculum appear to be short-lived (Collier, 1992; Genesee, 1985; W. P. Thomas, Collier, & Abbott, 1993).

In contrast, for non-English-speaking students who have recently immigrated to this country, total immersion in English may actually be detrimental to their academic progress. For these students, **bilingual education**—wherein instruction in academic subject areas is given in students' native language while they are simultaneously taught to speak and write in English—leads to higher academic achievement (e.g., in reading, mathematics, and social studies), greater self-esteem, and a better attitude toward school (Moll & Diaz, 1985; C. E. Snow, 1990; Willig, 1985; S. Wright & Taylor, 1995).

Why does immersion work better for some students while bilingual education is more effective for others? As discussed earlier, language is critical for children's cognitive development, promoting social interaction and providing a symbolic means through which they can mentally represent and think about their world. We therefore need a method of teaching a second language without losing the first language in the process. In this country, English-speaking students immersed in a second language at school still have many opportunities—at home, with their friends, and in the local community and culture—to continue using and developing their English. But recent immigrants to this country often have little opportunity outside their immediate families to use their native language. If these students are taught exclusively in English, they may very well lose proficiency in one language (their native tongue) before developing proficiency in another (Willig, 1985).

Given the many advantages of second-language learning and bilingualism, perhaps we should begin to think about promoting bilingualism in *all* students (Navarro, 1985; NCSS Task Force on Ethnic Studies Curriculum Guidelines, 1992). Doing so would not only promote our students' cognitive and linguistic development but also enhance communication, interaction, and interpersonal understanding among students with diverse linguistic and cultural backgrounds (Minami & Ovando, 1995).

For English-speaking students still living in an English-speaking society, provide total immersion in the second language.

For non-English-speaking students now living in an English-speaking society, teach them to speak and write in English while simultaneously providing other instruction in their native tongue.

Promote bilingualism in *all* students.

INTO THE CLASSROOM: Facilitating Language Development

Teach vocabulary related to topics being studied. Look for and correct students' misconceptions of word meanings.

> A science teacher explains and illustrates the concepts *speed* and *acceleration* and corrects students who erroneously use one term in place of the other.

Teach conventions with regard to syntax.

> A high school English teacher describes the situations in which it is appropriate to use *who* and *whom* and then gives her students practice using both terms correctly.

Help students understand that being good listeners involves understanding and remembering as well as paying attention.

> A fourth-grade teacher invites a police officer to speak to her class about bicycle safety. Following the officer's departure, she asks her students to summarize the important things to remember when riding a bicycle.

Give students lots of practice presenting their ideas orally to others. Provide specific and constructive feedback about how well they are communicating.

> A high school history teacher has each student give an oral report on a topic related to early American history. After each report, he speaks with the student individually, identifying parts of the report that were especially effective and providing suggestions for giving a better report the next time.

Spend time looking at the nature of language itself.

> A sixth-grade teacher asks, "Has anyone ever heard the expression 'A stitch in time saves nine'? What does that expression mean? Is it only about sewing?"

Encourage all students to learn a second language.

> A second-grade teacher spends a few minutes each day teaching her students some simple French vocabulary and phrases.

Considering Diversity in Cognitive and Linguistic Development

As previously noted, the *order* in which children acquire specific cognitive and linguistic capabilities is often similar, but the *rate* at which they acquire these abilities may differ considerably from one child to the next. As a result, we are likely to find considerable diversity in the level of development that each student has reached. From the perspective of Piaget's theory, we may see signs of both preoperational and concrete operational thinking in the primary grades; for example, some students may demonstrate conservation while others do not conserve. Similarly, we may find evidence of both concrete and formal operational thinking at the middle school and high school levels; for example, some students will think more abstractly than others, and students will differ in such abilities as hypothetical reasoning, separation and control of variables, and proportional thought. From Vygotsky's point of view, we will inevitably have students with different zones of proximal development: The cognitive challenges necessary for optimal cognitive development will vary from one student to the next. And from an information processing perspective, we will find diversity in the learning strategies that our students use, as well as in the background knowledge and experiences from which they can draw as they try to understand and elaborate on new information.

To some extent, children's cognitive development differs as a function of the culture in which they've been raised. For instance, some of the logical reasoning abilities that Piaget described (e.g., conservation, separation and control of variables) and some of the learning strategies (e.g., rehearsal) that information processing theorists have identified appear earlier in children raised in Western communities than in some Third World communities (Berk, 1997; Cole, 1990; Trawick-Smith, 1997). Presumably such cognitive processes are more highly valued and more systematically promoted in Western culture. When we consider cognitive abilities that other cultures value more than we do (e.g., the ability to judge the right amount of clay to use in making a pot, or the ability to locate food in a barren desert), our own children definitely fall short (Kearins, 1981; Price-Williams, Gordon, & Ramirez, 1969; Rogoff & Waddell, 1982).

We will find diversity in students' language capabilities as well. For example, our students will vary considerably in the size of their vocabulary and in their knowledge of complex syntactical structures. Some students may express themselves using a **dialect**— a form of English that is characteristic of a particular ethnic group or region of the country—other than the one that we ourselves use. Other students may have **limited English proficiency (LEP)**—they will be fluent in their native language but not in English—and so have difficulties both in communicating their ideas and in understanding others. And finally, our students are likely to have acquired varying social conventions when conversing with others—varying pragmatic skills—depending on the families and cultures in which they've been raised. We will identify strategies for accommodating some of these differences in our discussion of ethnicity in Chapter 4.

As teachers, we must continually be aware of the specific cognitive and linguistic abilities and weaknesses that individual students possess and then tailor instruction accordingly. For example, our students will display more advanced reasoning skills when we ask them to deal with topics with which they are familiar. And students with limited English proficiency will achieve at higher levels in a bilingual education program.

Keep individual students' cognitive and linguistic capabilities in mind as you plan and deliver instruction.

Accommodating Students with Special Needs

We are especially likely to see differences in cognitive and linguistic development in our students with special needs. For example, we may have a few students who show especially advanced cognitive development (e.g., students who are gifted), and perhaps we may have one or two who have not yet acquired the cognitive abilities typical of their age group (e.g., students with mental retardation). We may also have students with exceptional difficulties in specific aspects of cognition despite otherwise normal cognitive development (e.g., students with learning disabilities or attention-deficit hyperactivity disorder). Finally, we may have students who display abnormalities in speech that significantly interfere with their classroom performance (e.g., students with speech and communication disorders). Chapter 5 looks more closely at all of these students with special needs.

Table 2–4 presents specific characteristics related to cognitive and linguistic development that we may see in students with a variety of special educational needs. It also presents numerous strategies for helping such students achieve academic success.

TABLE 2.4

STUDENTS IN INCLUSIVE SETTINGS

Promoting Cognitive and Linguistic Development in Students with Special Educational Needs

STUDENTS WITH SPECIAL NEEDS	CHARACTERISTICS THAT THESE STUDENTS MAY EXHIBIT	CLASSROOM STRATEGIES THAT MAY BE BENEFICIAL FOR THESE STUDENTS
Students with specific cognitive or academic difficulties	Distractibility, difficulty paying and maintaining attention Few effective learning strategies Difficulties in listening comprehension Difficulties in expressive language (e.g., in syntax)	Make sure you have students' attention before giving instructions or presenting information. Keep distracting stimuli to a minimum. Teach learning strategies within the context of classroom lessons. Encourage students to use self-talk as a way of helping them deal with challenging situations.
Students with social or behavioral problems	Lack of attention, as reflected in restlessness, daydreaming, etc. (students with emotional or behavioral problems) Delayed language development (some autistic students) Uneven performance on cognitive tasks (some autistic students)	Capture students' attention by gearing instruction toward their personal interests. Provide intensive instruction and practice for any delayed cognitive or linguistic skills. (Also use strategies presented above for students with specific cognitive or academic difficulties.)
Students with general delays in cognitive and social functioning	Reasoning abilities characteristic of younger children (e.g., preoperational thought in the upper elementary grades, inability to think abstractly in the secondary grades) Absence of learning strategies such as rehearsal or organization Less developed knowledge base to which new information can be related Delayed language development (e.g., in vocabulary, listening comprehension)	Present new information in a concrete, hands-on fashion. Teach simple learning strategies (e.g., rehearsal) within the context of classroom lessons. Give instructions in concrete and specific terms.

The Big Picture: Recurring Themes in Cognitive and Linguistic Development

As you look back on the topics of this chapter, you may notice several recurring themes that seem to characterize both cognitive and linguistic development:

Development of increasingly more complex and abstract abilities. As we have seen, children become capable of more sophisticated thought processes, learning strategies, and language as they grow older. For example, young children often think illogically and concretely about isolated pieces of information, whereas many adolescents think logically and abstractly about integrated bodies of knowledge. Elementary students depend primarily on rehearsal to learn new information; secondary students are better able to organize and elaborate on that information. Students also become increasingly able to use and understand complex syntactical structures and to understand the nonliteral meanings of language as they progress through the grade levels.

continued

STUDENTS WITH SPECIAL NEEDS	CHARACTERISTICS THAT THESE STUDENTS MAY EXHIBIT	CLASSROOM STRATEGIES THAT MAY BE BENEFICIAL FOR THESE STUDENTS
Students with physical or sensory challenges	Less developed knowledge base to which new information can be related, due to limited experiences in the outside world Possible cognitive and/or language deficiencies (if brain damage is present) Delayed language development (if students have long-term hearing loss) Difficulties with articulation (if students have difficulties with muscular control or are congenitally deaf)	Provide the basic life experiences that students may have missed because of their disabilities. Identify any specific cognitive and/or language deficiencies that students may be lacking, and adjust instruction and assessment practices accordingly. Provide intensive instruction in the cognitive and/or language skills that students are lacking.
Students with advanced cognitive development	Appearance of formal operational thinking (e.g., abstract thought) at an earlier age Tendency for many regular classroom tasks to be below students' zone of proximal development Greater knowledge base to which new information can be related Advanced vocabulary More sophisticated expressive language	Provide opportunities through which students can explore classroom topics in greater depth or complexity. Provide opportunities for students to proceed through the curriculum at a more rapid pace.

Sources: Butterfield & Ferretti, 1987; Carter & Ormrod, 1982; Cone, Wilson, Bradley, & Reese, 1985; Diaz & Berk, 1995; Mercer, 1991; Morgan & Jenson, 1988; Patton, Beirne-Smith, & Payne, 1990; Patton, Payne, Kauffman, Brown, & Payne, 1987; Piirto, 1994; Pressley, 1995; Turnbull, Turnbull, Shank, & Leal, 1999; Winner, 1997.

Note: Compiled with the assistance of Dr. Margie Garanzini-Daiber and Dr. Margaret Cohen, University of Missouri—St. Louis.

Dependence of later knowledge and skills on earlier ones. Children rarely learn new knowledge and skills in isolation from the things they have already learned; instead, they use what they know to help them acquire more complex understandings and processes. Early experiences and accomplishments therefore provide an essential foundation for later cognitive and linguistic development. As teachers, we must make sure that our students master basic cognitive and linguistic knowledge and skills before we ask them to proceed to more difficult tasks.

Constructive processes. We encountered the process of construction not only in all three theories of cognitive development, but also in theoretical perspectives regarding language development. In recent years, theorists and practitioners have come increasingly to the conclusion that children do not simply absorb what they see and hear in a straightforward, perhaps verbatim fashion. Instead, they construct their *own* knowledge—knowledge both about the world and about the nature of language. Chapter 7 explores the process of knowledge construction in greater depth.

Importance of challenge. Challenge is critical for development. We saw this idea most clearly in Vygotsky's concept of the zone of proximal development. But the importance of challenge appears in other perspectives as well. From Piaget's view, children modify their schemes and develop new ones only when they cannot easily interpret new events using their existing schemes. From an information processing view, children develop more sophisticated learning strategies only when their present ones are not sufficiently effective. And children are likely to develop more sophisticated receptive and expressive language capabilities only if specific tasks require them to do so.

Challenges are critical for cognitive and linguistic development.

CALVIN AND HOBBES © Watterson. Reprinted with permission of UNIVERSAL PRESS SYNDICATE. All rights reserved.

Development within a social context. Both Piaget and Vygotsky have emphasized the importance of social interaction for cognitive development. Language development also depends heavily on social interaction: Children can learn to understand speech only if they hear others speak, and they can learn to speak themselves only if given an opportunity to do so. In fact, a child's social world has ramifications far beyond cognitive and linguistic development; it has ramifications for personal, social, and moral development as well, as we shall discover in the next chapter.

CASE STUDY: In the Eye of the Beholder

Ms. Kontos is teaching a unit on vision to her fifth-grade class. She shows her students a diagram of the various parts of the human eye—lens, cornea, retina, and so on. She then explains that people can see objects because light from the sun or another light source bounces off those objects and into the eye. To illustrate this idea, she shows them this picture:

"Do you all understand how our eyes work?" she asks. Her students nod that they do.

The next day, Ms. Kontos gives her students the following picture:

She asks them to draw how light travels so that the child can see the tree. More than half of the students draw lines something like this:

Obviously, most of Ms. Kontos' students have not really learned what she thought she had taught them.

- What went wrong? Can you explain the students' inability to learn within the context of Piaget's theory of cognitive development? Can you explain it using some of Vygotsky's ideas? Can you explain it from an information processing perspective?

- In what ways might students' language capabilities have been insufficient to enable them to understand?

- What things might Ms. Kontos have done differently?

Summing Up

Developmental Principles in the Classroom

Children develop skills and abilities in a somewhat predictable sequence, although not always at the same rate, and their development is a function of environment as well as heredity. As teachers, we need to monitor the growth and development of our students and be sure they acquire the skills necessary for future learning. We must also remember that what we do in the classroom will likely affect our students' development over the long run.

Piaget's Theory

Piaget's four stages give us a rough idea of when various logical thinking capabilities will emerge, and Piagetian tasks (e.g., conservation problems) can provide valuable insights about how our students are reasoning. Regardless of developmental stage, all learners benefit from building on prior knowledge, discovering relationships among concepts and ideas, and exercising their natural curiosity. As teachers, we should challenge students' beliefs about the world and expand their experiences to help them progress to more complex levels of thought.

Vygotsky's Theory

Vygotsky's theory encourages us to share with growing children the ways that we, as adults, think about and interpret the events around us. It also encourages us to help students develop by challenging them and stretching the limits of what they know and can do. As we do so, we must give them the guidance and support (the scaffolding) they need to perform difficult tasks successfully.

Information Processing Theory

Information processing theorists believe that cognitive capabilities improve over time, but not necessarily in the discrete stages that Piaget proposed. We must remember that our students will often be less efficient learners than we are; for example, they will have shorter attention spans, less knowledge to which they can relate school subject matter, and less sophisticated learning strategies.

Linguistic Development

We see continuing development in language—for instance, in vocabulary, syntax, listening comprehension, oral communication, and metalinguistic awareness—throughout the school years. Whether we have English-speaking students, bilingual students, or nonnative speakers of English, we need to be aware of the ways in which language can foster or hinder classroom performance. We must adapt our instruction and instructional materials to our students' existing linguistic knowledge and skills. At the same time, we can do many things to promote students' language development; for instance, we can explicitly teach vocabulary and grammar, give students many opportunities to practice oral communication skills, and teach them one or more foreign languages.

Diversity in Cognitive and Linguistic Development

Our students are likely to vary considerably in terms of their logical thinking skills, learning strategies, background knowledge, and English proficiency, and different students will find different tasks optimally challenging. Some students may be different enough from their classmates in either cognitive or language skills that they will need specially adapted instructional materials and practices.

General Themes

Several themes have appeared throughout our discussion of cognitive and linguistic development. As students develop, more sophisticated thought processes, language capabilities, and understandings of the world emerge from and build upon existing mental capabilities and knowledge; hence, we must remember that the knowledge and skills developed in the early years provide an essential foundation for later development. Students construct their own knowledge, rather than absorb it directly from the environment, and misinterpretations are likely to be common, especially in the early years. We should offer ample opportunities for students to acquire new knowledge and skills through challenging academic and social contexts.

KEY CONCEPTS

developmental milestones (p. 27)
universals (in development) (p. 27)
stages (p. 28)
maturation (p. 28)
sensitive period (p. 28)
constructivism (p. 30)
schemes (p. 30)
assimilation (p. 30)
accommodation (p. 30)
equilibrium (p. 31)
disequilibrium (p. 31)
equilibration (p. 32)
sensorimotor stage (p. 33)
object permanence (p. 33)
preoperational stage (p. 33)
symbolic thinking (p. 33)
preoperational egocentrism (p. 33)
egocentric speech (p. 33)
conservation (p. 35)

operations (p. 35)
concrete operations stage (p. 35)
multiple classification (p. 35)
deductive reasoning (p. 35)
formal operations stage (p. 37)
formal operational egocentrism (p. 39)
sociocultural perspective (p. 43)
internalization (p. 44)
self-talk (private speech) (p. 44)
inner speech (p. 44)
actual developmental level (p. 45)
level of potential development (p. 45)
zone of proximal development (ZPD)
  (p. 45)
guided participation (p. 46)
scaffolding (p. 46)
apprenticeship (p. 47)
cognitive apprenticeship (p. 48)
cognitive processes (p. 50)

learning strategies (p. 51)
rehearsal (p. 51)
organization (p. 52)
elaboration (p. 52)
knowledge base (p. 52)
metacognition (p. 54)
receptive language (p. 59)
expressive language (p. 59)
semantics (p. 59)
undergeneralization (p. 60)
overgeneralization (p. 60)
syntax (p. 61)
overregularization (p. 61)
pragmatics (p. 63)
metalinguistic awareness (p. 63)
immersion (p. 65)
bilingual education (p. 65)
dialect (p. 67)
limited English proficiency (LEP) (p. 67)

3

Personal, Social, and Moral Development

W hat people in your life have had a significant impact on the kind of person you are today? To what extent have parents or other family members influenced the ways that you think about yourself, the manner in which you interact with others, or the moral values that guide your decisions? Can you think of teachers who've had a major effect on your self-confidence, your interpersonal skills, or your moral values? In what ways have your friends and classmates also played a role in the development of these characteristics?

School is not just a place where students learn reading, writing, and arithmetic. It is also a place where they develop greater or lesser degrees of self-esteem, acquire strategies for getting along with other people, and explore various perspectives on the difference between right and wrong. In other words, school is a place where students grow personally, socially, and morally, as well as academically.

In this chapter we will consider children's personal development (their emerging personalities and self-concepts), social development (their increasing ability to interact effectively with other people), and moral development (their evolving understanding of right and wrong behavior). In particular, we will address questions such as these:

- How does the environment influence students' personal, social, and moral development?
- What do we mean by the term *personality*? To what extent are students' personalities influenced by heredity and environment, and to what extent are they likely to change as students develop?
- How do students' self-concepts and self-esteem affect their classroom performance and academic achievement, and how can we help students think positively about themselves?
- Under what conditions and in what contexts are students most likely to learn appropriate social skills?
- How can we promote social interaction among diverse groups of students?
- In what ways do students' moral reasoning and prosocial behavior change over time, and how can we promote their moral and prosocial development?
- In what ways are students likely to differ from one another in terms of their personal, social, and moral development, and how can we accommodate such differences?

CASE STUDY: The Bad Apple

Adam seems to cause problems wherever he goes. In the classroom, he is rude and defiant. On a typical school day, he comes to class late, slouches in his seat, rests his feet on his desk, yells obscenities at classmates and his teacher, and stubbornly refuses to participate in classroom activities.

Away from his teacher's watchful eye, Adam's behavior is even worse. He shoves and pushes students in the hall, steals lunches from smaller boys in the cafeteria, and frequently initiates physical fights on the school grounds.

For obvious reasons, no one at school likes Adam very much. His classmates describe him as a bully, and their parents describe him as a "bad apple," rotten to the core. Even his teacher, who tries to find the best in all of her students, has seen few redeeming qualities in Adam and is beginning to write him off as a lost cause.

Adam doesn't seem to be bothered by the hostile feelings he generates. He's counting the days until he can legally drop out of school.

- Why does Adam behave the way he does? What possible factors in his environment—perhaps at home, at school, or among his peers—might have contributed to his aggressiveness, impulsiveness, and apparent self-centeredness?

- How could a teacher help Adam develop more appropriate and productive behavior?

How the Environment Influences Personal, Social, and Moral Development

You might have formed several different hypotheses about why Adam behaves as he does. Perhaps a parent encourages aggressive behavior, or at least does nothing to *discourage* it. Perhaps Adam lives in an inner-city neighborhood in which violence is commonplace and aggression is the best means of self-defense. Perhaps his family can't afford to provide breakfast at home or lunch at school or perhaps has never taught him that stealing infringes on the rights of others. At school, perhaps previous teachers have tolerated Adam's obscene language. Perhaps classmates have learned to stay away from him because of his inappropriate social skills, and he now finds that pushing, shoving, and picking fights are the only ways he can get their attention.

Without a doubt, the most important contributors to children's personal, social, and moral development are *other people,* including parents, teachers, and fellow students. Of these, parents are perhaps the most influential. They reward their children for some behaviors and punish them for others. They also serve as models for their children, providing examples of how one should behave. And they often control the specific activities that their children will engage in, thereby influencing the information that their children encounter and the other people with whom they associate (R. D. Hess & McDevitt, 1989).

But the school environment, including the teachers and peers with whom children interact on a daily basis, also plays a major role in how children develop personally, socially, and morally. For example, teachers are instrumental in helping their students develop a strong sense of self-esteem and in teaching behaviors that are acceptable both inside and outside the classroom. Students' classmates provide innumerable opportunities to practice social skills and to learn how to look at situations from someone else's point of view. And as we will soon discover, many classroom activities and events provide a context in which students must critically examine their own notions of what actions constitute moral and immoral behavior.

Personal Development

Psychologists disagree regarding how to define **personality** (Mischel, 1993), but in general we can think of personality as a set of relatively enduring traits that characterize the way in which a person typically interacts with his or her physical and social environments. In a classroom context, personality includes the extent to which our students are outgoing or shy, independent or dependent, energetic or "laid back," self-confident or full of self-doubt.

Research tells us that some aspects of our students' personalities may be, at least in part, the result of heredity. For example, we see differences in infants' temperaments— their activity level, adventurousness, shyness, irritability, and distractibility—almost from birth (Bouchard, Lykken, McGue, Segal, & Tellegen, 1990; Kagan, Snidman, & Arcus, 1992; Lanthier & Bates, 1997; Plomin, 1989). But contemporary developmentalists believe that environmental factors also play a critical role in determining the kinds of individuals that children become—whether they are friendly and self-confident, unhappy and unsure of their own capabilities, or perhaps even as angry and rebellious as Adam. Parents are among the most important environmental influences on children's personalities, as we shall see now.

How Parents Influence Their Children's Personal Development

Parents' behaviors begin to influence their children's personalities even in the first few weeks and months of life. For example, when parents and their infants form a strong, affectionate bond (a process called **attachment**), the infants are likely to develop into amiable, cooperative, and independent children. In contrast, those who do not become closely attached to a parent or some other individual early in life are apt to become immature, unpopular, dependent, and prone to disruptive and aggressive behaviors later on (Hartup, 1989; Jacobson & Wille, 1986; Sroufe, 1983).

Patterns of childrearing also appear to play a significant role in children's personal development. Researchers have identified four different **parenting styles** that are correlated with children's social behaviors and personalities (Baumrind, 1971, 1989; Maccoby & Martin, 1983). These four parenting styles—authoritative, authoritarian, permissive, and uninvolved—are summarized in Table 3–1. Here you will also find suggestions for dealing with children from each type of home.

As you can see from Table 3–1, an authoritative style seems to be most beneficial. Children from authoritative homes are well-adjusted, happy, energetic, self-confident, curious, and independent. They are motivated to do well in school; as a result, they are often high achievers (L. S. Miller, 1995; L. Steinberg et al., 1989). They are likable and cooperative, make friends easily, and show strong leadership skills. They also exhibit self-control and concern for the rights and needs of others.

As you read about the four parenting styles in Table 3–1, you may notice that these styles differ from one another in the degree of control that parents exert over their children. At one extreme is the excessively controlling, authoritarian parent; at the other extreme is the noncontrolling (either permissive or uninvolved) parent. The authoritative home appears to be the happy medium: Children thrive when parents establish and consistently enforce standards for acceptable behavior while at the same time considering their children's individual rights and needs. Ideally, adults should tailor the degree of control to the developmental level of the child, gradually loosening restrictions as children become capable of greater responsibility and independence (Maccoby & Martin, 1983). Too much control may lead to a lack of self-confidence and initiative; too little may lead to selfish, impulsive, and possibly delinquent behavior. Thinking back to the opening case study, we might wonder whether Adam's aggressiveness, impulsiveness, and self-centeredness result from too little control at home.

Parent-child interactions are, to some extent, a two-way street. Although children's behaviors are often the result of how their parents treat them, sometimes the reverse is true as well: Parents' behaviors may be the result of how *they are treated by their children* (Clarke-Stewart, 1988; Maccoby & Martin, 1983; Scott-Jones, 1984). Temperament is, in part, genetically determined: Some children appear to be naturally quieter and more easygoing, whereas others are more lively or irritable. When children are quick to comply with their parents' wishes, parents may have no reason to be overly controlling. When children are hot-tempered, parents may have to impose more restrictions on behavior

Think about some television shows that depict family life (e.g., *Roseanne, Full House, Married with Children*). Which parenting styles best characterize each of these shows?

TABLE 3.1

COMPARE/CONTRAST

Parenting Styles and Implications for Teachers

WHEN PARENTS EXHIBIT THIS PARENTING STYLE . . .	CHILDREN TEND TO BE . . .	AS TEACHERS WE SHOULD . . .
Authoritative: Provide a loving, supportive, home environment Hold high expectations and standards for their children's behaviors Enforce household rules consistently Explain why some behaviors are acceptable and others are not Include children in family decision making	Happy Self-confident Curious Independent Likable Respectful of others Successful in school	Adopt an authoritative style similar to that of their parents
Authoritarian: Convey less emotional warmth than authoritative parents Hold high expectations and standards for their children's behaviors Establish rules of behavior without regard for the children's needs Expect rules to be obeyed without question Allow little give-and-take in parent-child discussions	Unhappy Anxious Low in self-confidence Lacking initiative Dependent on others Lacking in social skills and altruistic behaviors Coercive in dealing with others Defiant	Adopt an authoritative style, with particular emphasis on: • conveying emotional warmth • soliciting students' perspectives on classroom rules and procedures • considering students' needs in developing classroom rules
Permissive: Provide a loving, supportive, home environment Hold few expectations or standards for their children's behaviors Rarely punish inappropriate behavior Allow their children to make many of their own decisions (e.g., about eating, bedtime)	Selfish Unmotivated Dependent on others Demanding of attention Disobedient Impulsive	Adopt an authoritative style, with particular emphasis on: • holding high expectations for behavior • imposing consequences for inappropriate behavior
Uninvolved: Provide little if any emotional support for their children Hold few expectations or standards for their children's behaviors Have little interest in their children's lives Seem overwhelmed by their own problems	Disobedient Demanding Low in self-control Low in tolerance for frustration Lacking long-term goals	Adopt an authoritative style, with particular emphasis on: • conveying emotional warmth • holding high expectations for behavior • imposing consequences for inappropriate behavior

Sources: Baumrind, 1971, 1989; Maccoby & Martin, 1983; Simons, Whitbeck, Conger, & Conger, 1991; L. Steinberg, 1993; L. Steinberg, Elmen, & Mounts, 1989.

and administer consequences for misbehaviors more frequently. We must be careful that we don't always place total credit or blame on parents for their parenting styles.

As teachers, we can serve as valuable resources to parents about possible strategies for promoting their children's personal development. With newsletters, parent-teacher conferences, and parent discussion groups, we can share ways of helping children develop increasingly more appropriate and mature behaviors. The important thing is to communicate information *without* pointing fingers or being judgmental about parenting styles.

In our own classrooms, we should adopt a style similar to that of the authoritative parent. For example, we should exert some control in the classroom by holding high ex-

Offer yourself as a resource to parents about strategies for promoting more appropriate behaviors, but don't pass judgment about the parenting styles you observe.

pectations for student behavior and enforcing classroom rules consistently. At the same time, we should explain to students why some behaviors are acceptable and others are not, provide a supportive environment, and recognize each student's legitimate needs and point of view. We can include students in classroom decision making and encourage them to be independent and self-reliant. And we should gradually loosen the reins as students demonstrate increasing independence and self-control.

One aspect of personal development in which teachers play an especially important role is the development of students' self-concepts and self-esteem. Let's look at this area of development and find out how we can definitely make a difference.

Self-Concept and Self-Esteem

Experiencing Firsthand
Describing Yourself

On a sheet of paper, list twenty adjectives or phrases that describe the kind of person you think you are.

How did you describe yourself? Are you a good student? Are you physically attractive? Are you friendly? likable? moody? intelligent? test-anxious? strong? uncoordinated?

Your answers to these questions tell you something about your **self-concept**—your beliefs about yourself, your personality, your strengths and weaknesses. They may also tell you something about your **self-esteem**—the extent to which you believe yourself to be a capable and worthy individual.

Students tend to have an overall general feeling of self-worth: They believe either that they are good, capable individuals or that they are somehow inept or unworthy (Harter, 1990; H. W. Marsh & Craven, 1997). At the same time, they are usually aware that they have both strengths and weaknesses, that they do some things well and other things poorly (Harter, 1982; Marsh & Craven, 1997; H. W. Marsh & Yeung, 1997). For example, students may have somewhat different views about themselves in these three areas (Harter, 1982):

- *Cognitive competence.* Students have general beliefs about their academic ability and performance. For example, they may describe themselves as being smart and performing academic tasks successfully, or perhaps instead as being stupid and doing poorly in school.

- *Social competence.* Students have general beliefs about their ability to relate with other people, especially their peers. For example, they may describe themselves as having many friends and being liked, or instead as having trouble making friends and being unpopular.

- *Physical competence.* Students have general beliefs about their ability to engage in physical activities such as sports and outdoor games. For example, they may describe themselves as doing well at sports and often being selected for athletic teams, or instead as being uncoordinated and frequently excluded from team sports.

Many students, older ones especially, may make still finer distinctions when judging themselves (Harter, 1990; H. W. Marsh, 1990b; Schell, Klein, & Babey, 1996). For example, students may define themselves as poor readers but good in mathematics. And they are likely to see a difference between at least two aspects of their physical selves—their athletic capabilities and their physical attractiveness to others. Thus, self-concept appears to have several levels of specificity, as Figure 3–1 illustrates.

Students may even have differing beliefs about themselves regarding specific tasks and situations within a particular domain. For instance, although I don't think of myself

Adopt an authoritative style in the classroom.

Can you think of specific situations in which it might be appropriate to include students in classroom decision-making?

In which of these three areas is your own self-esteem highest?

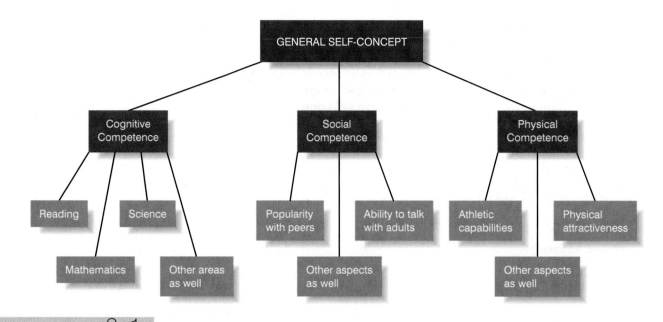

Self-concept is multifaceted and hierarchical in nature.

as being a very good athlete—I'm not very strong, and I have little endurance—I know that I'm a fairly decent water-skier and racquetball player. And although I'm generally shy around people I've never met, I can be quite friendly once I've gotten to know them. When we talk about people's self-beliefs at this level of specificity, we are talking about *self-efficacy,* a topic we will consider in greater depth in Chapter 11.

As students grow older, and especially as they reach adolescence, their self-concepts begin to include a sense of **identity:** a self-constructed definition of who they are, what things they find important, and what goals they want to accomplish in life. Memberships in various groups—perhaps informal cliques at school, organized clubs or teams, or eth-nic neighborhoods or communities—often play a key role in adolescents' identities (Trawick-Smith, 1997; Wigfield, Eccles, & Pintrich, 1996). Not only do such groups help students define who they are, but they also endorse values and goals that students may adopt for themselves. Furthermore, a strong sense of ethnic or racial identity and pride can often help students from minority groups deal with the racist behaviors that they sometimes face (McAdoo, 1985; Spencer & Markstrom-Adams, 1990). Consider this statement by Eva, an African American high school student, as an example:

> I'm proud to be black and everything. But, um, I'm aware of, you know, racist acts and racist things that are happening in the world, but I use that as no excuse, you know. I feel as though I can succeed. . . . I just know that I'm not gonna let [racism] stop me. . . . Be-ing black is good. I'm proud to be black but you also gotta face reality. And what's going on, you know, black people are not really getting anywhere in life, but I know I will and I don't know—I just know I will. Well, I'm determined to . . . and with God's help, you can't go wrong. (Way, 1998, p. 257)

Self-concept and self-esteem are important factors influencing behavior and achieve-ment in school: Students tend to behave in ways that are consistent with their beliefs about themselves (Pintrich & Garcia, 1994; Yu, Elder, & Urdan, 1995). Those who see themselves as "good students" are more likely to pay attention, follow directions in class, use effective learning strategies, work independently and persistently to solve difficult problems, and enroll in challenging courses. In contrast, those who believe they are "poor students" are likely to misbehave in class, study infrequently or not at all, neglect to turn in homework assignments, and avoid taking difficult subjects. Along a similar vein, students who see themselves as friendly and likable are apt to seek the company of their classmates and to run for student council, whereas those who believe they are disliked by classmates may keep to themselves or perhaps even act with hostility and aggression toward their peers. Student with a high sense of physical competence will go out for extracurricular athletics, whereas those who see themselves as total klutzes probably will not.

Clearly, students who have a positive self-concept and high self-esteem are those most likely to succeed academically, socially, and physically (Assor & Connell, 1992; Ma & Kishor, 1997; Pintrich & Schunk, 1996). Let's look at the factors that influence self-concept and then at several reasons why students' self-concepts become increasingly more stable over time.

Factors Influencing the Development of Self-Concept and Self-Esteem

Simply telling students that they are "good" or "smart" or "popular" is unlikely to make much of a dent in low self-esteem (Damon, 1991; L. Katz, 1993; H. W. Marsh & Craven, 1997). However, at least three factors definitely *do* influence the degree to which students form positive or negative self-concepts:

- Their own prior behaviors and performance
- The behaviors of other individuals toward them
- The expectations that others hold for their future performance

Each one offers insights as to how, as teachers, we can enhance our students' self-concepts.

Students' prior behaviors and performance. As noted earlier, students' self-concepts influence the ways in which they behave. Yet the reverse is true as well: To some extent, students' self-concepts and self-esteem depend on how successfully they have behaved in the past (Damon, 1991; H. W. Marsh, 1990a). Students are more likely to believe that they have an aptitude for mathematics if they have been successful in previous math classes, to believe they are capable athletes if they have been victorious in athletic competitions, or to believe they are likable individuals if they have been able to establish and maintain friendly peer relationships.

The interplay between self-concept and behavior can create a vicious downward cycle: A poor self-concept leads to less productive behavior, which leads to fewer

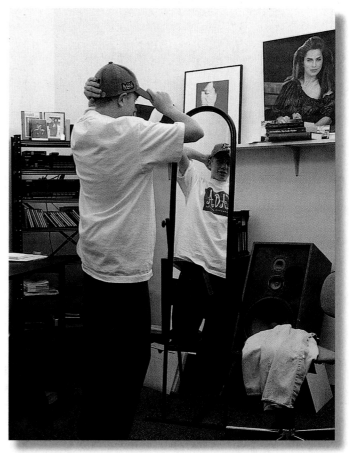

Students who have a positive self-concept and high self-esteem are more likely to succeed academically, socially, and physically.

successes, which perpetuates the poor self-concept. To break the cycle, we must make sure that our students have numerous opportunities to succeed at academic, social, and physical tasks (Damon, 1991; L. Katz, 1993; H. W. Marsh & Craven, 1997). For example, we can gear assignments to their developmental levels and cognitive capabilities. We can make sure they have mastered the necessary prerequisite knowledge and skills *before* we assign new tasks. But we must remember that success in very *easy* activities is unlikely to have much of an impact, as Figure 3–2 so clearly illustrates. Instead, we should assign challenging tasks, giving students the structure and support (the scaffolding) they need to accomplish those tasks successfully.

Give students the opportunities and support they need to succeed at challenging academic, social, and physical tasks.

FIGURE 3.2

We are unlikely to boost students' self-esteem by rewarding easy accomplishments.

DOONESBURY © G. B. Trudeau. Reprinted with permission of UNIVERSAL PRESS SYNDICATE. All rights reserved.

How students evaluate their own performance also depends to some extent on how the students around them are performing (H. W. Marsh, 1990b; H. W. Marsh, Chessor, Craven, & Roche, 1995; Nicholls, 1984). Older students in particular are likely to judge themselves in terms of how they compare with their peers. When students see themselves performing better than other students in their class, they are likely to develop a relatively positive self-concept. When their own performance is poorer than that of their classmates, they develop a more negative self-concept. To help our students develop positive self-concepts, then, we probably want to minimize competitive and other situations in which students might compare themselves unfavorably with their classmates.

Behaviors of others. The behaviors of other people, both adults and peers, also play a crucial role in the development of students' self-concepts (Durkin, 1995; Harter, 1983; Hartup, 1989). How these individuals behave toward a child communicates their evaluations of the child and their beliefs about his or her worth as a person. For example, parents who accept their children as they are and who treat their children's interests and problems as important are likely to have children with positive self-concepts and high self-esteem. Parents who punish their children for the things they cannot do, without also praising them for the things they do well, are likely to have children with low self-esteem (Griffore, 1981; Harter, 1983). Teacher behaviors undoubtedly have a similar effect; for example, the relative proportion of positive and negative feedback from a teacher tells students a great deal about their academic capabilities. And students' classmates communicate information about their social competence through a variety of behaviors—for example, by seeking out their companionship or by ridiculing them in front of others.

Obviously we can't always control how other people treat our students. But we *can* make sure we respond to students in ways that will boost rather than lower their self-

🍎 Minimize competitive and other situations in which students might compare themselves unfavorably with their classmates.

▪ Have you ever heard one student say something that threatens another student's self-esteem? How might a teacher intervene in such a situation?

esteem. Students who misbehave usually capture our attention more readily than those who behave appropriately, so it is often easier to criticize undesirable behavior rather than praise desirable behavior. As teachers, we must make a concerted effort to catch students in the act of doing something well and praise them accordingly. We must be specific about what we are praising, because we will usually be more successful in improving particular aspects of our students' self-concepts than in improving their overall sense of self-worth (H. W. Marsh, 1990b). More generally, we must treat our students with respect—for example, by asking them about their personal views and opinions about academic subject matter, by seeking their input in important classroom decisions, and by communicating a genuine interest in their well-being (e.g., L. Katz, 1993).

Give positive feedback about students' accomplishments, and communicate a genuine interest in students' feelings, opinions, and general well-being.

At the same time, our students will only learn what academic responses are incorrect and what classroom behaviors are unacceptable if we let them know when they are doing something wrong. It is inevitable, then, that we occasionally give negative feedback. The trick is to give that negative feedback while at the same time also communicating respect and affection for our students as human beings. For example, when students make mistakes in their academic work, we can point out that errors are a natural part of the learning process and can provide valuable information about how to improve in knowledge and skills. When students behave inappropriately in the classroom, we can communicate that, although we like them, we disapprove of their present actions—for example, by saying something such as, "You're generally a very kind person, Gail, but you hurt Jenny's feelings just now by making fun of her new outfit."

Provide negative feedback when necessary, but only while also communicating respect and affection for students.

Expectations for students' future performance. People in a student's life often communicate expectations for that student through their behaviors. When parents and teachers have high expectations and when they offer support and encouragement for the attainment of challenging goals, students tend to have more positive self-concepts (Griffore, 1981; M. J. Harris & Rosenthal, 1985). When parents and teachers expect children to achieve academically, those children are more likely to have confidence in their own academic capabilities (Eccles, Jacobs, Harold-Goldsmith, Jayaratne, & Yee, 1989; Eccles [Parsons] et al., 1983).

Hold realistically high expectations for students' performance.

The result of all this feedback from others is that students' perceptions of themselves are usually similar to how others perceive them (Harter, 1990; Shaffer, 1988). For example, students' beliefs about their academic ability are similar to their classroom teachers' beliefs about their intelligence and aptitude. Their beliefs about their physical ability are correlated with the perceptions of their physical education teachers. And their sense of their own competence in social situations is likely to be a reflection of their actual popularity with peers.

The Increasing Stability of the Self-Concept

Students' self-concepts become increasingly stable—and therefore increasingly resistant to change—as they grow older (H. W. Marsh & Craven, 1997; O'Malley & Bachman, 1983; Savin-Williams & Demo, 1984). Students with the most positive self-concepts in the early years also tend to have the most positive self-concepts in later years. Conversely, students who think poorly of themselves in elementary school also have lower self-esteem in high school. Hence, it is especially important to help students develop positive self-concepts in the early elementary school years.

Speculate on possible reasons for this trend before you read further.

There are probably several reasons why students' self-concepts eventually become so resistant to change. First, as mentioned earlier, people usually behave in ways that are consistent with what they believe about themselves, so their behaviors are likely to produce reactions from others that confirm their self-concepts. To illustrate, a student who thinks of herself as a class clown is likely to continue "entertaining" her class and thus to evoke the continuing laughter of her classmates. Second, people tend to seek out information that confirms what they already believe about themselves: Students with positive self-concepts are more likely to seek out positive feedback, whereas those with negative self-concepts may

Remember that
improving a student's
self-esteem may take
time, especially at the
secondary level.

actually look for information about their weaknesses and limitations (Swann, 1997). Third, people seldom put themselves in situations where they believe they won't succeed, thereby eliminating any possibility of discovering that they *can* succeed. For example, if a student believes he is a poor athlete and so refuses to go out for the baseball team, he may never learn that, in fact, he has the potential to become a skillful player. And fourth, many outside factors that contribute to one's self-concept—for example, parental behaviors, socioeconomic circumstances, and one's physical attractiveness—usually remain relatively stable throughout childhood (O'Malley & Bachman, 1983).

As we have seen, older students have more differentiated self-concepts, as well as more stable ones, than younger students. Let's look at some additional ways in which students of different ages are likely to exhibit certain personality traits.

Developmental Differences in Personality

The preceding chapter described some ways in which students' cognitive and linguistic abilities change as they grow older. Students' personal characteristics are also likely to vary somewhat at different age levels. As we consider developmental differences in personality, we will draw from a theory of personal development proposed by Erik Erikson (1963, 1972); his eight stages of "psychosocial" development are described in Figure 3–3. We will also draw from research findings related to child and adolescent development.

The Preschool Years

Erikson described the preschool years as a period of *initiative versus guilt.* Preschoolers become increasingly capable of accomplishing tasks on their own, rather than depending on adults to do those tasks for them. With this growing independence, they begin to make their own decisions about the activities they want to pursue. Sometimes they initiate projects that they can readily accomplish, but at other times they undertake projects that are beyond their limited capabilities or that interfere with the plans and activities of others. Erikson recommended that, as teachers, we can help young children develop *initiative*—independence in planning and undertaking activities—by encouraging and supporting them in their efforts to plan and carry out their own activities, while at the same time helping them make realistic choices that do not conflict with the needs of others. When adults instead discourage the pursuit of these activities or dismiss them as silly and bothersome, then children may instead develop *guilt* about their desires to pursue projects independently.

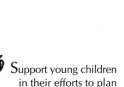 Support young children
in their efforts to plan
and carry out their
own activities.

Most preschoolers have positive self-concepts and high self-esteem. In fact, they often believe they are more capable than they actually *are* (Flavell et al., 1993). To some extent, this overconfidence may be due to the fact that they have few opportunities to compare their own performance to that of their age-mates. Instead, their self-assessments are probably based primarily on the progress they continue to make in accomplishing "big boy" and "big girl" tasks.

The Elementary School Years

Erikson proposed that the elementary school years are critical for the development of self-confidence and described this period as one of *industry versus inferiority.* Ideally, elementary school provides many opportunities for children to achieve the recognition of teachers, parents, and peers by producing things (*industry*)—for example, by drawing pictures, solving addition problems, and writing sentences. When children are encouraged to make and do things and are then praised for their accomplishments, they begin to demonstrate industry by being diligent, persevering at tasks until they complete them, and putting work before pleasure. If children are instead ridiculed or punished for their efforts or if they find that they are incapable of meeting their teachers' and parents' expectations, they may develop feelings of *inferiority* and inadequacy about their own capabilities.

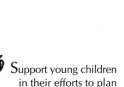 Encourage elementary
students to make and do
things, and praise them for
their accomplishments.

FIGURE 3.3

Erikson's eight stages of psychosocial development

Erik Erikson (1963, 1972) described a series of eight "psychosocial" stages through which people proceed over the course of development. Each stage presents a unique developmental task, and the way in which an individual deals with each task has a particular impact on that individual's personal development.

TRUST VERSUS MISTRUST (INFANCY)

According to Erikson, the major developmental task of infants is to learn whether or not other people can be trusted to satisfy basic needs. A child's parents and other primary caretakers play a key role here. When caretakers can be depended on to feed a hungry stomach, change an uncomfortable diaper, and provide physical affection at regular intervals, an infant learns *trust*—that others are consistently dependable and reliable. When caretakers ignore the infant's needs, are inconsistent in attending to them, or are even abusive, the infant may instead learn *mistrust*—that the world is an undependable, unpredictable, and possibly dangerous place.

AUTONOMY VERSUS SHAME AND DOUBT (TODDLER YEARS)

With the increased muscular coordination that results from physiological maturation and the increased mobility that accompanies learning to crawl and walk, toddlers become capable of satisfying some of their own needs. They are learning to feed themselves, wash and dress themselves, and use the bathroom. When parents and other caretakers encourage self-sufficient behavior, toddlers develop a sense of *autonomy*—a sense of being able to handle many problems on their own. But when caretakers demand too much too soon, refuse to let children perform tasks of which they are capable, or ridicule early attempts at self-sufficiency, children may instead develop *shame and doubt* about their ability to handle the problems that the environment presents.

INITIATIVE VERSUS GUILT (PRESCHOOL YEARS)

During the preschool years, children begin to get their own ideas about the activities they want to pursue; for example, they may undertake simple art projects, make houses and roadways in the sandbox, or play "house" with other children. When parents and preschool teachers encourage and support such efforts, children develop *initiative*—independence in planning and undertaking activities. In contrast, when adults discourage such activities, children may develop *guilt* about their needs and desires.

INDUSTRY VERSUS INFERIORITY (ELEMENTARY SCHOOL YEARS)

When they reach elementary school, children are expected to master many new academic skills, and they soon learn that they can gain the recognition of adults through their written assignments, art projects, dramatic productions, and so on. When children are allowed and encouraged to make and do things and when they are praised for their accomplishments, they begin to demonstrate *industry*—a pattern of working hard, persisting at lengthy tasks, and putting work before pleasure. But when children are punished for their efforts or when they find that they can't meet their teachers' and parents' expectations for their performance, they may develop feelings of *inferiority* about their own abilities.

IDENTITY VERSUS ROLE CONFUSION (ADOLESCENCE)

As they make the transition from childhood to adulthood, adolescents ponder the roles they will play in the adult world. Initially, they are likely to experience some *role confusion*—mixed ideas and feelings about the specific ways in which they will fit into society—and may experiment with a variety of behaviors and activities (e.g., tinkering with cars, baby-sitting for neighbors, engaging in extracurricular activities at school, affiliating with particular political or religious groups). Eventually, most adolescents achieve a sense of *identity* regarding who they are and where their lives are headed.

(continued)

Figure 3.3 (continued)

INTIMACY VERSUS ISOLATION (YOUNG ADULTHOOD)

Once people have established their identities, they are ready to make commitments to one or more other individuals. They become capable of forming *intimate,* reciprocal relationships with others (e.g., through marriage or close friendships) and willingly make the sacrifices and compromises that such relationships require. When people cannot form these intimate relationships (perhaps because of their reluctance or inability to forego the satisfaction of their own needs), then a sense of *isolation* may result.

GENERATIVITY VERSUS STAGNATION (MIDDLE AGE)

During middle age, the primary developmental task is one of contributing to society and helping to guide future generations. When an individual makes a contribution during this period, perhaps by raising a family or by working toward the betterment of society, a sense of *generativity*—a sense of productivity and accomplishment—results. In contrast, an individual who is self-centered and unable or unwilling to help society move forward develops a feeling of *stagnation*—a dissatisfaction with the relative lack of production.

INTEGRITY VERSUS DESPAIR (RETIREMENT YEARS)

According to Erikson, the final developmental task is a retrospective one. Individuals look back on their lives and accomplishments. They develop feelings of contentment and *integrity* if they believe that they have led a happy, productive life. They may instead develop a sense of *despair* if they look back on a life of disappointments and unachieved goals.

Children in the elementary grades learn that, by producing things, they can achieve the recognition of teachers and parents.

Research tells us that, in general, children's self-esteem often drops soon after they first reach elementary school (Harter, 1990; Stipek, 1981), perhaps because of the many new challenges—both academic and social—that school presents. As they have more and more opportunities to compare themselves with their classmates during the elementary grades, their self-assessments become increasingly more realistic (Flavell et al., 1993; Paris & Cunningham, 1996; Pintrich & Schunk, 1996).

Adolescence

Another drop in self-esteem occurs at about the time that students move from elementary school to junior high school—a drop that is especially pronounced for girls (Eccles & Midgley, 1989; H. W. Marsh, 1990b; Sadker & Sadker, 1994; Simmons & Blyth, 1987). The physiological changes that occur with puberty may be a factor: Students' self-esteem depends increasingly on their beliefs about their appearance and their popularity, yet boys and girls alike tend to think of themselves as being somewhat less attractive once they reach adolescence (Bender, 1997; Cornell et al., 1990; Harter, 1990). The changing school environment probably also has a negative impact on self-esteem. Junior high schools often differ from elementary schools in several ways (Eccles & Midgley, 1989). For one thing, students don't have the opportunity to form the close-knit, supportive relationships with teachers that many of them had in elementary school. Students may also discover that their school grades are based more on competitive criteria—that is, on how well they perform in comparison with their classmates. Furthermore, at a time when they probably have an increased need for close friendships, students may find themselves in classes with many people they don't know. Because all of these unsettling changes occur simultaneously, it is not surprising that we see a temporary drop in self-esteem. Fortunately, once they have successfully adjusted to the junior high school environment, most adolescents enjoy positive self-concepts and general mental health (Durkin, 1995; Nottelmann, 1987; S. I. Powers, Hauser, & Kilner, 1989).

Erikson described adolescence as a period of *identity versus role confusion.* As students move from childhood to adulthood, they begin to wrestle with the question of who they are and how they will eventually fit into the adult world; in other words, they strive to achieve a sense of *identity* regarding the role they will play as adults. In the meantime, they often experience a state of *role confusion*—uncertainty about the direction that their lives will take. In their ongoing search for identity, they may adopt temporary "identities," aligning themselves strongly with a particular peer group, adhering rigidly to a single brand of clothing, or insisting on a certain hairstyle. For example, as a fifteen-year-old, my son Alex described himself as a "skater"—someone for whom skateboarding becomes a way of life as well as a form of transportation—and insisted on wearing the oversized shirts and hip-hugging baggy pants (revealing at least six inches' worth of boxer shorts!) that came with the territory.

Erikson believed that most people achieve a sense of identity by the end of adolescence. But more recent evidence indicates that, even by the high school years, only a small minority of students have begun to think seriously about the eventual role they will play in society and to identify some lifelong goals (Archer, 1982; Durkin, 1995; Marcia, 1980). It appears that adolescents need a period of time to explore various options for themselves, in terms of both possible careers and ideological belief systems, before they can achieve a true sense of their adult identity (Marcia, 1980). But once they have done so, they will have a commitment to a particular career, a set of self-chosen social, political, and religious beliefs, and a strong sense of direction about where their own lives are likely to take them (Marcia, 1980).

There are two additional aspects of adolescent self-perceptions of which we should be aware (Elkind, 1981). First, many adolescents believe that, in any social situation, everyone else's attention is focused squarely on themselves. This self-centered aspect of the adolescent self-concept is sometimes called the **imaginary audience.** Because they believe themselves to be the center of attention, teenagers are often preoccupied with their physical appearance and are quite critical of themselves, assuming that everyone else is going to be equally observant and critical. Their extreme sensitivity to embarrassment may, in some situations, lead them to respond with undue violence to the insults or verbal attacks of their peers (Lowry, Sleet, Duncan, Powell, & Kolbe, 1995).

A second noteworthy characteristic of adolescent self-concepts is the **personal fable:** Teenagers often believe themselves to be completely unlike anyone else. For instance, they often think that their own feelings are completely unique—that those around them have never experienced such emotions. Hence, they may insist that no one else, least of all parents and teachers, can possibly know how they feel. They may also have a sense of immortality, believing that they are not susceptible to the normal dangers of life. It is not surprising, then, that many adolescents take seemingly foolish risks, such as driving at high speeds, experimenting with drugs and alcohol, or having unprotected sexual intercourse (Arnett, 1995; DeRidder, 1993; Packard, 1983; S. P. Thomas, Groër, & Droppleman, 1993).

The development of both the imaginary audience and personal fable may to some extent reflect students' changing cognitive abilities during the adolescent years. For instance, some theorists have proposed that both the imaginary audience and the personal fable are a symptom of the *adolescent egocentrism* that Piaget described (e.g., Elkind, 1981). Others suggest that they may result from adolescents' increasing ability to look at the world from other people's perspectives (Lapsley, Milstead, Quintana,

Take special pains to enhance students' self-esteem during early adolescence.

Provide opportunities for adolescents to explore various career options and belief systems.

Do you remember being overly concerned about your clothes, hair, or complexion as a teenager?

To let students know that you understand their personal concerns, describe instances in your own life in which you felt insecure, embarrassed, confused, or frustrated.

Flannery, & Buss, 1986). Whatever the origins of these phenomena, however, they appear to peak in early adolescence and then slowly decline (Durkin, 1995; Lapsley, Jackson, Rice, & Shadid, 1988).

FOR BETTER OR FOR WORSE / Lynn Johnston

Elizabeth's excessive concern about her appearance is seen frequently in teenagers. Adolescents often believe that they are the focus of everyone else's attention—a belief known as the *imaginary audience.*

FOR BETTER OR FOR WORSE © 1994 Johnston. Dist. by United Media. Reprinted with permission. All rights reserved.

INTO THE CLASSROOM: Promoting Personal Development

Promote success on classroom tasks.

> A teacher provides a format (scaffolding) for writing an expository paragraph: a sentence expressing the main idea, three sentences that support that idea, and a concluding sentence.

Hold reasonably high expectations for students' performance.

> A junior high school swimming coach encourages students to come out for the swim team regardless of prior experience. She works as closely with newcomers as with experienced swimmers, so that all team members can improve.

Give positive feedback for students' accomplishments. Provide negative feedback within the context of overall positive regard.

> The same swimming coach tells a student, "Your crawl stroke has really improved. Your timing on the butterfly is a bit off; let's work on that today."

Give students opportunities to examine and try out a variety of adultlike roles.

> A third-grade teacher develops a list of classroom chores, such as getting a hot lunch count, delivering messages to the main office, and feeding the class goldfish and rabbit. He assigns these chores to students on a rotating basis.

Communicate a genuine interest in students' well-being.

> When a new seventh-grade student is visibly teary-eyed during class, her teacher invites her to take a walk with him during lunchtime. She describes the trouble she is having making friends at her new school, and together they develop some strategies to address the problem.

Social Development

Let's return to the case study presented at the beginning of the chapter. Adam engages in several socially inappropriate behaviors: He pushes other students in the corridor, picks fights in the schoolyard, and yells obscenities in class. As a result, his peers want little to do with him, and his teacher has just about given up on him.

As our students grow older, they should be learning how society as a whole expects them to behave. They should also be acquiring strategies for getting along with their classmates. In the next few pages, we will identify strategies for promoting such social development as we consider the topics of socialization and peer relationships.

Socialization

Beginning early in their lives, most children learn that there are certain things that they can or should do and other things that they definitely should *not* do. For example, many parents teach their toddlers not to hit other children, first-grade teachers ask their students to sit quietly rather than interrupt when someone else is speaking, and high school teachers expect their students to turn in homework assignments on time.

The process of shaping behavior so that children fit in with society is called **socialization.** Through socialization, children learn society's **norms**—the rules determining acceptable and unacceptable behavior. They also learn the specific **roles** that different people occupy within their society—the patterns of behavior acceptable for people having various functions within the group. For example, children usually learn that different behaviors are considered appropriate for the teachers and students in a classroom. And many children develop the notion that boys and girls should behave differently and that men and women should do likewise. Norms and roles are, to some extent, culture-specific: Each culture has its own norms regarding acceptable behavior and defines the roles of various individuals (e.g., teachers vs. students, males vs. females) in a somewhat unique fashion.

Children typically learn their earliest lessons about society's expectations from their parents, who teach them personal hygiene, table manners, rudimentary interpersonal skills (e.g., saying "please" and "thank you"), and so on. Yet teachers become equally important socialization agents once children reach school age. For example, teachers typically expect and encourage behaviors such as these (Helton & Oakland, 1977; R. D. Hess & Holloway, 1984):

- Obeying school rules
- Behaving in an orderly fashion
- Showing respect for authority figures
- Controlling impulses
- Following instructions
- Working independently
- Completing assigned tasks
- Helping and cooperating with classmates
- Striving for academic excellence
- Delaying the satisfaction of immediate needs and desires in order to attain long-term goals

When behaviors expected of students at school differ from those expected at home, children may become confused, nonproductive, sometimes even resistant (R. D. Hess & Holloway, 1984). In other words, they may experience some **culture shock** when they first enter school.

In Chapter 4, we will ▲ find that boys and girls, as well as children from various ethnic groups, are often socialized quite differently.

Expect and encourage 🍎 behaviors essential for long-term school success.

Children may experience some culture shock when they first enter school, especially if behaviors expected at school are very different from those expected at home.

As teachers, we must especially encourage our students to exhibit those behaviors essential for long-term school success—behaviors such as obeying school rules, following instructions, and working independently. For example, when we expect students to work independently, even those students who have not had this expectation placed on them at home show improved work habits (J. L. Epstein, 1983). At the same time, students will need our guidance in meeting any new expectations for their behavior; they will undoubtedly need our patience and understanding as well.

Peer Relationships

Students' social development is affected not only by their parents and teachers but also by their **peers**—their friends and classmates. The classroom is very much a "social" place, a place where students interact regularly with one another. In fact, for many students, socializing with their friends is more important than accomplishing classroom assignments (B. B. Brown, 1993; Doyle, 1986a).

A number of years ago, I asked my three children, "What are friends for?" Here are their responses:

Jeff (at age 6):   To play with.

Alex (at age 9):   Friends can help you in life. They can make you do better in school. They can make you feel better.

Tina (at age 12):   To be your friend and help you in good times and bad times. They're there so you can tell secrets. They're people that care. They're there because they like you. They're people you can trust.

Like Jeff, students in the early elementary grades view their age-mates primarily as a source of entertainment; thus, their relationships with peers are relatively superficial. When students reach the later elementary years, as in the case of Alex, friendships take on an element of trust: Friends begin to believe that they can depend on one another (Damon, 1977). Adolescents like Tina develop increasingly more intimate friendships as they start to share their innermost dreams and secrets with one another (Berndt, 1992; Damon, 1977; G. P. Jones & Dembo, 1989).

Peers become more influential as children grow and gain greater independence from home and family (R. D. Hess & McDevitt, 1989). In fact, people who have few close friends growing up are those who, later in life, are those most likely to drop out of school, have marital problems, and engage in criminal behavior (McCallum & Bracken, 1993). Peer relationships, especially friendships, provide at least three things important for a child's development:

- Emotional support
- Information about acceptable behaviors and values
- An arena for developing social skills

Emotional Support

Students frequently turn to their peers for emotional support in times of trouble or confusion (Asher & Parker, 1989; Buhrmester, 1992; Seltzer, 1982). Furthermore, close friendships foster self-esteem and, especially at the secondary school level, provide a sense of identity for students—a sense that they "belong" to a particular group (Berndt, 1992; Knapp & Woolverton, 1995).

Because adolescence is a particularly confusing time, it's not surprising that friendships become especially important during the teenage years (Csikszentmihalyi, 1995; Wigfield et al., 1996). Friends often understand a teenager's perspective—the preoccupation with physical appearance, the concerns about the opposite sex, and so on—when no one else seems to. By sharing their thoughts and feelings with one another, students may discover that they aren't as unique as they once thought, thereby poking holes in the personal fable I spoke of earlier (Elkind, 1981).

Make sure students have opportunities during the school day to converse with one another about personal matters.

Unfortunately, not all students are readily accepted by their peers; some are ignored or even overtly rejected. Students with few social skills—for example, those who are overly aggressive and those who are exceptionally fearful or withdrawn—often experience peer rejection (Coie & Cillessen, 1993; Juvonen, 1991; McCallum & Bracken, 1993). And students from minority groups frequently find themselves the targets of derogatory remarks and other forms of racism and discrimination, as do students from low-income families (Nieto, 1995; Olneck, 1995; Pang, 1995; Phelan, Yu, & Davidson, 1994).

In the face of widespread rejection by their peers, some students turn to street gangs or deviant subcultures (e.g., Satanism, neo-Nazi groups) to get the emotional support they can find nowhere else (C. C. Clark, 1992; Parks, 1995). As teachers, we can definitely make a difference in the lives of these students (Parks, 1995). We must, first and foremost, show these students that we truly care about them and their well-being—for instance, by being willing listeners in times of trouble and by providing the support they need to achieve both academic and social success. We must also have some awareness of the backgrounds from which they come—their cultural values, economic circumstances, and so on—so that we can better understand the issues with which they may be dealing.

Reach out to students who seem to have little peer support.

Peers are a major source of emotional support, especially during the adolescent years.

Information About Acceptable Behaviors and Values

Most students want to be accepted by their classmates. They look to their friends for approval and may alter their behaviors—for instance, the ways they dress, the language they use, and the activities in which they engage—in order to fit in (Hartup, 1983; Owens, 1996).

Students' peers tend to encourage some behaviors and discourage others, with such **peer pressure** having its strongest effect during the junior high school years (Berndt, Laychak, & Park, 1990; Erwin, 1993; Urdan & Maehr, 1995).

Fortunately, peer groups often encourage such desirable qualities as truthfulness, fairness, cooperation, and a sense of humor (Damon, 1988; McCallum & Bracken, 1993). But they may also encourage students to engage in gender-stereotypical behavior; for example, boys who engage in traditionally "masculine" activities (e.g., playing football) and girls who engage in traditionally "feminine" activities (e.g., putting on makeup) are usually more popular than those who pursue counter-stereotypical activities (Huston, 1983). And violent behavior is much more likely when a student's peer group expects or demands it (Lowry et al., 1995).

Sadly, many peer groups convey the message that academic achievement is undesirable, perhaps by making fun of "brainy" students or by encouraging such behaviors as cheating on homework, cutting class, and skipping school (Berndt, 1992; B. B. Brown, 1993; Knapp & Woolverton, 1995). In fact, in some ethnic minority groups, a student who achieves good grades is "acting White"—a label some students want to avoid at all costs (B. B. Brown, 1993; Ogbu, 1992). Consider what happened to the professional basketball player Kareem Abdul-Jabbar when, as a nine-year-old African-American student, he enrolled in a new school:

> I got there and immediately found I could read better than anyone in the school. . . . When the nuns found this out they paid me a lot of attention, once even asking me, a fourth grader, to read to the seventh grade. When the kids found this out I became a target. . . . I got all A's and was hated for it; I spoke correctly and was called a punk. I had to learn a new language simply to be able to deal with the threats. I had good manners and was a good little boy and paid for it with my hide. (Abdul-Jabbar & Knobles, 1983, p. 16)

To cope with such pressure, some students lead "double lives" that enable them to attain academic success while maintaining the acceptance of their peers; for example, although they attend class and do their homework faithfully, they may feign disinterest in certain activities, disrupt class with jokes or goofy behaviors, and express surprise at receiving high grades (B. B. Brown, 1993; Covington, 1992). We can often help these students maintain their "image" by minimizing the occasions in which they must demonstrate their achievements in front of their classmates; instead, we might ask them to show us what they've accomplished through written assignments or in one-on-one conversations.

An Arena for Developing Social Skills

A child's relationships with parents and teachers are usually lopsided, unequal ones, such that the adults have the upper hand and control the nature of interactions. But in most relationships with peers, each individual is an equal partner. This equality provides a situation in which a child can begin to develop cooperative behaviors, a sense of reciprocity ("You do me a favor, and I'll do you one"), and strategies for resolving conflicts (Asher & Parker, 1989; Erwin, 1993; Maxmell, Jarrett, & Dickerson, 1998).

As noted earlier, students with poor social skills (such as Adam in the chapter's opening case study) typically have few friends. But by not interacting frequently with their peers, they rarely get the opportunities they need to develop the skills they are lacking (Coie & Cillessen, 1993). When they do interact with their classmates, their behaviors are often counterproductive, leaving them more isolated than ever. Consider the plight of a seventh-grader named Michelle:

> Michelle is an extremely bright student, and her academic accomplishments have earned her much teacher praise over the years. But despite her many scholastic successes, Michelle has few friends. To draw attention to herself, she talks incessantly about her academic achievements. Her classmates interpret such bragging as a sign

Provide opportunities for students associating with the "wrong crowd" to interact with students who have more productive attitudes and values.

When friends or classmates discourage high academic achievement, ask students to demonstrate what they have learned privately rather than publicly.

Provide opportunities for students to practice cooperation, reciprocity, and conflict resolution skills.

of undeserved arrogance, and so they insult her frequently as a way of knocking her down a peg or two. In self-defense, Michelle begins hurling insults at her classmates as soon as she sees them—beating them to the punch, so to speak.

When students routinely offend or alienate others, their peers seldom give them the kind of constructive feedback that allows them to improve their behavior on future occasions. It may be up to us, as teachers, to give them the guidance they so desperately need. Let's look at some strategies for doing so.

Think back to our discussion of self-concept. What do Michelle's behaviors tell us about her self-perceptions of social competence?

Fostering Social Skills

Social skills are the things that we do to interact effectively with other people—cooperating, sharing, showing courtesy, initiating conversations, and so on. Some social skills are aimed at benefiting someone else more than ourselves; such **prosocial behaviors** include helping, comforting, and showing empathy for another person's feelings. Schools and classrooms, as complex social situations, provide the ideal context in which social skills and prosocial behaviors can develop (Deutsch, 1993; S. N. Elliott & Busse, 1991).

Students such as Adam and Michelle may be unaware of how socially counterproductive their behaviors really are. As teachers, we can help them develop ways of forming positive and productive interpersonal relationships. Here are several strategies we can use for promoting social skills and prosocial behaviors:

• *Teach specific social skills, provide opportunities for students to practice them, and give feedback.* We can teach students appropriate ways of behaving both through explicit verbal instructions and through modeling desired behaviors for them. Such instruction is especially likely to be effective when we also ask students to practice their newly learned social skills (perhaps through role playing) and give them concrete feedback about how they are doing (S. N. Elliott & Busse, 1991; S. Vaughn, 1991; Zirpoli & Melloy, 1993).

Teach specific social skills.

• *Label and praise appropriate behaviors when they occur.* We should identify and praise the specific social skills that our students exhibit (Vorrath, 1985; Wittmer & Honig, 1994). For example, we might say, "Thank you for being so helpful," or, "I'm glad that you two were able to cooperate so well as you worked on your project."

Label and praise appropriate behaviors.

• *Describe students as having desirable social behaviors.* We can openly describe our students as being helpful, courteous, or generous (Grusec & Redler, 1980; Wittmer & Honig, 1994). For example, eight-year-olds who are told, "You're the kind of person who likes to help others whenever you can," are more likely to share their belongings with others at a later date (Grusec & Redler, 1980).

Describe students as being helpful, courteous, and so on.

• *Teach social problem-solving strategies.* Some students lack productive strategies for solving social problems; for example, they may barge into a game without asking or respond to any provocation in an aggressive fashion (Hughes, 1988; Neel, Jenkins, & Meadows, 1990; Zirpoli & Melloy, 1993). One strategy we can teach them is to think carefully about a situation before responding and then talk themselves through the appropriate behaviors for dealing with it (Hughes, 1988). A strategy we can use for our classroom as a whole is *mediation training,* teaching students how to mediate conflicts among classmates by asking the opposing sides to express their differing points of view and then working together to devise a reasonable resolution (Deutsch, 1993; Sanchez & Anderson, 1990; Stevahn, Johnson, Johnson, & Real, 1996). We will discuss both of these strategies in more depth when we consider self-regulation in Chapter 11.

Teach social problem solving.

• *Plan cooperative activities.* When students participate in cooperative games, rather than in competitive ones, their aggressive behaviors toward one another decrease (Bay-Hinitz, Peterson, & Quilitch, 1994). And when they engage in cooperative learning

Plan cooperative activities.

activities, they can learn and practice help-giving, help-seeking, and conflict-resolution skills, and they develop a better sense of justice and fairness with regard to their classmates (Damon, 1988; Lickona, 1991; N. M. Webb & Farivar, 1994). Chapter 14 describes characteristics of effective cooperative learning activities.

Establish and enforce rules regarding appropriate behavior.

• *Establish and enforce firm rules regarding acceptable classroom behavior.* In addition to encouraging appropriate social behaviors, we must actively *dis*courage such inappropriate behaviors as inconsiderateness, aggression, and prejudicial remarks (Bierman, Miller, & Stabb, 1987; Braukmann, Kirigin, & Wolf, 1981; Schofield, 1995). We must have clear guidelines for classroom behavior and impose consequences when such guidelines are not followed (see Chapters 10 and 15). By establishing and enforcing firm rules about aggressive behavior while simultaneously teaching appropriate social skills, we often see noticeable improvements in behavior.

But even when our students are able to relate effectively with one another, we may find that many of them interact almost exclusively within a small, close-knit group and that a few others remain socially isolated. Yet students have much of value to learn from their classmates, including those very different from themselves. So let's also consider how we can facilitate social interaction among diverse groups of students.

Promoting Social Interaction Among Diverse Groups

Simply putting students in the same school building is rarely sufficient to promote interaction among individual students or among groups of students. For example, students often divide themselves along ethnic lines when they eat lunch and interact in the schoolyard (Schofield, 1995). Immigrant students rarely interact with long-term residents (Olneck, 1995). And students with special needs are often poorly accepted or even rejected by their classmates (Hymel, 1986; Juvonen & Hiner, 1991; Yuker, 1988).

As teachers, we must often take proactive steps to broaden the base of our students' social interactions. Here are some strategies that seem to be effective in doing so:

Foster cross-group friendships.

• *Set up situations in which students can form new friendships.* We can do many simple things to encourage students to get to know one another. We can arrange situations that compel them to work or play cooperatively with their classmates; for example, we can develop structured cooperative learning activities in which all group members must share equal responsibility, or we can provide play equipment that requires the participation of several students (Banks, 1994a; Schofield, 1995). We can assign a partner to a student with special needs—a classmate who can provide assistance when needed, perhaps reading to a student with a visual impairment, signing to a student with hearing loss, tutoring a student with a learning disability, or taking notes for a student with a physical impairment. And the very simple practice of giving students assigned seats in class and then occasionally changing those assignments increases the number of friends that they will make (Schofield, 1995).

Assigning partners to students with special needs is one mechanism through which we can facilitate the development of new friendships.

• *Minimize or eliminate barriers to social interaction.* Students are less likely to interact with their classmates when there are physical, linguistic, or social barriers to doing so. For example, I am reminded of a junior high girl who could not negotiate the cafeteria steps with her wheelchair and so always ended up eating lunch alone. Obviously, we must be on the lookout for any physical impediments to the mobility of students with special needs and campaign for the removal of such obstacles. We can also teach groups of students who speak different languages (including American Sign Language, with which many students with hearing loss communicate) some basic vocabulary and simple phrases in one another's native tongues. And we must actively address the prejudices and tensions that sometimes separate diverse ethnic groups (Ulichny, 1994); we will identify specific strategies for doing so in our discussion of multicultural education in Chapter 4.

Minimize barriers to interaction.

- *Encourage and facilitate participation in extracurricular activities.* Extracurricular activities provide additional opportunities for students to interact and work cooperatively with a wide range of classmates (Genova & Walberg, 1984; Phelan et al., 1994; Schofield, 1995). We must be careful, however, that no single group of students dominates in membership or leadership in any particular activity (Sleeter & Grant, 1994). Schools may need to make special arrangements for after-school transportation for some students (Schofield, 1995).

Encourage participation in extracurricular activities.

- *Develop nondisabled students' understanding of students with special needs.* Nondisabled students sometimes feel resentment or anger about inappropriate behaviors that they believe a classmate with special needs should be able to control (Juvonen, 1991; Juvonen & Weiner, 1993). For example, they are less likely to be tolerant of students with cognitive difficulties or emotional and behavioral disorders than they are of students with obvious physical disabilities (Madden & Slavin, 1983; Ysseldyke & Algozzine, 1984). As teachers, we must help nondisabled students become aware of any difficulties that students with special needs may have as a result of a disability. At the same time, we must also show them the many ways in which such students are normal children with the same thoughts, feelings, and needs as anyone else their age.

Help nondisabled students better understand students with special needs.

- *Help change the reputations of formerly antisocial students.* Unfortunately, students' bad reputations often live on long after their behavior has changed for the better. Even after students show dramatic improvements in behavior, their classmates may continue to dislike and reject them (Bierman et al., 1987; Juvonen & Hiner, 1991; Juvonen & Weiner, 1993). For example, in the case of formerly aggressive students, the perception of many classmates is "once a bully, always a bully." So when we work to improve the behaviors of antisocial students, we must work to improve their reputations as well—for example, by placing them in cooperative learning groups where they can use their newly developed social skills or by encouraging their active involvement in extracurricular activities. In one way or another, we must help them show their peers that they have changed and are worth getting to know better.

Help change students' reputations.

- *Encourage a general feeling of respect for others.* Teachers who effectively facilitate friendships among diverse groups of students are often those who communicate a consistent message over and over again: We must all respect one another as human beings (Turnbull, Pereira, & Blue-Banning, in press). Fernando Arias, a high school vocational education teacher, has put it this way:

Encourage respect for others.

> In our school, our philosophy is that we treat everybody the way we'd like to be treated. . . . Our school is a unique situation where we have pregnant young ladies who go to our school. We have special education children. We have the regular kids, and we have the drop-out recovery program . . . we're all equal. We all have an equal chance. And we have members of every gang at our school, and we hardly have any fights, and there [are] close to about 300 gangs in our city. We all get along. It's one big family unit it seems like. . . . (Turnbull et al., in press, pp. 7–8)

Truly productive interpersonal relationships depend on students' ability to respect one another's rights and privileges, to see things from one another's perspective, and to support classmates who are going through hard times. Such capabilities are aspects of students' moral development, a topic we turn to now.

INTO THE CLASSROOM: Promoting Social Development

Expect and encourage behaviors essential for students' long-term success.

On Monday, a seventh-grade teacher gives homework assignments for the entire week as a way of promoting students' responsibility and independence regarding their schoolwork.

Give students numerous opportunities to interact with one another in pairs or small groups.

A middle school teacher has students work in groups of three on a complex library research project. She structures the assignment in such a way that each group member has a clearly defined role to perform.

When appropriate to do so, let students work out their own interpersonal difficulties.

When several students argue about whose turn it is to use the classroom computer, their teacher encourages them to work out a plan that will allow fair and equitable use of the computer each week.

Teach and provide practice in ways of interacting effectively with others.

A teacher notices that one girl in his class rarely speaks to her classmates except to insult them. He schedules several after-school meetings with her, and together they role-play appropriate ways of initiating social interactions. In the weeks that follow, he monitors her interactions with classmates and gives her feedback about her progress.

Promote social interaction among diverse groups.

A science teacher decides how students will be paired for weekly lab activities. She changes the pairings every month and frequently pairs students from different ethnic backgrounds.

Consistently model both acceptance of and respect for diversity.

A teacher listens patiently and attentively as a student with a speech impediment stumbles over his words. At one point, she gives a stern look to a classmate who is giggling at the student's plight.

Moral and Prosocial Development

In our opening case study, we found Adam engaging in immoral behavior: He was routinely stealing lunches in the cafeteria. When we speak of immoral behavior more generally, we are talking about actions that are unfair, cause physical or emotional harm, or violate the rights of others (Smetana, 1983; Turiel, 1983).

Students' beliefs about moral and immoral behavior—their beliefs about what's right and wrong—affect their actions at school and in the classroom. For example, we will have fewer instances of theft or violence when students respect the property and safety of their classmates. We will have fewer infractions of school and classroom rules when students recognize the importance of obeying such rules. We will have fewer cases of cheating when students believe that cheating is morally unacceptable.

Students' beliefs about morality also affect how they think about and understand the topics they study in school. For instance, students' moral values are likely to influence their reactions when, in history, they read descriptions of the holocaust during World War II. Their sense of human dignity may enter in when they read the anti-Semitic statements that some characters in Shakespeare's *The Merchant of Venice* make about a Jewish money-lender. And the importance of fairness and respect for the rights of others certainly come into play in any discussions about good sportsmanship on the athletic field. Students simply cannot avoid moral issues as they study school subject matter.

As teachers, we play a significant role in the moral and prosocial development of our students (Pollard, Kurtines, Carlo, Dancs, & Mayock, 1991; Rushton, 1980). Consider the teacher who prepares a class for the arrival of a new student, first by discussing the feelings of uncertainty, apprehension, and loneliness that the student is likely to have, and then by helping the class identify steps it can take to make the student feel at home. This teacher is facilitating perspective taking and setting the stage for students to behave prosocially toward the newcomer. Now consider the teacher who ignores incidents of selfishness and aggression in class and on the playground, perhaps using the rationale that students should always work things out among themselves. This teacher is doing little to promote students' social and moral growth and in fact may inadvertently be sending them the message that antisocial behavior is quite acceptable.

In the pages that follow, we will look at the multidimensional nature of moral development. We will consider the emotional underpinnings of moral behavior and then examine the development of moral reasoning, perspective taking, and prosocial behavior. Finally, we will identify a number of strategies for promoting the moral and prosocial development of our students.

How Emotions Reflect Moral Development

THINKING ABOUT WHAT YOU KNOW

How do you feel when you inadvertently cause inconvenience for someone else? when you hurt someone else's feelings? when a friend has a death in the family?

Three distinct emotions are associated with moral development. By the time children reach the middle elementary grades, most of them occasionally feel **shame:** They feel embarrassed or humiliated when they fail to meet the standards for moral behavior that parents and teachers have set for them (Damon, 1988). Shortly thereafter, as they begin to develop their own standards for behavior, they sometimes experience **guilt**—a feeling of discomfort when they know that they have caused someone else pain or distress (Damon, 1988; Hoffman, 1991). Both shame and guilt, though unpleasant in nature, are good signs that students are developing a sense of right and wrong and that their future behaviors will improve.

A third emotion involved in moral development is **empathy**—experiencing the same feelings as someone in unfortunate circumstances (Damon, 1988; Eisenberg, 1982; Hoffman, 1991). Empathy continues to develop throughout the elementary school years, and sometimes into the high school years as well (Eisenberg, 1982). In the primary grade levels, empathy is confined to people that students know, such as friends and classmates. But by the late elementary school years, students may also begin to feel empathy for people they *don't* know—perhaps for the poor, the homeless, or those living in war-torn nations (Damon, 1988; Hoffman, 1991). Empathy may be especially instrumental in the development of prosocial behavior: Students are more likely to act on someone else's behalf if they share that person's feelings of sadness or frustration. As we consider the topics of perspective taking and induction later in the chapter, we will identify teaching strategies that should help our students develop empathy for others.

Look for signs of shame, guilt, and empathy as indicators that students are developing morally.

See "Assessing
Moral Reasoning" in
*Simulations in
Educational
Psychology.*

Development of Moral Reasoning: Kohlberg's Theory

▢ Experiencing Firsthand
Heinz's Dilemma

In Europe, a woman was near death from a rare form of cancer. There was one drug that the doctors thought might save her, a form of radium that a druggist in the same town had recently discovered. The druggist was charging $2,000, ten times what the drug cost him to make. The sick woman's husband, Heinz, went to everyone he knew to borrow the money, but he could only get together about half of what the drug cost. He told the druggist that his wife was dying and asked him to sell it cheaper or let him pay later. But the druggist said no. So Heinz got desperate and broke into the man's store to steal the drug for his wife. (Kohlberg, 1984, p. 186)

- Should Heinz have stolen the drug? What would *you* have done if you were Heinz? Which is worse, stealing something that belongs to someone else or letting another person die a preventable death? Why?

- Do you think that people younger than yourself might answer the same questions differently? How do you think a typical fifth grader might respond? a typical high school student?

The story of Heinz and his dying wife illustrates a **moral dilemma**—a situation to which there is no clear-cut right or wrong response. Lawrence Kohlberg presented a number of moral dilemmas to people of various ages and asked them to propose solutions for each one. Here are three solutions to Heinz's dilemma proposed by school-age students. I have given the students fictitious names so that we can refer to them again later.

James (a fifth grader):
Maybe his wife is an important person and runs a store, and the man buys stuff from her and can't get it any other place. The police would blame the owner that he didn't save the wife. He didn't save an important person, and that's just like killing with a gun or a knife. You can get the electric chair for that. (Kohlberg, 1981, pp. 265–266)

Jesse (a high school student):
If he cares enough for her to steal for her, he should steal it. If not he should let her die. It's up to him. (Kohlberg, 1981, p. 132)

Jules (a high school student):
In that particular situation Heinz was right to do it. In the eyes of the law he would not be doing the right thing, but in the eyes of the moral law he would. If he had exhausted every other alternative I think it would be worth it to save a life. (Kohlberg, 1984, pp. 446–447)

Each student offers a different reason to justify why Heinz should steal the lifesaving drug. James bases his decision on the possible advantages and disadvantages of stealing or not stealing the drug for Heinz alone; he does not consider the perspective of the dying woman at all. Likewise, Jesse takes a very self-serving view, proposing that the decision to either steal or not steal the drug depends on how much Heinz loves his wife. Only Jules considers the value of human life in justifying why Heinz should break the law.

After obtaining hundreds of responses to moral dilemmas, Kohlberg proposed that the development of moral reasoning is characterized by a series of stages (e.g., Colby, Kohlberg, Gibbs, & Lieberman, 1983; Kohlberg, 1984). These stages, as in any stage theory, form an invariant sequence: An individual progresses through them in order, without skipping any. Each stage builds upon the foundation laid by earlier stages but reflects a more integrated and logically consistent set of moral beliefs than those before it.

Level I: Preconventional Morality	Stages	Nature of Moral Reasoning
Age range: Seen in preschool children, most elementary school students, some junior high school students, and a few high school students.	Stage 1: Punishment-avoidance and obedience	Individuals make moral decisions based on what is best for themselves, without regard for others' needs or feelings. They obey rules only if established by more powerful individuals; they disobey when they can do so without getting caught.
	Stage 2: Exchange of favors	Individuals begin to recognize that others also have needs. They may attempt to satisfy others' needs if their own needs are also met in the process. They continue to define right and wrong primarily in terms of consequences to themselves.
Level II: Conventional Morality Age range: Seen in a few older elementary school students, some junior high school students, and many high school students.	Stage 3: Good boy/good girl	Individuals make moral decisions based on what actions will please others, especially authority figures. They are concerned about maintaining interpersonal relationships through sharing, trust, and loyalty. They now consider someone's intentions in determining innocence or guilt.
	Stage 4: Law and order	Individuals look to society as a whole for guidelines concerning what is right or wrong. They perceive rules to be inflexible and believe that it is their "duty" to obey them.
Level III: Postconventional Morality Age range: Rarely seen before college.	Stage 5: Social contract	Individuals recognize that rules represent an agreement among many people about appropriate behavior. They recognize that rules are flexible and can be changed if they no longer meet society's needs.
	Stage 6: Universal ethical principle	Individuals adhere to a small number of abstract, universal principles that transcend specific, concrete rules. They answer to an inner conscience and may break rules that violate their own ethical principles.

FIGURE 3.4

Kohlberg's three levels and six stages of moral reasoning
Sources: Colby & Kohlberg, 1984; Colby et al., 1983; Kohlberg, 1976, 1984, 1986; Reimer, Paolitto, & Hersh, 1983.

Kohlberg grouped his stages into three *levels* of morality: the preconventional, conventional, and postconventional levels. These three levels and the two stages within each one are summarized in Figure 3–4. Let's look at each level more closely.

Level I: Preconventional Morality

We see preconventional morality in preschool children, most elementary school students (especially those in the primary grades), some middle and junior high school students, and a few high school students (Colby & Kohlberg, 1984; Reimer et al., 1983). Preconventional morality is the earliest and least mature form of morality, in that the

Why is this level called *preconventional?*

🍎 Describe the
consequences for
appropriate and
inappropriate classroom
behavior and apply them
consistently, especially
when dealing with a largely
"preconventional" class.

individual has not yet adopted or internalized society's conventions regarding what is morally right or wrong. The preconventional individual's judgments about the morality of behavior are determined primarily by the consequences of those behaviors. Behaviors that lead to rewards and pleasure are "right"; behaviors that lead to punishment are "wrong." Preconventional individuals will obey people who have control of rewards and punishments; they will not necessarily obey people without such control over consequences. Here we see one reason why, as teachers, we should tell students the consequences for appropriate and inappropriate classroom behavior and apply those consequences consistently.

Stage 1: Punishment-avoidance and obedience. Stage 1 individuals (including our friend James) make moral decisions based on what they think is best for themselves, without regard for the needs or feelings of other people. For these individuals, the only "wrong" behaviors are ones that will be punished. Stage 1 individuals follow rules of behavior that are established by people more powerful than themselves, whether these people are parents, teachers, or stronger peers. But they may disobey rules if they think that they can avoid punishment in doing so. In a nutshell, individuals in Stage 1 will do anything if they can get away with it.

In making moral decisions, Stage 1 individuals seldom consider the intentions or feelings of other people. "Badness" is defined strictly in terms of physical or material consequences. To illustrate, consider the cases of John and Henry:

- John was in his room when his mother called him to dinner. John went down and opened the door to the dining room. But behind the door was a chair, and on the chair was a tray with fifteen cups on it. John did not know the cups were behind the door. He opened the door, the door hit the tray, bang went the fifteen cups, and they all got broken.

- One day when Henry's mother was out, Henry tried to get some cookies out of the cupboard. He climbed up on a chair, but the cookie jar was still too high, and he couldn't reach it. But while he was trying to get the cookie jar, he knocked over a cup. The cup fell and broke. (based on stories originally used by Piaget, 1932; adapted from Bandura & McDonald, 1963, p. 276)

🍎 Talk about people's
well-meaning intentions in
situations where their
actions have inadvertently
led to an undesirable
consequence.

Even though John's intentions were more honorable than Henry's, the Stage 1 person would declare John to be the naughtier of the two boys because he broke more cups.

Stage 2: Exchange of favors. Individuals in Stage 2 (which Kohlberg has often called the *instrumental-relativist* stage) are beginning to recognize that others have needs just as they do. They sometimes address the needs of others by offering to exchange favors ("You scratch my back, and I'll scratch yours"), but they usually try to get the better end of the bargain. To Stage 2 individuals, being "fair" means that everybody gets the same opportunities or the same amount of whatever is being handed out. As teachers, we might hear "That's not fair!" from Stage 2 students who think that they're being short-changed.

🍎 Make things as fair as
you can, providing the
same opportunities to
all students.

Like Stage 1 individuals, Stage 2 individuals focus on the physical consequences of behavior, rather than on more abstract, less observable consequences. For example, if a boy at this stage is thinking about insulting a classmate, he may refrain from doing so if he thinks that the classmate will beat him up, but the thought that the insult might hurt the classmate's feelings will not be a deterrent. Kohlberg classified Jesse's response to the Heinz dilemma as a Stage 2 response. Jesse is beginning to recognize the importance of saving someone else's life, but the decision to do so ultimately depends on whether or not Heinz loves his wife; in other words, it depends on *his* feelings alone.

Level II: Conventional Morality

A few older elementary school students, some middle and junior high school students, and many high school students exhibit conventional morality (Colby & Kohlberg, 1984; Reimer et al., 1983). Conventional morality is characterized by an acceptance of society's conventions concerning right and wrong: The individual obeys rules and follows society's norms even when there is no reward for obedience and no punishment for disobedience. Adherence to rules and conventions is somewhat rigid; a rule's appropriateness or fairness is seldom questioned.

Stage 3: Good boy/good girl. Stage 3 individuals look primarily to the people they know, and especially to authority figures (e.g., parents, teachers, popular classmates), for guidance about what is right and wrong. Stage 3 individuals want to please others and gain their approval; they like being told that they are a "good boy" or a "good girl." They are also concerned about maintaining interpersonal relationships through sharing, trust, and loyalty. For example, they believe in the Golden Rule ("Do unto others as you would have them do unto you") and in the importance of keeping promises and commitments.

Stage 3 individuals can put themselves in another person's shoes and consider the perspectives of others in making decisions. They also acknowledge that someone's *intentions* must be considered in determining guilt or innocence. In examining the John and Henry situations I described earlier, the Stage 3 individual would identify Henry as being naughtier than John because of his dishonorable intention: He tried to get cookies behind his mother's back. John, who broke many more cups, would be less naughty because he "meant well."

Stage 4: Law and order. Stage 4 individuals look to society as a whole, rather than just to the people they know, for guidelines (conventions) as to what is right and wrong. They know that rules are necessary for keeping society running smoothly and believe that it is their "duty" to obey them. They see these rules as set in concrete, however; they do not yet recognize that it may occasionally be more "moral" to break laws (perhaps those legitimizing racial segregation or interfering with basic human rights) than to follow them. Nor do they recognize that, as society's needs change, rules should be changed as well.

Level III: Postconventional Morality

Postconventional morality is rarely observed in students before they reach college, and in fact most people never reach this level of moral reasoning at all (Colby & Kohlberg, 1984; Reimer et al., 1983). Postconventional individuals have developed their own set of abstract principles to define what actions are morally right and wrong—principles that typically include such basic human rights as life, liberty, and justice. Postconventional individuals obey rules consistent with their own abstract principles of morality, and they may *dis*obey rules inconsistent with those principles.

Stage 5: Social contract. Stage 5 individuals view rules that are determined through a democratic process as a *social contract*—an agreement among many people about how they should all behave. They think of such rules as being useful mechanisms that maintain the general social order and protect individual human rights, rather than as absolute dictates that must be obeyed simply because they are "the law." They also recognize the flexibility of rules; rules that no longer serve society's best interests can and should be changed. An example of Stage 5 thinking can be seen in Jules's response to the Heinz dilemma: Jules proposed that the woman's well-being would be better served by breaking the law than by obeying it.

Stage 6: Universal ethical principle. Kohlberg described Stage 6 as an "ideal" stage that few people ever reach. This stage represents adherence to a few abstract, universal principles that transcend specific norms and rules for behavior. Such principles typically include respect for human dignity and basic human rights, the belief that all people are truly equal, and a commitment to justice and due process. Stage 6 individuals answer to a strong inner conscience, rather than to authority figures or concrete

Communicate your approval when students behave in a morally desirable fashion.

With Stage 4 students, begin to talk about situations in which breaking laws may be morally appropriate.

At the high school level, begin to talk with students about such abstract principles as justice and human rights.

In high school social studies classes, identify situations in which a society's laws or conventions might be counterproductive. In physical education classes, explain why the rules of a game sometimes change over time.

laws, and they willingly disobey laws that violate their own ethical principles. Martin Luther King Jr.'s "Letter from a Birmingham Jail," excerpted here, illustrates Stage 6 reasoning:

> One may well ask, "How can you advocate breaking some laws and obeying others?" The answer lies in the fact that one has not only a legal but a moral responsibility to obey just laws. One has a moral responsibility to disobey unjust laws, though one must do so openly, lovingly and with a willingness to accept the penalty. An individual who breaks a law that conscience tells him is unjust, and accepts the penalty to arouse the conscience of the community, is expressing in reality the highest respect for law. An unjust law is a human law not rooted in eternal law and natural law. A law that uplifts human personality is just; one which degrades human personality is unjust. (King, 1965; cited in Kohlberg, 1981, pp. 318–319)

Factors Affecting Progression Through Kohlberg's Stages

As you undoubtedly just noticed, students at any particular age are not always reasoning at the same level and stage. We see the greatest variability in high school students, some of whom may show Stage 4 reasoning while others are still reasoning at Stage 1. Why do students of the same age sometimes show very different stages of moral reasoning? Kohlberg proposed that two aspects of Piaget's theory of cognitive development—his stages of cognitive development and his concept of disequilibrium—affect the progression to more advanced stages of moral reasoning.

Stage of cognitive development. Kohlberg proposed that moral reasoning is somewhat dependent on Piaget's stages of cognitive development. Postconventional morality, because it involves reasoning with abstract principles, cannot occur until an individual has acquired formal operational thought, and even conventional morality probably involves some formal operational thinking capabilities (Kohlberg, 1976). Thus, conventional and postconventional levels of moral reasoning do not usually appear until adolescence. At the same time, progression to an advanced stage of cognitive development does not guarantee equivalent moral development; for example, it is quite possible to be formal operational in logical reasoning but preconventional in moral reasoning. In other words, Kohlberg maintained that cognitive development is a *necessary but insufficient* condition for moral development to occur.

Do you know anyone who is very intelligent yet reasons at a preconventional level?

Disequilibrium. As you should recall from Chapter 2, Piaget proposed that children progress to a higher stage of cognitive development when they experience *disequilibrium*—that is, when they realize that their knowledge and schemes do not adequately explain the events around them. Because disequilibrium is an uncomfortable feeling, children begin to reorganize their thoughts and ideas into a more complex and better integrated system, one that more adequately accounts for their experiences.

Kohlberg proposed that a similar process promotes moral development. Individuals become increasingly aware of the weaknesses of a particular stage of moral reasoning, especially when their moral judgments are challenged by people reasoning at the next higher stage. By struggling with these challenges and with moral dilemmas, individuals begin to restructure their thoughts about morality and so gradually move from one stage to the next.

Challenge the moral reasoning of students in a particular stage by presenting reasoning at the next higher stage.

As teachers, we can best create disequilibrium regarding moral issues when we present a moral argument just one stage above the stage at which a student is currently reasoning—for instance, when we present "law and order" logic (Stage 4) to a student concerned primarily about gaining the approval of others (Stage 3). If we present a moral argument that is too much higher than the student's current stage, then the student is unlikely to understand and remember what we are saying (e.g., Narvaez, 1998) and so is unlikely to experience disequilibrium.

What Research Tells Us About Kohlberg's Stages

Many research studies of moral development have followed on the heels of Kohlberg's theory. Some research supports Kohlberg's sequence of stages: Generally speaking, people seem to progress through the stages in the order Kohlberg proposed (e.g., Colby & Kohlberg, 1984; Reimer et al., 1983). At the same time, it appears that people are not always completely in one stage: Their moral thought usually reflects a particular stage, but they also show occasional instances of reasoning in the two surrounding stages. And to some extent, students' levels of moral reasoning may be situation-specific (Durkin, 1995; Krebs, Vermeulen, Carpendale, & Denton, 1991; Turiel, Smetana, & Killen, 1991). For example, students are more likely to think of lying as immoral if it causes someone else harm than if it has no adverse effect (if it is just a "white lie"). And moral reasoning plays a role in students' decisions about using drugs only when they view drug use as potentially harmful to others (Berkowitz, Guerra, & Nucci, 1991).

Kohlberg's theory has been criticized because it focuses on moral *thinking* rather than on moral *behavior.* Some researchers have found that people at higher stages of moral reasoning do tend to behave more morally as well (Bear & Richards, 1981; Blasi, 1980; Reimer et al., 1983). For example, students at the higher stages are less likely to cheat in the classroom, more likely to help people in need, and more likely to disobey orders that would cause harm to another individual (Kohlberg, 1975; Kohlberg & Candee, 1984). However, the relationship between moral reasoning and moral behavior is a weak one at best (Durkin, 1995). Obviously, then, Kohlberg's theory cannot give us the total picture of how morality develops.

The "fishing" study described in Chapter 2 illustrated how logical reasoning may be somewhat content-specific. Here we find that moral reasoning may be content-specific as well.

Gender Differences in Moral Reasoning: Gilligan's Theory

Kohlberg developed his stages after studying how people solved moral dilemmas, but consider this quirk in his research: Subjects in his studies were almost exclusively males. Carol Gilligan (1982, 1987; Gilligan & Attanucci, 1988) believes that Kohlberg's theory does not adequately describe female moral development. Kohlberg's stages emphasize issues of fairness and justice but omit other aspects of morality, especially compassion and caring for those in need, that Gilligan suggests are more characteristic of the moral reasoning and behavior of females. She argues that females are socialized to stress interpersonal relationships and to take responsibility for the well-being of others to a greater extent than males; therefore, females develop a morality that emphasizes a greater concern for others' welfare. The dilemma that follows illustrates a morality based on compassion.

▪ Experiencing Firsthand
The Porcupine Dilemma

A group of industrious, prudent moles have spent the summer digging a burrow where they will spend the winter. A lazy, improvident porcupine who has not prepared a winter shelter approaches the moles and pleads to share their burrow. The moles take pity on the porcupine and agree to let him in. Unfortunately, the moles did not anticipate the problem the porcupine's sharp quills would pose in close quarters. Once the porcupine has moved in, the moles are constantly being stabbed. The question is, what should the moles do? (Meyers, 1987, p. 141; adapted from Gilligan, 1985)

According to Gilligan, males are more likely to look at this situation in terms of someone's rights being violated. For example, they might point out that the burrow belongs to the moles, and so the moles can legitimately throw the porcupine out. If the porcupine refuses to leave, some may argue that the moles are well within their rights to kill him. In contrast, females are more likely to show compassion and caring when dealing with the dilemma. For example, they may suggest that the moles simply cover the porcupine with a blanket; this way, his quills won't annoy anyone and everyone's needs will be met (Meyers, 1987).

Gilligan raises a good point: Males and females are often socialized quite differently, as you will discover in Chapter 4. Furthermore, by including compassion for other human beings as well as consideration for their rights, she broadens our conception of what morality *is* (Durkin, 1995). Keep in mind, however, that many research studies do *not* find major gender differences in moral reasoning (Eisenberg et al., 1996; Nunner-Winkler, 1984; Walker, 1991).

The theories of Kohlberg and Gilligan both describe the development of moral reasoning. Let's turn now to recent findings in two other aspects of moral development: perspective taking and prosocial behavior.

Remember that morality includes compassion and caring as well as respect for the rights of others.

Development of Perspective Taking: Selman's Theory

To make moral decisions and behave in morally appropriate ways, a child must be able to look at a situation from someone else's perspective—to imagine what someone else may be thinking or feeling. Consider the following situation as an example.

Experiencing Firsthand
Holly's Dilemma

Holly is an eight-year-old girl who likes to climb trees. She is the best tree climber in the neighborhood. One day while climbing down from a tall tree she falls off the bottom branch but does not hurt herself. Her father sees her fall. He is upset and asks her to promise not to climb the trees any more. Holly promises.

Later that day, Holly and her friends meet Sean. Sean's kitten is caught up in a tree and cannot get down. Something has to be done right away or the kitten may fall. Holly is the only one who climbs trees well enough to reach the kitten and get it down, but she remembers her promise to her father.

- Does Holly know how Sean feels about the kitten?
- Does Sean know why Holly cannot decide whether or not to climb the tree?
- What does Holly think her father will think of her if he finds out?
- Does Holly think her father will understand why she climbed the tree? (Selman & Byrne, 1974, p. 805)

To answer these questions, you must look at the situation from the perspectives of three different people: Sean, Holly, and Holly's father.

By presenting situations like the "Holly" story and asking children to view them from various perspectives, Robert Selman (1980; Selman & Schultz, 1990) found that children show an increasing ability to take the perspective of others as they grow older. He described a series of five levels that characterize the development of perspective taking; these levels are summarized in the left column of Table 3–2.

According to Selman, most preschoolers are incapable of taking anyone else's perspective (they are at Level "0"); thus, we see the preoperational egocentrism that Piaget described. But by the time children reach the primary grades, most have begun to realize that people have different thoughts and feelings as well as different physical features (Level 1). They view someone else's perspective as a relatively simplistic, one-dimensional entity, however; for example, another person is simply happy, sad, or angry. Furthermore, they tend to equate behavior with feelings: A happy person will smile, a sad person will pout or cry, and so on. Their interpretations of someone else's actions are also overly simplistic, as this scenario illustrates:

How is Selman's Level 0 similar to Piaget's preoperational stage of cognitive development?

The Development of Perspective Taking and Prosocial Behavior

SELMAN'S LEVELS OF PERSPECTIVE-TAKING*	EISENBERG'S LEVELS OF PROSOCIAL BEHAVIOR*
Level 0: Egocentric perspective taking (most preschool and a few early elementary students) Students are incapable of taking anybody else's perspective. They don't realize that others have thoughts and feelings different from their own.	**Level 1: Selfish and self-centered orientation** (most preschool and many early elementary students) Students show little interest in helping others apart from serving their own interests. They exhibit prosocial behavior primarily to benefit themselves.
Level 1: Subjective perspective taking (most early and middle elementary students) Students realize that others have thoughts and feelings different from their own but perceive these in a simplistic, one-dimensional fashion.	**Level 2: Superficial "needs of others" orientation** (some preschool and many elementary school students) Students show some concern for another's physical and emotional needs, but their concern is simplistic and lacks true understanding of the other's situation.
Level 2: Second-person, reciprocal perspective taking (many upper elementary school students) Students realize that others may have mixed and possibly contradictory feelings about a situation. They also understand that people may feel differently from what their behaviors indicate and that they sometimes do things they didn't intend to do.	**Level 3: Approval and stereotypic good boy/girl orientation** (some elementary and secondary school students) Students advocate prosocial behavior on the grounds that it's the "right" thing to do and that they will be liked or appreciated if they help. They hold stereotypical views of what "good boys and girls" and "bad boys and girls" do.
Level 3: Third-person, mutual perspective taking (many middle school and junior high school students) Students not only see things from their own and another's perspective but also can take an "outside" perspective of the two-person relationship. They appreciate the need to satisfy both oneself and another simultaneously and therefore understand the advantages of cooperation, compromise, and trust.	**Level 4: Empathic orientation** (a few elementary and many secondary students) Students have true empathy for another's situation and a desire to help a person in need. They seem genuinely concerned with the well-being of others.
Level 4: Societal, symbolic perspective taking (some junior high and many high school students) Students recognize that people are a product of their environment—that past events and present circumstances contribute to personality and behavior. They begin to develop an understanding of the *unconscious*—the idea that people are not always aware of why they act as they do.	**Level 5: Internalized values orientation** (a few high school students) Students have internalized values about helping other people—values that reflect a belief in the dignity, rights, and equality of all human beings. They express a strong desire to help others in need and to improve the conditions of society as a whole.

The level numbers are those used by Selman and Eisenberg.

Sources: Eisenberg, 1982; Eisenberg, Lennon, & Pasternack, 1986; Eisenberg, Lennon, & Roth, 1983; Selman, 1980; Selman & Schultz, 1990.

Donald is a new student in a second-grade classroom. A group of boys in the class openly ridicule his unusual hairstyle and shun him at lunch and on the playground. After school, one of the boys makes a cruel remark about Donald's hair, and Donald responds by punching him. The boys decide that Donald is a "mean kid."

The boys at Donald's new school are interpreting his behavior in a simplistic, Level 1 fashion. They do not yet appreciate the many feelings that Donald may be experiencing: anxiety about a new school and community, shame about a hairstyle that was "cool" at his previous school, and frustration at his inability to make new friends.

What might you do to ease the transition of a new student into your classroom? How might you help other students see things from a new student's point of view?

As they approach the upper elementary grades, students are likely to show signs of Level 2 perspective taking. They now know that other people can have mixed, possibly conflicting feelings about a situation. They also realize that people may feel differently from what their behaviors indicate—that they may try to hide their true feelings. At this point, too, students recognize the importance of intentions: They understand that people may do things that they didn't really want or intend to do. For example, Level 2 children would be more likely to appreciate Donald's predicament and to understand that his aggressive behavior might reflect something other than a mean streak. They might also recognize that Donald's punch was an unintended reaction to a thoughtless insult.

In middle and secondary school, most students are at Selman's two highest levels of perspective taking, in which they are able to take an "outsider's" perspective of interpersonal relationships. Students at Levels 3 and 4 appreciate the need to satisfy both oneself and another simultaneously and therefore understand the advantages of cooperation, compromise, and trust. Not surprisingly, then, students' friendships become relationships of mutual sharing and support beginning in middle and junior high school. Additional aspects of perspective taking emerge at Level 4: Students begin to recognize that an individual's behavior is likely to be influenced by many factors—including one's thoughts, feelings, present circumstances, and past events—and that other people are not always aware of why they act as they do. Level 4 perspective taking, then, relies on understanding the true complexity of human behaviors, thoughts, and emotions.

How can we promote greater perspective taking in our students? One strategy is to create disequilibrium by presenting perspective taking one level above that of our students. For example, with preschoolers, we can continually point out how their classmates' feelings differ from their own (Level 1). In the early and middle elementary grades, we can begin to discuss situations in which students may have mixed feelings or want to hide their feelings—situations such as going to a new school, trying a difficult but enjoyable sport for the first time, or celebrating a holiday without a favorite family member present (Level 2). At the middle and secondary school levels, we can explore aspects of psychology, so that students begin to understand the many ways in which people really are a product of their environment (Level 4).

A second strategy is to create opportunities for students to encounter multiple, and often equally legitimate, perspectives. For example, at the upper elementary grades, we can provide opportunities for students to work more closely with one another on school projects so that they begin to discover the advantages of cooperation, compromise, and trust (Level 3). Students at all grade levels benefit from hearing a variety of perspectives, including those of different genders, races, cultures, religions, and political belief systems.

When children are better able to take the perspective of another individual, they are also more likely to behave in altruistic and socially beneficial ways—that is, to exhibit prosocial behavior in the classroom. We turn to the development of such behavior now.

Present perspective taking one level above that of students.

Create opportunities in which students hear the perspectives of different genders, races, cultures, religions, and political belief systems.

Development of Prosocial Behavior: Eisenberg's Theory

In most cultures, one intended outcome of children's socialization is the development of such prosocial actions as sharing, helping, cooperating, and comforting—behaviors that promote the well-being of other individuals. People will be more productive adult citizens if, as children, they learn the advantages and good feelings associated with occasionally putting the needs of others before their own. School, because it is often the most social environment in children's lives, provides a perfect medium in which children can learn prosocial behavior.

As a general rule, children act in more prosocial ways as they grow older; for example, they become increasingly generous with age (Eisenberg, 1982; Rushton, 1980). Nancy Eisenberg and her colleagues (Eisenberg, 1982; Eisenberg et al., 1986; Eisenberg et al., 1983) have identified five levels of reasoning about prosocial behavior that can

Children tend to act in more prosocial ways as they grow older; for example, they become increasingly empathic with age.

help us predict how children at different ages are likely to behave. Eisenberg's levels of prosocial behavior are summarized in the right column of Table 3–2.

As you may notice from looking at Table 3–2, there are several parallels between the development of perspective taking and the development of prosocial behavior. When students are incapable of taking someone else's perspective (Selman's Level 0), they are likely to exhibit prosocial behavior only when such behavior simultaneously benefits themselves (Eisenberg's Level 1). When students have a simplistic, one-dimensional view of another person's perspective (Selman's Level 1), they also show an overly simplistic and superficial concern for others' needs—one without any true empathy for another person's situation (Eisenberg's Level 2). As students increasingly recognize the complexity of human emotions and interpersonal relationships (Selman's Levels 2, 3, and 4), they also begin to show increasing empathy for the situations of others and a greater desire to help fellow human beings (Eisenberg's Levels 3, 4, and 5).

How can we promote greater empathy and prosocial behavior in our students? Certainly we can encourage our students to engage in such prosocial behavior as cooperating and sharing with one another and comforting classmates whose feelings have been hurt. We can also acknowledge and reward such behaviors when we see them. And as the curriculum gives our students an increasingly broader view of the country and world in which they live, we can expose them to situations in which other people's needs may be far greater than their own.

In what ways is Eisenberg's Level 3 similar to Kohlberg's Stage 3?

Encourage prosocial behavior and acknowledge it when it occurs.

Expose students to situations in which others' needs are far greater than their own.

Integrating the Stages of Moral Reasoning, Perspective Taking, and Prosocial Behavior

The theories of Kohlberg, Selman, and Eisenberg portray various aspects of moral development in terms of stages or levels. Let's pull together the work of these three theorists to get an overall picture of the moral and prosocial characteristics of children in different grade ranges.

Elementary School Years

In the elementary grades, most children are more concerned about the consequences of their behaviors for themselves than for other people. But we should also see evidence that they are capable of looking at events from another person's perspective, albeit very simplistically in the early grades. And some elementary school children do behave prosocially toward their classmates, although with some fairly stereotypical notions of what "good boys and girls" should do to help others.

Middle School and Junior High School Years

In middle and junior high school, many students are in Kohlberg's Stages 2 and 3. Some students (those in Stage 2) define acceptable behavior as being "anything I can get away with"; for example, copying another's homework assignment is justifiable if the teacher doesn't find out, even though the assignment might help a student learn valuable new skills. Other students (those in Stage 3) adhere to internalized rules or group norms but follow those rules or norms primarily to attain the approval of teachers, popular and influential classmates, or other real or imagined authority figures. Many junior high school students are capable of taking an "outside" perspective of a two-person relationship; thus, they appreciate the need for cooperation, compromise, and mutual trust. Many of these students still behave prosocially to gain the approval of those around them, but others are now motivated more by true feelings of empathy for a person in need.

High School Years

At the high school level, encourage discussions about human rights issues and get students involved in working toward solutions to human problems.

By high school, most students reason at Kohlberg's conventional level of development; they have internalized society's views (or perhaps the views of a particular subgroup) of what is right and wrong. But they still see rules in a somewhat rigid manner—as absolute and inflexible entities, rather than as socially agreed on and therefore changeable mechanisms for protecting human rights and promoting the advancement of society. In taking the perspective of someone else, many high school students now understand that a person's behaviors, thoughts, and emotions are often the product of a complex interaction among past events and present circumstances. And most students now have a sense of empathy for the needs of other individuals, with a resulting desire to help those people. A few students in this age range (those in Eisenberg's Level 5) are beginning to show a true commitment to preserving and enhancing the dignity, rights, and equality of all human beings.

Summarize what you have just learned about the age-group that you will be teaching.

In all the theories of moral development we've discussed, we find a common thread: a gradual progression away from self-centeredness toward increased awareness of the needs and perspectives of others and an increased desire to help fellow human beings. What factors in a child's environment affect the development of moral and prosocial behavior? Let's find out.

Promoting Moral Development in the Classroom

As we have discovered, students in the early stages of moral development make behavior choices based largely on the consequences they anticipate for various actions. Because we certainly cannot be there to impose consequences for students' entire lives, we must hope that by the time students finish high school, they are following their own internal guidelines for behavior. Yet it does little good to "lecture" to students about morally appropriate behavior (Damon, 1988). Several other conditions *do* seem to make a difference in the development of moral reasoning and behavior, however. Five important ones are these:

- An authoritative environment
- Reasons why some behaviors are unacceptable
- Practice in recognizing others' emotional states

- Models of moral and prosocial behavior
- Moral issues and dilemmas

These conditions are summarized in Table 3–3. Let's look more closely at each one.

An Authoritative Environment

Earlier in the chapter, I described an *authoritative* environment—one in which adults hold high expectations and standards for children's behavior within the context of an accepting and supportive environment—as the one most likely to produce happy, well-adjusted, and self-confident children. An authoritative environment promotes moral development as well: Children become more sensitive to others' needs and are more willing to accept responsibility for wrongdoings (Damon, 1988; Hoffman, 1970, 1975). As teachers, then, we must hold firm regarding our expectations that students show consideration for classmates, respect for others' property, and tolerance for diverse cultures, religions, and political views.

Insist that students respect the feelings, rights, and property of others.

Reasons Why Some Behaviors Are Unacceptable

Although it is important to impose consequences for immoral or antisocial behaviors, punishment by itself often focuses children's attention primarily on their own hurt and

TABLE 3.3

PRINCIPLES/ASSUMPTIONS

Conditions that Promote Moral Development

FACTOR	EDUCATIONAL IMPLICATION	EXAMPLE
Authoritative environment	Insist that students show consideration and respect for the rights and needs of others; do so within the context of a firm, yet supportive environment.	When teaching art in the lower elementary grades, provide one set of art supplies (e.g., crayons, scissors, glue) for each table, so that children sitting at the same table must share. Give the children some guidelines about how to share the materials in an equitable manner.
Reasons why some behaviors are unacceptable	When students behave in an immoral or antisocial manner, help them recognize that they have caused distress or inconvenience to someone else.	If a student maliciously ruins a classmate's work (e.g., a homework assignment or an art project), we might point out that the classmate spent quite a bit of time completing the work and insist that the student make amends.
Practice in recognizing others' emotional states	Using both real-life and fictional situations, encourage students to deduce how particular individuals must be feeling.	As high school students read classic works of literature, occasionally ask them to speculate about the emotional states of various characters.
Models of moral and prosocial behavior	Model moral and prosocial behaviors; expose students to other good models as well.	During a school-wide food drive, bring in bags of canned goods that you have collected from your neighbors.
Moral issues and dilemmas	Discuss moral dilemmas as they arise during the school day. Also, include moral issues and dilemmas in the curriculum.	Hold a classroom debate on the pros and cons of capital punishment, perhaps after first having students conduct library research to support their perspectives.

Are you more likely to obey rules when you know the reasons behind them?

Explain why some behaviors are inappropriate, especially in terms of the harm or inconvenience those behaviors have caused.

Help students learn to recognize the specific feelings that others are experiencing.

Model moral and prosocial behavior, and present additional models through literature.

We will consider modeling in more detail in Chapter 11.

distress (Hoffman, 1975). To promote moral development, we must focus students' attention on the hurt and distress their behaviors have caused *others*. Thus, we should give them reasons that certain behaviors are unacceptable—an approach known as **induction** (Hoffman, 1970, 1975). For example, we might describe how a behavior harms someone else either physically ("Having your hair pulled the way you just pulled Mai's can really be painful") or emotionally ("You probably hurt John's feelings when you call him names like that"). We might also show students how they have caused someone else inconvenience ("Because you ruined Marie's jacket, her parents are making her work around the house to earn the money for a new one"). Still another approach is to explain someone else's perspective, intention, or motive ("This science project you've just ridiculed may not be as fancy as yours, but I know that Michael spent many hours working on it and is quite proud of what he's done").

Induction is victim-centered: It helps students focus on the distress of others and recognize that they themselves have been the cause of it (Hoffman, 1970). The consistent use of induction in disciplining children, particularly when accompanied by *mild* punishment for misbehavior, appears to promote cooperation with rules (Baumrind, 1971) and facilitate the development of such prosocial characteristics as empathy, compassion, and altruism (G. H. Brody & Shaffer, 1982; Hoffman, 1975; Maccoby & Martin, 1983; Rushton, 1980).

Practice in Recognizing Others' Emotional States

We will have less of a need to explain someone else's feelings if our students are able to recognize those feelings on their own. Yet many students, young ones especially, are poor judges of the emotional states of others. At the preschool level, it may be helpful actually to label a classmate's feelings as "sadness," "disappointment," or "anger" (Chalmers & Townsend, 1990; Wittmer & Honig, 1994). In later years, we might ask students to describe to one another exactly how they feel about particular misbehaviors directed toward them (Doescher & Sugawara, 1989). Or we might ask them how they themselves would feel in the same situation (Hoffman, 1991). And, as teachers, we should describe our own emotional reactions to any inappropriate behaviors (Damon, 1988).

Models of Moral and Prosocial Behavior

Children and adolescents are more likely to exhibit moral and prosocial behavior when they see others behaving in morally appropriate ways. For example, when parents are generous and show concern for others, their children tend to do likewise (Rushton, 1980). Yet by the same token, when children see their peers cheating, they themselves are more likely to cheat (Sherrill, Horowitz, Friedman, & Salisbury, 1970). Television, too, provides both prosocial and antisocial models for children. When children watch television shows that emphasize prosocial behavior (e.g., *Sesame Street* or *Mister Rogers' Neighborhood*), they are more likely to exhibit prosocial behavior themselves; when they see violence on television, they, too, are more likely to be violent (Rushton, 1980).

As teachers, we teach by what we do as well as by what we say. When we model compassion and consideration of the feelings of others, such behaviors may rub off on our students. When we are instead self-centered and place our own needs before those of others, our students may follow suit.

We can also make use of models of moral behavior that we find in literature (Ellenwood & Ryan, 1991). For example, in Harper Lee's *To Kill a Mockingbird*, set in the highly segregated and racially charged Alabama of the 1930s, a lawyer defends an obviously innocent African American man who is charged with murder; in doing so, he exemplifies a willingness to fight for high moral principles in the face of strong social pressure to let the man hang for the crime. In John Gunther's *Death Be Not Proud*, a young boy is generous and considerate despite his impending death from cancer (Ellenwood & Ryan, 1991).

Moral Issues and Dilemmas

Kohlberg proposed that children develop morally when they are challenged by moral dilemmas they cannot adequately deal with at their current stage of moral reasoning. Research confirms his belief: Classroom discussions of controversial topics and moral issues appear to promote the transition to more advanced moral reasoning and increased perspective taking (DeVries & Zan, 1996; D. W. Johnson & Johnson, 1988; Power, Higgins, & Kohlberg, 1989; Schlaefli, Rest, & Thoma, 1985).

Social and moral issues often arise at school. Sometimes these issues relate to inappropriate student behaviors that occur in most classrooms at one time or another (e.g., cheating, plagiarism, theft, interpersonal conflicts). And sometimes moral issues are intrinsic in course content. Consider the following questions that might emerge in discussions related to history, science, social studies, or literature:

Is it appropriate to engage in armed conflict, and hence to kill others, when two groups of people disagree about political or religious issues?

Should laboratory rats be used to study the effects of cancer-producing agents?

How can a capitalistic society encourage free enterprise while at the same time protecting the rights of citizens and the ecology of the environment?

Was Hamlet justified in killing Claudius to avenge the murder of his father?

Social and moral issues will not always have right or wrong answers. Nevertheless, as teachers, we can facilitate student discussions of such issues in a variety of ways (Reimer et al., 1983). First, we can provide a trusting and nonthreatening classroom atmosphere in which students feel free to express their ideas without censure or embarrassment. Second, we can help students identify all aspects of a dilemma, including the needs and perspectives of the various individuals involved. Third, we can help students explore their reasons for thinking as they do—that is, to clarify and examine the principles on which their moral judgments are based.

Incorporate moral issues and dilemmas into classroom discussions.

What specific moral dilemmas might you incorporate into your own curriculum?

Help students identify all aspects of a dilemma, including the needs and perspectives of each person involved.

Considering Diversity in Personal, Social, and Moral Development

These are not easy times in which to grow up, and many of our students will have experienced challenges that we ourselves may never have imagined as children. More than half of our students are likely to spend at least part of their childhood in a single-parent home; for example, some will have been raised by unwed mothers, and many others will have lived through a divorce (Brough, 1990; Nielsen, 1993). Violence in schools and on the streets is on the rise, especially in low-income areas (Gorski & Pilotto, 1993; Lowry et al., 1995; Parks, 1995). Temptations to experiment with drugs and alcohol are everywhere (G. R. Adams, Gullotta, & Markstrom-Adams, 1994; S. P. Thomas et al., 1993). For students facing such challenges, we must be especially supportive, acting as willing listeners and communicating regularly how much we value each and every one of them (Ogden & Germinario, 1988; Parks, 1995).

Even when our students haven't experienced personal challenges, their personalities, social skills, and moral beliefs will vary considerably from one student to the next. To some extent, these differences will be a product of their diverse ethnic backgrounds. For instance, different ethnic groups value and encourage different personality traits. Chinese and Japanese parents often raise their children to be shy, cautious, and self-restrained, and many Mexican American parents encourage obedience rather than self-assertiveness (Chen, Rubin, & Sun, 1992; Ho, 1994; Trawick-Smith, 1997). In such cases,

Be especially supportive of students who face difficult challenges in their personal lives.

INTO THE CLASSROOM: Promoting Moral and Prosocial Development

Remember that standards for what is "moral" and "immoral" differ somewhat from one culture to another.

A teacher sees a student inadvertently knock a classmate's jacket off its hook. The teacher mentions the incident to the student, but he denies that he had anything to do with the fallen jacket. Remembering that in this student's culture, lying is an acceptable way of saving face, the teacher doesn't chastise the student; instead, she asks him to do her the "favor" of returning the jacket to its hook. A short time later, she engages her class in a conversation about the importance of being careful around other people's belongings.

Model appropriate moral and prosocial behavior.

A junior high school teacher mentions that he will be working in the annual canned food drive on Saturday and asks if any of his students would like to help.

Talk about reasons why some behaviors are inappropriate, especially in terms of the harm or inconvenience that those behaviors have caused.

A second-grade teacher explains to Sarah that because she has thoughtlessly left her chewing gum on Margaret's chair, Margaret's mother must now pay to have Margaret's new pants professionally cleaned.

Incorporate moral issues and dilemmas into classroom discussions.

When discussing the Vietnam War, a high school history teacher mentions that many young men in the United States escaped the draft by going to Canada. She asks her students to decide whether they think such behavior was appropriate and to explain their reasoning.

Foster perspective taking.

A sixth-grade teacher prepares his class for the arrival of a new student, first by discussing the feelings of uncertainty, apprehension, and loneliness that the student is likely to have and then by helping the class identify steps they can take to make the student feel at home.

Encourage prosocial behavior and acknowledge and reward it when it occurs.

The same teacher asks Alberto to be a buddy to the new student—for example, by showing him classroom procedures and including him in group games at recess.

Communicate your approval when students behave in a morally desirable fashion.

A kindergarten teacher commends a student for consoling a classmate whose feelings have been hurt.

---

we may see less of the initiative that, according to Erikson, is characteristic of many elementary school children (Trawick-Smith, 1997).

In addition, some ethnic groups encourage a strong sense of identity with one's family, and possibly with one's ethnicity as well; students from such backgrounds may take more pride in the accomplishments of their families or communities than in their own, individual achievements (Olneck, 1995; Pang, 1995; Trawick-Smith, 1997). We may find, too, that many minority students, while often having high self-esteem in general, have little faith in their ability to achieve academic success (Covington, 1992; Elrich, 1994;

Remember that some students value group accomplishments more than individual achievement.

Graham, 1994). As teachers, we will often need to make a special effort to foster positive self-concepts in students from minority backgrounds. For example, we can help them explore their cultural backgrounds as a way of fostering an appreciation of their ethnic roots (Phinney, 1989; S. Wright & Taylor, 1995). And we must certainly provide whatever scaffolding they need to be successful on academic tasks.

We will see diversity in students' social development as well. Some students may have had few opportunities to form friendships and, as a result, few opportunities to develop effective ways of interacting with their peers. For instance, children in some families are encouraged to stay close to home, perhaps to perform household chores, care for younger brothers and sisters, or play with older siblings (Trawick-Smith, 1997). Children who have recently immigrated from a non-English-speaking country may have only a limited ability to communicate with other children in their neighborhoods and classrooms (A. Doyle, 1982).

Definitions of what is "moral" behavior are also likely to differ somewhat depending on students' backgrounds. For example, although lying is generally discouraged in our own culture, it is a legitimate way of saving face in many others (Triandis, 1995). Furthermore, some ethnic groups (including many from Asia and South America) value loyalty and foster prosocial behavior more than others do (Greenfield, 1994; Markus & Kitayama, 1991; P. B. Smith & Bond, 1994; Triandis, 1995). Whereas some ethnic groups emphasize the importance of being considerate of other people (e.g., "Please be quiet so that your sister can study"), others emphasize the importance of tolerating inconsiderate behavior (e.g., "Please try not to let your brother's radio bother you when you study"; C. A. Grant & Gomez, 1996). As teachers, we must remember that our students' notions of moral behavior will not always be identical to our own.

Accommodating Students with Special Needs

Some of our students will undoubtedly have special educational needs related to their personal, social, or moral development. For example, many of our students with special needs will have lower self-esteem than their classmates (e.g., Brown-Mizuno, 1990; T. Bryan, 1991; H. W. Marsh & Craven, 1997). Students with mental retardation will typically have less understanding of how to behave in social situations than their nondisabled peers (Greenspan & Granfield, 1992). Students with emotional and behavioral disorders—for example, those with a history of aggressive and violent behavior—will frequently have poor perspective taking and social problem-solving abilities, and they may perceive hostile intentions in the most innocent of their classmates' actions (Hughes, 1988; Lind, 1994). Additional characteristics that you may see in students with special needs, along with strategies for promoting the personal, social, and moral development of such students, are presented in Table 3–4.

The Big Picture: Recurring Themes in Personal, Social, and Moral Development

Three themes have appeared repeatedly in our discussion of personal, social, and moral development:

• *Standards for acceptable behavior and the reasons behind them.* Standards for acceptable behavior, along with reasons why these standards must be upheld, are essential for promoting children's development. Well-adjusted children are typically those who grow up in an authoritative environment—one in which rules are set for appropriate behavior, reasons are provided regarding *why* the rules are necessary, and infractions of the rules are punished. Moral development is promoted when punishment

Foster students' understanding and appreciation of their own ethnic backgrounds.

Remember that some students' backgrounds have probably been more conducive to promoting social skills than those of other students.

Remember that your students' notions of moral behavior may differ from your own.

Communicate clearly what behaviors are and are not acceptable at school, and explain why certain behaviors cannot be tolerated.

TABLE 3.4

Promoting Personal, Social, and Moral Development in Students with Special Educational Needs

STUDENTS WITH SPECIAL NEEDS	CHARACTERISTICS THAT THESE STUDENTS MAY EXHIBIT	CLASSROOM STRATEGIES THAT MAY BE BENEFICIAL FOR THESE STUDENTS
Students with specific cognitive or academic difficulties	Low self-esteem related to areas of academic difficulty Greater susceptibility to peer pressure (if students have learning disabilities or ADHD) Difficulty in perspective taking (if students have learning disabilities or ADHD) In some cases, poor social skills and few friendships (especially if students have ADHD)	Promote academic success (e.g., by providing extra scaffolding for classroom tasks). Give students the opportunity to "show off" the things that they do well. Use induction to promote perspective taking (e.g., focus students' attention on how their behaviors have caused harm or distress to others). Teach any missing social skills.
Students with social or behavioral problems	Poor social skills Difficulties in social problem solving Rejection by peers; few friendships Misinterpretation of social cues (e.g., perceiving hostile intent in innocent interactions) Less ability to recognize the emotional states of others Less empathy for others Difficulty in perspective taking	Explicitly teach social skills, provide opportunities to practice them, and give feedback. Establish and enforce firm rules regarding acceptable classroom behavior. Label and praise appropriate behaviors when they occur. Teach social problem-solving strategies (e.g., through mediation training). Provide opportunities for students to make new friends (e.g., through cooperative learning activities). Help students recognize the outward signs of various emotions. Use induction to promote empathy and perspective taking.
Students with general delays in cognitive and social functioning	Generally low self-esteem Social skills typical of younger children Difficulty identifying and interpreting social cues Concrete, often preconventional, ideas of right and wrong	Promote academic and social success. Teach social skills, provide opportunities to practice them, and give feedback. Specify rules for classroom behavior in specific, concrete terms. Label and praise appropriate behaviors when they occur.
Students with physical or sensory challenges	Fewer friends, and possible social isolation Fewer opportunities to develop appropriate social skills	Maximize opportunities for students to interact with their classmates. Assign "buddies"—classmates who can assist students with tasks that they cannot perform themselves due to a disability. Teach any missing social skills.

continued

STUDENTS WITH SPECIAL NEEDS	CHARACTERISTICS THAT THESE STUDENTS MAY EXHIBIT	CLASSROOM STRATEGIES THAT MAY BE BENEFICIAL FOR THESE STUDENTS
Students with advanced cognitive development	Above-average social development and emotional adjustment (although some extremely gifted students may have difficulty because they are so *very* different from their peers) High self-esteem with regard to academic tasks (more typical of males than females) Conflicts (especially for females) between the need to develop and display abilities on the one hand, and to gain peer acceptance on the other For some students, more advanced moral reasoning Concerns about moral and ethical issues at a younger age than peers Greater perspective taking	Talk with students regarding their concerns about their exceptional abilities. Engage students in conversations about ethical issues and moral dilemmas. Involve students in projects that address social problems at a community, national, or international level.

Sources: Asher & Coie, 1990; Barkley, 1995b; Bassett et al., 1996; Bierman et al. 1987; Brown-Mizuno, 1990; T Bryan, 1991; Cartledge & Milburn, 1995; Coie & Cillessen, 1993; Coleman & Minnett, 1992; DuPaul & Eckert, 1994; E. S. Ellis & Friend, 1991; Flavell et al., 1993; Genshaft, Greenbaum, & Borovosky, 1995; Greenspan & Granfield, 1992; Gresham & MacMillan, 1997; Heward, 1996; Hughes, 1988; Juvonen & Hiner, 1991; Juvonen & Weiner, 1993; B. K. Keogh & MacMillan, 1996; Licht, 1992; Lind, 1994; Maker & Schiever, 1989; H. W. Marsh & Craven, 1997; McCormick & Wolf, 1993; C. D. Mercer, 1991; Neel et al., 1990; Patton et al., 1990; Piirto, 1994; Schonert-Reichl, 1993; Schumaker & Hazel, 1984; Turnbull et al., 1999; S. Vaughn, 1991; Winner, 1997; Zeaman & House, 1979; Zirpoli & Melloy, 1993.

Note: *Compiled with the assistance of Dr. Margie Garanzini-Daiber and Dr. Margaret Cohen, University of Missouri—St. Louis.*

for rule infractions is accompanied by induction—by descriptions of how one's misbehavior has caused physical or emotional harm to someone else. As teachers, we must communicate clearly to students what behaviors are and are not acceptable at school and explain why some behaviors will not be tolerated.

• *Social interaction.* Social interaction is critical not only for children's cognitive and linguistic development (Chapter 2), but also for personal, social, and moral development. For example, the way that others behave toward students significantly affects their self-concepts. Social skills develop within the context of interactions with others, and especially with peers. Conversations about controversial topics and moral issues help students see things from other viewpoints and create disequilibrium for many students; thus, such conversations are critical for the development of perspective taking and moral reasoning. Classroom discussions and other opportunities for social interaction must therefore be an important and frequent component of classroom life.

Provide numerous opportunities for social interaction.

• *A warm, supportive environment.* Development is most effectively fostered within the context of a generally warm and supportive environment. We first saw the importance of a loving yet firm environment in our discussion of authoritative parenting. We also discovered the very important role that positive feedback plays in the development of students' self-concepts and self-esteem. And we learned that students are more likely to express their ideas about moral issues in a classroom in which they feel free to express their ideas openly and honestly.

Provide a warm, supportive classroom environment.

It would be naive for us to think of schools only as places where students learn academic skills. Whether we like it or not, our schools, including the teachers and classmates within them, play an important and influential role in children's personal, social, and moral development as well. It is critical that we not leave these important aspects of children's development to chance.

C A S E   S T U D Y : A Discussion of Runaway Slaves

Mr. Dawson's eighth-grade American history class is learning about the large cotton plantations prevalent in the Southern states before the Civil War. Mr. Dawson explains that such plantations probably would not have been possible without the thousands of slaves who picked the cotton.

"Sometimes the slaves would run away," he says. "And when they did, White people who believed that slavery was wrong would hide them or help them escape to the North. But helping runaway slaves was against the law; a person could be put in jail for doing so. Was it right for these people to help the slaves? Would *you* have helped a slave run away?"

"I don't think I would," says Mark. "Some of the plantation owners might have been my friends, and I wouldn't want them to get angry at me."

"I don't think I would either," says Lacy. "After all, it was against the law. I'd get punished if I broke the law. I wouldn't want to end up in jail."

"I think I might do it," says Kevin, "but only if I was sure I wouldn't get caught."

"I agree with Kevin," says Pam. "Besides, if I were really nice to the slave, he might help me around the house or in my garden."

Mr. Dawson is appalled at what his students are telling him. Where is their sense of injustice about the enslavement of human beings? Isn't the very notion of slavery inconsistent with the idea that all people are created equal?

- Are you as surprised as Mr. Dawson is? What stages of moral reasoning are evident in the opinions of these four students? Are these stages typical or atypical for eighth graders?

Summing Up

Personal Development

Some aspects of students' personalities are inherited; others will have been formed early in life. Yet the school environment, including teachers and classmates, also influences students' personal development; for example, students' self-concepts and self-esteem are affected by the expectations that teachers have for their behavior and by the ways that teachers and classmates treat them. We can promote students' personal development by holding high yet realistic expectations for performance, helping them be successful in classroom tasks, providing positive feedback for things well done, and giving negative feedback while still communicating that we care about students as human beings. We must also consider students' ages; for example, we can (1) support preschoolers in their efforts to initiate activities, (2) encourage elementary school students to produce things and praise them for their accomplishments, and (3) provide opportunities for secondary school students to explore various career options and a variety of social and political belief systems.

Social Development

Schools are important socialization agents; for example, teachers teach students to control impulses, follow directions, work independently, cooperate with classmates, and delay gratification. As teachers, we must expect and encourage those behaviors essential for students' long-term life success.

Classmates are equally important in students' social development; peer relationships provide emotional support, information about acceptable behaviors and values, and an arena for developing social skills. We can help students develop supportive peer relationships by teaching productive interpersonal skills and by encouraging interaction among diverse groups.

Moral Development

As students progress through the grade levels, most of them become less self-centered in their solutions to moral problems, gain an increasing ability to see situations from someone else's viewpoint, and demonstrate prosocial behavior more frequently. As teachers, we can promote the development of more advanced moral reasoning, perspective taking, and prosocial behavior by providing an authoritative classroom environment, giving students reasons why certain behaviors are unacceptable, encouraging them to recognize how others feel in various situations, challenging their thinking with moral issues and dilemmas, and modeling moral behavior ourselves.

Diversity in Personal, Social, and Moral Development

Some students will face extra challenges in their lives (e.g., family problems, violence, drug addiction) that will invariably affect their personal, social, and moral development. We will also see differences among our students because of the cultural contexts in which they have been raised; for example, some students' sense of identity may include pride in their ethnic heritage, and their sense of morality is likely to reflect the values of their local community. Students with special needs may need additional support to enhance their self-esteem, social skills, and moral development.

General Themes

Three themes appeared repeatedly in our discussion of personal, social, and moral development. First, students need standards for acceptable behavior as well as reasons as to why some behaviors are unacceptable. Second, social interaction plays a critical role in students' lives; among other things, it affects students' self-concepts and promotes the development of social skills, moral reasoning, and perspective taking. And third, students need a warm, supportive environment in which they feel comfortable expressing their views and in which they get positive feedback for their successes.

KEY CONCEPTS

personality (p. 76)
attachment (p. 77)
parenting style (p. 77)
authoritative parenting style (p. 78)
authoritarian parenting style (p. 78)
permissive parenting style (p. 78)
uninvolved parenting style (p. 78)
self-concept (p. 79)
self-esteem (p. 79)

identity (p. 80)
imaginary audience (p. 87)
personal fable (p. 87)
socialization (p. 89)
norms (p. 89)
roles (p. 89)
culture shock (p. 89)
peers (p. 90)

peer pressure (p. 92)
social skills (p. 93)
prosocial behaviors (p. 93)
shame (p. 97)
guilt (p. 97)
empathy (p. 97)
moral dilemma (p. 98)
induction (p. 110)

4

Individual and Group Differences

As you discovered in Chapters 2 and 3, students change in many ways as they grow older, and so students at one age level are often quite different from those at another age level. But what differences have you observed among students of the *same* age? For instance, have you noticed that some students seem to learn more quickly and easily than their classmates, or that some are more creative than others when they complete assigned tasks? When we talk about how students of the same age often differ from one another, perhaps in ways that reflect intelligence or creativity, we are talking about **individual differences.**

Sometimes we find consistent differences among various groups of students. For example, you have undoubtedly observed that different ethnic groups often use different words, pronunciations, and grammatical structures—in other words, different *dialects*—even though all groups are using the English language. But have you also noticed that females tend to form closer, more intimate friendships than males, or that students from lower-income families have lower educational and career aspirations than their classmates from middle-income families? When we talk about how students of one group typically differ from those of another group, we are talking about **group differences.**

This chapter describes how we can adapt our classroom practices to accommodate individual and group differences. More specifically, we will address questions such as these:

- To what extent will knowledge about individual and group differences enable us to draw conclusions about individual students?

- What do we mean by the term *intelligence*, and how can we promote intelligent behavior in all of our students?

- How can we foster creativity in the classroom?

- In what ways are students from various ethnic groups likely to be different from one another, and what implications do such differences have for classroom practice?

- In what ways are males and females alike and different? What can we do to provide equitable educational opportunities for both boys and girls?

- How can we accommodate the unique needs of students from lower socioeconomic groups?

- What characteristics can help us identify students at risk for school failure, and how can we help these students achieve academic success?

- What happens when we form unwarranted expectations for students' performance? How can we guard against jumping to premature and inaccurate conclusions about our students?

CASE STUDY: Hidden Treasure

Six-year-old Lupita has just enrolled in Ms. Padilla's kindergarten classroom. The daughter of migrant workers, Lupita has been raised by her grandmother in Mexico, where she has had little experience with toys, puzzles, paper, crayons, or scissors, and few opportunities to interact with other children. Ms. Padilla rarely calls on Lupita in class because of her apparent lack of academic skills; she is afraid of embarrassing Lupita in front of her classmates. By midyear, Ms. Padilla is thinking about holding Lupita back for a second year of kindergarten.

Lupita is always quiet and well behaved in class; in fact, she's so quiet that Ms. Padilla sometimes forgets she's even there. Yet a researcher's video camera captures a different side to Lupita. On one occasion, Lupita is quick to finish her Spanish assignment and so begins to work on a puzzle during her free time. A classmate approaches, and he and Lupita begin playing with a box of toys. A teacher aide asks the boy whether he has finished his Spanish assignment, implying that he should return to complete it, but the boy does not understand the aide's subtle message. Lupita gently persuades the boy to go back and finish his work. She then returns to her puzzle and successfully fits most of it together. Two classmates having difficulty with their own puzzles request Lupita's assistance, and she competently and patiently shows them how to assemble puzzles and how to help each other.

Ms. Padilla is amazed when she views the videotape, which shows Lupita to be a competent girl with strong teaching and leadership skills. Ms. Padilla readily admits, "I had written her off . . . her and three others. They had met my expectations and I just wasn't looking for anything else." Ms. Padilla and her aides begin working closely with Lupita on academic skills, and they often allow her to take a leadership role in group activities. At the end of the school year, Lupita obtains achievement test scores indicating exceptional competence in language skills and mathematics, and she is promoted to first grade.

- Why might one jump to the conclusion that Lupita has poor academic skills? Might Lupita's background be a reason? Might her classroom behavior be a reason?

- How might teachers' expectations for their students affect the way they behave toward students? How might teachers' expectations affect students' academic achievement?

- What might have happened to Lupita if her behavior with classmates had gone unnoticed? How might her academic life have been different?

Based on a case study in Carrasco, 1981.

Keeping Individual and Group Differences in Perspective

We will inevitably find that some students learn more easily than others. For example, Lupita finishes assignments and completes puzzles more quickly than some of her classmates. We will also find differences in how accurately our students remember information, how readily they connect ideas with one another, and how easily and creatively they apply their knowledge to new situations and problems.

Some of Lupita's behaviors may be partly due to either her Mexican heritage or her gender. For example, she is proficient in Spanish and displays the cooperative attitude encouraged in many Hispanic cultures. She is so quiet in class that her teacher often forgets she's there; as we will discover later, girls are typically less assertive in whole-class situations than boys.

In observing our students day after day, we are likely to draw inferences about their academic capabilities, just as Ms. Padilla did for Lupita. Yet we must be careful that such inferences are never set in stone—that we keep an open mind about how each student is likely to perform in future situations. For example, we will soon discover that creativity is domain-specific: Some students may be creative in science, whereas others are more creative in fine arts. We will find, too, that intelligence can change over time, especially during the early years, and that students often behave more intelligently in some contexts than in others.

When considering group differences, such as those among diverse ethnic groups and those between males and females, we need to keep in mind two very important points. First, *there is a great deal of individual variability within any group.* I will be describing how students of different groups behave *on the average,* yet some students may be very different from that "average" description. Second, *there is almost always a great deal of overlap between two groups.* Consider gender differences in verbal ability as an example. Research studies often find that girls demonstrate slightly higher verbal performance than boys (Halpern, 1992; Lueptow, 1984; Maccoby & Jacklin, 1974). This difference is sometimes statistically significant; in other words, we cannot explain it as something that happens just by chance in one particular study. Yet the average difference between girls and boys in verbal ability is quite small, with a great deal of overlap between the two groups. Figure 4–1 shows the typical overlap between boys and girls on measures of verbal ability: Notice how many of the boys are *better* than some of the girls despite the average advantage for girls.

Be careful not to make predictions about individual students based on group differences alone.

Remember that average group differences are often quite small, with a great deal of overlap between any two groups.

As we shall discover in this chapter, teachers' preconceived notions about how students will behave may actually *increase* the differences among those students. At the same time, if we are to maximize the learning and development of all students, then we should be aware of individual and group differences that influence students' classroom performance. Several general principles regarding student diversity are presented in Table 4–1.

This chapter identifies many differences that are likely to affect our students' academic achievement, as well as strategies for accommodating those differences. As teachers, we should never ask ourselves whether particular students can learn. We should instead ask how we can most effectively help every student master the knowledge and skills essential for school and lifelong success.

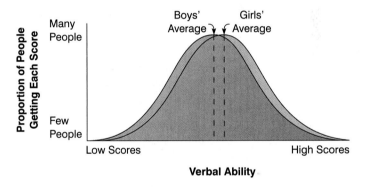

FIGURE 4.1
Typical "difference" between boys and girls on tests of verbal ability

Intelligence

THINKING ABOUT WHAT YOU KNOW

What kinds of behaviors make you think that someone is "intelligent"? Do you believe that intelligence is a general ability that contributes to success in many different areas? Or is it possible for an individual to be intelligent in one area yet not in another?

What exactly is **intelligence?** Unfortunately, psychologists have not yet reached consensus on the answer to this question. But here are several components of what many theorists construe to be intelligent behavior:

- It is *adaptive.* It involves modifying and adjusting one's behaviors to accomplish new tasks successfully.

General Principles Regarding Student Diversity

GENERAL PRINCIPLE	EDUCATIONAL IMPLICATION	EXAMPLE
Differences among students are subject to change over time; they are not necessarily *permanent* differences.	Never make long-range predictions about students' future success or failure based on their present behaviors.	Although a student currently shows little creativity, believe that creative behavior is possible, and plan instructional activities that promote such creativity.
There is a great deal of variability within any group of seemingly similar students.	Be careful not to draw conclusions about students' characteristics and abilities simply on the basis of their gender, ethnic background, or other group membership.	Encourage students from low-income neighborhoods to strive for a college education, and support them in their efforts to achieve one.
When two groups differ *on the average* in terms of a particular characteristic, considerable overlap usually exists between the two groups with respect to that characteristic.	Remember that average differences between groups don't necessarily apply to individual members of those groups.	Although boys have historically developed their athletic abilities more than girls, nevertheless provide equal opportunities for both genders to achieve athletic success.
Students achieve at higher levels when instruction takes individual and group differences into account.	Consider students' unique backgrounds and abilities when planning instructional activities.	Use cooperative learning activities more frequently when students' cultural backgrounds emphasize the value of cooperation and group achievement.

- It is related to *learning ability*. Intelligent people learn information more quickly and easily than less intelligent people.
- It involves the *use of prior knowledge* to analyze and understand new situations effectively.
- It involves the complex interaction and coordination of *many different mental processes*.
- It may be seen in *different arenas*—for example, on academic tasks or in social situations.
- It is *culture-specific*. What is "intelligent" behavior in one culture is not necessarily intelligent behavior in another culture. (Laboratory of Human Cognition, 1982; Neisser et al., 1996; Sternberg, 1997; Sternberg & Detterman, 1986)

For most theorists, intelligence is somewhat distinct from what an individual has actually learned (e.g., as reflected in school achievement). At the same time, intelligent thinking and intelligent behavior are to some extent *dependent* on prior learning. The more students know about their environment and about the tasks they need to perform, the more intelligently they can behave. Intelligence, then, is not necessarily a permanent, unchanging characteristic. As you will soon discover, it can be modified through experience and learning.

Measuring Intelligence

Curiously, although psychologists cannot pin down exactly what intelligence *is*, they have been trying to measure it for almost a century. In the early 1900s, school officials in France asked Alfred Binet to develop a method of identifying those students unlikely

Think of someone you consider intelligent. Does that individual's behavior fit these criteria?

to benefit from regular school instruction and therefore in need of special educational services. To accomplish the task, Binet devised a test that measured general knowledge, vocabulary, perception, memory, and abstract thought. In doing so, he designed the earliest version of what we now call an **intelligence test.** To get a flavor for what intelligence tests are like, try the following exercise.

Experiencing Firsthand
A Mock Intelligence Test

Answer each question.

1. What does the word *quarrel* mean?
2. How are a goat and a beetle alike?
3. What should you do if you get separated from your family in a large department store?
4. Three kinds of people live on the planet Zircox: bims, gubs, and lops. All bims are lops. Some gubs are lops. Which one of the following must also be true?
   a. All bims are gubs.
   b. All lops are bims.
   c. Some gubs are bims.
   d. Some lops are bims.
5. Complete the following analogy:

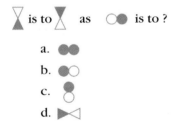

These test items are modeled after items on many modern-day intelligence tests. Think, for a moment, about the capabilities you needed to answer them successfully. Does general knowledge about the world play a role? Is knowledge of vocabulary important? Is abstract thought involved? The answer to all three questions is yes. Although intelligence tests have evolved considerably since Binet's time, they continue to measure many of the same abilities that Binet's original test did.

IQ Scores

Scores on intelligence tests were originally calculated by using a formula involving division; hence, they were called "intelligence quotient," or **IQ**, scores. Even though we still use the term *IQ,* intelligence test scores are no longer based on the old formula. Instead, they are determined by comparing a student's performance on the test with the performance of others in the same age-group. A score of 100 indicates average performance: Students with this score have performed better than half of their age-mates on the test and not as well as the other half. Scores below 100 indicate below-average performance on the test; scores above 100 indicate above-average performance.

Figure 4–2 shows the percentage of students getting scores at different points along the scale (e.g., 12.9% get scores between 100 and 105). Notice how the curve is high in the middle and low at both ends. This tells us that many more students obtain scores close to 100 than scores very much higher or lower than 100. For example, if we add the percentages in different parts of Figure 4–2, we find that approximately two-thirds (68%)

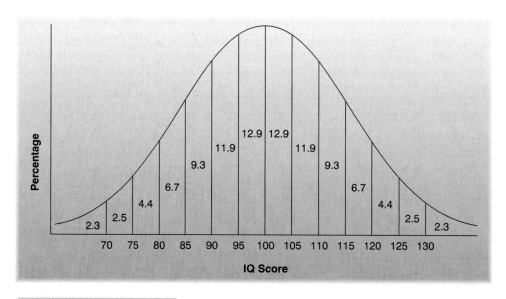

FIGURE 4.2
Percentage of IQ scores in different ranges

Is this description consistent with your previous beliefs about IQ scores?

of students score within 15 points of 100 (i.e., between 85 and 115). In contrast, only 2 percent of students score as low as 70, and only 2 percent score as high as 130. This symmetric and predictable distribution of scores happens by design rather than by chance; psychologists have created a method of scoring intelligence test performance that intentionally yields such a distribution. (You can find a more detailed explanation of IQ scores in the discussion of *standard scores* in Appendix C.)

IQ and School Achievement

Modern intelligence tests have been designed with Binet's original purpose in mind: to predict how well individual students are likely to perform in the classroom. Studies repeatedly show that performance on intelligence tests is correlated with school achievement (N. Brody, 1997; Gustafsson & Undheim, 1996; Neisser et al., 1996). On average, children with higher IQ scores do better on standardized achievement tests, have higher school grades, and complete more years of education. In other words, IQ scores *do* predict school achievement to some extent. As a result, intelligence tests are often used by school psychologists and other specialists to identify those students who may have special educational needs.

Under what circumstances might it be appropriate for a teacher to use intelligence test results? What potential dangers are there in relying solely on IQ scores as a measure of students' abilities?

While recognizing the relationship between intelligence test scores and school achievement, we must also keep three points in mind about this relationship. First, intelligence does not necessarily *cause* achievement; it is simply correlated with it. Even though students with high IQs typically perform well in school, we cannot say conclusively that their high achievement is actually the result of their intelligence. Intelligence probably does play an important role in school achievement, but many other factors are also involved—factors such as motivation, quality of instruction, family economics, parental support, and peer group norms.

Remember that, at best, IQ scores are imprecise predictors of school achievement.

Second, the relationship between IQ scores and achievement is not a perfect one; there are exceptions to the rule. For a variety of reasons, some students with high IQ scores do not perform well in the classroom. And other students achieve at higher levels than we would predict from their IQ scores alone. Therefore, we should never base our expectations for students' achievement solely on intelligence test scores.

Third and most important, we must remember that IQ scores simply reflect a student's performance on a particular test at a particular time and that some change is to be expected over the years. In fact, the longer the time interval between two measures of intelligence, the greater the change in IQ we are likely to see, especially with young children (Hayslip, 1994; McCall, 1993; C. E. Sanders, 1997).

Limitations of Intelligence Tests

As you can see, intelligence tests are hardly instruments that can determine a person's "true" intelligence (if, in fact, such a thing even exists). Yet on some occasions, we might find ourselves considering IQ scores along with other information as we make instructional decisions about some of our students—for example, as we meet with colleagues and parents to identify the most appropriate instructional program for a student with special educational needs. It is critical, then, to be aware of these limitations of traditional intelligence tests:

- Different kinds of intelligence tests often lead to somewhat different results.
- A student's performance on any test is inevitably affected by many temporary factors present at the time the test is taken, including general health, mood, fatigue, time of day, and the number of distracting stimuli. (Such temporary factors affect a test's *reliability*—a concept we will consider in Chapter 16.)
- Test items focus on a limited set of skills that are important in mainstream Western culture, and particularly in school settings; they do not necessarily tap into skills that may be more highly valued in other contexts or other societies.
- Some students may be unfamiliar with the content or types of tasks involved in particular test items and perform poorly on those items as a result.
- Students with limited English proficiency (LEP) are at an obvious disadvantage when an intelligence test is administered in English.
- Some students (e.g., minority students who want to avoid "acting White") may not be motivated to perform at their best and so may obtain scores that underestimate their capabilities.
- Some students (e.g., those from certain ethnic groups) may not be familiar with the question-answer format that predominates in a typical testing situation; others may continually respond with "I don't know" as a way of ending a seemingly unpleasant situation as quickly as possible. (Dirks, 1982; Heath, 1989; Neisser et al., 1996; Ogbu, 1994; Perkins, 1995; Sternberg, 1996b; Zigler & Finn-Stevenson, 1992)

Used within the context of other information, IQ scores can, in many cases, give a general idea of a student's current cognitive functioning. But as you can see from the limitations just listed, we should always maintain a healthy degree of skepticism about the accuracy of IQ scores, especially when students come from diverse ethnic backgrounds or have acquired only limited proficiency in English.

How Theorists Conceptualize Intelligence

Up to this point, we have been talking about intelligence in terms of a single IQ score. Yet not all theorists believe that intelligence is a single entity that people "have" in varying degrees; some theorists instead propose that people may behave more or less intelligently in different situations and on different kinds of tasks. Here we will look at four very different perspectives regarding the nature of intelligence. We'll first consider the traditional idea that intelligence is a single, generalized trait—a concept often referred to as the *g* factor. We will then examine two theories, developed by Howard Gardner and Robert Sternberg, that portray intelligence as a multidimensional and context-dependent entity. Finally, we will address the concept of "distributed" intelligence.

Remember that IQ scores are never "permanent" indicators of a student's ability.

Do you have any prior beliefs about intelligence tests that are inconsistent with what you've just read? If so, can you resolve the inconsistencies?

Spearman's Concept of g

Whenever we use an IQ score as an estimate of a person's cognitive ability, we are, to some extent, buying into the notion that intelligence is a single entity. Historically, considerable evidence has supported this idea (McGrew, Flanagan, Zeith, & Vanderwood, 1997; Neisser et al., 1996; Spearman, 1927). Although different types of intelligence tests yield somewhat different scores, they all correlate with one another to some degree: People who score high on one test tend to score high on others as well. Charles Spearman (1904, 1927) called this single entity a *general factor,* or *g.* Some contemporary information processing theorists believe that *g* is a reflection of the speed and efficiency with which people can process information, learning tasks, and problem situations (Vernon, 1993).

Gardner's Theory of Multiple Intelligences

In addition to a general factor in intelligence, many researchers have found evidence for more specific abilities as well, and measures of these abilities can sometimes predict performance on particular school tasks more accurately than general intelligence tests do (McGrew et al., 1997; Neisser et al., 1996; Thurstone, 1938). Howard Gardner (1983, 1995, 1998; Gardner & Hatch, 1990) believes there are eight different abilities, or *intelligences,* that are relatively independent of one another (see Table 4–2). Gardner's perspective presents the possibility that most, and quite possibly all, of our students may be quite intelligent in one way or another. Some students may show exceptional promise in language, others may be talented in music, and still others may be able to learn mathematics more easily than their classmates.

Gardner proposes that intelligence is reflected somewhat differently in different cultures. For example, in our culture, spatial intelligence might be reflected in painting, sculpture, or geometry. But among the Kikuyu people in Kenya, it might be reflected in one's ability to recognize every animal within one's own herd of livestock and to distinguish one's

Some theorists, such as Howard Gardner, believe that there are a number of distinctly different "intelligences," such that a person may be more intelligent in one area than in another.

T A B L E 4.2   Gardner's Eight Intelligences

TYPE OF INTELLIGENCE	EXAMPLES OF RELEVANT BEHAVIORS
Linguistic Intelligence The ability to use language effectively	Making persuasive arguments Writing poetry Being sensitive to subtle nuances in word meanings
Logical-Mathematical Intelligence The ability to reason logically, especially in mathematics and science	Solving mathematical problems quickly Generating mathematical proofs Formulating and testing hypotheses about observed phenomena*
Spatial Intelligence The ability to notice details of what one sees and to imagine and "manipulate" visual objects in one's mind	Conjuring up mental images in one's mind Drawing a visual likeness of an object Making fine discriminations among very similar objects
Musical Intelligence The ability to create, comprehend, and appreciate music	Playing a musical instrument Composing a musical work Having a keen awareness of the underlying structure of music
Bodily-Kinesthetic Intelligence The ability to use one's body skillfully	Dancing Playing basketball Performing pantomime
Interpersonal Intelligence The ability to notice subtle aspects of other people's behaviors	Reading another's mood Detecting another's underlying intentions and desires Using knowledge of others to influence their thoughts and behaviors
Intrapersonal Intelligence Awareness of one's own feelings, motives, and desires	Discriminating among such similar emotions as sadness and regret Identifying the motives guiding one's own behavior Using self-knowledge to relate more effectively with others
Naturalist Intelligence The ability to recognize patterns in nature and differences among natural objects and life forms	Identifying members of various species Classifying natural forms (e.g., rocks, types of mountains) Applying one's knowledge of nature in such activities as farming, landscaping, or hunting

In which of Gardner's eight kinds of intelligence are you most "intelligent"?

This example may remind you of Piaget's theory of cognitive development. Many of the stage-relevant characteristics that Piaget described fall within the realm of logical-mathematical intelligence.

Present classroom subject matter using a variety of approaches to capitalize on students' diverse abilities.

own animals from those of other families. And among the Gikwe bushmen of the Kalahari Desert, it might be reflected in one's ability to recognize and remember many specific locations over a large area (perhaps over several hundred square miles), identifying each location in terms of the rocks, bushes, and other landmarks found there (Gardner, 1983).

Gardner's theory encourages us to use many different approaches to teach classroom subject matter—approaches that are likely to capitalize on the diverse abilities that different students may have (Armstrong, 1994; L. Campbell, Campbell, & Dickinson, 1998; Gardner, 1995). For example, when my son Jeff took high school biology, he had to write a short story that included at least four examples of living things (either plants or animals) changing energy from one form into another—an assignment in which his linguistic intelligence obviously played a substantial role. Consider, too, how an eighth-grade teacher took advantage of two girls' musical intelligence to teach spelling:

> . . . both [girls] enjoyed playing the piano. [I] asked the girls to label the piano keys with the letters of the alphabet, so that the girls could "play" the words on their keyboards. Later, on spelling tests, the students were asked to recall the tones and sounds of each word and write its corresponding letters. Not only did spelling scores improve, but the two pianists began thinking of other "sound" texts to set to music. Soon, they performed each classmate's name and transcribed entire sentences. (Campbell et al., 1998, p. 142)

Gardner presents some evidence to support the existence of multiple intelligences. For instance, he describes people who are quite skilled in one area (perhaps in composing music) and yet have seemingly average abilities in the other areas. He also points out that people who suffer brain damage sometimes lose abilities that are restricted primarily to one intelligence; for instance, one person might show deficits primarily in language, whereas another might have difficulty with tasks that require spatial skills. Nevertheless, some psychologists believe that Gardner's evidence is not sufficiently compelling to support the notion of eight distinctly different abilities; many are taking a "wait and see" attitude until more research is conducted (e.g., Berk, 1997; Feldman & Goldsmith, 1991).

Sternberg's Triarchic Theory

Whereas Gardner focuses on different kinds of intelligence, Robert Sternberg of Yale University focuses on the nature of intelligence itself. Sternberg (1984, 1985) suggests that intelligent behavior involves an interplay of three factors, all of which may vary from one occasion to the next: (1) the environmental *context* in which the behavior occurs, (2) the way in which one's prior *experiences* are brought to bear on a particular task, and (3) the *cognitive processes* required by that task. These three dimensions are summarized in Figure 4–3. Let's look at each one in more detail.

Role of environmental context. Earlier in the chapter, we noted that intelligence is both *adaptive* and *culture-specific.* Sternberg proposes that intelligent behavior involves adaptation: Individuals must adapt their behaviors to deal successfully with specific environmental conditions, modify the environment to better fit their own needs, or select an alternative environment more conducive to success. He also proposes that behavior may be more or less intelligent in different cultural contexts. For example, learning to read is an adaptive response in some cultures yet may be an irrelevant skill in others.

Sternberg has identified three general skills that may be particularly adaptive in Western culture. One such skill is *practical problem-solving ability*—for example, one's ability to identify exactly what the problem *is* in a particular situation, to reason logically (both deductively and inductively), and to generate a multitude of possible problem solutions. A second skill is *verbal ability*—for example, one's ability to speak and write clearly, to develop and use a large vocabulary, and to understand and learn from what one reads. A third skill is *social competence*—for example, one's ability to relate effectively with other human beings, to be sensitive to others' needs and wishes, and to provide leadership.

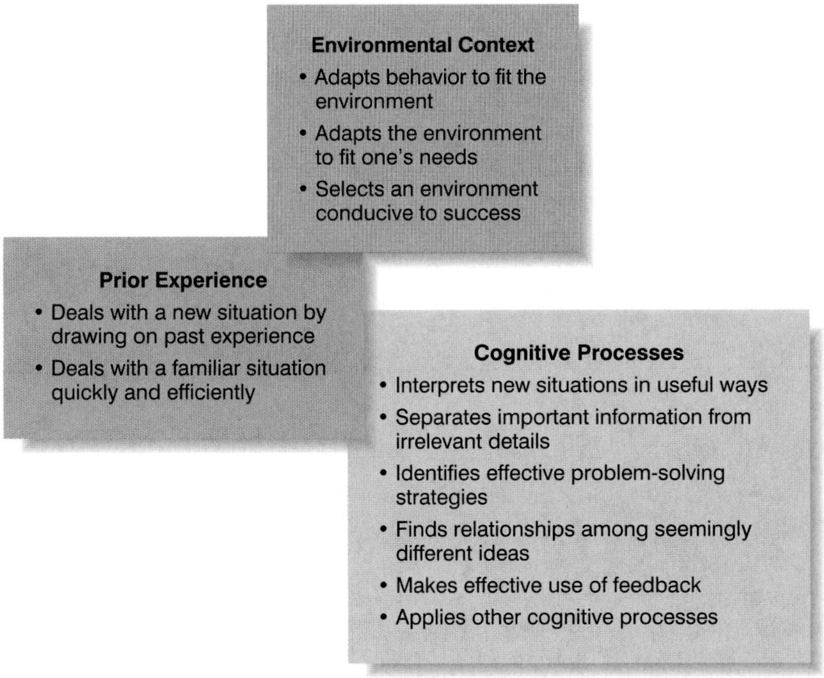

Environmental Context
- Adapts behavior to fit the environment
- Adapts the environment to fit one's needs
- Selects an environment conducive to success

Prior Experience
- Deals with a new situation by drawing on past experience
- Deals with a familiar situation quickly and efficiently

Cognitive Processes
- Interprets new situations in useful ways
- Separates important information from irrelevant details
- Identifies effective problem-solving strategies
- Finds relationships among seemingly different ideas
- Makes effective use of feedback
- Applies other cognitive processes

FIGURE 4.3
Sternberg's three dimensions of intelligence

Role of prior experiences. Sternberg proposes that intelligent behavior sometimes reflects one's ability to deal successfully with a brand new task or situation. At other times, it reflects one's ability to deal with more familiar tasks and situations in a rapid and efficient manner. In both cases, one's prior experiences play a critical role.

When dealing with a new task or situation, people must make some sort of new response. But to do so, they must draw on their past experiences, considering the kinds of responses that have been effective in similar situations. Try the following exercise as an illustration.

■ Experiencing Firsthand
Finding the Bus Station

You and two friends, Bonnie and Clyde, drive to a small city about two or three hours away to do some sight-seeing. Once there, Bonnie and Clyde decide to spend the night so that they can attend a concert scheduled for the following day. You, however, want to return home the same day. You've been traveling in Bonnie's car, and now the only way you can get back home is to take a bus. How might you find your way to the bus station? What strategies have you used in other situations that might help you in your efforts?

One strategy is to find a telephone book and look up *bus lines.* Another is to ask directions of a police officer, hotel clerk, or other seemingly knowledgeable person. Still another is to find the city's central business district and wander around; bus stations in most cities are located somewhere in the downtown area. Each of these strategies may be similar to an approach you've used in the past—perhaps to find a friend's house, a suitable place to eat, or a pharmacy open on Saturday nights.

When people deal with more familiar situations, intelligent behavior involves developing **automaticity**—an ability to respond quickly and efficiently—in either

Remember that students can behave more "intelligently" when they have prior experiences from which to draw.

mentally processing or physically performing a task. As an example, try the following exercise.

■ Experiencing Firsthand
Solving for x

How quickly can you solve for *x* in this problem?

$$\frac{4}{5} = \frac{x}{30}$$

If you were able to identify the correct answer (24) very quickly and without a great deal of thought and effort, then you show some automaticity (and hence some intelligence) in your ability to solve mathematical problems involving proportions. Automaticity results from experience—from performing certain tasks over and over again. (Chapter 6 discusses automaticity in more depth.)

Role of cognitive processes. In addition to considering how context and prior experience affect behavior, we must also consider how an individual thinks about (mentally processes) a particular task. Sternberg proposes that numerous cognitive processes are involved in intelligent behavior: interpreting new situations in ways that promote successful adaptation, separating important and relevant information from unimportant and irrelevant details, identifying possible strategies for solving a problem, finding relationships among seemingly different ideas, making effective use of external feedback about one's performance, and so on. Different cognitive processes are likely to be involved to a greater or lesser degree in different behaviors, and an individual may behave more or less "intelligently" on a task, depending on the specific cognitive abilities and processes needed in that situation.

To date, research neither supports nor refutes Sternberg's belief that intelligence has this "triarchic" nature. At the same time, Sternberg's theory reminds us that an individual's ability to behave "intelligently" may vary considerably, depending on the particular context and on the specific knowledge, skills, and cognitive processes that a task requires. Some theorists believe that context makes all the difference in the world—a belief that is clearly evident in the concept of *distributed intelligence*.

The Concept of Distributed Intelligence

Implicit in our discussion so far is the assumption that intelligent behavior is something that people engage in with little if any help from the objects or people around them. But some theorists point out that people are far more likely to think and behave intelligently when they have the support of their physical and social environments (Pea, 1993; Perkins, 1992, 1995; Sternberg & Wagner, 1994). For example, it's easier for many people to solve for *x* in $\frac{4}{5} = \frac{x}{30}$ if they have pencil and paper, or perhaps even a calculator, with which to work the problem out. It should be easier to find the local bus station if one can debate the pros and cons of various strategies with a few friends. As noted in Chapter 2, virtually anyone can perform more difficult tasks when he or she has the support structure, or *scaffolding,* to do so.

This idea that intelligent behavior depends on people's physical and social support systems is sometimes referred to as **distributed intelligence.** People can "distribute" their thinking (and therefore think more intelligently) in at least three ways (Perkins, 1992, 1995). First, they can use physical objects, and especially technology (e.g., calculators, computers), to handle and manipulate large amounts of information. Second, they can work with other people to explore ideas and solve problems; after all, two heads are usually better than one. And third, they can represent and think about the sit-

Identify physical, social, and symbolic supports that can help students think more intelligently.

uations they encounter using the various symbolic systems that their culture provides—for instance, the words, diagrams, charts, mathematical equations, and so on, that help them simplify or summarize complex topics and problems. As teachers, rather than asking the question, "How intelligent are our students?" we should instead be asking, "How can we help our students think as intelligently as possible? What tools, social networks, and symbolic systems can we provide?"

Heredity, Environment, and Group Differences

THINKING ABOUT WHAT YOU KNOW

In 1994, Richard Herrnstein and Charles Murray published *The Bell Curve.* What have you heard about this book? Why is it so controversial?

Three fairly consistent research findings are that, on average, African American families have lower incomes than Caucasian families, students from lower-income families get lower IQ scores than students from upper- and middle-income families, and Caucasian students get higher IQ scores than African American students (N. Brody, 1992; McLoyd, 1998; Neisser et al., 1996). In *The Bell Curve,* Herrnstein and Murray proposed that these differences are due largely to heredity—in other words, that, genetically speaking, Caucasians have the advantage over African Americans. As you might guess, the book generated considerable controversy and a great deal of outrage.

Scholars have poked so many holes in *The Bell Curve* that it doesn't seem to hold much water (Jacoby & Glauberman, 1995; Marks, 1995). For instance, they find numerous weaknesses in the research and statistical analyses that Herrnstein and Murray described; as one simple example, they remind us that we can ultimately never draw conclusions about causation by looking only at correlational studies. They point out, too, that the concept of *race,* although widely used to categorize people in our society, actually has no basis in biology: It is virtually impossible to identify a person's "race" by analyzing his or her DNA. And as we have seen, many theorists question the notion of a general factor (*g*) in intelligence—a notion on which traditional IQ scores are based.

Research tells us that heredity probably does play some role in intelligence. For instance, identical twins, even when they are raised in different homes, tend to have more similar IQ scores than fraternal twins do (Plomin, 1994). And in many respects, the cognitive development of adopted children more closely resembles that of their biological parents than that of their adoptive parents, particularly as the children grow older (McGue, Bouchard, Iacono, & Lykken, 1993; Plomin, Fulker, Corley, & DeFries, 1997).

Yet the environment clearly has a large effect on IQ scores. For instance, poor nutrition in the early years of development (including the prenatal period) leads to lower IQ scores, as does a mother's excessive use of alcohol during pregnancy (D'Amato, Chitooran, & Whitten, 1992; Neisser et al., 1996; Ricciuti, 1993). Attending school has a consistently positive effect on IQ scores (Ceci & Williams, 1997; Ramey, 1992). Permanently changing a child's environment from an impoverished one to an enriched, stimulating one can lead to increases in intelligence of up to 20 or 25 points in measured IQ score (Bloom, 1964; Capron & Duyme, 1989; Scarr & Weinberg, 1976; Skeels, 1966; Zigler & Seitz, 1982). Furthermore, researchers are finding that, worldwide, there is a slow but steady increase in people's IQ scores—a trend that is almost certainly due to better nutrition, better schooling, an increased amount of daily stimulation (through increased access to television, reading materials, etc.), and other improvements in people's environments (Flynn, 1987; Neisser et al., 1996).

Most theorists now believe that it is ultimately impossible to separate the effects of heredity and environment. The two combine to influence children's cognitive development and measured IQ in ways that we can probably never disentangle (Bouchard et al., 1990; Rutter, 1997; A. H. Yee, 1995). Yet we have considerable evidence that IQ differences between African American and Caucasian children are due largely to differences in environment—more specifically, to economic circumstances that affect the quality of prenatal and postnatal nutrition, availability of stimulating books and toys, access to educational opportunities, and so on (Brooks-Gunn, Klebanov, & Duncan, 1996; McLoyd, 1998). We find, too, that African American and Caucasian children have, in recent years, become increasingly *similar* in IQ; this trend can only be attributed to more equitable environmental conditions for the two groups (Neisser et al., 1996). Furthermore, we must remember that IQ scores are definitely *not* perfect measures of intelligence. As noted earlier, scores are influenced by students' familiarity with the content and nature of IQ tests and by their motivation to perform well on these tests—factors that are almost certainly different for different ethnic and socioeconomic groups. In general, then, we should assume that African American and Caucasian children (and presumably other racial and ethnic groups as well) have equivalent potential with respect to intelligence and cognitive development.

🍎 Assume that children from all racial and ethnic groups have equivalent potential with respect to intelligence and cognitive development.

Being Optimistic about Students' Potential

Contemporary views of intelligence give us reason to be optimistic about our students' abilities. If intelligence is as multifaceted as theorists such as Gardner and Sternberg believe, then scores from any single IQ test cannot possibly give a complete picture of our students' "intelligence" (Neisser et al., 1996). In fact, we are likely to see intelligent behavior in many of our students—perhaps in *all* of them—in one way or another (Gardner, 1995). One student may show promise in mathematics, another may be an exceptionally creative writer, a third may be skillful in interpersonal relationships, and a fourth may show talent in art, music, or physical education. The notion of distributed intelligence tells us that intelligent behavior should be relatively commonplace when students have the right tools, social groups, and symbolic systems with which to work.

🍎 Remember that different students may be intelligent in different ways.

For optimal intellectual development, children need a variety of stimulating experiences throughout the childhood years, including age-appropriate toys and books, frequent verbal interactions with adults and other children, and numerous opportunities to practice important behavioral and cognitive skills (R. H. Bradley & Caldwell, 1984; Brooks-Gunn et al., 1996; Ericsson & Chalmers, 1994; R. D. Hess & Holloway, 1984; McGowan & Johnson, 1984). When parents and other primary caretakers cannot provide such experiences, most welcome the availability of enriched preschool and after-school programs. Access to such programs on an ongoing basis can greatly enhance a child's cognitive development and potential to lead a productive adult life.

🍎 Be on the lookout for behaviors that are "intelligent" within the context of students' cultural backgrounds.

We must remember, too, that to the extent that intelligence is culture-dependent, intelligent behavior is likely to take different forms in children from different ethnic backgrounds (Gardner, 1995; Neisser et al., 1996; Perkins, 1995; Sternberg, 1985). For example, in our case study of Lupita, we saw a kindergarten girl with an exceptional ability to work cooperatively with others; cooperation is a valued skill among many Mexican Americans. As another example, the intelligence of Navajo students may be reflected in their ability to help their family and tribe, to perform cultural rituals, or to demonstrate expert craftsmanship (Kirschenbaum, 1989). We must be careful not to limit our conception of intelligence only to students' ability to succeed at traditional academic tasks.

Finally, intelligence—no matter *how* we define it—can never be the only characteristic that affects our students' academic achievement. Learning strategies, motivation, and creativity also play important roles. It is to the last of these three, creativity, that we turn now.

Creativity

Bugs are big,
Bugs are small.
Bugs are black,
Bugs are all . . .
    NEAT!

My critter-happy son Alex wrote this poem as a second grader. His teacher thought the poem reflected a certain degree of creativity; so did his not-so-objective mother. What do *you* think?

What exactly do we mean by the term **creativity?** Like intelligence, creativity is often defined differently by different people. But most definitions of creativity (Ripple, 1989; Runco & Chand, 1995) usually include two components:

■ *New and original behavior:* behavior that has not specifically been learned from someone else

■ *An appropriate and productive result:* a useful product or effective problem solution

Both criteria must be met before we identify behavior as creative.

To illustrate these two criteria, let's say that I am giving a lecture on creativity and want a creative way of keeping my students' attention. One possible solution would be to come to class stark naked. This solution certainly meets the first criterion for creativity: It is new and original behavior, and I did not learn it from any other teacher. It does not, however, meet the second criterion: It isn't appropriate or productive within the context of our culture. A second possible solution might be to give my students several challenging problems that require creative thinking. This approach is more likely to meet both criteria. Not only is it a relatively original way of teaching, but it is also appropriate and productive for students to learn about creativity by exploring the process firsthand.

Although a certain degree of intelligence is probably necessary for creative thinking, intelligence and creativity are somewhat independent abilities (Sternberg, 1985; I. A. Taylor, 1976; Torrance, 1976). In other words, highly intelligent students are not always the most creative ones. Many theorists believe that the cognitive processes involved in intelligence and creativity may be somewhat different (e.g., see Kogan, 1983). Tasks on intelligence tests often involve **convergent thinking**—pulling several pieces of information together to draw a conclusion or to solve a problem. In contrast, creativity often involves **divergent thinking**—starting with one idea and taking it in many different directions. To see the difference firsthand, try the following exercise.

> Can you recall a situation in which you met both criteria for creativity?

■ Experiencing Firsthand
Convergent and Divergent Thinking

On a sheet of paper, write your responses to each of the following:

• Why are houses more often built with bricks than with stones?

• What are some possible uses of a brick? Try to think of as many different and unusual uses as you can.

• Add improvements to the wagon drawing so that the object will be more fun to play with. (modeled after Torrance, 1970)

To answer the first question, you pull together the things you know about several different objects (bricks, stones, and houses) in a convergent fashion. But the other two items require divergent thinking about a single object: You consider how a brick might be used in many different contexts and how a child's wagon might be embellished in a wide variety of ways.

Creativity is probably *not* a single entity that people either have or don't have (e.g., Hocevar & Bachelor, 1989). Rather, it is probably a combination of many specific characteristics, thinking processes, and behaviors. Among other things, creative individuals tend to:

- Interpret problems and situations in a flexible manner
- Possess a great deal of information relevant to a task
- Combine existing information and ideas in new ways
- Evaluate their accomplishments in accordance with high standards
- Have a passion for—and therefore invest considerable time and effort in—what they are doing (Csikszentmihalyi, 1996; Glover, Ronning, & Reynolds, 1989; Runco & Chand, 1995; Russ, 1993; Weisberg, 1993)

Furthermore, creativity is probably somewhat specific to different situations and different content areas (R. T. Brown, 1989; Feldhusen & Treffinger, 1980; Ripple, 1989). Students may show creativity in art, writing, or science, but they aren't necessarily creative in all those areas. As teachers, we must be careful not to label particular students as "creative" or "not creative." Instead we should keep our eyes and minds open for instances of creative thinking or behavior in many (perhaps *all*) of our students.

Look for signs of creativity in a variety of situations and within many different content areas.

Fostering Creativity in the Classroom

Environmental factors play an important role in the development of creativity (Esquivel, 1995; Ripple, 1989; Torrance, 1976). Research studies suggest several strategies for promoting creativity in the classroom:

- *Show students that creativity is valued.* We are more likely to foster creativity when we show students that we value creative thoughts and behaviors. One way we can do this is to encourage and reward unusual ideas and responses. For example, we can express excitement when students complete a project in a unique and unusual manner. And, as we grade assignments and test papers, we should look for responses that, though not what we were expecting, are legitimately correct. Engaging in creative activities ourselves also shows students that we value creativity (Feldhusen & Treffinger, 1980; Hennessey & Amabile, 1987; Parnes, 1967; Torrance & Myers, 1970).

Make it clear that you value creativity.

- *Focus students' attention on internal rather than external rewards.* Students are more creative when they engage in activities because they enjoy them and take pride in what they have done; they are less creative when they work for external rewards such as grades (Hennessey, 1995; Lubart, 1994). Therefore, we can foster creativity by giving students opportunities to explore their own special interests—interests that they will gladly pursue without having to be prodded. For example, we might encourage students to choose a topic about which they are genuinely curious when planning for the science fair. We can also foster creativity by downplaying the importance of grades, instead focusing students' attention on the internal satisfaction that their creative efforts bring (Hennessey, 1995; Hennessey & Amabile, 1987; Perkins, 1990; Pruitt, 1989). For example, we might tell students in an art class:

Focus students' attention on the internal rewards that creative activities bring.

> Please don't worry too much about grades. As long as you use the materials appropriately and give each assignment your best shot, you will do well in this class. The important thing is to find an art form that you enjoy and through which you can express yourself.

Creativity is specific to different content domains. Some students may be creative artists, others creative writers, and still others creative scientists.

• *Promote mastery of a subject area.* Creativity in a particular subject area is more likely to occur when students have considerable mastery of that subject; it is unlikely to occur when students have little or no understanding of the topic. One important way of fostering creativity, then, is to help students master course content (Amabile & Hennessey, 1992; Perkins, 1990; Sternberg, 1985). For example, if we want our students to apply scientific principles in a creative manner—perhaps as they conduct a science fair experiment or develop a solution to an environmental problem—we should make sure that they first have those principles down pat.

Help students master the subject area in which you want them to think creatively.

• *Ask thought-provoking questions.* Students are more likely to think creatively when we ask them questions that require them to use previously learned information in a new way (these are frequently called **higher-level questions**). Questions that ask students to engage in divergent thinking may be particularly helpful (Feldhusen & Treffinger, 1980; Feldhusen, Treffinger, & Bahlke, 1970; Perkins, 1990; Torrance & Myers, 1970). For example, during a unit on the Pony Express, we might ask:

Ask questions that require students to use information in new ways.

- What are all the ways mail might have been transported across the United States at that time?
- Can you think of some very unusual way that no one else has thought of to transport mail today? (Feldhusen & Treffinger, 1980, p. 36)

• *Give students the freedom and security to take risks.* Creativity is more likely to appear when students feel comfortable taking risks; it is unlikely to appear when they are afraid of failing (Houtz, 1990). To encourage risk taking, we can allow students to engage in certain activities without evaluating their performance. We can also urge them to think of their mistakes and failures as an inevitable—but usually temporary—aspect of the creative process (Feldhusen & Treffinger, 1980; Hennessey & Amabile, 1987; Parnes, 1967; Pruitt, 1989). For example, when students are writing a creative short story, we might give them several opportunities to get our feedback, and perhaps the feedback of their peers, before they turn in a final product.

Create an environment in which students feel comfortable taking risks.

• *Provide the time that creativity requires.* Students need time to experiment with new materials and ideas, to think in divergent directions, and occasionally to make mistakes. A critical aspect of promoting creativity, then, is to give them that time

Give students time to experiment, to think in divergent directions, and to make mistakes.

(Feldhusen & Treffinger, 1980; Pruitt, 1989). For example, when teaching a foreign language, we might ask small groups of students to create and videotape a television commercial spoken entirely in that language. This is hardly a project that students can do in a day; they may need several weeks to brainstorm various ideas, write and revise a script, find or develop the props they need, and rehearse their lines. Creative ideas and projects seldom emerge overnight.

Like intelligence, creativity is often perceived differently in different cultures: What constitutes a work of art or "good music" might vary from one cultural perspective to another. As we shall see now, the diverse ethnic backgrounds among our students will manifest themselves in numerous other ways as well.

Ethnic Differences

◻ Experiencing Firsthand
Ruckus in the Lunchroom

In the following passage, a young teenager named Sam is describing an incident at school to his friend Joe:

> I got in some trouble at lunch today. Classes went at their usual slow pace through the morning, so at noon I was really ready for lunch. I got in line behind Bubba. As usual the line was moving pretty slow and we were all getting pretty restless.
>
> For a little action Bubba turned around and said, "Hey Sam! What you doin', man? You so ugly that when the doctor delivered you he slapped your face!"
>
> Everyone laughed, but they laughed even harder when I shot back, "Oh yeah? Well, you so ugly the doctor turned around and slapped your momma!"
>
> It got even wilder when Bubba said, "Well, man, at least my daddy ain't no girl scout!"
>
> We really got into it then. After a while more people got involved—four, five, then six. It was a riot! People helping out anyone who seemed to be getting the worst of the deal.
>
> All of a sudden Mr. Reynolds, the gym teacher, came over to try to quiet things down. The next thing we knew we were all in the office. The principal made us stay after school for a week; he's so straight! On top of that, he sent word home that he wanted to talk to our folks in his office Monday afternoon. Boy! Did I get it when I got home. That's the third notice I've gotten this semester.
>
> As we were leaving the principal's office, I ran into Bubba again. We decided we'd finish where we left off, but this time we would wait until we were off the school grounds. (adapted from Reynolds, Taylor, Steffensen, Shirey, & Anderson, 1982, p. 358)

Exactly what happened in the school cafeteria? Were the boys fighting? Or were they simply having a good time?

The story you just read is actually about "sounding," a friendly exchange of insults common among male youth in some African American communities (e.g., DeLain, Pearson, & Anderson, 1985; Reynolds et al., 1982). Some boys engage in sounding to achieve status among their peers—those throwing out the greatest insults are the winners—whereas others do it simply for amusement. If you interpreted the cafeteria incident as a knock-down-drag-out fight, you're hardly alone; many eighth graders in a research study did likewise (Reynolds et al., 1982). When we don't understand the culture in which our students have been raised, we will inevitably misinterpret some of their behaviors.

An **ethnic group** is a group of individuals with the following characteristics:

- Its roots either precede the creation of or are external to the country in which it resides; for example, it may be comprised of people of the same race, national origin, or religious background.
- It has a common set of values, beliefs, and behaviors that influence the lives of its members.
- Its members share a sense of interdependence—a sense that their lives are intertwined. (NCSS Task Force on Ethnic Studies Curriculum Guidelines, 1992)

It is important to note that we cannot always determine a student's ethnicity strictly on the basis of physical characteristics (e.g., race) or birthplace (Wlodkowski & Ginsberg, 1995). For instance, my daughter Tina, although she was born in Colombia and has Hispanic and Native American ancestors, was raised by two Caucasian parents; ethnically speaking, Tina is probably more "White" than anything else.

It is becoming more and more apparent that our schools are not adequately meeting the needs of the diverse ethnic groups they serve. Students from ethnic minorities are often *at risk*: They achieve at levels far below their actual capabilities, and an alarming number never graduate from high school (Ford, 1996; García, 1992; Losey, 1995; Santiago, 1986). One probable reason for the low success rates of such students is the problem of cultural mismatch, as we shall see now.

The Problem of Cultural Mismatch

Recall from Chapter 3 that children entering school for the first time experience some degree of culture shock. This culture shock is more intense for some groups of students than for others (Casanova, 1987; Ramsey, 1987). Most schools in North America and western Europe are based largely on White, middle-class, "mainstream" culture, so students from White, middle-class homes often adjust quickly to the classroom environment. But students who come from other cultural backgrounds, sometimes with very different norms regarding acceptable behavior, may find school a confusing and incomprehensible place. For example, recent immigrants may not know what to expect from others or what behaviors others expect of them (C. R. Harris, 1991). Children raised in a society where gender roles are clearly differentiated—where males and females are expected to behave very differently—may have difficulty adjusting to a school in which similar expectations are held for boys and girls (Kirschenbaum, 1989; Vasquez, 1988). Any such **cultural mismatch** between home and school cultures can interfere with students' adjustment to the school setting, and ultimately with their academic achievement as well (García, 1995; C. D. Lee & Slaughter-Defoe, 1995; Ogbu, 1992; Phelan et al., 1994).

Cultural mismatch is compounded when teachers misinterpret the behaviors of students from ethnic minority groups. For example, we may misinterpret the nature of students' verbal exchanges, just as you might have misinterpreted Sam's behavior in the cafeteria. Certain Native American communities find it unnecessary to say hello or good-bye (Sisk, 1989), yet a teacher from another culture may misunderstand when he or she isn't greeted in the morning. In other Native American communities, people rarely express their feelings through facial expressions (Montgomery, 1989), giving some teachers the mistaken impression that students are bored or disinterested. When students' behaviors differ enough from our own and we misinterpret them as inappropriate, unacceptable, or just plain "odd," we may jump to the conclusion that these students are unable or unwilling to be successful in the classroom (B. T. Bowman, 1989; Hilliard & Vaughn-Scott, 1982). Perhaps this was the case for Ms. Padilla, Lupita's teacher in our opening case study.

As teachers, we will rarely, if ever, have a classroom in which all students share our own cultural heritage. Clearly, then, we must educate ourselves about the ways in which

Can you think of any ways in which your own school environment was mismatched with the culture in which you were raised?

students from various ethnic backgrounds are likely to be different from one another and from ourselves.

Examples of Ethnic Diversity

We must keep in mind that African Americans, Asian Americans, Hispanics, Native Americans, and European Americans are all culturally very heterogeneous populations (Irvine & York, 1995; Maker & Schiever, 1989; Santiago, 1986; A. H. Yee, 1992). Thus, we must be careful not to form hard and fast stereotypes about *any* group. At the same time, we must be aware of differences that may exist so that we can better understand why our students sometimes behave as they do.

Researchers have identified a variety of ways in which the cultures of some ethnic minority students may be different from the culture of a typical North American classroom. In the next few pages, we will consider potential differences in eight areas:

- Language and dialect
- Sociolinguistic conventions
- Cooperation versus competition
- Private versus public performance
- Eye contact
- Conceptions of time
- Types of questions
- Family relationships and expectations

Before you read further, can you predict what some of these cultural differences might be?

Language and Dialect

An obvious cultural difference is in language. For example, in the United States, more than six million students speak a language other than English at home (McKeon, 1994; National Association of Bilingual Education, 1993). Children who have not encountered English before they begin school will naturally have difficulty with schoolwork in an English-based classroom (McKeon, 1994; Olneck, 1995; Pang, 1995).

Even when children speak English at home, they may use a form of English different from the **Standard English** that is typically considered acceptable in school. More specifically, they may speak in a different **dialect**—a form of English that includes some unique pronunciations and grammatical structures. For example, some African American children speak in an **African American dialect,** using sentences such as these:

> He going home.
>
> She have a bike.
>
> He be workin'.
>
> Ask Albert do he know how to play basketball. (Dale, 1976, pp. 274–275)

At one time, researchers believed that the African American dialect represented an erroneous and less complex form of speech than Standard English and urged educators to teach students to speak "properly" as quickly as possible. But we now realize that African American dialects are, in fact, very complex language systems with their own predictable grammatical rules and their own unique idioms and proverbs. Furthermore, these dialects promote communication and complex thought as readily as Standard English (De-Lain et al., 1985; Durkin, 1995; Fairchild & Edwards-Evans, 1990; Owens, 1996).

For many students, their native language or dialect is part of their cultural identity (McAlpine, 1992; Ulichny, 1994). The following incident among rural Native American students at a boarding school in Alaska is an example:

> Many of the students at the school spoke English with a native dialect and seemed unable to utter certain essential sounds in the English language. A new group of speech

teachers was sent in to correct the problem. The teachers worked consistently with the students in an attempt to improve speech patterns and intonation, but found that their efforts were in vain.

One night, the boys in the dormitory were seeming to have too much fun, and peals of laughter were rolling out from under the door. An investigating counselor approached cautiously, and listened quietly outside the door to see if he could discover the source of the laughter. From behind the door he heard a voice, speaking in perfect English, giving instructions to the rest of the crowd. The others were finding the situation very amusing. When the counselor entered the room he found that one of the students was speaking. "Joseph," he said, "You've been cured! Your English is perfect." "No," said Joseph returning to his familiar dialect, "I was just doing an imitation of you." "But if you can speak in standard English, why don't you do it all of the time?" the counselor queried. "I can," responded Joseph, "but it sounds funny, and I feel dumb doing it." (Garrison, 1989, p. 121)

Most educators recommend that all students develop proficiency in Standard English because success in mainstream adult society will be difficult to achieve without such proficiency (Casanova, 1987; Craft, 1984; Terrell & Terrell, 1983). At the same time, we should also recognize that other languages and dialects are very appropriate means of communication in many situations (Fairchild & Edwards-Evans, 1990; García, 1995; C. K. Howe, 1994; C. D. Lee & Slaughter-Defoe, 1995; Ulichny, 1994; Vasquez, 1990). For example, although we may wish to encourage Standard English in most written work or in formal oral presentations, we might find other dialects quite appropriate in creative writing or informal classroom discussions.

> **W**ork toward improving Standard English in some situations but allow other dialects in other, less formal ones.

Sociolinguistic Conventions

In our discussion of linguistic development in Chapter 2, I introduced the concept of *pragmatics,* general behavioral skills important for conversing effectively with others. Pragmatics include **sociolinguistic conventions:** specific language-related behaviors that appear in some cultures or ethnic groups but not in others. For example, in some Native American groups, silence is valued, and in some Hispanic and rural southern African American communities, children are expected to speak only when spoken to (Menyuk & Menyuk, 1988; Owens, 1996). Yet people from European American backgrounds may feel uncomfortable with silence and say things just to fill in gaps in a conversation (Irujo, 1988). And in many African American, Puerto Rican, and Jewish families, adults and children alike sometimes speak spontaneously and simultaneously; in such settings, waiting for one's turn may mean being excluded from the conversation altogether (Trawick-Smith, 1997).

> **R**emember that some students may be unaccustomed to verbalizing their thoughts freely.

We also see ethnic differences in the amount of time that individuals wait before they respond to other people's comments or questions. For instance, students from some Native American communities pause before answering a question as a way of showing respect, as this statement by a Northern Cheyenne illustrates:

> Even if I had a quick answer to your question, I would never answer immediately. That would be saying that your question was not worth thinking about. (Gilliland, 1988, p. 27)

Teachers frequently ask questions of their students and then wait for an answer. But exactly how long *do* they wait? Research indicates that most teachers wait a second or even less for students to reply. Research also indicates that when teachers wait for longer periods of time—for three seconds or even longer—students, especially those from ethnic minority groups, are more likely to answer teachers' questions and participate in class discussions (C. A. Grant & Gomez, 1996; Mohatt & Erickson, 1981; Rowe, 1987; Tharp, 1989). Not only does such an extended **wait time** allow students to show respect, but it also gives students with limited English proficiency some mental "translation" time (Gilliland, 1988). (Chapter 6 identifies additional advantages of a longer wait time.)

> **I**ncrease wait time after asking a question or posing a problem.

Yet we should also be aware that some native Hawaiian students, rather than wanting time to think or show respect, may have a preference for **negative wait time:** They often interrupt teachers or classmates who haven't finished speaking. Such interruptions, which many might interpret as rude, are instead a sign of personal involvement in the community culture of those students (Tharp, 1994).

Cooperation Versus Competition

School achievement in a traditional classroom is often a solitary, individual endeavor. Students receive praise, stickers, and good grades when they perform at a high level, regardless of how their classmates are performing. Sometimes, though, school achievement is quite competitive: A student's performance is evaluated in comparison with the performance of classmates. For example, some teachers may identify the "best" papers or drawings in the class; others may grade "on a curve," with some students doing very well and others inevitably failing.

Yet in some cultures, it is neither individual achievement nor competitive achievement that is recognized, but rather *group* achievement: The success of the village or community is valued over individual success. Students from such cultures (including many Native American, Mexican American, Southeast Asian, and Pacific Islander students) are more accustomed to working cooperatively than competitively, and for the benefit of the community rather than for themselves (García, 1992; C. A. Grant & Gomez, 1996; Greenfield, 1994; Lomawaima, 1995; Suina & Smolkin, 1994; Tharp, 1994; Triandis, 1995; Vasquez, 1990). They may therefore resist when asked to compete against their classmates. They may also be confused when teachers scold them for helping one another on assignments or for "sharing" answers. And they may feel uncomfortable when their individual achievements are publicly acknowledged. Group work, with an emphasis on cooperation rather than competition, often facilitates the school achievement of these students (García, 1995; C. A. Grant & Gomez, 1996; Losey, 1995; McAlpine & Taylor, 1993; L. S. Miller, 1995).

Private Versus Public Performance

In many classrooms, learning is a very public enterprise. Individual students are often asked to answer questions or demonstrate skills in full view of their classmates, and they are encouraged to ask questions themselves when they don't understand. Such practices, which many teachers take for granted, may confuse or even alienate the students of some ethnic groups (Crago, Annahatak, & Ningiuruvik, 1993; Eriks-Brophy & Crago, 1994; García, 1994; Hidalgo, Siu, Bright, Swap, & Epstein, 1995; Lomawaima, 1995). For example, children raised in the Yup'ik culture of Alaska are expected to learn by close, quiet observation of adults; they rarely ask questions or otherwise interrupt what the adults are doing (García, 1994). Children from some ethnic backgrounds, including many Puerto Ricans and Native Americans, have been taught that speaking directly and assertively to adults is downright rude (Hidalgo et al., 1995; Lomawaima, 1995). Many Native American children are also accustomed to practicing a skill privately at first, performing in front of a group only after they have attained a reasonable level of mastery (García, 1994; S. Sanders, 1987; Suina & Smolkin, 1994). Native Hawaiian students willingly respond as a group when their teacher asks a question yet often remain silent when called on individually; apparently, these one-on-one interactions with adults remind many students of scoldings they have received from their parents at home (Au, 1980). As you might guess, then, many students from diverse ethnic

Why do you think some teachers encourage competition among their students?

Use cooperative learning techniques involving group interaction and activities. Reward students for helping one another learn and achieve.

In some cultures, such as in many Mexican American and Native American communities, group achievement is valued over individual or competitive achievement. Children from such cultures are therefore more accustomed to working cooperatively than competitively.

Interact with students frequently in small groups or on a private, one-to-one basis. Give students a chance to practice skills in private until they have mastered them.

backgrounds perform better when they can work one-on-one with the teacher or in a co-operative setting with a small group of classmates (Cazden & Leggett, 1981; Vasquez, 1990). They may also feel more comfortable practicing new skills in privacy until they have sufficiently mastered them (C. A. Grant & Gomez, 1996).

Eye Contact

For many of us, looking someone in the eye is a way of indicating that we are trying to communicate with that person or that we are listening intently to what the person is saying. But in many Native American, African American, Mexican American, and Puerto Rican communities, a child who looks an adult in the eye is showing disrespect. In these communities, children are taught to look down in the presence of adults (Gilliland, 1988; Irujo, 1988). The following anecdote shows how a teacher's recognition of this culturally learned behavior can make a difference:

> A teacher [described a Native American] student who would never say a word, nor even answer when she greeted him. Then one day when he came in she looked in the other direction and said, "Hello, Jimmy." He answered enthusiastically, "Why hello Miss Jacobs." She found that he would always talk if she looked at a book or at the wall, but when she looked at him, he appeared frightened. (Gilliland, 1988, p. 26)

Don't rely on eye contact as the only indicator that students are paying attention.

Conceptions of Time

Many people regulate their lives by the clock: Being on time to appointments, social engagements, and the dinner table is important. This emphasis on punctuality is not characteristic of all cultures, however; for example, many Hispanic and Native American communities don't observe strict schedules and timelines (H. G. Burger, 1973; Garrison, 1989; Gilliland, 1988). Not surprisingly, children from these communities may be chronically late for school and have difficulty understanding the need for school tasks to be completed within a certain time frame.

To succeed in mainstream Western society, students eventually need to learn punctuality. At the same time, we must recognize that not all of our students will be especially concerned about clock time when they first enter our classrooms. Certainly we should expect students to arrive at class on time and to turn in assignments when they are due. But we must be patient and understanding when, for cultural reasons, students do not develop such habits immediately.

Teach students the importance of clock time at school, but be patient when some students are slow to conform.

Types of Questions

Here are some typical questions that elementary school teachers ask beginning students:

- What's this a picture of?
- What color is this?
- What's your sister's name?

These questions seem simple enough to answer. But in fact, different cultures teach children to answer different kinds of questions. Parents from European American backgrounds frequently ask their children to identify objects and their characteristics. Yet in some other ethnic groups, parents rarely ask their children questions that they themselves know the answers to (Crago et al., 1993; Heath, 1980, 1989; Rogoff & Morelli, 1989). For example, parents in African American communities in parts of the southeastern United States are more likely to ask questions involving comparisons and analogies; rather than asking "What's that?" they may instead ask "What's that like?" (Heath, 1989). And children in these same communities are specifically taught *not* to answer questions that strangers ask about personal and home life—questions such as "What's your name?" and "Where do you live?" The complaints of parents in these communities illustrate how much of a cultural mismatch there can be between the children and their Caucasian teachers:

- "My kid, he too scared to talk, 'cause nobody play by the rules he know. At home I can't shut him up."

- "Miss Davis, she complain 'bout Ned not answerin' back. He says she asks dumb questions she already know about." (Heath, 1980, p. 107)

Teachers' comments about these children reflect their own lack of understanding about the culture from which the children come:

- "I would almost think some of them have a hearing problem; it is as though they don't hear me ask a question. I get blank stares to my questions. Yet when I am making statements or telling stories which interest them, they always seem to hear me."

- "The simplest questions are the ones they can't answer in the classroom; yet on the playground, they can explain a rule for a ballgame or describe a particular kind of bait with no problem. Therefore, I know they can't be as dumb as they seem in my class." (Heath, 1980, pp. 107–108)

Be aware that some students may not be accustomed to answering the kinds of questions that teachers usually ask.

Family Relationships and Expectations

In some ethnic groups—for example, in many Hispanic, Native American, and Asian communities—family bonds and relationships are especially important. Students raised in these cultures are likely to feel responsibility for their family's well-being and a strong sense of loyalty to other family members; they will also go to great efforts to please their parents (Abi-Nader, 1993; Delgado-Gaitan, 1994; García, 1994; C. A. Grant & Gomez, 1996; Hidalgo et al., 1995; Vasquez, 1990).

In many cultures, school achievement is valued highly, and parents encourage their children to do well in school (Delgado-Gaitan, 1992; Duran & Weffer, 1992; Hidalgo et al., 1995; Hossler & Stage, 1992; Nieto, 1995; Pang, 1995; Yee, 1992). But in a few cases, classroom achievement may be less valued than achievement in other areas. For example, in some very traditional Native American and Polynesian communities, children are expected to excel in art, dance, and other aspects of their culture, rather than in more academic pursuits such as reading or mathematics (Kirschenbaum, 1989; Reid, 1989). We must certainly be sensitive to situations in which the achievements that *we* think are important are not those that are valued by students' families. To the extent that we can do so, we must show our students how the school curriculum and classroom activities relate to their own cultural environment and their own life needs.

Relate the school curriculum to students' home environments and cultures.

We must also maintain open lines of communication with our students' parents. Because some parents, especially parents of minority children, may be intimidated by school personnel, teachers often need to take the first step in establishing a productive parent-teacher relationship. When teachers and parents realize that both groups want students to succeed in the classroom, they are more likely to work cooperatively to promote student achievement (García, 1995; Hidalgo et al., 1995; C. K. Howe, 1994; Salend & Taylor, 1993; R. L. Warren, 1988). Chapter 15 identifies some specific strategies for working effectively with parents.

Establish and maintain open lines of communication with parents, and jointly identify ways in which home and school can work together to help students succeed in the classroom.

Creating a More Multicultural Classroom Environment

Clearly, we must be sensitive to the ways in which students of various ethnic groups are likely to be different from one another. Yet it is just as important that we help our students develop the same sensitivity: As adults, they will inevitably have to work cooperatively with people from a wide variety of backgrounds. It is in our students' best interests, then, that we promote awareness of numerous cultures in every classroom. To promote a truly multicultural classroom environment, we must:

- Incorporate the values, beliefs, and traditions of many cultures into the curriculum
- Work to break down ethnic and cultural stereotypes
- Promote social interaction among students from various ethnic groups
- Foster democratic ideals

Incorporating the Values, Beliefs, and Traditions of Many Cultures into the Curriculum

Multicultural education should not be limited to cooking ethnic foods, celebrating Cinco de Mayo, or studying famous African Americans during Black History Month. Rather, effective **multicultural education** includes the perspectives and experiences of numerous cultural groups on a regular basis (Banks, 1995; García, 1995; NCSS Task Force on Ethnic Studies Curriculum Guidelines, 1992).

As teachers, we can incorporate content from different ethnic groups into many aspects of the school curriculum. Here are some examples:

- In literature, read the work of minority authors and poets.
- In music, learn songs from many cultures and nations.
- In physical education, learn games or folk dances from other countries and cultures.
- In history, look at wars and other major events from diverse perspectives (e.g., the Spanish perspective of the Spanish-American War, the Japanese perspective of World War II, the Native American perspective of the pioneers' westward migration in North America).
- In art, consider the creations and techniques of artists from around the world.
- In current events, consider such issues as discrimination and oppression. (Asai, 1993; Boutte & McCormick, 1992; Casanova, 1987; Cottrol, 1990; Freedman, 1996; Koza, 1996; NCSS Task Force on Ethnic Studies Curriculum Guidelines, 1992; Pang, 1995; Sleeter & Grant, 1994; Ulichny, 1994)

Incorporate multicultural content into the curriculum.

As we explore various cultures, we should look for commonalities as well as differences. For example, we might study how various cultural groups celebrate the beginning of a new year, discovering that "out with the old and in with the new" is a common theme among many such celebrations (Ramsey, 1987). At the secondary level, it can be beneficial to explore issues that adolescents of all cultures face: gaining the respect of elders, forming trusting relationships with peers, and finding a meaningful place in society (Ulichny, 1994). One important goal of multicultural education should be to communicate that, underneath it all, people are more alike than different.

Look for commonalities as well as differences among people from different cultural backgrounds.

Breaking Down Ethnic Stereotypes

Experiencing Firsthand
Picture This #1

Form a picture in your mind of someone from each of the following three places. Use the *first* image that comes to mind in each case.

The Netherlands (Holland)

Mexico

Hawaii

Now answer yes or no to each of these questions:

- Was the person from the Netherlands wearing wooden shoes?
- Was the person from Mexico wearing a sombrero?
- Was the person from Hawaii wearing a hula skirt or flowered lei?

If you answered yes to any of the three questions, then one or more of your images reflected an ethnic stereotype. Most people in the Netherlands, Mexico, and Hawaii do *not* wear wooden shoes, sombreros, or hula skirts and leis on a regular basis.

Although we and our students should certainly be aware of true differences among various ethnic groups, it is counterproductive to hold a **stereotype**—a rigid, simplistic, and inevitably erroneous caricature—of any particular group. As teachers, we must make a concerted effort to develop and select curriculum materials that represent all cultural groups in a positive and competent light; for example, we should choose textbooks, works of fiction, and videotapes that portray people of diverse ethnic backgrounds as legitimate participants in mainstream society, rather than as exotic "curiosities" who live in a separate world from the rest of us. And we must definitely avoid or modify curriculum materials that portray members of minority groups in an overly simplistic, romanticized, exaggerated, or otherwise stereotypic fashion (Banks, 1994a; Boutte & McCormick, 1992; Ladson-Billings, 1994b; Pang, 1995).

Stereotypes don't exist only in curriculum materials; they also exist in society at large. We can help break down ethnic stereotypes in several simple yet effective ways. For one thing, we can arrange opportunities for students to meet and talk with successful minority models. We can also explore the historical roots of stereotypes with our students—for example, by explaining that cultural differences sometimes reflect the various economic and social circumstances in which particular ethnic groups have historically found themselves. And finally, we must emphasize the notion of individual differences—that members of any single ethnic group will often be very different from one another (García, 1994; C. D. Lee & Slaughter-Defoe, 1995; McAlpine & Taylor, 1993; Spencer & Markstrom-Adams, 1990; Trueba, 1988).

> ♥ **U**se curriculum materials that represent all cultural groups in a positive and competent light.

> ♥ **E**xpose students to successful minority models.

> ♥ **P**rovide opportunities for students to get to know one another better.

Promoting Social Interaction among Students from Various Ethnic Groups

Students are more likely to be tolerant of one another's differences when they have the opportunity to interact on a regular basis. Such interactions can sometimes occur within the context of planned classroom activities; for example, we can hold classroom discussions in which our students describe the traditions, conventions, and perceptions of their own ethnic groups. We can also promote friendships among students of diverse ethnic backgrounds by using some of the strategies identified in Chapter 3—for instance, by using cooperative learning activities, teaching the rudiments of other students' native languages, and encouraging schoolwide participation in extracurricular activities. By learning to appreciate the multicultural differences that exist within a single classroom, our students take an important first step toward appreciating the multicultural nature of the world at large (Casanova, 1987; Craft, 1984; Pettigrew & Pajonas, 1973).

Unfortunately, not all schools have a diverse enough population to foster students' awareness and appreciation of cultural differences on a firsthand basis. In such culturally homogeneous schools, we may have to take our students, either physically or vicariously, beyond school boundaries. For example, we can engage our students in community action projects that provide services to particular ethnic groups—perhaps in preschools, nursing homes, or city cultural centers. Or we can initiate a "Sister

By discussing the different traditions, conventions, and perceptions of various cultural groups, students can begin to understand why others sometimes behave differently than they themselves do.

Schools Program" in which students from two ethnically different communities regularly communicate through the mail or the Internet, possibly exchanging news, stories, photographs, art projects, and various artifacts from the local environment (Koeppel & Mulrooney, 1992).

Fostering Democratic Ideals

Ultimately, any multicultural education program must include such democratic ideals as human dignity, equality, justice, and tolerance for diverse points of view (Cottrol, 1990; NCSS Task Force on Ethnic Studies Curriculum Guidelines, 1992; Sleeter & Grant, 1994). We better prepare our students for functioning effectively in a democratic society when we help them understand that virtually any nation includes a diversity of cultures and that such diversity provides a richness of ideas and perspectives that will inevitably yield a more creative, productive society overall.

Foster such democratic ideals as human dignity, equality, justice, and tolerance for diverse viewpoints.

INTO THE CLASSROOM: Accommodating Ethnic Differences

Build on students' background experiences.

A teacher asks a classroom of inner-city African American students to vote on their favorite rap song. She puts the words to the song on an overhead transparency and asks students to translate each line for her. In doing so, she shows students how their local dialect and Standard English are interrelated, and she gives them a sense of pride in being bilingual (Ladson-Billings, 1994a).

Use curriculum materials that represent all ethnic groups in a positive and competent light.

A high school history teacher peruses a history textbook to make sure that it portrays members of all ethnic groups in a nonstereotypical manner. He supplements the text with readings that highlight the important roles that members of various ethnic groups have played in history.

Expose students to successful models from various ethnic backgrounds.

A sixth-grade teacher invites several successful professionals from minority groups to speak with her class about their careers. When some students seem especially interested in one or more of these careers, she arranges for the students to spend time with the professionals in their workplaces.

Provide opportunities for students of different backgrounds to get to know one another better.

For a cooperative learning activity, a middle school teacher forms groups that integrate students from various neighborhoods and ethnic groups.

Educate yourself about the cultures in which students have been raised.

A teacher accepts an invitation to have dinner with several of his students and their families, all of whom are dining together one evening at one family's home on the Navajo Nation in western New Mexico. During his visit, the teacher discovers why his students are always interrupting one another and completing one another's sentences: Their parents converse with one another in a similar manner (Jackson & Ormrod, 1998).

A democracy involves **equity**—freedom from bias or favoritism—as well as equality. To help students achieve maximal classroom success, we must be equitable in our treatment of them; in other words, we must tailor instruction to meet the unique characteristics of each and every one. The notion of equitable treatment applies not only to students of diverse ethnic backgrounds but also to both boys and girls. Let's consider how boys and girls are likely to be different and how we can help students of both genders achieve academic success.

Gender Differences

THINKING ABOUT WHAT YOU KNOW

- In what ways do you think males and females are alike and different? Do they have different academic abilities? different motives? different interests? different expectations for themselves?
- How might the environment contribute to gender differences? Do parents treat boys and girls differently? Do classmates? Do teachers?

Are the findings in Table 4–3 consistent with your own observations of males' and females' behaviors? If not, can you resolve the discrepancies?

In terms of academic abilities, boys and girls are probably more similar than you think. But in other respects, they may be more different than you realize. Researchers have investigated possible differences between males and females in numerous areas; general trends in their findings, along with educational implications, are presented in Table 4–3.

TABLE 4.3   COMPARE/CONTRAST

Gender Differences and Their Educational Implications

CHARACTERISTIC	SIMILARITIES AND DIFFERENCES	EDUCATIONAL IMPLICATION
Scholastic abilities	Boys and girls have similar general intellectual ability (e.g., IQ scores). Girls are often slightly better at verbal (language-based) tasks; boys may be somewhat better at tasks involving visual-spatial skills. Researchers report mixed findings regarding males' vs. females' achievement in such areas as mathematics and science; any gender differences are usually quite small. In recent years, boys and girls have become increasingly more *similar* in their academic performance.	Expect boys and girls to have similar aptitudes for all academic subject areas.
Physical and motor skills	Before puberty, boys and girls have similar physiological capability, but boys tend to develop their physical and motor skills more than girls. After puberty, boys have the advantage in height and muscular strength.	Assume that both genders have similar potential for developing physical and motor skills, especially during the elementary school years.
Motivation	Girls are generally more concerned about doing well in school: They tend to work harder on school assignments, take fewer risks when doing their assignments, get higher grades, and are more likely to graduate from high school. Boys exert more effort in stereotypically "masculine" areas such as mathematics, science, and mechanical skills; girls work harder in stereotypically "feminine" areas such as reading, literature, art, and music.	Encourage both boys and girls to achieve in all areas of the curriculum.

As Table 4–3 shows, girls and boys are similar in general intellectual ability; any differences in aptitudes for specific academic areas are small, with a great deal of overlap between the two groups (e.g., refer back to the gender differences in verbal ability depicted in Figure 4–1). Girls are generally more concerned about doing well in school, yet boys have greater confidence in their *ability* to succeed. Boys and girls alike tend to be more motivated to achieve in gender-stereotypical areas, and they have greater self-confidence about their chances for success in these areas. As teachers, we should expect our male and female

Expect boys and girls to have similar academic aptitudes for different subject areas.

continued

CHARACTERISTIC	SIMILARITIES AND DIFFERENCES	EDUCATIONAL IMPLICATION
Self-esteem	Boys are more likely to have self-confidence in their ability to control the world and solve problems; girls are more likely to see themselves as competent in interpersonal relationships. Boys and girls also tend to have greater self-esteem in areas consistent with society's stereotypes about what males and females should do. In general, boys tend to rate their own performance on tasks more positively than girls do, even when actual performance is the same for both genders.	Show students that they can be successful in counterstereotypical subject areas. For example, show girls that they have just as much potential for learning mathematics and science as boys do.
Explanations for success and failure	Boys and girls interpret their successes and failures somewhat differently. Boys tend to attribute their successes to an enduring ability (e.g., they're "smart" or "naturally athletic") and their failures to a lack of effort (they didn't try hard enough). In contrast, girls attribute their successes to effort (they worked very hard) and their failures to a lack of ability (e.g., they "can't do math" or are "not very good at sports"). Boys' beliefs in greater natural ability make them more optimistic about their chances for future success.	Convince girls that their past and present successes indicate an ability to succeed and that they can avoid or overcome failure with sufficient effort.
Expectations and career aspirations	Although girls are more likely to see themselves as college-bound, boys have higher long-term expectations for themselves, especially in stereotypically "masculine" areas. Career aspirations tend to be consistent with gender stereotypes; furthermore, girls (but not boys) tend to choose careers that will not interfere with their future roles as spouses and parents.	Expose students to successful male and female models in a variety of roles and professions. Also, provide examples of people successfully juggling careers with marriage and parenthood.
Interpersonal relationships	Boys exhibit more physical aggression, although girls can be just as aggressive as boys in more subtle and less physical ways (e.g., by tattling, gossiping, or snubbing peers). Girls are more affiliative—they form closer and more intimate interpersonal relationships—and they seem to be more sensitive to the subtle, nonverbal messages ("body language") that others give them. Boys feel more comfortable than girls in competitive situations; girls prefer cooperative environments that offer social support.	Teach both genders less aggressive and more prosocial ways of interacting with one another. To accommodate girls' more affiliative nature, provide opportunities for cooperative group work and frequent interaction with classmates.

Sources: N. S. Anderson, 1987; Berndt, 1992; Binns, Steinberg, Amorosi, & Cuevas, 1997; Bjorkqvist, Osterman, & Kaukiainen, 1992; Block, 1993; Bornholt, Goodnow, & Cooney, 1994; Brodzinsky, Messer, & Tew, 1979; Burkam, Lee, & Smerdon, 1997; P. A. Campbell, 1986; Chipman, Brush, & Wilson, 1985; Deaux, 1984; Durkin, 1995; Eagly, 1987; Eccles, 1989; Eccles [Parsons], 1984; Eisenberg et al., 1996; Fennema, 1987; Fennema, Carpenter, Jacobs, Franke, & Levi, 1998; Fennema & Peterson, 1985; Gustafsson & Undheim, 1996; Halpern, 1997; Hedges & Nowell, 1995; Huston, 1983; Hyde & Linn, 1988; Inglehart, Brown, & Vida, 1994; Jacklin, 1989; G. P. Jones & Dembo, 1989; Kahle, 1983; Kelly & Smail, 1986; Law, Pellegrino, & Hunt, 1993; M. C. Linn & Hyde, 1989; M. C. Linn & Petersen, 1985; Loeber & Stouthamer-Loeber, 1998; Lueptow, 1984; Maccoby & Jacklin, 1974; H. W. Marsh, 1989; McCall, 1994; McCallum & Bracken, 1993; Neisser et al., 1996; Nemerowicz, 1979; K. Paulson & Johnson, 1983; Sadker & Sadker, 1994; J. Smith & Russell, 1984; Stipek, 1984; J. R. Thomas & French, 1985; Wigfield et al., 1996; Yu et al., 1995.

students to have similar academic aptitudes for different subject areas; furthermore, we should encourage both groups to achieve in all areas of the curriculum.

We must convince girls that they have just as much potential for learning such subjects as mathematics and science as boys do.

Origins of Gender Differences

Obviously heredity determines the differences in physical characteristics we see in males and females both at birth and when they reach puberty. Because of heredity, girls reach puberty earlier than boys, and after puberty, boys are taller and have more muscle tissue than girls. Adolescent males are better than their female age-mates at tasks involving strength—an advantage that probably results from genetics (J. R. Thomas & French, 1985).

Aside from such physical differences, many theorists believe that biology plays a relatively minor role in the development of gender differences (Harway & Moss, 1983; Huston, 1983; R. Rosenthal & Rubin, 1982; Ruble, 1988). One likely explanation for many of the gender differences we see is socialization. Boys and girls are taught that some behaviors are more appropriate for males and that others are more appropriate for females. To see what I mean, try the following exercise.

■ Experiencing Firsthand
Picture This #2

Form a picture in your mind of each of the following individuals. Use the *first* image that comes to mind in each case.

Bank president

Kindergarten teacher

Fashion model

Scientist

Building contractor

Secretary

Now answer this question: Which of the individuals that you pictured were male, and which were female?

If you are like most people, your bank president, scientist, and building contractor were males, and your kindergarten teacher, fashion model, and secretary were females. Gender stereotypes—rigid ideas about how males and females "typically" behave—persist throughout our society, and even preschool children are aware of them (Bornholt et al., 1994; Eisenberg et al., 1996).

Many aspects of society conspire to teach growing children to conform to gender stereotypes. For example, parents are more likely to encourage their sons to be independent, athletic, and aggressive, and they tend to have higher career expectations for their sons than for their daughters, especially in stereotypically masculine professions (Block, 1983; Eccles & Jacobs, 1986; Fagot, Hagan, Leinbach, & Kronsberg, 1985; Olneck, 1995; Parsons, Adler, & Kaczala, 1982; Ruble, 1988; J. R. Thomas & French, 1985). In addition, girls and boys have different toys and play different games (Block, 1983; P. A. Campbell, 1986; Etaugh, 1983). Girls get dolls and stuffed animals, and they play "house" and board games—toys and activities that foster the development of verbal and social skills. Boys get blocks, model airplanes, and science equipment, and they play football, basketball, and video games—toys and activities that foster greater development of visual-spatial skills (Liss, 1983; Sprafkin et al., 1983). Although gender-stereotypical expectations for males and females are evident in virtually any society, they are more pronounced in some cultures than in others (C. A. Grant & Gomez, 1996).

The media promote gender-stereotypical behavior as well. Movies, television programs, and books (including many elementary reading primers) often portray males and females in gender-stereotypical ways: Males are aggressive leaders and successful problem solvers, whereas females are domestic, demure, and obedient followers (Durkin, 1987; Huston, 1983; Ruble & Ruble, 1982; Sadker & Sadker, 1994). Furthermore, males appear far more prominently in history and science textbooks than females do (Eisenberg et al., 1996; Sadker, Sadker, & Klein, 1991). As teachers, we must make a concerted effort to develop and select curriculum materials that represent both genders in a positive and competent light; nonsexist curriculum materials reduce gender stereotypes when students are exposed to them on a continual and consistent basis (Fennema, 1987; Horgan, 1995; Sadker & Miller, 1982).

As noted in Chapter 3, schools are important socialization agents for children, and such socialization often includes further encouragement of gender-stereotypical behaviors. Let's look at how the behaviors of two particularly influential groups of people—peers and teachers—promote the development of gender differences.

> Use nonsexist curriculum materials that portray both genders in a competent, successful light.

Peer Behaviors

Playmates and classmates do many things to ensure that children adhere to traditional gender stereotypes. Peers often respond more positively to children who play in "gender appropriate" ways and more negatively to those who do not (Eisenberg et al., 1996; Fagot & Leinbach, 1983; Huston, 1983). They may also ridicule or avoid students who enroll and excel in "gender inappropriate" subjects, such as high school girls who excel in science and mathematics (Casserly, 1980; Sadker & Sadker, 1994; Schubert, 1986). As a result, many students will engage in counterstereotypical activities only when their successes in such activities can be hidden from peers (Eccles, 1989; Huston, 1983; Ruble, 1988). As teachers, we can do a great deal to keep student achievement out of the public eye—for example, by keeping grades confidential[1] and perhaps by allowing students to demonstrate their achievement through written assignments rather than through oral responses to in-class questions.

> When students feel a need to "hide" their achievements, keep those achievements private and confidential.

Remember how quiet and passive Lupita was in our opening case study? Boys often take a more active role in class than girls, especially when the two are asked to work together; for example, when paired in a science lab, boys perform experiments while girls take notes (Arenz & Lee, 1990; Eccles, 1989; Kahle & Lakes, 1983; Schubert, 1986; Théberge, 1994). For this reason, it may sometimes be beneficial to group girls with girls, and boys with boys, to ensure that girls become more active participants in classroom activities (Kahle & Lakes, 1983; MacLean, Sasse, Keating, Stewart, & Miller, 1995). Girls are also more likely to assume the role of leader in same-sex groups and, in the process, to value leadership skills (Fennema, 1987).

> Occasionally form same-sex groups for cooperative classroom activities.

Teacher Behaviors

During the past twenty years, schools have shown increasing efforts to treat boys and girls similarly (Eccles, 1989). For example, girls' sports are enjoying more publicity and financial support than ever before. Nevertheless, differences in the treatment of boys and girls

---

[1] In the United States, there are legal as well as pedagogical reasons for keeping grades confidential. The Family Educational Rights and Privacy Act (1974) mandates that a student's records, including grades, be shared only with the student, his or her parents or legal guardians, and school personnel directly involved in the student's education and well-being.

🍎 Give equal attention to
males and females.
Equally encourage
both males and females to
think through questions
and problems on their own.

continue to exist. For instance, teachers tend to give more attention to boys—partly because, on average, boys ask more questions and present more discipline problems (Brophy, 1985; Dweck, 1986; Sadker & Sadker, 1994; L. C. Wilkinson & Marrett, 1985). Teachers interact more with high-achieving boys than with high-achieving girls, perhaps because boys seek out more interaction (Fennema, 1987; Sadker & Sadker, 1994). When girls cannot answer a question, their teachers tend to tell them the correct answer; but when boys have equal difficulty, their teachers usually help them think through the correct answer on their own (Sadker & Sadker, 1985). Boys are told to try harder when they fail; girls are simply praised for trying (P. A. Campbell, 1986; Eccles & Jacobs, 1986; L. H. Fox, 1981).

In most cases, teachers are probably unaware that they discriminate between boys and girls the way they do. The first step toward ensuring more equitable treatment of males and females is to become aware of existing inequities. Then we can try to correct those inequities—for example, by interacting frequently with *all* of our students, by helping them think through correct answers, by encouraging them to try harder when they experience difficulty, and by holding high expectations for everyone.

In the last few pages, we have considered numerous strategies for treating male and female students, as well as students from diverse ethnic backgrounds, in an equitable fashion. Yet equity must be extended to students of different socioeconomic circumstances as well. Let's look at some of the specific characteristics that students from lower-income families, including those growing up in true poverty, are likely to have, as well as at some strategies for helping these students achieve classroom success.

INTO THE CLASSROOM: Promoting Gender Equity

Use your knowledge of typical gender differences to create greater equity for males and females, *not* to form expectations about how successful males and females are likely to be in various activities.

> A physical education teacher realizes that most of the girls in her class have probably not had as much experience throwing overhand as the boys have, so she gives them basic instruction and extra practice in the overhand throw.

Be on the lookout for gender stereotypes in classroom materials, and use some materials that portray both genders in a counterstereotypical fashion.

> An English teacher assigns Harper Lee's *To Kill a Mockingbird,* in which an attorney named Atticus Finch is portrayed as a gentle, affectionate, and compassionate man, and his daughter Scout is portrayed as a courageous and adventuresome eight-year-old. The teacher also assigns Zora Neale Hurston's *Their Eyes Were Watching God,* in which an African American woman grows from a teenager dependent entirely on others to meet her needs into a self-sufficient woman who can easily fend for herself.

Occasionally ask students to work together in single-sex pairs or groups.

> A science teacher has students work in groups of three boys or three girls to conduct an assigned laboratory activity.

Monitor yourself to see if you are unintentionally treating boys and girls differently.

> A French teacher decides to count the number of times that he calls on boys and girls during class. He finds that he calls on boys more than three times as often as on girls, partly because the boys raise their hands more frequently. To combat his bad habit, he institutes a new procedure: He alternates between boys and girls when he calls on students, and he sometimes calls on students who are not raising their hands.

Socioeconomic Differences

The concept of **socioeconomic status** (often abbreviated as **SES**) encompasses a number of variables, including family income, parents' occupations, and the degree to which parents have received a formal education. Students' school performance is correlated with socioeconomic status: Higher-SES students tend to have higher academic achievement, and lower-SES students tend to be at greater risk for dropping out of school (McLoyd, 1998; Miller, 1995; Portes, 1996; H. W. Stevenson, Chen, & Uttal, 1990).

Factors Interfering with School Success

Several factors probably contribute to the generally lower school achievement of low-SES students. These are described in the following paragraphs.

Poor nutrition. Some lower-SES families cannot afford nutritional meals for their children. As noted earlier, poor nutrition in the early developmental years is associated with lower IQ scores; it is also associated with poorer attention and memory, impaired learning ability, and lower school achievement (D'Amato et al., 1992; L. S. Miller, 1995). Furthermore, when students are chronically hungry, they may have little interest in school learning (Maslow, 1987). As teachers, we must take any necessary steps to ensure that our students are adequately fed; for instance, we can make sure that all eligible children have access to the free and reduced-cost meal programs that the school district offers.

Connect students with free or reduced-cost meal programs.

Emotional stress. Students function less effectively when they are under stress, and many low-SES families live in chronically stressful conditions (McLoyd, 1998). Obviously, the economic problems of the poor family are a source of anxiety; children may wonder where their next meal is coming from or how long it will be before their landlord evicts them for not paying the rent. The preponderance of single-parent homes among low-SES families is another source of stress; a single parent may be overwhelmed with worries about supporting the family (Scott-Jones, 1984). We must continually be on the lookout for signs that our students are undergoing unusual stress at home and provide whatever support we can for these students. In some instances, such support may involve nothing more than being a willing listener; in other cases, we may want to consult with a school district social worker about possible support systems and agencies in the local community.

Provide emotional support for students under stress; seek out community resources when appropriate.

Fewer early experiences that foster school readiness. Many students from lower-SES families lack some of the basic skills (e.g., familiarity with letters and numbers) on which successful school learning so often depends (McLoyd, 1998; Portes, 1996). Access to early educational opportunities—books, educational toys, trips to zoos and museums, and so on—is always somewhat dependent on a family's financial resources. Furthermore, low-income parents may often be so preoccupied with the basic necessities of life— food, warm clothing, and so on—that they have little time or energy to consider how they might promote their children's cognitive development (Trawick-Smith, 1997). And many low-SES parents have poor reading skills and so can provide few early reading experiences for their children. Such experiences, as we will discover in Chapter 9, are critical for children's reading development during the elementary years (R. D. Hess & Holloway, 1984; Laosa, 1982). As teachers, it is essential that we identify and teach any missing basic skills; when we do so, we are likely to see significant improvements in our students' classroom performance (S. Griffin, Case, & Capodilupo, 1995; McLoyd, 1998).

Identify and address any missing basic skills.

Peer rejection. Students from lower-income families are often rejected by their more economically fortunate classmates; as a result, they may have fewer opportunities to

Facilitate peer acceptance.

become actively involved in school activities (Knapp & Woolverton, 1995). The strategies described in Chapter 3 in the sections "Fostering Social Skills" and "Promoting Social Interaction Among Diverse Groups" should prove useful in helping these students forge new friendships.

Lower aspirations. Students from low-SES backgrounds, and particularly girls, typically have lower aspirations for educational and career achievement (Knapp & Woolverton, 1995; S. M. Taylor, 1994). Teachers, too—even those who teach kindergarten and first grade—often have lower expectations for students from lower-income families (McLoyd, 1998; Portes, 1996). Certainly, we must encourage *all* of our students to aim high in their educational and professional goals. We must also provide the extra support they need to achieve such goals; offering help sessions for challenging classroom material, finding low-cost academic enrichment programs available during the summer, and helping students fill out applications for college scholarships are just a few of the forms that such support might take.

Less parental involvement in children's education. The great majority of parents at all income levels want their children to get a good education (H. W. Stevenson et al., 1990). But parents in many lower-SES households have had little education themselves, so they may not be capable of helping their children with assigned schoolwork (Finders & Lewis, 1994). Furthermore, economic factors may prevent parents from becoming actively involved in their children's schooling; lower-income parents often have difficulty getting off work, finding suitable child care, and arranging transportation to visit school and meet with teachers (Finders & Lewis, 1994; Salend & Taylor, 1993). In addition, some parents may have had bad experiences when they themselves were students and so feel uncomfortable in a school setting (Finders & Lewis, 1994). As teachers, we should be especially flexible about when and where we meet with the parents of lower-income students; we should also be especially conscientious about establishing comfortable, trusting relationships with them (Finders & Lewis, 1994; Salend & Taylor, 1993).

Working with Homeless Students

Children of homeless families typically face far greater challenges than other low-SES students. Many will have health problems, low self-esteem, a short attention span, poor language skills, and inappropriate behaviors (Coe, Salamon, & Molnar, 1991; McLoyd, 1998; Pawlas, 1994). Some may be reluctant to come to school because they lack bathing facilities and appropriate clothing (Gollnick & Chinn, 1994). And some may have moved so frequently from one school to another that there are large gaps in the academic skills they have mastered (Pawlas, 1994).

As teachers, we, too, will face unusual challenges when teaching students living in homeless shelters. Here are several suggestions for giving them the extra support they may need to achieve both academic and social success at school (Pawlas, 1994):

- Pair new students with classmates who can "show them the ropes" around school—for example, by explaining school procedures and making introductions to other students.
- Provide a notebook, clipboard, or other portable "desk" on which students can do their homework at the shelter.
- Find adult or teenage volunteers to serve as tutors at the shelter.
- Enlist the help of civic organizations to collect clothing and school supplies for the students.
- Meet with parents at the shelter rather than at school.
- Share copies of homework assignments, school calendars, and newsletters with shelter officials.

Hold high expectations for students' academic and professional achievement.

Remember that students may have few resources at home to help them with their schoolwork.

Be flexible about when and where to meet with parents, and establish comfortable, trusting relationships with them.

Fostering Resilience

Fortunately, many students of low-income families succeed in school despite exceptional hardship (Humphreys, 1992; Nieto, 1995; B. Williams & Newcombe, 1994). Some seem to be **resilient students:** They develop characteristics and coping skills that help them rise above their adverse circumstances. As a group, resilient students have likable personalities, positive self-concepts, strong motivation to succeed, and high yet realistic goals. They believe that success comes with hard work, and their bad experiences serve as constant reminders of the importance of getting a good education (Masten & Coatsworth, 1998; McMillan & Reed, 1994; Werner, 1995).

Resilient students usually have one or more individuals in their lives whom they trust and know they can turn to in difficult times (McLoyd, 1998; Werner, 1995). Such individuals may be family members, neighbors, or school personnel; for example, resilient students often mention teachers who have taken a personal interest in them and been instrumental in their school success (McMillan & Reed, 1994; Paris & Cunningham, 1996). As teachers, we are most likely to promote resilience in low-SES students when we show them that we like and respect them, are available and willing to listen to their views and concerns, hold high expectations for their performance, and provide the encouragement and support they need to succeed both inside and outside the classroom (Masten & Coatsworth, 1998; McMillan & Reed, 1994; Werner, 1995).

Building on Students' Strengths

Although many students from lower-SES backgrounds may lag behind their classmates in such basic academic skills as reading, writing, and computation, they bring other strengths to the classroom. For example, they are often more clever at improvising with everyday objects (Torrance, 1995). If they work part-time to help their families make ends meet, they may have a good understanding of the working world. If they are children of single, working parents, they may know far more than their classmates about cooking, cleaning house, and taking care of younger siblings. If financial resources have been particularly scarce, they may know firsthand what it is like to be hungry for days at a time or to live in an unheated apartment in the winter; they may therefore have a special appreciation for basic human needs and true empathy for victims of war or famine around the world. As teachers, then, we must remember that students who have grown up in poverty may, in some respects, have more knowledge and skills than their more economically advantaged peers. Such knowledge and skills can often provide a basis for teaching classroom subject matter. Furthermore, students who are willing to talk about the challenges they've faced can sensitize their classmates to the serious inequities that currently exist in our society.

Students at Risk

THINKING ABOUT WHAT YOU KNOW

Do you remember classmates in elementary school who never seemed to complete assignments or get their homework done? Do you remember classmates in high school who did poorly in most of their classes and rarely participated in extracurricular activities? How many of those students eventually graduated from high school? What are they doing now?

Students at risk are students with a high probability of failing to acquire the minimum academic skills necessary for success in the adult world. Many of them drop out

---

Remember that many bright students come from low-income families.

Help low-SES students develop resiliency by being a trustworthy individual on whom they can depend in difficult times.

Provide opportunities for lower-SES students to build on and share their knowledge, skills, and life experiences.

before high school graduation; many others graduate without basic skills in reading or mathematics (National Assessment of Educational Progress, 1985; Slavin, 1989). Such individuals are often ill-equipped to make productive contributions to their families, communities, or society at large.

Characteristics of Students at Risk

Some students at risk are those with identified special educational needs; for example, they may have learning disabilities or emotional and behavioral problems that interfere with learning and achievement. Others may be students whose cultural backgrounds don't mesh easily with the dominant culture at school. Still others may be students from home environments in which academic success is neither supported nor encouraged.

Students at risk come from all socioeconomic levels, but children of poor, single-parent families are especially likely to leave school before high school graduation. Boys are more likely to drop out than girls. African Americans, Hispanics, and Native Americans are more likely to drop out than European American and Asian American students. Students at greatest risk for dropping out are those whose families speak little or no English and whose own knowledge of English is also quite limited (Frazer & Wilkinson, 1990; García, 1995; L. S. Miller, 1995; Nieto, 1995; Portes, 1996; Raber, 1990; Rumberger, 1995; L. Steinberg, Blinde, & Chan, 1984; U.S. Department of Education, 1997).

In addition, students at risk, especially those who eventually drop out of school, typically have some or all of the following characteristics:

- *A history of academic failure.* High school dropouts often have a history of poor academic achievement going back as far as third grade (Garnier, Stein, & Jacobs, 1997; Lloyd, 1978). On the average, they have less effective study skills, earn lower grades, obtain lower achievement test scores, and are more likely to repeat a grade level than their classmates who graduate (Jozefowicz, Arbreton, Eccles, Barber, & Colarossi, 1994; Lloyd, 1978; Raber, 1990; L. Steinberg et al., 1984; L. D. Wilkinson & Frazer, 1990).

- *Older age in comparison with classmates.* Because low achievers are sometimes retained at the same grade level from one year to the next, they are often older than their classmates (Raber, 1990; Wilkinson & Frazer, 1990). Some (though not all) research studies find that students who are overage in comparison with classmates are those most likely to drop out of school (D. C. Gottfredson, Fink, & Graham, 1994; Roderick, 1994; Rumberger, 1995).

- *Emotional and behavioral problems.* Potential dropouts tend to have lower self-esteem than their more successful classmates. And they are more likely to exhibit disruptive behavior, create discipline problems, use drugs, and engage in criminal activities (Finn, 1991; Garnier et al., 1997; Jozefowicz et al., 1994; Rumberger, 1995; U.S. Department of Education, 1992).

- *Lack of psychological attachment to school.* Students who are at risk for academic failure are less likely to identify with their school or to perceive themselves as a vital part of the school community; for example, they engage in fewer extracurricular activities, and they are more likely to express dissatisfaction with school in general (Finn, 1989; Rumberger, 1995).

- *Increasing disinvolvement with school.* Dropping out is not really an all-or-none thing. In fact, many high school dropouts show lesser forms of "dropping out" many years before they officially leave school. For example, future dropouts are absent from school more frequently than their peers, even in the early elementary grades (Finn, 1989; G. A. Hess, Lyons, & Corsino, 1990; Jozefowicz et al., 1994). They are more likely to have been suspended from school, and they are more likely to show a long-term pattern of dropping out, returning to school, and dropping out again (Raber, 1990).

What are possible reasons why some students don't participate in their school's extracurricular activities?

Over time, then, we see decreasing involvement—physical, academic, and social—in school activities.

Why Some Students Drop Out

Students typically drop out for one of three reasons. Some have little family support or encouragement for school success. Others have extenuating life circumstances; for example, they may have medical problems, take an outside job to help support the family, or become pregnant. Still others become dissatisfied with school: They don't do well in their classes, have trouble making and keeping friends, or find the curriculum boring and irrelevant to their needs (Portes, 1996; Raber, 1990; Rumberger, 1995; L. Steinberg et al., 1984).

Helping Students at Risk Stay in School

Students who are at risk for academic failure are a diverse group of individuals with a diverse set of needs, and there is probably no quick fix to keep every student in school until high school graduation (Finn, 1991). Nevertheless, we can do several things to help students at risk succeed and stay in school:

- *Identify students at risk as early as possible.* We begin to see indicators of "dropping out," such as low school achievement and high absenteeism, as early as elementary school. And such other signs as low self-esteem, disruptive behavior, and lack of involvement in school activities often appear years before students officially withdraw from school. So it is quite possible to identify at-risk students early in their school careers and to take steps to prevent or remediate academic difficulties before those difficulties become insurmountable. Research indicates clearly that, for students at risk, prevention and early intervention are more effective than later intervention efforts (Ramey & Ramey, 1998).

Identify at-risk students as early as possible and intervene on their behalf.

- *Make the curriculum relevant to students' lives and needs.* Students are more likely to stay in school if they find the curriculum relevant to their own cultural values, life experiences, and future needs (Knapp, Turnbull, & Shields, 1990; Ramey & Ramey, 1998). To increase the relevance of school for students at risk, we should place academic skills within the context of real-world tasks, and particularly within the context of students' local cultural environments. For example, we might teach reading skills by using magazines related to students' interests (e.g., magazines dealing with sports or teen fashions). We might teach writing skills by asking students to write a letter to the editor of a local newspaper. We might teach basic arithmetic by having students calculate the price of soft drinks when purchased individually versus in a six-pack.

Make the curriculum relevant to students' life experiences and future needs.

- *Communicate high expectations for academic success.* Although many students at risk have a history of academic failure, under no circumstances should we write these students off. On the contrary, we should communicate to them that school success is both possible and expected (García, 1994; Garibaldi, 1993; C. K. Howe, 1994; Ladson-Billings, 1994a). We can acknowledge past learning problems but let students know that there are ways to overcome those problems, and that furthermore we will help them acquire the knowledge and skills they need for classroom success (Alderman, 1990).

Help students set high yet realistic goals.

It is often more effective to focus students' attention on short-term, specific goals (e.g., learning to do long division or spell a list of one hundred words) rather than long-term, general ones (e.g., becoming an expert mathematician or a gifted writer). Students at risk will perceive short-term goals to be more easily accomplishable than long-term goals, and they will achieve success more quickly (Alderman, 1990).

• *Provide extra support for academic success.* Because students at risk often have a history of academic failure and may have little support for academic achievement at home, these students may need more than the usual amount of assistance from teachers and other school personnel to succeed. Here are some specific ways to facilitate their academic success:

- Help them develop more effective reading and learning strategies.
- Adapt instruction to their current skills and knowledge.
- Give them relatively structured tasks and tell them exactly what is expected.
- Develop mastery of one skill before moving to a more difficult one.
- Assess their progress frequently and give them specific criteria for measuring their own success.
- Increase one-on-one teacher-student interactions.
- Deliver as much instruction as possible within the context of general education; make any necessary instruction in self-contained settings as brief as possible.
- Solicit parent and community cooperation with the school program. (Alderman, 1990; Covington & Beery, 1976; Garibaldi, 1993; Slavin, Karweit, & Madden, 1989)

As you may have noticed, these recommendations would be helpful for *any* student. Research indicates that the most effective programs for students at risk are those that incorporate normal, educationally sound teaching practices (Slavin, Madden, & Karweit, 1989).

• *Show students that they are the ones who have made success possible.* When students at risk improve academically, we must help them recognize that *they them-*

Provide support for academic success by using educationally sound teaching practices.

Help students recognize their personal responsibility for success.

Students are more likely to stay in school when they feel as if they truly belong there.

selves are responsible for their success (Alderman, 1990). For example, we might give messages such as this: "You really deserved this A. You are writing in complete sentences now, and you are checking your work for spelling and punctuation errors." Here we are talking about increasing students' *self-efficacy* through the *attributions* we give for their success. We'll discuss these concepts in Chapters 11–12.

• *Encourage and facilitate identification with school.* Students at risk may need extra encouragement to become involved in academic and social school activities. To help them become more involved in, and feel more psychologically attached to, the school community, we can:

Encourage and facilitate identification with school.

- Establish close working relationships with students.
- Include instructional techniques that promote active class involvement (e.g., class discussions, cooperative learning).
- Encourage participation in athletic programs, extracurricular activities, and student government. (This is especially important when students are having

INTO THE CLASSROOM: Helping Students at Risk for Academic Failure and Dropping Out

Identify at-risk students as early as possible.

A second-grade teacher speaks with the principal and school counselor about possible ways to help a student who is frequently absent from school and seems to have little interest in her schoolwork.

Use students' strengths to promote high self-esteem.

A school forms a singing group (the "Jazz Cats") for which students in a low-income, inner-city elementary school must try out. The group performs at a variety of community events, and the students enjoy considerable visibility for their talent. Group members exhibit increased self-esteem, improvement in other school subjects, and greater teamwork and leadership skills (Jenlink, 1994).

Communicate high expectations for students' performance.

A mathematics teacher tells a group of junior high school students, "Yes, I know that you're finding fractions difficult right now. But I also know that you can learn fractions if you try hard and practice using them. Why don't we try a different approach to learning them today—one that might work a little better for us?"

Provide extra support for academic success.

A high school English teacher meets with a small group of low-reading-level students to read and discuss reading materials in areas of interest to them.

Show students that they are personally responsible for their successes.

A teacher tells a student, "Wow, look how much you've improved! That extra practice really helped."

Facilitate students' identification with school.

A teacher encourages a student with a strong throwing arm to go out for the school baseball team and introduces the student to the baseball coach.

academic difficulties, because it provides an alternative way of experiencing school success.)

- Involve students in school policy and management decisions.
- Give students positions of responsibility in managing school activities.
- Provide rewards (e.g., trips to a local amusement park) for good attendance records. (Finn, 1989; Garibaldi, 1992; Newmann, 1981; M. G. Sanders, 1996)

Students are far more likely to stay in school and try to succeed in school activities when they feel as if they truly belong there.

Although particular groups of students may have characteristics in common, it is critical to remember this: *We must never make predictions about individual students on the basis of group differences alone.* A teacher's expectations for a student, either positive or negative, can have a profound impact on how that student ultimately behaves. Let's look at some of the effects of teacher expectations.

Teacher Expectations

Teachers typically draw conclusions about their students relatively early in the school year, forming opinions about each one's strengths, weaknesses, and potential for academic success. In many instances, teachers size up their students fairly accurately: They know which ones need help with reading skills, which ones have short attention spans, which ones have trouble working together in the same cooperative group, and so on. But even the best teachers inevitably make errors in their judgments; for example, teachers often underestimate the abilities of students who speak in a dialect other than Standard English (Bowie & Bond, 1994; McLoyd, 1998; J. Taylor, 1983). Such erroneous judgments can significantly affect how well students perform in the classroom.

Effects of Teacher Expectations

Teachers' expectations for students have at least three effects:

- *Teacher expectations tend to perpetuate themselves.* In the opening case study, we found Ms. Padilla jumping to the conclusion that Lupita had few academic skills and probably needed a second year of kindergarten. She was quite surprised to see a very different, and very competent, side of Lupita captured by a researcher's video camera. Ms. Padilla readily admitted that her early expectations had colored her assessment of Lupita: "I had written her off . . . her and three others. They had met my expectations and I just wasn't looking for anything else." As we will discover in our discussion of knowledge construction in Chapter 7, people tend to remember things that are consistent with what they already know or believe about the world, and they tend to distort or forget things inconsistent with previously held ideas. Thus, people are likely to confirm and perpetuate their own previously formed beliefs and expectations, just as Ms. Padilla did, and may turn a blind eye and a deaf ear to any evidence to the contrary.

This biasing factor in what people learn and remember is evident in teachers' perceptions of students of different genders and ethnic groups. For example, teachers often underestimate the ability and achievement of minority students and students from low-income families (Commins & Miramontes, 1989; Gaines & Davis, 1990; García, 1994; Graham, 1990; L. P. Jones, 1990; Knapp & Woolverton, 1995). They also may interpret the successful academic performance of both minorities and females as being the result of short-term, unstable factors such as high effort or good luck while simultaneously attributing poor performance to long-term, stable factors such as low intelligence (Deaux, 1984; Murray & Jackson, 1982/1983).

• *Teacher expectations influence how teachers treat students.* Teachers frequently treat their students in ways consistent with their expectations for those students, and such differential treatment is not necessarily a bad thing (Goldenberg, 1992; Good & Brophy, 1994). For example, a teacher who expects a student to have difficulty learning to read, perhaps because that student has illiterate parents or comes from a non-English-speaking home, may spend extra time with the student to develop basic reading skills.

Yet expectations can lead teachers to behave in ways that create a **self-fulfilling prophecy;** in other words, what teachers expect students to achieve becomes what students actually *do* achieve. For example, when teachers have high expectations for their students' performance, they create a warmer classroom climate, interact with students more frequently, provide more opportunities for students to respond, and give more positive feedback; they also present more course material and more challenging topics. In contrast, when teachers have low expectations for certain students, they offer fewer opportunities for speaking in class (remember Ms. Padilla's reluctance to call on Lupita for fear of embarrassing her), ask easier questions, give less feedback about students' responses, and present few if any challenging assignments (Babad, 1993; Good & Brophy, 1994; Graham, 1990; M. J. Harris & Rosenthal, 1985; R. Rosenthal, 1994).

• *Teacher expectations affect students' self-concepts.* Students are often well aware of how their teachers expect them to perform (Olneck, 1995; R. S. Weinstein, 1993). When they receive the same message repeatedly—perhaps that they are incapable of learning difficult materials or perhaps that they can't do *anything* right— they may begin to see themselves as others see them. Their behavior will tend to mirror the self-concepts they form. For example, boys are more likely to hear comments about male-stereotypical characteristics ("My goodness, how strong you're getting!"), whereas girls hear female-stereotypical remarks ("My goodness, you've become such a lady!"). When boys think of themselves as strong and girls think of themselves as ladylike, very different behaviors can result (Bem, 1984). Differences among students from different cultural and socioeconomic groups may be partially a result of similar influences. For example, when African American boys are scolded more frequently than Caucasian boys (e.g., L. Grant, 1985), their self-concepts are likely to be adversely affected.

Certainly teacher expectations don't always affect what students think of themselves. Research indicates that teacher expectation effects are most likely to appear in the early elementary school years (Grades 1 and 2) and again about the time that students first enter junior high school (Grade 7) (Raudenbush, 1984). They are also most likely to appear when false expectations have been formed within the first few weeks of school (Raudenbush, 1984). In general, then, teacher expectations have their strongest effect at transition points in students' academic careers—when they first enter a new school environment.

Guarding Against Unwarranted Expectations

Sometimes teacher expectations are based on completely erroneous information. More frequently, however, teachers' initial impressions of students are reasonably accurate. In the latter case, a problem emerges when teachers don't *change* their expectations in the light of new data (H. M. Cooper & Good, 1983; Good & Brophy, 1994). As teachers, we must keep in mind what we have learned about intelligence and creativity: Ability can

Continually ask yourself whether you are giving inequitable treatment to students for whom you have low expectations.

Can you think of a teacher who did not have as much faith in you as you had in yourself? How did you react to that teacher?

Be especially careful not to form unwarranted expectations for students at transition points in their academic careers.

Remember that ability changes over time; don't assume that current deficiencies portend long-term difficulty.

and does change over time, especially when environmental conditions are conducive to such change. Accordingly, we must continually reassess our expectations for individual students, modifying them as new evidence presents itself. Several strategies can keep unwarranted expectations to a minimum:

Learn more about your students' backgrounds.

- *Learn more about students' backgrounds and home environments.* Teachers are most likely to have low expectations for students' performance when they have formed rigid stereotypes about students from certain ethnic or socioeconomic groups (McLoyd, 1998; R. E. Snow, Corno, & Jackson, 1996). And such stereotypes are often the result of ignorance about students' cultures and home environments (K. L. Alexander, Entwisle, & Thompson, 1987). So education is the key here: We must learn as much as we can about our students' backgrounds and local communities. When we have a clear picture of their activities, their habits, their values, and their families, we are far more likely to think of them as *individuals* than as stereotypical members of any particular group.

Look for *every* student's strengths.

- *Look for strengths in every student.* Sometimes students' weaknesses are all too evident. But as noted earlier, it is essential that we also look for the many unique qualities and strengths that our students will inevitably have (C. A. Grant & Gomez, 1996; Knapp et al., 1990). For instance, children from some African American communities are accustomed to high-spirited group singing and other vocalizations, especially in weekly church services (Lein, 1975). And many African American students show considerable creativity when they converse; they joke, tease, and tell lively stories (Hale-Benson, 1986). (As an example, consider the "sounding" incident in the "Ruckus in the Lunchroom" exercise presented earlier in the chapter.) Certainly we can take advantage of such playfulness in students' speech, perhaps by having students create songs, jokes, or short stories that relate to classroom subject matter.

Assess students' progress objectively.

- *Assess students' progress regularly and objectively.* Because our expectations for students' performance are likely to color our informal evaluations of what they actually accomplish, we need to identify more objective ways of assessing learning and achievement. Furthermore, we should assess students' progress frequently, so that we have ongoing and reasonably accurate information with which to make instructional decisions (Goldenberg, 1992). Chapter 16 identifies a wide variety of strategies for assessing classroom learning with a reasonable degree of objectivity and accuracy.

Remember that you *can* make a difference.

- *Remember that teachers can definitely make a difference.* We are more likely to have high expectations for students when we are confident in our own abilities to help *all* of our students achieve academic and social success (Ashton, 1985; R. S. Weinstein, Madison, & Kuklinski, 1995).

Taking Individual and Group Differences into Account

Clearly, different students have different needs. It is often helpful to know how individual differences (e.g., intelligence, creativity) and group differences (e.g., those associated with being female or growing up in a particular ethnic group) potentially affect the behaviors and beliefs that different students bring with them to the classroom. At the same time, we must be careful not to jump to conclusions about our students on the basis of insufficient data. Table 4–4 reviews some of the individual and group differences described in this chapter and provides several ideas about how to accommodate such differences without letting them bias our judgments.

Accommodating Students with Special Needs

We will, of course, see differences among our students with special educational needs, and some of these differences will be related to the individual and group difference variables examined in this chapter. For instance, students from lower socioeconomic backgrounds

Taking Individual and Group Differences into Account

GENERAL PRINCIPLE	EDUCATIONAL IMPLICATION	EXAMPLE
Intelligence is partly a function of environment and can change over time. In addition, different students are likely to be intelligent in different ways.	Never jump to conclusions about what students will or will not be able to do, and do not assume that a student having difficulty in one area will necessarily have difficulty in another.	Never use IQ scores as the sole indicator of students' potential for academic success. Factors such as quality of instruction, student motivation, parental support, and peer group norms will also have a significant effect.
Students tend to be creative in specific content domains rather than to show creativity in every aspect of their behavior. Furthermore, students' level of creativity is influenced by environmental conditions.	Foster students' creativity in a particular area by valuing creative products, encouraging students to take risks, and giving them the time they need to generate new ideas.	Form small, cooperative groups that work together over several days or weeks to develop a play, short story, scientific invention, or new team sport.
Each ethnic group has its own norms for appropriate behavior. People from one culture sometimes misinterpret the behaviors of those from a different culture.	Be careful not to interpret students' actions in terms of your own cultural standards for behavior.	When students share answers, don't assume they are intentionally cheating; their culture may value group achievement over individual achievement. Provide opportunities for both group and individual accomplishments, and make it clear when each is expected.
On the average, male and female students have similar or equal abilities in all academic areas; however, most have greater self-confidence in areas consistent with traditional gender stereotypes.	Encourage males and females equally in all areas of the curriculum—in science, mathematics, language arts, art, music, physical education, and so on—and in all extracurricular activities.	Expose students to successful individuals in different professions, making sure they see both men and women in these roles.
Low-income parents sometimes have difficulty giving their children the resources and educational experiences on which successful school learning often builds.	When necessary, provide additional support and experiences at school (perhaps in terms of needed school supplies, one-on-one assistance with homework, field trips, and so on) to help students achieve academic success. At the same time, remember that students from low-SES backgrounds have probably had valuable experiences that their wealthier classmates have not.	Incorporate enriching outside experiences into the curriculum; for example, take students to museums, the zoo, and the city library.

are more likely to be identified as having either cognitive or behavioral difficulties that require special educational services (U.S. Department of Education, 1996). Some cultures discourage females, even those with high IQ scores and considerable academic promise, from pursuing advanced educational opportunities; as a result, some gifted female students are reluctant to make the most of their advanced cognitive abilities (Nichols & Ganschow, 1992). Other gender differences exist as well; for example, we will more often see specific cognitive or academic difficulties (e.g., learning disabilities) among boys than girls,

TABLE 4.5

Considering Individual and Group Differences in Students with Special Educational Needs

STUDENTS WITH SPECIAL NEEDS	CHARACTERISTICS THAT THESE STUDENTS MAY EXHIBIT	CLASSROOM STRATEGIES THAT MAY BE BENEFICIAL FOR THESE STUDENTS
Students with specific cognitive or academic difficulties	In most cases, average or above-average scores on traditional intelligence tests Greater frequency in males than females (students with learning disabilities) Higher than average dropout rate (students with learning disabilities)	Remember that students with difficulties in one area (e.g., those with specific learning disabilities) may nevertheless be capable of average or above-average performance in other areas.
Students with social or behavioral problems	Gender differences in the nature of the problems exhibited, with males more likely to demonstrate overt misbehaviors (e.g., aggressive or antisocial behaviors) and females more likely to have internalized problems (e.g., social withdrawal or excessive anxiety) Greater frequency in lower-SES students Higher dropout rate than any other category of special needs (students with emotional or behavior disorders)	Be on the lookout for possible emotional problems when students (especially girls) are exceptionally quiet or withdrawn. Take steps to decrease the likelihood of students dropping out (e.g., by making the curriculum relevant, providing extra support for academic success, and facilitating identification with school).
Students with general delays in cognitive and social functioning	Low scores on traditional intelligence tests Gender differences and socioeconomic differences, with general cognitive and social delays (e.g., mental retardation) more common in males and in students from lower-SES backgrounds Higher than average dropout rate	Look for and nurture individual students' strengths in terms of Gardner's multiple intelligences. Remember that the great majority of students from low-SES backgrounds have average or above-average intelligence.
Students with physical or sensory challenges	Average intelligence in most cases Chronic illness more common in students from lower-income families	Assume an average ability to learn classroom subject matter unless there is compelling evidence to the contrary.

and we are likely to observe different kinds of problems in boys and girls with emotional and behavioral disorders (Caseau, Luckasson, & Kroth, 1994; Halpern, 1997; U.S. Department of Education, 1992). Table 4–5 presents numerous instances of individual and group differences among students with special needs, along with classroom strategies specifically related to such differences.

All students have strengths and talents that we can foster, and *all* students have the potential to develop new skills and abilities. Furthermore, the unique background and qualities that each student brings to class—for example, the realization by many girls that career aspirations must ultimately be balanced against dedication to family, the preference of students from some ethnic backgrounds for cooperative rather than competitive endeavors, and the firsthand awareness of some students from low-income homes regarding such social issues as poverty and homelessness—together create a situation in which we and our students have much to learn from one another.

continued

STUDENTS WITH SPECIAL NEEDS	CHARACTERISTICS THAT THESE STUDENTS MAY EXHIBIT	CLASSROOM STRATEGIES THAT MAY BE BENEFICIAL FOR THESE STUDENTS
Students with advanced cognitive development	High scores on traditional intelligence tests (less true for students from culturally diverse backgrounds, due to the cultural-specific nature of such tests) For many students, presence of specific areas of giftedness (e.g., in language, mathematics, music), with other areas being less advanced Divergent thinking (e.g., asking unusual questions, giving novel responses) Giftedness manifested in different ways in different cultures (e.g., possible richness of oral language among African American students, possible exceptional sensitivity to the feelings and perspectives of others among Native American students) More self-doubt about own abilities among females than males In some cultures, discouragement of females from acting too "intelligently" or pursuing advanced education Little exposure to female and minority role models	Accept and encourage divergent thinking, including responses that you haven't anticipated. Help students accurately appraise their own abilities. Encourage females as well as males to achieve at high levels, while also identifying avenues whereby students can demonstrate their talents in ways that their families and local cultures value.

Sources: Alderman, 1990; American Psychiatric Association, 1994; Barga, 1996; Barkley, 1995b; Davis & Rimm, 1998; Finn, 1989; Garibaldi, 1993; Halpern, 1997; Heward, 1996; Knapp et al., 1990; Maker & Schiever, 1989; McLoyd, 1998; Nichols & Ganschow, 1992; Patton et al., 1990; Piirto, 1994; Pressley, 1995; Sadker & Sadker, 1994; Torrance, 1989; Turnbull et al., 1999; U.S. Department of Education, 1992, 1997.

Note: Compiled with the assistance of Dr. Margie Garanzini-Daiber and Dr. Margaret Cohen, University of Missouri—St. Louis.

C A S E   S T U D Y : The Active and the Passive

Ms. Stewart has noticed that only a few students actively participate in her junior high school science classes. When she asks a question, especially one that requires students to draw inferences from information presented in class, the same hands always shoot up. She gives the matter some thought and realizes that all of the active participants are White and that most of them are boys.

She sees the same pattern in students' involvement in lab activities. When she puts her classes into small groups for particular lab assignments, the same students (notably the White males) always take charge. The females and minority males take more passive roles, either providing assistance to the group "leaders" or else just sitting back and watching.

Ms. Stewart is a firm believer that students learn much more about science when they participate in class and when they engage in hands-on activities. She is concerned about the lack of involvement of many of her students. She wonders whether they really even care about science.

- What are some possible reasons why the girls and minority students are not participating in classroom activities? What strategies might Ms. Stewart use to increase their participation?

Summing Up

Individual and Group Differences

The students in any single classroom will be diverse in terms of both individual differences (e.g., those based on intelligence or creativity) and group differences (e.g., those based on ethnicity, gender, or SES). As teachers, we must remember that there is considerable individual variability within any group and a great deal of overlap between any two groups.

Intelligence

Intelligence involves adaptive behavior and may manifest itself differently in different cultures. Many psychologists believe that intelligence is a single entity (a *general factor,* or *g*) that influences students' learning and performance across a wide variety of tasks and subject areas; this belief is reflected in the widespread use of IQ scores as general estimates of academic ability. But other theorists (e.g., Gardner, Sternberg) propose that intelligence consists of many, somewhat independent abilities and therefore cannot be accurately reflected in a single IQ score. Furthermore, there is a growing conviction that people are more likely to behave "intelligently" when they have physical and social support systems (e.g., computers, cooperative groups) to help them in their efforts—in other words, that intelligence can be *distributed.* In general, one's environment has a significant effect on intelligence and intelligent behavior; as teachers, we must remember that intelligence may change over time, especially during the early years.

Creativity

Creativity is new and original behavior that produces an appropriate and productive result; it is probably a combination of many thinking processes and behaviors that reflect themselves differently in different situations and content areas. We are likely to see more creative behavior when we show students that we value creativity, focus their attention on internal rather than external rewards, promote mastery of the subject matter, and encourage them to take risks.

Ethnic Differences

For students from ethnic minority groups, there is often some degree of cultural mismatch between the home and school environments. We may see cultural differences in language, sociolinguistic conventions, cooperation, private versus public performance, eye contact, conceptions of time, familiarity with the types of questions typically asked at school, and family relationships and expectations. All students benefit when we promote increased awareness of cultural differences and foster social interaction among students from diverse ethnic groups.

Gender Differences

Males and females have very similar academic abilities, but they differ somewhat in terms of motivation, self-esteem, explanations for success and failure, expectations for themselves, and interpersonal relationships. Many gender differences appear to be largely the result of the differing environmental conditions that boys and girls experience as they develop. As teachers, we should hold equally high expectations for both boys and girls and make sure that both genders have equal educational opportunities.

Socioeconomic Differences

Factors such as poor nutrition, emotional stress, little access to early academic experiences, low aspirations, and homelessness may all contribute to the generally lower achievement of students from low-SES families. As teachers, we can help such students succeed in the classroom by providing the academic and emotional support they need and by building on students' many strengths.

Students at Risk

Students at risk are those with a high probability of failing to acquire the minimum academic skills necessary for success in the adult world; they may graduate from high school without having learned to read or write, or they may drop out before graduation. To help such students succeed at school, we should identify them as early as possible, make the curriculum relevant to their needs, provide support for their academic success, and encourage greater involvement in school activities.

Teacher Expectations

Premature and unwarranted expectations for students tend to be self-perpetuating; they influence teachers' behaviors toward students and ultimately also influence students' self-concepts and academic achievement. We must remember that students' current deficiencies are not necessarily indicative of long-term difficulty, and we must be careful that we don't give inequitable treatment based on low expectations for performance. As teachers, we must use our knowledge of individual and group differences to help all of our students, including those with special educational needs, to achieve their maximum potential.

KEY CONCEPTS

individual differences (p. 119)
group differences (p. 119)
intelligence (p. 121)
intelligence test (p. 123)
IQ scores (p. 123)
g (in intelligence) (p. 126)
automaticity (p. 129)
distributed intelligence (p. 130)
creativity (p. 133)

convergent thinking (p. 133)
divergent thinking (p. 133)
higher-level questions (p. 135)
ethnic group (p. 137)
cultural mismatch (p. 137)
Standard English (p. 138)
dialect (p. 138)
African American dialect (p. 138)
sociolinguistic conventions (p. 139)

wait time (p. 139)
negative wait time (p. 139)
multicultural education (p. 143)
stereotype (p. 144)
equity (in instruction) (p. 145)
socioeconomic status (SES) (p. 151)
resilient students (p. 153)
students at risk (p. 153)
self-fulfilling prophecy (p. 159)

5

Students with Special Educational Needs

W hat weaknesses do you have in comparison with your fellow students? Perhaps you sometimes have more difficulty remembering course material, or perhaps you are so shy that you rarely talk to your classmates. Yet at the same time, can you think of ways in which you surpass most of your peers? Perhaps you are someone for whom learning a foreign language comes easily, or perhaps you are an exceptional softball player or long-distance runner.

All students are unique individuals, with different patterns of strengths and weaknesses. They differ considerably in cognitive abilities; for instance, some learn complex classroom material quickly and easily, while others struggle just to master basic concepts and skills. They also show a wide variety of social and emotional characteristics; for example, some may be friendlier and more outgoing than others, and some may appear more self-confident about their own capabilities than their classmates are. And students have varying physical capabilities—varying degrees of physical strength, muscular coordination, eyesight, and hearing ability. Most of the time we can accommodate students' individual differences within general education classroom practices and activities. But once in a while students have characteristics that require specially adapted instructional materials or practices; in other words, they are **students with special needs.**

In the United States, federal legislation now protects the civil rights of students with special educational needs. This legislation supports inclusive education, whereby most students with exceptionalities spend part or all of the school day in regular classrooms. In this chapter, we will focus on the things that regular classroom teachers need to know to meet the unique educational needs of these students. In particular, we will consider questions such as these:

- Why are most students with special needs educated in general education classrooms rather than in "special" classes or schools?
- What laws protect the rights of students with disabilities?
- How do educators typically categorize various kinds of special needs, and what characteristics are associated with each category?
- How can we help students with specific cognitive or academic difficulties learn and achieve effectively?
- How can we help students with social or behavioral problems behave more appropriately in the classroom?
- What can we do to promote the development of students with general delays in cognitive and social functioning?
- How can we adapt curricular materials and instructional practices for students with physical or sensory challenges?
- What can we do to maximize the growth of students who show exceptional gifts and talents—in other words, students with advanced cognitive development?
- Why are disproportionate numbers of students from diverse backgrounds receiving special educational services?
- What general principles can guide us as we try to provide maximally beneficial classroom experiences for *all* students with special needs?

C A S E   S T U D Y : Four Students

Jonathan is a boy with many strengths: He is friendly and outgoing, enjoys playing the trumpet, and is the star pitcher on his Little League baseball team. Academically, Jonathan does average work in mathematics, but he has unusual difficulty with any subject that involves quite a bit of reading. A recent score on a standardized reading achievement test indicates that Jonathan's reading ability is well below that of other students at his grade level.

Andrea is a very aggressive student. When she speaks to other girls, it is usually to insult them, and she frequently starts fights for no apparent reason. Not surprisingly, Andrea has no real friends among her classmates. Furthermore, she has trouble relating with her teachers: She refuses to participate in classroom discussions, doesn't complete assignments, and resists all efforts to help her.

Midori shows great promise in art; her clay sculptures and pen-and-ink drawings often bring awards at local art shows. But Midori has difficulty with language. She must look closely at people's faces when they speak to her and yet still does not always understand their meaning correctly. When she speaks, her voice has a strange monotone and hollow sound to it.

Angelo has an unusually rich vocabulary for a boy his age, using words such as *inordinate* and *commensurate* in his everyday speech. And he seems to know more than most adults do about certain subjects; for example, he reads every book about astronomy and space travel that he can get his hands on. But Angelo is getting poor grades in school because he doesn't complete his classroom assignments; he'd much rather read Carl Sagan's *Cosmos* than do his math homework. Angelo insists that schoolwork is too "boring" to bother with.

- ■ Each of these students is exceptional in one way or another. Can you guess what the "special need" of each student might be?

Inclusion: Educating All Students in General Education Classrooms

Despite normal intelligence (e.g., as evidenced in his average performance in mathematics and his strengths in social skills, music, and baseball), Jonathan has a *learning disability* that hinders his progress in learning to read. Andrea, who has difficulty relating effectively with others, has an *emotional or behavioral disorder.* Midori has trouble understanding and producing spoken language because she is *deaf.* And Angelo finds typical classroom activities boring because he long ago mastered many of the skills now being taught in his classroom; he is intellectually *gifted.*

In the United States, more than two-thirds of students with special educational needs are educated in general education classrooms for part or all of the school day (U.S. Department of Education, 1996). In fact, recent U.S. legislation mandates a practice known as **inclusion:** School districts must educate students with special needs, even those with severe and multiple disabilities, in regular classrooms in their neighborhood schools to the greatest extent possible. Let's look briefly at the history of the inclusion movement in the United States and at federal legislation that lends its support to this movement.

An Historical Overview of the Inclusion Movement

Until the late 1960s, children with significant disabilities—for example, those who were blind, used a wheelchair, or had severe mental retardation—were educated in almost complete isolation from their nondisabled peers (if, in fact, they were educated at all). During the 1800s, the most common approach was to place such students in separate, specialized institutions. In the first half of the twentieth century, students with disabilities began to be educated in public schools, but usually within special classrooms designed for their particular needs. Such **self-contained classes** were smaller than regular classes, were taught by specially trained teachers, and had a curriculum adapted to specific disabilities. It was widely believed that such classes could better promote the educational achievement of students with special needs.

But beginning in the late 1960s, many parents and educators began to question the removal of students with special needs from regular classrooms. In an era of increasing concern for human rights and the equal treatment of people from all racial and ethnic groups, students from ethnic minority groups were nevertheless being placed in special classes (and therefore taken *out* of the typical classroom environment) in greater proportions than nonminorities. Furthermore, researchers frequently found that students did not benefit from special classroom placement: Their academic and social development was no better, and in fact was sometimes worse, than that of similar students who remained in regular classrooms (e.g., Madden & Slavin, 1983).

Laws passed within the past three decades have mandated the increasing integration of students with special needs into classrooms with their nondisabled peers. Initially, such integration often took the form of **mainstreaming:** having students with special needs join regular classes only when their abilities enabled them to participate in normally scheduled activities as successfully as other students. Under such conditions, some students remained in regular classrooms for a good part of the school day but went to "resource rooms" for specialized instruction in areas of particular difficulty (e.g., for reading or mathematics). Other students were nothing more than occasional "visitors" in regular classes, joining their peers primarily for such specialized activities as art, music, and physical education.

Yet many people were concerned—in fact, some were outraged—that such practices gave students a fragmented, inconsistent educational experience and interfered with students' ability to develop normal peer relationships and social skills (e.g., Hahn, 1989; Will, 1986). Others argued that *all* students, even those with severe and multiple disabilities, have the right to be educated in general education classrooms and in their neighborhood schools with their nondisabled peers (e.g., Kunc, 1984; S. Stainback & Stainback, 1985, 1990). They proposed that students with special needs should be able to participate in all aspects of regular school life; in addition to receiving academic instruction with their nondisabled peers, they should be able to join their peers on the playground, in the cafeteria, and in extracurricular activities. This practice of integrating all students with special needs into the overall community and "life" of the neighborhood school embodies the spirit of the inclusion movement.

What additional concerns might people have had about self-contained classes?

Public Law 94–142: The Individuals with Disabilities Education Act (IDEA)

Supporting the inclusion movement, at least in the United States, is key federal legislation that mandates including all students in general education classrooms to the greatest extent possible. In 1975 the U.S. Congress passed Public Law 94–142, which is now known as the **Individuals with Disabilities Education Act (IDEA).** IDEA has been amended several times, in 1983 (P.L. 98–199), 1986 (P.L. 99–457), and 1990 (P.L. 101–476), and it was reauthorized in 1997 (P.L. 105–17). IDEA now grants educational rights to people with cognitive, emotional, or physical disabilities from birth until age 21, and it guarantees several rights for students with disabilities:

- A free and appropriate education
- Fair and nondiscriminatory evaluation
- Education in the least restrictive environment
- An individualized education program
- Due process

These are summarized in Table 5–1. Let's look at each one more closely.

A Free and Appropriate Education

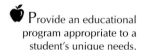
Provide an educational program appropriate to a student's unique needs.

All students with disabilities are entitled to a free educational program designed specifically to meet their unique educational needs. For example, a student with a learning disability who has unusual difficulty with reading is entitled to a special educational program designed to promote greater development of reading skills. This program might involve additional instructional time in reading, a different instructional approach, or tailor-made reading materials. A student who uses a wheelchair may not be able to participate physically in the school's traditional unit on basketball, but she can possibly benefit from some aspects of the unit (for example, practice in dribbling or shooting baskets) and from certain modifications of the sport (e.g., playing in district-wide wheelchair basketball games).

Underlying the guarantee of a free and appropriate education is the concept of *zero reject:* A school district must enroll all students regardless of their disabilities and provide appropriate educational services no matter how severe the disabilities might be. Furthermore, a school district cannot expel students whose inappropriate behavior is caused by their disabilities.

Fair and Nondiscriminatory Evaluation

Why is it important for parents to be included on the multidisciplinary team?

When determining whether a student has a particular disability that requires special services, a team of individuals is formed to conduct an evaluation of that student's specific needs. This multidisciplinary team typically consists of the student's parents or guardians, at least one general education teacher, at least one special education teacher, and often one or more specialists who can appropriately administer evaluation instruments and interpret the results that they yield. If the student is at least 18 years old, he or she is also a member of the evaluation team; in some cases, students younger than 18 may participate in team decision making as well. The exact makeup of each team depends on the needs of the student and varies somewhat from state to state.

To avoid a biased assessment, school personnel use tests and other evaluation tools that can provide an accurate, meaningful, and complete indication of the specific disabling conditions. Evaluation instruments must be administered by individuals trained in their use, and evaluation procedures must take students' backgrounds and any suspected physical or communication difficulties into account. Tests must be administered in students' primary language (e.g., if a student is learning English but has been raised in a Spanish-speaking home, all tests are given in Spanish). Students must be assessed in all areas related to their potential disability and so may be assessed with regard to any one or more of the following characteristics: general intelligence, specific academic aptitude, social and emotional status, communication skills, vision, hearing, health, and motor skills. As a final safeguard, students must be evaluated on the basis of multiple assessment methods, *never* on the basis of a single test score.

PRINCIPLES/ASSUMPTIONS

Five Assumptions on Which the Individuals with Disabilities Education Act (IDEA) Is Based

ASSUMPTION	EXPLANATION	EDUCATIONAL IMPLICATION
A free and appropriate education	Students with disabilities are entitled, free of cost, to an educational program designed to meet their unique educational needs.	Students must be given instruction and materials adapted to their abilities and disabilities. For example, a student who is blind may have reading material in Braille. A student with mental retardation may be given intensive instruction in basic arithmetic and considerable practice working with money.
Fair and nondiscriminatory evaluation	School personnel must use evaluation methods that give a complete, accurate, and meaningful indication of each student's specific educational needs.	Students must be assessed in all areas related to potential disabilities. Evaluation methods must take the student's native language, cultural background, and any suspected physical or communication difficulties into account.
Education in the least restrictive environment	Students with disabilities are entitled to the most typical and standard educational environment that can reasonably meet their specific needs They must also be given sufficient supplementary aids and support services to make success in that environment possible.	Many students with disabilities attend a regular classroom for most or all of the school day, although some of their instruction, materials, and assignments may be adapted to meet their unique educational abilities and needs.
An individualized education program (IEP)	An instructional program for each student must be identified and described in written form. Several things must be specified, including short- and long-term educational goals, the methods used to accomplish these goals, appropriate educational placements, any specialized services that the school will provide, and the procedures used to evaluate the student's progress.	After identifying a particular student's educational needs, a team comprised of teachers, related service providers, and the student's parents or legal guardians (and sometimes the student) collaborate to develop an IEP that addresses how the school district will address those needs. Members of the team touch base regularly to ensure that the student is making reasonable progress. They modify the IEP at least once a year, but more frequently if new needs or issues arise.
Due process	Students' rights, as well as those of parents acting on behalf of their children, must be preserved throughout the decision making process.	Parents (as well as any student who has reached the age of majority) can give or withhold permission to have a student evaluated for special services, and they have the right to see all school records concerning a student. Furthermore, any disagreements between parents and the school district regarding the most appropriate educational program for a student should be addressed through mediation and/or a formal hearing.

Education in the Least Restrictive Environment

The **least restrictive environment** is the most typical and standard educational environment that can reasonably meet a student's needs. Students with disabilities should not be segregated from their classmates; instead, they should be included in the same academic environment, extracurricular activities, and social interactions as their nondisabled peers. The general rule here is that educators must begin by assuming that a student *will*

Provide as typical an educational experience as possible for *all* students in your classes.

be educated within a regular classroom context and given sufficient supplementary aids and support services to make success in that context possible. Exclusion from general education is warranted only when teachers or other students are clearly jeopardized (e.g., as would be the case when a student with an emotional or behavioral disorder is extremely violent) or when, even with proper support and assistance, the student cannot make appreciable progress in meeting educational goals in a general education classroom (Turnbull et al., 1999).

Individualized Education Program (IEP)

An instructional program tailored to the student's strengths and weaknesses, called an **individualized education program (IEP),** must be developed and described in written form for each student identified as having a special educational need. The IEP is typically developed by the same multidisciplinary team (including the regular classroom teacher) that has evaluated the student. All team members agree to and sign the IEP and then continue to review and (if appropriate) revise it at least once a year—more frequently if conditions warrant doing so or if a parent or teacher requests a review.

Use IEPs to plan and implement instruction.

An IEP typically has the following components:

- A description of the student's current educational performance
- Short-term objectives and long-term instructional goals for the student
- The methods to be used in accomplishing the instructional objectives, including the services of any specialists that may be required and any curricular and instructional supports that the school will provide
- Criteria and procedures to be used in evaluating the success of the prescribed methods

If applicable, the team must also describe the extent to which the student will receive some educational programming outside the context of the regular classroom and justify why such placement is in the student's best interests. Figure 5–1 presents a more detailed description of the components of an IEP.

Due Process

Implicit in IDEA is the assumption that a student with disabilities has the same rights as any other U.S. citizen. IDEA mandates several practices that ensure that the student's rights, as well as those of the parents acting on behalf of their child, are preserved throughout the decision making process (Heward, 1996):

- Parents must be notified in writing before the school takes any action (e.g., testing, change in educational placement) that may change their child's educational program.
- Parents can give or withhold permission to have their child evaluated for special education services.
- At their request, parents can see all school records about their child.
- If parents and the school system disagree regarding the most appropriate placement for a child, mediation or a hearing before an impartial individual (someone who is not an employee of the school district) can be used in an attempt to resolve the differences.
- Either parents or the school district may appeal the result of a due process hearing to the state department of education.

Is Inclusion in the Best Interest of Students?

Despite the clear mandates of IDEA, inclusion continues to be a controversial and hotly debated practice among both theorists and practitioners (Brantlinger, 1997; B. K.

FIGURE 5.1

INCLUSION: EDUCATING
ALL STUDENTS IN
GENERAL EDUCATION
CLASSROOMS

173

Typical components of an IEP

The IEP is a written statement for a student, age 3 to 21, who has been identified as having a special educational need. Any IEP that is developed or revised should contain the following:

- The student's present levels of educational performance, including:
  - How the student's disability affects his or her involvement and progress in the general curriculum (for students 6–21 years old), *or*
  - How the child's disability affects his or her participation in appropriate activities (for children 3–5 years old)
- Measurable annual goals, including "benchmarks" or short-term objectives, related to:
  - Meeting needs resulting from the disability, to ensure that the student is involved in and can progress through the general curriculum
  - Meeting each of the student's other disability-related needs
- The special education, related services, supplementary aids, program modifications, and supports that will be provided so that the student can:
  - Advance appropriately toward attaining the annual goals
  - Be involved in and progress through the general curriculum
  - Participate in extracurricular and other nonacademic activities
  - Be educated and participate in general education with other students with disabilities and with students who do not have disabilities
- The extent, if any, to which the student will *not* participate with nondisabled students in general education classes and in extracurricular and other nonacademic activities of the general curriculum, as well as justifications for such exclusion
- How the student's progress toward annual goals will be assessed and how the student's parents will be regularly informed of the student's progress toward those goals
- The projected date for beginning services and program modifications and the anticipated frequency, location, and duration of each
- Any individual modifications in the administration of state or district-wide assessments of student achievement, so that the student can participate in those assessments; moreover, if the IEP determines that the student will not participate in a particular state or district-wide assessment or any part of an assessment, why that assessment is not appropriate for the student and how the student will be alternatively assessed
- Transition plans, including:
  - Beginning at age 14 and each year thereafter, a statement of the student's needs that are related to transition services, including those that focus on the student's courses of study (e.g., the student's participation in advanced-placement courses or in a vocational education program)
  - Beginning at age 16 (or sooner, if the IEP team decides it is appropriate), a statement of needed transition services, including, when appropriate, a statement of the interagency responsibilities or any other needed linkages
  - Beginning at least one year before the student reaches the age of majority under state law (usually at age 18), a statement that the student has been informed of those rights under IDEA that will transfer to the student from the parents when the student becomes of age

Source: Adapted from Exceptional Lives: Special Education in Today's Schools *(2nd ed.) by A. Turnbull, R. Turnbull, M. Shank, and D. Leal, 1999, Upper Saddle River, NJ: Merrill/Prentice Hall. Copyright © 1999. Reprinted with permission of Prentice Hall, Inc., Upper Saddle River, NJ.*

Keogh & MacMillan, 1996; W. Stainback & Stainback, 1992). Some experts worry that when students with special needs are in a regular classroom for the entire school day, they cannot possibly get the intense specialized instruction that many need to achieve essential basic skills in reading, mathematics, and so on (Manset & Semmel, 1997; Zigmond et al., 1995). Others voice the concern that the trend to educate all students in regular classrooms is based more on philosophical grounds than on research results (Lieberman, 1992).

Yet many research studies have yielded results indicating that placement in general education classrooms may have several benefits for students with special needs:

- It often promotes academic achievement equivalent to, and sometimes higher than, the achievement of students in self-contained classes.
- It sometimes promotes more appropriate classroom behavior.
- It clearly provides more frequent opportunities for interaction with nondisabled peers.
- It often leads to more positive self-concepts and greater self-esteem.
- It often leads to more positive attitudes about school.

We are especially likely to see such benefits when regular classroom materials and instruction are tailored to students' specific educational needs and academic levels (Hunt & Goetz, 1997; Madden & Slavin, 1983; Scruggs & Mastropieri, 1994; Semmel, Gottlieb, & Robinson, 1979; Slavin, 1987; S. Stainback & Stainback, 1992). It is important to note, however, that many studies comparing the effectiveness of regular class versus special class placement are correlational rather than experimental studies, making it difficult to draw firm conclusions about causal relationships (Madden & Slavin, 1983; Murphy, 1996; Semmel et al., 1979). Furthermore, research has focused more on students with mild disabilities than severe disabilities and more on students in the elementary grades rather than secondary grades (B. K. Keogh & MacMillan, 1996).

Students with special needs are probably not the only ones who benefit from inclusive practices. Nondisabled students often benefit as well: They develop an increasing awareness of the very heterogeneous nature of the human race and discover that individuals with special needs, apart from some obvious disabilities, are in many respects very much like themselves (Gearheart, Weishahn, & Gearheart, 1992; Hunt & Goetz, 1997; Lewis & Doorlag, 1991). As an example, I think of my son Jeff's friendship with a boy named Evan during their third-grade year:

Why do you think students placed in regular classrooms often have more appropriate classroom behavior? Why do you think they may have better self-concepts and more positive attitudes about school?

Inclusion has benefits for students both with and without disabilities.

Evan was a 10-year-old boy with severe physical and cognitive disabilities. Wheelchair-bound, he had only minimal use of his arms and legs. He was fed by means of a tube inserted into his throat, and a teacher aide was by his side throughout the school day to tend to his health needs. The only recognizable word in Evan's oral vocabulary was *hi*; more often, he simply communicated by making the sound "aaaahhh."

Early in the school year, the third-grade teacher asked Jeff to be a "special friend" to Evan. Jeff sat with Evan in class and at lunch and would talk to him whenever the schedule allowed time for conversation. Jeff would also give Evan things to feel and manipulate; Evan especially liked feeling and playing with the pieces of Velcro on Jeff's winter gloves. The boys' teacher marveled at how Jeff could convince Evan to perform assigned tasks when no one else could.

As Jeff's mother, I saw an additional benefit of Jeff's friendship with Evan. Normally a very shy child, Jeff became increasingly self-confident that he was, indeed, a genuinely likable person. When the two boys passed in the hallway, Evan always made it clear through his gestures and facial expressions that he was delighted to see

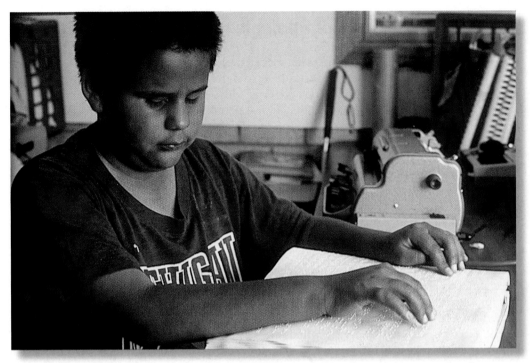

Students with special needs are more successful in the regular classroom when instruction is adapted to meet their individual needs.

Jeff. And on one occasion, when Evan was given the opportunity to invite a friend to accompany him on his weekly trip to the swimming pool, he chose Jeff—an invitation that Jeff considered to be a high honor indeed.

Now, several years later, Jeff's reflections on his friendship are these: "It made me realize that Evan was a person too. It made me realize that I could have a friendship with a boy with disabilities. Doing things that made Evan happy made me happy as well. I knew that *Evan* knew that we were friends."

The Current Conception of Inclusion

In the early years of IDEA—in particular, in the late 1970s and throughout the 1980s—many classroom teachers continued to use regular curriculum and methods for their nondisabled students and adapted the curriculum and methods as necessary to accommodate students with special needs. In such a situation, one or more special education teachers would visit the classroom periodically to give guidance and support or perhaps to provide individualized instruction to students with special needs. But within the past few years, two notable changes have occurred (Turnbull et al., 1999). First, truly inclusive practices require individualization of instruction for *all* students, not just those with identified needs. Such individualization must necessarily entail a major overhaul of traditional curriculum materials and instructional practices, rather than just occasional "add-ons" and modifications. Second, effective teaching is seen as involving an equal, collaborative partnership between regular classroom teachers and special educators; thus, we are likely to see a great deal of **cooperative teaching,** in which at least two teachers teach all students—both those with disabilities and those without—throughout the school day (e.g., Thousand, Villa, & Nevin, 1994).

Before identifying the kinds of curricular materials and instructional practices that are likely to be most effective for students with special educational needs, it may help us to consider how various disabilities are categorized in special education.

General Categories of Students with Special Needs

Why do you think it is so difficult to define some categories of special needs?

The practice of classifying students with special needs has some inherent difficulties. For one thing, experts often disagree about how to define categories of special needs; categories that cannot be described in terms of a readily observable physical condition (e.g., learning disabilities, emotional and behavioral problems, giftedness) are especially difficult to pin down with precise definitions (e.g., Chalfant, 1989; Landesman & Ramey, 1989; Reis, 1989; Turnbull et al., 1999). Experts also disagree about the best ways of identifying members of those categories, yet different methods of identification sometimes lead to different conclusions as to which students have special needs (Kirschenbaum, 1983; Kontos, Carter, Ormrod, & Cooney, 1983; Reis, 1989; Ysseldyke & Algozzine, 1984). Even when experts do agree on such issues, any category of students with special needs includes students who are often as different as they are similar, so these students often require different types of support and services (Adelman, 1996; MacMillan & Meyers, 1979). A final concern is that labels such as "mentally retarded" or "learning disabled" may unintentionally communicate the message that students with special needs are somehow inferior; thus, these labels may adversely affect self-esteem. It is important to note, however, that some students with special needs develop low self-esteem as a result of their disabilities (perhaps because other people treat them as "different") before any label is ever applied to them at school (M. C. Reynolds, 1984).

Despite these disadvantages, most educators continue to classify students with special needs because of the advantages in doing so. Although members of the same category are in some respects very different from one another, they also tend to have characteristics in common; these similarities allow educators to make certain generalizations about how to foster the academic and social development of students in any given category. In addition, special needs categories provide a rallying point around which social and political forces can promote the interests of these students. For example, over the years such organizations as the American Association on Mental Retardation and the Autism Society of America, and such journals as the *Journal of Learning Disabilities* and *Gifted Child Quarterly*, have emerged to support these students. Special interest groups are often instrumental in collecting information, supporting and publishing research, and facilitating federal and state legislation to help students with special needs (Hobbs, 1980).

But probably the most influential factor affecting educators' use of categories and labels, at least in the United States, is that federal funds, available to support special educational services for up to 12 percent of the student population, are provided only when students have been formally identified as having a particular disabling condition. In accordance with IDEA, federal funds are provided to support special services for students who fall within the following categories of special needs:

- Specific learning disabilities
- Speech or language impairments
- Emotional disturbance
- Autism
- Mental retardation, including severe and multiple disabilities
- Orthopedic impairments (physical disabilities)
- Traumatic brain injury
- Hearing impairments, including deafness
- Visual impairments, including blindness
- Other health impairments

Special educators do not necessarily use the classification system and labels of IDEA (e.g., Heward, 1996; Turnbull et al., 1999). In the remainder of the chapter, we will be using terminology and categories that are more broadly used in the field of special education. For example, rather than talk about "emotional disturbance," we will use the term *emotional or behavioral disorder*. And rather than discuss traumatic brain injury as a separate disability, we will include it under our discussion of *physical and health impairments*.

Using People-First Language

▣ Experiencing Firsthand
The Importance of Being Fatheaded

The person who sold you this book told me that you have an unusually large head. I consulted with your professor and a few of your classmates, who confirmed the report: You do indeed have a big head.

So, you fatheaded person, continue reading. As a fathead, you will undoubtedly learn a great deal about students with special needs in the pages that follow. You will not, however, learn anything about fatheaded people, because little research has been conducted on fatheads, and there is no evidence to indicate that fatheads require special educational services.

At the same time, you may want to seek out other fatheads who attend the same institution that you do. You will undoubtedly find that you have a great deal in common with them; for instance, all of you cast big shadows and have very strong neck muscles. Furthermore, you can consult with the other fatheads about places to shop for extra-large hats and giant-size bottles of shampoo.

Did I offend you just now? If so, why? Look back at the passage and try to identify what I might have said to rub you the wrong way. But at the same time, assume that my assessment is accurate—that you do, indeed, have a large head.

One thing that may have offended you is the fact that once I determined that you were a fathead, that label dominated everything that I thought and said about you. In reality, even though you are fatheaded, you have many other traits as well, including, almost certainly, some very admirable ones. Perhaps you are intelligent, likable, considerate, and honest, with a good sense of humor and high moral standards. The label *fatheaded* dominated my characterization of you, to the exclusion of your many other qualities.

Special educators worry that attaching certain labels to students may have this kind of effect—that it may focus our attention on a particular disabling condition rather than on the many ways in which students are in other respects just ordinary human beings. To minimize such an effect, special educators urge us all to use **people-first language** whenever we refer to students with disabilities—in other words, to mention the person *before* the disability. For instance, we might say *students with mental retardation* rather than *mentally retarded student* or *student who is blind* rather than *blind student*. Placing the person before the disability when we speak can help us remind both ourselves and others that a disability is only one of many characteristics that a particular student has.

Use people-first language.

An Overall Organizational Scheme

In the next five sections of the chapter, I will organize our discussion of students with various special needs using the five general categories that appear in the "Students in Inclusive Settings" tables throughout the book. Table 5–2 lists the specific kinds of special needs that fall within each category.

Note that two of the special needs listed in Table 5–2—attention-deficit hyperactivity disorder (ADHD) and giftedness—are not specifically covered by IDEA. A few children

TABLE 5.2

General and Specific Categories of Students with Special Needs

GENERAL CATEGORY	SPECIFIC CATEGORIES	DESCRIPTION
Students with specific cognitive or academic difficulties	Learning disabilities	Difficulties in specific cognitive processes (e.g., in perception, language, memory, or metacognition) that cannot be attributed to such other disabilities as mental retardation, emotional or behavioral disorders, or sensory impairments.
	Attention-deficit hyperactivity disorder (ADHD)	Disorder marked by either or both of these characteristics: (a) difficulty focusing and maintaining attention and (b) frequent hyperactive and impulsive behavior.
	Speech and communication disorders	Abnormalities in spoken language (e.g., mispronunciations of certain sounds, stuttering, or abnormal syntactical patterns) or language comprehension that significantly interfere with classroom performance.
Students with social or behavioral problems	Emotional or behavioral disorders	Emotional states or behaviors that are present over a substantial period of time, to the point where they significantly disrupt academic learning and performance.
	Autism	Condition marked by varying degrees of impaired social interaction and communication, repetitive behaviors, and restricted interests; a strong need for a predictable environment is also commonly observed.
Students with general delays in cognitive and social functioning	Mental retardation	Condition marked by significantly below-average general intelligence and deficits in adaptive behavior (i.e., in practical and social intelligence).
Students with physical or sensory challenges	Physical and health impairments	Physical or medical conditions (usually long-term) marked by one or more of these three characteristics: limited energy and strength, reduced mental alertness, or little muscle control.
	Visual impairments	Malfunctions of the eyes or optic nerves that prevent normal vision even with corrective lenses.
	Hearing loss	Malfunctions of the ear or associated nerves that interfere with the perception of sounds within the frequency range of normal speech.
	Severe and multiple disabilities	Presence of two or more of the disabilities listed above, the combination of which requires significant adaptations and highly specialized educational services.
Students with advanced cognitive development	Giftedness	Unusually high ability or aptitude in one or more of these areas: general intellectual ability, aptitude in a specific academic field, creativity, visual or performing arts, or leadership.

with ADHD may fall within the IDEA category "other health impairments" (Heward, 1996); others are entitled to reasonable educational accommodations under other federal legislation (Section 504 of the Rehabilitation Act [P.L. 93–112] and the Americans with Disabilities Act [P.L. 101–336]). The Jacob K. Javits Gifted and Talented Student Education Act (P.L. 103–382) encourages, but does not necessarily mandate, school districts to provide special educational services for students who are gifted. Most gifted students are unlikely to reach their full potential within the context of regular classroom assignments and activities; for this reason, many school districts *do* provide special programs for these students.

Students with Specific Cognitive or Academic Difficulties

Some students with special educational needs may show few if any outward signs of physical disability and yet still appear to have cognitive difficulties that interfere with their ability to learn academic material or perform typical classroom tasks. This section describes three categories of special needs that involve specific cognitive or academic difficulties: learning disabilities, attention-deficit hyperactivity disorder, and speech and communication disorders.

Learning Disabilities

Remember Jonathan, the first student in the case study at the beginning of the chapter? Jonathan exhibits average performance in mathematics and has notable strengths in social skills, music, and baseball. Yet Jonathan's reading skills are well below grade level. Despite his ability to handle many aspects of his life, Jonathan has a learning disability that hinders his progress in learning to read.

Students with **learning disabilities** comprise the largest single category of students with special needs (U.S. Department of Education, 1996). Educators have not reached complete agreement about how best to define this category. Nevertheless, most apply the following criteria when classifying a student as having a learning disability (Mercer, Jordan, Allsopp, & Mercer, 1996; National Joint Committee on Learning Disabilities, 1994):

- *The student has significant difficulties in one or more specific cognitive processes.* For instance, the student may have difficulties in perception, language, memory, or metacognition. Such difficulties are typically present throughout the individual's life and are assumed to result from a specific, possibly inherited dysfunction of the central nervous system (J. G. Light & Defries, 1995; Manis, 1996). Figure 5–2 lists some of the forms that a student's learning disability may take.

- *The student's difficulties cannot be attributed to other disabilities, such as mental retardation, an emotional or behavioral disorder, hearing loss, or a visual impairment.* Many students with learning disabilities have average or above-average intelligence. For example, they may obtain average scores on an intelligence test, or at least on most of its subtests.

- *The student's difficulties interfere with academic achievement to such a degree that special educational services are warranted.* Students with learning disabilities invariably show poor performance in one or more specific areas of the academic curriculum; their achievement in those areas is much lower than we would expect based on their overall intelligence level. At the same time, they may exhibit achievement consistent with their intelligence in other subjects. Consider once again Jonathan's average performance in math but below-average performance in reading. This uneven pattern in Jonathan's achievement is typical of students with learning disabilities.

FIGURE 5.2

Examples of cognitive processing deficiencies in students with learning disabilities

Perceptual difficulty: Students may have difficulty understanding or remembering the information they receive through a particular sensory modality. For example, they may have trouble perceiving subtle differences between similar sounds in speech (a difficulty in auditory discrimination), retaining a clear image of letters they have seen (a difficulty in visual-spatial perception), or remembering the correct order of letters in a word (a difficulty in memory for a visual sequence).

Memory difficulty: Students may appear to have less capacity to remember the information they receive, either over the short or long run; more specifically, they may have problems with either *working memory* or *long-term memory* (see Chapter 6).

Metacognitive difficulty: Students may have difficulty using effective learning strategies, monitoring their progress toward learning goals, and in other ways directing their own learning.

Difficulty processing oral language: Students may have trouble understanding spoken language or remembering what they have been told.

Reading difficulty: Students may have trouble recognizing printed words or comprehending what they read. An extreme form of this condition is known as *dyslexia*.

Written language difficulty: Students may have problems in handwriting, spelling, or expressing themselves coherently on paper. An extreme form of this condition is known as *dysgraphia*.

Mathematical difficulty: Students may have trouble thinking about or remembering information involving numbers. For example, they may have a poor sense of time or direction or they may have difficulty learning basic number facts.

Difficulty with social perception: Students may have trouble interpreting the social cues and signals that others give them (for example, they may have difficulty perceiving another person's feelings or reactions to a situation) and therefore may respond inappropriately in social situations.

Sources: *Conte, 1991; Eden, Stein, & Wood, 1995; Landau & McAninch, 1993; Lerner, 1985; H. L. Swanson, 1993; H. L. Swanson & Cooney, 1991; Turnbull et al., 1999; Wong, 1991a, 1991b.*

Common Characteristics

Students identified as having a learning disability are a particularly heterogeneous group—they are probably far more different than they are similar (Bassett et al., 1996; Chalfant, 1989; National Joint Committee on Learning Disabilities, 1994). Students with learning disabilities typically have many strengths; however, some may display such characteristics as these:

- Distractibility (i.e., inability to sustain attention when confronted with competing stimuli)
- A "passive" approach to learning rather than active involvement in a learning task (for example, staring at a textbook page without thinking about the meaning of the words printed on the page)
- Ineffective learning and memory strategies and resulting difficulties in remembering information
- Poor self-concept and low motivation regarding academic tasks (especially when they receive no remedial assistance in their areas of difficulty)
- Poor motor skills
- Poor social skills
  (T. Bryan, 1991; Chapman, 1988; Gearheart et al., 1992; Gresham & MacMillan, 1997; Mercer, 1991; Ormrod & Lewis, 1985; H. L. Swanson, 1993; H. L. Swanson & Cooney, 1991; Turnbull et al., 1999; Wong, 1991a)

It is important to remember that the characteristics listed in Figure 5–2 are typical of many students with learning disabilities, but they certainly do not describe *all* of these students. For instance, some students with learning disabilities are attentive in class and work diligently on assignments, and some are socially skillful and quite popular with their peers (Heward, 1996).

Learning disabilities may also manifest themselves somewhat differently in elementary and secondary school students (Lerner, 1985). At the elementary level, students with learning disabilities are likely to exhibit poor attention and motor skills and often have trouble acquiring one or more basic skills. As these students reach the upper elementary grades they may also begin to show emotional problems, due at least partly to frustration about their repeated academic failures.

At the secondary school level, difficulties with attention and motor skills may diminish. But at this level, students with learning disabilities may be particularly susceptible to emotional problems. On top of dealing with the usual emotional issues of adolescence (e.g., dating, peer pressure), they must also deal with the more stringent demands of the junior high and high

Students with learning disabilities often have less effective learning and memory skills, lower self-esteem, and less motivation to succeed at academic tasks.

school curricula. Learning in secondary schools is highly dependent on reading and learning from relatively sophisticated textbooks, yet the average high school student with a learning disability reads at a third- to fifth-grade level and has acquired few if any effective study strategies (Alley & Deshler, 1979; E. S. Ellis & Friend, 1991). To get a sense of how these students may feel under such circumstances, try the following exercise.

Experiencing Firsthand
A Reading Assignment

Read the following passage carefully. I will be testing you on its contents later in the chapter.

> Personality research needs to refocus on global traits because such traits are an important part of everyday social discourse, because they embody a good deal of folk wisdom and common sense, because understanding and evaluating trait judgments can provide an important route toward the improvement of social judgment, and because global traits offer legitimate, if necessarily incomplete, explanations of behavior. A substantial body of evidence supporting the existence of global traits includes personality correlates of behavior, interjudge agreement in personality ratings, and the longitudinal stability of personality over time. Future research should clarify the origins of global traits, the dynamic mechanisms through which they influence behavior, and the behavioral cues through which they can most accurately be judged. (Funder, 1991, p. 31)

How well do you think you will perform on the upcoming test covering the passage?

You probably found the passage more challenging to read than the rest of the chapter. In fact, this passage is a fairly typical one from *Psychological Science,* a professional journal written for people with advanced educations; many of its readers hold doctoral degrees. Essentially, I was asking you to read something that was written well above your usual reading level. (If it's any consolation, I won't *really* be testing you on its contents.)

I hope that, during the exercise, you experienced just a little bit of the frustration that high school students with learning disabilities probably experience on a daily basis. Yet secondary school teachers rarely teach reading or study skills as a part of their course content (Lerner, 1985). For many students with learning disabilities, school success may constantly feel like an uphill battle. Perhaps for this reason, students with learning disabilities are among those most at risk for dropping out of school (Barga, 1996).

Adapting Instruction

As we have seen, students with learning disabilities comprise a very heterogeneous group, and instructional strategies must be tailored to their specific strengths and weaknesses. Nevertheless, there are several strategies that should benefit a broad range of students:

🍎 Minimize distractions.

• *Minimize potentially distracting stimuli.* Because many students with learning disabilities are easily distracted, we should minimize the presence of other stimuli likely to compete for their attention. For example, we might make sure that the classroom is fairly quiet during seatwork time. Or we might pull down window shades when students in other classes are playing in the schoolyard.

🍎 Present the same idea in several different ways.

• *Use multiple modalities to present information.* Some students with learning disabilities have difficulty learning information through a particular modality—for example, through seeing or listening. We therefore need to be flexible in the modalities we use to communicate information to these students. In different situations, we might want to use visual, auditory, tactile (touch), or even kinesthetic (movement) approaches (J. W. Wood, 1989). For example, when teaching a student how to read and spell a particular word, we might write the word for the student (visual input), say its letters aloud (auditory input), have the student feel the word spelled with letters cut out of sandpaper (tactile input), have the student trace or write the word (kinesthetic), and have the student repeat the word's letters (both kinesthetic and auditory). In our lectures to secondary students, we may want to incorporate videos, graphics, and other visual materials; we might also encourage students to audiotape the lectures (J. W. Wood & Rosbe, 1985).

🍎 Look at errors for clues about processing difficulties.

• *Analyze students' errors for clues about their processing difficulties.* Like anyone else, students with learning disabilities are likely to make errors in responding to questions, problems, and other academic tasks. Rather than thinking of certain responses simply as being wrong, we can look closely at errors for clues about the specific difficulties students are having (Lerner, 1985). For example, a student who solves a subtraction problem this way:

$$\begin{array}{r} 65 \\ -28 \\ \hline 43 \end{array}$$

may be applying an inappropriate rule (*always subtract the smaller number from the larger one*) to subtraction. A student who reads the sentence:

I drove the car.

as "I drove the *cat*" may be having trouble using context clues in reading words and sentences. A student who reads the same sentence as "I drove the *cab*" may be overly dependent on context and not attending closely enough to the words that actually appear on the page. Analyzing a student's errors, then, is an important step in identifying the knowledge and skills that may require remediation.

- *Teach learning and memory strategies.* Still another way of helping students with learning disabilities is to provide specific strategies for helping them learn information. For example, we might teach students to give themselves mental "instructions" that help them follow the appropriate steps of a task (Turnbull et al., 1999). We might teach them how to take notes and then periodically monitor their notes for accuracy and completeness (J. W. Wood & Rosbe, 1985). We might also teach them certain **mnemonics,** or "memory tricks," to help them learn new information (Mastropieri & Scruggs, 1992). As an example, Figure 5–3 presents one very simple mnemonic—a way of helping students remember the difference between the letters *b* and *d.* Additional strategies likely to help students with learning disabilities are described in Chapters 6 and 8.

Teach learning
strategies.

- *Provide study aids.* In addition to teaching more effective study strategies, we can also provide scaffolding that facilitates the sometimes overwhelming task of studying classroom material. For instance, we can provide study guides that help students identify important ideas (Mastropieri & Scruggs, 1992). We can show how material is organized, perhaps with outlines that enumerate major and subordinate ideas or with graphics that show how key concepts are interrelated (Brigham & Scruggs, 1995; J. W. Wood & Rosbe, 1985). We can let students copy the notes of a classmate who is a particularly good note taker (Turnbull et al., 1999).

Providing scaffolding
to facilitate effective
studying.

These teaching strategies don't necessarily apply only to students with learning disabilities. Many of them should also be helpful when working with students with attention-deficit hyperactivity disorder, a category of special needs that we turn to now.

Attention-Deficit Hyperactivity Disorder (ADHD)

Distractibility and impulsive behavior were two of the characteristics I listed as being sometimes associated with a learning disability. These characteristics are even more frequently observed when a student has **attention-deficit hyperactivity disorder.** This category of special needs is marked by either or both of the following characteristics (American Psychiatric Association, 1994; Landau & McAninch, 1993; Turnbull et al., 1999):

- *Inattention.* The student may have considerable difficulty focusing and maintaining attention on whatever task is at hand; he or she is easily distracted either by external stimuli or by internal thought processes. Such inattentiveness may manifest itself in such behaviors as daydreaming, difficulty listening to and following directions, frequent and careless mistakes, and an inability to persist at tasks that require sustained mental effort.

- *Hyperactivity and impulsivity.* The student may seem to have an excess amount of energy; for instance, he or she is likely to be fidgety, move around the classroom at inappropriate times, talk excessively, and have difficulty working or playing quietly. In addition, the student may show such impulsive behaviors as blurting out answers, interrupting others, and acting without thinking about the potential consequences of behaviors. Such impulsive behaviors may reflect a general inability to delay responses to external stimuli (Barkley, 1994).

The lowercase letters *b* and *d* are frequently confused by young students with learning disabilities. Clenched fists, with the palms facing away from the student and the little fingers pointing upward, form rough representations of these two letters. By "reading" their hands in the normal left-to-right fashion, students can more easily remember the difference between *b* and *d*—*b* comes first in both the alphabet and the fists.

FIGURE 5.3

A mnemonic for remembering the letters *b* and *d*

It is important to note that some students with ADHD have only *one* of these characteristics. For instance, some students with attention difficulties may be *under-* rather than overactive, to the point where they actually appear listless and apathetic (Barkley, 1990; Turnbull et al., 1999).

ADHD is assumed to have a biological and possibly genetic origin (Barkley, 1995b; Landau & McAninch, 1993). It seems to run in families and is three times as likely to be identified in boys as in girls (Conte, 1991; Faraone et al., 1995). But once identified as having ADHD, many students can be helped to control the symptoms through medication (e.g., Ritalin).

Common Characteristics

In addition to inattentiveness, hyperactivity, and impulsivity, students identified as having ADHD may have characteristics such as these:

- Information processing difficulties
- Exceptional imagination and creativity
- Classroom behavior problems (e.g., disruptiveness, noncompliance with classroom rules)
- Difficulty making smooth transitions from one classroom activity to another
- Few friendships with peers, and possible outright rejection by them (Barkley, 1995b; Gresham & MacMillan, 1997; Grodzinsky & Diamond, 1992; Hallowell, 1996; Lahey & Carlson, 1991; Landau & McAninch, 1993)

Some students with ADHD may also be identified as having a learning disability or an emotional or behavioral disorder, yet others may be gifted (Conte, 1991; Hallowell, 1996; Reeve, 1990). The characteristics associated with ADHD typically last throughout the school years and into adulthood (Claude & Firestone, 1995); perhaps as a result of the difficulties that such characteristics may create in school, students with ADHD are at greater risk than normal for dropping out of school (Barkley, 1995b).

Adapting Instruction

Researchers and practitioners have offered several suggestions for helping students with attention-deficit hyperactivity disorder:

Teach attention-
focusing strategies.

- *Teach strategies that help students focus their attention on classroom tasks.* As is true for students with learning disabilities, we can certainly remove stimuli that are likely to compete for a student's attention. But in addition, we can teach the student strategies for specifically keeping his or her attention on a task at hand (Buchoff, 1990). For instance, we can ask the student to keep his or her eyes on us when we're giving directions or providing new information. We can also tell the student what specifically to listen for; for instance, we might say, "Listen carefully while I explain the things you should include in your essay." And we can encourage the student to move to a new location if the current one presents too many distracting sights or sounds.

Teach strategies for
controlling hyperactivity
and impulsivity.

- *Teach strategies for controlling hyperactivity and impulsivity.* To help students control excess energy, we might give them a "settling-in" time after recess or lunch before we ask them to engage in any activity that involves quiet concentration (Pellegrini & Horvat, 1995); for instance, many elementary teachers begin the afternoon by reading a chapter from a high-interest storybook. We can also teach students strategies for resisting the tendency to respond too quickly and impulsively to questions and problems; for example, Chapter 11 describes *self-instructions* as a way of controlling impulsive behavior. And we must certainly make sure that our students have regular opportunities to release pent-up energy, such as during recess and physical education.

Help students use time
effectively.

- *Teach strategies for organizing and using time effectively.* As noted earlier, many students with ADHD are daydreamers, and so the school day may often slip by without their having accomplished assigned tasks. These students may overestimate

INTO THE CLASSROOM: Helping Students with Specific Cognitive or Academic Difficulties

Give students the extra structure they may need to succeed on academic tasks.

A teacher provides a particular format for writing an expository paragraph: one sentence expressing the main idea, followed by three sentences that support the idea and a final, concluding sentence.

Help students pay attention.

A teacher has a student with attention-deficit hyperactivity disorder sit near her desk, away from distractions that classmates may provide; she also encourages the student to keep his desk clear of all objects and materials except those with which he is presently working (Buchoff, 1990).

When reading difficulties are evident, minimize dependence on reading materials or provide materials written at a lower level.

For two high school students reading well below grade level, a teacher finds some supplementary reading materials related to the topics the class is studying; although written for adults, these materials use simpler language than the class textbook. The teacher also meets with the students once a week for verbal explanations of class material and a hands-on exploration of scientific principles.

Look at students' errors for clues about possible processing difficulties.

When a student spells *refrigerator* as "refegter" and *hippopotamus* as "hepopoms," her teacher hypothesizes that she has difficulty relating written words to the phonetic sounds they represent.

the time available to them; they may perceive time to move more slowly than it actually does (Barkley, 1995a). We can do several things to help students use class time more effectively. We can show them how to establish a daily routine (including times to sharpen pencils, gather work materials together, etc.) and post that routine on their desks (Buchoff, 1990). We can break large tasks into smaller ones and set a deadline for each subtask (Barkley, 1995a). We can provide daily or weekly "to-do" lists on which students check off completed assignments (Buchoff, 1990; J. W. Wood & Rosbe, 1985). And we can provide a folder in which students can transport their homework assignments to and from school (Buchoff, 1990).

• *Teach and encourage appropriate classroom behaviors.* A structured environment with clear expectations for behavior and definite consequences for appropriate and inappropriate actions is often effective when dealing with students who have ADHD (Barkley, 1990; Buchoff, 1990; Landau & McAninch, 1993; N. Nussbaum & Bigler, 1990). Our discussion of *applied behavior analysis* and *positive behavioral support* in Chapter 10 will provide many useful strategies for creating such an environment.

Teach appropriate behaviors.

Speech and Communication Disorders

THINKING ABOUT WHAT YOU KNOW

If you have studied a foreign language, think back to your early attempts to speak the language. Did you feel awkward, knowing that your pronunciation and grammar were almost certainly flawed? Did you sometimes worry that your imperfect speech might make you look foolish to your teacher or classmates? If you had such feelings, then you perhaps have an inkling of how many students with speech and communication disorders feel when they are asked to speak in class.

Speech and communication disorders are abnormalities in spoken language or in language comprehension that significantly interfere with students' classroom performance. Examples include persistent articulation problems (mispronunciations of certain sounds and words), stuttering, abnormal syntactical patterns, and difficulty understanding the speech of others. Speech and communication disorders are also suspected when students fail to demonstrate age-appropriate language (e.g., a kindergartner who communicates only by pointing and gesturing, or a third grader who says, "Him go," instead of, "He's gone"). In many cases, the exact causes of these disorders are unknown (Wang & Baron, 1997).

The great majority of students with speech and communication disorders are in general education classrooms for most or all of the school day (U.S. Department of Education, 1996). Some of these students may have other disabilities as well, such as hearing loss or mental retardation (Turnbull et al., 1999). But many others are, in all other respects, just typical students.

Common Characteristics

Several characteristics are frequently, although not always, observed in students with speech and communication disorders:

- Reluctance to speak
- Embarrassment and self-consciousness when speaking
- Difficulties in reading and writing
  (Fey, Catts, & Larrivee, 1995; LaBlance, Steckol, & Smith, 1994; Patton et al., 1987; Rice, Hadley, & Alexander, 1993)

Adapting Instruction

Typically a trained specialist will work with students to help them improve or overcome their speech and communication difficulties—perhaps within the regular classroom context or perhaps in a separate setting. Nevertheless, regular classroom teachers can assist in several ways:

Gently encourage students to talk.

- *Encourage regular oral communication.* Because students with speech and communication disorders need as much practice in classroom-based "public" speaking as their classmates, we can encourage them to talk in class, provided that doing so does not produce exceptional stress for them (Patton et al., 1987).

Listen patiently.

- *Listen patiently.* When students have difficulty expressing themselves, we may be tempted to assist them—for example, by finishing their sentences. But we better help students with speech and communication disorders when we allow them to complete their own thoughts, no matter how long it takes them to do so. We must learn to listen attentively and politely to students with speech problems without criticizing or ridiculing them, and we must encourage other students to do likewise (Lewis & Doorlag, 1991; Patton et al., 1987; J. W. Wood, 1989).

Ask for clarification when necessary.

- *Ask for clarification when the message is unclear.* On occasions when we haven't understood what students are saying, we should explain the things we *did* understand and ask them to clarify the rest. Honest feedback helps students learn how well they are communicating (Patton et al., 1987).

General Recommendations for Students with Specific Cognitive or Academic Difficulties

In addition to the instructional strategies described in the previous pages, there are several more general strategies we can use to help students with specific cognitive or academic difficulties:

- *Promote success on academic tasks.* Many of the students just described, especially those with learning disabilities or attention-deficit hyperactivity disorder, perform poorly on academic tasks and assignments. They may lack some of the basic concepts and skills that their nondisabled peers have already acquired and so need individualized instruction and practice to fill in the gaps. Many theorists suggest that one or another form of *direct instruction,* whereby students are specifically taught the things they need to learn, is the most effective approach (E. S. Ellis & Friend, 1991; Tarver, 1992; Turnbull et al., 1999); Chapter 13 presents instructional strategies involved in direct instruction. Other theorists recommend that we also teach students specific ways of *thinking* about classroom tasks. For example, when we teach students how to write stories or essays, we should give them extensive instruction and practice in each phase of the writing process: planning, drafting, editing, and revising (Hallenbeck, 1996).

- *Clearly describe expectations for academic performance.* Students will have an easier time performing classroom tasks successfully when they know exactly what we expect them to do. We may sometimes need to explain in very concrete and precise terms what an assigned task entails. For instance, before students begin a science lab activity, we may want to remind them about how they should carefully follow the steps described on the lab sheet, what safety precautions they should take while using the equipment, and what components they should be sure to include in their lab reports.

- *Consider students' reading skills when assigning reading materials.* Many students with specific cognitive or academic difficulties have poor reading skills. We may therefore need to consider methods of presenting academic content other than using standard grade-level textbooks. As alternatives, we might reduce the amount of reading required of these students, substitute materials written at a simpler (yet not "babyish") level, or present information through some medium other than written text (E. S. Ellis & Friend, 1991; Lewis & Doorlag, 1991; Semmel et al., 1979; Turnbull et al., 1999).

- *Take steps to enhance self-confidence and motivation.* Because students with specific cognitive or academic difficulties have typically had a history of failure at certain kinds of tasks—especially tasks that seem to come easily to their classmates—they are likely to have little self-confidence and little motivation with regard to those tasks. It may be especially important, then, that we help students recognize that they are making progress and that they do some things very well (Buchoff, 1990). For example, we can set daily goals for them that we know they can attain. We can have them keep journals in which they describe the successes they have achieved each day. And we can give them opportunities to do tasks that they enjoy and usually perform successfully (Buchoff, 1990).

Some students with learning disabilities or ADHD may have social or behavioral problems as well as academic difficulties. It is to this general category of special needs that we turn now.

Promote academic success from the very beginning.

Describe expectations for academic performance.

Reduce dependence on grade-level reading materials for teaching academic content.

Enhance students' self-confidence.

Chapters 11 and 12 describe the nature of self-confidence (or *self-efficacy*) and its role in motivation.

Students with Social or Behavioral Problems

Many students have minor social, emotional, or behavioral difficulties at one time or another, especially during times of unusual stress or major life changes. Such difficulties are often temporary, especially when the students have the support of caring adults. Yet a few students show a pattern of behavioral problems that seriously interfere with their academic learning and performance, to the point where they require special educational services. This section looks at two groups of students who fall into this category: those with emotional and behavioral disorders and those with autism.

Emotional and Behavioral Disorders

Our opening case study introduced Andrea, a particularly aggressive student who has difficulty relating effectively with others and refuses to become involved in classroom activities. Students with an **emotional or behavioral disorder** become identified as students with special needs—and therefore as students who qualify for special educational services—when their problems have a substantial negative effect on classroom success and achievement. As is true for students with learning disabilities, students with emotional and behavioral disorders exhibit a wide variety of problems and are often more different from one another than they are similar. Examples of such problems include an inability to establish and maintain satisfactory interpersonal relationships with adults and peers, excessive and long-term depression or anxiety, exaggerated mood swings, and exceptionally aggressive or antisocial behavior.

Emotional and behavioral disorders are often divided into two broad categories. **Externalizing behaviors** have direct or indirect effects on other people; examples are aggression, defiance, disobedience, lying, stealing, and lack of self-control. **Internalizing behaviors** primarily affect the student with the problem; examples are anxiety, depression, withdrawal from social interaction, eating disorders, and suicidal tendencies. Although students with externalizing behaviors are those that teachers are more likely to refer for evaluation and possible special services (M. M. Kerr & Nelson, 1989), students with internalizing behaviors are often at just as much risk for school failure.

Many emotional and behavioral disorders are believed to result from environmental factors, such as child abuse, inconsistent parenting practices, stressful living conditions, exposure to violence, and family drug or alcohol abuse (H. C. Johnson & Friesen, 1993; Patterson, DeBaryshe, & Ramsey, 1989; Shaffer, 1988). At the same time, biological causes, such as heredity, chemical imbalances, brain injuries, and illnesses, may also contribute to emotional and behavioral problems (Hallowell, 1996; H. C. Johnson & Friesen, 1993). Some students with genetic predispositions for emotional or behavioral disorders exhibit few if any signs of a problem until adolescence; consider the case of Kirk:

> As a high school freshman, Kirk was a well-behaved, likable student who was getting As and Bs in his classes and showed particular promise in science and mathematics. During his sophomore year, however, his grades began to slip, and he occasionally exhibited mildly hostile or defiant behaviors. Concerned, Kirk's parents and teachers imposed stricter limits on his behavior, but Kirk increasingly resisted such attempts to keep him in line. By the end of his junior year, Kirk was hanging out regularly with high school dropouts who engaged in minor criminal activities, and his grades had fallen to Cs and Ds.
>
> When Kirk failed three classes during the fall of his senior year, thereby jeopardizing his chances of graduating with his class, the school principal called him, his parents, and his faculty advisor to a meeting to determine how to help Kirk get back on track. At the meeting, the principal described several occasions on which Kirk had acted disoriented, belligerent, and seemingly "high" on marijuana or some other illegal substance. At this point, an appropriate and constructive response on Kirk's part would have been to appear contrite and willing to change his behavior so that he could graduate—an essential goal given his strong desire to attend college the following year. Instead, Kirk sat at the meeting smirking (seemingly gleeful about the anger he had instilled in others) and focusing his attention on picking the peanuts

Have you ever had a classmate who had emotional or behavioral problems severe enough to interfere with his or her academic achievement?

out of a bowl of trail mix on the conference room table. By the end of the meeting, the principal was so infuriated by his behavior that she expelled him from school.

A few days after his expulsion, Kirk was arrested for carrying an illegal weapon (a knife) on school property. Over the next two weeks, as he waited in the juvenile detention facility for his court hearing, his mental condition deteriorated rapidly, and the judge eventually ordered his hospitalization in the state mental institution. Kirk was eventually diagnosed with bipolar disorder, a condition (often inherited) characterized by excessive mood swings (hence, the disorder is sometimes called manic depression) and, in some cases, distorted (psychotic) thought processes.

Factors at school may exacerbate the problems that these students already have. Their inappropriate behaviors not only interfere with academic achievement but also incur rejection by their classmates, thus leading to social as well as academic failure. Many students, especially those with externalizing behaviors, may eventually seek the companionship of the few peers who *will* accept them—peers who typically behave in similarly inappropriate ways. Antisocial students often provide mutual support for one another's antisocial behavior and may introduce one another to drugs, alcohol, or criminal activity (Patterson et al., 1989). Such difficulties undoubtedly contribute to the high dropout rate of students with emotional and behavioral disorders: Fewer than 50 percent graduate from high school (Bassett et al., 1996; Koyanagi & Gaines, 1993).

Why are these students so often disliked by their classmates?

Common Characteristics

Although students with emotional and behavioral disorders are a very heterogeneous group indeed, several characteristics are often observed in students in this category:

- Difficulty interacting with others in socially acceptable ways
- Difficulty establishing and maintaining satisfactory interpersonal relationships
- Poor self-concept
- Frequent absences from school
- Deteriorating academic performance with increasing age
  (DuPaul & Eckert, 1994; Leiter & Johnsen, 1997; Morgan & Jenson, 1988; Richards, Symons, Greene, & Szuszkiewicz, 1995; Semmel et al., 1979; Turnbull et al., 1999; J. W. Wood, 1989)

Some students with emotional or behavioral disorders have other special needs as well, including learning disabilities, mental retardation, or giftedness (Fessler, Rosenberg, & Rosenberg, 1991; Turnbull et al., 1999).

Adapting Instruction

Effective educational programs for students with emotional and behavioral disorders are usually individualized and tailored to the unique needs of each student. Nevertheless, several strategies may benefit many of these students:

- *Show an interest in students' well-being.* Many students with emotional and behavioral disorders have few positive and productive relationships with individuals outside school; we can often help these students simply by showing them that we care about their welfare (Diamond, 1991). For example, we can greet them warmly when we see them in the hallway. We can express concern when they seem upset, worried, or overly stressed. We can lend a ready and supportive ear when they want to share their ideas, opinions, feelings, or frustrations. And we can let them know that such sharing is welcome by sharing aspects of our own personal lives (Diamond, 1991).
- *Make classroom activities relevant to students' interests.* Students with emotional or behavioral disorders are more likely to get involved in their schoolwork

Show an interest in students' well-being.

Take students' interests 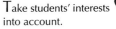 into account.

Give students some
sense of control.

Be alert for signs of
possible abuse or neglect.

Be alert for indications
that a student is
contemplating suicide.

when teachers take their personal interests into account (Clarke et al., 1995; McWhiter & Bloom, 1994). Chapter 12 identifies several ways we can meet important instructional objectives while also addressing students' interests.

• *Give students a sense that they have some control.* Some students—especially those who exhibit defiance toward authority figures—respond to efforts to control them by behaving even *less* appropriately than they have previously. With such students, it is important to avoid power struggles—situations where only one person "wins" and the other inevitably loses. Instead, we must create situations in which we ensure that the students conform to classroom expectations and yet the students feel that they have some control over what happens to them. For instance, we can teach them techniques for observing and monitoring their own actions with the goal of developing more productive classroom behavior (Kern, Dunlap, Childs, & Clark, 1994). We can also give them choices (within reasonable limits) about how to proceed in particular situations (Knowlton, 1995). We will examine such approaches in more depth in our discussions of *self-regulation* in Chapter 11 and *self-determination* in Chapter 12.

• *Be alert for signs of possible child abuse or neglect.* Possible indicators of abuse or neglect are frequent or serious physical injuries (e.g., bruises, burns, broken bones), untreated medical needs, obvious hunger, lack of warm clothing in cold weather, and exceptional knowledge about sexual matters (Turnbull et al., 1999). As teachers, we are both morally and legally obligated to report any cases of suspected child abuse to the proper authorities. You should consult with your principal about the specific policy in your own school district.

• *Be alert for signs that a student may be contemplating suicide.* Seriously depressed students often exhibit behaviors indicating that they may be thinking about taking their own lives. Warning signs include (Kerns & Lieberman, 1993):

Sudden withdrawal from social relationships

Disregard for personal appearance

A dramatic personality change

A sudden elevation in mood

A preoccupation with death and morbid themes

Overt or veiled threats (e.g., "I won't be around much longer")

Actions that indicate "putting one's affairs in order" (e.g., giving away prized possessions)

As teachers, we must take any of these warning signs seriously. We must show potentially suicidal students that we care very much about what happens to them, and we should seek trained help, such as the school psychologist or counselor, immediately (K. McCoy, 1994).

It is also essential that we help students with emotional and behavioral disorders acquire more appropriate behaviors—both those important for interacting effectively with others and those essential for maintaining a classroom environment conducive to learning. Strategies that can facilitate behavior improvement are likely to help students with autism as well; accordingly, I will describe such strategies after we discuss autism in the section that follows.

Autism

Autism is a condition that is almost certainly caused by a brain abnormality (Gillberg & Coleman, 1996). Perhaps the most central characteristic of this disability is a marked impairment in social interaction. Some students with autism form weak if any emotional attachments to other people and prefer to be alone (Denkla, 1986; Schreibman, 1988). Several other characteristics are also frequently seen in individuals with this condition: communication impairments (e.g., absent or delayed speech), repetitive behaviors (e.g., continually rocking or waving fingers in front of one's face), narrowly focused and odd interests (e.g., an unusual fascination with watches), aggression toward self or others, and a strong need for a predictable environment (American Psychiatric Association, 1994; E. G. Carr et al., 1994; Dalrymple, 1995; Turnbull et al., 1999). Some theorists have speculated that underlying autism may be either an undersensitivity or oversensitivity to sensory stimulation and that the abnormal behaviors so commonly observed reflect various attempts to make the environment more tolerable (R. C. Sullivan, 1994; Williams, 1996). Although the majority of students with autism are educated in self-contained classrooms or special schools, approximately one-fifth of them are enrolled in regular classrooms for part or all of the school day (U.S. Department of Education, 1996).

Common Characteristics

In addition to the traits just listed, students with autism often have these characteristics:

- A lack of basic social skills (e.g., making eye contact, seeking comfort from others when hurt or upset)
- Echolalia (i.e., continually repeating a portion of what someone has just said)
- Strong attachments to certain inanimate objects
- Abnormal movements (e.g., an awkward gait, repetitive gestures)
- Strong visual-spatial thinking skills
  (Denkla, 1986; Grandin, 1995; Koegel, 1995; Leary & Hill, 1996; Schreibman, 1988; Williams, 1996)

Although some students with autism have average or above-average intelligence, others have varying degrees of mental retardation (Ritvo & Freeman, 1978). Nevertheless, individuals with autism often show great variability in their abilities. In a few instances, a student with autism possesses an extraordinary ability (such as exceptional musical talent) that is quite remarkable in contrast to other aspects of mental functioning; this is called **savant syndrome** (Cheatham, Smith, Rucker, Polloway, & Lewis, 1995).

Have you seen the movie *Rain Man*? Dustin Hoffman plays a man with autism and mental retardation who is especially adept at calculating probabilities.

Adapting Instruction

Just as is true for other students in our classes, a high priority for students with autism is that they master academic content and skills commensurate with their ability. Many of the strategies I describe for helping students with learning disabilities, ADHD, and mental retardation learn academic subject matter may help students with autism as well. In addition, the following three strategies may be especially useful:

- *Change the arrangement of the classroom as infrequently as possible.* Many students with autism apparently find security in the predictability of their environment (Dalrymple, 1995) and so may become excessively upset when objects or pieces of furniture in a familiar environment are rearranged. If we know that we will have a student with autism in class, we should identify a physical layout for the classroom that will be serviceable throughout the school year and change it later only if absolutely necessary.

Keep the classroom's physical arrangement constant.

- *Follow a regular daily or weekly schedule.* To the extent possible, we should schedule certain activities at the same time each day or on a particular day of each week (Dalrymple, 1995). When there is a change in the schedule (perhaps because of a fire drill or school assembly), we should prepare the student well in advance of the change and indicate when the schedule will be back to normal again (Dalrymple, 1995).

Follow a predictable schedule.

Use visual aids to
enhance communication.

• *Use visual approaches to instruction.* Because students with autism often have strong visual-spatial skills but difficulties in oral communication, a heavy emphasis on visual materials is often beneficial (Hogdon, 1995; Quill, 1995). For instance, we might use objects, pictures, and photographs to convey ideas about academic topics. We might also provide a visual depiction of a student's daily schedule and give some sort of visual cue to indicate the start of a new activity.

General Recommendations for Students with Social or Behavioral Problems

Although the causes of emotional and behavioral disorders and those of autism are probably quite different, both groups of students may nevertheless benefit from some of the same teaching strategies. Certainly we want to promote success on academic tasks, perhaps by using some of the instructional strategies recommended earlier for students with specific cognitive or academic difficulties. In addition, students with social or behavioral problems may need extra assistance in learning appropriate and productive classroom behaviors:

Teach interpersonal
skills.

• *Teach interpersonal skills.* Many students with social and behavioral problems have never really learned appropriate ways of interacting with other people or perhaps are unable to process the nonverbal information that promotes social development. For example, some students may lack even the most basic social skills, whereas others need skills in cooperating, communicating, or resolving interpersonal conflicts (Shaffer, 1988). Directly teaching these students how to interact effectively with others is one obvious approach (see "Fostering Social Skills" in Chapter 3). Frequent opportunities to interact with both peers and adults, such as through cooperative learning activities in the classroom or through "partner" programs with young adults in the community, may also be valuable (Slavin, 1990; Turnbull et al., 1999). And many research studies have shown that applied behavior analysis and positive behavioral support (described in Chapter 10) can be quite powerful in bringing about behavior change in students with social and behavioral problems (E. G. Carr et al., 1994; DeVault, Krug, & Fake, 1996; Koegel, Koegel, & Dunlap, 1996; Landau & McAninch, 1993; D. P. Morgan & Jenson, 1988; Turnbull et al., 1999).

Communicate
expectations for behavior.

• *Communicate clear expectations for behavior.* When students exhibit serious behavior problems, it is especially important to specify exactly which behaviors are acceptable and unacceptable in precise and concrete terms (e.g., Landau & McAninch, 1993). For example, we can provide specific guidelines about when students can speak in class and when they are free to move about the classroom. Students are more likely to behave appropriately in the classroom when they are given reasonable limits for their behavior.

Try to anticipate
problems.

• *Try to anticipate problems and then nip them in the bud.* After we have gotten to know our students fairly well, we can in some cases predict the circumstances that are likely to precede, and possibly to trigger, undesirable behaviors. For instance, I think of Ben, a 9-year-old boy who, although usually mild-mannered, had occasional unpredictable temper tantrums that would disrupt the entire class. Eventually his teacher discovered that Ben's ears always turned red just before an outburst; this discovery allowed her to divert Ben's tantrums to a punching bag, where he could unleash his feelings with only minimal distraction to the rest of the class (Jackson & Ormrod, 1998). As another example, consider the case of Samantha:

Samantha was a 9-year-old third grader who had been identified as having autism and moderate speech disabilities. She frequently ran out of the classroom, damaging school property and other students' belongings in her flight. When the teacher aide or another adult tried to intervene, she would fight back by biting, scratching, hitting, kicking, and pulling hair.

The multidisciplinary team working with Samantha eventually discovered that Samantha's destructive and aggressive behaviors were more likely to occur when she was given a difficult academic assignment or had reason to anticipate such an assignment. Departures from the routine schedule or the absences of favorite teachers further increased the probability of such responses (DeVault et al., 1996).

Once Samantha's team had determined the circumstances that were likely to provoke her inappropriate behaviors, it was in a better position to deal with those behaviors. We will find out just what the team did to help Samantha in our discussion of positive behavioral support in Chapter 10.

• *Specify and follow through on consequences.* When working with students with social or behavioral problems, it is especially important that we describe the consequences—either reinforcing or punishing—to which various behaviors will lead; it is equally critical that we follow through with those consequences (Barkley, 1990; Landau & McAninch, 1993; Knowlton, 1995). At the same time, we should also give students explicit feedback about their behavior (Patton et al., 1987). When praising desirable behavior, rather than saying "Well done" or "Nice job," we should describe exactly what behaviors we are praising. When imposing punishment for inappropriate behavior, we should tell students exactly what they have done wrong. For example, we might say, "You borrowed Austin's book without asking him first. You know that taking other students' possessions without their permission is against class rules."

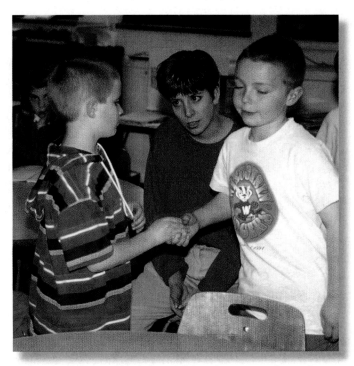

Students with emotional or behavioral disorders may need considerable guidance on how to interact appropriately with their peers.

Specify and follow through on consequences.

You should be aware that the job of helping students with social and behavioral problems is often a challenging one. Many of these students will at first resist any efforts to help them. It may only be when they themselves can observe the natural consequences of their changing behavior—for example, when they start to make new friends or when they get along better with their teachers—that they begin to recognize the value of the assistance that you are giving them (Patton et al., 1987).

Students with General Delays in Cognitive and Social Functioning

One of the categories I've included in the "Students in Inclusive Settings" tables located throughout the book is *students with general delays in cognitive and social functioning.* I intentionally used this term so that it might include any student who had a pattern of developmental delays in all areas, whether the student was specifically identified as having a disability or not. For instance, educators sometimes use the term *slow learner* to describe a student who obtains intelligence test scores in the 70s and has difficulties with virtually all aspects of the academic curriculum yet does not qualify for special educational services. A student with more pronounced developmental delays may be specifically identified as having *mental retardation*—a diagnosis that, in the United States, falls under the auspices of IDEA.

INTO THE CLASSROOM: Helping Students with Social or Behavioral Problems

Make expectations for classroom behavior clear and specific.

A teacher reminds a student, "You cannot borrow Mary's bottle of glue without asking. Check with Mary first to make sure it's all right for you to use her things. If Mary says no, ask another student."

Give feedback about specific behaviors rather than general areas of performance.

A teacher tells a student, "You did a good job in study hall today. You focused your attention on your homework, and you didn't retaliate when Jerome accidentally brushed past you on his way to my desk."

Specify and follow through on consequences for appropriate and inappropriate behaviors.

A teacher tells a student, "Sam, you know that certain four-letter words, such as the two that you just used, are unacceptable in this classroom. You also know the consequence for such behavior, so please go to the time-out corner for ten minutes."

Teach interpersonal skills.

When a student's only comments to classmates are derogatory remarks, her teacher meets with her after school to demonstrate more appropriate ways of initiating interaction. Together, they practice the new strategies through various role-playing situations.

Show an interest in students' well-being.

A teacher who sees a girl weeping quietly every day in class takes her aside when the other students have gone to lunch. As the student describes the nasty divorce proceedings in which her parents are involved, the teacher empathizes, explaining that his own parents divorced in an equally unpleasant fashion. He also connects her with a weekly support group that the school psychologist has formed for students whose parents are going through divorce.

Expect gradual improvement rather than immediate perfection.

A teacher is pleased that a student who once refused to participate in classroom activities now gets involved in activities two or three days a week, even though that student still has some days when little is accomplished.

Mental Retardation

Students with **mental retardation** show developmental delays in most aspects of their academic and social functioning. Students must exhibit *both* significantly below-average general intelligence and deficits in adaptive behavior before they are identified as having mental retardation (American Association on Mental Retardation, 1992):

- *Significantly below-average general intelligence.* Intelligence test scores of students with mental retardation are quite low—usually no higher than 65 or 70, reflecting performance in the bottom 2 percent of their age-group (B. K. Keogh & MacMillan, 1996; Turnbull et al., 1999). These students show other signs of

FIGURE 5.4

Adaptive skills used in identifying students with mental retardation

Communication: Skills related to understanding and expressing ideas through spoken and written language and through body language.

Self-care: Skills related to hygiene, eating, dressing, and grooming.

Home-living: Skills related to general functioning at home, including housekeeping, laundry, food preparation, budgeting, and home safety.

Social: Skills related to social interaction, including adhering to social conventions for interaction, helping others, recognizing feelings, forming friendships, controlling impulses, and abiding by rules.

Community use: Skills related to using community resources effectively, including shopping, using local transportation and facilities, and obtaining services.

Self-direction: Skills related to making choices, following a schedule, initiating activities appropriate to the context, completing required tasks, seeking needed assistance, and solving problems.

Health and safety: Skills related to personal health maintenance, basic first aid, physical fitness, basic safety, and sexuality.

Functional academics: Skills acquired in the academic curriculum that have direct application to independent living, such as reading, writing, and basic arithmetic.

Leisure: Skills related to initiating self-chosen leisure and recreational activities based on personal interests, playing socially with others, and abiding by age and cultural norms for activities undertaken.

Work: Skills related to holding a job, including specific job skills, appropriate social behavior, completion of tasks, awareness of schedules, and money management.

Derived from the ten adaptive skills described by the American Association on Mental Retardation, 1992.

below-average intelligence as well; for instance, they learn slowly and perform quite poorly on school tasks in comparison with their age-mates. And they show consistently poor achievement across virtually all academic subject areas.

- *Deficits in adaptive behavior.* Low intelligence test scores and poor academic performance are insufficient evidence to classify students as having mental retardation. An additional criterion is a deficit in **adaptive behavior:** These students show limitations in *practical intelligence*—managing the ordinary activities of daily living—and *social intelligence*—conducting themselves appropriately in social situations. In these respects, students with mental retardation often exhibit behaviors typical of children much younger than themselves. Figure 5–4 lists the kinds of adaptive skills with which students may have difficulty.

Mental retardation is often caused by genetic conditions; for example, most children with Down syndrome have delayed cognitive development. Other cases are due to biological but noninherited causes, such as severe malnutrition during the mother's pregnancy or oxygen deprivation associated with a difficult birth (B. K. Keogh & MacMillan, 1996). In still other situations, environmental factors, such as parental neglect or an extremely impoverished and unstimulating home environment, may be at fault; accordingly, children from

Have you ever interacted with individuals who have mental retardation? In what ways did their social skills seem immature? What particular strengths did these people have?

poor, inner-city neighborhoods are overrepresented in the students who are identified as having mental retardation (Batshaw & Shapiro, 1997; Baumeister, 1989; M. Wagner, 1995).

Although usually a long-term condition, mental retardation is not necessarily a life-long disability, especially when the presumed cause is environmental rather than genetic (Landesman & Ramey, 1989; Patton, Payne, & Beirne-Smith, 1990). As an example, I think of 12-year-old Steven:

> Steven had no known genetic or other organic problems but had been officially labeled as "mentally retarded" based on his low scores on a series of intelligence tests. His prior schooling had been limited to just part of one year in a first-grade classroom in inner-city Chicago. His mother had pulled him out after a bullet grazed his leg while he was walking to school one morning; fearing for her son's safety, she would not let him outside the apartment after that, not even to play, and certainly not to walk the six blocks to school.
>
> When a truant officer finally appeared at the door one evening in May five years later, Steven and his mother quickly packed their bags and moved to a small town in northern Colorado. They found residence with Steven's aunt, who persuaded Steven to go back to school. After considering Steven's intelligence and achievement test scores, the school psychologist recommended that he attend a summer school class for students with special needs.
>
> Steven's summer school teacher soon began to suspect that Steven's main problem might simply be a lack of the background experiences necessary for academic success. One incident in particular stands out in her mind. The class had been studying nutrition, and so she had asked her students to bring in some fresh vegetables to make a large salad for their morning snack. Steven brought in a can of green beans. When a classmate objected that the beans weren't fresh, Steven replied, "The hell they ain't! Me and Momma got them off the shelf this morning!"
>
> If Steven didn't know what *fresh* meant, the teacher reasoned, then he might also be lacking many of the other facts and skills on which any academic curriculum is invariably based. She and the teachers who followed her worked hard to help Steven make up for all those years in Chicago when he had experienced and learned so little. By the time Steven reached high school, he was enrolling in regular classes and maintaining a 3.5 grade-point-average. (adapted from Jackson & Ormrod, 1998, pp. 63–66)

Common Characteristics

Although most students with mental retardation are educated in self-contained classrooms or at separate schools or other facilities, a small proportion of them attend regular classes for part or all of the school day (U.S. Department of Education, 1996). Students with mental retardation are likely to display many or all of the following characteristics:

- A desire to "belong" and fit in at school
- Less general knowledge about the world
- Poor reading and language skills
- Lack of metacognitive awareness and few, if any, effective learning and memory strategies
- Difficulty with abstract ideas
- Difficulty generalizing something learned in one situation to a new situation
- Difficulty filling in details when instructions are incomplete or ambiguous
- Poor motor skills
- Immature interpersonal skills
- Excessive dependence on others in decision making
  (Butterfield & Ferretti, 1987; DuPaul & Eckert, 1994; Gresham & MacMillan, 1997; Kail, 1990; Patton et al., 1990; Patton et al., 1987; Turnbull et al., 1999.)

Adapting Instruction

Many of the strategies I've previously described in this chapter are likely to be useful for helping students with mental retardation. Here are some additional strategies to keep in mind:

- *Pace instruction slowly enough to ensure a high rate of success.* When working with a student who has mental retardation, we should move through topics and assign new tasks slowly enough that the student experiences a high degree of success (Patton et al., 1987). Students with mental retardation typically have a long history of failure at academic tasks; hence they need frequent success experiences to learn that they *can* succeed in school.

Pace instruction more slowly.

- *Explain tasks concretely, specifically, and completely.* As noted earlier, students with mental retardation have difficulty filling in details correctly when instructions are ambiguous or incomplete. If we tell a student only to "Take this absentee sheet to the principal's office," it may not occur to the student to return to the classroom after completing the errand. Instead, we should provide concrete, specific, and complete instructions; for example, we might say, "Go to the principal's office, give Mrs. Smith the absentee sheet, and come back here" (Patton et al., 1987, p. 64).

Explain tasks concretely and completely.

- *Provide considerable scaffolding to facilitate effective cognitive processing.* Students with mental retardation often have little awareness of how to direct and regulate their own learning. So it is often helpful to provide extra guidance in terms of cognitive processing. For instance, we can help students focus their attention by using such phrases as "get ready," "look," or "listen" (Turnbull et al., 1999). We can teach them a few simple, concrete memory strategies, such as repeating instructions to themselves or physically rearranging a group of items that they need to remember (Fletcher & Bray, 1995; Turnbull, 1974). We can also give them simple, structured study guides that quite specifically tell them what to focus on when they study (Mastropieri & Scruggs, 1992).

Scaffold effective cognitive processing.

- *Include vocational and general life skills in the curriculum.* Most students with mental retardation join the adult work force rather than go on to higher education. Accordingly, an important part of any high school curriculum for students with mental retardation is training in general life and work skills. Because of students' limited ability to generalize what they have learned from one situation to another, it is especially important to teach life and work skills in realistic settings that closely resemble the situations in which students will find themselves once they leave school (Turnbull et al., 1999).

Teach vocational and general life skills.

- *Encourage independence rather than dependence on others.* When we notice a student with mental retardation being overly dependent on other people, we should discourage such dependence as much as possible (Patton et al., 1987). If a student comes to class without a pencil, we might ask the student to purchase one from the classroom supply cabinet, rather than simply hand out a pencil. And we might give specific instructions about what a student should do *independently* with any free time after assigned tasks are completed.

Encourage independence.

At this point, we turn our attention to a very different group of students—those with physical and sensory challenges. Yet as you will soon discover, some (although by no means all) of these students may also have some of the cognitive or social difficulties that characterize other students with special needs.

INTO THE CLASSROOM: Helping Students with General Delays in Cognitive and Social Functioning

Introduce new material at a slower pace, and provide many opportunities for practice.

A teacher gives a student only two new addition facts a week because any more than two seem to overwhelm him. Every day, the teacher has the student practice writing the new facts and review addition facts learned in previous weeks.

Explain tasks concretely and in very specific terms.

An art teacher gives a student explicit training in the steps he needs to take at the end of each painting session: (1) Rinse the paintbrush out at the sink, (2) put the brush and watercolor paints on the shelf in the back room, and (3) put the painting on the counter by the window to dry. Initially the teacher needs to remind the student of every step in the process; however, with time and practice, the student eventually carries out the process independently.

Give students explicit guidance about how to study.

A teacher tells a student, "When you study a new spelling word, it helps if you repeat the letters out loud while you practice writing the word. Let's try it with *house*, the word you are learning this morning. Watch how I repeat the letters—H...O...U...S...E— as I write the word. Now you try doing what I just did."

Encourage independence.

A high school teacher teaches a student how to use her calculator to figure out what she needs to pay for lunch every day. The teacher also gives the student considerable practice in identifying the correct bills and coins to use when paying various amounts.

Students with Physical and Sensory Challenges

Some of our students with special needs will have physical or sensory disabilities caused by medically detectable physiological conditions. In this section, we will look at four kinds of physical or sensory disabilities: physical and health impairments, visual impairments, hearing loss, and severe and multiple disabilities.

Physical and Health Impairments

Physical and health impairments are general physical or medical conditions (usually long-term) that interfere with school performance to such an extent that special instruction, curricular materials, equipment, or facilities are necessary. Students in this category may have limited energy and strength, reduced mental alertness, or little muscle control. Examples of specific conditions that may qualify students for special services include traumatic brain injury, spinal cord injury, cerebral palsy, muscular dystrophy, epilepsy, cystic fibrosis, asthma, heart problems, arthritis, cancer, and AIDS. The majority of students with physical and health impairments attend general education classrooms for part or all of the school day (U.S. Department of Education, 1996).

Common Characteristics

It is difficult to generalize about students with physical and health impairments because their conditions are so very different from one another. Nevertheless, there are four

Students with mental retardation should have the same opportunities to participate in extracurricular activities that their classmates have. Such activities can help promote the development of independence and appropriate social skills.

noteworthy characteristics common to many of these students (Patton et al., 1987; Wood, 1989):

- Learning ability similar to that of nondisabled students
- Fewer opportunities to experience and interact with the outside world in educationally important ways (for example, less use of public transportation, fewer visits to museums and zoos, and fewer family trips)
- Low stamina and a tendency to tire easily
- Possible low self-esteem, insecurity, embarrassment, or overdependence (depending partly on how parents and others have responded to their impairments)

Adapting Instruction

To get a small glimpse of the kinds of challenges that students with physical disabilities may face on a daily basis, try the following exercise.

▪ Experiencing Firsthand
Stiffen Up

Stand up, and then make your arms and legs totally straight and stiff. Also stiffen your wrists, fingers, and neck. While keeping all of these body parts totally stiff, try the following activities:

1. Skip around the room.
2. Bend over and touch your toes.
3. Find a tissue or handkerchief and blow your nose.
4. Go back to your chair and sit down.
5. Take a piece of scrap paper and use it to mark this page. Turn back to the first page of the chapter (p. 167) and read the first paragraph, then return to this page.

6. While continuing to keep your elbows, wrists, and fingers completely stiff, try "cutting" an imaginary sheet of paper using an imaginary pair of scissors. Then "glue" two pieces of paper together using an imaginary bottle of rubber cement. Remember to "unscrew" the top off the bottle before you use it.

Now return your body to its usual, more relaxed state.

What kinds of difficulties did you encounter in your stiffness? You were probably able to skip around the room, although not as quickly and gracefully as you would otherwise. You may have been able to touch your toes as well, but did you find that your stiff neck made the task more difficult? And how did you blow your nose? I myself found that I couldn't do it in any way that would be presentable in a public place.

You may have experienced varying degrees of difficulty with the last three activities as well. Can you think of special equipment that might help you perform these activities more successfully? Would a different kind of chair be more comfortable? Would a metal book holder help you keep the textbook open while you read it? Might specially shaped scissors better fit your stiff fingers?

Although we will not always need to modify the general classroom curriculum for students with physical and health impairments, we will want to make other special accommodations:

Be flexible in accommodating students' limitations.

• *Be sensitive to specific needs and disabilities, and accommodate them flexibly.* Despite normal learning capabilities, students with physical and health impairments may not be able to perform certain tasks as easily as their classmates. For example, one student may require extra time with a writing assignment, and perhaps should not be held to the same standards of neatness and legibility. Another may need to respond to test questions orally rather than on paper. Still another may tire easily and need to take frequent breaks from school tasks. In your previously "stiffened" condition, you may have needed all of these accommodations. Consider the case of Wesley as another example:

> During his junior year in high school, Wesley sustained a serious head injury in a motorcycle accident. Although he had previously been an excellent student, he returned to school his senior year with special educational needs. It took him much longer to read and process information than it used to. He tended to forget things that weren't written down for him. And he grew tired after only an hour or two of class.
>
> Wesley's teachers did several things to accommodate his needs that year. They let him finish in-class assignments at home. They allowed him to take tests by himself in a room near the main office and gave him as much time as he needed to respond to test items. They wrote instructions on the chalkboard where he could see and copy them, and they alerted him to crucial course content by saying, "This is important, so put it in your notes." Furthermore, the school counselor scheduled no classes during the third and fourth class periods so that Wesley could take a nap in the nurse's office. (adapted from Jackson & Ormrod, 1998, pp. 91–93)

Be prepared for emergencies.

• *Know what to do in emergency situations.* Some students have conditions that may result in occasional, potentially health-threatening situations. For example, a student with diabetes may go into insulin shock, a student with asthma may have trouble breathing, or a student with epilepsy may have a *grand mal* seizure. We should consult with school medical personnel to learn ahead of time exactly how to respond to such emergencies.

Help classmates understand the disability.

• *Educate classmates about the nature of the disability.* Although many classmates are apt to treat a student with a physical or health impairment with kindness and respect, others may be less considerate and tolerant. In some situations, such mistreatment may be due to ignorance regarding the nature of the disability, and accurate information must be made available. For example, in one widely publicized case, Ryan White, a student with AIDS, was initially barred from his neighborhood school because of classmates' and parents' unwarranted fear that other children would be infected. Ryan was able to return to school only after the public was convinced that AIDS was not a condition that could be contracted through normal activities or bodily contact (R. White & Cunningham, 1992).

Visual Impairments

Students with **visual impairments** have malfunctions of their eyes or optic nerves that prevent them from seeing normally even with corrective lenses, to the point where their classroom performance is affected. Some students are totally blind; others have limited sensitivity to light, seeing fuzzy patterns of light and dark. Still others have a restricted visual field (sometimes called *tunnel vision*), whereby they can see only a very small area at a given time. Visual impairments are caused by congenital abnormalities in, or later damage to, either the eye or the visual pathway to the brain.

Common Characteristics

Students with visual impairments are likely to have many or all of these characteristics:

- Normal functioning of other senses (hearing, touch, etc.)
- General learning ability similar to that of nondisabled students
- Fewer opportunities to experience and interact with the outside world in educationally important ways (for example, less exposure to maps, films, and other visual material); as a result, less general knowledge about the world
- Reduced capability to imitate the behaviors of others
- Inability to observe the body language and other nonverbal cues often present in human interactions, leading to occasional misperceptions of intended meanings
- Occasional confusion, particularly in chaotic situations such as on the playground or in the lunchroom
- A general feeling of uncertainty and anxiety as a result of having no visual knowledge of the events happening within the classroom
  (Patton et al., 1987; M. C. Reynolds & Birch, 1988; Turnbull et al., 1999; Tuttle & Tuttle, 1996)

Adapting Instruction

Specialists will typically give students who are blind or have limited vision the training they need in Braille, orientation and mobility, and specially adapted computer technology. Apart from such additions to the curriculum, regular classroom content and objectives are usually appropriate for these students.

At the same time, we can help students with visual impairments learn and achieve successfully with these strategies:

- *Orient students ahead of time to the physical layout of the classroom.* Students with serious visual impairments should be given the chance to explore the classroom before other students have arrived—ideally, well before the first day of class. We can help students locate various objects in the classroom (wastebasket, pencil sharpener, etc.) and can point out special sounds (such as the buzzing of a clock on the wall) so students get their bearings (Wood, 1989).
- *Use visual materials with sharp contrast for partially sighted students.* Students with visual impairments will obviously have limited success in learning from

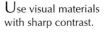 Orient students to the classroom's physical layout.

Use visual materials with sharp contrast.

ordinary printed materials such as textbooks, posters, charts, and maps. Some students can benefit from visual materials provided that the various features of those materials are easily distinguishable from one another. For example, some students with partial sight may be able to read large print books (available at most public libraries). But students' eyes will tend to tire quickly; thus, we should limit the use of visual materials to short periods of time (Patton et al., 1987).

Use modalities other than vision.

• *Find ways of transmitting information through other modalities.* For students who are blind, we must find viable alternatives for presenting classroom material. We can obtain Braille copies of required books and assignments and audiotapes of novels and other literature. We can engage students in hands-on activities involving objects they can feel and manipulate. Plastic relief maps that portray mountains, valleys, and coast-lines three-dimensionally can be embellished by making pin pricks along borders or by placing small dabs of nail polish on major cities. When exclusively visual material must be used for large-group instruction, this material should be described in detail to students with visual impairments—perhaps by their teacher, an aide, or a fellow student.

Allow extra time.

• *Allow extra time for learning and performance.* Learning by hearing often takes more time than learning by seeing: When students *look* at something, they can perceive a great deal of information all at once, but when they *listen* to it, they receive it just one piece at a time. Hence we may often need to give students with visual impairments extra time to learn classroom material and complete their assignments (Rowe, 1978).

Hearing Loss

Our opening case study profiled Midori, a girl with exceptional talent in art. Midori has trouble understanding what others say to her, and her own voice has a monotonous and hollow sound to it. Midori has never actually heard the sound of human language be-cause she has been deaf since birth.

Students with **hearing loss** have a malfunction of the ear or associated nerves that interferes with the perception of sounds within the frequency range of normal human speech. Students who are completely *deaf* have insufficient sensation to understand any spoken language, even with the help of a hearing aid. Students who are *hard of hearing* understand some speech but experience exceptional difficulty in doing so. Approxi-mately 50 percent of the students identified as having hearing loss are in regular class-rooms for part or all of the school day (U.S. Department of Education, 1995).

THINKING ABOUT WHAT YOU KNOW

Think about how difficult it is to hear what someone else is saying to you when you are at a noisy party. Might the frustration you feel be similar to the way a student with hear-ing loss feels?

Common Characteristics

Most students with hearing loss have normal intellectual abilities (Braden, 1992; Schirmer, 1994). In addition, they are likely to have these characteristics:

• Delayed language development, especially if the hearing impairment was pres-ent at birth or occurred early in life, because of reduced exposure to spoken language

• Less oral language than hearing classmates

• Some ability to read lips (*speechreading*)

Many students with hearing loss have proficiency in American Sign Language. ASL is not a word-for-word representation of English; it has its own unique vocabulary and syntax.

- Proficiency in sign language, such as American Sign Language (ASL) or finger spelling (a manual alphabet through which words can be spelled)
- Less developed reading skills, especially if other aspects of language development have been delayed
- Less general knowledge about the world than their peers, due to reduced exposure to verbal information
- In some cases, social isolation and more limited social skills due to the reduced ability to communicate, and therefore to interact, with others
  (Bassett et al., 1996; Gearheart et al., 1992; Patton et al., 1987; M. C. Reynolds & Birch, 1988; Rowe, 1978; Turnbull et al., 1999)

Adapting Instruction

Specialists typically provide training in such communication skills as American Sign Language, finger spelling, and speechreading. Aside from the addition of these topics, the regular school curriculum is appropriate for most students with hearing loss. Teachers can do a number of things to help these students learn and achieve successfully:

- *Minimize irrelevant noise.* Even when students with hearing loss wear hearing aids, what they hear is apt to be somewhat distorted or diminished. For students who have some ability to hear sounds, then, it is helpful to minimize any irrelevant and potentially distracting noises in the classroom. For instance, carpet on the floor and multiple bulletin boards on the walls can absorb some of the extraneous noises that will inevitably be present. And students may be better able to focus on important auditory messages if such noisy devices as pencil sharpeners and fans are as far away as possible (Turnbull et al., 1999).

 Minimize irrelevant noise.

- *Supplement auditory presentations with visual information and hands-on experiences.* For obvious reasons, we should supplement any auditory presentations (such as

 Use visual aids and hands-on experiences.

directions, lectures, or classroom discussions) with information provided through other (especially visual) modalities. For example, we can write important points on the chalkboard. We can illustrate key ideas with pictures and other graphics. We can make reading materials available that duplicate lectures. We can ask a classroom aide or student volunteer to take notes on in-class discussions. And we can use concrete activities (e.g., role playing, experiments, field trips) to make potentially abstract ideas come alive.

Help students speechread.

* *Take steps to maximize students' hearing capabilities and ability to speechread.* Students who are hard-of-hearing are most likely to understand words spoken in a normal tone of voice (not overly loud) and with a distinct but otherwise normal pronunciation (Gearheart et al., 1992; J. W. Wood, 1989). They should sit in places where they can clearly see the speaker's face. Furthermore, we should speak only while facing students, and never while sitting in a dark corner or standing in front of a window or bright light (Patton et al., 1987; Turnbull et al., 1999).

Check for understanding.

* *Occasionally check for understanding by asking students to repeat what you've said.* Even the most skillful speechreaders won't always get our messages exactly as we've transmitted them. To make sure that students correctly understand what we are telling them, we can occasionally ask them to repeat what we've said. By doing so, we can identify and correct misunderstandings (Gearheart et al., 1992; Patton et al., 1987).

Address reading and other language difficulties.

* *Address deficiencies in reading and other language skills.* We must be sure to address any language and reading deficiencies that students may have (Bassett et al., 1996). In some cases, a special educator or other specialist can give us guidance and assistance in this regard. Many of the strategies in Chapter 2 (see the section on language development) and Chapter 9 (see the sections on reading and writing) may also be helpful.

Teach ASL and finger spelling to classmates.

* *Teach elements of American Sign Language and finger spelling to other class members.* Some students with hearing loss, because of their reduced ability to communicate, may feel relatively isolated from their peers and teachers. One effective way of opening the lines of communication is for other class members, ourselves included, to gain some competence in American Sign Language and finger spelling. For instance, I once taught at a school where *every* student—those with hearing loss and those without—received some instruction in signing. One girl in my class was totally deaf yet was quite popular with her classmates; I often observed her and her friends communicating freely and easily both before and after (and, unfortunately, sometimes at inappropriate times *during*) class.

Severe and Multiple Disabilities

Students with **severe and multiple disabilities** have two or more of the disabilities already described and require significant adaptations and highly specialized services in their educational program. These disabilities are almost always due to organic causes, such as genetic abnormalities or serious complications before or during birth. Despite their extensive need for special services, some students with severe and multiple disabilities (such as my son Jeff's friend Evan, whom I described earlier in the chapter) may be in general education classrooms for part of the school day.

Common Characteristics

Students who have severe and multiple disabilities often have these characteristics:

* Varying degrees of intellectual functioning (some students may have normal intelligence that is hidden beneath a limited ability to communicate)
* Limited awareness of surrounding stimuli and events; periods of alertness and responsiveness in some cases

- Limited communication skills (often consisting of gestures, facial expressions, or other nonverbal means), which can sometimes be facilitated by technology
- Limited adaptive behaviors (e.g., social skills, self-care skills)
- Significant delays in motor development
- Mild or severe sensory impairments
- Extensive medical needs (e.g., medications, intravenous tubes) (Guess, Roberts, Siegel-Causey, & Rues, 1995; Turnbull et al., 1999)

Adapting Instruction

Should we have students with severe and multiple disabilities in our classrooms, we will almost certainly have one or more specialists or teacher aides that assist us in their education. Yet we must keep in mind that, despite extensive disabilities, these students are full-fledged members of the class and should participate in all curricular activities to the extent that they can do so. In addition to using the many strategies described earlier in the chapter, we can accommodate students with severe and multiple disabilities in ways such as these:

- *Identify and teach those behaviors and skills most essential for a student's general welfare and successful inclusion in the classroom.* Almost any student with special needs, no matter how serious his or her disabilities, has some capacity to adapt to a new environment. We should therefore identify those behaviors that will enhance the student's learning and performance for the time that we will have them— behaviors that may include more effective ways of communicating, rudimentary word recognition or arithmetic skills, or the use of new technologies specially designed for certain disabling conditions. In teaching a basic skill, we may find it useful to guide the student slowly through the skill one step at a time, verbally or manually guiding (i.e., scaffolding) his or her actions, and then gradually removing such guidance as the student develops increasing competence, self-confidence, and independence.

Teach skills essential for general welfare and successful class inclusion.

- *Pair students with and without disabilities in the same activity, having different objectives for different students.* It may sometimes be appropriate to pair a nondisabled student with a student who has disabilities and have the two of them work cooperatively on a classroom task. In some cases, they might be working to achieve different objectives within the same content area; for example, when two students conduct a science experiment, one might be learning methods of scientific experimentation while the other is mastering basic scientific concepts. In other cases, the pair might be working to achieve objectives in two completely different areas; for example, while one is learning experimentation techniques, the other may be practicing basic communication skills (Giangreco, 1997).

Have students with and without disabilities work together on classroom tasks.

- *Keep the mind-set that all students can and should participate in regular classroom activities to the fullest extent possible.* As we have moved toward greater inclusion of students with disabilities in recent years, many educators have found that when they keep open minds about what their students can accomplish, and especially when they think creatively and collaboratively about how they can adapt regular classroom activities to accommodate students with special needs, almost all students can participate in some meaningful fashion in virtually all classroom activities (Logan, Alberto, Kana, & Waylor-Bowen, 1994; Salisbury, Evans, & Palombaro, 1997).

Keep an inclusive mind-set.

General Recommendations for Students with Physical and Sensory Challenges

Like other students with special needs, students with physical and sensory challenges should have as normal an education as we can reasonably provide for them. We have identified a number of specific ways to help students in the various disability categories adjust successfully to the classroom environment. Several more general strategies also can facilitate the classroom success of students with physical and sensory challenges:

Provide equal access to educational opportunities.

- *Provide access to the same educational opportunities that other students have.* Partly as a result of federal legislation, individuals with physical and sensory challenges now have greater access to educational opportunities than they did twenty years ago; for example, the now commonplace wheelchair ramps leading into schools and other public buildings were virtually nonexistent when I was a child. Nevertheless, we must consider how the physical conditions within our own classrooms may possibly interfere with students' access to important educational facilities and materials, and we may have to make a concerted effort to ensure equal access. For example, to accommodate children in wheelchairs, we may need to widen the aisles between classroom desks and place items taped to walls or posted on bulletin boards at their eye level (Stephens, Blackhurst, & Magliocca, 1988). We may also need to make special arrangements that allow students with disabilities to accompany our classes on field trips.

Treat students as normally as possible.

- *Treat students in the same way that you treat their classmates without disabilities.* Students with physical and sensory disabilities adjust to their conditions more successfully when other individuals treat them normally—for example, by expecting them to perform the same tasks as other students when they are capable of doing so, and by avoiding behaviors that reflect pity or patronization. As one simple example, we should speak to students directly, rather than asking a third person (such as a parent or therapist), "How is Johnny doing today?"

Give assistance only when needed.

- *Provide assistance only when students really need it.* In their eagerness to help students with physical or sensory challenges, many adults inadvertently perform tasks and solve problems that these students are perfectly capable of dealing with on their own. Yet one of our goals for these students is to promote their independence, not their dependence on others. So when we see that students are having difficulty with a task, we should ask them if they need assistance before we try to help them.

Use available technology.

- *Use technological innovations to facilitate student learning and performance.* There has been a virtual explosion of technological aids to help students with physical and sensory challenges in their daily school activities. For example, many computers have been adapted for the visually impaired: Some calculators "talk" as buttons are pushed and answers are displayed, some computers "tell" a student what appears on the computer screen, and some computer printers print in Braille. Specially adapted joysticks or voice recognition systems can help students with limited muscle control use a classroom computer. Machines known as augmentative communication devices can provide synthesized speech to facilitate the communication of individuals incapable of normal speech (Stephens et al., 1988; Turnbull et al., 1999).

We have considered many ways of helping students with a variety of disabilities adapt successfully to a general education environment. Yet an additional group of students—those who show exceptional ability in one or more areas—may also have special educational needs. The next section addresses the specific needs of these students.

Students with Advanced Cognitive Development

THINKING ABOUT WHAT YOU KNOW

As a child, what special talents did you have that might have benefited from individualized instruction? For instance, did you show a strong aptitude for reading or math? exceptional creativity in your art? an unusual flair for music, dance, or drama?

INTO THE CLASSROOM: Helping Students with Physical or Sensory Challenges

Provide equal access to educational opportunities.

A teacher who has two students with impaired vision in her class constructs a bulletin board in both printed letters and Braille. She then adds pictures that she has outlined with a ridge of clear, dry glue, so that the students who can't see the pictures can feel the shapes within them.

Treat students in the same way you treat their classmates without disabilities.

A teacher talks with a student who has multiple disabilities about the basketball game they both attended last weekend.

Provide assistance only when students truly need it.

A teacher allows a student who is blind to find his way to the school library, knowing that he has done so successfully on several previous occasions.

Use technological innovations to facilitate instruction and performance.

A teacher obtains a specially adapted joystick so that a student with muscular dystrophy can use the computer.

As you examine the "Students in Inclusive Settings" tables that appear throughout the book, you should think of *students with advanced cognitive development* as being on a continuum of abilities rather than being contained within a distinct category separate from their classmates. Many of our students are likely to have advanced cognitive abilities, either in specific subject areas or across the board, that warrant our attention and nurturance. In fact, it may be just as important to encourage the development of gifts and talents in *all* students as it is to identify the particular gifts and talents that some of our students bring with them to the classroom (Council for Exceptional Children, 1995).

In the United States, providing special educational services for gifted students, although not required under IDEA, is encouraged by other legislation—more specifically, by the Jacob K. Javits Gifted and Talented Students Education Act of 1988 (P.L. 100–297, IV[B]), which was reauthorized in 1994 (P.L. 103–382, XIV). Furthermore, most state governments in the United States have passed legislation that either mandates or encourages special educational services for students whom local school districts have identified as being gifted (Council for Exceptional Children, 1995). Let's look at what the term *giftedness* typically means, as well as at some instructional strategies especially suited for gifted students.

Giftedness

Giftedness is unusually high ability or aptitude in one or more areas, to the point where special educational services are necessary to help a student meet his or her full potential.

Students who are gifted (sometimes called *gifted and talented*) show exceptional achievement or promise in one or more of the following areas:

- General intellectual ability
- Aptitude in a specific academic field
- Creativity
- Visual or performing arts
- Leadership
  (Jacob K. Javits Gifted and Talented Students Education Act of 1988 [P.L. 100–297, IV(B); P.L. 103–382, XIV]; U.S. Department of Education, 1993a).

When we try to pin down giftedness more precisely, we find considerable disagreement about how to do so (Carter, 1991; B. K. Keogh & MacMillan, 1996). Although many school districts identify gifted students primarily on the basis of general IQ scores, often using 125 or 130 as a cutoff point (B. K. Keogh & MacMillan, 1996; J. T. Webb, Meckstroth, & Tolan, 1982), some experts argue that multiple criteria should be applied when determining students' eligibility for special services (Renzulli, 1978; Renzulli & Reis, 1986; Sternberg & Zhang, 1995). For instance, one theorist has argued that we should consider creativity and task commitment as well as IQ scores (Renzulli, 1978). Furthermore, scores on general intelligence tests may be largely irrelevant when identifying students who show exceptional promise in specific academic fields, creativity, the arts, or leadership.

In addition, giftedness is likely to take different forms in different cultures (you may recall Chapter 4's discussion of the culture-dependent nature of intelligence). For example, among African American students, giftedness may be reflected in oral language, such as in colorful speech, creative storytelling, or humor (Torrance, 1989). Among Native Americans, giftedness may be reflected in interpersonal skills, such as in sensitivity to the feelings of others or skill at effectively mediating disagreements (Maker & Schiever, 1989). Our tendency to rely heavily on traditional intelligence tests for identifying gifted students is probably a key reason that many minority populations are underrepresented in the students that we identify (C. R. Harris, 1991; Maker & Schiever, 1989; U.S. Department of Education, Office of Civil Rights, 1993).

We must note, too, that gifted students often hide their talents to some degree, making their identification even more difficult. Many students fear that peers will ridicule them for their high academic abilities and enthusiasm for academic topics, especially at the secondary school level (Covington, 1992; DeLisle, 1984). Girls in particular are likely to hide their talents, especially if they have been raised in cultures that do not value high achievement in females (Covington, 1992; Davis & Rimm, 1998). Gifted Asian Americans, because of cultural traditions of obedience, conformity, and respect for authority, may be reluctant to engage in creative activities and may willingly comply when asked to perform unchallenging assignments (Maker & Schiever, 1989).

Common Characteristics

Angelo, whom we met in our opening case study, exhibits several characteristics common in students who are gifted: a rich vocabulary, extensive knowledge about certain topics, a fondness for reading, and boredom with unchallenging tasks.

Students who are identified as being gifted show exceptional achievement or promise in general intellectual ability, aptitude in a specific academic field, creativity, leadership, or visual and performing arts.

Although students who are gifted tend to be quite different from one another in terms of their unique strengths and talents, they often have characteristics such as these:

- Large vocabulary
- Extensive knowledge and expertise in certain areas
- Ability to learn more quickly and easily than their age-mates
- More advanced and effective cognitive processing and metacognitive skills
- Greater flexibility in ideas and approaches to tasks
- Appearance of formal operational thought processes (e.g., abstract thinking) at an earlier age
- High standards regarding their performance (in a minority of cases, to the point of unhealthy perfectionism)
- High motivation to achieve on challenging tasks; feelings of boredom about easy tasks
- Positive self-concept, especially with regard to academic endeavors
- Above-average social development and emotional adjustment (although a few extremely gifted students may have difficulties because they are so *very* different from their peers)
  (Candler-Lotven, Tallent-Runnels, Olivárez, & Hildreth, 1994; Carter & Ormrod, 1982; Clark, 1997; Cornell et al., 1990; Hoge & Renzulli, 1993; Janos & Robinson, 1985; Lupart, 1995; Parker, 1997; Rabinowitz & Glaser, 1985; Winner, 1997)

We should note here that a student can be gifted and also have a disability. For example, some gifted students have learning disabilities, ADHD, emotional or behavioral disorders, or physical or sensory challenges (Brown-Mizuno, 1990). In such situations, we must address the students' disabilities as well as their unique gifts when we plan instruction.

Adapting Instruction

Why do students who are gifted need special services? Critics of gifted education argue that students with high abilities can certainly achieve normal school objectives without assistance. They also propose that special services for these students foster a certain degree of "elitism": They convey the message that some students are somehow more privileged than others.

But consider this statement from a gifted individual:

> People like me are aware of their so-called genius at ten, eight, nine. . . . I always wondered, "Why has nobody discovered me? In school, didn't they see that I'm more clever than anybody in this school? That the teachers are stupid, too? That all they had was information that I didn't need?" It was obvious to me. Why didn't they put me in art school? Why didn't they train me? I was different, I was always different. Why didn't anybody notice me? (cited in H. Gardner, 1983, p. 115)

This individual was a well-known public figure in the 1960s and 1970s. Can you guess who he was?

Many students with special gifts and talents become frustrated when their school experiences don't provide tasks and assignments that challenge them and help them develop their unique abilities. Recalling Lev Vygotsky's view of cognitive development from Chapter 2, we could say that gifted students are unlikely to be working within their zone of proximal development if we limit them to the tasks we assign to other students; thus, they are unlikely to develop new cognitive skills. Furthermore, many of these students report being bored by typical classroom activities: Instruction seems too slow and often

Why else might some individuals oppose special services for gifted students? How do you feel about such programs?

Did you participate in a gifted program in school? If so, was the curriculum appropriate for your particular talents?

deals with what they already know (Feldhusen & Kroll, 1985; Winner, 1997). As a result, they may lose interest in school tasks and put in only minimal effort (Feldhusen, 1989). In fact, gifted students are among our schools' greatest underachievers; when required to progress at the same rate as their nongifted peers, they achieve at levels far short of their capabilities (Carter, 1991; Gallagher, 1991; Reis, 1989). (By the way, the gifted individual I quoted earlier was John Lennon.)

We can foster students' special abilities and talents in numerous ways. Here are several strategies that theorists and practitioners recommend:

Individualize tasks based on students' unique talents.

- *Provide individualized tasks and assignments.* Even though students who are gifted are a very heterogeneous group, many schools provide the same curriculum and materials for all students whom they've identified as being gifted. In fact, no single program can meet the specific needs of each and every gifted student. Different students may need special services in very different areas—for example, in mathematics, creative writing, or studio art. Some gifted students—especially those with limited English background—may even need training in certain basic skills (C. R. Harris, 1991; Udall, 1989).

Form study groups of students with similar abilities and interests.

- *Form study groups of students with similar interests and abilities.* In any school building, there are likely to be several students who have common interests and abilities, and it may sometimes be helpful to pull them together into study groups where they can cooperatively pursue a particular topic or task (Fiedler, Lange, & Winebrenner, 1993; Stanley, 1980). Forming homogeneous study groups has several advantages. First, a single teacher can meet the needs of several students simultaneously. Second, students appear to benefit from increased contact with other students who have similar interests (McGinn, Viernstein, & Hogan, 1980). And third, students are less likely to try to hide their talent and enthusiasm for the subject matter when they work with classmates who share similar ability and motivation (Feldhusen, 1989).

In some cases, a study group may explore a topic with greater depth and more sophisticated analysis than other students do (an *enrichment* approach). For example, in a geometry class those students who show high ability might be asked to work together on an exceptionally challenging geometric proof. In other cases a study group may simply move through the standard school curriculum at a more rapid pace (an *acceleration* approach). For example, students reading well above the level of their classmates might be assigned books not ordinarily encountered until more advanced grade levels.

Teach complex cognitive skills related to specific subject areas.

- *Teach complex cognitive skills within the context of specific subject areas.* Some programs for the gifted have tried to teach complex thought processes like creativity and problem solving as skills totally separate from school subject matter. But this approach tends to have minimal impact on the development of gifted students; in fact, it often focuses on skills that many students have already acquired. Instead, we are better advised to teach complex thinking skills within the context of specific topics—for example, reasoning and problem solving skills in science, or creativity in writing (M. C. Linn et al., 1989; Moon, Feldhusen, & Dillon, 1994; Pulos & Linn, 1981; Stanley, 1980).

Assign independent study projects.

- *Provide opportunities for independent study.* Many students who are gifted have advanced learning and metacognitive skills and a strong motivation to learn academic subject matter (Candler-Lotven et al., 1994; Lupart, 1995). Accordingly, independent study in topics of interest may be especially appropriate for these students. When we provide opportunities for independent study, however, we should teach students the study habits and research skills they will need to use their time and resources effectively.

Encourage high goals.

- *Encourage students to set high goals for themselves.* Just as gifted students are capable of higher performance in specific areas, so they should also be setting higher goals for themselves in those areas. We should encourage students to aim high, while at the same time not asking them to expect perfection for themselves (Parker, 1997;

INTO THE CLASSROOM: Helping Gifted Students

Individualize instruction in accordance with students' specific talents.

A middle school student with exceptional reading skills and an interest in Shakespeare is assigned several Shakespearean plays; he then discusses each play with his student teacher, who is an English major at a nearby university.

Form study groups of students with similar abilities and interests.

A music teacher forms and provides weekly instruction to a quartet of exceptionally talented music students.

Teach complex cognitive skills within the context of specific school topics rather than separately from the normal school curriculum.

A teacher has an advanced science study group conduct a series of experiments related to a single topic. To promote critical thinking, the teacher gives students several questions to ask themselves as they conduct these experiments.

Encourage students to set high goals for themselves.

A teacher encourages a student from a lower socioeconomic background to consider going to college and helps the student explore possible sources of financial assistance for higher education.

Seek outside resources to help students develop their exceptional talents.

A student with a high aptitude for learning foreign language studies Russian at a local university.

Patton et al., 1987; Sanborn, 1979). For instance, some students may have given little or no thought to attending college, perhaps because their families have never expected them to pursue higher education; under such circumstances, we might give them the opportunity to visit a college campus and explore possible means of funding a college education (Spicker, 1992).

• *Seek outside resources.* A single school is likely to have students with exceptional potential in so many different areas that no single adult—not even a specialist in gifted education—can reasonably meet all of their needs (L. H. Fox, 1979; Stanley, 1980). It might sometimes be appropriate to identify suitable *mentors,* individuals with expertise in a particular area who help students develop their own talent in that area. In other circumstances, outside agencies—for example, laboratories, government offices, private businesses, volunteer community groups, theater groups, and art and videotaping studios—may provide an arena in which students can develop their unique talents (Ambrose, Allen, & Huntley, 1994; Piirto, 1994; Seeley, 1989).

Seek mentors who can foster specific talents.

Considering Diversity When Identifying and Addressing Special Needs

A disproportionately large number of students identified as having disabilities are from ethnic minority groups and low-income neighborhoods (Halpern, 1997; McLoyd, 1998; U.S. Department of Education, 1996, 1997). At the same time, relatively few students from some minority groups, especially African Americans and Hispanic Americans, are enrolled in programs for the gifted (U.S. Department of Education, Office of Civil Rights, 1993).

Most theorists believe that differences in environment account for the disproportionate numbers of students from certain ethnic backgrounds found in special education programs (McLoyd, 1998; H. W. Stevenson et al., 1990). Students from some ethnic minority groups are more likely than their classmates to grow up in lower-income neighborhoods, where lack of adequate medical care, poor prenatal and infant nutrition, maternal drug and alcohol abuse, increased exposure to lead paint (which, if ingested, can cause brain damage), more stressful and violent living conditions, and less access to early educational resources can contribute to lower intellectual functioning and more serious behavior problems (Conlon, 1992; McLoyd, 1998).

The inequitable representation of particular groups in various categories of disabilities poses a dilemma for educators. On the one hand, we don't want to use categories such as *mental retardation* or *emotional or behavioral disorder* for students whose classroom performance and behavior may be due primarily to the adverse environmental conditions in which they have been raised. On the other hand, we also don't want to deprive these students of special educational services that might very well help them learn and achieve more successfully over the long run. In such situations, we need to conduct fair and nondiscriminatory evaluations of students' needs and, if students qualify under a special needs category, create individualized education programs (IEPs) to meet those needs. We should consider the categories of special needs as *temporary* classifications—ones that may no longer be applicable as students' classroom performance improves. The case of Steven, the boy with the "fresh" can of green beans described earlier in the chapter, is a classic example of this approach: Although Steven was initially identified as having mental retardation, he eventually acquired the background knowledge and skills of which he had been deprived during his early years, and by high school he was attending regular high school classes as a student with no disability classification whatsoever. It's important to remember that students are identified under a special education category because they need specialized services; all students, with and without disability classifications, have changing needs that evolve over time.

We have already noted some possible reasons for the underrepresentation of some ethnic minority groups in gifted programs. As teachers, it is important to remember that many students from minority groups may not be identified as gifted when traditional intelligence tests and other standardized measures are used. It is critical that we be on the lookout for students who show other signs of special abilities and talents and so are likely to benefit from enriched educational experiences. Here are some examples of traits that may indicate giftedness in students from diverse cultural backgrounds:

- Ability to learn quickly from one's experiences
- Exceptional communication skills (e.g., articulateness, richness of language)
- Originality and resourcefulness in thinking and problem solving
- Ability to generalize what one has learned to other, seemingly unrelated, tasks and ideas
- Unusual sensitivity to the needs and feelings of others
  (Frasier, 1989; Maker & Schiever, 1989; Torrance, 1989)

For the growth of our society over the long run, it is imperative that we nurture the many gifted and talented students that we find in *all* ethnic groups.

Be alert for signs that students from diverse backgrounds may have exceptional gifts or talents.

The Big Picture: Helping All Students with Special Needs

In addition to using strategies specific to various special needs categories, we can do several things to help *all* students with special needs develop both academically and socially:

- *Obtain as much information as possible about each student.* We must remember that students identified as having a particular special educational need are *individuals* first, each with a unique set of strengths and weaknesses. The more we know about students' specific needs—whether academic, social, or medical—the better our position to help each and every student succeed at classroom tasks and activities (e.g., B. A. Keogh & Becker, 1973; Stephens, Blackhurst, & Magliocca, 1988).

- *Consult and collaborate with specialists.* To help students with special needs, school districts usually employ a variety of educational specialists, including counselors, school psychologists, nurses, speech pathologists, physical and occupational therapists, and specialists in such areas as mental retardation and learning disabilities. Although some students leave the classroom for part of the day to work with such specialists, the movement toward greater inclusion means that more and more special services are now being provided within the regular classroom context. As classroom teachers, we need to work closely and collaboratively with educational specialists to develop and deliver an appropriate program for each student (B. L. Driver, 1996; Scruggs & Mastropieri, 1994).

- *Communicate regularly with parents.* In accordance with IDEA, parents are part of the multidisciplinary team that determines the most appropriate program for a student with special needs. A student's parents can provide invaluable information for helping us identify and carry out strategies that are likely to facilitate the student's academic and social growth. Parents can often tell us what works and what does not, and they can alert us to certain conditions or events at home that may trigger problem behaviors in class. Furthermore, we can more effectively bring about desired behavioral changes if we have the same expectations for behavior both at school and at home. We should keep in mind, however, that some parents, especially those from certain cultural backgrounds, may believe that they have little to contribute to decision making with regard to their child—that decisions are better left in the hands of "experts" (DeGangi, Wietlisbach, Poisson, Stein, & Royeen, 1994; Harry, Allen, & McLaughlin, 1995). In some situations, then, we may need to make an extra effort to be sure that parents *are* actively involved in planning for their child's educational success. And in cultures in which extended families play a key role in children's lives, we may want to get other family members (perhaps grandparents, aunts, or uncles) involved as well.

- *When reasonable, hold the same expectations for a student with special needs as for other students.* Sometimes disabilities make it difficult or even impossible for students to accomplish particular school tasks. Aside from such tasks, we should generally hold the same expectations for our students with special needs as we hold for other students. Rather than thinking of reasons why a student *cannot* do a particular task, we should instead be thinking about how we can help that student *do* it. In fact, if we think about it, we can identify many people who've achieved great success despite major disabilities. Here are just a few examples (Armstrong, 1994):

  Albert Einstein had a learning disability (dyslexia).

  Vincent Van Gogh and Edgar Allan Poe had emotional problems.

  In the latter part of his career, Ludwig von Beethoven was completely deaf.

  Helen Keller was both deaf and blind.

  Franklin Delano Roosevelt was confined to a wheelchair.

  Stephen Hawking, the world-renowned astrophysicist, has amyotrophic lateral sclerosis (Lou Gehrig's disease), a progressive neuromuscular disorder that has left him unable to walk, talk, or use pencil and paper.

- *Identify prerequisite knowledge and skills a student may not have acquired.* Some students lack knowledge and skills essential for their school success, perhaps

Get as much information as possible about a student.

Collaborate with specialists.

Communicate frequently with parents.

Hold "normal" expectations for performance when appropriate.

Identify and remediate any gaps in basic knowledge and skills.

because of inexperience or perhaps as a direct result of a disability. Students from impoverished home environments may have had little or no exposure to things that many of us take for granted; for instance, if they have never been to a zoo or a farm and if they have never looked at picture books with their parents, then they may have no idea what a lion, elephant, cow, or horse is. Students with reduced physical mobility have probably not had as many opportunities to manipulate objects in their environment. Students with visual impairments have not been able to observe many of the cause-effect relationships that form a foundation for learning science—for instance, the change in wood's appearance when it is burned (Rowe, 1978). And students who have had few opportunities to interact with other children may have poorly developed interpersonal skills.

Be flexible.

- *Be flexible in approaches to instruction.* Some instructional methods may work better than others for teaching students with special needs, and we cannot always predict which methods will be most effective for individual students. For example, special educators often try a variety of strategies for helping students with learning disabilities practice and learn their spelling (e.g., having students spell the word aloud, trace the letters with their fingers, type each word on a typewriter). If we don't succeed with a particular approach, we should try again. But each time, we might want to try *differently*.

Involve students in decision making.

- *Provide opportunities for students to be involved in decision making.* Although gifted programs often give students a fair amount of autonomy to choose topics and methods of study, educational programs for students with other special needs are often highly structured, to the point where students have little say regarding what and how they learn (Wehmeyer, 1996). But increasingly, special educators are recognizing the importance of letting students with special needs make some choices about academic goals and curriculum (Abery & Zajac, 1996; L. E. Powers et al., 1996; Wehmeyer, 1996). Student decision making can ultimately promote greater *self-regulation*—increasing independence from, and less need for, the guidance of other people. It can also lead to a greater feeling of *self-determination*—a sense of being able to set one's own life course, which many theorists believe is essential for intrinsic motivation (see Chapters 11 and 12).

Promote interaction between students with and without disabilities.

- *Promote interaction between students with special needs and their nondisabled classmates.* One feature often found in classrooms where students with special needs function effectively is frequent interaction between these students and their nondisabled classmates (Scruggs & Mastropieri, 1994). Such interaction is likely to enhance the social skills of our nondisabled students as well as those with special needs. Yet positive social interaction does not necessarily happen on its own (Hymel, 1986; Juvonen & Hiner, 1991; Yuker, 1988). Some students with special needs are readily welcomed by their nondisabled peers. Others are poorly accepted or even rejected by their classmates (Aiello, 1988; Hannah, 1988; Semmel et al., 1979).

For a variety of reasons, some students may not know how, or may be less able, to develop and maintain friendly relationships. And nondisabled classmates may feel resentment or anger about inappropriate behaviors that they believe a special needs classmate should be able to control (Juvonen, 1991; Juvonen & Hiner, 1991). Thus, nondisabled students are often willing to accept students with obvious physical or sensory disabilities (such as cerebral palsy or deafness) but may reject students who behave differently without an obvious physical reason for doing so (Madden & Slavin, 1983; Semmel et al., 1979; Ysseldyke & Algozzine, 1984).

To pave the way for a smooth integration of students with special needs into our classrooms, we must take steps to promote appropriate social interactions between these students and their nondisabled peers. Here are some suggestions:

1. **Teach effective social skills.** Some students may need explicit instruction in how to share, how to cooperate in work and play, how to initiate a conversation, or how to respond appropriately to the statements and questions of others (Bassett et al., 1996; S. Vaughn, 1991).

2. **Provide examples of effective interaction.** It is often helpful to illustrate effective social interaction taking place. For instance, we can use books, plays, or puppet shows to show people with and without disabilities forming friendships, working cooperatively, or being mutually helpful (Aiello, 1988).

3. **Ask students with and without disabilities to assist their classmates.** We might ask a hearing student to take notes for a student with hearing loss or a physical disability, or we might ask a student who is blind to help a nondisabled classmate identify the sounds of particular instruments in a musical score. In addition to promoting greater social interaction, such "giving," prosocial behaviors are also consistent with the spirit of the *community of learners* that we will consider in Chapter 14.

4. **Provide opportunities for cooperative work on academic tasks and in play situations.** We can encourage interaction through such instructional strategies as cooperative learning and peer tutoring (described in Chapter 14). We can also provide toys and games that require the participation of several students (Madden & Slavin, 1983; S. S. Martin, Brady, & Williams, 1991).

5. **Encourage students with special needs to participate in extracurricular activities and community events.** Activities outside the classroom provide an additional arena in which friendships between students with and without disabilities can form (Turnbull et al., in press). For instance, I think of Gabe, a student with Down syndrome and mild mental retardation who attended school in my hometown when I lived in Colorado. Gabe was an avid sportsman, participating in his school's swimming and football teams. I remember once seeing him at a swim meet; although he was clearly in last place in his event, Gabe's teammates cheered him on throughout the race and, after he finished, congratulated him and gave him "high fives" for his performance.

6. **Develop nondisabled students' understanding of students with special needs.** Many of our nondisabled students may need to be educated not only about students' difficulties but also about the *strengths* that these students have. We must communicate the message that, in many ways, students with special needs are normal children with the same thoughts, feelings, and needs as other children their age. As an example, consider Mr. Fields, a teacher who had Danny—a boy with mental retardation—in his classroom. Mr. Fields often publicly described Danny as someone who had better manners than many of his classmates and was, in general, "hard not to like." When he asked Danny questions about classroom subject matter, Mr. Fields would discourage other students from providing the answers for Danny by saying something such as, "No, no, no, I'm asking him. I want to know what *he's* thinking" (Turnbull et al., in press).

• *Look for gradual improvement rather than overnight success.* Because many students with disabilities are likely to improve slowly and gradually, we should look for small, day-to-day improvements rather than expect immediate perfection. By focusing on small improvements, we and our students alike can be encouraged by the changes we do see rather than being discouraged by any problems that persist (Gearheart et al., 1992; Patton et al., 1987).

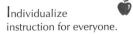 Be encouraged by small changes.

• *Individualize instruction for all students.* Students with special needs blend in better with their classmates when instruction is individualized for everyone. This way, they are not singled out by virtue of any special attention or help they receive. Thus, to the extent that our time and resources allow us to do so, we should try to individualize instruction for *all* students (T. Bryan, 1991; Madden & Slavin, 1983; M. C. Reynolds & Birch, 1988). When instruction is individually tailored to each and every student's unique needs, everyone benefits.

Individualize instruction for everyone.

CASE STUDY: Quiet Amy

Mr. Mahoney has been teaching kindergarten for fifteen years, and he has learned through experience that many kindergartners have some temporary difficulty adjusting to the school environment, especially if they haven't previously attended daycare or preschool. But Amy is giving him cause for concern; after being in school for almost two months, her behavior has changed very little from what it was on the first day of school. Amy never speaks, either to him or to the other children, even when she is directly spoken to; on the infrequent occasions when she wants to communicate—perhaps to express her desire for a particular object or her distress about a classroom event—she does so primarily by looking and pointing at something or someone in the room. She has trouble following even the simplest directions, almost as if she hasn't heard what she's been instructed to do. And she appears distracted during the daily storybook readings and science lessons. The only activities that seem to give her pleasure are arts and crafts; she enjoys working with construction paper, crayons, scissors, and glue, and her creations are often among the most inventive in the class.

To see if he can identify the root of Amy's difficulties, Mr. Mahoney visits her mother, a single woman raising five other children in addition to Amy. "Amy doesn't talk at home, either," the mother admits. "I work two jobs to make ends meet, and I haven't been able to spend as much time with her as I'd like. Her brothers and sisters take good care of her, though. They always seem to know what she wants, and they make sure that she has it."

"My conversation with Mom didn't give me any ideas about how to help Amy," Mr. Mahoney thinks as he drives home after his visit. "It does seem, though, that Amy's primary caretakers are her brothers and sisters, who probably mean well by always responding to her nonverbal behaviors but are doing nothing to encourage her to speak. When I get to school tomorrow morning, my first order of business will be to refer Amy for an in-depth evaluation."

- Mr. Mahoney suspects that Amy may qualify for special educational services. If she does, in what category of special needs might she fall? Can you develop at least three *different* hypotheses as to where her difficulties may lie?

- Amy's evaluation will undoubtedly take several weeks to complete. In the meantime, what strategies might Mr. Mahoney try to improve Amy's classroom performance?

Summing Up

Trend Toward Inclusion

More and more students with special needs are being educated in the regular classroom for part or all of the school day. Such students often show greater academic achievement, better self-concepts, and more appropriate social skills than students with special needs who are educated in self-contained classrooms or separate facilities. In the United States, inclusive practices are encouraged by the *Individuals with Disabilities Education Act* (IDEA), which mandates that public schools: (1) provide a free and appropriate education for any student identified as

having one or more disabilities; (2) evaluate the student accurately, thoroughly, and without discrimination; (3) provide as typical an educational experience as possible for the student; (4) develop and implement an individualized education program (IEP) that addresses the student's unique needs; and (5) ensure due process in decision making.

Categories of Students with Special Needs

Despite some disadvantages of assigning categories and labels to students with special needs, several factors contribute to their continuing use. Although students within any single category often have similar characteristics and needs, we must be careful not to overgeneralize about these students. In this chapter, we organize the various kinds of special educational needs into five general groups: specific cognitive or academic difficulties, social or behavioral problems, general delays in cognitive and social functioning, physical and sensory challenges, and advanced cognitive development.

Students with Specific Cognitive or Academic Difficulties

This broad category encompasses three groups of students. Students with *learning disabilities* often have average or above-average overall scores on intelligence tests but experience difficulty with one or more specific cognitive processing skills. Students with *attention-deficit hyperactivity disorder* (ADHD) either have trouble focusing and maintaining their attention or act in a hyperactive, impulsive fashion; some students with ADHD exhibit both inattention and hyperactive, impulsive behavior. Students with *speech and communication disorders* have abnormalities in speech or language comprehension that significantly interfere with classroom performance.

To some extent, the instructional strategies that we use must be tailored to students' specific difficulty areas. Yet several strategies are applicable to many or all of these students: providing sufficient scaffolding to maximize the likelihood of students' classroom success, clearly communicating expectations for students' classroom performance, and enhancing students' self-confidence and motivation with regard to academic tasks.

Students with Social or Behavioral Problems

This category includes two groups of students. Students with *emotional or behavioral disorders* exhibit either externalizing behaviors (e.g., aggression, defiance) or internalizing behaviors (e.g., depression, withdrawal from all social interaction) that significantly interfere with their classroom learning and performance. Students with *autism* have marked impairments in social interaction and communication, repetitive behaviors, and narrowly focused interests; such characteristics may be due to an abnormal sensitivity to environmental stimuli. Both groups of students are likely to benefit from training in interpersonal skills. They may also perform more successfully in a structured environment in which desired behaviors are clearly identified and consequences for desired and undesired behaviors are consistently administered.

Students with General Delays in Cognitive and Social Functioning

Many students who fall into this category have been identified as having *mental retardation,* a condition characterized by low general intellectual functioning and deficits in adaptive behavior. Strategies for working effectively with such students include pacing instruction more slowly than usual, explaining tasks concretely and in very specific terms, and encouraging independent and self-reliant behaviors.

Students with Physical and Sensory Challenges

Included in this general category are students with *physical and health impairments* (conditions that result in reduced energy, alertness, or muscle control), *visual impairments, hearing loss,* and *severe and multiple disabilities.* Although our instructional strategies will depend to a great extent on students' specific challenges, strategies beneficial to most students in this category include maximizing access to general educational opportunities, making use of technological innovations that can facilitate communication and learning, and providing assistance only when students really need it.

Students with Advanced Cognitive Development

Students identified as being *gifted* often require special educational services to meet their full potential. We must be open-minded about how we identify such students, keeping in mind that giftedness may reflect itself differently in different cultures. Strategies for promoting the achievement of students with gifts and talents include forming study groups of students with similar abilities, teaching complex cognitive skills within the context of various academic subject areas, and providing opportunities for independent study.

General Strategies for Students with Special Needs

Numerous educational strategies apply to virtually all students with special needs. For instance, we should: (1) obtain as much information as possible about each student; (2) consult and collaborate with specialists; (3) communicate regularly with parents; (4) hold the same expectations for a special needs student that we hold for other students (to the extent that's reasonable); (5) identify prerequisite knowledge and skills that a student, perhaps because of a disability, may not have acquired; (6) be flexible in our approaches to instruction; (7) engage students in educational decision making; and (8) facilitate students' social integration into the classroom.

KEY CONCEPTS

Learning and Cognitive Processes

W hat do you mean when you say that you have *learned* something? Do you think differently about some aspect of the world than you did previously? Has your behavior improved or otherwise changed in some way? What specific changes have actually taken place as a result of your learning?

We are always learning new things. As children, we learn a variety of motor skills, such as eating with a fork, holding a pencil, and writing the letters of the alphabet. We also learn innumerable pieces of information, such as the spelling of the word *cat,* the meaning of *atom,* and the location of the Panama Canal. Furthermore, we learn patterns and relationships among pieces of information, such as the "at" pattern found in words like *cat* and *sat,* the relationship between atoms and molecules, and the role that the Panama Canal plays in world trade. And we learn that certain situations call for certain behaviors; for instance, we raise our hands when we wish to speak in class, turn in an assignment on the day it is due, and apologize when we have hurt someone else's feelings.

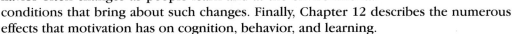

Human learning—a complex, multifaceted process that often involves changes in both thinking and behavior—is the topic of Part 2 of the book: "Understanding How Students Learn." The first four chapters examine the cognitive processes involved in learning, focusing on basic principles of cognition (Chapters 6 and 7), complex thinking skills (Chapter 8), and the forms that thinking and learning often take in various content domains (Chapter 9). Chapters 10 and 11 look at the ways in which behavior often changes as people learn and at the environmental conditions that bring about such changes. Finally, Chapter 12 describes the numerous effects that motivation has on cognition, behavior, and learning.

This chapter addresses the following questions:

- What is *learning,* and what general theoretical perspectives can we use to describe and explain it?
- What basic assumptions and concepts are central to cognitive psychologists' beliefs about learning?
- What is the nature of human memory?
- What cognitive processes are involved in learning (*storing*) something new, and how can we, as teachers, facilitate these processes in students?
- What factors influence students' ability to remember (*retrieve*) information over the long run, and why do students sometimes forget what they've previously learned?
- What are the advantages of giving students time to process classroom material?
- How can we accommodate student diversity in cognitive processing?

CASE STUDY: Darren's Day at School

At the dinner table one night, Darren's mother asks him, "How was your day at school?"

Darren shrugs, thinks for a moment, and says, "Okay, I guess."

"What did you learn?" his father asks.

"Nothing much," Darren replies.

Nothing much, indeed! Let's look at several slices of Darren's school day and see how much he actually *did* learn.

During his daily math lesson, Darren is studying the multiplication tables for the number 9. He finds that some multiplication facts are easy to learn because he can relate them to things he already knows; for example, $9 \times 2 = 18$ is like adding 9 plus 9, and $9 \times 5 = 45$ can be derived from counting by fives. Others, such as $9 \times 4 = 36$ and $9 \times 8 = 72$, are more difficult because he can't connect them to any number facts he has learned before. When Ms. Caffarella finds Darren and a few of his classmates struggling, she teaches the class two tricks for learning the nines multiplication table:

1. The first digit in the product is 1 less than the number by which 9 is being multiplied. For 9×6, the first digit in the product must be $6 - 1$, or 5.

2. The two digits of the product, when added together, equal nine. Because 5 plus 4 equal 9, the product of 9×6 must be 54.

With these two tricks, Darren discovers a pattern in the nines table that helps him recite the table correctly.

During a geography lesson, Ms. Caffarella describes the trip she took to Greece last summer. She holds up a picture postcard of the Parthenon and explains that the building is constructed entirely of marble. Darren is sitting near the back of the room and can't see the picture very clearly; he envisions a building made entirely of *marbles* and silently wonders how the ancient Greeks managed to glue them all together.

In physical education, Darren's class has begun a unit on soccer. Darren has never played soccer before, and his first attempts to move and control the ball with his feet are clumsy and inept. His teacher watches his footwork closely, praising him when he moves his feet appropriately, and eventually Darren is dribbling and passing the ball successfully to his classmates.

In the afternoon's art lesson, Darren's class is making papier-mâché masks. His friend Carla gives her mask a very large nose by adding a crumpled wad of paper below the eye holes and then covering and shaping the wad with several pieces of glued paper. Darren watches her closely throughout the process and then makes his own mask's nose in a similar fashion.

■ What has Darren learned during his math, geography, physical education, and art lessons? Can you identify one or more principles of learning that might describe what has happened in each situation?

Looking at Learning from Different Perspectives

Despite his apparent amnesia at the dinner table, Darren has clearly learned a number of things at school that day, including the nines table in multiplication, the "fact" that the Parthenon was made with marbles, some rudimentary techniques for moving a soccer ball, and a strategy for sculpting with papier-mâché.

But exactly what do we mean by the word **learning?** Theorists disagree about how to define the term. Some theorists propose a definition such as this one:

Definition 1:

Learning is a relatively permanent change in behavior due to experience.

Others propose a definition along these lines:

Definition 2:

Learning is a relatively permanent change in mental associations due to experience.

How are these two definitions similar? How are they different?

You may notice two ways in which the definitions are similar. First, both describe learning as a *relatively permanent change*—something that lasts for a period of time. Second, the change is *due to experience*. It results from specific experiences that students have had—perhaps a lesson in multiplication, a teacher's description of the Parthenon, soccer instruction, or the opportunity to watch a classmate work with papier-mâché.

But now look at how our two definitions differ. The first one describes learning as a change in *behavior,* the second one as a change in *mental associations.* In Darren's day at school, we see several examples of learning as a change in behavior: Darren recites the nines tables correctly for the first time, shows improvement in his ability to dribble a soccer ball, and tries a new way of shaping papier-mâché. We also see several examples of learning as a change in mental associations: Darren relates $9 \times 2 = 18$ to $9 + 9 = 18$, relates the marble in the Parthenon to the marbles he has at home, and remembers the steps that his friend Carla has used to make a nose.

Some learning theories focus on how people's behaviors change over time and on the environmental conditions that bring such changes about. Other theories focus more on internal mental processes—on thinking—than on observable behaviors. Let's look briefly at each of these approaches.

Learning as a Change in Behavior

A problem we encounter when we study "thinking" is that we can never actually *see* thought processes. All we can really observe is behavior: what people do and say. For example, we can't really observe Karl "remember"; we can only hear him say, "Oh, yes, now I remember . . . the capital of Spain is Madrid." We can't truly determine whether Karen is "paying attention"; we can only see whether she is focusing her eyes on the teacher.

Before the turn of the century, many psychologists attempted to study thinking and learning through a method known as *introspection:* They asked people to "look" inside their own minds and describe what they were "thinking." But beginning in the early 1900s, some psychologists began to criticize the introspective approach for its lack of objectivity or scientific rigor. They proposed that, to study learning in an objective, scientific manner, theorists must focus on two things that can be observed: people's behaviors **(responses)** and the environmental events **(stimuli)** that precede and follow those responses. Since then, many psychologists have attempted to describe and understand learning and behavior primarily through an analysis of stimulus-response relationships. Such psychologists are called *behaviorists,* and their theories of learning are collectively known as **behaviorism.**

Not all changes reflect ▲ learning; some are short-lived and unrelated to specific experiences. For example, feelings of fatigue, stomachaches, and eye blinks are temporary, and students soon return to their original alert, healthy, and open-eyed states.

From a teacher's perspective, what are the potential advantages of defining learning as a change in behavior? as a change in mental associations?

We see an example of the behaviorist perspective in action in Darren's physical education class. The teacher watches Darren's *footwork* (his responses) and gives him *praise* (a stimulus) when he makes the right moves. Rather than worry about what Darren might be thinking about soccer, the teacher focuses exclusively on Darren's behavior and provides a desirable consequence when it shows improvement. The teacher is applying a simple behaviorist principle: *A response that is followed by a desired (reinforcing) stimulus is more likely to occur again.*

Learning as a Change in Mental Associations

During the first half of the twentieth century, many psychologists adhered to the behaviorist perspective, especially in North America. As the years went by, however, it became increasingly clear that behaviorism alone could not give us a complete picture of learning. For example, early behaviorists believed that learning can occur only when learners actually behave in some way—perhaps when they make a response and experience the consequences of that response. But in the 1940s, some psychologists proposed that people can also learn a new behavior simply by watching and imitating what *other* people do (N. E. Miller & Dollard, 1941). This idea of *modeling* provided the impetus for an alternative perspective that considers how people learn from observing those around them. Originally called *social learning theory,* this perspective has increasingly incorporated cognitive processes into its explanations of learning; it is now more commonly called **social cognitive theory.**

We find an example of modeling in Darren's experience with the papier-mâché masks. Darren watches Carla as she makes a nose for her mask; after she finishes, he follows the same steps. Notice that Darren imitates what Carla has done only after she has already completed her nose; hence, he makes his nose by using his *memory* of what he has previously observed Carla do. According to social cognitive theorists, learning itself occurs at the time that observation takes place; a behavior change as a result of that learning may or may not occur. For example, Darren might possibly watch Carla and remember what she has done, yet choose *not* to make his nose in the same way.

By the 1960s, many learning theorists were beginning to realize that they could not completely understand learning unless they considered thinking as well as behavior, and they began to conceptualize learning as a mental change rather than a behavioral one. These psychologists shifted their attention away from a detailed analysis of stimulus-response relationships and focused more on the thought processes involved in learning new knowledge and skills. A perspective known as **cognitive psychology**—one that addressed such mental phenomena as memory, attention, concept learning, problem solving, and reasoning—soon emerged (e.g., Neisser, 1967). Some cognitive psychologists have incorporated the ideas of such early theorists as Jean Piaget and Lev Vygotsky into their explanations of how people learn. (My description of the evolution of learning theories is depicted graphically in Figure 6–1.)

What about behaviorists' concern that thinking cannot be studied objectively? Cognitive and social cognitive theorists propose that, by observing people's responses to various stimuli, it is possible to draw *inferences*—to make educated guesses—about the internal mental events that probably underlie those responses. As an example of how we might learn about thought processes by observing people's behaviors, try this simple exercise.

Can you think of examples of how scientists in other disciplines have drawn inferences about unobservable phenomena?

Experiencing Firsthand
Twenty Words

Read these twenty words silently. Read each word carefully, but read each one *only once.*

goat	car	fork	pig	boat
shirt	plate	pants	cup	horse
plane	cow	bus	hat	sock
knife	shoe	spoon	truck	sheep

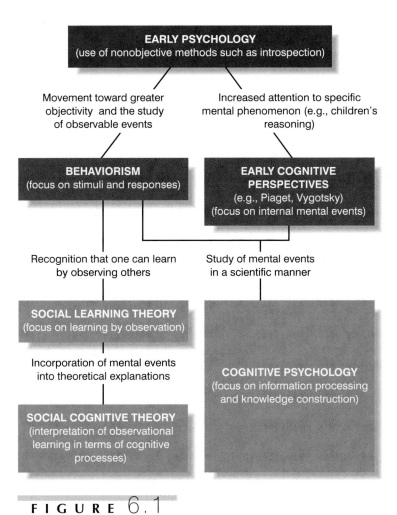

FIGURE 6.1
The evolution of learning theories

Now cover the page and write down as many of the words as you can in whatever order the words come to mind.

Did you write the words down in the order in which you read them? Probably not. If you are like most people, then you remembered many of the words in categories. Perhaps you remembered the clothing items, then the vehicles, then the eating utensils, and then the farm animals. From the order in which you wrote down the words (from your *behavior*), we can draw an inference about an internal cognitive process that occurred as you learned the words: You mentally *organized* them into categories.

Researchers are certainly not the only ones who can draw inferences about cognitive processes from observable behaviors; we, as teachers, can do likewise. By observing what our students say and write, by asking them to explain their reasoning, by looking closely at their mistakes, and so on, we can make some reasonable guesses about what and how they are thinking about classroom topics.

Look at students' behaviors for indications of how they are thinking about classroom subject matter.

Keeping an Open Mind About Theories of Learning

Behaviorism, social cognitive theory, and cognitive psychology encompass different views of several fundamental issues. As a result, each perspective will take us in a

Cognitive theories of learning can help us understand how students think about and process classroom subject matter.

somewhat different direction as we explore the nature of human learning. Yet keep in mind that no single theoretical orientation can give us a complete picture of how people learn. All three perspectives offer valuable lessons for helping students achieve in the classroom.

In terms of the number of articles published in professional journals and the number of presentations given at professional conferences, cognitive psychology's view of learning is the one most in vogue at the present time. Hence, this is the perspective we will take as we begin our exploration of how we can help our students learn effectively in classroom settings, and we will rely on it almost exclusively in Chapters 6 through 9. When we shift our attention to behaviorism in Chapter 10, we will find that we can help students learn more appropriate and productive behaviors if we identify environmental stimuli that promote such behaviors. I have saved social cognitive theory for Chapter 11 because it integrates elements of both cognitive psychology and behaviorism; at that point, we will consider several topics that have implications for classroom practice, including modeling, self-efficacy, and self-regulation. As we discuss motivation in Chapter 12, we will find that all three perspectives—cognitive psychology, behaviorism, and social cognitive theory—provide useful strategies for helping our students *want* to learn.

Basic Assumptions of Cognitive Psychology

Underlying cognitive psychology are several basic assumptions about how people learn. These assumptions, summarized in Table 6–1, are as follows:

Chapter 2 describes cognitive development from the perspective of information processing theory. What concepts and principles can you recall from that discussion?

• *Cognitive processes influence the nature of what is learned.* As noted earlier, cognitive psychologists view learning as an internal mental phenomenon, not an external behavior change. Furthermore, how people think about and interpret their experiences determines what they learn from those experiences. Cognitive psychologists have offered numerous explanations for how people mentally process information; many of these theories are collectively known as **information processing theory.**

As an illustration of the role that cognitive processes play, consider how Darren relates $9 \times 2 = 18$ to $9 + 9 = 18$ and relates $9 \times 5 = 45$ to counting by fives. Consider, too, how the teacher's description of a pattern in the nines table helps Darren remember more difficult facts such as $9 \times 8 = 72$. These two examples illustrate two principles from cognitive psychology: (1) *People learn new information more easily when they can relate it to something they already know,* and (2) *People learn several pieces of new information more easily when they can relate them to an overall organizational structure.*

This focus on the nature of cognitive processes can be extremely helpful to us as teachers. We must consider not only *what* we want our students to learn but also *how* they can most effectively learn it.

Encourage students to think about class material in ways that will help them remember it.

• *People are selective about what they process and learn.* People are constantly bombarded with information. For example, consider the various stimuli that you are

Basic Assumptions of Cognitive Psychology and Their Educational Implications

ASSUMPTION	EDUCATIONAL IMPLICATION	EXAMPLE
Influence of cognitive processes	Encourage students to think about class material in ways that will help them remember it.	When introducing the concept *mammal,* ask students to identify numerous examples.
Selectivity about what is learned	Help students identify the most important things for them to learn. Also help them understand why these things are important.	Give students questions that they should try to answer as they read their textbooks. Include questions that ask them to apply what they read to their own lives.
Construction of meaning	Provide experiences that will help students make sense of the topics they are studying.	When studying Nathaniel Hawthorne's *The Scarlet Letter,* ask students to get together in small groups to discuss why Reverend Arthur Dimmesdale refuses to acknowledge that he is the father of Hester Prynne's baby.
Role of prior knowledge and beliefs	Relate new ideas to what students already know and believe about the world.	When introducing the vocabulary word *debut* to Mexican American students, relate it to *quinceañera,* a "coming-out" party that many Hispanic families hold for their 15-year-old daughters.
Active involvement in learning	Plan classroom activities that get students actively thinking about and using classroom subject matter.	To help students understand latitude and longitude, ask them to track the path of a hurricane using a series of latitude-longitude coordinates that they obtain on the Internet.

encountering at this very moment. How many separate stimuli appear on these two open pages of your textbook? How many objects do you see right now *in addition to* your textbook? How many sounds are reaching your ears? How many objects do you feel—objects on your fingertips, on your toes, at your back, around your waist, and so on? I suspect that you had been ignoring most of these stimuli until just now; you were not processing them until I asked you to do so. People can handle only so much information at a given time, and so they must be selective: They focus on what they think is important and ignore everything else.

As an analogy, consider the hundreds of items a typical household receives in the mail each year—packages, letters, bills, brochures, catalogs, fliers, advertisements, requests for donations, and sweepstakes announcements. Do *you* open, examine, and respond to all the mail you receive? Probably not. If you're like me, then you "process" only a few key items (e.g., packages, letters, bills, and a few miscellaneous things that happen to catch your eye). You may inspect other items long enough to know that you don't need them; you may even discard some items without opening them at all.

In much the same way, our students will encounter a great deal of new information every day—information delivered by way of teacher instruction, textbooks, worksheets, classroom bulletin boards, classmates' behaviors, and so on. They will inevitably make choices as to which pieces of information are most important. They will select a few stimuli to examine and respond to in depth, give other stimuli just a cursory glance, and ignore other stimuli altogether. As teachers, we must help our

It is useful to distinguish ▲ between *sensation*—one's ability to sense stimuli in the environment—and *perception*—one's interpretation of stimuli. What the body senses is not always perceived (interpreted).

Help students identify 🍎 what is most important for them to learn.

students make wise decisions about the pieces of information they choose to attend to, process, and save.

• *Meaning is constructed by the learner, rather than being derived directly from the environment.* The process of **construction** lies at the core of many cognitive theories of learning: People take many separate pieces of information and use them to create an understanding or interpretation of the world around them (e.g., Bransford & Franks, 1971; Hegland & Andre, 1992; Marshall, 1992; Neisser, 1967). To experience the process of construction firsthand, try the following exercise.

▣ Experiencing Firsthand
Three Faces

Figure 6–2 contains three pictures. What do you see in each one? Most people perceive the picture on the left as being that of a woman even though many of her features are missing. Enough features are visible—an eye, parts of the nose, mouth, chin, and hair— that you can construct a meaningful perception from them. Is enough information available in the other two figures for you to construct two more faces? Construction of a face from the figure on the right may take you a while, but it can be done.

Objectively speaking, the three sets of black splotches in Figure 6–2, and especially the two rightmost sets, leave a lot to the imagination. For example, the woman in the middle is missing half of her face, and the man on the right is missing the top of his head. Yet you know enough about how human faces typically appear that you were probably able to add the missing features yourself (mentally) to perceive a complete picture. Curiously, once you have constructed faces from the figures, they then seem obvious. If you were to close this book now and not pick it up again for a week or more, you would probably see the faces almost immediately even if you had had considerable difficulty perceiving them originally.

We see the process of construction in our case study as well. When Ms. Caffarella describes the Parthenon as being made of marble, Darren envisions a building made of marbles similar to the ones he has at home (such a misconception has been described

FIGURE 6.2

Can you construct a person from each of these pictures?

From "Age in the Development of Closure Ability in Children," C. M. Mooney, 1957, Canadian Journal of Psychology, 11, *p. 220. Copyright 1957. Canadian Psychological Association. Reprinted with permission.*

by Sosniak & Stodolsky, 1994). He combines new information with what he already knows to construct meaning.

Some cognitive theories focus primarily on the ways that learners construct knowledge; many of these theories are collectively known as **constructivism.** We first encountered the constructivist perspective in Chapter 2; for example, Piaget proposed that children construct their own body of knowledge about the world, and Vygotsky described how a child can work jointly with an adult to devise an approach to tackle a difficult task.

As teachers, we must remember that our students won't necessarily learn information exactly as we present it to them; in fact, they will each interpret classroom subject matter in their own, idiosyncratic ways. In some cases our students, like Darren, may even learn *mis*information. Accordingly, we should frequently monitor students' understanding by asking questions, encouraging dialogue, and listening carefully to students' ideas and explanations.

Check individual students' understanding of classroom material.

- *Prior knowledge and beliefs play a major role in the meanings that people construct.* Perhaps the major reason that different students in the same classroom learn different things is that they have different bodies of knowledge and beliefs from which to draw as they interpret new information and events. Students all have their own personal histories, and they are likely to come from a wide variety of neighborhoods and cultural backgrounds. Most cognitive psychologists believe that existing understandings of the world have a major influence on what and how effectively people can learn from their experiences. We will be seeing the effects of prior knowledge and beliefs frequently throughout the next few chapters.

Remember that students' background experiences will influence their ability to understand and learn classroom subject matter.

- *People are actively involved in their own learning.* As should be clear by now, cognitive psychologists do not believe that people simply "absorb" knowledge from their surroundings. Instead, people are, and in fact *must be,* active participants in their own learning. Cognitive processing and knowledge construction require a certain amount of mental "work." In our discussion of memory in the pages ahead, we will begin to find out what this "work" involves—in other words, what our students must do (mentally) to learn effectively.

Get students actively involved in thinking about classroom topics.

Basic Terminology in Cognitive Psychology

Four concepts—memory, storage, encoding, and retrieval—will be important in our upcoming discussions of the cognitive processes involved in learning.

Memory

The term **memory** refers to learners' ability to "save" things (mentally) that they have previously learned. In some instances, we will use the term to refer to the actual process of saving learned knowledge or skills over a period of time. In other instances, it will refer to a "location," such as *working memory* or *long-term memory,* where learners "put" what they learn.

Storage

The term **storage** refers to the acquisition of new knowledge—the process of putting what is learned into memory in the first place. For example, you have, I hope, been *storing* the ideas that you have been reading in this chapter. And each time you

Can you make sense of this situation based on your prior knowledge about the world?

go to class, you undoubtedly store some of the ideas presented in lecture or class discussion. You may store other information from class as well—perhaps the name of the person sitting next to you (George), the shape and size of the classroom (rectangular, about 15 by 30 meters), or the pattern of the instructor's shirt (orange and purple horizontal stripes).

Encoding

We don't always store information exactly as we receive it. We usually change it in some way as we store it; in other words, we **encode** it. For example, when you listen to a story, you may picture some of the story's events in your mind. When you see that orange and purple striped shirt, you may think, "Hmmm, this instructor has really bad taste."

People frequently store information in a different way from how it was presented to them. For example, they may change information from auditory to visual form, as is true when they form a mental picture of a story they are listening to. Or they may change information from visual to auditory form, as is true when they read aloud a passage from a textbook. Furthermore, encoding frequently involves assigning specific *meanings* and *interpretations* to stimuli and events. As an illustration, try this exercise.

Experiencing Firsthand
The Old Sea Dog at the Admiral Benbow Inn

Read the following passage *one time only:*

> He was a very silent man by custom. All day he hung round the cove, or upon the cliffs, with a brass telescope; all evening he sat in a corner of the parlour next the fire, and drank rum and water very strong. Mostly he would not speak when spoken to; only look up sudden and fierce, and blow through his nose like a fog-horn; and we and the people who came about our house soon learned to let him be. Every day, when he came back from his stroll, he would ask if any seafaring men had gone by along the road. At first we thought it was the want of company of his own kind that made him ask this question; but at last we began to see he was desirous to avoid them. When a seaman put up at the "Admiral Benbow" (as now and then some did, making by the coast road for Bristol), he would look in at him through the curtained door before he entered the parlour; and he was always sure to be as silent as a mouse when any such was present. For me, at least, there was no secret about the matter; for I was, in a way, a sharer in his alarms. He had taken me aside one day, and promised me a silver fourpenny on the first of every month if I would only keep my "weather-eye open for a seafaring man with one leg," and let him know the moment he appeared. Often enough, when the first of the month came round, and I applied to him for my wage, he would only blow through his nose at me, and stare me down; but before the week was out he was sure to think better of it, bring me my fourpenny piece, and repeat his orders to look out for "the seafaring man with one leg." (from Robert Louis Stevenson's *Treasure Island*)

Now that you have finished the passage, take a few minutes to write down as much of the passage as you can remember.

Think of an exam you have taken recently. Which student would have done better on that exam: one who had encoded information verbatim or one who had encoded it in terms of meanings?

As you reflected back on the passage you had just read, you probably remembered that the man was afraid of a one-legged seafarer. You may also have recalled that the man paid the story's narrator some money to keep an eye out for such an individual. But could you remember *each and every detail* about the events that took place? Could you recall the *exact words* that the author used to describe the man's behavior? If you are like most people, you stored the gist of the passage (its general meaning) without necessarily storing the specific words (e.g., Brainerd & Reyna, 1992).

Retrieval

Once you have stored information in your memory, you may later discover that you need to use that information. The process of remembering previously stored information—that is, "finding" the information in memory—is called **retrieval.** Try your hand at retrieval in the following exercise.

◻ Experiencing Firsthand
Retrieval Practice

See how quickly you can answer each of the following questions.

1. What is your name?
2. In what year did World War II end?
3. What is the capital of Spain?
4. What did you have for dinner three years ago today?
5. When talking about serving appetizers at a party, we sometimes use a French term instead of the word *appetizer.* What is that French term, and how is it spelled?

As you probably just noticed when you tried to answer these questions, retrieving information from memory is sometimes an easy, effortless process; for example, you undoubtedly had little difficulty remembering your name. But other things stored in memory can be retrieved only after some thought and effort; for example, it may have taken you some time to remember that World War II ended in 1945 and that the capital of Spain is Madrid. And still other things, even though they may have been stored in memory at one time, may never be retrieved at all; perhaps a dinner menu three years ago and the correct spelling of *hors d'oeuvre* fall into this category.

How is information stored and encoded in memory? And what factors influence the ease with which we can retrieve it later? Let's look at a model of how human memory might work.

A Model of Human Memory

Cognitive psychologists do not agree about the exact nature of human memory. But many theorists believe that memory may have three components: a sensory register, a working (short-term) memory, and a long-term memory. A three-component model of human memory, based loosely on one proposed by Atkinson and Shiffrin in 1968 but modified to reflect more recent research findings, is presented in Figure 6–3. Please note that, in referring to three components of memory, I am *not* necessarily referring to three separate parts of the brain. The model of memory that I describe here has been derived from studies of human behavior, not from studies of brain physiology.

In the pages that follow, we will look at the characteristics of each component of memory and at how information is moved from one component to the next.

The Nature of the Sensory Register

If you have ever played with a lighted sparkler at night, then you've undoubtedly noticed the "tail" of light that follows a sparkler as you wave it about. And if you have ever daydreamed in class, then you may have noticed that when you tune back in to the lecture, you can still "hear" three or four words spoken just *before* you've started paying attention

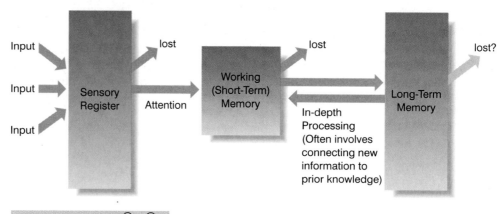

F I G U R E   6.3

A model of the human memory system

to your instructor again. The sparkler's tail and the words that you can still "hear" after they have already been spoken are not "out there" in the environment—they are recorded in your sensory register.

The **sensory register** is the component of memory that holds the information you receive—*input*—in more or less its original, *un*encoded form. Probably everything that your body is capable of seeing, hearing, and otherwise sensing is stored in the sensory register. In other words, the sensory register has a *large capacity*; it can hold a great deal of information at one time.

That's the good news. The bad news is that information stored in the sensory register doesn't last very long (Cowan, 1995; Wingfield & Byrnes, 1981). Visual information—what you *see*—probably lasts for less than a second. As a child, I never could spell out my entire name with a sparkler; the J had always faded before I got to the final E, no matter how quickly I wrote. Auditory information—what you *hear*—probably lasts slightly longer, perhaps for two or three seconds. To keep information for any time at all, then, we need to move it to *working memory*. Whatever information isn't moved is probably lost, or "forgotten."

Moving Information to Working Memory: The Role of Attention

How does information move from the sensory register into working memory? Many theorists believe that **attention** plays a key role here: *Whatever people pay attention to (mentally) moves into working memory.* Anything in the sensory register that does not get a person's attention disappears from the memory system. For example, imagine yourself reading a textbook for one of your classes. Your eyes are moving down each page, but meanwhile you are thinking about something altogether different—a recent fight with a friend, a high-paying job advertised in the paper, or your growling stomach. What have you learned from the textbook? Absolutely nothing. Even though your eyes were focused on the words in your book, you weren't really paying attention to those words. And now imagine yourself in class the following day. Your mind is not on the class discussion, but on something else—a fly on the wall, the instructor's orange and purple shirt, or (again) your growling stomach. As a result, you will remember nothing about that class discussion.

Unfortunately, people can attend to only a very small amount of information at any one time. In other words, attention has a *limited capacity.* For example, if you are in a room where several conversations are occurring at once, you can usually attend to—and

Keep in mind that students won't remember the information they receive unless they process it in some way—at a minimum, by paying attention to it.

therefore can learn from—only *one* of those conversations; this phenomenon is some-times called the *cocktail party phenomenon* (Cherry, 1953; Norman, 1969). If you are sitting in front of the television set with your textbook open in your lap, you can attend to the *I Love Lucy* rerun *or* to your book, but not to both simultaneously. If you are pre-occupied in class with your instructor's ghastly taste in clothing, you are unlikely to be paying attention to the content of the instructor's lecture.

Exactly *how* limited is the limited capacity of human attention? People can often per-form two or three well-learned, automatic tasks at once; for example, you can walk and chew gum simultaneously, and you can probably drive a car and drink a Coke at the same time. But when a stimulus or event is detailed and complex (this is the case for both text-books and *I Love Lucy* reruns) or when a task requires considerable thought (under-standing a lecture and driving a car on an icy mountain road are examples of tasks re-quiring one's utmost concentration), then people can usually attend to only *one* thing at a time (J. R. Anderson, 1990; Reisberg, 1997).

Because of the limited capacity of human attention, only a very small amount of in-formation stored in one's sensory register ever moves on to working memory. The vast majority of information that the body initially receives is quickly lost from the memory system, much as we might quickly discard all that junk mail we receive every day.

Attention in the Classroom

Obviously, it is critical that our students pay attention to the things we want them to learn. To some extent, we can tell which students are paying attention by their overt be-haviors (Grabe, 1986; Piontkowski & Calfee, 1979). But appearances can be deceiving. For example, you can probably think of times when, as a student, you looked at a teacher without really hearing anything the teacher said. You can probably also think of times when you looked at a textbook without a single word on the page sinking in. Attention is not just a behavior, it is also a mental process. It is not enough that students' eyes and ears are directed toward their classroom material. Their minds must be directed toward it as well.

How can we be sure our students are really paying attention? For one thing, we can ask questions in class that test students' understanding of the ideas we are presenting; our students are more likely to keep their minds on a lecture or assignment if they know that they will be immediately accountable for it (Grabe, 1986; Piontkowski & Calfee, 1979). We can also ask students to put classroom material to use—for example, by hav-ing them draw an inference or solve a problem using new information. A third strategy is to encourage students to take notes; research tells us that note taking usually helps students learn information, partly because it makes them pay attention to what they are hearing or reading (Di Vesta & Gray, 1972; Kiewra, 1989).

Every classroom has students who are easily distracted. Such students are more likely to pay attention when they are seated near their teacher (Schwebel & Cherlin, 1972). We can also help these students by providing a stimulating classroom environ-ment in which everyone *wants* to pay attention. Our students are more likely to pay at-tention when they find exciting new things to learn every day, when we use a variety of methods to present classroom material, and when we are lively and obviously enthusi-astic about our subject matter. They are less likely to keep their minds on their work when they study the same topics and follow the same routine day after day, and when, as teachers, we seem to be as bored with the subject matter as they are (Berlyne, 1960; Good & Brophy, 1994; Zirin, 1974).

Of course, students cannot keep their minds on any particular topic forever. They need occasional breaks from intensive mental activity (Pellegrini & Bjorklund, 1997). Some breaks are built into the daily school schedule in such forms as recess, passing pe-riods, and lunch. But we may want to give students additional mental "breathers" as

Remember that students can usually attend to—and thus learn from—only one thing at a time.

Ask students to do something with the information you present.

What things do your favorite instructors do to keep your attention?

Provide a stimulating classroom, one in which students *want* to pay attention.

Chapter 15 identifies additional strategies for keeping students on task.

well—perhaps by asking them to perform a physical task related to the topic at hand or perhaps, after an intensive work session, just by giving them a chance to take a one-minute stretch.

The Nature of Working (Short-Term) Memory

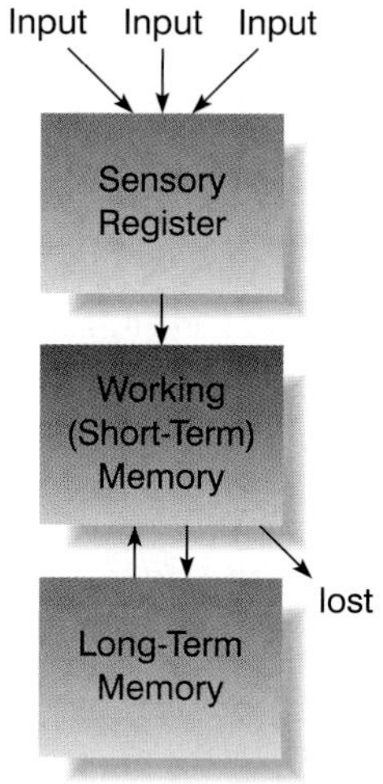

Working memory—sometimes known as **short-term memory**—is the component of memory where new information is held while it is mentally processed; in other words, it is a temporary "holding bin" for new information. Working memory is also where much of our thinking, or cognitive processing, occurs. It is where we try to make sense of a lecture, understand a textbook passage, or solve a problem.

Generally speaking, working memory is the component that probably does most of the "work" of the memory system. It has two characteristics that are particularly worth noting: a short duration and a limited capacity.

Short Duration

THINKING ABOUT WHAT YOU KNOW

Imagine that you need to call a friend, so you look up the friend's telephone number in the phone book. Once you have the number in your head, you discover that someone else is using the phone. You have no paper and pencil handy. What do you do to remember the number until the phone is available?

Because you've paid attention to the number, it is now in your working memory. But working memory, as its alternative name "short-term memory" implies, is *short*. Unless you do something further with the number, it will probably last only five to twenty seconds at the most (e.g., L. R. Peterson & Peterson, 1959).

To keep the telephone number in your head until the phone is available, you might simply repeat it to yourself over and over again. This process, known as **maintenance rehearsal,** keeps information in working memory for as long as you're willing to continue talking to yourself. But once you stop, the number quickly disappears (e.g., Landauer, 1962; G. Sperling, 1967).

I sometimes hear students talking about putting class material in "short-term memory" so that they can do well on an upcoming exam. Such a statement reflects the common misconception that this component of memory lasts for several days, weeks, or even months. Now you know otherwise: Information stored in working memory lasts less than half a minute unless it is processed further. Working memory is obviously *not* the "place" to leave information that you need to know for an exam later in the week, or even for information that you'll need for a class later today.

Limited Capacity

Let's put your working memory to work for a moment.

Experiencing Firsthand
A Divisive Situation

Try computing the answer to this division problem in your head:

$$59\overline{)49{,}383}$$

Did you find yourself having trouble remembering some parts of the problem while you were dealing with other parts? Did you ever arrive at the correct answer of 837? Most

---

Margin notes (left column):

Input   Input   Input

Sensory
Register

Working
(Short-Term)
Memory

Long-Term
Memory

lost

Do you see why this process is called *maintenance* rehearsal?

Did you have this misconception about short-term memory before you read this section?

people cannot solve a division problem with this many numbers unless they can write the problem on paper. The fact is, working memory just doesn't have room to hold all that information at once—it has a *limited capacity* (G. A. Miller, 1956; Simon, 1974).

Just like other human beings, our students will have limited space in their working memories, so they can only learn so much so fast. We must keep this in mind as we plan classroom lessons and activities. A mistake that many new teachers make is to present too much information too quickly, and their students' working memories simply can't keep up. Instead, we should present new information at a pace that gives students time to process it. We can accomplish this in numerous ways—for example, by repeating the same idea several times (perhaps rewording it each time), by stopping to write important points on the chalkboard, and by providing numerous examples and illustrations.

Even when the pace of learning is appropriate, our students can probably never learn *everything* presented to them in class or in a textbook. Most teachers and textbooks present much more information than students can possibly store (Calfee, 1981). For example, one psychologist (E. D. Gagné, 1985) has estimated that students are likely to learn only about one to six new ideas from each minute of a lecture—a small fraction of the ideas that are typically presented during that time! Although they must continually make choices about what things to learn and what things *not* to learn, students aren't always the best judges of what is important (Garner, Alexander, Gillingham, Kulikowich, & Brown, 1991; Mayer, 1984; R. E. Reynolds & Shirey, 1988). We must help our students make the right choices—perhaps by telling them what information is most important, giving them guidelines on how and what to study, or omitting details that really aren't very important after all.

> Remember that students can process only so much information at a time, and pace instruction accordingly.

> Give students guidance about where to focus their learning efforts.

Moving Information to Long-Term Memory: Connecting New Information with Prior Knowledge

In the memory model depicted in Figure 6–3, you will notice that the arrows between working memory and long-term memory go in both directions. The process of storing new information in long-term memory usually involves drawing on "old" information already stored there; in other words, it necessitates using prior knowledge. Here are three examples:

> When Patrick reads about the feuding between the Montagues and the Capulets in *Romeo and Juliet,* he thinks, "Hmmm . . . sounds a lot like the relationship my family has with our next-door neighbors."

> Paolo discovers that the initial letters of each of the five great lakes—Huron, Ontario, Michigan, Erie, and Superior—spell the word *HOMES.*

> Like many young children, Priscilla believes that the world is flat. When her teacher tells her that the world is round, Priscilla pictures a flat, circular disk (which is, of course, round *and* flat).

Each student is connecting new information with something that he or she already knows or believes. Patrick finds a similarity between *Romeo and Juliet* and his own neighborhood. Paolo connects the five Great Lakes with a common, everyday word. And Priscilla relates the idea that the world is round to her previous conception of a flat world and to the many flat, circular objects (e.g., coins, pizzas) she has encountered over the years.

THE FAR SIDE   By GARY LARSON

"Mr. Osborne, may I be excused? My brain is full."

Working memory is a bottleneck in the human memory system.

Later in the chapter we will look more specifically at the processes through which information is stored in long-term memory. But before we do so, we need to examine the characteristics of long-term memory and the nature of the "old" information stored within it.

The Nature of Long-Term Memory

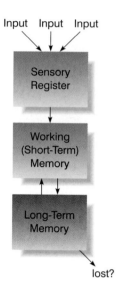

Input   Input   Input

Sensory
Register

Working
(Short-Term)
Memory

Long-Term
Memory

lost?

Long-term memory is the final component of the human memory system. This component holds information for a relatively long period of time—perhaps a day, a week, a month, a year, or one's entire lifetime. Your own long-term memory is where you've stored such pieces of information as your name, a few frequently used telephone numbers, your general knowledge about the world, and the things that you've learned in school—perhaps the year in which World War II ended, the capital of Spain, or the correct spelling of *hors d'oeuvre*. It is also where you've stored your knowledge about how to perform various behaviors—perhaps how to ride a bicycle, swing a baseball bat, or write a cursive letter *G*.

Long-term memory has three characteristics that are especially worth noting: a long duration, an essentially unlimited capacity, and a rich network of interconnections.

(Indefinitely) Long Duration

As you might guess, information stored in long-term memory lasts much longer than information stored in working memory. But exactly *how* long is long-term memory? As you well know, people often forget things that they have known for a day, a week, or even longer. Some psychologists believe that information may slowly "weaken" and possibly disappear from long-term memory, especially if it is not used on a regular basis (J. R. Anderson, 1990; Reisberg, 1997). Others instead believe that, once information is stored in long-term memory, it remains there permanently but may in some cases be extremely difficult to retrieve (Loftus & Loftus, 1980). The exact duration of long-term memory has never been determined, and perhaps never can be (Eysenck & Keane, 1990).

Unlimited Capacity

Long-term memory seems to be capable of holding as much information as an individual needs to store there—there is probably no such thing as a person "running out of room." In fact, for reasons that you will discover shortly, the more information already stored in long-term memory, the easier it is to learn new things.

Interconnectedness

Theorists have discovered that the information stored in long-term memory is organized and interconnected to some extent. To see what I mean, try this simple exercise.

☐ Experiencing Firsthand
Horse #1

What is the first word that comes to your mind when you hear the word *horse*? And what word does that second word remind you of? And what does that third word remind you of? Beginning with the word *horse,* follow your train of thought, letting each word remind you of another one, for a sequence of at least eight words. Write down your sequence of words as each word comes to mind.

You probably found yourself easily following a train of thought from the word *horse,* perhaps something like the route I followed:

horse → cowboy → lasso → rope → knot →
Girl Scouts → cookies → chocolate

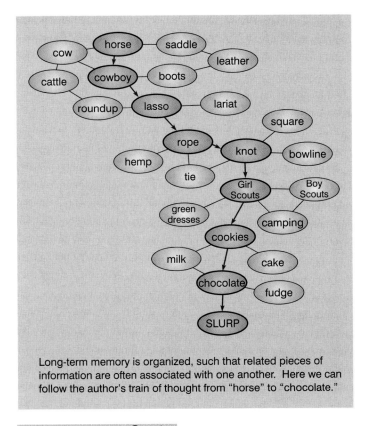

Long-term memory is organized, such that related pieces of
information are often associated with one another. Here we can
follow the author's train of thought from "horse" to "chocolate."

FIGURE 6.4
Interconnectedness in long-term memory

The last word in your sequence might be one with little or no obvious relationship to
horses. Yet you can probably see a logical connection between each pair of words in the
sequence. Cognitive psychologists believe that related pieces of information in long-
term memory are often connected with one another, perhaps in a network similar to the
one depicted in Figure 6–4.

Critiquing the Three-Component Model

In the last few pages, we have considered the sensory register, working memory, and
long-term memory. But are there really three separate components of human memory,
and are they as distinctly different from one another as I have portrayed them? Not all
cognitive psychologists agree that the three-component model is an accurate representation of how human memory works, and research yields mixed results as to whether we
can neatly distinguish among the different components of memory (Cowan, 1995;
R. Crowder, 1993; Eysenck & Keane, 1990).

  Some psychologists (e.g., J. R. Anderson, 1995; A. M. Collins & Loftus, 1975; Cowan,
1995) have proposed that working and long-term memory are not separate components
but instead simply reflect different **activation** states of a single memory. According to
this view, all information stored in memory is in either an active or inactive state. Information that is currently active, which may include both incoming information and information previously stored in memory, is the information that people are paying attention to and processing—information that I have previously described as being in
working memory. As attention shifts, other pieces of information in memory become

Can you summarize
the model of memory
described in the last few
pages?

activated, and the previously activated information gradually becomes inactive. The bulk of the information stored in memory is in an inactive state, so that we are not consciously aware of it; this is information that I have previously described as being in long-term memory.

The three-component model, though perhaps not perfect, is similar to how many cognitive psychologists conceptualize human memory. This model also emphasizes aspects of memory that are important for us to keep in mind as we teach. For example, it highlights the importance of *attention* in learning, the *limited capacity* of attention and working memory, the *interconnectedness* of the knowledge that learners acquire, and the importance of *relating* new information with things learned on previous occasions.

Regardless of whether there are three truly distinct components of memory, some aspects of memory are definitely "long-term." Certainly we remember many things for a considerable length of time, and in this sense, at least, these things are in long-term memory. Let's look more closely at the nature of long-term memory storage.

Long-Term Memory Storage

What forms does "knowledge" take in long-term memory? How do people think about and process new information and skills so they can remember them later? And as teachers, what can we do to help our students engage in effective long-term memory storage processes? These are issues that we turn to now.

The Various Forms of Knowledge

▲ Human memories are undoubtedly stored in some neurological ("brain") form. The forms of encoding described are how memories *appear* to us, rather than how they are in a physiological sense.

Information is probably encoded in long-term memory in a number of different forms (e.g., J. R. Anderson, 1995; J. M. Clark & Paivio, 1991; E. D. Gagné, 1985). For example, some information is stored in a *verbal* form, in terms of actual words. Things that you remember word for word—for example, your name, your address, the nursery rhyme "Jack and Jill," Hamlet's soliloquy ("To be or not to be, that is the question . . . ")—are all verbally encoded. Other information is encoded in the form of *imagery*—that is, in terms of how that information appears on the surface. For example, if in your mind you can "see" the face of a relative or friend or "hear" that individual's voice, then you are retrieving images. Finally, a great deal of information in long-term memory is encoded *semantically,* in terms of its underlying meanings. For example, when you listen to a lecture or read a textbook, you probably store the "gist" of the message more frequently than you store the words themselves. All of these examples are instances of **declarative knowledge**—knowledge that relates to the nature of *how things are.*

Yet people acquire **procedural knowledge** as well; in other words, they learn *how to do things* (e.g., J. R. Anderson, 1983; Phye, 1997; Tulving, 1983). For example, you probably know how to ride a bicycle, wrap a birthday present, and multiply a three-digit number by a two-digit number. To perform such actions successfully, you must adapt your behavior to changing conditions; for example, when you ride a bicycle, you must be able to turn left or right when you find an object directly in your path, and you must be able to come to a complete stop when you reach your destination. Accordingly, procedural knowledge must include information about how to respond under different circumstances.

In many situations, information may be encoded in more than one form simultaneously. For example, stop and think about your last educational psychology class session. Can you recall some of the ideas (meanings) that were presented at that class? Can you recall what your instructor looked like that day (an image)? Can you recall some of the specific words that were spoken or written on the chalkboard (verbal encoding)?

Present the same information in more than one form—for example, as both a verbal explanation and a diagram.

Research evidence indicates that information encoded in multiple ways is more easily retrieved from long-term memory than information encoded in just one way. For example, students learn and remember information more readily when they receive that information in both a verbal form (e.g., a lecture or textbook passage) and a visual form (e.g., a picture, map, or diagram) (Denis, 1984; Kulhavy, Lee, & Caterino, 1985; Winn, 1991). Thus, by presenting information to students in multiple modalities, we increase the likelihood that they will be able to remember it over the long run.

How Declarative Knowledge Is Learned

Consider this situation:

> In biology class Kanesha has been struggling to learn the names of all the bones in the human body from head (*cranium*) to toe (*metatarsus*). She has learned a few bones quickly and easily; for example, it makes sense that the *nasal bone* is near the nose, and she remembers the *humerus* (upper arm bone) by thinking of it as being just above one's "funny (humorous?) bone." But she is still confused about a few bones; for example, the *tibia* and *fibula* are similar-sounding names and are located in the same place (the lower leg). And she keeps thinking that the *sternum* (at the front of the chest) is in back just like the stern of a boat. She has trouble remembering many of the other bones—the coccyx, ulna, sacrum, clavicle, patella—because she's never encountered these words before and can't relate them to anything she knows.
>
> To prepare for her upcoming biology quiz, Kanesha looks at a diagram of the human skeleton and whispers the name of each bone to herself several times. She also writes each name down on a piece of paper. "These terms should certainly sink in if I repeat them enough times," she tells herself.
>
> Kanesha scores only 70 percent on the biology quiz. As she looks over her incorrect answers, she sees that she confused the tibia and the fibula, labeled the ulna as "clavicle," put the sternum in the wrong place, and completely forgot to label the coccyx, sacrum, and patella.

Why are some of the bones easier for Kanesha to remember than others? Which of Kanesha's strategies for learning the bones are probably most effective?

Kanesha is thinking about different bones in different ways. She makes some kind of logical "sense" of the nasal bone and humerus; she also tries to make sense of the sternum, but her strategy backfires when she relates this bone to the stern of a boat. Kanesha does little if any thinking about why the other bones have the names they do. The extent to which Kanesha mentally processes the material she needs to learn and the *ways* in which she processes it affect her performance on the biology quiz.

The specific cognitive processes that a person uses when trying to learn new information affects the individual's ability to remember and use that information at a later time. In the next few pages, we will consider five processes (summarized in Table 6–2) that people may use in storing declarative information in long-term memory:

- Rehearsal
- Meaningful learning
- Organization
- Elaboration
- Visual imagery

Rehearsal

Earlier I described how maintenance rehearsal—repeating something over and over again verbally—helps us keep information in working memory indefinitely. Early theorists (e.g., Atkinson & Shiffrin, 1968) believed that **rehearsal** is also a means through

Five Possible Ways of Learning Declarative Knowledge

PROCESS	DEFINITION	EXAMPLE	EFFECTIVENESS	EDUCATIONAL IMPLICATION
Rehearsal	Repeating information verbatim, either mentally or aloud	Repeating a word-for-word definition of *inertia*	Relatively ineffective: Storage is slow, and later retrieval is difficult	Suggest rehearsal only when more effective strategies are not possible.
Meaningful learning	Making connections between new information and prior knowledge	Putting a definition of *inertia* into one's own words or identifying examples of inertia in one's own life experiences	Effective if associations made with prior knowledge are appropriate ones	Help students understand new information in terms of the things that they already know.
Organization	Making connections among various pieces of new information	Studying how one's lines in a play relate to the overall plot	Effective if organizational structure is legitimate and if it consists of more than a "list" of separate facts	Present material in an organized fashion, and point out the organizational structure and interrelationships in the material.
Elaboration	Adding additional ideas to new information based on what one already knows	Thinking about possible reasons why historical figures behaved as they did	Effective if added ideas are appropriate inferences	Encourage students to go beyond the information itself—for example, to draw inferences and to speculate about possible implications.
Visual imagery	Forming a mental "picture" of information	Imagining how various characters and events in *Ivanhoe* might have looked	Individual differences in effectiveness; especially beneficial when used as a supplement to semantic encoding	Illustrate verbal instruction with visual materials (e.g., pictures, maps, diagrams).

which information is stored in long-term memory. In other words, if we repeat something often enough, it might eventually sink in.

The main disadvantage in using rehearsal is that we make few if any connections between new information and the knowledge that we already have in long-term memory. Thus, we are engaging in **rote learning:** We are learning information in a strictly verbatim fashion, without attaching any meaning to it. Contrary to what many students think, rote (meaningless) learning is a slow and relatively ineffective way of storing information in long-term memory (J. R. Anderson, 1995; Ausubel, 1968; Craik & Watkins, 1973). Furthermore, for reasons you will discover later, information stored in a rote fashion is more difficult to retrieve later on.

If you have already read the discussion of cognitive development in Chapter 2, then you may remember that rehearsal is one of the first learning strategies that students develop (usually in early elementary school). Verbally rehearsing information is probably better than not processing it at all. And in cases where students have little if any prior knowledge to draw on to help them understand new material (as was the case when Kanesha was trying to learn the tibia, fibula, coccyx, ulna, etc.), rehearsal may be one of the few strategies that they can use (E. Wood, Willoughby, Reilley, Elliott, & DuCharme, 1994).

If we teach young children, we should expect that rehearsal will be a predominant method through which they will attempt to learn new information. For secondary students, however, we should promote the use of other, more effective methods, such as meaningful learning, organization, elaboration, and visual imagery.

Meaningful Learning

The process of **meaningful learning** involves recognizing a relationship between new information and something else already stored in long-term memory. When we use words like *comprehension* or *understanding,* we are talking about meaningful learning. Here are some examples:

> When Juan reads that World War II ended on August 10, 1945, he thinks, "Hey, August tenth is my birthday!"

> Students in a German class notice that the German word *Buch* is pronounced similarly to its English equivalent: *book*.

> Jane encounters a new subtraction fact: $4 - 2 = 2$. "That makes sense," she thinks. "After all, two plus two are four, and this is just doing the same thing backward."

> When Julian reads J. D. Salinger's *Catcher in the Rye,* he sees similarities between Holden Caulfield's emotional struggles and his own adolescent concerns.

Research clearly indicates that meaningful learning is more effective than rote learning (Ausubel et al., 1978; Mayer, 1996; Bransford & Johnson, 1972). As illustrations of the effectiveness of meaningful learning, try the following two exercises.

Experiencing Firsthand
Two Letter Strings, Two Pictures

1. Study each of the following strings of letters until you can remember them perfectly:

   AIIRODFMLAWRS   FAMILIARWORDS

2. Study each of the two pictures below until you can reproduce them accurately from memory.

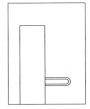 

Figures are from "Comprehension and Memory for Pictures" by G. H. Bower, M. B. Karlin, and A. Dueck, 1975, Memory and Cognition, 3, *p. 217. Reprinted by permission of Psychonomic Society, Inc.*

No doubt the second letter string was easier for you to learn because you could relate it to something that you already knew: "familiar words." How easily were you able to learn the two pictures? Do you think that you could remember them well enough to draw them from memory a week from now? Do you think that you would be able to remember them more easily if they had meaningful titles such as "a short person playing a trombone in a telephone booth" and "an early bird who caught a very strong worm"? The answer to the latter question is a very definite yes (Bower et al., 1975).

Encourage younger students to use rehearsal if they know no other learning strategies. Support older students in using more effective storage methods whenever possible.

Meaningful learning is similar to Piaget's concept of *assimilation* (see Chapter 2).

Encourage students to relate new information to things they already know.

Some students approach school assignments with meaningful learning in mind: They try to make sense of new information in terms of what they already know. These students are likely to be the high achievers in the classroom. Other students instead use such rote learning strategies as repeating something over and over to themselves without really thinking about what they are saying. As you might guess, these students have more difficulty in school (e.g., C. E. Weinstein, 1978).

Yet we cannot always blame students when they take a relatively meaning*less* learning approach to their studies. Inadvertently, many teaching practices encourage students to learn school subjects in a rote fashion. Think back to your own experiences in school. How many times were you allowed to define a word by repeating a dictionary definition, rather than being expected to explain it in your own words? In fact, how many times were you *required* to learn something word for word? And how many times did an exam test your knowledge of facts or principles without ever testing your ability to relate those facts and principles to everyday life or to things learned in previous courses? When students expect a test to focus on the recall of unrelated facts, rather than on the understanding and application of an integrated body of knowledge, many of them will rely on rote learning, believing that such an approach will yield a higher test score and that meaningful learning would be counterproductive (Crooks, 1988). It is little wonder that meaningful learning is the exception rather than the rule in many classrooms (Cooney, 1991; McCaslin & Good, 1996; Novak & Musonda, 1991; Schoenfeld, 1985b).

Why do some students learn things meaningfully, whereas others persist in their attempts at rote memorization? At least three conditions probably facilitate meaningful learning (Ausubel et al., 1978):

• *The student has a meaningful learning set.* When students approach a learning task believing they can make sense of the information—that is, when they have a **meaningful learning set**—they are more likely to learn that information meaningfully. For example, students who recognize that chemical reactions occur in accordance with familiar mathematical principles are more likely to make sense of those reactions. Students who realize that historical events can often be explained in terms of human personality are more likely to understand why World War II occurred.

My daughter Tina once came home from school with an assignment to learn twelve of the gods and goddesses of ancient Greece (e.g., Zeus was the king of gods, Athena was the goddess of the city and civilization, Apollo was the god of light, Aphrodite was the goddess of love). Unfortunately, there had been little discussion in school of the relevance of these gods and goddesses to anything else Tina knew—for example, to the city of Athens or to the Apollo space flights. And I was reluctant to introduce my daughter to the word *aphrodisiac* simply to help her remember Aphrodite. As a result, Tina had no meaningful learning set for the twelve gods and goddesses—no expectation of connecting them with their domains in any meaningful way. Refusing my motherly offers to help yet determined to do well on an upcoming quiz, she confined herself to her room and rehearsed those gods and goddesses over and over until she could recite all twelve. A month later, I asked her how many she could still recall. She remembered only Zeus.

Do we present information merely as "something to be learned" or instead as something that can help students better understand their world? Do we ask students to define new terminology by using the exact definitions presented in the textbook or instead require them to define terms in their own words? When asking students to give examples of a concept, do we expect examples already presented in the textbook or instead request that students generate new examples? How we present a learning task clearly affects the extent to which our students are likely to adopt a meaningful learning set (Ausubel et al., 1978). Ideally, we must communicate our belief that students *can* and *should* make sense of the things they study.

Communicate the belief that students can and should make sense of the things they study.

Meaningful learning is more likely to occur when learners have had experiences to which new information can be related.

• *The student has previous knowledge to which the new information can be related.* Meaningful learning can occur only when long-term memory contains a relevant **knowledge base**—information to which a new idea can be connected. Students will better understand scientific principles if they have already seen those principles in action, either in their own lives or in the laboratory. They will more easily learn the events of an important battle if they have previously visited the battlefield. They will better understand how large the dinosaurs really were if they have seen actual dinosaur skeletons at a museum of natural history. The more information a student has already stored in long-term memory, the easier it is for that student to learn new information, because there are more things with which that new information can be associated.

• *The student is aware that previously learned information is related to new information.* Students often have prior information that relates to something new without ever making the connection; as a result, they often resort to rote learning strategies unnecessarily. Thus, we can facilitate meaningful learning by reminding students of things they know that have a direct bearing on a topic of classroom study (Machiels-Bongaerts, Schmidt, & Boshuizen, 1991; Resnick, 1989; Spires & Donley, 1998). For example, we can relate works of literature to students' own thoughts, feelings, and experiences. We can explain historical events in terms of the foibles of human personality. We can point out instances when foreign language vocabulary is similar to words in English. We can tie science to students' day-to-day observations and experiences. And we can relate mathematics to such commonplace activities as cooking, building a treehouse, or throwing a ball.

The two storage processes that follow—organization and elaboration—also involve relating new information to prior knowledge; hence, both of these processes incorporate meaningful learning. Yet each one has an additional twist as well.

Find out whether students have sufficient knowledge to understand new topics; for example, give a pretest or ask questions informally in class.

What implications does this second condition—relevant prior knowledge—have for teaching students from diverse cultural backgrounds?

Remind students of things they know that have a direct bearing on classroom material.

Calvin and Hobbes   by Bill Watterson

Calvin is trying to learn new information meaningfully, but his efforts are in vain because the word *feudal* is not in his knowledge base.

CALVIN AND HOBBES ©1995, 1990 Watterson. Dist. by UNIVERSAL PRESS SYNDICATE. Reprinted with permission. All rights reserved.

Organization

▢   THINKING ABOUT WHAT YOU KNOW

Have you ever had an instructor who came to class and spoke aimlessly for an hour, flitting from one idea to another in an unpredictable sequence? Have you ever read a textbook that did the same thing, so that you never knew how ideas related to one another? In general, how easily can you learn in a situation where information is disorganized?

The fact is, we learn and remember a body of new information more easily when we **organize** it (e.g., Bjorklund et al., 1994; G. Mandler & Pearlstone, 1966; Tulving, 1962). By organizing information, we make connections among various pieces of information rather than learn each piece in isolation; in the process, we often make connections with existing knowledge as well. Consider these examples of how students might organize school learning tasks:

> Giorgio is given a list of eleven events leading up to the American Revolution: the Navigation Acts, the Sugar Act, the Stamp Act, the Tea Act, the Boston Massacre, the Boston Tea Party, the attack of the *Gaspee,* the Battle of Lexington, the Battle of Concord, the Battle of Bunker Hill, and the signing of the Declaration of Independence. He puts them into three groups: British legislation, acts of colonial defiance, and pre-war battles.

> Genevieve's ten spelling words end with a "long e" sound. She decides to group the words based on their endings (*y, ey,* or *ie*) like this:

body	key	movie
family	donkey	cookie
party	monkey	calorie
gravy		

> When Greg is trying to learn the components of the human memory system, he makes a chart indicating their capacity and duration, like the following:

	Sensory Register	Working Memory	Long-term Memory
Capacity	large	small	large
Duration	very short: <1 second—visual 2–3 sec.—auditory	5–20 seconds	indefinitely long

Learners are more likely to organize information if the material fits an organizational structure with which they are already familiar—for example, if the material can be placed into discrete categories or into a hierarchical arrangement (Bousfield, 1953; Bransford & Franks, 1971; DuBois, Kiewra, & Fraley, 1988; Gauntt, 1991). They are also more likely to learn new material in an organized fashion if that material has been presented to them with its organizational structure laid out for them. As an illustration, let's consider the results of a classic experiment (Bower et al., 1969). College students were given four study trials in which to learn 112 words falling into four categories (e.g., minerals, plants). For some students, the words were arranged in an organized fashion (Figure 6–5 is an example). For other students, the words were arranged randomly. Look at the average number of words that each group remembered after studying them for one study period (about four minutes) and again after three additional study periods:

Number of Study Periods	Organized Words	Unorganized Words
1	73 (65%)	21 (19%)
4	112 (100%)	70 (63%)

Notice that, after studying the words one time, students with organized words remembered more than three times as many words as students who received them in mixed-up order. And after four study periods, students with the organized words remembered the entire list of 112!

Unfortunately, many students tend to "organize" the things they study in school merely as a list of separate facts, rather than as a set of interrelated ideas (Kletzien, 1988; B. J. F. Meyer, Brandt, & Bluth, 1980). As teachers, how can we help our own students organize class material more effectively? Obviously, we should present material in an organized fashion to begin with. For example, we can tell students ahead of time exactly what organizational structure the new material is likely to take—the categories that we will be talking about, the hierarchical nature of certain concepts, and so on. We can also present related pieces of information close together in time; students are more likely to associate related ideas when they encounter those ideas together (Glanzer & Nolan, 1986; Hayes-Roth & Thorndyke, 1979). And we can point out important interrelationships among various concepts and ideas.

Present information in an organized fashion.

We will identify some specific techniques for helping students organize information when we discuss *concept mapping* in Chapter 8 and *advance organizers* in Chapter 13.

Elaboration

People sometimes use their prior knowledge to expand on a new idea, thereby actually storing *more* information than was actually presented to them. This process of adding to newly acquired information in some way is called **elaboration**. Here are some examples:

Maria learns that an allosaur had powerful jaws and sharp, pointed teeth. "Allosaurs must have been meat eaters," she deduces.

Marcus gets a note from a friend who writes, "Meat me by the bak door after skool." Marcus translates his friend's message as, "Meet me by the back door after school."

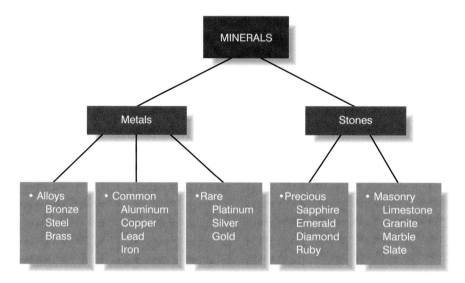

FIGURE 6.5

Storing information through organization

From "Hierarchical Retrieval Schemes in Recall of Categorized Word Lists" by G. H. Bower, M. C. Clark, A. M. Lesgold, and D. Winzenz, 1969, Journal of Verbal Learning and Verbal Behavior, 8, *p. 324. Copyright 1969 by Academic Press. Adapted by permission.*

When I took a Chinese course in high school, I learned that the Chinese word *wǒmen* means "we." "Aha," I thought to myself, "that's the sign on the rest room that *we* girls use."

In most cases, the more students elaborate on new material—the more they use what they already know to help them understand and interpret the material—the more effectively they will store it in long-term memory (J. R. Anderson, 1995). I remember very little of my two years of Chinese instruction, but the meaning of the word *wǒmen* remains indelibly stored in my long-term memory. Students who elaborate on the things they learn in school are usually better students than those who simply take information at face value (M. A. McDaniel & Einstein, 1989; Pressley, 1982; Waters, 1982).

As teachers, we will often want our students to get in the habit of going beyond the information actually presented to them. We can help them to elaborate in numerous ways. For example, we can ask frequent questions along these lines:

- Why do you think this happens?
- Can you think of some examples of this concept?
- Where might this idea be useful? How could we use it in our everyday lives?
- What things can you conclude from this information?

We can also foster elaboration by allowing students to talk about a topic among themselves, asking them to explain an idea on paper, or simply giving them time to think about new information.

Visual Imagery

Earlier in the chapter, I mentioned imagery as one possible way in which information might be encoded in long-term memory. Numerous research studies indicate that **visual imagery**—forming mental "pictures" of objects or ideas—can be an effective method of storing information (J. M. Clark & Paivio, 1991; Dewhurst & Conway, 1994; Sadoski,

*C*an you think of situations in which you learned and remembered something more effectively by elaborating on it?

*E*ncourage students to elaborate—to use their prior knowledge and experiences to expand on the new things they learn.

Goetz, & Fritz, 1993). To show you how effective visual imagery can be, let me teach you a few of the Chinese words I studied in high school.

Experiencing Firsthand
Five Chinese Words

Try learning these five Chinese words by forming the visual images I describe:

Chinese Word	English Meaning	Image
fáng	house	Picture a *house* with *fangs* growing on its roof and walls.
mén	door	Picture a rest room *door* with the word "*MEN*" painted on it.
ké	guest	Picture someone giving someone else (the *guest*) a *key* to the house.
fàn	food	Picture a plate of *food* being cooled by a *fan.*
shū	book	Picture a *shoe* with a *book* sticking out of it.

At this point, find something else to do for a couple of minutes. Stand up and stretch, get a glass of water, or use the bathroom. But be sure to come back to your reading in just a minute or two. . . .

Now that you're back, cover the list of Chinese words, English meanings, and visual images. Try to remember what each word means:

ké

fàn

mén

fáng

shū

Did the Chinese words remind you of the visual images that you stored? Did the images help you remember the English meanings of the Chinese words?

You may have remembered all five words easily, or you may have remembered only one or two. People differ in their ability to use visual imagery: Some form visual images quickly and easily, whereas others form them only slowly and with difficulty (J. M. Clark & Paivio, 1991; Kosslyn, 1985; Riding & Calvey, 1981). For those in the former category, imagery can be a powerful means of storing information in long-term memory.

As teachers, we can promote the use of visual imagery in several ways. We can ask students to imagine how certain events in literature or history might have looked. We can demonstrate abstract ideas with concrete objects. And we can provide visual materials—pictures, charts, graphs, and so on—that illustrate important ideas.

The last three storage processes—organization, elaboration, and visual imagery—are clearly *constructive* in nature: They all involve combining several pieces of information into a meaningful whole. When we organize information, we rearrange the specific items we need to learn so that they fit within a familiar framework (categories, a hierarchy, or the like). When we elaborate on new information, we use what we already know to help us make better sense of it. And when we use visual imagery, we construct mental pictures (perhaps a house with fangs, or a rest room door with *MEN* painted on it) based on how we know certain objects typically look. In Chapter 7, we will examine the constructive nature of long-term memory storage more closely.

Have students form visual images that capture the things they are studying.

Present ideas in a visual manner—for example, with pictures, charts, or graphs.

INTO THE CLASSROOM: Helping Students Learn New Information

Let students know what information is most important to learn.

When a history teacher prepares his students for an upcoming exam on World War I, he reminds them, "When you study for the test, you should try to understand how the specific events that we discussed contributed to the progress and eventual outcome of the war. Know when each event occurred in relation to other events, but don't try to learn each and every date."

Present the same ideas in more than one form.

A biology teacher shows her class a diagram of the human heart. She traces the flow of blood with her finger as she describes how the heart pumps blood through the body.

Show students how new material relates to things they already know.

When describing the law of gravity, a teacher asks, "What happens when you let go of something? Which way does it fall? Have you ever seen anything fall *up*?"

Present information in an organized fashion.

A teacher groups new spelling words according to their letter patterns. For example, she gives students a list of *uff* words (e.g., *buff, muff, stuff*) and *ough* words (e.g., *rough, tough, enough)*.

Encourage students to elaborate on class material.

A social studies teacher describes a general principle of geography: New settlements often spring up at the junctions of two or more major transportation routes. She then asks her class, "Why do you think that might be so?"

Encourage students to form visual images that capture the things they are studying.

An elementary teacher is reading a short story to his class. After reading a description of the story's main character, he stops and asks his class to imagine the person just as the author has described her—a woman with tousled gray hair, twinkling brown eyes, and a warm, welcoming smile.

Begin at a level consistent with students' existing knowledge base.

At the beginning of the school year, a mathematics teacher gives her students a pretest covering the mathematical concepts and operations they studied the year before. She finds that many students still have difficulty computing the perimeter and area of a rectangle. She reviews these procedures and gives students additional practice with them before beginning a unit on computing the volume of objects with rectangular sides.

How Procedural Knowledge Is Learned

Some of the procedures that people learn—for example, driving a stick shift, baking a cake, and serving a volleyball—consist primarily of overt behaviors. Many others—for instance, solving for *x* in an algebraic equation, making sense of difficult reading material, and surfing the Internet—are largely mental in nature. Most procedures obviously involve a combination of physical behaviors and mental activities.

Procedural knowledge ranges from relatively simple actions (e.g., holding a pencil correctly or using scissors) to far more complex ones. Complex procedures are usually not learned in one fell swoop. Instead, they are acquired slowly over a period of time, often only with a great deal of practice (J. R. Anderson, 1983; Ericsson & Chalmers, 1994; Proctor & Dutta, 1995).

Researchers are only beginning to identify the cognitive processes involved in storing procedural knowledge. To some extent, of course, learners store procedures in terms of actual behaviors. Yet many procedures, particularly complex ones, may begin largely as declarative knowledge—in other words, as *information* about how to execute a procedure rather than as the actual *ability* to execute it (J. R. Anderson, 1983, 1987). When learners use declarative knowledge to guide them as they carry out a new procedure, their performance is slow and laborious, the activity consumes a great deal of mental effort, and they often talk themselves through their actions (using the *self-talk* that Vygotsky described). As they continue to perform the activity, however, their declarative knowledge gradually evolves into procedural knowledge. This knowledge becomes fine-tuned over time and eventually allows learners to perform an activity quickly, efficiently, and effortlessly (J. R. Anderson, 1983, 1987).

Researchers have identified several general teaching strategies that seem to help students learn and remember procedures more effectively. For instance, we can demonstrate a procedure or show pictures of the specific behaviors it involves (R. Gagné, 1985). We can encourage students to use verbal rehearsal as they learn a new skill—in other words, to repeat the required steps over and over to themselves (Weiss & Klint, 1987). And as you might guess, our students will be more likely to remember a procedure when we give them a chance to carry it out themselves and when we give them regular feedback about how they are doing (R. L. Cohen, 1989; Heindel & Kose, 1990; Proctor & Dutta, 1995).

Many of the instructional strategies we derived from Vygotsky's theory (see Chapter 2) are also useful for helping students acquire procedural knowledge; in particular, we can show students how we ourselves think as we perform a difficult task, and we can provide the scaffolding students may initially need to perform the same task successfully. Chapters 8 and 9 describe additional strategies for facilitating the acquisition of procedural knowledge within the context of problem solving, metacognition, and the various content domains.

Demonstrate a new procedure and encourage students to rehearse it verbally.

Give students the opportunity to execute a procedure themselves, and provide feedback about their performance.

Prior Knowledge and Working Memory in Long-Term Memory Storage

Occasionally, students' prior knowledge interferes with something they need to learn; as examples, consider Darren's confusion about the marble Parthenon and Kanesha's difficulty learning where the sternum is located. But in general, a relevant knowledge base helps students store classroom subject matter much more effectively (P. A. Alexander, 1996; P. A. Alexander, Kulikowich, & Schulze, 1994; Hamman et al., 1995; W. Schneider, 1993). Students' prior knowledge facilitates their learning in several ways:

- It helps them determine what is most important to learn; thus, it helps them direct their *attention* appropriately.
- It enables them to understand something—that is, to engage in *meaningful learning*—instead of learning it at a rote level.
- It provides a framework for *organizing* new information.
- It helps them *elaborate* on information—for example, by filling in missing details, clarifying ambiguities, or drawing inferences. (Ausubel et al., 1978; Carpenter & Just, 1986; Rumelhart & Ortony, 1977; West, Farmer, & Wolff, 1991; P. T. Wilson & Anderson, 1986)

Do you now see why Kanesha had such difficulty remembering the coccyx, ulna, sacrum, clavicle, and patella?

Yet as we noted in our earlier discussion of meaningful learning, it is not enough that our students have the knowledge they need to interpret new material; they must also be *aware* that the knowledge is relevant. They must then retrieve it from their long-term memories at the same time that they are thinking about new material, such that they have both the "old" and the "new" in working memory simultaneously and can make appropriate connections between them (Bellezza, 1986; Glanzer & Nolan, 1986).

As teachers, we should keep students' existing knowledge in mind and use it as a starting point whenever we introduce a new topic. For example, we might begin a first-grade unit on plants by asking students to describe what their parents do to keep flowers or vegetable gardens growing. Or, in a secondary English literature class, we might introduce Sir Walter Scott's *Ivanhoe* by asking students to tell the tale of Robin Hood as they know it. We should also remember that students from diverse cultural backgrounds are likely to have different knowledge bases and modify our starting points accordingly.

🍎 Introduce a new topic by asking students to retrieve things they already know about the topic.

Using Mnemonics in the Absence of Relevant Prior Knowledge

THINKING ABOUT WHAT YOU KNOW

Can you think of topics you studied in school that would have been difficult to learn meaningfully no matter how much prior knowledge you had? Can you think of examples in science? mathematics? history? music? a foreign language?

When you were in elementary and secondary school, there were probably many times when you had difficulty making sense of material that you needed to learn. Perhaps you had trouble learning the chemical symbols for some of the elements because those symbols seemed unrelated to the elements' names. (Why is Au the symbol for gold?) Perhaps you couldn't remember words in a foreign language because those words were very different from their English meanings. Or perhaps you couldn't remember lists of things (e.g., four things you should do when treating a victim of shock, eleven events leading up to the American Revolution) because they always contained several seemingly unrelated items, and one item didn't help you remember any of the others.

When students are likely to have trouble finding relationships between new material and their prior knowledge or when a body of information has an organizational structure with no apparent logic behind it (e.g., as is true for many lists), special memory "tricks" known as **mnemonics** can help them learn classroom material more effectively. Three commonly used mnemonics are:

🍎 Give students mnemonics to use when new information is difficult to learn meaningfully.

- Verbal mediation
- Keyword method
- Superimposed meaningful structures

Verbal Mediation

A **verbal mediator** is a word or phrase that forms a logical connection, or "bridge," between two things. Verbal mediators can be used for such "paired" pieces of information as foreign language words and their English meanings, countries and their capitals, chemical symbols for the elements, and words and their spellings. Here are some examples:

Information to be learned	Verbal mediator
Handschuh is German for "glove."	A glove is a *shoe* for the *hand*.
Quito is the capital of Ecuador.	Mos*quito*s at the equator.
Au is the symbol for gold.	*Ay, you* stole my gold watch!
The word principal ends in *pal* (not *ple*).	The principal is my *pal*.

In our earlier case study, Kanesha uses a verbal mediator to help her remember one of the bones: She thinks of the humerus as being just above the "funny (*humorous*) bone."

Keyword Method

Like verbal mediation, the keyword method is a technique for making a connection between two things. This method is especially helpful when there is no logical verbal mediator to fill the gap—for example, when there is no obvious sentence or phrase to relate a foreign language word to its English meaning. The keyword method involves two steps, which I will illustrate using the Spanish word *amor* and its English meaning *love*:

1. Identify a concrete object to represent each piece of information. The object may be either a commonly used symbol (e.g., a heart to symbolize *love*) or a "sound alike" word (e.g., a suit of armor to represent *amor*). Such objects are **keywords.**

2. Form a picture in your mind of the two objects together. To remember that *amor* means *love,* you might picture a knight in a suit of armor with a huge red heart painted on his chest.

You used the keyword method when you did the "Five Chinese Words" exercise earlier. Here are some additional examples:

Information to be learned	Visual image
Das Pferd is German for "horse."	A *horse* driving a *Ford*.
Augusta is the capital of the state of Maine.	A *gust of* wind blowing through a horse's *mane*.
Tchaikovsky composed "Swan Lake."	A *swan* swimming on a *lake*, wearing a *tie* and *cough*ing.

Superimposed Meaningful Structure

A larger body of information (e.g., a list of items) can often be learned by superimposing a meaningful structure—a familiar shape, word, sentence, poem, or story—on that information. Here are some examples of such **superimposed meaningful structures:**

Information to be learned	Superimposed meaningful structure
The shape of France	A "bearskin rug"
The Great Lakes (Huron, Ontario, Michigan, Erie, Superior)	HOMES
Lines on the treble clef (EGBDF)	Elvis's guitar broke down Friday, *or* every good boy does fine.
The distinction between stalagmites and stalactites	When the "mites" go up, the "tites" come down.
The number of days in each month	Thirty days has September . . .

Superimposed meaningful structures can be used to remember procedures as well as declarative information. Here are three examples that my students have shared with me:

Procedure to be learned	Superimposed meaningful structure
Turning a screw (clockwise to tighten it, counterclockwise to loosen it)	Righty, tighty. Lefty, loosey.
Throwing a free throw in basketball	BEEF: *b*alance the ball, *e*lbows in, *e*levate the arms, *f*ollow through
Multiplying a mathematical expression of the form $(ax + b)(cx + d)$	FOIL: multiply the *f*irst terms within each set of parentheses, then the two *o*uter terms, then the two *i*nner terms, and finally the *l*ast terms

Research consistently supports the effectiveness of mnemonics in student learning (Bower & Clark, 1969; Bulgren, Schumaker, & Deshler, 1994; Higbee, 1977; Pressley, Levin,

What mnemonics might be useful for the subject matter you will be teaching?

INTO THE CLASSROOM: Helping Students Acquire New Procedures

Help students understand the logic behind the procedures they are learning.

As a teacher demonstrates the correct way to swing a tennis racket, she asks her students, "Why is it important to have your feet apart rather than together? Why is it important to hold your arm straight as you swing?"

When skills are especially complex, break them into simpler tasks that students can practice one at a time.

Knowing how overwhelming the task of driving a car can initially be, a driver education teacher begins behind-the-wheel instruction by having students practice steering and braking in an empty school parking lot. Only later, after students have mastered these skills, does he have them drive in traffic on city streets.

Provide mnemonics that can help students remember a sequence of steps.

In a unit on basketball, a teacher coaches her students on an effective approach to making a free throw. "Just remember BEEF," she says. "*B*alance the ball, put your *el*bows in, *e*levate your arms, and *f*ollow through."

Give students many opportunities to practice new skills, and provide the feedback they need to help them improve.

A science teacher asks his students to write lab reports after each week's lab activity. Many of his students have had little or no previous experience in scientific writing, so when he grades the reports, he writes numerous comments as well. Some comments describe the strengths that he sees, and others provide suggestions for making the reports more objective, precise, or clear.

& Delaney, 1982; Scruggs & Mastropieri, 1989; C. E. Weinstein, 1978). In addition to helping students store information and skills in long-term memory, mnemonics also appear to help students retrieve what they stored at an earlier time. We turn to the topic of retrieval now.

Long-Term Memory Retrieval

As you learned earlier in the chapter, some information is easily retrieved from long-term memory. No doubt you can quickly retrieve your birthday, the name of your college or university, or a close friend's telephone number. But it may take you longer to "find" some of the other pieces of information stored in your long-term memory. Try the following exercise as an example.

■ Experiencing Firsthand
More Retrieval Practice

The answer to each of the following questions has appeared earlier in this chapter. See how many answers you can retrieve from your long-term memory and how quickly you can retrieve each one.

1. What are the five Great Lakes?
2. What is the German word for "book"?

3. In what year did World War II end?

4. Who wrote *Catcher in the Rye*?

5. About how long does information remain in working memory before it disappears?

6. How do you spell the French term for "appetizer"?

Did you find yourself unable to remember one or more of the answers even though you know you "processed" the information at the time you read it? If so, then you have just discovered firsthand that, in some cases, information is retrieved from long-term memory only with great difficulty, or perhaps not at all.

The Nature of Long-Term Memory Retrieval

Retrieving information from long-term memory appears to be a process of following a "pathway" of associations. One idea reminds us of another idea, which reminds us of still another, and so on, just as we saw in the "Horse #1" exercise earlier in the chapter. Retrieval is successful only when we eventually stumble on the information we are looking for. We are most likely to do so if we have connected the desired information to something else—presumably something that is logically related to it—in long-term memory.

To illustrate this idea, I return once again to all those packages, letters, bills, brochures, catalogs, fliers, advertisements, requests for donations, and sweepstakes announcements that arrive in your mailbox every year. Imagine that, on the average, you receive ten important items—things that you really need to save—every day. At six postal deliveries a week and 52 weeks a year, you have been saving 3,120 pieces of mail each year. If you have been saving your mail for the last fifteen years, then you have 46,800 really important things stashed somewhere in your home.

One day you hear that stock in a clothing company (Mod Bod Jeans, Inc.) has tripled in value. You remember that your wealthy Aunt Agnes sent you some Mod Bod stock certificates for your birthday several years ago, and you presumably decided that they were important enough to save. But where in the world did you put them? How long will it take you to find them among all those important letters, bills, brochures, catalogs, fliers, and sweepstakes announcements?

How easily you find the certificates and, in fact, whether you find them at all depends on how you have been storing all your mail as you've accumulated it over the years. If you've stored your mail in a logical, organized fashion—for example, by putting all paid bills on a shelf in your closet, all mail order catalogs on the floor under the window, and all items from relatives in a file cabinet (in alphabetical order by last name)—then you should quickly retrieve Aunt Agnes's gift. But if you simply tossed each day's mail randomly around the house, you will be searching your home for a long, long time, possibly without ever finding any evidence that you own Mod Bod stock.

Like a home with fifteen years' worth of mail, long-term memory also contains a great deal of information. And like finding the Mod Bod certificates, the ease with which information is retrieved from long-term memory depends to some extent on whether that information is stored in a logical "place"—that is, whether it is connected with related pieces of information. By making those important connections with existing knowledge, we will know where to "find" the information we store when we need it later on. In contrast, learning something at a rote level is like throwing Aunt Agnes's gift randomly among thousands of pieces of unorganized mail: We may never retrieve it again.

Can you still remember what the Chinese words *ké, fàn, mén, fáng,* and *shū* mean? Can you retrieve the visual images you stored to help you remember these words?

Factors Affecting Retrieval

Even when we connect new information with our existing knowledge base, we can't always find it when we need it. At least four factors promote our ability to retrieve information from long-term memory:

- Making multiple connections with existing knowledge
- Learning information to mastery and "beyond"
- Using knowledge frequently
- Having a relevant retrieval cue

Making Multiple Connections with Existing Knowledge

If retrieving information from long-term memory is a process of following a pathway of associations, what happens if we take the wrong "route" and go in an inappropriate "direction"? In such a situation, we may never find what we are looking for.

We are more likely to retrieve information when we have many possible pathways through which we might get to it—in other words, when we have associated it with many other things in our existing knowledge base. Making multiple connections is like having a cross-referencing system in the way that you store your mail. You may have filed the Mod Bod stock in the "items from relatives" file cabinet, but you've also left numerous notes in other places about where that stock is—perhaps with your birth certificate (after all, you received the stock on your birthday), with your income tax receipts, or in your safe-deposit box. By looking in any one of these logical places, you will discover the location of your valuable stock.

As teachers, we can help students more effectively remember classroom subject matter over the long run if we help them connect it to numerous pieces of information in their existing knowledge base. For example, we can show them how new material relates to:

- Concepts and ideas within the same subject area (e.g., showing them how multiplication is related to addition)
- Concepts and ideas in other subject areas (e.g., talking about how scientific discoveries have affected historical events)
- Students' general knowledge of the world (e.g., drawing parallels between the "Black Death" of the fourteenth century and the current AIDS epidemic)
- Students' personal experiences (e.g., finding similarities between the family feud in *Romeo and Juliet* and students' own interpersonal conflicts)

The more interrelationships our students form among pieces of information in long-term memory, the more easily they can retrieve those pieces later on.

Learning Things to Mastery and Beyond

Is it enough for students to demonstrate mastery of information or skills—for example, to recite all their addition facts—on just one occasion? Probably not. Research tells us that people are far more likely to retrieve the material they have learned if they continue to study and practice it (Krueger, 1929; Semb & Ellis, 1994; Underwood, 1954).

When students continue to practice information and skills they have already mastered, they eventually achieve **automaticity:** They can retrieve what they've learned quickly and effortlessly and can use it almost without thinking (J. R. Anderson, 1983; P. W. Cheng, 1985; Proctor & Dutta, 1995; Schneider & Shiffrin, 1977). As an example, think of a complicated skill—perhaps driving a car—that you can perform easily. Your first attempts at driving probably required a great deal of mental effort. But now you can drive without having to pay much attention to what you are doing—you execute the skill automatically.

Help students relate new information to many different things that they already know.

If you have already read Chapter 4, then you may recall that automaticity plays a role in Robert Sternberg's theory of intelligence.

Certainly education must be more than the drill and practice of isolated facts and procedures. But some things need to be retrieved quickly and automatically, especially if students need to use them in complicated tasks (LaBerge & Samuels, 1974; Proctor & Dutta, 1995; Resnick, 1989). For example, second graders reading a story can better focus their efforts on understanding it if they don't have to stop and sound out words like *before* and *after*. Fourth graders faced with a multiplication problem such as this one:

$$\begin{array}{r} 87 \\ \times\ 59 \\ \hline \end{array}$$

can solve it more easily if they can quickly retrieve such basic multiplication facts as $9 \times 8 = 72$ and $5 \times 7 = 35$. High school chemistry students can more easily interpret Na_2CO_3 (sodium carbonate) if they don't have to stop to think about what the symbols Na, C, and O represent. Remember, working memory has a very limited capacity: It can only do so much at one time. When much of its capacity must be used for retrieving single facts or executing simple procedures, there is little room left over for understanding more complex situations or dealing with more difficult tasks.

Using Knowledge Frequently

Frequently used knowledge is retrieved more easily than knowledge that is used rarely or not at all (e.g., R. Brown & McNeill, 1966; Yarmey, 1973). It is easier to remember your own birthday than the birthday of a friend or relative. It is easier to remember the current year than the year in which World War II ended. And it is definitely easier to remember the spelling of *information* than the spelling of *hors d'oeuvre*, even though both terms have the same number of letters.

As teachers, we should occasionally have classroom activities that require students to review the things they have learned earlier in the year or in previous years. For example, we might have occasional "refresher" discussions of "old" material, or we might ask students to use the material to understand new topics or solve new problems. Research is clear on this point: Occasional review enhances students' memory for information over the long run, especially when review sessions are spaced out over several months or years (Bahrick, Bahrick, Bahrick, & Bahrick, 1993; Dempster, 1991; Di Vesta & Smith, 1979; M. A. McDaniel & Masson, 1985).

Having a Relevant Retrieval Cue

If you were educated in North America, then you probably learned the names of the five Great Lakes at one time or another. Yet you may have trouble retrieving all five names, even though they are all still stored in your long-term memory. Perhaps Lake Michigan doesn't come to mind when you retrieve the other four. The *HOMES* mnemonic provides a **retrieval cue**—a hint about where to "look" in long-term memory. The mnemonic tells you that one lake begins with the letter M, and so you search among the "M" words in your long-term memory until (we hope) you find "Michigan." Learners are more likely to retrieve information when relevant retrieval cues are present to start their search of long-term memory in the right direction (e.g., Tulving, 1983; Tulving & Thomson, 1973).

For another example of how retrieval cues can facilitate retrieval, try the following exercise.

Experiencing Firsthand
Recall Versus Recognition

Earlier in the chapter, I described a process that keeps information in working memory for longer than the usual five to twenty seconds. Can you retrieve the name of that process from your long-term memory? See if you can before you read any further.

When classroom subject matter must be retrieved rapidly, provide drill and practice exercises that can help students learn it to a level of automaticity.

Periodically review important information and skills; for example, incorporate them into later lessons.

If you can't remember the term to which I am referring, then try answering the same question posed in a multiple-choice format:

What do we call the process that keeps information in working memory for longer than the usual five to twenty seconds?

   a.   facilitative construction

   b.   internal organization

   c.   short-term memorization

   d.   maintenance rehearsal

Did you experience an "Aha, now I remember" feeling? The correct answer is *d.* Perhaps the multiple-choice format provided a retrieval cue for you, directing you to the correct answer you had stored in long-term memory. Generally speaking, remembering is easier in a **recognition task** (in which you simply need to recognize correct information among irrelevant information or incorrect statements) than in a **recall task** (in which the correct information must be retrieved in its entirety from long-term memory) (Semb, Ellis, & Araujo, 1993). A recognition task is easier because it provides more retrieval cues to aid you in your search of long-term memory.

As teachers, we won't always want to help students retrieve information by putting that information right in front of them. Nevertheless, there will be occasions when providing hints is certainly appropriate. For example, when Sheri asks how the word *liquidation* is spelled, we might respond by saying, "*Liquidation* means to make something liquid. How do you spell *liquid*?" When Shawn wants to know what the chemical symbol *Au* stands for, we might help him retrieve the answer for himself with a hint like this one: "In class, we talked about how *Au* comes from the Latin word *aurum.* Can you remember what aurum means?"

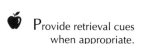

Provide retrieval cues when appropriate.

In the early grades, teachers typically provide many retrieval cues for their students: They remind students about the tasks they need to do and when they need to do them ("I hear the fire alarm. Remember, we all walk quietly during a fire drill"; or "It's time to go home. Do you all have the field trip permission slip you need to take to your parents?"). But as they grow older, students must develop greater independence, relying more on themselves and less on their teachers for the things they need to remember. At all grade levels, we can teach students ways of providing retrieval cues for *themselves.* For example, if we expect first graders to bring back those permission slips tomorrow, we might ask them to write a reminder on a piece of masking tape that they put on their jackets or lunch boxes. If we give junior high school students a major assignment due several weeks later, we might suggest that they help themselves remember the due date by taping a note to the bedside table or by making an entry on the kitchen calendar.

Teach students to develop their own retrieval cues for things they need to remember.

When you attempted my multiple-choice question a few minutes ago, did you have trouble remembering "maintenance rehearsal" even though it was staring you in the face? If so, why do you think you had difficulty? Let's look at some possible explanations—some possible reasons why people forget.

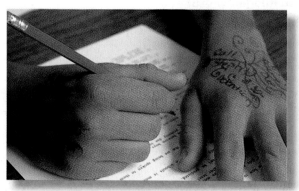

Students should learn to develop their own retrieval cues.

Why People Sometimes "Forget"

Fortunately, we don't need to remember *everything.* For example, we probably have no reason to remember the phone number of a florist we called yesterday, the plot of last week's *I Love Lucy* show, or the due date of an assignment we turned in last semester. Much of the information we encounter is—like our junk mail—not worth keeping.

But as we have just seen, we sometimes have trouble recalling what we *do* need. Psychologists have several explanations for why people seem to "forget":

- Failure to retrieve
- Reconstruction error
- Interference
- Decay
- Failure to store

Let's consider each one in turn.

Failure to Retrieve

A man at the supermarket looks familiar, but you can't remember who he is or when you met him. He smiles at you and says, "Hello. Nice to see you again." Gulp. You desperately search your long-term memory for his name, but you have clearly forgotten who this man is.

A few days later, you have a bowl of chili for dinner. The chili reminds you of the "Chili for Charity" supper at which you worked a few months back. Of course! You and the man at the supermarket stood side by side serving chili to hundreds of people that night. Oh yes, you recall, his name is Melville Herman.

One reason we "forget" is an **inability to retrieve:** We can't locate information stored in long-term memory. Sometimes we stumble on the information at a later time, perhaps by accident when we are "looking" for something else. But sometimes we never do retrieve the information, perhaps because we learned it at a rote level or perhaps because there are insufficient retrieval cues to guide our search in long-term memory.

Reconstruction Error

Retrieval isn't necessarily an all-or-nothing phenomenon. Sometimes we retrieve only part of the information we are seeking from long-term memory. In such situations, we sometimes fill in the gaps by using our general knowledge and assumptions about the world (Kolodner, 1985; Loftus, 1991; Rumelhart & Ortony, 1977; P. T. Wilson & Anderson, 1986). Even though the gaps are filled in "logically," they aren't always filled in correctly—a form of forgetting called **reconstruction error.** The next chapter looks at the reconstructive nature of retrieval in greater detail.

Interference

Experiencing Firsthand
Seven Chinese Words

Here are six more Chinese words and their English meanings (for simplicity, I've omitted the "tone" marks on the words). Read them two or three times and try to store them in your long-term memory. But don't do anything special to learn the words; for example, don't intentionally develop mnemonics to help you remember them.

Chinese	English
jung	middle
ting	listen
sung	deliver
peng	friend
ching	please
deng	wait

Now cover up the list of words and test yourself. What was the word for *friend? please? listen? wait?*

Did you find yourself getting confused, perhaps forgetting which English meaning went with each Chinese word? If you did, then you were the victim of **interference.** The various pieces of information in your long-term memory were interfering with one another; in a sense, the pieces were getting "mixed up." Notice that I told you *not* to use mnemonics to learn the Chinese words. Interference is especially likely to occur when pieces of information are similar to one another and when they are learned at a rote level (e.g., Dempster, 1985; Postman & Underwood, 1973; Underwood, 1948, 1957).

Think back to the earlier case study involving Kanesha. The similarity between *tibia* and *fibula* is yet another reason why she confuses the names of the two bones.

Decay

As noted earlier, some psychologists believe that information remains in long-term memory forever. But others propose that information may weaken over time and perhaps disappear altogether, especially if it is not used on a regular basis (J. R. Anderson, 1990; Reisberg, 1997). Theorists sometimes use the word **decay** when describing this gradual fading process.

Failure to Store

Last on my list of reasons for "forgetting" is **failure to store:** Information never reached long-term memory to begin with. Perhaps a person receiving a piece of information didn't pay attention to it, so it never went beyond the sensory register. Or perhaps the learner, after attending to it, didn't process it any further, so it went no farther in the memory system than working memory. Obviously, failure to store is not an explanation of information loss; however, it is one possible reason why students who *think* they have learned something cannot recall it later on.

All five explanations for forgetting underscore the importance of instructional strategies we've identified earlier: We must help students relate new material to things they already know, and we must give them opportunities to review and practice that material frequently.

▲ When students informally test themselves as they learn and study, such "failure to store" is less likely to occur. We will consider this process of *monitoring comprehension* in Chapter 8.

One possible explanation of "forgetting" is that the student doesn't store the information to begin with.

INTO THE CLASSROOM: Maximizing Retrieval and Minimizing Forgetting

Where important information is concerned, never assume that once is enough.

A language arts teacher introduces the parts of speech (e.g., nouns, verbs, adjectives) early in the school year. Because these concepts will be important for students to know when they study a foreign language in later grades, he continues to review them throughout the year—for example, by frequently incorporating them into classroom activities.

When information must be retrieved rapidly, provide drill and practice exercises that enable students to learn the information to automaticity.

An elementary school teacher continues to give practice in the addition and subtraction facts until each student can answer every single-digit addition and subtraction fact quickly and accurately.

Teach students to develop their own retrieval cues for things they need to remember.

A teacher suggests that students tape a note to their jackets, reminding them to return their permission slips tomorrow.

When important details are difficult to fill in logically, make sure students learn them well.

A teacher gives students extra practice in "problem" spelling words—words that are spelled differently than they are pronounced (e.g., *people, February)*.

Provide retrieval cues when appropriate.

When a student puzzles over how to compute the area of a circle, her teacher says, "We studied this last week. Do you remember the formula?" When the student shakes her head, the teacher continues, "Because the problem involves a circle, the formula probably includes π, doesn't it?"

Long-term memory storage and retrieval processes don't always happen instantaneously. For example, it may take time for our students to relate new material to their existing knowledge and, at some later date, to retrieve all the "pieces" of what they have learned. What happens when teachers give students more time to process and retrieve information? The results can be quite dramatic, as we shall see now.

Giving Students Time to Process: Effects of Increasing Wait Time

Consider the following situation.

Mr. Smith likes to ask questions in his classroom. He also likes to keep class sessions going at a rapid pace. A typical day goes something like this:

Mr. Smith: Why is it warmer in summer than in winter?

Amelia: Because the sun is hotter.

Mr. Smith: Well, yes, the sun *feels* hotter. What changes in the earth make it feel hotter?

Arnold:	The earth is closer to the sun in the summer.
Mr. Smith:	That's a possibility, Arnold. But there's something we need to consider here. When it's summer in the Northern Hemisphere, it's winter in the Southern Hemisphere. When North America is having its warmest days, Australia is having its coldest days. Can we use the earth's distance from the sun to explain that?
Arnold:	Uh . . . I guess not.
Mr. Smith:	So . . . why is it warmer in summer than in winter? (No one responds.) Do you know, Angela? (She shakes her head.) How about you, Andrew?
Andrew:	Nope.
Mr. Smith:	Can you think of anything we discussed yesterday that might help us with an explanation? (No one responds.) Remember, yesterday we talked about how the earth changes its tilt in relation to the sun throughout the year. This change in the earth's tilt explains why the days get longer throughout the winter and spring and why they get shorter during the summer and fall. (Mr. Smith continues with an explanation of how the angle of the sun's rays affects temperature on earth.)

Mr. Smith is hoping that his students will draw a connection between information they learned yesterday (changes in the earth's tilt) and today's topic (the seasons). Unfortunately, Mr. Smith is moving too quickly from one question to the next and from one student to another. His students don't make the connection he expects because he simply doesn't give them enough time to do so.

The problem with Mr. Smith's lesson is one seen in many classrooms: too short a **wait time.** When teachers ask students a question, they typically wait one second or less for a response. If students don't respond in that short time interval, teachers tend to speak again—sometimes by asking different students the same question, sometimes by rephrasing the question, sometimes even by answering the question themselves (Rowe, 1974, 1987). Teachers are equally reluctant to let much time lapse after students answer questions or make comments in class; once again, they typically allow *one second or less* of silence before responding to a statement or asking another question (Rowe, 1987).

If we consider basic principles of cognitive psychology—for example, the importance of relating new information to prior knowledge and the difficulty often associated with retrieving information from long-term memory—then we realize that one second is a very short time indeed for students to develop their responses. When teachers increase their wait time by allowing at least *three seconds* to elapse (instead of just one) after their own questions and after students' comments, dramatic changes occur in both students' and teachers' behaviors:

Changes in students' behaviors:

- *More class participation.* More students participate in class; this is especially true for females and students from ethnic minority groups. Students are more likely to answer questions correctly and to contribute spontaneously to a class discussion, perhaps by asking their own questions, presenting their own perspectives, and responding to one another's comments.

- *Better quality of responses.* Students give a greater variety of responses to the same question, and their responses are longer and more sophisticated. They are more likely to support their reasoning with evidence or logic and more likely to speculate when they don't know an answer.

- *Better overall classroom performance.* Students are more likely to feel confident that they can master the material and are more motivated to learn it. Academic achievement increases, and discipline problems decrease.

How much wait time do your own instructors exhibit? Is it long enough to promote good classroom discussions?

When teachers increase wait time to three seconds or longer, students participate more actively and give more complex responses to questions.

Changes in teachers' behaviors:

- *Different kinds of questions.* Teachers ask fewer "simple" questions (e.g., those requiring recall of facts) and a greater number of complex questions (e.g., those requiring students to elaborate or develop alternative explanations).

- *Increased flexibility in teaching.* Teachers modify the direction of discussion to accommodate students' comments and questions, and they allow their classes to pursue a topic in greater depth than they had originally anticipated.

- *Higher expectations.* Teachers' expectations for many students, especially previously low-achieving students, begin to improve. (Mohatt & Erickson, 1981; Rowe, 1974, 1987; Tharp, 1989; Tobin, 1987)

From the perspective of cognitive psychology, increasing wait time appears to have two benefits for student learning (Tobin, 1987). First, it allows students more time to process classroom subject matter. Second, it appears to change the very nature of teacher-student discussions; for example, teachers are more likely to ask challenging, thought-provoking questions. In fact, the nature of the questions that teachers ask is probably as important as—and perhaps even more important than—the amount of wait time per se (Giaconia, 1988).

When our objective is simple recall—when students need to retrieve classroom material very quickly, to "know it cold"—then wait time should be short. There is a definite advantage to rapid-fire drill and practice for information and skills that students must learn to a level of automaticity. But when our objectives include more complex processing of ideas and issues, longer wait time may provide both teachers and students the time that they need to think things through.

Incorporate a wait time of at least three seconds into question-answer sessions and classroom discussions.

Accommodating Diversity in Cognitive Processes

As we've explored basic principles of cognitive psychology in this chapter, we've considered many factors—attention, working memory capacity, long-term memory storage processes, prior knowledge, retrieval, and so on—that influence what and how well our students are likely to learn and remember classroom material. Naturally, our students will differ considerably with regard to these factors; for example, they will have unique knowledge bases on which to draw, and they will elaborate differently on the ideas we present (e.g., Cothern, Konopak, & Willis, 1990; C. A. Grant & Gomez, 1996). They may also have had varying experiences with different kinds of memory tasks. For instance, students from traditional North American classrooms are likely to have had more experience learning lists of things, whereas students from some African countries may have an easier time remembering stories, and students from some Australian communities may have an easier time remembering the locations of objects (Flavell et al., 1993). And as we noted both here and in Chapter 4, students from diverse backgrounds will benefit from more wait time; for instance, some Native American students may wait several seconds before responding as a way of showing respect for an adult, and those with limited proficiency in English may require some "mental translation" time.

Facilitating Cognitive Processing in Students with Special Needs

Some of our students with special educational needs may have particular trouble processing classroom subject matter in an effective manner. This will certainly be true for students with learning disabilities: By definition, these students have difficulty with certain cognitive processes. Furthermore, students with mental retardation will typically process information more slowly than their classmates, and students with emotional and behavioral disorders may have trouble keeping their attention on the task at hand (Turnbull et al., 1999). In contrast, gifted students are likely to process new ideas more rapidly and in a more complex manner than many of their classmates (B. Clark, 1997; Heward, 1996). Table 6–3 identifies cognitive processing differences we are likely to see in students with special educational needs.

TABLE 6.3

STUDENTS IN INCLUSIVE SETTINGS

Facilitating Information Processing in Students with Special Educational Needs

STUDENTS WITH SPECIAL NEEDS	CHARACTERISTICS THAT THESE STUDENTS MAY EXHIBIT	CLASSROOM STRATEGIES THAT MAY BE BENEFICIAL FOR THESE STUDENTS
Students with specific cognitive or academic difficulties	Deficiencies in one or more specific cognitive processes (e.g., perception, encoding) Distractibility, inability to sustain attention in some students Difficulty screening out irrelevant stimuli Less working memory capacity, or less efficient use of working memory Impulsivity in responding	Analyze students' errors as a way of identifying possible processing difficulties. Identify weaknesses in specific cognitive processes and provide instruction that enables students to compensate for these weaknesses. Present information in an organized fashion and make frequent connections to students' prior knowledge as ways of promoting more effective long-term memory storage. Teach mnemonics to facilitate long-term memory storage and retrieval. Encourage greater reflection before responding—for instance, by reinforcing accuracy rather than speed, or by teaching self-instructions (see Chapter 11).

continued

STUDENTS WITH SPECIAL NEEDS	CHARACTERISTICS THAT THESE STUDENTS MAY EXHIBIT	CLASSROOM STRATEGIES THAT MAY BE BENEFICIAL FOR THESE STUDENTS
Students with social or behavioral problems	Lack of attention because of off-task thoughts and behaviors Difficulty shifting attention quickly (students with autism) Possible difficulties in other specific cognitive processes	Make sure you have students' attention before giving instructions or presenting information. Refer students to a school psychologist for evaluation and diagnosis of possible learning disabilities.
Students with general delays in cognitive and social functioning	Slower information processing Difficulty with attention to task-relevant information Reduced working memory capacity, or less efficient use of working memory Smaller knowledge base on which to build new learning	Keep instructional materials simple, emphasizing relevant stimuli and minimizing irrelevant stimuli. Provide clear instructions that focus students' attention on desired behaviors (e.g., "Listen," "Write," "Stop"). Pace instruction to allow sufficient time for students to think about and process information adequately (e.g., provide ample wait time after questions). Assume little prior knowledge about new topics (i.e., "begin at the beginning").
Students with physical or sensory challenges	Normal cognitive processing ability in most students Less general knowledge due to limited experiences in the outside world	Assume equal ability for learning and understanding new information and skills, but consider how students' physical and sensory challenges may interfere with some learning processes. Expose students to life experiences they may have missed due to their disabilities.
Students with advanced cognitive development	More rapid information processing Larger knowledge base (the nature of which will vary, depending on students' cultural backgrounds) More interconnections among ideas in long-term memory More rapid retrieval of information from long-term memory	Proceed through topics more quickly or in greater depth. Study topics in an interdisciplinary fashion to foster cross-disciplinary integration of material in long-term memory.

Sources: *Bulgren et al., 1994; Butterfield & Ferretti, 1987; B. Clark, 1997; Courchesne et al., 1994; Heward, 1996; Landau & McAninch, 1993; Mercer, 1991; Morgan & Jenson, 1988; Patton et al., 1990; Piirto, 1994; Pressley, 1995; Rabinowitz & Glaser, 1985; H. L. Swanson, 1992; H. L. Swanson & Cooney, 1991; Turnbull et al., 1999; Zeaman & House, 1979.*

Note: *Compiled with the assistance of Dr. Margie Garanzini-Daiber and Dr. Margaret Cohen, University of Missouri—St. Louis.*

Virtually all of our students, including those without any identified special needs, will occasionally have difficulty learning or remembering class material. Accordingly, many of the instructional strategies in Table 6–3—getting students' attention, analyzing their errors, teaching them mnemonics, and so on—need not be limited to use with students who have special needs. *All* of our students can benefit from help in processing information more effectively.

CASE STUDY: How Time Flies

Ms. Llewellyn is a first-year social studies teacher at Madison High School; she recently completed her degree in United States history and knows her subject matter well. Her history classes begin in September with a study of early explorers of the Western Hemisphere. By early October, students are reading about the colonial settlements of the 1600s. By December, they have covered the French and Indian War, the Revolutionary War, and the Declaration of Independence. The winter months are spent studying the nineteenth century (e.g., the Industrial Revolution, the Civil War), and the spring is spent studying the twentieth century (including both world wars, the Korean War, the Vietnam War, and the Persian Gulf crisis).

Ms. Llewellyn has high expectations for her students. In her daily class lectures, she describes historical events in detail, hoping to give her students a sense of how complex many of these events really were. In addition to having students read the usual high school textbook, she also assigns articles in the historical journals that she herself reads.

Occasionally, Ms. Llewellyn stops a lecture a few minutes before the bell rings to ask questions that check her students' recall of the day's topics. Although her students can usually remember the main gist of her lecture, they have difficulty with the details, either mixing them up or forgetting them altogether. A few students remember so little that she can hardly believe they were in class that day. Her students perform even more poorly on monthly essay exams; it's obvious from their written responses that they can remember little of what Ms. Llewellyn has taught them.

"I explained things so clearly to them," she tells herself. "Perhaps these kids just don't want to learn."

- What are some possible reasons why Ms. Llewellyn's students are having difficulty learning and remembering the things that she teaches them? Can you think of possible reasons related to the class curriculum? to Ms. Llewellyn's style of teaching? to Ms. Llewellyn's reading assignments?

- From the perspective of cognitive psychology, what would you do differently than Ms. Llewellyn?

Summing Up

Looking at Learning from Different Perspectives

Theorists define learning as a relatively permanent change due to experience. Our students' learning and achievement will include changes both in their behavior and in their ways of thinking.

Behaviorists describe learning in terms of the observable responses that people make and the environmental stimuli that influence how those responses change over time. Cognitive psychologists describe learning in terms of such internal mental processes as attention, memory, and problem solving. Social cognitive theorists build on elements of both behaviorism and cognitive psychology as they describe what and how

people learn by observing and imitating those around them. As teachers, we will find that each of the three perspectives—behaviorism, cognitive psychology, and social cognitive theory—has numerous implications for how we can most effectively help students learn and achieve.

Assumptions of Cognitive Psychology

Cognitive psychologists believe that learners often process the same situation in different ways, in part because they all draw on unique bodies of knowledge and experiences to understand and interpret the situation. Most cognitive psychologists propose that learning does not involve absorbing information directly from the environment; instead, it involves constructing one's own understanding of the world. The things our students do mentally with the subject matter we present in class will determine how effectively they learn and remember it.

Basic Terminology

The term *memory* refers to learners' ability to "save" things (mentally) that they have previously learned. *Storage* refers to the acquisition of new information, and *encoding* involves changing that information in some way as it is stored. *Retrieval* is the process of "finding" previously stored information when it is needed.

Components of Memory

Many theorists propose that human memory has three components. The *sensory register* provides temporary storage for incoming information, holding new input for two or three seconds at most. By paying attention to information, learners move it to *working memory,* where they actively think about and make sense of it. Attention and working memory have a limited capacity; hence, our students can pay attention to and think about only a limited amount of information at any one time. The third component—*long-term memory*—has an extremely large capacity and an indefinitely long duration.

Long-Term Memory Storage

Both information (*declarative knowledge*) and skills (*procedural knowledge*) are stored in long-term memory. To store declarative knowledge effectively, learners should engage in meaningful learning, organization, elaboration, and visual imagery. To learn a new skill effectively, learners may, in many situations, first have to store it in a declarative form (e.g., as a list of steps to be followed) and then practice it over time, gradually gaining increasing competence as they do so. We can do many things to help our students process and learn classroom subject matter; for instance, we can show them how it relates to things they already know, present it in an organized fashion, ask them to draw inferences, give them many opportunities to practice, and provide mnemonics for seemingly "meaningless" pairs and lists.

Retrieval and Wait Time

Retrieving information from long-term memory appears to be a process of following a pathway of associations. Our students' attempts at retrieving what they have learned are more likely to be successful if they have learned classroom subject matter to mastery and connected it with numerous other things they know, if they use it frequently, and if relevant retrieval cues are present in their environment. Increasing wait time—in other words, giving students more time to respond to the questions and comments of others—promotes greater retrieval and enhances students' overall academic performance.

Diversity in Cognitive Processing

Students' cognitive processes will differ, in part, as a function of their cultural backgrounds, English proficiency, and any special educational needs that they might have. At one time or another, all of our students are likely to have difficulty processing and learning classroom subject matter. By considering the specific cognitive processes involved in learning effectively, we can help *everyone* achieve classroom success.

KEY CONCEPTS

learning (p. 221)
responses (p. 221)
stimuli (p. 221)
behaviorism (p. 221)
social cognitive theory (p. 222)
cognitive psychology (p. 222)
information processing theory (p. 224)
construction (p. 226)
constructivism (p. 227)
memory (p. 227)
storage (p. 227)
encoding (p. 228)
retrieval (p. 229)
sensory register (p. 230)
attention (p. 230)

working memory (short-term memory) (p. 232)
maintenance rehearsal (p. 232)
long-term memory (p. 234)
activation (p. 235)
declarative knowledge (p. 236)
procedural knowledge (p. 236)
rehearsal (p. 237)
rote learning (p. 238)
meaningful learning (p. 239)
meaningful learning set (p. 240)
knowledge base (p. 241)
organization (p. 242)
elaboration (p. 243)
visual imagery (p. 244)

mnemonics (p. 248)
verbal mediator (p. 248)
keyword (p. 249)
superimposed meaningful structure (p. 249)
automaticity (p.252)
retrieval cue (p. 253)
recognition task (p. 254)
recall task (p. 254)
inability to retrieve (p. 255)
reconstruction error (p. 255)
interference (p. 256)
decay (p. 256)
failure to store (p. 256)
wait time (p. 258)

Knowledge Construction

T hink back to a time when you tried to carry on a conversation with someone in a noisy room—perhaps at a party, in a bar where a band was playing, or in a workshop with loud machinery operating nearby. You probably couldn't hear everything the other person was saying. But perhaps you were able to hear enough to get the gist of what he or she was trying to tell you. You combined what you *did* hear with things that you could see (e.g., gestures and facial expressions) and with things that you already knew about the topic under discussion. We often construct meanings from the stimuli around us—meanings that aren't necessarily obvious from the stimuli themselves, and meanings that may or may not be accurate.

As we discovered in the preceding chapter, many cognitive psychologists do not believe that learning is a simple process of absorbing information from the environment. Instead, learning involves constructing one's own knowledge from one's experiences. This chapter focuses on constructive processes in learning and memory. More specifically, we will address these questions:

- In what ways are both storage and retrieval constructive in nature?
- How do learners organize their knowledge?
- Why do students sometimes acquire misconceptions about the world, and how do such beliefs affect later learning?
- What strategies can we use to help students construct accurate and useful knowledge about classroom topics?
- What strategies can we use to encourage students to correct any misconceptions they have about the world? In other words, how can we promote *conceptual change*?
- How are constructive processes likely to be different in students with diverse backgrounds and needs?

CASE STUDY: Pulling It All Together

Rita is a fourth grader who attends school in Michigan. Her class has recently had a unit on Michigan's state history. Rita still knows little about American history; she will study this subject as a fifth grader next year. Despite her limited background in history, Rita responds eagerly to an interviewer's question about the New World.

Interviewer:	Our country is in the part of the world called America. At one time, America was called the New World. Do you know why it was called the New World?
Rita:	Yeah. We learned this in social studies.
Interviewer:	What did you learn?

Rita:	Because they used to live in England, the British, and they didn't know about . . . they wanted to get to China 'cause China had some things they wanted. They had some cups or whatever—no, they had furs. They had fur and stuff like that and they wanted to have a shorter way to get to China so they took it and they landed in Michigan, but it wasn't called Michigan. I think it was the British that landed in Michigan and they were there first and so they tried to claim that land, but it didn't work out for some reason so they took some furs and brought them back to Britain and they sold them, but they mostly wanted it for the furs. So then the English landed there and they claimed the land and they wanted to make it a state, and so they got it signed by the government or whoever, the big boss, then they were just starting to make it a state so the British just went up to the Upper Peninsula and they thought they could stay there for a little while. Then they had to fight a war, then the farmers, they were just volunteers, so the farmers went right back and tried to get their family put back together again.
Interviewer:	Did you learn all this in state history this year?
Rita:	Um hum. (VanSledright & Brophy, 1992, p. 849; reprinted by permission)

- Which parts of Rita's response accurately describe the history of the New World? Which parts are clearly *in*accurate?
- Can you identify at least two instances in which Rita has pulled together unrelated ideas in her construction of "knowledge" of history?

Constructive Processes in Learning and Memory

Rita has taken bits and pieces of information learned in school and pulled them into a scenario that makes sense to her. In the process, she has developed some unique interpretations of historical events. For example, she knows that the British wanted something that could be obtained in the Far East; she also knows that there was once a high demand for animal furs in England. Put them together and *voilà!*—the Chinese had the furs that the British wanted. (In reality, it was the spices of the Far East that the British were after.) Notice, too, how Rita maintains that the British found a shorter way to get to China—one that apparently went right through Michigan. Although Rita's description of historical events has a few elements of truth, these elements have been combined to form an overall "knowledge" of history that could give any historian heart failure.

Rita may have constructed her unique view of history at the time she learned it—that is, during storage. But she may also be constructing it while the adult is interviewing her—in other words, while she is retrieving the things she's previously learned. Let's consider how construction can occur during both storage and retrieval.

Construction in Storage

Experiencing Firsthand
Rocky

Read the following passage *one time only*.

Rocky slowly got up from the mat, planning his escape. He hesitated a moment and thought. Things were not going well. What bothered him most was being held, especially since the charge against him had been weak. He considered his present situation. The lock that held him was strong but he thought he could break it. He knew, however, that his timing would have to be perfect. Rocky was aware that it was because of his early roughness that he had been penalized so severely—much too severely from his point of view. The situation was becoming frustrating; the pressure had been grinding on him for too long. He was being ridden unmercifully. Rocky was getting angry now. He felt he was ready to make his move. He knew that his success or failure would depend on what he did in the next few seconds. (R. C. Anderson, Reynolds, Schallert, & Goetz, 1977, p. 372)

Now summarize what you've just read in two or three sentences.

Were you able to make sense of the passage? What did you think it was about? A prison escape? A wrestling match? Or perhaps something else altogether? The passage about Rocky includes a number of facts but leaves a lot unsaid; for example, it tells us nothing about where Rocky was, what kind of "lock" was holding him, or why timing was of the utmost importance. Yet you were probably able to use the information you were given to construct an overall understanding of Rocky's situation. Most people do find meaning of one sort or another in the Rocky passage (R. C. Anderson et al., 1977).

Different people often construct different meanings from the same stimuli, in part because they each bring their own unique prior experiences and knowledge bases to the same situation. For example, when the Rocky passage was used in an experiment with college students, physical education majors frequently interpreted it as a wrestling match, but music education majors (most of whom had little or no knowledge of wrestling) were more likely to think that it was about a prison break (R. C. Anderson et al., 1977).

Furthermore, people often interpret what they see and hear based on what they *expect* to see and hear. As an example, try the following exercise.

Experiencing Firsthand
Hamlet's Soliloquy

Here is the first part of a well-known soliloquy from William Shakespeare's *Hamlet*. Read it *as quickly as you can,* and read it *one time only.*

> To be, or not to be, that is the quastion—
> Whether 'tis nobler in the mind to suffer
> The slings annd arrows of outrageous fortune,
> Or to take arms against a sea of troubles,
> And by opposing end them. To die, to sleep—
> No more; and by a sleep to say we end
> The heart-ache, and the thousand naturel shocks
> That flesh is heir to; 'tis a consummation
> Devoutly to be wished. To die, to sleep—
> To sleep, perchance to dream, ay there's the rubb,
> For in that sleep of death what dreams may come
> When we have shuffled off this mortal coil,
> Must give us pause; there's tha respect
> That makes calamity of so long life.

You may have noticed one or two typographical errors in the passage. But did you catch them all? Altogether, there were *five* mistakes: *quastion* (line 1), *annd* (line 3), *naturel*

F I G U R E 7.1

What do you see in this picture?

From "The Role of Frequency in Developing Perceptual Sets" by B. R. Bugelski & D. A. Alampay, 1961, *Canadian Journal of Psychology, 15*, p. 206. Copyright 1961. Canadian Psychological Association. Reprinted with permission.

Adult readers often skip over letters, and even over entire words, as they read, yet may still understand what they are reading quite accurately (e.g., F. Smith, 1988). Can you explain this phenomenon using the idea of knowledge construction?

Make sure messages to students are clear and unambiguous.

(line 7), *rubb* (line 10), and *tha* (line 13). If you didn't notice all the errors—and many people don't—then your perception of the passage was influenced by what words you *expected* based on your general knowledge of English spelling and perhaps (if you once memorized Hamlet's soliloquy) on your recollection of what Hamlet actually said.

Prior knowledge and expectations are especially likely to influence learning when new information is ambiguous (e.g., Eysenck & Keane, 1990). To see what I mean, try another exercise.

Experiencing Firsthand
A Pen-and-Ink Sketch

Take a look at Figure 7–1. Look at the details carefully. Notice the shape of the head, the facial features, and the relative proportion of one part to another. But what exactly *do* you see?

Did you see a picture of a rat or mouse, or did you see a bald-headed man? In fact, the drawing isn't a very good picture of *anything*; too many details have been left out. Despite the missing pieces, people can usually make sense of Figure 7–1. Whether they see a man or a rodent depends, in large part, on whether they expect to see a human being or a nonhuman creature (Bugelski & Alampay, 1961). People's interpretations of ambiguous information are particularly susceptible to biases and expectations because so much of the information necessary for an "accurate" perception (if such is possible) is simply not available.

As teachers, we will find our students constructing their own idiosyncratic meanings and interpretations for virtually all aspects of the classroom curriculum. For example, as the Rocky exercise illustrates, the activity of reading is often quite constructive in nature: Students combine the ideas that they read with their prior knowledge and then draw logical conclusions about what the text is trying to communicate (Dole, Duffy, Roehler, & Pearson, 1991; Otero & Kintsch, 1992; F. Smith, 1988). So, too, will we find constructive processes in such subject areas as mathematics, science, and social studies (Driver, Asoko, Leach, Mortimer, & Scott, 1994; Resnick, 1989; VanSledright & Brophy, 1992). When we want our students to interpret classroom subject matter in particular ways, we must be sure to communicate clearly and unambiguously, so that there is little room for misinterpretation.

Construction in Retrieval

THINKING ABOUT WHAT YOU KNOW

Have you ever remembered an event very differently than someone else did? Were you and the other person both equally convinced of the accuracy of your memories? How might you explain this difference of opinion in terms of constructive processes?

As noted in Chapter 6, retrieval isn't always an all-or-nothing phenomenon. Sometimes we retrieve only certain parts of whatever information we are looking for in long-term memory. In such situations, we may construct our "memory" of an event by combining the tidbits we can retrieve with our general knowledge and assumptions about the world (Kolodner, 1985; Loftus, 1991; Rumelhart & Ortony, 1977). As an example of how retrieval of a specific event or idea often involves drawing on our knowledge about other things as well, try the following exercise.

▪ Experiencing Firsthand
Missing Letters

Can you fill in the missing letters of these five words?

1. sep - rate
2. exist - nce
3. adole - - - nce
4. retr - - val
5. hors d'o - - - - -

Were you able to retrieve the missing letters from your long-term memory? If not, then you may have found yourself making reasonable guesses, using either your knowledge of how the words are pronounced or your knowledge of how words in the English language are typically spelled. For example, perhaps you used the *i before e except after c* rule for word 4; if so, then you reconstructed the correct spelling of *retrieval.* Perhaps you used your knowledge that *ance* is a common word ending. Unfortunately, if you used this knowledge for word 2, then you spelled *existence* incorrectly. Neither pronunciation nor typical English spelling patterns would have helped you with *hors d'oeuvre,* a term borrowed from the French. (The correct spellings for words 1 and 3 are *separate* and *adolescence.*)

When people fill in the gaps in what they've retrieved based on what seems "logical," they often make mistakes—a form of forgetting called **reconstruction error.** Rita's version of what she learned in history is a prime example: She retrieved certain facts from her history lessons (e.g., the British wanted furs; they eventually settled in what is now Michigan) and constructed a scenario that made some sort of sense to her. So, too, will our own students sometimes fall victim to reconstruction error, pulling together what they can recall in ways that we may hardly recognize. If important details are difficult to fill in logically, we must make sure our students learn them well enough that they can retrieve them directly from their long-term memories.

Knowledge Construction: An Individual Activity and a Social Process

Up to this point, we have been talking about construction as a process that occurs within a single learner. Theories that focus on how people, as individuals, construct meaning from events are collectively known as **individual constructivism.** Our opening case study in which Rita weaves an idiosyncratic picture of early American history illustrates this perspective. Piaget's theory of cognitive development has an element of individual constructivism, as do many theorists' perspectives of how children's knowledge of vocabulary and syntax develops over the years (see Chapter 2).

Yet people often construct meaning by working together rather than by working alone, and the knowledge they create results from their combined efforts to interpret their experiences. Unlike individually constructed knowledge, which may differ considerably from one individual to another, socially constructed knowledge is shared by two or more people simultaneously. A perspective known as **social constructivism** focuses on such collective efforts to impose meaning on the world. If you have read Chapter 2, then you have already encountered one social constructivist—Lev Vygotsky.

Sometimes meaning is constructed by a group of people at a single point in time. For example, this would be the case if, by working together in a study group, you and a few classmates made sense of confusing course material. But at other times, the social

W hat implications does the notion of reconstruction error have for the credibility of eyewitness testimony?

W hen important details are difficult to fill in logically, make sure students learn them well.

T hink about times when you were confused about material in one of your classes. In such situations, did you ever work cooperatively with one or more classmates, who perhaps were equally confused, to make sense of the material *together*?

construction of meaning may take weeks, years, or even centuries. We find the latter situation in the development of such academic disciplines as history, social studies, science, and mathematics. Through these disciplines, people have developed such concepts as *revolution, democracy, molecule,* and *square root* and such principles as *supply-and-demand* and the *Pythagorean Theorem* to simplify, organize, and explain the very diverse nature of the world. Literature, music, and fine arts help us to impose meaning on the world as well—for example, by trying to describe the thoughts and feelings that characterize human experience. Here we see the very critical role that *culture* plays in knowledge construction: To the extent that different groups of people use different concepts and principles to explain their physical experiences, and to the extent that they have unique bodies of literature, music, and art to capture their psychological experiences, they will inevitably see the world in very diverse ways (e.g., Banks, 1991).

Think of novels that have given you new insights into human nature.

Organizing Knowledge

In the process of constructing knowledge, people also organize it in a variety of ways, thereby creating the interconnected long-term memory described in Chapter 6. This section introduces several ways in which people appear to organize the things they learn: *concepts, schemas, scripts,* and *personal theories.* Of these, we will spend the most time looking at concepts, not because they are the most important, but simply because researchers have been studying them for a longer time and so know more about them.

Concepts

A **concept** is a way of mentally grouping or categorizing objects or events. For instance, the concept *furniture* encompasses such objects as chairs, tables, beds, and desks. And the concept *swim* encompasses a variety of actions—breast stroke, crawl, butterfly—that all involve propelling oneself through water.

Students learn thousands of concepts during their school years. They learn some concepts quickly and easily. They acquire others more gradually and continue to revise them over time; in the meantime, they may have an "almost-but-not-quite" understanding of what the concepts are. Here are several examples of such partial understanding:

Lonnigan thinks of an *animal* as something with four legs and fur. He is quite surprised when his teacher says that fish, birds, and insects are also animals.

Lisa correctly defines a *rectangle* as a geometric figure composed of two sets of parallel lines that are joined by right angles; this definition correctly includes squares as examples of rectangles. Yet when she is shown a variety of shapes and asked to pick out all the rectangles, she doesn't identify the squares as being rectangles (P. S. Wilson, 1988).

Luis learns that a *noun* is "a person, place, or thing." Using this definition, he classifies words like *you* and *me* as nouns because they refer to people. Only later, when Luis learns about other parts of speech, does he realize that *you* and *me* are pronouns rather than nouns.

Be on the lookout for partial understanding of concepts, as reflected in undergeneralization or overgeneralization.

In some cases, students **undergeneralize** a concept: They have too narrow a view as to which objects or events are included. Lonnigan undergeneralizes when he excludes fish, birds, and insects from his concept of *animal.* And Lisa's current conception of a *rectangle* is an undergeneralization because she doesn't realize that squares can be rectangles. On other occasions, students may **overgeneralize** a concept: They may identify objects and events as examples of a concept when in fact they are nonexamples. For example, Luis overgeneralizes when he identifies *you* and *me* as nouns. Students don't fully understand what a concept is until they can identify both examples (**positive instances**) and nonexamples (**negative instances**) of the concept with complete accuracy.

Theorists have differing opinions regarding what people actually learn when they acquire a new concept. Let's consider how a concept might be learned as a *feature list,* a *prototype,* or a set of *exemplars*; let's also consider how numerous concepts are often interconnected in long-term memory.

Concepts as Feature Lists

Some theorists propose that learning a concept involves learning the specific attributes, or *features,* that characterize positive instances of the concept. **Defining features** are characteristics present in *all* positive instances. For example, a *circle* must be round, a *square* must have four equal sides connected at 90° angles, and an *animal* must be a consumer of food (rather than produce its own food through photosynthesis).

The task of identifying a concept's defining features is not always an easy one. As an example, consider this situation:

> A father goes to work. On the way home from work in the evening he stops at a bar to have a drink. His friends there are drunkards and he becomes a drunkard too. Is he still a father? (Saltz, 1971, p. 28)

Most eight-year-old children deny that a drunkard can still be a father (Saltz, 1971). Their response reflects their ignorance about the defining features of the concept *father.* Rather than recognize that fatherhood is defined simply in terms of a biological or adoptive relationship, many young children believe that a defining feature of fatherhood is "goodness," so a "bad" drunkard is automatically disqualified. "Goodness" is a **correlational feature** of fatherhood—a feature present in many positive instances of the concept but not essential for concept membership.

A concept is most easily learned when its defining features are concrete and obvious—in other words, when they are **salient**—rather than when they are abstract or difficult to pin down. As an example, the concept *red* has a single defining feature—a particular range of light wavelengths—that is easily seen by anyone who isn't color-blind. But what about the defining feature of *plant*? The process of photosynthesis is not readily observable. Instead, we are more apt to notice other characteristics of plants (e.g., that they have leaves or that they grow in gardens) that are correlational rather than defining features.

When children first encounter concepts, they are sometimes led astray by correlational features, particularly if those features are more salient than the defining ones (Anglin, 1977; Keil, 1989; Mervis, 1987). Thus, we should not be surprised to find Lisa omitting squares from her concept of *rectangle.* Most of the rectangles that Lisa has seen have probably had noticeably different widths and lengths. Nor is it surprising that Lonnigan excludes fish and birds from his concept of *animal.* Two very obvious correlational features—fur and four legs—have undoubtedly characterized many of the critters that people in Lonnigan's life have specifically labeled as "animals."

How do people learn a concept's defining features? The following exercise illustrates one possible mechanism.

Fur and four legs are features of many of the animals that young children encounter and so may be misconstrued as defining features of the concept *animal.*

What is the difference between squerkles and nonsquerkles?

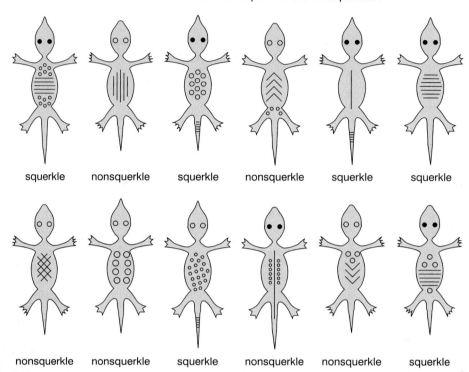

FIGURE 7.2
Learning the concept *squerkle*

▣ Experiencing Firsthand
Squerkles

Figure 7–2 shows a bird's-eye view of some positive and negative instances of a lizard-like creature known as a *squerkle.* Before you read any further, look at the figure and see whether you can determine what defines a squerkle.

While trying to learn what a squerkle is, you may have noticed yourself forming various hypotheses about its defining features. For example, when you saw four pointy-nosed squerkles and two round-nosed nonsquerkles on the top row, you may have thought that nose shape determines whether a critter is a squerkle. But then you would have found a pointy-nosed nonsquerkle and a round-nosed squerkle, thus squashing that hypothesis. And perhaps you thought that all squerkles had black eyes—until you reached the bottom row. I hope that you eventually discovered the defining feature of a squerkle: horizontal lines on either the body or the tail. Black eyes and pointy noses are correlational features of squerkles: Most squerkles have them, and only a few nonsquerkles have them. Other characteristics, such as dots, tail length, and number of toes, are features that are totally irrelevant to squerkleness.

To some extent, learning a concept may be similar to the process you just went through: Learners form hypotheses about a concept's defining features and then test them against the positive and negative instances they encounter (Bruner, Goodnow, & Austin, 1956; M. Levine, 1966). As new examples disprove a particular hypothesis, learners continue to revise their idea of what the concept is. By providing a variety of positive

🍎 Present both positive and negative instances of a concept, and also ask students to generate their own examples.

and negative instances of concepts, and also by asking students to generate their *own* examples of concepts, we enable students to test and refine their hypotheses about—and hence to develop a more accurate understanding of—those concepts (H. C. Ellis & Hunt, 1983; M. D. Merrill & Tennyson, 1977; Tennyson & Cocchiarella, 1986).

We can often short-circuit the hypothesis-testing process by simply telling students what a concept's defining features are—in other words, by presenting a definition (R. M. Gagné, 1985; Tennyson & Cocchiarella, 1986). Definitions are especially effective when a concept's defining features are nonsalient or abstract. Children can usually learn what *red* means and what a *circle* is even without a definition because redness and roundness are fairly obvious characteristics. But the defining features of *father* and *plant* are far less salient; for concepts like these, a definition can be quite helpful.

Concepts as Prototypes

Experiencing Firsthand
Visual Images

Close your eyes and picture a *bird.* Take a good look at the visual image you create.
    Now close your eyes again and picture a *vehicle.* Once again, look closely at your image.

What came to mind when I asked you to picture a bird? If you are like most people, then you probably visualized a relatively small bird, perhaps one about the size of a robin or sparrow, rather than a penguin or an ostrich. Likewise, your picture of a *vehicle* probably resembled a car or a truck, rather than a skateboard or an elevator.

For many concepts, learners seem to construct a mental **prototype:** an idea (perhaps a visual image) of a "typical" example (Rosch, 1973a, 1973b, 1977; Tennyson & Cocchiarella, 1986). Prototypes are usually based on the positive instances that learners encounter most frequently. For instance, people see small birds, cars, and trucks more frequently than they see large birds, skateboards, and elevators.

Once learners have formed a prototype for a particular concept, they compare new objects and events against the prototype. Objects or events similar to the prototype are easily identified as positive instances of the concept. Objects or events very different from the prototype are sometimes mistakenly identified as negative instances of the concept. As an illustration, let's say that your prototype of an *animal* looks something like a small dog, perhaps similar to Figure 7–3. How likely are you to recognize that the following critters are also animals?

horse   whale
grizzly bear   earthworm
frog   sponge
person

The more different the critter is from your doglike prototype, the less likely you are to identify it as an animal.

In some cases, a single "best example" represents a concept fairly accurately. In such situations, it makes sense to present the example to students as a way of helping them construct a mental prototype for the concept. Yet we must make sure that our students also know the concept's defining features so that they can correctly recognize any positive instances that *don't* closely resemble the prototype—so that they can identify an ostrich as a bird, a square as a rectangle, and so on.

Concepts as Exemplars

We probably cannot explain all concept learning strictly in terms of feature lists and prototypes. For one thing, how we categorize an object depends on the context in which we

---

Provide a definition that identifies a concept's defining features.

Are definitions likely to be effective when students learn them at a rote level? Why or why not?

What is your prototype for the concept *house? chair? plant?* Can you think of positive instances of these concepts that don't resemble your prototypes?

FIGURE 7.3
A possible prototype for the concept *animal*

Present a "best example" of a concept—one similar to most positive instances—as a prototype.

find it. For instance, if a cuplike object contains flowers, we might identify it as a *vase* rather than a *cup*; if it contains mashed potatoes, we might instead identify it as a *bowl* (Labov, 1973; Schwartz & Reisberg, 1991). Furthermore, not all concepts lend themselves readily to a specific set of defining features or a single prototype (Eysenck & Keane, 1990; Hampton, 1981; McCloskey & Glucksberg, 1978). For instance, I myself have a difficult time identifying the defining features or a typical example of *music*: Classical, rock, jazz, country-western, and Oriental music are all quite different from one another.

In some cases, knowledge of a concept may be based more on a variety of examples, or **exemplars,** than on a set of defining features or a single prototype (Reisberg, 1997; B. H. Ross & Spalding, 1994). Exemplars can give learners an idea of the variability they are likely to see in any category of objects or events. For instance, the concept *fruit* may bring to mind many different things: Apples, bananas, raspberries, mangos, and kiwi fruit are all possibilities. If you encounter a new instance of fruit—a blackberry, let's say—you could compare it to the variety of exemplars you have already stored and find one (a raspberry, perhaps) that is relatively similar.

Students typically learn concepts more effectively when they are given many examples rather than only one or two. The examples we provide should illustrate the full range of the concept so that students do not undergeneralize; for example, we might illustrate the concept *mammal* with whales and platypuses as well as with cats and dogs (E. V. Clark, 1971; M. D. Merrill & Tennyson, 1978; Tennyson & Cocchiarella, 1986).

It is possible that prototypes or exemplars are used to identify positive instances in clear-cut situations, whereas defining features are used in other, more ambiguous ones (e.g., Is a sponge an animal?) (Andre, 1986; Glass & Holyoak, 1975; Glass, Holyoak, & Santa, 1979). It may also be that children rely on prototypes or exemplars in the early years and then discover defining features later on. For example, as a preschooler, my son Jeff adamantly denied that the concept *animal* includes people, fish, and insects. When he began studying the animal kingdom in school, he learned a biology-based definition of an animal that incorporates some of its major features: a form of life that derives its food from other organisms, responds immediately to its environment, and can move its body. At that point Jeff acknowledged that people, fish, and creepy-crawlies are legitimate animals. (Someday, however, he may learn that biologists do not completely agree on a definition of *animal* and that true defining features of the concept are difficult to identify.)

Interconnectedness of Concepts

In addition to learning concepts, students also learn how concepts are interrelated. In many situations, concepts are nested within one another in a hierarchical fashion. For instance, as a student, you learned that *dogs* and *cats* are both *mammals,* that *mammals* and *birds* are both *vertebrates,* and that *vertebrates* and *invertebrates* are both *animals.* The more general, all-encompassing concepts (those near the top of the hierarchy) tend to be relatively abstract, whereas the more specific ones (those near the bottom of the hierarchy) tend to be fairly concrete (Flavell et al., 1993; Rosch, Mervis, Gray, Johnson, & Boyes-Braem, 1976). Given what we learned about cognitive development in Chapter 2, we can predict that in many instances, children are going to learn the specific (concrete) concepts earlier than they learn the more general (abstract) ones.

As you discovered in Chapter 2, Piaget described young children as being unable to view objects as belonging to two or more categories at the same time—a phenomenon known as *single classification.* As children reach the concrete operational stage, they become capable of *multiple classification.* From the perspective of concept learning, however, multiple classification is not an ability that children either have or don't have. Instead, children become able to categorize objects in two or more ways simultaneously when they learn how various concepts are interrelated—knowledge that is likely to evolve, at least in part, as a result of formal education (Flavell et al., 1993).

P̃resent positive instances that illustrate the full range of the concept.

S̃how students how concepts are interrelated.

INTO THE CLASSROOM: Facilitating Concept Learning

Provide a definition of the concept.

A geometry teacher defines a *sphere* as "the set of points in three-dimensional space that are equidistant from a single point."

Make defining features as concrete and salient as possible.

A teacher illustrates the concept *insect* with a line drawing that emphasizes the defining features, such as three body parts and three pairs of legs, in bold black lines. At the same time, the drawing downplays other, irrelevant characteristics that students might see, such as the insect's color or the presence of wings.

Present a variety of positive instances.

A music teacher plays a *primary chord* in several keys.

Present a "best example," or prototype.

To illustrate the concept *democracy,* a social science teacher describes a hypothetical, "ideal" government.

Present negative instances—especially "near misses"—to show what the concept is not.

When a teacher describes what a *mammal* is, he shows students frogs and lizards and explains why these animals are *not* mammals.

Ask students to identify positive and negative instances from among numerous possibilities.

A language arts teacher gives students a list of sentences and asks them to identify the sentences containing a *dangling participle.*

Ask students to generate their own positive instances of the concept.

A teacher asks students to think of examples of *adjectives* that they use frequently in their own conversations.

Show students how various concepts are related to one another.

A science teacher explains that the concepts *velocity* and *acceleration* have somewhat different meanings, even though they both relate to speed.

Schemas and Scripts

Experiencing Firsthand
Horse #2

Take a moment to think about what you know about horses. For instance, what do they look like? How do they spend their time? Where are you most likely to see them? Write down as many things about a horse as you can think of.

Some theorists propose that much of the information stored in long-term memory is organized as **schemas**—organized bodies of knowledge about specific topics (e.g., Rumelhart & Ortony, 1977). Schemas give us an idea of how things "typically" are. For example, you probably had little difficulty retrieving many different things about horses, perhaps including their elongated heads, tendency to graze in pastures, and frequent appearance at race tracks. The various things you know about horses are closely interrelated in your long-term memory in the form of a "horse" schema.

Not only do schemas provide a means for organizing information, but they also influence how we interpret new situations. As an example, try the following exercise.

Experiencing Firsthand
John

Read the following passage *one time only*.

> John was feeling bad today so he decided to go see the family doctor. He checked in with the doctor's receptionist, and then looked through several medical magazines that were on the table by his chair. Finally the nurse came and asked him to take off his clothes. The doctor was very nice to him. He eventually prescribed some pills for John. Then John left the doctor's office and headed home. (Bower, Black, & Turner, 1979, p. 190)

You probably had no trouble understanding the passage because you have been to a doctor's office yourself and have a schema for how those visits usually go. You can therefore fill in a number of details that the passage doesn't ever tell you. For example, you probably inferred that John must have *gone* to the doctor's office, although the story omits this essential step. Likewise, you probably concluded that John took his clothes off in the examination room, *not* in the waiting room, even though the story never makes it clear where John did his striptease. When a schema involves a predictable sequence of events related to a particular activity, as is the case in a visit to the doctor's office, it is sometimes called a **script.**

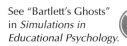 What is a typical script for a trip to the grocery store? to the movies? to a fast-food restaurant?

Students from diverse cultural backgrounds may sometimes come to school with different schemas and scripts and so may interpret the same classroom materials or activities differently (Lipson, 1983; R. E. Reynolds et al., 1982; Steffensen, Joag-Dev, & Anderson, 1979). As an illustration, try the next exercise.

Experiencing Firsthand
The War of the Ghosts

Read the following story *one time only*.

See "Bartlett's Ghosts" in *Simulations in Educational Psychology.*

> One night two young men from Egulac went down to the river to hunt seals, and while they were there it became foggy and calm. Then they heard war-cries, and they thought, "Maybe this is a war-party." They escaped to the shore, and hid behind a log. Now canoes came up, and they heard the noise of paddles, and saw one canoe coming up to them. There were five men in the canoe, and they said:
>
> "What do you think? We wish to take you along. We are going up the river to make war on the people."
>
> One of the young men said: "I have no arrows."
>
> "Arrows are in the canoe," they said.
>
> "I will not go along. I might be killed. My relatives do not know where I have gone. But you," he said, turning to the other, "may go with them."
>
> So one of the young men went, but the other returned home.
>
> And the warriors went on up the river to a town on the other side of Kalama. The people came down to the water, and they began to fight, and many were killed. But presently the young man heard one of the warriors say, "Quick, let us go home: that Indian has been hit." Now he thought: "Oh, they are ghosts." He did not feel sick, but they said he had been shot.

So the canoes went back to Egulac, and the young man went ashore to his house, and made a fire. And he told everybody and said, "Behold I accompanied the ghosts, and we went to fight. Many of our fellows were killed, and many of those who attacked us were killed. They said I was hit, and I did not feel sick."

He told it all, and then he became quiet. When the sun rose he fell down. Something black came out of his mouth. His face became contorted. The people jumped up and cried.

He was dead. (F. C. Bartlett, 1932, p. 65)

Now cover the pages and write down as much of the story as you can remember.

Compare your own rendition of the story with the original. What differences do you notice? Your version is almost certainly the shorter of the two, and you probably left out a number of details. But did you also find yourself distorting certain parts of the story so that it made more sense to you?

The War of the Ghosts is a Native American ghost story—one that is probably not totally consistent with the schemas and scripts you've learned if you were raised in another culture. In an early study of long-term memory (F. C. Bartlett, 1932), students at England's Cambridge University were asked to read the story twice and then to recall it at various times later on. The students' recollections of the story often included additions and distortions that made the story more consistent with English culture. For example, people rarely go "to the river to hunt seals" because seals are salt-water animals. Students might therefore say that the men went to the river to *fish*. Similarly, the ghostly element of the story did not fit comfortably with the religious beliefs of most Cambridge students and so was often modified. For example, one student was asked to recall the story six months after he had read it; notice how the version he remembers leaves out many of the story's more puzzling aspects (puzzling, at least, from the perspective of mainstream Western culture):

Different students will inevitably construct somewhat different meanings from the same classroom material, in part because they have different schemas and scripts for organizing their experiences.

Four men came down to the water. They were told to get into a boat and to take arms with them. They inquired, "What arms?" and were answered "Arms for battle." When they came to the battle-field they heard a great noise and shouting, and a voice said: "The black man is dead." And he was brought to the place where they were, and laid on the ground. And he foamed at the mouth. (F. C. Bartlett, 1932, pp. 71–72)

As teachers, we need to find out whether students have the appropriate schemas and scripts—the organized bodies of knowledge about specific topics and events—to understand the subject matter we are teaching. When our students *don't* have such knowledge, we may sometimes need to "back up" and help them develop it before we forge full-steam ahead with new material.

Begin instruction at a level consistent with students' existing knowledge base.

Personal Theories

Experiencing Firsthand
Coffeepots and Raccoons

Consider each of the following situations (adapted from Keil, 1989, p. 184).

1. Doctors took a coffeepot that looked like this:

They sawed off the handle, sealed the top, took off the top knob, sealed closed the spout, and sawed it off. They also sawed off the base and attached a flat piece of metal. They attached a little stick, cut a window in it, and filled the metal container with birdseed. When they were done, it looked like this:

After the operation, was this a coffeepot or a bird feeder?

2. Doctors took this raccoon:

and shaved away some of its fur. They dyed what was left all black. Then they bleached a single stripe all white down the center of its back. Then, with surgery, they put in its body a sac of super smelly odor, just as a skunk has. After they were all done, the animal looked like this:

After the operation, was this a skunk or a raccoon?

Chances are, you concluded that the coffeepot had been transformed into a bird feeder but that the raccoon was still a raccoon despite its radical surgery; even fourth graders come to these conclusions (Keil, 1986, 1989). Now how is it possible that the coffeepot could be made into something entirely different, whereas the raccoon could not?

Learners seem to acquire general belief systems—**personal theories**—about how the world operates (Keil, 1989; Neisser, 1987). These theories include many concepts and the relationships (e.g., correlational and cause-effect relations) among them. For example, even children as young as eight or nine seem to make a basic distinction between human-made objects (e.g., coffeepots, bird feeders) and biological entities (e.g., raccoons, skunks). Furthermore, they seem to conceptualize the two categories in fundamentally different ways: Human-made objects are defined largely by the *functions* they serve (e.g., keeping coffee warm, feeding birds), whereas biological entities are defined primarily by their origins (e.g., the parents who brought them into being, their DNA). Thus, when a coffeepot begins to hold birdseed rather than coffee, it becomes a bird feeder because its function has changed. But when a raccoon is surgically altered to look like a skunk, it still has raccoon parents and raccoon DNA and so cannot possibly *be* a skunk (Keil, 1987, 1989). Thinking along similar lines, even preschoolers will tell you that you can't change a yellow finch into a bluebird by giving it a coat of blue paint or dressing it in a "bluebird" costume (Keil, 1989).

People's personal theories about the world seem to guide them as they identify potential defining features of the concepts they are learning (Keil, 1987). For example, if you were trying to learn what a *horse* is, knowing it's an animal would lead you to conclude that its location (in a stable, a pasture, a shopping mall, or whatever) is irrelevant. In contrast, if you were trying to learn what the *equator* is, knowing that it's something on a map of the world should lead you to suspect that location is of the utmost importance.

By the time they reach school age, children have developed some preliminary theories and beliefs about the physical world, the biological world, and, to some extent, even the mental world (i.e., theories about the nature of thinking) (Flavell et al., 1993; Wellman & Gelman, 1992). These theories and beliefs have typically evolved with little or no guidance from other, more knowledgeable individuals; as a result, they may include some erroneous beliefs, or **misconceptions,** about how the world operates. Let's look at the origins and effects of such misconceptions.

When Knowledge Construction Goes Awry: Origins and Effects of Misconceptions

When learners construct their own understandings, there is, of course, no guarantee that they will construct accurate ones. For example, recall how Rita (in our opening case study) thinks that the British went to China to get furs and that they traveled through Michigan along the way. And consider how seven-year-old Rob thinks that mountains are formed:

Interviewer:	How were the mountains made?
Rob:	Some dirt was taken from outside and it was put on the mountain and then mountains were made with it.
Interviewer:	Who did that?
Rob:	It takes a lot of men to make mountains, there must have been at least four. They gave them the dirt and then they made themselves all alone.
Interviewer:	But if they wanted to make another mountain?
Rob:	They pull one mountain down and then they could make a prettier one. (Piaget, 1929, p. 348)

Construction workers apparently play a major role in Rob's mental theory about the physical world.

Research tells us that children and adolescents typically have many misconceptions about the world around them; Figure 7–4 lists a few common ones. Such misconceptions probably have a variety of sources. Sometimes they result from how things *appear* to be (Byrnes, 1996; diSessa, 1996; Duit, 1991); for example, from our perspective on the earth's surface, the sun looks as if it moves around the earth, rather than vice versa. Sometimes misconceptions are encouraged by common expressions in language; for instance, we often talk about the sun "rising" and "setting" (Duit, 1991; Mintzes, Trowbridge, Arnaudin,

FIGURE 7.4
Common student misconceptions

ASTRONOMY

Fact: The earth revolves around the sun.
Misconception: The sun revolves around the earth. It "rises" in the morning and "sets" in the evening, at which point it "goes" to the other side of the earth.

Fact: The earth is shaped more or less like a sphere.
Misconception: The earth is shaped like a round, flat disk.

BIOLOGY

Fact: A living thing is something that carries on such life processes as metabolism, growth, and reproduction.
Misconception: A living thing is something that moves and/or grows. The sun, wind, clouds, and fire are living things.

Fact: A plant is a food producer.
Misconception: A plant grows in a garden and is relatively small. Carrots and cabbage are vegetables, not plants. Trees are plants only if they are small.

PHYSICS

Fact: An object remains in uniform motion until a force acts upon it; a force is needed only to *change* speed or direction.
Misconception: Any moving object has a force acting upon it. For example, a ball thrown in the air continues to be pushed upward by the force of the throw until it begins its descent.

Fact: Gravity is the force whereby any two masses are attracted together.
Misconception: Gravity is the "glue" that holds people to the earth. There is no gravity without air.

GEOGRAPHY

Fact: The Great Lakes contain fresh water.
Misconception: The Great Lakes contain salt water.

Fact: Rivers run from higher elevation to lower elevation.
Misconception: Rivers run from north to south. For example, rivers can run from Canada into the United States, but not vice versa.

EDUCATIONAL PSYCHOLOGY

Fact: Meaningful learning is more effective than rote learning.
Misconception: Rote learning is more effective than meaningful learning.

Fact: Negative reinforcement is the removal of a stimulus (usually an aversive, or unpleasant, one). It increases the frequency of the behavior it follows. (We'll study negative reinforcement in Chapter 10.)
Misconception: Negative reinforcement is the presentation of an aversive stimulus (e.g., a scolding, a spanking). Its effect, if any, is to decrease the frequency of a behavior that it follows. Essentially, the term is just a nicer way of saying "punishment."

Sources: S. Carey, 1986; Kyle & Shymansky, 1989; Lennon et al., 1990; J. Nussbaum, 1985; Sneider & Pulos, 1983; Vosniadou, 1994; Vosniadou & Brewer, 1987; geography misconceptions courtesy of R. K. Ormrod.

& Wandersee, 1991). Sometimes learners infer incorrect cause-effect relationships be-tween two events simply because those events often occur at the same time (Byrnes, 1996; Keil, 1991). Perhaps even fairy tales and television cartoon shows play a role in promoting misconceptions (Glynn, Yeany, & Britton, 1991); as an example, think of cartoon "bad guys" who run off a cliff and remain suspended in air until they realize that there's noth-ing holding them up. And unfortunately, students may also learn erroneous ideas from oth-ers, including, in some instances, teachers and textbook authors (Begg, Anas, & Farinacci, 1992; Duit, 1991).

Unfortunately, students' existing misconceptions can wreak havoc on new learning. Thanks to the processes of meaningful learning and elaboration—processes that usually facilitate learning—students may change or distort new information to fit their existing misbeliefs. As a result, students can spend a great deal of time learning the wrong thing! Consider the case of Kevin (K. J. Roth & Anderson, 1988). Kevin's fifth-grade class was studying photosynthesis, the process through which plants produce their own food. On a pretest, Kevin indicated his misconception that plants get food from other sources:

> Food (for plants) can be sun, rain, light, bugs, oxygen, soil and even other dead plants. Also warmth or coldness. All plants need are at least three or four of these foods. Plus minerals. (Roth & Anderson, 1988, p. 117)

At the end of the instructional unit, his definition of the process of photosynthesis is fairly accurate (excuse the grammar):

> Well, in the leaves, in the green plants, they have little chloroplasts which inside that have chlorophyll. When the sun shines on it, it does photosynthesis which changes, well it doesn't really change, but the plant has certain chemicals that change the sunlight . . . well, they have certain chemicals that the sunlight changes into food which is energy for the plant. (K. J. Roth & Anderson, 1988, p. 117)

Nevertheless, the unit on photosynthesis didn't put much of a dent in Kevin's original belief about sources of food for plants, as revealed by his response when asked how a plant gets its food:

> Whew, from lots of places. From the soil for one, for the minerals and water, and from the air for oxygen. The sunlight for sun and so it would change chemicals for sugars. It sort of makes its own food and gets food from the ground. And from air. (K. J. Roth & An-derson, 1988, p. 118)

Kevin had learned that photosynthesis provides a source of food for plant life. Thanks to his prior misconception, however, Kevin had not learned a critical point of the lesson: Photosynthesis provides the *only* source of food for plants.

As teachers, our job is twofold: Not only must we help students construct accurate understandings of the world around them, but we must also encourage them to discard any erroneous beliefs they have previously constructed. As we consider how to promote both knowledge construction and conceptual change in the next two sections, we will identify some strategies for accomplishing both of these goals.

> Even college students ▲ have been known to ignore information presented in class when it is inconsistent with their prior beliefs (Holt-Reynolds, 1992).

Promoting Effective Knowledge Construction

Knowing that learning is probably a constructive process does not necessarily tell us how we can most effectively promote such learning (K. R. Harris & Alexander, 1998; Hirsch, 1996; Nuthall, 1996). In fact, cognitive psychologists believe there are many ways to help students construct an increasingly richer and more sophisticated knowledge base. A few possibilities are:

- Providing opportunities for experimentation
- Presenting the ideas of others

- Emphasizing conceptual understanding
- Promoting dialogue
- Using authentic activities

Providing Opportunities for Experimentation

Provide opportunities for students to experiment with the physical world.

By interacting and experimenting with the objects around them, students can discover many characteristics and principles of the world firsthand (e.g., Fosnot, 1996). As teachers, we can create numerous hands-on opportunities for students to touch, manipulate, modify, combine, and recombine concrete objects. For example, at the elementary school level, we might use beads or pennies to help students discover basic addition and subtraction facts, or we might use two balls of clay and a scale to promote the realization that an object's weight remains the same despite changes in its shape (Piaget's notion of *conservation*). At the secondary level, such activities as science labs, in-class demonstrations, and computer simulations should also help our students construct knowledge about the world around them.

Teachers often teach clearly delineated, step-by-step procedures for accomplishing certain tasks. Yet on some occasions, it might be more helpful to let students develop such procedures *on their own* through experimentation. For example, when teaching cooking, it may sometimes be more productive to cast aside recipes and instead let students try different combinations and proportions of ingredients (Hatano & Inagaki, 1993). As another example, let's consider a study in which kindergarten students had one of two different experiences raising animals (Hatano & Inagaki, 1993). Some students had pet rabbits in their classrooms; they took turns feeding and taking care of the rabbits by using procedures their teacher had carefully prescribed for them. Others were raising goldfish at home; these students had to make their own decisions about how best to care for their pets and, in doing so, could experiment with feeding schedules, water purity, and other variables that might affect the fish's welfare. The students who raised the goldfish appeared to develop a more accurate understanding of animals in general—for example, learning that baby animals grow bigger over time—and were able to apply what they learned from their own pets to other species. One goldfish owner, when asked whether one could keep a baby frog the same size forever, said, "No, we can't, because the frog will grow bigger as the goldfish grew bigger. My goldfish were small before, but now they are big" (Hatano & Inagaki, 1993, p. 121).

Unfortunately, the researchers didn't eliminate several other possible explanations for their results. Besides the fact that one group of children used teacher-prescribed procedures and the other used self-chosen procedures, what other differences between the two groups might account for the results obtained in this study? (You may want to refer to the Chapter 1 section, "Drawing Conclusions from Research.")

Hands-on activities are a key component of an instructional strategy known as *discovery learning*. We will consider this approach in more depth in Chapter 13.

Presenting the Ideas of Others

Expose students to the ways in which other people interpret physical and social events.

As noted earlier, knowledge is constructed not only by people working independently but also by people working together over the course of years or centuries to make sense of complex phenomena. Although it may sometimes be beneficial to have our students discover basic principles for themselves (reinventing the wheel, so to speak), we must also provide opportunities for them to hear and read about the ideas of others—the concepts, principles, theories, and so on, that society has developed to explain both the physical and psychological aspects of human experience (R. Driver, 1995; Vygotsky, 1962). Our students are most likely to construct a productive view of the world when they have the benefit of experiencing the world firsthand *and* the benefit of learning how those before them have interpreted such experience.

Emphasizing Conceptual Understanding

Let's look again at our opening case study. Rita acquired a few miscellaneous facts in her history lessons, but she clearly had no idea about how those facts were interconnected.

Students can more effectively construct meaningful interpretations of events when they examine how others have interpreted similar events. For example, by reading classic works of literature, they view daily life from the perspectives of numerous authors.

Unfortunately, such learning of isolated facts, without any sense of how they fit together, is all too common at both the elementary and secondary grade levels (Brophy & Alleman, 1992; J. Hiebert & Lefevre, 1986; Hollon, Roth, & Anderson, 1991; McCaslin & Good, 1996; McRobbie & Tobin, 1995).

Without a doubt, students benefit more from acquiring facts, concepts, and ideas in an integrated, interrelated, and meaningful fashion; in other words, they benefit from developing a **conceptual understanding** of academic subject matter (L. M. Anderson, 1993; Bédard & Chi, 1992; J. J. White & Rumsey, 1994). For example, rather than simply memorizing basic computation procedures, students should also learn how these procedures reflect underlying principles of mathematics (J. Hiebert & Lefevre, 1986). Rather than memorize historical facts as a list of unrelated people, places, and dates, students should place those facts within the context of major social and religious trends, migration patterns, economic considerations, characteristics of human personality, and so on.

Here are several specific strategies for helping students develop a conceptual understanding of classroom subject matter:

- Organize units around a few core ideas and themes, always relating specific content back to this core.
- Explore each topic in depth—for example, by considering many examples, examining cause-effect relationships, and discovering how specific details relate to more general principles.
- Explain how new ideas relate to students' own experiences and to things they have previously learned.

Help students learn material in an integrated, interrelated fashion.

- Show students—through the things we say, the assignments we give, and the criteria we use to evaluate learning—that conceptual understanding of classroom subject matter is far more important than knowledge of isolated facts.

- Ask students to teach what they have learned to others—a task that encourages them to focus on main ideas and pull them together in a way that makes sense. (L. M. Anderson, 1993; Brophy & Alleman, 1992; Hatano & Inagaki, 1993; Prawat, 1993; VanSledright & Brophy, 1992; J. J. White & Rumsey, 1994)

Construction of an integrated understanding of any complex topic will inevitably take time. Accordingly, many educators advocate a *less is more* principle: *Less* material presented more thoroughly is learned *more* completely and with greater understanding (Brophy & Alleman, 1992; Kyle & Shymansky, 1989; Marshall, 1992; Sizer, 1992).

🍎 Address fewer topics and spend more time on each one.

Promoting Dialogue

🍎 Encourage students to exchange their views through frequent classroom dialogues.

Students are more likely to remember new information and experiences when they talk about these things with others (Schank & Abelson, 1995; Tessler & Nelson, 1994; Wasik, Karweit, Burns, & Brodsky, 1998). Furthermore, students are often more successful in making sense of the world when they work *together* to construct meaning from the phenomena they observe. Frequent conversations are essential for such mutually constructed meanings to develop (Hatano & Inagaki, 1993; Marshall, 1992; Paris & Cunningham, 1996; Sosniak & Stodolsky, 1994).

As an example of how members of a classroom might work together to construct meaning, let's consider an interaction in Keisha Coleman's third-grade classroom (P. L. Peterson, 1992). The class has been studying positive and negative numbers, and the students are now specifically addressing how they might solve the problem $-10 + 10 = ?$ with this number line:

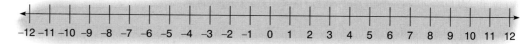

One student, Marta, gives the answer "Zero" and explains herself by saying, "You have to count ten numbers to the right." A second student, Tessa, agrees with Marta's answer of zero but disagrees with her explanation. The following conversation among Ms. Coleman and two of her students, Tessa and Chang, ensues:

Ms. Coleman: What do you disagree with?

Tessa: You have to count numbers to the right. If you count numbers to the right, then you couldn't get to zero. You'd have to count to the left.

Ms. Coleman: Could you explain a little bit more about what you mean by that? I'm not quite sure I follow you. And the rest of *you need to listen very closely so you can make comments about what she's saying* or say whether or not you agree or disagree. Tessa?

Tessa: Because if you went that way [points to the right] then it would have to be a higher number.

Ms. Coleman: Any comments about what Tessa's trying to say? Chang?

Chang: I disagree with what she's trying to say.

Ms. Coleman: O.K. Your disagreement is?

Chang: Tessa says if you're counting right, then the number is—I don't really understand. She said, "If you count right, then the number has to go smaller." I don't know what she's talking about. Negative ten plus negative ten is zero.

Ms. Coleman:	You said that you don't understand what she's trying to say?
Chang:	No.
Ms. Coleman:	Do you want to ask her?
Chang:	[Turns to Tessa and asks]: What do you mean by counting to the right?
Tessa:	If you count from ten up, you can't get zero. If you count from ten left, you can get zero.
Chang:	[to Tessa]: Well, negative ten is a negative number—smaller than zero.
Tessa:	I know.
Chang:	Then why do you say you can't get to zero when you're adding to negative ten, which is smaller than zero?
Tessa:	OHHHH! NOW I GET IT! This is positive.
Ms. Coleman:	Excuse me?
Tessa:	You have to count right.
Ms. Coleman:	You're saying in order to get to zero, you have to count to the right? From where, Tessa?
Tessa:	Negative 10. (P. L. Peterson, 1992, pp. 165–166; reprinted by permission)

Ms. Coleman's class continues to struggle with Marta's incomplete explanation of counting "ten numbers to the right" as a way of determining that $-10 + 10 = 0$. Eventually, Tessa offers a revised and more complete explanation. Pointing to the appropriate location on the number line, she says, "You start at negative 10. Then you add 1, 2, 3, 4, 5, 6, 7, 8, 9, 10." She moves one number to the right for each number she counts. She reaches the zero point on the number line when she counts "10" and concludes, "That equals zero."

By asking our students to explain, discuss, and debate classroom subject matter openly, we accomplish several things simultaneously:

- We encourage students to clarify and organize their ideas sufficiently so that they can verbalize them to others.

- We provide opportunities for students to *elaborate* on what they have learned—for example, by drawing inferences, generating hypotheses, and asking questions.

- We enable students to discover flaws and inconsistencies in their own thinking, thereby helping them identify gaps in their understanding.

- We expose students to the views of others—views that may reflect a more accurate understanding of the topics under discussion.

- We help students discover how different individuals, perhaps from various cultures, may interpret the world in different, yet perhaps equally valid, ways. (L. M. Anderson, 1993; Banks, 1991; Barnes, 1976; Fosnot, 1996; Hatano & Inagaki, 1993; E. H. Hiebert & Raphael, 1996; N. M. Webb & Palincsar, 1996)

Classroom dialogues provide an additional benefit to us as teachers. By listening carefully to students' comments and questions, we can identify and remediate any misconceptions that might interfere with students' ability to acquire further knowledge and skills (Presseisen & Beyer, 1994; Sosniak & Stodolsky, 1994).

Using Authentic Activities

Many theorists suggest that students can construct a more useful and productive knowledge base if they learn classroom subject matter within the context of **authentic activities**—activities similar to those encountered in the outside world. For example, rather than have students practice writing skills through short, artificial writing exercises, we might ask them to write stories or essays or to send letters to real people. Students' writing improves

If you have read Chapters 2, 3, and 4, try to recall additional benefits of classroom interaction that those chapters identify.

Chapter 14 describes how classroom discussions, cooperative learning, and reciprocal teaching can promote student dialogue.

Many cognitive psychologists advocate authentic activities that resemble tasks students will eventually encounter in the outside world.

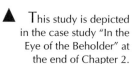

Incorporate classroom subject matter into "real world" activities.

See "Intuitive Physics" in *Simulations in Educational Psychology.*

▲ This study is depicted in the case study "In the Eye of the Beholder" at the end of Chapter 2.

in both quality and quantity when they engage in such authentic writing tasks (E. H. Hiebert & Fisher, 1992). Likewise, rather than have students develop map interpretation skills (e.g., interpreting symbols, scale, and latitude and longitude) by answering a series of unrelated questions in a workbook, we might instead have them construct their own maps, asking them to choose appropriate symbols and scale and to integrate information about latitude and longitude. Although students may sometimes feel a bit overwhelmed by the complexity of such map-making activities, they are likely to gain a more complete understanding of how to use and interpret maps effectively than do those who simply engage in workbook exercises (Gregg & Leinhardt, 1994a).

Authentic activities can relate to virtually any area of the curriculum. For example, we might ask students to:

Give an oral report	Converse in a foreign language
Write an editorial	Play in an athletic event
Participate in a debate	Complete an art project
Find information in the library	Perform in a concert
Conduct an experiment	Tutor a classmate
Graph data	Make a videotape
Construct a chart or model	Perform a workplace routine
Create and distribute a class newsletter	Develop a "home page" for the Internet

In many cases, these activities may require considerable support (scaffolding) to ensure that students carry them out successfully. As such, they may remind you of the *guided participation* that I described within the context of Vygotsky's theory in Chapter 2.

By placing classroom activities in "real world" contexts, we help our students discover the reasons why they are learning academic subject matter; we also increase the likelihood that, later on, they will actually use the information and skills we have taught them (A. Collins et al., 1989; De Corte et al., 1996). We will revisit the importance of authentic activities when we discuss *transfer* in Chapter 8 and *instructional strategies* in Chapter 13, and we will consider a related topic, *authentic assessment,* in Chapter 16.

Promoting Conceptual Change

Teachers often present new information in class thinking that such information will replace any erroneous beliefs that students currently have. Yet research indicates that students of all ages often hold quite stubbornly to their misconceptions, even after considerable instruction that explicitly contradicts those misconceptions (Carey, 1986; Chambliss, 1994; Chinn & Brewer, 1993; Shuell, 1996). Consider this situation (Eaton, Anderson, & Smith, 1984):

A class of fifth graders was about to study a unit on light and vision. Based on results of a pretest, it was clear that most students believed incorrectly that vision occurs simply as the result of light shining on an object and making it bright. During the unit, the correct explanation of human vision was presented: Light must be reflected off an object *and then travel to the eye* before the object can be seen. Even though students both read and heard the correct explanation of how people see objects,

INTO THE CLASSROOM: Promoting Knowledge Construction

Focus on an in-depth understanding of a few key ideas instead of covering many topics superficially.

A teacher tells his class, "As we study the geography of South America, we aren't going to worry about memorizing a lot of place names. Instead, we will look at how topography and climate have influenced the economic and cultural development of different regions of the continent."

Provide opportunities for experimentation.

A teacher has students experiment with clay and water to discover the principle that a certain quantity of a solid displaces the same amount of water regardless of the shape that the solid takes.

Expose students to others' interpretations of the world.

A teacher has students read poetry from a variety of countries and cultures.

Promote classroom discussions in which students can freely exchange their views.

A teacher asks students to speculate on how the Japanese people must have felt after the atomic bomb was dropped over Hiroshima.

Include authentic activities in the curriculum.

A teacher has students develop and cook a menu that includes all the basic food groups.

most of them "learned" what they already believed: that an object can be seen as soon as light hits it. Posttest results indicated that only 24 percent of the class had learned the correct explanation.

Why are students' misconceptions often so resistant to change? Theorists have offered several possible explanations:

- As noted earlier, students' existing misconceptions may often color their understanding of new information. Learners are likely to interpret new information in ways that are consistent with what they already "know" about the world, to the point where they continue to believe what they have always believed.

- Students also tend to look for information that confirms their existing beliefs and to ignore any *dis*confirming evidence (Duit, 1991; Gunstone & White, 1981; Kuhn, Amsel, & O'Loughlin, 1988).

- Students' existing beliefs are often consistent with their everyday experiences; in contrast, more accurate explanations (perhaps commonly accepted scientific principles or theories) may be fairly abstract and difficult to relate to everyday reality (P. A. Alexander, 1997; Driver et al., 1994; M. C. Linn, Songer, & Eylon, 1996). For example, although the law of inertia tells us that force is needed to *start* an object in motion but not to *keep* it in motion, we know from experience that if we want to move a heavy object across the floor, we have to continue to push it (Driver et al., 1994).

- Some erroneous beliefs are integrated into cohesive personal theories, with many interrelationships existing among various ideas; in such a situation, changing misconceptions involves changing an entire organized body of knowledge rather than a single belief (Chambliss, 1994; Derry, 1996; C. Smith, Maclin, Grosslight, & Davis, 1997). For example, the belief that the sun revolves around the earth may be part of a more general "earth-centered" view of things, perhaps one that includes the moon, stars, and various other heavenly bodies revolving around the earth as well. In reality, of course, the moon revolves around the earth, the earth revolves around the sun, and the other stars are not directly involved with the earth one way or the other. Yet the earth-centered view is a much easier one to understand and accept (on the surface, at least), and everything fits so nicely together.

- In many situations, students learn new information without letting go of their prior beliefs, so that two inconsistent ideas are kept in memory simultaneously (Chambliss, 1994; Keil & Silberstein, 1996; Mintzes et al., 1991; Winer & Cottrell, 1996). Sometimes this happens because students learn the new information at a rote level, without relating it to what they already know and believe (Chambliss, 1994; Strike & Posner, 1992). In other cases, it may occur because existing misconceptions are not easily retrievable from long-term memory (Keil & Silberstein, 1996). In either situation, students will not realize that the new things they have learned contradict what they already believe.

When our students hold misconceptions about the world, we must help them revise their thinking to undergo **conceptual change.** Psychologists have identified several principles regarding how conceptual change may come about. These principles can guide us as we face the often difficult challenge of helping our students correct stubborn misconceptions:

- Conceptual change is more likely to occur when existing misconceptions are identified before instruction begins.

- Students are most likely to revise their current beliefs about the world when they become convinced that these beliefs are incorrect.

- Students must be motivated to learn correct explanations for the phenomena they observe.

- Some misconceptions may persist despite instruction designed to contradict them.

These principles are summarized in Table 7–1. Let's look at the implications of each one.

Identifying Existing Misconceptions Before Instruction Begins

Check for
misconceptions about
the topic at hand.

As teachers, we can more easily address students' misconceptions when we know what those misconceptions *are* (Kyle & Shymansky, 1989; Putnam, 1992; K. J. Roth & Anderson, 1988; Vosniadou & Brewer, 1987). Thus, we should probably begin any new topic with some sort of assessment of students' current beliefs about the topic—perhaps simply by asking a few informal questions. The following conversation illustrates the kinds of misconceptions that questioning may reveal:

Adult: What is rain?

Child: It's water that falls out of a cloud when the clouds evaporate.

Adult: What do you mean, "clouds evaporate"?

Child: That means water goes up in the air and then it makes clouds and then, when it gets too heavy up there, then the water comes and they call it rain.

Adult: Does the water stay in the sky?

Child: Yes, and then it comes down when it rains. It gets too heavy.

Adult: Why does it get too heavy?

Child: 'Cause there's too much water up there.

Adult: Why does it rain?

Child: 'Cause the water gets too heavy and then it comes down.

Principles for Promoting Conceptual Change

PRINCIPLE	EDUCATIONAL IMPLICATION	EXAMPLE
Conceptual change is more likely to occur when existing misconceptions are identified before instruction begins.	Probe students' understanding of a topic through a short pretest or a series of discussion questions.	When beginning a unit on gravity, ask, "If we were to drop a penny and a golf ball from a second-story window at exactly the same time, would one of them land sooner than the other, or would they both land at the same time?"
Students are most likely to revise their current beliefs about the world when they become convinced that these beliefs are incorrect.	Show students how new information contradicts the things they currently believe.	If students predict that a golf ball would land sooner than a penny, have them conduct an experiment to test their prediction. This experiment should show them that, although a golf ball is heavier than a penny, both objects actually fall at the same rate.
Students must be motivated to learn correct explanations for the phenomena they observe.	Show students how correct explanations have relevance to their own personal interests.	Demonstrate how the laws of physics relate to auto mechanics and, indirectly, to auto repair.
Some misconceptions may persist despite instruction designed to contradict them.	Carefully scrutinize what students say and write, not only during a lesson but after the lesson as well, for signs of partial or total misunderstanding.	When a student says that a spider is an *insect*, respond: "A spider is actually an *arachnid*, not an insect. Think back to what we learned about insects. Why don't spiders fit in that category?"

Adult: Why doesn't the whole thing come down?

Child: Well, 'cause it comes down at little times like a salt shaker when you turn it upside down. It doesn't all come down at once 'cause there's little holes and it just comes out.

Adult: What are the little holes in the sky?

Child: Umm, holes in the clouds, letting the water out. (adapted from Stepans, 1991, p. 94)

This conception of a cloud as a "salt shaker" of sorts is hardly consistent with the scientifically accepted view of how and why rain comes about.

Such informal "pretesting" will be particularly important in your first few years of teaching. As you gain experience teaching a particular topic year after year, you may eventually find that you can anticipate what your students' prior beliefs and misbeliefs about the topic are likely to be.

Convincing Students That Existing Beliefs Are Inadequate

As teachers, we can more effectively promote conceptual change when we show our students how new information contradicts what they currently believe and when we

Show students how new information contradicts the things they currently believe.

289

demonstrate why their existing conceptions are inadequate. To accomplish these ends, we might use strategies such as these:

- Asking questions that challenge students' current beliefs
- Presenting phenomena that students cannot adequately explain within their existing perspectives
- Engaging students in discussions of the pros and cons of various explanations
- Pointing out, explicitly, the differences between students' beliefs and "reality"
- Showing how the correct explanation of an event or phenomenon is more plausible (i.e., makes more sense) than anything students themselves can offer (Chan, Burtis, & Bereiter, 1997; G. J. Posner, Strike, Hewson, & Gertzog, 1982; Prawat, 1989; K. J. Roth, 1990; Slusher & Anderson, 1996; Vosniadou & Brewer, 1987)

Students will notice inconsistencies between new information and their previously acquired beliefs only if they try to make connections between the "new" and the "old"—in other words, if they engage in meaningful learning (Chinn & Brewer, 1993; O. Lee & Anderson, 1993; Pintrich, Marx, & Boyle, 1993; Slusher & Anderson, 1996). In Chapter 6, we found that students who engage in meaningful rather than rote learning acquire new information more quickly and retrieve it more easily. Here we see an additional reason to encourage meaningful learning: It helps "undo" existing misconceptions.

Motivating Students to Learn Correct Explanations

Students are most likely to engage in meaningful learning and undergo conceptual change when they are motivated to do so (O. Lee & Anderson, 1993; Pintrich et al., 1993). For example, students should be interested in the subject matter they are studying, set their sights on mastering it, and believe that they are actually *capable* of mastering it (Pintrich et al., 1993). Chapter 12 identifies a variety of strategies for fostering such motivation.

Monitoring for Persistent Misconceptions

Because of students' natural tendency to reinterpret new information within the context of what they already know and believe, some misconceptions may be especially resistant to change despite our best efforts. These misconceptions are sometimes blatantly incorrect; at other times, they may be sort-of-but-not-quite correct. As an example of the latter situation, students sometimes define the concept *transparent* as "something you can see through" (K. J. Roth & Anderson, 1988). Although such a definition is consistent with how we speak about transparency on a day-to-day basis, it may nevertheless reflect the erroneous belief that sight originates with the eye and goes outward to and through the transparent object. *Transparent* is more accurately defined as "something light passes through."

Throughout a lesson, we should continue to check students' beliefs about the topic at hand, looking for subtle signs that their understanding is not quite accurate and giving corrective feedback when necessary. As an example, consider this classroom discussion about vision and opaque objects:

Ms. Ramsey:	(Projects an overhead transparency on the wall) Why can't the girl see around the wall?
Annie:	The girl can't see around the wall because the wall is opaque.
Ms. Ramsey:	What do you mean when you say the wall is opaque?
Annie:	*You can't see through it. It is solid.*
Brian:	(calling out) The rays are what can't go through the wall.
Ms. Ramsey:	I like that answer better. Why is it better?
Brian:	The rays of light bounce off the car and go to the wall. They can't go through the wall.

Promote meaningful learning, especially when new material contradicts existing misconceptions.

Give students reasons to want to revise their thinking about a topic.

Monitor students' understanding throughout a lesson.

Ms. Ramsey:	Where are the light rays coming from originally?
Students:	The sun.
Annie:	*The girl can't see the car because she is not far enough out.*
Ms. Ramsey:	So you think her position is what is keeping her from seeing it. (She flips down the overlay with the answer.) Who was better?
Students:	Brian.
Ms. Ramsey:	(to Annie) Would she be able to see if she moved out beyond the wall?
Annie:	Yes.
Ms. Ramsey:	Why?
Annie:	*The wall is blocking her view.*

INTO THE CLASSROOM: Promoting Conceptual Change

Check for prior misconceptions that may lead students to interpret new information incorrectly.

A fourth-grade teacher describes *gravity* as "a force that pulls you down." He then points to Australia on a globe and asks, "What do you think would happen if we traveled to Australia? Would gravity pull us off the earth and make us fall into space?"

Show how new information contradicts the things that students currently believe.

When several students express their stereotypical beliefs that new immigrants to the country are "lazy," their teacher invites several recent immigrants to visit the class and describe their experiences in adapting to a new culture.

Ask questions that challenge students' misconceptions.

A physics teacher has just begun a unit on inertia. Several students assert that when a baseball is thrown in the air, some force continues to act upon the ball, pushing it upward until it begins to drop. The teacher asks, "What force in the air could possibly be pushing that ball upward once it leaves the thrower's hand?"

Show students how your alternative explanation is more plausible and useful than their original misconception.

The same physics teacher points out that the baseball continues to move upward even though no force pushes it in that direction. He explains the concept of *inertia* within this context: The ball needs a force only to get it *started* in a particular direction. Once the force has been exerted, other forces (gravity and air resistance) alter the ball's speed and direction.

Give students corrective feedback about responses that reflect misunderstanding.

A psychology teacher says to a student, "Hmmm, you just told me that you could learn a foreign language by playing audiotapes while you sleep. But didn't we just discover last week that attention is essential for effective cognitive processing?"

When pointing out misconceptions that students have, do so in a way that maintains their self-esteem.

When a student expresses an erroneous belief, her teacher says, "You know, many of my students come to class thinking exactly that. It's a very logical thing to think. But the truth of the matter is . . . ."

Ms. Ramsey:	Is it blocking her view? What is it blocking?
Student:	Light rays.
Ms. Ramsey:	Light rays that are doing what?
Annie:	If the girl moves out beyond the wall, then the light rays that bounce off the car are not being blocked. (K. J. Roth & Anderson, 1988, pp. 129–130)

Notice how Ms. Ramsey is not satisfied with Annie's original answer that the wall is opaque. With further questioning, it becomes clear that Annie's understanding of opaqueness is off target: She talks about the girl being unable to "see through" the wall, rather than about light's inability to pass through the wall. With Ms. Ramsey's continuing insistence on precise language, Annie eventually begins to bring light rays into her explanation (K. J. Roth & Anderson, 1988).

Ask students to apply what they have learned.

Assessment of students' comprehension is important *after* a lesson as well. We are more likely to detect misconceptions when we ask students to *use* and *apply* what they have learned (as Ms. Ramsey does in the conversation I just presented), rather than just to spit back memorized facts, definitions, and formulas (K. J. Roth, 1990; K J. Roth & Anderson, 1988). For example, if we want students in a social studies class to understand that there are usually valid and compelling perspectives on both sides of any controversial issue, rather than to believe that controversy is always a matter of the "good guys" versus the "bad guys," we might ask them to engage in a debate in which they must convincingly present a perspective contrary to their own beliefs. If students in a creative writing class have previously learned that complete sentences are always essential in good writing and we want to convince them otherwise, we might ask them to find examples of how incomplete sentences are sometimes used quite effectively in short stories and novels.

Considering Diversity in Constructive Processes

As we have seen, our students will inevitably interpret classroom subject matter in unique, idiosyncratic ways. Different students will have different knowledge bases—including different concepts, schemas, scripts, and personal theories—that they will use to make sense of any new situation. For instance, students of different cultural backgrounds may come to us with somewhat different concepts and, therefore, with somewhat different ways of categorizing and interpreting their experiences. For example, when giving directions, natives of Hawaii rarely speak in terms of north, south, east, and west; instead, they are more likely to talk about going toward the sea (*makai*) or toward the mountains (*mauka*). Some students may even have concepts that we ourselves don't have; for example, many Mexican Americans have different names for several varieties of peppers that, for me, all fall into one category—hot peppers. Furthermore, some schemas and scripts are likely to be specific to particular cultures, and subject matter that incorporates those schemas and scripts will cause difficulty for students from other cultural backgrounds. This is a principle that you may have discovered firsthand when you did *The War of the Ghosts* exercise.

Remember that students from diverse cultural backgrounds will have somewhat different concepts, schemas, and scripts. Such diversity will influence how students interpret classroom subject matter.

Have students consider multiple perspectives of the same situation.

As we help our students construct a meaningful understanding of the world around them, we can increase their multicultural awareness by promoting *multiple constructions* of the same situation. For example, we might present the western migration across North America during the 1700s and 1800s from two different perspectives—that of the European settlers and that of the Native Americans already residing on the land. One simple way to do this is to point out that the migrating peoples are referred to as *pioneers* or *settlers* by most United States history books, but might instead have been called *foreigners* or *invaders* by Native Americans (Banks, 1991). Ultimately, we must help our students to understand the very complex nature of human "knowledge" and to appreciate the fact that there may be several, equally valid interpretations of any single event.

How might you introduce multiple perspectives into the subject matter you will be teaching?

Accommodating Students with Special Needs

We will see evidence of diversity in constructive processes in our students with special educational needs. To illustrate, students with learning disabilities may construct inappropriate meanings from stories that they hear (Pressley, 1995; J. P. Williams, 1991). Students with emotional and behavioral disorders may construct counterproductive interpretations of social situations (Hughes, 1988); for example, they might "see" an act of aggression in an innocent gesture or "hear" an insult when none was intended. Table 7–2 identifies some patterns that researchers have found in the constructive processes of students with special needs; it also presents suggestions for helping these students acquire appropriate meanings from academic and social situations.

TABLE 7.2 **STUDENTS IN INCLUSIVE SETTINGS**

Promoting Knowledge Construction in Students with Special Educational Needs

STUDENTS WITH SPECIAL NEEDS	CHARACTERISTICS THAT THESE STUDENTS MAY EXHIBIT	CLASSROOM STRATEGIES THAT MAY BE BENEFICIAL FOR THESE STUDENTS
Students with specific cognitive or academic difficulties	Possible holes in students' knowledge base that may limit meaningful understanding of some classroom topics Occasional unusual or inappropriate interpretations of prose Occasional misinterpretations of social situations	Determine the extent to which students have prior knowledge about a new topic; remind them of what they *do* know about the topic. Monitor students' comprehension of prose; correct misinterpretations. Present alternative interpretations of others' behaviors.
Students with social or behavioral problems	Frequent misinterpretations of social situations	Present alternative interpretations of others' behaviors and identify suitable courses of action based on the most reasonable interpretation of a given situation.
Students with general delays in cognitive and social functioning	Smaller knowledge base from which to draw Difficulty constructing an accurate interpretation when information is ambiguous or incomplete	Assume little if any prior knowledge about topics unless you have evidence to the contrary; remind students of what they *do* know about a topic. Present information clearly and unambiguously.
Students with physical or sensory challenges	Limited knowledge base to which students can relate new information, due to fewer opportunities to interact with the outside world	Provide the background experiences (e.g., field trips) that students need to make sense of classroom subject matter.
Students with advanced cognitive development	Larger knowledge base from which to draw Rapid concept learning Greater conceptual understanding of classroom material (e.g., greater understanding of cause-effect relationships) Greater ability to draw inferences	Assign challenging tasks that enable students to develop and use their advanced understanding of topics. Ask thought-provoking questions that encourage inference drawing.

Sources: Butterfield & Ferretti, 1987; Patton et al., 1987; Piirto, 1994; Pressley, 1995; Schumaker & Hazel, 1984; Turnbull et al., 1999; J. P. Williams, 1991.

Note: Compiled with the assistance of Dr. Margie Garanzini-Daiber and Dr. Margaret Cohen, University of Missouri—St. Louis.

As we've noted before, all of our students—those with special needs and those without—will construct their own unique interpretations of the ideas and events they encounter in the classroom. Many of their interpretations, though perhaps different from one another, may be equally valid and appropriate. But other interpretations—for example, beliefs that the earth is flat, that rote learning is more effective than meaningful learning, or that a classmate is trying to pick a fight—may interfere with students' future success in the outside world. As teachers, we must help our students interpret the world around them in ways that are likely to be productive over the long run.

CASE STUDY: Earth-Shaking Summaries

Ms. Jewell spends the first half hour of her seventh-grade geography class describing how earthquakes occur. She introduces the theory of *plate tectonics*—the notion that the earth's crust is made up of many separate pieces (*plates*) that rest upon a layer of hot, molten rock (the *mantle*). She explains that plates occasionally shift and rub against each other, making the immediate area shake and leaving *faults* in the earth's surface.

Her students listen attentively throughout her explanation. When she finishes, she asks whether there are any questions. Finding that there are none, she says, "Great! I'm glad you all understand. What I'd like you to do now is to take out a piece of paper and write a paragraph answering this question: *Why do we have earthquakes?*" She has read in a professional journal that asking students to summarize what they've learned often helps them to remember it better later on, and she figures that the task she's just assigned is an excellent way to encourage summarization.

Ms. Jewell collects students' papers as they leave for their next class. As she glances quickly through the stack, she is distressed by what she sees. Some of her students have provided a relatively complete and accurate description of plate tectonics. But the responses of others are vague enough to make her uneasy about how thoroughly they understood her explanation; here are two examples:

Frank: The earth's crust shifts around and shakes us up.
Mitchell: Earthquakes happen when really big plates on the earth move around.

And three of her students clearly have made little sense of the lesson:

Adrienne: Scientists use technology to understand how earthquakes happen. They use computers and stuff.
Toni: When there are earthquakes, people's plates move around the house.
Jonathan: Earthquakes aren't anybody's fault. They just happen.

Ms. Jewell sighs, clearly discouraged by the feedback she's just gotten about her lesson. "I guess I still have a lot to learn about teaching this stuff," she concludes.

- Why is Ms. Jewell not convinced that Frank and Mitchell have mastered the material? What critical aspects of the lesson did each boy omit in his response?

- What pieces of information from the lesson did Adrienne, Toni, and Jonathan apparently use when answering Ms. Jewell's question? Can you explain their responses using the concept of knowledge construction?

- What instructional strategies might Ms. Jewell have used to help her students gain a more conceptual understanding of plate tectonics?

Summing Up

Construction in Storage and Retrieval

Many cognitive psychologists believe that individuals *construct* knowledge from their experience, rather than simply absorb it in the form presented to them; the resulting "reality" they perceive is not necessarily identical to the reality of the external world. Constructive processes may occur both when information is being received (during long-term memory storage) and when it is later recalled (during long-term memory retrieval). Some theorists describe the processes by which people construct their own personal understandings of the world; this perspective is sometimes called *individual constructivism.* Other theorists focus more on people's collective efforts to impose meaning on the world around them; this perspective is frequently called *social constructivism.*

Organizing Knowledge

People organize what they learn in a variety of ways. A *concept* provides a way of mentally grouping or categorizing objects or events. Students truly understand a concept when they know its defining features and can accurately identify both positive and negative instances. We can help our students learn concepts more effectively by giving definitions, presenting numerous and varied positive and negative instances, and asking students to generate their own examples.

Schemas are organized bodies of knowledge about specific topics; *scripts* are schemas that involve a predictable sequence of events. Schemas and scripts often enable learners to fill in missing details and so to understand classroom subject matter more completely. Some schemas and scripts are culture-specific—a point to keep in mind when teaching students from diverse cultural backgrounds.

Personal theories are general belief systems about the world; they include numerous concepts and the interrelationships among them. Students' personal theories provide guidance in concept learning. At the same time, they may include many misconceptions that interfere with students' learning of academic subject matter.

Promoting Effective Knowledge Construction

As teachers, we can help students construct accurate interpretations of the world around them by (1) providing opportunities for them to experiment with the physical world, (2) presenting others' interpretations of various phenomena (e.g., through the concepts and principles of academic disciplines, through art and literature), (3) emphasizing conceptual understanding, (4) promoting classroom dialogue, and (5) using authentic activities.

Promoting Conceptual Change

Students' misconceptions often persist despite instruction regarding more accurate explanations. We are more likely to promote conceptual change when we (1) determine what misconceptions students have before instruction, (2) show students that their existing beliefs are inadequate, (3) motivate them to develop a more accurate understanding of the topic in question, and (4) monitor their written work, as well as their questions and comments in class, for any especially persistent misconceptions.

Diversity in Constructive Processes

Different students are likely to interpret classroom events and subject matter differently, in part because they each bring diverse experiences and knowledge bases into play when trying to make sense of the things they see and hear. We can increase our students' multicultural awareness by promoting *multiple constructions* of the same situation—by encouraging them to look at events from the perspectives of different groups. At the same time, we must be on the lookout for counterproductive constructions that some of our students (including those with special needs) may derive from their classroom experiences.

KEY CONCEPTS

reconstruction error (p. 269)
individual constructivism (p. 269)
social constructivism (p. 269)
concept (p. 270)
undergeneralization (p. 270)
overgeneralization (p. 270)
positive instances (p. 271)

negative instances (p. 271)
defining features (p. 271)
correlational features (p. 271)
salience (of features) (p. 271)
prototype (p. 273)
exemplars (p. 274)
schema (p. 275)

script (p. 276)
personal theory (p. 278)
misconceptions (p. 279)
conceptual understanding (p. 283)
authentic activities (p. 285)
conceptual change (p. 288)

8

Higher-Level Thinking Skills

T ake a moment to reflect on your years as a college student. You've certainly spent a great many hours studying the information and skills that are central parts of the college curriculum, and you have probably learned a great deal. But how effectively do you *think about* the material that you study in your college courses? Can you apply it to situations and problems in your own life? Do you evaluate it with a critical eye, rather than simply take it at face value? And after so many years of practice as a student, have you finally learned how to study effectively?

The preceding two chapters described how people learn and remember declarative and procedural knowledge. In this chapter, we will focus on some of the complex ways that learners *use* that knowledge to interpret and respond to situations and tasks in their daily lives. We will also consider effective ways of studying academic subject matter. In particular, we will address the following questions:

- What do we mean by the term *higher-level thinking?*
- Under what circumstances are learners most likely to apply (*transfer*) what they've learned to new situations?
- What cognitive processes are involved in effective *problem solving,* and how can we help students solve problems more successfully?
- What is *critical thinking,* and how can we promote it in our students?
- How does *metacognition*—knowledge and beliefs about one's own cognitive processes—influence students' ability to learn successfully?
- What *study strategies* seem to facilitate academic achievement, and how can we help our students acquire these strategies?
- How can we promote higher-level thinking skills in students with diverse backgrounds and educational needs?

As we address these questions, I hope that you, as a student yourself, will learn more effective ways of applying, evaluating, and studying the subject matter you encounter in your *own* college classes.

CASE STUDY: A Question of Speed

Mary is studying for tomorrow's exam in her physics class. As she looks over her class notes, she finds the following statement in her notebook:

Velocity equals acceleration times time.

She also finds a formula expressing the same idea:

$v = a \times t$

Mary dutifully memorizes the statement and formula until she knows both by heart.

The following day, Mary encounters this problem on her physics exam:

An automotive engineer has designed a car that can reach a speed of 50 miles per hour within 5 seconds. What is the car's rate of acceleration?

She puzzles over the problem for several minutes. She thinks about a car reaching 50 miles per hour: Is this the car's acceleration, its velocity, or something else altogether? She realizes that she doesn't know the difference between acceleration and velocity. She finally turns in her exam with this and several similar questions unanswered.

She later confides to a classmate, "I really blew that test today, but I don't know why. I mean, I really studied *hard*!"

- How does Mary study for her physics exam? What things does she *not* do as she studies—things that might have led to better performance?

- If you were Mary's physics teacher, how might you help Mary study more effectively for the next exam?

The Nature of Higher-Level Thinking

One critical mistake that Mary makes is to use only rote learning as she studies for her exam. Although she memorizes "velocity equals acceleration times time," she never really learns what velocity and acceleration *are*. (*Velocity* is the speed at which an object travels in a particular direction. *Acceleration* is the rate with which an object's velocity changes.) As a result, she is unable to apply her knowledge in any meaningful way.

From Chapters 6 and 7 you have already learned a great deal about learning. For example, from the discussion of long-term memory storage in Chapter 6, you've discovered that people store new information more effectively when they relate it to things they have previously learned—that is, when they engage in such cognitive processes as meaningful learning and elaboration. From the discussion of knowledge construction in Chapter 7, you've discovered that learning may be a process of creating one's own, idiosyncratic knowledge base by combining both new and old information into something that makes some sort of "sense." Let's now put to work some of the things that you know about learning. Let's see what you can learn about a new topic, the world's diminishing rain forests.

▪ Experiencing Firsthand
Rain Forests

Read this passage, then answer the questions that follow.

Rain forests are home to nearly half of all the plants, animals, and insects in the world. Tropical plants produce chocolate, nuts, tannins, fruits, gums, coffee, waxes, wood and wood products, rubber and petroleum substitutes, and ingredients found in toothpaste, pesticides, fibers, and dyes. In addition, several medical wonders of the twentieth century have come from plants found only in rain forests. These plants have been used to treat high blood pressure, Hodgkin's disease, multiple sclerosis, and Parkinson's disease. A study of the Costa Rican rain forest found that 15 percent of the plants studied had "potential as anticancer agents."

But the rain forests, which provide food and fuel for millions of people in the developing world, are increasingly losing ground. Each year, millions of the developing world's poor head into the rain forest to eke out a subsistence living on plots recently cleared for farming. Rain forest soil is usually too poor to support a farmer's crops for more than a few years, and the land is soon depleted of nutrients. Peasant farmers must then head farther into the rain forest, slashing and burning still more land for farming, and starting the cycle all over. In many cases, cattle ranchers buy up the land abandoned by peasant farmers. But after only a few years, the land is unable to support even herds of cattle.

Every day, nearly 75,000 acres of rain forest disappear from the globe. In a year, 27 million acres of tropical rain forest—a land area the size of Austria or Pennsylvania—vanish. (adapted from Hosmer, 1989, pp. 70–71)

1. What are three illnesses that can be treated by using rain forest plants?

2. How does peasant farming change the nature of rain forest land?

3. Why do peasants continue to farm more and more rain forest land despite the environmental consequences of doing so?

4. What things might be done to halt the destruction of rain forests?

5. What are the most useful ideas to be gained from the passage?

Which of the five questions were the easiest ones to answer? Which questions were the most *important* ones to answer? You may have found Questions 1 and 2 relatively easy because the answers were clearly stated in the passage. These two **lower-level questions** ask you to retrieve information that was specifically given to you. You may have found the last three questions more difficult because you had to go beyond the information itself. To answer Question 3, you had to apply something that you know about people in general—the fact that people usually do whatever they need to do in order to survive—to your understanding of the peasant farmers' plight. To answer Question 4, you had to combine your prior knowledge with information in the passage to generate possible solutions to a difficult problem. And to answer Question 5, you needed to make a judgment about what information was most likely to be useful to you at a later point in time. Such **higher-level questions,** which ask you to go *beyond* the information actually presented, are usually more difficult than lower-level questions. Yet these higher-level questions are often the most important ones for learners to address.

Most theorists and practitioners find value in having students master basic facts and skills. At the same time, they argue that students should also apply, analyze, synthesize, evaluate, and in other ways mentally manipulate information; in other words, students should engage in **higher-level thinking** on a regular basis. The ideal school curriculum should address both lower-level and higher-level objectives (Bloom, Englehart, Furst, Hill, & Krathwohl, 1956; Cole, 1990; Onosko & Newmann, 1994).

Transfer, problem solving, critical thinking, and metacognition are all examples of higher-level thinking. As we explore these topics, we will identify numerous strategies for helping students think about and use classroom subject matter in new, productive, and otherwise "intelligent" ways.

Unfortunately, many classes devote most of their time to lower-level learning tasks at the expense of higher-level, "thinking" tasks (Blumenfeld, 1992; Freiberg, 1987; Tobin, 1987).

Transfer

Consider these four students:

Elena is bilingual: She speaks both English and Spanish fluently. She begins a French course in high school and immediately recognizes many similarities between French and Spanish. "Aha," she thinks, "my knowledge of Spanish will help me learn French."

In his psychology class, Larry learns the principle of reinforcement: A response followed by a reinforcing stimulus is more likely to occur again. Later that day, he thinks about playing a video game before doing his homework. "Oh, no," he says to himself, "that would be backward. I need to do my homework *first.* Playing the video game can be my reinforcer."

In her history class, Stella discovers that she does better on exams when she takes more notes. She decides to take more notes in her geography class as well, and once again the strategy pays off.

Ted's mathematics class has been working with decimals for several weeks. His teacher asks, "Which number is larger, 4.4 or 4.14?" Ted recalls something that he knows about whole numbers: Numbers with three digits are larger than numbers with only two digits. "The larger number is 4.14," he mistakenly concludes.

People often use information and skills they have learned in one situation to help them in another situation. What students learn in school and at home can potentially help them later on—perhaps in more advanced classwork, in their personal lives, or in their later careers. But occasionally students (like Ted) learn something at one time that, rather than helping, actually *interferes* with something they need to learn or do later.

When something students have previously learned affects how they learn or perform in another situation, **transfer** is occurring. Ideally, transfer of knowledge should be a major objective for classrooms at all grade levels. When people cannot use their basic arithmetic skills to compute correct change or balance a checkbook, when they cannot use their knowledge of English grammar in a job application or business report, and when they cannot apply their knowledge of science to an understanding of personal health or environmental problems, then we have to wonder whether the time spent learning the arithmetic, the grammar, and the science might have been better spent doing something else.

How can we help students successfully apply information from the classroom to new situations and problems, both in class and in the outside world? We will discover numerous answers to this question as we explore the topic of transfer in the pages that follow.

How often do your instructors ask you to apply what you learn in class to a new situation?

Basic Concepts in Transfer

Let's begin our discussion by looking at different kinds of transfer that may occur:

- Positive versus negative transfer
- Specific versus general transfer

Positive Versus Negative Transfer

Positive transfer occurs when something that a person has learned in one situation *helps* that person learn or perform in another situation. Positive transfer took place when Elena's Spanish helped her learn French, when Larry's knowledge of reinforcement influenced his decision to do his homework before playing a video game, and when Stella's experiences with note taking in history class improved her performance in geography.

In contrast, **negative transfer** occurs when prior knowledge *hinders* a person's learning or performance at a later time. This was the situation for poor Ted: He transferred a principle related to whole numbers (one number is always larger than another if it has more digits) to a situation where it didn't apply: the comparison of decimals. Another case of negative transfer occurs when students confuse the facts related to the various wars they study in history. For example, some students in the United States believe that the American Revolution was a battle between the English and the French (thus confusing it with the French and Indian War) or between the Northern and Southern states (thus confusing it with the American Civil War) (McKeown & Beck, 1990).

Can you think of a recent situation in which you exhibited positive transfer? negative transfer?

Obviously, negative transfer is the "bad guy" here. Later in the chapter, as we consider theoretical perspectives of transfer, we will identify a strategy for minimizing the extent to which our students fall victim to negative transfer.

Specific Versus General Transfer

Transfer from one situation to another often occurs when the two situations overlap in content. Consider Elena, the student fluent in Spanish who is now taking French. Elena should have an easy time learning to count in French because the numbers (*un, deux, trois, quatre, cinq*) are very similar to the Spanish she has already learned (*uno, dos, tres, cuatro, cinco*). When transfer occurs because the original learning task and the transfer task overlap in content, we have **specific transfer.**

Now consider Stella's strategy of taking more notes in geography because note taking was beneficial in her history class. History and geography don't necessarily overlap in content, but a strategy that she developed in one class has been effectively applied in the other. Here is an instance of **general transfer:** Learning in one situation affects learning and performance in a somewhat dissimilar situation.

Research tells us that specific transfer occurs more frequently than general transfer (Gray & Orasanu, 1987). In fact, the question of whether general transfer occurs at all has been the subject of considerable debate, as you will discover shortly.

Factors Affecting Transfer

All too often, students *don't* transfer the knowledge and skills they learn in school on occasions when such knowledge and skills are clearly applicable (Mayer & Wittrock, 1996; Perkins, 1992; Renkl, Mandl, & Gruber, 1996). Research reveals a number of factors that influence the extent to which transfer is likely to occur:

- Amount of instructional time
- Extent to which learning is meaningful rather than rote
- Extent to which principles rather than facts are learned
- Variety of examples and opportunities for practice
- Degree of similarity between two situations
- Length of time between the two situations
- Extent to which information is seen as context-free rather than context-bound

These factors are summarized as general principles in Table 8–1. Let's look briefly at each one.

Amount of Instructional Time

Instructional time is clearly an important variable affecting transfer: The more time students spend studying a particular topic, the more likely they are to transfer what they learn to a new situation (Gick & Holyoak, 1987; Schmidt & Bjork, 1992; Voss, 1987). Conversely, when students study a great many topics without learning very much about any one of them, they are unlikely to apply what they have learned at a later date. Here we see the principle of *less is more* once again: Our students are more likely to transfer their school learning to new situations, including those beyond the classroom, when we have them study a few things in depth and learn them *well*, rather than study many topics superficially (Brophy, 1992b; Porter, 1989).

Examine a few topics in depth rather than many topics superficially; be sure that students learn each topic thoroughly.

Extent to Which Learning Is Meaningful

In Chapter 6, we identified two advantages of meaningful learning over rote learning: Information is stored more quickly and is retrieved more easily. An additional advantage is that information learned in a meaningful fashion is more likely to be transferred or applied to a new situation (Bereiter, 1995; Brooks & Dansereau, 1987; Mayer & Wittrock, 1996).

Remember, meaningful learning involves connecting information with what one already knows. The more associations our students make between new information and the various other things in their long-term memories, the more likely it is that they will "find" (retrieve) that information at a time when it will be useful.

Promote meaningful rather than rote learning of classroom material.

Basic Principles of Transfer

PRINCIPLE	EDUCATIONAL IMPLICATION	EXAMPLE
As **instructional time** increases, the probability of transfer also increases.	To promote transfer, teach a few topics in depth, rather than many topics superficially.	When teaching a unit on the geography of South America, focus on cultural similarities and differences across the continent, instead of presenting a lengthy, encyclopedia-like list of facts about each country.
Meaningful learning leads to greater transfer than rote learning.	Encourage students to relate new material to the things they already know.	When introducing the concept *gravity* to third graders, ask them to think about what happens whenever they throw an object into the air (i.e., it comes back down).
Principles transfer more readily than facts.	Teach general principles (e.g., cause-effect relationships) related to each topic, along with general strategies based on those principles.	When teaching a unit on softball, basketball, soccer, or tennis, tell students, "Keep your eye on the ball," and explain why such vigilance is important.
Numerous and varied **examples** and **opportunities for practice** promote transfer.	Illustrate new concepts and principles with a variety of examples, and engage students in activities that let them practice new skills in different contexts.	After teaching students what a *complete sentence* is, have them practice writing complete sentences in essays, short stories, and class newsletter articles.
As the **similarity** between two situations increases, so does the probability of transfer from one situation to the other.	Make school tasks as similar as possible to the tasks that students are likely to encounter in the outside world.	When teaching students about the foods that make a balanced diet, have them prepare a healthful lunch with groceries from a local food store.
Transfer is more likely when only a **short amount of time** has elapsed after students have studied a topic.	Present topics as close in time as possible to the occasions when students will need to use those topics.	After having students learn and play the F Major scale in an instrumental music class, have them practice several musical pieces in the key of F Major.
Transfer is more likely when students perceive classroom material to be **context-free** rather than context-bound.	Relate topics in one discipline to topics in other disciplines and to tasks in the outside world.	When teaching students how to solve for x in algebra, give them word problems in which they must solve for an unknown in such contexts as physics, building construction, and sewing.

Experiencing Firsthand
Central Business Districts

Consider these two ideas from geography:

- Boston's central business district is located near Boston Harbor.
- The central business districts of most older cities, which were settled before the development of modern transportation, are found in close proximity to a navigable body of water, such as an ocean or a river.

Which statement would be more helpful to you if you were trying to find your way around Liverpool, Toronto, or Pittsburgh?

No doubt the second statement would prove more useful to you. The first one is a fact about a particular city, whereas the second one reflects a general principle applicable to many different cities. People can transfer general (and perhaps somewhat abstract) principles more easily than specific, concrete facts (J. R. Anderson, Reder, & Simon, 1996; Judd, 1932; Perkins & Salomon, 1987).

Specific facts have an important place in the classroom; for example, students should know what two plus three equal, what the Berlin Wall signified, and where to find Africa on a globe. Yet facts themselves have limited utility in new situations. The more we can emphasize general principles instead of specific facts—for example, that two whole numbers added together always equal a larger number, that a country's citizens sometimes revolt when their government officials act unjustly, and that the cultures of various nations are partly a function of their location and climate—the more we facilitate students' ability to transfer what they learn.

Teach general principles.

Provide many and different examples and opportunities for practice.

Variety of Examples and Opportunities for Practice

Students are more likely to apply something they learn if, within the course of instruction, they are given many examples and have numerous opportunities to practice in different situations (Cox, 1997; Reimann & Schult, 1996; J. A. Ross, 1988; Schmidt & Bjork, 1992). For example, students will be more apt to use their knowledge of fractions and ratios in the future if they practice using this knowledge in such activities as cooking, converting dollars to a foreign currency, and drawing objects to scale. By using knowledge in many contexts, students store that knowledge in association with all those contexts and so are more likely to retrieve the information on a future occasion (Perkins & Salomon, 1987; Voss, 1987).

Similarity of the Two Situations

Let's return to the problem that Mary encounters in our case study at the beginning of the chapter:

> An automotive engineer has designed a car that can reach a speed of 50 miles per hour within 5 seconds. What is the car's rate of acceleration?

Imagine that Mary eventually learns how to solve this problem by using the $v = a \times t$ principle. Because the velocity (v) is *50 miles*

Children are more likely to transfer their knowledge of fractions and ratios to future situations if they practice using fractions and ratios in a variety of contexts.

per hour and the time (*t*) is 5 seconds, the rate of acceleration (*a*) must be *10* miles per hour per second.

Now Mary encounters two additional problems:

A car salesperson tells a customer that a particular model of car can reach a speed of 40 miles per hour within 8 seconds. What is the car's rate of acceleration?

A biologist reports that a cheetah she has been observing can attain a speed of 60 kilometers per hour within a 10-second period. How quickly does the cheetah increase its speed?

Which problem do you think Mary will find easier to solve?

Transfer is more likely to occur when a new situation appears to be similar to a previous situation (Bassok, 1990; Blake & Clark, 1990; Di Vesta & Peverly, 1984). Mary will probably have an easier time solving the problem involving the car salesperson because it superficially resembles the problem about the automotive engineer: Both problems involve cars, and both use miles as the unit of measure. The cheetah problem, even though it can be solved using the same approach as the other two, involves a different domain (animals) and a different unit of measure (kilometers).

Here we see the value of *authentic activities* in the curriculum. Of the many examples and opportunities for practice that we give our students, some should be very similar to the situations that students are likely to encounter in future studies or in the outside world. The more that school tasks resemble students' later life experiences, the more likely it is that our students will put their school learning to use (Perkins, 1992).

Yet we should note that the similarity of two situations, while promoting positive transfer, may promote negative transfer as well. Try the following exercises as an example.

🍎 *Make school tasks similar in appearance to future situations students are likely to encounter.*

▢ Experiencing Firsthand
A Division Problem

Consider this division problem:

$$20 \div 0.38$$

Is the answer larger or smaller than 20?

_____

If you applied your knowledge of division by whole numbers here, you undoubtedly concluded that the answer is smaller than 20. In fact, the answer is 52.63, a number *larger* than 20. And remember Ted's erroneous conclusion—4.14 is larger than 4.4—based on his knowledge of how whole numbers can be compared. Many students, even at the university level, show negative transfer of whole number principles to situations involving decimals (Tirosh & Graeber, 1990). Working with decimals appears, on the surface, to be similar to working with whole numbers; the only difference is a tiny decimal point.

To help prevent negative transfer, we, as teachers, should make a special effort to point out differences between two superficially similar topics. For example, Ted's teacher could have identified some of the specific ways in which decimals are *not* like whole numbers.

🍎 *Emphasize differences between topics if negative transfer is likely to occur.*

As another example, I find that my own students in educational psychology often have trouble using the term *maturation* correctly in our discussions of child development because the term has a different meaning in their everyday conversations. Therefore, when I first introduce the concept of maturation, I take great pains to show students how psychology's meaning of the word (the unfolding of genetically controlled developmental changes) differs from the meaning they are familiar with (developmental changes in general).

Length of Time Between the Two Situations

People are most likely to apply new information soon after they have learned it. They are less likely to use that information as time goes on (Gick & Holyoak, 1987). To the extent that we can, then, we should try to present topics to students as close in time as possible to the occasions when students will need to use those topics.

To illustrate, consider again the physics principle that Mary learns in the opening case study: $v = a \times t$ (velocity equals acceleration times time). The formula tells Mary how to calculate velocity when she knows both the acceleration and the time. But let's say that she instead wants to calculate the rate of acceleration, as she needed to do for the "car" and "cheetah" problems. If Mary is studying algebra concurrently with her physics class, or else has studied it very recently, she is more likely to see the usefulness of algebra in rearranging the formula like so: $a = \frac{v}{t}$

Perception of Information as Context-Free Rather Than Context-Bound

In many cases, we would like our students to transfer their knowledge in one content domain to a different domain—for example, to transfer mathematics to physics, grammar to creative writing, history to current events, and health to personal eating habits. Yet students tend to think of academic subject areas as being separate, unrelated disciplines; they also tend to think of their school learning as being unrelated to real-world concerns (Perkins & Simmons, 1988; Rakow, 1984). When students see what they learn in school as being *context-bound*—as being related only to a particular topic or discipline—they are unlikely to transfer it to situations outside that context (P. A. Alexander & Judy, 1988; J. R. Anderson et al., 1996; Bassok, 1996; diSessa, 1982; Renkl et al., 1996).

When we teach material within a particular academic discipline, then, we should relate that material to other disciplines and to the outside world as frequently as possible (Blake & Clark, 1990; Perkins, 1992). For example, we might show students how human digestion provides a justification for categorizing food into several basic food groups or how economic issues affect tropical rain forests. We can also encourage students to brainstorm specific situations in which they could apply what they are learning in class (J. R. Anderson et al., 1996).

As you can see, a variety of factors influence the extent to which transfer is likely to occur. But why do such factors make a difference? Let's turn to several theoretical perspectives as to when and why transfer occurs.

> Present topics as close in time as possible to the occasions when students will need to use those topics.

> Relate topics in one academic discipline to other academic disciplines and to the nonacademic world.

Theories of Transfer

Over the years, educators and psychologists have held differing views as to when and why transfer occurs. In the next few pages, we will consider three perspectives of transfer with a distinctly cognitivist flavor:

- In past years, some theorists have emphasized the value of general *mental "exercise"*: Studying difficult and rigorous subject matter strengthens the mind.
- More recently, cognitive psychologists have stressed the importance of *retrieval*: Transfer occurs only when conditions within a new situation facilitate the retrieval of previously learned information and skills.
- Many theorists now speak of *situated cognition:* Knowledge and thinking skills are typically acquired in specific contexts and are unlikely to be used outside those contexts.

Mental "Exercise"

As a beginning high school sophomore in the fall of 1963, my guidance counselor recommended that I take the two languages that my high school offered: French and Latin. Taking French made a great deal of sense: Growing up in Massachusetts, I was within a

By GARY LARSON

Brain aerobics

The formal discipline view of transfer portrays the mind as a muscle that benefits from general mental exercise.

🍎 Teach class material in a way that promotes multiple connections to other things in students' lives.

🍎 When appropriate, provide retrieval cues that remind students of information relevant to the transfer situation.

day's drive of French-speaking Quebec. "But why should I take Latin," I asked? "I can only use it if I attend Catholic mass or run across phrases like 'caveat emptor' or 'in Deo speramus.' Hardly anyone speaks the language anymore." My guidance counselor pursed her thin red lips and gave me a look that told me that she knew best. "Latin will discipline your mind. It will help you learn better."

My guidance counselor's advice reflects an early view of transfer known as **formal discipline.** According to this view, students should study such rigorous subjects as Latin, Greek, mathematics, and logic primarily because such subjects "strengthen" the mind. By undergoing such mental "exercise," the theory proposes, students become capable of learning many other, unrelated things more easily.

But research results have generally discredited this "mind as muscle" notion of transfer (Perkins & Salomon, 1989; E. L. Thorndike, 1924). For example, practice in memorizing poems does not necessarily make one a faster poem memorizer (James, 1890). And studying computer programming, though often a worthwhile activity in its own right, does not necessarily help a person with dissimilar kinds of logical tasks (Mayer & Wittrock, 1996; Perkins & Salomon, 1989).

Retrieval

Many cognitive psychologists propose that information learned in one situation helps in another situation only if the information is *retrieved* within the context of that second situation (Cormier, 1987; Gick & Holyoak, 1987; Halpern, 1998). For example, Elena's knowledge of Spanish will help her learn French only if she remembers relevant Spanish words while studying her French words. Larry will apply the principle of reinforcement to his own behavior only if he happens to think of reinforcement while planning the rest of his day.

As you should recall from Chapter 6, information is most easily retrieved when it is associated with many other items in long-term memory. At least four of the factors we have identified as promoting transfer—the amount of instructional time, the extent to which learning is meaningful rather than rote, the extent to which general principles rather than facts are learned, and the number of examples and opportunities to practice—should affect our students' ability to make multiple connections between class material and other aspects of their world. Students are *un*likely to apply information they have not previously connected to other things (information they have learned at a rote level), partly because they probably won't retrieve it when they need it and partly because they won't see its relevance even if they do retrieve it.

As noted earlier, people are also more likely to transfer what they've learned in one situation to very *similar* situations. One explanation for this principle is that a similar situation presents helpful *retrieval cues*—reminders of relevant information stored in long-term memory (Gick & Holyoak, 1987; Perkins & Salomon, 1989; Sternberg & Frensch, 1993). A second explanation lies in the concept of *situated cognition,* a concept that we turn to now.

Situated Cognition

Earlier, I mentioned that studying computer programming does not necessarily help a person with other kinds of logical tasks (Perkins & Salomon, 1989). Some theorists propose that knowledge and thinking skills are typically acquired in specific contexts and are unlikely to be used outside those contexts (Hirschfeld & Gelman, 1994; Lave & Wenger, 1991; Light & Butterworth, 1993; Singley & Anderson, 1989; however, also see J. R. Anderson et al., 1996). This principle is often referred to as **situated cognition:** Knowledge and thinking skills are *situated* within the context in which they develop.

If you have read the discussion of cognitive development in Chapter 2, then you have already seen evidence of situated cognition. As you may recall, Piaget proposed that such thinking abilities as abstract thought, proportional reasoning, and separation and control of variables emerge at about eleven or twelve years of age (at the onset of the formal operations stage) and are then used in a wide variety of tasks. Yet we reviewed evidence in Chapter 2 to indicate that students do not acquire formal operational abilities in one fell swoop and then apply them equally across all subject domains. Instead, students are more likely to exhibit formal operational reasoning in some domains than in others, and they are especially likely to exhibit them in contexts where they have the most experience.

The principle of situated cognition provides additional justification for using authentic activities in the classroom. If we want our students to use what they learn at school in real-world situations, we should teach classroom subject matter within the context of such situations. Furthermore, we may occasionally be able to have students practice their knowledge and skills in so many different contexts that what they've learned is no longer confined to certain contexts; in other words, it becomes context-free (A. Collins et al., 1989).

Researchers have found that learning in one situation can help in a very different situation if, in the process, one *learns how to learn.* When a student acquires effective learning strategies within the context of one academic discipline, those strategies often transfer positively to learning in a very different discipline (Brooks & Dansereau, 1987; Perkins, 1995; Pressley, Snyder, & Cariglia-Bull, 1987). Later in the chapter, when we consider metacognition and study strategies, we will examine such potentially transferable strategies in more depth.

The recommendations presented in this section can help us facilitate one very important form of transfer: solving problems. Cognitive psychologists have provided additional insights about problem solving as well, as you shall see now.

See "Intuitive Physics" in *Simulations in Educational Psychology.*

 Is this an instance of specific transfer or general transfer?

Problem Solving

Experiencing Firsthand
Four Problems

How many of these problems can you solve?

1. You buy two apples for 25¢ each and one pear for 40¢. How much change will you get back from a dollar bill?

2. You are building a treehouse with the shape and dimensions illustrated in Figure 8–1. You need to buy planks for a slanted roof. How long must those planks be to reach from one side of the treehouse to the other?

3. You want to demonstrate the fact that metal battleships float even though metal is denser (and so heavier) than water. You don't have any toy boats made of metal. What can you use instead to illustrate the principle that a metal object with a hollow interior can float on water?

4. Every day, almost 75,000 acres of tropical rain forest disappear. What steps might be taken to curtail this alarming rate of deforestation?

How long do the roof planks of this treehouse need to be?

FIGURE 8.1
Building a treehouse

Sometimes problems are straightforward and relatively easy to solve. For example, Problem 1 requires only simple addition and subtraction; you probably had little difficulty finding the correct solution, *10¢*. Problem 2 (Figure 8–1) is more difficult, partly because you don't encounter such problems very often. But if you have studied geometry, then you undoubtedly learned the Pythagorean theorem, which leads to the correct problem solution: In any right triangle, the square of the hypotenuse equals the sum of the squares of the other two sides. Looking at the top part of the treehouse (from the dotted line upward) as a triangle, we can find the length for the roof planks (x) this way:

$$x^2 = (5 - 2)^2 + 4^2$$
$$x^2 = 9 + 16$$
$$x^2 = 25$$
$$x = 5$$

Yet problems don't always have a single correct solution. For example, if you are looking for a metal object with a hollow interior to float on water (Problem 3), you might use a number of different objects to solve your problem—possibly a pie plate, a bucket, or a thimble. And you might identify several possible ways of addressing rain forest deforestation (Problem 4), but you probably wouldn't know which of these (if any) are correct solutions (i.e., which ones would successfully help preserve tropical rain forests) until you actually implemented them.

This section of the chapter explores the multifaceted nature of human problem solving. After defining several basic concepts, we will examine several cognitive factors that help or hinder successful problem solving; in the process, we will also identify strategies for helping students become more successful problem solvers. As we go along, you may find places where you can apply (*transfer!*) your knowledge of transfer.

Basic Concepts in Problem Solving

As the four problems you just tackled illustrate, the problems that people need to solve may differ widely in their content and scope; for example, one problem may relate to a backyard treehouse and another to the devastation of tropical rain forests. The four problems also differ widely with respect to the particular strategies that can be used to solve them; for example, one problem might be solved by using the Pythagorean theorem, whereas another might be solved only by a world summit conference. Yet virtually all problems can be considered to be either *well-defined* or *ill-defined* (or perhaps somewhere in between), and virtually all problem-solving strategies can be categorized as either *algorithms* or *heuristics*. Let's consider these two distinctions.

Well-Defined and Ill-Defined Problems

Problems differ in the extent to which they are clearly specified and structured. A **well-defined problem** is one in which the goal is clearly stated, all information needed to solve the problem is present, and only one correct answer exists. Problem 1 (calculating the amount of change one gets from a dollar) and Problem 2 (determining the length of planks needed for a treehouse roof) are examples of well-defined problems. In both cases, we know exactly what is required to solve the problem.

In contrast, an **ill-defined problem** is one in which the desired goal is unclear, information needed to solve the problem is missing, or several possible solutions to the prob-

▲ The distinction between well-defined and ill-defined problems is better conceptualized as a continuum than an "either-or" situation.

lem exist. To some extent, finding a suitable substitute for a metal ship (Problem 3) is an ill-defined problem: A number of objects might serve as a ship substitute, and some might work better than others. The rain forest deforestation problem (Problem 4) is even less defined. First, the goal—curtailing deforestation—is ambiguous. Do we want to stop deforestation altogether or just slow it down a bit? If we just want to decrease the rate, what rate is acceptable? Second, we undoubtedly need more information to solve the problem. For example, it would be helpful to determine whether previously cleared and farmed lands can be reclaimed, and to identify economically reasonable alternatives to slash-and-burn farming practices. Some of this needed information may require extensive research. Finally, there is no single "correct" solution for Problem 4: Curtailing deforestation will undoubtedly require a number of steps taken more or less simultaneously. Ill-defined problems, then, are usually more difficult to solve than well-defined ones.

Most problems presented in school are well-defined: A question clearly specifies a goal, all needed information is present (no more, no less), and there is only one correct answer. Consider this typical mathematics word problem as an example:

> Old MacDonald has planted potatoes in a field 100 meters long and 50 meters wide. If the field yields an average of 5 pounds of potatoes in each square meter, how many pounds of potatoes can MacDonald expect to harvest from his field?

In this problem, the goal is clear: Determine how many pounds of potatoes the field will yield. We also have all the information needed to solve the problem, with no irrelevant information to distract us. And there is only one correct answer, with no room for debate.

But the real world presents ill-defined problems far more often than well-defined ones, and students need practice in dealing with them. Consider this problem as an example:

> Old MacDonald's son wants to go to a small, coeducational college 200 miles away. MacDonald does not know whether he can afford the college tuition; it all depends on how well his potato crop does this summer. What should MacDonald tell his son?

Notice how the problem has a rather vaguely stated goal: determining what MacDonald should say to his son. It does not identify the specific questions he needs to address before he gives an answer. And we don't have all the information we need to solve the problem: We don't know the size of MacDonald's potato field, the predicted size of his crop, the probable value of the potatoes, the family's day-to-day living expenses, or the cost of college tuition. Finally, there may be no single correct answer: Whether MacDonald encourages his son to go to college depends not only on finances but also on his beliefs about the value of a college education and on the extent to which the son's contribution to the farm necessitates his staying at home next autumn.

One way of helping our students learn to solve problems is to teach them techniques for better defining ill-defined problems. For example, we can teach them how to break large problems into smaller, well-defined ones (e.g., determining the probable size of the potato crop, calculating the farmer's daily living expenses). We can also teach them to distinguish information they need (e.g., the size of the farmer's potato field) from information they may *not* need (e.g., the fact that the college is coeducational). And we can teach techniques for finding missing information (e.g., how to measure distance, how to use the library to find the current price of potatoes, how to obtain information about tuition rates at different colleges).

Problem-Solving Strategies: Algorithms and Heuristics

Some problems can be successfully solved by following specific, step-by-step instructions—that is, by using an **algorithm**. For example, we can put a new bicycle together by following the "Directions for Assembly" that come with it. We can calculate the length of a slanted roof by using the Pythagorean theorem. When we follow an algorithm faithfully, we invariably arrive at a correct solution.

Can you think of problems you've encountered recently that were well-defined? ill-defined?

Give students practice in dealing with ill-defined problems.

Show students ways of making ill-defined problems more well-defined.

Calvin and Hobbes   by Bill Watterson

Some problems can be solved by an algorithm—a set of step-by-step instructions that guarantees a correct solution.

CALVIN AND HOBBES © Watterson. Reprinted with permission of UNIVERSAL PRESS SYNDICATE. All rights reserved.

Yet not all problems come equipped with directions for assembly. There are no rules we can follow to identify a substitute metal ship, no list of instructions to help us solve the deforestation problem. When there is no algorithm for solving a problem, people may instead use a **heuristic**—a general problem-solving strategy that may or may not yield a workable solution. For example, one heuristic that we might use in solving the deforestation problem is this: Identify a new behavior that adequately replaces the problem behavior (in particular, find something else that peasant farmers can do to meet their survival needs). As another example of a heuristic, consider the addition problem in the exercise that follows.

Experiencing Firsthand
Grocery Shopping

Solve this addition problem *as quickly as you possibly can:*

You are purchasing three items at the store, at these prices:

$19.95

$39.98

$29.97

About how much money are you spending? (Don't worry about a possible sales tax.)

Using the subject matter you will be teaching, develop two problems, one well-defined and one ill-defined. Do your problems require algorithms or heuristics to be solved?

The fastest way to solve the problem is to round off and approximate. The first item costs about $20, the second about $40, and the third about $30; therefore, you are spending about $90 on your shopping spree. Rounding is often an excellent heuristic for arriving quickly at approximate answers to mathematical problems.

Students in our schools get far more practice solving well-defined problems than ill-defined ones, and they are taught many more algorithms than heuristics. For example, they are likely to spend more school time learning problem-solving strategies useful in determining the length of planks needed for a treehouse roof than strategies applicable to the problem of deforestation. And they are likely to spend more time using laws of physics to make predictions about when battleships will float on water than wrestling with ways of preventing the conflicts that require those battleships in the first place. Yet many real-world problems—problems that our students will encounter after gradua-tion—probably cannot be solved with cut-and-dried algorithms.

Problem-solving strategies, algorithms and heuristics alike, are often specific to a particular content domain. But here are three general problem-solving heuristics that our students may find helpful in a variety of contexts.

- *Identify subgoals.* Break a problem into two or more subproblems that can be better defined and more easily solved.
  Example: Students wrestling with the problem of diminishing rain forests identi-fies several smaller problems: poor economic circumstances of local residents, lack of good agricultural land, and lack of government regulation of deforestation practices. They then discuss possible ways to solve each problem.

- *Work backward.* Begin at the goal of the problem (at the solution needed) and work backward, one step at a time, toward the initial problem statement.
  Example: A student is given this problem:

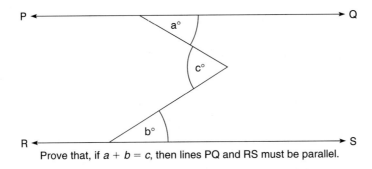

Prove that, if $a + b = c$, then lines PQ and RS must be parallel.

To prove this statement, the student decides to start with the idea that the two lines are, in fact, parallel and then work backward, step by step, to show that $a + b$ must equal c.

- *Draw an analogy.* Identify an analogous situation to the problem situation and derive potential problem solutions from that analogy.
  Example: A student attempting to calculate the volume of an irregularly shaped object recognizes that, just as she herself displaces water when she steps into the bathtub, the object will displace its volume when immersed in water. She places the object into a container filled to the brim with water, collects the water that sloshes out, and measures the amount.

Teaching problem-solving strategies. How can we help our students acquire effective problem-solving strategies? Here are a number of possibilities:

For teaching algorithms:

- Describe and demonstrate specific algorithms and situations in which they can be used.
- Provide worked-out examples of algorithms being applied.
- Help students understand why particular algorithms are relevant and effective in certain situations.
- When a student's application of an algorithm yields an incorrect answer, look closely at the specific steps the student has taken until the trouble spot is located.

For teaching heuristics:

- Give students practice in defining ill-defined problems.
- Teach heuristics that students can use in situations where no specific algorithms apply; for example, encourage such strategies as rounding, identifying subgoals, working backward, and drawing analogies.

For teaching both algorithms and heuristics:

- Teach problem-solving strategies within the context of specific subject areas (*not* as a topic separate from academic content).
- Provide scaffolding for difficult problems—for example, by breaking them into smaller and simpler problems, giving hints about possible strategies, or providing partial solutions.
- Have students solve problems in small groups, sharing ideas about problem-solving strategies, modeling various approaches for one another, and discussing the merits of each approach. (Heller & Hungate, 1985; Mayer, 1985, 1992; Noddings, 1985; Reimann & Schult, 1996; Resnick, 1983)

▲ If necessary, review the discussion of *scaffolding* in Chapter 2. Scaffolding will also be relevant to our discussion of study strategies later in the chapter.

As we have seen, well-defined problems are usually more easily solved than ill-defined ones, and problems that can be solved with algorithms are generally easier than those that require heuristics. But there are several other factors, all cognitive in nature, that affect problem-solving success as well.

Cognitive Factors Affecting Problem Solving

Cognitive psychologists have identified at least four factors that affect a person's success in solving a problem:

- Working memory capacity
- Encoding of the problem
- Depth and integration of one's knowledge relevant to the problem
- Retrieval of relevant information from long-term memory

Before you read further, can you guess how each of these factors affects problem solving?

As we consider each factor, we will identify additional ways to help our students become more effective problem solvers.

Working Memory Capacity

You may recall from an exercise in Chapter 6 how difficult it is to solve a long division problem in your head. Remember, working memory has a limited capacity: It can only hold a few pieces of information and can only accommodate so much cognitive processing at any one time. If a problem requires an individual to deal with too much information at once or to manipulate that information in a very complex fashion, working memory capacity may be insufficient for effective problem processing. Once working memory capacity is exceeded, the problem cannot be solved (Johnstone & El-Banna, 1986; Perkins, 1995).

Our students can overcome the limits of their working memories in at least two ways. One obvious way is to create an external record of information relevant to the problem—for example, by writing that information on a piece of paper. (This is typically our strategy when we do long division problems, so that we don't have to hold all the numbers in working memory at once). Another way to overcome working memory capacity is to learn some skills to a level of automaticity—in other words, to learn them to a point where they can be retrieved quickly, easily, and almost without conscious thought (N. Frederiksen, 1984a; Mayer & Wittrock, 1996; Rabinowitz & Glaser, 1985; W. Schneider & Shiffrin, 1977).

🍎 Encourage students to write parts of the problem on paper.

🍎 Teach the information and skills essential in problem solving to a level of automaticity.

As an illustration of the role that automaticity plays in problem solving, try the following exercise.

▣ Experiencing Firsthand
A Multiplication Problem

See whether you can do this multiplication problem *in your head*. Look at it once, then close your eyes and try to solve it:

$$
\begin{array}{r}
23 \\
\times\, 9 \\
\hline
\end{array}
$$

Were you able to remember the problem at the same time that you were calculating the answer? If so, it was probably because you could remember basic multiplication facts (*9 × 2* and *9 × 3*) without having to think very hard about them. But imagine instead that once you had put the problem in your working memory, you had to stop and think about what *9 × 3* equals: "Hmm, let me see . . . 9 plus 9 is 18 . . . and I need to add 9 more, so that's 19, 20, 21, 22, 23, 24, 25, 26, 27 . . . and now what was the second top number again?" When people must use a significant portion of working memory capacity for retrieving or reconstructing basic skills and information (e.g., for recalling multiplication facts, spelling, or the meaning of *deforestation*), they may not have enough capacity left to solve the problems (e.g., solving complex mathematical questions, writing a persuasive essay, or identifying methods of curtailing deforestation) that require such skills and information.

Encoding of the Problem

When we discussed cognitive processes in Chapter 6, we talked about *encoding,* changing the form of new information as we store it in memory. Encoding is clearly a factor affecting our ability to solve problems successfully. Sometimes we encode a problem ineffectively or incorrectly; at other times, we have trouble encoding a problem at all. Let's consider each of these two circumstances. We will then identify some strategies for helping our students encode problems more effectively.

Encoding a problem ineffectively or incorrectly. Consider the following situation:

▣ Experiencing Firsthand
Two Trains and a Bird

Two train stations are fifty miles apart. At 2 P.M. one Saturday afternoon two trains start toward each other, one from each station. Just as the trains pull out of the stations, a bird springs into the air in front of the first train and flies ahead to the front of the second train. When the bird reaches the second train it turns back and flies toward the first train. The bird continues to do this until the trains meet.

If both trains travel at the rate of 25 miles per hour and the bird flies at 100 miles per hour, how many miles will the bird have flown before the trains meet? (M. I. Posner, 1973, pp. 150–151)

See whether you can solve the problem. Don't read any further until you have either solved the problem or else spent five minutes *trying* to solve it.

If, after five minutes, you are still having trouble solving the problem, try answering this question first: *How long must the bird fly before the trains meet?* Can you *now* determine how far the bird must fly?

Because the two train stations are 50 miles apart and the trains are traveling at 25 miles per hour, the trains will meet in 1 hour. The bird is flying at a speed of 100 miles per hour; therefore, it will fly 100 miles before the trains meet.

We can solve the trains/bird problem more easily if we encode it as a "time" problem (how *long* must the bird fly?) rather than as a "distance" problem (how *far* must the bird fly?). There are often different ways of encoding the same problem in memory—different ways of representing the problem mentally—and some forms of encoding may promote easier problem solution than others.

For a very different example of how encoding affects problem-solving success, try solving the next problem.

■ Experiencing Firsthand
The Candle Problem¹

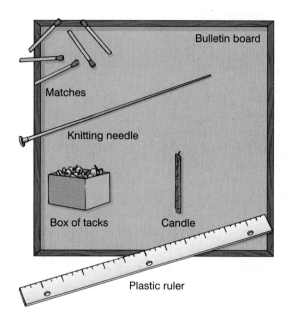

Bulletin board

Matches

Knitting needle

Box of tacks   Candle

Plastic ruler

You are in a room with a bulletin board firmly affixed to the wall about four feet above the floor. Your task is to *stand a candle upright* in front of the bulletin board. You do not want the candle touching the bulletin board, because the candle's flame must not singe the bulletin board. Instead, you need to place the candle about a centimeter away. How can you accomplish the task with the following materials?

  small candle

  metal knitting needle

  matches

  box of thumbtacks

  twelve-inch plastic ruler

See whether you can solve the problem before you read further.

_____

As it turns out, the ruler and knitting needle are useless in solving the candle problem (if you try to puncture the candle with the knitting needle, you will probably break the candle; if you try to balance the ruler on a few tacks, it will probably fall down). The easiest solution is to fasten the thumbtack box to the bulletin board with tacks and then attach the candle to the top of the box with either a tack or some melted wax. Many people don't consider this solution, however, because they encode the box only as a *container of tacks,* thereby overlooking its potential use as a candle stand. When we encode a problem in a particular way that excludes potential solutions, we are the victims of a **mental set.**

As you may know from your own experience, many students have trouble solving mathematical word problems. One reason is that they often have difficulty encoding a problem in terms of the operation (e.g., addition or subtraction) required (e.g., Mayer, 1992). When students have limited knowledge about a certain topic (e.g., limited conceptual understanding of mathematics), they are likely to encode a problem related to that topic on the basis of superficial problem characteristics (Chi, Feltovich, & Glaser, 1981; Schoenfeld & Hermann, 1982). For example, I remember being taught in elementary school that the word *left* in a problem indicates that subtraction is called for. Encoding a "left" problem as a subtraction problem works well in some instances, such as this one:

> Tim has 7 apples. He gives 3 apples to Emily. How many apples does he have left?

But it is inappropriate in other instances, such as this one:

> Ana went shopping. She spent $3.50 and then counted her money when she got home. She had $2.35 left. How much did Ana have when she started out? (Resnick, 1989, p. 165)

▲   The candle problem illustrates a particular kind of mental set—*functional fixedness*—whereby an individual thinks of an object as having only one possible function and therefore overlooks another function that it might serve.

_____
¹ Adapted from Duncker, 1945.

The latter problem requires addition, not subtraction. Obviously, words alone can be deceiving.

When students encode a problem incorrectly, they are less likely to solve it successfully. But sometimes students have difficulty encoding a problem in *any* way, as we shall see now.

Failing to encode a problem. See whether you can solve the following problem:

▣ Experiencing Firsthand
Pigs and Chickens

Old MacDonald has a barnyard full of pigs and chickens. Altogether there are 21 heads and 60 legs in the barnyard (not counting MacDonald's own head and legs). How many pigs and how many chickens are running around the barnyard?

Can you figure out the answer? If you are having difficulty, try thinking about the problem this way:

Imagine that the pigs are standing in an upright position on only their two hind legs; their front two legs are raised over their heads. Therefore, all the animals—pigs and chickens alike—are standing on two legs. Can you now figure out how many legs are on the ground and how many must be in the air? From this, can you determine the number of pigs and chickens there must be?

In case you are still having difficulty with the problem, follow this logic:

* Obviously, because there are 21 heads, the number of pigs plus the number of chickens must equal 21.

* Because each animal has 2 legs on the ground and because there must be twice as many legs on the ground as there are number of heads, there are 42 (21 × 2) legs on the ground.

* Because there are 42 legs on the ground, there must be 18 (60 − 42) pigs' legs in the air.

* Because each pig has 2 front legs, there must be 9 (18 ÷ 2) pigs.

* Because there are 9 pigs, there must be 12 (21 − 9) chickens.

▣ How could you use algebra to solve this problem?

Some ways of encoding a problem promote more successful problem solving than others.

If you initially had trouble solving the Old MacDonald problem, your difficulty may have been the result of your inability to encode the problem in any way that allowed you to solve it. Students often have trouble solving mathematical word problems because they don't know how to translate those problems into procedures or operations with which they are familiar (Mayer, 1982, 1986; Resnick, 1989; Reusser, 1990).

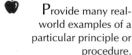

Help students develop useful ways of encoding problems in memory.

Facilitating problem encoding. As you have just seen, encoding a problem appropriately is an essential yet often difficult step in problem solving. How can we help students encode problems more effectively? Here are some things we can do:

- Present the problem in a concrete way; for example, provide real objects that students can manipulate or an illustration of the problem's components (Luchins & Luchins, 1950; Mayer, 1992).

- Encourage students to make a problem concrete *themselves;* for example, encourage them to draw a picture or diagram of the problem (Anzai, 1991; Mayer, 1986; Prawat, 1989; K. Schultz & Lochhead, 1991).

- Point out any features of problems that students *can* solve, and when those features appear again in a different problem, indicate that the same information can be applied or the same approach to problem solution can be used (Prawat, 1989).

- Have students work in cooperative groups to identify several different ways of representing a single problem—perhaps as a formula, a table, and a graph (Brenner et al., 1997).

Depth and Integration of Knowledge Relevant to the Problem

Let's return once again to Mary, our case study at the beginning of the chapter. Mary learned a principle of physics (velocity equals acceleration multiplied by time) at a rote level, without really comprehending what she was studying. As a result, she is unable to use her knowledge to solve a problem about a car's rate of acceleration.

Research consistently indicates that when people have a thorough, conceptual understanding of a topic—when they have stored a great deal of information about that topic, with various pieces of information appropriately organized and interrelated in long-term memory—they can more easily use their knowledge to solve problems (P. A. Alexander & Judy, 1988; Heller & Hungate, 1985; Voss, Greene, Post, & Penner, 1983). For example, students are more likely to apply a principle of physics to a specific situation if they understand the concepts underlying that principle and the situations to which it relates. They are more likely to apply the Pythagorean theorem to the calculation of a diagonal roof if they have learned that theorem at a meaningful level and have associated it with such ideas as "diagonal" and "measurement." And when proposing possible solutions to the problem of rain forest destruction, they are more likely to draw from their knowledge of several disciplines (e.g., from ecology, economics, and psychology) if they have stored ideas from those disciplines in an interrelated, cross-disciplinary fashion.

This facilitation of problem-solving skills is yet another reason for teaching a few topics thoroughly, rather than many topics superficially (the *less is more* notion once again). It also justifies providing many and different examples and opportunities for practice. Students can study arithmetic by using such diverse examples as balancing a checkbook, calculating change, or predicting the possible profits and necessary supplies for a lemonade stand (e.g., number of cups, amount of lemonade mix). They can learn basic principles of geography (e.g., that large cities are almost always located near major transportation junctions) by examining maps of different countries, as well as by exploring their own local geographic environment. Only by spending time with a certain topic and studying a variety of examples can our students learn that topic in a meaningful fashion

In what areas do you have the depth of knowledge necessary for solving problems successfully? In what areas has your relative lack of knowledge been a handicap?

Provide many real-world examples of a particular principle or procedure.

and make multiple connections with situations to which that subject matter applies. All too often, students don't have these critical opportunities (e.g., Porter, 1989).

We should note here that students are also more likely to make connections between classroom material and its potential applications when they anticipate situations in which they might need to use the material to solve problems (J. R. Anderson et al., 1996). Not only should we focus more of our classroom instruction on the application of information, but we should focus more of our assessment procedures on application as well (Bransford et al., 1989; Sternberg & Frensch, 1993). Here is an example of an assessment task in which students must apply their knowledge of geographic principles:

Include applications in assessment techniques.

> A map of a hypothetical country includes information as to where bodies of water (e.g., river, lakes) and various forms of vegetation (grasslands, forests, etc.) are located. It also includes information about elevation, rainfall, and temperature ranges. A particular spot on the map is marked X. Students are asked questions such as these:
>
> - If people living at the point marked X on the map began to migrate *or* expand, where would they go, and what direction might they take?
> - What would be the distribution of population in country X; that is, where would many people live, and where would very few people live?
> - Where would large cities develop in country X?
> - How would you judge the country's economic potential; that is, which areas might be best for development, which might be worst, and so on? (adapted from Massialas & Zevin, 1983)

By incorporating the application of classroom material into our classroom assignments and tests, we indirectly teach students that this information can be used in a variety of contexts and furthermore *should* be used in these contexts. We will revisit the importance of assessing higher-level thinking skills in our discussion of classroom assessment in Chapter 16.

How many exams have you taken that have tested your ability to remember but not *apply* information? Did such exams give you the message that knowing something was important but using it was not?

Retrieval of Relevant Information from Long-Term Memory

Obviously, people cannot solve a problem unless they retrieve from long-term memory the information necessary to solve it. But as we discovered in Chapter 6, long-term memory contains a great deal of information, and people cannot possibly retrieve it all in any given situation. Successful problem solving therefore requires that an individual search the right "places" in long-term memory at the right time.

The parts of long-term memory that a person searches depends on how the individual encoded the problem in the first place. For example, if a student sees the word *left* in a word problem and thinks "subtraction," that student will retrieve rules of subtraction even when addition is required. If a student encodes a box only as a container for tacks, that student will not retrieve other characteristics of boxes (e.g., their flat surfaces, their relative sturdiness) that might be useful in solving the candle problem. When people have a mental set about a problem, they may unnecessarily restrict their search of long-term memory, overlooking stored information that is critical for problem solution.

Situated cognition influences problem-solving success in much the same way that it affects other forms of transfer: Our students may learn how to solve problems in certain contexts yet *not* solve problems requiring similar algorithms or heuristics once they find themselves in a different context (Lave, 1993; Saljo & Wyndhamn, 1992; Schliemann & Carraher, 1993). As an illustration, let's consider a study with 15- and 16-year-old students (Saljo & Wyndhamn, 1992). The students were asked to figure out how much postage they should put on an envelope that weighed a particular amount, and they were given a table of postage rates that would enable them to determine the correct amount. When students were given the task in a social studies class, most of them used the postage table to find the answer. But when students were given the task in a math class, most of them tried to *calculate* the postage in some manner, sometimes figuring it to several decimal places. Curiously, the students in the social studies class were more likely to solve the problem correctly; as a former social studies teacher myself, I suspect that, in class, they were well accustomed to finding information in tables and charts. In contrast, many of the students in the math class apparently never considered pulling the correct postage directly from the table. Instead, they tried to apply some of the complex mathematical operations that served them so well in their daily assignments—operations that were counterproductive in this situation.

INTO THE CLASSROOM: Promoting Successful Transfer and Problem Solving

---

Teach important topics in depth and be sure students learn them thoroughly.

A teacher of a second-year Spanish class teaches only two new verb tenses (preterit and imperfect) during fall semester, saving other tenses (e.g., near past, near future) for later instruction.

Tie class material to what students already know.

After teaching the fact that water expands when it freezes, a science teacher explains that many of the bumps seen in country roads are frost heaves caused by freezing water.

Give students practice in dealing with ill-defined problems and show them how to make such problems more well-defined.

A teacher asks students in an interdisciplinary class to wrestle with the problem of diminishing rain forests. He starts them off by asking, "What should be the final goal of preservation efforts?" and "What are some of the biological, social, and political factors that you need to consider as you try to solve this problem?"

Teach the information and skills essential in problem solving to a level of automaticity.

An elementary school teacher makes sure that his students have thoroughly mastered the basic multiplication and division facts before teaching them long division.

Provide opportunities for students to apply what they have learned to new situations and problems.

A geography teacher asks students to apply their knowledge of human settlement patterns in explaining why the populations of various countries are distributed as they are.

Ask students to apply what they know in tests and other assessment activities.

A science teacher asks students to use principles of physics to describe how they might move a 500-pound object to a location twenty feet away.

Make school tasks similar to the tasks that students are likely to encounter in the real world.

An English teacher teaches persuasive writing skills by having students write editorials for the school newspaper.

Once again we see the value of authentic activities—in this case, authentic activities that have a problem-solving component. When students use certain principles and skills to solve problems in authentic contexts, they will be more likely to retrieve those principles and skills later on when they encounter similar problems in similar contexts in the adult world. Authentic activities will be important not only in promoting effective problem solving, but also in promoting critical thinking skills. We turn to the latter topic now.

Provide practice with authentic problem-solving activities to promote later retrieval of principles and problem-solving strategies relevant to various contexts.

Critical Thinking

▣ Experiencing Firsthand
Happiness Is a Well-Behaved Classroom

Here is a research finding presented at the annual conference of the American Educational Research Association in 1994:

> Teachers who feel happy when they teach are more likely to have well-behaved students (Emmer, 1994).

If you want to have well-behaved students, then, should you try to feel happy when you enter the classroom each morning?

If you answered yes to my question, then you made a mistake that I warned you about in Chapter 1: You drew a conclusion about a cause-effect relationship (i.e., teacher happiness causes good behavior in students) on the basis of a correlational research study. Although Dr. Emmer found that teacher happiness and student behavior are *associated* with one another, he did not necessarily find that teacher happiness *causes* good behavior. In fact, there are other possible explanations for the correlation. For instance, perhaps good student behavior makes teachers feel happy (rather than vice versa), or perhaps teachers who use effective teaching techniques feel happy *and* keep students on task as the result of using those techniques (Emmer, 1994).

Evaluating research findings as you read about them is an example of critical thinking. More generally, **critical thinking** involves evaluating information or arguments in terms of their accuracy and worth (Beyer, 1985). Critical thinking may take a variety of forms, depending on the context. For instance, it may involve any one or more of the following (Halpern, 1998):

- *Verbal reasoning:* Understanding and evaluating the persuasive techniques to be found in oral and written language. For example, consider this:

  Aren't you tired of sniffles and runny noses all winter? Tired of always feeling less than your best? Get through a whole winter without colds. Take Eradicold Pills as directed. (R. J. Harris, 1977, p. 605)

  Do Eradicold Pills reduce cold symptoms? The passage provides no proof that they do. Instead, it simply includes the suggestion to "Take Eradicold Pills as directed" within the context of a discussion of undesirable symptoms—a common ploy in persuasive advertising.

- *Argument analysis:* Discriminating between reasons that do and do not support a particular conclusion. For example, imagine this situation:

  You have a beat-up old car and have several thousand dollars to get the car in working order. You can sell the car in its present condition for $1,500, or you can invest a

Critical thinking takes different forms in different content domains.

couple of thousand dollars on more repairs and then sell it for $3,000. What should you do? (modeled after Halpern, 1998)

Obviously, it makes more sense to sell the car now: If you sell the car for $3,000 after making $2,000 worth of repairs, you make $500 less than you would otherwise. Yet many people mistakenly believe that their *past* investments justify making additional ones, when in fact past investments are irrelevant to the present state of affairs (Halpern, 1998).

- *Hypothesis testing:* Evaluating the value of data and research results in terms of the methods used to obtain them and their potential relevance to particular conclusions. When hypothesis testing includes critical thinking, it involves considering such questions as these:

  Was an appropriate method used to measure a particular outcome?

  Are the data and results derived from a relatively large number of people, objects, or events?

  Have other possible explanations or conclusions been eliminated?

  Can the results obtained in one situation be reasonably generalized to other situations?

  The "Happiness" exercise provides an example of this form of critical thinking.

- *Decision making:* Identifying several alternatives and selecting the best alternative. For example, when we choose a particular approach to teaching a topic by considering several possible approaches and weighing the pros and cons of each one, we are engaging in critical thinking.

The nature of critical thinking will obviously be different in different content domains. For instance, in writing, critical thinking may involve reading the first draft of a persuasive essay to look for errors in logical reasoning or for situations in which opinions have not been sufficiently justified. In science, critical thinking may involve revising present theories or beliefs to account for new evidence; in other words, it may involve conceptual change. In history, it may involve drawing inferences from various historical documents, attempting to determine whether things *definitely* happened a particular way or only *maybe* happened that way.

Perhaps because the term *critical thinking* encompasses such a variety of different skills, research regarding how to promote critical thinking skills in the classroom is sketchy at best. Nevertheless, here are a few suggestions that theorists have offered:

- Teach fewer topics, but in greater depth—the *less is more* principle yet again (Onosko, 1989; Onosko & Newmann, 1994).

- Encourage some degree of intellectual skepticism—for instance, by urging students to question and challenge the ideas that they read and hear (Onosko, 1989).

- Model critical thinking—for instance, by thinking aloud while analyzing a persuasive argument or scientific report (Onosko & Newmann, 1994).

- Show students that critical thinking involves considerable mental effort, but that the benefits often make the effort worthwhile (Halpern, 1998).

- Give students many and varied opportunities to practice critical thinking—for instance, by identifying flaws in the logical arguments presented in persuasive essays and by evaluating the quality and usefulness of scientific findings (Halpern, 1998).

- Embed critical thinking skills within the context of authentic activities as a way of helping students retrieve those skills later on, both in the workplace and in other aspects of adult life (Halpern, 1998).

- Ask questions such as these to encourage critical thinking:
  - What additional information do I need?
  - What information is relevant to this situation? What information is irrelevant?
  - What persuasive technique is the author using? Is it valid, or is it designed to mislead the reader?
  - What reasons support the conclusion? What reasons do *not* support the conclusion?
  - What actions might I take to improve the design of this study? (adapted from Halpern, 1998, p. 454)

- Have students debate controversial issues from several perspectives, occasionally asking them to take a perspective quite different from their own (Reiter, 1994).

Critical thinking is one form of *elaboration,* whereby learners use their prior knowledge to expand on new information, in essence storing *more* than the information actually presented. Do our students realize how important it is to elaborate on classroom material and in other ways learn it in a meaningful fashion? Or, like Mary in our opening case study, do they believe that rote memorization is a better approach to take? We will answer questions such as these as we discuss metacognition and study strategies.

Encourage and model critical thinking, and give students numerous opportunities to practice critical thinking skills.

Metacognition and Study Strategies

THINKING ABOUT WHAT YOU KNOW

- How and when did you learn how to study? Did your teachers give you suggestions as to how you might best learn classroom material? Did your parents provide guidance about your study habits? Did you observe and adapt any of the study strategies that you saw your classmates using? Did you learn how to study mostly through your own trial and error?

- What specific study strategies do you use? For example, do you take notes? Do you outline course material? Do you summarize what you read in your textbooks? What does your current grade point average tell you about the effectiveness of your study strategies?

Students vary considerably in the study strategies they use. Consider these three students:

Kate is studying for a biology exam. She moves her eyes down each of the assigned pages in the textbook, but all the while she is thinking about the upcoming school dance. Kate seems to think that as long as her eyes are looking at the page, the information printed on it will somehow sink in.

Ling is studying for the same exam. She spends most of her time memorizing terms and definitions in her textbook. Eventually, she can recite many of them word for word.

Sarah is also studying for the biology exam. She focuses her efforts on trying to understand basic biological principles and on generating new examples of those principles.

Which student is likely to do best on the biology exam? Considering what we now know about learning and memory, we can predict that Sarah will get the highest score of the three girls. Unfortunately, Ling has not yet discovered that she learns better when she relates new ideas to her prior knowledge than when she memorizes things at a rote level. And poor Kate knows even less about how to learn effectively: She's not even paying attention to what she thinks she is reading!

When we talk about students' knowledge and beliefs regarding their own cognitive processes and students' attempts to regulate their cognitive processes to maximize learning and memory, we are talking about **metacognition.** Metacognition includes:

- Knowing the limits of one's own learning and memory capabilities
- Knowing what learning tasks one can realistically accomplish within a certain amount of time
- Knowing which learning strategies are effective and which are not
- Planning an approach to a learning task that is likely to be successful
- Using effective learning strategies to process and learn new material
- Monitoring one's own knowledge and comprehension—in other words, knowing when information has been successfully learned and when it has not
- Using effective strategies for retrieval of previously stored information

To illustrate, you have undoubtedly learned by now that you can only acquire so much information so fast; you cannot possibly absorb the contents of an entire textbook in one hour. You have also learned that you can store information more quickly and retrieve it more easily when you organize it logically. And perhaps you have also discovered the advantage of checking yourself as you read a textbook, stopping every so often to make sure that you've understood what you've just read. In other words, you are metacognitively aware of some things that you need to do (mentally) to learn new information effectively.

The more students know about effective learning strategies—the greater their metacognitive awareness—the higher their classroom achievement is likely to be (L. Baker, 1989; Perkins, 1995; P. L. Peterson, 1988). Furthermore, students who use more sophisticated metacognitive strategies are more likely to undergo conceptual change when such change is warranted (Gunstone, 1994; Wittrock, 1994).

Unfortunately, many students are unaware of how they can best learn and remember information. Younger children (those in the elementary grades) are especially naive about effective learning strategies (see the discussion of developmental changes in information processing in Chapter 2). But older students are also prone to misconceptions about how they can best learn and remember. For example, many students at all grade levels (even those in college!) erroneously believe that rote learning is an effective study strategy (Pintrich & De Groot, 1990; Prawat, 1989; Schommer, 1994a).

With each transition to a higher educational level—for example, from elementary school to middle school, from junior high to high school, or from high school to college—teacher expectations for student learning and performance are also higher. At each successive level, students are asked to learn more information and to process it in a more sophisticated fashion. Thus, the simple learning strategies that students develop in grade school (e.g., rehearsal) become less and less effective with each passing year.

Yet all too often, teachers teach academic content—history, biology, mathematics, and so on—without also teaching students how to *learn* that content (Pressley et al., 1990; J. E. Wilson, 1988). Because students often have little knowledge of how they can best study and learn, they may have difficulty mastering the content that teachers teach. And when students *don't* learn successfully, they may not know why they have failed, nor may they know how to improve their chances of succeeding the next time around (e.g., Horgan, 1990; O'Sullivan & Joy, 1990).

We can better help our students be successful learners if, when teaching specific academic content, we also teach them how to study that content (e.g., Alexander & Judy, 1988; Holt-Reynolds, 1992). But to help students develop and use effective learning and study strategies, we first need to determine which strategies actually work and which do not. Let's see what research tells us about this issue.

D id you have misconceptions about how best to study before you read this book?

A re teachers' expectations for your learning more demanding at the college level than they were in high school? If so, have you been able to adapt your study strategies accordingly?

Effective Study Strategies

Research studies point to a number of effective study strategies, including these:

- Identifying important information
- Taking notes
- Retrieving relevant prior knowledge
- Organizing
- Elaborating
- Summarizing
- Monitoring comprehension

As we consider these strategies in the pages that follow, you will undoubtedly find some that you yourself use as you study course material.

Identifying Important Information

THINKING ABOUT WHAT YOU KNOW

What cues do you use to identify important ideas in your textbooks? Are you more likely to believe that something is important if it's printed in *italics* or **boldface**? Do you look for important points in headings, introductions, concluding paragraphs, or summaries? Do you focus on definitions, formulas, or lists of items?

People rarely learn everything they read in a textbook or remember everything they hear in the classroom. Obviously, then, students must be selective in studying course content. The things they choose to study—whether main ideas and critical pieces of information, or isolated facts and trivial details—inevitably affect their learning and school achievement (Dee-Lucas & Larkin, 1991; Dole et al., 1991; R. E. Reynolds & Shirey, 1988).

Students often have difficulty separating central and important information from the trivial and unimportant. Here are some features of books and classroom lectures on which students often focus:

Look through this textbook. Can you find paragraphs in which the main idea is located in the middle or near the end of the paragraph, rather than at the beginning?

- *The first sentence of a lesson or paragraph.* Many students erroneously believe that the main idea (and perhaps *only* idea) of a paragraph is always found in the first sentence (Mayer, 1984). (In writing instruction, students are often taught to put the main idea first; hence, it is not surprising that they expect to find the same pattern in the writings of others.)
- *Items that look different.* Definitions and formulas often stand out visually in a textbook. They may appear in *italics* or **boldface** type or may be

set apart

from the rest of the text. As a result, students often focus on them to the exclusion of other, perhaps more important information (Mayer, 1984). For example, when reading scientific proofs, students often focus their attention on specific equations, rather than on the verbal text that makes those equations meaningful (Dee-Lucas & Larkin, 1991).
- *Items presented in more than one way.* Students are more likely to view material as important when it is presented in several different ways. For example, they are more likely to pay attention to things that teachers describe verbally *and* write on the chalkboard (Kiewra, 1989).
- *Items that are intrinsically interesting.* Students at all levels attend more to interesting statements than to uninteresting ones even if the most interesting statements are relatively unimportant ones (P. A. Alexander & Jetton, 1996; Garner, Brown, Sanders, & Menke, 1992; R. E. Reynolds & Shirey, 1988).

When important ideas are presented within the middle of a lesson or paragraph, without any obvious cues to make them stand out, and especially when those ideas do not grab students' immediate interest, then students often overlook them.

As teachers, we can facilitate our students' academic success by letting them know what things are most important for them to learn. We could, of course, simply tell them exactly what to study. But we can also get the same message across through more subtle means:

Let students know what things are most important to learn.

- Provide a list of objectives for a lesson.
- Write key concepts and major ideas on the chalkboard.
- Ask questions that focus students' attention on important ideas.

Do such prompts remind you of the concept of *scaffolding?*

Students (especially low-achieving ones) are more likely to learn the important points of a lesson when such "prompts" are provided for them (Kiewra, 1989; R. E. Reynolds & Shirey, 1988; Schraw & Wade, 1991). As our students become increasingly able to distinguish important from unimportant information on their own, we can gradually phase out our guidance.

Taking Notes

No doubt you have at one time or another missed a class and therefore had to rely on a classmate's notes from the class lecture. And no doubt you discovered that the classmate's notes were different (perhaps *very* different) from the notes that you yourself usually take. For twenty students in the same classroom, we will find twenty different sets of notes. Each student makes unique assumptions about what is important, what is useful, and what is likely to be on an upcoming exam, and these assumptions influence the amount and type of notes that the student takes.

In general, note taking is associated with more successful classroom learning; in fact, when students have *no* opportunity either to take or review notes, they may recall very little of what they hear in a lecture (Hale, 1983; Kiewra, 1989). The process of note taking seems to serve two very important functions (Barnett, Di Vesta, & Rogozinski, 1981; Di Vesta & Gray, 1972; Kiewra, 1989):

When teachers write major concepts and ideas on the chalkboard, they cue students about what things are important to learn.

- *Encoding.* Note taking helps students remember information *even when they have no opportunity to review those notes.* Apparently, the process of taking notes helps students encode information in long-term memory. Furthermore, students who are actively engaged in taking notes are less likely to let their minds wander from what they are reading or listening to in class.

- *External storage.* As we discovered in Chapter 6, retrieval of information from long-term memory is a somewhat undependable process: Even when we have effectively stored information in long-term memory, we can't always find it again. Notes provide an additional means of storing information—in this case, through a mechanism external to the memory system. Whereas memory is often unreliable, notebooks are fairly dependable: Our notes are present in their original form many days, weeks, or even months after we've written them. And reviewing those notes on one or more later occasions does help us remember the information better.

How useful are the notes you take in your classes? Can you think of ways you might improve your notes?

The extent to which note taking helps students learn and achieve naturally depends on the quantity and quality of the notes taken, as the following exercise illustrates.

Experiencing Firsthand
Two Notebooks

Here are two students' notes from the same introductory lesson on dinosaurs.

What differences do you notice in the two sets of notes? From which set could you study more effectively?

No doubt you preferred the first set of notes. The first set provides a relatively coherent set of statements about dinosaurs, whereas the second set is too brief and disjointed to make much sense. In general, quantity of notes is positively correlated with achievement: Students who take more notes do better (Kiewra, 1989). But the quality of notes is equally critical: Notes must reflect the main ideas of a lecture or reading assignment (A. L. Brown, Campione, & Day, 1981; Kiewra, 1985; B. M. Taylor, 1982). Good notes seem to be especially valuable for students who have little prior knowledge about the subject matter they are studying (Shrager & Mayer, 1989).

As teachers, we should encourage students to take notes on their class material. We should also give them suggestions as to what is most important to include in those notes (Pressley, Yokoi, van Meter, Van Etten, & Freebern, 1997; Yokoi, 1997). And we might occasionally ask to look at students' notebooks, to make sure that their notes accurately reflect the material they should be emphasizing as they study.

> **Encourage students to take notes, give suggestions as to what information is most important to include, and occasionally check notes for accuracy.**

Retrieving Relevant Prior Knowledge

Students can engage in meaningful learning only to the extent that they have previous knowledge to which new information can be related and are also *aware* of the potential relationship. How can we encourage students to think about the things they already know as they encounter new information? One approach is to model this strategy for our students. For example, we might read aloud a portion of a textbook, stopping occasionally to tie an idea in the text to something previously studied in class or to something in our own personal experiences. We can then encourage our students to do likewise, giving suggestions and guiding their efforts as they proceed (Spires et al., 1990). Especially when working in the elementary grades, we might also provide specific questions that remind students to think about what they already know about a topic as they read and study:

> **Model the strategy of making connections to existing knowledge as you read.**

- What do you already know about your topic?
- What do you hope to learn about your topic?
- Do you think what you learn by reading your books will change what you already know about your topic? (Thompson & Carr, 1995, p. 9).

> **Does this approach also remind you of scaffolding?**

With time and practice, our students should eventually be able to retrieve their relevant prior knowledge with little or no assistance from us (Spires et al., 1990).

Organizing

As we discovered in Chapter 6, organized information is stored and retrieved more easily than unorganized information. When students engage in study activities that help them organize information, they learn more effectively (DuBois et al., 1988; M. A. McDaniel & Einstein, 1989; Mintzes, Wandersee, & Novak, 1997). For example, one useful way of organizing information is *outlining* the material—a strategy that may be especially helpful to low-achieving students (L. Baker, 1989; M. A. McDaniel & Einstein, 1989; Wade, 1992).

> **Encourage students to organize classroom material.**

Another strategy that facilitates organization is making a **concept map,** a diagram that depicts the concepts of a unit and their interrelationships (Novak & Gowin, 1984). Figure 8–2 shows concept maps constructed by two fifth-grade students after they watched a slide lecture on Australia. The concepts themselves are in circles; their interrelationships are designated by lines and phrases that link pairs of concepts. As an example of concept mapping in action, try the following exercise.

◧ Experiencing Firsthand
Mapping Concepts About Concepts

Quickly review the section on concept learning in Chapter 7 (especially pp. 270–271). The section contains numerous concepts concerning the topic of concept learning:

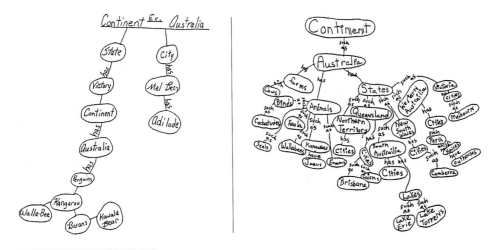

FIGURE 8.2

Concept maps constructed by two fifth-grade students after watching a slide lecture on Australia.

From Learning How to Learn *(pp. 100–101) by J. D. Novak and D. B. Gowin, 1984, Cambridge, England: Cambridge University Press. Copyright 1984 by Cambridge University Press. Reprinted with the permission of Cambridge University Press.*

undergeneralization	defining features
overgeneralization	correlational features
positive instances	salient features
negative instances	

The section also talks about how these concepts are related to one another; for example, *overgeneralization* is a case of incorrectly identifying *negative instances* as examples of a concept, and a concept is easier to learn when its *defining features* are *salient*.

On a separate sheet of paper, make a concept map with the seven "concepts about concepts" just listed. Write the concepts down in an arrangement that makes sense to you, circle each one, and then add lines and phrases to describe the interrelationships between pairs of concepts.

There is certainly more than one "correct" way to map the seven concepts; the concept map shown in Figure 8–3 on page 328 is just one of many possibilities. I hope that the exercise helped you organize some of the things you learned about concepts in the preceding chapter. I hope that it also gave you a better understanding of the process of concept mapping.

Students benefit in numerous ways from constructing their own concept maps for classroom material. By focusing on how concepts relate to one another, students organize material better. They are also more likely to notice how new concepts are related to concepts they already know; thus, they are more likely to learn the material meaningfully. Furthermore, when students construct a concept map from verbal material (e.g., from a lecture or a textbook), they can encode that material in long-term memory visually as well as verbally. And the very process of concept mapping may promote a more sophisticated perspective of what learning *is;* more specifically, students may begin to realize that learning is not just a process of "absorbing" information but instead

In this map, connections are correctly interpreted by starting at the top and following the lines downward.

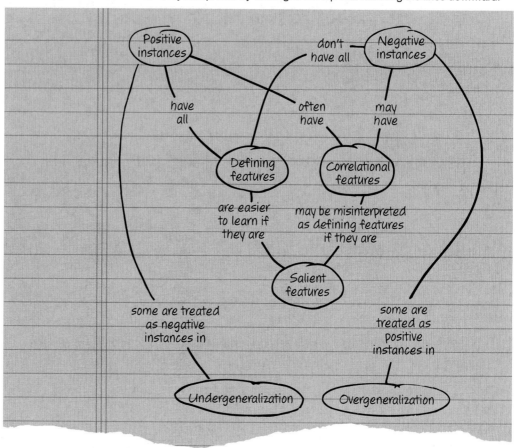

FIGURE 8.3

One possible concept map for concepts related to concept learning

involves actively making connections among ideas (Holley & Dansereau, 1984; Mintzes et al., 1997; Novak & Gowin, 1984).

Not only do concept maps help students, they may also help teachers. When we ourselves develop a concept map for a lesson, the organizational scheme of that lesson becomes clearer, and we have a better idea about how to sequence the presentation of ideas. And when we examine the concept maps that our students have constructed, students' understanding of a lesson becomes readily apparent, as do any misconceptions that students may have (Novak & Gowin, 1984; Novak & Musonda, 1991). For example, if you look once again at Figure 8–2, you should notice how very different the two children's knowledge of Australia appears to be, even though both children received the same information. The concept map on the left reveals several misconceptions that the student has; for instance, Adelaide is *not* part of Melbourne; it is a different city altogether! If geographic knowledge about Australia is an instructional objective, then this student clearly needs further instruction to correct such misinformation.

Elaborating

Whether they are reading, taking notes in a lecture, or studying for an exam, students typically do better when they elaborate on course material—for example, when they

🍎 Assign concept-mapping exercises both to help students organize material and to help you assess what they have learned.

draw inferences from that material or consider its implications. To illustrate, imagine that Pai and Paulo are studying the same reading passage in history. Pai focuses on facts presented in the passage, trying to remember who did what and when. Paulo tries to go beyond the material he actually reads, speculating upon possible reasons for people's actions, thinking about how a historical event has relevance to current events, and so on. Pai and Paulo may do equally well on simple fact-based questions about the passage. But Paulo will do better on tasks that involve drawing inferences; he will also explain and integrate the material more effectively (Van Rossum & Schenk, 1984).

How can we encourage our students to elaborate as they study class material? For one thing, when we model retrieval of relevant prior knowledge, we can model elaboration as well—for example, by stopping to identify our own examples of a concept we are reading about, to consider the implications of a new principle, and so on. Another approach is to give students questions such as these to consider as they listen to a lecture or read their textbook:

- Can I think of any additional examples of . . . ?
- What is the difference between . . . and . . . ?
- How are . . . and . . . similar?
- What are the strengths and weaknesses of . . . ?
- What conclusions can I draw about . . . ?
- How might I use . . . ?
- What might happen if . . . ? (adapted from A. King, 1992)

Yet another approach is to teach our students to develop and answer their *own* elaborative questions—a strategy sometimes known as **elaborative interrogation** (Kahl & Woloshyn, 1994; A. King, 1992, 1994; Rosenshine, Meister, & Chapman, 1996; E. Wood et al., 1994). For example, if our students are studying this fact:

The Gulf Stream warms the British Isles.

we might encourage them to ask themselves, *"Why* does the Gulf Stream warm the British Isles?" and then generate a reasonable answer to the question. Or if our students are studying two or more related concepts (e.g., series vs. parallel circuits; monarchies, theocracies, and democracies), we might encourage them to ask questions concerning the similarities and differences among the concepts. Elaborative interrogation is not necessarily an easy strategy for students to develop; accordingly, they may sometimes use it more effectively, at least at first, when they work in pairs or small groups to develop and answer questions (A. King, 1994; Rosenshine et al., 1996; E. Wood et al., 1994).

Summarizing

Another important study strategy is summarizing the material being studied (Dole et al., 1991; Hidi & Anderson, 1986; A. King, 1992). Effective summarizing usually entails at least three processes (Hidi & Anderson, 1986; Spivey, 1997):

- Separating important from unimportant information
- Condensing details into more general ideas
- Identifying important relationships among those general ideas

Many students have trouble summarizing material even at the high school level (V. Anderson & Hidi, 1988/1989). Probably the best way of helping students develop this strategy is to ask them to summarize what they hear and read on a regular basis. For example, we might occasionally give homework assignments asking them to write a

Model elaboration.

Give students higher-level questions to consider as they read.

Teach students how to generate their own elaborative questions.

Reciprocal teaching, a teaching strategy we will examine in Chapter 14, provides an effective means of showing students how to elaborate as they read.

Give students practice in summarizing bodies of information.

summary of a textbook chapter. Or we might ask them to work in cooperative groups to develop a brief oral presentation that condenses the information they have learned about a particular topic. At the beginning, we should restrict summarizing assignments to short, simple, and well-organized passages involving material with which students are familiar; we can assign more challenging material as students become more proficient summarizers (V. Anderson & Hidi, 1988/1989).

Monitoring Comprehension

▣ Experiencing Firsthand
Looking Back

Stop for a minute and ask yourself this question:

> *What have I learned from the last five pages of this textbook?*

Write your answer on a piece of scrap paper.

Now go back and look at the five pages just before this one. Does your answer include all the major points covered in these pages? Is there something that you thought you understood but realize now that you didn't? Is there something that you never learned at all—perhaps something that you were "reading" when your mind was someplace altogether different?

Successful students engage in **comprehension monitoring:** They periodically check themselves to make sure they understand what they are reading or hearing. Furthermore, successful students take steps to correct the situation when they *don't* comprehend; for example, they reread a section of a textbook or ask a question in class (L. Baker, 1989; Hacker, 1995; Haller, Child, & Walberg, 1988). In contrast, low achievers seldom check themselves or take appropriate action when they don't comprehend. Poor readers, for instance, rarely reread paragraphs that they haven't sufficiently understood the first time around (L. Baker & Brown, 1984).

Many students at all grade levels engage in little if any comprehension monitoring (Dole et al., 1991; Markman, 1979; J. W. Thomas, 1993a). When students don't monitor their own comprehension, they don't know what they know and what they don't know: They may think they have mastered something when they really haven't (Butler & Winne, 1995; Horgan, 1990; Schraw, Potenza, & Nebelsick-Gullet, 1993). This **illusion of knowing** is seen in students at all levels, even college students (L. Baker, 1989). Perhaps you have a friend who has difficulty on exams despite many hours of reading and studying the textbook. Perhaps you even find yourself in this predicament on occasion. If so, then your friend and you may not be adequately monitoring your comprehension—for example, by asking yourselves questions periodically to make certain you are learning the things you read. Our case study at the beginning of the chapter provides another example of the illusion of knowing: When Mary studies, she fails to realize that she doesn't understand the difference between *velocity* and *acceleration,* so she is later quite surprised to find herself doing poorly on her test.

To be successful learners—and more specifically, to *know what they know*—students should monitor their comprehension both *while* they study and *after* they study (Horgan, 1990; T. O. Nelson & Dunlosky, 1991; Spires, 1990). As teachers, we can promote better comprehension-monitoring skills by teaching students **self-questioning.** Not only might we provide questions that students can answer as they go along, but we can also encourage students to formulate and ask *themselves* questions; such questions might include both simple, fact-based questions and the elaborative questions described

🍎 Encourage students to "test" themselves by asking themselves questions both as they study and at a later time.

▢ As you read a textbook, when is the information in working memory? in long-term memory? With your answers in mind, explain why students should monitor their comprehension both as they read and also at a later time.

T A B L E 8.2   Which Study Strategies Do You Use, and When?

STUDY STRATEGY	IN WHICH CLASSES OR SUBJECTS DO YOU USE THIS STRATEGY FREQUENTLY?	IN WHICH CLASSES OR SUBJECTS MIGHT YOU BENEFIT FROM USING THIS STRATEGY MORE OFTEN?	WHAT FACTORS AFFECT YOUR ABILITY TO USE THIS STRATEGY SUCCESSFULLY?
Identifying important information			
Taking notes			
Retrieving relevant prior knowledge			
Organizing			
Elaborating			
Summarizing			
Monitoring comprehension			

earlier. When students "test" themselves over the material they are studying, they have a better sense of what they do and don't know, and as a result they ultimately learn the material more completely and meaningfully (Rosenshine et al., 1996; Wong, 1985). Because students are often better judges of what they have learned *after* they have studied, rather than during the study session itself (T. O. Nelson & Dunlosky, 1991; Weaver & Kelemen, 1997), we should also suggest that they follow up their studying with a self-test at a later time.

Experiencing Firsthand
Self-Reflection

Which study strategies do you use frequently? Which do you use seldom or not at all? Take a minute to fill in the empty boxes in Table 8–2.

Judging from the entries you made in Table 8–2, do you think you are using effective study strategies? Do you see areas for improvement? Study strategies are complex metacognitive skills that are not easily acquired; your own strategies will undoubtedly continue to improve over time as you study increasingly more challenging material in your college courses.

Some of the study strategies just described, such as taking notes and making outlines, are behaviors we can actually see. Others, such as retrieving relevant prior knowledge and monitoring comprehension, are internal mental processes that we *can't* see. It is probably the latter set of strategies—those internal mental processes—that ultimately affect students' learning (Kardash & Amlund, 1991). As we help students develop study strategies, we must remember that behavioral strategies (e.g., taking notes) will be useful only to the extent that they facilitate more effective cognitive processing.

Remember that behavioral study strategies are only helpful when they facilitate more effective cognitive processing.

Factors That Affect Strategy Use

At least three factors appear to influence students' choice and use of strategies: knowledge base, beliefs about what knowledge *is,* and training.

Knowledge base.   Students are more likely to use effective strategies when they have a fair amount of prior knowledge about a topic (B. A. Greene, 1994; W. Schneider, 1993; E. Wood et al., 1994). Considering what you've learned about long-term memory storage processes, this principle should hardly surprise you. Such processes as meaningful learning, organization, and elaboration all involve making connections between new material and things already stored in long-term memory—connections that are more likely to be made when long-term memory contains information directly relevant to the topic at hand.

Beliefs about the nature of knowledge and knowledge acquisition.   Different students have different views regarding the nature of knowledge and knowledge acquisition—different **epistemological beliefs**—and such views influence the ways in which they study and learn (Hofer & Pintrich, 1997; Purdie, Hattie, & Douglas, 1996; Schommer, 1997). For example, many students believe that knowledge is black-and-white (ideas are indisputably either right or wrong) and that you either have that knowledge or you don't. But other students recognize that there may be different, equally valid viewpoints on the same topic that could all legitimately be called "knowledge" (Schommer, 1994b). The former group of students is more likely to believe that learning should be a relatively rapid process, and so they will give up quickly if they find themselves struggling to understand classroom material (Schommer, 1994b).

As another example of how students' epistemological beliefs may differ, some students believe that when they read a textbook, information is directly transmitted in a relatively unaltered fashion from the page to themselves; they may also believe that studying a textbook simply means learning isolated facts, perhaps in a relatively passive manner. In contrast, other students believe that learning from reading requires them to construct their own meanings from the information presented in the textbook, and that they should actively attempt to organize and apply the subject matter about which they are reading. It is the latter students—those who think of reading as a constructive process—who are most likely to process what they read in a meaningful and effective fashion (Purdie et al., 1996; Schommer, 1994b).

As teachers, we must communicate to our students—not only in what we *say,* but also in what we *do* (e.g., what activities we assign, how we assess students' learning)—what we ourselves have already learned about knowledge and knowledge acquisition (Hofer & Pintrich, 1997; Schommer, 1994b):

> That knowledge does not always mean having clear-cut answers to difficult, complex issues
>
> That knowledge involves knowing the interrelationships among ideas, as well as the ideas themselves
>
> That learning involves active construction of knowledge, rather than just a passive "reception" of it
>
> That understanding a body of information and ideas sometimes requires persistence and hard work

In doing so, we increase the likelihood that our students will apply effective study strategies, engage in critical thinking, and undergo conceptual change when they study classroom subject matter (Hofer & Pintrich, 1997; Purdie et al., 1996; Schommer, 1994b; Strike & Posner, 1992).

Foster productive epistemological beliefs.

Study strategies training. Can students be taught to study more effectively? Research studies answer this question with a firm *yes* (see the reference list at the bottom of Table 8–3). Effective study skills training programs often include components such as these:

Time management (e.g., planning when and how long to study)

Effective learning and reading strategies

Note-taking strategies

Specific memory techniques (e.g., mnemonics)

Comprehension-monitoring strategies

Test-taking strategies

Do you study a little bit each day or procrastinate until the last minute? Why is the former approach more likely to be effective?

INTO THE CLASSROOM: Helping Students Learn to Learn

Teach study skills within the context of academic subject areas.

When a health teacher tells students to read Chapter 3 of their textbook, he also describes strategies they might use to help them remember what they read.

Model effective study strategies.

A student reads aloud a passage describing how, during Columbus's first voyage across the Atlantic, many members of the crew wanted to turn around and return to Spain. The teacher says, "Let's think of some reasons why the crew might have wanted to go home. Do you think some of them might have been homesick? Do you think some of them might have been afraid of what lay ahead in uncharted waters? What other possible reasons can we identify?"

Identify situations in which various strategies are likely to be useful.

A science teacher says to her class, "We've studied several features of the nine planets in our solar system—size, color, composition, distance from the sun, and duration of revolution around the sun. This sounds like a situation where a two-dimensional chart might help us organize the information better."

Give students opportunities to practice using specific study strategies.

An elementary school teacher has members of a reading group take turns summarizing the passages that the group reads.

Scaffold students' initial efforts at using various study strategies, and gradually remove the scaffolding as they become more proficient.

A social studies teacher encourages her students to take notes, gives suggestions as to what to include in those notes, and occasionally checks students' notes for accuracy.

Encourage students to "test" themselves by asking themselves questions both as they study and at some later time.

An elementary school teacher instructs his students to study their spelling words as soon as they get home from school and then to make sure they can still remember how to spell those words after they have eaten dinner. "You might also want to call another student on the telephone and ask that person to test you on the words," he suggests.

Promoting More Effective Study Strategies

PRINCIPLE	EDUCATIONAL IMPLICATION	EXAMPLE
Study strategies are most effectively learned within the context of particular content domains.	When presenting academic content to students—through lectures, reading assignments, and so on—simultaneously teach them how to study that content.	Give students specific questions to ask themselves (thereby facilitating comprehension monitoring) as they read their textbooks.
Group learning situations often promote the development of effective strategies, perhaps because students verbalize and model various ways to think about classroom subject matter.	Occasionally ask students to study instructional materials in pairs or small cooperative learning groups.	Have students work in pairs to develop and answer questions that require them to elaborate on textbook content.
Students are more likely to acquire sophisticated study strategies when their initial efforts are scaffolded to promote success. Such *metacognitive scaffolding* should be phased out as students become more proficient in strategy use.	Scaffold students' attempts to use new strategies in a number of ways—for example, by modeling such strategies, giving clues about when certain strategies are appropriate, providing opportunities for group study (allowing students to observe one another's strategies), requiring mastery of increasingly more complex material, and giving feedback regarding appropriate and inappropriate strategy use.	To encourage students to organize material in a particular way, provide an organizational chart that cooperative learning groups fill out.
Students learn more effectively when their study strategies are numerous and varied.	As appropriate opportunities arise, continue to introduce new strategies—note taking, elaboration, self-questioning, mnemonics, and so on— throughout the school year.	Suggest that students use such mnemonics as verbal mediation and the keyword method to learn the capitals of South American countries or the meanings of Japanese vocabulary words.
Students are more likely to use effective study strategies when they understand why those strategies are useful.	Explain the usefulness of various strategies in ways that students understand.	Show students how note taking helps them keep their minds from wandering during class and how comprehension monitoring enables them to identify weak spots in their knowledge of class material.
Students use strategies more effectively if they know when each one is most appropriate.	Point out situations in which particular strategies are likely to be helpful.	Give students opportunities to elaborate on material—by drawing implications, generating new examples, and so on—when they must apply it to new situations and problems.

PRINCIPLE	EDUCATIONAL IMPLICATION	EXAMPLE
Students are most likely to master effective strategies when they can practice them over a long period of time and across a wide variety of tasks.	Give students numerous and varied opportunities to apply metacognitive strategies.	Ask students' previous teachers what study strategies they have taught and then explain how such strategies are applicable for current learning tasks as well.
Students are likely to use effective strategies only when they believe that such strategies can ultimately help them learn classroom material more successfully.	When teaching various study strategies, make sure each student is eventually able to apply them successfully. Also, expose students to peers who use the strategies effectively.	After a lecture, place students in small groups where they look at the notes each group member has taken and then combine all notes into a single, comprehensive set.

Sources: P. A. Alexander, Graham, & Harris, 1998; Barnett et al., 1981; Borkowski, Carr, Rellinger, & Pressley, 1990; Butler & Winne, 1995; A. Collins et al., 1989; Hattie, Biggs, & Purdie, 1996; Kahl & Woloshyn, 1994; A. King, 1992, 1994; Kucan & Beck, 1997; Mayer & Wittrock, 1996; Meloth & Deering, 1994; Nist, Simpson, Olejnik, & Mealey, 1991; Palincsar & Brown, 1984; Paris, 1988; Paris & Winograd, 1990; Pintrich, Garcia, & De Groot, 1994; Pressley, Borkowski, & Schneider, 1987; Pressley, El-Dinary, Marks, Brown, & Stein, 1992; Pressley, Harris, & Marks, 1992; Rosenshine & Meister, 1992; Rosenshine et al., 1996; J. W. Thomas, 1993a; Vygotsky, 1978; C. E. Weinstein, Goetz, & Alexander, 1988; West, Farmer, & Wolff, 1991; Winne, 1995; E. Wood et al., 1994.

Graduates of successful study skills training programs are more confident about their ability to succeed in the classroom and, in fact, do achieve at higher levels (Paris, 1988; Pressley et al., 1992; J. E. Wilson, 1988).

How can we help students "learn how to learn"? Researchers have identified several principles that describe the conditions under which students are most likely to acquire and use effective study skills. Table 8–3 presents these principles, as well as their implications for classroom practice.

Considering Diversity in Higher-Level Thinking Processes

We have noted the importance of a solid knowledge base for both successful problem solving and effective study strategies. Students with different backgrounds will, of course, have different knowledge bases, and such diversity will naturally affect their ability to deal with specific classroom tasks. For instance, our students will use more effective study strategies when they read textbook materials consistent with their own cultural experiences (Pritchard, 1990).

Furthermore, students' previous experiences may have influenced the particular thinking skills that they have developed. For example, thanks to the phenomenon of situated cognition, some students may have developed effective problem-solving strategies within the contexts of their own home and neighborhood environments (e.g., easily performing complex mathematical calculations while selling gum and candy on the street) yet have difficulty transferring what they've learned to more formal classroom tasks involving similar skills (Carraher et al., 1985; Gay & Cole, 1967). In some cultures, respect for one's elders may be highly valued, and so critical thinking and analysis of elders' beliefs may be strongly discouraged (Delgado-Gaitan, 1994). And students whose previous

Remember that students' problem-solving skills may be somewhat context-bound. Remember, too, that not all cultures encourage critical thinking or effective study strategies.

Promoting Higher-Level Thinking Skills in Students with Special Educational Needs

STUDENTS WITH SPECIAL NEEDS	CHARACTERISTICS THAT THESE STUDENTS MAY EXHIBIT	CLASSROOM STRATEGIES THAT MAY BE BENEFICIAL FOR THESE STUDENTS
Students with specific cognitive or academic difficulties	Difficulties in problem solving, perhaps because of limited working memory capacity, inability to identify important aspects of a problem, or inability to retrieve appropriate problem-solving strategies Less metacognitive awareness or control of learning Use of few and relatively inefficient learning strategies Increased strategy use after training	Present simple problems at first, then gradually move to more difficult ones as students gain proficiency and self-confidence. Teach techniques for minimizing the load on working memory during problem solving (e.g., writing the parts of a problem on paper, making a diagram of the problem situation). Teach more effective learning strategies (e.g., taking notes, using mnemonics) and identify occasions when each strategy is likely to be useful. Scaffold students' use of new learning strategies (e.g., provide outlines to guide note taking, ask questions that encourage retrieval of prior knowledge).
Students with social or behavioral problems	Deficiencies in social problem-solving skills Limited learning strategies (for some students)	Teach social problem-solving skills (see Chapter 11 for ideas). Provide guidance in using effective learning and study strategies (e.g., give outlines that guide note taking, ask questions that encourage retrieval of prior knowledge).
Students with general delays in cognitive and social functioning	Difficulty in transferring information and skills to new situations Few effective problem-solving strategies Lack of metacognitive awareness or control of learning Lack of learning strategies, especially in the absence of strategies training	Teach new information and skills in the specific contexts and situations in which you want students to be able to use them. Present simple problems and guide students through each step of the solutions. Teach relatively simple learning strategies (e.g., rehearsal, specific mnemonics) and give students ample practice using them.

continued

STUDENTS WITH SPECIAL NEEDS	CHARACTERISTICS THAT THESE STUDENTS MAY EXHIBIT	CLASSROOM STRATEGIES THAT MAY BE BENEFICIAL FOR THESE STUDENTS
Students with physical or sensory challenges	No consistent deficits in higher-level thinking processes; the deficits observed may be due to students' limited experiences with tasks that require higher-level thinking	Address any deficits in higher-level thinking skills using strategies that you would use with nondisabled students, making appropriate accommodations for physical and sensory limitations.
Students with advanced cognitive development	Greater transfer of learning to new situations Greater effectiveness in problem solving; more sophisticated problem-solving strategies; greater flexibility in strategy use; less susceptibility to mental sets Use of relatively sophisticated learning strategies	Place greater emphasis on higher-level thinking skills (e.g., transfer, problem solving) within the curriculum. Teach higher-level thinking skills within the context of specific classroom topics rather than in isolation from academic content.

Sources: Brownell, Mellard, & Deshler, 1993; Candler-Lotven et al., 1994; B. Clark, 1997; Campione et al., 1985; DuPaul & Eckert, 1994; N. R. Ellis, 1979; E. S. Ellis & Friend, 1991; Frasier, 1989; Grodzinsky & Diamond, 1992; K. R. Harris, 1982; Heward, 1996; M. C. Linn et al., 1989; Maker, 1993; Maker & Schiever, 1989; Meichenbaum, 1977; C. D. Mercer, 1991; Patton et al., 1990; Piirto, 1994; Porath, 1988; Pressley, 1995; Pulos & Linn, 1981; Scruggs & Mastropieri, 1992; Stanley, 1980; H. L. Swanson, 1993; Torrance, 1989; Turnbull et al., 1999; Wong, 1991b; Yell, 1993.

Note: Compiled with the assistance of Dr. Margie Garanzini-Daiber and Dr. Margaret Cohen, University of Missouri—St. Louis.

educational experiences have focused on drills and rote memorization (e.g., as is true in some Asian schools) may have little awareness of the value of such learning strategies as meaningful learning and elaboration (Ho, 1994; Purdie & Hattie, 1996).

Accommodating Students with Special Needs

We are especially apt to find diversity in the higher-level thinking skills of our students with special needs. Table 8–4 presents some characteristics we are likely to see in these students.

Particularly noteworthy in this context is the diversity that we are apt to find in students' metacognitive awareness and use of study strategies. Many of our students with learning disabilities will demonstrate little knowledge or use of effective strategies (E. S. Ellis & Friend, 1991; H. L. Swanson, 1993; Wong, 1991b). Students with mental retardation are likely to show even greater deficits in metacognitive skills; in addition, they will often have difficulty transferring any strategies they learn to new situations (Campione, Brown, & Bryant, 1985). In contrast, our gifted students will typically have more sophisticated study strategies than their classmates (Candler-Lotven, Tallent-Runnels, Olivárez, & Hildreth, 1994).

For many students with special needs, we may have to teach complex cognitive skills explicitly and with considerable **metacognitive scaffolding**—that is, with close guidance and assistance in the use of specific learning strategies. For example, we might provide partially filled-in outlines to guide students' note taking (Heward, 1996); Figure 8–4 presents an example of such an outline. We might also indicate

For students with special needs, teach higher-level skills explicitly and with considerable scaffolding.

MUSCLES

A. *Number of Muscles*

    1.   There are approximately _____ muscles in the human body.

B. *How Muscles Work*

    1.   Muscles work in two ways:

        a.   They _____, or shorten.

        b.   They _____, or lengthen.

C. *Kinds of Muscles*

    1.   _____ muscles are attached to the bones by _____.

        a.   These muscles are _____(voluntary/involuntary).

        b.   The purpose of these muscles is to _____

            _____.

    2.   _____ muscles line some of the body's _____.

        a.   These muscles are _____(voluntary/involuntary).

        b.   The purpose of these muscles is to _____

            _____.

    3.   The _____ muscle is the only one of its kind; it is also called the _____.

        a.   This muscle is _____ (voluntary/ involuntary).

            The purpose of this muscle is to _____

            _____.

FIGURE 8.4

An example of metacognitive scaffolding: A partially filled-in outline that can guide students' note taking

when particular strategies (e.g., elaboration, comprehension monitoring) are appropriate and model the use of such strategies with specific classroom subject matter (E. S. Ellis & Friend, 1991). Finally, we must give students opportunities to practice their newly acquired strategies, along with feedback about how effectively they are using each one (E. S. Ellis & Friend, 1991).

The Big Picture: Promoting Higher-Level Thinking in the Classroom

Teach higher-level thinking skills within the context of specific topics.

As teachers, we will occasionally run across packaged curricular programs designed to teach complex thought processes such as problem solving, critical thinking, or study strategies in relative isolation from school subject matter. But our discussion of situated cognition tells us that such programs are likely to have little if any long-term benefit for our students. Instead, we are better advised to teach higher-level thinking skills within the context of specific topics—for example, teaching reasoning and problem-solving skills in science or teaching creativity in writing (M. C. Linn et al., 1989; Porath, 1988; Pulos & Linn, 1981; Stanley, 1980).

If you have already read the discussion of individual differences in Chapter 4, then you are familiar with Robert Sternberg's theory of intelligence. Sternberg proposes that specific cognitive processes are one critical aspect of human intelligence. To the extent that our students are able to process information in sophisticated ways—to separate important information from irrelevant details, find relationships among seemingly different ideas, interpret new situations in useful ways, identify effective problem solving strategies, critically analyze the things that they read, and so on—they all become more "intelligent" human beings.

If we focus classroom activities on the learning of isolated facts, and if we also use assessment techniques that emphasize students' knowledge of those facts, our students will naturally begin to believe that school learning is a process of absorbing information in a rote, meaningless fashion and then regurgitating it later on. In contrast, if we focus class time on *processing* information—on understanding, organizing, elaborating, applying, analyzing, and evaluating it—and if we also assess students' ability to transform classroom material, rather than simply to repeat it in its original form, then our students must begin to develop learning and memory strategies that will serve them well in the world beyond the classroom.

This chapter, as well as the preceding two chapters, has emphasized the cognitive processes that influence students' learning. In the next chapter, we will apply what we have learned about cognition to various content domains—in particular, to reading, writing, mathematics, science, and social studies.

Demonstrate both by what you say and by what you do that school is more than just a place for learning isolated facts at a rote level.

CASE STUDY: Checks and Balances

Mr. Chen has just finished a unit on the three branches of the United States Government: executive, legislative, and judicial. He is appalled at some of his students' responses to an essay question he gives. Here are some examples of his students' responses to this question:

> How do the three branches of government provide a system of "checks and balances"? Use an example to illustrate how one branch might serve as a check and balance for another branch. Do *not* use an example that was presented in class.

Debra: The judicial branch finds out if people are innocent or guilty. The executive branch executes the sentences that guilty people get.

Mark: The system of checks and balances is when one branch of government makes sure another branch doesn't do something wrong. I can't think of any examples.

Seth: I don't have anything about this in my notes. Checks and balances have something to do with the way the government spends money.

Karen: I did all the reading, honest I did! But now I can't remember anything about this.

- To what extent have these students learned the material that Mr. Chen was trying to teach them? Why are they apparently unable to identify new examples of checks and balances?

- What evidence do you see that Mr. Chen's students have poor study skills? If you were teaching Mr. Chen's class, what might you do to help the students study and learn more effectively?

Summing Up

Transfer

Transfer occurs when something learned in one situation either helps (for positive transfer) or hinders (for negative transfer) learning or performance in another situation. Transfer is more likely to occur when relevant information and skills are retrieved in the transfer situation. Unfortunately, most information and skills are acquired in specific contexts (a phenomenon known as *situated cognition*), decreasing the likelihood that they will be retrieved outside those contexts. We can do many things to help students apply what they learn in school to new situations; for instance, we can explore topics in depth rather than superficially, show students the many ways in which classroom material can be applied, and give them numerous opportunities to practice using that material, especially in real-world situations.

Problem Solving

Solving problems is one form of transfer. Schools more frequently teach students how to solve well-defined problems, rather than ill-defined ones, yet real-world problems are often quite ill-defined in nature. We can help students become more effective problem solvers in a number of ways: by teaching algorithms and heuristics relevant to various problem situations, helping students understand the meaning and rationale underlying particular problem-solving procedures, providing practice in dealing with and defining ill-defined problems, and promoting automaticity with regard to fundamental knowledge and skills.

Critical Thinking

Critical thinking involves evaluating information in terms of its accuracy and worth. It takes a variety of forms, depending on the situation; for instance, it may involve analyzing persuasive arguments, determining whether data support a particular conclusion, or choosing the best of several alternatives. As teachers, we should encourage and model a certain amount of intellectual skepticism, provide many opportunities for students to engage in critical analysis of classroom subject matter, and ask questions that guide students in their analyses.

Metacognition and Study Strategies

Metacognition includes both the beliefs that students have about their own cognitive processes and their attempts to regulate those processes to maximize learning and memory. Many students of all ages have misconceptions about how they can best learn and remember information; in other words, they are metacognitively naive. In addition to teaching academic content, we should concurrently teach students effective strategies for studying that content (e.g., elaborating, summarizing, monitoring comprehension) and give them sufficient practice and scaffolding to ensure their success in applying such strategies. Ultimately, we must help our students discover that school is more than just a place for learning isolated facts at a rote level.

Diversity in Higher-Level Thinking Processes

Our students will exhibit considerable diversity in their higher-level thinking skills. For example, students from diverse cultural backgrounds, although they may have developed effective problem-solving strategies within the contexts of their own home and neighborhood environments, may have difficulty transferring what they've learned to more formal classroom tasks involving similar skills. And many of our students with special needs may have acquired few if any effective study strategies and so may need considerable scaffolding in their early attempts at using such strategies.

KEY CONCEPTS

9

Learning in the Content Areas

W hat subjects have you especially enjoyed studying in your many years as a student? Do you enjoy classroom topics more when your teachers present them as ideas to be understood, applied, and critically analyzed, rather than just as facts and procedures to be memorized?

When I went to school in the 1950s and 1960s, the general public, as well as many teachers and educational theorists, thought that classroom instruction should be largely a process of teaching specific facts and procedures. But in recent years, theorists and practitioners alike have radically changed their thinking about how school subject matter can most effectively be taught. Although students continue to learn facts and procedures, classroom curricula increasingly focus on helping students develop higher-level thinking skills (transfer, problem solving, critical thinking, metacognitive strategies, etc.) as well (Alleman & Brophy, 1997; Glynn et al. 1991; Lester, Lambdin, & Preston, 1997; Newmann, 1997).

In this chapter, we will apply principles we have learned about cognition, knowledge construction, and higher-level thinking to learning and instruction in five areas: reading, writing, mathematics, science, and social studies. As we do so, we will consider questions such as these:

- What general principles seem to hold true regardless of the subject matter we are teaching?
- How do students' reading skills change across the school years, and how can we encourage students at various grade levels to read more effectively?
- What specific processes are involved in writing, and how can we help students develop these processes?
- How can we promote a true understanding and application of mathematics, rather than meaningless memorization of mathematical facts and procedures?
- How can we foster scientific reasoning skills, so that students apply scientific concepts and principles to address real-world problems?
- How can we encourage students to use the things they learn in social studies—in particular, in history and geography—to understand and interpret the societies and cultures in which they live?
- What things should we keep in mind when we teach various content areas to students from diverse populations?

CASE STUDY: The Birth of a Nation

Ms. Jackson recently asked her second graders to write an answer to this question: *The land we live on has been here for a very long time, but the United States has only been a country for a little more than 200 years. How did the United States become a country?* Here are some of the children's responses:

Bill: The United States began around two hundred years ago, when an Inglish ship from Ingland accadently landed on a big State that wasn't named yet. They named it America, but they didn't know there was already Indians ashore. Soon they found out, and they had a big fight. The Indians trying to fight the Inglish off, and the Inglish trying to fight off the Indians. So finally they talked and after they worked out their problems then they had a big feast for friendship and relationship.

Matt: It all staredid in eginggind they had a wore. Thein they mad a bet howevery wone the wore got a ney country. Called the united states of amarica and amaricins wone the wore. So they got a new country.

Sue: The pilgrums we're sailing to some place and a stome came and pushed them off track and they landed we're Amaraca is now and made friends with the indens and coled that spot AMARACA!

Lisa: We wone the saver wore. It was a wore for fradam and labrt. One cind of labraty is tho stashow of labrt. We got the stashew of labraty from england. Crastaver calbes daskaved Amaraca.[1]

Meg: The United States began around two hundred years ago. The dinosors hav ben around for six taosine years ago. Christfer klumbis salde the May flowr.

Ben: 2000 Days oh go George Washington gave us the Country to Live on.

■   What writing skills have all of the second graders mastered? What skills are most of them still developing? In what ways are all of these compositions very different from something a high school student might write?

■   What things have the second graders learned about American history? What misconceptions do you see in their responses? In what ways does their knowledge of history fall short of a true understanding of the birth of the United States?

[1]This student's spelling is sufficiently "creative" that a translation is probably in order: "We won the Civil War. It was a war for freedom and liberty. One kind of liberty is the Statue of Liberty. We got the Statue of Liberty from England. Christopher Columbus discovered America."

Responses courtesy of Dinah Jackson.

Applying General Principles to Teaching Classroom Subject Matter

These second graders clearly have a basic understanding of the nature of written language. For instance, they know that, at least in English, writing proceeds from left to right and from the top of the page to the bottom. They are aware that written language needs to follow certain conventions with regard to capitalization and punctuation. They have mastered the spellings of many simple words. They know, too, that how a word is spelled is, to some extent, a function of how it is pronounced—in other words, that different letters correspond to different sounds. For example, when Lisa spells *liberty* as "labrt," she is probably thinking that her word would be pronounced "LAB R T."

At the same time, the children do not yet know how to spell many words, and they are still learning the situations in which capitalization and punctuation are and are not appropriate. For instance, Matt spells *England* as "eginggind" and puts a period in the middle of what should be a sentence. By the time these students reach high school, however, they should be writing multiple-paragraph compositions that reflect a logical sequence of events. For now, only Bill's response comes close to telling a story; most of the other responses consist of short, choppy sentences that are strung together like beads.

The children have also learned a few things about American history. They know that Columbus sailed across the ocean, that people from England (the Pilgrims) were early settlers who found Native Americans already living on the land, and that George Washington was a prominent figure when the country was formed. But they don't always have their facts straight. For example, the American Revolution did not involve making a bet, Columbus did not sail on the Mayflower, and George Washington did not "give" us the country. In general, the children's knowledge of American history consists of only a few isolated pieces of information; they have little or no understanding of how the country actually came into being.

Like Ms. Jackson's assignment, many classroom tasks involve both language skills, such as reading or writing, and knowledge related to one or more academic disciplines, such as mathematics, science, or social studies. As we explore how students learn and achieve in reading, writing, math, science, and social studies, we will repeatedly run into the concepts and principles of learning and development that we have studied in previous chapters. But there are several general principles that will feature prominently in our upcoming discussions:

What other misconceptions do you see in the children's responses?

- *Constructive processes.* Learners use the information they receive from various sources to build their own, unique understandings of the world.

- *Influence of prior knowledge.* Learners' interpretations of new information and events are influenced by what they already know and believe about the world.

- *Role of metacognition.* Over time, learners develop cognitive strategies and epistemological beliefs that influence their thinking and performance within a particular content domain.

- *Qualitative changes with development.* The ways in which learners think about and understand academic subject matter are qualitatively different at different points in their cognitive development.

We see two of these principles—constructive processes and prior knowledge—at work in the second graders' history compositions. For instance, Lisa uses her knowledge of letter sounds to construct what is, to her, a reasonable spelling of *liberty*, and Meg knows that *someone* sailed on the Mayflower and assumes (incorrectly) that it must have been Columbus. As Lisa and Meg move to higher grade levels, they will construct more accurate and abstract understandings of historical events, express their thoughts on paper more thoroughly and completely, and have greater metacognitive awareness of what they are doing as they write. Furthermore, their success in learning history and other content areas will increasingly depend on their ability to learn through reading textbooks and other printed materials. Accordingly, virtually *all* teachers should teach reading to some extent, even if they are teaching courses in history, science, or mathematics.

Reading

As a topic of instruction per se, reading is taught primarily in elementary school. Many middle school and high school teachers assume that their students have achieved sufficient reading proficiency to learn successfully from textbooks and other printed materials. Such an assumption is not always warranted, however; even at the high school level, many students have not yet mastered all of the skills involved in reading effectively.

In this section, we will examine the many skills that contribute to reading ability and consider how the quality of students' reading changes over time. We will also identify a number of teaching strategies that researchers and practitioners recommend for enhancing students' ability to read and learn from written language. But first, let's look at the things that many children learn about reading and writing long before they enter school—knowledge and skills that are collectively known as *emergent literacy.*

Emergent Literacy

When you were a young child, perhaps three or four years old, you may have spent many hours listening to parents or other adults read you storybooks. What might you have learned about the nature of written language from these storybook sessions?

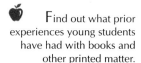
Find out what prior experiences young students have had with books and other printed matter.

Researchers have consistently found that children who are read to frequently during the preschool years, and especially children who associate reading with pleasure and enjoyment, learn to read more easily once they reach kindergarten and first grade (L. Baker, Scher, & Mackler, 1997; Crain-Thoreson & Dale, 1992; Sulzby & Teale, 1991; Whitehurst et al., 1994). Through storybook reading and other home activities that focus on either oral or written language (storytelling, object and picture identification, practice with the alphabet, rhyming games, etc.), children acquire considerable knowledge and skills essential to the reading process. For instance, they learn that:

- Reading proceeds from left to right and from the top of the page to the bottom
- Spoken language is represented in a consistent fashion in written language
- Each letter of the alphabet is associated with one or more sounds in spoken language

They may also learn to recognize their own name in print, and many children begin to recognize the logos of popular products and commercial establishments, such as Coke, Pepsi, McDonalds, and Burger King. Taken together, such knowledge and skills lay a foundation for reading and writing—a foundation that theorists call **emergent literacy.**

The Nature of Skilled Reading

Storybook reading in the early years promotes the development of emergent literacy—basic knowledge about written language and literature that provides the foundation for learning how to read and write.

Reading is a complex process that involves considerable knowledge and abilities:

- Recognizing individual sounds and letters
- Using word decoding skills
- Recognizing most words quickly and automatically
- Using context clues to facilitate word recognition
- Constructing an understanding of the writer's intended meaning
- Metacognitively regulating the reading process

Sound and Letter Recognition

A growing body of research indicates that **phonological awareness**—hearing distinct sounds, or *phonemes,* within a spoken word (e.g., detecting the sound "guh" in the word *gate*—is an essential element of successful reading. Children who have trouble identifying the specific phonemes contained in words have more difficulty reading than their classmates. Furthermore, specifically teaching students to hear the individual sounds in words enhances later reading ability (Foorman, Francis, Fletcher, Schatschneider, & Mehta, 1998; Lonigan, Burger, Anthony, & Barker, 1998; Pennington, Groisser, & Welsh, 1993). We can use strategies such as these to promote students' phonological awareness:

- Ask students to identify objects that all begin with the same sound.
- Show pictures of several objects and ask students to choose the one that begins with a different sound from the others.
- Say several words and ask students which one ends in a different sound.
- Play rhyming games. (Bradley & Bryant, 1991)

Obviously, another prerequisite for learning to read is learning to distinguish individual letters of the alphabet in uppercase and lowercase forms. Although some students will already have learned the written alphabet before they begin school, others may know few if any letters. Especially when we are teaching at the kindergarten or early elementary grade levels, one of our first orders of business must be to determine whether our students have mastered the upper- and lowercase alphabets. Before they begin reading in earnest, our students should be able to identify every letter of the alphabet quickly and effortlessly and associate each letter with one or more sounds that it "makes" in spoken language. To help students learn to recognize letters and their corresponding sounds, we can:

- Read alphabet books that embed individual letters in colorful pictures and meaningful stories.
- Ask students to make letters with their bodies (e.g., a single student stands with arms outstretched like a Y, or two students bend over and clasp hands to form an M).
- Have students practice writing the letters, first by copying them and eventually by retrieving them from memory.

Help students learn to hear the distinct sounds in words.

Make sure students achieve automaticity for letter recognition.

Word Decoding Skills

When people see a word for the first time, they often engage in **word decoding:** They identify the sounds associated with the word's letters and blend them together to determine what the word probably is. To do this, they must, of course, know how particular letters and letter combinations are typically pronounced. Here are examples of how we can promote word decoding skills:

- Teach generalizations that apply most of the time (e.g., an *e* at the end of a word is usually silent).
- Show patterns in similarly spelled and pronounced words (e.g., the *end* in *bend, mend,* and *fender*).
- Have students create nonsense words and poems using common letter combinations (e.g., *I know an old lady who swallowed a zwing, I don't why she swallowed the zwing, I guess she'll die;* Reutzel & Cooter, 1999, p. 146).
- Give students lots of practice sounding out unfamiliar words.
- Teach students how to spell the words they are learning to read. (Adams, 1990; Ehri, 1992; Ehri & Wilce, 1987; Reutzel & Cooter, 1999)

Teach word decoding strategies.

Automatic Word Recognition

Try this simple exercise.

▢ Experiencing Firsthand
An Excerpt from Webster's Dictionary

Read the following sentence as quickly as you can while also trying to make as much sense of it as you can (*Webster's Ninth,* 1991).

A *zymogram* is an electrophoretic strip or a representation of it exhibiting the pattern of separated proteins or protein components after electrophoresis.

Did you find yourself slowing down at certain points in the sentence? If so, what particular words slowed you down?

I am guessing that three words slowed you down: *zymogram, electrophoretic,* and *electrophoresis.* Unless you are a biologist, you had probably never encountered these words before. But I suspect that you read the other words—even *representation,* which has fourteen letters—with virtually no effort because you've read each of them on many previous occasions.

When students must use their limited working memory capacity to decode and interpret individual words, they have little "room" left to understand the overall meaning of what they are reading. It is essential, then, that our students develop automaticity with regard to word recognition. Ultimately, word recognition must become automatic in two ways. First, students must be able to *sight-read* words: They must be able to recognize them in a split second, without having to decode them letter by letter. Second, they must be able to *retrieve the meanings* of words immediately—for example, to know without hesitation what *pattern* and *protein* mean when those words appear in a sentence (M. J. Adams, 1990; R. G. Anderson & Freebody, 1981; Goldberg, Schwartz, & Stewart, 1977; W. S. Hall, 1989).

As you may recall from Chapter 6, automaticity develops primarily through practice, practice, and more practice. In some instances—perhaps with young children or with students who have particular difficulty learning to read (e.g., those with certain learning disabilities)—we might promote more automatic word recognition by using flashcards of individual words. And we can certainly teach the meanings of words through explicit vocabulary lessons. But probably most effective (and certainly more motivating) for promoting automatic word recognition is to encourage students to read as frequently as they possibly can.

Promote automatic recognition of words and their meanings.

Context Clues

▢ Experiencing Firsthand
A Sense of Urgency

What is the blurry word in this sentence?

I need to make sure that I get to the ▨▨▨ on time today.

Even when people have learned words to a level of automaticity, they recognize them faster and more easily when they see them within the context of a sentence than when they see them in isolation (R. F. West & Stanovich, 1978). Probably both the syntax and the overall meaning of the sentence provide context clues that help. For instance, when you read the sentence in the exercise just now, you undoubtedly concluded that the blurry word toward the end must be a noun (only a noun would be syntactically correct between *the* and *on*) and that the noun in question must be something that people attend and something for which punctuality is important. These clues, plus the general length and shape of the word, should have led you to identify the blurry word as *meeting.*

Effective use of context clues seems to be especially important for young readers (e.g., those in the elementary grades), perhaps, in part, because these students have not fully developed automaticity in word recognition (Goldsmith-Phillips, 1989; R. F. West & Stanovich, 1978). As teachers, we must remember that the English language isn't completely dependable when it comes to letter-sound correspondences; for example, the letters *ough* are pronounced differently in *through, though, bough,* and *rough.* Accordingly, we should encourage students to use context clues whenever they encounter a word they don't know, perhaps simply by posing the question, "What do you know about the word just by looking at the words around it?"

Encourage students to use the context to identify unfamiliar words.

Meaning Construction

Most reading theorists today believe that reading is very much a constructive process (e.g., E. H. Hiebert & Raphael, 1996; Weaver & Kintsch, 1991). When people read, they usually go beyond the words themselves: They identify main ideas, draw inferences, make predictions about what the author is likely to say next, and so on. Fairly sophisticated readers may also find symbolism in a work of fiction, evaluate the quality of evidence in a persuasive essay, or identify assumptions or philosophical perspectives that underlie a particular piece of writing.

Effective meaning construction in reading is, of course, enhanced by the amount of knowledge that the reader already has about the topic in question (Beck, McKeown, Sinatra, & Loxterman, 1991; Lipson, 1983). For instance, if you were a biologist who knew what *electrophoretic* and *electrophoresis* were, then you would have little difficulty comprehending the *zymogram* definition I gave you earlier. Similarly, second graders who already know a lot about spiders remember more when they read a passage about spiders and can draw inferences more readily than their less knowledgeable classmates (Pearson, Hansen, & Gordon, 1979). Helpful, too, is knowledge about the structures that various types of literature typically follow; for example, the events described in works of fiction usually follow a chronological sequence, and persuasive essays usually begin with a main point and then present evidence to support that point (Byrnes, 1996; Dryden & Jefferson, 1994; Graesser, Golding, & Long, 1991; J. M. Mandler, 1987).

Here are several suggestions that experts have offered for helping students construct meaning from the things they read:

- Remind students of the things they already know about the topic.
- Give students specific training in drawing inferences from reading material.
- Relate events in a story to students' own lives.
- Ask students to form mental images of the people or events depicted in a reading passage.
- Ask students to retell or summarize what they have read, perhaps after each sentence, paragraph, or section. (Chi, de Leeuw, Chiu, & LaVancher, 1994; Gambrell & Bales, 1986; Hemphill & Snow, 1996; Morrow, 1989; Oakhill & Yuill, 1996)

Support (scaffold) students' efforts to make sense of what they read.

Metacognitive Processes

Not only do good readers work actively to construct meaning from what they read, they also "supervise" their own reading at a metacognitive level. Many of the metacognitive strategies identified in Chapter 8—for instance, elaborating, summarizing, and comprehension monitoring—are particularly important in reading. Good readers also spend more time on parts of a passage that are likely to be critical to their overall understanding, and they frequently make predictions about what they will read next (Gernsbacher, 1994; Hyona, 1994; Palincsar & Brown, 1984). And good readers typically set goals for their reading; for example, they may ask themselves questions that they hope to answer as they read (W. S. Hall, 1989; N. M. Webb & Palincsar, 1996).

In Chapter 8, we identified several ways of promoting effective metacognitive strategies, and many of them are certainly applicable to teaching reading. We can further encourage metacognitive processing by explicitly teaching students strategies that good readers use; for instance, we can teach them to

What goal(s) are *you* trying to accomplish by reading this section on reading?

- Delete trivial information
- Delete redundant information
- Identify general ideas that incorporate several more specific ideas (Bean & Steenwyk, 1984)

🍎 Teach students
strategies that help them
learn from what they read.

We can also teach them to make predictions as they read—perhaps by looking at the title and section headings, and perhaps later by considering the ideas that have already been presented—and then to reflect back on the accuracy of their predictions (Pressley et al., 1994). Group discussions of reading material provide yet another way of enhancing students' metacognitive skills; I will describe some techniques along this line later in this section, as well as in the discussion of *reciprocal teaching* in Chapter 14.

Developmental Changes in Reading

As students grow older and gain more experience as readers, their reading processes and skills improve in several ways. A major accomplishment during the kindergarten and early elementary grades is the development of phonological awareness; by second grade, most students are able to divide words into syllables and into the specific phonemes that make up each syllable (Lonigan et al., 1998; Owens, 1996). Reading instruction in the early elementary years typically focuses on word recognition and basic comprehension skills, often within the context of reading simple stories (Chall, 1983; Owens, 1996).

In the upper elementary grades, most students have acquired sufficient linguistic knowledge and reading skills that they can focus almost exclusively on reading comprehension (Owens, 1996). They are more adept at drawing inferences, and they become increasingly able to learn new information from what they read (Chall, 1983; Paris & Upton, 1976). At this point, they tend to take the things they read at face value, with little attempt to evaluate them critically and little sensitivity to obvious contradictions (Chall, 1983; Johnston & Afflerbach, 1985; Markman, 1979).

As students move into the secondary grades, they become more skillful at identifying main ideas, summarizing passages of text, monitoring their comprehension, and backtracking when they don't understand something the first time they read it (Alvermann & Moore, 1991; Byrnes, 1996; Garner, 1987). They also begin to recognize that different authors sometimes present different viewpoints on a single issue, and they read written material with a critical eye instead of accepting it as absolute truth (Chall, 1983; Owens, 1996). Furthermore, they become more cognizant of the subtle aspects of fiction—for example, the underlying theme and symbolism of a novel (Chall, 1983). We must keep in mind, however, that students' general knowledge of the world and their experiences with a variety of both fictional and nonfictional literature will definitely have an impact on their ability to read challenging material successfully (Byrnes, 1996).

When students reach high school, they begin to read text with a critical eye; they no longer take everything they read at face value.

🍎 Make sure that
reading materials and
assigned tasks are
developmentally
appropriate for students'
reading skills.

General Strategies for Teaching Reading

As we identified the various processes involved in effective reading, we also identified instructional strategies that should promote the development of those processes. Here are several more general strategies to keep in mind:

🍎 Use authentic
reading materials, and give
students some choices
about what they read.

• *Make frequent use of authentic reading materials, and give students some choices about what they read.* In Chapter 8, we noted the importance of using *authentic activities* for promoting real-world transfer of the knowledge and skills that students learn in the classroom. Many reading theorists advocate the frequent use of authentic reading materials as well—having students read storybooks, novels, magazine articles, newspaper articles, poems, and so on—rather than a heavy reliance on the traditional "reading" textbooks so common in the 1970s and 1980s. Furthermore, research consistently tells us that students read more energetically and persistently, use more sophisticated metacognitive strategies, and remember more content when they are interested in what they are reading (R. C. Anderson, Shirey, Wilson, & Fielding, 1987; Guthrie et al., 1998; Sheveland, 1994).

In its most extreme form, this approach is known as **whole language instruction:** teaching reading exclusively by using authentic reading materials (Goodman, 1989; Goodman & Goodman, 1979; Weaver, 1990). Basic knowledge and skills related to reading, such as letter-sound correspondences and word recognition, are taught solely within the context of real-world reading and writing tasks, and far less time is devoted to instruction of such skills than is true in more traditional reading programs. Instead, students spend a great deal of time writing and talking with their classmates about what they have read.

Numerous research studies have been conducted comparing the effectiveness of whole-language and basic-skills approaches to reading instruction; taken together, these studies do not tell us conclusively that one approach is better than the other (Byrne, Freebody, & Gates, 1992; McKenna, Stratton, Grindler, & Jenkins, 1995; Purcell-Gates, McIntyre, & Freppon, 1995; Sacks & Mergendoller, 1997; Stahl, McKenna, & Pagnucco, 1994). As a result of such research, as well as the research indicating the importance of early phonological awareness for later reading success, many theorists urge us to strike a balance between whole-language activities and basic-skills instruction (Mayer, 1999).

• *Use meaningful contexts to teach basic reading skills.* Even when we do teach basic skills such as letter-sound correspondences, word decoding, and use of context clues, we do not necessarily need to teach them through dry, drill-and-practice workbooks. Such workbooks are often not terribly motivating for students, who may see assignments in such books primarily as exercises to complete as quickly as possible (E. H. Hiebert & Raphael, 1996). With a little thought, we can create meaningful contexts to teach almost any basic skill. Here are just three examples:

Playing a game of "Twenty Questions" that begins with a hint such as, "I'm thinking of something in the classroom that begins with the letter B"

Giving students a homework assignment to bring in three objects that begin with the letter T and three more that end with the letter T

Using children's poems that illustrate common letter patterns (e.g., Dr. Seuss's *The Cat in the Hat* or *Green Eggs and Ham*)

And we can teach these and other basic skills, such as using context clues to identify unfamiliar words and making predictions about what will happen next, while students read interesting storybooks with simple language and colorful illustrations (Clay, 1985).

• *Engage students in group discussions about the things they read.* Students can often construct meaning more effectively when they discuss their readings with their classmates. For instance, we can form "book clubs" in which students lead small groups of classmates in discussions about specific books (McMahon, 1992). We can hold "grand conversations" about a particular work of literature, asking students to share their responses to questions with no single right answers—perhaps questions related to interpretations or critiques of various aspects of a text (Eeds & Wells, 1989; E. H. Hiebert & Raphael, 1996). And we can encourage students to think about a piece of literature from the author's perspective, posing such questions as "What's the author's message here?" or "Why do you think the author wants us to know about this?" (Beck, McKeown, Worthy, Sandora, & Kucan, 1996).

Teach basic skills within meaningful contexts.

Promote meaning construction through group discussion.

Students develop additional insights about both reading and writing when they become authors themselves and share their writing with classmates. We turn our attention now to the nature of writing and to strategies for helping students become proficient writers.

Writing

The second graders in our opening case study clearly had a long way to go in terms of writing development. This is hardly surprising, because writing is a very complex and multifaceted skill. In addition to mastering the vocabulary and syntax of the English language, students must also master elements of written language—spelling, punctuation, capitalization—that aren't directly evident in speech. Yet good writing goes far beyond knowing how to spell words, where to put periods and commas, and when to capitalize; more importantly, it involves putting words together in such a way that readers can construct a reasonable understanding of the author's intended message. Let's look more closely at the processes that skilled writing involves.

The Nature of Skilled Writing

THINKING ABOUT WHAT YOU KNOW

How much planning do you do for a term paper before you actually begin writing? What strategies do you use as you write so that you can create a message that the reader will be able to understand? How much time do you spend revising what you've written, and what kinds of errors do you specifically look for when you edit your work?

As you might guess, students who are better readers also tend to be better writers; this correlation is undoubtedly due, at least in part, to the fact that general language ability—knowledge and effective use of grammar, vocabulary, and so on—provides a foundation for both reading and writing (Perfetti & McCutchen, 1987; Shanahan & Tierney, 1990). In addition to proficiency in English, the following processes are also central to effective writing:

Planning:
Setting one or more goals for a writing project
Identifying relevant knowledge
Organizing ideas

Drafting:
Writing a first draft
Addressing mechanical issues

Metacognition:
Metacognitively regulating the writing process

Revision:
Editing (i.e., identifying weaknesses)
Rewriting

These processes are summarized in Table 9–1. Skilled writing probably typically involves moving back and forth among them throughout a writing project (Benton, 1997; Flower & Hayes, 1981; Kellogg, 1994). Let's look more closely at each one.

T A B L E 9.1 Components of Skilled Writing

COMPONENT	SPECIFIC PROCESSES INVOLVED	CHALLENGES THAT STUDENTS FACE	INSTRUCTIONAL STRATEGIES
Planning	Setting goals	Students must decide what they want to accomplish through their writing.	Ask students to answer questions such as "Why am I writing this?" and "Who am I writing for?" before they begin to write.
	Identifying relevant knowledge	Students must identify what they already know about a topic. In some cases, they must also conduct research to obtain the information they need.	Have students brainstorm ideas before they begin writing. Teach essential research strategies (e.g., finding information in the library or on the Internet).
	Organizing ideas	Students must create a logical sequence in which to present their ideas.	Have students develop an outline before they begin writing. Teach specific structures that students might follow as they write (e.g., a structure for a persuasive essay, the typical elements of a short story).
Drafting	Writing a first draft	Students must get their ideas on paper in a reasonably logical and coherent fashion.	Remind students that they must communicate their ideas in a way that their readers can understand. Give students some strategies for communicating effectively (e.g., using examples, analogies, rhetorical questions). Ask students not to worry too much about spelling, punctuation, and capitalization in the first draft. When students know how to spell few if any words (especially in the early elementary grades), let them dictate their stories.
	Addressing mechanics	Students must use correct word spellings and apply rules and conventions regarding grammar, punctuation, and capitalization.	Provide some systematic instruction in spelling, grammar, punctuation, and capitalization. Allow students to use spell and grammar checkers on word processing programs.
Metacognition	Metacognitively regulating the writing process	Students must continually monitor their writing for clarity and logical sequencing, and they must continually keep both their goals and audience in mind.	Give students a list of questions to consider as they write (e.g., "Am I achieving my goal?" "Am I following a logical train of thought?"). Ask students to write for a specific, concrete audience (e.g., for a younger child or for a member of Congress). Have students write in pairs as a way of encouraging them to verbalize issues related to writing effectively.
Revising	Editing	Students must find mechanical errors; they must also identify problems in organization, clarity, and style.	Provide frequent, concrete, and constructive feedback about both content and mechanics. Have students meet to edit one another's work.
	Rewriting	Students must address the errors and problems they've identified during editing and eventually produce a clear, cohesive, and error-free text.	Encourage students to use a word processor so that they can make changes more easily. Have students collaborate with one another as they make revisions.

Setting Goals

Certainly the first step in any writing project is to determine what one wants to accomplish by writing. For example, I have two primary goals as I write this textbook: (1) to provide an accurate synthesis of what psychologists and educators have discovered about how students learn and develop, and (2) to help my readers learn this information meaningfully, so that they can easily transfer it to their future instructional practices. But writers may have other goals instead—perhaps to entertain, describe, report, or persuade. I suspect that many students have only one, not terribly useful goal when they complete written classroom assignments: to write something that will earn them a good grade.

Expert writers identify specific goals before they begin writing, but beginning writers rarely give much thought to their objectives (Scardamalia & Bereiter, 1986). As teachers, we must help our students establish clear goals for themselves before they begin to write, and such goals should focus more on conveying intended meanings successfully than on addressing such writing mechanics as spelling and punctuation (Langer & Applebee, 1987). For instance, we might ask our students to address questions such as these before they put pen to paper: Why am I writing this? Who am I writing for? (Englert, Raphael, Anderson, Anthony, & Stevens, 1991). By encouraging students to clarify their writing goals, we will almost certainly help them write more effectively (Byrnes, 1996; MacArthur & Ferretti, 1997).

Help students clarify their goals for writing.

Identifying Relevant Knowledge

Whether they write fiction or nonfiction, writers can write about only the things they know or believe. Thus, they must identify what they have already learned about a topic—knowledge acquired, perhaps, through formal instruction, independent reading, or personal experience—and then, if necessary, supplement it with additional research. Effective writers typically have a solid understanding of the content about which they are writing: They have learned it in a meaningful, well-organized, and elaborated fashion (Benton, 1997; Kellogg, 1994).

Encourage students to write about things they know well.

In some situations, we will, of course, need to teach our students various strategies for locating needed information in newspapers, at the library, or on the Internet. In other situations, we may simply need to help them retrieve helpful information from their long-term memories. For instance, as a prewriting activity we might conduct small-group or whole-class discussions on the topics that students will be writing about (Boiarsky, 1982).

Conduct discussions and ask questions that promote broad searches of long-term memory.

Organizing

After identifying what they know or believe about a topic, good writers typically spend a fair amount of time organizing their ideas (Berninger, Fuller, & Whitaker, 1996; Scardamalia & Bereiter, 1987). For instance, students can organize their thoughts using such tried-and-true methods as making a list, forming clusters of related ideas, or developing an outline (Kellogg, 1994). Furthermore, we can scaffold their first attempts at particular forms of writing by providing a structure for them. For instance, when asking students to write a persuasive essay, we can suggest that they follow four steps:

Help students organize their thoughts before they begin to write.

1. Develop a topic sentence.
2. List several reasons that support the topic sentence.
3. Determine whether each reason is likely to be convincing to readers; if necessary, modify it so that it is more convincing.
4. Develop an appropriate ending or conclusion. (adapted from Graham & Harris, 1988)

When we have students write short stories, we can teach them to incorporate the features that most stories have: a setting, a main character with certain thoughts and feelings, a problem situation, an outcome, and so on (Gambrell & Chasen, 1991; Graham & Harris, 1992).

Writing a First Draft

Converting one's ideas into written language—a process known as **translating**—is possibly the most challenging part of effective writing. A good writer uses a wide variety of words and sentence structures to convey ideas, takes into account the prior knowledge that readers are likely to have, and puts words together in such a way that readers can easily construct the intended meaning (Burnett & Kastman, 1997; Byrnes, 1996; Spivey, 1997).

Many students at all grade levels think of writing as a process of putting ideas on paper, rather than as a process of presenting ideas in a way that enables their readers to *understand* those ideas. Furthermore, students rarely elaborate in writing on the ideas they present; for instance, they are reluctant to analyze, synthesize, and evaluate them. In general, students' writing tends to be *knowledge telling* rather than *knowledge transforming* (Bereiter & Scardamalia, 1987; C. A. Cameron, Hunt, & Linton, 1996; S. Greene & Ackerman, 1995; McCutchen, 1996). As examples, consider these two essays, each one written by a small group of fourth graders; both essays were supposedly written to help younger children learn about electric circuits:

Example of knowledge telling:

Electric circuits are wires that when it's closed electricity flows through and it's circular. A generator is a magnet that spins around in coils. It powers up a city or town. A conductor is what makes electricity. It powers up electrical things. (Chambliss, 1998, p. 8; reprinted by permission.)

Example of knowledge transforming:

Electric Circuits They'll Shock You

You have energy inside of you that allows you to walk, run, jump, etc. There's also another source of energy, electrical energy. It lets you turn on your light, run your computer, listen to the radio, and many other things.

But before you experiment let us caution you that electricity can be very dangerous so don't experiment without adult supervision. Here are some safety precautions for when you experiment: Never touch the copper part of a wire. Do NOT leave liquid substances near electrical equipment. Do not open a battery without protection (it contains acid).

Now that you know the rules let me tell you about electricity. When you turn on your light that means you have made a circuit flow, when you turn off the light that means you broke the circuit. How does a light bulb light you ask? Well you have to have a complete circuit. Let all the equipment touch each other. The wires must touch the battery. The battery must touch the light. The light must touch the battery.

If you don't understand how the circuit breaks, here is an example. When you are using the refrigerator, you open it, and all the air comes out. When you are not using the refrigerator, you close it, and the air no longer comes out.

Now that you know about electricity it won't shock you the way it works. (Chambliss, 1998, p. 8; reprinted by permission.)

When students engage in knowledge telling, they are likely to write their thoughts in the order in which they retrieve them from long-term memory, with little regard to constructing a cohesive, logical, and complete piece of written work. In contrast, when students engage in knowledge transforming, they tailor their presentation to the things that their intended audience is likely to know and systematically lead their readers toward a better understanding of the topic in question.

Students may knowledge-tell, rather than knowledge-transform, partly because they must consider *so* many different things—the content, the audience, spelling, grammar, punctuation, handwriting, and so on—when they write that their working memories simply cannot handle the load (Benton, 1997; Flower & Hayes, 1981; McCutchen, 1996). It is usually beneficial, then, to have students address only one aspect of the writing process at

Portray writing as a process of knowledge transforming rather than knowledge telling.

The translation aspect of writing involves many things: considering what the reader is likely to know already, expressing thoughts coherently, spelling words correctly, adhering to conventions of grammar and punctuation, and so on. Most students probably don't have the working memory capacity to handle all of these tasks simultaneously.

a time; for instance, we might ask them to plan and organize their thoughts *before* they actually begin writing and ignore the mechanics of writing until after they have written their first draft (K. R. Harris & Graham, 1992; Treiman, 1993). We may also want to brainstorm with students about strategies for communicating ideas effectively—for instance, using examples, analogies, graphics, and rhetorical questions—to a particular audience (Chambliss, 1998). And we can illustrate knowledge transforming by showing students actual examples of how expert writers communicate their ideas (Byrnes, 1996; Englert et al., 1991).

Addressing Writing Mechanics

Expert writers have typically learned the mechanical aspects of writing—spelling, punctuation, capitalization, and proper syntax (correct word order, subject-verb agreement, etc.)—to a level of automaticity. Yet it makes little sense to postpone writing tasks until students have completely mastered writing mechanics; if we did so, our students might never have a chance to write!

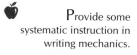
Downplay the importance of mechanics in early stages of writing.

Too much emphasis on writing mechanics is likely to discourage our students from wanting to write very much in the future. When we put writing mechanics aside for awhile—for the first draft in the case of older students and perhaps altogether in the case of very young ones—we are likely to see our students write more frequently and create longer and more complex texts (L. K. Clarke, 1988; Leu & Kinzer, 1995; Treiman, 1993). For instance, kindergartners and first graders can write a great deal using "invented spellings" that often only vaguely resemble actual words. Consider this kindergartner's creation entitled "My Garden" (note that "HWS" is *house*):

THIS IS A HWS

THE SUN

WL SHIN

ND MI

GRDN

WL GRO

(Hemphill & Snow, 1996, p. 192)

If time and resources allow, and especially if we are teaching in the early elementary grades, we might even have our students initially *dictate* stories and compositions for someone else to write down (Scardamalia, Bereiter, & Goelman, 1982).

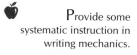
Provide some systematic instruction in writing mechanics.

Eventually, of course, we must teach our students the conventions of written language and stress the importance of using those conventions for effective communication (Treiman, 1993). For instance, we should teach general rules of punctuation and capitalization, stress the importance of subject-verb agreement, and introduce various kinds of simple and complex sentences. And we will undoubtedly want to provide some explicit instruction in spelling. Theorists and practitioners have offered several strategies for spelling instruction:

- Point out letter-sound correspondences in how words are spelled.
- Draw analogies among words that are spelled similarly.
- Have students write each word several times as they study it.
- Stress the importance of correct spelling for enhancing a writer's credibility. (K. J. Brown, Sinatra, & Wagstaff, 1996; Kernaghan & Woloshyn, 1994; M. H. Thomas & Dieter, 1987)

Metacognition

Throughout the writing process, writers must monitor their progress and the effectiveness of what they have written, addressing questions such as these:

- Am I achieving my goal(s) for writing this piece?
- Am I explaining myself clearly?
- Am I following a logical train of thought?
- Am I giving examples to illustrate my ideas?
- Am I supporting my opinions with valid arguments?

Answers to such questions influence the course of action that the writer takes next.

Furthermore, skillful writers continually keep their anticipated readers in mind (Kellogg, 1994; Paris & Cunningham, 1996). When we converse with other people, we get constant verbal and nonverbal feedback from them; for instance, they ask questions when they don't understand and let us know when they disagree with us. But when we write, we do so in isolation from our audience. We must therefore make assumptions about our readers' prior knowledge, vocabulary level, cognitive maturity, and motivation for reading what we have written.

All too often, elementary and secondary students write without giving much thought to who their audience might be; this is not surprising given the fact that, in most cases, the only person who *does* read their work is their teacher. Yet our students are more likely to write effectively when they adapt their writing to a particular audience, as did the fourth graders who wrote the "Electric Circuits They'll Shock You" essay (Burnett & Kastman, 1997; C. A. Cameron et al., 1996; M. Sperling, 1996). For example, we might ask our students to write a letter to people their own age who live in environments very different from their own—perhaps in a large city or in farm country (Benton, 1997; Kroll, 1984). Or we might ask them to imagine themselves in particular roles—perhaps as reporters investigating a news story or travelers hoping to spread peace throughout the world (J. J. Schneider, 1998). Students as young as seven or eight can adapt their writing to different audiences when they understand who those audiences are (J. J. Schneider, 1998).

Ask students to write for a particular audience.

Editing

▢ Experiencing Firsthand
What's Wrong?

Here is how one eighth-grade girl responded to the question: *How did the United States become a country?* As you read it, mark places that need revision.

> The first people here were what we called the Native Americans they crossed over to America on a land Bridge or as some people say.
>
> In Europue people where thinking the world was flat and if you sailed on and on you would fall of the world but Christopher Columbus did not beleave that he believed it was round. So Christopher Columbus sailed to America. Soon after Pilgrims came to get away from the Cathalic religion. More people came over and keept pushing the Indians off their land and taking what was not theirs the Indians where willing to share it but americans just took it. Then the people wanted to break away from Brittany. Then Americans fought with each other over many things like slaver. And North won. (courtesy of Dinah Jackson)

Now count how many times you marked these kinds of errors:

Spelling errors	_____	Indentation errors	_____
Punctuation errors	_____	Run-on sentences	_____

Capitalization errors	_____	Unclear writing	_____
Factual errors	_____	Problems of style	_____

What kinds of problems did you focus on when you edited the student's composition?

How much did you focus on writing mechanics (spelling, capitalization, etc.) in your editing? Did you identify any problems *other* than mechanical errors? Did you find the two factual errors? The Pilgrims wanted to leave the Church of England, not the Catholic church, and they left Britain, not Brittany (a region in France). Did you note any instances of unclear writing? For instance, in the phrase "taking what was not theirs" in the second paragraph, the meanings of *what* and *theirs* are not clear. And what about the overall style of the piece? The phrase "or as some people say" serves no purpose, and the last sentence is short and choppy. In general, the student has engaged in knowledge telling rather than knowledge transforming: She has simply written down her thoughts, apparently in the order in which she retrieved them from long-term memory, and made no attempt to tie them together into a coherent whole.

Unfortunately, when teachers provide feedback about students' writing, they tend to focus more on mechanical errors than on problems with style, clarity, or cohesiveness (Byrnes, 1996). So it is not surprising that when students edit their own work, they, too, focus on mechanics (Berninger et al., 1996; McCutchen, Kerr, & Francis, 1994). Many students, especially those in the elementary grades, believe that they are expressing themselves more clearly than they actually are; they have difficulty reading their own writing as another person might read it (E. J. Bartlett, 1982; Beal, 1996).

Our students can identify weaknesses in their writing more successfully when we give them criteria that they can use to judge their work (C. B. McCormick, Busching, & Potter, 1992). It is essential, too, that we provide feedback that addresses style, clarity, and cohesiveness as well as mechanics (Benton, 1997; Covill, 1997). (We should be careful, of course, that we balance criticism with a healthy dose of feedback about what students are doing *well,* so that we don't discourage them from writing altogether!) Furthermore, we can ask students to read and respond to one another's work (Benton, 1997; C. A. Cameron et al., 1996; M. Sperling, 1996); in the process, they may become better able to examine their own writing from the perspective of potential readers.

Rewriting

Good writers almost invariably revise the things they write; in the process, they tend to focus on problems of clarity and organization while keeping in mind the overall goals of their writing (Fitzgerald, 1992; Scardamalia & Bereiter, 1986). In contrast, children and adolescents rarely revise unless a teacher or other adult specifically urges them to do so; when they *do* rewrite, they tend to make only small, superficial changes (Beal, 1996; Fitzgerald, 1987).

Sometimes students fail to address problems in clarity and organization because they haven't located these problems to begin with (Fitzgerald, 1987). But our students may also not know *how* to revise their work. Researchers have identified several strategies through which we can help our students as they revise the things they've written:

- Schedule in-class time for revising so that students can get assistance as they need it.

- Before students begin rewriting, ask them to list five things that they can do to make their writing better.

- Provide questions students should ask themselves as they rewrite (e.g., "Is this confusing?" "Do I need another example here?" "Who am I writing this for?").

Why is it so difficult for people to detect ambiguities in their own writing?

Provide the guidance and feedback students need to edit their writing.

Give students the scaffolding they need to revise their writing effectively.

- Occasionally have students work in pairs or small groups to help one another revise. (Benton, 1997; Bereiter & Scardamalia, 1987; C. A. Cameron et al., 1996; Graham, MacArthur, & Schwartz, 1995; Graves, 1983; Kish, Zimmer, & Henning, 1994; N. M. Webb & Palincsar, 1996)

Writing as a Facilitator of Learning

As you must surely have noticed in the preceding discussion, writing involves several cognitive processes that promote learning. Writers must retrieve from long-term memory the things that they already know about a topic. They must clarify and organize their thoughts sufficiently to communicate them to their readers. And a knowledge-transforming approach to writing requires writers to elaborate on the things they know—for instance, to put ideas in language that the intended audience can understand, to think of good examples, and to anticipate readers' questions. So it is not surprising that writing about a topic enhances students' understanding of that topic (Benton, 1997; S. Greene & Ackerman, 1995; Kellogg, 1994). As teachers, then, we should ask students to write frequently for two reasons: to enhance their writing ability *and* to enhance their learning more generally.

Assign writing projects as a way of promoting students' learning.

Developmental Changes in Writing

The nature and quality of students' writing changes in many ways throughout the elementary and secondary school years. In the early elementary years, writing projects typically involve narratives: Students write about their own personal experiences and create short, fictional stories (Hemphill & Snow, 1996). They have a hard time writing for an imaginary audience and, as a result, engage in knowledge telling (rather than knowledge transforming) almost exclusively (Knudson, 1992; Perfetti & McCutchen, 1987). And of course, as was evident in the second graders' compositions in the opening case study, students in the lower elementary grades are still working on the "basics" of spelling, grammar, punctuation, and capitalization.

In the later elementary grades, writing mechanics (e.g., many word spellings) are beginning to become automatic, enabling students to use more complex sentence structures and to devote more effort to communicating their thoughts effectively on paper (Owens, 1996). Furthermore, they begin to think about how their readers might respond to what they have written and so are more likely to proofread and revise their work (Owens, 1996). At this point, however, they do very little planning before they begin to write, and their writing continues to involve knowledge telling rather than knowledge transforming (Berninger et al., 1996).

We see several changes as students move through the secondary grades. First, students are more capable of analyzing and synthesizing their thoughts when they write, and so they are better able to write research papers and argumentative essays (Knudson, 1992; McCann, 1989; Spivey, 1997). They are more likely to consider specific goals when they write and therefore to include only content directly relevant to those goals (Scardamalia & Bereiter, 1987). When asked to write about a particular topic, they retrieve and generate many more ideas than students in the elementary grades do (Scardamalia & Bereiter, 1986). Their sentences are more likely to vary in structure and frequently contain one or more dependent clauses (Byrnes, 1996). And in general, they compose more cohesive, integrated texts (Berninger et al., 1996; Byrnes, 1996; Owens, 1996; Spivey, 1997). At this point, too, although many students continue to engage in knowledge telling, we start seeing regular signs of knowledge transforming as well (Spivey, 1997). As an example, consider how this eighth grader answered the question: *How did the United States become a country?*

> We became a country by way of common sense. The inhabitants on American soil thought it rather silly and ridiculus to be loyal to, follow rules and pay taxes to a ruler

who has never seen where they live. King George III had never set foot (as far as I know) on American soil, but he got taxes and other things from those who lived here. When America decied to unit and dishonnor past laws and rules, England got angry. There was a war. When we won, drew up rules, and accepted states America was born.

In a more poetic sense, we became a country because of who lived here and what they did. They actions of heros, heroines, leaders, followers, and everyday people made America famous, an ideal place to live. The different cultures and lifestyles made America unique and unlike any other place in the world. If you think about it, it's like visiting the worlds at Epcot in Florida. You can go from country to country without leaving home. (courtesy of Dinah Jackson)

The student's analogy between the United States and Disney World's Epcot Center is knowledge transforming at its finest.

General Strategies for Teaching Writing

We've already identified numerous strategies for helping students develop specific aspects of the writing process. Here are several additional strategies to promote writing development in general:

Assign authentic writing tasks.

- *Assign authentic writing tasks.* Although we would like students to be able to write for a variety of audiences, in reality most of them write primarily for one person: their teacher (Benton, 1997). By giving our students authentic, real-world writing tasks—having them write short stories for their classmates, letters to businesses and lawmakers, editorials for the local newspaper, e-mail messages to people in distant locations, and so on—we can encourage them to consider the language abilities and prior knowledge of their readers (e.g., Sugar & Bonk, 1998). Such tasks can also prompt students to set specific goals for writing and to acquire the writing skills they need to achieve those goals.

Give choices about writing topics.

- *Offer students some choices regarding writing topics.* Students write more frequently, and in a more organized and logical fashion, when they are interested in what they are writing about (Benton, 1997; Garner, 1998). For instance, one high school English teacher, who noticed that several very capable students were failing his class because they weren't completing assigned writing tasks, began having his students write about their own personal experiences and share them on the Internet with students in other classrooms; the teacher monitored their compositions for vulgar language but imposed no other restrictions. The students suddenly began writing regularly, presumably because they could write for a real audience and could now choose their own topics (Garner, 1998). As we will discover in Chapter 12, choices enhance students' sense of *self-determination,* which in turn enhances their intrinsic motivation to complete assigned tasks and, hence, to develop their academic skills.

Have students collaborate on writing projects.

- *Use peer groups to promote effective writing skills.* Earlier we noted the value of using peer groups to help students edit and revise their writing. In fact, we may want to have our students actually *write* together as well. Several studies have shown that when students collaborate on writing projects, they produce longer and more complex texts, revise more, and enhance one another's writing skills (Daiute, 1986, 1989; Daiute & Dalton, 1993).

Encourage word processing.

- *Encourage students to use word processing programs.* Word processing programs encourage students to revise; after all, it is much easier to change words and move sentences when one is working on a computer rather than on paper (Cochran-Smith, 1991; Kellogg, 1994). Word processing may also lessen students' working memory load by taking over some of the mechanical aspects of writing, thus leaving more working memory capacity to devote to the overall quality of writing (I. Jones & Pellegrini, 1996). As an illustration, consider what the same first grader wrote by hand and by computer (I. Jones & Pellegrini, 1996):

By hand:

Some busy wut to play boll But thay cnat play Boll Be cus the Big Busys and the grul wit to tale on them (p. 711)

By computer:

The man cooks some soup and he cooks carrots in the soup and the king gives the man a big hat, and the man goes to the house and the man shows the hat cap to the children. (p. 711)

A big difference, wouldn't you say?

• *Include writing assignments in all areas of the curriculum.* Writing shouldn't be a skill that only elementary teachers and secondary English teachers teach. In fact, writing takes different forms in different disciplines; for instance, writing fiction is very different from writing a science laboratory report, which in turn is very different from writing an analysis of historical documents. Ideally, *all* teachers should teach writing to some degree, and, especially at the secondary level, they should teach the writing skills specific to particular academic disciplines (Burnett & Kastman, 1997; M. Sperling, 1996).

Not only is writing often very different in different subject areas, but the very nature of thinking and learning can also be quite different as well. You will see what I mean as we explore mathematics, science, and social studies.

Have students write in all areas of the curriculum.

INTO THE CLASSROOM: Promoting Reading and Writing Skills

Help young children develop phonological awareness.

A kindergarten teacher suggests to his class, "Let's see how many words we can think of that rhyme with the word *gate*. I'll write the words on the chalkboard. Let's see if we can think of at least eight words that rhyme with *gate*."

Help students develop automaticity in word recognition and spelling, but do so within the context of authentic reading and writing activities as much as possible.

A second-grade teacher has her students read Dr. Seuss's *The Cat in the Hat*, a book that repeats many of the same words (e.g., *cat, hat, thing*) over and over again.

Have students discuss with their classmates the things they are reading and writing.

A middle school teacher has his students meet in small groups to read their short stories to one another. As each student reads his or her story, other group members ask questions for clarification and make suggestions about how to make the story better. Later, students consider their classmates' comments as they revise their stories.

Scaffold students' efforts as they work on increasingly more challenging reading and writing tasks.

A high school English teacher gives students a format to follow when writing a research paper: an introductory paragraph that describes the topic of the paper, at least three different sections within the paper that address different aspects of the topic (each one beginning with a new heading), and a "Conclusion" section that summarizes and integrates the main ideas of the paper.

Address reading and writing skills in all areas of the curriculum.

An eighth-grade social studies teacher gives her students an article to read from *Newsweek* magazine. Knowing that the reading level of the article may be challenging for many of her students, she gives them specific questions to answer as they read the article.

Mathematics

Mathematics probably causes more confusion and frustration, for more students, than any other subject in the school curriculum. The hierarchical nature of the discipline may be partly to blame for this phenomenon: To the extent that students don't completely master mathematical concepts and procedures at one grade level, they lack necessary prerequisites for learning math successfully in later grades. As increasingly more complex and abstract concepts and procedures are introduced over the years, students must resort more and more frequently to rote, meaningless learning.

Mathematics is actually a cluster of domains—arithmetic, algebra, geometry, and statistics and probability—that comprise somewhat different methods of representing situations and strategies for solving problems (De Corte, Greer, & Verschaffel, 1996). Nevertheless, we can identify several key components that underlie effective mathematical reasoning across the board. As we do so, we will also identify many strategies that can help our students become successful mathematical thinkers.

The Nature of Mathematical Reasoning

Mathematical thinking and problem solving typically require the following:

- Understanding numbers and counting
- Understanding central mathematics concepts and principles
- Encoding problem situations appropriately
- Mastering a variety of problem-solving procedures
- Relating problem-solving procedures to mathematical concepts and principles
- Relating mathematical principles to everyday situations
- Developing effective metacognitive processes and beliefs

Understanding Numbers and Counting

Many children begin counting before their third birthday, and most three- and four-year-olds can count to ten correctly (Geary, 1994). Five-year-olds can often count far beyond ten (perhaps to 50), but they may get confused about the order of such numbers as 70, 80, and 90 (Fuson & Hall, 1983). Most five-year-olds have also mastered several basic principles of counting, including these:

- *One-one principle.* Each object in the group being counted must be assigned one and only one number word; in other words, you say "one" while pointing to one object, "two" while pointing to another, and so on, until every object has been counted once.

- *Cardinal principle.* The last number word counted indicates the number of objects in the group; in other words, if you count up to five when counting objects, then there are five objects in the group.

- *Order-irrelevance principle.* A group of objects has the same number regardless of the order in which they are counted. (Gallistel & Gelman, 1992; Gelman & Gallistel, 1978)

Many five-year-olds have also developed some simple procedures for adding and subtracting—procedures that, in most cases, they have developed on their own (Bermejo, 1996; Correa, Nunes, & Bryant, 1998; Geary, 1994). For instance, if they want to add a group of five objects and a group of three objects, they won't necessarily begin counting with *one*; instead, they may begin with *five* and then count the smaller group: "Five, six, seven, eight." They might do something similar for subtracting, starting with the original number of objects and then counting down the number of objects removed: "Eight, seven, six, five." Even-

Do you sometimes use your fingers when doing simple math? In what way do your fingers help you?

tually, children no longer need to have the objects in front of them when they add and subtract; instead, they use their fingers to represent the objects (Bermejo, 1996).

Certainly not all young children acquire the basic understanding of counting, numbers, addition, and subtraction just described. Yet such understanding forms the basic foundation for the arithmetic that we teach in the early elementary years. Especially if we are teaching kindergartners or first graders, we must determine what our students do and do not know about numbers and remediate any weaknesses in their understanding. Numerous activities and games involving counting, comparing quantities, adding, and subtracting—always using concrete objects—are likely to be helpful. We may also want to use a number line to help young children develop an understanding of how numbers relate to one another (Greeno, Collins, & Resnick, 1996; S. Griffin et al., 1995; S. A. Griffin, Case, & Siegler, 1994).

Determine whether children can count and have a true understanding of what numbers are.

Understanding Central Concepts and Principles

In addition to a basic understanding of numbers, mathematical reasoning requires an understanding of numerous concepts and principles. For instance, students must master such concepts as *negative number, right angle,* and *variable* and such principles as these:

- Multiplying a positive number by a negative number always yields a negative number.
- The three angles of a triangle always have a total of 180°.
- When an equation of the form $ax + by + c = 0$ is plotted on a graph, all possible solutions for x and y form a straight line.

Growing children are unlikely to develop most of these concepts and principles on their own; instead, some degree of formal instruction seems to be essential (De Corte et al., 1996; Geary, 1994; Ginsburg, Posner, & Russell, 1981).

The more abstract mathematical concepts and principles are, the more difficulty our students are likely to have understanding them (Byrnes, 1996). With a little creativity, we can translate abstract mathematical ideas into concrete form; Figure 9–1 presents three examples.

Encoding Problems Appropriately

As noted in Chapter 8, an essential step in solving a problem is to encode it—that is, to think of it as being a certain *kind* of problem. For instance, you would immediately categorize this problem:

We must be sure that children have a basic understanding of numbers and counting before we introduce more advanced mathematical concepts and principles.

> Mary has five marbles. John gave her seven more. How many does she have altogether?

as an addition problem. And you should recognize this problem:

> I have a carpet that is 45 square feet in area. It is 4 feet longer than it is wide. What are the dimensions of my carpet?

as an area-of-a-rectangle problem. You might also identify it as an algebra problem, because the two numbers you need to calculate the area (the width and length) are unknowns.

At the high school level, encoding algebra problems poses a challenge for many students (Clement, 1982; Geary, 1994). And students of all ages tend to have difficulty

Use concrete situations to illustrate abstract ideas.

How might you set up (encode) the "carpet" problem using algebra?

encoding *relational problems*—problems in which only comparative numbers are given—and hence are often unable to solve problems such as this one:

> Laura is 3 times as old as Maria was when Laura was as old as Maria is now. In 2 years Laura will be twice as old as Maria was 2 years ago. Find their present ages. (Mayer, 1982, p. 202)

Even college students have trouble encoding and solving this problem (Mayer, 1982). (Laura is 18 and Maria is 12.)

TEACHING FRACTIONS

Pizza A is divided into six equal pieces. Each piece is $\frac{1}{6}$ of the pizza.

Pizza B is divided into eight equal pieces. Each piece is $\frac{1}{8}$ of the pizza.

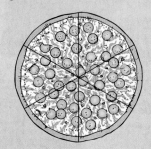

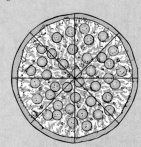

- *Which is bigger, $\frac{1}{6}$ or $\frac{1}{8}$?*

$$\frac{1}{6} > \frac{1}{8}$$

- *How many pieces equal $\frac{1}{2}$ of each pizza?*

3 pieces $= \frac{1}{2}$ 4 pieces $= \frac{1}{2}$

$\frac{1}{6} + \frac{1}{6} + \frac{1}{6} = \frac{3}{6}$ $\frac{1}{8} + \frac{1}{8} + \frac{1}{8} + \frac{1}{8} = \frac{4}{8}$

In other words, $\frac{3}{6} = \frac{1}{2}$ In other words, $\frac{4}{8} = \frac{1}{2}$

- *Which is more, $\frac{2}{3}$ of a pizza or $\frac{5}{8}$ of a pizza?*

Four pieces of Pizza A are more pizza than five pieces of Pizza B.

So $\frac{2}{3} > \frac{5}{8}$

TEACHING NEGATIVE NUMBERS

(Based on a strategy used by Jaime Escalante in *Stand and Deliver* [Musca & Menendez, 1988])

Imagine that you dig a hole in the ground like this:

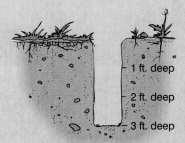

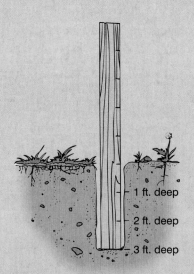

The bottom of the hole is 3 feet below ground level. If you think of the ground as 0, then the bottom of the hole is –3.

You want to put a wooden post in the hole so that it rises 5 feet above the ground. *How long does the post need to be?*

The pole needs to be 8 feet long.
–3 + 8 = 5

FIGURE 9.1

Illustrating abstract mathematical concepts and principles in concrete ways

Chapter 8 offered several suggestions for helping students encode problems more effectively: We can give them real objects or pictures that can help them think about a problem in concrete terms, encourage them to draw their *own* pictures or diagrams, and point out features of a problem that should remind them of similar problems. Several additional strategies are useful as well (Mayer, 1999). We can give students a large number of problems and ask them only to categorize the problems, not to solve them. We

Give students practice 🍎 in encoding problems correctly.

TEACHING THE AREA OF A PARALLELOGRAM

(Modeled after Sayeki, Ueno, & Nagasaka, 1991)

Imagine that you have a pile of paper. You look at it from the side, like this:

The side of the pile forms a rectangle that is 11 inches across and 5 inches high. We know that the area of a rectangle is its length × its height.

$$11 \times 5 = 55$$

The area of this rectangle is 55 square inches.

Now we push the pile of papers from one end so that the side forms a parallelogram, like this:

There is still the same amount of paper, so the area of the parallelogram is still the same.

$$11 \times 5 = 55$$

We push the papers sideways even more, like this:

Even though the shape of the parallelogram is different than before, there is *still* the same amount of paper. The area of a parallelogram is always its length × its height.

$$11 \times 5 = 55$$

FIGURE 9.1
continued

can give them problems with irrelevant as well as relevant information (e.g., in the "carpet" problem presented earlier, we might include information about how old the carpet is or how much it cost). And we should definitely mix different kinds of problems together (e.g., problems requiring addition, subtraction, multiplication, and division) so that students get in the habit of encoding different problems differently (Mayer, 1999).

Mastering Problem-Solving Procedures

Many mathematical problem-solving procedures involve specific algorithms that, when correctly applied, always yield a correct answer. For instance, students learn algorithmic procedures for doing long division, multiplying and dividing fractions, and solving for x in algebraic equations. Problem-solving heuristics sometimes come into play as well. For instance, there aren't always specific algorithms that students can use in geometric proofs. As an illustration, let's use this problem from Chapter 8:

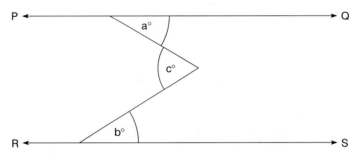

Prove that, if $a + b = c$, then lines PQ and RS must be parallel.

There is no single "right" way to prove this point. Instead, we might experiment with the situation, perhaps extending some of the lines and considering other angles, like this:

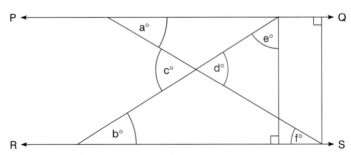

By using principles related to the angles of triangles and intersecting lines, we can eventually prove that, yes, lines PQ and RS must be parallel.

As teachers, there are several things we can do to help students master mathematical procedures. In some cases—for instance, in basic addition, subtraction, multiplication, and division—we may want to replace algorithms with quickly retrievable facts; after all, retrieving $5 + 3 = 8$ uses less working memory capacity than an algorithm such as counting "five . . . and six, seven, eight." We should also encourage students to use external forms of "storage" to reduce the working memory load—perhaps using their fingers or paper and pencil to keep track of numbers or other elements of a problem. We can use concrete manipulatives to illustrate what might otherwise be fairly abstract procedures (Fuson & Briars, 1990). For example, we might demonstrate the rationale behind "borrowing" in subtraction by using toothpicks, some of which have been bundled into groups of ten or one hundred (see Figure 9–2). We can provide worked-out examples to illustrate such complex procedures as solving quadratic equations (Mayer & Wittrock, 1996; Mwangi & Sweller, 1998; Zhu & Simon, 1987). Ultimately, however, we must help our students understand

 Promote automaticity in essential mathematical facts and skills.

 Provide worked-out examples.

We have two thousand toothpicks. Many of them are bundled into groups of 10. Some bundles of 10 are bundled a second time into groups of 100. We demonstrate regrouping by changing a bundle of 100 into ten bundles of 10, or by changing a bundle of 10 into ten "singles," as illustrated in the following examples:

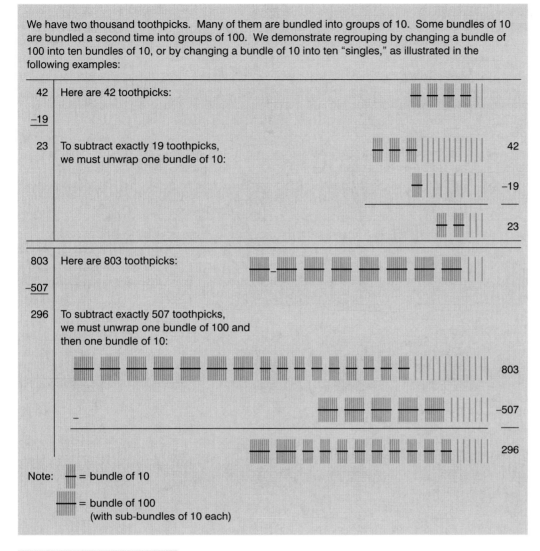

Note: = bundle of 10

 = bundle of 100
   (with sub-bundles of 10 each)

FIGURE 9.2

Illustrating a problem-solving algorithm with concrete manipulatives

why the mathematical procedures they use are appropriate. This particular point is so important that I address it separately in the following discussion.

Relating Procedures to Concepts and Principles

Experiencing Firsthand
Quarters and Dimes

See whether you can solve this problem before you read further.

> The number of quarters a man has is seven times the number of dimes he has. The value of the dimes exceeds the value of the quarters by two dollars and fifty cents. How many has he of each coin? (Paige & Simon, 1966, p. 79)

If you found an answer to the problem—any answer at all—then you overlooked an important point: Quarters are worth more than dimes. If there are more quarters than dimes, the value of the dimes cannot possibly be greater than the value of the quarters. The problem makes no sense, and so it cannot be solved.

Unfortunately, when our schools teach mathematical problem solving, they often focus on teaching procedures for solving problems while omitting explanations of why the procedures work; in other words, they don't relate the procedures to basic concepts and principles of mathematics (Cooney, 1991; J. Hiebert & Lefevre, 1986; Perkins & Salomon, 1989). For example, perhaps you can recall learning how to solve a long division problem, but you probably don't recall learning *why* you multiply the divisor by each digit in your answer and write the product in a particular location below the dividend. Or perhaps you were taught that the words *all together* in a word problem indicate that addition is called for and that the word *left* means you should subtract.

When students learn mathematical procedures at a rote level, without understanding the concepts, principles, and general logic behind them, they may often apply them "unthinkingly" and inappropriately (Perkins & Simmons, 1988; Prawat, 1989; Resnick, 1989; Schoenfeld, 1982, 1985a; Silver, Shapiro, & Deutsch, 1991). As a result, they may obtain illogical or physically impossible results. Consider these instances of meaningless mathematical problem solving as examples:

> A student is asked to figure out how many chickens and how many pigs a farmer has if the farmer has 21 animals with 60 legs in all. The student adds 21 and 60, reasoning that, because the problem says "how many in all," addition is the logical operation (Lester, 1985).

> A student uses subtraction whenever a word problem contains the word *left*—even when a problem actually requiring addition includes the phrase "John left the room to get more apples" (Schoenfeld, 1982).

> A student learns the process of regrouping ("borrowing") in subtraction. In subtracting a number from 803, the student may "borrow" from the hundreds column, but only add 10 to the ones column (Resnick, 1989). Here is an example:

$$\begin{array}{r} \overset{7}{8}\ \overset{1}{0}\ 3 \\ -\ 5\ 0\ 7 \\ \hline 2\ 0\ 6 \end{array}$$

(The correct answer, of course, is 296.)

🍎 Show students the logic underlying problem-solving procedures.

Rather than simply teach mathematical procedures at a rote level, we should help students understand *why* they do the things they do to solve problems (Greeno, 1991; S. A. Griffin & Case, 1996; J. Hiebert & Wearne, 1993; Kerkman & Siegler, 1993; M. Perry, 1991). For instance, we can relate regrouping procedures ("carrying" and "borrowing") in addition and subtraction to the concept of *place value*—the idea that a number in the second column from the right indicates the number of *tens,* the number in the third column indicates the number of *hundreds,* and so on (Byrnes, 1996). By showing our students the logic behind problem-solving procedures, we increase the likelihood that they will apply those procedures at appropriate times and obtain plausible results.

Relating Mathematics to Everyday Situations

Ultimately, learning mathematics is of little use unless students can apply it to real-world situations. Word problems are often used to help students make the connection between formal mathematics and everyday life. Yet traditional word problems alone are probably insufficient to enable most students to bridge the gap between classroom math and everyday situations (De Corte et al., 1996). First, word problems are typically well-defined: they provide all the information students need to know and pose a specific question that students must answer. In contrast, the real world rarely presents such well-defined problems: Some necessary numbers or measures may be missing, irrelevant information may be present, and perhaps the exact question to be answered is not clearly specified.

We can illustrate a second difficulty with word problems with the following exercise.

Experiencing Firsthand
Busing the Band

Take a minute to solve the following problem. Feel free to use a calculator if you have one handy.

> The Riverdale High School marching band is traveling to Hillside High School to perform in the half-time show at Saturday's football game. The school buses owned by the Riverdale School District can transport 32 passengers each. There are 104 students in the Riverdale band. How many buses will the band director need to request to transport the band to Hillside on Saturday?

Did you get the answer 3.25? If so, think about it for a moment. How is it possible to have 3.25 *buses*? What in the world is .25 of a bus? In actuality, the band director must request four buses for Saturday's game. If you fell into my trap, you're not alone. Many students develop the habit of solving word problems based on numerical information alone and overlook the realities of the situation with which they are dealing (De Corte et al., 1996).

In addition to using word problems, then, many theorists suggest that we engage students in tasks that require them to identify, on their own, the specific mathematical problems they need to solve to complete the tasks successfully (De Corte et al., 1996; J. Hiebert et al., 1996; Lester et al., 1997; W. Roth, 1996). For example, we might have our students collect and then analyze large sets of data while studying their local ecology (W. Roth, 1996). We might take them grocery shopping, asking them to consider not only the "best buys" for various products but also how much cupboard space they have for storage (Lave, 1988). And we can ask them to bring to class some of the mathematical problems they encounter at home (Resnick, Bill, Lesgold, & Leer, 1991).

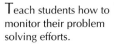 Have students apply math to real-world situations.

Developing Metacognitive Processes and Beliefs

Like virtually any other complex cognitive task, mathematical problem solving involves metacognition: The successful student must choose one or more appropriate problem-solving strategies, monitor progress toward the problem goal, and recognize when a solution has been reached (Schoenfeld, 1992). Rather than assume that our students will acquire these metacognitive processes on their own, we should probably teach such processes explicitly (Cardelle-Elawar, 1992). For instance, we can give students practice in identifying situations in which they don't have all the information they need to answer a question. And we can give them problems requiring two or more separate procedures, ask them to list the specific steps necessary to solve the problems, and then cross off each step as they accomplish it.

Teach students how to monitor their problem solving efforts.

We must make sure, too, that our students' beliefs about mathematics are conducive to effective learning and problem solving in math. Unfortunately, many students, even at the high school level, have several counterproductive beliefs:

- Mathematics is a collection of meaningless procedures—procedures that must inevitably be learned in a rote fashion.
- Mathematical problems always have one and only one right answer.
- One will either solve a problem within a few minutes or else not solve it at all.
- There's only one right way to solve any particular math problem. (Schoenfeld, 1988, 1992)

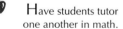

Present experiences that contradict inaccurate beliefs about the nature of mathematics.

Encourage students to use the strategies they have developed on their own.

Relate abstract ideas to concrete examples even at the high school level.

Have students tutor one another in math.

When we teach mathematics, we must certainly be aware of students' beliefs about math and take steps to correct any erroneous ones. For instance, as mentioned before, we can make mathematical procedures meaningful by relating them to concepts and principles that students have already learned. We can present problems that have multiple answers or that require considerable time and persistence to solve. And as we will see shortly, we can engage students in discussions about the variety of approaches possible with any particular problem.

Developmental Changes in Mathematical Understanding

As noted earlier, many (although not all) students first enter school having some proficiency in counting and some understanding of number. In the early elementary grades, we need to solidify these capabilities and extend them to work in addition and subtraction, and eventually to multiplication and division. But rather than ignore any strategies that students may have developed on their own—for instance, using their fingers to keep track of numbers or to add and subtract—we should probably encourage them to use those strategies that seem to work for them. They will eventually discard relatively "immature" strategies as they acquire more efficient ones (Geary, 1994; Siegler, 1989).

The mathematics curriculum at the upper elementary grades typically includes an introduction to such proportions as fractions and decimals. Yet the ability to reason effectively about proportions typically does not appear until students are, on average, about eleven or twelve years old (see Chapter 2). If school district objectives give us little choice about teaching proportions or other concepts that, from a developmental perspective, are going to be especially challenging for our students, then we must present as many concrete and real-world examples of these concepts as possible.

In the middle school, junior high, and high school grades, mathematics instruction focuses increasingly on abstract ideas such as negative and irrational numbers, *pi* (π), *infinity,* and *variable.* Over time, mathematical concepts and principles gradually become more and more removed from the concrete realities with which students are familiar. Perhaps it is no surprise, then, that students' anxiety about mathematics peaks during the high school years (Geary, 1994). Two general strategies can help us keep math anxiety within reasonable limits. First, we must continue to use concrete examples and experiences to illustrate mathematical ideas even in high school. And second, we must make sure that our students truly master the concepts and procedures they will need as they proceed to more difficult topics.

General Strategies for Teaching Mathematics

Throughout this section, we have identified specific strategies for helping students learn and use mathematics more effectively. Here are three more general strategies:

• *Have students tutor one another in mathematics.* When students tutor one another in math, both the tutor and the student being tutored seem to learn from the interaction. Peer tutoring can occur within a single classroom, with students pairing off differently on different occasions, depending on which students have and have not mastered a particular idea (L. S. Fuchs et al., 1995; L. S. Fuchs et al., 1996). But it can also happen in a cross-age fashion, with older students tutoring younger ones. In one situation, for instance, fourth graders who were doing relatively poorly in math served as arithmetic tutors for first and second graders; the tutors themselves showed a substantial improvement in arithmetic problem-solving skills (Inglis & Biemiller, 1997).

Why does peer tutoring help the tutors as well as the students being tutored? Theorists believe that by explaining something to someone else, the tutors must first clarify it in their own minds. Furthermore, tutors may have to provide several examples to help their partners understand a concept or procedure; developing such examples requires the tutors to *elaborate* on what they know—always a good strategy from a cognitive processing perspective.

• *Hold small-group or whole-class discussions about mathematical problems.* A growing body of research supports the effectiveness of group discussions for enhancing students' mathematical understanding (Cobb et al., 1991; J. Hiebert & Wearne, 1992; Lampert, 1990). One common strategy is to ask students to identify and defend various ways of solving a particular problem (Brenner et al., 1997; J. Hiebert & Wearne, 1996; Lampert, 1990). For example, at the second grade level, students might develop their own strategies for adding two- and three-digit numbers (J. Hiebert & Wearne, 1996). At the high school level, they might derive their own set of geometric theorems (Healy, 1993).

Many theorists believe that when we encourage students to invent and justify new procedures and principles within a group context, we also encourage them to construct a more meaningful understanding of mathematics (Cobb, 1994; Lampert, Rittenhouse, & Crumbaugh, 1996; Resnick, 1989). Furthermore, if particular students have misconceptions that lead them to develop inappropriate procedures or principles, then their classmates may quickly object to their ideas. But to create a climate in which students feel free to argue with one another about mathematics, we must communicate two messages very clearly—that as a group, we "agree to disagree" and that, as lifelong learners, we are all apt to be wrong some of the time (Lampert et al., 1996).

C onduct class discussions in which students identify and justify new procedures and principles.

Students develop a better understanding of mathematics when they must explain and justify their ideas to their classmates.

• *Have students use calculators and computers frequently.* On some occasions, we will probably want students to do calculations by hand; for instance, this will often be the case when students are first mastering such operations as addition, subtraction, multiplication, and division. But eventually, especially as students begin dealing with complex mathematical situations and problems, we may want to help them ease the load on working memory by encouraging them to use calculators or computers to do simple calculations. Calculators and computers also enable students to experiment with mathematics—for example, to graph an equation and then see how the graph changes when the equation is modified in particular ways (De Corte et al., 1996; Pressley, 1995).

E ncourage the use of calculators and computers, especially for complex problems.

In Chapter 4, I introduced the notion of *distributed intelligence*—the idea that people can perform more complex tasks, and therefore can behave in a more "intelligent" fashion, when they have the support of their social and physical environments. Peer groups and technology are two examples of such environmental support. There is no reason why we or our students should think of mathematics as something that must be done in isolation from other people and without the use of modern technology. The same is true for science as well, and we turn to this subject area now.

Science

Historically, science as a discipline has had two major goals: to describe and to explain what people observe in nature (Mayer, 1999). Some of the things you studied in science were primarily descriptive in content. For instance, you probably studied characteristics of the planets in our solar system, discovered that water expands when it freezes, and examined the ways in which vertebrates and invertebrates are different. But you probably also studied possible explanations—*theories*—regarding natural phenomena. For instance, you may have considered theories about how the universe began, why water expands when it freezes, or how various animal species evolved.

Actually, you began learning science long before you entered school as a kindergartner or first grader. In your early explorations of the world, you learned that objects usually fall toward the earth when you let go of them, that water freezes when it gets cold, and that dogs and cats have four legs whereas birds have two legs and fish have none. Children rarely come to school as "blank slates" when it comes to science.

Not only have young learners already made numerous observations about the world, but they have also constructed their own explanations—their **personal theories**—for those observations. In some cases, these theories are reasonably accurate. For instance, by the time children are six years old, most of them have an intuitive understanding of differences between living things and inanimate objects: Both plants and animals grow and reproduce, and animals can typically move themselves around, whereas inanimate objects can neither grow nor go of their own accord (Hatano & Inagaki, 1996; Massey & Gelman, 1988). Yet children also acquire many misconceptions about the world around them. For instance, most of them initially believe that the earth is flat and motionless and that the sun and stars revolve around it (Vosniadou, 1991).

Most contemporary theorists believe that learning science is very much a constructive process: As learners gather more and more information about the world around them, they construct increasingly complex and integrated theories (diSessa, 1996; R. Driver, 1995; Wellman & Gelman, 1992; Wittrock, 1994). Children's early observations of the world provide a foundation upon which formal science instruction in school can more effectively build. At the same time, the misconceptions that emerge in the early years often hinder children's ability to develop more scientifically acceptable understandings of natural phenomena.

Identify and address existing misconceptions about scientific phenomena.

The Nature of Scientific Reasoning

Ideally, a school science curriculum must help students begin to think about the phenomena they observe in the same ways that adult scientists do. Here are some of the abilities that such reasoning includes:

- Investigating scientific phenomena objectively and systematically
- Constructing theories and models
- Revising theories and models in light of new evidence or better explanations
- Applying scientific principles to real-world problems
- Metacognition

Investigating Scientific Phenomena

See "The Pendulum Experiment" in *Simulations in Educational Psychology*

Do you recall the "Pendulum Problem" exercise you completed in Chapter 2? (If you have not already read Chapter 2, do the exercise on page 38.) If you performed the exercise like a true scientist, then you engaged in two processes essential to scientific reasoning: *formulation and testing of hypotheses* and *separation and control of variables*. In particular, you identified several possible causes of a pendulum's oscillation rate (your hypotheses), perhaps including the *weight* of the hanging object, the *length* of the string, the *force* with which the pendulum is pushed, and the *height* from which the object is dropped. You then tested your hypotheses by changing one variable at a time and keeping the other three constant. For instance, you might have varied the weight at the bottom of the pendulum while always keeping the length of string, force of push, and height of drop the same. If the oscillation rate changed each time you changed the weight, then you would know that weight has an effect; if it *didn't* change, then you would know that weight is irrelevant. You might have experimented with length, force, and height in a similar manner (always keeping the other three variables constant) and once again looked for resulting differences in oscillation rate.

To study a phenomenon objectively scientists follow a systematic series of steps, or a *scientific method,* that commonly includes formulating and testing hypotheses as well as separating and controlling variables. Furthermore, scientists must make observations that specifically relate to their hypotheses. This task is not necessarily as easy as it might seem, as the following exercise demonstrates.

Experiencing Firsthand
Four Cards

Each of the cards above has a letter on one side and a number on the other side. Consider the following rule, which may or may not be true about the cards:

If a card has a vowel on one side, then it has an even number on the other side.

Which one or more cards *must* you turn over to determine whether the rule is true for this set of cards? Don't turn over any more cards than you have to. Make your selection(s) before you continue reading. (modeled after Wason, 1968)

Which card or cards did you turn over to test the rule? You probably identified the E card as one that you should turn over; after all, if the other side has an odd number, then the rule is false. If you are like most people, then you also decided that you need to turn over the 4 card (Wason, 1968). But in fact, you do *not* need to turn over the 4 card. If it has a consonant on the other side, you haven't disproved the rule, which says nothing about what cards with consonants have on the flip side. Instead, you need to turn over the 7 card: If you find a vowel on the other side, then you have a card that violates the rule. In other words, then, you need to look both for evidence that confirms the rule and for evidence that *contradicts* it.

Many students, especially those in the elementary grades, fail to separate and control variables when they test their hypotheses (e.g., they might change weight and length simultaneously when dealing with the pendulum problem), making their observations essentially uninterpretable (Pulos & Linn, 1981; Schauble, 1990). Furthermore, students of all ages (even college students) have a tendency to look for evidence that confirms their hypotheses but to ignore evidence that runs counter to their hypotheses—a phenomenon known as **confirmation bias** (Kuhn et al., 1988; Minstrell & Stimpson, 1996; Schauble, 1990). For example, when students in a high school science lab observe results that contradict what they expected to happen, they might complain that "Our equipment isn't working right" or "I can never do science anyway" (Minstrell & Stimpson, 1996).

In our science lessons and courses, we want our students to be able to separate and control variables so that they can test various hypotheses in a systematic fashion. We also want them to be able to determine whether the information they obtain confirms or disconfirms their existing hypotheses and beliefs. One obvious way to accomplish both objectives, of course, is to engage them regularly in experimentation. Such experiments can occur in both traditional school laboratories and outside (field) settings. A growing body of research tells us, however, that students often need considerable scaffolding to conduct meaningful experiments and to interpret the results appropriately. Here are some ways to provide such scaffolding:

🍎 Provide sufficient
guidance to enable
students to conduct
meaningful experiments.

- Present situations in which only two or three variables need to be controlled, especially when working with elementary students.

- Use situations with which students are familiar (e.g., the fishing situation depicted in Figure 2–4 in Chapter 2).

- Ask students to identify several possible hypotheses about cause-effect relationships before beginning to experiment.

- Provide regular guidance, hints, and feedback regarding the need to control variables and evaluate observations objectively.

- Ask questions that encourage students to make predictions and reflect appropriately on their observations (e.g., "What do you think will happen?" "What is your evidence?" "Do you see things that are inconsistent with what you predicted?")

- Point out occasions when students obtain information that contradicts the hypotheses they are testing.

- Ask students to summarize their findings. (S. Carey, Evans, Honda, Jay, & Unger, 1989; C. Howe, Tolmie, Greer, & Mackenzie, 1995; Kuhn et al., 1988; Metz, 1995; Minstrell & Stimpson, 1996; Ruffman, Perner, Olson, & Doherty, 1993; B. Y. White & Frederiksen, 1998)

Constructing Theories and Models

An essential part of learning science is acquiring increasingly complex and integrated understandings of various natural phenomena. Scientific understanding sometimes takes the form of a **theory**—an organized body of concepts and principles that have been developed to explain certain scientific phenomena. For example, when you studied biology, you probably studied the theory of evolution, a theory that encompasses interrelationships among such concepts as *mutation, adaptation,* and *natural selection.* Scientific understanding may also take the form of a **model**—knowledge of the components of a particular scientific entity and the interrelationships among those components. For instance, you probably have a mental model of our solar system that includes the sun and nine planets revolving around it at varying distances. If you look at Figure 3–1 (p. 80), Figure 4–3 (p. 129), and Figure 6–3 (p. 235), you will see physical representations of the models that some educational psychologists have developed for *self-concept, intelligence,* and *human memory.*

🍎 Encourage students to
find interrelationships
among concepts and
principles.

To some extent, students may acquire their knowledge of science through their own experimentation. But they must also study the concepts, principles, theories, and models that professional scientists currently use to make sense of the physical world (R. Driver, 1995; Hatano & Inagaki, 1996; M. C. Linn et al., 1996). The trick is for students to pull all of the things they learn into integrated, meaningful bodies of knowledge. Theorists have offered several suggestions for helping students learn science as integrated, cohesive theories and models:

- Introduce a new unit with a lesson or experiment that illustrates the important issues that the unit will address (i.e., a **benchmark lesson** or **benchmark experiment**).

- Use analogies that help students relate new ideas to prior knowledge.

- Present physical models of the phenomena being described, perhaps in the form of diagrams, flowcharts, or physical replicas.

- Ask students to organize the material they have learned (e.g., by drawing diagrams, making concept maps, or writing summaries). (D. E. Brown, 1992; A. L. Brown & Campione, 1994; Minstrell & Stimpson, 1996; Mayer, 1999; Mayer & Wittrock, 1996; Wittrock, 1994)

Experiencing Firsthand
Water and Earth

Complete these problems before you read further.

1. A glass half full of water is lifted from the table on which it is resting and tilted at a 45-degree angle. Draw a line in the glass to mark the water's surface.

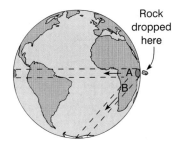

Rock dropped here

A
B

2. A rock is dropped at the equator, at the entrances to two tunnels that go through the earth. Tunnel A comes out at the equator on the opposite side of the earth. Tunnel B comes out at the South Pole. Into which tunnel will the rock fall?

Your water line in the tilted glass should be parallel to the top of the table; in other words, it should be horizontal. Did you instead draw a line that slanted one way or the other? If so, you're hardly alone; many adults have difficulty with this task (Pulos, 1997). I hope that you had an easier time with the "tunnels" question: The rock will fall into Tunnel A, toward the center of the earth.

Many middle school students have difficulty with both of these problems related to gravity (Pulos, 1997). They draw a slanted line to indicate that the water's surface tilts upward toward one side of the glass or the other, and they answer that the rock will fall into Tunnel B, thinking, apparently, that gravity always pulls something "down." They respond in these ways despite many personal experiences with tilted water glasses and despite explicitly learning that gravity pulls objects toward the center of the earth (Pulos, 1997).

Just as scientific theories and models evolve over time as new evidence emerges, so, too, must our students continually revise their understanding of natural phenomena as they acquire more information; in other words, they must undergo conceptual change. Yet students often cling tenaciously to their naive ideas about scientific phenomena despite considerable experience and instruction to the contrary (diSessa, 1996; Keil & Silberstein, 1996; McCloskey, 1983; Vosniadou, 1991).

In Chapter 7, we identified several strategies for promoting conceptual change. Here are some additional ones that relate specifically to science:

■ Portray science as a dynamic, evolving collection of theories and models to be understood, rather than as a collection of discrete facts to be memorized.

See "Intuitive Physics" in *Simulations in Educational Psychology*

Encourage students to revise their knowledge and beliefs as they encounter new evidence.

Any science curriculum should help students make connections between scientific principles and real-world situations.

- Identify and discuss students' existing scientific beliefs (e.g., the idea that gravity pulls objects toward the South Pole), so that such beliefs are in working memory and, as a result, more likely to be modified.

- Relate abstract ideas to concrete and familiar experiences; for instance, illustrate the abstract concept *density* by showing how a can of diet soft drink floats in water while a can of regular soft drink sinks.

- Give students opportunities to discuss competing perspectives within a classroom environment that communicates the message, "It's OK to make errors and to change our minds." (Brandes, 1996; Byrnes, 1996; Duit, 1991; Keil & Silberstein, 1996; Minstrell & Stimpson, 1996)

Applying Science to Real-World Problems

All too often, students have trouble relating the things they learn in science to real-world situations (M. C. Linn et al., 1996; Mayer, 1996). For instance, despite formal instruction about the nature of heat and insulation, it never occurs to many students that they can use wool to keep something *cold* as well as to keep it warm (M. C. Linn et al., 1996).

Ideally, any science curriculum should make frequent connections between school science and everyday situations (M. C. Linn et al., 1996; B. Y. White & Frederiksen, 1998). Accordingly, we should provide numerous opportunities for students to apply scientific principles to the kinds of problems they are likely to encounter in their outside lives.

Ask students to make frequent connections between scientific principles and everyday situations.

Metacognition

Students' beliefs about the nature of science (i.e., their epistemological beliefs) will undoubtedly affect the approaches that they take (mentally) when they study science. Students who believe that "knowing" science means understanding how various concepts and principles fit together and using those concepts and principles to explain everyday phenomena are going to study and learn more effectively than students who think that learning science means memorizing facts (M. C. Linn et al., 1996). And students who recognize that scientific theories will inevitably change over time are more likely to evaluate theories with a critical eye (Bereiter, 1994; Kuhn, 1993; M. C. Linn et al., 1996). It is essential, therefore, that, through both our lessons and our assessment techniques, we continually communicate the message that "mastering" science means understanding concepts and principles in a meaningful fashion, integrating concepts and principles into a cohesive whole, revising personal theories in the light of new evidence, and applying science to real-world situations (Schauble, 1996; Vosniadou, 1991; Wittrock, 1994).

Developmental Changes in Science

As noted earlier, children acquire considerable knowledge about science long before they begin school. But their ability to *think about* science is likely to be limited throughout the elementary grades. As we discovered in Chapter 2, abstract and hypothetical reasoning capabilities and the ability to separate and control variables all appear to be fairly limited until adolescence. Perhaps for this reason, elementary school teachers focus most science instruction on descriptions of natural phenomena rather than explanations of why those phenomena occur (Byrnes, 1996). Yet even at the elementary level, it is probably counterproductive to portray science as nothing more than a collection of facts. By having students engage in simple experiments almost from the very beginning of the science curriculum, we can convey the message that science is an ongoing, dynamic process of unraveling the mysteries of our world.

At the middle school level, students' increasing ability to think about abstract ideas enables us to begin addressing some of the causal mechanisms that underlie natural phenomena. Yet even at this point, we may not want to introduce ideas completely removed from students' everyday, concrete experiences (M. C. Linn & Muilenburg, 1996; M. C. Linn et al., 1996). For instance, when teaching eighth graders about heat, we may have better success if we talk about heat as something that "flows" from one object to another rather than as something that involves molecules moving and colliding with one another at particular rates. Although the heat-flow model is, from a chemical perspective, not entirely accurate, students can effectively apply it to a wide variety of everyday situations; for instance, they can use it to explain why a bathtub filled with warm water heats the air around it, why packing food in ice helps to keep it cold, and why using a wooden spoon is safer than using a metal one to stir something cooking on the stove (M. C. Linn & Muilenburg, 1996).

When students reach high school, they are more likely to have acquired the scientific knowledge they need to begin thinking in truly abstract ways about natural phenomena (M. C. Linn et al., 1996). Nevertheless, it is wise to continue to engage students in frequent hands-on science activities—not only through systematic laboratory experiments but also through informal, exploratory activities that relate scientific concepts and principles to everyday experiences. Secondary students in general, but especially females, are likely to achieve at higher levels when they have regular hands-on experiences with the phenomena they are studying (Burkam et al., 1997).

General Strategies for Teaching Science

Throughout this section we have identified specific strategies for helping students learn various aspects of science more effectively. Here are three more general strategies to keep in mind:

• *Engage students regularly in authentic scientific investigations.* Historically, most science laboratory activities have been little more than cookbook recipes: Students are given specific materials and instructions to follow in a step-by-step manner (Committee on High School Biology Education, 1990). Although such activities can certainly help make scientific phenomena more concrete for students, they are unlikely to encourage

Portray mastery of science as involving meaningful learning, integration of ideas, ongoing revision of knowledge, and application to real-world contexts.

In elementary school, focus more on description than on explanation.

In middle school, use relatively concrete models to explain scientific phenomena.

In high school, introduce more abstract theories, but continue to relate them to everyday life.

🍎 Have students conduct experiments in which they choose their own procedures and address questions with no predetermined answers.

students to engage in thinking processes—testing and formulating hypotheses, separating and controlling variables, and so on—that characterize true scientific reasoning (Keil & Silberstein, 1996; Padilla, 1991). So in addition, we must give students many opportunities to conduct investigations in which the procedures and outcomes are not necessarily predetermined. In some cases, we can provide materials that allow students to explore phenomena closely related to known scientific principles; for instance, we might ask them to address questions such as "How does the amount of electric current affect electromagnetic strength?" or "How does temperature affect the germination rate of seeds?" (Padilla, 1991). In other situations, we can have students apply their developing experimentation skills to address everyday problems; for instance, we might pose a question such as "Does one fast food chain provide more meat in a hamburger than others?" or "Is one brand of paper towel stronger or more absorbent than the others?" (Padilla, 1991). We may also want to engage our students in long-term, outdoor field work, perhaps studying the vegetation of the local environment or analyzing the bacterial content of neighborhood rivers and lakes.

🍎 Provide opportunities for students to explain and justify their reasoning to one another.

• *Use class discussions to promote conceptual change.* A growing body of research indicates that class discussions help students acquire more accurate and integrated understandings of scientific phenomena (Bereiter, 1994; Greeno et al., 1996; Hatano & Inagaki, 1991; Minstrell & Stimpson, 1996). For example, we might use a *hypothesis-experiment-instruction* approach:

1. Present a question or issue with three or four possible answers; here is one possibility:

   Suppose that you have a clay ball on one end of a spring. You hold the other end of the spring and put half of the clay ball into water. Will the spring (a) become shorter, (b) become longer, or (c) retain its length? (Hatano & Inagaki, 1991, p. 337)

2. Solicit students' responses to the question and ask them to explain their reasoning.

3. As a class, conduct an experiment that enables students to test their predictions.

4. Finally, have students discuss possible explanations as to why the experiment yielded the results that it did (Hatano & Inagaki, 1991).

If many students have initially made inaccurate predictions, the experiment will encourage them to revise their thinking and acquire a more accurate understanding of the scientific principles involved.

• *Make use of computer technology.* Many software programs now enable students to explore scientific phenomena in ways that might not be possible in real life. Some programs let students "explore" human anatomy—the heart, the lungs, the eye, and so on—or conduct "dissections" of frogs, cats, and other species. Other programs create "virtual" environments that allow students to manipulate and experiment with such phenomena as friction, gravity, and thermodynamics, allowing them to separate and control variables in ways that the real world would prohibit (Greeno et al., 1996; Schauble, 1990; B. Y. White & Frederiksen, 1998). Furthermore, electronic mail and the Internet provide the means through which students can communicate with one another and with outside experts, enabling them to share information and test their hypotheses and ideas (Pea, 1992).

🍎 Use computer technology to create "virtual" phenomena and to promote communication.

Over the past few decades, many psychologists and educators have studied how students learn mathematics and science and how teachers can help them master these content domains more effectively. Only recently, however, has a significant number of theorists and researchers turned their attention to that part of the school curriculum known collectively as *social studies.* In the next section, we will explore some of the ideas that are beginning to emerge in this area.

INTO THE CLASSROOM: Promoting Mathematical and Scientific Reasoning Skills

Take students' cognitive development into account when teaching concepts and principles.

A fourth-grade teacher asks his students to conduct experiments to find out what kinds of conditions influence the growth of sunflower seeds. He knows that his students probably have only a limited ability to separate and control variables, so he asks them to study the effects of just two things: the amount of water and the kind of soil. He has the students keep their growing plants by the window, where temperature and amount of sunlight will be the same for all of the plants.

Use concrete manipulatives and analogies to illustrate abstract ideas.

A high school physics teacher has learned from experience that, even though her students are, in theory, capable of abstract thought, they are still likely to have trouble understanding this principle: *When an object rests on a surface, the object exerts a force on the surface, and the surface also exerts a force on the object.* To illustrate the principle, she places a book on a large spring. The book compresses the spring somewhat, but not completely. "So you see, class," she says, "the book pushes downward on the spring, and the spring pushes upward on the book. An object compresses even a hard surface, such as a table, a little bit, and the surface pushes back up in response" (based on D. E. Brown & Clement, 1989).

Ask students to apply math and science to real-world problems.

A third-grade teacher gives his students copies of a menu from a local family restaurant. He tells them, "Imagine that you have eight dollars to spend. Figure out what you might order for lunch so that your meal includes each of the food groups we've discussed."

Ask students to identify several strategies or hypotheses regarding a particular task or situation, and to explain and justify their ideas to one another.

A middle school math teacher is beginning a unit on how to divide numbers by fractions. After students convene in small groups, she says, "You've already learned how to multiply a number by a fraction. For example, you've learned that when you multiply 1/3 by 1/2, you get 1/6. But now imagine that you want to *divide* 1/3 by 1/2. Do you think you'll get a number smaller than 1/3 or larger than 1/3? And what kind of number might you get? Talk within your groups about how you might answer these questions. In a few minutes we'll all get back together to talk about the ideas you've come up with."

Foster metacognitive strategies that students can use to regulate their experimentation and problem solving.

When a high school science teacher has his students conduct lab experiments, he always has them keep several questions in mind as they work: (1) As I test the effects of one variable, am I controlling for possible effects of other variables? (2) Am I seeing anything that supports my hypothesis? (3) Am I seeing anything that contradicts my hypothesis?

Have students use mathematics and scientific methods in other content domains.

A junior high school social studies teacher asks his students to work in small groups to conduct experiments regarding the effects of smiling on other people's behavior. As the groups design their experiments, he reminds them about the importance of separating and controlling variables, and he insists that each group identify an objective means of measuring the specific behavior or behaviors that it intends to study. Later, he has the groups tabulate their results and report their findings to the rest of the class.

An important goal of any social studies curriculum should be to promote tolerance and understanding of diverse perspectives and cultures.

Social Studies

Many theorists believe that the ultimate goal of social studies education should be to help students make informed decisions about matters of public policy, social welfare, and personal growth (Alleman & Brophy, 1997; Byrnes, 1996). In my own mind, social studies should also promote tolerance for diverse perspectives and cultures, with the understanding that such diversity of ideas is essential for the social, moral, and cultural advancement of the human race over time.

If we want our students to draw on the things they learn in social studies when they make decisions as adult citizens, it is essential that we focus on meaningful learning and higher-level thinking skills—transfer, problem solving, and so on—in the social studies curriculum, rather than on the learning of discrete facts (Alleman & Brophy, 1997; Newmann, 1997). In this section of the chapter, we will consider how we might focus the curriculum of two specific areas: history and geography.

The Nature of Historical Knowledge and Thinking

A true understanding of history, both as a body of knowledge and as an academic discipline, requires several abilities and processes:

- Understanding the nature of historical time
- Drawing inferences from historical documents
- Identifying cause-effect relationships among events
- Recognizing that historical figures were real people

Understanding Historical Time

In the case study at the beginning of the chapter, Ben accounts for America's origins as follows:

2000 Days oh go George Washington gave us the Country to Live on.

As a second grader, Ben obviously has little sense of how long a time span "2000 days" is. Like Ben, children in the early elementary grades have little understanding of historical time (Barton & Levstik, 1996). For instance, they might refer to events that happened "a long, long time ago" or "in the old days" yet tell you that such events happened in 1997. And they tend to lump historical events into two general categories: those that happened very recently and those that happened many years ago. Not until about fifth grade do students show a reasonable ability to sequence historical events and to attach them to particular periods of time (Barton & Levstik, 1996).

Perhaps it is not surprising, then, that systematic history instruction typically does not begin until fifth grade (Byrnes, 1996). In the earlier grades, any instruction about history should probably focus on students' own, personal histories and on events that have occurred locally and in the recent past (Byrnes, 1996).

Remember that historical dates have little meaning for students in the early elementary grades.

Drawing Inferences from Historical Documents

History textbooks often describe historical events very matter-of-factly, communicating the message that "This is what actually happened" (Britt, Rouet, Georgi, & Perfetti, 1994; Wineburg, 1994). In reality, however, historians often don't know *exactly* how particular events occurred. Instead, they construct a reasonable interpretation of these events after looking at a variety of historical documents, which frequently provide differing perspectives of what transpired (Leinhardt, 1994; Leinhardt & Young, 1996; Seixas, 1996; Wineburg, 1994).

The idea that history is often as much a matter of perspective as it is a matter of fact is a fairly abstract notion that students may not be able to wrestle with before they reach adolescence (Byrnes, 1996; Seixas, 1996). At the secondary level, we can begin to have them read multiple accounts of significant historical events and then draw conclusions both about what *definitely* happened and about what *might* have happened (Britt et al., 1994; Leinhardt, 1994; Seixas, 1996; Wineburg, 1994). For instance, when students study racial strife in the American South, they might learn about the Montgomery, Alabama, bus boycott of 1955 both by reading newspaper articles published at the time and by reading Rosa Parks's own account of why she refused to give up her bus seat for a white person (Banks, 1994b). When they study the Mexican-American War, they should be exposed to the Mexican perspective as well as that of the United States. Ultimately, students at the secondary grade levels must discover that history is not as cut-and-dried as some present it—that learning history involves constructing a reasonable interpretation of events based on the evidence at hand and that some aspects of history may never be known for certain.

At the secondary level, have students read multiple and varying accounts of particular historical events.

Identifying Cause-Effect Relationships Among Events

To some extent, an integrated knowledge of history includes an understanding of how some events led to others. For instance, it might be helpful for students to learn that economic hardship in the Southern states was a contributing factor to the Northern victory in the American Civil War, and that paranoia about growing empires was partly responsible for World War II, the Korean War, and the Vietnam War. One way we can help students learn such cause-effect relationships is, of course, to describe them ourselves. But we can also engage students in discussions in which they develop their *own* explanations of why certain events must have occurred (Leinhardt, 1993). And we can indirectly help them discover causal relationships by asking them to consider how things might have been different if certain events had *not* taken place (Byrnes, 1996).

Help students discover cause-effect relationships among events.

Thinking of Historical Figures as Real People

Students will learn historical events in a more meaningful fashion when they discover that historical figures had particular goals, motives, and personalities and that these individuals often had to make decisions based on incomplete information—in other words, that they were, in many respects, just ordinary human beings. As an example, we might ask students to read Rosa Parks's explanation as to why she refused to give up her bus seat:

> People always say that I didn't give up my seat because I was tired, but that isn't true. I was not tired physically, or no more tired than I usually was at the end of a working day. I was not old, although some people have an image of me being old then. I was 42. No, the only tired I was, was tired of giving in. (Parks, 1992, cited in Banks, 1994b)

As another example, we might ask students to read newspaper accounts of World War II just prior to Harry Truman's decision to drop an atomic bomb on Hiroshima—accounts that give students a better feel for what Truman probably did and did not know at the time (Yeager et al., 1997). When students understand why historical figures behaved as they did, they are more likely to empathize with them, and such empathy makes historical events just that much more understandable (Seixas, 1996; Yeager et al., 1997).

🍎 Help students
understand why historical
figures behaved as
they did.

The Nature of Geographic Knowledge and Thinking

Many people conceive of geography as consisting of little more than the locations of various countries, capital cities, rivers, and so on. In fact, the discipline of geography involves not only *where* things are but also *why* and *how* they got there (National Geographic Education Project, 1994). For instance, geographers study why and how rivers and mountain ranges end up where they do, why people are more likely to settle in some locations than in others, and how people in various locations interact with one another.

Mastering geography involves at least three things:

- Understanding maps as symbolic representations
- Identifying interrelationships among people, places, and environments
- Appreciating cultural differences

Understanding Maps as Symbolic Representations

Central to geographic thinking is the realization that maps depict the arrangement and characteristics of particular locations. Yet young children have trouble interpreting maps and using them effectively (Blades & Spencer, 1987; Liben & Downs, 1989b). Children in the early elementary grades don't truly appreciate the *symbolic* nature of maps: They take what they see on a map too literally (H. Gardner, Torff, & Hatch, 1996; Liben & Downs, 1989b). For instance, they may think that roads depicted in red are paved with red concrete and that the lines separating states and countries are actually painted on the earth. Young children also have difficulty maintaining a sense of scale and proportion (Liben & Downs, 1989b). For instance, they might deny that a road could actually be a road because it's "too skinny for two cars to fit on" or insist that mountains depicted on a three-dimensional plastic relief map can't possibly be mountains because "they aren't high enough."

One major goal of any geography curriculum, especially in the elementary grades, must be to foster an understanding of the symbolic nature of maps. Students probably need explicit instruction in map interpretation skills (Liben & Downs, 1989a). We can certainly do this by giving students practice in interpreting a wide variety of maps, including maps that depict different kinds of information (e.g., maps that depict physical landforms, maps that depict roads and highways, maps that depict varying elevations) and maps that use different kinds of symbols (Liben & Downs, 1989a). We can also teach map interpretation skills by having students create their *own* maps, perhaps of their neighborhoods or even of the entire country (Forbes, Ormrod, Bernardi, Taylor, & Jackson, 1999; Gregg & Leinhardt, 1994a).

🍎 Give students practice
in interpreting a wide
variety of maps.

Students must learn, too, that different maps are drawn to different scales, reflecting various proportions between graphic representation and reality (Liben & Downs, 1989b).

🍎 Introduce scale after
students have developed
proportional reasoning
capabilities.

We must keep in mind that, because proportional reasoning typically does not emerge until adolescence (see Chapter 2), we probably do not want to study scale in any systematic way until the middle school years. At this point, we can specifically talk about the scales used in different maps (one inch per mile, one centimeter per ten kilometers, etc.).

Identifying Interrelationships Among People, Places, and Environments

Much of geography centers on principles that identify how people, places, and environments interact. Consider these geographic principles as examples:

- People are more likely to settle in areas that are easily accessible—for instance, along navigable rivers or near major roadways.
- People tend to migrate from places with limited or decreasing resources to places with more plentiful resources.
- People who are separated by significant physical barriers—mountain ranges, large rivers, deserts, and so on—interact with one another rarely, if at all, and so may develop distinctly different cultural patterns.

We can teach our students to use maps as tools not only to help them locate places but also to look for patterns in what they see and to speculate about why those patterns exist (Gregg & Leinhardt, 1994b; Liben & Downs, 1989a). For instance, we can ask them to consider questions such as these as they peruse maps like those in Figures 9–3 and 9–4:

> Why did Chicago become the major railroad center of the American Midwest in the middle of the nineteenth century? (Use Figure 9–3.)

> Why are the languages of the Far East so distinctly different from those of the Middle East? (Use Figure 9–4.)

Ask students to use geographic principles to interpret patterns in maps.

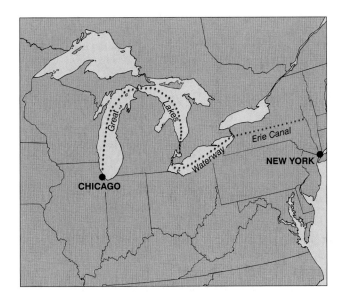

FIGURE 9.3
Why did Chicago become the major railroad center of the American Midwest in the middle of the nineteenth century?

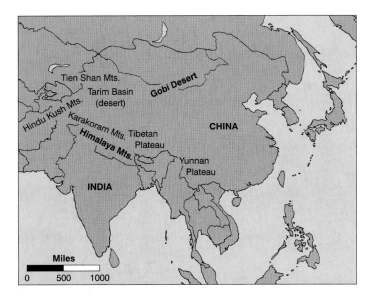

FIGURE 9.4
Why are the languages of the Far East so distinctly different from those of the Middle East?

🍎 Foster an appreciation of cultural diversity.

Appreciating Cultural Differences

An important goal of any geography curriculum must be to help students develop an understanding and appreciation of cultural diversity. In our discussion of "Creating a More Multicultural Classroom Environment" in Chapter 4, I identified general strategies for promoting cultural awareness and tolerance. Those strategies are probably worth repeating again in this context:

- Incorporate the values, beliefs, and traditions of many cultures into the curriculum
- Work to break down ethnic and cultural stereotypes
- Promote social interaction among students from various ethnic groups
- Foster democratic ideals

Although not all of these strategies fall within the discipline of geography, certainly they all fall within the more general domain of social studies.

🍎 Find similarities among diverse cultures.

An additional strategy is to show students that, despite superficial differences among cultures, human beings often behave in similar ways and for similar reasons. I found an excellent example of this strategy a few years ago when I visited Colorado's Mesa Verde National Park, once the home of cliff-dwelling Native Americans now called the Anasazi (a Navajo word meaning "ancient ones"). The National Park Service distributed a pamphlet that compared the Anasazi lifestyle in the thirteenth century with that of people living in Europe during the same time period. Here are some excerpts from the pamphlet:

> The romantic notion that the Middle Ages were filled with knights in shining armor and ladies-in-waiting is exaggerated. In reality, 80 to 90 percent of Europeans at that time were serfs or peasants. The thirteenth-century peasant was surrounded by a world just as difficult for him to understand as it was for the average Anasazi. In Europe famines, plagues and diseases were rampant and decimated populations almost overnight. . . . During a lunar eclipse, many Europeans might spend a night in terror behind their cottage walls of mud and wattle. It is no wonder that religion played a major role in the lives of both cultures, influencing a great deal of their daily activities. Given the problems of drought and overuse of natural resources, it is understandable that the Anasazi would seek outside assistance in the form of ceremonies and special rites, just as the Europeans were governed by their superstitious beliefs. In certain respects, the way the two cultures looked at their world was not so different at all.
>
> . . . Sanitation was a major problem for both cultures. Today's visitors [to Mesa Verde National Park] think it is appalling that the Anasazi would throw their refuse—broken pottery vessels, used sandals, food remnants, etc.—right out in front of the dwelling. However, European city dwellers threw their trash out their windows and onto the streets. . . . Since the humidity levels in the American Southwest are less than most areas of Europe, the stench and decay may have been worse in Europe than it was for the Anasazi. (Mesa Verde Museum Association, n.d.)

Developmental Changes in Thinking About History and Geography

Students' understanding of social studies is, of course, dependent on their growing cognitive abilities. At the elementary level, students tend to think in relatively concrete terms. For example, in history, they may conceptualize the birth of the United States as resulting from a single, specific event (e.g., the Boston Tea Party) or as involving nothing more than constructing new buildings and towns (Ormrod, Jackson, Kirby, Davis, & Benson, 1999). In geography, they may think that an airplane symbol on a map represents an airport with only one airplane (Liben & Downs, 1989b).

🍎 Keep general trends in cognitive development in mind when planning lessons in history and geography.

As students develop the ability to think abstractly, so, too, can they more readily comprehend the abstract principles that underlie historical events and geographical patterns. Furthermore, as they acquire an increasing ability to look at events from other people's perspectives (see Selman's and Eisenberg's theories in Chapter 3), they become more capable of empathizing with historical figures (Ormrod et al., 1999). And as they develop proportional reasoning, they can more effectively consider the concept of scale in map making.

General Strategies for Teaching Social Studies

In addition to the specific strategies we've considered for teaching history and geography, here are three more general strategies for teaching social studies:

- *Choose content that helps students discover important principles and ideas within the discipline.* Social studies cover a broad range of topics—far too many to include in just twelve or thirteen years of schooling. So what exactly *do* we include in a social studies curriculum? Theorists suggest that we develop lessons and units that help students discover the key principles—the "big ideas"—that underlie social studies (Alleman & Brophy, 1997; Newmann, 1988; Olsen, 1995). For instance, when teaching students about various wars, we might focus on cause-effect relationships and general trends (e.g., the role of women on the homefront and in the military) rather than on the details of specific battles (Olsen, 1995). Or, when exploring the geography of Africa, we might consider how different environments (tropical rain forests, desert plains, etc.) lead to very different lifestyles among the residents of various regions.

Choose content that illustrates important principles and ideas.

- *Determine what students do and do not already know about a new topic.* Many history textbook writers assume their readers have knowledge that the students probably *don't* have (Beck, McKeown, & Gromoll, 1989; McKeown & Beck, 1994). For instance, textbook writers may assume that fifth graders can appreciate why the early American colonists resented the British policy of "taxation without representation," yet such a situation is far removed from students' own personal experiences. In the history compositions presented earlier in the chapter, we saw numerous errors of fact—errors that might easily lead to confusion as students study history in later grades. For example, one second grader in the opening case study believed that the dinosaurs were around as recently as six thousand years ago. And the eighth grader whose composition appeared in the "What's Wrong?" exercise didn't know that Britain and Brittany are two different places. When we begin with what our students definitely know, not with what we think they *should* know, and proceed from there, our students' comprehension of social studies will improve (McKeown & Beck, 1994).

Consider what students already do and do not know.

- *Have students conduct their own research using primary source materials.* Our students must eventually learn that history and geography, like science, are evolving, dynamic disciplines and that, even as students, they can contribute to the knowledge bases in these disciplines. For instance, we might have them study the history of their own community using old newspapers, brochures, personal letters, and other artifacts; they can then display their findings in a local museum (A. Collins, Hawkins, & Carver, 1991). Or we might have them compile specific information about the populations of people living in various parts of their state, province, or country (perhaps voting records, occupations, or health patterns) and then construct maps that depict this information.

Have students conduct their own social studies research.

As you have seen, each of the content domains considered in this chapter—reading, writing, mathematics, science, and social studies—involves numerous skills and abilities that are somewhat domain-specific. Accordingly, different teaching strategies may be more or less applicable for each of them.

Before we close, we need to consider how we can accommodate student diversity as we teach various content areas. And we need to look once again at the four general principles identified at the beginning of the chapter.

INTO THE CLASSROOM: Facilitating Learning in Social Studies

Help students organize the things that they learn.

During a unit on ancient civilizations (e.g., Mesopotamia, Egypt, Greece, Rome), a middle school teacher has her students mark the location of each civilization on a map of the Eastern Hemisphere. She also has them develop a time line that depicts the rise and fall of the various civilizations.

Ask students to draw inferences.

A geography teacher displays a map showing European countries and their capital cities. "Notice how almost all of the capital cities are located either by seaports or on major rivers," he points out. "Why do you suppose that is?"

Identify cause-effect relationships.

A history teacher asks her students to consider the question, "What effects did the Japanese bombing of Pearl Harbor have on the course and final outcome of World War II?"

Encourage empathy for people from diverse cultures and different periods of time.

A fourth-grade teacher encourages his students to imagine themselves as Native Americans who are seeing Europeans for the first time. "You see some strange-looking men sail to shore on big boats—boats much larger than the canoes your own people use. As the men disembark from their boats and approach your village, you see that they have very light skin; in fact, it is almost white. And they have yellow hair and blue eyes. 'Funny colors for hair and eyes,' you think to yourself. How might you feel as these people approach?"

Taking Student Diversity into Account

As we teach reading and writing, we must remember that students' early experiences with language and literature are likely to vary considerably. For instance, students in some African American families may have had few experiences reading storybooks but a great deal of experience with storytelling, jokes, rhymes, and other creative forms of oral language (Trawick-Smith, 1997). And some Native American communities may value nonlinguistic forms of expression, such as art and dancing, more than reading and writing (Trawick-Smith, 1997). We must be sensitive to what students' early literacy experiences have been and use the specific knowledge and skills that they *have* developed as the basis for future instruction in reading and writing.

When teaching mathematics and science, we must keep in mind that these two disciplines have, historically, been considered "male" domains. As a result, the boys in our classes are more likely to believe that they can be successful in these areas; this will be the case even though there are no substantial gender differences in *ability* in these areas (see Chapter 4). We must make a concerted effort to convey the message that mathematics and science are important for girls as well as boys. We should also use instructional strategies—small-group discussions, hands-on activities, cooperative learning, and so on—that encourage males and females alike to become actively involved in studying, talking about, and mastering math and science.

As we teach social studies, we must remember that students' perspectives on history and geography will, in part, be a function of the cultures in which they have been raised

Build on students' early language and literacy experiences.

Take extra steps to motivate and encourage females to achieve in math and science.

and the early family experiences that they have had. For instance, a student with a Japanese heritage is likely to have a very different perspective on Truman's decision to bomb Hiroshima than a student with English ancestors. And students who, as young children, have traveled extensively are apt to have a greater appreciation of distance, a greater knowledge of differing environmental landscapes, and a better understanding of how maps are used (Trawick-Smith, 1997). A friend of mine once described her experience taking children raised in a lower-income, inner-city Denver neighborhood on a field trip into the Rocky Mountains. Even though these children had seen the Rockies many times from downtown Denver, some of them, upon seeing the mountains up close for the very first time, were amazed at how big they were. And a few children were quite surprised to discover that the white stuff on the mountaintops was snow!

Remember that differences in students' cultural backgrounds and early experiences may influence their understanding of history and geography.

Accommodating Students with Special Needs

When we teach various content domains, we must often make special accommodations for those students who have special educational needs. Table 9–2 presents some specific strategies that may be helpful when we work with these students.

The Big Picture: Revisiting the Four General Principles

Although the various domains considered in this chapter involve cognitive processes that are, to some degree, quite specific to those content areas, many of the principles of learning and development that we identified in earlier chapters kept popping up in our discussion. Four principles have been especially prominent:

- *Learners use the information they receive from various sources to build their own, unique understandings of the world.* We've seen this principle at work in how students construct meaning from what they read, engage in knowledge-transforming as they write, and build increasingly complex and integrated understandings as they study mathematics, science, and social studies.

Table 9-3 (pp. 389–390) presents these four principles within each of the content domains.

- *Learners' interpretations of new information and events are influenced by what they already know and believe about the world.* Students draw on their prior knowledge to interpret what they read, and they write more effectively about the things they know well. Their success in learning mathematics depends on the extent to which they've mastered prerequisite concepts and procedures. Their ability to learn and apply scientific principles is influenced by their personal theories about scientific phenomena. And their understanding of social studies is enhanced when they relate historical events and geographical phenomena to their personal experiences.

- *Over time, learners develop cognitive strategies and epistemological beliefs that influence their thinking and performance within a particular content domain.* Good readers, writers, mathematicians, and scientists continually monitor their progress toward goals and ask themselves questions that guide their thinking. Furthermore, certain epistemological beliefs—for example, beliefs that mathematical procedures make logical sense and that much of history is interpretive rather than factual—increase the likelihood that students will learn and achieve at high levels.

- *The ways in which learners think about and understand academic subject matter are qualitatively different at different points in their cognitive development.* Several trends in cognitive development influence students' learning and performance in the content domains, including the increasing automaticity of basic skills and growing abilities to think abstractly, separate and control variables, reason about proportions, and take the perspectives of others.

TABLE 9.2

STUDENTS IN INCLUSIVE SETTINGS

Helping Students with Special Needs Achieve in Various Content Domains

STUDENTS WITH SPECIAL NEEDS	CHARACTERISTICS THAT THESE STUDENTS MAY EXHIBIT	CLASSROOM STRATEGIES THAT MAY BE BENEFICIAL FOR THESE STUDENTS
Students with specific cognitive or academic difficulties	Difficulties in word recognition and reading comprehension Difficulties in spelling and handwriting Tendency to focus on mechanics (rather than meaning) during the revision stage of writing Greater than average difficulty learning basic facts in math, science, and social studies	Assign reading materials appropriate for students' reading skills. Provide extra scaffolding for reading assignments (e.g., shorten assignments, identify main ideas, have students look for answers to specific questions). Provide extra scaffolding for writing activities (e.g., give students a specific structure to follow as they write, encourage use of word processing programs with grammar and spelling checkers). Use concrete manipulatives to teach math and science. Use mnemonics to help students remember basic facts.
Students with social or behavioral problems	Less motivation to achieve academic success in some or all content domains	Have students read and write about topics of personal interest. Ask students to apply math, science, and social studies to situations relevant to their own lives. (Also use strategies listed for students with specific cognitive or academic difficulties.)
Students with general delays in cognitive and social functioning	Delayed language development (e.g., in reading, writing) Less developed knowledge base to which new information can be related Difficulty remembering basic facts Lack of learning strategies such as rehearsal or organization Reasoning abilities characteristic of younger children (e.g., inability to think abstractly in the secondary grades)	Minimize reliance on reading materials as a way of presenting new information. Provide experiences that help students learn the basic knowledge and skills that other students may have already learned on their own. Have students conduct simple scientific experiments in which they need to consider only one or two variables at a time. (Also use strategies listed for students with specific cognitive or academic difficulties.)
Students with physical or sensory challenges	Possibly lower reading skills, especially if students have hearing loss Fewer outside experiences and less general world knowledge upon which instruction in math, science, and social studies can build	Locate Braille texts for students with visual impairments. When students have difficulty with motor coordination, allow them to dictate the things that they write. Conduct demonstrations and experiments to illustrate basic scientific concepts and principles. Use drama and role playing to illustrate historical events. If students have visual impairments, use three-dimensional relief maps and embellish two-dimensional maps with dried glue or nail polish.
Students with advanced cognitive development	Development of reading at an early age Advanced reading comprehension ability More sophisticated writing abilities Greater ability to construct abstract and integrated understandings	Provide challenging tasks (e.g., higher-level reading assignments, more advanced writing assignments). Form study groups in which students can pursue advanced topics in particular domains.

Sources: Bassett et al., 1996; Butterfield & Ferretti, 1987; Cone et al. 1985; Garner, 1998; Graham, Schwartz, & MacArthur, 1993; Hallenbeck, 1996; Mastropieri & Scruggs, 1992; Piirto, 1994; Salend & Hofstetter, 1996; Swanson & Cooney, 1991; Turnbull et al., 1999.

TABLE 9.3

Applying Four General Principles in Different Content Domains

CONTENT DOMAIN	CONSTRUCTIVE PROCESSES	INFLUENCE OF PRIOR KNOWLEDGE	ROLE OF METACOGNITION	QUALITATIVE CHANGES WITH DEVELOPMENT
Reading	Students construct an understanding of an author's intended meaning using the clues that the text provides. Good readers go beyond the specific things that they read, drawing inferences, making predictions, finding symbolism, and so on.	Students use what they already know about a topic to help them construct meaning from text. Their knowledge of typical text structures (e.g., the usual sequence of events of stories, the usual structure of expository text) also assists them in comprehension.	Good readers monitor their comprehension and engage in processes that are likely to increase their comprehension (setting goals, asking questions that they try to answer, etc.).	In the preschool and early elementary years, students begin to develop and use word decoding skills, and they are capable of comprehending simple text. At the upper elementary grades, word recognition is largely automatic, enabling students to focus almost exclusively on comprehension. In the secondary years, students acquire more sophisticated metacognitive skills and become more critical of the things they read.
Writing	Effective writing is a process of knowledge transforming rather than knowledge telling.	Students write more effectively about things that they know well.	Good writers set goals for their writing, consider what their audience is likely to know about their topic, and think consciously about how to help the audience understand the message they are trying to communicate.	Young writers have difficulty writing for an imaginary audience and engage almost exclusively in knowledge telling. As writing mechanics become more automatic in the upper elementary grades, students begin to use complex sentence structures and to focus on communicating effectively. Secondary school students produce more comprehensive and organized texts, and many of them engage in knowledge transforming.
Mathematics	Beginning with a basic understanding of numbers and counting, students build an increasingly complex and integrated understanding of mathematical concepts and principles.	Mathematics is an especially hierarchical discipline—one in which advanced concepts and principles almost always build on ideas learned in earlier years.	Effective problem solvers monitor their progress toward problem solutions. They also have epistemological beliefs conducive to problem-solving success; for instance, they recognize that mathematical procedures make logical sense and know that they may need to try several different approaches before they are successful.	In the elementary grades, students' understanding of mathematics is limited to concrete situations and focuses on simple operations (e.g., addition, multiplication). In the middle and secondary school years, students become increasingly able to think about abstract concepts and procedures (e.g., solving for an unknown x in algebra).

(continued)

continued

CONTENT DOMAIN	CONSTRUCTIVE PROCESSES	INFLUENCE OF PRIOR KNOWLEDGE	ROLE OF METACOGNITION	QUALITATIVE CHANGES WITH DEVELOPMENT
Science	Learning science effectively involves constructing an integrated understanding of concepts and principles related to a particular topic.	Students often develop personal theories about natural phenomena long before they have formal instruction about these phenomena. To the extent that such theories represent inaccurate understandings, they may interfere with students' ability to learn more scientifically acceptable explanations.	Students' beliefs about what science is influence how they study and learn science; for instance, those who believe that science consists of isolated facts are likely to focus on meaningless memorization. Furthermore, students' ability to conduct meaningful experiments is influenced by the extent to which they ask themselves questions about their observations and interpretations (e.g., "Have I confirmed my prediction?").	In the elementary grades, students have difficulty thinking about abstract scientific concepts, and they can separate and control variables only in simple and familiar situations. In the middle school grades, students still have limited abstract reasoning capabilities and so may benefit from concrete models of scientific phenomena (e.g., the idea of heat "flow"). High school students can comprehend abstract scientific explanations, especially after they have studied a topic in depth.
Social Studies	Mastery of history and geography involves constructing integrated understandings of cause-effect relationships.	Students learn social studies more effectively when they can relate historical events and geographical phenomena to their own personal experiences.	A true understanding of history involves the recognition that a great deal of historical "knowledge" is interpretive rather than factual.	Elementary school students (especially those in the lower grades) have difficulty comprehending the nature of historical time and appreciating the symbolic nature of maps. At the secondary level, students' understanding of both history and geography becomes increasingly more abstract. Secondary students are more capable of empathizing with historical figures; in addition, they can apply their proportional reasoning skills to interpreting the scales of various maps.

In this chapter, as well as in the preceding three chapters, we have emphasized the cognitive processes that influence students' learning. But learning involves more than just cognition; it involves behavior as well. In the next chapter, we will consider the behavioral side of human learning as we turn our attention to the *behaviorist* perspective.

CASE STUDY: All Charged Up

Jean, Greg, Jack, and Julie are working on a laboratory assignment in Mr. Hammer's high school physics class. They are using a ball of crumpled aluminum hanging from a piece of string (a device known as a *pith ball*) to determine whether various objects have an electric charge; objects that are charged will make the aluminum ball swing either toward or away from them, and objects that aren't charged will have no effect on the ball. The students have attached two plastic straws—one wrapped in aluminum foil—to opposite sides of an aluminum pie plate, which they have placed on a Styrofoam cup. The materials before them look like this:

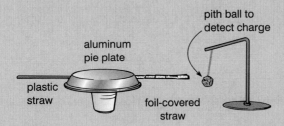

The students put a charge on the aluminum pie plate and discover that the aluminum-covered straw becomes electrically charged (it attracts the pith ball), but the uncovered plastic straw remains uncharged. As Mr. Hammer approaches, Greg explains what the group thinks it has just observed:

Greg: The plate is aluminum, right? And the foil-covered straw is the same thing. The plate charges the foil straw because they're both aluminum.

Mr. Hammer: Hmmm . . . do you think that if the plate were plastic, then the plastic straw would become charged?

Greg: If the plate was charged and if it was plastic, then yes.

Mr. Hammer: So your idea is that one object can charge another only if both objects are made of the same kind of material—that aluminum charges aluminum, and plastic charges plastic?

Greg agrees with Mr. Hammer's statement, as do Julie and Jack. Jean is hesitant, however, and suggests another experiment.

Jean: I don't know; could we try it with the foam? Charge a foam plate, maybe, and then put a foam cup on it.

Mr. Hammer: That's a great experiment.

Mr. Hammer is delighted. He knows that Styrofoam does not conduct electricity, so a foam plate cannot possibly share a charge with a foam cup. He fully expects that the experiment that Jean has proposed will force the students to discard their hypothesis that any object can be charged but will transfer its charge only to other objects of the same material. He gives the group a couple of foam plates to add to their experimental materials and then moves on to converse with other students.

Later in the lab session, Mr. Hammer returns to the foursome to inquire about their observations in the second experiment. He is quite taken aback at what they tell him.

Jack: It worked. The charge on the foam plate spread to the foam cup.

Julie: We even tried it in a different way. We put one foam plate on top of another one, and it gave us the same result.

(continued)

All four students are quite confident about the conclusion they have drawn from their experiments: Charge moves from foam to foam in the same way that it moves from aluminum to aluminum.

- Why do the students draw an erroneous conclusion from their experiments with the foam objects? What common error in scientific reasoning are they making?

- What strategies might Mr. Hammer use to encourage the students to reject their current hypothesis and adopt one more consistent with the laws of physics?

Adapted from Hammer, 1997, p. 486.

Summing Up

Reading

Most children learn some things about literacy (e.g., that particular words are always spelled in the same way) before they begin school; such knowledge is called *emergent literacy.* Skilled reading involves knowing letter-sound correspondences, recognizing both individual letters and entire words quickly and automatically, using context clues to facilitate decoding, constructing meaning from the words on the page, and metacognitively regulating the reading process. Strategies for helping students become proficient readers include promoting phonological awareness, scaffolding students' efforts to make sense of what they read, giving students many opportunities to read authentic literature, and engaging students in discussions about what they are reading.

Writing

Skilled writing involves planning, drafting, metacognition, and revising; good writers move back and forth among these processes. We can help students learn to write effectively by asking them to clarify their goals for writing and the audience for whom they are writing, organize their thoughts before they begin to write, and focus more on clear communication than on writing mechanics in early drafts. We should also assign writing tasks in all areas of the curriculum and provide sufficient criteria and feedback to guide students as they revise their written work.

Mathematics

To master mathematics, students must understand key mathematical concepts and principles, encode problems in ways that facilitate correct solutions, understand problem-solving procedures in terms of the mathematical concepts and principles that underlie them, and acquire appropriate metacognitive processes and beliefs. We can facilitate students' mathematics learning by using concrete situations to illustrate abstract concepts, promoting automaticity in basic facts and skills, giving students a great deal of practice solving a wide variety of problems, and teaching students how to monitor their problem-solving efforts.

Science

Scientific reasoning involves investigating natural phenomena objectively and systematically, constructing theories and models that explain these phenomena, revising those theories and models in light of new evidence or better explanations, and metacognitively overseeing the reasoning process. We can help students learn science and scientific methods by scaffolding their efforts to conduct meaningful and authentic investigations, encouraging them to learn how scientific concepts and principles are interconnected and how they are related to everyday situations, and engaging them in discussions about their hypotheses and predictions.

Social Studies

Effective learning in history involves understanding the nature of historical time, drawing inferences from historical documents, identifying causal relationships among events, and recognizing that historical figures were real people. Effective learning in geography involves understanding that maps are symbolic representations of places, identifying interrelationships among people and their environments, and appreciating cultural differences. When we teach social studies, we should choose topics that encompass important general principles, point out cause-effect relationships, identify similarities among diverse cultures, and have students conduct some of their own social studies research.

General Principles Related to Teaching in the Content Domains

Four key ideas are common to all of the content domains discussed in the chapter: constructive processes, the influence of prior knowledge, the role of metacognition, and qualitative changes with development. Table 9–3 (pp. 389–390) summarizes how these principles play out in each of the content domains.

KEY CONCEPTS

emergent literacy (p. 346)
phonological awareness (p. 346)
word decoding (p. 347)
whole language instruction (p. 351)

translating (p. 355)
personal theories (p. 372)
confirmation bias (p. 373)

theories (p. 374)
models (p. 374)
benchmark lesson or experiment (p. 374)

10

Behaviorist Views of Learning

As we grow from young infants into mature adults, we learn thousands of new behaviors. As toddlers, we learn to walk, feed ourselves, and ask for what we want. As preschoolers, we learn to brush our teeth, ride a tricycle, and use scissors. During the elementary school years, we begin to use a calculator, write in cursive letters, and play team sports. As adolescents, we may learn how to drive a car, ask someone for a date, or perform in an orchestra. In many cases, we develop such behaviors because our environment encourages us—perhaps even requires us—to do so.

Chapter 6 introduced a theoretical perspective known as **behaviorism**—a perspective that focuses on how environmental stimuli bring about changes in the behaviors that people exhibit. In this chapter, we will use behaviorist theories to understand how, as teachers, we can help students acquire behaviors that are perhaps more complex, productive, or prosocial than the ones they exhibit when they first enter our classrooms. In particular, we will address these questions:

- What basic assumptions are central to behaviorists' beliefs about learning?
- How can we explain students' emotional responses to classroom events using the behaviorist notion of classical conditioning?
- How might students acquire a variety of behaviors—both productive ones and undesirable ones—through operant conditioning?
- How can we help students acquire new behaviors and skills using the concepts of reinforcement, shaping, and antecedent stimuli and responses?
- What behaviorist principles can assist us in our efforts to reduce students' inappropriate classroom behaviors?
- What strategies can we use to maintain desirable student behaviors over the long run?
- How can we apply behaviorist principles systematically to address especially difficult classroom behaviors?
- How can we accommodate student diversity in our application of behaviorist principles?

CASE STUDY: The Attention Getter

James is the sixth child in a family of nine children. He likes many things; for example, he likes rock music, comic books, basketball, and strawberry ice cream. But more than anything else, James likes attention.

James is a skillful attention getter. He gets his teacher's attention by blurting answers out in class, throwing paper clips and erasers in the teacher's direction, and refusing to turn in classroom assignments. He gets the attention of classmates by teasing them, poking them, or writing obscenities on the rest room walls. By the middle of the school year, James is getting an extra bonus as well: His antics send him to the main office often enough that he has the school principal's attention at least once a week.

It's true that the attention James gets is often in the form of a teacher's scolding, a classmate's angry retort, or the principal's admonishment that "We can't have any more of this behavior, young man." But after all—attention is attention.

■ Why do you think James chooses such inappropriate behaviors (rather than more appropriate ones) as a way of getting the attention of others? Can you speculate on possible reasons?

■ Exactly what has James learned? Can you derive a principle of learning from James's attention-getting behavior?

Basic Assumptions of Behaviorism

As you consider James's situation, think back to your own experiences as a student in elementary and secondary school. Which students received the most attention, those who behaved appropriately or those who behaved inappropriately? Chances are that it was the *mis*behaving students to whom your teachers and classmates paid the most attention (e.g., J. C. Taylor & Romanczyk, 1994). James has undoubtedly learned that if he wants to be noticed—if he wants to stand out in a crowd—then he must behave in ways that other students are *not*.

THE FAR SIDE   By GARY LARSON

© 1986 FarWorks, Inc./Dist. by Universal Press Syndicate

8-28   Larson

**"Stimulus, response! Stimulus, response!
Don't you ever *think*?"**

THE FAR SIDE © FARWORKS, INC. Used by permission. All rights reserved.

Our case study illustrates a basic assumption of behaviorism: People's behaviors are largely the result of their experiences with environmental stimuli. Several key assumptions that underlie behaviorist views of learning (summarized in Table 10–1) are as follows:

• *People's behaviors are largely the result of their experiences with environmental stimuli.* Many behaviorists believe that, with the exception of a few simple reflexes, a person is born as a "blank slate" (sometimes referred to by the Latin term *tabula rasa*), with no inherited tendency to behave one way or another. Over the years, the environment "writes" on this slate, slowly molding, or **conditioning,** the individual into an adult who has unique characteristics and ways of behaving.

As teachers, we must keep in mind the very significant effect that students' past and present environments are likely to have on the behaviors they exhibit. We can use this basic principle to our advantage: By changing the environmental events that our students experience, we may also be able to change their behaviors.

• *Learning can be described in terms of relationships among observable events—that is, relationships among stimuli and responses.* As mentioned in Chapter 6, behaviorists have traditionally believed that the processes that occur inside a person (thoughts, beliefs, attitudes, etc.) cannot be observed and so cannot be studied scientifically. Many behaviorists describe a person as a "black box"—something that cannot be opened for inspection. Psychological inquiry should instead focus on things that can be observed and

TABLE 10.1

PRINCIPLES/ASSUMPTIONS

Basic Assumptions of Behaviorism and Their Educational Implications

ASSUMPTION	EDUCATIONAL IMPLICATION	EXAMPLE
Influence of the environment	Develop a classroom environment that fosters desirable student behaviors.	When a student often has trouble working independently, inconspicuously praise her every time she completes an assignment without having to be prompted.
Focus on observable events (stimuli and responses)	Identify specific stimuli (including your own behaviors) that may be influencing the behaviors that students exhibit.	If a student frequently engages in disruptive classroom behavior, consider whether you might be encouraging such behavior by giving the student attention every time it occurs.
Learning as a behavior change	Do not assume that learning has occurred unless students exhibit a change in classroom performance.	Look for concrete evidence that learning has taken place, rather than assume that students have learned simply because they say they understand what they are studying.
Contiguity of events	If you want students to associate two events (stimuli and/or responses) with each other, make sure the events occur close together in time.	Include enjoyable yet educational activities in each day's schedule as a way of helping students associate school subject matter with pleasurable feelings.
Similarity of learning principles across species	Remember that research with nonhuman species often has relevance for classroom practice.	Reinforce a hyperactive student for sitting quietly for successively longer periods of time—a *shaping* process based on early research studies with rats and pigeons.

studied objectively; more specifically, it should focus on the responses that learners make (symbolized as *R*s) and the environmental stimuli (*S*s) that bring those responses about.

Not all behaviorists hold firmly to the black box assumption, however. In recent years, some have begun to incorporate cognitive processes into their theoretical explanations (Rachlin, 1989, 1991; Rescorla, 1988; Schwartz & Reisberg, 1991; A. R. Wagner, 1981). It is becoming increasingly evident, even to behaviorists, just how difficult it is to omit thought from our explanations of learning and behavior.

• *Learning involves a behavior change.* From a behaviorist perspective, learning itself should be defined as something that can be observed and documented; in other words, it should be defined as a change in behavior. This definition can be especially useful for us as teachers. To illustrate, consider this scenario:

> Your students look at you attentively as you explain a difficult concept. When you finish, you ask, "Any questions?" You look around the room, and not a single hand is raised. "Good," you think, "they all understand."

Assume that learning has occurred only when you see changes in student behavior.

But *do* your students understand? On the basis of what you've just observed, you really have no idea whether they do or not. Only observable behavior changes—perhaps an improvement in test scores, a greater frequency of independent reading, or a reduction in hitting and kicking—can ultimately tell us that learning has occurred.

• *Learning is most likely to take place when stimuli and responses occur close together in time.* For stimulus-response relationships to develop, certain events must occur in conjunction with other events. When two events occur at more or less the same time, we say that there is **contiguity** between them. These two examples illustrate contiguity:

> One of your instructors scowls at you as she hands back the exam she has just corrected. You discover that you have gotten a D− on the exam, and you get an uncomfortable feeling in the pit of your stomach. The next time your instructor scowls at you, that same uncomfortable feeling returns.

> Another instructor smiles and calls on you every time you raise your hand. Although you are fairly quiet in your other classes, you find yourself raising your hand and speaking up more and more frequently in this one.

In the first situation, the instructor's scowl and the D− on your exam are presented more or less simultaneously; here we see contiguity between two stimuli. In the second situation, your response of raising your hand is followed immediately by the instructor's smile and his calling on you; in this case, we see contiguity between a response and two stimuli (although smiling and calling on you are responses that the instructor makes, they are *stimuli* for *you*). In both situations, your behavior has changed: You've learned to respond with an unpleasant feeling in your stomach every time a particular instructor scowls, and you've learned to raise your hand and speak up more frequently in another instructor's class.

• *Many species of animals, including humans, learn in similar ways.* Behaviorists are well known for their experiments with such animals as rats and pigeons. They assume that many species share similar learning processes; hence, they apply the learning principles that they derive from observing one species to their understanding of how many other species (including humans) learn.

Students in my own educational psychology classes sometimes resent having their own learning compared to the learning of rats and pigeons. But the fact is that behaviorist theories developed from the study of nonhuman animals often *do* explain human behavior. In the pages that follow, we will focus on two behaviorist theories—classical conditioning and operant conditioning—that have been derived largely from animal research, yet can nevertheless help us understand many aspects of human learning and behavior.

What animals have you observed learning something new? Can you think of any similarities in the ways that animals and people learn?

Classical Conditioning

Consider this situation:

> Alan has always loved baseball. But in a game last year, he was badly hurt by a wild pitch while he was up at bat. Now, although he still plays baseball, he gets anxious whenever it is his turn at bat, to the point where he often backs away from the ball instead of swinging at it.

One possible explanation of Alan's learning is **classical conditioning,** a theory that explains how we sometimes learn new responses as a result of two stimuli (in this case, the sight of a baseball coming toward him and the pain of the ball's impact) being present at approximately the same time. Alan's current responses to a pitched ball—anxiety and backing away—are ones that he didn't exhibit before his painful experience with a baseball; thus, learning has occurred.

Classical conditioning was first described by Ivan Pavlov (e.g., 1927), a Russian physiologist who was conducting research related to the physiology of salivation. Pavlov often used dogs as his research subjects and presented meat to get them to salivate. He noticed that the dogs frequently began to salivate as soon as they heard the lab assistant coming down the hall, even though they could not yet smell the meat the assistant was carrying. Curious about this phenomenon, Pavlov conducted an experiment to examine more systematically how a dog learns to salivate to a new stimulus. His experiment went something like this:

1. Pavlov flashes a light. The dog does not salivate to the light stimulus. Using S for stimulus and R for response, we can symbolize Pavlov's first observation like so:

$$S \text{ (light)} \longrightarrow R \text{ (none)}$$

2. Pavlov flashes the light again and presents meat immediately afterward. He repeats this procedure several times, and the dog salivates every time. The dog is demonstrating something that it already knows how to do—salivate to meat—so it has not yet learned anything new. We can symbolize Pavlov's second observation like so:

$$\left. \begin{array}{l} S \text{ (light)} \\ \\ S \text{ (meat)} \end{array} \right\} \longrightarrow R \text{ (salivation)}$$

3. Pavlov flashes the light once more, but this time without any meat. The dog salivates; in other words, it has learned a new response to the light stimulus. We can symbolize Pavlov's third observation this way:

$$S \text{ (light)} \longrightarrow R \text{ (salivation)}$$

In more general terms, classical conditioning proceeds as follows:

1. It begins with a stimulus-response association that already exists—in other words, with an *unconditioned* stimulus-response association. For example, Pavlov's dog salivates automatically whenever it smells meat, and Alan becomes anxious and backs away whenever he encounters a painful stimulus; no learning is involved in either case. When a stimulus leads to a particular response without prior learning, we say that an **unconditioned stimulus (UCS)** *elicits* an **unconditioned response** (UCR). The unconditioned response is typically an automatic, involuntary one—one over which the individual has little or no control.

2. Conditioning occurs when a **neutral stimulus**—one that doesn't elicit any particular response—is presented immediately before the unconditioned stimulus. For example, in the case of Pavlov's dog, a light is presented immediately before the meat; in the case of Alan, a baseball is pitched immediately before the painful hit. Conditioning is especially likely to occur when both stimuli are presented together on several occasions and when the neutral stimulus occurs *only* when the unconditioned stimulus is about to follow (R. R. Miller & Barnet, 1993; Rachlin, 1991; Rescorla, 1967).

3. Before long, the new stimulus also elicits a response, usually one very similar to the unconditioned response. The neutral stimulus has become a **conditioned stimulus (CS)**, and the response to it is called a **conditioned response (CR)**. For example, Pavlov's dog acquires a conditioned response of salivation to a new, conditioned stimulus—the light. Likewise, Alan acquires conditioned

The word *elicit*, meaning "draw forth or bring out," is frequently used in descriptions of classical conditioning.

responses of anxiety and backing away to a pitched baseball. Like the unconditioned response, the conditioned response is an involuntary one; it occurs automatically every time the conditioned stimulus is presented.

Classical Conditioning of Emotional Responses

Experiencing Firsthand
"Classical" Music

Some songs make people feel certain ways. For example, Handel's "Water Music" always elicits especially "happy" feelings in me, perhaps because it's the music that was played at my wedding. The theme from the television show *Dragnet* still elicits tinges of anxiety in me because the show frightened me when I was a young child. Take a minute and think about particular songs you might listen to if you wanted to experience each of the following feelings:

Feeling	Song
Happiness	_____
Relaxation	_____
Anxiety	_____
Sadness	_____

Why do the songs bring out such feelings? Can you trace those feelings to significant occasions in your life when each song was playing?

In some cases, your emotional reactions to a song may be attributable simply to the mood that the song conveys. But in other cases, a song may make you feel the way you do because you associate it with particular events. Consider the case of Brenda:

At the school dance, Brenda has one dance with Joe, a boy she has a tremendous crush on. They dance to "Michelle," an old Beatles song. Later, whenever Brenda hears "Michelle," she feels happy.

In this situation, Joe is initially the source of Brenda's good feelings. A second stimulus— "Michelle"—is associated with Joe, and so the song begins to elicit those same feelings. From a classical conditioning perspective, we can analyze the situation this way:

UCS: Joe $\rightarrow$ UCR: good feelings about Joe

CS: "Michelle" $\rightarrow$ CR: good feelings about "Michelle"

Here are some other examples of how emotional responses might be learned through classical conditioning. Notice that in every case, two stimuli are presented together. One stimulus already elicits a response, and as a result of the pairing, the second stimulus begins to elicit a similar response.

Bernard falls into a swimming pool and almost drowns. A year later, when his mother takes him to the local recreation center for a swimming lesson, he cries hysterically as his mother tries to drag him to the side of the pool.

UCS: inability to breathe $\rightarrow$ UCR: fear of being unable to breathe

CS: swimming pool $\rightarrow$ CR: fear of the swimming pool

Bobby misses a month of school because of illness. When he returns to school, he does not know how to do his long division assignments. After a number of frustrating experiences in which he fails long division problems, he begins to feel anxious whenever he encounters a division task.

| UCS: | failure/frustration | $\rightarrow$ | UCR: | anxiety about failure |
| CS: | long division | $\rightarrow$ | CR: | anxiety about long division |

Beth's teacher catches Beth writing a letter to one of her classmates during class. The teacher reads the note to the entire class, revealing some very personal and private information about Beth. Beth now feels embarrassed whenever she goes into that teacher's classroom.

| UCS: | humiliation | $\rightarrow$ | UCR: | embarrassment in response to humiliation |
| CS: | teacher/classroom | $\rightarrow$ | CR: | embarrassment in response to teacher/classroom |

Classical conditioning is frequently used to explain why people sometimes respond emotionally to what might otherwise be fairly "neutral" stimuli. When a particular stimulus is associated with something that makes us happy or relaxed, it may begin to elicit those same feelings of happiness or relaxation. When a stimulus is associated with something that makes us fearful or anxious, it, too, may begin to elicit feelings of fear and anxiety.

As teachers, we must maintain a classroom whose stimuli (including our own behaviors toward students) are those likely to elicit such responses as enjoyment or relaxation, *not* fear or anxiety. When students associate school with pleasant stimuli—positive feedback, enjoyable activities, and so on—they soon learn that school is a place where they want to be. But when they instead encounter unpleasant stimuli in school—negative comments, public humiliation, or constant frustration and failure—they may eventually learn to fear or dislike a particular activity, subject area, teacher, or (perhaps) school in general.

Generalization

When people learn a conditioned response to a new stimulus, they may also respond in the same way to similar stimuli—a phenomenon known as **generalization.** For example, a boy who learns to feel anxious about long division tasks may generalize that anxiety to other aspects of mathematics. And a girl who experiences humiliation in one classroom may generalize her embarrassment to other classrooms as well. Here we see

Do you remember the earlier example of learning to respond negatively to an instructor's scowl? Can you explain your learning from the perspective of classical conditioning?

 Create a pleasant, upbeat classroom atmosphere.

Remember that the feelings students develop in response to you, your classroom, and school subject matter may generalize to situations far beyond the classroom itself.

When students associate school with pleasant stimuli, they learn that school is a place where they want to be.

one more reason why students should associate pleasant feelings with classroom subject matter. Students' reactions to school and class activities may generalize to situations far beyond the classroom itself.

Extinction

Pavlov discovered that conditioned responses don't necessarily last forever. By pairing a light with meat, he conditioned a dog to salivate to the light alone. But later, when he flashed the light repeatedly without ever again following it with meat, the dog salivated less and less. Eventually, the dog no longer salivated when it saw the light flash. When a conditioned stimulus occurs repeatedly *in the absence of* the unconditioned stimulus—for example, when a light is never again associated with meat, when mathematics is never again associated with failure, or when a teacher is never again associated with humiliation—the conditioned response may decrease and eventually disappear. In other words, **extinction** has occurred.

Many conditioned responses fade over time. Unfortunately, many others do not; a person's fear of water or anxiety about mathematics may persist for years. One reason that fears or anxieties regarding certain stimuli are likely to persist over time is that people tend to avoid those situations that cause such emotional reactions. If they stay away from a stimulus that makes them fearful, they never have a chance to experience that stimulus in the absence of the unconditioned stimulus with which it was originally paired. As a result, they have no opportunity to learn *not* to be afraid—they have no opportunity for the response to undergo extinction.

As teachers, how can we reduce the counterproductive conditioned responses that our students may exhibit—for example, their fear of water or their mathematics anxiety? Psychologists have learned that one way to extinguish a negative emotional reaction to a particular conditioned stimulus is to introduce that stimulus *slowly and gradually* while the student is happy or relaxed (M. C. Jones, 1924; Wolpe, 1969). For example, if Bernard is afraid of water, we might begin his swimming lessons someplace where he feels at ease—perhaps on dry land or in the baby pool—and move to deeper water only as he begins to feel more comfortable. If Bernice gets overly anxious every time she attempts a mathematics problem, we might revert back to easier problems—those she can readily solve—and gradually increase the difficulty of her assignments only as she demonstrates greater competence and self-confidence.

There is nothing like success to help students feel good about being in the classroom. One thing we can do to facilitate student success is structure the classroom environment so that appropriate behaviors are reinforced and inappropriate behaviors are not. It is to the role that reinforcement plays in learning—to operant conditioning—that we turn now.

▲ We will consider the nature and effects of anxiety in more detail in our discussion of motivation in Chapter 12.

🍎 When a particular subject matter or task arouses anxiety in students, present it slowly and gradually while they are happy and relaxed.

Operant Conditioning

Mark is a student in Ms. Ferguson's geography class. This is what happens to Mark during the first week in October:

Monday: Ms. Ferguson asks the class to locate Colombia on the globe. Mark knows where Colombia is, and he sits smiling, with his hands in his lap, hoping that Ms. Ferguson will call on him. Instead, Ms. Ferguson calls on another student.

Tuesday: Ms. Ferguson asks the class where Colombia got its name. Mark knows that Colombia is named after Christopher Columbus, so he raises his hand a few inches. Ms. Ferguson calls on another student.

Wednesday: Ms. Ferguson asks the class why people in Colombia speak Spanish, rather than English or French. Mark knows that Colombians speak Spanish because

INTO THE CLASSROOM: Applying Principles of Classical Conditioning

Create a positive classroom environment.

A third-grade teacher plans many activities that make classroom learning fun. He never ridicules students for mistakes they may make.

Be sure that students associate success with all areas of the curriculum.

A high school mathematics teacher takes a mastery approach to teaching algebra, making sure that her students master each concept and procedure before moving to more advanced material.

When a particular subject or task arouses anxiety in students, present it slowly and gradually while they are happy and relaxed.

When teaching a water-phobic child to swim, a swimming instructor begins the first lesson by playing games in the baby pool, moving to deeper water very gradually as the child seems comfortable about doing so.

the country's early European settlers came from Spain. He raises his hand high in the air. Ms. Ferguson calls on another student.

Thursday: Ms. Ferguson asks the class why Colombia grows coffee but Canada does not. Mark knows that coffee can only be grown in certain climates. He raises his hand high and waves it wildly back and forth. Ms. Ferguson calls on him.

Friday: Whenever Ms. Ferguson asks a question that Mark can answer, Mark raises his hand high and waves it wildly about.

Notice how several of Mark's behaviors in geography class, such as sitting quietly, smiling, and raising his hand politely, bring no results. But waving his hand wildly does bring Mark the result that he wants: his teacher's attention. The response that has attracted Ms. Ferguson's attention continues. Other responses disappear.

The change in Mark's behavior illustrates **operant conditioning,** a form of learning described by many behaviorists and most notably by B. F. Skinner (e.g., 1953, 1954, 1968). The basic principle of operant conditioning is a simple one:

A response that is followed by a reinforcing stimulus (a reinforcer) is more likely to occur again.

When behaviors are followed by desirable consequences, they tend to increase in frequency. When behaviors don't produce results, they typically decrease and may even disappear altogether.

Students often learn and demonstrate new behaviors for the consequences that those behaviors bring. Here are some examples:

Sergio brings a fancy new bicycle to school and finds himself surrounded by classmates who want to ride it. Suddenly Sergio has several new "friends."

Sharon decreases the number of steps that she takes when she bowls. She now gets more strikes and spares than she used to.

Steven studies hard for his French vocabulary quiz. He gets an A on the quiz.

Samirah copies her answers to the French quiz from Steven's paper. She gets an A on the quiz.

Many appropriate and productive behaviors—such as studying French or trying a new approach to bowling—are acquired because of the desirable consequences to which they lead. Many inappropriate and undesirable behaviors—such as cheating on a quiz or waving one's hand wildly about—may be acquired for the same reason.

As teachers, we should be sure to reinforce the behaviors we want our students to learn. If we want students to read frequently, to volunteer in class, to demonstrate good form in dribbling and passing a soccer ball, or to work cooperatively with their classmates, we should reinforce such behaviors as they occur. At the same time, we should be careful *not* to reinforce any inappropriate and counterproductive behaviors that students exhibit. If we repeatedly allow Jane to turn in assignments late because she tells us she forgot her homework and if we often let Jake get his way by bullying his classmates on the playground, then we are reinforcing (and hence increasing) Jane's excuse making and Jake's aggressiveness.

Contrasting Classical and Operant Conditioning

Like classical conditioning, operant conditioning involves both a stimulus and a response. But operant conditioning is different from classical conditioning in two important ways:

- *The order of the stimulus and response.* In classical conditioning, certain stimuli lead to certain responses, like this:

$$S \rightarrow R$$

But in operant conditioning, the response comes first, followed by a reinforcing consequence. The reinforcing consequence is actually a stimulus, so we will use the notation S_{Rf}. We can symbolize the relationship between stimulus and response this way:

$$R \rightarrow S_{Rf}$$

- *The nature of the response.* In classical conditioning, a response occurs as a result of a particular stimulus; in other words, the stimulus elicits the response. The learner often has little or no control over whether the response occurs. But in operant conditioning, the response is usually a voluntary one: The learner can control whether or not it occurs. As an example, consider James, the attention getter in our opening case study. Several of James's responses, such as blurting out answers, throwing erasers across the room, and teasing classmates, increased as a result of the attention (a stimulus) that such responses brought. Yet James willingly made these responses; no particular stimulus forced him to do so.

Three Essential Conditions for Operant Conditioning

Operant conditioning can occur only under three conditions:

- *The individual must make a response.* To be reinforced—to *learn*—the learner must first make a response. Behaviorists believe that little is accomplished by having students sit quietly and listen passively to their teacher. Instead, students are more likely to learn when they are making active, overt responses in the classroom (e.g., Drevno et al., 1994). For example, Pamela will learn her cursive letters most easily by writing them. Peter will learn how to make a good cake only by actually making cakes. Paula will be able to solve mathematical word problems easily only when she works with such problems on a regular basis.

- *A reinforcer must follow the response.* Operant conditioning occurs only when a reinforcer comes *after* a response. A teacher who gives students several minutes of free time after they have completed an assignment or who lets students go to lunch only after they have cleaned their desks is following this principle. A teacher who gives

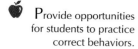

Do you have any bad habits that the environment has in some way reinforced?

Reinforce desirable behaviors; don't inadvertently reinforce *un*desirable ones.

Provide opportunities for students to practice correct behaviors.

Make sure reinforcers *follow* desired behaviors, rather than vice versa.

students five minutes of free time before they begin working on an assignment or who tells students that they must clean up their mess after they come back from lunch has things in the wrong order.

To be most effective, reinforcement should occur *immediately* after a desired response has occurred; in other words, the response and the reinforcing stimulus should occur in close contiguity. If students find the country of Colombia on a globe, or pronounce "*Comment allez vous?*" like a Frenchman, or execute a good tennis serve, they should experience some form of immediate reinforcement—perhaps a smile, words of praise ("*Très bien!*"), or a tennis opponent's failure to return a serve. The more closely a reinforcer follows a response, the more effective it is likely to be (J. A. Kulik & Kulik, 1988; Rachlin, 1991). Delayed reinforcers sometimes have an effect on behavior, but they are most likely to be effective with older students, and especially with learners who immediately realize that a particular behavior will eventually lead to reinforcement (Fowler & Baer, 1981; Green, Fry, & Myerson, 1994).

- *The reinforcer must be presented only when the response has occurred.* For successful operant conditioning, the reinforcer should occur *only* after a particular response has occurred; it should never occur in the absence of that response. In other words, the reinforcer must be **contingent** on the desired behavior. A teacher who praises students only when they behave appropriately is making reinforcement contingent on desired responses. In contrast, the teacher who laughs at the antics of a chronically misbehaving student is providing reinforcement even when an acceptable response hasn't occurred, so the student's behavior is unlikely to improve.

Make sure desired behaviors are reinforced immediately in some fashion.

Present a reinforcer *only* when a student has made a desired response.

How is the concept of *contingency* different from *contiguity*?

Reinforcement in the Classroom

Experiencing Firsthand
What Would It Take?

Imagine this scenario:

You are currently enrolled in my educational psychology class. As your instructor, I ask you to spend an hour after class tutoring two classmates who are having difficulty understanding the course material. You have no other commitments for that hour; however, you'd really rather spend the time at a nearby coffee shop, where you know several of your friends are having lunch. What would it take for you to spend the hour tutoring your classmates instead of joining your friends? Would you do it as a way of gaining my approval? Would you do it if I gave you a candy bar? Would you do it if I gave you five dollars? Would you do it simply because it made you feel good inside to be helping someone else? Write down a reward—one that I have listed or a different one altogether—that would persuade you to help your classmates instead of meeting your friends.

And now imagine this second scenario:

A few weeks later, I ask you to spend the weekend (eight hours a day on both Saturday and Sunday) tutoring the same two struggling classmates. What would it take this time to convince you to do the job? Would my approval do the trick? a candy bar? five dollars? five *hundred* dollars? Or would your internal sense of satisfaction be enough? Once again, write down what it would take for you to agree to help your classmates.

Obviously, there are no "right" answers for the exercise you just completed. Different people would agree to tutor their classmates for different reasons. But you were probably able to identify at least one consequence in each situation that would entice you to give up your own personal time to help your classmates.

We often talk about giving students rewards for their academic achievements and for appropriate classroom behaviors. But as you may have noticed, I have not used the term *reward* in my description of operant conditioning. I have been using the term *reinforcer* for a very important reason. The word *reward* brings to mind things that we would all agree are pleasant and desirable—things like candy, praise, money, trophies, or special privileges. But some individuals increase their behavior for consequences that others would not find so appealing. A **reinforcer** is *any consequence that increases the frequency of a particular behavior,* whether other people find that consequence pleasant or not. The act of following a particular response with a reinforcer is called **reinforcement.**

Let's return once again to our attention-getting student. James learned that he could get his teacher's attention by blurting out answers in class, throwing objects around the room, and refusing to turn in classroom assignments. We can assume that James's teacher is not smiling or praising him for such behavior. Probably the teacher is frowning, scolding, or even yelling. We don't usually think of frowning, scolding, and yelling as rewards. Yet those consequences are leading to an increase in James's misbehaviors, so they are apparently reinforcing for James.

Some students may thrive on teacher scoldings even though others dislike them. Some students may respond well to praise, but others (perhaps those who don't want to be labeled "teacher's pet" by their peers) may view a teacher's praise as a fate worse than death (e.g., Pfiffner, Rosen, & O'Leary, 1985). Some students may work at academic tasks simply for the feelings of success and accomplishment that such activities bring, but others may work diligently at the same tasks only if doing so leads to social reinforcers—perhaps the respect of classmates or the opportunity to spend time with friends. Some students like getting As, but others (perhaps those afraid of being labeled a "nerd") may actually prefer Cs. An important principle of operant conditioning, then, is that *different stimuli are reinforcing for different individuals.* We must never make assumptions about what specific events are reinforcing for particular students.

Reinforcement comes in all shapes and sizes. In the next few pages we will look at two basic distinctions that operant conditioning theorists make: primary versus secondary reinforcers, and positive versus negative reinforcement. As we do so, we will identify a number of potentially effective reinforcers that we can use in classroom settings.

Primary Versus Secondary Reinforcers

A **primary reinforcer** satisfies a basic physiological need; food, water, warmth, and oxygen are all examples. To some extent, physical affection and cuddling may address biological needs as well (Harlow & Zimmerman, 1959). And for an adolescent addicted to an illegal substance, the next "fix" is also a primary reinforcer.

In contrast, a **secondary reinforcer** does not satisfy any physiological need yet becomes reinforcing over time through its association with another reinforcer. For example, perhaps praise was once associated with a special candy treat from mother, or a good grade was associated with a hug from father. Through such associations, consequences such as praise, good grades, money, feelings of success, and perhaps even scolding become reinforcing in their own right: They become secondary reinforcers.

Secondary reinforcers are far more common in classrooms than primary reinforcers. But we must remember that secondary reinforcers are *learned* reinforcers, and not everyone has come to appreciate them. Although most of our students will probably respond positively to such consequences as praise or a good grade, a few students may not.

How do *you* feel when a teacher praises you in front of your classmates?

Don't make assumptions about what specific events will be reinforcing for particular students.

Can you think of other examples of primary and secondary reinforcers?

Remember that not all students have learned to appreciate such secondary reinforcers as praise and good grades.

Positive Versus Negative Reinforcement

Up to this point, we have been speaking of reinforcement as the *presentation* of a particular reinforcing stimulus. But in some cases, we can also reinforce a behavior through the *removal* of a stimulus. Operant conditioning theorists distinguish between these two situations by using the terms *positive reinforcement* and *negative reinforcement*.

Positive Reinforcement

Whenever a particular stimulus is *presented* after a behavior, and the behavior increases as a result, **positive reinforcement** has occurred. This is the case whether or not the presented stimulus is one that others would agree is pleasant and desirable. For instance, some students will make a response to get a teacher's praise, but others (like James in our case study) may behave to get themselves a scolding. Most students will work for As, but a few may actually prefer Cs or even Fs. Depending on the individual, any one of these stimuli—the praise, the scolding, the A, or the F—may be a positive reinforcer.

A variety of positive reinforcers can increase the frequency of desired student behaviors; these are described in the following paragraphs.

Concrete reinforcers. A concrete reinforcer is an actual object—something that can be touched. Snacks, stickers, and toys are all examples of concrete reinforcers. Such reinforcers are especially likely to be effective with young children (e.g., Rimm & Masters, 1974).

Social reinforcers. A social reinforcer is a gesture or sign that one person gives another regarding a recently performed response. A smile, a hug, attention, praise, and "thank you" are all social reinforcers; coming from a teacher, they are often effective reinforcers for students (L. Katz, 1993; Piersel, 1987; Schepis, Reid, & Fitzgerald, 1987). The approval of a student's friends and classmates can also be very reinforcing (G. W. Evans & Oswalt, 1968; Lovitt, Guppy, & Blattner, 1969). As teachers, we can often use simple social gestures—smiles, compliments, nods of approval, and expressions of appreciation—as classroom reinforcers. We can also provide opportunities for students to reinforce one another for desirable academic and social behaviors (T. R. McDaniel, 1987; Northup et al., 1995).

Activity reinforcers. An activity reinforcer is an opportunity to engage in a favorite activity. Students will often do one thing—perhaps something they don't like to do—if doing so allows them to do something they do enjoy. This phenomenon is sometimes called the **Premack principle** (Premack, 1959, 1963). For example, third graders are more likely to sit quietly if being quiet enables them to go to lunch. High school students

Remember that some consequences that you think of in "negative" terms (e.g., scoldings, bad grades) may nevertheless be *positively* reinforcing for some students.

If necessary, use concrete reinforcers, especially with young children.

Show your approval of appropriate behavior; give students opportunities to reinforce one another as well.

Follow less enjoyable activities with more enjoyable ones.

GARFIELD / Jim Davis

Attention can be a very effective reinforcer.

are more likely to do their homework if their parents make extracurricular activities contingent on getting schoolwork done first. And students at risk for dropping out of school are more likely to come to school regularly if a good attendance record will earn them a trip to a local amusement park (Sanders, 1996).

🍎 Make some reinforcers contingent on group performance.

Group contingencies. A group contingency is a situation in which students are reinforced only when *everyone* in a particular group (perhaps everyone in the classroom) achieves at a certain level or behaves in an appropriate fashion. Group contingencies are clearly effective in improving academic achievement and classroom behavior, provided that everyone in the group is capable of making the desired response (Barbetta, 1990; Lentz, 1988). Consider these two examples as evidence:

> A class of 32 fourth graders was not doing very well on weekly spelling tests. On the average, only 12 students (38%) had perfect spelling tests in any given week. Hoping for improvement, their teacher announced that any student with a perfect test score would get free time later in the week. The new reinforcement program had a noticeable effect: The average number of perfect spelling tests rose to 25 a week (80%). But then the teacher added a group contingency: Whenever the entire class achieved perfect spelling tests by Friday, the class could listen to the radio for 15 minutes. The group contingency produced an average of 30 perfect spelling tests (94%) a week (Lovitt et al., 1969).

> Another fourth-grade teacher was dealing with an unusually unruly class: In any given minute, chances were that one or more students would be talking out of turn or getting out of their seats. In a desperate move, the teacher divided the class into two teams that competed in a "good behavior game." Each time a student was observed talking out of turn or getting out of his or her seat, the student's team received a chalk mark on the chalkboard. The team that received fewer marks during a lesson won special privileges—for example, being first in the lunch line or having free time at the end of the day. When both teams had five marks or fewer, everyone won privileges. Misbehaviors in the class dropped almost immediately to less than 20 percent of their initial frequency (Barrish, Saunders, & Wolf, 1969).

Group contingencies are probably effective for at least two reasons. One reason may be peer pressure: Students encourage their classmates to achieve and to behave themselves, and then reinforce those classmates for doing so (O'Leary & O'Leary, 1972). Furthermore, students begin to tutor one another in academic subjects, a practice that enhances achievement (e.g., Pigott, Fantuzzo, & Clement, 1986). Group contingencies play an important role in *cooperative learning,* an instructional strategy we will discuss in Chapter 14.

🍎 Tell students exactly what they have done well and how they can improve their performance further.

Playing a team sport is an example of a behavior reinforced by a group contingency: The team wins together or loses together.

Positive feedback. Sometimes the simple message that an answer is correct or that a task has been done well—positive feedback—is reinforcement enough. For example, you can probably think of times when you were happy about getting an answer right even though knowing the answer did not affect your class grade the tiniest bit. Many students want to do well in school, so feedback that they have been successful may be a sufficient consequence to increase desired classroom behaviors. Feedback is most effective when it tells students in explicit terms what they are doing well and what they can do to improve their performance even further (Bangert-Drowns, Kulik, Kulik, & Morgan, 1991; Butler & Winne, 1995).

Intrinsic reinforcers. Until now, we've been talking about **extrinsic reinforcers**—reinforcers provided by the external environment (often by other people). In contrast, intrinsic reinforcers are supplied by learners themselves or inherent in the task being performed. Students engage in some activities simply because they enjoy those activities or because they like to feel competent and successful. When students perform certain behaviors in the absence of any observable reinforcers—when they read an entire book without putting it down, when they do extra classwork without being asked, when they practice on their electric guitars into the wee hours of the morning—they are probably working for the intrinsic reinforcement that such behaviors yield.

It is important to note that intrinsic reinforcers are *not* observable events; as such, they do not fit comfortably within traditional behaviorist theory. Yet people clearly do engage in some behaviors solely for the intrinsic satisfaction that those behaviors bring. We will talk more about such *intrinsic motivation* in Chapter 12.

Some reinforcers, such as praise, are concrete and visible. Others, such as feelings of accomplishment and pride, are less noticeable but equally effective.

From our perspective as teachers, positive feedback and the intrinsic reinforcers that such feedback brings are probably the most desirable forms of classroom reinforcement. But we must remember that consistent positive feedback and the resulting feelings of success and mastery can occur only when classroom instruction has been carefully tailored to individual skill levels and abilities, and only when students have learned to value academic achievement. When students are not motivated to achieve academic success (for whatever reasons), then social reinforcers, activity reinforcers, group contingencies, and (if necessary) even concrete reinforcers can be used to increase desired classroom behaviors.

Provide opportunities for students to pursue intrinsically reinforcing activities.

How might you determine which reinforcers are most effective for your students?

Experiencing Firsthand
Take Two on "What Would It Take?"

In a preceding exercise, you considered what would entice you to spend time tutoring classmates when you'd really rather join your friends at the local coffee shop. Classify each one of these consequences of tutoring your classmates in terms of the kind of reinforcer it reflects:

Consequence	Kind of reinforcer
You gain my approval.	_____
You get a candy bar.	_____
You get five dollars.	_____
You feel good about helping somebody else.	_____

You can find the correct answers at the bottom of the page.[1] But no peeking until you've made your own decisions!

---

[1]My approval is a social reinforcer, the candy bar and the money are concrete reinforcers, and feeling good about what you have done is an intrinsic reinforcer. Of these, only the candy bar is a primary reinforcer; the other three are secondary reinforcers.

Negative Reinforcement

As we have just seen, positive reinforcement involves the presentation of a stimulus. In contrast, **negative reinforcement** brings about the increase of a behavior through the *removal* of a stimulus (typically an unpleasant one). The word *negative* here is not a value judgment; it simply refers to the act of taking away a stimulus.[2] When people make a response to get rid of something, they are being negatively reinforced. We saw an example of negative reinforcement in our opening case study. When James misbehaved, he was often sent to the principal's office; this negatively reinforced his misbehavior because it enabled him to *get out of class* (to remove a stimulus—the class environment—that may have been aversive for him).

Here are additional examples of negative reinforcement:

A rat is getting an electric shock through the floor of its cage. It learns to press a metal bar to terminate the shock.

Rhonda must read *Ivanhoe* for her English literature class before the end of the month. She doesn't like having this assignment hanging over her head, so she finishes it early. When she's done, she no longer has to worry about it.

Reuben is in the same literature class. Whenever he sits down at home to read *Ivanhoe,* he finds the novel confusing and difficult to understand. He quickly ends his study sessions by finding other things that he "needs" to do instead—things like playing basketball with his friends, washing his hair, or folding his socks.

Ms. Randolph yells at her rowdy seventh graders. They quiet down. By yelling, Ms. Randolph has stopped a noisy and unpleasant stimulus (if only temporarily), and so her yelling has been negatively reinforced.

In the examples just presented, notice how negative reinforcement sometimes promotes desirable behaviors—such as completing an assignment early—and at other times promotes undesirable behaviors—such as procrastination. And notice, as well, how students are not the only ones who respond to reinforcement in the classroom. After all, teachers are human beings too!

As teachers, we will use negative reinforcement rarely if at all; ideally, we want to create a classroom environment in which there are few stimuli that students want to be rid of. Nevertheless, we should recognize that negative reinforcement *does* have an effect on behavior. Some students may finish an assignment more to "get it out of the way" than for any intrinsic satisfaction that the assignment brings. Others may engage in inappropriate classroom behavior as a way of avoiding the assignment altogether. When certain responses enable students to remove unpleasant stimuli—perhaps classroom assignments or perhaps even the classroom itself—those responses will increase in frequency.

Using Reinforcement Effectively

As teachers, we may often want to use reinforcement to promote desired student behaviors. Several strategies will increase the likelihood that our use of reinforcement brings about desired behavior changes in our students. In particular, we should:

• *Specify desired behaviors at the beginning.* Behaviorists recommend that we describe the form and frequency of the behaviors we want students to demonstrate—the **terminal behaviors**—at the very beginning of the operant conditioning process. Furthermore, they urge us to describe these behaviors in *specific, concrete, observable*

margin notes:
What stimulus is being removed in each of these situations? What response is being reinforced as a result?

Did you previously think of negative reinforcement as something that leads to a *decrease* in behavior? If so, have you now changed your mental definition of this concept?

When students consistently behave in ways that enable them to escape or avoid certain classroom activities, identify and address the reasons that students find those activities unpleasant.

Specify desired terminal behaviors in specific, concrete, observable terms.

[2]You might draw an analogy between positive and negative reinforcement and positive and negative numbers. Positive numbers and positive reinforcement both *add* something to a situation. Negative numbers and negative reinforcement both *subtract* something from a situation.

terms. Rather than talk about the need for students to "learn world history," we might instead talk about students being able to describe the antecedents and consequences of World War I. Rather than say that students should "learn responsibility," we might instead talk about their need to follow instructions, bring the necessary books and supplies to class every day, and turn in assignments by the due date. An advantage of describing terminal behaviors in such concrete terms is that we know exactly when these behaviors have been learned and when they have not.

When educators describe desired terminal behaviors in concrete, measurable terms, they are identifying *behavioral objectives* for their students. Chapter 13 examines behavioral objectives more closely.

• *Choose an appropriate reinforcer for each student.* As noted earlier, different students will find different consequences reinforcing. How can we determine which reinforcers are likely to be effective with particular students? One approach is to ask students themselves (or perhaps their parents) about the consequences they find especially appealing. Another approach is to observe students' behaviors, keeping a lookout for consequences that students seem to appreciate. The one thing that we don't want to do is *guess* about the reinforcers we should use. Operant conditioning is far more effective when reinforcers are tailored to individual students than when the same consequences are used for everyone (e.g., Pfiffner et al., 1985).

In some cases, we may want to give students the opportunity to choose their own reinforcers, and possibly to choose different reinforcers on different occasions (L. G. Bowman, Piazza, Fisher, Hagopian, & Kogan, 1997; Fisher & Mazur, 1997). One mechanism through which we can do this is the **token economy,** whereby students who exhibit desired behaviors receive *tokens* (poker chips, specially marked pieces of colored paper, etc.) that they can later use to "purchase" a variety of reinforcers—perhaps small treats, free time in the reading center, or a prime position in the lunch line.

Whenever possible, we should stay away from concrete reinforcers such as toys and candy. Such reinforcers can be expensive, and they also distract students' attention away from the task at hand—their schoolwork. Fortunately, many nontangible reinforcers can be effective with school-age children and adolescents, including positive feedback, special privileges, favorite activities, and parental reinforcement at home for school behaviors (Ormrod, 1999).

• *Make response-consequence contingencies explicit.* Reinforcement is more likely to be effective when students know exactly what consequences will follow various behaviors. For example, kindergarten students are more likely to respond appropriately when they are told that, "The quietest group will be first to get in line for lunch." High school students are more likely to complete their Spanish assignments if they know that by doing so they will be able to take a field trip to a local *Cinco de Mayo* festival.

One explicit way of communicating our expectations is through a **contingency contract.** To develop such a contract, the teacher meets with a student to discuss a problem behavior (e.g., perhaps the student has a tendency to talk to friends when independent seatwork has been assigned, or displays an inability to get along with classmates). The teacher and student then identify and agree on desired behaviors that the student will demonstrate (e.g., completing seatwork assignments within a certain time frame, or speaking with classmates in a friendly manner and pleasant tone of voice). The two also agree on one or more reinforcers for those behaviors (e.g., a certain amount of free time, or points earned toward a particular privilege or prize) that the student values. Together the teacher and the student write and sign a contract that describes both the behaviors that the student will perform and the reinforcers that will result. Contingency contracts have consistently been shown to be an effective strategy for improving a wide variety of academic and social behaviors

Identify consequences that are truly reinforcing for each student.

Minimize your reliance on concrete reinforcers.

Make response-reinforcement contingencies explicit.

When trying to increase a desired behavior, reinforce it every time you see it occur.

Determine the baseline level of desired behaviors and then continue to monitor their frequency during the reinforcement process.

(Brooke & Ruthren, 1984; D. L. Miller & Kelley, 1994; Rueger & Liberman, 1984; Welch, 1985).

• *Administer reinforcement consistently.* As you might guess, responses increase more quickly when they are reinforced each and every time they occur—that is, when they are subject to **continuous reinforcement.** As teachers, we will see more rapid improvements in our students' behavior if we reinforce desired responses whenever we observe them.

• *Monitor students' progress.* When we use reinforcement in the classroom, behaviorists urge us to determine, as objectively as possible, whether our efforts are bringing about the desired results. More specifically, they urge us to assess the frequency of the terminal behavior both before and during our attempts to increase it through operant conditioning. The frequency of a behavior *before* we intentionally use reinforcement to increase it is called the **baseline** level of that behavior. Some behaviors occur frequently even when they are not being explicitly reinforced, whereas other behaviors occur rarely or not at all.

By comparing the baseline frequency of a response with its frequency after we begin reinforcing it, we can determine whether the reinforcer we are using is actually bringing about a behavior change. As an example, let's look once again at James in the opening case study. James rarely turns in classroom assignments; this is a behavior with a low baseline. An obvious reinforcer to use with James is attention, a consequence that, until now, has effectively reinforced such counterproductive behaviors as blurting out answers in class and throwing objects across the room. When we make our attention contingent on James's turning in assignments, rather than on his refusals to do so, we should see an almost immediate increase in the number of assignments we receive from James. If we see no significant change in James's behavior, we need to consider alternative reinforcers; in other words, we need to find out what it will take for James to work productively in the classroom.

But what if a desired behavior has a baseline level of *zero*? How can we encourage behaviors that students never exhibit at all? Operant conditioning theorists provide a solution to this problem: the process of shaping.

Shaping New Behaviors

Consider this situation:

> Donald seems very shy and withdrawn. He rarely interacts with other students, either in class or on the playground. When he is in a situation where he must interact with a classmate, he doesn't seem to know how to behave.

Donald has apparently not learned how to interact effectively with his classmates. How might we help Donald develop appropriate social behaviors when the baseline level for such behaviors is essentially zero?

When a desired behavior occurs rarely or not at all, we can use a procedure called **shaping.** Shaping is a process of reinforcing a series of responses that increasingly resemble the desired terminal behavior—a process of reinforcing successively closer and closer approximations to that behavior. To shape a new response, we:

Shape a low-frequency response by reinforcing closer and closer approximations over time.

1. First reinforce any response that in some way resembles the terminal behavior

2. Then reinforce a response that more closely approximates the terminal behavior (no longer reinforcing the previously reinforced response)

3. Then reinforce a response that resembles the terminal behavior even more closely

1   2   3   4

Donald is extremely shy and rarely interacts with his classmates. We can teach him social skills through a process of *shaping*—that is, by reinforcing a series of successively more social behaviors. For example, we can reinforce Donald for: (1) smiling at a classmate, (2) responding appropriately to a classmate's question, (3) initiating a conversation with a single classmate, then (4) initiating interaction with a larger group.

F I G U R E 10.1

Shaping Donald's social behavior

4. Continue reinforcing closer and closer approximations to the terminal behavior

5. Finally reinforce only the terminal behavior

Each response in the sequence is reinforced every time it occurs until we see it regularly. Only at that point do we begin reinforcing a behavior that more closely approaches the terminal behavior.

To illustrate this process, let's consider how we might shape Donald's social behavior. We might first reinforce him for something that he occasionally does, such as smiling at a classmate. After we begin to see him smiling frequently (perhaps after a few days or weeks), we might reinforce him only when he makes a verbal response to the comments or questions of a classmate. When that behavior occurs frequently, we might reinforce him only when he initiates a conversation. Later steps to take would be reinforcing Donald for approaching a group of peers, for suggesting a group activity, and so on (see Figure 10–1).

As teachers, we must remember that it may often be unreasonable to expect students to make drastic changes in their behavior overnight. When we want them to exhibit responses radically different from the things they are doing now, we may need to shape their behavior by first reinforcing one small step in the right direction, then by reinforcing another small step, and then yet another, until eventually the desired terminal behavior is achieved. If we want rambunctious Bernadette to sit still for twenty-minute periods, we may first have to reinforce her for staying in her seat for just *two* minutes, gradually increasing the "sitting" time required for reinforcement as she makes progress. In much the same way, we can use shaping (and often do) to teach students to work independently on classroom assignments. We begin by giving first graders short, structured tasks—tasks that may only take five to ten minutes to complete. As students move through the elementary school years, we expect them to work independently for longer periods of time, and we also give them short assignments to do at home. By the time they reach high school, students have extended study halls (where, with luck, they study independently) and complete lengthy assignments at home. In the college years, student assignments require a great deal of independence and self-direction.

How might you use shaping to teach an eight-year-old to write in cursive? a twelve-year-old to swing a baseball bat? an aggressive high school student to behave prosocially?

Effects of Antecedent Stimuli and Responses

On what occasions are you most likely to:

- Look up a word that you don't know how to spell?
- Express your beliefs about effective teaching?

Up to this point, we have focused on the consequences of desired behaviors. Yet you have undoubtedly learned that some of your behaviors are more likely to be reinforced in some situations than in others. For example, the response of looking up a word to find its correct spelling is more likely to be reinforced when you are writing a research paper than when you are taking a spelling test; we could diagram the situation this way:

$$S_{Paper} \quad \rightarrow \quad R \quad \rightarrow \quad S_{Rf}$$
$$S_{Test} \quad \rightarrow \quad R \quad \rightarrow \quad \text{nothing}$$

Similarly, the response of talking about effective teaching practices is more likely to be reinforced when you are sitting in your educational psychology class than when you are sitting in an opera house watching *The Barber of Seville.*

You may also have noticed that you are more likely to make a particular response when you are already making similar kinds of responses. For example, you are more likely to look up an unknown word when you have just looked up a different word and so have the dictionary lying open in front of you. And you are more likely to volunteer your opinions about teaching practices when you have already made a few comments in class—when you are "on a roll," so to speak.

Researchers have found that the stimuli and responses that precede a particular desired response (i.e., the **antecedent stimuli** and **antecedent responses**) often influence the frequency of the response. Here we will look at four phenomena—generalization, discrimination, cueing, and setting events—that involve antecedent stimuli and one—behavioral momentum—that involves antecedent responses.

Generalization

Expect that students will sometimes generalize responses learned in one situation to very similar situations.

Once people have learned that a response is likely to be reinforced in one set of circumstances (in the presence of one antecedent stimulus), they are likely to make the same response in a similar situation. In other words, they show **generalization** from one stimulus to a similar stimulus. For example, after Lindsey has learned to sit quietly in her kindergarten class, she may generalize that behavior to her first-grade class. After Donald has learned how to make friends at one school, he may generalize his skills to a new town and new school the following year. Our students are likely to generalize frequently from their experiences, exhibiting certain responses in situations similar to ones in which those responses have previously been reinforced.

This process of generalization should remind you of the generalization that occurs in classical conditioning. In fact, the two processes are similar: In both cases, an individual learns a response to one stimulus and then responds in the same way to a similar stimulus. The major difference is one of control: Generalization involves an automatic, involuntary response in classical conditioning but a voluntary response in operant conditioning.

Discrimination

Sometimes people learn that responses are reinforced only when certain stimuli (certain environmental conditions) are present. For example, Donald might learn that a class-mate who smiles at him is more likely to reinforce his attempts at being friendly than a classmate with a scowl. Lindsey might learn that she can get up and leave the classroom only after her teacher has given her permission to do so. When people learn that responses are reinforced in the presence of one stimulus but not in the presence of an-other (and perhaps very similar) stimulus, they have learned **discrimination** between the two stimuli.

Occasionally, our students may overgeneralize, exhibiting responses they have learned in situations where such responses are inappropriate. In such cases, we must teach them to discriminate between suitable and unsuitable stimulus conditions. For instance, we should describe in very concrete terms the circumstances in which certain behaviors are and are not acceptable and productive. And we must be sure that we reinforce students for exhibiting behaviors *only* in situations where those behaviors are appropriate.

Describe the conditions under which certain behaviors are appropriate; reinforce those behaviors only when they *are* appropriate.

Cueing

As teachers, we may frequently find it helpful to use a strategy known as **cueing**, whereby we remind students, either directly or more subtly, about the behaviors we ex-pect of them. For example, we might occasionally say things along these lines:

Give students occasional verbal cues to remind them of what they need to do.

- "I hear the signal for a fire drill. Everyone *line up quietly and then walk in single file to the outside door.*
- "Students who *have their desks clear* go to lunch first."
- "After you have all *read pages fourteen through nineteen in your textbooks,* I will hand out information about the school ski trip."
- "I see some *art supplies that still need to be put back on the shelves* before you can go home."

Such reminders, often called *cues* or *prompts,* serve as antecedent stimuli that increase the likelihood that students will behave appropriately.

Setting Events

Thus far, we have focused our discussion on specific stimuli that encourage students to behave in particular ways. Yet some theorists talk not about specific stimuli, but instead about complex environmental conditions—**setting events**—under which certain be-haviors are most likely to occur. For example, young children are more likely to interact with their classmates during free play time if they have a relatively small area in which to play and if the toys available to them (balls, puppets, toy housekeeping materials) en-courage group activity (W. H. Brown, Fox, & Brady, 1987; S. S. Martin et al., 1991). Sim-ilarly, the nature of the games that children are asked to play influences the behaviors that they exhibit: Cooperative games promote cooperative behavior, whereas competi-tive games promote aggressive behavior (Bay-Hinitz et al., 1994). In general, then, we should create the kinds of environments that are likely to encourage the very behaviors we want our students to exhibit.

Create an environment that encourages desired behaviors.

Behavioral Momentum

In many cases, people are more likely to make desired responses if they are already mak-ing similar responses—a phenomenon sometimes called **behavioral momentum**

(Belfiore, Lee, Vargas, & Skinner, 1997; Mace et al., 1988; Nevin, Mandell, & Atak, 1983). Consider this situation as an example:

> Two high school students, Allison and Roberta, have a history of refusing to do the academic tasks that their teachers assign. A researcher finds that the girls more willingly attempt difficult three-digit multiplication problems after they have first worked on a few simple one-digit problems (Belfiore et al., 1997).

Similarly, we might ask students to tidy up a messy classroom after they have already cleaned their own desktops, or to try a backward roll after they have already executed a forward roll successfully. And in general, we can promote behavioral momentum by assigning relatively easy or enjoyable tasks that lead naturally into more complex and potentially frustrating ones.

🍎 Assign easy tasks that pave the way for similar, more challenging ones.

INTO THE CLASSROOM: Encouraging Productive Classroom Behaviors Through Operant Conditioning

Reinforce desirable behaviors.

To a student who has just completed an excellent oral book report, a teacher says, "Nice job, Monica. You made the book sound so interesting. I think we *all* want to read it now."

Give feedback about specific behaviors rather than general areas of performance.

A teacher tells a student with mental retardation, "You did a good job taking the absentee sheet to Mrs. Smith. You went directly to the office and you came straight back" (Patton et al., 1987, p. 65).

Provide opportunities for students to practice correct behaviors.

In a unit on basketball, a physical education teacher makes sure that every student has several successful shots at the basket.

Remember that different things are reinforcing to different students.

A teacher allows students to do the various things they enjoy during the free time they earn that day. For example, some students work on the classroom computer, others work on favorite art projects, and still others converse with friends.

When the baseline level of a desired behavior is low, gradually shape the behavior over time by reinforcing closer and closer approximations.

A teacher praises a shy and withdrawn boy for smiling or making eye contact with his classmates. After such behaviors become more frequent, the teacher begins praising him when he responds to classmates' questions or comments. As those behaviors also become a frequent occurrence, the teacher praises the boy only when he initiates a conversation with someone else.

Cue appropriate behaviors.

As students are busily working on cooperative group projects, their teacher sees that one group's discussion is being dominated by a single student. He announces to the class, "Please remember a point that I made earlier: You are more likely to create a good product when *all* group members contribute their ideas."

Once students are exhibiting desired behaviors frequently, continue to reinforce them intermittently.

After a formerly aggressive student has developed appropriate social skills and is using them consistently in the classroom, her teacher occasionally commends her for her prosocial behavior.

Reducing and Eliminating Undesirable Behaviors

So far, we have been talking primarily about strategies for promoting desirable behaviors. Yet our students may sometimes exhibit *un*desirable behaviors—those that interfere with their own learning and achievement, and possibly with the learning and achievement of their classmates as well. How do we decrease, perhaps even eliminate, such behaviors? Behaviorists offer several possible strategies: extinction, cueing inappropriate behaviors, reinforcing incompatible behaviors, and punishment.

Extinction

What happens when a response is no longer reinforced? As you might guess, a nonreinforced response decreases in frequency and usually returns to its baseline level—a phenomenon known as **extinction.** For example, the class clown whose jokes are ignored may stop telling jokes. The aggressive child who never gets what she wants by hitting or shoving others may become less aggressive. One way of reducing the frequency of an inappropriate behavior, then, is simply to make sure it is never reinforced.

Extinguish undesirable behaviors by removing reinforcing consequences.

Unfortunately, teachers and other adults often inadvertently reinforce the very behaviors they want to eliminate. For example, a girl who copies her homework assignment word for word from a classmate and then receives a high grade for that assignment is reinforced for representing someone else's work as her own. A boy whose comments in class are so obnoxious that his teacher has no choice but to give him the attention that he seeks is also being reinforced for inappropriate behavior. As teachers, we must look reflectively at our own behaviors in the classroom, being careful *not* to reinforce, either intentionally or unintentionally, those responses that are not likely to help our students over the long run.

How is extinction similar in classical and operant conditioning? How is it different?

There are several points to keep in mind about extinction, however. First of all, once reinforcement stops, a previously reinforced response doesn't always decrease immediately. Sometimes there is a temporary *increase* in behavior (Lerman & Iwata, 1995). To illustrate how this might occur, imagine that you have a cantankerous television set that gives you a clear picture only when you bang its side once or twice. Eventually, something changes in the inner workings of your set, so that banging is no longer an effective remedy. As you desperately try to get a clear picture, you may bang your television a number of times in succession (more times than you usually do) before giving up that response. In much the same way, the class clown who is now being ignored may increase the frequency of joke telling at first, and the aggressive child may initially become more aggressive, before learning that such behaviors are not producing the desired results.

Don't be surprised to see a temporary increase in behaviors you have stopped reinforcing.

Second, we may sometimes find situations in which a response does not decrease even when we remove a reinforcer. In such situations—when extinction doesn't occur—chances are that we haven't been able to remove *all* reinforcers of the response. Perhaps the behavior is leading to a naturally reinforcing consequence; for example, a class clown's classmates may continue to snicker even when the teacher ignores his jokes. Or perhaps the response is intrinsically reinforcing; for example, a student's physically aggressive behavior may release pent-up energy (and so may "feel good") even if it doesn't otherwise get her what she wants. Only when all reinforcers are removed will extinction occur.

Finally, we must remember that extinction may occur with desirable behaviors as easily as with undesirable ones. The student who is never called on in class may stop raising his hand. The student who never passes a paper-pencil test no matter how hard she studies may eventually stop studying. As teachers, we must be very careful that, while counterproductive classroom behaviors are not being reinforced, productive responses *are* being reinforced, either through such extrinsic reinforcers as attention,

Make sure you don't inadvertently extinguish desired behaviors.

Simple body language is often an effective cue. When this teacher is temporarily preoccupied, her hand on a student's shoulder provides a subtle reminder about what he should and should not be doing.

praise, or favorite activities or through the intrinsic satisfaction that classroom accomplishments may bring.

Cueing Inappropriate Behaviors

Just as we can use cueing to remind students about what they should be doing, we can also use this strategy to remind them about what they should *not* be doing. Three cues that quickly and easily point out inappropriate responses are described in the following paragraphs.

Body language. Simple body language can serve as a subtle reminder to students about what they should and should not be doing. Making eye contact with a distracted student is often sufficient to get that student back on task. Such signals as a frown, a raised eyebrow, or a finger to the lips are additional ways of letting students know that we disapprove of their behavior and would like it to cease (Emmer, 1987; Palardy & Mudrey, 1973; Shrigley, 1979; Woolfolk & Brooks, 1985).

Physical proximity. When body language doesn't get the attention of a misbehaving student, a more obvious cue is to move closer to the student and stand there until the problem behavior stops (Emmer, 1987; Woolfolk & Brooks, 1985). Particularly if we are walking around the room anyway during a classroom activity, this strategy can attract the attention of the guilty party without at the same time drawing undue attention from classmates.

A brief verbal cue. Sometimes subtlety just doesn't work, and so we have to be more explicit. In such cases, a brief remark—stating a student's name, reminding a student about correct behavior, or (if necessary) pointing out an inappropriate behavior—may be in order (G. A. Davis & Thomas, 1989; Emmer, 1987; Northup et al., 1995). For example, we might say something as simple as, "Please keep your eyes on your own work," or, "Lucy, put the magazine away."

🍎 Use physical or verbal cues to discourage inappropriate behavior.

Reinforcing Incompatible Behaviors

Experiencing Firsthand
Asleep on Your Feet

Have you ever tried to sleep while you were standing up? Horses can do it, but most of us humans really can't. In fact, there are many pairs of responses that we can't possibly perform simultaneously. Take a minute and identify something that you cannot possibly do when you perform each of these activities:

When you:	You cannot simultaneously:
Sit down	_____
Eat crackers	_____
Take a walk	_____

Two behaviors are **incompatible** when they cannot be performed simultaneously; in a sense, the two behaviors are opposites. For example, sitting is incompatible with standing. Eating crackers is incompatible with singing, or at least with singing *well.* Taking a walk is incompatible with taking a nap. In each case, it is physically impossible to perform both activities at exactly the same time.

When our attempts at extinction or cueing are unsuccessful, another way to reduce an inappropriate behavior is to reinforce an incompatible (and presumably more desirable) one; the inappropriate response must inevitably decrease as the incompatible one increases. This is the approach we are taking when we reinforce a hyperactive student for sitting down: Sitting is incompatible with getting-out-of-seat and roaming-around-the-room behaviors. It is also an approach that we might use to deal with forgetfulness (we reinforce students when they remember to do what they were supposed to do), being off-task (we reinforce on-task behavior), and verbal abusiveness (we reinforce prosocial statements). And consider how we might deal with a chronic litterbug (Krumboltz & Krumboltz, 1972):

> Walt is a junior high school student who consistently leaves garbage—banana peels, sunflower seed shells, and so on—on the lunchroom floor, in school corridors, and on the playground. When the school faculty establishes an "anti-litter" committee, it decides to put Walt on the committee. The committee eventually elects Walt as its chairperson.
>
> Under Walt's leadership, the committee institutes a massive anti-litter campaign, complete with posters and lunchroom monitors, and Walt receives considerable recognition for the campaign's success. Curiously (or perhaps not), school personnel no longer find Walt's garbage littering the school grounds.

Reinforce behaviors 🍎
that are incompatible with
undesirable behaviors.

Punishment

Some misbehaviors require an immediate remedy—not only do they interfere significantly with students' learning, but they may threaten students' physical safety or psychological well-being as well—and so we cannot simply wait for gradual improvements over time. Consider this student as an example:

> Bonnie doesn't handle frustration very well. Whenever she encounters a difficulty or obstacle that she cannot immediately overcome, she responds by hitting, kicking, or breaking something. Over the course of the school year, she has knocked over several pieces of furniture, smashed two windows, made several dents in the wall, and broken innumerable pencils. Not only is Bonnie's behavior hindering her academic progress, but it's also getting very expensive.

Bonnie's inappropriate behaviors are difficult to extinguish because they aren't really being reinforced to begin with (not extrinsically, at least). They are also behaviors with no obvious incompatible responses that we can reinforce. And we can reasonably assume that Bonnie's teacher has already cued her about her inappropriate behaviors on many occasions. When other strategies are inapplicable or ineffective, punishment may be our only alternative.

Earlier in the chapter, we defined reinforcement as a consequence that increases the frequency of a particular behavior. We will define **punishment** in a similar fashion—as a consequence that *decreases* the frequency of the response it follows.

All punishing consequences fall into one of two groups. **Presentation punishment** involves presenting a new stimulus, presumably something that a student finds unpleasant and doesn't want. Spankings, scoldings, and teacher scowls, if they lead to a reduction in the behavior they follow, are all instances of presentation punishment. **Removal punishment** involves removing a previously existing stimulus, presumably one that a student finds desirable and doesn't want to lose. The loss of a privilege, a fine (involving the loss of money or points), and "grounding" (when certain pleasurable outside activities are missed) are all possible examples of removal punishment.

Over the years, I have observed many occasions when people have used the term *negative reinforcement* when they were really talking about punishment. Remember, negative reinforcement increases a response, whereas punishment has the opposite effect. Table 10–2 should help you understand how negative reinforcement, presentation punishment, and removal punishment are all very different concepts.

Use punishment only 🍎
when alternative
approaches are ineffective.

Can you describe
positive reinforcement,
negative reinforcement,
presentation punishment,
and removal punishment in
your own words? Can you
think of examples of each
concept?

TABLE 10.2

Distinguishing Among Positive Reinforcement, Negative Reinforcement, and Punishment

CONSEQUENCE	EFFECT	EXAMPLES
Positive reinforcement	Response *increases* when a new stimulus (presumably one that the person finds desirable) is *presented*.	A student *is praised* for writing an assignment in cursive. She begins to write other assignments in cursive as well. A student *gets his lunch money* by bullying a girl into surrendering hers. He begins bullying his classmates more frequently.
Negative reinforcement	Response *increases* when a previously existing stimulus (presumably one that the person finds undesirable) is *removed*.	A student *no longer has to worry* about a research paper that he has completed several days before the due date. He begins to do his assignments ahead of time whenever possible. A student *escapes the principal's wrath* by lying about her role in a recent incident of school vandalism. She begins lying to school faculty whenever she finds herself in an uncomfortable situation.
Presentation punishment	Response *decreases* when a new stimulus (presumably one that the person finds undesirable) is *presented*.	A student *is scolded* for taunting other students. She taunts others less frequently after that. A student *is ridiculed by classmates* for asking a "stupid" question during a lecture. He stops asking questions in class.
Removal punishment	Response *decreases* when a previously existing stimulus (presumably one that the person finds desirable) is *removed*.	A student *is removed from the softball team for a week* for showing poor sportsmanship. She rarely shows poor sportsmanship in future games. A student *loses points on a test* for answering a question in a creative but unusual way. He takes fewer risks on future tests.

Strictly speaking, punishment is not a part of operant conditioning. Many early behaviorists believed that punishment is a relatively *in*effective means of changing behavior—that it might temporarily suppress a response but can never eliminate it—and suggested that teachers focus their efforts on reinforcing desirable behaviors, rather than on punishing undesirable ones. More recently, however, many behaviorists have found that some forms of punishment can be quite effective in reducing problem behaviors.

Effective Forms of Punishment

As a general rule, we will want to use relatively mild forms of punishment in the classroom; severe consequences may lead to such unwanted side effects as resentment, hostility, or truancy (Ormrod, 1999). Researchers and educators have identified several forms of mild punishment that are often effective in reducing classroom misbehaviors; these are described in the following paragraphs.

Verbal reprimands (scolding). Although some students seem to thrive on teacher scolding because of the attention that it brings, most students, particularly if they are scolded relatively infrequently, find verbal reprimands to be unpleasant and punishing

(Pfiffner & O'Leary, 1987; Van Houten, Nau, MacKenzie-Keating, Sameoto, & Colavecchia, 1982). Softly spoken reprimands are sometimes more effective than loud ones, possibly because they are less likely to be noticed and so less likely to draw the attention of other students (O'Leary, Kaufman, Kass, & Drabman, 1970). Reprimands should be given in private whenever possible: Some students may relish the peer attention they receive when they are scolded in front of their classmates, and others (e.g., many Native American and Hispanic students; C. A. Grant & Gomez, 1996) may feel totally humiliated.

Response cost. Response cost involves the loss either of a previously earned reinforcer or of an opportunity to obtain reinforcement; thus, it is an instance of removal punishment. For example, teachers of students with chronic behavior problems sometimes use a point system in their classrooms, awarding points, check marks, or plastic chips for good behavior (reinforcement) and subtracting points for bad behavior (response cost). Students who accumulate a sufficient number of points can use them to "buy" objects, privileges, or enjoyable activities that are otherwise not available. Response cost is especially effective when coupled with reinforcement of appropriate behavior (Iwata & Bailey, 1974; Lentz, 1988; Rapport, Murphy, & Bailey, 1982).

Logical consequences. A logical consequence is a consequence that follows naturally or logically from a student's misbehavior; in other words, the punishment fits the crime. For example, if a student destroys a classmate's possession, a reasonable consequence is for the student to replace it or pay for a new one. If two close friends talk so much that they aren't getting their assignments done, a reasonable consequence is for them to be separated. If a student intentionally makes a mess in the cafeteria, a reasonable consequence is to clean it up. The use of logical consequences makes "logical" sense, and numerous research studies and case studies vouch for its effectiveness (Dreikurs, 1998; Lyon, 1984; Schloss & Smith, 1994; L. S. Wright, 1982).

Time-out. In time-out, a misbehaving student is placed in a dull, boring (but not scary) situation—perhaps a separate room designed especially for time-outs, a little-used office, or a remote corner of the classroom. A student undergoing time-out has no opportunity to interact with classmates and no opportunity to obtain reinforcement. The length of the time-out is often quite short (perhaps two to ten minutes, depending on the age of the student), but the student is not released from the time-out situation until inappropriate behavior (e.g., screaming, kicking) has stopped. Time-outs have been used successfully to reduce a variety of noncompliant, disruptive, and aggressive behaviors (Ormrod, 1999; Rortvedt & Miltenberger, 1994; A. G. White & Bailey, 1990). Although some theorists argue that time-out is not really punishment, most students find the boredom of a time-out to be somewhat unpleasant.

In-school suspension. In-school suspension is similar to time-out in that the student is placed in a quiet, boring room within the school building; however, it often lasts one or more school days and involves close adult supervision. Students receiving in-school suspension spend the day working on the same assignments that their nonsuspended peers do and so are able to keep up with their schoolwork. But they have no opportunity for interaction with classmates and friends—an aspect of school that is reinforcing to most students. Although in-school suspension programs have not been investigated through controlled research studies, practitioners report that these programs are often effective in reducing chronic misbehaviors, particularly when part of the suspension session is devoted to teaching appropriate behaviors and tutoring academic skills and when the supervising teacher acts as a supportive resource rather than as a punisher (Gootman, 1998; Huff, 1988; J. S. Sullivan, 1989).

Just as we must use different reinforcers for different students, we must also individualize our use of punishment. For example, some students enjoy the attention that

Use such mild forms of punishment as reprimands, response cost, time-out, logical consequences, and if necessary, in-school suspension.

Suspension from school may actually reinforce inappropriate school behavior rather than punish it.

verbal reprimands bring. A few may even appreciate the peace and quiet of an occasional time-out (Solnick, Rincover, & Peterson, 1977). If we find that a particular form of punishment produces no substantial decrease in a student's behavior, we should conclude that it isn't really a punishing consequence for that student and that a different form of punishment for future misbehaviors is called for.

Ineffective Forms of Punishment

Four forms of punishment are typically *not* recommended: physical punishment, psychological punishment, extra classwork, and out-of-school suspension.

Physical punishment. Physical punishment is generally not advised for school-age children (Doyle, 1990; Zirpoli & Melloy, 1993); furthermore, its use in the classroom is *illegal* in many places. Even mild physical punishment, such as a spank or slap with a ruler, can lead to such undesirable behaviors as resentment of the teacher, inattention to school tasks, lying, aggression, vandalism, avoidance of school tasks, and truancy. And when carried to extreme lengths, physical punishment constitutes child abuse and may cause long-term or possibly even permanent physical damage.

Psychological punishment. Psychological punishment is any consequence that seriously threatens a student's self-esteem. Embarrassing remarks and public humiliation have the potential to inflict long-term psychological harm. Psychological punishment can lead to some of the same side effects as physical punishment: resentment of the teacher, inattention to school tasks, and truancy from school. To the extent that it lowers students' self-esteem, it may also lower students' expectations for future performance and their motivation to learn.

Extra classwork. Asking a student to complete make-up work for time missed in school is a reasonable and justifiable request. But assigning extra classwork or homework beyond that which is required for other students is inappropriate if it is assigned simply to punish a student's wrongdoing (H. Cooper, 1989; Corno, 1996). In this case, we have a very different side effect: We inadvertently communicate the message that "schoolwork is unpleasant."

Stay away from physical or psychological punishment, extra classwork, or out-of-school suspension.

Out-of-school suspension. Teachers and administrators are negatively reinforced when they suspend a problem student. After all, they get rid of something they don't want—the student! But out-of-school suspension is usually *not* an effective means of changing a student's behavior (Doyle, 1990; Moles, 1990). In the first place, being suspended from school may be exactly what the student wants, in which case inappropriate behaviors are being reinforced rather than punished. And second, because many students with chronic behavior problems also tend to do poorly in their schoolwork, suspension involves a loss of valuable instructional time, thereby decreasing even further their chances for academic success (e.g., Skiba & Raison, 1990).

An additional form of punishment is *missing recess,* which gets mixed reviews regarding its effectiveness. In some situations, missing recess may be a logical consequence for students who fail to complete their schoolwork during regular class time due to off-task behavior. Yet research tells us that, at least at the elementary level, students can more effectively concentrate on school tasks when they have occasional breaks from academic activities (Maxmell et al., 1998; Pellegrini, Huberty, & Jones, 1995). Perhaps the best piece of advice here is to withdraw recess privileges infrequently, if at all, and to monitor the effectiveness of such a consequence on students' classroom behavior over the long run.

Using Punishment Humanely

A frequent criticism of using punishment is that it is "inhumane," or somehow cruel and barbaric. And certain forms of punishment, such as physical abuse or public humiliation, do indeed constitute inhumane treatment. We must be *extremely careful* in our use of punishment in the classroom. When administered judiciously, however, some forms of mild punishment can lead to a rapid reduction in misbehavior without causing physical or psychological harm. And when we can decrease counterproductive classroom behaviors quickly and effectively—especially when those behaviors are harmful to self or others—then punishment may, in fact, be one of the most humane approaches that we can take. Here are several guidelines for using punishment effectively and humanely:

• *Inform students ahead of time that certain behaviors will be punished, and explain how those behaviors will be punished.* When students are informed of response-punishment contingencies ahead of time, they are less likely to engage in the forbidden behaviors; they are also less likely to be surprised or resentful if punishment must be administered (G. D. Gottfredson & Gottfredson, 1985; Moles, 1990). Ultimately, students should learn that their behaviors influence the consequences that they experience—that, to some extent, they can control what happens to them. We will consider this idea of control more closely in our discussion of *attribution theory* in Chapter 12.

Give students advance notice as to what responses are unacceptable and how they will be punished.

• *Follow through with specified consequences.* One mistake that many teachers make is to continue to threaten possible punishment without ever following through. One warning is desirable, but repeated warnings are not. The teacher who says, "If you bring that rubber snake to class one more time, Tommy, I'm going to take it away," but never does take the snake away, is giving the message that no response-punishment contingency really exists.

Follow through with specified consequences.

• *Administer punishment privately.* By administering punishment in private, we protect our students from public embarrassment or humiliation. We also eliminate the possibility that the punishment will draw the attention of classmates—a potential reinforcer for the very behavior that we are trying to eliminate.

Administer punishment in private.

• *Explain why the punished behavior is unacceptable.* We must explain exactly why a certain behavior cannot be tolerated in the classroom—perhaps because it interferes with learning, threatens the safety or self-esteem of other students, or damages school property. Punishment is far more effective when accompanied by one or more reasons why the punished behavior is unacceptable (Cheyne & Walters, 1970; Parke, 1974; D. G. Perry & Perry, 1983).

Explain why the behavior is unacceptable.

• *Emphasize that it is the* behavior *that is undesirable, not the* student. As teachers, we must emphasize to students that certain behaviors interfere with their success in learning—that they are preventing themselves from becoming the very best that they can be.

Place emphasis on the behavior rather than the student.

• *Simultaneously teach and reinforce desirable alternative behaviors.* Punishment of misbehavior is almost always more effective when appropriate behaviors are being reinforced at the same time (Ruef, Higgins, Glaeser, & Patnode, 1998; G. C. Walters & Grusec, 1977). Furthermore, by reinforcing "good" behavior as well as punishing the "bad," we give students a far more positive and optimistic message that, yes, behavior can and will improve. Ultimately, the overall "atmosphere" we create must be a positive one that stresses the good things that students do rather than the bad (e.g., R. E. Smith & Smoll, 1997).

Set an overall positive tone that emphasizes reinforcement rather than punishment.

INTO THE CLASSROOM: Decreasing and Eliminating Undesirable Behaviors

Don't inadvertently reinforce undesirable behaviors.

A teacher realizes that a particular "problem" student, a girl who makes frequent inappropriate remarks in class, seems to thrive on any kind of attention. He also realizes that the girl's behavior has gotten worse instead of better. Rather than continue to reinforce the girl by scolding her publicly, he meets with her after school and together they develop a contingency contract designed to improve her behavior.

Cue students when you see them behaving inappropriately.

As she describes the morning's assignment, a teacher notices that two boys on the other side of the classroom are whispering, giggling, and obviously not paying attention. While continuing her description of the assignment, she walks slowly across the room and stands next to the boys.

Reinforce behaviors that are incompatible with undesirable behaviors.

A student is out of her seat so frequently that she gets little of her own work done and often distracts her classmates from doing theirs. Her teacher discusses the problem behavior with her, and together they decide that she will earn points for staying in her seat and keeping on task; she may use the points to "buy" time with her friends at the end of the day.

When a misbehavior must be suppressed quickly, choose a mild punishment, yet one that is likely to deter the behavior in the future.

When members of the school soccer team have an unexcused absence from team practice, they are not allowed to play in that week's soccer game.

Describe both appropriate and inappropriate behaviors, as well as their consequences, in concrete and explicit terms.

The soccer coach reminds students that, whereas students who miss practice will sit out at the next game, all students who *do* make practice every day will play at least part of the game.

When misbehaviors continue despite all reasonable efforts to correct them, seek the advice of experts.

A teacher consults with the school psychologist about three students who are often physically aggressive in their interactions with classmates. Together, using applied behavior analysis, they develop a strategy to help these students.

Maintaining Desirable Behaviors over the Long Run

As noted in our discussion of extinction, responses that are no longer reinforced decrease in frequency and often return to their baseline level; in some cases, the responses disappear altogether. Yet we cannot continue to reinforce every student each time that he or she engages in appropriate behavior. And we won't be able to reinforce our students at all after they leave our classrooms at the end of the school year. So how can we ensure that our students will continue to behave in ways that are in their own best interests over the long run? There are at least two viable strategies: promoting intrinsic reinforcement and using intermittent reinforcement.

Promoting Intrinsic Reinforcement

The advantage of intrinsic reinforcers is that they come from within individuals themselves, rather than from some outside source. Students will often engage in activities that are enjoyable or satisfy their curiosity. They will also exhibit behaviors that lead to success and to feelings of mastery, accomplishment, and pride. Ideally, it is such internal consequences that are most effective in sustaining productive behaviors both in the classroom and in the outside world.

Yet success is not always achieved easily and effortlessly. Many of the tasks that our students will tackle in school—reading, writing, solving mathematical problems, reasoning scientifically, understanding historical and social events, participating skillfully in team sports, learning to play a musical instrument—are complex, challenging, and often frustrating, especially at first. When students struggle with a challenging task and encounter frequent little failures, we should probably provide extrinsic reinforcement for the little improvements they make. And when we find that we must break down a complex task into smaller pieces that, though easier to accomplish, are less rewarding in their own right (e.g., when we assign drill-and-practice exercises related to basic reading or math skills), we will probably need to reinforce students' many seemingly "meaningless" successes. Once our students have mastered tasks and skills to a level that brings them frequent successes and feelings of mastery, however, extrinsic reinforcers should no longer be necessary (Covington, 1992; Lepper, 1981). In fact, for reasons that you will discover in Chapter 12, it is actually counterproductive to provide extrinsic reinforcers when students are already finding intrinsic reinforcement in the things they are doing.

Using Intermittent Reinforcement

I have been talking about reinforcement as an all-or-nothing occurrence, implying, perhaps, that a response is always reinforced or else never reinforced. But you can probably think of many behaviors that are reinforced inconsistently: Sometimes they are reinforced, and sometimes they are not. Whenever a response is reinforced only occasionally, with some occurrences of the response going unreinforced, we have **intermittent reinforcement.**

Continuous reinforcement and intermittent reinforcement produce somewhat different results. To show you what I mean, let's consider Molly and Maria, two students with low baseline levels for volunteering in class. Their teacher, Mr. Oliver, decides to reinforce the girls for raising their hands. Every time Molly raises her hand, Mr. Oliver calls on her and praises her response; she is receiving continuous reinforcement. But when Maria raises her hand, Mr. Oliver doesn't always notice her. He calls on Maria whenever he sees her hand in the air, but he doesn't often look in her direction; she is therefore receiving intermittent reinforcement. Which girl will more quickly increase her frequency of volunteering?

If you chose Molly, you are correct. One difference that we see between continuous and intermittent reinforcement is in their effect on the *acquisition* of new responses. As noted earlier, responses increase most rapidly when they are continuously reinforced.

But let's move ahead in time a few months. Thanks to Mr. Oliver's attentiveness to Molly and Maria, both girls are now volunteering frequently in class. Mr. Oliver turns his attention to several other students who have been failing to participate. Foolishly, he no longer reinforces either Molly or Maria for raising her hand. As you might expect, the girls' level of class participation goes down; in other words, we see signs of extinction. But for which girl will class participation extinguish more rapidly?

If you predicted that Molly's volunteering will decrease more rapidly than Maria's, you are correct. Responses that have previously been reinforced continuously tend to extinguish relatively quickly once reinforcement stops. But because Maria has been receiving intermittent reinforcement, she is accustomed to being occasionally ignored. It may take

Use extrinsic reinforcers only until students have mastered subject matter sufficiently to find intrinsic reinforcement in what they are doing.

One statement in this paragraph is based on the concept of *shaping.* Another statement reflects the concept of *scaffolding,* described in Chapter 2. Can you identify each of these statements?

Which of your behaviors are reinforced only on an intermittent basis?

🍎 Once students have acquired desired behaviors, continue reinforcing them on an intermittent basis.

Which form of reinforcement—continuous or intermittent—would you use to teach your students to persist at difficult tasks?

her longer to realize that she is no longer going to be called on when she raises her hand. Behaviors that have previously been reinforced intermittently decrease slowly (if at all) once reinforcement stops; in other words, they are more *resistant to extinction.*

Once students have acquired a desired terminal behavior, we should continue to reinforce that response on an intermittent basis, especially if it does not otherwise lead to intrinsic reinforcement. Mr. Oliver doesn't need to call on Molly and Maria every time they raise their hands, but he should certainly call on them once in a while. In a similar manner, we should occasionally reinforce diligent study habits, completed homework assignments, prosocial behaviors, and so on, even for the best of students, as a way of encouraging such responses to continue.

Addressing Especially Difficult Classroom Behaviors

Educators sometimes apply behaviorism in a very systematic fashion, especially when they want to address difficult and chronic behavior problems. Let's consider two systematic approaches for modifying especially challenging behaviors: *applied behavior analysis* and *positive behavioral support.*

Applied Behavior Analysis

When we apply traditional behaviorist principles in a systematic fashion, we have a group of procedures collectively known as **applied behavior analysis** (also called *behavior modification, behavior therapy,* or *contingency management*). Applied behavior analysis, or **ABA,** is based on the assumptions that behavior problems result from past and present environmental circumstances and that modifying a student's present environment will promote more productive responses. When teachers and therapists use ABA to help a student acquire more appropriate classroom behavior, they typically use strategies such as these:

- Describe both the present behaviors and the desired terminal behaviors in observable, measurable terms.
- Identify one or more effective reinforcers.
- Develop a specific intervention or treatment plan—one that may involve reinforcement of desired behaviors, shaping, extinction, reinforcement of incompatible behaviors, punishment, or some combination of these.
- Measure the frequency of desired and/or undesirable behaviors both before treatment (i.e., at baseline level) and during treatment.
- Monitor the treatment program for effectiveness by observing how various behaviors change over time, and modify the program if necessary.
- Take steps to promote generalization of newly acquired behaviors (e.g., by having the student practice the behaviors in a variety of realistic situations).
- Gradually phase out the treatment (e.g., through intermittent reinforcement) after the desired behaviors are acquired.

Hundreds of research studies tell us that the systematic use of behaviorist principles can lead to significant improvements in academic performance and classroom behavior. For example, when we reinforce students for successful achievement, we find improvements in such subjects as mathematics, reading, spelling, and creative writing (Piersel, 1987). When we reinforce appropriate classroom behaviors, such as paying attention and interacting cooperatively and prosocially with classmates, misbehaviors decrease (S. N. Elliott & Busse, 1991; McNamara, 1987; Ormrod, 1999). In many situations, ABA is effective when other approaches have not been (Emmer & Evertson, 1981; O'Leary & O'Leary, 1972; Piersel, 1987).

One probable reason that ABA often works so well is that students know exactly what is expected of them. Consistent use of reinforcement for appropriate responses informs students in a very concrete way which behaviors are acceptable and which are not. Another likely reason is that, through the gradual process of *shaping,* students attempt to learn new behaviors only when they are truly ready to acquire them. They therefore find that their learning efforts usually lead to success (i.e., to reinforcement). And after all, everyone likes to be successful!

Can you think of other possible reasons for the success of behaviorist techniques?

Positive Behavioral Support

In recent years, some theorists have advocated a modification of the traditional ABA approach called **positive behavioral support,** or **PBS** (DeVault et al., 1996; Koegel et al., 1996; Ruef et al., 1998). In this approach, teachers and therapists place particular emphasis on identifying one or more *purposes* that certain undesirable behaviors serve for a student. They also determine how the environment may inadvertently be encouraging those behaviors. They then use several strategies to promote more appropriate behavior (Ruef et al., 1998):

- Teach desirable behaviors that can serve the same purpose as—and can therefore replace—the inappropriate behaviors.
- Consistently reinforce desired behaviors in ways that the student truly appreciates.
- Modify the classroom environment to minimize conditions that might trigger inappropriate behaviors.
- Establish a predictable daily routine as a way of minimizing anxiety and making the student feel more comfortable and secure.
- Give the student frequent opportunities to make choices; in this way, the student can often gain desired outcomes without having to resort to inappropriate behaviors.
- Make adaptations in the curriculum and/or instruction to maximize the likelihood of academic success (e.g., by building on the student's interests and preferred activities, presenting material at a slower pace, or interspersing challenging tasks among easier and more enjoyable ones).

I'll illustrate the use of positive behavioral support with Samantha, a student that I first described in Chapter 5:

Samantha was a 9-year-old third grader who had been identified as having autism and moderate speech disabilities. She frequently ran out of the classroom, damaging school property and other students' belongings in her flight. When a teacher or other adult tried to intervene, she would fight back by biting, scratching, hitting, kicking, and pulling hair. On such occasions, school personnel would often call her parents and ask that they come to take her home.

The multidisciplinary team working with Samantha eventually discovered that her destructive and aggressive behaviors were more likely to occur when she was given a difficult academic assignment or had reason to anticipate such an assignment. Departures from the routine schedule or the absences of favorite teachers further increased the probability of such responses.

The team hypothesized that Samantha's undesirable behaviors served two purposes: They helped her avoid unpleasant academic tasks and enabled her to gain the attention of valued adults. The team suspected, too, that Samantha felt as if she had little or no control over classroom activities and that she yearned for social interaction with her teachers and classmates. (DeVault et al., 1996)

The team took several steps to address the roots of Samantha's inappropriate behaviors and help her acquire more productive ones (DeVault et al., 1996):

- Samantha was given a consistent and predictable daily schedule that included frequent breaks from potentially challenging academic tasks and numerous opportunities to interact with others.

- When Samantha felt that she needed a break from her academic work, she could ask to spend some time in the "relaxation room," a quiet and private space where she could sit in a beanbag chair and listen to soothing audiotapes.

- When a teacher observed behaviors that might escalate into aggression or flight from the classroom, he or she would remind Samantha that she could best deal with frustration and stress by spending some time in the relaxation room.

- On occasions when Samantha attempted to leave the classroom, an adult would place her immediately in the relaxation room, where she could calm down without a great deal of adult attention.

- Samantha was given "goal sheets" from which she could choose the academic tasks she would work on, the length of time she would work on them, and the specific reinforcer she would receive for achieving any particular goal.

- Samantha was taught how to ask for assistance when she needed it—a strategy that she could use instead of fleeing from the classroom when she encountered a challenging task.

- Samantha was given explicit instruction in how to interact appropriately with her classmates. Initially, she earned points for appropriate social behaviors, and she could trade these points for weekend family trips to Dairy Queen or a video store. Eventually, however, the behaviors themselves led to natural consequences—friendly interactions with her peers—that made such concrete reinforcers unnecessary.

Samantha's behavior changed dramatically within the course of a few months. By the time she was twelve years old and in sixth grade, her grades consistently earned her a place on the honor roll, and she had a group of friends with whom she participated in several extracurricular activities. Her teachers described her as sociable, inquisitive, and creative; her principal called her a "model student" (DeVault et al., 1996).

Positive behavioral support clearly has elements of behaviorist theory, including its focus on structuring an environment that reinforces desired behaviors and extinguishes undesirable ones. At the same time, it also incorporates contemporary theories of motivation, as reflected in its attempts to minimize anxiety, provide opportunities for choice making, and promote mastery of classroom tasks. The importance of doing all of these things will become clearer when we discuss motivation in Chapter 12.

Potential Limitations of Behaviorist Techniques

Before you conclude that behaviorist techniques will always provide the perfect solution to your students' classroom behavior problems, I should point out some potential drawbacks to using these approaches. First, as we will discover in Chapter 12, extrinsic reinforcement for a particular behavior may undermine any intrinsic motivation a student has for engaging in that behavior. A second potential side effect is that, when students increase the responses that lead to reinforcement, other desirable responses may decrease as a result. Students receiving extrinsic reinforcers for their academic work sometimes show less interest in *non*reinforced school activities, less desire to perform beyond minimal standards of performance, and less risk taking and creativity in assignments (Brophy, 1986; Clifford, 1990; Lepper & Hodell, 1989). For these reasons, before using extrinsic reinforcers to increase certain behaviors, we should be sure such reinforcers are truly necessary—that students show no intrinsic motivation to develop the academic or social skills essential for their school success.

Finally, we should note that, particularly when dealing with chronic misbehaviors, applied behavior analysis and positive behavioral support may take a fair amount of our instructional time (Hughes, 1988). Ideally, we should *prevent* misbehaviors as often as

Why do you think extrinsic reinforcers might have such effects? Can you form some hypotheses before you read Chapter 12?

we can, rather than having to correct them after they have already developed. Chapter 15 describes numerous preventive strategies.

Obviously, we can learn a great deal about human learning and behavior simply by looking at stimulus-response principles, and we can bring about major behavior changes by applying these principles in a systematic fashion. At the same time, such principles do not by any means give us a complete picture of human learning. For example, although reinforcement may increase the amount of time that students study, it does not necessarily increase the effectiveness of that study time; cognitive psychology provides more guidance as to how we can help students learn information more effectively, remember it longer, and apply it to new situations more readily. Furthermore, it appears that people learn not only the behaviors that they themselves are reinforced for but also the behaviors that they see *others* exhibit. A third perspective of learning, social cognitive theory, provides more guidance about how we can help students learn through their observations of others. We will consider this perspective in the next chapter.

In a number of places throughout the chapter, I have sneaked unobservable phenomena (e.g., thoughts, feelings) into my description of behaviorist principles. Can you find some places where I have done so?

Considering Diversity in Student Behaviors

When we take a behaviorist perspective, we realize that our students bring their own unique set of prior experiences to the classroom; such diversity in previous environments is undoubtedly one of the reasons for the different behaviors we see in the classroom. For one thing, our students will have been reinforced and punished—by their parents, siblings, previous teachers, peers, and so on—for different kinds of behaviors. Some students may have been reinforced for completing tasks in a careful and thorough manner, whereas others may have been reinforced for completing tasks quickly but sloppily. Some students may have been reinforced for initiating interactions with age-mates; others may have been punished (perhaps in the form of peer rejection) for similar outgoing behavior. Some diversity in students' classroom responses will also be due to the different behaviors that varying cultures encourage (reinforce) and discourage (punish) in their children.

Furthermore, we will see differences in the secondary reinforcers to which students respond. Remember, secondary reinforcers are those that become reinforcing over time through their association with other reinforcing stimuli; thus, the relative effectiveness of such reinforcers as praise and positive feedback will depend on the extent to which such associations have been made. For example, some Native American students may feel uncomfortable when praised for their work as *individuals* yet feel quite proud when they receive praise for *group* success (C. A. Grant & Gomez, 1996). Such preference for group praise is consistent with the cooperative spirit in which these students have been raised (see the discussion of ethnic differences in Chapter 4).

Finally, our students will have had varying experiences with the stimuli they will encounter at school. For example, when they throw a softball for the first time at school, some may be able to generalize from previous experiences throwing a baseball, whereas others may have to start from scratch in developing the skill. When they find themselves in an argument with a classmate, some may try to resolve the conflict through negotiation and compromise, whereas others may decide to engage in a knock-down-drag-out fight.

With such diversity in mind, we will inevitably need to tailor our strategies to the particular students with whom we are working. Effective reinforcers, baseline rates of desired behaviors, and responses to particular stimuli will all be different for each student.

Accommodating Students with Special Needs

A behaviorist approach allows us to consider characteristics of students with special needs from a somewhat different angle than we have in previous chapters. Table 10–3 illustrates how responses, reinforcement, generalization, and discrimination may be somewhat different in some of our students with special needs.

TABLE 10.3

Encouraging Appropriate Behaviors in Students with Special Educational Needs

STUDENTS WITH SPECIAL NEEDS	CHARACTERISTICS THAT THESE STUDENTS MAY EXHIBIT	CLASSROOM STRATEGIES THAT MAY BE BENEFICIAL FOR THESE STUDENTS
Students with specific cognitive or academic difficulties	Inappropriate classroom behaviors (in some students) Difficulty discriminating among similar stimuli, especially when perceptual deficits exist Difficulty generalizing responses from one situation to another	Reinforce desired classroom behaviors. Emphasize differences among similar stimuli and provide opportunities to practice making subtle discriminations. Promote generalization of new responses (e.g., by pointing out similarities among different situations and by teaching skills in real-world contexts).
Students with social or behavioral problems	Inappropriate responses, especially in social situations; difficulty determining when and where particular responses are appropriate A history of inappropriate behaviors being reinforced (e.g., intrinsically or by teacher attention) Responsiveness to teacher praise if given in private (students with emotional or behavioral disorders) Difficulty generalizing appropriate responses to new situations	Describe desired behaviors clearly. Give precise feedback regarding students' behavior. Reinforce desired behaviors using teacher attention, private praise, activity reinforcers, group contingencies (students with emotional or behavioral disorders). Reinforce accomplishments immediately using concrete reinforcers, activity reinforcers, praise (some students with autism). Shape desired behaviors over time; expect gradual improvement rather than immediate perfection. Punish inappropriate behaviors (e.g., using time-out or response cost); consider positive behavioral support for persistent, challenging behaviors. Promote generalization of new responses to appropriate situations (e.g., by teaching skills in real-world contexts and providing opportunities to role-play new responses).
Students with general delays in cognitive and social functioning	High reinforcing value of extrinsic reinforcers Behaviors more likely to increase when reinforcement is immediate rather than delayed Inappropriate responses in social situations Difficulty discriminating between important and unimportant stimuli Difficulty generalizing responses from one situation to another	Cue students regarding appropriate behaviors. Provide immediate feedback regarding specific behaviors. Reinforce accomplishments immediately (e.g., using concrete reinforcers, activity reinforcers, praise). Use continuous reinforcement during the acquisition of new responses. Shape desired behaviors over time; expect gradual improvement rather than immediate perfection. Reprimand minor misbehaviors; use time-out or response cost for more serious and chronic misbehaviors. Highlight the stimuli to which you want students to attend. Promote generalization of new responses (e.g., by teaching skills in real-world contexts and by reinforcing generalization).
Students with physical or sensory challenges	Loss of some previously learned behaviors if students have had a traumatic brain injury	Shape desired behaviors over time; expect gradual improvement rather than immediate perfection.
Students with advanced cognitive development	Unusual and sometimes creative responses to classroom tasks	Keep an open mind regarding acceptable responses to classroom assignments. Encourage and reinforce creative responses.

Sources: Barbetta, 1990; Barbetta, Heward, Bradley, & Miller, 1994; Buchoff, 1990; E. S. Ellis & Friend, 1991; Gearheart et al., 1992; Heward, 1996; Landau & McAninch, 1993; Mercer, 1991; Morgan & Jenson, 1988; Patton et al., 1987; Patton et al., 1990; Piirto, 1994; Pressley, 1995; Turnbull et al., 1999.

Note: Compiled with the assistance of Dr. Margie Garanzini-Daiber and Dr. Margaret Coben, University of Missouri—St. Louis.

CASE STUDY: Hostile Helen

Mr. Washington has a close-knit group of friends in one of his high school vocational education classes. He is concerned about one particular student in this group, a girl named Helen. Helen uses obscene language in class. She is rude and disrespectful to Mr. Washington. She taunts and insults classmates outside her own circle of friends. And she is physically aggressive toward classroom facilities—defacing furniture, kicking equipment, punching walls, and so on.

At first, Mr. Washington tries to ignore Helen's hostile and aggressive behaviors, but this strategy doesn't lead to any improvement in her behavior. He then tries praising Helen on those rare occasions when she does behave appropriately, but this strategy doesn't seem to work either.

- In behaviorist terminology, what is Mr. Washington trying to do when he ignores Helen's inappropriate behavior? What are some possible reasons why this approach isn't working?

- In behaviorist terminology, what is Mr. Washington trying to do when he praises Helen's appropriate behavior? What are some possible reasons why this approach isn't working either?

- How might *you* use behaviorist learning principles to bring about a behavior change in Helen?

Summing Up

Behaviorism

Behaviorists focus on the role that the environment (i.e., stimuli) plays in bringing about changes in behavior (i.e., responses). It is clear from behaviorist principles that the classroom environments we create have a significant effect on our students' learning and behavior.

Classical Conditioning

Classical conditioning is one way through which people acquire emotional responses to stimuli in the environment. Classical conditioning occurs when (1) one stimulus (the unconditioned stimulus) already elicits a particular response (the unconditioned response) and (2) that stimulus is presented in conjunction with another stimulus, usually on several occasions. Under these circumstances, the second (conditioned) stimulus begins to elicit a (conditioned) response as well. As teachers, we should strive to create a classroom environment that conditions pleasure and relaxation responses to academic tasks, not an environment that elicits fear and anxiety.

Operant Conditioning

Operant conditioning occurs when a learner's response is followed by a reinforcing stimulus, thereby increasing the likelihood that the learner will repeat the response. We can increase the frequency of appropriate and productive student behaviors by reinforcing those behaviors whenever they occur or by gradually reinforcing closer and closer approximations to those behaviors (in other words, by shaping them); furthermore, we should describe desired behaviors clearly, individualize reinforcers according to students' preferences, and make response-consequence contingencies explicit and consistent. We must also be careful that we *don't* reinforce undesirable or counterproductive student behaviors.

Effects of Antecedent Stimuli and Responses

Students' behaviors are influenced not only by the consequences of those behaviors but also by antecedent events. For instance, once students have learned a response to a particular stimulus, they will tend to make the same response to similar stimuli (i.e., they will generalize). Seemingly similar situations may sometimes call for very different responses, however; in such situations, it is important to help students discriminate between occasions when particular behaviors are and are not appropriate, perhaps by providing cues regarding the responses we expect them to make. It is important, too, that we put students in situations in which desired behaviors are most likely to occur (i.e., that we create setting events) and that we engage students in easy tasks that will lead naturally to more difficult and challenging ones (through the phenomenon of behavioral momentum).

Reducing and Eliminating Undesirable Behaviors

Behaviorist principles offer several strategies for reducing and possibly eliminating nonproductive or counterproductive classroom behaviors. As teachers, we might remove the consequences that reinforce an unwanted behavior (resulting in the behavior's extinction), provide cues regarding inappropriate behavior, or reinforce responses incompatible with those we wish to eliminate. In some situations, we may need to punish students for inappropriate behaviors, particularly when those that interfere significantly with classroom learning or jeopardize students' physical safety or psychological well-being. Yet we should think of punishment as a last resort and abide by strict guidelines in its use, keeping in mind that consequences such as physical punishment, public humiliation, and out-of-school suspension are neither effective nor in our students' long-term best interests.

Maintaining Productive Behaviors

Ideally, desired behaviors are most likely to continue when they lead to such intrinsically reinforcing consequences as feelings of mastery or pride. When intrinsic reinforcement seems unlikely, we can instead maintain productive behaviors over the long run by reinforcing them on an intermittent basis.

Applying Behaviorism Systematically

Applied behavior analysis and positive behavioral support are two approaches through which we can apply behaviorist principles in a systematic fashion. Research indicates that such techniques are often effective in promoting greater academic success and more appropriate classroom behavior. We must be careful that we don't provide extrinsic reinforcement unnecessarily, however; in doing so, we may undermine any intrinsic reinforcers that are currently operating.

Diversity in Student Behaviors

Our students will have different histories of reinforcement and different experiences with the various stimuli in the classroom; hence, they will inevitably display different reactions to the same tasks and situations. Some students with special needs will exhibit counterproductive classroom behaviors; behaviorist principles may be especially useful in working with such students.

KEY CONCEPTS

behaviorism (p. 395)
conditioning (p. 396)
contiguity (p. 398)
classical conditioning (p. 398)
unconditioned stimulus (UCS) (p. 399)
unconditioned response (UCR) (p. 399)
neutral stimulus (p. 399)
conditioned stimulus (CS) (p. 399)
conditioned response (CR) (p. 399)
generalization (in classical conditioning) (p. 401)
extinction (in classical conditioning) (p. 402)
operant conditioning (p. 403)
contingency (p. 405)
reinforcer (p. 406)
reinforcement (p. 406)
primary reinforcer (p. 406)
secondary reinforcer (p. 406)
positive reinforcement (p. 407)

concrete reinforcer (p. 407)
social reinforcer (p. 407)
activity reinforcer (p. 407)
Premack principle (p. 407)
group contingency (p. 408)
positive feedback (p. 408)
intrinsic reinforcer (p. 409)
extrinsic reinforcer (p. 409)
negative reinforcement (p. 410)
terminal behavior (p. 410)
token economy (p. 411)
contingency contract (p. 411)
continuous reinforcement (p. 412)
baseline (p. 412)
shaping (p. 412)
antecedent stimulus (p. 414)
antecedent response (p. 414)
generalization (in operant conditioning) (p. 414)

discrimination (p. 415)
cueing (p. 415)
setting event (p. 415)
behavioral momentum (p. 415)
extinction (in operant conditioning) (p. 417)
incompatible behaviors (p. 418)
punishment (p. 419)
presentation punishment (p. 419)
removal punishment (p. 419)
response cost (p. 421)
logical consequence (p. 421)
time-out (p. 421)
in-school suspension (p. 421)
psychological punishment (p. 422)
intermittent reinforcement (p. 425)
applied behavior analysis (ABA) (p. 426)
positive behavioral support (PBS) (p. 427)

11

Social Cognitive Views of Learning

W hat behaviors have you learned by watching other people do them first? Can you think of any academic skills you've learned by watching someone else? Perhaps you learned a mathematical procedure or the correct conjugation of *estudiar*. What about social skills? Perhaps you observed how to answer the telephone or how to apologize to someone whose feelings you've hurt. And what about psychomotor skills? Perhaps you discovered how to swing a softball bat or write letters in cursive. We learn many behaviors—academic, social, and motor skills alike—by watching our parents, our teachers, our peers, people we see in the media, and a variety of other individuals we encounter in our daily lives. We also learn which behaviors are likely to get us ahead—and which behaviors are not—by observing the consequences of those behaviors for ourselves and others. Eventually, we develop a sense of what we ourselves are capable of doing, and we begin to direct our behavior toward goals that we value and think we can achieve.

This chapter explores **social cognitive theory** (also called *social learning theory*), a perspective that can help us understand what, when, and how people learn by watching others, and how people ultimately begin to assume some control over their own behavior. In particular, we will address these questions:

- What basic assumptions are central to the social cognitive perspective of learning?
- How do cognitive processes influence the effects that reinforcement and punishment have on behavior?
- How can we effectively use modeling to facilitate students' learning?
- What role does *self-efficacy* play in learning, and how can we enhance it in our students?
- How can we help our students take control of their own behavior and learning? In other words, how can we promote *self-regulation*?
- How do personal characteristics, environmental variables, and learners' behaviors interact with one another (a set of interactions collectively known as *reciprocal causation*)?
- How can social cognitive theory help us accommodate student diversity?

CASE STUDY: Parlez-Vous Français?

Nathan isn't taking French because he wants to; he has enrolled in French I only because his mother insisted. Although he does well in his other high school courses, he's convinced that he will be a failure in French. After all, three friends who took French last year got mostly Ds and Fs on quizzes and homework, and two of them dropped the class after the first semester.

On the first day of French class, Nathan notices that most of his classmates are girls; the few boys in the class are students he doesn't know very well. He sits sullenly in the back row, convinced that he will do no better in French than his friends did. "I do OK in math and science, but I'm just no good at learning languages," he tells himself. "Besides, learning French is a 'girl' thing."

Although Nathan comes to class every day, his mind usually wanders to other topics as his teacher explains simple syntactical structures and demonstrates the correct pronunciation of new vocabulary words. He makes feeble attempts at homework assignments but quickly puts them aside whenever he encounters anything he doesn't immediately understand.

Sure enough, Nathan is right: He can't do French. He gets a D− on his first exam.

- What has Nathan learned about French by observing other people?
- Why does Nathan's belief lead to a self-fulfilling prophecy?

Basic Assumptions of Social Cognitive Theory

You might initially think that Nathan has learned nothing from observing others because he has apparently not benefited from his teacher's explanations and demonstrations. Yet at second glance, you might realize that Nathan *has* learned something through observation after all: He has seen what happened to his three friends and concluded that *he* probably won't succeed in French class either. As we proceed through the chapter, you will discover some reasons why Nathan has apparently learned more from his friends than he has from his teacher.

Social cognitive theory has its roots in behaviorism, but over the past few decades it has increasingly incorporated cognitive processes into its explanations of learning; it now provides a nice blend of ideas from behaviorism and cognitive psychology. It has developed in large part through the research efforts of Albert Bandura at Stanford University. You will find references to Bandura and others who build on his ideas (e.g., Dale Schunk, Barry Zimmerman) throughout the chapter.

In our case study of Nathan, we can see one basic assumption underlying social cognitive theory: People can learn from observing others. This and several other assumptions are summarized in Table 11–1. Let's look at them more closely:

- *People can learn by observing others.* In our discussion of operant conditioning in the preceding chapter, we found that learning is sometimes a process of trial and error: People try many different responses, increasing the ones that bring about desirable consequences and eliminating the unproductive ones. Social cognitive theorists contend that people don't always have to "experiment" in this way; instead, they can acquire many new responses simply by observing the behaviors of the people around them. For example, a student might learn how to solve a long division problem, spell the word *synonym* correctly, or mouth off at the teacher simply by watching someone else do these things first.

- *Learning is an internal process that may or may not result in a behavior change.* Some of the things people learn appear in their behavior immediately, other things affect their behavior at a later point in time, and still others may never influence their behavior at all. For example, you might attempt to swing a tennis racket as soon as you learn the correct form. But you probably

Social cognitive theorists propose that people can sometimes learn more quickly and easily by watching how others behave and noticing which behaviors lead to reinforcement and which lead to punishment.

TABLE 11.1

PRINCIPLES/ASSUMPTIONS

Basic Assumptions of Social Cognitive Theory and Their Educational Implications

ASSUMPTION	EDUCATIONAL IMPLICATION	EXAMPLE
Learning by observation	Help students acquire new behaviors more quickly by demonstrating those behaviors yourself.	Demonstrate appropriate ways to deal with and resolve interpersonal conflicts. Then ask students to role-play conflict resolution in small groups, and commend those who use prosocial strategies.
Learning as an internal process that may or may not be reflected in behavior	Remember that learning does not always appear immediately, but may instead be reflected in students' later behaviors.	When one student engages in disruptive classroom behavior, take appropriate steps to discourage it. Otherwise, classmates who have witnessed the misbehavior may be similarly disruptive on future occasions.
Goal-directed behavior	Encourage students to set goals for themselves, especially goals that are challenging yet achievable.	When teaching American Sign Language to students to help them communicate with a classmate who is deaf, ask them to predict how many new words and phrases they can learn each week.
Self-regulation of behavior	Teach students strategies for helping themselves learn effectively and behave appropriately.	Give students some concrete suggestions about how they can remind themselves to bring needed supplies to school each day.
Indirect effects of reinforcement and punishment	Ensure that the consequences that students experience for various responses communicate the right messages as to which behaviors are and are not acceptable in the classroom.	To encourage students to speak in German, respond to questions only if students make a reasonable attempt to ask the questions in German.

won't demonstrate that you have learned how to apologize tactfully until some later time when an apology is necessary. And you might *never* walk barefoot over hot coals, no matter how many times you see someone else do it. Social cognitive theory, like cognitive psychology, defines learning as an internal mental process that may or may not be reflected in the learner's behavior.

• *Behavior is directed toward particular goals.* Because you are reading this book, you probably want to become a teacher or enter some related profession, and you are taking an educational psychology class to help you attain that goal. Social cognitive theorists propose that people often set goals for themselves and direct their behavior accordingly. Students are likely to have a variety of goals—perhaps a high grade point average, a college scholarship, popularity with classmates, athletic prowess, or a reputation as the class clown. Throughout the chapter we will see the relevance of such goals for learning and behavior.

• *Behavior eventually becomes self-regulated.* From a behaviorist perspective, people's behaviors are governed largely by the things that happen *to* them—the stimuli they encounter, the reinforcers that follow their behaviors, and so on. In contrast, social cognitive theorists believe that people eventually begin to regulate their *own* learning and behavior. As an example, let's consider Shih-tai, a third grader who is learning to write in cursive. A traditional behaviorist might tell us that Shih-tai can best learn cursive if her teacher reinforces her for increasingly more appropriate responses, thereby shaping skillful penmanship over a period of several weeks or months. But a social cognitive theorist might suggest that Shih-tai can learn to write cursive letters just as easily by looking carefully at the examples her teacher has written on the chalkboard, copying those letters as closely as possible, and then comparing the letters she has written with those on the board. If she is happy with her work, she will give herself a mental pat on the back; if she is not, she may continue to practice until her letters are comparable with those of the teacher. From the social cognitive perspective, people often set their own standards for acceptable and unacceptable behavior and then strive to behave in accordance with those standards.

- *Reinforcement and punishment have several indirect effects (rather than a direct effect) on learning and behavior.* Operant conditioning theorists believe that reinforcement is necessary for learning, because responses increase only when they are reinforced. Some behaviorists have also argued that punishment is an effective counterpart to reinforcement, decreasing the frequency of a behavior it follows. Implied in the behaviorist perspective is the idea that reinforcement and punishment are directly responsible for the behavior changes we see.

Reinforcement and punishment are less critical in social cognitive theory, but they have several indirect effects on learning and behavior. In the section that follows, we will find out exactly how reinforcement and punishment fit into the social cognitive perspective.

> Do you think your own behaviors are regulated more by the environment or by your own standards regarding what is acceptable and what is not?

The Social Cognitive View of Reinforcement and Punishment

According to social cognitive theorists (e.g., Bandura, 1977, 1986; T. L. Rosenthal & Zimmerman, 1978), both reinforcement and punishment influence learning and behavior in a number of ways:

- People form *expectations* about the likely consequences of future responses based on how current responses are reinforced or punished.
- People's expectations are also influenced by their observations of the consequences that follow other people's behaviors—in other words, by *vicarious experiences.*
- Expectations about probable future consequences affect the extent to which people *cognitively process* new information.
- Expectations also affect how people *choose to behave.*
- The *nonoccurrence of an expected consequence* may have a reinforcing or punishing effect in and of itself.

Let's see how each of these factors plays out in social cognitive theory.

Expectations

THINKING ABOUT WHAT YOU KNOW

- Perhaps you have taken a course in which all the exam questions were based on the textbook, without a single question coming from class lectures. After the first exam, did you find yourself studying the textbook very carefully but skipping class frequently?

- On the other hand, perhaps you have taken a course in which exams were based on the lectures and the assigned textbook readings seemed irrelevant. In that situation, did you go to class regularly but never bother to open your textbook?

According to social cognitive theory, people form expectations about the consequences that are likely to result from various behaviors. When we find that a particular response is reinforced every time we make it, we typically expect to be reinforced for behaving that way in future situations. When we discover that a response frequently leads to punishment, we expect that response to be punished on later occasions as well. For example, you use your own experiences with classroom tests to form expectations as to what specific behaviors (e.g., reading your textbook, going to class) are likely to be reinforced on future tests.

Students sometimes form their expectations about what things will be reinforced and punished on the basis of very little hard data. For example, one student might believe (perhaps erroneously) that, by bragging about his high test scores, he will gain the admiration of his classmates (a reinforcer). Another student might believe that her classmates will ridicule and reject (i.e., punish) her for being smart, regardless of whether they would actually do so.

Can you think of an occasion when you chose not to do something because of the ridicule you thought it might bring you?

From the social cognitive perspective, reinforcement increases the frequency of a behavior only when students know what behavior is actually being reinforced—that is, when they are *aware* of actual response-reinforcement contingencies (Bandura, 1986). As teachers, then, we should be very clear about what we are reinforcing, so that our students know the real response-reinforcement contingencies operating in the classroom. For example, if Sam gets an A on an essay but we don't let him know *why* he earned that grade, he won't necessarily know how to get an A the next time. To improve Sam's performance, we might tell him that the essay earned an A because he supported his opinion with a logical train of thought. Similarly, if we praise Sandra for her "good game" at the basketball tournament even though she scored only one basket, she may understandably be a bit confused. We might instead tell her that we were pleased with her high energy level throughout the game.

Specify response-reinforcement contingencies.

Vicarious Experiences

When I was in third grade, I entered a Halloween costume contest dressed as a tooth. I didn't win the contest; a "witch" won first prize. So the following year, I entered the same contest dressed as a witch, figuring that I was a shoo-in for first place. Our expectations about the consequences of certain responses come not only from making those responses ourselves but also from observing what happens when others make them. In other words, we sometimes experience reinforcement and punishment *vicariously*.

People who observe someone else getting reinforced for a particular behavior tend to exhibit that behavior more frequently themselves—a phenomenon known as **vicarious reinforcement.** For example, by watching the consequences that their classmates experience, students might learn that studying hard leads to good grades, that being elected to class office brings status and popularity, or that neatness counts.

Conversely, when we see someone else get punished for a certain behavior, we are *less* likely to behave that way ourselves—a phenomenon known as **vicarious punishment.** For example, when a coach benches a football player for poor sportsmanlike conduct, other players will be less likely to repeat such behavior. But unfortunately, vicarious punishment may suppress desirable behaviors as well. For example, when a teacher

Remember that the consequences you administer to one student may vicariously influence other students' behavior as well.

belittles a student for asking a seemingly silly question, other students may be reluctant to ask questions of their own.

As teachers, we must be extremely careful that we don't vicariously reinforce undesirable behaviors or vicariously punish desirable behaviors. If we give too much attention to a misbehaving student, others who want our attention may misbehave as well. If we ridicule a student who unwittingly volunteers an incorrect answer or erroneous belief, classmates will hardly be eager to respond to our questions or express their ideas and opinions.

Cognitive Processing

Experiencing Firsthand
Planning Ahead

Quickly skim the contents of Chapter 16 to get a general sense of the topics it includes. Once you have done so, imagine yourself in each of these situations:

1. Your educational psychology instructor announces, "Chapter 16 won't be on your test, but please read it anyway." How thoroughly and carefully will you read the chapter? Jot down a brief answer to this question.

2. The following day, your educational psychology instructor announces, "I gave you some incorrect information yesterday. In reality, half of next week's test will be based on the ideas presented in Chapter 16." *Now* how thoroughly and carefully will you read the chapter? Once again, jot down a brief answer.

___

If you don't expect to be reinforced for reading Chapter 16, you may very well *not* read it very carefully (perhaps you'll read it later, you think to yourself, but you have too many other things to do right now). But if, instead, you discover that getting an A in your educational psychology course depends on your knowing the material in Chapter 16 like the back of your hand, you are apt to read it slowly and carefully, possibly trying to learn and remember each and every detail.

When we believe that we will be reinforced for learning something, we are more likely to pay attention to it and mentally process it in an effective fashion. When we *don't* expect to be reinforced for learning it, we are far less likely to think about or process it in any significant way. As an example of the latter situation, let's return to Nathan, from our opening case study. Convinced that he can't learn French, Nathan pays little attention to what his teacher says in class, and he makes only half-hearted efforts to complete his homework assignments.

Choice of Behavior

People learn many things that they never demonstrate because there is no reinforcement for doing so. To see what I mean, try this short exercise.

Experiencing Firsthand
Dr. X

How many of the following questions can you answer about your educational psychology instructor? For lack of a better name, I'm going to call your instructor "Dr. X."

1. Is Dr. X right-handed or left-handed?

2. Is Dr. X a flashy dresser or a more conservative one?

3. What kind of shoes does Dr. X wear to class?

4.   Does Dr. X wear a wedding ring?
5.   Does Dr. X bring a briefcase to class each day?

If you've been going to class regularly, you probably know the answers to at least two of the questions, and possibly you can answer all five, even though you never thought you'd have a reason to know such information. Every time I teach educational psychology, I take a minute sometime during the semester to hide my feet behind the podium; I then ask my students to tell me what my shoes look like. My students first look at me as if I have two heads; information about my shoes is something that many of them have learned, but until now they have had absolutely no reason to demonstrate their knowledge. After a few seconds of awkward silence, at least a half dozen students (usually those sitting in the first two rows) begin to describe my shoes, right down to the rippled soles, scuffed leather, and beige stitching.

Students learn many things in the classroom. They learn facts and figures, they learn ways of getting their teacher's attention, and they may even learn such tiny details as which classmate stores Twinkies in his desk and what kind of shoes the teacher wears to school. Of all the things they learn, students will be most likely to demonstrate the ones they think will bring them reinforcement. The things they think will *not* be reinforced may remain hidden forever. As teachers, we should be sure that our students believe they will be reinforced for demonstrating their knowledge and skills related to important educational objectives.

Make sure students believe that they will be reinforced for demonstrating what they have learned.

Working for Incentives

When you work diligently for a reinforcer that you hope to obtain in the future, you are working for an **incentive.** Incentives are never guaranteed: You never know that you are going to get an A on a test when you study for it or that you are going to win a Halloween costume contest when you enter it. An incentive is an expected or hoped-for consequence, one that may or may not actually occur.

People don't work for incentives they don't believe they can achieve. For example, in a classroom of thirty students, a competition in which one prize will be awarded for the highest test score provides an incentive to just a handful of top achievers. An incentive is effective only to the extent that it is obtainable and that a student perceives it as such. Therefore, when we provide incentives for student achievement, we should find out whether our students believe they have some chance of achieving those incentives.

Make sure students believe that they can achieve the incentives offered in the classroom.

Nonoccurrence of Expected Consequences

When I entered the Halloween costume contest as a witch, I lost once again. (First prize went to a girl with a metal colander over her head. She was dressed as Sputnik, the first Soviet satellite launched into space.) That was the last time I entered the contest. I had expected reinforcement and felt cheated when I didn't get it. Social cognitive theorists propose that the nonoccurrence of expected reinforcement is a form of punishment (e.g., Bandura, 1986). When people think that a certain response is going to be reinforced, yet the response is *not* reinforced, they are less likely to exhibit that behavior in the future.

Perhaps you can think of a time when you broke a rule, expecting to be punished, but got away with your crime. Or perhaps you can remember seeing someone else break a rule without being caught. When nothing bad happens after a forbidden behavior, people may actually feel as if they have been reinforced for that behavior. Just as the nonoccurrence of reinforcement is a form of punishment, the nonoccurrence of punishment is a form of reinforcement (Bandura, 1986).

Can you recall an occasion when, as a student, you did not receive the reinforcement you expected? How did you feel and behave when that happened?

When a forbidden behavior goes unpunished, it is actually reinforced and so is likely to occur again.

Follow through with the consequences that students expect for certain behaviors. See Chapter 10 for guidelines and cautions on the use of punishment.

When students work hard to achieve a desired end result—perhaps a compliment, a certificate, or a special privilege—and the anticipated result doesn't materialize, they will be unlikely to work as hard the next time. And when students break school rules yet are not punished for doing so, they are more likely to break those rules again. As teachers, it is important that we follow through with promised reinforcements for desirable student behaviors. It is equally important that we impose the consequences students have come to expect for undesirable behaviors.

As we have seen, students learn many behaviors from observing those around them. But they don't necessarily model everything they see someone else do. When do students imitate the behaviors they see? And what kinds of people are they most likely to imitate? It is to such questions about *modeling* that we turn now.

Modeling

Consider these research findings:

- In one experiment, young children were taught not to speak to strangers through one of two techniques. One group of children heard a lecture about the dangers of following strangers and about the things they should do if a stranger tried to entice them; nevertheless, very few of these children tried to resist a friendly stranger who later appeared on the playground. A second group of children actually observed another child demonstrate techniques for resisting strangers; most of these children resisted the stranger's advances (Poche, Yoder, & Miltenberger, 1988).

- When children see aggressive models—whether those models are people the children know, people on television, or cartoon characters—they are more likely to be aggressive themselves. Boys in particular are likely to model the aggressive behaviors they observe (Bandura, 1965; Bandura, Ross, & Ross, 1961, 1963; Friedrich & Stein, 1973; Lowry et al., 1995; Steuer, Applefield, & Smith, 1971).

- After watching adults demonstrate such behaviors as cooperation, sympathy, sharing, and generosity, children are more likely to demonstrate similar

INTO THE CLASSROOM: Administering Consequences from a Social Cognitive Perspective

Describe the specific behaviors you are reinforcing, so that students are aware of the response-reinforcement contingencies operating in the classroom.

A teacher tells his class, "Because everyone got at least 80 percent of the math problems correct this morning, we will have ten minutes of free time at the end of the day."

Make sure students believe that they can achieve the incentives offered in the classroom.

A teacher realizes that if she were to grade her students' science projects on a curve, only a few students could possibly get As. Instead, she gives her students a checklist of the specific criteria she will use to grade the science projects; she tells her class that any project meeting all the criteria will get an A.

Tell students what behaviors are unacceptable in the classroom and describe the consequences that will result when those behaviors occur.

A teacher reminds students that anyone seen pushing in the lunch line will go to the end of the line.

Follow through with the reinforcements that you have promised for desirable student behaviors; also follow through with the adverse consequences that students expect for undesirable behaviors.

When announcing tryouts for an upcoming school play, a teacher tells students that only those who sign up ahead of time may try out. When she holds tryouts the following week, she sticks to her word, turning away any student whose name does not appear on her sign-up sheet.

Remember that the consequences you administer for a particular student's behavior have a potential effect on any students who observe those consequences.

The student council president, even though she is well liked and highly respected by both students and teachers, is nevertheless punished in accordance with school rules when she is caught cheating on an exam.

prosocial behaviors (R. Elliott & Vasta, 1970; Friedrich & Stein, 1973; Radke-Yarrow, Zahn-Waxler, & Chapman, 1983; Rushton, 1980).

- When a model preaches one set of moral values and practices another, observers are more likely to do what the model *does* than what the model *says* (J. H. Bryan, 1975).

We learn many different things through modeling. We learn such motor skills as holding a pencil, whittling a piece of wood, and dribbling a basketball by seeing how other people do these things. We also acquire skills in such academic areas as arithmetic and reading more readily by observing others. And we develop interpersonal skills and moral values, at least in part, by watching and imitating the people around us.

Most of the models from which we learn are **live models**—real people that we actually see doing something. In a classroom setting, students may learn something by watching their teacher solve an algebraic equation, observing a visiting police officer demonstrate important rules of bicycle safety, or seeing a classmate perform a flawless hook shot on the basketball court. But we are also influenced by **symbolic models**—real or fictional characters portrayed in books, in films, on television, and through various other media. For example,

Think of specific people who might serve as positive role models (either real or symbolic) for your own students.

When a teacher punishes a student, the consequence doesn't just affect the future behavior of that student. It also affects the future behavior of other students who observe the punishment.

students can learn valuable lessons from studying the behaviors of important figures in history or reading stories about people who accomplish great things in the face of adversity.

How Modeling Affects Behavior

Social cognitive theorists (e.g., Bandura, 1977, 1986; T. L. Rosenthal & Zimmerman, 1978) propose that modeling has several possible effects on human behavior; these are described in the following paragraphs.

Observational learning. The observational learning effect is one in which *the observer acquires a new behavior demonstrated by the model.* By seeing and hearing models, students learn how to dissect an earthworm, swim the elementary back stroke, and pronounce *¿Estudia usted español?* correctly. They may also acquire the political and religious beliefs that they hear their parents advocate. And they may adopt the attitudes of their teachers—perhaps enthusiasm about baseball, fear of mathematics, or disdain for the study of history (e.g., Rushton, 1980).

Response facilitation. The response facilitation effect is one in which *the observer displays a previously learned behavior more frequently after seeing a model being rein-*

forced for that behavior (i.e., after receiving vicarious reinforcement). As an example, consider this situation:

> Billy returns to school in September to discover that his expensive new jeans are no longer in style. All his classmates are now wearing old, well-worn jeans; those with holes in the knees are especially fashionable. When he arrives home after his first day of school, Billy digs through his dresser drawers and the family rag bag, looking for old jeans. The next day, much to his parents' dismay, Billy goes to school wearing a pair of jeans with one large hole in the left knee and a three-inch rip running up the right thigh. The brand new jeans that Billy's mother has purchased for him are relegated to the top shelf of his closet, where they remain for the rest of the school year.

Our students are more likely to wear ragged old jeans if their classmates appear to be winning popularity with this attire. Similarly, they are more likely to complete their reading assignments on time and to work cooperatively rather than competitively with classmates—behaviors they may have learned long ago—if they see others being reinforced for doing so.

Response inhibition. The response inhibition effect is one in which *the observer displays a previously learned behavior less frequently after seeing a model being punished for that behavior* (i.e., after receiving vicarious punishment). Students tend to inhibit (*not* engage in) behaviors that result in adverse consequences for those around them. For example, students are less likely to be aggressive on the playground if they see their friends being punished for aggression. They are less likely to cheat on assignments if their peers are caught in the act. And they are less likely to volunteer to answer questions in class when the incorrect answers of their classmates are ridiculed.

Response *disinhibition*. The response disinhibition effect is one in which *the observer displays a previously forbidden or punished behavior more frequently after seeing a model exhibit the behavior without adverse consequences.* Just as students will inhibit behaviors leading to punishment, they will also engage in previously inhibited behaviors more frequently if they observe those behaviors going unpunished for other people. For example, students are more likely to chew gum, copy homework from classmates, or fight in the corridors if they see other students getting away with such behaviors. Remember, the nonoccurrence of expected punishment is reinforcing, so naturally any forbidden activities that seem to have no adverse effects for others may easily increase.

> Why is this called the disinhibition effect?

> How are the response facilitation and response disinhibition effects similar? How are they different?

Yet students don't always model the individuals around them. What factors determine when students are most likely to imitate the behaviors they see? A look at characteristics of effective models will help us with the answer.

Characteristics of Effective Models

Experiencing Firsthand
Five People

Write down the names of five people whose behaviors you would like to imitate in some fashion. Then, beside each name, write down one or more of the reasons *why* you admire these individuals.

Social cognitive theorists have found some consistency in the types of models that others are most likely to imitate (Bandura, 1986; T. L. Rosenthal & Bandura, 1978). Effective models typically exhibit one or more of the following four characteristics—characteristics that you probably see reflected in the list you just created.

Show competence as
you model behavior.

Have students observe
prestigious or powerful
models, either live or
symbolic, engaging in
desirable behaviors.

Expose students to
successful models of both
genders.

Show students how
the behaviors you model
are relevant to their
own lives.

Expose students to
successful models from
diverse cultural
backgrounds. Expose them
also to models who have
become successful despite
disabilities.

Competence. Students will typically try to imitate people who do something well, not those who do it poorly. They will try to imitate the basketball skills of a professional basketball player, rather than those of the class klutz. They will copy the fashions of a popular classmate, rather than those of a student who is socially isolated. They will adopt the mathematical problem-solving procedures of teachers who clearly know what they are doing, rather than the procedures of teachers who make frequent mistakes at the chalkboard.

Prestige and power. Children and adolescents often imitate people who are famous or powerful. Some effective models—a world leader, a renowned athlete, a popular rock star—are famous at a national or international level. The prestige and power of other models—a head cheerleader, the captain of the high school hockey team, a gang leader—may be limited to a more local environment.

In addition to modeling desired behaviors ourselves, we can expose our students to a variety of models that they are likely to view as prestigious and powerful. For example, we might invite respected professionals (e.g., police officer, nurse, newspaper reporter) to visit our classroom and talk with students about topics within their areas of expertise. We might also have students read and learn about appropriate models through such media as books and films—for example, by reading Helen Keller's autobiography or watching news clips of Martin Luther King, Jr.

"Gender appropriate" behavior. Remember our friend Nathan's belief that French is a "girl" thing? Students are most likely to model behaviors they believe are appropriate for their gender (with different students inevitably defining *gender appropriate* somewhat differently). For example, many girls and boys limit their academic choices and career aspirations to the subjects and professions they believe are "for women" and "for men." Some girls may shy away from careers in mathematics as being too "masculine." Some boys may not take keyboarding because they perceive it to be a secretarial skill, and most secretaries are women. Yet mathematics and keyboarding are useful skills for both genders. Exposure to numerous examples of people in "nontraditional careers"—female mathematicians and engineers, male secretaries and nurses—can help broaden students' perceptions as to what behaviors are gender appropriate. In the process, such models can also broaden students' academic choices and possibly enhance their career aspirations.

Behavior relevant to the learner's own situation. Students are most likely to model the behaviors they believe will help them in their own circumstances. A boy may wear the torn jeans that his popular classmates wear if he thinks he can become popular by doing so; however, he will have less reason to dress this way if he thinks that his thick glasses and adolescent acne will prevent him from ever being popular regardless of his clothing. A teenage girl may be tempted to join her friends in drinking beer if she thinks that doing so helps her become more accepted by them; she is less likely to indulge if she is the "designated driver" and knows that her friends are depending on her to stay sober.

In the classroom, we are likely to model a variety of behaviors throughout the day. But our students will adopt these behaviors only if they believe that such responses will truly be useful and productive for them. Therefore, we must show them how the problem-solving methods we teach, the writing skills we demonstrate, and the physical fitness regimen we advocate are all applicable to their own situations.

Our students are less likely to perceive the relevance of modeled behaviors when the model is different from them in some obvious way. For example, students from cultures other than our own may think that some of the things we try to teach them don't apply to their own cultural circumstances. Similarly, students with disabilities may believe that they are incapable of accomplishing the things a nondisabled teacher demonstrates. So it is important that we include individuals from minority cultures and individuals with disabilities in the models we present to our students. Minority students benefit from observing successful minority adults, and students with disabilities become more optimistic about their own futures when they meet adults successfully coping with and overcoming their own disabilities (Pang, 1995; L. E. Powers, Sowers, & Stevens, 1995).

For better or worse, students tend to emulate models who are attractive and prestigious and who behave in traditionally gender-appropriate ways.

You can probably think of teachers you admired and wanted to be like. Most teachers have one or more characteristics of an effective model; for example, students typically view their teachers as being competent and having power, at least within the school environment. So as teachers, we "teach" not only by what we say but also by what we do. It is critical that we model appropriate behaviors and *not* model inappropriate ones. Do we model fairness to all students, or favoritism to a small few? Do we model enthusiasm and excitement about the subject matter being taught, or merely tolerance for a dreary topic? Do we expound on the virtues of innovation and creativity yet use the same curriculum materials year after year? Our actions often speak louder than our words.

But even when models are competent and prestigious and even when they exhibit behaviors that students think are appropriate for themselves as well, successful modeling does not necessarily occur. What must students do to learn modeled behavior effectively? Let's find out.

Helping Students Learn from Models

According to social cognitive theorists (e.g., Bandura, 1986), four conditions are necessary before a student can successfully model someone else's behavior: attention, retention, motor reproduction, and motivation.

Attention. In the opening case study, Nathan paid little attention to his French teacher. Yet to learn effectively, *the learner must pay attention to the model.* Before imitation is possible, our students must observe carefully as we demonstrate proper procedures in the science lab, watch closely as we demonstrate the elementary backstroke, or listen attentively as we pronounce *Comment allez-vous?*.

Retention. After paying attention, *the learner must remember what the model does.* If you have already read the discussion of cognitive processes in Chapter 6, then you know that students are more likely to remember information they have encoded in memory in more than one way—perhaps both as a visual image and as a verbal representation. As teachers, then, we may often want to describe what we are doing as we demonstrate behaviors (Hughes, 1988). We may also want to give descriptive labels to complex behaviors that might otherwise be difficult to remember (Gerst, 1971; T. L. Rosenthal, Alford, & Rasp, 1972). To illustrate, an easy way to help students learn the three arm movements of the elementary backstroke in swimming is to teach them "chicken" (arms bent with hands tucked under armpits), "airplane" (arms straight out to the side), and "soldier" (arms straight and held close to the torso; see Figure 11–1).

It may be especially helpful for students to repeat such labels aloud as they copy a model's actions (R. L. Cohen, 1989; Mace, Belfiore, & Shea, 1989; Schunk, 1989c). As an example, consider the following set of self-instructions taught to students who are first learning a basic tennis stroke:

Avoid modeling undesirable behaviors.

Make sure students are paying attention as you model the behaviors you want them to learn.

Describe what you are doing as you model desired behaviors. Provide descriptive labels for complex behaviors.

Have students repeat the descriptive labels as they perform the behavior.

"Chicken"   "Airplane"   "Soldier"

FIGURE 11.1

Students can often more easily remember a complex behavior, such as the elementary backstroke, when those behaviors have verbal labels.

1. Say *ball* to remind yourself to look at the ball.
2. Say *bounce* to remind yourself to follow the ball with your eyes as it approaches you.
3. Say *hit* to remind yourself to focus on contacting the ball with the racket.
4. Say *ready* to get yourself into position for the next ball to come your way. (adapted from Ziegler, 1987)

Tennis students taught to give themselves these simple instructions—*ball, bounce, hit,* and *ready*—improve the accuracy of their returns more quickly than students not taught to do so (Ziegler, 1987).

Motor reproduction. In addition to attending to and remembering, *the learner must be physically capable of reproducing the modeled behavior.* When a student lacks the ability to reproduce an observed behavior, motor reproduction obviously cannot occur. For example, first graders who watch a high school student throw a softball do not possess the muscular coordination to mimic that throw. Secondary school students who haven't yet learned to roll their *R*s will have trouble repeating the Spanish teacher's tongue twister:

> Erre con erre cigarro, erre con erre barril.
> Rápido corren los carros del ferrocarril.

It will often be useful to have students imitate a desired behavior immediately after they watch us demonstrate it. When they do so, we can give them the feedback they need to improve their performance. Modeling accompanied by verbal guidance and frequent feedback—a technique known as *coaching*—is often more effective than modeling alone (S. N. Elliott & Busse, 1991; Schunk & Swartz, 1993; Zirpoli & Melloy, 1993). At the same time, we must keep in mind a point made in Chapter 4: Students from some ethnic groups (e.g., many Native Americans) may prefer to practice new behaviors in private at first, showing us what they have learned only after they have achieved sufficient mastery.

🍎 As students practice modeled behaviors, give guidance and feedback.

🍎 Remember that students from some ethnic groups may prefer to practice new skills in private at first.

Motivation. Finally, *the learner must be motivated to demonstrate the modeled behavior.* Some students may be eager to show what they have observed and remembered; for example, they may have seen the model reinforced for a certain behavior and so have already been vicariously reinforced. But other students may not have any motivation to demonstrate something they have seen a model do, perhaps because the model was punished or perhaps because they don't see the model's actions as being appropriate for themselves. Increasing students' motivation to engage in classroom activities and strive for important instructional objectives is a topic we will consider at length in Chapter 12.

When all four factors—attention, retention, motor reproduction, and motivation—are present, modeling can be an extremely powerful teaching technique (S. N. Elliott & Busse, 1991; Hughes, 1988; Schloss & Smith, 1994; Zirpoli & Melloy, 1993). Modeling has an additional benefit as well: It frequently boosts students' self-confidence that they themselves can accomplish the things they observe models accomplishing. For example, when a student from an inner-city ghetto meets someone from the same neighborhood who has since grown up to become a physician, and when a student with a physical disability meets an individual who, despite cerebral palsy, is a top executive at the local bank, these students may begin to believe that they also are capable of such achievements. Students who believe in their own abilities have developed *self-efficacy,* a topic we turn to now.

Make sure students are motivated to demonstrate the modeled behavior.

INTO THE CLASSROOM : Making Effective Use of Models

Model desired behaviors.

A teacher shows compassion for a student whose pet dog has just died.

Make sure students are paying attention as you model desired behaviors.

A science teacher makes sure all eyes are on her as she demonstrates the proper procedure for lighting a Bunsen burner.

Provide descriptive labels for modeled actions.

A swimming instructor describes the arm movements of the elementary backstroke as "chicken, airplane, soldier."

Make sure students are physically capable of doing what you ask.

A Spanish teacher works with students individually on the proper mouth and tongue movements for rolling *R*s in the pronunciation of many Spanish words.

Make sure students have a reason to demonstrate the modeled behavior.

The same Spanish teacher gives students credit in his grade book when they show that they can roll their *R*s correctly.

Avoid modeling undesirable behaviors.

A teacher who has not yet kicked her smoking habit refrains from smoking on school grounds or in public places where she is likely to run into her students.

Expose students to a variety of exemplary live and symbolic models, including females, minorities, and individuals with disabilities.

A history teacher has students read *The Diary of Anne Frank.*

Self-Efficacy

- Do you believe that you'll be able to understand educational psychology by reading this textbook and thinking carefully about its content? Or do you believe that you're going to have trouble with the material regardless of how much you study?

- Do you think you could learn to execute a reasonable swan dive from a high diving board if you were shown how to do it and given time to practice? Or do you believe you're such a klutz that no amount of training and practice would help?

- Do you think you could walk barefoot over hot coals unscathed? Or do you think the soles of your feet would be burned to a crisp?

People are more likely to engage in certain behaviors when they believe they are capable of executing those behaviors successfully—that is, when they have high **self-efficacy** (e.g., Bandura, 1982). For example, I hope you believe that, with careful thought about what you read, you will be able to understand the ideas in this textbook; in other words, I hope you have high self-efficacy for learning educational psychology. You may or may not believe that, with instruction and practice, you will eventually be able to perform a passable swan dive; in other words, you may have high or low self-efficacy about learning to dive. You are probably quite skeptical that you could ever walk barefoot over hot coals, so my guess is that you have low self-efficacy regarding this activity.

The concept of self-efficacy is similar to the concept of self-esteem, but with an important difference. Self-esteem is conceptualized as something that pervades a wide variety of activities; for instance, we tend to describe people as having generally high or low self-esteem. Self-efficacy is more situation-specific; for example, people may have high self-efficacy about reading an educational psychology text but not about reading a text on neurosurgery. They may have high self-efficacy about learning to perform a swan dive but not about swimming the entire length of a swimming pool underwater.

■ $\quad$ Can you predict possible answers to these questions before you read on?

How do students' feelings of self-efficacy affect their behavior? And how do feelings of high or low self-efficacy develop? In the next few pages, we will identify several answers to these two questions.

How Self-Efficacy Affects Behavior

According to social cognitive theorists, people's sense of self-efficacy affects their choice of activities, their effort and persistence, and their learning and achievement (Bandura, 1982; Schunk, 1989c; Zimmerman, Bandura, & Martinez-Pons, 1992).

Choice of activities. Imagine yourself on registration day, perusing the hundreds of courses in the semester schedule. You fill most of your schedule with required courses, but you have room for an elective. Only two courses are offered at the time slot you have open. Do you sign up for Advanced Psychoceramics, a challenging seminar taught by the famous Dr. Josiah S. Carberry? Or do you sign up for an English literature course known across campus as being an "easy A"? Perhaps you find the term *psychoceramics* a bit intimidating, and you think

A student must believe that she has the ability to make friends before she will actually try to make them.

that you can't possibly pass such a course, especially if Dr. Carberry is as grouchy a man as everybody claims. So you settle for the literature course, knowing it is one in which you can succeed.

People tend to choose tasks and activities at which they believe they can succeed and to avoid those at which they think they will fail. Students who believe that they can succeed at mathematics are more likely to take math courses than students who believe that they are mathematically incompetent. Students who believe that they can win a role in the school musical are more likely to try out than students with little faith in their acting or singing ability.

Effort and persistence. Think back once again to our case study of Nathan. As you may recall, Nathan was convinced that he couldn't learn French. Because of his low self-efficacy, he gave up quickly on his French homework assignments whenever he encountered something he didn't understand.

Students with a high sense of self-efficacy are more likely to exert effort in attempting to accomplish a task. They are also more likely to persist (to "try, try again") when faced with obstacles to their success. In contrast, students with low self-efficacy about a particular task will put in little effort and will give up quickly when they encounter obstacles.

Learning and achievement. Students with high self-efficacy tend to learn and achieve more than students with low self-efficacy even when actual ability levels are the same (Bandura, 1986; J. L. Collins, 1982). In other words, among students of equal ability, those students who *believe* that they can do a task are more likely to accomplish it successfully than those who do not believe that they are capable of success. To some extent, students with high self-efficacy may achieve at superior levels because they engage in cognitive processes that promote learning—paying attention, organizing, elaborating, and so on (Pintrich & Schunk, 1996). As teachers, then, we should do whatever we can to enhance our students' beliefs that they can be successful at school tasks.

Factors in the Development of Self-Efficacy

Perceptions of self-efficacy are usually fairly accurate: Students typically have a good sense of what they can and cannot do (Bandura, 1986). But sometimes students underestimate their chances of success, perhaps because of a few bad experiences. For example, a girl who gets a C in science from a teacher with exceptionally strict grading criteria may erroneously believe that she is "no good" in science. A new boy at school whose attempts at being friendly are rejected by two or three thoughtless classmates may erroneously believe that no one likes him.

According to social cognitive theorists (e.g., Bandura, 1986, 1989; Schunk, 1989a; Schunk, Hanson, & Cox, 1987), at least three factors affect the development of self-efficacy:

- One's own previous successes and failures
- Messages from others
- The successes and failures of others

Previous Successes and Failures

Students feel more confident that they can succeed at a task—that is, they have greater self-efficacy—when they have succeeded at that task or at similar ones in the past (Bandura, 1986). For example, Edward is more likely to believe that he can learn to divide fractions if he has already mastered the process of multiplying fractions. Elena will be more confident about her ability to play field hockey if she has already developed skills in soccer. One important strategy for promoting our students' self-efficacy, then, is to help them be successful in various academic disciplines—for instance, by teaching important basic

Interpret reluctance and lack of persistence as possible indicators of low self-efficacy.

Such effort and persistence reflect the fact that students with high self-efficacy are *intrinsically motivated* (more about this in the next chapter).

What factors in Nathan's situation may have contributed to his low self-efficacy for learning French?

Teach basic skills to mastery (see Chapter 13). Help students make noticeable progress on difficult tasks (e.g., through *scaffolding*).

🍎 Present some tasks that are challenging yet achievable so that students succeed only with effort and perseverance. (This strategy should promote cognitive development as well; see Chapter 2.)

🍎 Assure students that they can be successful.

🍎 Communicate your confidence in students' abilities by what you do as well as by what you say.

🍎 Tell students that others like themselves have succeeded.

skills to mastery and by providing the necessary instructional support that enables students to make noticeable progress on difficult and complex tasks.

Once students have developed a high sense of self-efficacy, an occasional failure is unlikely to dampen their optimism. In fact, when students encounter small setbacks on the way to achieving success, they learn that sustained effort and perseverance are key ingredients of that success; in other words, they develop **resilient self-efficacy** (Bandura, 1989). When students *consistently* fail at an activity, however, they tend to have little confidence about their ability to succeed at that activity in the future. For instance, students with learning disabilities, who typically have encountered failure after failure in classroom activities, often have low self-efficacy with regard to the things they study in school (Schunk, 1989c).

Messages from Others

To some extent, we can enhance students' self-efficacy by assuring them that they can, in fact, be successful. Statements such as "You can do this problem if you work at it" or "I bet Judy will play with you if you just ask her" do give students a slight boost in self-confidence. But this boost will be short-lived unless students' efforts at a task ultimately meet with success (Schunk, 1989a).

Sometimes the messages we give students are implied rather than directly stated, yet such messages can have just as much of an effect on self-efficacy. For example, by giving constructive criticism about how to improve a poorly written research paper—criticism that indirectly communicates the message that "I know that you can do better, and here are some suggestions how"—we can enhance students' self-confidence about writing such research papers (Parsons, Kaczala, & Meece, 1982; Pintrich & Schunk, 1996). But in some cases, actions speak louder than words. For example, if we give struggling students more help than they really need, we may inadvertently communicate the message that "I don't think you can do this on your own" (Schunk, 1989b).

Successes and Failures of Others

We often form opinions about our own self-efficacy by observing the successes and failures of other people, especially those similar to ourselves. For example, you are more likely to enroll in Dr. Carberry's Advanced Psychoceramics class if several of your friends have done well in the course. After all, if they can do it, so can you. But if your friends in the course have been dropping like flies, then (like Nathan) you may suspect that your own chances of succeeding are pretty slim.

In much the same way, students often consider the successes and failures of their classmates, especially those of similar ability, when appraising their own chances of success. So we can enhance students' self-efficacy by pointing out that others like themselves have mastered the task they are learning; when we do so, students are likely to complete more of the task themselves and have higher self-efficacy when doing so (Schunk, 1983, 1989c). For example, a class of chemistry students horrified about the number of chemical symbols they must learn can perhaps be reassured with a statement such as this: "I know it seems like a lot to learn in such a short amount of time. My students last year thought so too, but they found that they could learn the symbols within three weeks if they studied a few new symbols each day."

When students actually *see* others of similar age and ability successfully reaching a goal, they are especially likely to believe that they, too, can achieve that goal. Hence, students sometimes develop greater self-efficacy when they see a fellow student model a behavior than when they see their teacher model that same behavior. For example, in one study (Schunk & Hanson, 1985), elementary school children having trouble with subtraction were given 25 subtraction problems to complete. Children who had seen another student successfully complete the problems got an average of 19 correct, whereas those who saw a teacher complete the problems got only 13 correct, and those who saw no model at all solved only 8!

So another way to enhance our students' self-efficacy regarding academic tasks is to have them observe their peers successfully accomplishing those tasks. It may especially benefit students to see one or more peers struggling with a task or problem at first—something they themselves are likely to do—and then eventually mastering it (Hughes, 1988; Schunk & Zimmerman, 1997).

Although learning from another's example boosts self-efficacy, we don't want students to become excessively dependent, either on us or on classmates, as they strive to learn new things. Social cognitive theorists believe that people can and should ultimately regulate their own learning and behavior. We therefore turn to a topic gaining increasing prominence in psychological and educational literature: *self-regulation*.

Self-Regulation

Experiencing Firsthand
Self-Reflection About Self-Regulation

In each of the following situations, choose the alternative that most accurately describes your own attitudes and behavior as a college student. No one will see your answers except you, so be honest!

> Have students observe successful peer models, including peers who encounter failure in their initial attempts at a task.

> Think of a recent situation in which you had especially high or low self-efficacy. Which of the three factors just described affected your confidence in that situation?

INTO THE CLASSROOM: Enhancing Self-Efficacy

Teach basic skills to mastery.

A biology teacher makes sure all students clearly understand the basic structure of DNA before moving to mitosis and meiosis, topics that require a knowledge of DNA's structure.

Help students make noticeable progress on difficult tasks.

In November a creative writing teacher shows students samples of their work from September and points out ways in which each student has improved over the two-month period.

Present some tasks that are challenging but achievable so that students succeed at them only with effort and perseverance.

A physical education teacher tells her students, "Today we've seen how far each of you can go in the broad jump. We will continue to practice the broad jump a little bit every week. Let's see if each one of you can jump at least two inches farther when I test you again at the end of the month."

Assure students that they can be successful and remind them that others like themselves have succeeded before them.

Students in beginning band express frustration about learning to play their instruments. Their teacher reminds them that students in last year's beginning band—like themselves—started out with little knowledge but eventually mastered their instruments.

Have students see successful peer models.

The students in beginning band class hear the school's advanced band (last year's beginning band class) play a medley from *Phantom of the Opera*.

1. In terms of my final course grades, I am trying very hard to:
   a. Earn all As.
   b. Earn all As and Bs.
   c. Earn at least a C in every class.
   d. Keep my overall grade point average above the minimally acceptable level for the program I am in.

2. As I am reading or studying a textbook:
   a. I often notice when my attention is wandering, and I immediately get my mind back on my work.
   b. I sometimes notice when my attention is wandering, but not always.
   c. I often get so lost in my daydreams that I waste a lot of time.

3. Whenever I finish a study session:
   a. I write down how much time I have spent on my schoolwork.
   b. I make a mental note of how much time I have spent on my schoolwork.
   c. I don't really think much about the time I have spent.

4. When I turn in an assignment:
   a. I usually have a very good idea of the grade I will get on it.
   b. I have a rough idea of the grade I will get; I can usually tell when it will be either very good or very bad.
   c. I am often surprised by the grade I get.
   d. I don't really think much about the quality of what I have done.

5. When I do exceptionally well on an assignment:
   a. I feel good about my performance and often "treat" myself in some way (e.g., by going shopping, socializing with friends).
   b. I feel good about my performance but don't do anything special for myself afterward.
   c. I don't feel any differently than I had before I received my grade.

The standards we set for ourselves, the extent to which we monitor and evaluate our own behavior, and the consequences we impose on ourselves for our successes and failures are all aspects of **self-regulation**. By observing how our environment reacts when we behave in particular ways—by discovering that some behaviors are reinforced and that others are punished—we begin to distinguish between appropriate and inappropriate responses. Once we have developed an understanding about which responses are appropriate (for ourselves, at least) and which are not, we begin to regulate our own behavior (Bandura, 1986).

Ideally, our students should become increasingly self-regulated as they grow older. After all, once they leave the relatively structured and protective environments of home and school, they will make most of their own decisions about what they should accomplish and how they should behave. Ultimately, we want them to make wise choices that enable them to achieve their goals and make productive contributions to society.

In the pages that follow, we will identify some of the things that learners do when they engage in self-regulated behavior. We will then use what we have learned to consider how we might promote *self-regulated learning* and *self-regulated problem solving.*

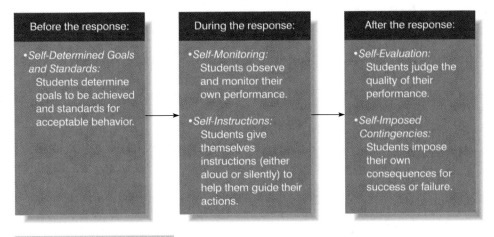

Before the response:	During the response:	After the response:
•*Self-Determined Goals and Standards:* Students determine goals to be achieved and standards for acceptable behavior.	•*Self-Monitoring:* Students observe and monitor their own performance. •*Self-Instructions:* Students give themselves instructions (either aloud or silently) to help them guide their actions.	•*Self-Evaluation:* Students judge the quality of their performance. •*Self-Imposed Contingencies:* Students impose their own consequences for success or failure.

FIGURE 11.2
Components of self-regulated behavior

Components of Self-Regulated Behavior

Five aspects of self-regulated behavior are summarized in Figure 11–2. Each one provides ideas about how to help students more successfully regulate and control their own behavior.

Self-Determined Goals and Standards

As human beings, we tend to identify certain goals for ourselves and then engage in the kinds of behaviors that can help us achieve those goals. We also set standards for our own behavior; in other words, we establish criteria regarding what constitutes acceptable performance.

Different students will inevitably adopt different goals and standards for themselves. For example, Robert may be striving for a report card with straight As, whereas Richard is content with Cs. Rebecca may be seeking out many friends of both sexes, whereas Rachel believes that a single, steady boyfriend is the best companion. To some extent, the goals and standards that students set for themselves are modeled after those that they see other people adopt (Bandura, 1986; Locke & Latham, 1990). For example, at the high school I attended, many students wanted to go to the best college or university they possibly could; in such an environment, others began to share the same academic aspirations. But at a different high school, getting a job after graduation (or perhaps even *instead* of graduation) might be the aspiration more commonly modeled by a student's classmates.

Students are more likely to be motivated to work toward goals—and thus are more likely to accomplish them—when they have set those goals for themselves, rather than when others have imposed goals on them (Schunk, 1996; Spaulding, 1992). So one way we can help students develop self-regulation is to provide situations in which they set their own goals. For example, we might ask them to decide how many addition facts they are going to learn by Friday, determine the topic they wish to study for a research project, or identify the particular gymnastic skills they wish to master.

Ideally, we should encourage our students to establish goals and standards that are challenging yet realistic. When students have goals and standards that are too low—for example, when intelligent students are content getting Cs on classroom assignments—then they will not achieve at maximal levels. In contrast, when students' standards are too high—for example, when they are satisfied only if every grade is 100 percent—then

Students from low-income families typically set low goals for themselves in terms of career aspirations (Durkin, 1995). Can you explain this fact in light of the discussion here?

Provide opportunities for students to set some of their own goals in the classroom. Encourage them to set challenging yet realistic ones.

they are doomed to frequent failure and equally frequent self-recrimination. Such students may become excessively anxious or depressed when they can't achieve the impossible goals they have set for themselves (Bandura, 1986; Covington, 1992).

To facilitate appropriate goal setting, we can show our students that challenging goals are attainable, perhaps by describing individuals of similar ability who have attained them with reasonable effort. In some situations, we might even want to provide incentives that encourage students to set and achieve challenging goals (Stipek, 1996). At the same time, we must help any overly ambitious students understand and accept the fact that no one is perfect and that an occasional failure is nothing to be ashamed of.

Self-Monitoring

An important part of self-regulation is to observe oneself in action—a process known as **self-monitoring** (sometimes known as *self-observation*). To make progress toward important goals, we must be aware of how well we are doing presently; we must know which aspects of our performance are working well and which need improvement. Furthermore, when we see ourselves making progress toward our goals, we are more likely to continue with our efforts (Schunk & Zimmerman, 1997).

Yet students are not always accurate observers of their own behavior. They aren't always aware of how frequently they do something wrong or how *in*frequently they do something right. To help students attend to the things that they do and don't do, we can have them observe and record their own behavior. If Raymond is speaking out of turn too frequently, we can bring the seriousness of the problem to his attention by asking him to make a check mark on a piece of paper every time he catches himself speaking out of turn. If Olivia has trouble staying on task during assigned activities, we can ask her to stop and reflect on her behavior every few minutes (perhaps with the aid of an egg timer), determining whether she was staying on task during each interval. Figure 11–3 provides an example of the type of form we might give Olivia to record her observations.

▲   Self-selected goals promote a greater sense of *self-determination,* a topic we will consider in Chapter12.

🍎   Have students observe and record their own behavior.

FIGURE 11.3
Example of a self-observation sheet for staying on task

Research indicates clearly that such self-focused observation and recording can bring about changes (sometimes dramatic ones) in student behavior. For example, self-observation can be used to increase the extent to which students pay attention to their work (their *time on task*) and the number of assignments they are likely to complete. It is also effective in reducing aggressive responses and such disruptive classroom behaviors as talking out of turn and getting out of one's seat (K. R. Harris, 1986; Mace & Kratochwill, 1988; Webber, Scheuermann, McCall, & Coleman, 1993).

Self-Instructions

Consider the formerly "forgetful" student who, before leaving the house each morning, now asks herself, "Do I have everything I need for my classes? I have my math homework for Period 1, my history book for Period 2, my change of clothes for P.E. during Period 3. . . ." And consider the once impulsive student who now pauses before beginning a new assignment and says to himself, "OK, what am I supposed to do? Let's see . . . I need to read the directions first. What do the directions tell me to do?" And consider as well the formerly aggressive student who has learned to count to ten every time she gets angry—an action that gives her a chance to cool off.

Sometimes students simply need a reminder about how to respond in particular situations. By teaching students how to talk themselves through these situations using **self-instructions,** we provide them with a means through which *they remind themselves* about appropriate actions, thereby helping them to control their own behavior. Such a strategy is often effective in working with students who otherwise seem to behave without thinking (Casey & Burton, 1982; Meichenbaum, 1985; Yell, 1993).

One effective way of teaching students to give themselves instructions involves five steps (Meichenbaum, 1977):

1. The teacher models self-instruction by repeating instructions aloud while simultaneously performing the activity.
2. The teacher repeats the instructions aloud while the student performs the activity.
3. The student repeats the instructions aloud while performing the activity.
4. The student whispers the instructions while performing the activity.
5. The student simply "thinks" the instructions while performing the activity.

Through these five steps, impulsive elementary school children can effectively learn to slow themselves down and think through what they are doing (Meichenbaum & Goodman, 1971). For example, notice how one formerly impulsive student was able to talk his way through a matching task in which he needed to find two identical pictures among several very similar ones:

> I have to remember to go slowly to get it right. Look carefully at this one, now look at these carefully. Is this one different? Yes, it has an extra leaf. Good, I can eliminate this one. Now, let's look at this one. I think it's this one, but let me first check the others. Good, I'm going slow and carefully. Okay, I think it's this one. (Meichenbaum & Goodman, 1971, p. 121)

Self-Evaluation

Both at home and in school, students' behaviors are frequently judged by others—their parents, teachers, classmates, and so on. But eventually our students should also begin to judge their *own* behavior by engaging in **self-evaluation.** Once they have developed appropriate goals and standards, and once they have developed some objective techniques for observing their own behavior, there are many ways in which we can allow and encourage them to evaluate their own performance. For example, we can have them

- Assemble portfolios of what they think is their best work, with self-evaluations of each entry

Teach students instructions that they can give themselves in troublesome situations.

Can you relate Steps 3, 4, and 5 to Vygotsky's notions of *self-talk* and *inner speech* (Chapter 2)?

How might you use this technique to help a student with sloppy work habits? to help a student who responds with uncontrolled anger in frustrating situations?

Once students have set appropriate standards and objective methods of self-observation, encourage them to evaluate their own performance.

Chapter 16 describes *portfolios* in greater depth.

- Write in daily or weekly journals, in which they address the strengths and weaknesses of their performance
- Participate in peer conferences, in which several students discuss their reactions to one another's work
  (Paris & Ayres, 1994)

We might also have students complete self-assessment instruments that show them what to look for as they judge their work (Paris & Ayres, 1994). For example, to evaluate a project they have just completed, students might respond to questions such as these:

- What did you like about this project?
- What would have made this project better?
- What grade do you feel you earned on this project? Justify your response. (adapted from Paris & Ayres, 1994, p. 78)

Students who hold different standards for themselves will naturally judge the same behavior in different ways. For example, if Robert and Richard both get all Bs on their report cards, Robert (with the straight-A standard) will judge his performance to be unacceptable, whereas Richard (with acceptability defined as "C") will go home and celebrate. It is essential, then, that we help our students use appropriate criteria for evaluating their performance (Yell, 1993; Zuckerman, 1994). For example, when asking them to analyze the quality of a summary they have just written, we might ask them to agree or disagree with statements such as these:

- I included a clear main idea statement.
- I included important ideas that support the main idea.
- My summary shows that I understand the relationships between important concepts.
- I used my own words rather than words copied from the text. (Paris & Ayres, 1994, p. 75)

Or, when asking students to evaluate their on-task behavior in class on a scale of one to five, we might reinforce them when their own self-assessments closely match the ones we ourselves give them (D. J. Smith, Young, West, Morgan, & Rhode, 1988).

Self-Imposed Contingencies

▢ THINKING ABOUT WHAT YOU KNOW

- How do you feel when you accomplish a difficult task—for example, when you earn an A in a challenging course, when you get elected president of an organization, or when you make a three-point basket in a basketball game?
- How do you feel when you fail in your endeavors—for example, when you get a D on an exam because you forgot to study, when you thoughtlessly hurt a friend's feelings, or when you miss an easy goal in a soccer game?

When you accomplish something you've set out to do, especially if the task is complex and challenging, you probably feel quite proud of yourself and give yourself a mental pat on the back. In contrast, when you *fail* to accomplish that task, you are probably unhappy with your performance; you may also feel guilty, regretful, or ashamed. Likewise, as our students become increasingly self-regulated, they will begin to reinforce themselves—perhaps by feeling proud or telling themselves they did a good job—when they accomplish their goals. And they will also begin to punish themselves—perhaps by feeling sorry, guilty, or ashamed—when they do something that does not meet their own performance standards.

Yet such **self-imposed contingencies** are not necessarily confined only to the emotional reactions that people have in response to their own behaviors. Many self-regulating individuals reinforce themselves in far more concrete ways when they accomplish something successfully. For example, I have a colleague who goes shopping every time she completes a research article or report (she has one of the best wardrobes in town!).

Thus, an additional way to help students become more self-regulating is to teach them self-reinforcement. When students begin to reinforce themselves for appropriate responses—perhaps by giving themselves some free time, allowing themselves to engage in a favorite activity, or simply praising themselves—their classroom behavior often improves significantly (K. R. Harris, 1986; S. C. Hayes et al., 1985). For instance, in one research study, students who were performing poorly in arithmetic were taught to give themselves points when they did well on their assignments; they could later use these points to "buy" a variety of items and privileges. Within a few weeks, these students were doing as well as their classmates on both in-class assignments and homework (H. C. Stevenson & Fantuzzo, 1986). On some occasions, self-reinforcement is just as effective as reinforcement administered by a teacher (Bandura, 1977).

Do you ever reinforce yourself in some tangible way for your accomplishments? If so, how?

Teach students to reinforce themselves for appropriate behavior.

Experiencing Firsthand
More Self-Reflection

Refer back to the previous self-reflection exercise on pp. 453–54. Evaluate your responses to each question in terms of what you have just learned about effective self-regulation.

Self-Regulated Learning

Social learning theorists and cognitive psychologists alike are beginning to realize that to be truly effective learners, students must engage in some of the activities just described. In fact, not only must students regulate their own behaviors, but they must also regulate their own cognitive processes. In particular, **self-regulated learning** involves such processes as these:

- *Goal-setting.* Self-regulated learners know what they want to accomplish when they read or study. For instance, they may want to learn specific facts, get an overall understanding of the ideas presented, or simply acquire sufficient knowledge to do well on a classroom exam (Nolen, 1996; Winne, 1995; Wolters, 1997; Zimmerman & Bandura, 1994).

- *Planning.* Self-regulated learners determine ahead of time how best to use the time they have available for a learning task (Zimmerman & Risemberg, 1997).

- *Attention control.* Self-regulated learners try to focus their attention on the subject matter at hand and to clear their minds of potentially distracting thoughts and emotions (Harnishfeger, 1995; Kuhl, 1985; Winne, 1995).

- *Application of learning strategies.* Self-regulated learners choose different learning strategies depending on the specific goal they hope to accomplish. For example, the way they read a magazine article depends on whether they are reading it for entertainment or studying for an exam (Linderholm, Gustafson, van den Broek, & Lorch, 1997; Winne, 1995).

- *Self-monitoring.* Self-regulated learners continually monitor their progress toward their goals, and they change their learning strategies or modify their goals if necessary (Butler & Winne, 1995; Carver & Scheier, 1990; Zimmerman & Risemberg, 1997). *Comprehension monitoring* (described in Chapter 8) is an example of such self-monitoring.

- *Self-evaluation.* Self-regulated learners determine whether what they have learned is sufficient for the goals they have set for themselves (Butler & Winne, 1995; Schraw & Moshman, 1995; Zimmerman & Risemberg, 1997).

In addition to these metacognitive activities, self-regulated learning also involves **intrinsic motivation**—motivation that comes from within the individual, rather than from such outside influences as extrinsic reinforcers (Zimmerman & Risemberg, 1997). One important factor in intrinsic motivation is high self-efficacy: Students must believe that they have the ability to accomplish the learning task successfully. Chapter 12 identifies numerous strategies for promoting intrinsic motivation.

When students are self-regulated learners, they set more ambitious academic goals for themselves, learn more effectively, and achieve at higher levels in the classroom (Butler & Winne, 1995; Zimmerman & Risemberg, 1997). Furthermore, a great deal of adolescent and adult learning—doing homework, reading, surfing the Internet, and so on—occurs in isolation from other people and so requires considerable self-regulation (Winne, 1995). Unfortunately, however, few students develop a high level of self-regulated learning, perhaps, in part, because traditional instructional practices do little to promote it (Paris & Ayres, 1994; Zimmerman & Risemberg, 1997).

To promote self-regulated learning, we must, of course, teach students the kinds of cognitive processes that facilitate learning and memory (see the discussion of metacognition in Chapter 8). In addition, theorists have suggested these strategies:

- Give students opportunities to learn without teacher assistance, including both independent learning activities in which students study by themselves (e.g., seatwork assignments, homework) and group activities in which students help one another learn (e.g., peer tutoring, cooperative learning).

- Occasionally assign activities (e.g., research papers, creative projects) in which students have considerable leeway regarding goals, use of time, and so on.

- Model self-regulating cognitive processes by "thinking aloud" about such processes, and then give students constructive feedback as they engage in similar processes.

- Consistently ask students to evaluate their own performance, and have them compare their self-assessments to teacher assessments. (A. King, 1997; McCaslin & Good, 1996; Schunk & Zimmerman, 1997; J. W. Thomas, 1993b; Zimmerman & Bonner, in press; Zimmerman & Risemberg, 1997)

As we consider how best to help our students become self-regulated learners, we should keep in mind a point that Lev Vygotsky made many years ago: Many complex cognitive processes have their roots in social interactions, including interactions with teachers and classmates. Over time, the things that students may initially do on a social level—setting group goals, planning the best use of learning time, identifying effective ways to approach a particular learning task, discussing appropriate evaluation criteria, and so on—eventually become internalized in the form of mental processes that students can use on their own.

Self-Regulated Problem Solving

Teach students the mental steps they can take to solve problems more effectively.

We can sometimes use self-regulation techniques (especially self-instructions) to help students develop more effective problem-solving skills. For example, to promote greater creativity in their solutions to academic problems, we might encourage them to give themselves instructions such as these:

> I want to think of something no one else will think of, something unique. Be freewheeling, no hangups. I don't care what anyone thinks; just suspend judgment. I'm not sure what I'll come up with; it will be a surprise. The ideas can just flow through me. . . . (Meichenbaum, 1977, p. 62)

To help students deal more effectively with social conflicts and other interpersonal problems, we might ask them to take steps such as these:

1. Define the problem.
2. Identify several possible solutions.

3. Predict the likely consequences of each solution.

4. Choose the best solution.

5. Identify the steps required to carry out the solution.

6. Carry the steps out.

7. Evaluate the results. (S. N. Elliott & Busse, 1991; Meichenbaum, 1977; Weissburg, 1985; Yell, 1993)

Such **self-regulated problem-solving strategies** often help students who have difficulty interacting appropriately with their peers (e.g., students who are either socially withdrawn or overly aggressive) to develop more effective interpersonal skills (K. R. Harris, 1982; Meichenbaum, 1977; Yell, 1993).

Another approach is **mediation training**—a strategy whereby we help students *help one another* solve interpersonal problems. More specifically, we teach students how to mediate conflicts among classmates by asking the opposing sides to express their differing points of view and then working together to devise a reasonable resolution (Deutsch, 1993; D. W. Johnson & Johnson, 1996). For example, in an experiment involving several classrooms at the second through fifth grade levels (D. W. Johnson, Johnson, Dudley, Ward, & Magnuson, 1995), students were trained to help their peers resolve interpersonal conflicts by asking the opposing sides to do the following:

Teach students strategies for effectively mediating classmates' interpersonal conflicts.

1. Define the conflict (the problem)

2. Explain their own perspectives and needs

3. Explain the *other* person's perspectives and needs

4. Identify at least three possible solutions to the conflict

5. Reach an agreement that addressed the needs of both parties

The students took turns serving as mediator for their classmates, such that everyone had experience resolving the conflicts of others. At the end of the training program, the students more frequently resolved their *own* interpersonal conflicts in ways that addressed the needs of both parties and were less likely to ask for adult intervention than students in an untrained control group. Similarly, in a case study involving adolescent gang members (Sanchez & Anderson, 1990), students were given mediation training and were asked to be responsible for mediating gang-related disputes. After only one month of training, rival gang members were exchanging friendly greetings in the corridors, giving one another the "high five" sign, and interacting at lunch; meanwhile, gang-related fights virtually disappeared from the scene.

Teachers sometimes intervene when students have an interpersonal conflict. But *mediation training,* whereby students learn how to help one another resolve their differences, is more likely to promote self-regulation.

When students set challenging goals for themselves and achieve those self-chosen goals through their own efforts, their self-efficacy is enhanced and their motivation to undertake new challenges increases (Bandura, 1989). And when students have a high sense of self-efficacy and engage in self-regulating activities, they are more likely to believe that they control their environment, rather than that their environment controls them. In fact, social cognitive theorists assert that people, their behaviors, and the environment all have a somewhat "controlling" influence on one another, as we shall see now.

INTO THE CLASSROOM: Fostering Self-Regulation

Help students set challenging yet realistic goals and standards.

A teacher encourages a pregnant student to stay in school until she graduates. Together they discuss strategies for juggling motherhood and schoolwork.

Have students observe and record their own behavior.

A student with attention-deficit hyperactivity disorder frequently tips his chair back to the point where he is likely to topple over. Concerned for the student's safety, his teacher asks him to record each instance of such behavior on a sheet of graph paper. Both student and teacher notice how quickly the behavior disappears once the student has become aware of his bad habit.

Teach students instructions they can give themselves to remind them of what they need to do.

To help a student control her impulsive behavior on multiple-choice tests, her teacher has her say this to herself as she reads each question: "Read the entire question. Then look at each answer carefully and decide whether it is correct or incorrect. Then choose the answer that seems most correct of all."

Encourage students to evaluate their own performance.

A science teacher gives students a list of criteria with which to evaluate their lab reports from yesterday. She assigns grades based on how accurately students have evaluated their own reports.

Teach students to reinforce themselves for appropriate behavior.

A teacher helps students develop more regular study habits by encouraging them to make a favorite activity—for example, shooting baskets, watching television, or calling a friend on the telephone—contingent on completing their homework first.

Give students opportunities to practice learning with little or no help from their teacher.

A middle school social studies teacher distributes various magazine articles related to current events in the Middle East, making sure that each student receives an article appropriate for his or her reading level. He asks students to read their respective articles over the weekend and prepare a one-paragraph summary to share with other class members. He also provides guidelines about what information students should include in their summaries.

Provide strategies that students can use to solve interpersonal problems.

A teacher teaches her students a sequence to follow when they find themselves in a conflict with a classmate: *identify* the source of the conflict, *listen* to each other's perspectives, *verbalize* each other's perspectives, and *develop* a solution that provides a reasonable compromise.

Reciprocal Causation

Throughout the chapter, we've discussed aspects of learners' environments and the behaviors that result from various environmental conditions. We have also talked about personal variables such as expectations and self-efficacy that learners bring with them to

Mutual Influences (Reciprocal Causation) Among Environment, Behavior, and Person

		A GENERAL EXAMPLE	AN EXAMPLE IN LORRAINE'S CASE (SCENE ONE)	AN EXAMPLE IN LORRAINE'S CASE (SCENE TWO)
Effect of Environment	On Behavior	Reinforcement and punishment affect future behavior	Teacher's ignoring Lorraine leads to future classroom failure	New instructional methods lead to improved academic performance
	On Person	Feedback from others affects sense of self-efficacy	Teacher's ignoring Lorraine perpetuates low self-efficacy	New instructional methods capture Lorraine's interest and attention
Effect of Behavior	On Environment	Specific behaviors affect the amount of reinforcement and punishment received	Poor classroom performance leads to the teacher meeting privately with Lorraine, then eventually ignoring her	Better academic performance leads to more reinforcement from the teacher
	On Person	Success and failure affect expectations for future performance	Poor classroom performance leads to low self-efficacy	Better academic performance leads to higher self-efficacy
Effect of Person	On Environment	Self-efficacy affects choices of activities and therefore the specific environment encountered	Attention to classmates rather than classroom activities affects environment experienced	Attention to classroom activities leads to greater influence of teacher's instruction
	On Behavior	Attention, retention, motor reproduction, and motivation affect degree to which one imitates modeled behavior	Attention to classmates rather than classroom activities leads to academic failure	Greater self-efficacy and increased motivation lead to more persistent study habits

a task. Now which one of these three factors—environment, behavior, or person—lays the foundation for learning? According to social cognitive theorists, all three are essential ingredients, and each one influences the other two. This interdependence among environment, behavior, and person is known as **reciprocal causation** (Bandura, 1989). Some examples of how each factor affects the other two are listed in Table 11–2.

As a concrete illustration of how environment, behavior, and personal factors can mutually influence one another, let's consider "Scene One" in the case of Lorraine:

Scene One

Lorraine, a student in Mr. Broderick's seventh-grade social studies class, often comes to class late and ill-prepared for the day's activities. In class, she spends more time interacting with her friends (e.g., whispering, passing notes) than getting involved in classroom activities. Lorraine's performance on most exams and assignments (when she turns the latter in at all) is unsatisfactory.

One day in mid-October, Mr. Broderick takes Lorraine aside to express his concern about her lack of classroom effort. He suggests that Lorraine could do better if she paid more attention in class; he also offers to work with her twice a week after school to help her understand class material. Lorraine is less optimistic, describing herself as "not smart enough to learn this stuff."

For a week or so after her meeting with Mr. Broderick, Lorraine seems to buckle down and exert more effort, but she never does stay after school for extra help. And before long, Lorraine is back to her old habits. Mr. Broderick eventually concludes that she is a lost cause and decides to devote his time and effort to helping more motivated students.

Lorraine's low self-efficacy (a *person* factor) is probably one reason that she spends so much class time engaged in task-irrelevant activities (*behaviors*). The fact that she devotes her attention (another *person* factor) to her classmates, rather than to her teacher, affects the particular stimuli that she experiences (her *environment*). Lorraine's poor performance on assignments and exams (*behaviors*) affects both her self-efficacy (*person*) and Mr. Broderick's treatment of her (*environment*). By eventually concluding that Lorraine is a lost cause, Mr. Broderick begins to ignore Lorraine (*environment*), contributing to her further failure (*behavior*) and even lower self-efficacy (*person*). (See Table 11–2 for a listing of these interactive effects under the column marked "Scene One.") Clearly, Lorraine is showing signs of being at risk for long-term academic failure.

But now imagine that, after learning more about how to deal with students at risk, Mr. Broderick develops greater optimism that he can break the vicious cycle of environment/behavior/person for students such as Lorraine. Midway through the school year, he makes the following changes in his classroom:

Can you think of occasions when you, like Lorraine, might have doomed yourself to failure through your own behaviors?

- He communicates clearly and consistently that he expects all students to succeed in his classroom.
- He incorporates students' personal experiences and interests into the study of social studies.
- He identifies specific, concrete tasks that students will accomplish each week.
- He provides guidance and structure for how each task should be accomplished.
- After consulting with the school's reading specialist and school psychologist, he helps students develop more effective reading and learning strategies.
- He gives a quiz every Friday so that students can assess their own progress.
- When students perform well on these quizzes, he reminds them that they themselves are responsible for their performance.

Let's see what happens next, as we consider "Scene Two":

Scene Two

By incorporating students' personal experiences and interests into his daily lesson plans, Mr. Broderick begins to capture Lorraine's interest and attention. She begins to realize that social studies has implications for her own life and becomes more involved in classroom activities. With the more structured assignments, better guidance about how to study class material, and frequent quizzes, Lorraine finds herself succeeding in a subject at which she has previously experienced only failure. Mr. Broderick is equally pleased with her performance, something he tells her frequently through his facial expressions, his verbal feedback, and his willingness to provide help whenever she needs it.

By the end of the school year, Lorraine is studying course material more effectively and completing her assignments regularly. She is eagerly looking forward to next year's social studies class, confident that she will continue to do well.

Once again, we see the interplay among environment, behavior, and person. Mr. Broderick's new instructional methods (*environment*) engage Lorraine's attention (*per-

son) and facilitate her academic performance (*behavior*). Lorraine's improved academic performance, in turn, influences Mr. Broderick's treatment of her (*environment*) and her own self-efficacy (*person*). And her improved self-efficacy, her greater attention to classroom activities, and her increased motivation to succeed (all *person* variables) affect the extent to which she is able to benefit from Mr. Broderick's instruction (*environment*) and her classroom success (*behavior*). (See the column marked "Scene Two" in Table 11–2 for a listing of such interactive effects.)

As you can see, then, the things we do in the classroom—the *environment* we create—affect both the behaviors that students exhibit and the personal factors that influence their learning. Students' behaviors and personal factors, in turn, influence the future classroom environment that they experience. As teachers, we must create and maintain a classroom environment that helps students develop the behaviors (e.g., academic and social skills) and personal characteristics (e.g., high self-efficacy and the expectation that their efforts will be rewarded) that are likely to bring them academic and personal success.

Can you explain reciprocal causation in your own words? Can you provide an example from your own experience?

Considering Diversity from a Social Cognitive Perspective

Social cognitive theory provides several insights regarding how we can adapt our classroom practices to serve students with diverse backgrounds, characteristics, and needs. The concepts of *modeling, self-efficacy,* and *self-regulation* can be especially useful in this context.

Using Diverse Models to Promote Success and Self-Efficacy

Two principles identified earlier are particularly pertinent when discussing diversity in the classroom:

- Students are most likely to model the behaviors they believe are relevant to their own situation.
- Students develop greater self-efficacy for a task when they see others like themselves performing the task successfully.

Both principles lead to the same conclusion: *Students need models who are similar to themselves in terms of race, cultural background, socioeconomic status, gender, and (if applicable) disability.* As teachers, we cannot possibly be all things to all students in this respect. We must therefore expose our students to as wide a variety of successful models—child and adolescent models as well as adults—as we possibly can. In some cases, we may be able to find such models within the school building itself. In other cases, we may be able to invite people from the region or the local community to visit the classroom. Occasionally, we may even find it effective to videotape students performing desired behaviors and then have them watch *themselves* being successful (Kehle, Clark, & Jenson, 1996).

Yet we need not limit ourselves to live models; students can learn a great deal from symbolic models as well. For example, we might ask our students to read biographies or autobiographies about such successful individuals as Maya Angelou (who, as an African American growing up in Arkansas in the 1930s, was raised in an environment of poverty and racial intolerance), Franklin D. Roosevelt (who had polio and was wheelchair-bound), and Stephen Hawking (who has a degenerative nerve disorder and can communicate only through computer technology). Or we might have students watch the video *Stand and Deliver,* the story of eighteen Mexican American high school students from a lower-income neighborhood in East Los Angeles who, through hard work and perseverance, earned college credit by passing the National Advanced Placement Calculus Exam.

Expose students to successful models who are similar to themselves in terms of cultural background, socioeconomic status, gender, and disability.

TABLE 11.3

STUDENTS IN INCLUSIVE SETTINGS

Promoting Social Learning in Students with Special Educational Needs

STUDENTS WITH SPECIAL NEEDS	CHARACTERISTICS THAT THESE STUDENTS MAY EXHIBIT	CLASSROOM STRATEGIES THAT MAY BE BENEFICIAL FOR THESE STUDENTS
Students with specific cognitive or academic difficulties	Difficulties predicting the consequences of specific behaviors Low self-efficacy for academic tasks in areas where there has been a history of failure Less self-regulation of learning and behavior	Help students form more realistic expectations regarding the consequences of their behaviors. Scaffold students' efforts on academic tasks to increase the probability of success. Identify students' areas of strength and give them opportunities to tutor other students in those areas. Promote self-regulation (e.g., by teaching self-observation, self-instructions, self-reinforcement).
Students with social or behavioral problems	Pronounced difficulty learning from the social environment (students with autism) Difficulties predicting the consequences of specific behaviors Friendships with peers who are poor models of effective social skills or prosocial behavior (students with emotional or behavioral disorders) Little self-regulation of behavior Deficits in social problem solving	Help students recognize and interpret social cues and nonverbal language (students with autism). Discuss possible consequences of various courses of action in social conflict situations (students with emotional or behavioral disorders) Model appropriate classroom behaviors; for students with autism, combine modeling with explicit verbal instruction and use visual aids to communicate desired behaviors. Provide opportunities for students to interact with peers who model effective social and prosocial behaviors. Videotape students exhibiting appropriate behaviors and then have them view *themselves* as models for such behavior. Teach self-regulation (e.g., self-observation, self-instructions, self-regulating problem-solving strategies).
Students with general delays in cognitive and social functioning	Low self-efficacy for academic tasks Tendency to observe others to find guidance about how to behave Low goals for achievement (possibly as a way of minimizing the likelihood of failure) Little if any self-regulation of learning and behavior	Scaffold students' efforts on academic tasks to increase the probability of success. Model desired behaviors; identify peers who can also serve as appropriate models. Encourage students to set high yet realistic goals for their own achievement. Promote self-regulation (e.g., by teaching self-observation, self-instructions, self-reinforcement).
Students with physical or sensory challenges	Few opportunities to develop self-regulation skills due to health limitations and/or a tightly controlled environment	Teach skills that promote self-sufficiency and independence. Teach students to make positive self-statements (e.g., "I can do it! ") as a way of enhancing their self-efficacy for acting independently.
Students with advanced cognitive development	High self-efficacy regarding academic tasks High goals for performance More effective self-regulated learning For some students, a history of easy successes and, hence, little experience dealing with failure effectively	Provide the academic support that students need to reach their goals. Provide opportunities for independent study. Provide challenging tasks at which students may sometimes fail; teach constructive strategies for dealing with failure (e.g., persistence, using errors to guide future practice efforts).

Sources: Balla & Zigler, 1979; Bandura, 1989; E. S. Ellis & Friend, 1991; Hughes, 1988; Kehle, Clark, Jenson, & Wampold, 1986; Lupart, 1995; Mercer, 1991; Morgan & Jenson, 1988; J. R. Nelson, Smith, Young, & Dodd, 1991; Patton et al., 1990; Piirto, 1994; Sands & Wehmeyer, 1996; Schumaker & Hazel, 1984; Schunk et al., 1987; Turnbull et al., 1999; Yell, 1993.

Note: Compiled with the assistance of Dr. Margie Garanzini-Daiber and Dr. Margaret Cohen, University of Missouri—St. Louis.

Although we may differ from our students in many ways, we are likely to be powerful models for them nonetheless. Regardless of our own heritage, we must *always* model acceptance and respect for people with diverse backgrounds and characteristics (Boutte & McCormick, 1992).

Promoting Self-Regulation in Students with Special Needs

Most of our students will probably stand to gain from teaching strategies that promote greater self-regulation. But students with special educational needs will often be among those in greatest need of becoming more self-regulated (Sands & Wehmeyer, 1996). Such students are especially likely to benefit when we encourage them to set and strive for their own goals, particularly when such goals are concrete, specific, and accomplishable within a short period of time. Students with special needs will also be well served when we teach them self-observation, self-regulated problem-solving skills, and self-reinforcement techniques (Abery & Zajac, 1996; E. S. Ellis & Friend, 1991; Powers et al., 1996; Schunk, 1991; Yell, 1993).

Table 11–3 presents a social cognitive perspective of characteristics commonly seen in students with special needs; it also presents a number of strategies for promoting the academic and social success of these students. As you will undoubtedly notice, such concepts as *modeling, self-efficacy,* and *self-regulation* appear repeatedly throughout the table.

The Big Picture: Comparing the Three Perspectives of Learning

If you have been reading the chapters of Part 2 in sequence, then you have now examined three different theoretical perspectives of learning: cognitive psychology, behaviorism, and social cognitive theory. At the beginning of Chapter 6, I briefly identified some ways in which these perspectives differ from one another. Now that you have studied each perspective in depth, it might be helpful to make additional comparisons. Table 11–4 identifies some of the major ways in which the three theories are similar and different.

It is important to reiterate a point made in Chapter 6: *No single theoretical orientation can give us a complete picture of how people learn.* All three perspectives provide valuable lessons about how to facilitate students' classroom achievement. For example, principles from cognitive psychology give us ideas about how we can help students learn, remember, and transfer information. Principles from behaviorism yield strategies for helping students develop and maintain more productive classroom behaviors. Principles from social cognitive theory show us how we can effectively model the skills we want students to acquire and how we can promote greater self-regulation. And principles from all three perspectives are useful for motivating students to succeed in the classroom, as you will discover in the next chapter.

Model tolerance and respect for diversity

Teach self-regulation strategies to students with special needs.

Before you look at Table 11–4, make some comparisons on your own.

Remember that different theoretical orientations may be useful for facilitating different types of learning.

TABLE 11.4

Comparing the Three Perspectives of Learning

ISSUE	COGNITIVE PSYCHOLOGY	BEHAVIORISM	SOCIAL COGNITIVE THEORY
Learning is defined as . . .	an internal mental phenomenon that may or may not be reflected in behavior.	a behavior change.	an internal mental phenomenon that may or may not be reflected in behavior.
The focus of investigation is on . . .	cognitive processes.	stimuli and responses that can be readily observed.	both behavior and cognitive processes.
Principles of learning describe how . . .	people mentally process the information they receive and construct knowledge from their experiences.	people's behaviors are affected by environmental stimuli.	people's observations of those around them affect behavior and cognitive processes.
Consequences of behavior . . .	are not a major focus of consideration.	must be experienced directly if they are to affect learning.	can be experienced either directly or vicariously.
Learning and behavior are controlled . . .	primarily by cognitive processes within the individual.	primarily by environmental circumstances.	partly by the environment and partly by cognitive processes; people become increasingly self-regulated (and therefore less controlled by the environment) over time.
Educational implications focus on how we can help students . . .	process information in effective ways and construct accurate and complete knowledge about classroom topics.	acquire more productive classroom behaviors.	learn effectively by observing others.

CASE STUDY: Teacher's Lament

"Sometimes a teacher just can't win," complains Mr. Adams, a fifth-grade teacher. "At the beginning of the year, I told my students that homework assignments would count for 20 percent of their grades. Yet some students hardly ever turned in homework, even though I continually reminded them about their assignments. After reconsidering the situation, I decided that I probably shouldn't use homework as a criterion for grading. After all, in this poor, inner-city neighborhood, many kids don't have a quiet place to study at home.

"So in November, I told my class that I wouldn't be counting homework assignments when I calculated grades for the first report card. Naturally, some students—the ones who hadn't been doing their homework—seemed relieved. But the students who *had* been doing it were absolutely furious! And now hardly anyone seems to turn in homework anymore."

- Why were the students who had been doing their homework regularly so upset? Can you explain their reaction in terms of social cognitive theory?

- From a social cognitive perspective, Mr. Adams inadvertently punished some students and reinforced others. Which students in the class were reinforced, and how? Which students were punished, and how?

- What might Mr. Adams have done instead of eliminating homework as a criterion for class grades? What might he do to encourage and help all students to complete homework assignments?

Summing Up

Social Cognitive Theory

Social cognitive theory focuses on the ways that people learn by observing others. Social cognitive theorists believe that both environmental conditions (e.g., the consequences of behavior, the presence of models) and personal variables (e.g., goals, expectations, self-efficacy) influence learning and behavior. In addition to creating a classroom environment conducive to learning, then, we must also foster those personal characteristics that will enable our students to achieve academic success.

Reinforcement and Punishment

From a social cognitive perspective, reinforcement and punishment affect learning indirectly rather than directly, and consequences to one student vicariously influence the behaviors of others as well. Students who observe a classmate being reinforced or punished for a particular behavior may conclude that engaging in that behavior will yield similar consequences for themselves. Furthermore, the nonoccurrence of expected reinforcement is punishing, and the nonoccurrence of expected punishment is reinforcing. As teachers, we should recognize that the consequences of students' behaviors are likely to influence the expectations that students form, the ways in which they process information, and the choices that they make.

Modeling

Students learn from both live and symbolic models. We should provide numerous opportunities for our students to observe us and others demonstrating important skills. We can also expose our students to exemplary characters portrayed in books, films, and other media.

Four processes are necessary for modeling to occur: *attention* to the model, *retention* (memory) of what the model does, capacity for *motor reproduction* of the modeled behavior, and *motivation* to exhibit the modeled behavior. We should make sure that all four factors are present when we use modeling as an instructional technique.

Self-Efficacy

Students are more likely to engage and persist in certain activities when they believe that they can be successful—when they have high self-efficacy. We can promote greater self-efficacy in our students by having them observe successful peer models, assuring them that they too can succeed, and giving them many opportunities to experience success.

Self-Regulation

As children and adolescents grow older, most of them become increasingly self-regulating; for example, they begin to set standards and goals for themselves, and they monitor, evaluate, and reinforce their own behavior. Principles of self-regulation can be applied not only to behavior but to learning and problem solving as well. We can promote the development of self-regulation by having students set some of their own goals, teaching them to guide their own performance through self-instructions and self-regulated problem-solving strategies, helping them monitor and evaluate their efforts accurately, encouraging them to reinforce themselves for good work, and, eventually, assigning activities in which students study and learn with little or no teacher assistance.

Reciprocal Causation

Environment, behavior, and personal characteristics all interact with one another in their effects on learning—a three-way interdependence known as *reciprocal causation*. As teachers, we must recognize that the environment we create affects both the behaviors that students exhibit and the personal factors that influence their learning. Those behaviors and personal factors will, in turn, influence the future classroom environment that students experience.

Diversity from a Social Cognitive Perspective

Students often benefit more from models who are similar to themselves in terms of cultural background, socioeconomic status, gender, and (if applicable) disability. Students with special needs will often be among those who need the greatest support in developing self-regulation strategies.

Contrasting the Three Perspectives of Learning/General Principles of Learning

The three theoretical perspectives of learning that we have examined—cognitive psychology, behaviorism, and social cognitive learning—differ somewhat with regard to such issues as reinforcement, cognition, control, and educational implications. As teachers, we must recognize that all three perspectives have useful applications for classroom practice.

KEY CONCEPTS

12

Motivating Students to Learn

What motivated you to open your textbook and read this chapter today? Perhaps you have an upcoming test on the material in the chapter. Perhaps you want to show that you've done the assigned reading when your instructor calls on you in class. Or perhaps you are simply curious about the topic of motivation and want to learn some strategies for motivating your *own* students when you become a teacher.

We have already touched on the topic of motivation in previous chapters. In our discussion of knowledge construction in Chapter 7, we learned that students are more likely to revise incorrect beliefs about a topic—to undergo conceptual change—when they are motivated to do so. In our discussion of behaviorism in Chapter 10, we noted that students are more likely to exhibit those behaviors that have been previously reinforced. In our discussion of social cognitive theory in Chapter 11, we discovered that students more frequently pursue those tasks for which they have high self-efficacy, and they will persist at such tasks even in the face of failure.

In this chapter, we will look at motivation in greater depth, considering questions such as these:

- What do psychologists mean by the term *motivation,* and how does motivation affect behavior and learning?
- What's the difference between intrinsic and extrinsic motivation, and what conditions seem to promote each kind of motivation?
- What strategies can we use to foster an intrinsic motivation to learn classroom subject matter?
- What social needs are our students likely to have, and how can we reasonably address these needs?
- What roles do emotions (*affect*) play in learning? How can we keep students' anxiety about classroom tasks at a level that facilitates classroom success?
- How do students' explanations for success and failure (their *attributions*) influence their thoughts and behaviors?
- What differences are we likely to see in students' motivation as a function of their age, ethnic background, gender, socioeconomic status, and special needs?

CASE STUDY: Quick Draw

Unlike her more socially oriented classmates, Anya is a quiet student who usually prefers to be alone. Whenever she has free time in class, she grabs a pencil and a piece of paper and begins to sketch. Her love of drawing appears at other times as well. For example, she decorates her notebooks with elaborate doodles. She embellishes stories and essays with illustrations. She even draws pictures of the words on each week's spelling list.

Not surprisingly, Anya looks forward to her art class, paying particularly close attention on those days when her art teacher describes or demonstrates a new drawing technique. She buries herself in each new drawing assignment, seemingly oblivious to the classroom around her. Anya's art teacher notes with pride how much Anya's skill at drawing has improved over the course of the school year.

Anya makes no bones about her interest. "When I grow up, I want to be a professional artist," she states emphatically. "In the meantime, I'm going to practice, practice, practice."

■ Which of Anya's behaviors reflect her interest in art? Are these behaviors likely to facilitate her performance in art class? If so, how?

The Nature of Motivation

When it comes to art, Anya is highly motivated. We can reasonably draw this conclusion based on her close attention in class, her eagerness to draw whenever she can, and her career goal. **Motivation** is something that energizes, directs, and sustains behavior; it gets students moving, points them in a particular direction, and keeps them going. We usually see it reflected in a certain amount of *personal investment* in particular activities (Maehr & Meyer, 1997).

Virtually all students are motivated in one way or another. One student may be keenly interested in classroom subject matter and so may seek out challenging coursework, participate actively in classroom discussions, complete assignments diligently, and earn high marks on classroom assignments. Another student may be more concerned with the social side of school, interacting with classmates frequently, attending extracurricular activities almost every day, and perhaps even running for a student government office. Still another may be focused on athletics, excelling in physical education classes, playing or watching sports most afternoons and weekends, and working out daily. And yet another student, perhaps because of an undetected learning disability, poor social skills, or a seemingly uncoordinated body, may be interested primarily in *avoiding* academics, social situations, or athletic activities.

Anya brings her strong interest in art with her when she enters the classroom. Yet motivation is not always something that people "carry around" inside of them; it can also be influenced by environmental conditions. When we talk about how the environment can enhance a person's motivation to learn particular things or behave in particular ways, we are talking about **situated motivation** (Paris & Turner, 1994; Rueda & Moll, 1994). As we proceed through the chapter, we will find that, as teachers, we can do many things to create a classroom environment that motivates students to learn and behave in ways that will promote their long-term success.

How is *situated motivation* similar to *situated cognition*, a concept discussed in Chapter 8?

How Motivation Affects Learning and Behavior

Motivation has several effects on students' learning and behavior, which I've summarized in Figure 12–1:

• *It directs behavior toward particular goals.* As we discovered in Chapter 11, social cognitive theorists propose that individuals set goals for themselves and direct their behaviors toward those goals. Motivation determines the specific goals toward which people strive (Maehr & Meyer, 1997; Pintrich et al., 1993). Thus, it affects the

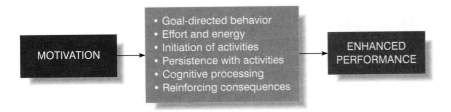

FIGURE 12.1
How motivation affects learning and behavior

choices that students make—whether to enroll in trigonometry or studio art,
whether to watch the Superbowl game or write an assigned research paper, whether
to try out for the lead in the school play or simply sit in the audience and watch the
performance.

  • *It increases effort and energy expended toward those goals.* Motivation
increases the amount of effort and energy that students expend in a particular activity
(Csikszentmihalyi & Nakamura, 1989; Maehr, 1984; Pintrich et al., 1993). It determines
the extent to which students pursue a task enthusiastically and wholeheartedly on the
one hand, or apathetically and lackadaisically on the other.

  • *It increases initiation of, and persistence in, activities.* Motivation determines
the degree to which our students will independently initiate and persist at activities
(Maehr, 1984; Pintrich et al., 1993; Wigfield, 1994). Students are more likely to begin a
task that they actually *want* to do. They are also more likely to continue that task until
they've completed it, even when they are occasionally interrupted or frustrated in
their efforts to do so.

  • *It enhances cognitive processing.* Motivation affects what and how information
is processed (Eccles & Wigfield, 1985; Pintrich et al., 1993; Voss & Schauble, 1992).
For one thing, motivated students are more likely to pay attention, and as we have
seen, attention is critical for getting information into both working memory and long-
term memory. They also try to understand material—to learn it meaningfully—rather
than simply "go through the motions" of learning in a superficial, rote fashion.
Furthermore, motivated students are more likely to seek help on a task when they
need it, perhaps by asking for clarification or additional practice opportunities.

  • *It determines what consequences are reinforcing.* The more students are
motivated to achieve academic success, the more proud they will be of an A and the
more upset they will be by an F or perhaps even a B (remember our discussion of self-
imposed contingencies in Chapter 11). The more students want to be accepted and
respected by their peers, the more meaningful membership in the "in group" will be,
and the more painful the ridicule of classmates will seem. To a student uninterested in
athletics, making the school football team is no big deal, but to a student whose life
revolves totally around football, making or not making the team may be a consequence of monumental importance.

  • *It leads to improved performance.* Because of these other effects—goal-
directed behavior, energy and effort, initiation and persistence, cognitive processing,
and reinforcement—motivation often leads to improved performance. As you might
guess, then, our students who are most motivated to learn and excel in classroom
activities will also tend to be our highest achievers (Gottfried, 1990; Schiefele, Krapp,
& Winteler, 1992; Walberg & Uguroglu, 1980).

What consequences
are reinforcing to you?
What consequences are
punishing? Can you tie
your preferences to
particular motives?

Can you find each
of these effects in the case
study of Anya?

Intrinsic Versus Extrinsic Motivation

Some researchers believe that our schools foster extrinsic motivation far more frequently than intrinsic motivation (Ryan, Connell, & Grolnick, 1992; Spaulding, 1992). Has this been true in your own experience?

Sometimes students are motivated **intrinsically,** by factors within themselves or inherent in the task they are performing. For example, they may engage in an activity because it gives them pleasure, helps them develop a skill they think is important, or is the ethically and morally right thing to do. At other times, students are motivated **extrinsically,** by factors external to themselves and unrelated to the task they are performing. For example, they may want the good grades, money, or recognition that particular activities and accomplishments bring.

Students are most likely to show the beneficial effects of motivation when they are *intrinsically* motivated to engage in classroom activities. Intrinsically motivated students tackle assigned tasks willingly and are eager to learn classroom material. They are also more likely to process information in effective ways—for example, by engaging in meaningful learning, elaboration, and visual imagery. In contrast, extrinsically motivated students may have to be enticed or prodded, are often interested in performing only easy tasks and meeting minimal classroom requirements, and may process information in a rote, superficial manner (Schiefele, 1991a; Spaulding, 1992; Tobias, 1994; Voss & Schauble, 1992).

Under what conditions are students most likely to be intrinsically motivated? One theorist, Abraham Maslow, has proposed that intrinsic motivation emerges only after other, more basic human needs have been satisfied. More recently, several theorists have suggested that intrinsic motivation is most likely to be present when both self-efficacy and self-determination are present. Let's consider how we might promote greater intrinsic motivation in our students by using each of these perspectives.

Maslow's Hierarchy of Needs

Abraham Maslow's work (e.g., 1973, 1987) has been a central aspect of the *humanist* movement, a perspective especially prominent in psychology during the 1960s and 1970s. Humanism, with roots in clinical and counseling psychology, focuses on how individuals acquire emotions, attitudes, values, and interpersonal skills. Humanist views tend to be grounded more in philosophy than in research, but they provide useful insights into human motivation nevertheless.

Maslow proposed that people have five basic kinds of needs that they try to satisfy:

1. *Physiological needs.* People are motivated to satisfy needs related to their physical survival (e.g., needs for food, water, oxygen, warmth, exercise, and rest). For example, thirsty students may request a trip to the drinking fountain, students needing to release pent-up energy may become restless and fidgety, and hungry students may be thinking more about their growling stomachs than a classroom activity.

2. *Safety needs.* People have a need to feel safe and secure in their environment. For instance, students like to know what things are expected of them and are happier when classroom routines are somewhat orderly and predictable.

3. *Love and belonging needs.* People seek affectionate relationships with others and like to feel that they are accepted as part of a group; in other words, they have a need for affiliation. For example, a fourth grader may place great importance on having a "best" friend. And many adolescents take great pains to fit in with the "cool" crowd—for example, by wearing a certain hairstyle or clothes emblazoned with a certain brand name.

4. *Esteem needs.* People have a need to feel good about themselves (a *need for self-esteem*) and to believe that other people also feel positively about them (a

need for esteem from others). To develop positive self-esteem, students will strive for achievement and mastery of their environment. To attain the esteem and respect of others, they will behave in ways that gain them recognition, appreciation, and prestige. For example, a second grader can partially satisfy the need for self-esteem by reading a book "all by myself" or by achieving a special merit badge in Cub Scouts or Campfire Girls. A high school student may try to satisfy the need for esteem from others by running for Student Council treasurer or becoming a star athlete.

5. *Need for self-actualization.* People have a need to **self-actualize**—to grow and become all they are capable of becoming. Individuals striving toward self-actualization seek out new activities as a way of expanding their horizons and strive to learn simply for the sake of learning. For example, one student may be driven by her own curiosity to learn everything she can about dinosaurs; another may pursue an active interest in ballet both as a means of developing her muscle tone and as an outlet for creative self-expression.

Maslow further proposed that the five sets of needs form a *hierarchy,* as illustrated in Figure 12–2. When two or more needs are unmet, people tend to satisfy them in a particular sequence. They begin with the lowest needs in the hierarchy, satisfying physiological needs first, safety needs next, and so on. They attempt to fulfill higher needs only when lower needs have already been met. For example, a boy with a need for exercise (a physiological need) may become excessively restless in class even though he is scolded by his teacher for his hyperactivity (thereby *not* satisfying his need for esteem from others). A girl with an unfulfilled need for love and belonging may decide not to enroll in intermediate algebra—a class that would satisfy her desire to learn more math—if the peers whose friendships she most values tell her the class is only for nerds. I once knew a boy living in a Philadelphia ghetto who had a strong interest in learning yet often stayed home from school to avoid the violent gangs that hung out on the local street corner. This boy's need for safety took precedence over any need for self-actualization that he might have had.

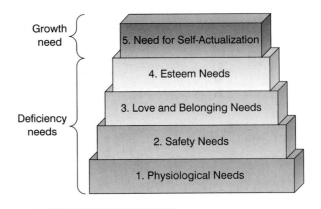

FIGURE 12.2
Maslow's hierarchy of needs

The first four needs in the hierarchy—physiological, safety, love and belonging, and esteem—result from things that a person *lacks*; hence, Maslow called them **deficiency needs.** Deficiency needs can be met only by external sources—by people and events in one's environment. Furthermore, once these needs are fulfilled, there is no reason to satisfy them further. The last need, self-actualization, is a **growth need:** Rather than simply addressing a deficiency in a person's life, it enhances the person's growth and development. The need for self-actualization is never completely satisfied; people seeking to self-actualize continue to strive for further fulfillment. Self-actualizing activities are intrinsically motivating: People engage in them because doing so gives them pleasure and satisfies their desire to know and grow.

According to Maslow, total self-actualization is rarely if ever achieved, and then typically only by mature adults. Nevertheless, as teachers we can help our students move in this direction by making sure their deficiency needs are at least partially satisfied. Our students may not show much intrinsic motivation to learn classroom material until they are rested and well-fed, feel safe and secure in their classroom, and enjoy the love and respect of their teachers and classmates.

How might Maslow's hierarchy come into play in an economically diverse classroom?

Help students meet their physiological, safety, love and belonging, and esteem needs.

Self-Efficacy and Self-Determination

Experiencing Firsthand
Enjoyable Activities

1. Make a list of five different things you like to do. You might list hobbies, favorite sports, or other activities in which you are intrinsically motivated to engage.

2. Using the following scale, rate each of the activities you've just listed in terms of *how successfully you usually perform it:*

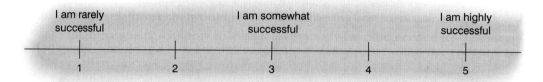

3. Using the following scale, rate each of your activities in terms of *how much choice you have regarding whether or not you engage in the activity:*

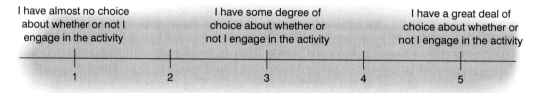

Take a close look at the numerical ratings you've just assigned to your favorite activities. Chances are, your ratings were almost exclusively 3 or higher on both of the scales. A number of theorists have proposed that people are most likely to be intrinsically motivated to perform a certain task when two conditions exist (Boggiano & Pittman, 1992; Corno & Rohrkemper, 1985; Deci & Ryan, 1985, 1992; Spaulding, 1992):

1. They have high **self-efficacy:** They believe that they are capable of successfully accomplishing the task.

2. They have a sense of **self-determination:** They believe that they are in control of their own destinies and can make choices regarding the directions that their lives will take.

Self-Efficacy

Our students are more likely to be intrinsically motivated to engage in classroom activities when they have high self-efficacy—what some motivation theorists call a *sense of competence*—about their ability to perform those activities successfully. In our discussion of social cognitive theory in the preceding chapter, we identified several strategies for enhancing students' self-efficacy:

- Make sure they master basic skills.
- Help them make noticeable progress on difficult tasks.
- Communicate confidence in students' abilities through both words and actions.
- Expose them to successful peers.

How is *self-efficacy* similar to Maslow's *need for self-esteem*? How are the two concepts different?

Motivation theorists have offered several additional recommendations for enhancing students' self-efficacy and, indirectly, increasing intrinsic motivation:

• *Provide competence-promoting feedback.* As we noted in Chapter 10, positive feedback is often an effective reinforcer for students. Positive feedback may also promote intrinsic motivation, especially if it conveys the message that students have the ability to perform the task successfully and thereby enhances their self-efficacy. In fact, even negative feedback can promote high self-efficacy if it tells students how they can improve their performance and communicates confidence that improvement is likely (Deci & Ryan, 1985; Pintrich & Schunk, 1996). Here are some examples of negative feedback that might positively influence student motivation:

When giving either positive or negative feedback, communicate the message that students have the ability to succeed.

> "I can see from the past few homework assignments that you're having trouble with long division. I think I know what the problem is. Here, let me show you what you need to do differently."

> "In the first draft of your research paper, many of your paragraphs don't lead logically to the ones that follow. A few headings and transitional sentences would make a world of difference. Let's find a time to discuss how you might use these techniques to improve the flow of your paper."

> "Your time in the 100-meter dash was not as fast as it could be. It's early in the season, though, and if you work on your endurance, I know you'll improve. Also, I think you might get a faster start if you keep low when you come out of the starting blocks."

• *Promote mastery on challenging tasks.* You might think of a **challenge** as a situation in which success is neither easy nor guaranteed but can be attained with a significant amount of effort. A challenge encourages people to stretch themselves to their limits—perhaps to experiment with new strategies or to think in new ways. In Chapter 2, we found that challenging activities promote cognitive development. In addition, mastery of such challenges enhances self-efficacy and, as a result, promotes intrinsic motivation. Students who master challenging tasks experience considerable pleasure, satisfaction, and pride in their accomplishments (Csikszentmihalyi & Nakamura, 1989; Deci & Ryan, 1992; Lan, Repman, Bradley, & Weller, 1994; A. G. Thompson & Thompson, 1989; Turner, 1995).

Encourage students to tackle challenging tasks.

Once students are intrinsically motivated, they frequently pursue further challenges of their own accord. They also exhibit considerable persistence in the face of difficulty, and they continue to remain interested in an activity even when they make frequent errors (Covington, 1992; Deci, 1992; Harter, 1992). As you can see, then, challenges and intrinsic motivation mutually enhance one another, leading to a "vicious" cycle of the most desirable sort.

As teachers, we are more likely to encourage students to tackle challenging tasks when, through the feedback we give and the criteria we use for evaluation, we create an environment in which our students feel free to take risks and make mistakes (Clifford, 1990). We can also provide greater rewards for succeeding at challenging tasks than for achieving an easy success; for example, we might give students a choice between doing an easy task or a more difficult one but give them more points for accomplishing the difficult one (Clifford, 1990; Lan et al., 1994). At the same time, however, we must tailor the level of challenge to students' current self-efficacy levels: Students who have little or no confidence in their ability to perform a particular activity may initially respond more favorably when we give them tasks that result in a high degree of success (Stipek, 1996).

Create an environment that encourages students to take risks, and then reinforce them for doing so.

Don't present exceptionally challenging tasks when students' self-efficacy is low.

• *Promote self-comparison rather than comparison with others.* If we define success in terms of task accomplishment, skill improvement, or academic progress,

🍎 Minimize competition, except on occasions when all students have an equal chance of being successful.

🍎 Define success as improvement over time.

🍎 Be sure mistakes and errors occur within an overall context of success—for instance, by balancing challenging tasks with easier ones.

then virtually all of our students can be successful. If we instead define success in terms of how well students perform in comparison with their peers, many will be doomed to failure. Such competition may motivate a few students who believe that they can rise to meet the challenge; however, it will undermine the intrinsic motivation of the majority of their classmates, who will see failure as the most likely outcome (Deci & Ryan, 1992; Stipek, 1996). Furthermore, some students (e.g., those from some Native American communities) may resist competing if they believe that their own success will contribute to their classmates' failures (C. A. Grant & Gomez, 1996).

As students progress through the elementary grades, they become increasingly aware of how their performance compares with that of their classmates (Feld, Ruhland, & Gold, 1979; Ruble, 1980). Inevitably, then, some students begin to believe that they simply don't measure up to their peers—in other words, that they are failures. As teachers, we shouldn't compound the problem. Most of our students will achieve at higher levels if we encourage them to define success in terms of their own improvement, rather than in terms of how they stack up against others (Covington, 1992; Graham & Golen, 1991).

We can do at least two things to encourage students to make self-comparisons rather than comparisons with others. First, we can minimize the degree to which they are even *aware* of the performance levels of their classmates. For example, we should assess their performance independently of how well others are doing, keep their performance on assignments confidential, and give them feedback in private. In addition, we should encourage them to assess their own performance in much the same way that we are assessing it—that is, in terms of their improvement. We must remember that children and adolescents are often impatient, expecting success overnight when in fact the development of knowledge and skills may take several days, months, or even years. We can help them focus on their successes rather than their imperfections by providing them with concrete mechanisms that highlight improvement—for example, by giving them occasional nongraded quizzes, progress charts that they can fill in themselves, or frequent verbal or written feedback about the "little things" they are doing well.

• *Be sure errors occur within an overall context of success.* At one time, many educators proposed that students should never be allowed to fail. But whether we like it or not, occasional failures are a normal, inevitable, and often beneficial part of the learning process, and students need to learn to take such failures in stride. When learners never make mistakes, we can reasonably assume that they are not being challenged by the tasks we are assigning. Furthermore, learners unaccustomed to failure in their school curriculum have difficulty coping with failure when they eventually do encounter it (Dweck, 1986).

Yet when students encounter failure *too* frequently, they will develop low self-efficacy, believing that nothing they do will produce positive results. Ideally, then, students should experience occasional failure within the context of overall success. This way, they learn that they *can* succeed if they try, while also developing a realistic attitude about failure—that it at worst is a temporary setback and at best can give them useful information about how to improve their performance. To keep failure from becoming too frequent an occurrence, we may often want to balance challenging classroom tasks with some that students can accomplish with relative ease (L. Katz & Chard, 1989; Spaulding, 1992).

Self-Determination

▣ Experiencing Firsthand
Painting Between the Lines

Imagine that I give you a set of watercolor paints, a paintbrush, two sheets of paper, and some paper towels. I ask you to paint a picture of your house, apartment building, or dormitory and then give you the following instructions:

Students are more likely to be intrinsically motivated when they have a sense of self-determination about classroom activities.

Before you begin, I want to tell you some things that you will have to do. They are rules that I have about painting. You have to keep the paints clean. You can paint only on this small sheet of paper, so don't spill any paint on the big sheet. And you must wash out your brush and wipe it with a paper towel before you switch to a new color of paint, so that you don't get the colors all mixed up. In general, I want you to be a good art student and not make a mess with the paints. (adapted from Koestner, Ryan, Bernieri, & Holt, 1984, p. 239)

How much fun do you think your task would be? After reading my rules about painting, how eager are you to begin painting?

My rules about painting are somewhat restrictive, aren't they? In fact, they are quite *controlling:* They make it clear that I am in charge of the situation and that you, as an art student, have little choice about how you go about your task. Chances are, you have little intrinsic motivation to paint the picture I've asked you to paint (Deci, 1992; Koestner et al., 1984). Furthermore, you would probably be less creative in your painting than if I had not been so controlling (Amabile & Hennessey, 1992).

Students are more likely to be intrinsically motivated when they have a sense of self-determination—when they believe that they have some choice and control regarding the things they do and the directions their lives take (Boggiano & Pittman, 1992; Corno & Rohrkemper, 1985; deCharms, 1972; Deci, 1992; Deci & Ryan, 1985, 1987, 1992; Spaulding, 1992; Turner, 1995). Motivation theorists have offered a number of suggestions for enhancing students' sense of self-determination about school activities and assignments:

• *Present rules and instructions in an informational rather than controlling manner.* Virtually any classroom needs a few rules and procedures to ensure that students act appropriately and that class activities run smoothly. Furthermore, there may be times when we must impose guidelines and restrictions related to how students carry out their assignments. The challenge is to present these rules, procedures, guidelines, and restrictions without communicating a message of *control* (like that in the "Painting Between the Lines" exercise). Instead, we can present them as *information*—for instance, as conditions that can help students accomplish classroom objectives (Deci, 1992; Koestner et al., 1984). Here are three examples of how we might describe rules or give instructions in an informational rather than controlling manner:

Present rules and instructions as mechanisms for helping students accomplish classroom objectives.

"We can make sure everyone has an equal chance to speak and be heard if we listen without interrupting and if we raise our hands when we want to contribute to the discussion."

▲ You can find additional examples in Figure 15–2 of Chapter 15.

🍎 Within reasonable limits, let students make choices.

"I'm giving you a particular format to follow when you do your math homework. If you use this format, it will be easier for me to find your answers and to figure out how I can help you improve."

"Let's remember that other students will be using the same paints and brushes later today, so as we work, we need to make sure everything we use now is still in tip-top shape when we're done. It's important, then, that we rinse our brushes in water and wipe them on a paper towel before we switch to a new color. We should also clean our brushes thoroughly when we're done painting."

• *Provide opportunities for students to make choices.* Sometimes there is only one way to accomplish a particular instructional objective. But more frequently there are several routes to the same destination. In such cases, why not let students choose how they want to get there? For example, we might allow them to make decisions, either individually or as a group, about some or all of the following:

Rules and procedures to make the class run more smoothly

Ways of achieving mastery of a classroom objective (e.g., which of several possible procedures to use, whether to work individually or in small groups)

Specific topics for research or writing projects

Specific works of literature to be read

Due dates for major assignments

The order in which specific tasks are accomplished during the school day

Ways of demonstrating that an objective has been mastered

Criteria by which some assignments will be evaluated
(Kohn, 1993; Meece, 1994; Stipek, 1993)

When students can make choices such as these, they are more likely to be interested in what they are doing, to work diligently, to complete assignments quickly and efficiently, and to take pride in their work (Deci & Ryan, 1992; Lepper & Hodell, 1989; Ross, 1988; Turner, 1995). Furthermore, students who are given choices—even those with serious behavior problems—are less likely to misbehave in class (Dunlap et al., 1994; S. Powell & Nelson, 1997; B. J. Vaughn & Horner, 1997).

In some situations, students' choices can be almost limitless; for example, in a unit on expository writing, a wide variety of student-selected research topics might be equally appropriate. In other situations, we may need to impose certain limits on the choices that students make; for example, if we allow a class to set its own due dates for major assignments, we might insist that the final schedule provide sufficient time for us to grade each assignment. In still other situations, we may want to provide a handful of options from which students can choose; for instance, we might allow them to choose from among several works of literature, specialize in one of several art media (e.g., watercolors, pastels, clay), or select a piece of equipment (e.g., parallel bars, rings, floor mats) on which to develop gymnastic skills.

🍎 Evaluate students in ways that help them improve.

• *Evaluate student performance in a noncontrolling fashion.* As teachers, we will inevitably need to evaluate students' accomplishments. But we must keep in mind that external evaluations may undermine students' intrinsic motivation, especially if those evaluations are communicated in a controlling manner (Deci & Ryan, 1992; Harter, Whitesell, & Kowalski, 1992). Ideally, we should present our evaluations of students' work, not in terms of a "judgment" of some sort (e.g., not in terms of how they *should* perform), but in terms of information that can help them improve their knowledge and skills (Stipek, 1996). Furthermore, we can give students criteria by which they can evaluate *themselves* in the self-comparative manner described earlier.

- *Minimize reliance on extrinsic reinforcers.* The discussion of behaviorism in Chapter 10 emphasized the importance of relying on intrinsic reinforcers—for example, on students' own feelings of pride and satisfaction about their accomplishments—as often as possible. A problem with using extrinsic reinforcers—praise, stickers, favorite activities, and so on—is that they may undermine intrinsic motivation, especially when students perceive them as controlling behavior and limiting choices (Deci, 1992; Gottfried, Fleming, & Gottfried, 1994; Lepper & Hodell, 1989).[1] Extrinsic reinforcers may also communicate the message that classroom tasks are unpleasant "chores" (why else would a reinforcer be necessary?), rather than activities to be carried out and enjoyed for their own sake (Hennessey, 1995; Stipek, 1993).

Yet there may be occasions when, despite our efforts, our students will have little interest in acquiring certain knowledge or skills critical for their later success in life. In such situations, we may have to provide extrinsic reinforcers—good grades, free time, special privileges—to encourage learning. How can we use such reinforcers without diminishing students' sense of self-determination? For one thing, we can use reinforcers such as praise to communicate information rather than to control behavior (Deci, 1992; Ryan, Mims, & Koestner, 1983); consider these statements as examples:

"Your description of the main character in your short story makes her come alive."

"I think you have finally mastered the rolling R sound in Spanish."

"This poster clearly states the hypothesis, method, results, and conclusions of your science project. Your use of a bar graph makes the differences between your treatment and control groups easy to see and interpret."

Furthermore, as noted in the discussion of self-regulation in Chapter 11, we may want to encourage *self*-reinforcement—a practice that clearly keeps control in the hands of students.

- *Help students keep externally imposed constraints in proper perspective.* Our students will often encounter circumstances that cast a "controlling" light on school activities; competitions, extrinsic rewards, and external evaluation are frequent events in most schools. For example, students often enter competitive events such as athletic contests, spelling bees, and science fairs. They may make the Honor Roll, win a first-place ribbon at an art exhibit, or receive a free pizza coupon for reading a certain number of books each month. And they will almost inevitably receive grades, in one form or another, that reflect their teachers' evaluations of their achievement.

To help our students keep such external constraints in perspective as they engage in a learning task, we should remind them that, although competition, extrinsic rewards, or evaluation may be present, the most important thing is for them to focus on the inherent value of the task itself (Amabile & Hennessey, 1992; Hennessey, 1995). For example, we might encourage them to tell themselves something along this line:

I like to get good grades, and when I bring home a good report card, my parents always give me money. But that's not what's really important. I like to learn a lot. There are a lot of things that interest me, and I want to learn about them, so I work hard because I enjoy it. (Amabile & Hennessey, 1992, p. 68)

As teachers, we would ultimately like our students to be motivated to acquire knowledge and skills simply because they *want* to learn them, rather than because we give them extrinsic reinforcers for doing so. Let's find out more about how we can promote one form of intrinsic motivation—the motivation to learn.

Avoid extrinsic reinforcers when students are intrinsically motivated.

Use praise to provide information rather than to control students' behavior.

Encourage self-reinforcement.

Encourage students to focus on the intrinsic value of the tasks they perform.

[1]Not everyone agrees that extrinsic reinforcers have this undermining effect. For alternative perspectives, see J. Cameron & Pierce (1994) and several follow-up articles in the Fall 1996, issue of *Review of Educational Research.*

Motivation to Learn

Consider these two students in a trigonometry class:

Sheryl detests mathematics and is taking the class for only one reason: a C or better in trigonometry is a requirement for a scholarship at State University, where she desperately wants to go to college.

Shannon has always liked math. Trigonometry will help her get a scholarship at State University, but in addition, Shannon truly wants to understand how to use trigonometry. She sees its usefulness for her future profession as an architect. Besides, she's discovering that trigonometry is actually a lot of fun.

Which student is going to learn more in class? We can reasonably predict that Shannon will achieve at a higher level than Sheryl. Sheryl is motivated only to get a C or better, not to learn trigonometry. She will do whatever she needs to do to get a passing grade, but she probably won't do much more than that. In contrast, Shannon has the **motivation to learn**—the tendency to find school-related activities meaningful and worthwhile and therefore to attempt to get the maximum benefit from them (Brophy, 1986, 1987; McCombs, 1988).

Students may have varying degrees of motivation to learn in different aspects of the school curriculum. Some students, like Shannon, may be particularly motivated in mathematics, whereas others may be eager to acquire knowledge or skills in art (remember our case study of Anya), history, athletics, or auto mechanics.

Characteristic of students like Shannon and Anya—students with a motivation to learn—is a focus on learning goals rather than performance goals. The distinction between these two types of goals is the topic we turn to now.

Learning Versus Performance Goals

Mr. Wesolowski, the physical education teacher, is teaching a unit on basketball. He asks Tim, Travis, and Tony to get on the court and try dribbling, passing, and shooting baskets. Consider what the three boys are thinking as they begin to practice:

Tim: This is my chance to show all the guys what a great basketball player I am. If I stay near the basket, Travis and Tony will keep passing to me, and I'll score a lot of points. I can really impress Wesolowski and my friends.

Travis: Boy, I hope I don't screw this up. If I shoot at the basket and miss, I'll look like a real jerk. Maybe I should just stay outside the three-point line and keep passing to Tim and Tony.

Tony: I'd really like to become a better basketball player. I can't figure out why I don't get more of my shots into the basket. I'll ask Wesolowski to give me feedback about how I can improve my game. Maybe some of my friends will have suggestions, too.

All three boys want to play basketball well, but for different reasons. Tim is concerned mostly about his performance—about looking good in front of his teacher and classmates—and so he wants to maximize opportunities to demonstrate his skill on the court. Travis is also concerned about the impression he will make, but he just wants to make sure he *doesn't* look *bad*. Unlike Tim and Travis, Tony isn't even thinking about how his performance will appear to others. Instead, he is interested mainly in developing his skill in the game and doesn't expect immediate success. For Tony, making mistakes is an inevitable part of learning a new skill, not a source of embarrassment or humiliation.

Tony's approach to basketball illustrates a **learning goal,** a desire to acquire additional knowledge or master new skills. In contrast, Tim and Travis are each setting a **per-**

TABLE 12.1

Students with Learning Versus Performance Goals

STUDENTS WITH LEARNING GOALS	STUDENTS WITH PERFORMANCE GOALS
Believe that competence develops over time through practice and effort.	Believe that competence is a stable characteristic; people either have talent or they don't.
Choose tasks that maximize opportunities for learning.	Choose tasks that maximize opportunities for demonstrating competence; avoid tasks and actions (e.g., asking for help) that make them look incompetent.
React to easy tasks with feelings of boredom or disappointment.	React to easy tasks with feelings of pride or relief.
View effort as something necessary to improve competence.	View effort as a sign of low competence; think that competent people shouldn't have to try very hard.
Are more likely to be intrinsically motivated to learn course material.	Are more likely to be extrinsically motivated—that is, by expectations of external reinforcement and punishment—and are more likely to cheat to obtain good grades.
Exhibit more self-regulated learning and behavior.	Exhibit less self-regulation.
Use learning strategies that promote true comprehension of course material (e.g., meaningful learning, elaboration, comprehension monitoring).	Use learning strategies that promote only rote learning (e.g., repetition, copying, word-for-word memorization).
Evaluate their own performance in terms of the progress they make.	Evaluate their own performance in terms of how they compare with others.
View errors as a normal and useful part of the learning process; use errors to help improve performance.	View errors as a sign of failure and incompetence.
Are satisfied with their performance if they try hard, even if their efforts result in failure.	Are satisfied with their performance only if they succeed.
Interpret failure as a sign that they need to exert more effort.	Interpret failure as a sign of low ability and therefore predictive of continuing failure in the future.
View their teacher as a resource and guide to help them learn.	View their teacher as a judge and as a rewarder or punisher.

Sources: *Ablard & Lipschultz, 1998; R. Ames, 1983; C. Ames & Archer, 1988; Anderman, Griesinger, & Westerfield, 1998; Anderman & Maehr, 1994; Dweck, 1986; Dweck & Elliott, 1983; Entwisle & Ramsden, 1983; Graham & Weiner, 1996; Jagacinski & Nicholls, 1984, 1987; McCombs, 1988; Meece, 1994; Newman & Schwager, 1995; Nolen, 1996; B. M. Powell, 1990; Schiefele, 1991a, 1992; Stipek, 1993; Urdan, Midgley, & Anderman, 1998.*

formance goal, a desire to look good and receive favorable judgments from others or else *not* look bad and receive unfavorable judgments. When we compare students who have learning goals with those who have performance goals, we find many differences in attitudes and behaviors (see Table 12–1).

As Table 12–1 illustrates, students with learning goals tend to engage in the very activities that will help them learn: They pay attention in class, process information in ways

Consider Sheryl and Shannon (our trigonometry students) and Anya from our "Quick Draw" case study. For which girl(s) do we see a learning goal? For which girl(s) do we see a performance goal?

483

that promote effective long-term memory storage, and learn from their mistakes. Furthermore, students with learning goals have a healthy perspective about learning, effort, and failure: They realize that learning is a process of trying hard and continuing to persevere even in the face of temporary setbacks. Consequently, it is usually these students who benefit the most from their classroom experiences.

In contrast, students with performance goals may stay away from some of the very tasks that, because of their challenging nature, would do the most to help them master new skills (Dweck, 1986). Furthermore, because these students may exert only the minimal effort necessary to achieve desired performance outcomes, they may learn only a fraction of what their teachers have to offer them (Brophy, 1987).

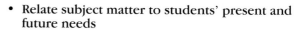

Fostering the Motivation to Learn

Unfortunately, performance goals seem to be far more prevalent than learning goals among today's students. Most students, if they are motivated to succeed in their schoolwork, are primarily concerned about getting good grades, and they prefer short and easy tasks to lengthier, more challenging ones (Blumenfeld, 1992; W. Doyle, 1983, 1986b).

How can we foster our students' motivation to learn? How can we help them focus more on learning than on simply looking good to others? Among other things, we can:

- Relate subject matter to students' present and future needs
- Capitalize on students' interests
- Model our own interest in the subject matter
- Communicate our belief that students want to learn
- Focus students' attention on learning goals rather than performance goals

Let's consider each of these strategies.

Relating Subject Matter to Students' Present and Future Needs

Some classroom activities will be naturally fun, interesting, or otherwise intrinsically motivating for students. But others—perhaps the drill and practice so essential for developing automaticity of basic skills, or perhaps complex ideas or procedures with which students must initially struggle—may sometimes be less than exciting. Our students are more apt to be motivated to learn relatively unenticing classroom subject matter, and more likely to use effective cognitive processes in learning it, when they see how it relates to their personal lives and professional aspirations (C. Ames, 1992; Brophy & Alleman, 1991; Pintrich et al., 1993). In other words, students learn classroom material more effectively when they have a self-perceived *need to know* that material. Thus, we might illustrate how mathematics plays a role in shopping and budgeting one's allowance, how science facilitates everyday problem solving, and how physical fitness helps one look and feel better. We might show our students how oral and written language skills are critical for making a favorable impression on future employers. We might point out how knowledge of current events and social studies will help them make informed decisions in the voting booth.

Students with learning goals recognize that competence comes only from effort and practice.

In what areas do you have learning goals? In what areas are you interested only in how you appear to others? How is your learning affected by the particular goals you have?

Relate activities to students' present needs and long-term goals.

▪ Experiencing Firsthand
The Doctor's Office

You have just arrived at the doctor's office for your annual physical checkup. The receptionist tells you that the doctor is running late and that you will probably have to wait an hour before you can be seen. As you sit down in the waiting room, you notice six magazines on the coffee table in front of you: *Better Homes and Gardens, National Geographic, Newsweek, People, Popular Mechanics,* and *Sports Illustrated.*

1. Rate each of these magazines in terms of how *interesting* you think its articles would be to you:

	Not at All Interesting	**Somewhat Interesting**	**Very Interesting**
Better Homes and Gardens	____	____	____
National Geographic	____	____	____
Newsweek	____	____	____
People	____	____	____
Popular Mechanics	____	____	____
Sports Illustrated	____	____	____

2. Even though you think that some of the magazines will be more interesting than others, you decide to spend ten minutes reading each one. Estimate how much you think you might *remember* from what you read in each of the six magazines:

	Hardly Anything	**A Moderate Amount**	**Quite a Bit**
Better Homes and Gardens	____	____	____
National Geographic	____	____	____
Newsweek	____	____	____
People	____	____	____
Popular Mechanics	____	____	____
Sports Illustrated	____	____	____

Now compare your two sets of ratings. Chances are, the magazines that you rated highest in interest to you are also the magazines from which you will learn and remember the most.

When students are interested in what they are studying, they are more likely to have positive feelings about their schoolwork, to set learning goals rather than performance goals, to engage in such storage processes as meaningful learning and elaboration, and, ultimately, to learn and remember more (Renninger, Hidi, & Krapp, 1992; Tobias, 1994). In contrast, students who have no interest in their school subjects are apt to approach learning at a rote level, perhaps by reading and rereading with little understanding or by memorizing facts in a word-for-word fashion (Schiefele, 1991b).

Sometimes students' interests reflect long-term, fairly stable predispositions toward certain topics (Alexander & Jetton, 1996); for example, my son Alex was interested in insects, arachnids, and similar creatures from his toddler days until sometime around puberty (at which point, his attention turned to cars and girls). As teachers, we can certainly capitalize on such interests by giving students some flexibility in the topics about which they read and write. Furthermore, we can tie traditional classroom subjects to things that students are naturally curious about; for example, we might explain how we could use latitude and longitude to help us locate the Titanic (Brophy, 1986). Students are often

Relate classroom material to existing student interests.

interested in topics related to people and culture (e.g., disease, violence, holidays), nature (e.g., dinosaurs, weather, the sea), and current events (e.g., television shows, popular music, substance abuse, gangs) (Zahorik, 1994).

On other occasions, we can pique students' interest, at least temporarily, by the activities we develop and the ways we present information. Among other things, we can:

🍎 Pique students' interest through active involvement, novelty, contradictions, and fantasy.

- Provide opportunities for students to get actively involved with the subject matter
- Include variety and novelty in classroom materials or procedures
- Present inconsistent or discrepant information
- Encourage occasional fantasy and make-believe
  (Brophy, 1987; Covington, 1992; Deci, 1992; Hidi & Anderson, 1992; Lepper & Hodell, 1989; Ross, 1988; Wade, 1992; Zahorik, 1994)

To illustrate, here are some specific things we might do:

☐ Can you explain the value of inconsistent or discrepant information using Piaget's concept of *disequilibrium* (see Chapter 2)?

- In a unit on musical instruments, let students experiment with a variety of simple instruments.
- In a lesson about sedimentary, metamorphic, and igneous rocks, give cooperative groups a bag of rocks and have them categorize each one.
- In a lesson about alcoholic beverages, have students role-play being at a party and being tempted to have a beer or wine cooler.
- In a reading group, turn a short story into a play, with each student taking a part.
- In biology, have a classroom debate about the ethical implications of conducting medical research on animals.
- In spelling, occasionally depart from the standard word lists, instead asking students to learn how to spell the names of favorite television shows or classmates' surnames.
- In an aerobics workout in physical education, incorporate steps from swing, hip-hop, or country line dancing.
- In an art class, have students make a mosaic from items they've found on a scavenger hunt around the school building and its grounds.
- In a unit on aerodynamics, have each student make several paper airplanes and then fly them to see which of their designs travels farthest.
- In arithmetic, have students play computer games to improve their automaticity for number facts.
- In history, have students read children's perspectives of historical events (e.g., Anne Frank's diary during World War II, Zlata Filipovic's diary during the Bosnian War).
- In geography, present household objects not found locally and ask students to guess where in the world they might be from.

Students learn more and are more likely to engage in meaningful learning and elaboration when they are interested in what they are learning.

Modeling Interest in the Subject Matter

Our students are more likely to develop an intrinsic motivation to learn classroom material if, as teachers, we model our own enthusiasm for the subject matter and our desire to learn more about it (Deci & Ryan, 1992; Pintrich & Schunk, 1996). For example, we can show students how a topic has enriched our own personal lives. We can let them see how we continue to study the topic ourselves, perhaps by bringing in current magazine articles we have found. We can present our own opinions regarding controversial issues. And we can share our curiosity and puzzlement about unresolved questions (Brophy, 1987; Wlodkowski, 1978; Zahorik, 1994).

Communicating the Belief That Students Want to Learn

Through our statements and actions, we can convey the message that we believe our students are genuinely interested in school subject matter and intrinsically motivated to master it (Brophy, 1987; Hennessey & Amabile, 1987). To illustrate, here is how one teacher conveyed such a message (Brophy, 1986):

> [She] communicated positive expectations routinely by announcing at the beginning of the year that her class was intended to make the students into "social scientists" and by referring back to this idea frequently throughout the year through such comments as "Since you are social scientists, you will recognize that the description of this area as a tropical rain forest has implications about what kinds of crops will grow there," or "Thinking as social scientists, what conclusions might we draw from this information?" (p. 46)

We should definitely *not* communicate the belief that our students will dislike a particular topic or are working only to get good grades (Brophy, 1986).

Model your own interest in the subject matter.

Openly make the assumption that students want *to learn.*

Focusing Students' Attention on Learning Goals

Many common teaching practices promote performance goals rather than learning goals. Grading on a curve, reminding students that they need to get good grades if they want to go to college, displaying grades for everyone to see—all of these strategies, though undoubtedly well intended, encourage students to focus their attention more on "looking good" than on learning. When we instead point out how school subject matter will be useful in the future, encourage students to engage in meaningful learning rather than rote memorization, demonstrate that students are making progress, and acknowledge that effective learning requires exerting effort and making mistakes, we are emphasizing learning goals that will help our students focus more on understanding and mastery of subject matter (C. Ames, 1992; Anderman & Maehr, 1994; Graham & Weiner, 1996; Meece, 1994). Focusing learners' attention on learning goals, especially when those goals relate to learners' own lives, may especially benefit students from diverse ethnic backgrounds and students at risk (Alderman, 1990; Garcia, 1992; Wlodkowski & Ginsberg, 1995).

Encourage students to focus on learning goals.

Yet despite our efforts to promote learning goals rather than performance goals, many of our students will continue to be concerned about making mistakes that cause them to look bad in front of their classmates. Students are motivated not only to attain academic goals but to attain social goals as well; for example, most students want to be accepted and respected by their peers. Let's turn our attention now to this very different side of human motivation.

Social Needs

THINKING ABOUT WHAT YOU KNOW

- How much time do you spend with other people? Do you enjoy being with others a good deal of the time? Or, like Anya, do you prefer to spend much of your time alone?
- How important is it for you to have the recognition and acceptance of your family, teachers, and peers? How often do you do things primarily to win the approval of someone else? How often do you act without concern for what others might think?

INTO THE CLASSROOM: Promoting Intrinsic Motivation to Learn Classroom Subject Matter

Make sure that basic needs have been met.

A teacher notices that one student comes to school chronically hungry and tired. The student admits that he is rarely given breakfast at home or money for lunch at school. Knowing that the student's mother has limited reading and writing skills, the teacher helps the woman fill out an application for the school's free breakfast and lunch program.

Define success as eventual, rather than immediate, mastery of class material, and acknowledge that occasional mistakes are to be expected.

A middle school teacher consoles a student who is disappointed in her mediocre performance on a difficult assignment. "You're a very talented student, and you're probably used to having your schoolwork come easily. But remember, as students move through the grade levels, assignments become increasingly more challenging. With a little more study and practice, I know you'll improve quite a bit."

Encourage self-comparison, rather than comparison with other students.

In January, an elementary school teacher asks his students to write a short story. After reading the stories that students have written, he hands them back to students; he also returns stories that his students wrote in early September. "Do you see how much your writing has improved over the past four months?" he asks. "The stories that you wrote this week are longer and better developed, and you made fewer spelling and grammatical errors."

Enhance students' sense of self-determination regarding classroom assignments and activities.

A science teacher tells her students, "I know you can't always complete your lab reports the same day that you did the lab in class. Let's see whether we can set some reasonable due dates for your reports so that *you* have the time you need to write them and *I* have the time I need to read them and give you feedback before the next lab activity."

Relate classroom material to students' interests.

An elementary school teacher asks students to bring in objects they use to celebrate holidays at home. He incorporates these objects into a lesson on how holiday traditions differ not only from religion to religion but also from family to family.

Communicate your belief that students want to learn.

A junior high school history teacher introduces the next reading assignment this way: "The chapter I've assigned for tonight is an exciting one. As the chapter unfolds, you will see the American colonists become increasingly discontented with British rule. You will also learn how the colonists eventually managed to break free and form the United States of America."

Encourage students to set learning goals.

A Spanish teacher often reminds his students, "The important thing in this class is to learn how to speak Spanish comfortably and with correct pronunciation. We'll all work together until we can communicate easily with one another in Spanish."

To some extent, we are all social creatures: We live, work, and play with our fellow human beings. Yet some people are more socially oriented and more concerned about what others think than other people are. As teachers, we are likely to see a variety of differences among our students' social needs, including their needs for affiliation and approval.

Need for Affiliation

What do all of these students have in common?

> Shaquita and Mary Elizabeth have declared themselves "best friends." They are together most of the time, both in school and out. When one girl gets sick or leaves town for a few days, the other is at a complete loss for something to do.

> Logan goes out for the roller hockey team, not so much because he likes to play roller hockey, but mainly because all his buddies are going out for the team and he doesn't want to be left out.

> Randall is on the telephone almost continually from the minute he arrives home from school until the minute he has to go to bed. He calls one friend to get his history reading assignment, another to set up a double date to the movies, and still another to share the latest gossip about a classmate. Between Randall's numerous calls out, others are calling *him*—perhaps to find out whether he is going to tomorrow night's jazz concert or to solicit his advice for the lovelorn.

These students all have a **need for affiliation:** They desire and actively seek out friendly relationships with others, and they want to be liked and accepted by their classmates. Other students, such as Anya in our opening case study, have a much lower need for affiliation: They may enjoy the company of others once in a while, but they are not as concerned about being accepted, and they may even prefer to be alone on some occasions.

Students' needs for affiliation will be reflected in the choices they make at school (Boyatzis, 1973; French, 1956; Wigfield et al., 1996). For example, students with a low need for affiliation may prefer to work alone, whereas students with a high need for affiliation may prefer to work in small groups. When choosing work partners, students with a low affiliation need are apt to choose classmates whom they believe to be competent at the task to be performed; students with a high affiliation need are apt to choose their friends even if such friends are relatively incompetent. Students with a low need for affiliation are likely to choose a class schedule that meets their own interests and ambitions, whereas students with a high need for affiliation are more likely to choose one that enables them to be with their friends. As you can see, then, a high need for affiliation often interferes with maximal classroom learning and achievement (Urdan & Maehr, 1995; Wentzel & Wigfield, 1998).

As teachers, we cannot ignore the high need for affiliation that many students bring to the classroom. On the contrary, as we plan our daily lessons and classroom activities, we must provide opportunities for students to interact with one another. Ideally, we should find ways to help students learn academic subject matter *and* meet their affiliation needs simultaneously (Wentzel & Wigfield, 1998). Although some classroom objectives may be best accomplished when students work independently, others can be accomplished just as easily (perhaps even more so) when students work together. Group-based activities, such as discussions, debates, role playing, cooperative learning tasks, and competitions among two or more teams of equal ability, all provide the means through which students can satisfy their need for affiliation while simultaneously acquiring new knowledge or skills (Brophy, 1987; Urdan & Maehr, 1995). Such activities may also give students a greater sense of "belongingness"; that is, they may help students feel that they are accepted and liked by their classmates and are valued members of the class. Students who have this sense of belongingness within their classroom are likely to

Provide opportunities for students to interact with one another.

🍎 Show students that you like them, enjoy being with them, and are concerned about their well-being.

☐ Which of Maslow's needs does the concept *need for affiliation* most resemble?

🍎 Give frequent praise to students with a high need for approval.

🍎 Keep students' successes and failures private and confidential unless you have their permission to do otherwise.

exhibit greater interest and self-efficacy with regard to their schoolwork, greater effort in class, and higher academic achievement (Goodenow, 1991).

We must remember, too, that many of our students will want to affiliate not only with their classmates but with us teachers as well. Therefore, we should show our students that we like them, enjoy being with them, and are concerned about their well-being (McKeachie, Lin, Milholland, & Isaacson, 1966; Stipek, 1996). We can communicate our fondness for students in numerous ways—for example, by expressing an interest in their outside activities and accomplishments, providing extra help or support when it is needed, or lending a sympathetic ear. These "caring" messages may be especially important for students from culturally different backgrounds: Such students are more likely to succeed in our classroom if we show interest in their lives and concern for their individual needs (Phelan, Davidson, & Cao, 1991).

Need for Approval

Another social need in which we see individual differences is the **need for approval,** a desire to gain the acceptance and positive judgments of other people (Igoe & Sullivan, 1991; Juvonen & Weiner, 1993; Urdan & Maehr, 1995). Students with a high need for approval are overly concerned with pleasing others and tend to give in easily to group pressure, for fear that they might otherwise be rejected (Crowne & Marlowe, 1964; Wentzel & Wigfield, 1998). Whereas other students might engage in a school task for the pleasure that success at the task brings, students with a high need for approval are likely to engage in the task primarily to please their teacher and will persist at it only to the extent that their teacher praises them for doing so (Harter, 1975; S. C. Rose & Thornburg, 1984).

When students have a high need for approval, we can promote their classroom achievement by praising them frequently for the things they do well. At the same time, we must keep in mind that some students (especially at the secondary level) may be more concerned about gaining the approval of their peers than that of their teacher (Juvonen & Weiner, 1993; Wigfield et al., 1996). If being a high achiever is not the socially acceptable thing to do, many students will prefer that their accomplishments be praised privately rather than publicly. Ultimately, how well our students are accomplishing instructional objectives is no one's business but theirs, their parents', and ours.

Relationships with peers and teachers are, for many students, a source of considerable pleasure and enjoyment. Conversely, difficulties in interpersonal relationships, which may lead to difficulties in satisfying affiliation and approval needs, are often a source of anxiety. Pleasure, enjoyment, anxiety—all of these are examples of feelings, emotions, or what psychologists call *affect,* a topic we turn to now.

Many students have a high need for affiliation: They want and seek out friendly relationships with others.

Role of Affect

When we speak of motivation, it is difficult not to talk about **affect**—the feelings and emotions that an individual brings to bear on a task—at the same time. As just noted, students may have different *affective responses,* depending on whether their needs for affiliation and approval are being satisfied through their relationships with their classmates and teachers. We've seen other instances of how motivation and affect are interrelated as well. For instance, we've discovered that people respond differently to easy tasks—either with feelings of disappointment, on the one hand, or with relief, on the other—depending on whether they have learning goals or performance goals. And we've learned that students who master challenging tasks experience considerable pleasure, satisfaction, and pride in their accomplishments. Affect takes other forms as well; love, excitement, anger, sadness, and guilt are all examples.

Hot Cognition

Experiencing Firsthand
Flying High

As you read each of the following statements, decide whether it evokes positive feelings (e.g., happiness, excitement), negative feelings (e.g., sadness, anger), or no feelings whatsoever. Check the appropriate blank in each case.

	Positive Feelings	Negative Feelings	No Feelings
1. The city of Denver opened DIA, its new international airport, in 1995.	____	____	____
2. In a recent commercial airline crash, ninety passengers and eight crew members lost their lives.	____	____	____
3. A dozen people survived that crash, including a three-month-old infant found in the rear of the plane.	____	____	____
4. The area of an airplane in which food is prepared is called the *galley*.	____	____	____
5. Several major airlines are offering $69 round-trip fares to Acapulco, Mexico.	____	____	____
6. Those $69 fares apply only to those flights leaving at 5:30 in the morning.	____	____	____
7. Some flights between North America and Europe now include two full-course meals.	____	____	____

You probably had little if any emotional reaction to statements 1 (the opening of DIA) and 4 (the definition of *galley*). In contrast, you may have had pleasant feelings when you read statements 3 (the surviving infant) and 5 (the low fares to Acapulco), and unpleasant feelings when you read statements 2 (the high number of fatalities) and 6 (the dreadful departure time for those Acapulco flights). Your response to statement 7 (the two full-course meals) may have been positive, negative, or neutral, depending on your previous experiences with airline cuisine.

Sometimes learning and cognitive processing are emotionally charged—a phenomenon known as **hot cognition** (e.g., Hoffman, 1991; P. H. Miller, 1993). For example, students might get excited when they read about advances in science that could lead to effective treatments of spinal cord injuries, cancer, or AIDS. They may feel sad when they read about the living conditions in certain parts of the world. They will, we hope, get angry when they learn about the atrocities committed against African American slaves in the pre–Civil War days of the United States or against millions of Jewish people during World War II.

Affect is clearly intertwined with learning and cognition. Students are more likely to pay attention to things that evoke strong emotions such as excitement, sadness, or anger (Reisberg & Heuer, 1992). Students who are interested in a topic about which they are reading

Get students
emotionally involved with
classroom subject matter.

(perhaps finding it exciting or upsetting) process information more effectively—for example by engaging in more meaningful learning and visual imagery (Hidi & Anderson, 1992; Tobias, 1994). And students can usually retrieve information with high emotional content more easily than they can recall relatively nonemotional information (Barkley, 1996; Reisberg & Heuer, 1992). In general, then, students will learn and remember more when they become involved in classroom subject matter not only cognitively but emotionally as well.

Problem solving also is easier when students enjoy what they're doing, and successful problem solutions are often accompanied by feelings of excitement, pleasure, and pride (McLeod & Adams, 1989; M. U. Smith, 1991). In contrast, students are likely to feel frustrated and anxious when they fail at an activity, especially if it appears to be an easy one, and they are apt to develop a dislike for what they've been doing (Carver & Scheier, 1990; Stodolsky, Salk, & Glaessner, 1991). Let's look more closely at the effects of anxiety on students' learning and performance.

Anxiety

Imagine that you are enrolled in Professor Josiah S. Carberry's course in advanced psychoceramics. Today is your day to give a half-hour presentation on the topic of psychoceramic califractions. You have read several books and numerous articles on your topic and undoubtedly know more about psychoceramic califractions than anyone else in the room. And you have prepared the note cards for your presentation carefully and meticulously. As you sit in class waiting for your turn to speak, you should be feeling calm and confident. But instead you're a nervous wreck: Your heart is pounding wildly, your palms are sweaty, and your stomach is in a knot. When Professor Carberry calls you to the front of the classroom and you begin to speak, you have trouble remembering the things you wanted to say, and you can't read your note cards because your hands are shaking so much.

It's not as if you *want* to be nervous about speaking in front of your psychoceramics class. Furthermore, you can't think of a single reason why you *should* be nervous. After all, you are an expert on your topic, you know your underwear isn't showing (you double-checked), and your classmates are not the type to giggle or throw rotten tomatoes if you make a mistake. So what's the big deal? What happened to the self-assured student who stood practicing in front of the mirror last night?

You are a victim of **anxiety**: You have a feeling of uneasiness and apprehension about an event because you're not sure what its outcome will be. This feeling is accompanied by a variety of physiological symptoms, including a rapid heartbeat, increased perspiration, and muscular tension (e.g., a "knot" or "butterflies" in the stomach). Anxiety is similar to fear, but different in one important respect: Although we are usually *afraid* of something in particular (a roaring lion, a lightning storm, or the bogeyman under the bed), we usually don't know exactly why we're *anxious*. And it's difficult to deal with anxiety when we can't pinpoint its cause.

State Anxiety Versus Trait Anxiety

Almost everyone is anxious at one time or another. Many students become anxious just before a test that they know is going to be difficult, and most get nervous when they have to give a prepared speech in front of their classmates. Such temporary feelings of anxiety are instances of **state anxiety**. State anxiety is often elicited by a **threat** of some sort—by a situation in which students believe that they have little or no chance of succeeding (Combs, Richards, & Richards, 1976; Csikszentmihalyi & Nakamura, 1989; Deci & Ryan, 1992).

But some students are anxious a good part of the time, even when the situation is not particularly dangerous or threatening. For example, some students may get excessively nervous even before very easy exams, and others may be so anxious about math-

How is the concept of
threat different from the
concept of *challenge*?

ematics that they can't concentrate on the simplest math assignment. When an individual shows a pattern of responding with anxiety even in nonthreatening situations, we have a case of **trait anxiety.** It is our trait-anxious students whose performance is most hampered by anxiety and for whom we may have to go the extra mile to convince them that they can succeed at classroom tasks.

How Anxiety Affects Classroom Performance

Imagine, for a moment, that you are not at all anxious—not even the teeniest bit—about your grade in Professor Carberry's psychoceramics class. Without any anxiety at all, will you study for Carberry's tests? Will you turn in the assigned research papers? If you have no anxiety whatsoever, you might not even buy the textbook or go to class. And you probably won't get a very good grade in your psychoceramics class.

A small amount of anxiety often improves performance: It is **facilitating anxiety.** A little anxiety spurs people into action; for instance, it makes them go to class, read the textbook, do assignments, and study for exams. It also makes them approach their classwork carefully and think about their responses in a thoughtful and reflective fashion (Shipman & Shipman, 1985). Yet too much anxiety often interferes with effective performance: It is **debilitating anxiety.** Excessive anxiety distracts people and interferes with their attention to the task at hand.

At what point does anxiety stop facilitating and begin debilitating performance? In general, very easy tasks—things that students can do almost without thinking (e.g., running)—are facilitated by high levels of anxiety. But more difficult tasks—those that require considerable thought and effort—are best performed with only a small or moderate level of anxiety (Kirkland, 1971; Yerkes & Dodson, 1908). An excessive level of anxiety in difficult situations can interfere with several processes critical for successful learning and performance:

- Paying attention to what needs to be learned
- Processing information effectively (e.g., engaging in meaningful learning, organization, or elaboration)
- Demonstrating skills that have already been learned (Covington, 1992; Eysenck, 1992; I. G. Sarason, 1980)

Anxiety is especially likely to interfere with such processes when a task places heavy demands on working memory or long-term memory—for instance, when a task involves creativity or problem solving (Eysenck, 1992; McLeod & Adams, 1989; Mueller, 1980; S. B. Sarason, 1972; Tobias, 1985).

As you might expect, highly anxious students tend to achieve at levels lower than those at which they are capable of achieving; in other words, they are underachievers (K. T. Hill, 1984; Tobias, 1980). Highly anxious students are often so preoccupied about doing poorly that they simply can't get their minds on what they need to accomplish (Eccles & Wigfield, 1985; Wine, 1980).

Sources of Anxiety

Under what circumstances are our students likely to experience debilitating anxiety? Some common sources of anxiety in school-age children and adolescents are these:

- *Physical appearance*—for example, students may be concerned about being too fat or thin or about reaching puberty either earlier or later than their classmates

Did you previously believe that *any* amount of anxiety is detrimental? If so, have you now revised your thinking about anxiety's effects?

When asking students to perform difficult tasks, encourage them to do their best, but don't make them unnecessarily anxious about their performance.

Difficult tasks are best performed with only a small or moderate level of anxiety.

- *A new situation*—for example, students may experience uncertainty when moving to a new community or making the transition from elementary school to junior high
- *Judgment or evaluation by others*—for example, students may be worried about being liked and accepted by classmates or about receiving a low grade from a teacher
- *Classroom tests*—for example, students may panic at the mere thought of having to take an exam
- *Excessive classroom demands*—for example, students are likely to feel anxious when teachers expect them to learn a great deal of material in a very short amount of time
- *The future*—for example, adolescents may worry about how they will make a living after they graduate from high school
- *Any situation in which self-esteem is threatened*—for example, students may feel anxious when they perform a task awkwardly or incorrectly in front of others (Covington, 1992; Eccles & Midgley, 1989; Eccles & Wigfield, 1985; Harter, 1992; Hembree, 1988; N. J. King & Ollendick, 1989; Phelan et al., 1994; I. G. Sarason, 1980; S. B. Sarason, 1972; Stipek, 1993; Stodolsky et al., 1991; Wigfield & Meece, 1988)

As we discovered in our discussion of behaviorism in Chapter 10, students may also develop feelings of anxiety about particular stimuli through the process of classical conditioning. For instance, a student may become especially anxious about mathematics if mathematics has often been associated with failure and frustration. A student may become anxious about taking classroom tests if previous testing situations have been connected with shame and humiliation. As teachers, then, we must make an exceptional effort to ensure that our students do *not* experience important classroom activities under anxiety-arousing circumstances, at least not on a regular basis.

Keeping Students' Anxiety at a Facilitative Level

As teachers, we probably can't eliminate all sources of anxiety for our students; things such as physical appearance, acceptance by peers, and students' future circumstances are often beyond our control. Nevertheless, we can take several steps to keep students' anxiety about classroom tasks and activities at a productive and facilitative level. For one thing, we can reduce the uncertainty of the classroom environment by communicating our expectations for students' performance clearly and concretely. Highly anxious students, in particular, are likely to perform better in a well-structured classroom, one in which expectations for academic achievement and social behavior are explicitly laid out (Hembree, 1988; Stipek, 1993; Tobias, 1977).

In addition, we must make sure our students have a reasonable chance of success and give them reasons to believe they can succeed with effort; in other words, we must make sure they have high self-efficacy about classroom tasks. Therefore, we are more likely to keep students' anxiety at a facilitative level when we:

Reduce the uncertainty of the classroom environment by clearly communicating expectations for student performance.

Reduce students' debilitating anxiety by enhancing their self-efficacy.

- Set realistic expectations for performance, taking such factors as students' ability and prior performance level into account
- Match the level of instruction to students' cognitive levels and capabilities—for example, by using concrete materials to teach mathematics to students not yet capable of abstract thought
- Teach strategies (e.g., effective study skills) that enhance learning and performance
- Provide supplementary sources of support for learning subject matter (e.g., additional practice or individual tutoring) until mastery is attained
- Provide feedback about specific behaviors, rather than global evaluations of students' performance

INTO THE CLASSROOM: Keeping Students' Anxiety at a Facilitative Level

Be aware of situations in which students are especially likely to be anxious, and take steps to reduce their anxiety on those occasions.

The day before students are scheduled to take a standardized college aptitude test, their teacher consults the test manual. In accordance with the manual's recommendation, she tells her students, "The best way to prepare for the test is to get a good night's sleep and eat a good breakfast in the morning. As you take the test tomorrow, you certainly want to do the very best that you can do. But keep in mind that you aren't expected to know the answers to *all* of the questions. If you find a question you cannot answer, just skip it and go on to the next one."

Develop classroom routines that help create a comfortable and somewhat predictable work environment.

An elementary teacher has a list of classroom "chores"—getting a lunch count, feeding the fish, handing out paper, and so on—that are assigned to individual students on a rotating basis.

Communicate expectations for student performance clearly and concretely.

A high school history teacher begins a unit on World War II this way: "We will focus on the major battles that contributed to the Allied Forces' victory. As you read your textbook, look for reasons why certain battles played a role in the war's final outcome. I will *not* expect you to memorize all the details—dates, generals, numbers of troops, and so on—of every single battle."

Make sure students have a reasonable chance of success and give them reasons to believe that they can succeed with effort.

A science teacher describes an upcoming test: "On the tests you've taken so far this year, you've only had to describe the basic principles of chemistry we've studied. But on the next test, I'm going to ask you to apply what you know about chemistry to new situations and problems. I'll give you several practice test questions this week so you'll know what to expect. I'll also give you two chances to take the test. If you don't do well the first time, we'll work together on your trouble spots, and then you can take the test again."

■ Allow students to correct errors, so that no single mistake is ever a "fatal" one (Brophy, 1986; L. P. McCoy, 1990; I. G. Sarason, 1980; Stipek, 1993; Tryon, 1980)

Obviously, students' past successes and failures will affect the extent to which they feel anxious about classroom tasks. It appears, however, that the effect of any particular success or failure depends on how students *interpret* that outcome. Different students often interpret their successes and failures very differently, as we shall see now in our exploration of attribution theory.

Attributions: Perceived Causes of Success and Failure

Experiencing Firsthand
Carberry and Seville #1

1. Professor Carberry has just returned the first set of exams, scored and graded, in your advanced psychoceramics class. You discover that you've gotten one of

the few high test scores in the class: an A−. Why did you do so well when most of your classmates did poorly? On a piece of paper, jot down several possible explanations as to why you might have received a high grade in Carberry's class.

2. An hour later, you get the results of the first test in Professor Barbara F. Seville's sociocosmetology class, and you learn that you *failed* it! Why did you do so poorly? Jot down several possible reasons for your F on Seville's test.

3. You will be taking second exams in both psychoceramics and sociocosmetology in about three weeks' time. How much will you study for each exam?

Here are some possible explanations for your A− in Carberry's class:

- You studied hard.
- You're smart.
- Psychoceramics just comes naturally to you.
- You were lucky. Carberry asked the right questions; if he'd asked different questions, you might not have done so well.
- Carberry likes you, so he gave you a good grade even though you didn't know what you were talking about.
- All those hours you spent in Carberry's office, asking questions about psycho-ceramics and requesting copies of the articles he's written (which you never actually read), really paid off.

And here are some possibilities as to why you failed the exam in Seville's class:

- You didn't study enough.
- You didn't study the right things.
- You didn't feel well when you took the test.
- The student next to you was sick, and the constant coughing and wheezing distracted you.
- You were unlucky. Seville asked the wrong questions; if she'd asked different questions, you would have done better.
- You're stupid.
- You've never been very good at sociocosmetology.
- It was a bad test: The questions were ambiguous and tested knowledge of trivial facts.
- Seville hates you and gave you a poor grade out of spite.

The amount of time you spend studying for your upcoming exams will, to some extent, depend on how you've interpreted your earlier performances (i.e., your success on Carberry's exam and your failure on Seville's exam). For example, let's consider your A− on Professor Carberry's exam. If you think you did well because you studied hard, you will probably spend a lot of time studying for the second test as well. If you think you did well because you're smart or because you're a whiz at psychoceramics, you may not study quite as much. If you believe that your success was a matter of luck, you may not study much at all, but you may consider wearing your lucky sweater when you take the next exam. And if you think the A− was a function of how much Carberry likes you, you may decide that time spent flattering him is more important than time spent studying.

Now let's consider your failing grade on Professor Seville's exam. Once again, the reasons you identify for your failure will influence the ways in which you prepare for her second exam—if, in fact, you prepare at all. If you believe that you didn't study enough or didn't study the right things, you may spend more time studying the next time. If you think that your poor grade was due to a temporary situation—you were ill, the student sitting next to you distracted you, or Seville asked the wrong questions—then you may study in much the same way as you did before, hoping and praying that you'll do better than before. And if you believe that your failure was due to your stupidity, your ineptitude in sociocosmetology, Seville's dislike of you, or the fact that she writes lousy tests, then you may study even less than you did the first time. After all, what good will it do to study when your poor test performance is beyond your control?

The various causal explanations for success and failure just described are **attributions.** The attributions that people assign to the things that happen to them—their beliefs about *what causes what*—do indeed guide their future behavior. The theoretical examination of these attributions and their influence on behavior is known as **attribution theory** (e.g., Dweck, 1986; Weiner, 1984, 1986, 1994).

Attributions are an example of knowledge construction in action. Students combine new information (in this case, a consequence they've just experienced) with their prior knowledge and beliefs about themselves and the world. They then construct what is, to them, a reasonable interpretation of what happened and why.

Dimensions Underlying Students' Attributions

Our students may form a variety of attributions about the causes of classroom events; they will have beliefs about why they do well or poorly on tests and assignments, why they are popular with their classmates or have trouble making friends, why they are skilled athletes or total klutzes, and so on. They may attribute their school successes and failures to such factors as aptitude or ability (how smart or proficient they are), effort (how hard they tried), other people (how well the teacher taught or how much their classmates like them), task difficulty (how "easy" or "hard" something is), luck, mood, illness, fatigue, or physical appearance (e.g., Schunk, 1990). These various attributions differ from one another in at least three ways—locus, stability, and controllability (Weiner, 1984, 1986)[2]:

1. *Locus ("place"): Internal versus external.* Students sometimes attribute the causes of events to *internal* things—to factors within themselves. Thinking that a good grade is due to your own hard work and believing that a poor grade is due to your lack of ability are examples of internal attributions. At other times, students attribute events to *external* things—to factors outside themselves. Concluding that you received a scholarship because you "lucked out" and interpreting a classmate's scowl as being due to her bad mood (rather than to anything you yourself might have done to deserve it) are examples of external attributions.[3]

2. *Stability: Stable versus unstable.* Sometimes students believe that events are due to *stable* factors—to things that probably won't change much in the near future. For example, if you believe that you do well in science because of your intelligence or that you have trouble making friends because you're overweight, then you are attributing events to stable, relatively unchangeable causes. But sometimes students instead believe that events are the result of *unstable* factors—things that can change from one time to the next. Thinking that winning a tennis game was just a matter of luck and believing that you got a bad test grade because you were tired when you took the test are examples of attributions involving unstable factors.[4]

▲ Intelligence is not necessarily a stable, unchanging characteristic (see Chapter 4), yet many students perceive it to be so (Dweck & Leggett, 1988; Weiner, 1994).

---

[2]Weiner has actually identified five different dimensions of attributions; see Weiner (1984) for more details.

[3]This dimension is sometimes referred to as *locus of control*; however, Weiner (1986) has pointed out that *locus* and *control* are probably two, somewhat different dimensions.

[4]Weiner (1986) has pointed out that people may think of *effort* and *luck* as being either unstable or relatively stable characteristics. In our discussion here, however, we will use both of these terms to refer to a temporary state of affairs.

3. *Controllability: Controllable versus uncontrollable.* On some occasions, students attribute events to *controllable* factors—to things they can influence and change. For example, if you believe that a classmate invited you to his birthday party because you always smile and say nice things to him, and if you think that you probably failed a test simply because you didn't study the right things, then you are attributing these events to controllable factors. On other occasions, students attribute events to *uncontrollable* factors—to things over which they themselves have no influence. For example, if you think that you were chosen for the lead in the school play only because the drama teacher likes you or that you played a lousy game of basketball because you were sick, then you are attributing these events to uncontrollable factors.

Generally speaking, people tend to attribute their successes to internal causes (e.g., high ability, hard work) and their failures to external causes (e.g., luck, behaviors of others) (H. W. Marsh, 1990a; Whitley & Frieze, 1985). By patting themselves on the back for the things they do well and putting the blame elsewhere for poor performance, they are able to maintain high self-esteem (Clifford, 1990; Paris & Byrnes, 1989). Attributions don't always reflect the true state of affairs, however; for example, a student may blame a low test grade on a "tricky" test or an "unfair" teacher when that low grade is really due to the student's own lack of effort or poor study skills (e.g., Horgan, 1990).

If students' attributions regarding the reasons for their failures are inaccurate, and especially if students erroneously attribute their failures to stable and uncontrollable causes, they are unlikely to change their future behaviors in ways that will lead to greater success. Let's look more closely at how students' attributions influence both their thoughts and their behaviors.

🍎 Be on the lookout for inaccurate attributions.

How Attributions Influence Cognition and Behavior

Attributions influence several aspects of cognition and behavior; these are described in the following paragraphs.

Emotional reactions to success and failure. Naturally, students will be happy when they succeed. But they will also have feelings of pride and satisfaction about their successes when they attribute those successes to internal causes—that is, to something they themselves have done. When they instead believe that their successes are due to the actions of another person or to some other outside force, they are apt to feel grateful rather than proud (Weiner, Russell, & Lerman, 1978, 1979). Along a similar vein, students will usually feel a certain amount of sadness after a failure. They will also feel guilty or ashamed if they believe that their failures are due to internal causes—for example, to their own lack of ability or effort. But when they instead believe that their failures are due to external causes—to events and people outside themselves—they are likely to be angry (Weiner et al., 1978, 1979).

Expectations for future success or failure. When students attribute their successes and failures to stable factors, they will expect their future performance to be similar to their current performance. In other words, successful students will anticipate that they will continue to succeed, and failing students will believe that they will always be failures. In contrast, when students attribute their successes and failures to *un*stable factors such as effort or luck, then their current success rate will have less influence on their expectation for future success (Dweck, 1978; Weiner, 1986). The most optimistic students—those who have the highest expectations for future success—are the ones who attribute their successes to stable factors such as innate ability and their failures to unstable factors such as lack of effort or inappropriate strategies (Fennema, 1987; Schunk, 1990; Weiner, 1984).

Here we should note a difference between boys and girls that appears consistently in research studies (Durkin, 1987; Fennema, 1987; Stipek & Gralinski, 1990). Boys are more likely to attribute their successes to a fairly stable ability and their failures to lack of effort, thus having the attitude that *I know I can do this.* But girls show the reverse pattern: They attribute their successes to effort and their failures to lack of ability, believing that *I don't know whether I can keep on doing it, because I'm not very good at this type of thing.* We see this difference between boys and girls even when their previous levels of achievement are the same, and we are especially likely to see it for stereotypically "male" domains such as mathematics or sports (Eccles & Jacobs, 1986; Eccles et al., 1989; Stipek, 1984). As a result, boys set higher expectations for themselves than girls, particularly in traditionally masculine activities.

Expenditure of effort. When students believe that their failures are due to their own lack of effort, they are likely to try harder in future situations and to persist in the face of difficulty (Dweck, 1975; Feather, 1982; Weiner, 1984). But when students instead attribute failure to a lack of innate ability (they couldn't do it even if they tried), they give up easily and sometimes can't even perform tasks they have previously accomplished successfully (Dweck, 1978; Eccles [Parsons], 1983).

Help-seeking behavior. Students who believe that success is a result of their own doing—those who attribute success to internal and controllable causes—are more inclined to engage in behaviors that facilitate future learning. These students are more likely to seek their teacher's assistance if they don't understand course material; they are also more likely to attend extra help sessions when they need them (R. Ames, 1983). In contrast, students who believe that their learning successes and failures are beyond their own control are unlikely to seek the help they need.

Classroom performance. We find consistent correlations between students' attributions and their academic achievement. For example, students who expect to succeed get better grades than students of equal ability who expect to fail (Eccles [Parsons], 1983). Students who expect to succeed are more likely to approach problem-solving tasks in a logical, systematic manner; students who expect to fail are apt to solve problems through random trial and error or memorize problem solutions at a rote, nonmeaningful level (Tyler, 1958).

Future choices. As you might expect, students whose attributions lead them to expect success in a particular subject area are more likely to pursue that area—for example, by enrolling in more courses in the same discipline (Eccles [Parsons], 1984; Stipek & Gralinski, 1990; Weiner, 1986). Students who believe that their chances for future success in an activity are slim will avoid that activity whenever they can. Naturally, when students don't continue to pursue an activity, they can't possibly get better at it.

Self-efficacy. Young children, especially those in kindergarten and first grade, tend to believe that they can do well in school if they expend a reasonable amount of effort (Covington, 1992; Dweck & Elliott, 1983). As students get older, many of them begin to attribute their successes and failures to inherited ability—in other words, to something they perceive to be fairly stable and beyond their control (Covington, 1992; Nicholls, 1990). If these students are usually successful at school tasks, then they will have high self-efficacy about such tasks. But if, instead, they experience frequent failure with their schoolwork, and especially if they attribute this failure to low ability rather than to lack of effort or to poor study strategies, they may develop low self-efficacy concerning their competence in academic subjects (Dweck, 1986; Eccles [Parsons], 1983; Schunk, 1990). Secondary students are particularly discouraged by their failure experiences, as are students with a history of learning problems (Eccles & Wigfield, 1985; Pressley, Borkowski, & Schneider, 1987; Stipek & Gralinski, 1990).

Why do different students attribute the same events to different causes? For instance, why does one student believe that a failure is merely a temporary setback due to her own

Have you observed this difference in the males and females you know? Can you think of individuals who are exceptions to the pattern?

Older students and those with a history of learning problems are more likely to attribute their failures to a lack of innate ability. Why might this be so?

lack of effort, whereas another student believes that the failure is due to her lack of ability and so an ominous sign of failures to come, and still another believes that the same failure is the result of the teacher's capricious and unpredictable actions? By looking at factors affecting the development of different attributions, we can identify ways in which to help our students form more productive and optimistic interpretations of their successes and failures.

Factors Influencing the Development of Attributions

Researchers have identified at least four factors that seem to influence the attributions that students form:

- The pattern of past successes and failures
- The degree to which successes and failures have been followed by reinforcement or punishment
- Adults' expectations for students' future performance
- Adults' messages regarding their own attributions for students' successes and failures

These factors are reflected in the four conditions for promoting productive attributions that are described in Table 12–2. Let's look more closely at each factor and its implications.

Past Successes and Failures

Students' attributions are partly the result of their previous success and failure experiences (Covington, 1987; Hong, Chiu, & Dweck, 1995; Klein, 1990). Students who usually succeed when they give a task their best shot are likely to believe that success is due to internal factors such as effort or high ability. Those who frequently fail despite their best efforts are likely to believe that success is due to something beyond their control—perhaps to an ability they don't possess or to such external factors as luck or a teacher's arbitrary judgment. Here we find yet another reason to promote student success on a regular basis: In doing so, we also promote more internal, and thus more productive, attributions.

When we know that our students have high self-efficacy about the subject matter in question, we may occasionally want to give them a series of tasks that they can perform successfully only if they exert considerable time and mental effort. In doing so, we can promote **learned industriousness**: They will begin to realize that they can succeed at some tasks only with effort, persistence, and well-chosen strategies (Eisenberger, 1992; Winne, 1995).

Reinforcement and Punishment

Generally speaking, children are more likely to attribute events to internal, controllable causes when adults reinforce their successes but don't punish their failures. Conversely, children are more likely to make external attributions when adults punish failures and ignore successes (Katkovsky, Crandall, & Good, 1967). It appears that our students will be more apt to accept responsibility for their failures if, as teachers, we don't make a big deal out of them.

As we noted in our discussion of behaviorism in Chapter 10, however, there may be times when some form of mild punishment may be necessary for discouraging behaviors that seriously interfere with classroom learning. On such occasions, we must make response-consequence contingencies clear—for example, by describing unacceptable behaviors in advance and by using punishment in a consistent, predictable fashion. In the process, we help students learn that their *own behaviors* lead to desirable and undesirable consequences and that they can therefore influence the events that occur by changing how they behave. Hence, we help them develop internal attributions regarding the consequences they experience and a greater sense of control over classroom events.

Facilitate student success as one way of promoting internal attributions.

How might learned industriousness be related to students' epistemological beliefs (see Chapter 8)?

Reinforce students' successes, but don't make a big deal of their failures.

Make response-consequence contingencies clear.

Conditions That Promote Productive Student Attributions

CONDITION	EDUCATIONAL IMPLICATION	EXAMPLE
A history of success on tasks when sufficient effort has been exerted	Scaffold students' attempts to master classroom subject matter so that they experience success far more often than failure.	When teaching long division, first give students simple problems that enable them to practice the procedure. As they show increasing proficiency, increase the difficulty of future problems gradually enough that students continue to carry out the division process successfully.
Reinforcement for success, but little if any punishment for failure	Provide extrinsic reinforcers for success if students have little intrinsic motivation to learn. Encourage students to use their mistakes to help themselves improve.	When high school students use a computer spreadsheet correctly, show pleasure and approval. When students obtain erroneous results with their spreadsheets, assign a cooperative group activity in which each group tries to determine what procedural errors might have led to each set of results.
High expectations for students' performance	Aim high in terms of what you want to accomplish during the school year and encourage your students to do likewise.	When students express their apprehension about a challenging writing assignment, assure them that you will help them develop the skills they need to complete the assignment successfully.
Messages that attribute students' successes and failures to internal and primarily controllable factors	Interpret students' successes as being partly the result of controllable factors such as effort and effective strategies and partly the result of a relatively long-term and stable ability. Interpret students' failures as being primarily the result of controllable and changeable factors.	When a soccer team loses its first match of the season by several points, announce that upcoming practices will focus on developing a more aggressive offense. When the team wins its next match two weeks later, say something like this: "See what a difference good strategies can make? I think you have the ability to make the conference playoffs this year. Let's shoot for them, OK?"

Adults' Expectations

Parents and teachers communicate their expectations for students' performance—whether high or low—in a variety of subtle ways. For example, teachers who have high expectations for students' performance are likely to:

- Teach more material
- Teach more difficult material
- Insist on high levels of achievement
- Give students more opportunities to respond to questions

Teachers who hold high expectations for their students are more likely to give specific feedback about the strengths and weaknesses of students' responses.

- Rephrase questions when students are having trouble answering them
- Give specific feedback about the strengths and weaknesses of students' responses

▲ Minority students with a history of academic failure are especially likely to be the recipients of such low-ability signals (Graham, 1990).

In contrast, teachers who hold low expectations for their students often:

- Give students more assistance on tasks than they really need
- Accept poor performance
- Criticize incorrect answers to questions
- Overlook good performance when it occurs
- Fail to encourage students to try new and challenging tasks (Brophy & Good, 1970; H. M. Cooper, 1979; Graham, 1991; Graham & Barker, 1990; M. J. Harris & Rosenthal, 1985; Schunk, 1989b)

🍎 Reflect reasonably high expectations for student performance in your behaviors toward students.

To some extent, parents' and teachers' expectations for students are related to students' past performances. Yet even when several students all have the same history of success and failure, adults may hold different expectations for each of these students (perhaps because of differences in students' classroom behavior, socioeconomic status, or gender), and such expectations, in turn, lead to different student attributions and varying levels of achievement (Brophy & Good, 1970; Eccles & Wigfield, 1985; D. K. Yee & Eccles, 1988). For example, when teachers communicate their belief that students are incapable of mastering subject matter, those students are likely to attribute their failures to low ability and may therefore conclude that there is little to be gained by trying harder. Furthermore, as we discovered in Chapter 4, when teachers expect students *not* to do well, students perform at lower levels than they would otherwise—a self-fulfilling prophecy.

Adults' Messages Regarding Attributions

Once students have either succeeded or failed in an activity, the adults around them may interpret that performance in a variety of ways. Consider the following adult interpretations of a student's success:

- "You did it! You're so smart!"
- "That's wonderful. Your hard work has really paid off, hasn't it?"
- "You've done very well. It's clear that you really know how to study."
- "Terrific! This is certainly your lucky day!"

And now consider these interpretations of a student's failure:

- "Hmmm, maybe this just isn't something you're good at. Perhaps we should try a different activity."
- "Why don't you practice a little more and then try again?"
- "Let's see whether we can come up with some study strategies that might work better for you."
- "Maybe you're just having a bad day."

All of these comments are presumably intended to make a student feel good. But notice the different attributions they imply. In some cases, the student's success or failure is attributed to uncontrollable ability—that is, to being smart or not "good at" something. In other cases, success or failure is attributed to controllable (and therefore changeable) student behaviors—that is, to hard work or lack of practice, or to the use of effective or ineffective study strategies. In still other cases, the student's success is attributed to external, uncontrollable causes—that is, to a lucky break or a bad day. Students' attributions for their own successes and failures are often similar to the attributions that parents and teachers assign to those successes and failures (Lueptow, 1984; Parsons, Adler, & Kaczala, 1982; Schunk, 1982; D. K. Yee & Eccles, 1988).

As teachers, we must be careful about the attributions we assign to student performance. Probably the optimal state of affairs is that we attribute success partly to a relatively stable ability (thus promoting optimism about future success) and partly to such controllable factors as effort and learning strategies (thereby underscoring the fact that continued success will only come as a result of hard work). When considering possible causes for failure, however, we should focus primarily on factors that are internal, unstable, and controllable; thus, attributions for failures should focus on effort and learning strategies, rather than on low ability (which students are likely to believe is stable and uncontrollable) or external factors.

We can communicate appropriate attributions and optimistic expectations for student performance through statements such as these:

- "You've done very well. Obviously you're good at this, and you've been trying very hard to get better."
- "Your project shows a lot of talent and a lot of hard work."
- "The more you practice, the better you will get."
- "Perhaps you need to study a little bit more next time. And let me give you some suggestions on how you might study a little differently, too."

Studies have shown that when students' failures are consistently attributed to ineffective learning strategies or a lack of effort, rather than to low ability or uncontrollable external factors, and when new strategies or increased effort *do* in fact produce success, then students work harder, persist longer in the face of failure, and seek help when they need it (Dweck & Elliott, 1983; Eccles & Wigfield, 1985; Graham, 1991). Yet we must be careful when we attribute either success or failure to a student's effort, as we shall see now.

When attributions to effort can backfire. Although attributions to effort are often beneficial, there are at least two occasions when such attributions can actually be counterproductive. To see what I mean, try the next exercise.

How are teacher expectations and teacher attributions likely to be related? For example, if a teacher expects a student to fail, how is he or she likely to interpret a successful performance? How is a teacher who expects a student to succeed likely to interpret a failure?

Attribute students' successes to a combination of high ability and controllable factors such as effort and learning strategies; attribute their failures solely to factors that are controllable and easily changed.

▣ Experiencing Firsthand
Carberry and Seville #2

1. Imagine that Professor Carberry wants you to learn to spell the word *psychoceramics* correctly. He gives you ten minutes of intensive training in the spelling of the word. He then praises you profusely when you are able to spell it correctly. In which of the following ways would you be most likely to respond?

   a. You are delighted that he approves of your performance.

   b. You proudly show him that you've also learned how to spell *sociocosmetology.*

   c. You wonder, "Hey, is this all he thinks I can do?"

2. Now imagine that you drop by Professor Seville's office to find out why you did so poorly on her sociocosmetology exam. Professor Seville is warm and supportive, suggesting that you simply try harder next time. But the fact is, you tried as hard as you could the *first* time. Which one of the following conclusions would you be most likely to draw?

   a. You need to try even harder next time.

   b. You need to exert the same amount of effort the next time and just keep your fingers crossed that you'll make some lucky guesses.

   c. Perhaps you just weren't meant to be a sociocosmetologist.

Research results tell us that you probably answered *c* to both questions. Let's first consider the situation in which Carberry spent ten minutes teaching you how to spell *psychoceramics.* When students succeed at a very easy task and are then praised for their effort, they may get the unintended message that their teacher doesn't have much confidence in their ability (Graham, 1991; Stipek, 1996). Attributing students' successes to effort is likely to be beneficial only when students have, in fact, exerted a great deal of effort.

And now consider the second scenario, the one in which Seville encouraged you to try harder even though you had already studied as hard as you could for the first exam. When students fail at a task at which they've expended a great deal of effort and are then told that they didn't try hard enough, they are likely to conclude that they simply don't have the ability to perform the task successfully (Curtis & Graham, 1991; Stipek, 1996). Attributing students' failures to a lack of effort is likely to be helpful only when they really haven't given classroom tasks their best shot.

Rather than attribute the failure of hardworking students to lack of effort, we should probably attribute it to a lack of effective strategies (Curtis & Graham, 1991; Pressley, Borkowski, & Schneider, 1987). As we discovered in our discussion of metacognition in Chapter 8, students can and do acquire more effective learning and study strategies over time, especially when they are specifically trained to use these strategies. By teaching effective strategies, not only do we promote our students' academic success, but we also promote their beliefs that they can control that success (C. E. Weinstein, Hagen, & Meyer, 1991).

🍎 Attribute students' successes to effort only when they have actually exerted that effort.

🍎 Attribute students' failures to a lack of effort only when they *haven't* exerted sufficient effort.

🍎 Attribute the failures of hardworking students to a lack of effective strategies and then help them acquire such strategies.

For reasons we've just identified, different students may interpret the same events in very different ways. Over time, students gradually develop predictable patterns of attributions and expectations for their future performance. Some remain optimistic, confident that they can master new tasks and succeed in a variety of endeavors. But others, either unsure of their own chances for success or else convinced that they *can't* succeed, begin to display a growing sense of futility. Psychologists have characterized this difference among students as being one of a *mastery orientation* versus *learned helplessness.*

Mastery Orientation Versus Learned Helplessness

Consider these two students, keeping in mind that *their actual academic ability is the same:*

> Jared is an enthusiastic, energetic learner. He seems to enjoy working hard at school activities and takes obvious pleasure in doing well. He is always looking for a challenge and especially likes to solve the "brain teaser" problems that his teacher assigns as extra credit work each day. He can't always solve the problems, but he takes failure in stride and is eager for more problems the following day.
>
> Jerry is an anxious, fidgety student. He doesn't seem to have much confidence in his ability to accomplish school tasks successfully. In fact, he is always underestimating what he can do: Even when he has succeeded, he doubts that he can do it again. He seems to prefer filling out drill-and-practice worksheets that help him practice skills he's already mastered, rather than attempting new tasks and problems. As for those daily brain teasers, he sometimes takes a stab at them, but he gives up quickly if the answer isn't obvious.

Attributions play a significant role in the approach that students take toward the activities and challenges they encounter every day in the classroom. Students like Jared attribute their accomplishments to their own abilities and efforts: They have an *I can do it* attitude known as a **mastery orientation.** Students like Jerry instead attribute successes to outside and uncontrollable factors and believe that their failures reflect a lack of ability: They have an *I can't do it* attitude known as **learned helplessness.** Obviously, students with a mastery orientation have a higher sense of self-efficacy about classroom tasks than do students with learned helplessness.

Even though students with a mastery orientation and those with learned helplessness may have equal ability initially, those with a mastery orientation behave in ways that lead to higher achievement over the long run: They set ambitious goals, seek challenging situations, and persist in the face of failure. Students feeling learned helplessness behave very differently: Because they underestimate their own ability, they set goals they can easily accomplish, avoid the challenges likely to maximize their learning and growth, and respond to failure in counterproductive ways that almost guarantee future failure as well. These and other differences between students with a mastery orientation and those with learned helplessness are presented in Table 12–3.

If you compare Table 12–3 with Table 12–1 (see p. 483), you should notice several parallels between students with a mastery orientation and those with learning goals; for example, both groups prefer challenges rather than easy tasks, persist in the face of difficulty, and have a healthy attitude about mistakes and failure. And in fact, we can reasonably guess that students with a mastery orientation, because they have higher self-efficacy about classroom tasks, will be those most likely to have learning goals rather than performance goals. As noted earlier in the chapter, high self-efficacy is one of two essential conditions for intrinsic motivation.

Many of the strategies suggested for enhancing self-efficacy—giving competence-promoting feedback, encouraging self-comparison rather than comparison with others, providing a realistic perspective as to what constitutes success, and so on—should promote a mastery orientation as well. Nevertheless, even when students are highly motivated to learn, they cannot always learn on their own. They should have a variety of resources to which they can turn in times of difficulty—their teacher, of course, and possibly such additional resources as supplementary readings, extra practice sheets, self-instructional computer programs, or outside tutoring (perhaps by classmates, older students, or community volunteers). Our students must have sufficient academic support to believe that *I can do this if I really want to.*

▲ Think of this distinction as a continuum of individual differences rather than a complete dichotomy. You might also look at it as a difference between *optimists* and *pessimists* (C. Peterson, 1990; Seligman, 1991).

🍎 Provide the academic support necessary to help students discover that they can learn successfully.

Students with a Mastery Orientation Versus Learned Helplessness

STUDENTS WITH A MASTERY ORIENTATION	STUDENTS WITH LEARNED HELPLESSNESS
Have self-confidence	Lack self-confidence
Set high goals for themselves	Set low, easy goals for themselves
Prefer new and challenging tasks	Prefer easy tasks and tasks they have already completed successfully
Strive for success	Try to avoid failure
Believe that prior successes indicate high ability and future success	Don't see prior successes as indicative of ability and future success; *do* see prior failures as an indication of future failure
Accurately estimate the number of prior successes	Underestimate prior successes; may even *forget* about them
View failure as a challenge to be met	Define themselves as a "failure" when they fail
Persist when facing difficulty; try to determine the source of difficulty; seek assistance if needed	Become anxious and discouraged when facing difficulty; give up quickly
Increase effort and concentration after failure	Decrease effort and concentration after failure; may withdraw from the task
Take pride in their accomplishments	Don't take pride in their accomplishments because they don't believe that they *caused* them
Achieve at higher levels	Achieve at lower levels

Sources: Diener & Dweck, 1978; Dweck, 1975, 1986; Dweck & Licht, 1980; Graham, 1989; D. K. Meyer, Turner, & Spencer, 1994; C. Peterson, 1990; C. Peterson & Barrett, 1987; Seligman, 1991; C. J. Wood, Schau, & Fiedler, 1990.

Considering Diversity in Student Motivation

We've encountered numerous instances of student diversity in our discussion of motivation. For instance, we've discovered that students are often very different in terms of their interests, their needs for affiliation and approval, and the degree to which they experience anxiety about classroom tasks. The extent to which our students have high self-efficacy, learning goals, internal attributions, and a mastery orientation will influence the extent to which they prefer challenges, persist at difficult tasks, and take failure in stride. Let's now consider some of the specific ways in which students' motivation is likely to vary as a function of age, culture, gender, socioeconomic background, and special educational needs.

Age Differences

We're apt to see several developmental differences in student motivation. For one thing, whereas young children often want to gain their teachers' approval, older ones are typically more interested in gaining the approval of their peers (Juvonen & Weiner, 1993;

INTO THE CLASSROOM: Promoting Productive Attributions

Communicate high expectations for student performance.

In September, a high school teacher tells his class, "Next spring, I will ask you to write a fifteen-page research paper. Fifteen pages may seem like a lot now, but in the next few months we will work on the various skills you will need to research and write your paper. By April, fifteen pages won't seem like a big deal at all!"

Attribute students' successes to a combination of high ability and controllable factors such as effort and learning strategies.

In a unit on basketball, a physical education teacher tells his class, "From what I've seen so far, you all have the capability to play a good game of basketball. And it appears that many of you have been practicing basketball regularly after school."

Attribute students' successes to effort only when they have actually exerted that effort.

A teacher observes that his students complete a particular assignment more quickly and easily than he expected. He briefly acknowledges their success and then moves on to a more challenging task.

Attribute students' failures to factors that are controllable and easily changed.

A high school student seeks his teacher's advice as to how he might do better in her class. "I know you can do better than you are, Frank," she replies. "I'm wondering if part of the problem might be that, with your part-time job and all your extracurricular activities, you just don't have enough time to study. Let's sit down before school tomorrow and look at what you're doing to prepare for class. I'm sure we can figure out what you might do to get a better handle on class material."

When students fail despite obvious effort, attribute their failures to a lack of effective strategies and then help them acquire such strategies.

A student in an advanced science class is having difficulty on the teacher's challenging weekly quizzes. She works diligently on her science every night and attends the after-school help sessions her teacher offers on Thursdays, yet to no avail. Her teacher observes that the student is trying to learn the material at a rote level—an ineffective strategy for answering the higher-level questions the quizzes typically ask—and helps the student develop strategies that promote more meaningful learning.

Urdan & Maehr, 1995). As teachers, we must be sensitive to the fact that students' friends and classmates sometimes disapprove of high academic achievement; for example, we must be careful that we don't draw unnecessary public attention to students' classroom successes, especially at the secondary level.

A second noteworthy developmental change is that students often become less intrinsically motivated, and more *ex*trinsically motivated, as they progress through the school years (Harter, 1992). Learning goals may go by the wayside as performance goals become more prevalent, and as a result, students will begin to exhibit a preference for easy rather than challenging tasks (Harter, 1992; Igoe & Sullivan, 1991). Increasingly, students will value activities that they believe will have usefulness for them in their personal and professional lives, and subjects that are not directly applicable will decrease in popularity (Wigfield, 1994).

Emphasize the value of the knowledge and skills students are learning, especially at the secondary level.

Furthermore, as noted earlier, there are developmental changes in the ways that students interpret success. Elementary students tend to attribute their successes to effort and hard work; therefore, they are likely to be relatively optimistic about their chances for success and to work harder when they fail. By adolescence, however, students attribute success and failure more to an ability that is fairly stable and uncontrollable. Effort becomes a sign of low ability; if they have to exert a great deal of effort when performing classroom tasks, they may conclude that they don't have "what it takes" to be successful and so may develop a sense of learned helplessness (Nicholls, 1990; Paris & Cunningham, 1996). If, as teachers, we praise adolescents for trying hard, we may inadvertently communicate the message that they have little "natural" ability (Nicholls, 1984). As teachers, we can certainly praise elementary students for effort ("You tried really hard!"), but for secondary students, we may want to make reference to ability ("You're really good at this!") as well as to effort.

🍎 At the elementary level, attribute success primarily to effort; at the secondary level, attribute it to ability as well as effort.

Whereas young children are likely to attribute their successes to hard work, adolescents are more likely to attribute success to a relatively stable ability over which they have little or no control.

Ethnic Differences

We will sometimes see different motivational patterns in students from different ethnic backgrounds. Some students from ethnic minority groups may feel under more pressure to perform well in school and so may be more prone to debilitating test anxiety; for instance, this is often the case for students of Asian American families (C. A. Grant & Gomez, 1996; Pang, 1995). With such students, we may need to take extra precautions that classroom tests and other evaluative situations are as relaxed and nonthreatening as we can possibly make them.

Furthermore, students from some ethnic groups (e.g., those from many Native American and Hispanic communities) have especially strong loyalties to their family and may have been raised to achieve for their community, rather than just for themselves as individuals (see Chapter 4). Motivating statements such as "Think how proud your family will be!" and "If you go to college and get a good education, you can really help your community!" are likely to be especially effective for such students (e.g., Abi-Nader, 1993; Suina & Smolkin, 1994).

🍎 Point out the value of students' school achievement for their families and communities.

🍎 Take extra measures to boost the self-efficacy of students from minority backgrounds.

Finally, students' cultural backgrounds can influence their attributions. For instance, students from Asian backgrounds are more likely to attribute to unstable factors—effort in the case of academic achievement, and temporary situational factors in the case of appropriate or inappropriate behaviors—than students brought up in mainstream Western culture (Lillard, 1997; Peak, 1993). And African American students are more likely to develop a sense of learned helplessness about their ability to achieve academic success (Graham, 1989; Holliday, 1985). To some extent, racial prejudice may contribute to the development of learned helplessness: Some students may begin to believe that, because of the color of their skin, they have little chance of success no matter *what* they do (Sue & Chin, 1983).

Gender Differences

Although in some respects males and females are more similar than they were two or three decades ago (see Chapter 4), research continues to show gender differences in motivation. For example, females are more likely than males to have a high need for affiliation (Block, 1983). Females are also more concerned about doing well in school: They work harder on assignments, earn higher grades, and are more likely to graduate from high school (Halpern, 1992; McCall, 1994). We will typically find more boys than girls among our "underachieving" students—those who are not achieving at levels commensurate with their ability (McCall, 1994).

Although females, on average, have higher school achievement, males have higher long-term aspirations for themselves (e.g., Durkin, 1995). Such high aspirations may develop, in part, because males interpret their successes and failures in ways that yield greater optimism about what they are ultimately capable of accomplishing; for instance, girls are more likely to be discouraged by their failures (Dweck, 1986). Females are making some headway in this area; for example, girls growing up now are more likely to have career plans than girls who, like me, grew up in the 1950s and 1960s (e.g., A. J. C. King, 1989). Nevertheless, many of the girls in our classrooms, especially those in some ethnic groups, will limit their aspirations to traditional "female" roles (Durkin, 1995; Olneck, 1995; S. M. Taylor, 1994).

As we work to encourage high levels of motivation in all of our students, we may want to focus our efforts in somewhat different directions for males and females. For boys, we may need to stress the relationship of high classroom achievement to their own long-term goals. For girls, we may need to provide extra encouragement to consider a wide variety of career options, including many that they previously have ruled out as being options only for their male counterparts.

Help boys see the relationship between their classroom performance and their long-term goals. Encourage girls to consider a wide range of career options.

Socioeconomic Differences

As we learned in Chapter 4, students from lower-income families are among those most likely to be at risk for failing and dropping out of school. A pattern of failure may start quite early for many lower-income students, especially if they have not had the early experiences (e.g., exposure to children's literature, visits to zoos and museums) upon which school learning often builds.

One critical strategy for motivating students from lower socioeconomic backgrounds is to make school activities relevant to their own lives and experiences (P. A. Alexander et al., 1994; Knapp et al., 1990; Tobias, 1994; Wlodkowski & Ginsberg, 1995). As we present new material, we should draw on the knowledge that the students are likely to have, thereby increasing the likelihood of meaningful learning; for instance, we might keep in mind that these students are more likely to have encountered dogs and cats than elephants and zebras, more likely to have seen a grocery store or city park than a dairy farm or airport. We should also relate classroom tasks and activities to the specific, day-to-day needs and interests of our students; for example, we should teach academic subject matter within the context of authentic activities as often as we can. And we can occasionally solicit students' ideas about issues and questions that they'd like to study in class.

When working with students from lower socioeconomic backgrounds, we should also remember the two essential conditions for intrinsic motivation: self-efficacy and self-determination. We are most likely to enhance students' self-efficacy if we have high (yet realistic) expectations for their performance and if we provide the academic support through which they can meet those expectations (Brophy & Evertson, 1976). And when we give students a sense of self-determination and control over their lives—for example, when we involve them in classroom decision making and when we teach them effective ways of bringing about change in their local communities—they will attend school more regularly and achieve at higher levels (deCharms, 1972; NCSS Task Force on Ethnic Studies Curriculum Guidelines, 1992).

Remember that relevance is especially important for motivating students from lower-income families.

Accommodating Students with Special Needs

Our students with special educational needs will typically be among those who show the greatest diversity in motivation to succeed in the classroom. Some students who are gifted may have high intrinsic motivation to learn classroom subject matter, yet they may become easily bored if class activities don't challenge their abilities (Friedel, 1993; Turnbull et al.,

1999). Students with specific or general academic difficulties (e.g., those with learning disabilities, those with mental retardation) may show signs of learned helplessness with regard to classroom tasks, especially if their past efforts have repeatedly met with failure (Deshler & Schumaker, 1988; Jacobsen, Lowery, & DuCette, 1986; Seligman, 1975). Students who have difficulty getting along with their classmates (e.g., those with emotional and behavioral disorders) may inappropriately attribute their social failures to factors beyond their control (Heward, 1996). Table 12–4 presents a summary of these and other motivational patterns in students with special needs.

TABLE 12.4   **STUDENTS IN INCLUSIVE SETTINGS**

Promoting Motivation in Students with Special Educational Needs

STUDENTS WITH SPECIAL NEEDS	CHARACTERISTICS THAT THESE STUDENTS MAY EXHIBIT	CLASSROOM STRATEGIES THAT MAY BE BENEFICIAL FOR THESE STUDENTS
Students with specific cognitive or academic difficulties	Less intrinsic motivation to succeed at academic tasks High test anxiety Tendency to attribute poor achievement to low ability rather than to more controllable factors; tendency to attribute successes to external causes (e.g., luck) Tendency to give up easily; learned helplessness regarding performance on some classroom tasks Reluctance of some students to ask questions or seek assistance, especially at the secondary level	Use extrinsic reinforcers to encourage students' classroom effort and achievement; gradually phase them out as students show signs of intrinsic motivation. Establish challenging yet realistic goals for achievement. Minimize anxiety-arousing statements and procedures during testing situations (see Chapter 14 for ideas). Teach effective learning strategies and encourage students to attribute their successes to such strategies. Encourage students to develop more productive attributions regarding their achievement difficulties (e.g., attributing failures to insufficient effort or ineffective strategies). Offer assistance when you think that students may really need it, but refrain from offering help when you know that students are capable of succeeding on their own.
Students with social or behavioral problems	Motivation to succeed in the classroom (although such motivation may be difficult to detect because of students' outward behaviors) Debilitating anxiety in new or unpredictable situations (for students with autism) A greater desire for power over classmates than for affiliation with them (for some students with emotional or behavioral disorders) Tendency to interpret praise as an attempt to control them (when students exhibit defiance or oppositional behavior) Tendency to attribute negative consequences to uncontrollable factors (things just "happen")	Provide choices about academic activities as a way of decreasing inappropriate classroom behavior. Create a structured and predictable classroom environment, especially for students with autism. Relate the curriculum to specific needs and interests that students may have. Help students discover the benefits of interacting appropriately with classmates. Teach behaviors that lead to desired consequences; stress cause-effect relationships between actions and outcomes. When students are concerned about control issues, use subtle reinforcers (e.g., leave notes describing productive behaviors) rather than more obvious and seemingly controlling ones.

continued

STUDENTS WITH SPECIAL NEEDS	CHARACTERISTICS THAT THESE STUDENTS MAY EXHIBIT	CLASSROOM STRATEGIES THAT MAY BE BENEFICIAL FOR THESE STUDENTS
Students with general delays in cognitive and social functioning	Less intrinsic motivation than peers; responsiveness to extrinsic motivators Tendency to attribute poor achievement to low ability or to external sources rather than to more controllable factors; in some situations, a sense of learned helplessness Tendency to give up easily in the face of difficulty	Set specific and realistic goals for performance. Use extrinsic reinforcers to encourage productive behaviors; gradually phase them out as students show signs of intrinsic motivation. Help students see the relationship between their own actions and the consequences that result. Reinforce persistence as well as success.
Students with physical or sensory challenges	Low sense of self-determination regarding the course that their lives are taking	Give students some choices within the curriculum. Teach self-regulating behaviors and independence skills.
Students with advanced cognitive development	High intrinsic motivation (e.g., curiosity, motivation to learn) Boredom when classroom tasks don't challenge students' abilities A variety of interests Strong commitment to specific tasks Persistence in the face of failure (although some may give up easily if they aren't accustomed to failure)	Encourage students to set high goals, but without expecting perfection. Provide opportunities for students to pursue complex tasks and activities over an extended period of time. Give assignments that students find stimulating and challenging. Promote learned industriousness by assigning a series of tasks that require considerable effort and persistence.

Sources: T. Bryan, 1991; M. Carr & Borkowski, 1989; B. Clark, 1997; Deshler & Schumaker, 1988; Duchardt, Deshler, & Schumaker, 1995; Dunlap et al., 1994; Dweck, 1986; E. S. Ellis & Friend, 1991; Foster-Johnson, Ferro, & Dunlap, 1994; Friedel, 1993; Good & Brophy, 1994; Heward, 1996; Jacobsen et al., 1986; Knowlton, 1995; Mercer, 1991; Morgan & Jenson, 1988; Patrick, 1997; Patton et al., 1987, 1990; Phillips, Pitcher, Worsham, & Miller, 1980; Piirto, 1994; S. Powell & Nelson, 1997; L. E. Powers et al., 1996; Renzulli, 1978; Sanborn, 1979; Sands & Wehmeyer, 1996; G. F. Schultz & Switzky, 1990; Seligman, 1975; Stipek, 1993; Turnbull et al., 1999; Winne, 1995; Winner, 1997.

Note: Compiled with the assistance of Dr. Margie Garanzini-Daiber and Dr. Margaret Cohen, University of Missouri—St. Louis.

In recent years, special educators have become especially concerned about the need for students with disabilities to develop a sense of self-determination—to believe that they have some control over the direction that their lives take (Sands & Wehmeyer, 1996). Many of these students, especially those with physical or sensory challenges, may live in sheltered environments in which other people are calling most of the shots (Wehmeyer, 1996). We can do many simple things to enhance the self-determination that these students feel; for instance, we can let them make choices and set some of their own goals, help them develop skills that enable them to gain increasing independence, and teach the many self-regulation strategies that we identified in Chapter 11 (Abery & Zajac, 1996; L. E. Powers et al., 1996).

The Big Picture: Motivation and Learning

In this chapter, we've considered many strategies for promoting students' motivation to learn and achieve in the classroom. Table 12–5 presents highlights of our discussion, listing several general principles of human motivation and their implications for classroom practice.

General Principles of Motivation

PRINCIPLE	EDUCATIONAL IMPLICATION	EXAMPLE
Students are more likely to be intrinsically motivated when they have high self-efficacy and a sense of self-determination.	Give students many opportunities to achieve the successes they need for high self-efficacy. Also, let them make choices regarding certain aspects of classroom tasks and activities.	Allow students to choose among several ways of accomplishing the same instructional objective, being sure that each choice provides sufficient scaffolding that students are likely to achieve success.
Students with learning goals rather than performance goals engage in those behaviors and mental processes most likely to promote effective learning.	Acknowledge that test scores and classroom grades are important, but focus students' attention more on the intrinsic value of acquiring new knowledge and skills.	Model enthusiasm for classroom material, showing how it has helped you better understand the world.
Students are most likely to succeed at challenging classroom tasks if they are eager to do well but not overly anxious about their performance.	Try to keep students' anxiety about classroom activities and assignments at a facilitating (low to moderate) level.	Hold realistic expectations for student performance and communicate those expectations clearly and concretely.
Students are most likely to put forth effort in the classroom when they attribute their successes and failures to factors over which they have control.	Foster students' beliefs that classroom success is a function of sufficient effort and appropriate strategies.	When students struggle with classroom material, teach them study strategies that will help them process the material more effectively.

In general, we've found that motivation facilitates learning and achievement in a variety of ways; for example, appropriately motivated students pay attention, process information meaningfully, persist in the face of failure, use their errors to help improve skills, and seek out ever more challenging tasks. Yet we have also seen how learning and achievement foster the development of productive motivational patterns: When students discover that they can usually accomplish academic tasks successfully, they bring a sense of self-confidence and a desire to learn when they come to class. So motivation and classroom learning go hand in hand, with each one playing a crucial role in the development of the other.

As we've proceeded through the chapter, we've been drawing ideas from each of the perspectives of learning examined in earlier chapters. Here are some examples of how cognitive psychology, behaviorism, and social cognitive theory have each entered into our discussion:

Cognitive psychology:

- Students who have learning goals rather than performance goals are more likely to engage in *meaningful learning* and *elaboration.*
- Students are more optimistic about the likelihood of future success when they attribute failure to ineffective *study strategies* rather than to a general and relatively permanent lack of ability.
- Students' attributions regarding events—their *constructed interpretations* regarding the causes of successes and failures—influence how they respond to those events.

Behaviorism:

- Motivation determines what particular things are *reinforcing* to different students.
- The degree to which students attribute success to internal factors is affected by the extent to which they are *reinforced* (e.g., praised) for success.

Social cognitive theory:

- Students are more likely to be intrinsically motivated to engage in and persist at classroom tasks when they have high *self-efficacy* about performing those tasks.
- We can foster the motivation to learn when we *model* our own interest in school subject matter.
- Students' *expectations* for future success and failure—expectations they've derived from their attributions regarding previous successes and failures—influence their behaviors.

The principles and theories of learning and motivation that we have examined in Chapters 6 through 12 have yielded innumerable strategies for helping our students learn and achieve more successfully in the classroom. In the chapters to come, we translate these same principles and theories more directly into classroom practice as we consider instruction, classroom management, and assessment.

CASE STUDY: Writer's Block

On the first day of school, Mr. Grunwald tells students in his English composition class, "I expect you all to be proficient writers by the end of the school year. In fact, you won't get a passing grade from me unless you can write a decent essay by May."

Mr. Grunwald's statement raises anxious thoughts in many of his students. After all, a passing grade in English composition is a requirement for high school graduation. Furthermore, the colleges and universities to which some students are applying prefer As and Bs in composition. A few students are beginning to worry that their straight A averages will be destroyed.

Mr. Grunwald is far less concerned than his students; he firmly believes that all students should be able to develop writing proficiency before the year is out. He gives his students a new writing assignment each Monday, making each one more challenging than those preceding it. When he finds poorly written work among the papers he grades at the end of the week, he tries to motivate his students to do better with such comments as, "Below average work this time—you can do better," or, "Try harder next week."

The writing skills of some students improve as the year progresses. But those of other students seem almost to be deteriorating. He questions Janis, one of his low-achieving students, about the problem and is startled to hear her response.

"No matter what I do, I seem to get poor grades in your class," she laments. "I've pretty much given up trying. I guess I just wasn't meant to be a writer."

- How is Mr. Grunwald defining success in his English composition class? How are his students defining success? Are they focusing their attention on learning or performance goals?

- To what does Janis attribute her writing failure? What effect has her attribution had on her behavior?

- What strategies might Mr. Grunwald use to help his students become more intrinsically motivated to develop proficient writing skills?

Summing Up

Nature and Effects of Motivation

Motivation energizes, directs, and sustains behavior. It influences learning and behavior in several ways: It focuses learners' attention on particular goals, instigates behaviors that help learners achieve those goals, influences how learners cognitively process information, determines the specific consequences that are likely to be reinforcing, and ultimately leads to higher achievement in the classroom.

Intrinsic and Extrinsic Motivation

Intrinsic motivation arises from conditions within students themselves or from factors inherent in the task being performed. Extrinsic motivation is based on factors external to students and unrelated to the task at hand. We are especially likely to see the positive effects of motivation when our students are intrinsically rather than extrinsically motivated.

Maslow has suggested that students will be intrinsically motivated (in his words, they will strive for self-actualization) only after more basic needs—physiological needs and the needs for safety, love and belonging, and esteem—have already been satisfied. More recently, several theorists have proposed that students are most likely to be intrinsically motivated when two conditions exist: (1) They have high self-efficacy regarding their ability to succeed at classroom tasks, and (2) they have a sense of self-determination—a sense that they have some control over the course that their lives will take. As teachers, we can promote students' self-efficacy by giving them competence-promoting feedback, helping them master challenging tasks, and defining success in terms of long-term improvement. We can promote a greater sense of self-determination by presenting rules and evaluations in an informational rather than controlling fashion, minimizing our reliance on extrinsic reinforcers, and occasionally allowing students to make choices and be involved in classroom decision making.

Motivation to Learn and Learning Goals

One form of intrinsic motivation is the motivation to learn—the tendency to find school-related activities meaningful and therefore worth pursuing for their own sake. Students with learning goals rather than performance goals are more likely to recognize that competence comes only through effort and practice, choose activities that maximize their opportunities for learning, and use their errors constructively to improve future performance. We can foster students' motivation to learn and focus their attention on learning goals by relating school subject matter to their personal needs and interests, modeling our own interest in what we teach, and communicating our belief that students genuinely want to learn class material.

Social Needs

Many students come to the classroom with strong social needs, including needs to affiliate with others and to gain their approval. We can accommodate our students' social needs by providing opportunities for group interaction, expressing our concern for students' welfare, and frequently indicating our approval of desirable student behaviors.

Affect and Anxiety

Sometimes learning and cognitive processing are emotionally charged—a phenomenon known as *hot cognition.* Students will learn and remember more when they become involved in topics emotionally as well as cognitively.

A small amount of anxiety often facilitates performance, but a great deal of anxiety typically debilitates it, especially when difficult tasks are involved. Under most circumstances, we should strive to keep our students' anxiety at a low or moderate level—for example, by clearly communicating our expectations for student performance and by ensuring that students have a good chance of succeeding in classroom activities.

Attributions

Attributions are the explanations students give for why they succeed or fail at tasks. They affect many aspects of behavior and cognition, including expectations for future success, expenditure of effort, help-seeking behavior, choice of activities, and, ultimately, classroom performance. We can give students reasons for optimism about their future chances of success by attributing both their successes and their failures to factors they can control, including effort (if it has, in fact, influenced the outcome) and cognitive strategies. We should also attribute students' successes (but not failures) to a stable ability on which they can depend. Ultimately, we can promote an *I can do it* attitude (a mastery orientation) by facilitating students' success on challenging classroom tasks.

Diversity in Motivation

We will typically see different motives and attributions in different students. The specific patterns we see will depend, in part, on students' age levels, as well as on their ethnic background, gender, socioeconomic status, and any special educational needs. As teachers, we must remember that different motivational strategies will be more or less effective, depending on the specific students with whom we are working.

Motivation and Learning

Just as motivation affects learning, so, too, does learning play a critical role in motivation. As teachers, we cannot realistically address either learning or motivation in isolation from the other.

KEY CONCEPTS

motivation (p. 472)

situated motivation (p. 472)

intrinsic versus extrinsic motivation (p. 474)

self-actualization (p. 475)

deficiency versus growth needs (p. 475)

self-efficacy (p. 476)

self-determination (p. 476)

challenge (p. 477)

motivation to learn (p. 482)

learning goals versus performance goals (pp. 482–483)

need for affiliation (p. 489)

need for approval (p. 490)

affect (p. 490)

hot cognition (p. 491)

anxiety (p. 492)

state versus trait anxiety (pp. 492–493)

threat (p. 492)

facilitating versus debilitating anxiety (p. 493)

attributions (p. 497)

attribution theory (p. 497)

learned industriousness (p. 500)

mastery orientation (p. 505)

learned helplessness (p. 505)

13

Choosing Instructional Strategies

nder what conditions do you best learn and achieve in your college classes? Do you learn more when your instructors have carefully identified what they want you to learn and have planned their lessons accordingly? What kinds of instructional methods—lectures, hands-on activities, class discussions, cooperative learning groups, and so on—effectively help you understand and remember classroom material? Does the general "climate" in the classroom—for instance, whether the instructor is aloof or friendly, whether the atmosphere is businesslike or more laid-back—make a difference for you? And how do your instructors' assessment practices (tests, papers, group projects, etc.) influence what you study and learn?

Such issues are the focus of Part 3 of the book: "Understanding Instructional Processes." Here we will consider how planning and carrying out instruction (Chapters 13 and 14), creating a productive classroom environment (Chapter 15), and assessing student learning (Chapter 16) are all essential aspects of effective teaching and have an impact on what students ultimately learn and achieve. Yet as we make decisions related to each of these areas, we must also keep in mind what we know about our *students*. As we proceed through this and the next three chapters, we will repeatedly see examples of how planning, instruction, the classroom environment, and assessment practices affect one another and how, in addition, they both influence and are influenced by student behaviors and characteristics (see Figure 13–1).

Throughout Part 3, we will revisit principles and concepts that we have encountered in previous chapters. For instance, as we consider planning and carrying out instruction, we will draw from cognitive, behaviorist, and social cognitive views of learning. As we discuss ways of creating a productive classroom environment, we will make use of such "old friends" as *scaffolding, socialization, cueing,* and *self-determination.* And as we explore various strategies for assessing student learning, we will discover that our assessment practices are likely to influence students' long-term memory storage processes, motivation, and self-regulation.

In this chapter, we will begin our discussion of planning and carrying out instruction, with a focus on these questions:

- How can we plan effectively for instruction, both on a daily basis and over the course of the school year?
- What instructional strategies may be useful for helping students learn new material?
- What instructional strategies may be especially suitable for helping students elaborate on, and in other ways better understand, classroom subject matter?
- How can we best accommodate students' diverse backgrounds, characteristics, and needs when we plan and implement classroom instruction?

This chapter will emphasize instructional methods in which students learn with relative independence from one another. We will explore methods that involve considerable student interaction—class discussions, cooperative learning, and so on—in the following chapter.

CASE STUDY: A Math Problem

After leaving behind elementary school last year, twelve-year-old Reggie is adjusting easily to middle school. He has made new friends and established good working relationships with his teachers. He has As in almost every subject. But Reggie has a problem—mathematics.

Reggie knows the usual routine in Ms. Keeney's math class. After reviewing the previous night's homework assignment, Ms. Keeney explains a new concept (e.g., *negative number, improper fraction*) or demonstrates a new procedure (e.g., finding prime factors, multiplying fractions) on the chalkboard. She then gives her students time during class to work on several textbook problems related to the day's lesson. Just before the bell rings, she lists additional textbook problems that students should complete at home that night.

Reggie knows that mathematics is important, so he attends closely to each day's lesson and works diligently on his in-class problems and homework assignments. Yet despite his efforts, Reggie feels completely lost in math class—a feeling that is confirmed by his declining quiz and test scores.

"I'm getting further and further behind," he complains to his friends. "I'm not sure what I'm supposed to be learning, but whatever it is, I'm obviously not learning it."

- Why is Reggie experiencing difficulty in his mathematics class? Can you think of possible explanations based on principles of cognitive development or human learning?

- What specific things might the teacher do to help students like Reggie experience greater success in mathematics?

Planning for Instruction

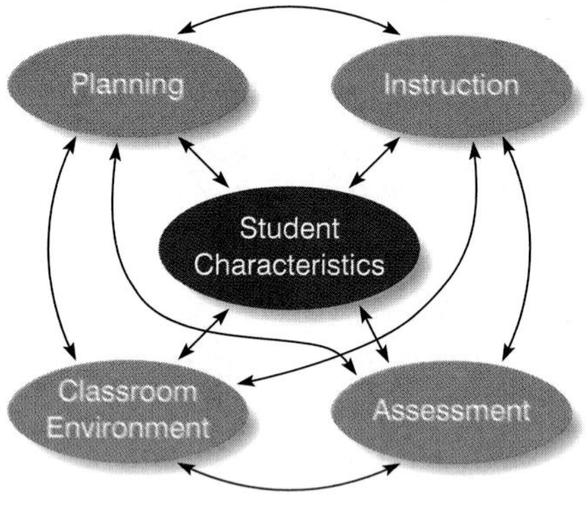

FIGURE 13.1

Planning, instruction, the classroom environment, assessment, and student characteristics are not independent; each one influences the others.

Perhaps Reggie doesn't know what he's supposed to be learning in math because Ms. Keeney has never told her students what *she* hopes they will learn. We might guess from Ms. Keeney's actions that she wants her students to acquire a variety of new mathematical concepts and procedures, but we have to wonder if she's given much thought to the specific things she wants her students to accomplish while they are in her class. We might suspect, too, that Ms. Keeney hasn't thought much about how she can best help her students learn class material effectively. Day after day, she relies almost exclusively on verbal explanations, chalkboard displays, and textbook problems to get her points across.

Effective teaching begins long before students enter the classroom. Effective teachers engage in a considerable amount of advance planning: They identify the knowledge and skills they want their students to acquire, determine an appropriate sequence in which to foster such knowledge and skills, and develop classroom activities that will promote maximal learning and keep students continually motivated and on task. Let's consider three aspects of instructional planning: identifying the goals of instruction, conducting a task analysis, and developing lesson plans.

Identifying the Goals of Instruction

An essential part of planning is identifying the specific things we want our students to learn during a lesson or unit, as well as the things we want them to accomplish over the course of the semester or school year. Educators often refer to such goals as **instructional objectives.**

When we identify our objectives before we begin teaching, we are in a better position to choose an effective method of instruction; we can also develop an appropriate means of evaluating our students' achievement. For example, if our objective for a unit on addition is the *knowledge* of number facts, then we may want to use drill and practice (perhaps flash cards) to enhance students' automaticity for these facts, and we may want to use a timed test to measure students' ability to recall them quickly and easily. But if our objective is the *application* of number facts, then we may want to focus our instruction and assessment methods on word problems, or perhaps on activities involving real objects, hands-on measurements, and so on.[1]

Students also benefit from knowing the objectives for a lesson or unit. When they know what their teacher hopes they will accomplish, they can make more informed decisions about how to focus their efforts and allocate their study time, and they can more effectively monitor their comprehension as they read and study (Gronlund, 2000; McAshan, 1979). For instance, if Ms. Keeney tells students in her math class that she expects them to "apply mathematics procedures to everyday situations," we would expect them to think about and study mathematics very differently than if she tells them to "know all the definitions by heart."

Have you ever been in a situation where you couldn't figure out what a teacher expected you to learn? Do you remember feeling confused, frustrated, or otherwise "lost" in that situation?

Choosing Appropriate Objectives

School districts typically identify a list of objectives for students at different grade levels. Yet as teachers, we will undoubtedly add our own objectives to any list that the school district provides. As we do so, we may want to consult national standards in the discipline as well as classifications, or *taxonomies,* of knowledge and skills that have been developed by educators.

If the objective is application, then students should engage in various application activities. As a science activity, this first grader uses his wind finder to determine the direction of the wind.

National standards in the discipline. Many discipline-specific professional groups have established **standards** for their discipline—general descriptions of the knowledge and skills that students should achieve and the characteristics that students' accomplishments should reflect. As illustrations, here are examples of recently published standards in science and geography:

Take into account any published *standards* for the discipline.

> **Example from the *National Science Education Standards* (1996):**
> As a result of their activities in grades 5–8, all students should develop understanding of
>
> - Structure and function in living systems
> - Reproduction and heredity
> - Regulation and behavior

---

[1]Some schools use an approach called *outcomes-based education* (OBE), in which the desired instructional objectives *(outcomes)* are specified before the school year begins, often at a district-wide level. Classroom assessment is tied directly to these outcomes, and decisions related to students' advancement and graduation are based on the specific knowledge and skills that each student can demonstrate (e.g., Boschee & Baron, 1993; Guskey, 1994).

- Populations and ecosystems

- Diversity and adaptations of organisms (p. 155)

**Example from *Geography for Life: National Geography Standards*
(National Geographic Education Project, 1994):**
By the end of the twelfth grade, the student should know and understand how to . . . systematically locate and gather geographic information from a variety of primary and secondary sources, as exemplified by being able to

- Gather data in the field by multiple processes—observing, identifying, naming, describing, organizing, sketching, interviewing, recording, measuring

- Gather data in the classroom and library from maps, photographs, videos, and other media (e.g., CD-ROM), charts, aerial photographs, and other nonbook sources, and then use the data to identify, name, describe, organize, sketch, measure, and evaluate items of geographic interest

- Gather data by spatial sampling in both secondary sources and the field . . .

- Use quantitative measures (e.g., means, medians, and modes) to describe data (p. 53)

Some sets of standards are more precise than others. For instance, in the two standards just presented, we see greater specificity for geography (and therefore probably have a better idea of the instructional techniques we should use) than is true for science.

Taxonomies of knowledge and skills. We don't necessarily want to limit our objectives just to the acquisition and use of information—in other words, to the **cognitive domain.** Other important objectives might involve body movements and actions (the **psychomotor domain**). And still others might involve students' feelings, attitudes, and values about what they learn (the **affective domain**). Educators have developed taxonomies in each of these domains that describe a variety of possible educational objectives; Table 13–1 presents three classic ones. Although certainly not exhaustive lists, such taxonomies can nevertheless give us some ideas about the kinds of objectives we may want to consider (Krathwohl, 1994).

Despite such standards and taxonomies, teachers, parents, taxpayers, and even experts cannot always agree on the instructional objectives that students of various age levels should achieve (Sosniak & Stodolsky, 1994; Stiggins, 1997). For example, some constituencies ask us to increase students' factual knowledge—a perspective sometimes referred to as "back to the basics" or "cultural literacy" (e.g., Hirsch, 1996). Yet others encourage us to foster higher-level thinking skills such as problem solving and critical thinking and to help students develop the "habits of mind" (e.g., scientific reasoning, inference-drawing from historical documents) central to various academic disciplines (P. A. Alexander, 1997; Berliner, 1997; Shulman & Quinlan, 1996). As teachers, we must remember that, at least at the present time, there is no definitive list of objectives for any age-group. We will ultimately have to tailor our instructional objectives to the particular characteristics of our students and to the particular expectations of the schools, communities, and larger society in which we teach.

Developing Useful Objectives

Experiencing Firsthand
Being a Good Citizen

Consider this instructional objective:

Students will learn and practice principles of good citizenship.

Write down at least three implications of this objective for your own classroom practice.

Consider objectives within the psychomotor and affective domains as well as within the cognitive domain.

Why is the third domain called *affective*? (See Chapter 12 for an explanation of *affect*.)

Consider student characteristics and community expectations as you develop objectives.

TABLE 13.1

Writing Objectives at Different Levels and in Different Domains

LEVEL AND DEFINITION	EXAMPLES
The Cognitive Domain (Bloom's Taxonomy) **(adapted from Bloom, Engelhart, Furst, Hill, & Krathwohl, 1956)**	
1. *Knowledge:* Rote memorizing of information in a basically word-for-word fashion	Reciting definitions of terms Remembering lists of items
2. *Comprehension:* Translating information into one's own words	Rewording a definition Paraphrasing a rule
3. *Application:* Using information in a new situation	Applying mathematical principles to the solution of word problems Applying psychological theories of learning to educational practice
4. *Analysis:* Breaking information down into its constituent parts	Discovering the assumptions underlying a philosophical essay Identifying fallacies in a seemingly logical argument
5. *Synthesis:* Constructing something new by integrating several pieces of information	Developing a theory Presenting a logical defense of a particular viewpoint within a debate
6. *Evaluation:* Placing a value judgment on data	Critiquing a theory Examining the internal and external validity of an experiment
The Psychomotor Domain **(adapted from Harrow, 1972)**	
1. *Reflex movements:* Responding to a stimulus involuntarily, without conscious thought	Ducking to avoid being hit by an oncoming object Shifting weight to help maintain one's balance
2. *Basic-fundamental movements:* Making basic voluntary movements directed toward a particular purpose	Walking Holding a pencil
3. *Perceptual abilities:* Responding appropriately to information received through the senses	Following a moving object with one's eyes Maintaining eye-hand coordination
4. *Physical abilities:* Developing general abilities in the areas of endurance, strength, flexibility, and agility	Running a long distance Exercising with weights Changing direction quickly
5. *Skilled movements:* Performing a complex action with some degree of proficiency or mastery	Swimming Throwing a football Sawing a piece of wood
6. *Nondiscursive communication:* Communicating feelings and emotions through bodily actions	Doing pantomime Dancing to communicate the mood of a musical piece

continued

continued

The Affective Domain (adapted from Krathwohl, Bloom, & Masia, 1964)	
1. *Receiving:* Being aware of, or paying attention to, something	Recognizing that there may be two sides to a story Knowing that there are differences among people of different cultural backgrounds
2. *Responding:* Making an active and willing response to something	Obeying playground rules Reading books for pleasure
3. *Valuing:* Consistently demonstrating interest in a particular activity so that ongoing involvement or commitment in the activity is reflected	Writing a letter to a newspaper regarding an issue one feels strongly about Consistently eating a balanced diet
4. *Organization:* Integrating a new value into one's existing set of values and building a value system	Forming judgments about the directions in which society should move Setting priorities for one's life
5. *Characterization by a value or value complex:* Consistently behaving in accordance with an organized value system and integrating that system into a total philosophy of life	Perceiving situations objectively, realistically, and with tolerance Relying increasingly on scientific methods to answer questions about the world and society

Certainly good citizenship is a goal toward which all students should strive. But did you find yourself having trouble translating the objective into specific things you might do in the classroom? Did you also find yourself struggling with what the term *good citizenship* means (honesty? empathy? involvement in school activities? all of the above?)? The "good citizenship" objective is nothing more than *word magic:* It looks great at first glance but really doesn't give us specific information about what we want students to achieve (Dyer, 1967).

Ideally, we should develop instructional objectives that can guide us as we plan instructional activities and assessment procedures. Here are several strategies for developing useful objectives:

• *Include objectives at varying degrees of complexity and sophistication.* The taxonomies presented in Table 13–1 include activities that range from very simple to fairly complex. For instance, the taxonomy for the cognitive domain (often called **Bloom's taxonomy**) includes both lower-level skills (knowledge, comprehension) and higher-level skills (application, analysis, synthesis, evaluation). We will undoubtedly want to include *both* kinds of skills in our objectives. As an illustration, consider these objectives for a lesson on the physics of light:

Students will describe laws related to the reflection and refraction of light.

Students will identify examples of reflection and refraction in their own lives (e.g., mirrors, eyeglasses).

Students will use the law of reflection and laws of geometry to determine the actual location of objects viewed in a mirror.

Students will use the law of refraction to explain how microscopes and telescopes make objects appear larger.

Include objectives that reflect several levels of knowing and using information and skills.

Although all four objectives lie within the cognitive domain, they reflect different levels of that domain. The first objective focuses exclusively on knowledge of separate facts—facts that students might conceivably learn at a rote level, in isolation from anything else they know. But the other three objectives, which involve application and analysis, should encourage students to engage in meaningful learning and can therefore promote effective concept learning, transfer, and problem solving.

- *Focus on what students should do, not what teachers should do.* Consider these goals for a unit on soccer:

Provide an overview of the rules of the game.

Show students how to kick, dribble, and pass the ball.

Teach the playing positions (e.g., center forward, goalkeeper) and the roles of players in each position.

The problem with these goals is that they tell us only what the teacher will do during instruction; they tell us nothing about what students should be able to do as a result of that instruction. Useful objectives focus on what students will do rather than on what teacher will do (Gronlund, 2000). With this point in mind, let's consider some alternative objectives for our soccer unit:

Students will describe the basic rules of the game and identify the procedures to be followed in various situations.

Students will demonstrate appropriate ways of kicking, dribbling, and passing the ball.

Students will identify the eleven playing positions and describe the roles of players in each position.

Here we have refocused our objectives on student accomplishments; in other words, we have described the knowledge and skills we want our students to acquire during their unit on soccer.

- *Describe the expected outcomes of instruction.* Objectives are often more useful when they describe learning outcomes rather than learning processes (Gronlund, 2000). To illustrate, consider these objectives for a French class:

Students will study the meanings of French words.

Students will practice pronouncing French words.

Students will learn how to conjugate French verbs.

These objectives describe what students will do during French class; in other words, they describe learning *processes*. But it is usually more important to determine what students can do at the end of instruction—that is, to describe what the *outcomes* of a class or lesson should be. Let's revise our objectives for French to reflect student outcomes:

Students will give the English meanings of French words.

Students will pronounce French words correctly.

Students will correctly conjugate common French verbs in the present and past tenses.

Now we know what to expect of students once they successfully complete their French class.

Many behaviorists recommend that our instructional objectives describe very specific behaviors that we want our students to exhibit—an idea that they've derived from the concept of *terminal behavior* (see Chapter 10). For instance, they recommend that we use verbs that reflect observable actions (e.g., *recite, explain,*

Focus on what students should accomplish as a result of instruction.

Describe learning outcomes, not learning processes.

choose) rather than verbs that reflect nonobservable cognitive processes (e.g., *know, understand, appreciate*). Instructional objectives that describe specific, observable behaviors are sometimes called **behavioral objectives** (e.g., Schloss & Smith, 1994).

Yet cognitive theorists point out that too much emphasis on describing specific behaviors can lead to very long lists of relatively trivial objectives (Newmann, 1997; Popham, 1995). They remind us, too, that how students cognitively process classroom subject matter is often just as important as what they learn; for instance, as we've noted many times before, students who engage in meaningful learning and elaboration learn more effectively than those who study at a rote level.

In fact, it is often possible for our instructional objectives to include descriptions of observable behaviors while also encouraging students to engage in the kinds of cognitive processes that promote effective learning over the long run. One way of doing so is to describe a few general and relatively abstract objectives (perhaps three to ten items) and then list examples of behaviors that reflect each one (Gronlund, 2000). To illustrate, if we want our students to engage in critical thinking as they read, we might develop an objective such as this one:

Students will demonstrate critical thinking skills in reading; for example, they will:

1. Distinguish between facts and opinions.
2. Distinguish between facts and inferences.
3. Identify errors in reasoning.
4. Distinguish between valid and invalid conclusions.
5. Identify assumptions underlying conclusions. (adapted from Gronlund, 2000, p. 52)

Obviously, not every facet of critical thinking is included here, but the six items listed give both us and our students a good idea of the specific kinds of behaviors that reflect achievement of the objective.

- *Identify both short-term and long-term goals.* Some instructional objectives can easily be accomplished within the course of a single lesson or unit. Pronouncing certain French words correctly and passing a soccer ball competently are examples of **short-term objectives.** But other objectives may require months or even years of instruction and practice before they are achieved (Brophy & Alleman, 1991; Cole, 1990; Gronlund, 2000). For example, we are talking about such **long-term objectives** when we want our students to use effective learning strategies as they study new subject matter, apply scientific methods as they try to understand and explain the world around them, or read critically rather than take everything at face value.

Some short-term objectives are "minimum essentials"—things that students *must* be able to do before they proceed to the next unit, course, or grade level (Gronlund, 2000). For example, elementary school students must know addition before they move to multiplication, and high school students must know the symbols for the chemical elements before they learn how chemical reactions are symbolized. In contrast, many long-term objectives can be thought of as "developmental" in nature: They include skills and abilities that continue to evolve and improve throughout the school years (Gronlund, 2000). Yet even when long-term objectives cannot be completely accomplished within the course of students' formal education, they are often among the most important ones for us to set for our students and must therefore have a prominent place in our list of objectives.

- *Incorporate opportunities for self-regulation and self-determination.* On some occasions, it is both appropriate and desirable for our students to identify their *own* objectives. For example, different students might choose different authors to read, different athletic skills to master, or different art media to use. By allowing students to

Especially when teaching a higher-level skill, list a few general (and perhaps not directly observable) objectives and then give examples of specific behaviors that reflect each one.

Consider both short-term and long-term objectives.

Occasionally let students identify their own objectives.

Long-term objectives, such as those related to writing and written expression, may require months or even years to master.

establish some of their own objectives, we are encouraging the *goal setting* that, from the perspective of social cognitive theory, is an important aspect of self-regulation. We are also fostering the sense of *self-determination* that many theorists believe is so critical for intrinsic motivation.

Experiencing Firsthand
Looking Ahead "Objectively"

1. On a sheet of paper, write down a grade level at which you might eventually teach.

2. Now write down the subject area(s) you are likely to be teaching at that grade level.

3. With both your grade level and subject area(s) in mind, write down at least five *important* objectives you might have for your students.

What kinds of objectives did you include in your list? Did you focus on student outcomes rather than on student learning processes or teacher activities? Did you identify accomplishments that reflect varying degrees of complexity? Did you include psychomotor outcomes (e.g., behaviors involving eye-hand coordination) and affective outcomes (e.g., particular attitudes toward classroom subject matter) as well as outcomes within the cognitive domain? Ultimately, the final list of objectives we develop for our students is likely to be quite broad in scope.

How do we break down a large instructional task—for example, a course in government, a unit on basketball, or a driver education class—into specific objectives? Several procedures known collectively as *task analysis* can help us analyze the components of a complex topic or skill.

Conducting a Task Analysis

Consider these five teachers:

Ms. Begay plans to teach her third graders how to solve arithmetic word problems. She also wants to help her students learn more effectively from the things they read.

Mr. Marzano, a middle school physical education teacher, is beginning a unit on basketball. He wants his students to develop enough proficiency in the sport that they will feel comfortable playing both on organized school basketball teams and in less formal games with friends and neighbors.

Ms. Flores, an eighth-grade social studies teacher, is going to introduce the intricacies of the federal judicial system to her classes.

Mr. Wu, a junior high school music teacher, needs to teach his new trumpet students how to play a recognizable version of *Seventy-Six Trombones* in time for the New Year's Day parade.

Mr. McKenzie must teach the students in his high school driver education class how to drive a car safely through the city streets.

These teachers have something in common: They want to teach complex topics or skills. All five should probably conduct a **task analysis**: They should identify the specific knowledge and behaviors necessary to master the subject matter in question. Such a task analysis can then guide them as they select the most appropriate methods and sequence in which to teach that subject matter.

Figure 13–2 illustrates three general approaches to task analysis (Jonassen, Hannum, & Tessmer, 1989):

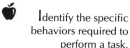
Identify the specific behaviors required to perform a task.

• *Behavioral analysis.* One way of analyzing a complex task is to identify the specific behaviors required to perform it (much as a behaviorist might do). For example, Mr. Marzano can identify the specific physical movements involved in dribbling, passing, and shooting a basketball. Mr. McKenzie can identify the actions required in driving an automobile with a standard transmission—turning on the ignition, steering, accelerating, stepping on the clutch, shifting gears, releasing the clutch, and braking. And Mr. Wu can identify the behaviors that students must master to play a trumpet successfully—holding the instrument with the fingers placed appropriately on the valves, blowing correctly into the mouthpiece, and so on.

Break down the subject matter in terms of specific topics, ideas, concepts, and so on.

• *Subject matter analysis.* Another approach to task analysis is to break down the subject matter in terms of the specific topics, concepts, and principles that it includes. To illustrate, Ms. Flores can identify various aspects of the judicial system (concepts such as "innocent until proven guilty" and "reasonable doubt," the roles that judges and juries play, etc.) and their interrelationships. Mr. Wu, who needs to teach his new trumpet students how to read music as well as how to play the instrument, can identify the basic elements of written music that students must know to interpret written music: the difference between the treble and bass clefs, the number of beats associated with different kinds of notes, and so on.

Subject matter analysis is especially important when the subject matter being taught includes many interrelated ideas and concepts. From the perspective of cognitive psychology, we can help students learn class material more meaningfully, organize it better in their long-term memories, and remember it more effectively if we teach them the interconnections among various ideas and concepts along with the ideas and concepts themselves.

• *Information processing analysis.* A third approach, using a cognitive perspective once again, is to specify the cognitive processes involved in a task. To illustrate,

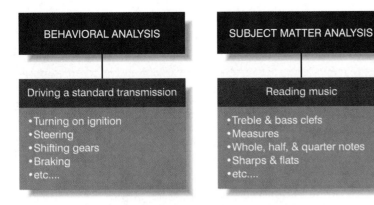

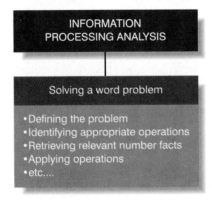

FIGURE 13.2
Three ways of analyzing a task

Ms. Begay can identify the mental processes involved in successfully solving an arithmetic word problem, such as correct classification (encoding) of the problem in terms of the operation required (e.g., addition, subtraction) and rapid retrieval of basic number facts. Similarly, she can identify some specific cognitive strategies useful in reading comprehension, such as finding main ideas, learning meaningfully, elaborating, and summarizing.

Break down a task in terms of the specific cognitive processes it involves.

■**Experiencing Firsthand**
   Making a Peanut Butter Sandwich

Conduct a task analysis for the process of making a peanut butter sandwich.

1. Decide whether your approach should be a behavioral analysis, a subject matter analysis, or an information processing analysis.

2. Now, using the approach you've selected, break the sandwich-making task into a number of small, "teachable" steps.

Conducting task analyses for complex skills and topics has at least two advantages (Desberg & Taylor, 1986; Jonassen et al., 1989). First, when we analyze a task's specific components—whether those components be behaviors, concepts and ideas, or cognitive processes—we have a better sense of what things our students need to learn and the order in which they can most effectively learn them. For example, Mr. McKenzie must

Use a task analysis to identify the specific things students need to learn and in what sequence.

INTO THE CLASSROOM: Identifying the Goals of Instruction

Describe objectives in terms of what students should be able to do at the end of instruction.

A Spanish teacher knows that students easily confuse the verbs *estar* and *ser* because both are translated in English as "to be." She identifies this objective for her students: "Students will correctly conjugate *estar* and *ser* in the present tense and use each one in appropriate contexts."

When desired goals involve complex topics or skills, list a few abstract objectives and then give examples of specific behaviors that reflect each one.

A junior high school principal identifies this objective for students at her school: "Students will demonstrate effective classroom listening skills—for example, by taking complete and accurate notes, answering teacher questions correctly, and seeking clarification when they don't understand."

Consider objectives within the cognitive, psychomotor, and affective domains.

A physical education teacher wants his students to know the basic rules of basketball, dribble and pass the ball appropriately, and develop a love for the game.

Develop objectives that reflect several levels of knowing and using information and skills.

A high school physics teacher wants students not only to understand the basic kinds of machines (e.g., levers, wedges) but also to recognize examples of these machines in their own lives and use them to solve real-world problems.

Identify both short-term and long-term objectives.

An elementary school teacher wants students to correctly spell a list of ten new words each week. She also wants them to write a coherent and grammatically correct short story by the end of the school year.

Analyze a complex task in terms of the specific behaviors, topics, and/or cognitive processes that it involves.

A gymnastics teacher identifies the specific sequence of movements required to execute forward and backward rolls. She also realizes that her students will have to learn basic spotting techniques to assist classmates who are practicing their rolls.

---

teach his driver education students how to control the clutch before he can teach them how to shift gears. At the same time, we may find that certain skills or topics we thought were important are actually *not* important. For example, a science teacher may realize that learning the history of science, though possibly having value in its own right, has little to do with how well students can apply scientific principles.

A second advantage in conducting a task analysis is that it helps us choose appropriate instructional strategies. Different tasks—and perhaps even different components of a single task—may require different approaches to instruction. For example, if one necessary component of solving arithmetic word problems is the rapid retrieval of math facts from memory, then repeated practice of these facts may be critical for developing automaticity. If another component of solving these problems is identifying the appropriate operation to apply in various situations, then promoting a true understanding of

 Use a task analysis to identify suitable instructional methods.

mathematical concepts and principles (perhaps by using concrete manipulatives or authentic activities) is essential.

Sometimes a task analysis will lead us to conclude that we can most effectively teach a complex task by teaching some or all of its components separately. For instance, Mr. Wu may ask his beginning trumpet students to practice blowing into the mouthpiece correctly without worrying about the specific notes they produce. Yet on other occasions, it may be more appropriate to teach the desired knowledge and behaviors entirely within the context of the overall task; by doing so, we make the subject matter more meaningful for our students. For instance, Ms. Begay should almost certainly teach her students the processes involved in learning effectively from reading materials—elaborating, summarizing, and so on—primarily within the context of authentic reading tasks.

Developing Lesson Plans

Once they have identified their goals for instruction and, in many cases, conducted a task analysis, effective teachers develop a lesson plan to guide them during instruction. A lesson plan typically includes the following:

- The objective(s) of instruction
- The instructional strategies used, and in what sequence
- Instructional materials (e.g., textbooks, handouts) and equipment required
- The assessment method(s) planned

Any lesson plan should, of course, take into account the students who will be learning—their developmental levels, prior knowledge, cultural backgrounds, and so on.

As a beginning teacher, you will probably want to develop a fairly detailed lesson plan that describes how you are going to help your students learn the subject matter in question (Calderhead, 1996; Sternberg & Horvath, 1995). For instance, when I taught middle school geography in Colorado, I spent many hours each week writing down the information, examples, questions, and student activities I wanted to use during the following week. Figure 13–3 presents a lesson plan I once used for a unit on culture and migration.

As you gain experience teaching certain topics, you will learn which strategies work effectively and which do not, and you may use some of the effective ones frequently enough that you can retrieve them quickly and easily from long-term memory. As time goes on, you will find that planning lessons becomes far less time-consuming than it once was and that you can do a lot of your planning in your head rather than on paper (Calderhead, 1996).

We should think of lesson plans more as guides than as recipes—in other words, as a general plan of attack that we can and should adjust as the situation warrants (Calderhead, 1996). For instance, during the course of a lesson, we may find that our students have less prior knowledge than we realized, and so we may have to "back up" and teach material we had thought they had already mastered. Or, if our students express curiosity or have intriguing insights about a particular topic, we may want to spend more time exploring that topic than we had originally intended.

As we proceed through the school year, our long-range plans will also change to some degree. For instance, we may find that our task analyses of desired knowledge and skills were overly simplistic. Or we may discover that the expectations we have for students' achievement, as reflected in the instructional objectives we've developed, are either unrealistically high or inappropriately low. We must continually revise our plans as instruction proceeds and as classroom assessments reveal the extent to which students are learning and achieving successfully.

FIGURE 13.3

A lesson plan for a middle school unit on culture and migration

OBJECTIVES

- Students will describe what the term *culture* means in their own words.
- Students will give several examples of the ways in which cultures are different from one another.
- Students will give several examples of how the United States is a multicultural nation.
- Students will identify several reasons why people may migrate from one location to another.

MATERIALS

- Chapter 11 of the class's geography textbook.
- An enlarged map of Colorado cut into eight pieces; each piece consists of two or more counties of the state.
- A Spanish dictionary.
- Transparency of a map of Colorado, with county lines marked in thick black lines.
- Overhead projector.
- Migration homework assignment, as follows:

  In the upcoming unit, we will be looking at migration of various cultures to the United States. We will also be looking at how many of our own families have migrated to Colorado from other states and other nations. To prepare for our discussion, please talk with a family member about the following questions. Fill in as many of the blanks as you can.

  1. In what state of the United States, or in what other country, were you born? _____

  2. In what state or country were your parents born?
     Mother _____ Father _____

  3. In what state or country were your grandparents born?
     Mother's parents: Grandmother _____ Grandfather _____
     Father's parents: Grandmother _____ Grandfather _____

INSTRUCTION—DAY 1

Homework

- Ask students to read Chapter 11 during free period today or at home tonight.

INSTRUCTION—DAY 2

Question/Explanation

- Ask the class, "What is *culture*?"

    Solicit several possible answers; write students' responses on the board.
    Integrate students' responses into the general notion that *culture* involves the ways that a particular group of people thinks and acts.

- Ask the class, "What are some ways in which cultures are different from one another?"

    Write students' responses on the board.
    List the following ways in which cultures may vary: food, recreation, family life, language, religion. Tie students' responses to these categories; add any other categories that their responses might reflect.
    Show the map in the textbook that illustrates how different religions are prominent in different parts of the world, and relate the distribution of religions to cultural differences.

- Say, "The United States is *multicultural*. In other words, it includes many different cultures. What are some examples of how the cultures of other countries have become a part of our way of life?"

    Write students' responses on the board.
    If students' responses have not been sufficiently diverse, add these examples:
       Mexico—food (e.g., tacos), Spanish words *(mesa)*; France—food (e.g., crepes), words *(rendezvous),* art; England—soccer (the English call it "football"), literature; China—food (e.g., egg rolls); Africa—fabric designs; Denmark—fairy tales (Hans Christian Andersen); and Japan—food (e.g., sushi).

Activity

- Divide the class into eight groups of three or four students each. Ideally, each group should consist of at least one sixth grader, one seventh grader, and one eighth grader. [The class was comprised of an approximately equal number of students from each grade.]
- Give each group one of the eight pieces of the Colorado map. Ask the groups to count the number of Spanish place names (towns, rivers, etc.) for each of the counties in their portion of the map. Tell them that they can refer to a Spanish dictionary if they aren't sure whether a particular name is Spanish.
- When all groups have completed the task, display the Colorado map transparency on the wall with the overhead projector. Ask the groups to give the number of Spanish names in each county, and write these numbers on the transparency.

Question/Explanation

- Ask, "What pattern do you see in these numbers?" Students' responses should reflect the fact that most Spanish names are in the south-central and southwestern portions of the state.
- Explain that the pattern reflects the history of migration to what is now Colorado. Most early settlers in the southern portions of the state came from the south—that is, from what was once Spanish territory. Aspects of Spanish culture (e.g., language) therefore "migrated" as well.

Homework

- Ask students to complete the migration homework assignment with their parent(s).

INSTRUCTION—DAY 3

Question/Explanation

- Ask, "How do cultures spread from one place to another? For instance, what kinds of experiences do we have that expose us to other cultures?"

  Write students' responses on the board.
  Summarize their responses by using the terms *migration, tourism, media, advertising,* and any other categories that seem appropriate.

- Ask, "Why do people migrate from one place to another? Can you remember some of the reasons that Chapter 11 in your textbook described? Can you think of other possible reasons as well?

  Solicit a variety of responses.
  Interpret the responses in terms of *push* and *pull* factors that promote migration.
  Explain that push and pull factors are likely to change over time.

Activity

- Have students take out their completed migration homework assignment from the night before. Put three columns on the board and label them *You, Parents,* and *Grandparents.* Have students go up to the board one table at a time and write the states or countries of origin in each column.
- When all students are seated, ask them to identify any patterns in the data.
- Ask, "If your parents or grandparents migrated to Colorado from another state or country, do you know *why* they did?" Relate students' responses to the push and pull factors identified earlier.

Class Discussion and Explanation

- Have students open their textbooks to the table of immigration figures for the United States. [This was a table that listed the major countries of origin for U.S. immigrants for each decade from the mid-1800s to the present.]
- Ask, "What patterns do you see in this table?"

  Solicit students' responses; they should reflect the fact that most early immigrants came from Europe, whereas many recent immigrants have come from Mexico and the Far East.

- Ask, "Why do you think the pattern of migration has changed over time? What might be some of the push and pull factors influencing the migration of different groups?"

  Solicit students' responses and tie them back to the earlier discussion of push and pull.

continued

continued

ASSESSMENT

- Informal assessment of students' understanding during class discussions.
- Brief essay asking students to:

  Describe three reasons that people migrate from one place to another and give an example to illustrate each reason.

  Describe three kinds of evidence to indicate that the United States is a multicultural nation.

As already noted, different instructional strategies are likely to be more or less appropriate for different objectives. We turn now to a discussion of the strategies we can use to help students learn classroom material effectively.

Overview of Instructional Strategies

In this and the following chapter, we will explore a wide variety of instructional strategies. To organize our discussion, I've grouped them into two general categories: those that introduce students to new material and those that help students elaborate on, and so more completely understand and more readily transfer, that material. I've further divided the second category into two subcategories: strategies for which the teacher usually assumes leadership *(teacher-directed)* and those for which students often assume leadership *(student-directed).* In the remainder of this chapter, we will address the first category and the teacher-directed strategies in the second category. Chapter 14 describes strategies that are typically student-directed and inevitably involve considerable student interaction. Figure 13–4 depicts the organizational scheme we will use.

Keep in mind, however, that our categories are overly simplistic. In fact, many of the strategies will, to some degree, enable us to introduce new material *and also* promote higher-level thinking skills. Furthermore, most of the strategies in the second category (those that foster elaboration and transfer) may vary considerably in the degree to which they are teacher-directed or student-directed.

Introducing New Material

There are numerous ways to help students acquire new knowledge and skills. Here we will consider several, commonly used strategies:

- Expository instruction
- Discovery learning
- Mastery learning
- Direct instruction
- Computer-based instruction

Expository Instruction

THINKING ABOUT WHAT YOU KNOW

- How often have your teachers used lectures to teach you something new? Which of your teachers were effective lecturers, and which were not? What did

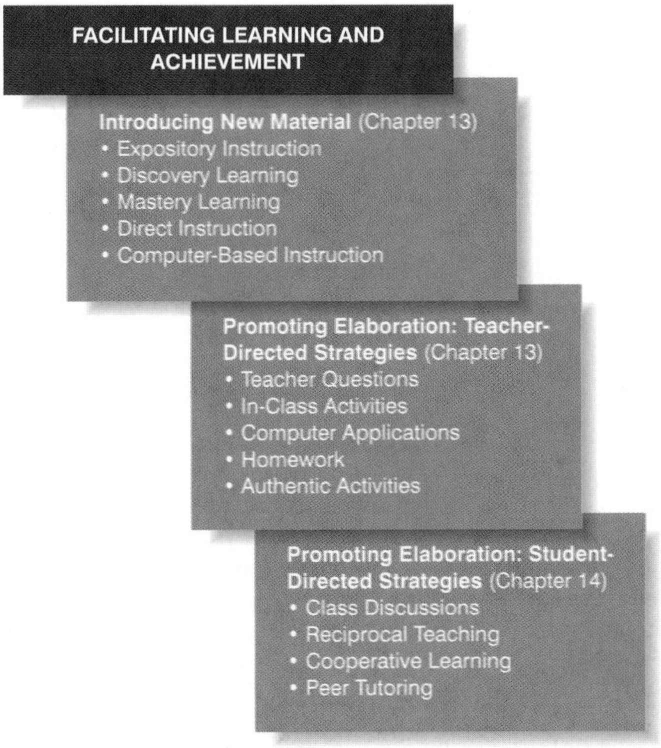

FACILITATING LEARNING AND ACHIEVEMENT

Introducing New Material (Chapter 13)
- Expository Instruction
- Discovery Learning
- Mastery Learning
- Direct Instruction
- Computer-Based Instruction

Promoting Elaboration: Teacher-Directed Strategies (Chapter 13)
- Teacher Questions
- In-Class Activities
- Computer Applications
- Homework
- Authentic Activities

Promoting Elaboration: Student-Directed Strategies (Chapter 14)
- Class Discussions
- Reciprocal Teaching
- Cooperative Learning
- Peer Tutoring

FIGURE 13.4

An organizational scheme for instructional strategies

the more effective lecturers specifically do to help you learn and understand classroom material?

- How much have you learned from textbooks you've read over the years? Were some textbooks easy to understand? Were others confusing and frustrating to read? What characteristics make for an effective textbook?

Reflecting on your past lectures and textbooks just now, you may have realized that much of your education over the years has taken the form of **expository instruction.** In other words, information was *exposed* to you in essentially the same form you were expected to learn it. Lectures, explanations, textbooks, and educational videos are all examples of expository instruction; in each case, the information that students need to know is explicitly laid out for them.

Some learning theorists, such as B. F. Skinner (e.g., 1968), have criticized expository instruction for putting students in a passive role. As you should recall from our discussion of behaviorism in Chapter 10, operant conditioning occurs when a response is reinforced; hence, students can learn only when they actually *make* a response. Yet students make very few observable responses when they simply sit quietly listening to a lecture, reading a textbook, or watching a video.

Many cognitivists argue, however, that students are often *mentally* active during such seemingly passive activities (Ausubel et al., 1978; Pressley, 1995; Weinert & Helmke, 1995). From the perspective of cognitive psychology, the degree to which students learn from expository instruction is a function of how they process information; in other words, it depends on the particular cognitive responses they make. The more students pay attention, and the more they engage in meaningful learning, organization, elabora-

Field trips can also be a form of expository instruction. What particular benefits might field trips have?

tion, and so on, the more they are likely to benefit from the lectures they hear and the textbooks they read.

Unfortunately, expository instruction doesn't always present information in ways that facilitate learning. For example, in our "Math Problem" case study at the beginning of the chapter, we see no evidence that Ms. Keeney's explanations and chalkboard demonstrations are helping Reggie and his classmates process the new information effectively. A similar problem exists for textbooks. Analyses in such diverse disciplines as history, geography, and science find that the focus of most school textbooks is on teaching specific facts, with little attention to helping students learn these facts in a meaningful fashion (Bochenhauer, 1990; Calfee & Chambliss, 1988; Chambliss, Calfee, & Wong, 1990; McKeown & Beck, 1990).

What specific techniques can we use to help our students learn from expository instruction? The following exercise might give you a few ideas about techniques that work for *you* as a student.

▣ Experiencing Firsthand
Finding Pedagogy in the Book

1. Look back at two or three of the chapters you've already read in this book. Find several places where specific things that I've done have helped you learn and remember the material more effectively. What specific techniques did I use to facilitate your cognitive processing?

2. In those same chapters, can you find places where you had difficulty processing the material presented? What might I have done differently in such instances?[2]

I'm hoping that the "Thinking About What You Know" questions and the "Experiencing Firsthand" exercises have helped you relate new topics to your own knowledge and experiences. Perhaps some of the graphics, tables, and summaries have helped you organize concepts and principles. Perhaps some of the questions in the margins have encouraged you to elaborate on what you were reading.

Researchers have identified a number of factors that facilitate students' learning from expository instruction, including these:

- Advance organizers
- Connections to prior knowledge
- Coherent organization
- Signals
- Visual aids
- Pacing
- Summaries

These factors are summarized in Table 13–2. Let's look at each one more closely.

Advance Organizers

Have you ever had teachers who presented information in such a disorganized and unpredictable manner that you never knew what they were going to say next? Perhaps you learned a few useful tidbits from those teachers, but you may have had little idea about how the tidbits fit together into a meaningful whole.

---

[2]I'm always eager to hear my readers' suggestions for improving the book (e-mail address: jormrod@ttlc.net).

Principles of Expository Instruction

PRINCIPLE	EDUCATIONAL IMPLICATION	EXAMPLE
An **advance organizer** helps students develop an overall organizational scheme for the material.	Introduce a new unit by describing the major ideas and concepts to be discussed and showing how they are interrelated.	When beginning a unit on mountains, briefly describe the four types—volcanic, dome, fold, and block mountains—before giving a detailed explanation of each one.
Connections to prior knowledge help students learn classroom material meaningfully.	Remind students of something they already know and point out how a new idea is similar.	When introducing new vocabulary words in a French class, identify English words that are spelled similarly and have similar meanings.
An **organized presentation** of material helps students make appropriate interconnections among ideas.	Present related ideas within the same lesson and at the same time.	To help students see how two poems have similar symbolism, discuss both poems on the same day.
Various **signals** built into expository instruction influence students' attention.	Stress important points.	During a lecture, write key concepts on the chalkboard.
Visual aids help students encode material visually as well as verbally.	Illustrate new material through pictures, diagrams, maps, models, and demonstrations.	When describing major battles of the American Civil War, present a map illustrating where each battle took place and how some battles were fought in especially strategic locations.
Appropriate **pacing** gives students adequate time to process information.	Pace a presentation slowly enough that students can engage in meaningful learning, elaboration, and other effective storage processes.	Intersperse lecture material with hands-on activities illustrating the principles presented.
Summaries help students review and organize material and identify main ideas.	After a lecture or reading assignment, summarize the key points of the lesson.	At the end of a unit on clouds, summarize the characteristics of the four types discussed: cumulus, cirrus, stratus, and cumulonimbus.

Unfortunately, many students try to learn a body of information as a list of isolated facts with little or no relationship to one another (B. J. F. Meyer et al., 1980). As teachers, we can help students better organize and interrelate the information in a lesson by providing an **advance organizer**—that is, by giving an introduction that describes an overall organizational scheme for the body of knowledge we are presenting (Ausubel et al., 1978; Corkill, 1992; Mayer, 1979a, 1979b). An advance organizer typically includes the major concepts and ideas of a lesson and shows how these concepts and ideas are related to one another. Here are some simple examples:

- "Today we are going to talk about the two different sounds for the letter *G*. Sometimes G is pronounced "guh," and sometimes it is pronounced "juh." Let's look at some examples."

Provide an advance organizer that gives a general organizational scheme for a lesson.

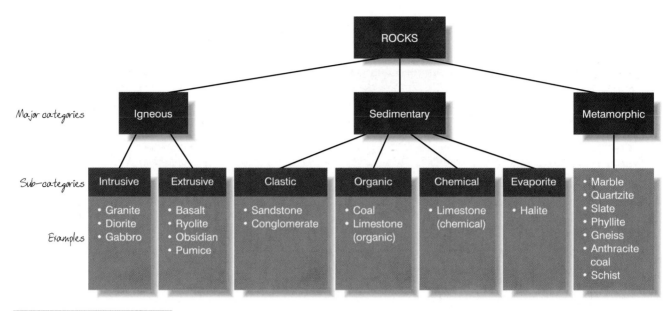

FIGURE 13.5
Graphic advance organizer for a unit on rocks
Adapted from a discussion by R. C. Scott, 1989.

- "During the next two weeks, we will be discussing animals known as *vertebrates*. Vertebrates are all similar in one very important respect: They have a backbone. We will be talking about five phyla of vertebrates: mammals, birds, reptiles, amphibians, and fish. And we will discover that animals in each of these phyla differ from one another in several ways, including whether they are warm-blooded or cold-blooded; whether they have hair, scales, or feathers; and whether they lay eggs or bear live young."

- "For tonight's homework, please read pages 110 through 124 in your history book. These pages describe Magellan's three-year expedition around the world. As you will discover in your reading, Magellan's ships left Spain in 1519. They sailed west and then south to the southernmost tip of South America, then north and west to the Philippines, south around Africa, and finally back up the Atlantic to Spain. As you read, you will learn about why Magellan made the trip, how he dealt with an attempted mutiny, what he called the ocean he found after leaving the Strait of Magellan, and how he died on Mactan Island before completing his expedition."

In some situations, an advance organizer might take a graphic, rather than strictly verbal, form. For example, Figure 13–5 shows how the overall organizational scheme of a unit on rocks might be presented. But regardless of how we do it, we can help students learn more effectively when we let them know ahead of time how the various concepts and ideas they will be studying are going to fit together.

Connections to Prior Knowledge

As we learned in our discussion of cognitive processes in Chapter 6, long-term memory storage and retrieval are easier when students relate new information to things they've already stored in long-term memory. Yet all too often, students fail to connect the new things they learn in school with the things they've previously learned (Perkins & Simmons, 1988; Prawat, 1989). When we begin a lesson by reminding students about the relevant information they already have—a strategy known as **prior knowledge activa-**

Begin instruction and introduce reading assignments by reminding students about what they already know about a topic.

tion—we help them make those critical, meaningful connections. For instance, we might briefly discuss a topic in class before students begin reading about the topic (Hansen & Pearson, 1983; P. T. Wilson & Anderson, 1986). Or, when material learned earlier in the year is important for understanding something new, we might provide a quick review of that "old" material.

Analogies provide an additional means of helping students connect new concepts and principles with what they already know. Here are some examples:

> *Radar is like an echo.* In both cases, waves (either radio waves or sound waves) travel from their source, bounce off a distant object, and return to the source. (Mayer, 1984)

> If we think of the *earth's history as a 24-hour day,* then humans have been in existence for only the last minute of that day. (Hartmann, Miller, & Lee, 1984)

> *Peristalsis,* the muscular contractions that push food through the digestive tract, *is like squeezing ketchup out of a single-serving packet.* "You squeeze the packet near one corner and run your fingers along the length of the packet toward an opening at the other corner. When you do this, you push the ketchup through the packet, in one direction, ahead of your fingers, until it comes out of the opening." (Newby, Ertmer, & Stepich, 1994, p. 4)

By using an analogy to compare new material to familiar material, we can help students store the new information more meaningfully and retrieve it more easily (Donnelly & McDaniel, 1993; Newby et al., 1994; Pittman & Beth-Halachmy, 1997; Zook, 1991). At the same time, we must also point out ways in which the two things are *different*; otherwise our students may take an analogy too far and draw some incorrect conclusions (Glynn, 1991; Zook & Di Vesta, 1991).

When we use expository instruction to build on students' existing knowledge base, we must remember that their "knowledge" is not always accurate: They may bring a number of misconceptions to a learning task. As noted in Chapter 7, students may impose such erroneous beliefs on what they are learning and inadvertently distort the new material as a result. Therefore, we must be sure to address students' misconceptions when we introduce new topics (see "Promoting Conceptual Change" in Chapter 7).

Coherent Organization

An advance organizer starts students on the right track toward organizing new material. But an equally important strategy is to introduce each new idea within the lesson in such a sequence that the important relationships among the various ideas are crystal clear. In other words, we can help students organize material in a particular way by presenting the information using that same organizational structure (Dansereau, 1995; Tennyson & Cocchiarella, 1986; Wade, 1992). For example, if we want students in an English literature class to discover similarities among various short stories, we should discuss several stories within the same lesson rather than talk about each one separately. If we want students to use principles from several subject areas simultaneously to analyze new situations or solve large-scale problems (e.g., the rain forest problem in Chapter 8), we should present these subject areas in an interdisciplinary manner, showing students how the ideas of each area tie in with the ideas of others.

One strategy for showing how the concepts and ideas of a lesson interrelate is to present a **concept map**—a diagram of the concepts or main ideas of a unit and the interrelationships among them (see Chapter 8). As an illustration, Figure 13–6 maps some of the key concepts in a lesson on ancient Egyptian art. Such organizational maps often help students learn, organize, and remember what they hear in a lecture or read in a textbook (R. H. Hall & O'Donnell, 1994; Krajcik, 1991; M. C. Linn et al., 1996).

Use analogies to compare new ideas and relationships to situations with which students are already familiar.

Address the typical misconceptions that students have when they encounter new topics.

Present information in an organized fashion, pointing out important interrelationships.

Does your instructor's organization of a lecture affect the quality of notes you take?

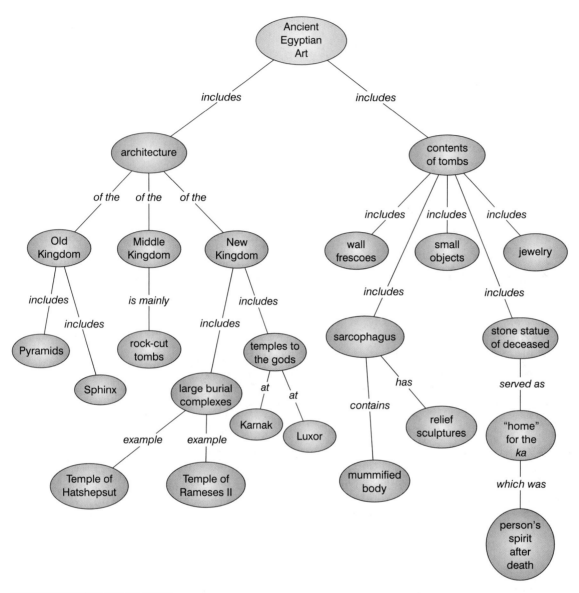

FIGURE 13.6

A concept map for a lesson on ancient Egyptian art

Signals

When, for whatever reason, we must present a great deal of information through expository instruction, our students may have trouble deciding which things are important and which things are not (P. A. Alexander & Jetton, 1996; Garner et al., 1991; R. E. Reynolds & Shirey, 1988). For example, students may focus their attention on interesting, relatively trivial details at the expense of less interesting but more central ideas (P. A. Alexander & Jetton, 1996; Garner et al., 1991; Ward, 1991). Or they may look at the equations they see in a textbook while ignoring any verbal explanations of those equations (Dee-Lucas & Larkin, 1991).

A variety of **signals** as to what information is most important can facilitate students' learning from expository instruction (Armbruster, 1984; Lorch, Lorch, & Inman, 1993). For example, we can emphasize key points by writing them on the chalkboard. We can

Give signals about what things are most important for students to learn.

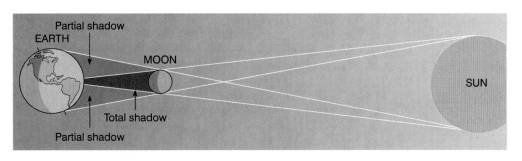

FIGURE 13.7
Model of a solar eclipse

draw students' attention to particular ideas by inserting appropriate questions through-out a lecture or reading assignment (Andre, 1979; M. A. McDaniel & Einstein, 1989). Even just telling students what's important probably makes a difference (R. E. Reynolds & Shirey, 1988).

Visual Aids

In our discussion of cognitive processes in Chapter 6, we discovered that visual imagery can be a highly effective way of storing information in long-term memory. We also dis-covered that information encoded in multiple ways is more easily retrieved from long-term memory than information encoded in just one way. Both principles point to the same conclusion: Supplementing verbal explanations with visual aids should promote more effective long-term memory storage and retrieval.

How might we incorporate a "visual" component into expository instruction? Here are some examples of techniques that research has shown to be effective:

- Live modeling (e.g., a demonstration of how to glaze a ceramic pot)
- Physical models (e.g., a concrete model of an atom)
- Pictures (e.g., a photograph of the Allied troops landing on Normandy Beach)
- Diagrams (e.g., a graphic depiction of the human digestive system)
- Maps (e.g., a series of maps showing the acreage of South American rain forest in 1970, 1980, and 1990)
  (Ferguson & Hegarty, 1995; J. R. Mayer, 1989; Mayer & Gallini, 1990; Scevak, Moore, & Kirby, 1993; M. Y. Small, Lovett, & Scher, 1993; Winn, 1991; also see the discussion of modeling in Chapter 11.)

As an example, Figure 13–7 provides a visual demonstration of how a solar eclipse oc-curs when the moon is aligned directly between the earth and the sun.

In most situations, visual aids should be simple and concise, and they should in-clude major ideas without overwhelming students with detail (Mayer, 1989). In addition to promoting visual imagery, many visual aids can also show students how major ideas relate to and affect one another; thus they provide one more way of helping students or-ganize the information they receive (B. F. Jones, Pierce, & Hunter, 1988/1989; J. R. Levin & Mayer, 1993; Winn, 1991).

Pacing

As you know, effective cognitive processing often takes time: Due to the limited capac-ity of working memory, students can learn only so much so fast. We must therefore pace our presentation of classroom subject matter to allow students the time they need to process it—for example, to think about how new ideas relate to what they already know,

Supplement verbal
explanations with visual
aids such as live models,
physical models, pictures,
diagrams, or maps.

Give students time to
process information.
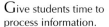

generate their own examples of new concepts, and draw their own conclusions and implications from what they are reading.

One strategy for providing this needed processing time is to build redundancy into an explanation or lecture—in other words, to present each important idea not just once, but several times, each time using different words to say essentially the same thing. To illustrate, perhaps we might first state the idea, then give an example to illustrate that idea, then state the idea again, then describe its relevance to students' own lives. If we present the same piece of information several times over, our students are bound to catch it at least one of those times! As an example, notice how redundant my discussion of redundancy is in this paragraph. I used the first three sentences to state and restate a single idea!

Another way of giving students the processing time they need is to stop a lecture at ten-minute intervals and give students a couple of minutes to meet in small groups to compare notes, ask one another questions, and share ideas (R. T. Johnson, 1989; Rowe, 1987). When we give students the opportunity to process lecture information in small groups, they are likely to produce more useful class notes, perform better on complex test questions, and remember information longer (Rowe, 1987).

Do your own instructors give you the time you need during a lecture to process new ideas sufficiently?

Summaries

Earlier, we noted the importance of providing an advance organizer before we begin a lesson: Students tend to learn more effectively when they are given advance notice of the things they will be learning and how those things are interrelated. Students also tend to benefit from summaries presented at the end of a verbal explanation or written passage: They learn more effectively when they hear or read a synopsis of the information they have just studied (Hartley & Trueman, 1982). Summaries are likely to serve multiple functions, helping students (1) review material, (2) determine which of the many ideas they have studied are most important, and (3) pull key ideas into a more cohesive organizational structure.

At the conclusion of a lesson or unit, summarize the material presented.

Perhaps the major advantage of expository instruction is that it enables students to explore a topic in an organized and relatively time-efficient manner. Yet expository instruction has a potential weakness as well: It often occurs in the absence of the actual objects or events under discussion. When students read a textbook passage about amphibians, they probably don't have a frog or toad to examine firsthand. When students listen to a lecture on the concepts of force and momentum, they may have trouble learning such abstract concepts without actually experiencing or witnessing them in action. Thus, many students—younger ones especially—are apt to have difficulty learning solely from lectures and textbooks. So we may also want to provide opportunities for them to interact directly with the topic at hand, perhaps through discovery learning.

Consider once again Reggie's "math problem" at the beginning of the chapter. What expository instruction techniques might the teacher use to help Reggie learn?

Discovery Learning

THINKING ABOUT WHAT YOU KNOW

Think about something you've learned through your own research or experimentation. How thoroughly did you learn that information or skill? Do you think you learned it more thoroughly than you would have if you had simply read about it in a book or heard about it from another person?

Unlike expository instruction, where information is presented in its final form, **discovery learning** is a process through which students interact with their physical or social environment—for example, by exploring and manipulating objects, performing experiments, or wrestling with questions and controversies—and derive information for themselves. Common examples of discovery learning are laboratory experiments, library research projects, and opportunities for students to learn by trial and error (e.g., as they "fiddle" with computer software, a soccer ball, or watercolor paints). Discovery learning can sometimes be incorporated into other forms of instruction; for example, the "Experiencing Firsthand" exercises in this very "expository" book have, I hope, helped you discover a number of important principles on your own.

Research studies indicate that people often remember and transfer information more effectively when they construct it for themselves rather than when they simply read it in expository material (M. A. McDaniel & Schlager, 1990; M. A. McDaniel, Waddill, & Einstein, 1988; D. S. McNamara & Healy, 1995). We can easily explain this finding using principles of cognitive psychology (Bruner, 1961, 1966; M. A. McDaniel et al., 1988; B. Y. White & Frederiksen, 1998). When learners discover something on their own, they typically have to think about (process) that information or skill to a greater extent than they might otherwise, and so they are more likely to engage in meaningful learning. In addition, learners often learn classroom subject matter in a more complete and integrated fashion (i.e., they achieve greater *conceptual understanding*) when they have opportunities to explore and manipulate their environment firsthand (see Chapter 7). Furthermore, when learners *see* something as well as hear or read about it, they can encode it in long-term memory visually as well as verbally. And from a developmental perspective, many students, especially those in the elementary grades, understand concrete experiences more easily than abstract ideas (see Chapter 2). For instance, from Piaget's perspective, twelve-year-old Reggie in our opening case study probably has not completely made the transition from concrete operational to formal operational thinking; accordingly, he may need many concrete experiences to help him understand the relatively abstract concepts (e.g., negative numbers, improper fractions) that Ms. Keeney has been trying to teach primarily through verbal (and presumably abstract) explanations.

How effective is discovery learning in a classroom context? Unfortunately, research does not always give us a clear answer to this question. Ideally, to determine whether discovery learning works better than other approaches, we would need to compare two groups of students who differ on only *one* variable: the extent to which discovery learning is a part of their instructional experience. Yet few research studies have made this crucial comparison, and the studies that have been conducted give us contradictory results. Nevertheless, some general conclusions about discovery learning can be gleaned from research findings:

- When we consider *overall academic achievement,* discovery learning is not necessarily better or worse than "traditional" (e.g., more expository) approaches to instruction; research yields mixed findings on this issue.

- When we consider *higher-level thinking skills,* discovery learning is often preferable for fostering transfer, problem solving, creativity, and self-regulated learning.

- When we consider *affective objectives,* discovery learning often promotes a more positive attitude toward teachers and schoolwork than does traditional instruction; in other

How might you make the concepts *negative number* and *improper fraction* concrete for students?

Students may better understand scientific principles when they actually observe those principles in action.

words, students like school better. (Ferguson & Hegarty, 1995; Giaconia & Hedges, 1982; Marshall, 1981; Mayer, 1974, 1987; P. L. Peterson, 1979; Roughead & Scandura, 1968; Shymansky, Hedges, & Woodworth, 1990; B. Y. White & Frederiksen, 1998)

At the same time, we should note two potential problems with discovery learning (Hammer, 1997; Schauble, 1990). First, students may sometimes construct incorrect understandings from their discovery activities. We saw an example of this in the "All Charged Up" case study at the end of Chapter 9, when four students in a physics lab concluded incorrectly that virtually any object can transfer an electrical charge to another object of the same material (e.g., a Styrofoam plate can transfer a charge to a Styrofoam cup). Second, discovery learning activities often take considerably more time than expository instruction, and teachers may sometimes feel torn between providing discovery experiences and "covering" all the school district's objectives for the year. In my own experience, I've found that my students typically remember what they've learned in hands-on discovery activities so much more effectively than what they've learned through expository instruction that the extra time I've devoted to those activities has been time well spent (another instance of the *less is more* principle).

Psychologists and educators have offered numerous suggestions for facilitating effective discovery learning. We can summarize these in terms of three general guidelines:

🍎 Make sure students have the necessary prior knowledge for interpreting what they observe.

- *Make sure students have the knowledge they need to interpret their findings appropriately.* Students are most likely to benefit from a discovery learning activity when they have relevant prior knowledge that they can draw on to interpret their observations (Bruner, 1966; N. Frederiksen, 1984a). For example, having students conduct experiments to determine the influence of gravity on the velocity of a falling object will typically be more beneficial if students are already familiar with the concepts *gravity* and *velocity*. As cognitive psychologists tell us, meaningful learning can occur only when students have appropriate prior knowledge to which they can relate new experiences.

- *Provide some structure to guide students' discovery activities.* Young children often learn from random exploration of their environment. For example, preschoolers can discover many properties of sand and water by manipulating dry sand, wet sand, and water in an unstructured setting—perhaps by scooping, pouring, scraping, pushing, digging, dropping, burying, or blowing. Through such play activities, children learn what physical objects do and what people can do *to* those objects (Hutt, Tyler, Hutt, & Christopherson, 1989).

🍎 Structure the experience so that students' explorations proceed in fruitful directions.

At the elementary and secondary school levels, however, students are more likely to benefit from carefully planned and structured activities (Hammer, 1997; Hickey, 1997; Mayer & Greeno, 1972; B. Y. White & Frederiksen, 1998). For example, high school chemistry students are rarely left to mix their own chemical concoctions; the results of their activities would be uninterpretable, wasteful, or even explosive. Instead, the chemistry teacher prescribes certain actions; students carry out those actions, observe the results, and try to explain them.

One simple way of structuring a discovery session is simply to pose a question and then let students develop their own procedure to answer it. For example, a high school biology teacher may ask the class, "How can we make a mealworm move backward?" Students can brainstorm a number of approaches to answering the question and then assemble items such as these:

flashlight	turpentine
smoke	burning match
pin	vinegar
hot iron	pencil
noisemaker	straw (for blowing with)
ammonia	wet ink

After watching a mealworm's reaction to each item, students make deductions about its ability to see, hear, and feel (Kuslan & Stone, 1972).

The degree to which a discovery session needs to be structured may depend to some extent on the scientific reasoning and problem-solving skills that students do or do not possess (B. Y. White & Frederiksen, 1998). For example, some students may have difficulty tackling vague, ill-defined problems (see Chapter 8). And many other students—perhaps those who have not yet acquired formal operational thinking capabilities—may have trouble formulating and testing hypotheses, or separating and controlling variables (see Chapter 2). Such students will probably work more effectively when they are given problems and questions that are concrete and well defined and when they are given specific suggestions regarding how to proceed.

• *Help students relate their procedures and observations to academic concepts and principles.* A discovery learning activity is most likely to be effective when students actively try to construct meaning from what they are doing and observing, and they may sometimes need scaffolding to help them construct appropriate meanings (e.g., Minstrell & Stimpson, 1996). Such scaffolding might take the form of questions that guide students' thinking; here are three examples:

In what ways has the culture in this petri dish changed since yesterday?

How can we measure a motorized vehicle's rate of acceleration in an objective way?

When we add these two chemicals together and then heat them, how can we be sure the *heat,* rather than some other variable, is bringing about the change that we see?

From Vygotsky's perspective, one important way that adults foster children's cognitive development is to convey how their culture typically interprets the world—perhaps through a *cognitive apprenticeship* in which an adult models and encourages culture-specific ways of thinking about a task or problem (see Chapter 2). A major part of Western culture is the concepts and principles that people in different academic disciplines have developed to explain a wide variety of human experiences. For example, look once again at the lesson plan in Figure 13–3. The lesson includes two structured discovery activities: calculating the number of Spanish place names in Colorado counties and identifying the various states and countries from which students and their ancestors have migrated. The activities are followed by class discussions and explanations that encourage the students to interpret their findings in terms of geographical concepts and principles—more specifically, *culture, migration,* and "push" and "pull" factors affecting migration.

As we have seen, students may benefit little from discovery learning sessions when they do not have the knowledge base to interpret their observations and discoveries accurately. When students need to learn knowledge or skills that are essential prerequisites for achieving later instructional objectives, a mastery learning approach is often recommended. We turn to this approach now.

Mastery Learning

Let's return once again to Ms. Keeney's math class. This class of twenty-seven students is beginning a unit on fractions. It progresses through several lessons as follows:

Lesson 1:

The class first studies the basic idea that a fraction represents parts of a whole: The denominator indicates the number of pieces into which the whole has been divided, and the numerator indicates how many of those pieces are present. By the end of the lesson, twenty-three children understand what a fraction is. But Sarah, LaShaun, Jason K., and Jason M. are either partly or totally confused.

Decrease the amount of structure as students' reasoning and problem-solving skills develop.

Model and encourage desired ways of thinking about procedures and observations.

Encourage students to relate their observations to specific concepts and principles in the discipline they are studying.

INTO THE CLASSROOM: Promoting
Discovery Learning

Identify a concept or principle about which students can learn through interaction with their physical or social environment.

> A mathematics teacher realizes that, rather than tell students how to calculate the area of a triangle, she can help them discover the procedure for themselves.

Make sure students have the necessary prior knowledge for discovering new ideas and principles.

> After students in a physics class have studied such concepts as velocity, acceleration, and gravity, their teacher has them measure the speed of a metal ball rolling down ramps of varying degrees of incline.

Structure the experience so that students proceed logically toward any discoveries you want them to make.

> To demonstrate the effects of prejudice, a social studies teacher creates a situation in which each student, because of an arbitrarily chosen physical characteristic that he or she possesses, experiences the prejudice of classmates.

Show puzzling results to arouse curiosity.

> A science teacher shows her class two glasses of water. In one glass, an egg is floating at the water's surface; in the other glass, an egg has sunk to the bottom. The students give a simple and logical explanation for the difference: One egg has more air inside, so it is lighter. But then the teacher switches the eggs into opposite glasses. The egg that the students believe to be "heavier" now floats, and the egg they think is "lighter" sinks to the bottom. The students are quite surprised to observe this result and demand to know what is going on. (Ordinarily, water is less dense than an egg, so an egg placed in it will quickly sink. But in this situation, one glass contains salt water—a mixture denser than an egg and therefore capable of keeping it afloat.) (adapted from Palmer, 1965)

Have students record their findings.

> A biology teacher has students make sketches of the specific organs they observe as they dissect an earthworm.

Help students relate their findings to concepts and principles in the academic discipline they are studying.

> After students in a social studies class have collected data on average incomes and voting patterns in different counties within their state, their teacher asks, "How can we interpret these data given what we've learned about the relative wealth of members of the two major political parties?"

Lesson 2:

The class then studies the process of reducing fractions to their lowest terms. For example, 2/4 can be reduced to 1/2, and 12/20 can be reduced to 3/5. By the end of the lesson, twenty children understand the process of reducing fractions. But Alison, Reggie, and Jason S. haven't mastered the idea that they need to divide both the numerator and denominator by the same number. And of course, Sarah, LaShaun, and the other two Jasons still don't understand what fractions *are* and so have trouble with this lesson as well.

Lesson 3:

Later, the class studies the process of adding two fractions together. At this point, the students look only at situations in which the denominators are the same. For example, 2/5 + 2/5 = 4/5 and 1/20 + 11/20 = 12/20. By the end of the lesson, nineteen children can add fractions with the same denominator. Matt, Charlie, Maria F., and Maria W. keep adding the denominators together as well as the numerators (thus figuring that 2/5 + 2/5 = 4/10). And Sarah, LaShaun, Jason K., and Jason M. still don't know what fractions actually *are*.

Lesson 4:

Finally, the class combines the processes of adding fractions and reducing fractions to their lowest terms. They must first add two fractions together and then, if necessary, reduce the sum to its lowest terms. For example, when they add 1/20 + 11/20 together, they must reduce the sum of 12/20 to 3/5. At this point, we lose Muhammed, Aretha, and Karen because they keep forgetting to reduce the sum to lowest terms. And of course, we've already lost Sarah, LaShaun, Alison, Reggie, Matt, Charlie, the two Marias, and the three Jasons on prerequisite skills. We now have thirteen of our original twenty-seven students understanding what they are doing— less than half the class! (See Figure 13–8.)

When we move through lessons without making sure that all students master the content of each one, we lose more and more students as we go along. To minimize the likelihood that such a situation will occur, we may want to implement an approach to instruction known as **mastery learning** (Block, 1980; Bloom, 1976, 1981; Guskey, 1985, 1994; Hunter, 1982; J. F. Lee & Pruitt, 1984). In a mastery learning situation, students must learn one lesson well (they must *master* the content) before proceeding to the next lesson. The approach is based on three underlying assumptions:

- Almost every student can learn a particular topic to mastery.
- Some students need more time to master a topic than others.
- Some students need more assistance (e.g., individualized tutoring or additional practice exercises) than others.

As you can see, mastery learning represents a very optimistic approach to instruction: It assumes that most children *can* learn school subject matter if they are given sufficient time and instruction to do so.

Mastery learning usually includes the following components:

1. *Small, discrete units.* Course content is broken up into a number of separate units or lessons, with each unit covering a limited amount of material and aimed at accomplishing a small number of instructional objectives (perhaps 1–3).

2. *A logical sequence.* Units are sequenced such that concepts and procedures that provide the foundation for later units are learned first. More complex concepts and procedures, including those that build on basic units, are learned later. For example, a unit in which students learn what a fraction is would obviously come before a unit in which they learn how to add two fractions together.

3. *Demonstration of mastery at the completion of each unit.* Before moving from one unit to the next, students must show that they have mastered the current unit—for example, by taking a test on the content of that unit. (Here is an example of how instruction and assessment often work hand in hand.)

4. *A concrete, observable criterion for mastery of each unit.* Mastery of a topic is defined in specific and concrete terms. For example, to "pass" a unit on adding fractions with the same denominator, students might have to answer at least 90 percent of test items correctly.

Can you recall a time when you were unable to master something that was critical for your later classroom success? How did you feel in that situation?

Conduct a task analysis to identify the content and sequence of each unit.

Make sure students demonstrate mastery of one unit before proceeding to the next.

Students	Lesson 1: Concept of Fraction	Lesson 2: Reducing to Lowest Terms (Builds on Lesson 1)	Lesson 3: Adding Fractions with Same Denominator (Builds on Lesson 1)	Lesson 4: Adding Fractions with Different Denominators (Builds on Lessons 2 & 3)
Sarah	−	−	−	−
LaShaun	−	−	−	−
Jason K.	−	−	−	−
Jason M.	−	−	−	−
Alison	+		+	−
Reggie	+		+	
Jason S.	+		+	
Matt	+	+		
Charlie	+	+		
Maria F.	+	+		
Maria W.	+	+		
Muhammed	+	+	+	
Aretha	+	+	+	−
Karen	+	+	+	−
Kevin	+	+	+	+
Nori	+	+	+	+
Marcy	+	+	+	+
Janelle	+	+	+	+
Joyce	+	+	+	+
Ming Tang	+	+	+	+
Georgette	+	+	+	+
LaVeda	+	+	+	+
Mark	+	+	+	+
Seth	+	+	+	+
Joanne	+	+	+	+
Rita	+	+	+	+
Shauna	+	+	+	+

Students become "lost" when they fail to master important building blocks on which later material depends. For these students, mastery is indicated by a solid line and nonmastery is indicated by a dotted line. Notice how we have lost 14 of the 27 students by the end of Lesson 4.

FIGURE 13.8
Sequential nature of mastery learning

Provide additional instructional activities for students who do not attain mastery on the first attempt.

5. *Additional "remedial" activities for students needing extra help or practice to attain mastery.* Students do not always demonstrate mastery on the first try. Additional support and resources (perhaps alternative approaches to instruction, different materials, workbooks, study groups, and individual tutoring) are provided for students who need them (e.g., Guskey, 1985).

Students engaged in mastery learning often proceed through the various units at their own speed; hence, different students may be studying different units at any given point in time. But it is also possible for an entire class to proceed through a sequence at the same time: Students who master a unit earlier than their classmates can pursue various enrichment activities, or they can serve as tutors for those still working on the unit (Block, 1980; Guskey, 1985).

We find justification for mastery learning in several theoretical perspectives. For example, operant conditioning theorists tell us that complex behaviors are often more easily learned through *shaping,* whereby a simple response is reinforced until it occurs frequently (i.e., until it is mastered), then a slightly more difficult response is reinforced, and so on. We see further justification in cognitive psychologists' concept of *auto-*

maticity: Information and skills that need to be retrieved rapidly or used in complex problem-solving situations must be practiced and learned thoroughly. Finally, as social cognitive theorists have noted, the ability to perform a particular task successfully and easily is likely to enhance students' sense of self-efficacy for performing similar tasks.

Research indicates that mastery learning has several advantages over nonmastery approaches. In particular, students tend to:

- Learn more and perform better on classroom assessments
- Maintain better study habits, studying regularly rather than procrastinating and cramming
- Enjoy their classes and teachers more
- Have greater interest in the subject
- Have more self-confidence about their ability to learn the subject
  (Block & Burns, 1976; Born & Davis, 1974; C. C. Kulik, Kulik, & Bangert-Drowns, 1990; J. A. Kulik, Kulik, & Cohen, 1979; Shuell, 1996)

Mastery learning is most appropriate when students must learn certain concepts or skills thoroughly (perhaps to a level of automaticity), and especially when, as in Ms. Keeney's math class, those concepts and skills provide the foundation for future educational tasks. When instructional objectives deal with such basics as reading word recognition, addition and subtraction, scientific concepts, or rules of grammar, instruction designed to promote mastery learning may be in order. Nevertheless, the very notion of mastery may be *in*appropriate for some of our long-term objectives. As noted earlier in the chapter, skills such as critical reading, scientific reasoning, and creative writing may continue to improve over the years without ever really being mastered.

Direct Instruction

An approach incorporating elements of both expository instruction and mastery learning is **direct instruction,** which uses a variety of techniques designed to keep students continually and actively engaged in learning and using classroom subject matter (Englemann & Carnine, 1982; R. M. Gagné, 1985; Rosenshine & Stevens, 1986; Tarver, 1992; Weinert & Helmke, 1995). To some extent, direct instruction is based on principles from behaviorist theories of learning; for instance, it requires learners to make frequent overt responses and provides immediate reinforcement of correct responses through teacher feedback. But it also considers principles from cognitive psychology, including the importance of attention and long-term memory storage processes in learning, the limited capacity of working memory, and the value of learning basic skills to automaticity (Rosenshine & Stevens, 1986).

Different theorists describe and implement direct instruction somewhat differently. But in general, this approach involves small and carefully sequenced steps, fast pacing, and a great deal of teacher-student interaction. Each lesson typically involves most or all of the following components (Rosenshine & Stevens, 1986):

1. *Review of previously learned material.* The teacher reviews relevant content from previous lessons, checks homework assignments involving that content and, if necessary, reteaches any information or skills that students have apparently not yet mastered.

2. *Statement of the goals of the lesson.* The teacher describes one or more objectives that students should accomplish during the new lesson.

3. *Presentation of new material in small, carefully sequenced steps.* The teacher presents a small amount of information or a specific skill in an expository fashion—perhaps through a verbal explanation, modeling, and one or more examples. The teacher may also provide an advance organizer, ask

Considering the subject matter you will be teaching, what important information and skills would you want your students to master?

INTO THE CLASSROOM: Promoting
Mastery Learning

Break course material into small, manageable units of instruction.

> A mathematics teacher breaks instruction on fractions into five units: the basic concept of a fraction, proper versus improper fractions, reducing to lowest terms, adding and subtracting fractions of like denominators, and adding and subtracting fractions of unlike denominators.

Identify the sequence in which these units should logically be arranged.

> An elementary school teacher recognizes that he must be sure students have mastered the four cardinal directions (north, south, east, and west) before he introduces the concepts of latitude and longitude.

Develop a concrete, observable criterion for mastery of each unit.

> In a German class, students demonstrate mastery of each textbook chapter by getting a score of at least 85 percent on the chapter quiz and engaging in oral recitations that incorporate the chapter's vocabulary and syntactical structures.

Make sure students demonstrate mastery of one unit before proceeding to the next.

> In the same German class, students must demonstrate mastery of each chapter before proceeding to the next.

Provide additional instructional activities for students who do not attain mastery on the first attempt.

> The teacher of the same German class provides additional exercises plus tutoring from more advanced students for those students unable to attain mastery after two attempts.

questions, or in other ways scaffold students' efforts to process and remember the material.

4. *Guided student practice and assessment after each step.* Students have frequent opportunities to practice what they are learning, perhaps by answering questions, solving problems, or performing modeled procedures. The teacher gives hints during students' early responses, provides immediate feedback about their performance, makes suggestions about how to improve, and, when necessary, provides remedial instruction.

5. *Assessment of student progress.* After students have completed guided practice, the teacher checks to be sure they have mastered the information or skill in question, perhaps by having them answer a series of follow-up questions or summarize what they've learned.

6. *Independent practice.* Once students have acquired some degree of mastery (e.g., by answering 80 percent of questions correctly), they engage in further practice either independently or in small, cooperative groups. By doing so, they work toward achieving automaticity for the material in question.

7. *Frequent follow-up reviews.* The teacher provides many opportunities for students to review previously learned material over the course of the school year—perhaps through homework assignments, writing assignments, or paper-pencil quizzes.

The teacher proceeds back and forth among these steps as necessary to ensure that all students are truly mastering the subject matter.

Like mastery learning, direct instruction is most suitable for teaching information and skills that are well-defined and should be taught in a step-by-step sequence (Rosenshine & Stevens, 1986). Because of the high degree of teacher-student interaction, it is often more easily implemented with small groups of students rather than with an entire classroom. Under such circumstances, research indicates that it can be a highly effective instructional technique, leading to substantial gains in achievement of both basic skills and higher-level thinking processes, high student interest and self-efficacy for the subject matter in question, and low rates of student misbehavior (Rosenshine & Stevens, 1986; Tarver, 1992; Weinert & Helmke, 1995).

One advantage of both mastery learning and direct instruction approaches is that, because students must demonstrate mastery at the completion of each unit, they receive frequent feedback about the progress they are making. Yet another approach—computer-based instruction—may provide even *more* frequent feedback, as we shall see now.

Direct instruction typically involves many opportunities to practice new skills, often with considerable teacher guidance in the early stages.

Computer-Based Instruction

As learning theories have evolved over the years, so, too, have ways of designing and delivering instruction through computers. Here we will consider two general approaches to computer-based instruction: an early approach derived from behaviorist principles and more recent approaches derived from principles within cognitive psychology.

A Behaviorist Approach

Experiencing Firsthand
A Shocking Lesson

Let's switch gears for a minute. Rather than studying instruction, take a few minutes to study a little first aid. What follows is a short lesson on treating victims of traumatic shock. The lesson is presented in a sequence of boxes known as *frames*. Use a sheet of blank paper to cover all but the first frame. Read the information presented in the first frame and then write the answer to the question at the top of your blank paper. Once you have done so, uncover the next frame and check your response against the answer presented in the upper left-hand corner. Read the new information and again respond to the question. Continue in this manner through all the frames, each time getting feedback to the question you just answered, reading the new information, and answering another question.

Frame 1

When the human body is seriously injured, a condition that frequently results is <u>traumatic shock.</u>
? A frequent result of serious injury is traumatic _____.

Frame 2

shock

Burns, wounds, and bone fractures can all lead to traumatic shock.

? Three common types of injuries can lead to traumatic shock:
burns, wounds, and bone _____.

Frame 3

fractures

Traumatic shock is a condition in which many normal bodily functions are depressed.

? When a person is suffering from traumatic shock, normal bodily functions become _____.

Frame 4

depressed

Bodily functions are depressed during shock because not enough blood is circulating through the body.

? The depression of bodily functions during shock is due to an insufficient amount of _____
circulating through the body.

Frame 5

blood

The more blood lost as a result of an injury, the greater the possibility of traumatic shock.

? The probability of shock increases when an injury results in the loss of more _____.

Frame 6

blood

An injured person who may be suffering from shock should be kept lying down and at a comfortable temperature.

? In a cold environment, it is probably best to do which of the following for a person possibly in shock?
   a. Cover the person with a blanket.
   b. Cover the person with cool, damp towels.
   c. Leave the person uncovered.

Frame 7

If you chose *a*, you are correct. Proceed to Frame 9.
If you chose *b* or *c*, you are incorrect. Continue with this frame.

A person who is possibly suffering from traumatic shock should be kept at a comfortable body temperature.

? A possible shock victim should be kept:
   a. as cool as possible
   b. as warm as possible
   c. at a comfortable body temperature

Frame 8

If you chose *c*, you are correct. Continue with this frame.
If you chose *a* or *b*, you are incorrect. Return to Frame 7.

In a cold environment, the person should be covered with a blanket in order to be kept warm. In a warm environment, little or no covering is needed.

? In a cold environment, it is probably best to do which of the following for a person who is possibly suffering from shock?
   a. Cover the person with cool, damp towels.
   b. Leave the person uncovered.
   c. Cover the person with a blanket.

Frame 9

If you chose *c*, you are correct. Continue with this frame.
If you chose *a* or *b*, you are incorrect. Return to Frame 7.

A possible shock victim should be kept lying down. This way, blood will more easily flow to the head and chest, where it is most needed.

? A shock victim should be placed in a _____ position.
   a. sitting
   b. lying-down
   c. standing

Frame 10

If you chose *b*, you are correct. Proceed to Frame 11.
If you chose *a* or *c*, you are incorrect. Continue with this frame.

It is best to keep a shock victim lying down. This way, blood circulates more readily to the head and chest.

? A shock victim should be kept _____.
   a. lying down
   b. sitting
   c. standing

Frame 11

If you chose *a*, you are correct. Continue with this frame.
If you chose *b* or *c*, you are incorrect. Return to Frame 4.

. . . the lesson continues . . .

As noted in our discussion of expository instruction, B. F. Skinner objected to instruction in which students, by making few if any overt responses, play a passive role. In addition, he was concerned that, in most schools, reinforcement (e.g., in the form of positive feedback for assignments completed appropriately or for test questions answered correctly) is intermittent at best, and it is often given days or even weeks after learning had actually occurred. In the "Shocking Lesson" you just studied, you saw an example of **programmed instruction** (Skinner, 1954, 1968), which incorporates these principles of operant conditioning:

1. *Active responding.* By answering questions or filling in blanks, you make an overt, observable response.

2. *Shaping.* Instruction begins with something you already know—in this case, the fact that human beings can suffer serious injuries. New information is broken into tiny pieces, and instruction proceeds through a gradual presentation of additional pieces in successive *frames* within the lesson. As more information is acquired and questions of increasing difficulty are answered, the terminal behavior is gradually shaped.

3. *Immediate reinforcement.* Because instruction involves a gradual shaping process, there is a high probability of responding correctly to the questions asked. Each answer is reinforced immediately when you receive feedback that the answer is correct.

The first part of the lesson on treating traumatic shock illustrates a **linear program:** All students progress through the same sequence of frames. Beginning with Frame 7, the lesson becomes a **branching program** (e.g., N. A. Crowder & Martin, 1961). At this point, instruction progresses more quickly, presenting larger amounts of information in each frame. As a result, questions are more difficult to answer, and students are more likely to make errors. Whenever students respond incorrectly to a question, they proceed to one or more remedial frames for further clarification or practice before continuing on with new information.

In the 1950s and 1960s, programmed instruction was typically presented through printed materials (e.g., books) in much the same way that I presented the first aid lesson to you just now. But with the wide availability of computer technology, it is now presented primarily by means of computers and so is often known as **computer-assisted instruction (CAI).** Most CAI programs are branching programs: They automatically switch to one frame or another depending on what response a student has made. Branching programs provide more flexibility than linear programs: Only those students having difficulty with a particular skill or concept proceed to remedial frames. Other students can move on to new information, without having to spend time on practice frames they do not need.

Cognitive Approaches

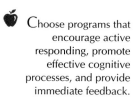
Choose programs that encourage active responding, promote effective cognitive processes, and provide immediate feedback.

Contemporary educational computer programs often incorporate cognitivist principles as well as those of behaviorism. For example, effective programs often take steps to capture and hold students' *attention,* elicit students' *prior knowledge* about a topic, and encourage long-term retention and transfer (R. M. Gagné, Briggs, & Wager, 1992; P. F. Merrill et al., 1996). Furthermore, some programs provide drill and practice of basic knowledge and skills (e.g., math facts, typing, fundamentals of music), helping students develop *automaticity* in these areas (P. F. Merrill et al., 1996). The term **computer-based instruction (CBI)** encompasses recent innovations in computer-delivered instruction as well as the more traditional CAI.

Although some computer-based instructional programs provide a fairly lock-step sequence of instruction, others do not. Perhaps, as a student, you have had experience with computer programs that allowed you to jump around from one topic to other, related topics, thereby enabling you to decide what things to study and in what order to study them. If so, then you have had experience with either hypertext or hypermedia (e.g., Jonassen, 1996; P. F. Merrill et al., 1996). **Hypertext** is a collection of computer-based verbal material that allows students to read about one topic and then proceed to related topics of their own choosing; for example, you might read a short, introductory passage about airplanes and then decide whether to proceed to more specific information about aerodynamics, the history of air travel, or military aircraft. **Hypermedia** include such other media as pictures, sound, animations, and videos as well as text; for example, some computer-based encyclopedias enable students to bounce from text to a voice message and then to a video about a particular topic.

Hypertext and hypermedia, when used for instructional purposes, are based on the assumption that students benefit from imposing their own organization on a subject area and selecting those topics that are most personally relevant (Jonassen, 1996; R. V. Small & Grabowski, 1992). Keep in mind, however, that not all students are capable of making wise choices about what to study and in what sequence to study it. For example, they may be overwhelmed by the large number of choices the computer offers, have trouble identifying important information, or lack sufficient comprehension-monitoring skills to determine when they have sufficiently mastered the material (Garhart & Hannafin, 1986; Lanza & Roselli, 1991; E. R. Steinberg, 1989).

Students' access to new information is not necessarily limited to the computer programs that we have in our own schools and classrooms. Through modems and telephone lines, our students will often have access to the *Internet,* a worldwide network of computers and computer databases that provide information on virtually any topic in which students are interested. Through such mechanisms as electronic mail (e-mail) and electronic bulletin boards, computer networks also enable students to communicate directly with people and agencies who may have the information they need.

Use hypertext and hypermedia when students are capable of making informed choices about what to study and learn.

Use computer networks to expand students' access to information located beyond school walls.

Effectiveness of Computer-Based Instruction

Numerous research studies have documented the effectiveness of CBI: Students often have higher academic achievement and better attitudes toward their schoolwork than is true for students taught with more traditional methods (J. A. Kulik, Kulik, & Cohen, 1980; Lepper & Gurtner, 1989; P. F. Merrill et al., 1996; Roblyer, Castine, & King, 1988; Tudor, 1995). Furthermore, students studying academic subject matter on a computer may gain an increased sense that they can control their own learning, thereby developing more intrinsic motivation to learn (Swan, Mitrani, Guerrero, Cheung, & Schoener, 1990).

Students gain easy access to a virtual "world" of information when they explore the Internet.

Computers offer several advantages for instruction that we often cannot achieve through any other medium. For one thing, instructional programs can include animations, video clips, and spoken messages—components that are, of course, not possible with traditional printed materials. Second, a computer can record and maintain ongoing data for each of our students, including such information as how far they have progressed in the program, how often they are right and wrong, how quickly they respond, and so on. With such data, we can monitor each student's progress through the program and identify students who are having particular difficulty with the material. And, finally, a computer can be used to provide instruction when flesh-and-blood teachers are not available; for example, CBI is often used to deliver instruction in rural areas far removed from traditional school settings.

Using a computer *in and of itself,* however, is not necessarily the key to better instruction (R. E. Clark, 1983). A computer can help our students achieve at higher levels only when it provides instruction that we cannot offer as easily or effectively by other means. There is little to be gained when a student is merely reading information on a computer screen instead of reading it in a textbook.

In what ways might CBI benefit Reggie in our opening case study?

When planned and implemented appropriately, all of the instructional strategies just examined—expository instruction, discovery learning, mastery learning, directed instruction, and CBI—should help students process classroom material in effective ways. But when our primary goal is to promote elaboration or transfer, we may want to consider some additional strategies as well, perhaps using them in combination with the approaches already described. Let's look at some of these strategies.

Promoting Elaboration of Classroom Material

Cognitive theories of learning emphasize that it's not enough for students simply to learn the information and skills presented or discovered in class. Students are far more likely to remember classroom material over the long run if they *elaborate* on it—that is, if they embellish on the material using things they already know.

This section presents several strategies that are likely to foster student elaboration and, in many cases, transfer as well:

- Teacher questions
- In-class activities
- Computer applications
- Homework
- Authentic activities

As noted earlier, these strategies tend to be somewhat teacher-directed. In Chapter 14, we'll consider student-directed strategies that also promote elaboration.

■ How can we best promote transfer? To refresh your memory, skim the section "Factors Affecting Transfer" in Chapter 8.

Teacher Questions

■ THINKING ABOUT WHAT YOU KNOW

Your instructors probably ask many questions in class. What kinds of teacher questions are most effective in helping you learn?

Questioning is a widely used teaching technique (e.g., Mehan, 1979). Many teacher questions are **lower-level questions:** They ask students to retrieve information they've presumably already learned. Such questions have several benefits (Airasian, 1994; Connolly & Eisenberg, 1990; P. W. Fox & LeCount, 1991; Wixson, 1984). First, they enable us to determine what students' prior knowledge and misconceptions about a topic are likely to be (see Chapter 7). Second, they tend to keep students' attention on the lesson in progress (see Chapter 6). Third, they help us ascertain whether students are learning class material successfully or are confused about particular points; even very experienced teachers sometimes overestimate what students are actually learning during expository instruction. Fourth, they give our students the opportunity to monitor their *own* comprehension—to determine whether they understand the information being presented or whether they should ask for help or clarification. Finally, when questions ask students about material they've studied earlier, they encourage review of that material, which should promote greater recall later on. Following is an example of how one eighth-grade teacher promoted review of a lesson on ancient Egypt by asking questions:

Teacher: The Egyptians believed the body had to be preserved. What did they do to preserve the body in the earliest times?

Student: They dried them and stuffed them.

Teacher: I am talking about from the earliest times. What did they do? Carey.

Carey: They buried them in the hot sands.

Teacher: Right. They buried them in the hot sands. The sand was very dry, and the body was naturally preserved for many years. It would deteriorate more slowly, at least compared with here. What did they do later on after this time?

Student: They started taking out the vital organs.

Teacher:	Right. What did they call the vital organs then?
Norm:	Everything but the heart and brain.
Teacher:	Right, the organs in the visceral cavity. The intestines, liver, and so on, which were the easiest parts to get at.
Teacher:	Question?
Student:	How far away from the Nile River was the burial of most kings? (Aulls, 1998, p. 62)

At the end of the dialogue, a *student* asks a question—one that requests information not previously presented. The student is apparently trying to elaborate on the material; perhaps he or she is thinking that only land a considerable distance from the Nile would be dry enough to preserve bodies for a lengthy period of time. We can encourage such elaboration, and therefore also encourage new knowledge construction, by asking **higher-level questions**—those that require students to go beyond the information they have learned (Meece, 1994; Minstrell & Stimpson, 1996). For instance, a higher-level question might ask students to think of their own examples of a concept, use a new principle to solve a problem, or speculate about possible explanations for a cause-effect relationship. As an illustration, consider these questions from a lesson on the telegraph:

> Was the need for a rapid communications system [in North America] greater during the first part of the nineteenth century than it had been during the latter part of the eighteenth century? Why do you think so? (Torrance & Myers, 1970, p. 214)

To answer these questions, students must recall what they know about the eighteenth and nineteenth centuries (including the increasing movement of settlers to distant western territories) and pull that knowledge together in a way they have perhaps never done before.

When we ask questions during a group lesson or provide follow-up questions to a reading assignment that students have completed on their own, we will often enhance our students' achievement (Allington & Weber, 1993; Liu, 1990; Redfield & Rousseau, 1981). This is especially likely when we ask higher-level questions that call for inferences, applications, justifications, or solutions to problems.

It is important to note that some students will be less eager to answer our questions than others; for example, many females and students from some ethnic minority groups may be reluctant to respond (B. Kerr, 1991; Sadker & Sadker, 1994; Villegas, 1991). If, in a classroom of thirty students, only a handful are responding to questions regularly, we have no way of knowing whether their answers reflect what the rest of the class has and has not learned. Thus, we must remember to direct our questions to the entire class, not just to the few who raise their hands (Airasian, 1994; Davis & Thomas, 1989). One approach that solicits *all* students' answers to a question is to conduct a class "vote" regarding several possible answers. Another is to have students write their answers on paper; we can either walk around the room and check individual responses or, if handwriting is large enough, we can ask students to hold up their responses for us to look at from the front of the room (Fairbairn, 1987; R. Gardner, Heward, & Grossi, 1994).

It is also important to give students adequate time to respond to the questions we ask. Just as students need time to process the information they are hearing or reading, they also need time to consider questions and to retrieve any information relevant to possible answers. As we discovered in our discussion of *wait time* in Chapter 6, when teachers allow at least three seconds to elapse after asking questions in class, a greater number of students volunteer answers, and their responses tend to be longer, more complex, and more accurate. Furthermore, even when students can retrieve an answer almost immediately, those from some ethnic backgrounds may allow several seconds to elapse before responding as a way of showing courtesy and respect (see Chapter 4).

Look at the teacher questions in the lesson plan in Figure 13–3. What purposes do the questions serve?

Ask questions both to assess students' learning and to encourage elaboration.

Allow sufficient wait time for students to formulate their answers, especially in a culturally diverse classroom.

In-Class Activities

Students are typically asked to accomplish a wide variety of tasks and assignments in class during the school year; for example, they might be asked to complete worksheets, solve problems, write short stories, draw pictures, practice basketball skills, and play musical instruments. Naturally, there are only so many things they can do in any single school year. How do we decide which activities are likely to be most beneficial to their long-term learning and achievement?

As teachers, we should, first and foremost, assign in-class activities that will help students accomplish our instructional objectives (Brophy & Alleman, 1992; W. Doyle, 1983). In some cases, these objectives may be at a "knowledge" level; for instance, we may want students to conjugate the French verb *être* ("to be"), know members of different biological classes and orders, and be familiar with current events around the globe. But in other cases, we may have higher-level objectives; for instance, we may want our students to write a persuasive essay, use scientific principles to interpret physical phenomena, or use arithmetic operations to solve real-world problems. Particularly when such higher-level objectives are involved, we will want to assign activities that help students learn classroom material in a meaningful and integrated fashion.

In addition to matching our in-class activities to our objectives, we are more likely to facilitate students' learning and achievement when we assign activities that:

- Accommodate student diversity in abilities and interests
- Clearly define each task and its purpose
- Generate students' interest in accomplishing the task
- Begin at an appropriate difficulty level for students—ideally, presenting a task that challenges students to "stretch" their knowledge and skills (a task within students' zone of proximal development)
- Provide sufficient scaffolding to promote success
- Progress in difficulty and complexity as students become more proficient
- Provide opportunities for frequent teacher monitoring and feedback regarding students' progress
- Encourage students to reflect on and evaluate the work they have completed (Brophy & Alleman, 1991, 1992; Brophy & Good, 1986)

The ways in which we assess students' performance will also have an impact on what our in-class activities actually accomplish (W. Doyle, 1983). For example, if we give full credit for completing an assignment without regard to the *quality* of responses, our students may focus more on "getting the work done" than on developing a conceptual understanding of what they are studying. Yet, if our criteria for acceptable performance are overly strict, we may discourage students from taking risks and making errors—risks and errors that are inevitable when students are seeking out and pursuing the challenges that are most likely to promote their cognitive growth.

Computer Applications

Earlier we talked about computer-based instruction as a means of introducing new material. We can use computers to foster elaboration and transfer as well—for instance, when we use games, simulations, and such tools as databases and spreadsheets.

Choose activities that facilitate accomplishment of important instructional objectives.

In-class activities should generate student interest while also helping students accomplish important instructional objectives.

Games and Simulations

Some computer programs promote higher-level thinking skills (e.g., problem solving) within the context of a gamelike task. One popular software program, *Where in the World Is Carmen San Diego?* teaches geography while the student acts as a detective. Other programs provide simulations of such events as running a lemonade stand, dissecting a frog, growing plants under varying environmental conditions, or conducting experiments in physics. Games and simulations are often both motivating and challenging, thereby keeping students on task for extended periods of time (P. F. Merrill et al., 1996; B. Y. White & Frederiksen, 1998).

Tool Applications

In today's society, students need to know not only about reading, writing, mathematics, science, and so on, but also need to know about how to use computers. For example, many professions may require expertise in such *computer tools* as word processing, desktop publishing, databases, and spreadsheets. Hence, our instructional objectives may sometimes include computer skills in addition to skills in more traditional academic areas.

As we teach students to use computer tools, we can simultaneously help them accomplish objectives in more traditional academic areas. Word processing programs can help students revise their short stories, essays, and other written work. Database programs can help students organize information about trees or planets. Spreadsheets enable students to predict changes in weather patterns or trends in the populations of endangered species. Tools known as *music editors* let students create musical compositions and experiment with different notes, keys, instrumental sounds, and time signatures (P. F. Merrill et al., 1996).

Homework

There is only so much that our students can accomplish during class time, and homework provides a means through which we can, in essence, extend the school day. Yet many students are likely to have few resources (equipment, people, etc.) to help them with their homework. In most cases, therefore, we should limit our homework assignments to tasks that require little or no adult scaffolding or to tasks that we can adequately scaffold ahead of time at school (H. Cooper, 1989).

On some occasions, we may want to use homework to give students extra practice with familiar information and procedures (perhaps as a way of promoting review and automaticity) or to introduce them to new yet simple material (H. Cooper, 1989). But in other situations, we can give homework assignments that ask students to apply classroom material to their outside lives (Alleman & Brophy, 1998). For example, in a second-grade unit on lifestyle patterns, we might ask children to

- Compare their own home with houses of different time periods (e.g., caves, stone huts, log cabins)
- Look through their closets and identify clothes that they use for different functions (e.g., household chores, formal occasions)
- Tour their homes (perhaps with a parent) and identify the modern conveniences that make their lives easier and more comfortable (e.g., sinks, electrical outlets, thermostats)
- Ask their parents to explain why they made the choices they did about where they live (e.g., considering the tradeoffs of renting versus purchasing a residence) (Alleman & Brophy, 1998)

And on other occasions, we might encourage students to bring items and ideas from home (e.g., tadpoles from the local pond, events that occurred over the weekend) and

Use games and simulations to motivate and challenge students.

What computer applications might be especially relevant to the subject matter you will be teaching?

Incorporate computer tools into instruction in more traditional academic areas.

Assign homework to enhance automaticity of basic knowledge and skills, encourage review, or introduce students to new yet relatively simple material.

Assign homework that helps students make connections between class material and the outside world.

use them as the basis for in-class activities (Corno, 1996; C. Hill, 1994). When we ask students to make connections between classroom material and the outside world through our homework assignments, we are, of course, promoting transfer.

Homework appears to be more beneficial for older students than for younger ones. Research tells us that doing homework has a small effect on the achievement of middle school and high school students but little if any effect on achievement at the elementary level (H. Cooper, 1989; H. Cooper, Lindsay, Nye, & Greathouse, 1998). I should point out, however, that research studies have typically not examined the *quality* of homework assignments (e.g., the extent to which they encourage meaningful learning and elaboration rather than rote memorization), which must obviously make a difference in the long-term effects that such assignments have.

We can maximize the benefits of homework by following a few simple guidelines (H. Cooper, 1989):

> ■ Use assignments primarily for instructional and diagnostic purposes; minimize the degree to which homework is used to assess learning and determine final class grades.
>
> ■ Provide the information and structure that students need to complete assignments without assistance from others.
>
> ■ Give a mixture of required and voluntary assignments (voluntary ones should help to give students a sense of self-determination and control, hence enhancing intrinsic motivation).

We must keep in mind that distractions, responsibilities, and parental involvement at home are likely to influence students' ability to complete the homework we assign. And we must *never* use homework as a form of punishment. Such a practice communicates the message that schoolwork is an unpleasant chore and so should be avoided whenever possible.

Authentic Activities

In our discussion of knowledge construction in Chapter 7, and again in our discussion of transfer and situated cognition in Chapter 8, we noted the value of activities similar to those that students are likely to encounter in the outside world. When we assign such *authentic activities,* we are more likely to promote meaningful connections between classroom subject matter and real-world contexts and, as a result, more likely to find students applying what they learn in school to their own personal and professional lives. Figure 13–9 presents examples of authentic activities in different academic disciplines.

It may occasionally be possible to assign authentic activities as homework; for example, we might ask students to write an editorial, design an electrical circuit, or plan a family budget while working at home in the evening. But many authentic activities may require considerable classroom dialogue, with students asking questions of one another, sharing their ideas, and offering explanations of their thinking (Hickey, 1997; Newmann & Wehlage, 1993; Paris & Turner, 1994). For example, creating a school newspaper, designing a model city, debating controversial social or political issues, and conversing in a foreign language may be activities that students can perform only as a group. Furthermore, because authentic activities are typically less structured and more complex than traditional classroom tasks, they may require considerable teacher scaffolding (Brophy, 1992a). For obvious reasons, then, many authentic activities can be accomplished more effectively in class than at home, or perhaps through a combination of group work during class and independent work after school hours.

Researchers have only begun to study the effects of authentic activities on students' learning and achievement, but preliminary results are encouraging (Cognition and Technology Group at Vanderbilt, 1993; Gregg & Leinhardt, 1994a; E. H. Hiebert & Fisher, 1992). For example, students' writing skills may show greater improvement in both qual-

Minimize your reliance on homework as a factor in assigning final grades.

Use authentic activities to promote meaningful connections between classroom subject matter and real-world tasks.

Remember that some authentic activities are more successfully accomplished when students work in groups rather than independently.

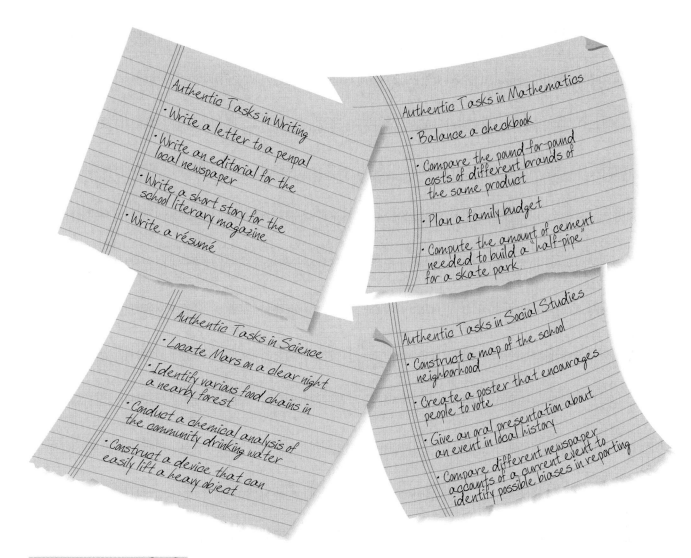

FIGURE 13.9

Examples of authentic tasks in different disciplines

ity and quantity when students write stories, essays, and letters to real people, rather than when they complete short, artificial writing exercises (Hiebert & Fisher, 1992). Likewise, students gain a more complete understanding of how to use and interpret maps effectively when they construct their own maps than when they engage in workbook exercises involving map interpretation (Gregg & Leinhardt, 1994a).

Theorists have suggested that an authentic activity is most likely to be effective when it has such characteristics as these:

- It requires a fair amount of background knowledge about a particular topic; in other words, students must know the subject matter thoroughly and have learned it in a meaningful fashion.

- It promotes higher-level thinking skills; for example, it may involve synthesizing information, forming and testing hypotheses, solving problems, and drawing conclusions.

- It requires students to seek out information in a variety of contexts and perhaps from a variety of academic disciplines.

- It conveys high expectations for students' performance, yet also encourages students to take risks and experiment with new strategies.
- Its final outcome is complex and somewhat unpredictable; there is not necessarily a single "right" response or answer. (Newmann & Wehlage, 1993; Paris & Turner, 1994)

It is not necessarily desirable to fill the entire school day with complex, authentic tasks, however. For one thing, students can often master basic skills more effectively when they practice them in relative isolation from other activities; for example, when learning to play the violin, they need to master their fingering before they join an orchestra, and when learning to play soccer, they need to practice dribbling and passing before they play in a game (Anderson et al., 1996). Second, some authentic tasks may be too expensive and time-consuming to warrant their regular use in the classroom (M. M. Griffin & Griffin, 1994). It is probably most important that classroom tasks encourage students to engage in such cognitive processes as meaningful learning, organization, and elaboration—processes that promote long-term retention and transfer of classroom subject matter—than that tasks always be authentic in nature (Anderson et al., 1996).

▨ Experiencing Firsthand
Thinking Authentically

Take a few minutes to think about and answer these questions:

- In what ways will the subject matter that you teach help your students be successful in their personal or professional lives? In other words, how would you like your students to use and apply school subject matter outside the classroom?
- How might you translate those long-term, real-world applications into activities your students can do in the classroom?

With your answers in mind, develop several authentic activities appropriate for the subject matter and age range of students whom you will be teaching.

Taking Student Diversity into Account

🍎 *When choosing instructional strategies, take into account students' developmental levels, background knowledge, and degree of self-regulated learning.*

As we consider which instructional strategies are most appropriate for our instructional objectives, we must also consider which strategies are most appropriate for the particular students we will be teaching. We should base our decisions, in part, on our students' ages and developmental levels. Our objectives themselves will, of course, differ for different age groups. Furthermore, strategies that involve teaching well-defined topics, require a great deal of active student responding, and provide frequent feedback (e.g., mastery learning, direct instruction, and CAI) will often be more appropriate for younger students than for older ones (Rosenshine & Stevens, 1986). Lectures (which are often somewhat abstract) and homework assignments appear to be more effective with older students (Ausubel et al., 1978; H. Cooper et al., 1998).

Yet we should definitely not base our instructional decisions on age alone. The background knowledge that our students bring to the topic at hand will also make a difference. Very structured and teacher-directed approaches (e.g., mastery learning, direct instruction, CAI, and some instances of expository instruction) may be particularly appropriate for students who know little or nothing about the subject matter (Gustafsson & Undheim, 1996; Rosenshine & Stevens, 1986). In contrast, students who already have some prior knowledge on which to draw as they explore new ideas may benefit considerably from engaging in discovery learning and working with hypertext, hypermedia, and the Internet. Computers can also come to our assistance when teaching students with limited ability to read and write in English; English-language tutorials, computer-based "books" that the computer "reads" to a student, and word processing programs with spell checkers and grammar checkers are all useful when working with these students (P. F. Merrill et al., 1996).

We should consider, too, the extent to which our students are *self-regulated learners*—that is, the extent to which they set their own learning goals, plan their study time effectively, continually monitor their progress and comprehension, and accurately determine when they have learned the subject matter successfully (see Chapter 11). Instructional strategies that provide relatively little structure—perhaps including discovery learning activities, authentic activities, hypertext and hypermedia, and explorations of the Internet—may prove invaluable with students who have shown themselves quite capable of self-regulated learning (Gustafsson & Undheim, 1996).

In general, however, virtually *any* student should have experience with a wide variety of instructional methods. For instance, although some students may need to spend considerable time on basic skills, too much time spent in structured, teacher-directed activities may minimize opportunities to choose what and how to study and learn and, as a result, may prevent students from developing a sense of self-determination (Battistich, Solomon, Kim, Watson, & Schaps, 1995). And authentic activities, though often unstructured and complex, may give students a greater appreciation for the relevance and meaningfulness of classroom subject matter than is possible with more traditional classroom tasks.

Furthermore, some instructional strategies adapt themselves readily to a wide variety of student abilities and needs. For example, mastery learning provides a means through which students can learn at their own pace. Computer-based instructional programs often tailor instruction to students' prior knowledge and skills. Homework assignments can be easily individualized for the amount and kinds of practice that different students need.

Accommodating Students with Special Needs

We may sometimes want to tailor our instructional objectives to students' specific cognitive abilities or disabilities; for example, we may need to modify our expectations in some academic areas for students with learning disabilities, and we may find it beneficial to set more challenging goals for students who are gifted. In addition, different instructional strategies may be more or less useful for students with special educational needs. For instance, strictly expository instruction (e.g., a lecture) may provide a quick and efficient means of presenting new ideas to students who think abstractly and process information quickly yet be incomprehensible and overwhelming to students with low cognitive ability. Similarly, discovery learning is often effective in enhancing the academic achievement of students with high ability; however, it may actually be detrimental to the achievement of students with less ability (Corno & Snow, 1986). And mastery learning and direct instruction have been shown to be effective with students who have learning difficulties, including many students with special educational needs, yet they may prevent rapid learners from progressing at a rate commensurate with their abilities (Arlin, 1984; Leinhardt & Pallay, 1982; Rosenshine & Stevens, 1986).

As teachers, we will often need to adapt instructional strategies to the particular strengths and weaknesses that our students with special needs have. For example, when students have difficulty processing information in one modality or another (e.g., when they have certain learning disabilities), it may be especially important to supplement verbal explanations with visual aids during expository instruction. When students have social or behavioral problems, we may find that we need to provide close supervision and frequent encouragement and feedback during independent seatwork assignments. Table 13–3 provides a "memory refresher" for some of the characteristics of students with special needs that we have considered in previous chapters; it also presents some of the instructional strategies that we can use to accommodate such characteristics.

Include your instructional strategies in the IEPs you develop for students with special needs.

TABLE 13.3

Identifying Objectives and Instructional Strategies Especially Suitable for Students with Special Educational Needs

STUDENTS WITH SPECIAL NEEDS	CHARACTERISTICS THAT THESE STUDENTS MAY EXHIBIT	CLASSROOM STRATEGIES THAT MAY BE BENEFICIAL FOR THESE STUDENTS
Students with specific cognitive or academic difficulties	Uneven patterns of achievement Difficulty with complex cognitive tasks in some content domains Difficulty processing or remembering information presented in particular modalities Poor listening and/or reading skills	Establish challenging yet realistic objectives; modify objectives in accordance with individual students' strengths and weaknesses. Use an information processing analysis to identify the specific cognitive skills involved in a complex task; consider teaching each of those skills separately. Be optimistic in your objectives for students; assume they can succeed, and help them achieve success. During expository instruction, provide information through multiple modalities (e.g., with videotapes, audiotapes, graphic materials). Supplement expository instruction with other instructional strategies. Use mastery learning, direct instruction, and computer-based instruction to provide additional instruction as needed. Have students use computer tools (e.g., grammar and spell checkers) that can help them compensate for areas of weakness. Use hypermedia to present information through multiple modalities. Assign homework that provides additional practice in basic skills; individualize assignments for students' unique abilities and needs. Use a mastery learning approach to ensure that students have achieved information and skills essential for later units.
Students with social or behavioral problems	Frequent off-task behavior Inability to work independently for extended periods of time	Provide direct instruction to a small group as a means of providing one-on-one attention and instruction. Keep unsupervised seatwork assignments to a minimum. (As appropriate, also use strategies presented above for students with specific cognitive or academic difficulties.)

continued

STUDENTS WITH SPECIAL NEEDS	CHARACTERISTICS THAT THESE STUDENTS MAY EXHIBIT	CLASSROOM STRATEGIES THAT MAY BE BENEFICIAL FOR THESE STUDENTS
Students with general delays in cognitive and social functioning	Difficulty with complex tasks Difficulty thinking abstractly Need for a great deal of repetition and practice of information and skills Difficulty transferring information and skills to new situations	Establish realistic objectives in both the academic and social arenas. Use task analysis to break complex behaviors into a number of simpler responses that students can more easily learn. Make sure students understand their assignments. Present information in as concrete a manner as possible (e.g., by engaging students in hands-on experiences). Use direct instruction, computer-assisted instruction, and in-class activities to provide extended practice in basic skills. Embed basic skills within authentic tasks to promote transfer to the outside world.
Students with physical or sensory challenges	Average intelligence in most cases Tendency to tire easily in some cases Limited motor skills in some cases	Aim for instructional objectives similar to those for nondisabled students unless there is a compelling reason to do otherwise. Allow frequent breaks from strenuous or intensive activities. Use computer-based instruction (perhaps with specially adapted input mechanisms) to allow students to progress through material at their own pace and make active responses during instruction.
Students with advanced cognitive development	Greater frequency of responses at higher levels of Bloom's taxonomy (e.g., analysis, synthesis) Rapid learning Greater ability to think abstractly; appearance of abstract thinking at a younger age Greater conceptual understanding of classroom material Ability to learn independently	Identify standards and objectives that challenge students and encourage them to develop their full potential. Ask predominantly higher-level questions. Provide opportunities to pursue topics in greater depth (e.g., through assigned readings or computer-based instruction). Teach strategies that enable students to learn on their own (e.g., library skills, scientific methods, use of hypermedia and the Internet).

Sources: *Carnine, 1989; DuNann & Weber, 1976; Heward, 1996; C. C. Kulik et al., 1990; Mercer, 1991; P. F. Merrill et al., 1996; Morgan & Jenson, 1988; Piirto, 1994; Ruef et al., 1998; Schiffman, Tobin, & Buchanan, 1984; Spicker, 1992; Turnbull et al., 1999; Tarver, 1992; J. W. Wood & Rosbe, 1985.*

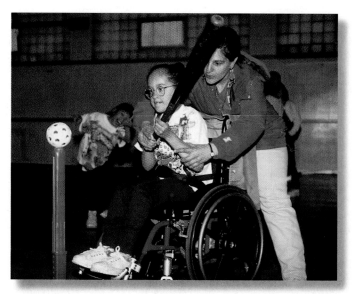

Instructional strategies may sometimes need to be adapted for students with special needs. Here a student receives extra scaffolding during direct instruction in physical education.

CASE STUDY: Round Robin

Mr. Lewis, an eighth-grade social studies teacher, is conducting a review session for a unit on ancient Egypt. He is using a technique that he calls a "round robin." Each row of students comprises a team, and the teams compete to see which one remembers the most about ancient Egyptian society. He presents a definition of a concept or a description of a certain location and then calls on a particular student to give the term or place to which he is referring. A student who fails to respond correctly must stand up beside his or her desk, indicating a "strike" for the team. After three strikes, the team is out of the competition.

Here is a portion of what transpires during the round robin.

Teacher:	Scott, "a society at an advanced stage of culture."
Scott:	Pass. [Strike one]
Teacher:	Stand up, please. Robert?
Robert:	*Civilization.*
Teacher:	"Shortage of food." Helen?
Helen:	That is a *drought.*
Teacher:	Marcy, "a substance used for making paper."
Marcy:	*Parchment.*
Teacher:	Fred, "a water-raising device."
Fred:	(No response) [Strike two]
Teacher:	Stand up, please. Remember the definitions you were given. Jeremy?
Jeremy:	*Shadoof.*
Teacher:	Rula, "a city along the rapids."
Rula:	Not sure. [Strike three]
Teacher:	The right side row has three strikes. OK, next row. . . .
	(Adapted from Aulls, 1998, p. 61)

- What purpose(s) does this activity serve? What instructional objective(s) does Mr. Lewis apparently have for his students?

- Contrast this scenario with the dialogue presented in the "Teacher Questions" section earlier in the chapter. The two teachers are teaching the same subject matter at the same grade level. Which teacher's technique do you prefer, and why?

Summing Up

Planning for Instruction

Effective teachers engage in considerable advance planning, and they continually evaluate and modify their plans as the school year progresses. They identify the goals (instructional objectives) that they would like their students to accomplish, conduct task analyses to break complex tasks into smaller and simpler components, and develop lesson plans that spell out activities they will use on a daily basis.

Introducing New Material

Virtually any instructional strategy may be used for multiple purposes simultaneously. Yet some instructional strategies—expository instruction, discovery learning, mastery learning, direct instruction, and computer-based instruction—are especially suited for helping students learn new material. In expository instruction, information is presented in essentially the same form that students are expected to learn it; lectures, textbooks, and other forms of expository instruction are more effective when we apply basic principles of cognitive psychology—for example, when we show students how new material relates to their prior knowledge and when we help them encode ideas in multiple ways. In discovery learning, students develop an understanding of a particular topic by interacting with their physical or social environment; it is more likely to be successful when we provide a structure that nudges students toward desired discov-

eries and when students have the necessary prior knowledge and guidance for appropriately interpreting those discoveries. Mastery learning, direct instruction, and computer-based instruction all provide structured contexts in which students learn and practice new information and skills and receive frequent feedback about how they are doing.

Promoting Elaboration and Transfer

Other instructional strategies, though sometimes appropriate for introducing new material, may be particularly useful in helping students go *beyond* material they've already learned. Some of these strategies—teacher questions, in-class activities, computer applications, homework, and authentic activities—are often controlled primarily by the teacher, and the extent to which they promote elaboration and transfer will differ considerably, depending on the exact nature of the activity. Additional elaborative strategies (those that tend to be more student-directed) are presented in Chapter 14.

Accommodating Student Diversity

Different instructional strategies are appropriate not only for different objectives but also for different students, depending on age, prior knowledge, capacity for self-regulated learning, and special educational needs.

KEY CONCEPTS

instructional objective (p. 519)
standards (p. 519)
cognitive domain (p. 520)
psychomotor domain (p. 520)
affective domain (p. 520)
Bloom's taxonomy (p. 522)
behavioral objectives (p. 524)
short-term versus long-term objectives (p. 524)

task analysis (p. 526)
expository instruction (p. 533)
advance organizer (p. 535)
prior knowledge activation (p. 536)
concept map (p. 537)
signals (in expository instruction) (p. 538)
discovery learning (p. 540)
mastery learning (p. 545)
direct instruction (p. 547)

programmed instruction (p. 551)
linear program (p. 552)
branching program (p. 552)
computer-assisted instruction (CAI) (p. 552)
computer-based instruction (CBI) (p. 552)
hypertext (p. 552)
hypermedia (p. 552)
lower-level versus higher-level questions (pp. 554–555)

14

Promoting Learning Through Student Interactions

W hat knowledge and skills have you learned primarily through discussions with your peers? Does a fellow student sometimes explain confusing course material more clearly than an instructor has? Do you sometimes understand course material better after *you* have explained it to someone else? Do classroom debates about controversial issues help you clarify your own thinking about those issues?

In this chapter we will focus on student-directed instructional strategies that involve considerable student interaction and, in many cases, considerable student leadership and direction as well. More specifically, we will address these questions:

- What are the potential benefits of student interaction during instruction and learning?

- What instructional strategies can we use to help students learn effectively by interacting with one another?

- How can we create a "community of learners" in the classroom—an environment in which students regularly support and facilitate one another's learning?

- How can we use interactive instructional methods to accommodate our students' diverse backgrounds and needs?

- What guiding principles can help us identify the most appropriate instructional strategies for different situations?

CASE STUDY: Crime and Punishment

In her high school social studies class, Ms. Steinway is using the topic *crime* to help students develop critical thinking and scientific reasoning skills. For instance, the students are looking for patterns in the distribution of various felonies across the nation, reviewing research studies and theoretical explanations regarding the possible causes of criminal behavior, and comparing the relative effectiveness of different forms of punishment.

When the unit begins, Ms. Steinway asks her students to write a brief essay presenting their opinions on the appropriateness of capital punishment as a consequence for first-degree murder—in other words, the appropriateness of killing someone who has intentionally killed someone else. She asks them, too, to describe how strongly they hold their opinions and to explain why they believe as they do.

On several occasions during the next few weeks, Ms. Steinway has her students pair off to discuss the pros and cons of capital punishment. She uses the essays to determine which students she pairs together, making sure that over the course of the discussion sessions, each student is exposed to diverse opinions. Her instructions at the beginning of each session are always the same: "As a pair, you should try to reach consensus about capital punishment. If you find that you cannot, then identify the nature of your disagreement." She gives the student pairs about ten minutes to exchange views and try to come to agreement.

At the end of the crime unit, Ms. Steinway again asks her students to write an essay describing and justifying their position on capital punishment. At home that night, she compares the two essays that each student has written. She discovers that only a few students have actually changed their opinions from "pro" to "con," or vice versa, as a result of their discussions. But she sees some interesting changes from the pre-unit essays to the post-unit essays. For one thing, students who had not provided a justification for their opinion at the beginning of the unit typically did so at the unit's conclusion; here are one student's essays:

> *Pre-unit:* I'm totally in favor of capital punishment. Yet I think that I could change my image of it if someone had a better opinion than I do because I'm not too sure if my opinion is correct.
>
> *Post-unit:* Capital punishment reduces crime. That's why I'm totally in favor of it. I strongly feel that it's the best method to reduce all types of crime.

Furthermore, many students who had previously provided some justification for their position expanded on their explanations in the post-unit essay, and some of them were also more likely to recognize that there were legitimate arguments both for and against capital punishment. One student wrote essays that illustrate both of these changes:

> *Pre-unit:* Capital punishment is the right thing to do because if someone does something, then the punishment fits the crime.
>
> *Post-unit:* I think that capital punishment is somewhat fair but at the same time I think that it is not right. It is fair for many reasons, but one of them is because if you killed a person, that person should get that same punishment that the other person went through. And at the same time, I think that it's unfair because sometimes they are framed, and I don't think that an innocent man should pay for it, and when they finally find the right person, that man had nothing to do with it. So I am not sure if I am more for one or the other.

- ■   Why have the discussions influenced students' thinking about capital punishment? Can you explain the changes using theories of learning or development that we've considered in earlier chapters?
- ■   Why does Ms. Steinway ask the pairs to try to reach consensus during their discussions? What purposes might this activity serve?

Based on Kuhn, Shaw, & Felton, 1997; essays are adapted from pp. 297 and 313.

Benefits of Student Interaction

Chapter 7 identified several advantages of student dialogue from the perspective of cognitive psychology, and these advantages are worth repeating here:

- • We encourage students to clarify and organize their ideas sufficiently so that they can verbalize them to others.
- • We provide opportunities for students to elaborate on what they have learned.
- • We enable students to discover flaws and inconsistencies in their own thinking, thereby helping them identify gaps in their understanding.
- • We expose students to classmates' views, which may reflect a more accurate understanding of the topics under discussion.

- We can help students discover how different cultures may interpret the world in different, yet perhaps equally valid, ways.

Other chapters identified additional advantages of interactive instruction:

- From the perspective of Piaget and Kohlberg, disagreements among peers are likely to promote progress to higher stages of cognitive and moral development (Chapters 2 and 3).

- From Vygotsky's perspective, many cognitive processes have their roots in social interactions. For instance, by arguing about issues with one another, children eventually internalize the "arguing" process and so acquire the ability to look at a single issue from multiple perspectives (Chapter 2). We see an example of such multi-sided thinking in the second post-unit essay in the opening case study.

- Students can acquire more sophisticated metacognitive strategies when they hear others verbalizing and modeling such strategies. Furthermore, discussions that involve debating controversial subject matter may promote more sophisticated epistemological beliefs, including the beliefs that acquiring "knowledge" involves developing an integrated set of ideas about a topic and that such knowledge is likely to evolve gradually over a lengthy period of time (Chapter 8).

When students must explain their thinking to someone else, they usually organize and elaborate on what they've learned. These processes help them develop a more integrated and thorough understanding of the material.

- Research by social cognitive theorists tells us that students often develop higher self-efficacy for performing a task when they see their peers accomplishing the same task successfully (Chapter 11).

- From a motivational standpoint, interactive instructional strategies provide a means through which students can meet their need for affiliation (Chapter 12).

Clearly, then, we have a great deal to gain from having our students interact with one another on a regular basis. Let's examine several specific instructional strategies we might use to promote effective student interactions.

Promoting Elaboration Through Student Interaction

At least four interactive instructional strategies can promote our students' classroom learning and performance.

- Class discussions
- Reciprocal teaching
- Cooperative learning
- Peer tutoring

Let's consider how we can implement these approaches in ways that maximize their effectiveness.

Class Discussions

As you know from reading Chapter 7, social constructivists propose that learners often work together to construct meaningful interpretations of their world. Class discussions in which students feel that they can speak freely, asking questions and presenting their

Use class discussions to promote more complete understanding of complex topics.

ideas and opinions in either a whole-class or small-group context, obviously provide an important mechanism for promoting such socially constructed understandings (e.g., Bruning, Schraw, & Ronning, 1995; Marshall, 1992).

Class discussions lend themselves readily to a variety of academic disciplines. For example, students may discuss various interpretations of classic works of literature, addressing questions that have no easy or "right" answers; when they do so, they are more likely to relate what they are reading to their personal lives and so to understand it better (Eeds & Wells, 1989; E. H. Hiebert & Raphael, 1996; McGee, 1992). In history classes, students may study and discuss various documents related to a single historical event and so begin to recognize that history is not necessarily as cut-and-dried as traditional history textbooks portray it (Leinhardt, 1994). In science classes, discussions of various and conflicting theoretical explanations of observed phenomena may help students come to grips with the idea that science is not "fact" as much as it is a dynamic and continually evolving understanding of the world (Bereiter, 1994). And in mathematics, class discussions that focus on alternative approaches to solving the same problem can promote a more meaningful understanding of mathematical principles and lead to better transfer of those principles to new situations and problems (Cobb et al., 1991; J. Hiebert & Wearne, 1996; Lampert, 1990).

Although students typically do most of the talking in classroom discussions, we teachers nevertheless play a critical role. Theorists have offered several guidelines for how we can promote effective classroom discussions:

• *Focus on topics that lend themselves to multiple perspectives, explanations, or approaches* (L. M. Anderson, 1993; E. H. Hiebert & Raphael, 1996; Lampert, 1990; Onosko, 1996). Controversial topics appear to have several benefits: Students are more likely to express their views to their classmates, seek out new information that resolves seemingly contradictory data, reevaluate their own positions on the issues under discussion, and develop a meaningful and well-integrated understanding of the subject matter (E. G. Cohen, 1994; D. W. Johnson & Johnson, 1985; K. Smith, Johnson, & Johnson, 1981).

• *Make sure students have sufficient prior knowledge about a topic to discuss it intelligently.* Such knowledge may come either from previous class sessions or from students' personal experiences (Bruning et al., 1995). In many cases, it is likely to come from studying a particular topic in depth (Onosko, 1996).

• *Create a classroom atmosphere conducive to open debate and the constructive evaluation of ideas.* Students are more likely to share their ideas and opinions if their teacher is supportive of multiple viewpoints and if disagreeing with classmates is socially acceptable (Cobb & Yackel, 1996; Eeds & Wells, 1989; Lampert et al., 1996; Onosko, 1996). To promote such an atmosphere in the classroom, we might do the following:

Communicate the message that understanding a topic at the end of a discussion is more important than having the "correct" answer at the beginning of the discussion (Hatano & Inagaki, 1993).

Communicate the beliefs that asking questions reflects curiosity, that differing perspectives on a controversial topic are both inevitable and healthy, and that changing one's opinion on a topic is a sign of thoughtful reflection (Onosko, 1996).

Encourage students to try to understand one another's reasoning and explanations (Cobb & Yackel, 1996).

Encourage students to be open in their agreement or disagreement with their classmates—in other words, to "agree to disagree" (Cobb & Yackel, 1996; Lampert et al., 1996).

Focus on controversial and other multifaceted topics.

Be sure students have some knowledge about the topic.

Create an open-minded and tolerant classroom atmosphere.

Depersonalize challenges to a student's line of reasoning by framing questions in a third-person voice—for example, by saying, "What if someone were to respond to your claim by saying . . .?" (Onosko, 1996).

Occasionally ask students to defend a position that is in direct opposition to what they actually believe (Onosko, 1996; Reiter, 1994).

Require students to develop compromise solutions that take opposing perspectives into account (Onosko, 1996). (We see this strategy in the opening case study when Ms. Steinway asks her students to reach consensus if possible.)

• *Use small-group discussions as a way of encouraging all students to participate.* Students are more likely to speak openly when their audience is a handful of classmates rather than the class as a whole; the difference is especially noticeable for females (Théberge, 1994). On some occasions, then, we may want to have our students discuss an issue in small groups first, thereby giving them the chance to test and possibly gain support for their ideas in a relatively private context; we can then bring them together for a whole-class discussion (Minstrell & Stimpson, 1996; Onosko, 1996).

Use small-group discussions to encourage participation.

• *Ask one or more thought-provoking questions to get the ball rolling.* By asking higher-level, thought-provoking questions, we can activate students' prior knowledge about a topic while simultaneously encouraging students to elaborate on what they have learned (Aulls, 1998; Pogrow & Londer, 1994). At the same time, however, we must recognize that an effective classroom discussion is one in which students eventually control the direction of the discussion to some extent—perhaps by asking their *own* questions and in other ways initiating new issues related to the topic (Aulls, 1998; Onosko, 1996).

Ask thought-provoking questions.

• *Provide a structure to guide the discussion.* Our class discussions are likely to be more effective when we structure them in some way. For example, we might ask the class to examine a textbook or other source of information with a particular goal in mind (Calfee, Dunlap, & Wat, 1994). Before conducting an experiment, we might ask students to make predictions about what will happen and to explain and defend their predictions; later, after students have observed the outcome of the experiment, we might ask them to explain what happened and why (Hatano & Inagaki, 1991). Another strategy, useful when the topic under discussion is especially controversial, is to follow a sequence such as this one:

Provide a structure for the discussion.

1. The class is divided into groups of four students apiece. Each group of four subdivides into two pairs.
2. Within a group, each pair of students studies a particular position on the issue and presents its position to the other two students.
3. The group of four has an open discussion of the issue, giving each student an opportunity to argue persuasively for his or her own position.
4. Each pair presents the perspective of the *opposing* side as sincerely and persuasively as possible.
5. The group strives for consensus on a position that incorporates all the evidence presented. (Deutsch, 1993)

By following such a procedure, and in particular by asking students to argue both sides of an issue, we encourage them to think critically about various viewpoints and to begin to recognize that opposing perspectives may *both* have some validity (Reiter, 1994). (The second post-unit essay in the opening case study shows some movement in this direction.)

• *Give students guidance about how to behave.* Our students are likely to have more productive discussions when we describe appropriate behaviors for discussion

Describe appropriate behaviors for class discussions.

sessions. We must take steps to ensure that our students' reactions to one another's ideas are not disparaging or mean-spirited (Onosko, 1996). And we may find it helpful to provide guidelines such as these for small-group discussions:

Encourage everyone to participate, and listen to everyone's ideas.

Restate what someone else has said if you don't understand.

Be critical of ideas rather than people.

Try to pull ideas from both sides together in a way that makes sense.

Focus not on winning, but on resolving the issue in the best possible way.

Change your mind if the arguments and evidence presented indicate that you should do so. (adapted from Deutsch, 1993)

Provide closure.

• *Provide some degree of closure at the end of the discussion.* Although students may sometimes come to consensus about a topic at the end of a class discussion, this will certainly not always be the case. Nevertheless, a class discussion should have some form of closure that helps students tie various ideas together. For instance, when I conduct discussions about controversial topics in my own classes, I spend about five minutes at the end of class identifying and summarizing the key issues that students have raised during the class period. Another strategy is to have students explain how a particular discussion has helped them understand a topic more fully (Onosko, 1996).

Class discussions are not necessarily stand-alone instructional strategies; for instance, we may often want to incorporate them into expository instruction or discovery learning sessions. Student dialogues not only encourage students to think about and process classroom subject matter more completely; they can also promote more effective learning strategies during reading and listening activities (A. L. Brown & Reeve, 1987; Cross & Paris, 1988; Palincsar & Brown, 1989; Paris & Winograd, 1990). One particular form of discussion, *reciprocal teaching,* is especially effective in this respect.

Reciprocal Teaching

As you may recall from our discussion of metacognition in Chapter 8, students typically know very little about how they can best learn information. As illustrations, here are three high school students' descriptions of how they study a textbook (A. L. Brown & Palincsar, 1987, p. 83):

". . . I stare real hard at the page, blink my eyes and then open them—and cross my fingers that it will be right here." [Student points at head.]

"It's easy, if she [the teacher] says study, I read it twice. If she says read, it's just once through."

"I just read the first line in each paragraph—it's usually all there."

None of these students mentions any attempt to understand the information, relate it to prior knowledge, or otherwise think about it in any way, so we might guess that they are *not* engaging in meaningful learning, organization, or elaboration. In other words, they are not using cognitive processes that should help them store and retain information in long-term memory.

Experiencing Firsthand
Metacogitating

Take a minute to think about what you've been doing in your head as you've been reading this chapter. Decide how frequently you've engaged in the following mental activities:

	Never	Occasionally	Frequently
Identifying and summarizing the main ideas	0	1	2
Asking yourself questions to check your understanding	0	1	2
Trying to clarify what you didn't initially understand	0	1	2
Predicting what you were likely to read next	0	1	2

One obvious objective of our educational system is that students learn to read. But an equally important objective is that students *read to learn*—in other words, that they acquire new information from the things they read. When we examine the cognitive processes that good readers (successful learners) often use, especially when reading challenging material, we find strategies such as these (A. L. Brown & Palincsar, 1987):

- *Summarizing.* Good readers identify the main ideas—the gist—of what they read.
- *Questioning.* Good readers ask themselves questions to make sure they understand what they are reading; in other words, they monitor their comprehension as they proceed through reading material.
- *Clarifying.* When good readers discover that they don't comprehend something—for example, when a sentence is confusing or ambiguous—they take steps to clarify what they are reading, perhaps by rereading it or making logical inferences.
- *Predicting.* Good readers anticipate what they are likely to read next; they make predictions about the ideas that are likely to follow the ones they are currently reading.

In contrast, poor readers (those who learn little from textbooks and other reading materials) rarely summarize, question, clarify, or predict. For example, many students cannot adequately summarize a typical *fifth*-grade textbook until high school or even junior college (A. L. Brown & Palincsar, 1987; Palincsar & Brown, 1984). Clearly, many students do not easily acquire the ability to read for learning.

Reciprocal teaching (A. L. Brown & Palincsar, 1987; Palincsar & Brown, 1984, 1989) is an approach to teaching reading through which students learn effective reading-to-learn strategies by observing and imitating what their teacher and fellow students do. The teacher and several students meet in a group to read a piece of text, occasionally stopping to discuss and process the text aloud. Initially, the teacher leads the discussion, asking questions about the text to promote summarizing, questioning, clarifying, and predicting. But gradually, he or she turns the role of "teacher" over to different students, who then take charge of the discussion and ask one another the same kinds of questions that their teacher has modeled. Eventually, the students can read and discuss a text almost independently of the teacher, working together to construct its meaning and checking one another for comprehension and possible misunderstandings.

As an illustration, the following is a reciprocal teaching session for a group of six first graders reading a passage about snowshoe rabbits. In this particular case, the classroom teacher reads the text in small segments (at higher grade levels, the students themselves take turns reading). After each segment, the teacher pauses while students discuss and process the segment. As you read the dialogue, look for examples of summarizing, questioning, clarifying, and predicting (there is at least one instance of each).

The children were reading about the snowshoe rabbit, and it was the sixteenth day of dialogue. The teacher had just read a segment of text describing the season in

Can you explain the value of these four strategies by relating them to effective memory storage processes?

Ask questions that promote summarizing, questioning, clarifying, and predicting in a group reading situation. Gradually turn the role of "teacher" over to students.

which baby rabbits are born and the ways in which the mother rabbit cares for her babies. A student named Kam is the dialogue leader.

Kam: When was the babies born?

Teacher: That's a good question to ask. Call on someone to answer that question.

Kam: Robby? Milly?

Milly: Summer.

Teacher: What would happen if the babies were born in the winter? Let's think.

Several children make a number of responses, including: "The baby would be very cold." "They would need food." "They don't have no fur when they are just born."

Kam: I have another question. How does she get the babies safe?

Kris: She hides them.

Kam: That's right but something else. . . .

Teacher: There is something very unusual about how she hides them that surprised me. I didn't know this.

Travis: They are all in a different place.

Teacher: Why do you think she does this?

Milly: Probably because I heard another story, and when they're babies they usually eat each other or fight with each other.

Teacher: That could be! And what about when that lynx comes?

Several children comment that that would be the end of all the babies.

Travis: If I was the mother, I would hide mine, I would keep them all together.

Kris: If the babies are hidden and the mom wants to go and look at them, how can she remember where they are?

Teacher: Good question. Because she does have to find them again. Why? What does she bring them?

Milly: She needs to bring food. She probably leaves a twig or something.

Teacher: Do you think she puts out a twig like we mark a trail?

Several children disagree and suggest that she uses her sense of smell. One child, recalling that the snowshoe rabbit is not all white in the winter, suggests that the mother might be able to tell her babies apart by their coloring.

Teacher: So we agree that the mother rabbit uses her senses to find her babies after she hides them. Kam, can you summarize for us now?

Kam: The babies are born in the summer. . . .

Teacher: The mother . . .

Kam: The mother hides the babies in different places.

Teacher: And she visits them . . .

Kam: To bring them food.

Travis: She keeps them safe.

Teacher: Any predictions?

Milly: What she teaches her babies . . . like how to hop.

Kris: They know how to hop already.

Teacher: Well, let's read and see. (dialogue courtesy of A. Palincsar)

Can you find at least one example each of summarizing, questioning, clarifying, and predicting in this dialogue? What strategies does the teacher use to elicit desired student responses?

Reciprocal teaching provides a mechanism through which both the teacher and students can model effective reading and learning strategies; hence, this approach has an element of social cognitive theory. But when we consider that we are encouraging effective cognitive processes by first having students practice them aloud in group sessions, then we realize that Vygotsky's theory of cognitive development is also at work here: Students should eventually *internalize* the processes that they first use in their discussions with others. Furthermore, the structured nature of a reciprocal teaching session scaffolds students' efforts to make sense of the things they read and hear. For example, in the previous dialogue, the teacher models elaborative questions and connections to prior knowledge ("What would happen if the babies were born in the winter?" "Do you think she puts out a twig like we mark a trail?") and provides general guidance and occasional hints about how students should process the passage about snowshoe rabbits ("Kam, can you summarize for us now?" "And she visits them . . ."). Also notice in the dialogue how students support one another in their efforts to process what they are reading; consider this exchange as an example:

Why is this approach called *reciprocal* teaching?

Kam: I have another question. How does she get the babies safe?

Kris: She hides them.

Kam: That's right but something else. . . .

Reciprocal teaching has been used successfully with a wide variety of students, ranging from first graders to college students, to teach effective reading and listening comprehension skills (Alfassi, 1998; Campione, Shapiro, & Brown, 1995; Palincsar & Brown, 1989; Rosenshine & Meister, 1994). For example, in an early study of reciprocal teaching (Palincsar & Brown, 1984), six seventh-grade students with a history of poor reading comprehension participated in twenty reciprocal teaching sessions, each lasting about thirty minutes. Despite this relatively short intervention, students showed remarkable improvement in their reading comprehension skills. They became increasingly able to process reading material in an effective manner and to do so independently of their classroom teacher. Furthermore, they generalized their new reading strategies to other classes, sometimes even surpassing the achievement of their classmates (A. L. Brown & Palincsar, 1987; Palincsar & Brown, 1984).

Do these findings surprise you? Why or why not?

Reciprocal teaching can be employed with an entire classroom of students almost as easily as in a small group. Although teachers are often very skeptical of such a radically different approach to teaching and learning, their enthusiasm grows once they've tried it themselves (A. L. Brown & Palincsar, 1987; Palincsar & Brown, 1989).

Cooperative Learning

Experiencing Firsthand
Purple Satin

Imagine yourself as a student in each of the three classrooms described here. Imagine how you would behave in each situation.

1. Mr. Alexander tells your class, "Let's find out which students can learn the most in this week's unit on the human digestive system. The three students getting the highest scores on Friday's unit test will get free tickets to the Purple Satin concert." Purple Satin is a popular musical group; you would give your eyeteeth to hear them perform, but the concert has been sold out for months.

2. Ms. Bernstein introduces her lesson this way: "Let's see whether each of you can learn all about the digestive system this week. If you can get a score of at least 90 percent on this Friday's test, then you will get a free ticket to the Purple Satin concert."

INTO THE CLASSROOM: Using Reciprocal Teaching

Model effective learning strategies—in particular, summarizing, questioning, clarifying, and predicting—in a group reading or listening situation.

As a junior high school teacher assigns a textbook chapter entitled "Exploring Outer Space," she asks students, "What do you think this chapter is about? Can you predict some things that you will probably learn about as you read the chapter?"

Gradually turn the role of "teacher" over to students, scaffolding their initial efforts.

An elementary school teacher working with a reading group asks one student, "Rachel, can you summarize what we have just read? Remember, the title of this section of the chapter is 'Habits of the Grizzly Bear'."

Eventually allow students to "teach" without your assistance.

A middle school teacher working with a group of low-achieving readers has students take turns serving as teacher for the group, addressing questions to other group members about the passage they are reading.

Provide praise and specific feedback about a student's participation.

A high school teacher commends a student, "That was an excellent question, Raul. You asked the group to clarify an idea that was not clearly explained in the book. Who can answer Raul's question?"

3. Mr. Camacho begins the same lesson like this: "Today we begin studying the human digestive system. Let's see how many students can get scores of 90 percent or better on Friday's test. I want you to work in groups of three to help one another learn the material. If all three members of a group score at least 90 percent on the test, then that group will get free tickets to the Purple Satin concert."

In which class(es) are you likely to work hard to get free tickets to Purple Satin? How might you work *differently* in the different situations?

The first classroom (Mr. Alexander's) is obviously a very competitive one: Only the three best students are getting tickets to the concert. Will you try to earn one of those tickets? It all depends on what you think your chances are of being a top scorer on Friday's test. If you have been doing well on tests all year, then you will undoubtedly study harder than ever for this week's unit. If, instead, you have been doing poorly in class despite your best efforts, then you probably won't work for something you are unlikely to get. But in either case, will you help your fellow students learn about the digestive system? If they express confusion about what the pancreas does, will you explain its function? If they forget the reading assignment, will you tell them the pages they need to read? Not if you want to go to the concert yourself!

In Ms. Bernstein's classroom, there's no competition for concert tickets. As long as you get a score of 90 percent or higher on the test, you get a ticket. Even if you think half the students in class are smarter than you are, you know that you have a good chance of going to the concert, and so you will probably study diligently for Friday's test. But will you help your classmates learn to distinguish between the large and small intestines? Maybe . . . *if* you have the time and are in a good mood.

In a cooperative learning environment, students sink or swim together.

Now consider Mr. Camacho's classroom. Whether or not you get a concert ticket depends on how well you *and two other students* score on Friday's test. Are you going to help those two students learn about salivation and digestive enzymes? And can you expect them, in turn, to help you understand where the liver fits into the whole system? Absolutely!

Cooperative learning (e.g., D. W. Johnson & Johnson, 1991; Slavin, 1990) is an approach to instruction in which students work in small groups to help one another learn. Unlike an individualistic classroom such as Ms. Bernstein's (where one student's success is unrelated to classmates' achievement) or a competitive classroom such as Mr. Alexander's (where one student's success actually depends on the failure of others), students in a cooperative learning environment such as Mr. Camacho's work together to achieve common successes. In other words, they *sink or swim together* (D. W. Johnson & Johnson, 1991).

We find justification for cooperative learning in several theoretical frameworks. From the perspective of cognitive psychology, cooperative learning yields the same benefits that emerge from class discussions: greater comprehension and integration of the subject matter, recognition of inadequacies or misconceptions in understanding, and increased perspective taking. Furthermore, when students help one another learn, they create scaffolding for one another's efforts, and they may jointly construct more sophisticated ideas and strategies than any single group member might be able to construct alone (Good et al., 1992; Hatano & Inagaki, 1991; O'Donnell & O'Kelly, 1994; N. M. Webb & Palincsar, 1996). From a behaviorist point of view, providing rewards for group success is consistent with the operant conditioning notion of a *group contingency*. From a social cognitive perspective, students are likely to have higher self-efficacy for performing a task when they know that they will have the help of other group members; furthermore, students can model effective learning and problem-solving strategies for one another (A. L. Brown & Palincsar, 1989; Good et al., 1992). And theorists of various theoretical persuasions point out that cooperative ventures are important elements of scientific inquiry and adult work environments (Greeno, 1997; D. W. Johnson & Johnson, 1991).

How often do adults need to work cooperatively in the workplace? Do you think they might have benefited from cooperative experiences during their school years?

Yet cooperative learning is not simply a process of putting students in groups and setting them loose to work on an assignment together. Oftentimes, our students will be more accustomed to competitive and individualistic classroom situations than they are to working cooperatively with their classmates. For a cooperative learning activity to be successful, we must structure the activity in such a way that cooperation is not only helpful for academic success but in fact even necessary for it (D. W. Johnson & Johnson, 1991). Here are several strategies that enhance the effectiveness of cooperative groups:

Group students who are likely to work together productively.

• *Choose group membership based on which students are likely to work effectively with one another.* Cooperative groups are typically comprised of two to six members; groups of three to four students are especially effective (Hatano & Inagaki, 1991; Lou et al., 1996). In most cases, *we* should form the groups (rather than letting students congregate into their own, self-chosen groups), identifying combinations of students that are likely to be productive (D. W. Johnson & Johnson, 1991).

Many advocates of cooperative learning suggest that each group be relatively heterogeneous in makeup—that each group include high achievers and low achievers, boys and girls, and children of various ethnic backgrounds (D. W. Johnson & Johnson, 1991; Shachar & Sharan, 1994; Stevens & Slavin, 1995). In recent years, however, some theorists have begun to question the practice of combining students of widely differing achievement levels, arguing that such a practice makes ability differences among students more obvious than they would be otherwise. High-achieving students may dominate discussions and discourage low-achieving students from fully participating; low-achieving students may be reluctant to ask for help in understanding the material being studied, or they may simply sit back and let other group members do most or all of the work (E. G. Cohen & Lotan, 1995; McCaslin & Good, 1996; O'Donnell & O'Kelly, 1994; S. E. Peterson, 1993; N. M. Webb & Palincsar, 1996).

Research regarding the effects of heterogeneous ability groupings has yielded mixed results. Some studies indicate that heterogeneous groups benefit both high-achieving students, who can sharpen their understanding of class material by explaining it to their classmates, and low-achieving students, who benefit from hearing such explanations (Lou et al., 1996; Stevens & Slavin, 1995; Webb & Palincsar, 1996). Yet other studies indicate that high-achieving students do not always gain from working with their low-achieving peers; in fact, these students occasionally even lose ground (Lou et al., 1996; Tudge, 1990). Furthermore, students of similar ability levels may sometimes be able to work more collaboratively than students of widely differing abilities (L. S. Fuchs, Fuchs, Hamlett, & Karns, 1998). Given such mixed messages from research, our best bet is probably to experiment with varying degrees of heterogeneity in our cooperative groups and to determine which approach works best for *our* students.

Give group members common goals.

• *Give group members one or more common goals toward which to work.* At the beginning of a cooperative group activity, we should specify clearly and concretely what each group should accomplish (Crook, 1995; D. W. Johnson & Johnson, 1991). For instance, when my daughter Tina was enrolled in high school Spanish, the goal of one cooperative activity was to write and videotape an episode of a television soap opera spoken entirely in Spanish. The students knew that these *telenovelas* would eventually be shown at an "Academy Awards" banquet for the students and parents, and "Oscars" would be presented for best picture, best screenplay, best leading and supporting actors and actresses, and so on.

Provide guidance about appropriate group behavior.

• *Provide clear guidelines about how to behave.* Without instruction about appropriate group behaviors, students may act in a decidedly uncooperative manner; for example, they may try to dominate discussions, ridicule one another's ideas, or exert pressure to complete the task in a particular way (Blumenfeld, Marx, Soloway, &

Krajcik, 1996; N. M. Webb & Palincsar, 1996). Instruction on such group skills as these seems to increase cooperative and productive group behaviors:

Listening to others politely and attentively

Giving encouragement to others

Making sure everyone has an equal chance to participate

Refraining from insulting or yelling at others

Offering assistance to those who need it

Asking clear, precise questions when one doesn't understand
(E. G. Cohen, 1994; Deutsch, 1993; Lou et al., 1996; O'Donnell & O'Kelly, 1994; N. M. Webb & Farivar, 1994; N. M. Webb & Palincsar, 1996)

- *Structure tasks so that group members are dependent on one another for their success.* We should structure cooperative learning activities in such a way that each student's success depends on the help and participation of other group members; furthermore, each student must believe it is to his or her advantage that *other* group members do well (Deutsch, 1993; Karau & Williams, 1995; Lou et al., 1996). For instance, tasks that involve creative problem solving and have more than one right answer are more likely to encourage students to work cooperatively with one another (Blumenfeld et al., 1996). In some situations, each student might have a unique and essential function within the group, perhaps serving as group leader, critic, bookkeeper, summarizer, and so on (A. L. Brown & Palincsar, 1989; D. W. Johnson & Johnson, 1991). In other situations, the **jigsaw technique** is useful: New information is divided equally among all group members, and each student must teach his or her portion to the other group members (Aronson & Patnoe, 1997). Still another approach is to assign projects that require such a wide range of talents and skills that every group member is likely to have something truly unique and useful to contribute to the group's overall success (E. G. Cohen, 1994; Schofield, 1995).

Structure the task to promote interdependence among students.

When students are novices at cooperative learning, it is often helpful to give them a set of steps (a "script" to follow) that guides their interaction (Fantuzzo, King, & Heller, 1992; Meloth & Deering, 1994; N. M. Webb & Palincsar, 1996). In one approach, known as **scripted cooperation,** students work together in pairs to read and study expository text (Dansereau, 1988). One member of the pair might act as "recaller," summarizing the contents of a textbook passage. The other student acts as "listener," correcting any errors and recalling additional important information. For the next passage, the two students switch roles. Such an approach can help students improve such learning strategies as elaboration, summarizing, and comprehension monitoring (Dansereau, 1988).

- *Serve more as a resource and monitor than as a "director."* During any cooperative learning activity, we should continually monitor each group to be sure that interactions are productive and socially appropriate (D. W. Johnson & Johnson, 1991); for instance, we may want to think about issues such as these:

Serve as a resource and monitor.

Are students working toward a common goal?

Are they all actively participating?

Are they listening to one another's perspectives?

Are they asking one another questions when they don't understand?

Are they criticizing ideas rather than people?

We might also provide assistance in situations where group members are unable to provide information or insights critical for accomplishing the group's goal. Too much intervention may be counterproductive, however: Students tend to talk less with one another when their teacher joins the group (E. G. Cohen, 1994).

Assess students' learning on an individual basis.

Provide rewards for group success.

Have students evaluate their group's effectiveness.

• *Make students individually accountable for their achievement, but also reinforce them for group success.* Students are more likely to learn assigned classroom subject matter during cooperative learning activities when they know that they will have to demonstrate individual mastery or accomplishment of the group's goal—for example, by taking a quiz or answering questions in class. Such an approach minimizes the likelihood that some students will do most or all of the work while others get a "free ride" (Karau & Williams, 1995; Slavin, 1990; N. M. Webb & Palincsar, 1996).

In addition to holding students accountable for their own learning and achievement, we should also reinforce group members for the success of the group as a whole—a group contingency in action (Lou et al., 1996; Slavin, 1990; Stipek, 1996). Such group rewards often promote higher achievement overall, perhaps because students have a vested interest in helping one another learn and so make a concerted effort to help fellow group members understand the material that the group is studying (Slavin, 1983; Stevens & Slavin, 1995). One commonly used approach is to give students a quiz over material they have studied in their cooperative groups and then award bonus points when all group members perform at or above a certain level.

• *At the end of an activity, have the groups evaluate their effectiveness.* Once our cooperative groups have accomplished their goals, we should have them look analytically and critically (perhaps with our assistance) at the ways in which they have functioned effectively and the ways in which they need to improve (E. G. Cohen, 1994; Deutsch, 1993; D. W. Johnson & Johnson, 1991). We might ask them to consider some of the same issues we kept in mind as we monitored the activity—for instance, whether everyone participated equally, whether group members asked one another questions when they didn't understand, and whether everyone criticized ideas rather than people.

Cooperative learning groups vary in duration, depending on the task to be accomplished. On some occasions, groups are formed on a short-term basis to accomplish specific tasks—perhaps to study new material, solve a problem, or complete an assigned project. On other occasions, groups are formed to work toward long-term classroom goals. For instance, **base groups** are cooperative groups that last the entire semester or school year; they provide a means through which students can clarify assignments for one another, help one another with class notes, and provide one another with a general sense of support and belonging in the classroom (e.g., D. W. Johnson & Johnson, 1991).

Numerous research studies indicate that cooperative learning activities, when designed and structured appropriately, are effective in many ways. For one thing, students of all ability levels show higher academic achievement; females, members of minority groups, and students at risk for academic failure are especially likely to show increased achievement (Lampe & Rooze, 1994; Lou et al., 1996; Qin, Johnson, & Johnson, 1995; Shachar & Sharan, 1994; Stevens & Slavin, 1995). Cooperative learning activities may also promote higher-level thinking skills: Students essentially "think aloud," modeling various learning and problem-solving strategies for one another and developing greater metacognitive awareness as a result (A. L. Brown & Palincsar, 1989; Good et al., 1992; Paris & Winograd, 1990).

The benefits of cooperative learning activities are not limited to gains in learning and achievement. Students have higher self-efficacy about their chances of being successful, express more intrinsic motivation to learn school subject matter, and participate more actively in classroom activities. They better understand the perspectives of others and more frequently engage in prosocial behavior—making decisions about how to divide a task fairly and equitably, resolving interpersonal conflicts, and encouraging and supporting one another's learning. Furthermore, they are more likely to believe that they are liked and accepted by their classmates, and increased numbers of friendships across racial and ethnic groups and between students with and without disabilities are likely to

Use cooperative learning to promote higher-level thinking skills as well as to facilitate learning.

Use cooperative learning to promote intrinsic motivation, prosocial behavior, and a wider range of friendships.

form (Lou et al., 1996; Marsh & Craven, 1997; Slavin, 1990; Stevens & Slavin, 1995; N. M. Webb & Palincsar, 1996).

However, there are also some potential disadvantages of cooperative learning. Students may sometimes be more interested in achieving a group reward with the least possible effort and so will focus more on getting the "right" answer than on ensuring that all group members understand the subject matter being studied (Good et al., 1992; Hatano & Inagaki, 1991; M. C. Linn et al., 1996). The students who do most of the work and most of the talking may learn more than other group members (Blumenfeld, 1992; Gayford, 1992; N. M. Webb, 1989). Students may occasionally agree to use an incorrect strategy or method that a particular group member has suggested, or they may share misconceptions about the topic they are studying (Good et al., 1992; Stacey, 1992). And in some cases, students may simply not have the skills to help one another learn (O'Donnell & O'Kelly, 1994). Clearly, then, we must keep a close eye on the discussions that cooperative groups have and the products that they create, providing additional structure and guidance when necessary to promote maximal learning and achievement.

One of the reasons that cooperative learning is so often effective is that students tutor one another in the subject matter they are studying. Such peer tutoring is our next topic of discussion.

Peer Tutoring

THINKING ABOUT WHAT YOU KNOW

Have you ever tutored or received tutoring from a fellow student? If so, what benefits did you gain from the experience?

As noted in our discussion of mastery learning in the preceding chapter, some of our students may need more time to master a topic than others; hence, they may need more instructional time, and perhaps more individualized instruction, than their classmates. As teachers, we can't always devote much time to one-on-one instruction. **Peer tutoring—** students who have mastered a topic teaching those who have not—can provide an effective alternative for teaching fundamental knowledge and skills. In some cases, we can have students within a single class tutor one another. In other situations, we might have older students teaching younger ones; for instance, fourth or fifth graders might tutor students in kindergarten or first grade (A. L. Brown & Campione, 1994; Inglis & Biemiller, 1997; Kermani & Moallem, 1997).

Like mastery learning, direct instruction, and computer-based instruction, peer tutoring sessions give students many opportunities to make the active responses that, from a behaviorist perspective, are so essential to learning. From the perspective of cognitive psychology, the process of tutoring someone else encourages students to organize and elaborate on what they have already learned sufficiently to make the material clear to someone else. And cross-age tutoring is consistent with Vygotsky's belief that older and more competent individuals are invaluable in promoting the cognitive development of younger children.

In some cases, peer tutoring leads to greater academic gains than either mastery learning or more traditional whole-class instruction (D. Fuchs, Fuchs, Mathes, & Simmons, 1997; Greenwood, Carta, & Hall, 1988). One possible reason for its effectiveness is that it provides a context in which struggling students may be more comfortable asking questions when they don't understand something. In one study (Graesser & Person, 1994), students asked 240 times as many questions during peer tutoring as they did during whole-class instruction!

INTO THE CLASSROOM: Promoting Cooperative Learning

Form groups of students who are likely to work together productively.

An elementary school teacher divides her class into cooperative groups of four or five students each. He makes sure that each group includes boys and girls, students of various ethnic backgrounds, and students who will be able to contribute different skills to the task at hand.

Provide clear goals toward which groups should work.

In a unit on Shakespeare, an English teacher asks cooperative groups to identify the attitudes toward Jewish people expressed in *The Merchant of Venice,* as reflected in the actions and statements of Shylock and other characters.

Give each group member a different role or task within the group.

A biology teacher asks cooperative groups to prepare for an upcoming classroom debate on the pros and cons of preserving tropical rain forests. She gives each student a unique function. One student acts as *reader* of information about rain forests, another acts as *recorder* of the arguments that group members present, a third acts as *checker* to determine whether all group members agree with each argument, and so on.

Monitor group interactions.

A junior high school social studies teacher asks cooperative groups to identify an effective way of helping the homeless find suitable housing. He observes the groups to be sure interactions within each group are productive and socially appropriate. When he hears a student insulting another because of a difference of opinion, he reminds the group that students should criticize ideas rather than people.

Provide critical information and insights when (but only when) a group is unlikely or unable to provide such information and insights for itself.

The same middle school teacher tells one group, "The solution you have developed assumes that most taxpayers would be willing to pay much higher taxes than they do now. Is that realistic?"

Make students individually accountable for their achievement.

A mathematics teacher has incorporated cooperative learning into a lesson on calculating the area of a triangle. She gives all students a quiz to assess their individual mastery of the subject.

Reinforce group success.

The same mathematics teacher awards bonus points to students whose entire group performs at or above a certain test score.

Ask students to evaluate their effectiveness in working as a group.

After cooperative groups have completed their assigned tasks, a social studies teacher asks the groups to answer questions such as these: "Did all group members actively participate?" "Did they ask questions when they didn't understand one another?" "Did they criticize ideas rather than people?"

Vary the duration of cooperative groups, depending on the task to be accomplished.

In September, a high school health teacher forms *base groups* of students who will provide support and assistance for one another throughout the school year. As the year progresses, he occasionally forms different, more short-term cooperative groups to accomplish specific tasks—for example, to identify the dangers of alcohol abuse or plan an inexpensive meal encompassing all major food groups.

Peer tutoring typically benefits tutors as well as those being tutored (D. Fuchs et al., 1997; Inglis & Biemiller, 1997; Semb et al., 1993; N. M. Webb & Palincsar, 1996). When students study material with the expectation that they will be teaching it to someone else, they are more intrinsically motivated to learn it, find it more interesting, process it in a more meaningful fashion, and remember it longer (Benware & Deci, 1984; Semb et al., 1993). Peer tutoring has nonacademic benefits as well. Cooperation and other social skills improve, classroom behavior problems diminish, and friendships develop between students of different ethnic groups and between students with and without disabilities (Greenwood et al., 1988).

Like other interactive approaches to instruction, peer tutoring is most effective when teachers follow certain guidelines in its use. Here are several suggestions for using peer tutoring effectively:

In many cases, when one student tutors another, the tutor learns as much from the experience as the student being tutored.

• *Make sure tutors have mastered the material they are teaching and use effective instructional techniques.* Good tutors have a meaningful understanding of the subject matter they are teaching and provide explanations that focus on such understanding; poor tutors are more likely to describe procedures without explaining why the procedures are useful (L. S. Fuchs et al., 1996). Good tutors also use teaching strategies that are likely to promote learning: They ask questions, give hints, scaffold responses when necessary, provide feedback, and so on (Lepper, Aspinwall, Mumme, & Chabey, 1990).

Students don't always have the knowledge and skills that will enable them to become effective tutors, especially at the elementary school level (Greenwood et al., 1988; Kermani & Moallem, 1997; Wood, Wood, Ainsworth, & O'Malley, 1995). It is essential, then, that tutoring sessions be limited to subject matter that the student tutors know well. Training in effective tutoring skills is also helpful; for example, we might show student tutors how to establish a good relationship with the students they are tutoring, how to break a task into simple steps, how and when to give feedback, and so on (Inglis & Biemiller, 1997; Kermani & Moallem, 1997).

 Make sure tutors have mastered the material they are teaching. Teach effective teaching strategies.

• *Provide a structure for students' interactions.* Providing a structure for tutoring sessions can often help students tutor their classmates more effectively (D. Fuchs et al., 1997; L. S. Fuchs et al., 1996; A. King, 1997, 1998). As an example, in one study (D. Fuchs et al., 1997), twenty second- through sixth-grade classrooms participated in a project called Peer-Assisted Learning Strategies (PALS), designed to foster more

Structure tutoring sessions to promote effective learning.

effective reading comprehension skills. In each classroom, students were ranked with regard to their reading performance, and the ranked list was divided in two. The first-ranked student in the top half of the list was paired with the first-ranked student in the bottom half of the list, the second student in the top half was paired with the second student in the bottom half, and so on down the line; through this procedure, students who were paired together had moderate but not extreme differences in their reading levels. Each pair read reading material at the level of the weaker reader and engaged in these activities:

Partner reading with retell. The stronger reader read aloud for five minutes, then the weaker reader read the same passage of text. Reading something that had previously been read presumably enabled the weaker reader to read the material easily. After the double reading, the weaker reader described the material that the pair had just read.

Paragraph summary. The students both read a passage one paragraph at a time. Then, with help from the stronger reader, the weaker reader tried to identify the subject and main idea of the paragraph.

Prediction relay. Both students read a page of text, and then, with help from the stronger reader, the weaker reader would summarize the text and also make a prediction about what the next page would say. The students would read the following page, then the weaker reader would confirm or disconfirm the prediction, summarize the new page, make a new prediction, and so on.

Such a procedure enabled students in the PALS program to make significantly greater progress in reading than students who had more traditional reading instruction, even though the amount of class time devoted to reading instruction was similar for both groups. The researchers speculated that the PALS students performed better because they had more frequent opportunities to make verbal responses to the things they were reading, received more frequent feedback about their performance, and, in general, were more frequently encouraged to use effective reading strategies.

At the secondary level, we can incorporate a tutoring component into paired study sessions by teaching students the kinds of questions they should ask one another as they jointly study science, social studies, and other academic disciplines. In one approach (A. King, 1997), students learn to ask their partners questions that promote meaningful learning, elaboration, and metacognition—for instance, questions such as these:

Describe . . . in your own words.

What is the difference between . . . and . . . ?

What do you think would happen to . . . if . . . happened?

How did you figure that out?

When we give students guidance about the kinds of questions that can help them promote one another's learning, highly effective tutoring sessions often result. Here is an example in which two seventh graders are following a prescribed questioning procedure as they study biology:

Jon: How does the muscular system work, Kyle?

Kyle: Well . . . it retracts and contracts when you move.

Jon: Can you tell me more?

Kyle: Um . . . well . . .

Jon: Um, why are muscles important, Kyle?

Kyle: They are important because if we didn't have them we couldn't move around.

Jon: But . . . how do muscles work? Explain it more.

Kyle: Um, muscles have tendons. Some muscles are called skeletal muscles. They are in the muscles that—like—in your arms—that have tendons that hold your muscles to your bones—to make them move and go back and forth. So you can walk and stuff.

Jon: Good. All right! How are the skeletal muscles and the cardiac muscles the same?

Kyle: Uhh—the cardiac and the smooth muscles?

Jon: The cardiac and the skeletal.

Kyle: Well, they're both a muscle. And they're both pretty strong. And they hold things. I don't really think they have much in common.

Jon: Okay. Why don't you think they have much in common?

Kyle: Because the smooth muscle is—I mean the skeletal muscle is voluntary and the cardiac muscle is involuntary. Okay, I'll ask now. What do you think would happen if we didn't have smooth muscles?

Jon: We would have to be chewing harder. And so it would take a long time to digest food. We would have to think about digesting because the smooth muscles—like the intestines and stomach—are *in*voluntary.

Kyle: Have you really thought about it?

Jon: Yeah.

Kyle: Yeah, well—um—but, do you think it would *hurt* you if you didn't have smooth muscles?

Jon: Well, yeah—because you wouldn't have muscles to push the food along—in the stomach and intestines—you'd get plugged up! Maybe you'd hafta drink liquid—just liquid stuff. Yuk. (King, Staffieri, & Adelgais, 1998, p. 141)

Notice how Kyle asks questions that encourage Jon to go beyond the material he has specifically learned (e.g., "How are the skeletal muscles and the cardiac muscles the same?" "Do you think it would hurt you if you didn't have smooth muscles?"). Kyle also asks questions that encourage Jon to think about his thinking and thereby may promote metacognition (e.g., "Why don't you think they have much in common?" "Have you really thought about it?"). Through such structured interactions, even students at the same grade and ability levels can provide valuable scaffolding for one another's learning efforts (A. King, 1998).

   • *Be careful that your use of higher-achieving students to tutor lower-achieving students is not excessive or exploitive.* As we have seen, tutors often gain just as much from tutoring sessions as the students they are tutoring. Nevertheless, we must not assume that high-achieving students will always learn from a tutoring session; we should therefore monitor the effects of a peer tutoring program to make sure that all of our students are reaping its benefits.

Don't exploit higher-achieving students.

   • *Use peer tutoring to help students with special educational needs.* Peer tutoring has been used effectively to help students with learning disabilities, physical disabilities, and other special educational needs (Cushing & Kennedy, 1997; D. Fuchs et al., 1997). For example, in one study (Cushing & Kennedy, 1997), low-achieving students were assigned as tutors for classmates who had moderate or severe intellectual or physical disabilities. The student tutors clearly benefited from their tutoring assignments: They became more attentive in class, completed classroom tasks more frequently, and participated in class more regularly. I suspect that the opportunity to tutor classmates less capable than themselves may have enhanced their own self-efficacy for learning classroom subject matter, which in turn would encourage them to engage in the kinds of behaviors that would ensure academic success.

Use peer tutoring to help students with special needs.

   • *Make sure that all students have experience tutoring their classmates.* Ideally, we should make sure that *all* of our students have an opportunity to tutor

Give everyone the chance to be a tutor.

their classmates at one time or another (Greenwood, 1991). This is often easier said than done, as a few of our students may show consistently lower achievement than most of their peers. One potentially effective strategy in such situations is to teach those students specific tasks or procedures that they can share with their higher-achieving, but in this case uninformed, classmates (E. G. Cohen, Lockheed, & Lohman, 1976; N. M. Webb & Palincsar, 1996). Another strategy is to create a *community of learners*—an approach we turn to now.

Creating a Community of Learners

In our earlier discussion of cooperative learning, I described an activity in which high school Spanish students created soap operas for which their teacher later awarded "Oscars" at an awards banquet. Obviously, the strategy incorporated an element of competition, as only one group could receive the award for "best picture," "best screenplay," and so on. Such competitions can be effective *if* all groups have equal ability and *if* the final outcome is determined more by student effort than by less controllable factors (Stipek, 1996).

Generally speaking, however, a competitive classroom environment is often counterproductive when we consider the principles of motivation presented in Chapter 12. For one thing, competitive situations focus students' attention on performance goals rather than learning goals (Nicholls, 1984; Spaulding, 1992); hence, students are more likely to worry about how good they appear to their teacher and classmates than about how effectively they are cognitively processing classroom material. Second, competition creates a situation in which most students become losers rather than winners; their self-efficacy decreases as a result, and their intrinsic motivation to learn is undermined (Deci & Ryan, 1985, 1992). Finally, when students consistently see others performing more successfully than themselves, they are more likely to attribute their own failures to a lack of ability: They conclude that they simply don't have what it takes to succeed at classroom tasks (C. Ames, 1984).

In contrast, a cooperative classroom environment enhances students' motivation to learn and achieve in the classroom because it increases the likelihood that students will be successful (C. Ames, 1984; Deci & Ryan, 1985). Furthermore, students who think and work together model effective learning and problem-solving strategies for one another, provide mutual scaffolding that enhances success on challenging tasks, and can construct a better understanding of a topic than any single student could alone. Some theorists (A. L. Brown et al., 1993; Hewitt & Scardamalia, 1998; Salomon, 1993) refer to such "group thinking" as **distributed cognition,** a concept similar to *distributed intelligence* (Chapter 4).

We can create a cooperative classroom environment when we incorporate elements of various interactive teaching methods into a **community of learners**—a classroom in which we and our students consistently work to help one another learn (A. L. Brown & Campione, 1994; Campione et al., 1995; Prawat, 1992; Rogoff, Matusov, & White, 1996). A classroom that operates as a community of learners is likely to have characteristics such as these:

Create a community of learners—a classroom in which you and your students actively and cooperatively work to help one another learn.

- All students are active participants in classroom activities.
- Discussion and collaboration among two or more students are common occurrences and play a key role in learning.
- Diversity in students' interests and rates of progress is expected and respected.
- Students and teacher coordinate their efforts at helping one another learn; no one has exclusive responsibility for teaching others.

- Everyone is a potential resource for the others; different individuals are likely to serve as resources on different occasions, depending on the topics and tasks at hand. (In some cases, students may "major" in a particular topic and thereby become local "experts" on that topic.)

- The teacher provides some guidance and direction for classroom activities, but students may also contribute to such guidance and direction.

- Constructive questioning and critique of one another's work is commonplace.

- The process of learning is emphasized as much as, and sometimes more than, the finished product. (A. L. Brown & Campione, 1994, 1996; Campione et al., 1995; Rogoff, 1994; Rogoff et al., 1996)

In one simple example of how a community of learners might be structured (A. L. Brown & Campione, 1994), students were divided into five groups to study five different subtopics falling within a general theme; for instance, subtopics for the theme *changing populations* were *extinct, endangered, artificial, assisted,* and *urbanized.* Each group conducted research and prepared teaching materials related to its subtopic. The class then reassembled into five new groups that included at least one representative from each of the previous groups; within these groups, the students taught one another the things they had learned. (Here we see an example of the *jigsaw technique* described in the section on cooperative learning.)

We can also use a computer network to promote a community of learners (Hewitt & Scardamalia, 1998). For instance, we might have all students place their classwork (short stories, essays, problem solutions, etc.) in computer files that their classmates can read and respond to. And we can create ongoing "chat rooms" in which students present questions or issues to which others respond. As an example, consider three students' on-line responses to another student's question, "How does heat affect solids?"; note that they use the terms "My theory" and "I need to understand" to structure their discussion:

In a *community of learners,* students actively and consistently work together to help one another learn.

JA: *My theory:* I think that heat makes solids burn or melt. I think that my prediction is right because I've seen solids melt and burn.

AR: *My theory:* I think that if a solid comes in contact with heat, it becomes hot. I also think it might change colour. Generally if any solid comes in contact with heat then it becomes hot. I think that the solid would become hot faster if it could conduct energy well. If an object didn't conduct energy well then it would heat up, but take a longer time than an object that conducts energy well. It might change colour because we think that if something is very hot it is white or red and sort of hot it is orange or yellow. There might be some truth to this.

AD: *My theory:* I think that it depends on how much heat there is. I also think that it depends on what sort of solid it is. For instance, the heat that might melt rubber might not melt metal. (This last sentence might be wrong, I'm just using it as an example.)
I need to understand: What makes wood burn instead of melt? (AD)
My theory: I think that it might have something to do with wood being organic, because I can't think of anything that is organic, and would melt. (adapted from Hewitt & Scardamalia, 1998, p. 85)

Such on-line discussions may be especially valuable for students who are shy or for other reasons feel uncomfortable communicating with their classmates in a more public fashion (Hewitt & Scardamalia, 1998).

As you can see, a community of learners incorporates several of the instructional strategies we've already considered, including class discussions, cooperative learning, peer tutoring, and discovery learning. Accordingly, we find justification for this approach in the various theoretical perspectives that support those other strategies. In addition, a community of learners is, in many respects, similar to the approach that scientists and other scholars take when they advance the frontiers of knowledge (conducting individual and collaborative research, sharing ideas, building on one another's findings, etc.) and so may help students acquire some rather sophisticated and adultlike knowledge-building skills (A. L. Brown & Campione, 1996; Hewitt & Scardamalia, 1998; Karpov & Haywood, 1998).

Researchers have not yet systematically compared the academic achievement of communities of learners to the achievement of more traditional classrooms. Case studies do indicate that classes structured as communities of learners have some positive effects, however. For one thing, these classes appear to promote higher-level thinking processes for extended periods of time (A. L. Brown & Campione, 1994). They are also highly motivating for students; for instance, students often insist on going to school even when they are ill, and they are disappointed when summer vacation begins (Rogoff, 1994). And they create an environment in which we can meet our students' needs for affiliation at the very same time that we encourage learning goals and an intrinsic motivation to learn classroom subject matter. To illustrate, one eighth-grade English teacher described her experiences with a community of learners this way:

> The classroom became . . . like a dining-room table, where people could converse easily about books and poems and ideas. I would watch my students leave the classroom carrying on animated conversations about which book was truly Robert Cormier's best, why sequels are often disappointing, which books they planned to reread or pack into their trunks for summer camp. Books became valuable currency, changing hands after careful negotiation: "Okay, you can borrow Adams's *So Long and Thanks for All the Fish* (Pocket), but you have to lend me the first two books in the Xanth series." The shelves neatly lined with class sets of books gradually gave way to a paperback library, stocked with books donated by students and their families, bonus copies from book clubs, and books I ordered with my budgeted allotment each year. (S. Moran, 1991, p. 439)

At the same time, we should note a couple of potential weaknesses that communities of learners may have (A. L. Brown & Campione, 1994). For one thing, what students learn will inevitably be limited to the knowledge that they themselves acquire and share with one another. Second, students may occasionally pass on their own misconceptions to their classmates. Obviously, then, when we structure our classrooms as communities of learners, we must carefully monitor student interactions to make sure that students ultimately acquire thorough and accurate understandings of the subject matter they are studying.

Taking Student Diversity into Account

Use cooperative approaches to enhance the achievement of females and students from ethnic minority groups.

Cooperative approaches to instruction may be especially suitable for the females in our classrooms. Small-group discussions encourage girls to participate more actively than they typically do during whole-class instruction (Théberge, 1994). We should note, however, that boys sometimes take control during small-group activities. If we regularly see such male "dominance," we may occasionally want to form all-female groups; by doing so, we are likely to increase girls' participation in group activities and encourage them to take leadership roles (Fennema, 1987; MacLean et al., 1995).

Furthermore, cooperative approaches often promote higher academic achievement for students whose backgrounds are equally cooperative in nature (Garcia, 1994, 1995; McAlpine & Taylor, 1993; N. M. Webb & Palincsar, 1996). As we discovered in Chapter 4, cooperative learning is more consistent with the cultures of many ethnic minority groups.

Interactive instructional strategies may also be our methods of choice when our objectives include promoting social development as well as academic achievement. Peer tutoring encourages friendly relationships across ethnic and racial lines (Greenwood et al., 1988). Cooperative learning groups, especially when students work on tasks involving a number of different skills and abilities, can foster an appreciation for the various strengths that students with diverse backgrounds are likely to contribute (E. G. Cohen, 1994; E. G. Cohen & Lotan, 1995). And virtually any "cooperative" approach to instruction—cooperative learning, reciprocal teaching, peer tutoring—may help students begin to recognize that despite the obvious diversity among them, they are ultimately more similar to one another than they are different (Schofield, 1995).

A community of learners may be especially valuable when we have a diverse classroom of students (Garcia, 1994; Ladson-Billings, 1995). Such a community values the contributions of all students, using everyone's individual backgrounds, cultural perspectives, and unique abilities to enhance the overall performance of the class. It also provides a context in which students can form friendships across the lines of ethnicity, gender, socioeconomic status, and disability—friendships that, as noted in Chapters 3 and 4, are so critical for students' social development and multicultural understanding.

Use cooperative approaches to instruction to promote students' social development.

Accommodating Students with Special Needs

Interactive approaches to instruction will often be helpful when working with students who have special educational needs. For instance, small-group activities can provide the scaffolding that some students need to achieve success at assigned tasks. And peer tutoring may provide a mechanism through which they can gain extra instruction and practice in basic skills. Table 14.1 provides a few suggestions for using and adapting interactive instructional strategies for students with special needs.

Have you ever tutored a student who had a disability? If so, what benefits did you gain from the experience?

The Big Picture: Choosing Instructional Strategies

THINKING ABOUT WHAT YOU KNOW

Historically, many theorists and practitioners have looked for—and in some cases decided that they've *found*—the single "best" way to teach students. The result has been a series of movements in which educators advocate a particular instructional approach and then, a few years later, advocate a very different approach (K. R. Harris & Alexander, 1998; Sfard, 1998). Why do you suppose the field of education lends itself so well to such "pendulum swings"?

I've often wondered about this pendulum-swinging trend myself, and I've developed several hypotheses. Perhaps some people are looking for a teaching *algorithm*— a specific procedure they can follow that will always guarantee high achievement. Perhaps they confuse theory with fact, thinking that the latest theoretical fad must inevitably be the "correct" explanation of how children learn or develop, and so

TABLE 14.1

Identifying Interactive Strategies Especially Suitable for Students with Special Educational Needs

STUDENTS WITH SPECIAL NEEDS	CHARACTERISTICS THAT THESE STUDENTS MAY EXHIBIT	CLASSROOM STRATEGIES THAT MAY BE BENEFICIAL FOR THESE STUDENTS
Students with specific cognitive or academic difficulties	Uneven patterns of achievement Poor listening and/or reading skills	Use cooperative learning and peer tutoring as possible means of supplementing instruction in students' areas of weakness. Use reciprocal teaching to promote listening and reading comprehension. Continually monitor students' progress to determine the effectiveness of your instructional strategies.
Students with social or behavioral problems	Poor social skills Frequent off-task behavior Inability to work independently for extended periods of time	Use cooperative learning to foster social skills and friendships. Give explicit guidelines about how to behave during interactive learning sessions. Use peer tutoring as a means of providing one-on-one attention and instruction. Continually monitor students' progress to determine the effectiveness of instructional strategies.
Students with general delays in cognitive and social functioning	Difficulty thinking abstractly Need for a great deal of repetition and practice of information and skills	Use peer tutoring as a means of promoting friendships with nondisabled classmates. Identify particular skills that students have mastered and can teach to their classmates.
Students with physical or sensory challenges	Average intelligence in most cases Tendency to tire easily in some cases Difficulty with speech in a few cases	Allow frequent breaks from strenuous or intensive activities. When students have difficulty speaking, provide another means of enabling them to participate actively in class discussions and cooperative learning groups (perhaps through technology).
Students with advanced cognitive development	Rapid learning Greater ability to think abstractly; appearance of abstract thinking at a younger age Greater conceptual understanding of classroom material Ability to learn independently	Provide opportunities to pursue topics in greater depth (e.g., through homogeneous cooperative learning or discussion groups). Encourage students to communicate via the Internet with others of similar interests and abilities. Use advanced students as peer tutors only to the extent that tutoring sessions help the tutors as well as those being tutored.

Sources: Fiedler et al., 1993; Greenwood et al., 1988; Heward, 1996; Mercer, 1991; Morgan & Jenson, 1988; Piirto, 1994; Robinson, 1991; Stevens & Slavin, 1995; Turnbull et al., 1999.

conclude that the teaching implications they derive from the theory must certainly be just as correct. Or maybe they just have an overly simplistic view of what the goals of our educational system should be.

When we consider which instructional strategies to use in our classrooms, we must remember that *there is no single best approach to classroom instruction.* Each of the strategies we've examined has its merits, and each is useful in different situations and for different students. Generally speaking, our choice of an instructional strategy must depend on at least three things: the objective of the lesson, the nature of the subject matter at hand, and the characteristics and abilities of our students. Table 14.2 presents general conditions and specific examples in which each strategy might be most appropriate.

In many instances, we can combine two or more strategies together quite effectively. For example, a mathematics or science lesson might include discovery learning experiences within an overall mastery learning approach. A social studies lesson might include expository instruction, class discussions, and reciprocal teaching within the context of a cooperative learning environment. A successful classroom—one in which students are acquiring and using school subject matter in a truly meaningful fashion—is undoubtedly a classroom in which a variety of approaches to instruction can be found.

As you gain experience as a classroom teacher, you will become increasingly adept at using a variety of instructional strategies. You will, I hope, experiment with different approaches to determine which ones work most effectively for your own objectives, academic disciplines, and students. Furthermore, as noted in Chapter 1, you can continue to grow as a teacher if you keep yourself up to date both on the subject matter you are teaching and on theoretical and research perspectives on effective classroom instruction.

Yet knowing how to plan and implement instruction is not enough. Effective teachers also create a classroom environment conducive to student learning. Furthermore, they regularly monitor their students' progress toward achieving classroom objectives and adapt instruction when warranted. We will consider the classroom environment and assessment in the next two chapters.

Consider the objective, the topic, and student characteristics when you choose your instructional strategies.

How might elements of cooperative learning and mastery learning be combined? In what way is computer-assisted instruction also expository instruction?

CASE STUDY: Uncooperative Students

Ms. Mihara is beginning a unit entitled "Customs in Other Lands" in her fourth-grade class. Having heard about the benefits of cooperative learning, she asks students to form groups of four that will work together throughout the unit. On Monday, she assigns each group a particular country: Australia, Colombia, Ireland, Israel, Greece, Japan, or South Africa. She then instructs the groups, "Today we will go to the school library, where you can find information on the customs of your country and check out materials you think will be useful. Over the next two weeks, you will have time every day to work as a group. You should learn all you can about the customs of your country. A week from Friday, each group will give an oral report to the rest of the class."

During the next few class sessions, Ms. Mihara runs into more problems than she ever imagined she would. For example, when the students form their groups, she notices that the high achievers have gotten together to form one group and that the socially oriented, "popular" students have flocked to three others. The remaining two groups are comprised of whichever students are left over. Some

(continued on p. 594)

Choosing an Instructional Strategy

YOU MIGHT USE . . .	WHEN . . .	FOR EXAMPLE, YOU MIGHT . . .
Expository instruction	The *objective* is to acquire knowledge within the cognitive domain. The *lesson* involves information best learned in terms of a specific organizational structure. *Students* are capable of abstract thought and possess a wealth of knowledge to which they can relate new material.	Enumerate the critical battles of World War I to advanced history students. Demonstrate several defensive strategies to the varsity soccer team.
Discovery learning	The *objective* is to develop firsthand knowledge of physical or social phenomena. The *lesson* involves information that can be correctly deduced from hands-on experimentation with concrete objects or from direct social interaction with others. *Students* have enough knowledge to interpret their findings correctly but sometimes have difficulty learning from strictly abstract material.	Ask students to find out what happens when two primary colors of paint (red and yellow, red and blue, or yellow and blue) are mixed together. Create a classroom situation in which students discover firsthand how it feels to experience "taxation without representation."
Mastery learning	The *objective* is to learn knowledge or skills to a level of mastery (perhaps to automaticity). The *lesson* provides critical information or skills for later instructional units. *Students* vary in the time they need to achieve mastery.	Have each student in band practice the C major scale until he or she can do so perfectly. Have students practice the one hundred single-digit addition facts until they can answer all the facts correctly within a five-minute period.
Direct instruction	The *objective* is to learn a well-defined body of knowledge and skills. The *lesson* provides critical information or skills for later instructional units. *Students* are likely to need considerable practice in order to learn successfully.	Explain how to add fractions with different denominators and give students practice in adding such fractions both in class and through homework. Demonstrate how to use a jigsaw and watch carefully as students use the tool to cut irregularly shaped pieces of wood.
Computer-based instruction	The *objective* is to acquire knowledge and skills within the cognitive domain. The *lesson* involves information that students can acquire in a piecemeal, step-by-step fashion *or* requires a simulation of real-world activities. *Students* have some familiarity with computers and can work with only minimal guidance from their teacher.	Have students locate information about a particular topic on the Internet. Have students "explore" human anatomy through a computer simulation that gives an inside "look" at various anatomical structures.
Teacher questions	The *objective* is to process a topic in greater depth. The *lesson* involves complex material, such that frequent monitoring of students' learning is essential and/or mental elaboration of ideas is beneficial. *Students* are not likely to elaborate spontaneously or to monitor their own comprehension effectively.	Ask questions that promote recall and review of the previous day's lesson. Ask students for examples of how nonrenewable resources are recycled in their own community.
In-class activities	The *objective* is to practice using new information or skills. The *lesson* requires considerable teacher monitoring and scaffolding. *Students* cannot yet work independently on the task.	Have beginning tennis students practice their serves. Have students work in pairs to draw portraits of one another.

YOU MIGHT USE . . .	WHEN . . .	FOR EXAMPLE, YOU MIGHT . . .
Computer applications	The *objective* is to acquire experience with computer tools. The *lesson* involves any task that lends itself to a computer application. *Students* have some familiarity with computers and can work with only minimal guidance from their teacher.	Assign a research project that requires the use of a computer-based encyclopedia. Have students write a résumé using a word processing program.
Homework	The *objective* is to learn new yet simple material, obtain additional practice with familiar information and procedures, or relate classroom subject matter to the outside world. The *lesson* is one that students can complete with little if any assistance. *Students* exhibit sufficient self-regulation to perform the task independently.	Have students read the next chapter in their health book. In a unit on migration, have students find out what state or country their parents and grandparents were born in.
Authentic activities	The *objective* is to apply classroom material to real-world situations. The *lesson* involves synthesizing and applying a variety of knowledge and skills. *Students* have mastered the knowledge and skills necessary to perform the task.	Have students grow sunflowers using varying amounts of water, plant food, and sunlight. Have students construct maps of their local community, using appropriate symbols to convey direction, scale, physical features, and so on.
Class discussion	The *objective* is to achieve greater conceptual understanding and/or acquire a multisided perspective of a topic. The *lesson* involves complex and possibly controversial issues. *Students* have sufficient knowledge about the topic to voice their ideas and opinions.	Ask students to discuss the ethical implications of the United States' decision to drop an atomic bomb on Hiroshima. Ask groups of four or five students to prepare arguments for an upcoming debate regarding the pros and cons of increasing the minimum wage.
Reciprocal teaching	The *objective* is to develop reading comprehension and learning strategies. The *lesson* requires students to cognitively process material in relatively complex ways. *Students* possess poor reading comprehension and learning strategies.	Model four types of questions—summarizing, questioning, clarifying, and predicting—as students read aloud a passage from the textbook. Ask students to take turns being "teacher" and ask similar questions of their classmates.
Cooperative learning	The *objective* is to develop the ability to work cooperatively with others on academic tasks. The *lesson* involves tasks that are too large or difficult for a single student to accomplish independently. *Students'* cultural backgrounds emphasize cooperation rather than competition.	Have groups of two or three students work together on mathematics "brain teasers." Have students in a Spanish class work in small groups to write and videotape a soap opera spoken entirely in Spanish.
Peer tutoring	The *objective* is to learn basic knowledge or skills. The *lesson* contains material that can effectively be taught by students. *Students* vary in their mastery of the material, yet even the most advanced can gain increased understanding by teaching it to someone else.	Have students work in pairs to practice conjugating irregular French verbs. Have some students help others work through simple mathematical word problems.

groups get immediately to work on their task, others spend their group time sharing gossip and planning upcoming social events, and still others flounder aimlessly for days on end.

As the unit progresses, Ms. Mihara hears more and more complaints from students about their task ("Janet and I are doing all the work; Karen and Mary Kay aren't helping at all." "Eugene thinks he can boss the rest of us around because we're studying Ireland and he's Irish." "We're spending all this time but just can't seem to get anywhere!"). And the group reports at the end of the unit differ markedly in quality: Some are carefully planned and informative, whereas others are disorganized and lack substantive information.

"So much for this cooperative learning stuff," Ms. Mihara mumbles to herself. "If I want students to learn something, I'll just have to teach it to them myself."

- Why have Ms. Mihara's cooperative learning groups not been as productive as she had hoped? Considering the features of cooperative learning that we examined in this chapter, what did Ms. Mihara do wrong?

- How might you orchestrate the cooperative learning unit differently than Ms. Mihara?

Summing Up

Benefits of Student Interaction

Interactive methods of instruction have numerous benefits. Such methods encourage students to clarify, organize, and elaborate on what they have learned sufficiently that they can explain it to their peers. Furthermore, when students present conflicting ideas, they must reexamine their own perspectives and perhaps revise their views to achieve a more accurate and complete understanding of the topic at hand. And active discussions of classroom topics provide a means through which students can observe and ultimately acquire higher-level thinking skills and metacognitive strategies.

Promoting Elaboration Through Student Interaction

Class discussions provide an arena in which students can explore and hear multiple perspectives on controversial topics. Reciprocal teaching promotes more sophisticated metacognition and study skills by modeling and providing practice in four processes important for learning expository material: summarizing, questioning, clarifying, and predicting. In cooperative learning activities, students are rewarded for helping one another accomplish assigned tasks but are also individually accountable for achieving instructional objectives. Peer tutoring helps both the tutor and the student being tutored gain a better understanding of classroom subject matter. Both cooperative learning and peer tutoring are

often more effective when students have a specific procedure or structure to follow.

Creating a Community of Learners

A *community of learners* is a classroom in which teacher and students actively and cooperatively work to help one another learn; it often incorporates such approaches as class discussions and cooperative learning. Although the teacher provides some guidance and direction for classroom activities, students assume much of the responsibility for facilitating one another's learning.

Accommodating Student Diversity

Interactive and cooperative instructional strategies may be especially effective for females, as well as for students whose cultural backgrounds encourage cooperation rather than competition. Interactive strategies may also be invaluable in facilitating the cognitive and social development of students with special educational needs.

Choosing Instructional Strategies

There is no single "best" instructional strategy. Ultimately, we must choose our strategies on the basis of our instructional objectives, the specific topics we are teaching, and the unique characteristics of the students in our classrooms.

KEY CONCEPTS

reciprocal teaching (p. 573)
cooperative learning (p. 577)
jigsaw technique (p. 579)

scripted cooperation (p. 579)
base group (p. 580)
peer tutoring (p. 581)

distributed cognition (p. 586)
community of learners (p. 586)

15

Creating and Maintaining a Productive Classroom Environment

Think back to your elementary and secondary school years. In which teachers' classrooms were you more likely to work hard and stay on task? In which teachers' classrooms were you more likely to misbehave? What strategies did the more effective teachers use to help you be productive?

Effective teachers not only choose instructional strategies that promote effective learning and cognitive processing, but they also create an environment that keeps students busily engaged in classroom activities. In this chapter, we will consider how we can plan and create a classroom environment conducive to students' learning and achievement. In particular, we will address the following questions:

- How can we create a classroom environment that promotes student learning and minimizes off-task behavior?
- How can we effectively deal with the misbehaviors that *do* occur?
- What strategies are especially important when we have students from diverse backgrounds?
- How can we coordinate our efforts with other teachers, community agencies, and students' parents?

CASE STUDY: A Contagious Situation

Ms. Cornell received her teaching certificate in May; soon after, she accepted a position as a fifth-grade teacher at Twin Pines Elementary School. She spent the summer planning her classroom curriculum: She identified the objectives she wanted her students to accomplish during the year and developed numerous activities to help them meet those objectives. She now feels well prepared for her first year in the classroom.

After the long, hot summer, most of Ms. Cornell's students seem happy to be back at school. So on the very first day of school, Ms. Cornell jumps headlong into the curriculum she has planned. But three problems quickly present themselves—problems in the form of Eli, Jake, and Vanessa.

These three students seem determined to disrupt the classroom at every possible opportunity. They move about the room without permission, making a point of annoying others as they walk to the pencil sharpener or wastebasket. They talk out of turn, sometimes being rude and disrespectful to their teacher and classmates and at other times belittling the classroom activities that Ms. Cornell has so carefully planned. They rarely complete their in-class assignments, preferring instead to engage in horseplay or practical jokes. They seem particularly prone to misbehavior at "down" times in the class schedule—for example, at the beginning and end of the school day, before and after recess and lunch, and on occasions when Ms. Cornell is preoccupied with other students.

Ms. Cornell continues to follow her daily lesson plans, ignoring her problem students and hoping they will begin to see the error of their ways. Yet, with the three of them egging one another on, the disruptive behavior continues. Furthermore, it

598

CHAPTER 15
CREATING AND
MAINTAINING A
PRODUCTIVE
CLASSROOM
ENVIRONMENT

begins to spread to other students. By the middle of October, Ms. Cornell's class is a three-ring circus, with general chaos reigning in the classroom and instructional objectives rarely being accomplished. The few students who still seem intent on learning something are having a difficult time doing so.

- In what ways has Ms. Cornell planned for her classroom in advance? In what ways has she *not* planned?

- Why are Eli, Jake, and Vanessa so disruptive right from the start? Can you think of possible reasons related to how Ms. Cornell has begun the school year? Can you think of possible reasons related to our discussion of motivation in Chapter 12? Can you think of possible reasons related to the classroom activities Ms. Cornell has planned?

- Why does the misbehavior of the three problem students continue? Why does it spread to other students in the classroom? Why is it particularly common during "down" times in the school day? Can you answer these questions using learning principles presented in earlier chapters?

Creating an Environment Conducive to Learning

As a first-year teacher, Ms. Cornell is well prepared in some respects but not at all prepared in others. She has carefully identified her objectives and the activities through which she intends to accomplish those objectives. But she has neglected to think about how she might keep students on task or how she might adjust her lesson plans based on how students are progressing. And she has not considered how she might nip behavior problems in the bud, before such misbehaviors begin to interfere with students' learning. In the absence of such planning, no curriculum—not even one grounded firmly in principles of learning and development—is likely to promote student achievement.

Students learn more effectively in some classroom environments than in others. Consider these four classrooms as examples:

Mr. Aragon's class is a calm, orderly one. The students are working independently at their seats, and all of them appear to be concentrating on their assigned tasks. Occasionally, students approach Mr. Aragon to seek clarification of an assignment or to get feedback about a task they've completed, and he confers quietly with them.

Mr. Boitano's class is chaotic and noisy. A few students are doing their schoolwork, but most are engaged in very nonacademic activities. One girl is painting her nails behind a large dictionary propped up on her desk, a boy nearby is picking wads of gum off the underside of his desk, several students are exchanging the latest school gossip, and a group of boys is re-creating the Battle of Waterloo with rubber bands and paper clips.

Mr. Cavalini's classroom is as noisy as Boitano's. But rather than exchanging gossip or waging war, students are debating (often loudly and passionately) about the pros and cons of nuclear energy. After twenty minutes of heated discussion, Cavalini stops them, lists their various arguments on the board, and then explains in simple philosophical terms why there is no easy or "correct" resolution of the issue.

Mr. Durocher believes that students learn most effectively when rules for their behavior are clearly spelled out. So he has rules for almost every conceivable occasion—53 rules in all. Following is a small sample:

Be in your seat before the bell rings.

Use a ballpoint pen with blue or black ink for all assignments.

Use white lined paper with straight edges; do not use paper with loose-leaf holes or spiral notebook "fringe."

Raise your hand if you wish to speak, and then speak only when called upon.

Do not ask questions unrelated to the topic being studied.

Never leave your seat without permission.

Durocher punishes each infraction severely enough that students follow the rules to the letter. So his students are a quiet and obedient, if somewhat anxious, bunch. Yet they never seem to learn as much as Durocher knows they are capable of learning.

Two of these classrooms are quiet and orderly; the other two are active and noisy. Yet as you can see, the activity and noise levels are not good indicators of how much students are learning. Students are learning in Mr. Aragon's quiet classroom, but also in Mr. Cavalini's rambunctious one. At the same time, neither the students in Mr. Boitano's loud, chaotic battlefield nor those in Mr. Durocher's peaceful military dictatorship seem to be learning much at all.

Effective **classroom management**—creating and maintaining a classroom environment conducive to learning and achievement—has little to do with the noise or activity level of the classroom. But it has everything to do with how much students are learning and achieving in that classroom. A well-managed classroom is one in which students are consistently engaged in productive learning activities. It is also one in which students' behaviors rarely interfere with the achievement of instructional objectives (W. Doyle, 1990; Emmer & Evertson, 1981; Munn, Johnstone, & Chalmers, 1990).

Creating and maintaining an environment in which students participate eagerly and actively in classroom activities can be a challenging task indeed. After all, we must tend to the unique needs of many different students, we must sometimes coordinate several activities at the same time, and we must often make quick decisions about how to respond to unanticipated events (W. Doyle, 1986a). So it is not surprising that beginning teachers usually mention classroom management as their number one concern (Veenman, 1984).

To create and maintain a productive learning environment, effective teachers typically:

* Physically arrange the classroom in a way that facilitates teacher-student interactions and keeps distracting influences to a minimum
* Create a classroom climate in which students have a sense of belonging and an intrinsic motivation to learn
* Set reasonable limits for student behavior
* Plan classroom activities that encourage on-task behavior
* Continually monitor what all students are doing
* Modify instructional strategies when necessary

In the pages that follow, we will consider specific ways to implement each of these strategies.

Remember that an effectively managed classroom does not necessarily have to be a quiet one.

Is it possible to *over*manage a classroom? If so, what might be the negative ramifications of doing so?

Arranging the Classroom

As we arrange the furniture in the classroom, decide where to put various instructional materials and pieces of equipment, and think about where each student

A well-managed classroom is one in which students are consistently engaged in learning. It is not necessarily one in which everyone is quiet.

600

CHAPTER 15
CREATING AND
MAINTAINING A
PRODUCTIVE
CLASSROOM
ENVIRONMENT

might sit, we should consider the effects that various arrangements are likely to have on students' behaviors. Ultimately, we want a situation in which we can:

- Keep distractions to a minimum
- Interact easily with any student
- Survey the entire class at any given point in time

Keeping Distractions to a Minimum

Stuart is more likely to poke a classmate with his pencil if he has to brush past the classmate to get to the pencil sharpener. Marlene is more likely to fiddle with instructional materials at an inappropriate time if they are within easy reach of her desk. David is more likely to gossip with a friend if that friend is sitting right beside him. As teachers, we should arrange our classrooms in ways that minimize the probability that such off-task behaviors will occur (Emmer, Evertson, Clements, & Worsham, 1994; Sabers, Cushing, & Berliner, 1991). For example, we can establish traffic patterns that allow students to move about in the classroom without disturbing one another, keep intriguing materials out of sight and reach until it is time to use them, and situate overly chatty friends on opposite sides of the room.

Arrange the classroom to minimize possible distractions.

Facilitating Teacher-Student Interaction

Ideally, we should arrange desks, tables, and chairs so that we can easily interact and converse with our students (G. A. Davis & Thomas, 1989). Students seated near their teacher are more likely to pay attention, interact with their teacher, and become actively involved in classroom activities; hence, we may want to place chronically misbehaving or uninvolved students close at hand (W. Doyle, 1986a; Schwebel & Cherlin, 1972; C. S. Weinstein, 1979; Woolfolk & Brooks, 1985).

Arrange your classroom so that you can easily interact with all your students. Place chronically misbehaving or uninvolved students close at hand.

Surveying the Entire Class

As we proceed through various lessons and activities—even when we're working with a single individual or small group—we should ideally be able to see *all* of our students (Emmer et al., 1994). By occasionally surveying the classroom for possible signs of confusion, frustration, or boredom, we can more easily detect minor student difficulties and misbehaviors before they develop into serious problems.

Situate yourself such that you can always see all of your students.

Creating an Effective Classroom Climate

THINKING ABOUT WHAT YOU KNOW

Think back to your many experiences as a student. Can you think of a class in which you were afraid of being ridiculed if you asked a "stupid" question? Can you think of one in which you and your fellow students spent more time goofing off than getting your work done because no one seemed to take the class seriously? Can you think of one in which you never knew what to expect because your instructor was continually changing expectations and giving last-minute assignments without warning?

In addition to the classroom's physical environment, we must also consider the psychological environment, or **classroom climate,** that we create. Ideally, we want a classroom in which students make their own learning a high priority and feel free to take the risks and make the mistakes so critical for long-term academic success. To create such a classroom climate, we should:

- Communicate acceptance of, respect for, and caring about our students as human beings
- Establish a businesslike, yet nonthreatening, atmosphere
- Communicate appropriate messages about school subject matter
- Give students some sense of control with regard to classroom activities
- Create a sense of community among the students

Showing Acceptance, Respect, and Caring

As you should recall from Chapter 12's discussion of social needs, many of our students are likely to have a high need for affiliation: They will actively seek out friendly relationships with others. Many will also have a high need for approval: They will attempt to gain the acceptance and high regard of those around them.

We can help our students meet such needs through our own actions, including the many little things we do daily. For example, we can give students a smile and warm greeting at the beginning of each class day. We can compliment them when they get a new haircut, excel in an extracurricular activity, or receive recognition in the local newspaper. We can ask them for information or advice when *they* know more than we do about a particular topic. We can offer our support when they struggle at challenging classroom tasks and let them know we're pleased when they eventually succeed at such tasks. We can be good listeners when they come to school angry or upset. And we can show them how we, too, are fallible human beings by sharing some of our own concerns, problems, and frustrations (Diamond, 1991; Spaulding, 1992). Research is clear on this point: Effective teachers are warm, caring individuals who, through a variety of statements and actions, communicate a respect for students, an acceptance of them as they are, and a genuine concern about their well-being (G. A. Davis & Thomas, 1989; C. B. Hayes, Ryan, & Zseller, 1994; Kim, Solomon, & Roberts, 1995; Wentzel & Wigfield, 1998).

Communicate your care and concern through the many "little things" you do each day.

Such teacher behaviors may be particularly beneficial for those students who have few caring relationships to draw on at home (Diamond, 1991).

Establishing a Businesslike, Nonthreatening Atmosphere

As we have just seen, an important element of effective classroom management is developing positive relationships with our students. At the same time, we must recognize that we and our students alike are in school to get certain things accomplished. Accordingly, we should maintain a relatively businesslike atmosphere in the classroom most of

Maintain a businesslike atmosphere, focusing on the achievement of instructional objectives, but refrain from behaviors that students will view as threatening.

the time (G. A. Davis & Thomas, 1989). This is not to say that our classroom activities must be boring and tedious; on the contrary, they can often be exciting and engaging. But excitement and entertainment should not be thought of as goals in and of themselves. Rather, they are means to a more important goal: achieving instructional goals.

Yet it is important that this businesslike atmosphere is not uncomfortable or threatening. As noted in Chapter 12, students who are excessively anxious about their class performance are unlikely to give us their best. How can we be businesslike without being threatening? Among other things, we can hold our students accountable for achieving instructional objectives yet not place them under continual surveillance. We can point out their mistakes yet not make them feel like failures (Rogers, 1983). We can admonish them for misbehavior yet not hold grudges against them from one day to the

The classroom climate should be one in which students believe that they can express their opinions and feelings openly and candidly.

602

CHAPTER 15
CREATING AND
MAINTAINING A
PRODUCTIVE
CLASSROOM
ENVIRONMENT

next (Spaulding, 1992). And, as we shall see now, we can give them a sense that they themselves have some control over the things that happen to them in the classroom.

Communicating Messages About School Subject Matter

In earlier chapters, we've stressed the importance of making school subject matter relevant to students' lives. Yet all too often, students view school activities and assignments more as things to "get done" than as things that will help them be successful over the long run (L. M. Anderson, Brubaker, Alleman-Brooks, & Duffy, 1985; Brophy & Alleman, 1991; Stodolsky et al., 1991).

As teachers, we give students messages about the value of school subject matter not only in what we say but also in what we do (e.g., W. Doyle, 1983). If we ask students to spend hours each day engaged in what seems like meaningless busy work, and if we assess learning primarily through tests that encourage rote memorization, we are indirectly telling students that classroom tasks are merely things that need to be "done." If, instead, we continually demonstrate how classroom topics have relevance to the outside world, and if we assess learning in ways that require meaningful learning, elaboration, and transfer, we show students that school subject matter isn't just something to be learned for its own sake—that it can enhance the quality of their lives.

Giving Students a Sense of Control

To make sure our students accomplish instructional goals, we must control the direction of classroom events to some extent. Nevertheless, we can give our students a sense that they, too, control some aspects of classroom life. For example, we can use strategies such as these (Spaulding, 1992):

- Give students advance notice of upcoming activities and assignments (enabling them to plan ahead).
- Create regular routines for accomplishing assignments (enabling students to complete the assignments successfully with minimal guidance from us).
- Allow students to set some of their own deadlines for completing assignments (enabling them to establish reasonable timelines for themselves).
- Provide opportunities for students to make choices about how to complete assignments or spend some of their class time (enabling them to set some of their own priorities).

By giving students opportunities to work independently and choose some of their own means of achieving classroom objectives, we promote the sense of self-determination so important for intrinsic motivation (see Chapter 12). We also promote the self-regulated learning that is so essential for students' long-term academic success (see Chapter 11).

Creating a Sense of Community

In Chapter 14, we considered the concept of a *community of learners*, a classroom in which teacher and students consistently work together to help one another learn. Ultimately, we want to create a **sense of community** in the classroom—a sense that we and our students have shared goals, are mutually respectful and supportive of one another's efforts, and believe that everyone makes an important contribution to classroom learning (Hom & Battistich, 1995; Kim et al., 1995; Lickona, 1991). Theorists have identified several strategies that can help create a sense of classroom community:

- Solicit students' ideas and opinions, and incorporate them into classroom discussions and activities.
- Create mechanisms through which students can help make the classroom run smoothly and efficiently (e.g., assign various "helper" roles to students on a rotating basis).

Consider the indirect messages you give students about the value of school and schoolwork.

Let students control some aspects of classroom life.

In what sense do Eli, Jake, and Vanessa have a sense of control in Ms. Cornell's class? What might Ms. Cornell do to help them control their classroom lives in more productive ways?

Create a sense of shared goals, interpersonal respect, and mutual support.

■ Emphasize such prosocial values as sharing and cooperation.

■ Provide opportunities for students to help one another (e.g., by asking, "Who has a problem that someone else might be able to help you solve?").

■ Provide public recognition of students' contributions to the overall success of the classroom. (Emmer et al., 1994; Kim et al., 1995; Lickona, 1991)

And when we build play time into the school day (as we typically do in the early elementary grades), we may want to institute the rule that "You can't say you can't play"—a rule that encourages children to include any and all of their classmates in play activities (Sapon-Shevin, Dobbelaere, Corrigan, Goodman, & Mastin, 1998). We may even want to encourage students to be on the lookout for classmates on the periphery of ongoing activities (perhaps students with disabilities) and to ask such children, "Do you want to play with us?" (Sapon-Shevin et al., 1998).

When students share a sense of community, they are more likely to exhibit prosocial behavior, stay on task, express enthusiasm about classroom activities, and achieve at high levels. Furthermore, a sense of classroom community is associated with lower rates of disruptive classroom behavior, truancy, violence, and drug use (Hom & Battistich, 1995; Kim et al., 1995).

Setting Limits

In the opening case study, Ms. Cornell provided no guidelines for how students should behave—something she should have done in the first week. A class without guidelines for appropriate behavior is apt to be chaotic and unproductive. And students must learn that certain behaviors—especially those that cause injury, damage school property, or interfere with classmates' learning and performance—will definitely not be tolerated. Reasonable limits regarding classroom behavior not only promote a more productive learning environment, but they also contribute to the socialization of students—to the development of those behaviors so essential for successful participation in the adult world.

Experienced educators have offered several suggestions for setting reasonable limits on students' classroom behavior. More specifically, they suggest that we:

• Establish a few rules and procedures at the beginning of the year

• Present rules and procedures in an informational rather than controlling manner

• Periodically review the usefulness of existing rules and procedures

• Acknowledge students' feelings about classroom requirements

As we consider these suggestions, we will also consider how we can preserve students' sense of control and self-determination.

Establishing a Few Rules and Procedures at the Beginning of the Year

The first few days and weeks of the school year are critical ones for establishing classroom procedures and setting expectations for student behavior. Effective classroom managers establish and communicate certain rules and procedures right from the start (Borko & Putnam, 1996; Davis & Thomas, 1989; W. Doyle, 1986a, 1990). They identify acceptable and unacceptable behaviors (e.g., see Figure 15–1). They develop consistent procedures and routines for such things as completing seatwork, asking for help, and turning in assignments. And they have procedures in place for nonroutine events such as school assemblies, field trips, and fire drills.

Ideally, our students should understand that rules and procedures are not merely the result of our personal whims but are designed to help the classroom run smoothly and efficiently. One way of promoting such understanding is to include students in decision

Establish some rules and procedures at the beginning of the year.

604   CHAPTER 15
      CREATING AND
      MAINTAINING A
      PRODUCTIVE
      CLASSROOM
      ENVIRONMENT

FIGURE 15.1

Beginning the school year with a few rules

Effective teachers typically begin the school year with a few rules that will help classroom activities run smoothly. Here are several examples of rules you might want to include in your list (adapted from Emmer et al., 1994):

Bring all needed materials to class. (Students should have books, homework assignments, permission slips, and any needed supplies for planned activities.)

Be in your seat and ready to work when the bell rings. (Students should be at their desks, have paper out and pencils sharpened, and be physically and mentally ready to work.)

Respect and be polite to all people. (Students should listen attentively when someone else is speaking, behave appropriately for a substitute teacher, and refrain from insults, fighting, and other disrespectful or hostile behavior.)

Respect other people's property. (Students should keep the classroom clean and neat, refrain from defacing school property, ask for permission to borrow another's possessions, and return those possessions in a timely fashion.)

Obey all school rules. (Students must obey the rules of the school building as well as the rules of the classroom.)

making about the rules and procedures by which the class will operate (Davis & Thomas, 1989; C. A. Grant & Gomez, 1996; Lickona, 1991). For example, we might solicit students' suggestions for making sure that unnecessary distractions are kept to a minimum and that everyone has a chance to speak during class discussions. By incorporating students' ideas and concerns regarding the limits we set, we help students understand the reasons for—and thereby help them adhere to—those limits (Emmer et al., 1994).

Once rules and procedures have been formulated, we should communicate them clearly and explicitly; we should also describe the consequences of noncompliance. Taking time to clarify rules and procedures seems to be especially important in the early elementary grades, when students may not be as familiar with "how things are done" at school (Evertson & Emmer, 1982; Gettinger, 1988).

Keep in mind that rules and procedures are easier to remember and therefore easier to follow if they are relatively simple and few in number (Davis & Thomas, 1989). Effective classroom managers tend to stress only the most important rules and procedures at the beginning of the school year; they introduce other rules and procedures later on as needed (W. Doyle, 1986a). Also keep in mind that, although a certain degree of order and predictability is essential for student productivity, *too much* order may make our classroom a rather boring, routine place—one without an element of fun and spontaneity. We don't necessarily need rules and procedures for everything!

Presenting Rules and Procedures in an Informational Manner

Describe rules and procedures in an informational manner.

As we learned in Chapter 12, we are more likely to maintain students' sense of self-determination if we present rules and procedures as items of information instead of as forms of control. Figure 15–2 lists several examples of how we might present rules and procedures in an informational rather than controlling manner. Notice how the informational statements on the left side of the figure include the reasons for imposing certain guidelines. The following case provides a simple illustration of how giving a reason can make all the difference in the world:

FIGURE 15.2
Describing classroom rules and procedures

Our students are more likely to be intrinsically motivated to follow classroom rules and procedures if we present them as items of information rather than as forms of control.

We might say this (information):	**. . . rather than this (control):**
"You'll get your independent assignments done more quickly if you get right to work."	"Please be quiet and do your own work."
"As we practice for our fire drill, it is important that we line up quickly and be quiet so that we can hear the instructions we are given and will know what to do."	"When the fire alarm sounds, line up quickly and quietly and then wait for further instructions."
"This assignment is designed to help you develop the writing skills you will need after you graduate. It is unfair to other authors to copy their work word for word, so we will practice putting ideas into our own words and giving credit to authors whose ideas we borrow. Passing off another's writing and ideas as your own can lead to suspension in college or a lawsuit in the business world."	"Cheating and plagiarism are not acceptable in this classroom."
"It's important that I can clearly read your writing. If your words are illegible and your cross-outs are confusing, I may not be able to give you as high a grade as you deserve on an assignment."	"Use good penmanship on all assignments and erase any errors carefully and completely. Points will be deducted for sloppy writing."

Gerard is a boy with a low tolerance for frustration. Whenever he asks Ms. Donnelly for assistance, he wants it *now*. If she is unable to help him immediately, he screams, "You're no good!" or "You don't care!" and shoves other students' desks as he walks angrily back to his seat.

At one point during the school year, the class has a unit on interpersonal skills. One lesson in the unit addresses *timing*—the most appropriate and effective time to ask for another person's assistance with a problem.

A week later, Gerard approaches Ms. Donnelly for help with a math problem. She is working with another student, but she turns briefly to Gerard and says, "Timing."

Ms. Donnelly waits expectantly for Gerard's usual screaming. Instead, he responds, "Hey, Ms. D., I get it! I can ask you at another time!" He returns to his seat with a smile on his face. (Adapted from Sullivan-DeCarlo, DeFalco, & Roberts, 1998, p. 81)

For additional benefits ▲ of providing reasons, see Chapter 3's discussion of *induction*.

Periodically Reviewing the Usefulness of Existing Rules and Procedures

As the school year progresses, we may occasionally want to revise the rules and procedures we've established in the first days or weeks. For instance, we may find that rules about when students can and cannot move around the room are overly restrictive or that procedures for turning in homework don't adequately accommodate students who must sometimes leave class early to attend athletic events.

606

CHAPTER 15
CREATING AND
MAINTAINING A
PRODUCTIVE
CLASSROOM
ENVIRONMENT

When it is necessary to change classroom rules and procedures, include students in decision making.

Regularly scheduled class meetings provide one mechanism through which we and our students can periodically review classroom rules and procedures (D. E. Campbell, 1996; Glasser, 1969; C. A. Grant & Gomez, 1996). Consider this scenario as an example:

Every Friday at 2:00, Ms. Ayotte's students move their chairs into one large circle, and the weekly class meeting begins. First on the agenda is a review of the past week's successes, including both academic achievements and socially productive events. Next, the group identifies problems that have emerged during the week and brainstorms possible ways to avert such problems in the future. Finally, the students consider whether existing classroom rules and procedures are serving their purpose. In some cases, they may modify existing rules and procedures; in other cases, they may establish new ones.

During the first few class meetings, Ms. Ayotte leads the group discussions. But once students have gotten the hang of things, she begins to relinquish control of the meetings to one or another of her students on a rotating basis.

Do you see parallels between an authoritative home (described in Chapter 3) and the guidelines for setting limits described in this chapter?

By providing such opportunities for students to revise classroom policies frequently, we find one more way of giving them a sense of ownership in such policies. Furthermore, perhaps because of the authoritative atmosphere and the conversations about moral dilemmas that student decision making may entail, more advanced levels of moral reasoning (as described in Chapter 3) may result (Power et al., 1989; Power & Power, 1992).

Acknowledging Students' Feelings

THINKING ABOUT WHAT YOU KNOW

As a student, have you ever resented restrictions placed on you? For example, were there times you had to sit quietly in your seat when you would rather have been talking with your classmates or getting up to stretch your legs? Were there times you had to devote an entire evening to a lengthy homework assignment when you would rather have been watching a favorite television show? Were there times you had to stay after school for extra help when you would rather have joined the neighborhood crowd in a game of softball?

Acknowledge students' feelings when you ask them to do something they would rather not do.

There will undoubtedly be times when we must ask our students to do something they would prefer not to do. Rather than pretend that such feelings don't exist, we are better advised to acknowledge them (Deci & Ryan, 1985). For example, we might tell students that we know how difficult it can be to sit quietly during an unexpectedly lengthy school assembly or to spend an entire evening on a particular homework assignment. At the same time, we can explain that the behaviors we request of them, though not always intrinsically enjoyable, do, in fact, contribute to the long-term goals they have set for themselves. By acknowledging students' feelings about tasks they would rather not do yet also pointing out the benefits of performing those tasks, we increase the likelihood that they will accept the limitations we impose on their behavior (Deci & Ryan, 1985).

Planning Activities That Keep Students on Task

As noted in Chapter 13, effective teachers plan their lessons ahead of time. Furthermore, they plan activities that not only facilitate students' learning and cognitive processing but also motivate students to *want* to learn. For instance, they think about how to make subject matter interesting and incorporate variety into lessons, perhaps by employing colorful audiovisual aids, using novel activities (e.g., small-group discussions, class debates), or moving to a different location (e.g., the media center or school yard) (Davis & Thomas, 1989; Munn et al., 1990).

As we plan our upcoming classroom activities, we should simultaneously plan specific ways of keeping our students on task. In addition to using the motivational strategies described in Chapter 12, we should:

- Be sure students will always be busy and engaged
- Choose tasks at an appropriate academic level
- Provide a reasonable amount of structure for activities and assignments
- Make special plans for transition times in the school day

Keeping Students Busy and Engaged

Experiencing Firsthand
Take Five

For the next five minutes, you are going to be a student who has nothing to do. *Remain exactly where you are,* put your book aside, and *do nothing.* Time yourself so that you spend exactly five minutes on this "task." Let's see what happens.

What kinds of responses did you make during your five-minute break? Did you fidget a bit, perhaps wiggling tired body parts, scratching newly detected itches, or picking at your nails? Did you "interact" in some way with something or someone else, perhaps tapping loudly on a table, turning on a radio, or talking to someone else in the room? Did you get out of your seat altogether—something I specifically asked you not to do?

The exercise I just gave you was a somewhat artificial one, to be sure, and the things I am defining as "misbehaviors" in this instance (e.g., wiggling your toes, tapping the table, getting out of your seat) won't necessarily qualify as misbehaviors in your classroom. Yet the exercise has, I hope, shown you that it is very difficult to do *nothing at all* for any length of time. Like us, our students will be most likely to misbehave when they have a lot of free time on their hands.

Effective classroom managers make sure there is little "empty" time in which nothing is going on in the classroom. As teachers, there are numerous strategies we can use to keep our students busy and engaged; as examples, we can:

- Have something specific for students to do each day, even on the first day of class
- Have materials organized and equipment set up before class
- Have activities that ensure *all* students' involvement and participation
- Maintain a brisk pace throughout each lesson (although not so fast that students can't keep up)
- Ensure that student comments are relevant and helpful but not excessively long-winded (perhaps by taking any chronic time-monopolizers aside for a private discussion about letting others have a chance to express their thoughts)
- Spend only short periods of time dealing with individual students during class unless other students are capable of working independently and productively in the meantime
- Have a system in place that ensures that students who finish an assigned task before their classmates have something else to do (perhaps writing in a class journal or reading a book)
(Davis & Thomas, 1989; W. Doyle, 1986a; Emmer et al., 1994; Evertson & Harris, 1992; Gettinger, 1988; Munn et al., 1990)

In your own classes, how can you tell when your instructors haven't adequately planned lessons ahead of time?

Keep students busy and engaged.

608

CHAPTER 15
CREATING AND
MAINTAINING A
PRODUCTIVE
CLASSROOM
ENVIRONMENT

Students who are busily engaged in classroom activities rarely exhibit problem behaviors.

Choosing Tasks at an Appropriate Level

Our students are more likely to get involved in their classwork, rather than in off-task behavior, when they have academic tasks and assignments appropriate for their current ability levels (W. Doyle, 1986a; Emmer et al., 1994). They are apt to misbehave when they are asked to do things that are probably too difficult for them—in other words, when they are incapable of completing assigned tasks successfully. Thus, classroom misbehaviors are more often observed in students who have a history of struggling in their coursework (W. Doyle, 1986a).

This is not to suggest that we should plan activities so easy that our students are not challenged and learn nothing new in doing them. One workable strategy is to *begin* the school year with relatively easy tasks that students can readily complete. Such early tasks enable students to practice normal classroom routines and procedures; they also give students a sense that they can enjoy and be successful in classroom activities. Once a supportive classroom climate has been established and students are comfortable with classroom procedures, we can gradually introduce more difficult and challenging assignments (W. Doyle, 1990; Emmer et al., 1994; Evertson & Emmer, 1982).

Providing Structure

■ Experiencing Firsthand
Take Five More

Grab a blank sheet of paper and a pen or pencil, and complete these two tasks:

   Task A: Using short phrases, list six characteristics of an effective teacher.

   Task B: Describe *schooling.*

Don't continue reading until you've spent a total of at least *five minutes* on these tasks.

   Once you have completed the two tasks, answer either "Task A" or "Task B" to each of the following questions:

Ensure that tasks and assignments are at an appropriate level for students. Begin the school year with easy and familiar tasks, introducing more difficult tasks once a supportive classroom climate has been established.

With this point in mind, how might Ms. Cornell (in the opening case study) have gotten the year off to a better start?

1. For which task did you have a better understanding of what you were being asked to do?

2. During which task did your mind more frequently wander to irrelevant topics?

3. During which task did you engage in more off-task behaviors (e.g., looking around the room, doodling on the paper, getting out of your seat)?

I am guessing that you found the first task to be relatively straightforward, whereas the second wasn't at all clear-cut. Did Task B's ambiguity lead to more irrelevant thoughts and off-task behaviors for you?

Just as may have been the case for you in the preceding exercise, off-task behavior in the classroom occurs more frequently when activities are so loosely structured that students don't have a clear sense of what they are supposed to do. Effective teachers tend to give assignments with some degree of structure. They also give clear directions about how to proceed with a task and a great deal of feedback about appropriate responses, especially during the first few weeks of class (W. Doyle, 1990; Evertson & Emmer, 1982; Munn et al., 1990; Weinert & Helmke, 1995).

Yet we need to strike a happy medium here. We don't want to structure classroom tasks to the point where students never make their own decisions about how to proceed or to the point where only lower-level thinking skills are required. Ultimately, we want our students to develop and use higher-level processes—for example, to think analytically, critically, and creatively—and we must have classroom assignments and activities that promote such processes (W. Doyle, 1986a; Weinert & Helmke, 1995).

The concept of *scaffolding* (first described in Chapter 2) is helpful here: We can provide a great deal of structure for tasks early in the school year, gradually removing that structure as students become better able to structure tasks for themselves. For example, when introducing students to cooperative learning, we might structure initial group meetings by breaking down each group task into several subtasks, giving clear directions as to how each subtask should be carried out, and assigning every group member a particular role to serve in the group. As the school year progresses and students become more adept at learning cooperatively with their classmates, we can become gradually less directive about how group tasks are accomplished.

Structure classroom activities to some extent, explaining the purpose of those activities and the nature of the performance you expect.

How much do your instructors structure your class assignments? What forms does such structure take?

Planning for Transitions

In the opening case study, Eli, Jake, and Vanessa often misbehaved at the beginning and end of the school day, as well as before and after recess and lunch. Transition times—as students end one activity and begin a second, or as they move from one classroom to another—are times when misbehaviors are especially likely to occur. Effective classroom managers take steps to ensure that such transitions proceed quickly and without a loss of momentum (Arlin, 1979; W. Doyle, 1984; Emmer et al., 1994). For example, they establish procedures for moving from one activity to the next. They ensure that there is little slack time in which students have nothing to do. And especially at the secondary level, where students change classes every hour or so, effective classroom managers typically have a task for students to perform as soon as class begins.

How might we plan for the various transitions that occur throughout the school day? Here are some examples:

Plan for a smooth and rapid transition from one activity to another.

Can you relate this strategy to behavioral momentum *(Chapter 10)?*

A physical education teacher has students begin each class session with five minutes of stretching exercises.

An elementary school teacher has students follow the same procedure each day as lunchtime approaches. Students must (1) place completed assignments in a basket on the teacher's desk, (2) put away classroom supplies (e.g., pencils, paint, scissors)

610

CHAPTER 15
CREATING AND
MAINTAINING A
PRODUCTIVE
CLASSROOM
ENVIRONMENT

they have been using, (3) get their lunch boxes from the coatroom, and (4) line up quietly by the classroom door.

A middle school mathematics teacher has students copy the new homework assignment as soon as they come to class.

A junior high school history teacher has formed long-term cooperative learning groups *(base groups)* of three or four students each. The groups are given a few minutes at the end of each class to compare notes on material presented that day and get a head start on the evening's reading assignment).

A high school English composition teacher writes a topic or question (e.g., "My biggest pet peeve," "Whatever happened to hula hoops?") on the chalkboard at the beginning of each class period. Students know that when they come to class, they should immediately take out pencil and paper and begin to write on the topic or question of the day.

All of these strategies, though very different in nature, share a common goal—to keep students focused on their schoolwork.

Monitoring What Students Are Doing

Effective teachers communicate something called **withitness:** They know (and their students *know* that they know) what students are doing at all times. In a sense, "with-it" teachers act as if they have eyes in the back of their heads. They make it clear that they are aware of what everyone is doing. They regularly scan the classroom and make frequent eye contact with individual students. They know what misbehaviors are occurring *when* those misbehaviors occur, and they know who the perpetrators are (Davis & Thomas, 1989; Emmer et al., 1994; Kounin, 1970). Consider this scenario as an example:

> An hour and a half of each morning in Mr. Rennaker's elementary school classroom is devoted to reading. Students know that, for part of this time, they will meet with Mr. Rennaker in their small reading groups. They spend the remainder of the time working on independent assignments tailored to the reading skills of individual students. As Mr. Rennaker works with each reading group in one corner of the classroom, he situates himself with his back to the wall so that he can simultaneously keep one eye on students working independently at their seats. He sends a quick and subtle signal—perhaps a stern expression, a finger to the lips, or a call of a student's name—to any student who begins to be disruptive.

When we demonstrate such withitness, especially at the beginning of the school year, our students are more likely to stay on task and display appropriate classroom behavior (W. Doyle, 1986a; Woolfolk & Brooks, 1985). And not surprisingly, they are also more likely to achieve at higher levels (W. Doyle, 1986a).

Modifying Instructional Strategies When Necessary

As we have repeatedly seen, principles of effective classroom management go hand in hand with principles of learning and motivation. When our students are learning and achieving successfully and when they clearly want to pursue the curriculum that the classroom offers, they are likely to be busily engaged in productive classroom activities for most of the school day (W. Doyle, 1990). In contrast, when they have difficulty understanding classroom subject matter or when they have little interest in learning it, they are likely to exhibit the nonproductive or even counterproductive classroom behaviors that result from frustration or boredom.

Research tells us that when students misbehave, beginning teachers often think in terms of what the students are doing wrong. In contrast, experienced, "expert" teachers are more apt to think about what *they themselves* can do differently to keep students on task (Sabers et al., 1991). So when behavior problems crop up, we should start thinking as the experts do, by considering questions such as the following:

INTO THE CLASSROOM: Creating and Maintaining an Environment Conducive to Learning

Physically arrange the classroom in a way that facilitates teacher-student interactions and keeps distracting influences to a minimum.

An elementary school teacher has arranged the twenty-eight student desks in his classroom into seven clusters of four desks each. The students who sit together in clusters form base groups for many of the classroom's cooperative learning activities. The teacher occasionally asks students to move their chairs into a large circle for whole-class discussions.

Show students that you care about and respect them as human beings, and give them some say about what happens in the classroom.

A high school teacher realizes that she is continually admonishing one particular student for his off-task behavior. To establish a more positive relationship with the student, she makes a point to greet him warmly in the hallway before school every day. And at the end of one day in which his behavior has been especially disruptive, she catches him briefly to express her concern, and the two agree to meet the following morning to discuss ways of helping him stay on task more regularly.

Set reasonable limits for student behavior.

After describing the objectives of an instrumental music class on the first day of school, a junior high school teacher tells his students, "There is one rule for this class to which I will hold firm. You must not engage in any behavior that will interfere with your own learning or with that of your classmates."

Plan classroom activities that encourage on-task behavior.

Before each class, a creative writing teacher writes the day's topic on the chalkboard. Her students know that when they arrive at class, they are to take out a pencil and paper and begin an essay addressing that topic.

Show students that you are continually aware of what they are doing.

While meeting with each reading group in one corner of the classroom, an elementary school teacher sits with his back to the wall so that he can keep an eye on those students who are working in centers or at their desks on independent assignments.

Modify your plans for instruction when necessary.

A teacher discovers that students quickly complete the activity she thought would take them an entire class period. She wraps the activity up after fifteen minutes and then begins the lesson she had originally planned for the following day.

- How can I alter instructional strategies to capture students' interest and excitement?
- Are instructional materials so difficult that students are becoming frustrated? Or are they so easy that students are bored?
- What are students really concerned about? For example, are they more concerned about interacting with their classmates than in gaining new knowledge and skills?
- How can I address students' motives (e.g., their need for affiliation) while simultaneously helping them achieve classroom objectives?

Answering such questions helps us focus our efforts on our ultimate goal: to help students *learn*.

612   CHAPTER 15
CREATING AND
MAINTAINING A
PRODUCTIVE
CLASSROOM
ENVIRONMENT

From your own
perspective, what are the
key ingredients of a
successfully managed
classroom?

Occasionally, current events on the international, national, or local scene (e.g., the bombing of Iraq, a president's impeachment trial, or a tragic car accident involving fellow students) may take priority. When students' minds are justifiably preoccupied with something other than the topic of instruction, they will have difficulty paying attention to that preplanned topic and are likely to learn little about it. In such extenuating circumstances, we may want to abandon our lesson plans altogether.

Despite our best efforts, students may sometimes behave in ways that disrupt classroom activities and interfere with student learning. Effective teachers not only plan and structure a classroom that minimizes potential behavior problems but they also deal with the misbehaviors that do occur (Doyle, 1990). What strategies are most effective in dealing with student misbehaviors? We turn to this topic now.

Dealing with Misbehaviors

THINKING ABOUT WHAT YOU KNOW

Considering your own experiences, what strategies do you think are most effective in dealing with students' misbehaviors? Do these strategies lead to a rapid reduction in inappropriate behavior? Do they lead to long-term improvement? Can you think of strategies that have *neither* of these effects?

For purposes of our discussion, we will define a **misbehavior** as any action that can potentially disrupt classroom learning and planned classroom activities (W. Doyle, 1990). Some classroom misbehaviors are relatively minor ones that have little long-term impact on students' achievement. Such behaviors as talking out of turn, writing notes to classmates during a lecture, and submitting homework assignments after their due date—particularly if such behaviors occur infrequently—generally fall in this category. Other misbehaviors are far more serious, in that they definitely interfere with the learning and achievement of one or more students. For example, when students scream at their teachers, hit their classmates, or habitually refuse to participate in classroom activities, then classroom learning—certainly the learning of the "guilty party," and often the learning of other students as well—may be adversely affected. Furthermore, such behaviors may, in some cases, threaten the physical safety or psychological well-being of others in the classroom.

As teachers, we need to plan ahead regarding how we are going to respond to the variety of misbehaviors that we may see in the classroom. As we do so, we must keep in mind that different strategies may be appropriate under different circumstances. In the following pages, we will consider six general strategies and the situations in which each is likely to be appropriate:

- Ignoring the behavior
- Cueing the student
- Discussing the problem privately with the student
- Promoting self-regulation
- Using applied behavior analysis and positive behavioral support
- Conferring with parents

These six strategies are summarized in Table 15–1.

Six Strategies for Dealing with Student Misbehavior

STRATEGY	SITUATION IN WHICH IT'S APPROPRIATE	POSSIBLE EXAMPLES
Ignoring the behavior	The misbehavior is unlikely to be repeated. The misbehavior is unlikely to spread to other students. Unusual circumstances elicit the misbehavior temporarily. The misbehavior does not seriously interfere with learning.	One student surreptitiously passes a note to another student just before the end of class. A student accidentally drops her books, startling other students and temporarily distracting them from their work. The entire class is hyperactive on the last afternoon before spring break.
Cueing the student	The misbehavior is a minor infraction yet interferes with students' learning. The behavior is likely to change with a subtle reminder.	A student forgets to close his notebook at the beginning of a test. A cooperative learning group is talking unnecessarily loudly. Several students are whispering to one another during an independent seatwork assignment.
Discussing the problem privately with the student	Cueing has been ineffective in changing the behavior. The reasons for the misbehavior, if made clear, might suggest possible strategies for reducing it.	A student is frequently late to class. A student refuses to do certain kinds of assignments. A student shows a sudden drop in motivation for no apparent reason.
Promoting self-regulation	The student has a strong desire to improve his or her behavior.	A student doesn't realize how frequently she interrupts her classmates. A student seeks help in learning to control his anger. A student wants to develop more regular study habits.
Using applied behavior analysis and positive behavioral support	The misbehavior has continued over a period of time and significantly interferes with student learning. The student seems unwilling or unable to use self-regulation techniques.	A student has unusual difficulty sitting still for reasonable periods of time. A student's obscene remarks continue even though her teacher has spoken with her about the behavior on several occasions. A member of the football team displays unsportsmanlike conduct that is potentially dangerous to other players.
Conferring with parents	The source of the problem may lie outside school walls. Parents are likely to work collaboratively with school personnel to bring about a behavior change.	A student does well in class but rarely turns in required homework assignments. A student is caught stealing, vandalizing school property, or engaging in other unethical or illegal behavior. A student falls asleep in class almost every day.

614

CHAPTER 15
CREATING AND
MAINTAINING A
PRODUCTIVE
CLASSROOM
ENVIRONMENT

Ignoring the Behavior

Consider these situations:

> Dimitra rarely breaks classroom rules. But on one occasion, after you have just instructed your students to work quietly and independently at their seats, you see her whisper briefly to the student beside her. None of the other students seems to notice that Dimitra has disobeyed your instructions.

> Herb is careless in chemistry lab and accidentally knocks over a small container of liquid (a harmless one, fortunately). He quickly apologizes and cleans up the mess with paper towels.

Are these misbehaviors likely to interfere with Dimitra's or Herb's academic achievement? Are they contagious behaviors that are likely to spread to other students, as the horseplay did in Ms. Cornell's class? The answer to both these questions is, "Probably not."

There are times when our best course of action is *no* action, at least nothing of a disciplinary nature (Davis & Thomas, 1989; Silberman & Wheelan, 1980). Whenever we stop an instructional activity to deal with a misbehavior, even for a few seconds, we run the danger of disrupting the momentum of the activity and possibly drawing students' attention to their misbehaving classmates (W. Doyle, 1986a). If we respond every time a student gets a little bit out of line, our own actions may be more distracting than the student actions we are trying to curtail. Furthermore, by drawing class attention to a particular student's behavior, we may actually be reinforcing that behavior rather than discouraging it.

Dimitra's misbehavior—whispering briefly to a classmate during independent seatwork—is unlikely to spread to her classmates (they didn't notice her behavior) and is probably not an instance of cheating (it occurred before she began working on the assignment). Herb's misbehavior—knocking over a container of liquid in chemistry lab—has, in and of itself, resulted in an unpleasant consequence for Herb; the natural consequence is that he has to clean up the mess. In both situations, *ignoring* the misbehavior is probably the best thing we can do. Generally speaking, here are the circumstances in which ignoring misbehavior may be the wisest course of action:

- When the behavior is a rare occurrence and probably won't be repeated
- When the behavior is unlikely to "spread"—that is, to be imitated by other students
- When unusual circumstances (e.g., the last day of school before a holiday, or an unsettling event in a student's personal life) elicit inappropriate behavior only temporarily
- When the behavior is typical for a particular age-group (e.g., when kindergartners become restless after sitting for an extended period of time, when fifth-grade boys and girls resist holding one another's hands during dance instruction)
- When the behavior's result (its natural consequence) is sufficiently unpleasant to deter a student from repeating the behavior
- When the behavior is not seriously affecting students' classroom learning (Davis & Thomas, 1989; W. Doyle, 1986a; Dreikurs & Cassel, 1972; Munn et al., 1990; Silberman & Wheelan, 1980; Wynne, 1990)

Ignore minor infractions that are unlikely to be repeated or to spread to other students.

Can you relate ignoring to a specific concept in operant conditioning?

Why is ignoring not an effective strategy in Ms. Cornell's classroom?

Cueing the Student

Consider these misbehaviors:

> As you are explaining a difficult concept to your class, Marjorie is busily writing. At first, you think she is taking notes, but then you see her pass the paper across the aisle to Kang. A few minutes later, you see the same sheet of paper being passed back to Marjorie. Obviously, the two students are spending class time writing notes to each other and probably not hearing a word you are saying.

You have separated your class into small groups for a cooperative learning exercise. One group seems to be more interested in discussing weekend plans than in accomplishing assigned work. The group is not making the progress that other groups are making and probably won't complete the assignment if its members don't get down to business soon.

In some situations, student misbehaviors, though not serious in nature, *do* interfere with classroom learning and must therefore be discouraged. Effective classroom managers handle such minor behavior problems as unobtrusively as possible: They don't stop the lesson, distract other students, or call unnecessary attention to the behavior they are trying to stop (W. Doyle, 1990; Emmer, 1987). In many cases, they use **cueing:** They let the students know, through a signal of one kind or another, that they are aware of the misbehavior and would like it to stop. (We previously discussed cueing within the context of behaviorism in Chapter 10.)

We can cue students about unacceptable behaviors in a variety of ways. One strategy is body language—perhaps frowning, making eye contact, or raising a finger to the lips to indicate "be quiet." A second is to use a signal of some kind—perhaps ringing a small bell or flicking the light switch on and off to get students' attention. We might also want to move closer to misbehaving students; such physical proximity communicates our withitness about what they are doing.

Cue students by using body language, signals, physical proximity, or verbal reminders.

In some situations, such subtle cues may not work, and so we will have to be more explicit. When we find that we must use explicit verbal cues, we should try to focus students' attention on what *should* be done, rather than on what *isn't* being done (Emmer et al., 1994; Good & Brophy, 1994). Here are some examples of simple yet potentially effective verbal cues:

- "Students who are quietest go to lunch first."
- "By now, all groups should have completed the first part of the assignment and should be working on the second part."
- "I see some art supplies that still need to be put back on the shelves before we can be dismissed."

Discussing the Problem Privately with the Student

Consider these misbehaviors:

Alonzo is almost always several minutes late to your third-period algebra class. When he finally arrives, he takes an additional two or three minutes pulling his textbook and other class materials out of his backpack. You have often reminded Alonzo about the importance of coming to class on time, yet the tardiness continues.

Trudy rarely completes classroom assignments; in fact, she often doesn't even *begin* them. On many occasions, you have tried unsuccessfully to get her on task with explicit verbal cues (e.g., "Your book should be open to page 27," "Your cooperative group is brainstorming possible solutions to a difficult problem, and they really could use your ideas"). A few times, when you have looked Trudy in the eye and asked her point-blank to get to work, she has defiantly responded, "I'm not going to do it. You can't make me!"

Sometimes in-class signals are insufficient to change a student's misbehavior. In such situations, talking with the student about the behavior is the next logical step. The discussion should be a *private* one for several reasons. First, as noted earlier, calling classmates' attention to a problem behavior may actually reinforce that behavior rather than discourage it. Or instead, the attention of classmates may cause a student to feel excessively embarrassed or humiliated—feelings that may make the student overly anxious about being in the classroom in the future. Finally, when we spend too much class time dealing with a single misbehaving student, other students are likely to get off task as well (J. Scott & Bushell, 1974).

Speak privately with students about chronic misbehaviors.

When we confer privately with students about chronic behavior problems, we should communicate our interest in their achievement and welfare over the long run.

Conversations with individual students give us, as teachers, a chance to explain why certain behaviors are unacceptable and must stop. (As noted earlier, students are more likely to obey rules when they understand the reasons behind the rules.) Furthermore, teacher-student conversations give students a chance to describe possible reasons why their misbehaviors continue despite our requests that they cease. To illustrate, when talking with Alonzo, we may discover that he is chronically tardy because, as a diabetic, he must check his blood sugar level between his second- and third-period classes. He can perform the procedure himself, but it takes a few minutes; besides, he would prefer to do it in the privacy of the nurse's office at the other end of the building. When speaking with Trudy about her inability and occasional refusal to do assigned work, she may tell you that she studied the subject matter you are teaching now when she lived in another school district last year, and she is tired of doing the same stuff all over again.

Students' explanations can sometimes provide clues about how best to deal with their behavior over the long run. For example, given Alonzo's diabetes, we may not be able to change his ongoing tardiness to class; instead, we might reassign him to a seat by the door so that he can join class unobtrusively each day, and we might ask the student next to him to fill him in quietly on what we have done before his arrival. Trudy's expressed boredom with classroom activities suggests that a workable strategy may be to find some enrichment activities for her to do until the rest of the class has completed the topics she has already mastered.

Yet our students won't always provide explanations that lead to such logical solutions. For example, it may be that Alonzo is late to class simply because he wants to spend a few extra minutes hanging out with his friends in the hall. Or perhaps Trudy tells you she doesn't want to do her assignments because she's sick and tired of other people telling her what to do all the time. In such circumstances, it is essential that we not get in a power struggle—a situation where one person "wins" by dominating over the other in some way (Diamond, 1991; Emmer et al., 1994). We can use several strategies to avoid such a power struggle:

- Listen empathically to what the student has to say, being openly accepting of the student's feelings and opinions (e.g., "I get the impression that you don't enjoy classroom activities very much; I'd really like to hear what your concerns are").

- Summarize what you believe the student has told you and seek clarification if necessary (e.g., "It sounds as if you'd rather not come across as a know-it-all in front of your friends. Is that the problem you're having, or is it something else?").

- Describe the effects of the problem behavior, including your own reactions to it (e.g., "When you come to class late every day, I worry that you are getting further and further behind, and sometimes I even feel a little hurt that you don't seem to value your time in my classroom").

- Give the student a choice of some sort (e.g., "Would you rather try to work quietly at your group's table, or would it be easier if you sat somewhere by yourself to complete your work?"). (based on Emmer et al., 1994)

Ultimately, we must communicate our interest in the student's long-term school achievement, our concern that the misbehavior is interfering with that achievement, and our commitment to working cooperatively with the student to alleviate the problem.

Promoting Self-Regulation

Sometimes, in addition to exploring reasons related to a student's misbehavior and its unacceptability in the classroom, we may also want to develop a long-term plan for changing the student's behavior. For instance, consider these situations:

> Brian doesn't seem to be making much progress toward instructional objectives; for instance, his performance on assignments and tests is usually rather low. As Brian's teacher, you are certain that he is capable of better work, because he occasionally turns in an assignment or test paper of exceptionally high quality. The root of Brian's problem seems to be that he is off task most of the time. When he should be paying attention to a lesson or doing an assignment, he is instead sketching pictures of sports cars and airplanes, fiddling with whatever objects he has found on the floor, or daydreaming. Brian would really like to improve his academic performance but doesn't seem to know how to go about doing so.

> Georgia frequently speaks out in class without permission. She blurts out answers to your questions, preventing anyone else from answering them first. She rudely interrupts other students' comments with her own point of view. And she initiates conversations with one or another of her classmates at the most inopportune times. You have talked with Georgia several times; she readily agrees that there *is* a problem and vows to restrain herself in the future. After each conversation with you, her behavior improves for a short time, but within a few days her mouth is off and running once again.

Brian's off-task behavior interferes with his own academic achievement, and Georgia's excessive chattiness interferes with the learning of her classmates. Cueing and private discussions haven't led to any improvement. But both Brian and Georgia have something going for them: They *want* to change their behavior. And when students genuinely want to improve their own behavior, why not teach them ways to bring about desired changes *themselves*?

Here we revisit the topic of self-regulation, which we first encountered within the context of social cognitive theory (Chapter 11). Social cognitive theorists offer several strategies for helping students begin to regulate and control their own behavior. *Self-monitoring* is especially valuable when students need a "reality check" about the severity of the problem behavior. Some students may underestimate the frequency with which they exhibit certain misbehaviors or the impact that those behaviors have on classroom learning. Georgia, for example, seems to blurt things out without even realizing that her actions interfere with her classmates' attempts to participate in classroom discussions. Other students may not be aware of how *in*frequently they exhibit appropriate behaviors. Brian, for instance, may think he is on task in the classroom far more often than he really is. To draw students' attention to the extent of their problem, we can ask them simply to record the frequency with which certain behaviors appear. For example, we might ask Georgia to make a check mark on a piece of paper every time she talks without permission. Or we might equip Brian with a timer that makes a small "beep" once every five minutes and ask him to write down whether or not he was paying attention to his schoolwork each time he hears the beep. Research studies tell us that some behaviors improve significantly when we do nothing more than ask students to record their own behavior. In fact, both Georgia's and Brian's problems have been successfully dealt with in just this way (Broden, Hall, & Mitts, 1971; K. R. Harris, 1986; Mace et al., 1989; Mace & Kratochwill, 1988).

Self-instructions and *self-regulated problem-solving strategies* provide students with methods of reminding themselves about appropriate actions. For instance, we

618

CHAPTER 15
CREATING AND
MAINTAINING A
PRODUCTIVE
CLASSROOM
ENVIRONMENT

might provide Georgia with a simple list of instructions that she can give herself whenever she wants to contribute to a classroom discussion:

1. "Button" my lips (by holding them tightly together)
2. Raise my hand
3. Wait until I'm called on

Likewise, as noted in Chapter 11, we might help overly aggressive students deal with their interpersonal conflicts more constructively by following a prescribed sequence of steps: defining the problem, identifying several possible solutions, predicting the likely outcome of each approach, choosing and carrying out the best solution, and evaluating the results.

Self-evaluation and *self-imposed contingencies* provide a means through which we can encourage students to evaluate their progress and reinforce themselves for appropriate behavior. For example, we might ask Brian to give himself one point for each five-minute period that he's been on task. We might instruct Georgia to give herself a check mark for every fifteen-minute period in which she has spoken only when given permission to do so. By accumulating a certain number of points or check marks, the students could earn the opportunity to engage in a favorite activity.

Self-regulatory strategies have several advantages. They enable us to avoid power struggles with students about who's "in charge." They are likely to increase students' sense of self-determination, hence also increasing students' intrinsic motivation to learn and achieve in the classroom. Furthermore, self-regulation techniques benefit students over the long run, promoting productive behaviors that are likely to continue long after students have moved on from a particular school or a particular teacher. And of course, when we teach our students to monitor and modify their own behavior, rather than to depend on us to do it for them, we become free to do other things—for example, to *teach!*

Using Applied Behavior Analysis and Positive Behavioral Support

There may occasionally be times when our students are either unwilling or unable to change their own behavior. Consider these situations:

> Tucker is out of his chair so often that, at times, you have to wonder whether he even knows where his chair *is.* He finds numerous reasons to roam about the room—he "has to" sharpen a pencil, he "has to" get his homework out of his backpack, he "has to" get a drink of water, and so on. Naturally, Tucker gets very little of his work done. Furthermore, his classmates are continually being distracted by his perpetual motion.

> Janet's verbal abusiveness is getting out of hand. She often insults her classmates by using sexually explicit language, and she frequently likens you to a female dog or a certain body part. You have tried praising her on occasions when she is pleasant with others, and she seems to appreciate your doing so, yet her abusive remarks continue unabated.

Imagine that both Tucker and Janet are in your class. As a teacher, you have already spoken with each of them about their inappropriate behaviors, yet you've seen no improvement. You have suggested methods of self-regulation, but the two students don't seem interested in changing for the better. So what do you do now?

When a particular misbehavior occurs so frequently that it is clearly interfering with a student's learning and achievement (and possibly with the learning and achievement of classmates as well) and when such other strategies as cueing and self-regulating techniques do not seem to decrease that misbehavior, then a more intensive intervention is in order. Two behaviorist approaches described in Chapter 10 may be especially useful here: *applied behavior analysis* (which is based on principles related to response-consequence contingencies, shaping, etc.) and *positive behavioral support* (which also addresses the purposes that misbehaviors may serve for students).

Encourage self-regulation by teaching such strategies as self-monitoring, self-instructions, self-regulated problem-solving strategies, self-evaluation, and self-imposed contingencies.

Use behaviorist principles to encourage more productive behavior when other, simpler interventions have been unsuccessful.

How might we use behaviorist techniques to bring about an improvement in Tucker's classroom behavior? Applying principles of operant conditioning, we might identify one or more effective reinforcers (given Tucker's constant fidgeting, opportunities for physical activity might be reinforcing) and then make those reinforcers contingent on Tucker's staying in his seat for a specified length of time. As Tucker improves, we would gradually reinforce longer and longer periods of sedentary behavior. At the same time, we should recognize that some out-of-seat responses (e.g., getting a reference book from the bookshelf, delivering a completed assignment to the teacher's "In" basket) are quite appropriate; we might therefore want to give Tucker a reasonable "allotment" of out-of-seats he can use during the day. Any out-of-seats that exceed this allotment should probably result in a mild yet punishing consequence—perhaps the logical consequence of spending time after school to make up uncompleted work.

It may be, however, that out-of-seat behavior serves a particular purpose for Tucker. Perhaps the behavior allows him to avoid tasks he has difficulty performing successfully. Or perhaps it enables him to release the energy that his body seems to overproduce. Following guidelines related to positive behavioral support, we would determine the kinds of situations in which Tucker is most likely to misbehave and then form and test hypotheses as to *why* he is occasionally hyperactive. If we discover that Tucker acts out only when he expects challenging assignments (as was true for Samantha in Chapter 10), then we need to provide the instruction and support he needs to accomplish those assignments successfully. If, instead, we find that Tucker's hyperactivity appears regularly regardless of the situation, we may instead suspect a physiological cause and so give him numerous opportunities to release pent-up energy throughout the school day.

Positive behavioral support and applied behavior analysis may be helpful with Janet as well. In this case, we might suspect that Janet has learned few social skills with which she can interact effectively with others; we might therefore need to begin by teaching her such skills through modeling, role playing, and so on (see "Fostering Social Skills" in Chapter 3 for additional ideas). Once we know that Janet possesses effective interpersonal skills, we can begin to reinforce her for using those skills (perhaps with praise, as she has responded positively to such feedback in the past). Meanwhile, we should also punish (perhaps by giving her a time-out) any relapses into her old, abusive patterns.

In our use of both reinforcement and punishment, we must keep in mind two guidelines that we identified in our discussion of behaviorism in Chapter 10. For one thing, we should be very explicit about response-consequence contingencies: We must let our students know ahead of time, in concrete terms, what behaviors will be followed by what consequences (e.g., we might use *contingency contracts,* described in Chapter 10). Furthermore, we should follow through with those consequences when the specified behaviors occur; effective classroom managers deal with inappropriate student behaviors quickly and consistently (W. Doyle, 1986a; Evertson & Emmer, 1982). Failing to follow through communicates the message that we were not really serious about the contingencies we described.

Conferring with Parents

Consider these problem behaviors:

You assign short homework assignments almost every night; over the past three months, Carolyn has turned in only about a third of them. You're pretty sure that Carolyn is capable of doing the work, and you know from previous teacher conferences that her parents give her the time and support she might need at home to get her assignments done. You have spoken with Carolyn about the situation on several occasions, but she shrugs you off as if she doesn't really care whether she does well in your class or not.

If need be, refresh your memory by rereading the sections on applied behavior analysis and positive behavioral support in Chapter 10.

What behaviorist techniques might Ms. Cornell use to help Eli, Jake, and Vanessa become more productive members of her classroom?

Social cognitive theorists also advocate following through with the consequences students are expecting. Do you recall their rationale?

620

CHAPTER 15
CREATING AND
MAINTAINING A
PRODUCTIVE
CLASSROOM
ENVIRONMENT

INTO THE CLASSROOM: Dealing with Misbehaviors

Ignore accidents and minor infractions that are unlikely to be repeated and unlikely to spread to other students.

A student accidentally knocks over a container of poster paint in art class. The art teacher, while watching to be sure the student cleans up the mess, continues working with other students.

Use physical signals or brief verbal cues to remind students about what they should or should not be doing.

A teacher looks pointedly at two students who are giggling during a standardized test, and they quickly stop.

Speak privately with students about chronic and clearly inappropriate behaviors.

A student continually teases a classmate who stutters. The teacher takes the student aside, points out that the classmate is not stuttering by choice, and voices her concern that such teasing may make the stuttering worse.

Teach self-regulating strategies when students are motivated to improve their behavior.

When a student too often speaks without thinking and, in doing so, unintentionally offends or hurts the feelings of classmates, her teacher gives her three mental steps to follow before speaking: (1) Button my lip, (2) think about what I want to say, and (3) think about how to say it nicely.

Use applied behavior analysis or positive behavioral support when students seem unwilling or unable to control their own behavior.

When a third-grade boy seems unable and unwilling to stay on task for more than two or three minutes at a time, his teacher sets up a system in which he can earn points toward free time or privileges at the end of the day. For now, he earns one point for every five minutes he remains on task; she will extend the required time gradually as the school year goes on.

Confer with parents if a collaborative effort might bring about a behavior change.

At a parent-teacher conference, a teacher expresses his concern that a student is not turning in her homework assignments. Her parents are surprised to hear this, saying that, "Marti usually tells us that she doesn't *have* any homework." Together they work out a strategy for communicating about what assignments have been given and when they are due.

Keep in mind that some behaviors considered unacceptable in your culture may be quite acceptable in the culture in which a student has been raised.

When two brothers are frequently late for school, their teacher recognizes that the boys are unaccustomed to living by the clock. He explains the importance of getting to school on time and praises them as they become increasingly more punctual in the weeks that follow.

Students have frequently found things missing from their tote trays or desks when Roger has been in the vicinity. A few students have told you that they've seen Roger taking things that belong to others. Many of the missing objects have later turned up in Roger's possession. When you confront him about your suspicion that he's been stealing from his classmates, Roger adamantly denies it. He says he has no idea how Cami's gloves or Marvin's baseball trading cards ended up in his desk.

As we deal with classroom misbehaviors, we may sometimes need to involve students' parents, especially when the misbehaviors show a pattern over a period of time and have serious implications for students' long-term success. In some instances, a simple telephone call may be sufficient (Emmer et al., 1994); for example, Carolyn's parents may be unaware that she hasn't been doing her homework (she's been telling them that she doesn't have any) and may be able to take the steps necessary to ensure that it is done from now on. In other cases, a school conference may be more productive; for example, you may want to discuss Roger's stealing habits with both Roger and his parent(s) together—something you can do more effectively when you all sit face-to-face in the same room. A little later in the chapter, we'll identify strategies for discussing problem behavior with students' parents.

Confer with parents about chronic problems that have serious implications for students' long-term success.

Taking Student Diversity into Account

As we plan for a productive classroom environment, we must always take the diverse characteristics and needs of our students into account. For instance, we should make an extra effort to establish a supportive classroom climate, especially for students of ethnic minority groups and for students from lower-income neighborhoods. We may also need to define and respond to misbehaviors in somewhat different ways, depending on the particular ethnic and socioeconomic groups that we have in our classrooms. Finally, we may often have to make special accommodations for students with special educational needs. Let's briefly consider each of these issues.

Creating a Supportive Climate

Earlier in the chapter, we noted the value of creating a warm, supportive classroom atmosphere. Such an atmosphere may be especially important for students from ethnic minority groups (García, 1995; Ladson-Billings, 1994a). For example, African American students in an eighth-grade social studies class were once asked why they liked their teacher so much. Their responses were very revealing:

"She listens to us!"

"She respects us!"

"She lets us express our opinions!"

"She looks us in the eye when she talks to us!"

"She smiles at us!"

"She speaks to us when she sees us in the hall or in the cafeteria!" (Ladson-Billings, 1994a, p. 68)

A warm, supportive classroom climate may be especially important for students from diverse ethnic backgrounds.

Simple gestures such as these go a long way toward establishing the kinds of teacher-student relationships that lead to a productive learning environment. It's essential, too, that we create a sense of community in the classroom—a sense that we and our students share common goals and are mutually supportive of everyone's reaching those goals. This sense of community is consistent with the cooperative spirit evident in many Hispanic, Native American, and African American groups (Cazden, 1988; Ladson-Billings, 1994a).

When working with students from lower-socioeconomic, inner-city backgrounds, we should also take special pains to create a classroom that feels safe and orderly (D. U. Levine & Lezotte, 1995). Many students from inner-city neighborhoods may be exposed to crime and violence on a daily basis; their world may be one in which they can rarely control the course of events. A classroom that is dependable and predictable can provide a sense of self-determination that students may not be able to find anywhere else; hence, it can be a place to which they look forward to coming each day.

When working with students from low-SES backgrounds, make an extra effort to create an environment that feels safe and orderly.

622   CHAPTER 15
CREATING AND
MAINTAINING A
PRODUCTIVE
CLASSROOM
ENVIRONMENT

 Remember that some behaviors considered unacceptable in your culture may be quite acceptable in a student's culture. When such behaviors interfere with classroom achievement, be patient and understanding as you help the student acquire behaviors consistent with school expectations.

Defining and Responding to Misbehaviors

As we determine which behaviors we do not want to allow in our classrooms, we must remember that some behaviors considered unacceptable in our own culture may be quite acceptable in the culture in which a particular student has been raised. Let's consider some examples based on the cultural differences we discussed in Chapter 4:

A student is frequently late for school, sometimes arriving more than an hour after the school bell has rung. A student who is chronically tardy may live in a community that does not observe strict schedules and timelines, a pattern common in some Hispanic and Native American communities.

Two students are sharing answers as they take a classroom test. Although this behavior may be cheating in your eyes, it may reflect the cooperative spirit and emphasis on group achievement evident in the cultures of many Native Americans and Mexican American students.

Several students are shouting at one another, hurling insults that become increasingly more derogatory and obscene. Such an interaction might seem to spell trouble, but it may instead be an instance of sounding, a friendly verbal interchange common in some African American communities.

Some of these behaviors are likely to have little if any adverse effect on students' learning. To the extent that some of them *do* have an effect, we must be patient and understanding as we help students acquire behaviors that are more conducive to academic productivity.

Accommodating Students with Special Needs

As we create a classroom environment that promotes student learning, we must take into account the special educational needs that some of our students are likely to have. Generally speaking, an orderly classroom—one in which procedures for performing certain tasks are specified, expectations for student behavior are clear, and misbehaviors are treated consistently—makes it easier for students with special needs to adapt comfortably to a general education classroom (M. C. Reynolds & Birch, 1988; Scruggs & Mastropieri, 1994).

When students have a history of behavior problems (e.g., as will often be the case for students with emotional or behavioral disorders), we may need to provide a great deal of guidance and support to help them develop productive classroom behavior. Furthermore, many students with special needs may need explicit feedback about their classroom performance. When praising desirable behavior, rather than saying "well done" or "nice work," we should describe exactly what responses we are praising. For example, we might say something like this to a student with mental retardation, "You did a good job taking the absentee sheet to Mrs. Smith. You went directly to the attendance office and you came straight back" (Patton et al., 1987, p. 65). Similarly, when students display inappropriate behavior, we should tell them exactly what they have done wrong. For example, when speaking with a student with chronic behavior problems, we might say, "You borrowed Austin's book without asking him first. You know that taking other students' possessions without their permission is against class rules." Additional suggestions for accommodating students with special needs are presented in Table 15–2.

The Big Picture: Coordinating Efforts with Others

As we work to promote students' learning and development, we must remember that we will be far more effective when we coordinate our efforts with the other people in students' lives. In particular, we must work cooperatively with other teachers, the community at large, and, most importantly, with parents.

TABLE 15.2

Planning for Students with Special Educational Needs

STUDENTS WITH SPECIAL NEEDS	CHARACTERISTICS THAT THESE STUDENTS MAY EXHIBIT	CLASSROOM STRATEGIES THAT MAY BE BENEFICIAL FOR THESE STUDENTS
Students with specific cognitive or academic difficulties	Difficulty staying on task In some students, misbehaviors such as hyperactivity, impulsiveness, disruptiveness, inattentiveness In some students, poor time management skills and/or a disorganized approach to accomplishing tasks	Closely monitor students during independent assignments. Make sure students understand their assignments; if appropriate, give them extra time to complete the assignments. Make expectations for behavior clear, and enforce classroom rules consistently. Cue students regarding appropriate behavior. Reinforce (e.g., praise) desired behaviors. For hyperactive students, plan short activities that help them settle down after periods of physical activity (e.g., recess, lunch, physical education). For impulsive students, teach self-instructions (see Chapter 11). Teach students strategies for organizing their time and work (e.g., tape a schedule of daily activities to their desks, provide folders they can use to carry assignments between school and home).
Students with social or behavioral problems	Frequent overt misbehaviors (e.g., acting out, aggression, noncompliance, destructiveness, stealing) in some students Misbehaviors triggered by changes in the environment or daily routine or by sensory overstimulation (for students with autism) Difficulty interacting effectively with classmates Difficulty staying on task Tendency for some students to engage in power struggles with their teacher	Specify in precise terms what behaviors are acceptable and unacceptable in the classroom; establish and enforce rules for behavior. Maintain a predictable schedule; warn students ahead of time about changes in the routine. Use self-regulation techniques, applied behavior analysis, and positive behavioral support to promote productive classroom behaviors. Teach social skills (see Chapter 3). Closely monitor students during independent assignments. Give students a sense of self-determination about some aspects of classroom life; minimize the use of coercive techniques. Make an extra effort to show students that you care about them as human beings.

(continued)

Coordinating Efforts with Other Teachers

Although teachers spend much of the school day working in individual classrooms, they are more effective when they:

- Communicate and collaborate regularly with one another
- Have common objectives regarding what students should learn and achieve

continued

STUDENTS WITH SPECIAL NEEDS	CHARACTERISTICS THAT THESE STUDENTS MAY EXHIBIT	CLASSROOM STRATEGIES THAT MAY BE BENEFICIAL FOR THESE STUDENTS
Students with general delays in cognitive and social functioning	Occasionally disruptive classroom behavior Dependence on others for guidance about how to behave More appropriate classroom behavior when expectations are clear	Establish clear, concrete rules for classroom behavior. Cue students regarding appropriate behavior; keep directions simple. Use self-regulation techniques, applied behavior analysis, and positive behavioral support to promote desired behaviors. Give explicit feedback about what students are and are not doing appropriately.
Students with physical or sensory challenges	Social isolation from classmates (for some students) Difficulty accomplishing tasks as quickly as other students Difficulty interpreting spoken messages (if students have hearing loss)	Establish a strong sense of community within the classroom. When appropriate, give extra time to complete assignments. Keep unnecessary classroom noise to a minimum if one or more students have hearing loss.
Students with advanced cognitive development	Off-task behavior in some students, often due to boredom during easy assignments and activities	Assign tasks appropriate to students' cognitive abilities.

Sources: Achenbach & Edelbrock, 1981; Barkley, 1990; Buchoff, 1990; B. Clark, 1997; Diamond, 1991; Friedel, 1993, D. A. Granger, Whalen, Henker, & Cantwell, 1996; Heward, 1996; Koegel et al., 1996; Landau & McAninch, 1993; Mercer, 1991; Morgan & Jenson, 1988; Ogden & Germinario, 1988; Patton et al., 1987, 1990; Pellegrini & Horvat, 1995; Piirto, 1994; M. C. Reynolds & Birch, 1988; Turnbull et al., 1999; Winner, 1997.

Note: Compiled with the assistance of Dr. Margie Garanzini-Daiber and Dr. Margaret Cohen, University of Missouri—St. Louis.

Communicate regularly with your building and district colleagues, and work cooperatively toward common goals.

- Work together to identify obstacles to students' learning and to develop strategies for overcoming those obstacles
- Are committed, as a group, to promoting equality and multicultural sensitivity throughout the school community (Battistich, Solomon, Watson, & Schaps, 1997; D. U. Levine & Lezotte, 1995)

Ideally, we should not only create a sense of community within our individual classrooms but also create an overall **sense of school community** (Battistich et al., 1995, 1997). Our students should get the same message from all of us—that we are working together to help them become informed, successful, and productive citizens, and that they can and should *help one another* as well.

When teachers and other school personnel communicate an overall sense of school community, students have more positive attitudes toward school, are more motivated to achieve at high levels, and exhibit more prosocial behavior, and students from diverse backgrounds are more likely to interact with one another. Furthermore, teachers have higher expectations for students' achievement and a greater sense of self-efficacy about their own teaching effectiveness (Battistich et al., 1995, 1997). Such a "team spirit" has an additional advantage for new teachers: It provides the support structure (the scaffolding) that many beginning teachers may need, especially when working with high-risk students. New teachers report greater confidence in their own ability to help their students learn and achieve when they collaborate regularly with their colleagues (Chester & Beaudin, 1996).

Working with the Community at Large

Students almost always have regular contact with other institutions besides school—possibly with youth groups, community organizations, social services, churches, hospitals, mental health clinics, or even parole boards. And many of them are probably growing up in cultural environments very different from our own.

We will be most effective if we understand the environment within which our students live and if we think of ourselves as part of a larger team that promotes their long-term development. For example, we must educate ourselves about students' cultural backgrounds, perhaps by taking coursework or getting involved in local community events after school hours (Hadaway, Florez, Larke, & Wiseman, 1993; Ladson-Billings, 1994a). We must also keep in contact with other people and institutions who play major roles in students' lives, coordinating our efforts whenever possible (Epstein, 1996).

Work cooperatively with other agencies that play a key role in students' lives.

Working Effectively with Parents

Above all, we must work cooperatively with students' parents or other primary caretakers. We can best think of our relationship with parents as a *partnership* in which we collaborate to promote students' long-term development and learning (Hidalgo et al., 1995). Such a relationship may be especially important when working with students from diverse cultural backgrounds (Hidalgo et al., 1995; Salend & Taylor, 1993). And as we discovered in Chapter 5, it is *essential* when working with students who have special educational needs.

Communicating with Parents

At the very minimum, we must keep in regular contact with parents about the progress that students are making. We must keep them informed about their children's accomplishments and alert them to any behaviors that are consistently interfering with their children's learning and achievement. Regular communication also provides a means through which parents can give *us* information. Such information might yield ideas about how we can best assist or motivate their children; at the least, it will help us understand why their children sometimes behave as they do. Finally, we can coordinate our classroom strategies with those that parents use at home; our own efforts to help students succeed will almost certainly yield greater returns if expectations for academic performance and social behavior are similar both in and out of school. The following paragraphs describe several ways in which we can communicate with parents.

Remember that communication with parents should be a two-way street, with information traveling in both directions.

Parent-teacher conferences. In most school districts, formal parent-teacher conferences are scheduled one or more times a year; several suggestions for conducting effective ones are presented in Figure 15–3. In many situations, we may want to invite students to their parent-teacher conferences (Popham, 1995; Stiggins, 1997). By doing so, we increase the likelihood that parents will come to the conference, and we encourage our students to reflect on their own academic progress. Furthermore, teachers, students, and parents alike are apt to leave such meetings with a shared understanding of the progress that has been made and the steps to be taken next.

Consider including students in parent-teacher conferences.

Written communication. Written communication can take a variety of forms. For example, it can be a regularly scheduled report card that documents a student's academic progress. It can be a quick, informal note acknowledging a significant accomplishment. Or it can be a general newsletter describing noteworthy classroom activities. All of these have something in common: Not only do they let parents know what is happening at school, but they also convey our intention to stay in touch on an ongoing basis.

Use informal notes and classroom newsletters in addition to more formal reports.

Telephone conversations. Telephone calls are useful when issues require immediate attention. We might call a parent to express our concern when a student's behavior

626

CHAPTER 15
CREATING AND
MAINTAINING A
PRODUCTIVE
CLASSROOM
ENVIRONMENT

FIGURE 15.3

Conducting effective parent-teacher conferences

Here are several suggestions for conducting smooth, productive conferences with students' parents:

- Schedule each conference at a time that accommodates parents' work schedules and other obligations.
- Prepare for the conference ahead of time; for example, organize your notes, review information you have about the student, plan an agenda for your meeting, and have examples of the student's work at hand.
- Create a warm, nonjudgmental atmosphere. For example, express your appreciation that the parents have come, and give them sufficient time to express their thoughts and perspectives. Remember that your objective is to work cooperatively and constructively together to create the best educational program possible for the student.
- Express your thoughts clearly, concisely, and honestly.
- Avoid educational jargon with which parents may be unfamiliar; describe the student's performance in ways a noneducator can understand.
- After the conference, follow through with anything you have said you will do.

Sources: Polloway & Patton, 1993; Salend & Taylor, 1993.

Make use of the telephone when issues require immediate attention.

deteriorates unexpectedly and without apparent provocation. But we might also call to express our excitement about an important step forward that a student has made. Parents, too, should feel free to call us. Keep in mind that many parents are at work during the school day; hence, it is often helpful to accept and encourage calls at home during the early evening hours.

Parent discussion groups. In some instances, we may want to assemble a group of parents to discuss issues of mutual concern. For example, we might use such a group as a sounding board when we can pick and choose among topics to include in our classroom curriculum, or perhaps when we are thinking about assigning controversial yet potentially valuable works of literature (e.g., Rudman, 1993). Alternatively, we might want to use a discussion group as a mechanism through which we can all share ideas about how best to promote students' academic, personal, and social development (e.g., J. L. Epstein, 1996).

Hold parent discussion groups for issues of general concern.

None of the communication strategies just described will, in and of itself, guarantee a successful working relationship with parents. Parent-teacher conferences and parent discussion groups typically occur infrequently. Written communication is ineffective with parents who have limited literacy skills. And, of course, not everyone has a telephone. Ideally, we want not only to communicate with parents but to get them actively involved in school activities as well.

Getting Parents Involved in School Activities

Plan activities that entice parents to become involved.

Effective teachers get parents and other important family members (e.g., grandparents, older siblings) actively involved in school life and in their children's learning (Davis & Thomas, 1989; J. L. Epstein, 1996; D. U. Levine & Lezotte, 1995). Students whose parents are involved in school activities have better attendance records, higher achievement, and more positive attitudes toward school (J. L. Epstein, 1996).

Most parents become involved in school activities only when they have a specific invitation to do so and when they know that school personnel genuinely *want* them to be involved (A. A. Carr, 1997; Hoover, Dempsey, & Sandler, 1997). For example, we might invite parents to an "open house" or choir performance in the evening, or we might request their help with a fund-raiser on a Saturday afternoon. We might seek volunteers to help with field trips, special projects, or individual tutoring during the school day. And we should certainly use parents and other family members as resources to give us a multicultural perspective of the community in which we work (Minami & Ovando, 1995).

Yet some parents, especially those from some minority groups, may not take our invitations seriously. Consider one African American parent's explanation of why she rarely attended school events:

> If we are talking about slavery times . . . the slaves were all around, plantation owner came to the plantation [and said] "Oh, we're having a party over next door, come on over!" He would say, "Come on over," there was an invitation without any qualification as to who was to come. The African Americans, the slaves would not come because they knew the invitation was not for them. . . . They were not expected to participate. . . . (A. A. Carr, 1997, p. 2)

In such cases, a *personal* invitation can often make the difference, as this parent's statement demonstrates:

> The thing of it is, had someone not walked up to me and asked me specifically, I would not hold out my hand and say, "I'll do it." . . . You get parents here all the time, black parents that are willing, but maybe a little on the shy side and wouldn't say I really want to serve on this subject. You may send me the form, I may never fill the form out. Or I'll think about it and not send it back. But you know if that principal, that teacher, my son's math teacher called and asked if I would. . . . (A. A. Carr, 1997, p. 2)

Issue personal invitations when necessary.

Encouraging "Reluctant" Parents

Despite our best efforts, a few parents will remain uninvolved in their children's education; for example, some parents may rarely if ever attend scheduled parent-teacher conferences. Before we jump too quickly to the conclusion that these parents are also *uninterested* in their children's education, we must recognize several possible reasons why parents might be reluctant to make contact with us. Some may have an exhausting work schedule or lack adequate child care. Others may have difficulty communicating in English (Salend & Taylor, 1993). Still others may believe that it's inappropriate to bother teachers with questions about their children's progress or to offer information as to why their children are having difficulty (Hidalgo et al., 1995; Olneck, 1995; U.S. Department of Education, 1993b). And a few may simply have had bad experiences with school when they themselves were children (Salend & Taylor, 1993).

Identify and address the reasons why some parents may be reluctant to attend school functions or otherwise communicate with you.

Educators have offered numerous suggestions for getting reluctant parents more involved in their children's schooling:

- Make an extra effort to establish parents' trust and confidence—for instance, by demonstrating that we value their input and would never make them appear foolish.
- Encourage parents to be assertive when they have questions or concerns.
- Invite other important family members (e.g., grandparents, aunts, uncles) to participate in school activities, especially if a student's cultural background is one that places high value on the extended family.
- Give parents suggestions on learning activities they can easily do with their children at home.
- Find out what different parents do exceptionally well (e.g., carpentry, cooking) and ask them to share their talents with the class.
- Provide opportunities for parents to volunteer for jobs that don't require them to leave home (e.g., to be someone whom students can call when they're not sure of their homework assignments).
- Identify individuals (e.g., bilingual parents) who can translate for those who speak little or no English.

628

CHAPTER 15
CREATING AND
MAINTAINING A
PRODUCTIVE
CLASSROOM
ENVIRONMENT

- Conduct parent-teacher conferences or parent discussions at times and locations more convenient for families.
- Make use of home visits *if* such visits are welcomed. (J. L. Epstein, 1996; Finders & Lewis, 1994; Hidalgo et al., 1995; C. K. Howe, 1994; Salend & Taylor, 1993; M. G. Sanders, 1996)

Discussing Problem Behaviors with Parents

As noted earlier, we may sometimes need to speak with parents about a chronic behavior problem at school. Put yourself in a parent's shoes in the following exercise.

Experiencing Firsthand
Putting Yourself in a Parent's Shoes

Imagine that you are the parent of a seventh grader named Tommy. As you and your son are eating dinner one evening, the telephone rings. You get up to answer the phone.

You:	Hello?
Ms. J.:	Hi. This is Ms. Johnson, Tommy's teacher. May I talk with you for a few minutes?
You:	Of course. What can I do for you?
Ms. J.:	Well, I'm afraid I've been having some trouble with your son, and I thought you ought to know about it.
You:	Oh, really? What seems to be the problem?
Ms. J.:	For one thing, Tommy hardly ever gets to class on time. When he does arrive, he spends most of his time talking and laughing with his friends, rather than paying attention to what I'm saying. It seems as if I have to speak to him three or four times every day about his behavior.
You:	How long has all this been going on?
Ms. J.:	For several weeks now. And the problem is getting worse rather than better. I'd really appreciate it if you'd talk with Tommy about the situation.
You:	I'll do it right now. And thank you for letting me know about this.
Ms. J.:	You're most welcome. Good night.
You:	Good night, Ms. Johnson.

Take a few minutes to jot down some of the things that, as a parent, you might be thinking after this telephone conversation.

You may have had a variety of reactions to your conversation with Ms. Johnson. Here are some of the possibilities:

- Why isn't Tommy taking his schoolwork more seriously?
- Isn't Tommy doing anything *right*?
- Has Ms. Johnson tried anything else besides reprimanding Tommy for his behavior? Or is she laying all of this on *my* shoulders?

Notice how Ms. Johnson focused strictly on the "negatives" of Tommy's classroom performance. As a result, you (as Tommy's parent) may possibly have felt anger at your son or guilt about your ineffective parenting skills. Alternatively, you may have maintained your confidence in your son's scholastic abilities and in your own ability to be a parent; if so, you may have begun to wonder about Ms. Johnson's ability to teach and motivate seventh graders.

We will be more effective when working with parents if we set a positive, upbeat tone in any communication. For one thing, we will always want to couch any negative

How might a chronically abusive parent react to the conversation with Ms. Johnson?

aspects of a student's classroom performance within the context of the many things that the student does *well.* (For example, rather than starting out by complaining about Tommy's behavior, Ms. Johnson might have begun by saying that Tommy is a bright and capable young man with many friends and a good sense of humor.) And we must be clear about our commitment to working *together* with parents to help a student succeed in the classroom.

Here are some additional suggestions for enhancing your chances for a successful outcome when you must speak with a parent about a problem behavior:

- *Don't place blame; instead, acknowledge that raising children is rarely easy.* Parents are more apt to respond constructively to your concerns if you don't blame them for their child's misbehavior.
- *Express your desire for whatever support they can give you.* Parents are more likely to be cooperative if you present the problem as one that can be effectively addressed if everyone works together to understand and solve it.
- *Ask for information and be a good listener.* If you show that you truly want to hear their perspective, parents are more likely to share their ideas regarding possible sources of the problem and possible ways of addressing it.
- *Agree on a strategy.* You are more likely to bring about an improvement in behavior if both you and a student's parents have similar expectations for behavior and similar consequences when those expectations are not met. Keep in mind that some parents, if making decisions on their own, may administer excessive or ineffective forms of punishment; agreement in your conference as to what consequences are appropriate may avert such a situation. (derived from suggestions by Emmer et al., 1994)

When a student's parents speak a language other than English, we will, of course, want to include in the conversation someone who can converse fluently with the parents in their native tongue (and ideally, someone whom the parents trust). We must be aware, too, that people from different cultural groups sometimes have radically different ideas about how children should be disciplined. For example, many Chinese American parents believe that Western schools are too lenient in the ways they attempt to correct inappropriate behavior (Hidalgo et al., 1995). In some Native American and Asian cultures, a child's misbehaviors may be seen as bringing shame on the family or community; thus, a common disciplinary strategy is to ignore or ostracize the child for an extended period of time (Pang, 1995; Salend & Taylor, 1993). As we confer with parents from cultures different from our own, we must listen with an open mind to the opinions they express and try to find common ground on which to develop strategies for helping their children become more productive students (Salend & Taylor, 1993).

Most parents ultimately want what's best for their children (e.g., Hidalgo et al., 1995). It's essential, then, that we not leave them out of the loop when we're concerned about how their children are performing in school.

Communicate your confidence in each student's ability to succeed, as well as your commitment to working cooperatively with parents.

Take parents' opinions about appropriate discipline into account.

CASE STUDY: Old Friends

Mr. Schulak has wanted to be a teacher for as long as he can remember. In his numerous volunteer activities over the years—coaching a girls' basketball team, assisting in a Boy Scout troop, teaching Sunday school—he has discovered how much he enjoys working with children. The children obviously enjoy working with him as well: Many of them occasionally call or stop by his home to shoot baskets, talk over old times, or just say hello. Some of them even call him by his first name.

630 CHAPTER 15
CREATING AND
MAINTAINING A
PRODUCTIVE
CLASSROOM
ENVIRONMENT

Now that he has completed his college degree and obtained his teaching certificate, Mr. Schulak is a first-year teacher at his hometown's junior high school. He is delighted to find that he already knows many of his students—he has coached them, taught them, or gone to school with their older brothers and sisters—and so he spends the first few days of class renewing his friendships with them. But by the end of the week, he realizes that he and his students have accomplished little of an academic nature.

The following Monday, Mr. Schulak vows to get down to business. He begins each of his six classes that day by describing the objectives for the weeks to come; he then begins the first lesson. He is surprised to discover that many of his students—students with whom he has such a good rapport—are resistant to settling down and getting to work. They want to move from one seat to another, talk with their friends, toss erasers across the room, and, in fact, do anything *except* the academic tasks that Mr. Schulak has in mind. In his second week as a new teacher, Mr. Schulak has already lost total control of his classroom.

- Why is Mr. Schulak having so much difficulty bringing his classroom to order? What critical things has Mr. Schulak not done in his first week of teaching?

- Given that Mr. Schulak has gotten the school year off on the wrong foot, what might he do now to remedy the situation?

Summing Up

Creating an Environment Conducive to Learning

Classroom management is a process of establishing and maintaining a classroom environment conducive to students' learning and achievement. As teachers, we want to create a classroom in which students are consistently engaged in classroom tasks and activities and in which few student behaviors interfere with those tasks and activities.

Several strategies are useful for establishing a productive classroom environment. In particular, we can (a) physically arrange the classroom in a way that facilitates our interactions with students and minimizes distractions, (b) create a classroom climate in which students have a sense of belonging and an intrinsic motivation to learn, (c) set reasonable limits for classroom behavior, (d) plan classroom activities that encourage on-task behavior, (e) continually monitor what students are doing, and (f) modify our instructional strategies when they are clearly ineffective.

Dealing with Student Misbehaviors

Some minor misbehaviors are usually best ignored, including those that probably won't be repeated, those that are unlikely to be imitated by other students, and those that occur only temporarily and within the context of unusual circumstances. Other minor infractions can be dealt with simply and quickly by cueing students about their inappropriate behaviors.

Chronic misbehaviors that significantly interfere with student learning often require greater intervention. In some cases, we may be able to address a problem behavior successfully by having a discussion with the student about the situation. In other circumstances, we may find that self-regulatory strategies, applied behavior analysis, or positive behavioral support bring about improvement. We may sometimes find it desirable to discuss chronic and serious misbehaviors with a student's parents so that we can coordinate our efforts and work toward a common solution.

Taking Student Diversity into Account

As we plan for a productive classroom, we must consider the characteristics of the students we are likely to have in our classroom. Creating a warm, supportive atmosphere and a sense of community among our students may be especially important for students from diverse cultural backgrounds, students from lower socioeconomic groups, and students with special needs. As we deal with classroom misbehavior, we must be especially understanding when students exhibit behaviors that are the product of a particular cultural upbringing or the result of a specific disability.

Coordinating Efforts with Other Individuals

We will be most effective when we work cooperatively with other teachers, other institutions, and parents to promote students' learning, development, and achievement. It is especially important that we keep in regular contact with parents, sharing information in both directions about the progress that students are making and coordinating efforts at school with those on the home front. We can keep the lines of communication open through a variety of mechanisms—for instance, by scheduling parent-teacher conferences, sending notes home, making frequent telephone calls, and getting parents actively involved in school activities. We may need to make an extra effort to establish productive working relationships with those parents who, on the surface, seem reluctant to become involved in their children's education.

KEY CONCEPTS

classroom management (p. 599)

classroom climate (p. 600)

sense of community (p. 602)

withitness (p. 610)

misbehavior (p. 612)

cueing (p. 615)

sense of school community (p. 624)

16

Assessing Student Learning

n your many years as a student, in what different ways have your teachers assessed your achievement? Generally speaking, has your performance on classroom assessments accurately reflected what you learned in class? Can you recall a situation in which a test or other classroom assessment seemed to have little relationship to important instructional objectives?

As teachers, we will often need to assess students' learning and achievement in order to make informed decisions in the classroom. For instance, when we begin a new topic, we will want to identify existing knowledge and skills so that we can gear instruction to an appropriate level. We will also want to monitor students' progress as we go along so that we can address any difficulties that arise. And ultimately, we will have to determine what each student has accomplished during the school year. According to one estimate, we may spend one-third of our time, possibly even more, in assessment-related activities (Stiggins & Conklin, 1992).

It is essential that we use assessment techniques that accurately reflect what our students know and can do; it is equally essential that such techniques promote our students' learning and achievement over the long run. In this chapter, we will examine a variety of potentially effective assessment strategies and identify the situations in which each one is appropriate. As we do so, we will address these questions:

- What do we mean by *assessment,* and what different forms can it take in classroom settings?
- For what purposes might we assess students' learning, and what kinds of assessment strategies are most useful in each case?
- What are the characteristics of good classroom assessments?
- In what situations is informal assessment most appropriate?
- What steps should we take as we plan a test, assignment, or other formal assessment of students' achievement?
- What guidelines can help us design valid paper-pencil measures of student learning?
- When is performance assessment more appropriate than a paper-pencil task, and how can we use such assessment effectively?
- How can we accommodate the abilities and needs of a diverse population of students in our assessment practices?
- In what different ways can we summarize students' achievement?
- How does assessment fit into the overall "big picture" of classroom instruction?

CASE STUDY : Studying Europe

Ellen and Roslyn are taking geography this year. Although they have different teachers, they both have the same textbook and often study together. In fact, they are each taking a test on Chapter 6 in their respective classes tomorrow. Here is a snippet of their conversation as they study the night before:

Ellen: Let's see . . . what's the capital of Sweden?

Roz: Stockholm, I think. Why?

Ellen: Because I need to memorize all the capitals of the countries in Europe. I know most of them, I guess. I'd better move on and study the rivers.

Roz: Geez, are you expected to know all those things?

Ellen: Oh, yeah. For our test, Ms. Peterson will give us a map of Europe and ask us to label all the countries, their capitals, and the rivers that run through them.

Roz: Wow! That's not what we're doing in Ms. Montgomery's class at all. We're supposed to learn the topography, climate, and culture of all the European countries. Ms. Montgomery says that she'll ask us to use what we know about these things to explain why each country imports and exports the products that it does.

Ellen: That sounds like a really hard test—much harder than mine.

Roz: Oh, I don't know. It all depends on what you're used to. Ms. Montgomery has been giving tests like this all year.

- What instructional objectives does each girl's test reflect? To what extent does it measure lower-level or higher-level skills?

- Are the two girls likely to study in different ways? If so, how will they study differently? Which girl is likely to remember what she has studied for a longer period of time?

The Various Forms of Classroom Assessment

Paper-pencil tests, such as those for which Ellen and Roz are preparing, provide one means through which we can assess student achievement. Yet not all classroom assessment involves paper and pencil. The statements our students make in class, the answers they give to our questions, the questions *they* ask—all of these tell us something about what they have learned. Nonverbal behaviors give us information as well: We can observe how well students use a pair of scissors, how carefully they set up laboratory equipment, or what kinds of scores they earn on physical fitness tests. Some forms of assessment take only a few seconds, whereas others may take several hours or even several days. Some are planned and developed in advance, whereas others occur spontaneously during the course of a lesson or classroom activities.

What exactly do we mean by the word *assessment*? This definition sums up its major features:

Assessment is a process of observing a sample of students' behavior and drawing inferences about their knowledge and abilities.

Several aspects of the definition are important to note. First, we are looking at students' *behavior.* As behaviorists have pointed out, it's impossible to look inside students' heads and see what knowledge lurks there; we can see only how students actually respond in the classroom. Second, we typically use just a *sample* of students' classroom behavior; we certainly cannot observe and keep track of every single thing that every single student does during the school day. And finally, we must draw *inferences* from the specific behaviors we do observe to make judgments about students' overall classroom achievement—a tricky business at best. As we proceed through the chapter, we will discover how to select behaviors that will give us a reasonably accurate estimate of what our students know and can do.

Can you think of classroom tests you've taken that were probably *not* good samples of what they were supposed to measure?

Figure 16–1 summarizes four distinctions that educators often make with regard to classroom assessment instruments. Let's look more closely at each one.

Standardized Tests Versus Teacher-Developed Assessment

Sometimes classroom assessments involve tests developed by test construction experts and published for use in many different schools and classrooms. Such assessment instruments are commonly called **standardized tests.** Many of them are *achievement tests* used to assess students' general academic progress in different areas of the school curriculum (e.g., reading, science, social studies). Other standardized tests, including both *intelligence* and *general scholastic aptitude* tests, are used to assess students' overall ability to learn and perform successfully in typical classroom situations (recall our discussion of intelligence tests in Chapter 4). Still others, known as *specific aptitude tests,* are used to assess students' ability to succeed in particular content domains (e.g., their ability to handle an accelerated mathematics course).[1]

Standardized tests typically come with test manuals that describe the instructions to give students, the time limits to impose, and explicit criteria for scoring responses. Furthermore, most standardized tests are accompanied by data regarding the typical performance **(norms)** of different groups of students on the test, and these norms are used in calculating students' overall test scores. We will learn more about such *norm-referenced scores* later in the chapter.

Most school districts administer standardized tests at one time or another. But these tests typically assess such broad abilities that they yield little information about what students specifically have and have not learned. When we want to assess students' learning and achievement related to specific instructional objectives—for example, whether students can do long division or whether they can apply what they've just learned in a social studies lesson—we will usually want to construct our own **teacher-developed assessment instruments.**

Some tests involve paper and pencil, but others do not. In this industrial arts class, the students have designed and constructed rockets, and their teacher is assessing how well each rocket performs.

Paper-Pencil Versus Performance Assessment

As teachers, we may sometimes choose **paper-pencil assessment,** in which we present questions to answer, topics to address, or problems to solve, and our students must write their responses on paper. Yet we may also find it helpful to use **performance assessment,** in which students demonstrate *(perform)* their abilities—for example, by giving an oral presentation, jumping hurdles, using a computer spreadsheet, or identifying acids and bases in a chemistry lab.

Some educators use the term *performance assessment* only when referring to complex, real-world tasks. Here we are using the term in a broader sense to refer to any non-paper-pencil assessment.

Traditional Versus Authentic Assessment

Historically, teachers' assessment instruments have focused on measuring basic knowledge and skills in relative isolation from tasks more typical of the outside world. Spelling

---

[1] A more detailed description of different types of standardized tests appears as a supplementary reading in the *Student Study Guide.*

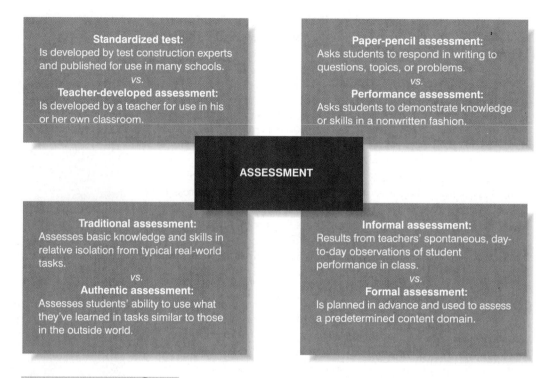

Standardized test:
Is developed by test construction experts and published for use in many schools.
vs.
Teacher-developed assessment:
Is developed by a teacher for use in his or her own classroom.

Paper-pencil assessment:
Asks students to respond in writing to questions, topics, or problems.
vs.
Performance assessment:
Asks students to demonstrate knowledge or skills in a nonwritten fashion.

ASSESSMENT

Traditional assessment:
Assesses basic knowledge and skills in relative isolation from typical real-world tasks.
vs.
Authentic assessment:
Assesses students' ability to use what they've learned in tasks similar to those in the outside world.

Informal assessment:
Results from teachers' spontaneous, day-to-day observations of student performance in class.
vs.
Formal assessment:
Is planned in advance and used to assess a predetermined content domain.

FIGURE 16.1

The many forms that classroom assessment can take

quizzes, mathematics word problems, and physical fitness tests are examples of such **traditional assessment.** Yet ultimately, our students must be able to apply their knowledge and skills to complex tasks outside the classroom. The notion of **authentic assessment**—measuring the actual knowledge and skills we want students to demonstrate in an "authentic," real-life context—is gaining increasing popularity among educators (Darling-Hammond, 1991; Lester et al., 1997; Paris & Ayres, 1994; Valencia, Hiebert, & Afflerbach, 1994).

In some situations, authentic assessment involves paper and pencil. For example, we might ask students to write a letter to a friend or develop a school newspaper. But in many cases, authentic assessment is performance based and closely integrated with instruction, such as with the *authentic activities* discussed in earlier chapters. For example, we might assess students' ability to present a persuasive argument, bake a cake, converse in a foreign language, design and build a bookshelf, or successfully maneuver a car into a parallel parking space. As teachers, we must consider what our students should be able to do when they join the adult world, and our assessment practices must, to some extent, reflect those real-life tasks.

Informal Versus Formal Assessment

Informal assessment results from our spontaneous, day-to-day observations of how students perform in class. When we conduct an informal assessment, we will rarely have a specific agenda as to what we are looking for, and we are likely to learn different things about different students. For instance, we may discover that Tony has a misconception about gravity when he asks, "How come people in Australia don't fall into space?" We may wonder if Jaffa needs an appointment with the eye doctor when we see her continually squinting as she looks at the chalkboard. And we may conclude that Marty has a high need for approval when he is constantly seeking our attention and praise.

In contrast, **formal assessment** is typically planned in advance and used for a specific purpose—perhaps to determine what students have learned from a certain unit in the geography curriculum, whether they can solve word problems requiring addition and subtraction, or how they compare with students nationwide in terms of physical fitness. It is "formal" in the sense that a particular time is set aside for it, students often study and prepare for it ahead of time, and we will get information about every student relative to the same instructional objectives. Paper-pencil tests (like those that Ellen and Roz are taking) are examples of formal assessment, as are such structured performance situations as oral reports and physical fitness tests.

Using Assessment for Different Purposes

On some occasions, we will engage in **formative evaluation:** We will assess what students know and can do *before or during instruction.* Ongoing formative evaluation can help us determine how well our students understand the topic at hand, what misconceptions they have, whether they need further practice on a particular skill, and so on. We can then develop or modify our lesson plans accordingly.

At other times, we will engage in **summative evaluation:** We will conduct an assessment *after instruction* to make final decisions about what students have ultimately achieved. Summative evaluations are used to determine whether students have mastered the content of a lesson or unit, what final grades to assign, which students are eligible for more advanced classes in a particular topic, and so on.

Let's consider how we might use assessment for the following purposes:

- To promote learning
- To promote self-regulation
- To determine whether instructional goals have been achieved

Using Assessment to Promote Learning

When we use formative evaluation to develop or modify our lesson plans, we are obviously using assessment to facilitate students' learning. But summative evaluation, too, may influence learning. For example, in the opening case study, Ellen and Roz are learning as they study for their geography tests, but they are learning different things and in different ways. Ellen is studying the names of capitals and rivers of various European countries; unless she can connect these names to something else she knows, she will probably learn them at a rote level. In contrast, Roz is trying to find relationships among the topography, climate, culture, imports, and exports of the countries; to do so, she must engage in meaningful learning, organization, and elaboration.

Research indicates that summative classroom assessments promote learning in several ways:

- They increase students' motivation to learn classroom material (although this motivation is usually extrinsic, rather than intrinsic, in nature).
- They encourage students to review previously learned information and therefore to process it further.
- They serve as learning experiences in and of themselves, particularly if they ask students to elaborate on the material in some way.
- They provide feedback about what students do and do not know; detailed feedback (e.g., pointing out misconceptions, giving constructive comments about how to improve) is especially effective in this regard. (Baron, 1987; Dempster, 1991; Foos & Fisher, 1988; N. Frederiksen, 1984b; Grolnick & Ryan, 1987; Krampen, 1987; Natriello & Dornbusch, 1984; Paris & Turner, 1994).

Students tend to study more for essay tests than for multiple-choice tests (D'Ydewalle, Swerts, & De Corte, 1983; G. Warren, 1979). Why might this be so?

Assess achievement in ways that encourage students to engage in effective cognitive processes as they study.

Construct an assessment instrument sufficiently difficult to reflect the level of performance you want students to achieve, but don't make it impossible.

Give students some leeway to make errors without penalty.

Whenever we assess students' performance as a way of facilitating their learning and achievement, our assessment instruments should:

• *Assess the specific behaviors and thought processes we want students to acquire.* Our students will draw inferences about our instructional objectives based on how we assess their learning. As a result, different kinds of assessment tasks will lead them to study and learn differently (J. R. Frederiksen & Collins, 1989; Lundeberg & Fox, 1991; Newmann, 1997; Poole, 1994).

Unfortunately, most teacher-developed classroom assessments focus primarily on knowledge of specific facts, perhaps because such assessments are the easiest to develop (J. R. Frederiksen & Collins, 1989; Nickerson, 1989; Poole, 1994; Silver & Kenney, 1995). If we want our students to do *more* than memorize facts, we must develop assessment techniques that reflect the things we actually want them to do when they study and learn. For example, we can use paper-pencil instruments that ask students to rephrase ideas in their own words, generate their own examples of concepts, use course material to solve problems, or examine ideas with a critical eye. We can use performance assessments that include complex behaviors and activities. And we can use authentic assessment to encourage students to transfer what they've learned to real-life situations.

• *Be at an appropriate difficulty level.* How difficult should our assessment instruments be? When they are too easy, students may not exert much effort (e.g., they may not study very much) and therefore may not learn as much as we would like. Furthermore, high scores based on little achievement may mislead us to believe that our students have learned something they haven't really learned at all. Yet when our assessment instruments are too difficult, students may become discouraged and believe that they are incapable of mastering the subject matter. As you can see, there are dangers in developing measures that are too easy *or* too difficult.

We should keep two things in mind when deciding just how difficult to make our assessment instruments. First, any assessment should reflect the level of performance we actually want our students to achieve. Second, it should be difficult enough that students must expend effort to succeed, but not so difficult that success is beyond reach. Classroom assessments are especially effective as motivators when students see them as good measures of class objectives and feel challenged to do their very best (Natriello & Dornbusch, 1984; Paris, Lawton, Turner, & Roth, 1991).

• *Encourage risk taking.* As noted in Chapter 12, students are more likely to tackle challenging tasks——tasks that will maximize learning and cognitive development——when they feel free to take risks and make mistakes. We encourage risk taking when our assessment strategies give students some leeway to be wrong without penalty (Clifford, 1990).

My colleague Dan Wagner, a high school mathematics teacher, uses what he calls a "mastery reform" as a way of allowing students to make mistakes and then learn from them. When it is clear from classroom assessments that students haven't demonstrated mastery of a mathematical procedure, Dan has them complete an assignment that includes the following:

1. *Identification of the error.* Students describe in a short paragraph exactly what it is that they do not yet know how to do.

2. *Statement of the process.* Students explain the steps involved in the procedure they are trying to master; in doing so, they must demonstrate their understanding by using words rather than mathematical symbols.

3. *Practice.* Students show their mastery of the procedure with three new problems similar to the problem(s) they previously solved incorrectly.

4. *Statement of mastery.* Students state in a sentence or two that they have now mastered the procedure.

By completing the four prescribed steps, students can replace a grade on a previous assessment with the higher one that they earn by attaining mastery. Such assignments may have longer-term benefits as well: Dan tells me that many of his students eventually incorporate the four steps into their regular, more internalized learning strategies.

• *Provide diagnostic information.* To be most helpful, our assessment procedures should indicate not only where students are going wrong but also *why* they are going wrong. In other words, we should get sufficient information that we know how to help our students improve (Baek, 1994; Baxter, Elder, & Glaser, 1996; Covington, 1992). Furthermore, we should pass such diagnostic information along to students, in the form of specific feedback, so that they know what they need to do differently. Such feedback can also promote greater self-regulation—our next topic of discussion.

 Use assessment procedures that provide information about possible sources of learning difficulties.

Using Assessment to Promote Self-Regulation

In our discussion of self-regulation in Chapter 11, we noted the importance of both *self-monitoring* (students must be aware of how well they are doing at any given time) and *self-evaluation* (students must be able to assess their own performance accurately). An important function of our classroom assessment practices should be to help students engage in such self-regulatory processes (Covington, 1992; Paris & Ayres, 1994; Stiggins, 1997).

Theorists have proposed several ways in which we can use classroom assessment procedures to promote greater self-observation and self-evaluation:

Give students the guidance they need to assess their own performance.

- We can provide students with our criteria for evaluating assignments and ask them to evaluate their own work using those criteria. For example, after writing a summary of a textbook chapter, students might judge what they've written using the following checklist:

  Components of a Good Summary

  _____ I included a clear main idea statement.

  _____ I included important ideas that support the main idea.

  _____ My summary shows that I understand the relationships between important concepts.

  _____ I used my own words rather than words copied from the text.
  (adapted from Paris & Ayres, 1994, p. 75)

- We can solicit students' ideas regarding the criteria we use in assessing their performance.
- We can provide examples of "good" and "poor" products and ask students to compare them with respect to a variety of criteria.
- We can have students reflect on and evaluate their performance by writing in a journal on a daily or weekly basis.
- We can have students write practice test items that are similar to those they expect to see on our tests.
- We can have students compare their recent work with their work from the beginning of the school year.
- We can have students create portfolios of their best work, making their own decisions about which products to include.
- We can conduct student-teacher conferences (similar to the more traditional parent-teacher conferences) in which our students describe their achievements. (A. L. Brown & Campione, 1996; Paris & Ayres, 1994; Stiggins, 1997; Valencia et al., 1994)

When we ask students to evaluate their own work, we promote greater self-regulation.

Assessing Achievement of Instructional Goals

We will almost certainly use one or more formal assessments to determine whether students have achieved our instructional goals. Such information will be essential if we are using a mastery-learning approach to instruction; it will also be important as we assign final grades. Furthermore, discovering what students have and have not learned will help us make decisions about the appropriateness of our objectives and the effectiveness of our instructional strategies. For example, if we find that almost all of our students are completing our assignments quickly and easily, we might set our sights higher regarding the things we expect them to accomplish. If we discover that many students are struggling with material we have presented through expository instruction, we might consider trying a different instructional approach—perhaps a more concrete, hands-on one.

Particularly when we use classroom assessments to make lasting decisions about individual students—decisions related to final grades, graduation, and so on—we must be sure our assessments accurately reflect what our students have actually achieved. How do we know when our assessment instruments and procedures are giving us accurate information? We'll answer this question as we consider four characteristics of good assessment.

Important Characteristics of Classroom Assessments

THINKING ABOUT WHAT YOU KNOW

As a student, have you ever been assessed in a way you thought was unfair? If so, *why* was it unfair? For example:

INTO THE CLASSROOM: Using Assessment to Promote Students' Learning and Achievement

Give a formal or informal pretest to determine where to begin instruction.

When beginning a new unit on cultural geography, a teacher gives his class a pretest designed to identify misconceptions that students may have about various cultural groups—misconceptions he can then address during instruction.

Choose or develop an assessment instrument that reflects the actual knowledge and skills you want students to achieve.

When planning how to assess his students' achievement, a teacher initially decides to use test questions from the test bank that comes with his textbook. When he looks more closely at the test bank, however, he discovers that the items measure only knowledge of isolated facts. Instead, he develops several authentic assessment tasks that better reflect his primary instructional objective: Students should be able to apply what they've learned to real-world problems.

Construct assessment instruments that reflect how you want students to process information when they study.

A teacher tells her students, "As you study for next week's vocabulary test, remember that the test questions will ask you to put definitions in your own words and give your own examples to show what each word means."

Use an assessment task as a learning experience in and of itself.

A high school science teacher has students collect samples of the local drinking water and test them for bacterial content. She is assessing her students' ability to use procedures she has taught them, but she also hopes they will learn something about their community's natural resources.

Use an assessment to give students specific feedback about what they have and have not mastered.

As he grades students' persuasive essays, a teacher writes numerous notes in the margins of students' papers to indicate places where they have analyzed a situation correctly or incorrectly, identified a relevant or irrelevant example, proposed an appropriate or inappropriate solution, and so on.

Provide criteria that students can use to evaluate their *own* performance.

The teacher of a "life skills" class gives her students a checklist of qualities to look for in the pies they have baked.

1. Did the teacher judge students' responses inconsistently?
2. Were some students assessed under more favorable conditions than others?
3. Was it a poor measure of what you had learned?
4. Was the assessment so time-consuming that, after a while, you no longer cared how well you performed?

In light of your experiences, what characteristics do *you* think are essential for a good classroom assessment instrument?

The four questions just posed reflect, respectively, four "RSVP" characteristics of good classroom assessment:

- Reliability
- Standardization
- Validity
- Practicality

A quick review: What do we call a memory aid such as *RSVP*? (You can find the answer in Chapter 6.)

These RSVP characteristics are summarized in Table 16–1. Let's look more closely at each one.

Reliability

Experiencing Firsthand
Fowl Play

Consider the following sequence of events:

Monday. After a unit on the bone structures of both birds and dinosaurs, Ms. Fowler asks her students to write an essay explaining why many scientists believe that birds are descended from dinosaurs. After school, she tosses the pile of essays in the back seat of her cluttered '57 Chevy.

Tuesday. Ms. Fowler looks high and low for the essays both at home and in her classroom, but she can't find them anywhere.

Wednesday. Because Ms. Fowler wants to use the essay to determine what her students have learned, she asks the class to write the same essay a second time.

Thursday. Ms. Fowler discovers Monday's essays in the back seat of her Chevy.

Friday. Ms. Fowler grades both sets of essays. She is surprised to discover that there is very little consistency between them: Students who wrote the best essays on Monday did not necessarily do well on Wednesday, and some of Monday's poorest performers did quite well on Wednesday.

Which results should Ms. Fowler use—Monday's or Wednesday's?

The **reliability** of an assessment technique is the extent to which it yields consistent information about the knowledge, skills, or abilities we are trying to measure. When we assess our students' learning and achievement, we must be confident that the conclusions we draw don't change much regardless of whether we give the assessment Monday or Wednesday, regardless of whether the weather is sunny or rainy, and regardless of whether we evaluate students' responses while in a good mood or a foul frame of mind. Ms. Fowler's assessment technique has poor reliability: The results are completely different from one day to another. So which day's results should she use? I've asked you a trick question. We have no way of knowing which set is more accurate.

The same assessment instrument will rarely give us *exactly* the same results for the same student, even if the knowledge or ability we are measuring (e.g., the extent to which a student knows basic addition facts, can execute a swan dive, or can compare the bone structures of birds and dinosaurs) remains the same. Many temporary conditions unrelated to what we are trying to measure—distractions in the classroom, variability in instructions and time limits, inconsistencies in rating students' responses, and so on—are likely to affect students' performance. Factors such as these almost invariably lead to some degree of fluctuation in assessment results.

What temporary conditions might have differentially affected students' performance on Ms. Fowler's essay on Monday and Wednesday? Following are a few possibilities:

TABLE 16.1

The RSVP Characteristics of Good Assessment

CHARACTERISTIC	DEFINITION	RELEVANT QUESTIONS TO CONSIDER
Reliability	The extent to which the assessment instrument yields consistent results for each student	How much are students' scores affected by temporary conditions unrelated to the characteristic being measured (*test-retest reliability*)? Do different parts of a single assessment instrument lead to similar conclusions about a student's achievement (*internal consistency reliability*)? Do different people score students' performance similarly (*scorer reliability*)?
Standardization	The extent to which assessment procedures are similar for all students	Are all students assessed on identical or similar content? Do all students have the same types of tasks to perform? Are instructions the same for everyone? Do all students have similar time constraints? Is everyone's performance evaluated using the same criteria?
Validity	The extent to which an assessment instrument measures what it is supposed to measure	Does the assessment tap into a representative sample of the content domain being assessed (*content validity*)? Does the instrument measure a particular psychological or educational characteristic (*construct validity*)? Do students' scores predict their success on a later task (*predictive validity*)?
Practicality	The extent to which an assessment is easy and inexpensive to use	How much class time does the assessment take? How quickly and easily can students' responses be scored? Is special training required to administer or score the assessment? Does the assessment require specialized materials that must be purchased?

- *Day-to-day changes in students*—for example, changes in health, motivation, mood, and energy level

    The 24-hour Netherlands Flu was making the rounds in Ms. Fowler's classroom that week.

- *Variations in the physical environment*—for example, variations in room temperature, noise level, and outside distractions

    On Monday, students who sat by the window in Ms. Fowler's classroom enjoyed peace and quiet; on Wednesday, those who sat by the window worked while noisy construction machinery tore up the pavement outside.

- *Variations in administration of the assessment*—for example, variations in instructions, timing, and the teacher's response to student questions

    On Monday, a few students had to write the essay after school because of play rehearsal during class time; Ms. Fowler explained the task more clearly than she had during class that day and gave students as much time as they needed to finish. On Wednesday, a different group of students had to write the essay after school because of a band concert during class time; on this occasion, Ms. Fowler explained the task very hurriedly and collected students' essays before they had finished.

- *Characteristics of the assessment instrument*—for example, the length of the task, and ambiguous or excessively difficult tasks (longer tasks tend to be more reliable because small errors have less of an impact on overall results; ambiguous and very difficult tasks increase students' tendency to guess randomly)

  The essay topic "Explain why many scientists believe that birds are descended from dinosaurs" was a vague one that students interpreted differently from one day to the next.

- *Subjectivity in scoring*—for example, tasks for which the teacher must make judgments about "rightness" or "wrongness," and situations in which students' responses are scored on the basis of vague, imprecise criteria

  Ms. Fowler graded both sets of essays while she watched "Chainsaw Murders at Central High" on television Friday night; she gave higher scores during kissing scenes, lower scores during stalking scenes.

Whenever we draw conclusions about students' learning and achievement, we must be confident that the information on which we've based our conclusions is not overly distorted by temporary factors irrelevant to what we are trying to measure. Probably no assessment technique is 100 percent reliable, but some instruments and procedures provide more reliable results than others, and it is helpful to know how dependable the results of any particular technique are likely to be.

It is often possible to determine a precise *reliability coefficient* that indicates how reliable an assessment technique is likely to be (see Appendix B, "Describing Relationships with Correlation Coefficients"). Yet even when we don't calculate the mathematical reliability of an instrument, we should take precautions to maximize the extent to which the instrument gives us reliable results. More specifically, we should:

- Include several tasks in each instrument and look for consistency in students' performance from one task to another
- Define each task clearly enough that students know exactly what they are being asked to do
- Identify specific, concrete criteria on which we will evaluate students' performance
- Try not to let our expectations for students' performance influence our judgments
- Avoid assessing students' learning when they are obviously ill, tired, or out of sorts
- Administer the assessment in similar ways and under similar conditions for all students

My last recommendation suggests that our assessment procedures be *standardized*—a second important characteristic of good assessment.

Standardization

A second important characteristic of good assessment is **standardization**: It involves similar content and format and is administered and scored in the same way for everyone. In most situations, all students should be given the same instructions, perform identical or similar tasks, have the same time limits, and work under the same constraints (making appropriate adjustments for students with special needs, however). And students' responses should be scored as consistently as possible; for example, we shouldn't use tougher standards for one student than for another.

Perhaps you can now see why the published tests described earlier are called *standardized* tests: They have explicit instructions for administration and scoring. Yet standardization is important in our teacher-developed assessment instruments as well. Standardization reduces some of the error in our assessment results, especially error due to variation in test administration or subjectivity in scoring. So the more an assessment is standardized for all students, the higher is its reliability. Equity is an additional consideration: Except in unusual situations, it is only fair to ask all students to be evaluated under similar conditions.

Validity

Experiencing Firsthand
FTOI

Just a few minutes ago, you read about *reliability*. Let's see whether you can apply (transfer) your understanding of that concept to this situation:

> I have developed a new test called the FTOI: the Fathead Test of Intelligence. It consists of only a tape measure and a table of norms describing how others have performed on the test. Administration of the FTOI is quick and easy: You simply measure a student's head circumference just above the eyebrows (firmly but not too tightly) and compare your measure against the table of norms. Large heads (comparatively speaking) receive high IQ scores. Smaller heads receive low scores.

Does the FTOI have high reliability? Answer the question before you read further.

No matter how often you measure a person's head circumference, you are probably going to get a very similar score: Fatheads will continue to be fatheads, and pinheads will always be pinheads. So the answer to my question is yes: The FTOI has high reliability because it yields consistent results. If you answered no, you were probably thinking that the FTOI isn't a very good measure of intelligence—but that's a problem with the instrument's *validity,* not with its reliability.

The **validity** of an assessment instrument is the extent to which it measures what it is supposed to measure. Does the FTOI measure intelligence? Are scores on a standardized, multiple-choice achievement test a good indication of how much students have learned during the school year? Does students' performance at a school concert reflect what they have achieved in their instrumental music class? To the extent that our assessments don't do these things—to the extent that they are poor measures of students' knowledge and abilities—then we have a problem with validity.

As noted earlier, numerous irrelevant factors are likely to influence how well our students perform in assessment situations. Some of these—students' health, distractions in the classroom, errors in scoring, and so on—are temporary conditions that lead to fluctuation in our assessment results and thereby lower reliability. But other irrelevant factors—perhaps reading ability, self-efficacy, trait anxiety—are more stable in nature, so their effects on our assessment results will be relatively constant. For example, if Joe has poor reading skills, then he may get consistently low scores on paper-pencil, multiple-choice achievement tests regardless of how much he has actually achieved in science, mathematics, or social studies. If Jane suffers debilitating anxiety whenever she performs in front of an audience, then her performance at a public concert may not be a good reflection of how well she can play the cello. When our assessment results continue to be affected by the same irrelevant variables, then we must question the validity of our instruments.

We should note here that reliability is a necessary condition for validity: Assessments can yield valid results only when they also yield reliable results—results that are only minimally affected by variations in administration, subjectivity in scoring, and so on. Reliability does not guarantee validity, however, as the FTOI exercise illustrates.

We should also note that an assessment tool may be valid for some purposes but not for others. A mathematics achievement test may be a valid measure of how well students can add and subtract but a terrible measure of how well they can apply addition and subtraction to real-life situations. A paper-pencil test regarding the rules of tennis may accurately assess students' knowledge of how many games are in a set, what *deuce* means, and so on, but it probably won't tell us much about how well students can actually play the game.

Psychologists distinguish among different kinds of validity, each of which is important in different situations. In some cases, we might be interested in **construct validity**—the extent to which an assessment accurately measures an underlying, nonobservable characteristic such as motivation, self-esteem, or visual-spatial ability.[2] For example, we might use our observations of students' on-task and off-task behavior in class to draw inferences about their motivation to learn academic subject matter. In other cases, we might be more interested in **predictive validity**—the extent to which the results of an assessment predict future behavior. For example, if the school psychologist tells us the IQ score a particular student has obtained on an intelligence test, we may be interested in knowing, as Alfred Binet once was, how well scores from the test predict students' future academic achievement. (As noted in Chapter 4, intelligence tests are often used to make such predictions.) But when we are measuring our students' achievement of instructional objectives, we will usually be concerned with **content validity**—the extent to which the tasks we ask students to perform are a representative sample of the knowledge and skills we are trying to assess. Content validity is especially important in formal assessment; we will discover how to maximize the validity of our formal assessment instruments later in the chapter.

Practicality

The last of the four RSVP characteristics is **practicality**—the extent to which assessment instruments and procedures are relatively easy to use. Practicality includes concerns such as these:

- How much time will it take to develop the instrument?
- How easily can the assessment be administered to a large group of students?
- Are expensive materials involved?
- How much time will the assessment take away from instructional activities?
- How quickly and easily can students' performance be evaluated?

There is often a trade-off between practicality and such other characteristics as validity and reliability. For example, a true-false test on tennis will be easier to construct and administer, but a performance assessment in which students actually demonstrate their tennis skills—even though it takes more time and energy—is probably a more valid measure of how well students have learned to play the game.

Of our four RSVP characteristics, validity is undoubtedly the most important of all: We *must* have an assessment technique that measures what we want it to measure. Reliability ensures the dependability of our assessment results (in doing so, it indirectly af-

---

[2]Psychologists use the term *construct* to refer to a hypothesized internal trait that cannot be directly observed but must instead be inferred from the consistencies we see in people's behavior. For example, *motivation, self-esteem, intelligence,* and *metacognition* are constructs; none of them can be seen directly.

fects their validity), and standardization is necessary to the extent that it enhances the reliability of those results. Practicality should be a consideration only when validity, reliability, and standardization are not jeopardized.

To what extent do different kinds of assessments meet our RSVP criteria? We will answer this question as we examine both informal and formal assessment in the upcoming pages.

Informal Assessment

As teachers, we need to monitor our students' performance on an ongoing basis. Through informal assessment—through our daily observations of students' verbal and nonverbal behaviors—we are likely to draw conclusions about what students have and have not learned, as well as about how future instruction should proceed. Here are just a few of the many forms that informal assessment can take:

Assessment of verbal behaviors:

- Asking questions
- Listening to whole-class and small-group discussions
- Holding brief conferences with individual students

Assessment of nonverbal behaviors:

- Observing how well students perform physical skills
- Looking at the relative frequency of on-task and off-task behaviors
- Identifying the activities in which students engage voluntarily
- Watching the "body language" that may reflect students' feelings about classroom tasks

Informal assessment has a number of advantages (Airasian, 1994; Stiggins, 1997). First and foremost, it provides continuing feedback about the effectiveness of the day's instructional tasks and activities. Second, it is easily adjusted at a moment's notice; for example, when students express misconceptions about a particular topic, we can ask follow-up questions that probe their beliefs and reasoning processes. Third, it provides information that may either support or call into question the data we obtain from more formal assessments such as paperpencil tests. Finally, informal procedures may often be the only means through which we can assess such affective objectives as "being interested in" or "valuing" something.

RSVP Characteristics of Informal Assessment

When we use informal assessment procedures to get information about students' learning and achievement, we must be aware of the strengths and limitations of these procedures in terms of the four RSVP characteristics of good assessment—reliability, standardization, validity, and practicality.

Reliability

Most informal assessments are quite short; for example, we may notice that Naomi is off task during an activity,

Without looking at Table 16–1, can you now describe each of the four RSVP characteristics of good assessment?

Why do you think affective outcomes are usually assessed informally rather than formally?

Informal assessment techniques, such as asking questions in class, allow us to continually monitor students' understanding of classroom material.

Base conclusions on many observations over a long period of time.

Keep written records of significant observations.

Never make comparisons among students solely on the basis of casual observations.

Remember that students' behaviors are not always accurate indicators of what they've learned.

Remember that your own biases and expectations may distort your interpretations of what you observe.

hear Manuel's answer to a question we've asked, or have a brief conversation with Jacquie after school. But brief snippets of students' behavior may be unreliable indicators of their overall achievement. Perhaps we happen to look at Naomi during the *only* time she is off task. Perhaps we ask Manuel one of the few questions to which he *doesn't* know the answer. Perhaps we misinterpret what Jacquie is trying to say during our conversation with her. When we use informal assessment to draw conclusions about what students have learned and achieved, we should base our conclusions on many observations over a long period of time (Airasian, 1994).

Furthermore, we should keep in mind a principle from cognitive psychology: Long-term memory is not a totally accurate or dependable record of previous experience. We will remember some student behaviors but not recall others. If we depend heavily on our in-class observations of students, we should probably keep ongoing, written records of the things we see and hear (Gronlund, 1993; Stiggins, 1997).

Standardization

Our informal assessments will rarely, if ever, be standardized; for example, we will ask different questions of different students, and we will probably observe each student's behavior in different contexts. Hence, such assessments will definitely *not* be giving us the same information for each student. As teachers, we will rarely be able to make comparisons among our students on the basis of casual observations alone.

Validity

Even when we see consistency in students' behavior over time, we will not always get accurate data about what they know and can do (Airasian, 1994; Stiggins, 1997). Tom may intentionally answer questions incorrectly so that he doesn't look too "smart" in front of his friends. Margot may be reluctant to say anything at all because of a chronic stuttering problem. Lamar may be listening carefully to an expository lesson even though we see him doodling in his notebook.

Principles from our discussion of knowledge construction (Chapter 7) are also important to recall here: We impose meanings on the things we see and hear, and those meanings are influenced by the things we already know or believe to be true. Our own biases and expectations will affect our interpretations of students' behaviors, inevitably affecting the accuracy of any conclusions we reach (Airasian, 1994; Ritts, Patterson, & Tubbs, 1992; Stiggins, 1997). We may expect academic or social competence from a student we like or admire and so are likely to perceive that student's actions in a positive light—a phenomenon known as the **halo effect.** In much the same way, we might expect inappropriate behavior from a student with a history of misbehavior, and our observations will be biased accordingly (we could call this the "horns effect").

As we discovered in Chapter 4, teachers' expectations for their students are often influenced by students' ethnicity, gender, and socioeconomic status, and such expectations may unfairly bias teachers' judgments of student performance. Let's look at an experiment by Darley and Gross (1983) as an example. Undergraduate students were told that they were participating in a study on teacher evaluation methods and were asked to view a videotape of a fourth-grade girl named Hannah. There were two versions of the videotape designed to give two different impressions about Hannah's socioeconomic status; Hannah's clothing, the kind of playground on which she played, and information about her parents' occupations indirectly conveyed to some students that she was from a low socioeconomic background and to others that she was from a high socioeconomic background. All students then watched Hannah taking an oral achievement test (one on which she performed at grade level) and were asked to rate Hannah on a number of characteristics. Students who had been led to believe that Hannah came from wealthy surroundings rated her ability well above grade level, whereas students believing that she lived in an impoverished environment evaluated her as being below grade level. The two groups of students also rated Hannah differently in terms of her work habits, motivation, social skills, and general maturity.

Practicality

A definite strength of informal assessment is practicality: We will typically make our observations spontaneously during the course of instruction. Informal assessment involves little if any of our time either beforehand or after the fact (except for any written records we decide to keep). An additional advantage is flexibility: We can adapt our assessment procedures on the spur of the moment, altering them as events in the classroom change.

Despite the practicality of informal assessment, we have noted serious problems regarding its reliability, standardization, and validity. Hence, we should treat any conclusions we draw only as *hypotheses* that we must either confirm or disconfirm through other means (Airasian, 1994). Ultimately, we should rely more heavily on formal assessment techniques to determine whether our students have achieved our instructional objectives.

> Treat the conclusions you draw from informal assessment as hypotheses that need confirmation through other means.

Planning a Formal Assessment

A valid and reliable formal assessment is usually one that has been carefully planned and thought out ahead of time. Here are three important questions to ask ourselves as we plan a formal assessment instrument:

- What content domain are we trying to assess?
- What type of tasks will best measure students' achievement?
- How can we get a representative sample of the domain?

Let's address each question in turn.

Identifying the Domain to Be Assessed

When planning and developing a formal assessment instrument, we first need to identify the specific content domain we want to assess and determine just how broad or narrow that domain is. For example, we may conceivably want to measure something as broad as "what students learned in history class this semester" or as narrow as "what students know about the Russian Revolution." Similarly, we may want to assess something as general as students' overall level of physical fitness or something as specific as their ability to do push-ups. We may be interested in determining whether students have learned enough algebra to move on to a pre-calculus class, or we may instead simply want to find out whether they can solve for x in a quadratic equation.

When we use a single assessment instrument to measure a very broad area of achievement (such as is usually the case when we administer a standardized achievement test), we get relatively little information about the specific things that students have and have not learned. When we devise separate assessments to measure narrower domains, we learn more about what knowledge and skills individual students have acquired, but at the expense of devoting a great deal of classroom time to assessment (Popham, 1990). Somewhere between these two extremes is a happy medium: We need to identify content domains small enough that our assessment instruments give us concrete information about what students have achieved, but not so small that we spend most of our classroom time assessing rather than teaching.

> For each assessment, identify content domains small enough to yield specific information about what students have achieved, but not so small that you spend most of your class time in assessment-related activities.

Selecting Appropriate Tasks

We maximize the content validity of our classroom assessment instruments when the tasks we ask students to perform are as similar as possible to the things we ultimately

Decide whether
paper-pencil or
performance tasks better
reflect your instructional
objectives.

What kinds of
performance tasks might be
appropriate in the subject
area you will be teaching?

want them to be able to do—in other words, when there is a match between assessment tasks and instructional objectives. In some situations, such as when the desired outcome is simple recall of facts, asking students to respond to multiple-choice or short-answer questions on a paper-pencil test may be both valid and practical. In other situations— for instance, when our objective is for students to explain everyday phenomena by using scientific principles or to critique a literary or artistic work—essay questions that require students to follow a logical line of reasoning may be appropriate. *If* we can truly measure a domain by having students respond to questions on paper, then a paper-pencil assessment is the most practical choice.

Yet there are many skills—cooking a hard-boiled egg, executing a front dismount from the parallel bars, identifying specific microorganisms through a microscope—that we cannot easily measure with paper and pencil. For skills such as these, performance assessments are likely to give us greater content validity. Performance assessment may be especially useful when we are concerned about students' ability to apply classroom subject matter to real-world situations.

In the end, we may find that the most valid yet practical approach to assessing our students' achievement is a combination of both paper-pencil and performance tasks (Messick, 1994; D. B. Swanson, Norman, & Linn, 1995). Paper-pencil assessments will allow us to assess students' knowledge in a relatively efficient manner; for example, short-answer questions will enable us to sample their knowledge of a broad topic fairly quickly. Performance assessments are far more time-consuming, yet they will often provide information related to our instructional objectives that we cannot acquire in any other way.

Obtaining a Representative Sample

Experiencing Firsthand
Ants and Spiders

Consider this situation:

> The students in Mr. Tyburczy's biology class are complaining about the quiz they just took. After all, the class spent two weeks studying insects and only one day studying arachnids, yet the quiz was entirely on arachnids. Students who forgot what arachnids were failed the quiz, even though some of them knew quite a bit about insects.

Why is Mr. Tyburczy's assessment strategy a poor one? Which aspect of Mr. Tyburczy's quiz are his students complaining about—reliability, standardization, validity, or practicality?

Most classroom assessment activities, even paper-pencil ones, can give us only a small sample of what students know and can do. It would be terribly impractical—and in most cases virtually impossible—to assess *everything* that a student has acquired from a unit on insects and arachnids, a chapter in a social studies textbook, or a semester of physical education. Instead, we must typically present a few questions or tasks to elicit behaviors that we hope are an accurate reflection of students' overall level of knowledge or skill.

Mr. Tyburczy's quiz does reflect a sample of what students have studied in his unit on insects and arachnids. The problem is that his questions are not representative of the unit as a whole: The focus of the quiz is exclusively on arachnids. The quiz, then, has poor *content validity*. Ideally, Mr. Tyburczy's quiz questions should reflect the various parts of the unit in appropriate proportions. His questions should also ask students to do the kinds of things that his instructional objectives describe—perhaps comparing arachnids to insects, identifying examples of each class, and so on.

How can we ensure that our test is truly a representative sample of the content domain? In other words, how can we ensure its content validity? The most widely recom-

Can you think of
occasions when a test you
took covered the entire
content domain?

Behaviors / **Topics**

Topics	Computation using number line	Rapid recall of sum	Regrouping ("carrying")	Estimation	Application to word problems
Single digits	2	6			4
Multiples of 10 and 100		2			2
Two-digit numbers			2	2	3
Three-digit numbers			2	2	3

This table provides specifications for a thirty-item paper-pencil test on addition. It assigns different weights (different numbers of items) to different topic-behavior combinations, with some combinations not being measured at all.

Topics	Make simple drawing of machine	Describe work that machine performs	Recognize examples among common objects	Solve problems by using machine
Inclined plane	5%	5%	5%	5%
Wedge	5%	5%	5%	5%
Lever	5%	5%	5%	5%
Wheel and axle	5%	5%	5%	5%
Pulley	5%	5%	5%	5%

This table provides specifications for a combination paper-pencil and performance assessment on simple machines. It assigns equal importance (the same percentage of points) to each topic-behavior combination.

FIGURE 16.2
Two examples of a table of specifications

mended strategy is to construct a *blueprint* that identifies the specific things we want to measure and the extent to which each one should be represented on the instrument. This blueprint frequently takes the form of a **table of specifications,** a two-way grid that indicates both the topics to be covered and the behaviors associated with them (i.e., the things that students should be able to *do* with each topic). In each cell of the grid, we indicate the relative importance of each topic-behavior combination in terms of a particular number or percentage of tasks or test items to be included in the overall assessment. Figure 16–2 illustrates such tables through two examples, one for a paper-pencil test on addition and a second for a combined paper-pencil and performance assessment on simple machines. Once we have developed a table of specifications, we can develop paper-pencil items or performance tasks that reflect both the topics and the behaviors we want to assess and have some confidence that our assessment instrument has content validity for the domain it is designed to represent.

Develop a table of specifications for the content domain you want to assess and then develop assessment tasks representative of that domain.

Sometimes the behaviors listed in a table of specifications are those in Bloom's taxonomy, such as "knowledge," "comprehension," and "application" (see Chapter 13).

Once we have determined the content domain to be assessed and the best way to assess it, we can then attend to more specific details, including considerations related to item construction, administration procedures, and scoring criteria. We'll address these issues separately for paper-pencil and performance assessment.

Paper-Pencil Assessment

We can often assess students' basic knowledge and skills with paper and pencil; for example, we might give our students a brief quiz to find out whether they can spell *dinosaur*, define *democracy*, or multiply 49×56. Written assignments and tests can sometimes help us assess students' higher-level thinking abilities as well; for example, we might ask students to compare the bone structures of birds and dinosaurs, write a persuasive essay about the advantages and disadvantages of a democratic government, or solve a complex mathematical word problem. But regardless of the objectives we use paper and pencil to assess, we must keep the four RSVP characteristics in mind.

Choosing Appropriate Tasks and Questions

If we believe that a paper-pencil instrument is appropriate for the situation at hand, what specific types of tasks or questions do we give? There are many options. We might ask students to write compositions, stories, poems, or research papers. We might ask them to solve well-defined or ill-defined mathematical or scientific word problems. We might ask questions in a variety of formats—perhaps short-answer, essay, true-false, matching, or multiple-choice. We might even want to combine several of these strategies. We can narrow down the possibilities by addressing several issues:

- Are we trying to assess lower-level or higher-level skills?
- Are recognition tasks or recall tasks more appropriate?
- Should students have access to reference materials?

Assessing Lower-Level or Higher-Level Skills

Test questions that require brief responses, such as short-answer, matching, true-false, and multiple-choice, are often suitable for assessing students' knowledge of single, isolated facts (Popham, 1995). Paper-pencil tasks that require extended responses—essays, for instance—lend themselves more easily to assessing such higher-level skills as problem solving, critical thinking, and the synthesis of ideas (J. R. Frederiksen & Collins, 1989; Stiggins, 1997). For example, we might assign tasks that require students to organize information, follow a line of reasoning, design an experiment, or justify their position on a controversial topic. Yet we can sometimes develop multiple-choice items that assess higher-level skills; here are two examples:

Example 1:

An inventor has just designed a new device for cutting paper. Without knowing anything else about his invention, we can predict that it is probably which type of machine?

    a. A lever

    b. A movable pulley

    c. An inclined plane

    d. A wedge

Example 2:

Which one of the following French sentences contains a grammatical error?

    a. Je vous aimez.

    b. Le crayon rouge est sur la table verte.

    c. Donnez-moi le crayon rouge, s'il vous plaît.

    d. Avez-vous un billet pour le théâtre ce soir?

What are ill-defined problems? (See Chapter 8.)

For higher-level skills, consider using questions that require extended responses.

Answers: (1) d; (2) a.

With a little ingenuity, we can even develop relatively "authentic" paper-pencil tasks that assess students' ability to apply classroom subject matter to real-world tasks (Gronlund, 1993; D. B. Swanson et al., 1995). Here are three examples:

Example 3:

You are shopping at your local discount store. You decide to buy a T-shirt that is regularly priced at $11.00 but now is marked 20% off. You also decide to buy two candy bars at 59¢ each. You know that the local sales tax is 6%. How much money will the store clerk ask you for when you get to the checkout counter?

Example 4:

You are to play the role of an advisor to President Nixon after his election to office in 1968. As his advisor, you are to make a recommendation about the United States involvement in Vietnam. Your paper should include:

(a) One or two introductory paragraphs that show an understanding of the Vietnam War up to this point (explaining who is involved in the war and what their objectives are) and make a specific recommendation to the President;

(b) Two or three paragraphs discussing the pros of your advice, including any statistics, dates, examples, and general information that support your case;

(c) Two or three paragraphs discussing the cons of your advice, describing at least two recommendations that others might make, and explaining why their recommendations would not be advisable;

(d) A concluding paragraph that makes a final appeal for your recommendation and sells the President on your advice. (adapted from Newmann, 1997, p. 368)

Example 5:

Following is a map of a small city named Riverdale. Indicate where in Riverdale you would be most likely to find a *steel mill*, and then explain why you chose the location you did.

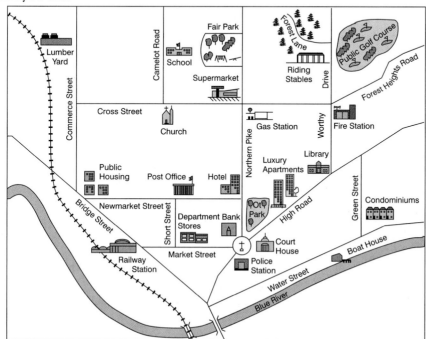

Adapted from "Reconceptualizing Map Learning" by J. E. Ormrod, R. K. Ormrod, E. D. Wagner, & R. C. McCallin, 1988, American Journal of Psychology, 101, *p. 428. Adapted with permission of the University of Illinois Press.*

Develop paper-pencil tasks that simulate real-world tasks.

Answers: (3) $10.58; (4) answers will vary but should adequately address parts a–d; (5) between the river and the railroad tracks, where both water and transportation are easily accessible.

As we noted in Chapter 6, recognition tasks are typically easier than recall tasks. Can you explain why this is so using the concepts of *retrieval* and *retrieval cues*?

Use recognition tasks to assess students' ability to recognize facts, especially when the content domain is large. Use recall tasks to assess students' ability to retrieve information on their own.

Allow students to use reference materials if your objective is application of information that does not need to be memorized.

Using Recognition or Recall Tasks

We should also consider whether a particular assessment task assesses recognition or recall. **Recognition tasks** ask students to identify correct answers within the context of incorrect statements or irrelevant information; examples include multiple-choice, true-false, and matching questions. **Recall tasks** require students to generate the correct answers themselves; examples include short-answer questions, essays, research papers, and word problems.

Recognition and recall tasks each have their advantages. Students can often answer many recognition questions in a limited period of time; hence, such questions allow us to sample a wide range of knowledge and skills. Furthermore, we can score students' responses quickly and consistently, thus addressing our needs for practicality and reliability. But when we want to assess our students' ability to remember knowledge and skills without the benefit of having the correct answer right in front of them, then recall tasks obviously have greater validity for assessing our instructional objectives.

Giving Students Access to Reference Materials

During some assessments, we may want our students to have only one resource—their own long-term memories—as they write a paper or take a test. But in other situations, it may be appropriate to let them use reference materials (perhaps a dictionary, an atlas, or a magazine article) as they work. An assessment task in which reference materials are allowed is especially appropriate when our objective is for students to locate and use information rather than memorize it. For example, we may not care whether students remember every principle in a geometry textbook, but we would like them to know how to use geometric principles to predict distances or angles. And we may not necessarily want students to know how to spell every word in the English language, but we would like them to be able to write a composition free of spelling errors if they have a dictionary to assist them.

Constructing and Administering the Assessment

Experiencing Firsthand
Assessing Assessment

Your educational psychology instructor gives you a test that includes these questions:

1. List four qualities of a good classroom assessment instrument.
2. Summarize the purposes of classroom assessment.

Take a few minutes to think about how you might answer each of these questions. Jot down your thoughts about what you would include in your responses.

Was your answer to Question 1 as simple as "reliability, standardization, validity, and practicality"? Did you think you would need to explain each of the RSVP characteristics? Did you identify legitimate qualities of "goodness" other than the four RSVP characteristics? And what about Question 2? What purposes would you have focused on, and how long do you think your summary might have been? Words such as *list, qualities,* and *summarize* are difficult to interpret and may even be misleading to students.

Having students use reference materials during a formal assessment allows them to demonstrate their ability to find and apply information.

Regardless of the kinds of tasks we ask our students to perform, we can follow several guidelines as we construct and administer a paper-pencil assessment instrument (the preceeding exercise illustrates the first guideline):

• *Define tasks clearly and unambiguously.* Contrary to what some teachers believe, there is little to be gained from assigning ambiguous tasks to assess students' learning and achievement (Sax, 1989). Whether or not students know how to respond to assessment tasks, they should at least understand what we are asking them to do. Therefore, we should define any paper-pencil task as clearly and precisely as we possibly can. As a double check, we might ask a colleague to read our assignments and questions for clarity; those that seem "obvious" to us may not be obvious at all to someone else.

Define tasks clearly.

• *Specify scoring criteria in advance.* We will typically want to identify correct responses at the same time that we develop our assessment tasks. In situations where there will be more than one correct answer (as may be true for an essay), we should at least identify the components of a good response. Furthermore, we should describe the scoring criteria to our students long before we give them the assessment; doing so gives them guidance about how they can best prepare. It is also a good idea to develop policies to guide our scoring when students give answers that are only partially correct, respond correctly to items but include additional *in*correct information, or write responses with numerous grammatical and spelling errors. We must be consistent about how we score students' responses in such situations.

Identify general scoring policies to which you will adhere, and describe them to the class.

• *Provide a quiet and comfortable environment.* Students are more likely to perform at their best when they complete a paper-pencil assessment in a comfortable environment—one with acceptable room temperature, adequate lighting, reasonable workspace, and minimal distractions. This comfort factor may be especially important for students who are easily distracted, unaccustomed to formal assessments, or relatively uninterested in performing well on them; for example, it may be especially important for our students at risk (Popham, 1990).

Provide a quiet and comfortable assessment environment.

• *Try to alleviate students' anxiety about the assessment.* How anxious do you get when you know you will be taking a test in class? For example, do you:

Worry the night before, wondering if you've read all the assigned readings?

Become nervous while the test is being handed out, thinking that maybe you don't know everything as well as you should?

Have a lot of trouble remembering things you knew perfectly well when you studied them?

Get in such a panic that you can barely read the test items at all?

If your answer to any of these questions is yes, then you, like most students, experience **test anxiety.**

Students are typically not anxious about learning new knowledge and skills. But as we discovered in Chapter 12, many of them *are* anxious at the thought that they will be evaluated and judged and perhaps found to be "stupid" or in some other way inadequate. A little bit of test anxiety may actually be a good thing: Students are more likely to prepare for an assessment and to respond to questions and tasks carefully if they are concerned about how well they are going to perform (Shipman & Shipman, 1985). But their performance is likely to be impaired when they are *very* test anxious, particularly when assigned tasks require them to use what they have learned in a flexible and creative manner (Kirkland, 1971). In cases of extreme test anxiety, students may have difficulty retrieving things from long-term memory and may not even be able to understand what we are asking them to do. We will see debilitating test anxiety more frequently in older students, students from some

TABLE 16.2 Keeping Students' Test Anxiety at a Facilitative Level

WHAT TO DO	WHAT *NOT* TO DO
Point out the value of the assessment as a feedback mechanism to improve learning.	Stress the fact that students' competence is being evaluated.
Administer a practice assessment or pretest that gives students an idea of what the final assessment instrument will be like.	Keep the nature of the assessment a secret until the day it is administered.
Encourage students to do their best.	Remind students that failing will have dire consequences.
Provide or allow the use of memory aids (e.g., a list of formulas or a single notecard containing key facts) when instructional objectives do not require students to commit information to memory.	Insist that students commit even trivial facts to memory.
Eliminate time limits unless speed is an important part of the skill being measured.	Give more questions or tasks than students can possibly respond to in the time allotted.
Be available to answer students' questions during the assessment.	Hover over students, watching them closely as they respond.
Use the results of several assessments to make decisions (e.g., to assign grades).	Evaluate students on the basis of a single assessment.

Sources: Brophy, 1986; Gaudry & Bradshaw, 1971; K. T. Hill, 1984; Popham, 1990; Sax, 1989; Sieber, Kameya, & Paulson, 1970.

minority groups, and students from lower socioeconomic backgrounds (K. T. Hill, 1984; Kirkland, 1971; Pang, 1995; Phillips et al., 1980). And, as noted in Chapter 12, students with a history of failure on academic tasks are particularly prone to such anxiety.

Avoid statements and behaviors that are apt to make students excessively anxious.

As teachers, we can make our students more or less anxious about our classroom assessments simply by how we present them (see Table 16–2). When we describe a classroom assessment as an occasion to "separate the men from the boys" or as "sudden death" for anyone who fails, students' anxiety levels are likely to go sky high. Instead, we should portray such assessments more as opportunities to increase knowledge and improve skills than as occasions for evaluation (Spaulding, 1992). For example, statements such as "We're here to learn, and you can't do that without making mistakes" (Brophy, 1986, p. 47) can help students keep their imperfections in perspective and their anxiety at a facilitating rather than debilitating level.

Encourage students to seek clarification when necessary.

• *Encourage students to ask questions when tasks are not clear.* As noted earlier, students need to know what we are asking them to do. Yet despite our best intentions, we may present a task or ask a question that is unclear, ambiguous, or even misleading. (Even after more than twenty years' experience writing exams, I still have students occasionally interpreting my assignments and test questions in ways I didn't anticipate.) To maximize the likelihood that our students will respond in the ways we are seeking, we should encourage them to ask for clarification whenever they are uncertain about a task. Such encouragement is especially important for students from ethnic minority groups, many of whom may be reluctant to ask questions during a formal assessment situation (L. R. Cheng, 1987).

■ Experiencing Firsthand
A Day Like Any Other

Imagine you are a middle school teacher. You have asked your class to write a short story written from the perspective of an animal. Here is a twelve-year-old boy's story:

> It was a day like any other, until I heard a strange sound. A sound like no other sound I had heard before. I hurried to my hole hoping nouthing had happened to my babys. They were all right so I gave them the food that was in my mouth.
>
> Then I heard the sound again. I huddled close to my baby rats so they wouldn't be to scared. I wish someone would huddle close to me so I wouldn't be scared.
>
> All of a sudden I started to hear some splashing noises. I looked up and saw that the sky was lite up. I was still standing close to my badys trying to calm them down. I wasn't shure what this was and what would happen to my family and me. And then, as soon as it had started, it stoped. My family and I walked out of the rat hole and discovered that the flowers in the flower box above our hole had bloomed. I knew that all that had scared me before, had happened for a reason.

If you had to give this story a letter grade—A, B, C, D, or F—what grade would you give? On what criteria would you base your decision?

Some paper-pencil tasks can be scored *objectively:* They have definite right and wrong answers, and there is little decision making involved in evaluating students' responses; this is the case for such recognition items as multiple-choice and true-false questions. Yet other paper-pencil tasks, such as short stories and essays, can be scored only *subjectively:* They require teacher judgment about how right or wrong any particular response is. How did you grade the story about the mother rat and her babies? What criteria did you use when you made your decision? To what extent was the student's development of the plot important? To what extent was creativity a factor? To what extent did grammar, spelling, and punctuation errors affect your judgment? Different teachers might weigh each of these criteria differently, and their grades for the same story would differ as a result. In fact, even *you* might grade the story differently next month than you graded it today.

The more variable and complex students' responses on a paper-pencil assessment instrument are, the greater difficulty we will have in scoring those responses objectively and reliably, and the more our expectations for students' performance may bias our judgments. As an example, imagine that Mr. Alexander has one student, Mary, who consistently performs well in her classwork, and another, Susan, who more typically turns in sloppy, incomplete assignments. Let's say that both girls turn in an essay of marginal quality. Mr. Alexander is likely to *over*rate Mary's performance and *under*rate Susan's.

We can use several strategies to maximize the likelihood that we score students' responses in an objective and reliable fashion:

- ■ Specify scoring criteria in concrete terms.
- ■ Score grammar and spelling separately from the *content* of students' responses.[3]
- ■ Skim a sample of students' responses ahead of time, looking for responses we didn't anticipate and revising our criteria if necessary.

Look again at our opening case study, "Studying Europe." Which test can be scored more objectively—Ms. Peterson's or Ms. Montgomery's?

Take steps to score students' responses as objectively as possible.

---

[3]This recommendation is especially important when assessing students with limited English proficiency (Hamp-Lyons, 1992; Scarcella, 1990).

- Score all responses to a single task or question at once (scoring task by task, rather than student by student).
- Score responses on a predefined continuum, rather than an all-or-none basis, if responses are likely to have varying degrees of correctness.
- Try not to let our expectations for students' performance influence our judgments of their *actual* performance.
- Score some or all responses a second time to check for consistency.

As we score students' responses, we should remember that our assessments should promote students' future learning as well as determine current achievement levels. Accordingly, we should give students detailed comments about their responses that tell them what they did well, where their weaknesses lie, and how they can improve (Bangert-Drowns et al., 1991; Deci & Ryan, 1985; Krampen, 1987).

RSVP Characteristics of Paper-Pencil Assessment

How do paper-pencil assessments measure up in terms of the RSVP characteristics? Let's consider each characteristic in turn.

Reliability

As just noted, when we have tasks and questions with definite right and wrong answers—that is, when we have objectively scorable responses—we can evaluate students' responses with a high degree of consistency and reliability. To the extent that we must make subjective judgments about the relative rightness or wrongness of students' responses, reliability will inevitably decrease.

Standardization

As a general rule, paper-pencil instruments are easily standardized. We can present similar tasks and instructions to all students, provide similar time limits and environmental conditions, and score everyone's responses in more or less the same way. At the same time, we probably don't want to go overboard in this respect. For example, we may sometimes allow students to choose a writing topic, perhaps as a way of increasing their sense of self-determination (see Chapter 12). We may also need to tailor assessment tasks to the particular abilities and disabilities of our students with special needs.

Validity

When we ask questions that require only short, simple responses—questions such as true-false, multiple-choice, and matching—we can sample students' knowledge about many topics within a relatively short period of time. In *this* sense, then, such questions may give us greater content validity. Yet in some situations, such items may *not* be an accurate reflection of our instructional objectives. If we want to assess our students' ability to apply what they've learned to new situations, or if we want to find out how well students can solve problems (especially the ill-defined ones so common in the adult world), we may need to be satisfied with a few tasks requiring lengthy responses, rather than with many tasks that merely assess what students know at a rote level.

Even when we're assessing students' knowledge of basic facts, recall items may sometimes be preferable because they more closely resemble real-world memory tasks. For example, when working adults need to recall certain information in order to perform their jobs, they rarely have the assistance of four multiple-choice alternatives to help them remember. Although recognition items may give us higher reliability, in many cases recall tasks will more closely resemble our instructional objectives.

Can you explain how each of these recommendations affects the reliability of the assessment instrument?

Remember that subjectively scorable tasks will inevitably have lower reliability than objectively scorable tasks.

Standardize your paper-pencil assessments as much as possible, but not at the expense of accommodating student diversity.

When evaluating the validity of your instrument, consider both the extent to which questions or tasks provide an adequate sample of the content domain *and* the extent to which they reflect your instructional objectives.

Practicality

Paper-pencil assessment is typically more practical than performance assessment; for instance, we will require no "equipment" other than paper and writing implements, and we can easily assess the knowledge and skills of all of our students at the same time. And some paper-pencil assessments have the additional advantage of being relatively quick and easy to score.

Because paper-pencil assessment is so practical, it should generally be our method of choice *if* it can also yield a valid measure of what students know and can do. But in situations where paper-pencil tasks are clearly *not* a good reflection of what students have learned, we may want to sacrifice such practicality to gain the greater validity that a performance assessment might provide.

Choose paper-pencil assessment over performance assessment if a paper-pencil instrument can yield a valid measure of your objectives.

Performance Assessment

Performance assessment typically takes one of two forms (Gronlund, 1993; E. H. Hiebert, Valencia, & Afflerbach, 1994; Messick, 1994). In some cases, we can look at tangible *products* that students have created—perhaps a pen-and-ink drawing, a scientific invention, or a poster depicting a particular foreign country. In other cases, there is no tangible product per se; in such instances, we must look at the specific *behaviors* that our students perform—perhaps an oral presentation, a forward roll, or an instrumental solo.

Some performance tasks allow us to examine students' thinking and learning processes; thus, they can be especially useful for formative evaluation. For instance, if we want to determine whether students have developed some of the concrete operational or formal operational abilities that Piaget described (conservation, multiple classification, separation and control of variables, etc.), we might present tasks similar to those that Piaget used and ask students to explain their reasoning (De Corte et al., 1996). Or if, from Vygotsky's perspective, we want to identify a student's zone of proximal development, we might present tasks of varying difficulty to identify those that the student can perform successfully only with considerable support (Calfee & Masuda, 1997; Phye, 1997). And we can often learn a great deal about how students conceptualize and reason about scientific phenomena when we ask them to manipulate physical objects (e.g., chemicals in a chemistry lab, electrical circuit boards in a physics class), make predictions about what will happen under varying circumstances, and then explain the results that they obtain (Magnusson, Boyle, & Templin, 1994; Quellmalz & Hoskyn, 1997). Psychologists sometimes use the term **dynamic assessment** to refer to situations in which we examine how students' knowledge or reasoning changes over the course of a performance task (Kozulin & Falik, 1995; Magnusson et al., 1994).

We will often want to use performance assessment for summative evaluation as well. Performance assessment allows us to assess students' mastery of instructional objectives in ways that may simply not be possible in a paper-pencil format. It lends itself especially well to the assessment of complex tasks, such as those that involve coordinating a number of skills simultaneously. It may also be especially useful in assessing such higher-level cognitive skills as problem solving, critical thinking, and creativity.

Choosing Appropriate Performance Tasks

A wide variety of performance tasks can be used to assess students' mastery of instructional objectives. Here are just a few of the many possibilities:

- Playing a musical instrument
- Conversing in a foreign language
- Identifying an unknown chemical substance

- Engaging in a debate about social issues
- Taking dictation in shorthand
- Fixing a malfunctioning machine
- Role-playing a job interview
- Performing a workplace routine
- Performing a computer simulation of a real-world task
  (Gronlund, 1993; C. Hill & Larsen, 1992; D. B. Swanson et al., 1995)

We might even consider placing students' knowledge of traditional academic subject matter in a performance-based context. For example, in a history class, rather than give a paper-pencil test, we might ask students to read old letters, speeches, newspaper articles, and so on, and then to draw conclusions about the events of the time period (E. L. Baker, 1994).

On some occasions, we may want to assess *extended performance*—that is, to determine what students are capable of doing over several days or weeks (Alleman & Brophy, 1997; De Corte et al., 1996; Lester et al., 1997). Extended performance tasks might provide opportunities for students to collect data, engage in collaborative problem solving, and edit and revise their work. As an example, we might assess high school students' mastery of a unit on urban geography using a field-based cooperative group task such as this one:

> Select one of the neighborhoods marked on the city map. Then do the following:
>
> 1. Identify the neighborhood's features by doing an inventory of its buildings, businesses, housing, and public facilities. Also, identify current transportation patterns and traffic flow.
>
> 2. Identify any special problems the neighborhood has, such as dilapidated housing, traffic congestion, or a high crime rate.
>
> 3. As a group, consider various plans for changing and improving the neighborhood. If there is a special problem, how will you address it? What kinds of businesses, if any, do you want to attract? What kind of housing do you want? Will there be parks and other recreation facilities? What transportation patterns do you want? Do you want to make the block attractive to different groups of people, such as senior citizens and young people?
>
> 4. After deciding on a plan, draw and label it on the overlap provided with your map. Describe the plan in a five- to ten-page narrative and explain how it will promote the neighborhood features you want. (adapted from Newmann, 1997, p. 369)

Such a task requires students to collect data systematically, use the data to draw conclusions and make predictions, and, more generally, think as an urban planner would think (Newmann, 1997).

As we select tasks for a performance assessment, we must have a clear purpose in mind; we must identify the specific conclusions we wish to draw from our observations of students' performance (Airasian, 1994). We must also consider the extent to which any particular task will enable us to make reasonable generalizations about what our students know and can do in the content domain in question (Popham, 1995; Wiggins, 1992).

Constructing and Administering the Assessment

Several of the guidelines presented in the section on paper-pencil assessment are equally relevant for summative performance assessment; in particular, we should:

- Define tasks clearly and unambiguously
- Specify scoring criteria in advance

In some situations, we can incorporate assessment into everyday instructional activities.

- Standardize administration procedures as much as possible
- Encourage students to ask questions

Yet there are additional guidelines to consider as well:

• *Consider incorporating the assessment into normal instructional activities.* Some theorists and practitioners recommend that we incorporate performance assessments into everyday instructional activities (Baxter et al., 1996; Boschee & Baron, 1993; Kennedy, 1992; Stiggins, 1997). There are a couple of advantages in doing so. First, we make more efficient use of the limited time we have with students if we can combine instruction and assessment into one activity. Second, we may reduce the "evaluative" climate in our classroom; you may recall from our discussion in Chapter 12 that external evaluation lowers students' sense of self-determination and may discourage risk taking.

We must recognize, however, that by instructing and assessing students in one fell swoop, we may not be able to standardize the conditions under which students are being assessed, and we will not necessarily see students' best work. Furthermore, although it is quite appropriate to give students assistance or feedback during instruction, it may often be *in*appropriate to do so during a summative evaluation of what they have achieved (L. M. Carey, 1994). In some situations, then, and especially in cases of important summative evaluations, we may want to conduct the assessment separately from instructional activities, announce it in advance, and give students some guidance as to how they can maximize their performance (Stiggins, 1997).

• *Provide an appropriate amount of structure.* We will probably want to structure performance tasks to some degree; for example, we can provide detailed directions about what we want students to accomplish, what materials and equipment they should use, and how we will evaluate their performance (Gronlund, 1993; E. H. Hiebert et al., 1994; Stiggins, 1997). Such structure helps to standardize the

Consider incorporating assessment into instructional activities.

Provide sufficient structure for a performance task to standardize the assessment, but not so much that you reduce the task's authenticity.

assessment and, hence, enables us to evaluate students' performance more reliably. Yet too much structure may reduce the authenticity of a task: It may lessen the extent to which it resembles expectations for performance in the outside world. Ultimately, we must consider both reliability and validity as we determine the appropriate amount of structure to impose in any performance assessment.

• *Plan classroom management strategies for the assessment activity.* As we conduct a performance assessment, we can put into practice two important principles of classroom management presented in Chapter 15: Effective teachers are continually aware of what their students are doing (the notion of *withitness*), and they make sure all students are busy and engaged. Particularly in situations when we must assess only a few students (or perhaps only one) at a time, we must make sure other students are actively involved in a learning activity (L. M. Carey, 1994). For example, in an English class, when one student is giving an oral presentation, we might have the other students jot down notes about the topic being presented, including facts they find interesting, ideas they disagree with, and questions they wonder about. In a unit on soccer, when a few students are demonstrating their ability to dribble and pass the ball as they run down the field, we might have other students work in pairs to practice their footwork.

> Make sure *all* students are busy and engaged throughout an assessment activity.

Scoring Students' Responses

Occasionally, responses to performance assessment tasks are objectively scorable; for example, we can easily count the errors on a typing test or time students' performance in a 100-meter dash. But more often than not, we will find ourselves making somewhat subjective decisions when we use performance assessment. There are no clear-cut right or wrong responses when students give oral reports, create clay sculptures, or engage in heated debates on controversial issues. If we aren't careful, our judgments may be unduly influenced by the particular expectations we hold for each student (L. M. Carey, 1994; Stiggins, 1997).

Especially when we are conducting summative rather than formative evaluations, we should carefully consider the criteria we want to use to evaluate students' responses. Our criteria should focus on the most important aspects of the desired performance—those aspects most essential to a "good" response (Wiggins, 1992). They should also be relatively few in number (perhaps no more than five or six) so that we can keep track of them as we observe each student's performance (Airasian, 1994; Gronlund, 1993; Popham, 1995).

> Can you use the concept of *working memory* (Chapter 6) to explain the value of having only a half dozen criteria?

In many cases, we may want a paper-pencil analysis of how each student has performed with respect to each of our criteria (L. M. Carey, 1994; Gronlund, 1993; Stiggins, 1997). Some tasks lend themselves well to **checklists,** whereby we describe our evaluation criteria in terms of specific qualities that a student's response either does or does not have. Other tasks are more appropriately evaluated with **rating scales,** whereby we describe each criterion as a continuum and determine where the student's response falls along the continuum (see Figure 16–3). Both types of analyses have instructional benefits as well: They identify any specific areas of difficulty for a student and so give feedback about how performance can be improved. Nevertheless, checklists and rating scales are rarely perfect. Whenever we analyze students' performance on a complex task in terms of discrete behaviors, we may lose valuable information in the process (Delandshere & Petrosky, 1998).

> Develop a checklist or rating scale when you are evaluating students' performance with respect to several different criteria.

RSVP Characteristics of Performance Assessment

Compared with paper-pencil assessment, performance assessment techniques are relative newcomers on the educational scene; hence, psychologists are only beginning to

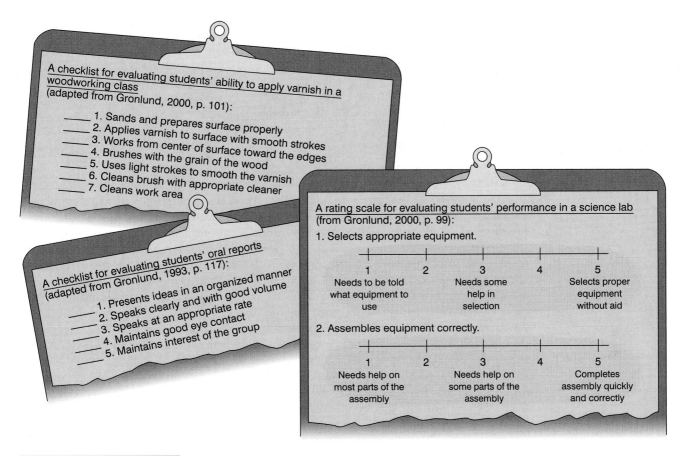

FIGURE 16.3

Examples of checklists and rating scales

address concerns related to reliability, standardization, validity, and practicality. Let's look at the data that researchers report, as well as at strategies for enhancing each of the four RSVP characteristics.

Reliability

Researchers have reported varying degrees of reliability in performance assessments; in many cases, results are inconsistent over time, and different teachers may rate the same performance very differently (S. Burger & Burger, 1994; R. L. Linn, 1994; Shavelson, Baxter, & Pine, 1992; D. B. Swanson et al., 1995). There are probably a couple of reasons why performance assessments often yield low reliability (L. M. Carey, 1994). For one thing, students don't always behave consistently; even in a task as simple as shooting a basketball, a student is likely to make a basket on some occasions but not on others. Second, we sometimes need to evaluate complex behaviors relatively rapidly; things may happen so quickly that we miss important aspects of a student's performance, and we will often have no tangible product to look back on and reevaluate.

Given these limitations, a single performance assessment may very well *not* be a reliable indicator of what our students have achieved. Accordingly, we should ask students to demonstrate behaviors related to important instructional objectives on more than one occasion (Airasian, 1994; L. M. Carey, 1994). And if possible, we should have more than one rater evaluate each student's performance (Stiggins, 1997; R. M. Thorndike, 1997).

Remember that a single performance assessment may not be a reliable indicator of what students have achieved.

663

Refrain from making comparisons among students when a performance assessment isn't standardized for everyone.

Remember that a single performance task may not provide a sufficiently representative sample of the content domain.

Consider whether the benefits of a performance assessment outweigh concerns related to practicality.

Standardization

Some performance assessments are easily standardized, but others are not (Airasian, 1994; E. H. Hiebert et al., 1994). For example, if we want to assess typing ability, we can easily make the instructions, time limits, and material to be typed the same for everyone. In contrast, if we want to assess artistic creativity, we may want to give students free rein with regard to the materials they use and the particular products they create. In such nonstandardized situations, it is especially important to use multiple assessments and look for consistency in students' performance across several occasions.

Validity

As previously noted, performance assessment tasks may sometimes provide more valid indicators of what our students have accomplished relative to instructional objectives. Researchers are finding, however, that students' responses to a *single* performance assessment task are frequently *not* a good indication of their overall achievement (Koretz, Stecher, Klein, & McCaffrey, 1994; R. L. Linn, 1994; Shavelson et al., 1992; D. B. Swanson et al., 1995). *Content validity* is at stake here: If we have time for students to perform only one or two complex tasks, we may not get a sufficiently representative sample of what they have learned and can do. In addition, any biases that affect our judgments (e.g., any beliefs that we have about particular students' abilities) may distort the conclusions we draw from their performance, further reducing the validity of our assessments (Airasian, 1994; L. M. Carey, 1994).

As a general rule, then, we will typically want to administer a variety of different performance assessments, or perhaps administer the same task under different conditions, to ensure a reasonable degree of validity in the conclusions we draw from the behaviors we observe (R. L. Linn, 1994; Messick, 1994; Stiggins, 1997; D. B. Swanson et al., 1995). For efficiency's sake, we may want to incorporate some of these assessment activities into everyday instructional activities (Shavelson & Baxter, 1992).

Practicality

Unfortunately, performance assessments are often less practical than more traditional paper-pencil assessments (L. M. Carey, 1994; Hambleton, 1996; Popham, 1995). For one thing, administration of an assessment can be quite time-consuming; this is especially true when we must observe students one at a time and when we ask them to perform relatively complex (perhaps authentic) tasks. In addition, we will often need equipment to conduct the assessment, perhaps enough that every student has his or her own set. Clearly, then, we must consider whether the benefits of a performance assessment outweigh any concerns we may have regarding its practicality (Messick, 1994; Worthen & Leopold, 1992).

As we've seen, performance assessments are often questionable with regard to reliability and practicality; furthermore, they may give us an insufficient sample of what students have learned. Yet in many situations, they may more closely resemble the long-term objectives we have for our students, and in this sense they may be more valid indicators of students' achievement. As educators gain experience in the use of performance assessment in the years to come, increasingly more valid, reliable, and practical measures of student performance will undoubtedly emerge. In the meantime, the most reliable, valid, and practical assessment strategy overall may be to use *both* paper-pencil and performance assessments when drawing conclusions about what our students have achieved (Gronlund, 1993; R. L. Linn, 1994).

Table 16–3 presents a summary of our RSVP analyses of informal assessment, formal paper-pencil assessment, and formal performance assessment. We now turn our attention to strategies for accommodating student diversity in our assessment practices.

Evaluating Different Kinds of Assessment in Terms of Their RSVP Characteristics

KIND OF ASSESSMENT	RELIABILITY	STANDARDIZATION	VALIDITY	PRACTICALITY
Informal assessment	A single, brief assessment is not a reliable indicator of achievement. We must look for consistency in a student's performance across time and in different contexts.	Informal observations are rarely, if ever, standardized. Thus, we should not compare one student to another on the basis of informal assessment alone.	Students' "public" behavior in the classroom is not always a valid indicator of their achievement (e.g., some may try to hide high achievement from peers).	Informal assessment is definitely practical: It is flexible and can occur spontaneously during instruction.
Formal paper-pencil assessment	Objectively scorable items are highly reliable. We can enhance the reliability of subjectively scorable items by specifying scoring criteria in concrete terms.	In most instances, paper-pencil instruments are easily standardized for all students. Giving students choices (e.g., about topics to write about or questions to answer), although advantageous from a motivational standpoint, reduces standardization.	Numerous questions that require short, simple responses maximize the degree to which the assessment is a representative sample of the content domain. But tasks requiring lengthier responses may sometimes more closely match objectives.	Paper-pencil assessment is usually practical: All students can be assessed at once, and no special materials are required.
Formal performance assessment	It is often difficult to score performance assessment tasks reliably. We can enhance reliability by specifying scoring criteria in concrete terms.	Some performance assessment tasks are easily standardized, whereas others may not be.	Performance tasks may sometimes be more consistent with instructional objectives than paper-pencil tasks. A single performance task may not provide a representative sample of the content domain; several tasks may be necessary to ensure content validity.	Performance assessment is typically less practical than other approaches: It may involve special materials, and it can take a fair amount of classroom time, especially if students must be assessed one at a time.

Taking Student Diversity into Account

As we develop and implement ways to assess learning and achievement, we must remember that students often differ from one another in ways that affect their performance in assessment situations. When two students have *learned equally* yet *perform differently* on our assessments, then the information we obtain from those assessments may have questionable validity. In the next few pages, we will look at the effects of student diversity from three angles:

- Cultural bias
- Language differences
- Testwiseness

We will then consider more specifically how we might adapt our classroom assessment procedures to accommodate students with special needs.

INTO THE CLASSROOM: Using Formal Assessments

Develop classroom assessments that reflect both the topics you want to assess and the things you expect students to do with those topics.

After his class completes a unit on cooking a balanced meal, a teacher develops a table of specifications for the unit. He uses the table to construct paper-pencil questions and performance tasks that reflect his instructional objectives.

Make sure students know what kinds of responses you are expecting.

When assessing her students' knowledge about color vision, a teacher gives students an essay question that indicates what a good response should include: "Describe the two major theories of color vision, explain how they are alike and different from a physiological standpoint, and cite evidence that supports each theory."

Maximize the reliability of your results by specifying your scoring criteria in specific, concrete terms.

When evaluating students' progress in their instrumental music class, a music teacher uses several rating scales (e.g., for pitch, tempo) to help him rate their performance consistently.

When holding some or all students to the same standards for achievement, be sure their assessment tasks are identical or equivalent in content, format, administration, and scoring criteria (making appropriate exceptions for students with disabilities).

When three students are absent on the day of a paper-pencil quiz, their teacher writes an alternative set of questions for them based on the same table of specifications he used in constructing the original quiz.

Choose an assessment procedure that will be as practical as possible without sacrificing reliability and validity.

When trying to decide whether to use paper-pencil or performance assessment at the end of a unit on scientific methods, a teacher realizes that a performance test is the only valid way to assess whether students have mastered the ability to separate and control variables. He identifies three performance tasks that he can administer to the class as a whole and that he believes will adequately reflect their ability to separate and control variables as they test various scientific hypotheses.

Avoid cultural bias in your assessment instruments.

A mathematics teacher creates an assignment in which she asks students to calculate the area of a tennis court. Later, she realizes that some of her students have probably never played tennis. She rewrites the assignment so that it involves a parking lot instead.

Cultural Bias

Experiencing Firsthand
Predicting the Future

Imagine you are taking a test designed to predict your success in future situations. Following are the first three questions on the test:

1. When you enter a hogan, in which direction should you move around the fire?
2. Why is turquoise often attached to a baby's cradleboard?

3. If you need black wool for weaving a rug, how can you obtain the blackest
    color? Choose one of the following:

    a. dye the wool by using a mixture of sumac, ochre, and piñon gum.

    b. dye the wool by using a mixture of indigo, lichen, and mesquite.

    c. use the undyed wool of specially bred black sheep.

Try to answer these questions before you read further.

Did you have trouble answering some or all of the questions? If so, your difficulty was
probably due to the fact that the questions are written from the perspective of a particular culture—that of the Navajos. Unless you have had considerable exposure to Navajo
culture, you would probably perform poorly on the test. By the way, the three answers
are: (1) clockwise; (2) to ward off evil; and (3) dye the wool by using a mixture of sumac,
ochre, and piñon gum (Gilpin, 1968).

Is the test culturally biased? That depends. If the test is designed to assess your ability to succeed in a Navajo community, then the questions may be very appropriate. But
if it's designed to assess your ability to succeed in a school system in which knowledge
of Navajo culture is totally irrelevant, then such questions are culturally biased.

An assessment instrument has **cultural bias** if any of its items either offend or unfairly penalize some students on the basis of their ethnicity, gender, or socioeconomic
status (e.g., Popham, 1995). For example, imagine a test question that implies that
boys are more competent than girls, and imagine another that has a picture in which
members of a particular ethnic group are engaging in criminal behavior. Such questions have cultural bias because some groups of students (girls, in the first situation,
and members of the depicted ethnic group, in the second) may be offended by the
questions and thus distracted from doing their best on the test. And consider these
two assessment tasks:

Task 1:

Would you rather swim in the ocean, a lake, or a swimming pool? Write a two-page
essay defending your choice.

Task 2:

Mary is making a patchwork quilt from 100 separate squares of fabric, like so:

Each square of fabric has a perimeter of 20 inches. Mary sews the squares together,
using a ½-inch seam allowance. She then sews the assembled set of squares to a large
piece of cotton that will serve as the flip side of the quilt, again using a ½-inch seam
allowance. How long is the perimeter of the finished quilt?

▲ Note that the term
cultural bias includes
biases related to gender
and socioeconomic status
as well as to culture.

🍎 Scrutinize your
assessment instruments
carefully for tasks that some
students might find
offensive or have difficulty
answering solely because
of their ethnicity, gender, or
socioeconomic status.

Look again at the treehouse problem depicted in Figure 8–1 (p. 308). Is this problem culturally biased? Why or why not?

When students have little facility with English, minimize your dependence on language to assess knowledge and skills that are not linguistic in nature.

Task 1 will obviously be difficult for students who haven't been swimming in all three environments, and even more difficult for those who haven't ever swum at all; students from low-income families might easily fall into one of these two categories. Task 2 assumes a fair amount of knowledge about sewing (e.g., about what a "seam allowance" is); this is knowledge that some students (especially girls) are more likely to have than others. Such tasks have cultural bias because some students will perform better than others because of differences in their background experiences, *not* because of differences in what they have learned in the classroom.

Language Differences

Students' facility with the English language will certainly affect their performance on classroom assessments. Poor reading and writing skills are likely to interfere with success on paper-pencil tasks; poor speaking skills will adversely influence students' ability to accomplish performance tasks such as classroom debates or oral reports. If we are trying to assess students' achievement in areas unrelated to the language arts—perhaps achievement in mathematics, music, or physical education—then we may in some cases want to minimize our dependence on language to assess those areas.

Testwiseness

Experiencing Firsthand
Califractions

Imagine you are enrolled in a course called Califractions. One day, your instructor gives you a surprise quiz before you've had a chance to do the assigned readings. Three quiz questions follow; see whether you can figure out the correct answers even though you *haven't* studied any califractions. Choose the single best answer for each item.

1. Because they are furstier than other califractions, califors are most often used to
    a. reassignment of matherugs
    b. disbobble a fwing
    c. mangelation
    d. in the burfews
2. Calendation is a process of
    a. combining two califors
    b. adding two califors together
    c. joining two califors
    d. taking two califors apart
3. The furstiest califraction is the
    a. califor
    b. calderost
    c. calinga
    d. calidater

You may have found that you were able to answer the questions even though you knew nothing whatsoever about califractions. Because the first quiz item says ". . . califors are most often used to . . . ," the answer must begin with a verb. Alternatives *a* and *c* apparently begin with nouns ("reassign*ment*" and "mangela*tion*"), and *d* begins with a preposition ("in"), so *b* is the only possible correct answer. Item 2 presents three alternatives (*a, b,* and *c*) that all say the same thing, so, because there can be only one right answer, the correct choice must be *d*. And the answer to Item 3 (the "furstiest califraction") must be *a* (a califor) because Item 1 has already stated that califors are furstier than other califractions.

If you did well on the califractions quiz, then you have some degree of **testwiseness**; that is, you use test-taking strategies that enhance your test performance. Testwiseness includes strategies such as these:

- *Using time efficiently:* for example, allocating enough time for each task and saving difficult items for last
- *Avoiding sloppy errors:* for example, checking answers a second time and erasing any stray pencil marks on a computer-scored answer sheet
- *Deductive reasoning:* for example, eliminating two alternatives that say the same thing and using information from one question to answer another
- *Guessing:* for example, eliminating obviously wrong alternatives and then guessing one of the others, and guessing randomly if time runs out and there is no penalty for guessing
  (Millman, Bishop, & Ebel, 1965; Petersen, Sudweeks, & Baird, 1990)

Even when we find no culturally biased content in our assessment instruments, we must remember that some students may not be familiar with certain types of assessment tasks; for example, students whose prior schooling has occurred within a different culture may be inexperienced in answering true-false, multiple-choice, or essay questions. In some instances, we may be able to make our assessment tasks similar to those with which students have had previous experience. In other situations—perhaps when the school district requests that we give a standardized, multiple-choice achievement test—we should be sure to explain the general nature of the tasks involved (Popham, 1990). For example, we might mention that we don't expect students to know all the answers and point out that many students will not have sufficient time to answer every question. We should also give students ample practice with the forms of any test items or performance tasks we use (Popham, 1990). For example, we might give them some simple multiple-choice tests covering content they know well, and we might give them practice in filling out computer-scored answer forms.

Familiarize students with assessment formats and procedures that are new to them.

The concerns about cultural bias, language differences, and testwiseness we've addressed point to the need for considerable flexibility in our approaches to classroom assessment; they also underscore the importance of assessing students' achievement in a variety of ways, rather than overly depending on a single instrument (Baek, 1994; Drake, 1993; C. Hill & Larsen, 1992). Ultimately, our assessment practices should be fair and equitable for *all* students, regardless of their ethnicity, gender, or socioeconomic status.

Accommodating Students with Special Needs

In some situations, we will have to adapt our classroom assessment instruments to accommodate students with special educational needs. For example, we may need to read paper-pencil test questions to students with limited reading skills (e.g., as is characteristic of some students with learning disabilities). We may need to break a lengthy assessment task into a number of shorter tasks for students with a limited attention span (e.g., for some students with ADHD or emotional and behavioral disorders). And we may have to devise individualized assessment instruments when we have different instructional objectives for some of our students with special needs (e.g., as may often be the case for students with mental retardation). Additional accommodations for students with special needs are presented in Table 16–4.

TABLE 16.4   **STUDENTS IN INCLUSIVE SETTINGS**

Assessing Classroom Achievement in Students with Special Educational Needs

STUDENTS WITH SPECIAL NEEDS	CHARACTERISTICS THAT THESE STUDENTS MAY EXHIBIT	CLASSROOM STRATEGIES THAT MAY BE BENEFICIAL FOR THESE STUDENTS
Students with specific cognitive or academic difficulties	Difficulty processing specific kinds of information Poor listening, reading, and/or writing skills Possibly inconsistent performance on classroom assessments due to off-task behaviors (e.g., hyperactivity, inattentiveness)	Look at students' errors for clues about processing difficulties. Make sure students understand what you are asking them to do. Minimize reliance on reading and/or writing skills. Provide extra time to complete assessments. Be sure students are motivated to do their best but are not overly anxious. Use informal assessments either to confirm or disconfirm results of formal assessments.
Students with social or behavioral problems	In some cases, inconsistent performance on classroom assessments due to off-task behaviors or lack of motivation	Be sure students are motivated to do their best but are not overly anxious. Use informal assessments either to confirm or disconfirm results of formal assessments.
Students with general delays in cognitive and social functioning	Slow learning and information processing Limited if any reading skills Poor listening skills	Make sure students understand what you are asking them to do. Make sure any reading materials are appropriate for students' reading level. Use performance assessments that require little reading or writing. Allow sufficient time for students to complete assigned tasks.
Students with physical or sensory challenges	Mobility problems (for some students with physical challenges) Tendency to tire easily (for some students with physical challenges) Less developed language abilities (for some students with hearing loss)	Provide extra time to complete assessments. Break lengthy assessments into segments that can be administered on separate occasions. Use simple language if students have language difficulties.
Students with advanced cognitive development	Greater ability to perform exceptionally complex tasks Unusual, sometimes creative, responses to classroom assessment instruments Tendency in some students to hide giftedness to avoid possible ridicule by peers (e.g., African American students may fear that they will be "acting White" if they demonstrate high performance)	Use performance assessments to assess complex activities. Establish criteria for "correct" responses that allow unusual and creative responses. Provide opportunities for students to demonstrate their achievements privately. Keep assessment results confidential.

Sources: Bassett et al., 1996; DeLisle, 1984; Eccles, 1989; Ford & Harris, 1992; Maker & Schiever, 1989; Mercer, 1991; Morgan & Jenson, 1988; Patton et al., 1990; Phillips et al., 1980; Piirto, 1994; Scarcella, 1990; Turnbull et al., 1999; Udall, 1989.

Note: Compiled with the assistance of Dr. Margie Garanzini-Daiber and Dr. Margaret Cohen, University of Missouri—St. Louis.

Whenever we modify our classroom assessment instruments for students with special needs, we must recognize that there is a trade-off between two of our RSVP characteristics. On the one hand, we are violating the idea that an assessment instrument should be equivalent in content, administration, and so on, for everyone—the idea that assessment should be standardized. On the other hand, if we fail to accommodate the particular disabilities that some of our students may have, we will inevitably obtain results that have little or no meaning—results with little validity regarding the knowledge and skills that our students have acquired. There is no magic formula for determining a reasonable balance between standardization and validity for students with special needs; as teachers, we must use our best professional judgment in each and every case.

Summarizing Students' Achievement

Many of our assessments will provide a considerable amount of information regarding students' strengths and weaknesses—information that we must eventually boil down into more general indicators of what our students have learned. Initially, we may simply want to determine *test scores* that reflect the overall quality of students' responses on either a paper-pencil or performance assessment. Eventually, we will need to summarize what they have achieved over the course of the semester or school year, perhaps through *final class grades* or *portfolios*. But regardless of how we summarize and report students' achievement, we must maintain *confidentiality* regarding our assessments. We turn to each of these topics now.

Assigning Test Scores

THINKING ABOUT WHAT YOU KNOW

In what different ways has your own performance on classroom assessments been summarized? How often has it been described in terms of the number or percentage of items you answered correctly? How often has it been described in terms of a percentile rank that told you how you compared with your peers? What other kinds of scores have you received? Have you ever had trouble figuring out just what a particular test score meant?

Students' performance on a particular assessment is often summarized in terms of a single *test score.* These scores typically take one of three forms: raw scores, criterion-referenced scores, and norm-referenced scores.

Raw Scores

Sometimes a test score is simply the number or percentage of tasks or questions to which a student has responded correctly. Sometimes it is the sum of all the points a student has earned—two points for one task, five for another, and so on. In situations such as these, we have a **raw score**, a score based solely on the number or point value of correct responses.

Raw scores are easy to calculate, and they appear to be easy to understand. But in fact, we sometimes have trouble knowing what raw scores really mean. For example, is 75 percent a good score or a bad one? Without knowing what kinds of tasks an assessment instrument includes or how other students have performed on the same assessment, there is no way to determine how good or bad a score of 75 percent really is. For this reason, raw scores are not always as useful as criterion-referenced or norm-referenced scores.

Use raw scores only when their meaning is easily understood.

Criterion-Referenced Scores

A **criterion-referenced score** tells us what students have achieved in relation to specific instructional objectives. Many criterion-referenced scores are "either-or" scores: They indicate that a student has passed or failed a unit, mastered or not mastered a skill, or met or not met an objective. Others indicate various levels of competence or achievement. For example, a criterion-referenced score on a fifth-grade test of written composition might reflect four levels of writing ability, three of which reflect mastery of essential writing skills, as follows:

In progress: Is an underdeveloped and/or unfocused message.

Essential: Is a series of related ideas. The pattern of organization and the descriptive or supporting details are adequate and appropriate.

Proficient: Meets Essential Level criteria and contains a logical progression of ideas. The pattern of organization and the transition of ideas flow. Word choice enhances the writing.

Advanced: Meets Proficient Level criteria and contains examples of one or more of the following: insight, creativity, fluency, critical thinking, or style. (adapted from "District 6 Writing Assessment, Narrative and Persuasive Modes, Scoring Criteria, Intermediate Level" [Working Copy] by School District 6 [Greeley/Evans, CO], 1993; adapted by permission)

If a particular assessment instrument is designed to assess only one instructional objective, then it may yield a single score. If it is designed to assess several objectives simultaneously, a student's performance may be reported as a checklist of the various objectives passed and not passed. As an example, a student's performance in a swimming class is often reported in a multiple-objective, criterion-referenced fashion (see Figure 16–4).

We will often want to use a criterion-referenced approach to summarize what our students have learned. Only through criterion-referenced assessment can we determine what specific objectives they have attained, what particular skills they have mastered, and where their individual weaknesses lie.

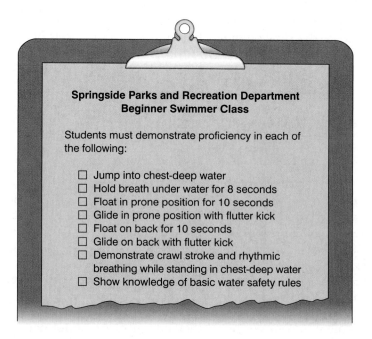

**Springside Parks and Recreation Department
Beginner Swimmer Class**

Students must demonstrate proficiency in each of the following:

☐ Jump into chest-deep water
☐ Hold breath under water for 8 seconds
☐ Float in prone position for 10 seconds
☐ Glide in prone position with flutter kick
☐ Float on back for 10 seconds
☐ Glide on back with flutter kick
☐ Demonstrate crawl stroke and rhythmic
   breathing while standing in chest-deep water
☐ Show knowledge of basic water safety rules

FIGURE 16.4

In this swimming class, students' performance is reported in a criterion-referenced fashion.

Norm-Referenced Scores

A **norm-referenced score** is derived by comparing a student's performance on an assessment task with the performance of other students (perhaps that of classmates or that of a nationwide *norm group*) on the same task. Rather than tell us specifically what a student has or has not learned, such a score tells us how well the student stacks up against others at the same age or grade level.

Norm-referenced scores are frequently used to report the results of standardized tests, and the norm group to which students are compared is often a large, national sample of students who have previously taken the same test. Norm-referenced scores for standardized tests take a number of different forms; some of the most common ones are described in Appendix C, "Interpreting Standardized Test Scores."

When we assign norm-referenced scores on our own teacher-developed assessments, the norm group is likely to be all the students we have in class at the present time: We give high scores to students who exhibit the best performance and low scores to students who, comparatively speaking, perform poorly. To use common lingo, we are "grading on the curve."

For teacher-developed assessments, norm-referenced scores may occasionally be appropriate. For example, such comparative scores may be necessary when designating "first chair" in an instrumental music class or choosing the best entries for a regional science fair. We may also need to resort to a norm-referenced approach when assessing complex skills that are difficult to describe in "mastery" terms (Gronlund & Linn, 1990). Some complex tasks—for example, writing poetry, demonstrating advanced athletic skills, or critically analyzing works of literature—can sometimes be evaluated more easily by comparing students with one another than by specifying an absolute level of accomplishment.

We should probably *not* assign norm-referenced test scores on a regular basis, however. For one thing, such scores tell us little about what we most need to know—whether our students have mastered our instructional objectives. Second, as we discovered in Chapter 12, competitive situations create many more losers than winners; such situations are likely to undermine students' self-efficacy, hence also undermining their intrinsic motivation to learn classroom material. And finally, norm-referenced scores are inconsistent with the *sense of community* discussed in Chapter 15.

Whenever we assign scores to students' performance on classroom assessments, we must also remember the important feedback function that such assessments serve. Accordingly, we should always accompany our test scores with specific, concrete feedback about the strengths and weaknesses of students' responses, as well as with suggestions that can help them improve over the long run.

Use norm-referenced scores only when you truly need to compare your students with one another.

Some educators believe that classroom assessment scores should *always* be criterion-referenced rather than norm-referenced. What do you think?

How do you feel when, as a student, you receive a low test score without any feedback about how you might improve?

Determining Final Class Grades

Teachers' grading practices have been a source of considerable controversy among educators. Fueling the controversy are several problems inherent in our attempts to assign final grades to students' achievement. First, to the extent that our individual assessment instruments have less than perfect validity and reliability, grades based on these measures also suffer from a certain degree of inaccuracy. Second, different teachers use different criteria to assign grades; for instance, some are more lenient than others, and some stress rote memorization, whereas others stress application. When an A in Ms. Peterson's geography class means something different from an A in Ms. Montgomery's geography class, we can't compare the performance of those two groups of students. A third problem is that typical grading practices promote performance goals rather than learning goals (see Chapter 12) and encourage students to go for the "easy A" rather than take risks (Stipek, 1993; S. Thomas & Oldfather, 1997). Finally, students under pressure to achieve high grades may resort to undesirable behaviors (e.g., cheating, plagiarism) to attain those grades.

Despite such problems, final grades continue to be the most common method of summarizing students' overall classroom achievement. As teachers, we must take steps to ensure that the grades we assign are as accurate a reflection of what each student has accomplished as we can possibly make them. We are most likely to do so when we:

- *Take the job of grading seriously.* Consider these scenarios:

A high school mathematics teacher who uses a formula to determine final grades makes numerous mathematical errors in his calculations. As a result, some students get lower grades than they've earned.

A middle school Spanish teacher asks her adolescent son to calculate her grades for her. Some of the columns in her grade book are for test scores that students have obtained when they've taken a test a second time to improve their record; students who did well on exams the first time have a blank in these columns. Not understanding the teacher's system, her son treats all blank spaces as a "zero." The highest achievers—those students who have many blank spots in the teacher's grade book—are quite surprised to find that they've earned Ds and Fs for the semester.

A mathematics teacher who makes mathematical errors? A Spanish teacher who relies on a teenager to determine final grades? Preposterous? No—both cases are true stories. Here we have teachers who assign grades that are totally meaningless. Students' final class grades are often the only data that appear in their school records. We must take the time and make the effort to ensure that those grades are accurate.

- *Base grades on hard data.* Subjective teacher judgments do correlate with actual student achievement, but they are imperfect assessments at best, and some teachers are better judges than others (Gaines & Davis, 1990; Hoge & Coladarci, 1989). Furthermore, although teachers can generally judge the achievement of high-ability students with some degree of accuracy, they are less accurate when they subjectively assess the achievement of low-ability students (Hoge & Coladarci, 1989). Teachers are especially likely to underestimate the achievement of students from minority groups and those from low socioeconomic backgrounds (Gaines & Davis, 1990). For these reasons and for the sake of our students (who learn more and achieve at higher levels when we tell them in concrete terms what we expect of them), we should base grades on objective and observable information derived from formal assessment instruments.

- *Be selective about the assessments used to determine grades.* Remember, no single source of information about students' achievement can be perfectly reliable and valid: Scores from some assessment instruments may be higher than they should be, and others may underestimate what students have actually learned. By combining scores from multiple assessments, we are likely to balance out the various measurement errors to some extent, thereby getting a reasonably accurate reflection of what each student has learned. An additional advantage in using numerous sources of data to determine final grades is that, with the pressure off to perform well on every single test and assignment, students are less likely to cheat to obtain good grades (E. D. Evans & Craig, 1990).

At the same time, we probably don't want to grade everything our students do. We have noted in previous chapters that, to maximize students' learning, we must provide an atmosphere in which students feel free to take risks and make mistakes. Thus, we may not want to consider students' initial efforts at new tasks, which are likely to involve some trial and error on their part (Canady & Hotchkiss, 1989). Many assessments may be more appropriately used for formative evaluation purposes—to help students learn—than for summative evaluation (Frisbie & Waltman, 1992).

What are students likely to conclude about these two teachers?

Make sure your calculations are accurate.

Base grades on objective and observable data, rather than on subjective impressions.

Use many sources of data to determine grades, but don't grade everything.

- *Identify a reasonable grading system and stick to it.* Consider this situation:

Ms. Gurney tells her middle school students that class grades will be based solely on quiz and test scores throughout the semester. After a couple of months, she realizes that most students are struggling with her exams and will probably get Ds or Fs as a result. So near the end of the semester, she asks students to turn in all their homework assignments; completed assignments will contribute 20 percent to students' final grades. Believing that she is being quite generous, she is surprised when her students protest loudly and angrily. Many of them, thinking that there was no reason to keep previous homework assignments, have already discarded them.

If most students are getting Ds and Fs, something is definitely wrong. Perhaps Ms. Gurney didn't take students' prior knowledge into account when she chose a starting point for instruction. Perhaps she's moving too quickly through the curriculum and so students never achieve mastery of a topic. Perhaps her instructional methods aren't as effective as other approaches might be. Perhaps her quizzes and tests are unnecessarily difficult (and therefore invalid) measures of what students are learning.

As teachers, we can't always anticipate how best to teach a new topic or how well our students will perform on our classroom assessment instruments. Nevertheless, if we want to give our students a sense that they have some control over the grades that they receive (recall Chapter 12's discussion of attribution theory), we must tell them early in the semester or school year what our grading criteria will be. If we find that our criteria are overly stringent, we may need to "lighten up" in some way, perhaps by adjusting cutoffs or by allowing retakes of critical assessments. But we must never change our criteria midstream in a way that unfairly penalizes some students or imposes additional expectations on them.

Tell students well in advance what the grading criteria will be.

Considering Improvement, Effort, and Extra Credit

Our discussion so far has been based on the assumption that class grades should reflect students' achievement of instructional objectives. Yet some educators suggest that students be graded on the basis of how much they improve, how hard they try, or how much extra work they do (e.g., Kane, 1983). Let's consider the implications of incorporating each of these factors into the grades we assign.

Grading improvement. There are at least two good arguments against basing final grades solely on students' improvement over the course of a semester or school year. Some students may come to the first day of class already possessing some of the knowledge and skills in the curriculum we've planned; there may be little room for them to improve if they've already mastered some of the topics they will be studying. Furthermore, when we use improvement as a criterion, students trying to "beat the system" may quickly learn that they can achieve high grades simply by performing as poorly as possible at the beginning of the year (Airasian, 1994; Sax, 1989).

Yet in our discussion of promoting self-efficacy and intrinsic motivation in Chapter 12, we noted the importance of focusing students' attention on their own improvement, rather than on how their performance compares with that of their classmates. One reasonable compromise is to assign greater weight to assessments conducted at the end of the semester or school year, after *all* students have had a reasonable opportunity to achieve instructional objectives (Lester et al., 1997). Another strategy is to use an approach similar to the *mastery reform* described earlier in the chapter: Students who initially receive low scores on certain assessments can replace those scores with higher ones after they demonstrate mastery of the objectives in question.

Consider improvement provided that final grades reflect students' actual achievement levels.

Grading effort. Most assessment experts recommend that we *not* base final grades on the amount of effort that students exert in the classroom. For one thing, students who begin the year already performing at a high level are penalized because they may not have to work as hard as their less knowledgeable classmates. Furthermore, "effort"

🍎 If you want to evaluate students' effort during the school year, evaluate it separately from achievement.

🍎 Be sure that any extra credit assignments relate to instructional objectives, and make them available to all students.

◻ Have you ever known a student who did little work all semester but was able to pull off a passing grade by doing an extra-credit project? Would such a student "learn a lesson" and develop more regular study habits over the long run? Why or why not?

🍎 Assign criterion-referenced grades unless there is a compelling reason to do otherwise.

is something that we can evaluate only subjectively and imprecisely at best (Sax, 1989; Stiggins, 1997).

When we want to communicate our impressions of students' effort in the classroom, we should do so separately from their achievement. For instance, some school systems have multidimensional grading systems that will allow us to assign separate grades to the various aspects of students' classroom performance (Popham, 1990). And such mechanisms as letters to parents, parent-teacher conferences, and letters of recommendation provide an additional means by which we can describe the multifaceted nature of students' classroom performance.

Giving extra credit. Every year, two or three of my students appear at my office door, asking, sometimes begging, for an opportunity to improve their grades by completing extra credit projects. Usually these students are failing one of my courses and are desperately trying to save their grade point average. My response to them is invariably no, and for a very good reason: My course grades are based on the extent to which students achieve my instructional objectives, as determined by their performance on tests and assignments that are the same or equivalent (therefore standardized and fair) for all students. Extra credit projects assigned to only a handful of students—typically those achieving at the lowest levels—neither meet my objectives nor are standardized for the entire class.

Certainly, we can consider some extra credit work as we assign grades, provided that the work relates to classroom objectives and all students are given the same opportunity to do it. But incorporating extra credit into final evaluations is not the most appropriate way to help a failing student—one who has not met course objectives—achieve a passing grade.

Choosing Criterion-Referenced or Norm-Referenced Grades

Many theorists and practitioners recommend that, as a general rule, the final grades we assign should reflect mastery of classroom subject matter and instructional objectives; in other words, our grades should be *criterion-referenced* (e.g., Stiggins, 1997; Terwilliger, 1989). Criterion-referenced grades are especially appropriate during the elementary years: Much of the elementary curriculum consists of basic skills that are either mastered or not mastered, and there is little need to use grades as a basis for comparing students to one another.

The issue becomes more complicated at the secondary level: Students' grades are sometimes used as indicators of achievement, but at other times they are used for comparative purposes—to choose college applicants, award scholarships, and so on. My personal recommendation is that high school grades be criterion-referenced to the extent that such is possible. For one thing, the most critical decisions for which grades are used—decisions about promotion and graduation—should be based on students' mastery or nonmastery of the school curriculum, not on their standing relative to others. Second, different classes of students often differ in ability level; if grading were strictly norm-referenced, then a student's performance in one class (e.g., honors math) might be graded as C, whereas the same performance in another class (e.g., general math) might warrant an A. (Under such circumstances, a student striving for a high grade point average would be a fool to enroll in the honors section.) And finally, only a very few students (the highest achievers) find a norm-referenced grading system motivating; most students quickly resign themselves to achieving at an average level at best (e.g., Wlodkowski, 1978).

When we set up a criterion-referenced grading system, we must decide as concretely as possible what we want each grade to communicate in terms of students' achievement. For example, if we are using traditional "ABCDF" grades, we might consider the letters to have meanings such as the following:

A portfolio of a student's work provides a way of summarizing the student's progress and achievements over a period of time.

A: The student has a firm command of both basic and advanced knowledge and skills in the content domain. He or she is well prepared for future learning tasks.

B: The student has mastered all basic knowledge and skills; mastery at a more advanced level is evident in some, but not all, areas. In most respects, he or she is ready for future learning tasks.

C: The student has mastered basic knowledge and skills but has difficulty with more advanced aspects of the subject matter. He or she lacks a few of the prerequisites critical for future learning tasks.

D: The student has mastered some but not all of the basics in the content domain. He or she lacks many prerequisites for future learning tasks.

F: The student shows little if any mastery of instructional objectives and cannot demonstrate the most elementary knowledge and skills. He or she lacks most of the prerequisites essential for success in future learning tasks. (based on criteria described by Frisbie & Waltman, 1992)

It can be quite a challenge to summarize students' many achievements in terms of a single class grade, and we inevitably lose a great deal of information in the process (Delandshere & Petrosky, 1998). Hence, some educators advocate that we communicate what students have achieved through other techniques that reflect the multifaceted nature of students' accomplishments. One strategy now gaining wide acceptance is the use of *portfolios.*

Using Portfolios

A **portfolio** is a systematic collection of a student's work over a lengthy period of time. For example, students might collect examples of their essays, poems, or artwork. A portfolio need not be limited to products that can be represented on paper; it might also include audiotapes, videotapes, or objects that the student has created.

Some portfolios are "developmental" in nature: Various products are included to show how a student has improved over a period of time. Others may include only the student's best work as a reflection of his or her final achievement (Spandel, 1997; Winograd & Jones, 1992).

Advocates of portfolios have offered several suggestions for using portfolios effectively:

- *Consider the specific purpose for which a portfolio will be used.* Different kinds of portfolios are useful for different purposes. Developmental portfolios, which include products from throughout the school year or perhaps from an even longer period of time, are most useful when we want to see whether our students are making reasonable progress toward long-term instructional objectives. Such portfolios are also invaluable for showing students *themselves* how much they've improved. In contrast, "best work" portfolios are more useful for summarizing students' final achievement, perhaps as a way of communicating students' accomplishments to parents, students' future teachers, or college admissions officers (Spandel, 1997).

- *Involve students in the selection of a portfolio's contents.* In most situations, students should decide for themselves which products to include in their portfolios (F. L. Paulson, Paulson, & Meyer, 1991; Popham, 1995; Spandel, 1997). Such practice allows them to have "ownership" of their portfolios and, as a result, can enhance their sense of self-determination and their intrinsic motivation to learn.

At the same time, we must give our students the scaffolding they need to make appropriate choices. One effective way of doing so is to schedule periodic conferences with each student in which we jointly discuss the products that best reflect his or her achievements (Popham, 1995). (My son Jeff's middle school advisor also included parents in such conferences—an excellent strategy for fostering a three-way communication among teacher, student, and parents.) We might also want to provide examples of portfolios that other students have created; however, we should do so only if those students and their parents have given permission or if a portfolio's creator can remain confidential (F. L. Paulson et al., 1991; Stiggins, 1997).

- *Identify the criteria by which products should be selected and evaluated.* As a way of providing additional guidance, it is essential that we identify both the criteria that students should use to make their selections and, if applicable, the criteria by which the entire portfolio will eventually be evaluated (Popham, 1995; Spandel, 1997; Stiggins, 1997). In some instances, we may want to include our students in the process of identifying these criteria (Popham, 1995). Such a strategy further enhances their sense of self-determination; it can also enhance their understanding of the qualities that are most important in future projects and assignments.

- *Encourage students to reflect on the products they include.* In addition to examples of students' work, many portfolios also include documentation that describes each product and the reason why it was included (Spandel, 1997; Stiggins, 1997). As an example, consider how a student in a creative writing class might explain the selection of two short stories for his portfolio:

> I wrote this first short story last October. It was my first attempt at creative writing. It includes a conflict, a protagonist and antagonist, a climax, and a final resolution. The basic elements of a story are there, but the main characters aren't developed very much. Also, I don't think the ending is likely to happen in real life.

> I wrote this second story in April. It is definitely better than the one I wrote in October. It has more characters, and each one has a personality. The first part of the story foreshadows some of the things that happen later on. The sequence of events is more realistic. It's not a case where everyone lives happily ever after.

Such documentation encourages students to reflect on and judge their own work in ways that we, as teachers, typically do (Airasian, 1994; Arter & Spandel, 1992; Popham,

1995). Thus, it is likely to promote the self-monitoring and self-evaluation skills that social cognitive theorists advocate; in other words, it will help them develop the self-regulatory capabilities so essential for their long-term success.

Using portfolios has a couple of advantages (C. Hill & Larsen, 1992; F. L. Paulson et al., 1991; Popham, 1995; Spandel, 1997). First, portfolios capture the complex nature of students' achievement, often over a prolonged period of time, in ways that single letter grades can't possibly do. Furthermore, they provide a mechanism through which we can easily intertwine assessment with instruction: Students are likely to include products that we may have assigned primarily for instructional purposes, and they will begin to apply fairly objective criteria when evaluating their own work. In fact, portfolios sometimes influence the very nature of the instruction that takes place; because the focus is on complex skills, teachers may be more likely to *teach* those skills (Koretz et al., 1994).

At the same time, we should note that our RSVP characteristics may be sources of concern. For one thing, when portfolios must be scored in some way, such scoring is often unreliable: There may be little agreement among teachers as to how any particular portfolio should be rated (Koretz et al., 1994; Popham, 1995). Furthermore, we have an obvious standardization problem: Because each portfolio will include a unique set of products, we will be evaluating each student on the basis of different information. We must consider a possible problem with validity as well: A portfolio must include a sufficient number of work samples to provide a representative sample of what our students have accomplished related to our instructional objectives (Arter & Spandel, 1992; Koretz et al., 1994). Last but not least, we must realize that portfolios, if used properly, are likely to take a great deal of a teacher's time, both during class and after hours (Airasian, 1994; Koretz et al., 1994; Popham, 1995); in this sense at least, they are less practical than other methods of summarizing achievement might be. All this is not to say that we should shy away from using portfolios. It *is* to say that we must use them cautiously when they serve as summative evaluations of what our students have accomplished.

Keeping Assessment Results Confidential

■ THINKING ABOUT WHAT YOU KNOW

Recall one or more occasions when your classmates knew exactly how you performed on a classroom assessment. Did you suffer any negative repercussions after your assessment results leaked out?

Regardless of how we summarize students' achievement—whether through test scores, final grades, portfolios, or some other means—we should keep such summaries *confidential,* known only to ourselves, individual students, their parents, and any school officials who reasonably need to be aware of students' assessment results. In some countries, such confidentiality is mandated by federal legislation: It is actually illegal to share students' test scores, grades, and school records with other students or with the general public.[4]

Keeping students' assessment results confidential makes educational as well as legal sense. Students may feel embarrassed or ashamed if their classmates are aware of their low test scores and grades, and they may become even more anxious about their future classroom performance than they would be otherwise. Students with high assessment

Use portfolios as a way of capturing the complex nature of students' achievement. Use them also as a means of integrating assessment with instruction.

Keep in mind the limitations of portfolios with respect to the RSVP characteristics.

Keep assessment results confidential.

---

[4]In the United States, the relevant legislation is the *Family Educational Rights and Privacy Act* (FERPA). This legislation, also known as the Buckley Amendment, was passed by the United States Congress in 1974.

INTO THE CLASSROOM: Summarizing Students' Achievement

Base final grades on objective and observable data.

Carolyn always sits passively at the back of the classroom and never contributes to class discussions. Her teacher is surprised when she earns high scores on his first two classroom tests. He eventually realizes that, despite her lack of class participation, Carolyn is definitely achieving his instructional objectives and so grades her accordingly.

Use as many sources of data as is reasonably possible to determine grades.

When determining semester grades, a teacher considers her students' performance on five paper-pencil tests, three formal performance assessments, a research paper, and numerous smaller assignments.

Don't count everything.

A teacher frequently assigns homework as a way of encouraging students to practice new skills. He gives students feedback on their work but does not consider these assignments when determining course grades.

Evaluate actual achievement separately from such other factors as effort, improvement, and extra-credit projects.

At a parent-teacher conference, a teacher describes Stan's performance this way: "Stan has gotten all Bs and Cs this term—grades that indicate adequate but not exceptional achievement. I have noticed a great deal of inconsistency in his classroom performance. When he puts forth the effort, he learns class material quite well; otherwise, he does poorly."

Assign criterion-referenced grades unless there is a compelling reason to do otherwise.

A teacher assigns criterion-referenced grades for Algebra I, knowing that those grades will be used by school counselors to determine an appropriate math class for each student next year.

Use portfolios to summarize students' accomplishment of complex, multifaceted tasks.

A teacher has students develop portfolios of their fiction and nonfiction writing. These portfolios are shared with parents at the end of the school year as a way of documenting students' mastery of some writing skills and progress on others.

Keep all assessment results confidential.

When handing back students' test papers, a teacher gives each test directly to its owner, folding the upper corner of the top sheet so that the test score cannot be seen by classmates.

scores may suffer from the revelation of these scores as well: In many classrooms, it isn't "cool" to be smart, and high achievers may actually perform at lower levels to avoid risking the rejection of their peers.

The Big Picture: Keeping Classroom Assessment in Perspective

As should be evident by now, there is no way we can reasonably separate assessment from planning and instruction. Our assessment tasks must reflect the specific objectives

Because no assessment instrument has perfect reliability or validity, we should never take the results of any single assessment too seriously.

we identified when we developed our lesson plans. Furthermore, classroom assessments often have instructional value in and of themselves. Regular assessment provides an opportunity for students to review, practice, and apply the things they have learned in the classroom; it also provides valuable feedback to both us and our students as to the next best steps to take—whether to spend more time on the same topics or to proceed to new ones, whether to stick with the instructional strategies we've been using or try different approaches, and so on. And the very nature of our assessment tasks affects both the things that students believe are most important to learn and the ways in which they study and process information.

As we have seen, the usefulness of various assessment techniques depends on how well matched they are to the situations in which we want to use them and how reliable and valid they are for those situations. Because no assessment instrument ever has perfect reliability or validity, we should never take the results of any single assessment too seriously. Nor should we interpret our assessment results as an indication that some students are permanently low-achieving or incapable. For the most part, we should think of our classroom assessment instruments as tools that can help us improve classroom instruction and maximize students' learning and achievement.

Think of classroom assessments primarily as tools that can help you improve classroom instruction and student performance.

CASE STUDY: Pick and Choose

Knowing that frequent review of class material leads to higher achievement and that a paper-pencil test is one way of providing such review, Mr. Bloskas tells his middle school science students that they will have a quiz every Friday. As a first-year teacher, he has had little experience developing test questions, so he decides to use the questions in the "test bank" that accompanies the class textbook. The night before the first quiz, Mr. Bloskas types thirty multiple-choice and true-false items from the test bank, making sure they cover the specific topics that he has covered in class.

(continued)

His students complain that the questions are "picky." As he looks carefully at his quiz, he realizes that his students are right: The quiz measures nothing more than rote memorization of trivial details. So when he prepares the second quiz, Mr. Bloskas casts the test bank aside and writes two essay questions asking students to apply scientific principles they have studied to real-life situations. He's proud of his efforts: His quiz clearly measures higher-level thinking skills.

The following Friday, his students complain even more loudly about the second quiz than they had about the first ("This is too hard!" "We never studied this stuff!" "I liked the first quiz better!"). And as Mr. Bloskas scores his students' essays, he is appalled to discover how poorly they have performed. "Back to the test bank," he tells himself.

- What mistakes does Mr. Bloskas make in developing the first quiz? What mistakes does he make in developing the second quiz? To what extent is each quiz likely to have content validity?

- Why do the students react as negatively as they do to the second quiz?

Summing Up

Assessment and Its Purposes

Assessment is a process of observing a sample of students' behavior and drawing inferences about their knowledge and abilities. On some occasions, we will use assessment primarily to facilitate students' future learning and perhaps to promote greater self-regulation. In other situations, we will use assessment to determine whether students have achieved our instructional objectives. Regardless of our primary purpose in assessing students' achievement, we must remember that the nature of our assessment instruments—for example, whether they measure lower-level or higher-level skills—will give students messages about what things are most important for them to learn and about how they should study and process information in the future.

Characteristics of Good Assessment

We should keep four "RSVP" characteristics in mind as we develop our classroom assessment strategies. First, an assessment instrument should be *reliable,* yielding consistent results regardless of the circumstances in which we administer and score it. Second, it should be *standardized,* in the sense that it has similar content and is administered and scored in a similar manner for everyone. Third, it should be *valid,* being an accurate reflection of the knowledge or skills we are trying to assess. And finally, it should be *practical,* staying within reasonable costs and time constraints.

Informal Versus Formal Assessment

As teachers, we may sometimes assess achievement in relatively informal ways, perhaps simply by observing what students do

and listening to what they say. At other times, we will assess achievement more formally, through either paper-pencil or performance-based instruments we have developed ahead of time. Whenever we must draw firm conclusions about what our students have and have not achieved—for example, when we are assigning final grades—we should base those conclusions largely on formal assessments that have some degree of validity and reliability. Especially important in this context is *content validity:* Our assessment tasks should provide a representative sample of what students have accomplished relative to our instructional objectives.

Accommodating Student Diversity

Students often differ from one another in ways that affect their performance on assessment tasks. Two students may have acquired identical knowledge and skills and yet perform differently on a classroom assessment—perhaps because they have difficulties in reading, writing, or processing certain kinds of information (e.g., as might be the case for a student with a learning disability) or perhaps because our assessment instrument is culturally biased. Whenever we suspect that such factors may be impeding students' performance, we should interpret our assessment results cautiously and look for other information that might either confirm or disconfirm those results.

Summarizing Students' Achievement

We will probably need to boil down the results of our assessments into more general indicators of what students have learned. Initially, we will simply want to determine test scores that reflect the overall quality of students' responses on either a paper-pencil or performance assessment. Such scores will usually have more meaning when they are either criterion-referenced (when they indicate whether certain objectives have been met) or, in some situations, norm-referenced (when they indicate how each student's performance compares with that of others). Eventually, we will also need to summarize what students have achieved over the course of the semester or school year, perhaps through final grades or portfolios. Ultimately, we must think of classroom assessment as an ongoing strategy that can help us maximize students' learning and achievement.

Key Concepts

assessment (p. 634)

standardized test versus teacher-developed assessment instrument (p. 635)

norms (p. 635)

paper-pencil versus performance assessment (p. 635)

traditional versus authentic assessment (p. 636)

informal versus formal assessment (p. 636)

formative versus summative evaluation (p. 637)

reliability (p. 642)

standardization (p. 644)

validity (p. 645)

construct validity (p. 646)

predictive validity (p. 646)

content validity (p. 646)

practicality (p. 646)

halo effect (p. 648)

table of specifications (p. 651)

recognition task (p. 654)

recall task (p. 654)

test anxiety (p. 655)

dynamic assessment (p. 659)

checklist (p. 662)

rating scale (p. 662)

cultural bias (p. 667)

testwiseness (p. 669)

raw score (p. 671)

criterion-referenced score (p. 672)

norm-referenced score (p. 673)

portfolio (p. 677)

The Seven Themes of the Book

Appendix A

CHAPTER	INTERACTION	COGNITIVE PROCESSES	RELEVANCE	CLASSROOM CLIMATE	CHALLENGE	EXPECTATIONS	DIVERSITY
Chapter 2: Cognitive and Linguistic Development	In Piaget's theory, interaction with the physical and social environments promotes cognitive development. In Vygotsky's theory, children work with more advanced individuals to accomplish tasks within their zone of proximal development.	In Piaget's theory, children construct knowledge of the world through assimilation and accommodation. According to Vygotsky, children acquire cognitive processes by internalizing their interactions with others. Information processing theorists study developmental changes in how children think about and remember information. Language provides a mechanism through which students can mentally represent their world.	Assimilation and accommodation can occur only when children relate new experiences to existing knowledge. Students show more advanced reasoning capabilities when classroom tasks are related to topics with which they are familiar. According to information processing theory, students' prior knowledge influences the degree to which they can understand, elaborate on, and remember new information.	Many students, especially younger ones, think it is unacceptable to ask their teacher for help, perhaps because they have previously been discouraged from asking questions at school.	Challenge promotes cognitive development, whether the challenge be in the form of disequilibrium (Piaget), a task within the zone of proximal development (Vygotsky), or the increasing need for sophisticated learning strategies (information processing theory). In a cognitive apprenticeship, teacher and students work together to accomplish a challenging task. Children are most likely to develop their linguistic capabilities when challenging tasks require them to do so.	Students may "hear" what they expect their teachers to say, rather than what teachers actually do say.	Students at any given age level vary in their cognitive and linguistic abilities. Some students have special educational needs related to their cognitive or linguistic development.
Chapter 3: Personal, Social, and Moral Development	Students' self-concepts and self-esteem are influenced by others' behaviors toward them. Social interaction promotes the development of social skills, moral reasoning, perspective taking, and prosocial behavior.	Some students have trouble looking at a situation from someone else's perspective. Some may also have difficulty interpreting other people's behaviors accurately.	Students may encounter numerous moral dilemmas relevant to the content domains they study in school.	Personal, social, and moral development is most effectively fostered within the context of a warm, supportive, and encouraging environment.	Discussions about controversial moral issues challenge students to think differently about such issues and hence may promote their moral development.	Students' self-concepts are partly the result of expectations that others have for them; their self-concepts, in turn, affect the expectations they have for themselves.	Students differ widely in their social skills, self-concepts, and moral behaviors. Teachers can promote friendships among students with diverse backgrounds by setting up situations in which such students must interact and work closely together.

A-1

CHAPTER	INTERACTION	COGNITIVE PROCESSES	RELEVANCE	CLASSROOM CLIMATE	CHALLENGE	EXPECTATIONS	DIVERSITY
Chapter 4: Individual and Group Differences	Students often behave more intelligently when they work with the cooperation and support of others. Teachers interact more frequently, and in different ways, with boys than with girls. Students are more tolerant of cultural differences when they interact in a multicultural social environment. Students at risk are less likely to drop out when they get involved in extracurricular activities.	According to Sternberg, numerous cognitive processes are involved in intelligent behavior.	Students are more likely to exhibit creativity when they have considerable knowledge related to the task at hand. Students at risk become more psychologically attached to their school when they believe that school activities are relevant to their own needs.	Creativity is more likely to appear when students feel free to take risks. When teachers have high expectations for students' performance, they create a warmer classroom climate, interact with students more frequently, and give more positive feedback. Students at risk are more likely to feel psychologically attached to school when teachers form close, trusting relationships with them.	Students are more likely to think creatively when teachers ask questions that require using information in new ways.	Teachers' expectations influence how they treat students and may ultimately lead to a self-fulfilling prophecy. Boys tend to have higher expectations for themselves than girls. Teachers should not form expectations about individual students based solely on their IQ scores or group membership. Teachers should communicate to at-risk students that school success is both possible and expected.	Considerable diversity is found even within a single ethnic group, gender, or socioeconomic group. Students may have trouble adjusting to the school environment when there is a mismatch between home and school cultures. On the average, boys and girls differ with respect to personality, motivation, and career aspirations.
Chapter 5: Students with Special Educational Needs	Many students with special needs achieve at higher levels when placed in classrooms with nondisabled classmates. Nondisabled students benefit from interacting with students who have special needs.	Some students with special needs have difficulties with specific cognitive processes. Gifted students may have more advanced cognitive processing capabilities.	Students with emotional and behavioral disorders are more likely to be motivated to learn when the curriculum is related to their personal interests and needs.	Teachers should make it clear that they care about students' welfare; this may be especially important for students with emotional and behavioral disorders. Some students with special needs are more successful when the classroom is orderly and predictable.	Students who are gifted often have a higher zone of proximal development than their classmates and so may need more challenging assignments to promote their cognitive development.	Students with special needs are often more successful when expectations for behavior are clearly specified. Teachers should hold similar expectations for all students, with and without special needs, unless there is a specific reason to do otherwise.	Students within any single category of special needs are often very different from one another and so have unique strengths, weaknesses, and educational needs.

CHAPTER	INTERACTION	COGNITIVE PROCESSES	RELEVANCE	CLASSROOM CLIMATE	CHALLENGE	EXPECTATIONS	DIVERSITY
Chapter 6: Learning and Cognitive Processes	Increasing teacher wait time can dramatically alter the nature of classroom interactions.	Cognitive psychologists incorporate such concepts as encoding, meaningful learning, elaboration, visual imagery, and retrieval into their explanations of learning. Increasing teacher wait time allows students more time to process information.	Meaningful learning is more likely to occur when students have existing knowledge to which they can relate new information. Making multiple connections between new information and existing knowledge facilitates later retrieval of the information.			When teachers increase their wait time, their expectations for many students, especially previously low-achieving ones, begin to improve.	Individual students encode and store information differently, in part because they have different knowledge bases to which they can relate the information.
Chapter 7: Knowledge Construction	Hands-on experimentation with physical objects helps students construct more complete understandings. Social constructivism focuses on how people can make more sense of an event or phenomenon when they work together to understand and interpret it.	Students construct their own meanings for the experiences they have and the information they receive.	Students may connect new information to prior misconceptions and misinterpret the information as a result. Authentic activities may help students understand how classroom learning relates to real-life situations.	A classroom dialogue in which students express their ideas openly with one another promotes a better understanding of the topic at hand.	Teachers can correct students' misconceptions by presenting information that conflicts with such misconceptions and by asking challenging questions.	Students and teachers alike may sometimes perceive events in a distorted fashion based on what they expect to see or hear.	Students' diverse backgrounds and knowledge bases lead them to interpret new experiences in different ways. Students from various cultures may derive different, yet equally valid, meanings from the same event.

continued

CHAPTER	INTERACTION	COGNITIVE PROCESSES	RELEVANCE	CLASSROOM CLIMATE	CHALLENGE	EXPECTATIONS	DIVERSITY
Chapter 8: Higher-Level Thinking Skills	When students study together in small groups, they are exposed to a variety of study strategies, including some that may be more effective than the ones they are currently using.	Information learned in one situation is transferred to another situation only when it is retrieved in the second situation. Working memory, encoding, and retrieval affect problem-solving success. Metacognition includes students' knowledge about their own cognitive processes and their attempts to regulate those processes.	Students are most likely to transfer their academic knowledge to real-world situations when they perceive its relevance to those situations. Successful problem solving is more likely to occur when students have thorough and integrated knowledge related to the topic in question. Study strategies are most effectively taught within the context of specific content domains.	Students are more likely to engage in critical thinking when teachers encourage them to view classroom subject matter with a skeptical eye.	The acquisition of complex study strategies can be facilitated when teachers scaffold students' initial studying efforts.	Students are likely to adopt complex study strategies only when they expect that such strategies will enhance their learning.	Some students have more effective study strategies than others; students with special needs often have few if any effective strategies. Students' differing background knowledge related to the topic at hand will affect their ability to solve problems and use effective study strategies.
Chapter 9: Learning in the Content Areas	Small-group discussions often promote development and achievement in reading, writing, mathematics, and science.	Meaning construction and metacognition are essential elements of learning in all of the content domains. Successful performance in reading, writing, and mathematics requires automaticity of basic skills.	Students benefit from authentic activities in all content domains. Teachers should incorporate reading and writing instruction into other academic disciplines. Students apply mathematical problem-solving procedures more appropriately when they know how those procedures relate to mathematical concepts and principles.				Students at different age levels exhibit qualitative differences in their ability to learn and perform in reading, writing, mathematics, science, and social studies. An important objective of any social studies curriculum should be to foster an appreciation for cultural differences.

CHAPTER	INTERACTION	COGNITIVE PROCESSES	RELEVANCE	CLASSROOM CLIMATE	CHALLENGE	EXPECTATIONS	DIVERSITY
Chapter 10: Behaviorist Views of Learning	Social reinforcers and positive feedback are often quite effective in changing behavior. In a group contingency, students are reinforced only when everyone exhibits desired behavior.	Some behaviorists incorporate cognitive processes into their theoretical explanations of learning.		Skinner recommended that teachers focus their efforts on reinforcing desirable behaviors, rather than on punishing undesirable ones.	Through the process of shaping, students are encouraged to exhibit increasingly more complex behaviors over time.	Cueing is a subtle strategy for reminding students about expectations for their behavior. One probable reason for the success of applied behavior analysis and positive behavioral support is that such techniques let students know exactly what is expected of them.	Because students have had unique previous experiences, they often respond to the same environmental stimuli in different ways.
Chapter 11: Social Cognitive Views of Learning	Students learn by observing others; for example, they may learn through vicarious reinforcement and punishment. Students' self-efficacy is affected by others' successes and failures.	Social cognitive theorists view learning as an internal mental process. Students process information more effectively when they expect to be reinforced for learning it. Attention and retention (memory) are necessary for successful imitation of a model's behavior.	Students are most likely to imitate behaviors they believe will help them in their own circumstances.		Students' self-efficacy is enhanced when they set and achieve challenging goals.	Students form expectations about the likely consequences of future responses on the basis of how current responses are reinforced and punished. Students are more likely to engage in certain behaviors when they believe that they can execute those behaviors successfully (i.e., when they have high self-efficacy).	Students differ considerably in their self-efficacy for performing school tasks and in their ability to regulate their own behaviors. Students benefit from observing a wide variety of models, including those of both genders and diverse cultural backgrounds.

continued

CHAPTER	INTERACTION	COGNITIVE PROCESSES	RELEVANCE	CLASSROOM CLIMATE	CHALLENGE	EXPECTATIONS	DIVERSITY
Chapter 12: Motivating Students to Learn	Most students prefer learning activities in which they can take an active, physical role. Students differ in their need for affiliation and their need for approval.	Motivation affects what and how information is processed. Students with learning goals and those who are interested in what they are studying are more likely to use such effective strategies as meaningful learning, elaboration, and comprehension monitoring. An excessive level of anxiety interferes with effective information processing. Attributions are students' beliefs about what causes what.	Students are more likely to have intrinsic motivation to learn school subject matter when they see its relevance for their personal lives and professional aspirations; such relevance may be especially important for students from lower socioeconomic backgrounds.	Students are more intrinsically motivated when they can control some aspects of classroom life—for example, when they are involved in classroom decision making. Students are more likely to develop the motivation to learn if their teachers commend successful performance but downplay the importance of mistakes. Many students have a strong need to affiliate with their teachers as well as with their classmates.	A challenge is a situation in which students believe there is some probability of success with effort; a threat is one in which students believe they have little or no chance of success. Students who are intrinsically motivated, and especially those who have a mastery orientation, are more likely to engage in challenging tasks.	Students are more likely to be intrinsically motivated when they expect that they will be able to accomplish a task successfully. Teachers can foster the motivation to learn by communicating the expectation that students *want* to learn. Communicating clear expectations for student performance lessens students' anxiety. Students' attributions affect their expectations for future success or failure.	Whereas young children often want their teachers' approval, many older ones may be more concerned about gaining the approval of their peers. Students' intrinsic motivation decreases and performance goals become more prevalent as students get older. Students from ethnic minority groups sometimes have more test anxiety than their classmates.
Chapter 13: Choosing Instructional Strategies	In discovery learning, students acquire firsthand knowledge through their interactions with the environment. Some authentic activities require considerable student interaction.	An information-processing task analysis involves identifying the specific cognitive processes that a skill or body of knowledge requires. Expository instruction is effective to the extent that it facilitates effective cognitive processing of the information presented. Teacher questions, in-class activities, authentic activities, and homework can promote elaboration of previously learned material.	Expository instruction should make frequent connections between new ideas and what students already know. Discovery learning is often most effective when students have relevant background knowledge they can draw on to interpret their observations. Hypermedia enable students to select topics that are relevant to them. Authentic activities are those that closely resemble real-life tasks.	Teachers should give students some leeway to take risks and make mistakes during in-class activities.	In-class activities should become increasingly challenging as students become more proficient.	Instructional objectives enable teachers to describe what they expect students to be able to do at the completion of a lesson. Mastery learning is based on the assumption that all students can eventually master course material.	Different instructional strategies may be appropriate for different students; for example, lectures are most appropriate for students who can think abstractly (e.g., gifted students), and mastery learning and direct instruction are more appropriate for students who need to work on basic skills. Computer-based instruction allows students to progress through material at their own speed.

CHAPTER	INTERACTION	COGNITIVE PROCESSES	RELEVANCE	CLASSROOM CLIMATE	CHALLENGE	EXPECTATIONS	DIVERSITY
Chapter 14: Promoting Learning Through Student Interactions	In class discussions, reciprocal teaching, cooperative learning, and peer tutoring, students learn through their interactions with one another.	When students explain what they know or think to someone else, they must clarify, organize, and often elaborate on their thoughts. Reciprocal teaching promotes development of metacognitive strategies.	Class discussions are more effective when students already know something about the topic at hand.	Class discussions are most effective when students believe that they can speak freely. Some theorists propose that classrooms are most effective when they function as a community of learners—that is, when teacher and students actively work to help one another learn.	In interactive instructional methods, students often challenge one another's perspectives. Reciprocal teaching provides a setting in which students can more effectively read challenging reading materials.	Cooperative learning enhances students' expectations that they will be successful (i.e., it enhances their self-efficacy).	Cooperative learning may be especially useful for females and students from diverse ethnic backgrounds. Interactive approaches promote friendships across diverse groups.
Chapter 15: Creating and Maintaining a Productive Classroom Environment	One strategy for dealing with a student's problem behavior is a private discussion between teacher and student.			Effective teachers create a classroom climate in which students have a sense of acceptance, belonging, and some degree of control. A productive classroom climate is businesslike without being uncomfortable or threatening. Effective teachers set reasonable limits for classroom behavior.	Some students are likely to behave in counterproductive ways when they are given challenging tasks; one workable strategy is to begin the school year with familiar and easily accomplishable tasks, moving to more difficult tasks after a supportive classroom climate has been established.	Effective teachers give clear directions about how to proceed with classroom tasks. Teachers should inform students in advance about behaviors that are unacceptable and the consequences that will follow such behaviors.	Classroom behaviors considered unacceptable in the dominant culture may be quite acceptable in the cultures of some students.

continued

continued

CHAPTER	INTERACTION	COGNITIVE PROCESSES	RELEVANCE	CLASSROOM CLIMATE	CHALLENGE	EXPECTATIONS	DIVERSITY
Chapter 16: Assessing Student Learning	Although students often decide which products to include in their portfolios, teacher guidance is essential for ensuring that they make appropriate choices.	The type of assessment students expect influences how they mentally process information as they study.	Content validity is maximized when assessment tasks are as similar to instructional objectives as possible. Authentic assessment involves asking students to perform in situations similar to "real life."	Teachers should portray classroom assessment tasks more as means to facilitate learning than as mechanisms to evaluate performance. Teachers' evaluation procedures must be consistent with an atmosphere in which students feel free to take risks and make mistakes.	Classroom assessment tasks should be difficult enough that students must expend effort to succeed, but not so difficult that success is beyond reach.	Assessment instruments never have perfect validity; thus, a single assessment should never be used as the sole basis on which to form expectations about students' future performance. Teachers' expectations for student performance may affect their evaluations of subjectively scorable assessment tasks.	It may sometimes be necessary and appropriate to tailor assessment methods to accommodate diverse cultural backgrounds or special educational needs.

Describing Relationships with Correlation Coefficients

Appendix B

- Do students with high self-esteem perform better in school than students with low self-esteem?
- Which students are more likely to answer questions correctly—those who answer questions quickly or those who are slow to respond?
- Do two different intelligence tests taken at the same time typically yield similar scores for the same student?
- Are intellectually gifted students more emotionally well-adjusted than their classmates of average intelligence?

Each of these questions asks about a relationship between two variables—whether it be the relationship between self-esteem and school achievement, between speed and accuracy in answering questions, between two sets of intelligence test scores, or between giftedness and emotional adjustment. The nature of such relationships is sometimes expressed in terms of a particular number—a statistic known as a **correlation coefficient.**

A correlation coefficient is a number between -1 and $+1$; most correlation coefficients are decimals (either positive or negative) somewhere between these two extremes. A correlation coefficient for two variables tells us about both the direction and strength of the relationship between those variables.

Direction. The direction of the relationship is indicated by the *sign* of the correlation coefficient—in other words, by whether the number is a positive or negative one. A positive number indicates a *positive correlation:* As one variable increases, the other variable also increases. For example, there is a positive correlation between self-esteem and school achievement: Students with higher self-esteem achieve at higher levels (e.g., Marsh, 1990a). In contrast, a negative number indicates a *negative correlation:* As one variable increases, the other variable decreases instead. For example, there is a negative correlation between speed and accuracy in answering questions: Students who take longer to answer questions tend to make fewer errors in answering them (e.g., Shipman & Shipman, 1985). Figure B–1 graphically depicts each of these relationships.

Strength. The strength of the relationship is indicated by the *size* of the correlation coefficient. A number close to either $+1$ or -1 (e.g., $+.89$ or $-.76$) indicates a *strong* correlation: The two variables are closely related, so knowing the level of one variable allows us to predict the level of the other variable with some degree of accuracy. For example, we often find a strong relationship between two intelligence tests taken at the same time: Students tend to get similar scores on both tests, especially if both tests cover similar kinds of content (e.g., McGrew et al., 1997). In contrast, a number close to 0 (e.g., $+.15$ or $-.22$) indicates a *weak* correlation: Knowing the level of one variable allows us to predict the level of the other variable, but we cannot predict with much accuracy. For example, there is a weak relationship between intellectual giftedness and emotional adjustment: Generally speaking, students with higher IQ scores show greater emotional maturity than students with lower scores (e.g., Janos & Robinson, 1985), but there are many students who are exceptions to this rule. Correlations in the middle range (for example, those in the .40s and .50s—whether positive or negative) indicate a *moderate* correlation.

As teachers, we will often find correlation coefficients in research articles in professional books and journals. For example, we might read that students' visual-spatial thinking ability is positively correlated with their success in a mathematics class or that

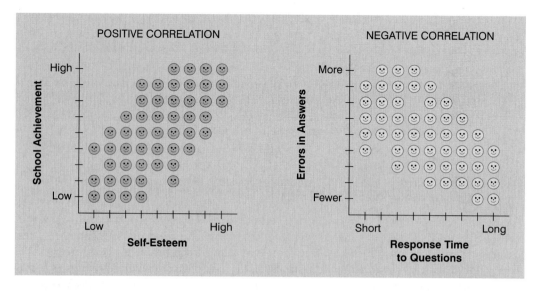

Imagine that each face in these two graphs represents one student in a group of fifty students. Each student is located at a place representing the extent to which the student is high or low on the two characteristics indicated. There is a *positive correlation* between self-esteem and school achievement: students with higher self-esteem tend to achieve at higher levels. There is a *negative correlation* between the length of time it takes for students to respond to questions and the number of errors in their answers: students who take longer to answer questions tend to have fewer errors in their responses.

FIGURE B.1
Positive and negative correlations

there is a negative correlation between class size and students' achievement test scores. Whenever we see such evidence of correlation, we must remember one very important point: *Correlation does not necessarily indicate causation.* For example, we cannot say that visual-spatial thinking ability specifically *leads to* greater mathematical ability, nor can we say that class size specifically *interferes with* classroom achievement; both of these italicized phrases imply a causal relationship between one variable and another that does not necessarily exist. As we discovered in Chapter 1, only carefully designed experimental studies enable us to draw conclusions about the extent to which one thing causes or influences another.

Using Correlation Coefficients to Determine Reliability

We sometimes use correlation coefficients as an index of the *reliability* of an assessment instrument (see Chapter 16 for an explanation of this concept). In most cases, we begin by getting two scores on the assessment for the same group of students—perhaps by having students perform the same task twice, computing two subscores based on different test questions, or scoring the same test papers at two different times. Each approach gives us a somewhat different angle on reliability; for example, scoring the same test papers twice tells us whether we are scoring our students' performance in a consistent manner.

Once we have two sets of scores for a group of students, we can determine how similar the scores are by computing a correlation coefficient. This coefficient will typically range from 0 to +1 (negative coefficients, though possible, are seldom obtained when calculating reliability). A number close to +1 indicates high reliability: The two sets of results are very similar. Although a perfect reliability coefficient of 1.00 is a rare occurrence, many standardized achievement and intelligence tests have reliabilities of .90 or above, reflecting a high degree of consistency in the scores they yield. As reliability coefficients become increasingly lower, they indicate more error in our assessment results—error due to temporary, and in most cases irrelevant, factors.

Many calculators are now programmed to compute correlation coefficients. Computing a correlation coefficient by hand is somewhat complicated but certainly not impossible. If you are curious, you can find the formula in most introductory statistics textbooks.

Interpreting Standardized Test Scores

Appendix C

Most scores on published standardized tests are norm-referenced scores. In some cases, the scores are derived by comparing a student's performance with the performance of students at a variety of grade or age levels; such comparisons give us grade- or age-equivalents. In other cases, the scores are based on comparisons only with students of the *same* age or grade; these comparisons give us either percentile scores or standard scores.

Grade- and Age-Equivalents

Imagine that Shantel takes the Mathematical Achievement Test (MAT) and gets 46 of the 60 test items correct (hence, 46 is her raw score). We turn to the norms reported in the test manual and find the average raw scores for students at different grade and age levels:

Normative Data for the MAT

NORMS FOR GRADE LEVELS		NORMS FOR AGE LEVELS	
Grade	Average Raw Score	Age	Average Raw Score
5	19	10	18
6	25	11	24
7	30	12	28
8	34	13	33
9	39	14	37
10	43	15	41
11	46	16	44
12	50	17	48

Shantel's raw score of 46 is the same as the average score of eleventh graders in the norm group, so she has a **grade-equivalent score** of 11. Her score is halfway between the average score of sixteen-year-old and seventeen-year-old students, so she has an **age-equivalent score** of about 16½. Shantel is actually only thirteen years old and in eighth grade, so she has obviously done well on the MAT.

In general, grade- and age-equivalents are determined by matching a student's raw score to a particular grade or age level in the norm group. A student who performs as well as the average second grader on a reading test will get a grade-equivalent of 2, regardless of what grade level the student is actually in. A student who gets the same raw score as the average ten-year-old on a physical fitness test will get an age-equivalent of 10, regardless of whether that student is five, ten, or fifteen years old.

Grade- and age-equivalents are frequently used because they seem so simple and straightforward. But they have a serious drawback: They give us no idea of the typical *range* of performance for students at a particular age or grade level. For example, a raw score of 34 on the MAT gives us a grade-equivalent of 8, but obviously not all eighth graders will get raw scores of exactly 34. It is possible, and in fact quite likely, that many "normal" eighth graders will get raw scores several points above or below 34, thus getting grade-equivalents of 9 or 7 (perhaps even 10 or higher, or 6 or lower). Yet grade-equivalents are often used inappropriately as a standard for performance: Parents, school personnel, government officials, and the public at large may believe that *all* students should perform at grade level on an achievement test. Given the normal variability within most classrooms, this goal is probably impossible to meet.

Expect variability in the grade- and age-equivalent scores that students obtain.

Percentile Ranks

A different approach is to compare our students only with others at the *same* age or grade level. One way of making such a peer-based comparison is by using a **percentile rank:** the percentage of people getting a raw score less than or equal to the student's raw score. To illustrate, let's look once again at Shantel's performance on the MAT. Because Shantel is in eighth grade, we turn to the eighth grade norms and discover that her raw score of 46 is at the 98th percentile. This means that Shantel has done as well as or better than 98 percent of eighth graders in the norm group on the Mathematical Achievement Test. Similarly, a student getting a percentile rank of 25 has performed better than 25 percent of the norm group, and a student getting a score at the 60th percentile has done better than 60 percent.

Because percentile ranks are relatively simple to understand, they are used frequently in reporting test results. But we need to be aware of a problem with percentiles: They distort actual differences among students. To illustrate, consider the percentile ranks of these four boys on the Basic Skills Test (BST):

Student	Percentile Rank
Ernest	45%ile
Frank	55%ile
Giorgio	89%ile
Nick	99%ile

In terms of the boys' *actual achievement* (as measured by the BST), Ernest and Frank are probably very similar to one another even though their percentile ranks are ten points apart. Yet ten points at the upper end of the scale probably reflect a substantial difference in achievement: Giorgio's percentile rank of 89 tells us that he knows quite a bit, but Nick's percentile rank of 99 tells us that he knows an exceptional amount. In general, percentiles tend to *over*estimate differences in the middle range of the characteristic being measured: Scores a few points apart reflect similar achievement or ability. At the same time, percentiles tend to *under*estimate differences at the lower and upper extremes: Scores only a few points apart often reflect significant differences in achievement or ability. We avoid this problem when we use a different type of norm-referenced score—a standard score.

▲ Percentile ranks refer to a percentage of *people.* They do *not* tell us the percentage of items that a student has answered correctly—a common misconception among teacher education students (Lennon et al., 1990).

🍎 Remember that percentile ranks overestimate differences between students near the middle of the distribution and underestimate differences between students at the extremes.

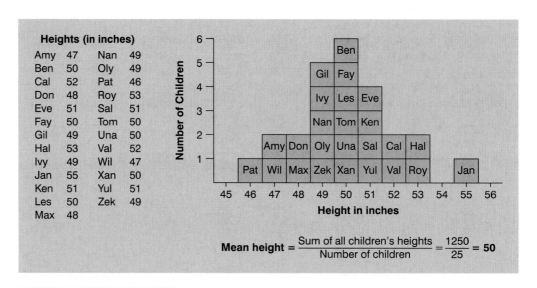

$$\text{Mean height} = \frac{\text{Sum of all children's heights}}{\text{Number of children}} = \frac{1250}{25} = 50$$

FIGURE C.1

Heights of children in Ms. Oppenheimer's third-grade class

Standard Scores

The school nurse measures the heights of all twenty-five students in Ms. Oppenheimer's third-grade class. The students' heights are presented on the left side of Figure C–1. The nurse then makes a bar graph of the children's heights, as you can see on the right side of Figure C–1.

Notice that the bar graph is high in the middle and low on both ends. This shape tells us that most of Ms. Oppenheimer's students are more or less average in height, with only a handful of very short students (e.g., Pat, Amy, and Wil) and just a few very tall ones (e.g., Hal, Roy, and Jan).

Many psychologists believe that educational and psychological characteristics (achievement and aptitude included) typically follow the same pattern we see for height: Most people are close to average, with fewer and fewer people as we move farther from this average. This theoretical pattern of educational and psychological characteristics is called the **normal distribution** (or **normal curve**) and looks like this:

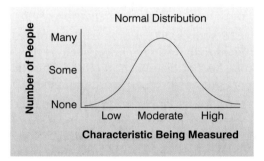

Standard scores are test scores that reflect this normal distribution: Many students get scores in the middle range, and only a few get very high or very low scores.

Before examining standard scores in more detail, we need to understand two numbers we use to derive these scores—the mean and standard deviation. The **mean (M)** is simply the average of a set of scores: We add all the scores together and divide by the number of scores (or people) there are. For example, if we add the heights of all 25 students in Ms. Oppenheimer's class and then divide by 25, we get a mean height of 50 (see the calculation at the bottom of Figure C–1). The average student in Ms. Oppenheimer's class, then, is 50 inches tall.

The **standard deviation (SD)** indicates the *variability* of a set of scores. In other words, it tells us how close together or far apart scores are from one another: A small number tells us they are close together, and a large number tells us they are far apart. For example, third graders tend to be more similar in height than eighth graders (some eighth graders are less than five feet tall, whereas other eighth graders may be almost six feet tall). The standard deviation for the heights of third graders is therefore smaller than the standard deviation for the heights of eighth graders. The procedure for computing a standard deviation is more complex than that for computing a mean. If you are curious, you can find the details in one of the supplementary readings in the *Student Study Guide*.

The mean and standard deviation can be used to divide the normal distribution into several parts, as shown in Figure C–2. The vertical line in the middle of the curve shows the mean; for a normal distribution, it is at the midpoint and highest point of the curve. The thinner lines to either side reflect the standard deviation: We count out a standard deviation's worth higher than the mean and draw a line and then count another standard deviation and draw another line. We do the same thing below the mean, drawing two lines to indicate the points at which scores are one or two standard deviations below the mean. When we divide the normal distribution in this way, the percentages of students getting scores in each part are always the same. Approximately two-thirds (68%) get scores within one standard deviation of the mean (34% in each direction). As we go farther away

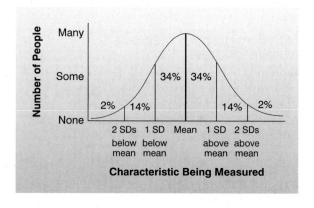

FIGURE C.2

Normal distribution divided by the mean and standard deviation

from the mean, we find fewer and fewer students, with 28 percent lying between one and two standard deviations away (14% on each side) and only 4 percent being more than two standard deviations away (2% at each end).

Now that we better understand the normal distribution and two statistics that describe it (the mean and standard deviation), let's return to the topic of standard scores. A standard score reflects a student's position in the normal distribution: It tells us how far the student's performance is from the mean in terms of standard deviation units. Unfortunately, not all standard scores use the same scale: Different scores have different means and standard deviations. Four commonly used standard scores, depicted graphically in Figure C–3, are the following:

IQ scores. IQ scores are frequently used to report students' performance on intelligence tests. They have a *mean of 100* and, for most tests, a *standard deviation of 15*.

ETS scores. ETS scores are used on tests published by the Educational Testing Service, such as the Scholastic Aptitude Test (SAT) and the Graduate Record Examination (GRE). They have a *mean of 500* and a *standard deviation of 100*; however, no scores fall below 200 or above 800.

Stanines. Stanines (short for *standard nines*) are often used to report standardized achievement test results. They have a *mean of 5* and a *standard deviation of 2*. Because they are always reported as whole numbers, each score reflects a *range* of test performance (reflected by the shaded and nonshaded portions of the upper right-hand curve in Figure C–3).

z-scores. Standard scores known as *z-scores* are often used by statisticians. They have a *mean of 0* and a *standard deviation of 1*.

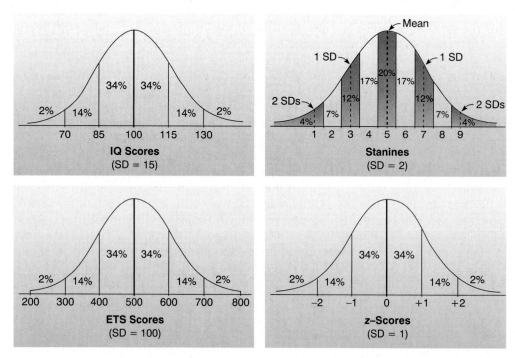

FIGURE C.3

Distributions of four types of standard scores

Glossary

Accommodation. In Piaget's theory, dealing with a new event by either modifying an existing scheme or forming a new one.

Activation. The degree to which a particular piece of information in memory is currently being attended to and mentally processed.

Activity reinforcer. An opportunity to engage in a favorite activity.

Actual developmental level. In Vygotsky's theory, the extent to which one can successfully perform a task independently.

Adaptive behavior. Behavior related to daily living skills and appropriate conduct in social situations; a deficit in adaptive behavior is used as a criterion for identifying students with mental retardation.

Advance organizer. An introduction to a lesson that provides an overall organizational scheme for the lesson.

Affect. The feelings and emotions that an individual brings to bear on a task.

Affective domain. The domain of learning tasks that includes attitudes and values about the things one learns.

African American dialect. A dialect of some African American communities that includes some pronunciations, grammatical constructions, and idioms different from those of Standard English.

Age-equivalent score. A test score that indicates the age level of students to whom a student's test performance is most similar.

Algorithm. A prescribed sequence of steps guaranteeing a correct problem solution.

Antecedent response. A response that increases the likelihood that another, particular response will follow.

Antecedent stimulus. A stimulus that increases the likelihood that a particular response will follow.

Anxiety. A feeling of uneasiness and apprehension concerning a situation with an uncertain outcome.

Applied behavior analysis. The systematic application of behaviorist principles in educational and therapeutic settings; sometimes known as *behavior modification*.

Apprenticeship. A situation in which a learner works intensively with an expert to learn how to accomplish complex tasks.

Assessment. The process of observing a sample of students' behavior and drawing inferences about their knowledge and abilities.

Assimilation. In Piaget's theory, dealing with a new event in a way that is consistent with an existing scheme.

Attachment. A strong, affectionate bond formed between a child and another individual (e.g., a parent); usually formed early in the child's life.

Attention. The focusing of mental processes on particular environmental stimuli.

Attention-deficit hyperactivity disorder (ADHD). A category of special needs marked either by inattention or by both hyperactivity and impulsive behavior (or by all three of these); such characteristics probably have a biological origin.

Attribution. A causal explanation for one's success or failure.

Attribution theory. A theoretical perspective that focuses on people's attributions concerning the causes of events that befall them, as well as on the behaviors that result from such attributions.

Authentic activities. Classroom activities similar to those that students are likely to encounter in the outside world.

Authentic assessment. Assessment of students' knowledge and skills in an authentic, real-life context; in many cases, an integral part of instruction rather than a separate activity.

Authoritarian parenting style. A parenting style characterized by rigid rules and expectations for behavior that children are expected to obey without question.

Authoritative parenting style. A parenting style characterized by emotional warmth, high expectations and standards for behavior, consistent enforcement of rules, explanations regarding the reasons behind these rules, and the inclusion of children in decision making.

Autism. A category of special needs characterized by impaired social interaction and communication, repetitive behaviors, restricted interests, and a strong need for a predictable environment; underlying the condition may be either an undersensitivity or oversensitivity to sensory stimulation.

Automaticity. The ability to respond quickly and efficiently while mentally processing or physically performing a task.

Base group. A cooperative learning group that lasts an entire semester or school year and provides a means through which students can be mutually supportive of one another's academic efforts and activities.

Baseline. The frequency of a response before operant conditioning takes place.

Behavioral momentum. An increased tendency for an individual to make a particular response immediately after making similar responses.

Behavioral objective. An instructional objective that describes a specific, observable behavior.

Behaviorism. A theoretical perspective in which learning and behavior are described and explained in terms of stimulus-response relationships. Adherents to this perspective are called **behaviorists.**

Behavior modification. See *applied behavior analysis.*

Benchmark lesson or experiment. Lesson or experiment that begins a new unit by illustrating the issues that the unit will address.

Bilingual education. An approach to second-language instruction in which students are instructed in academic subject areas in their native language while simultaneously being taught to speak and write in the second language. The amount of instruction delivered in the native language decreases as students become more proficient in the second language.

Bloom's taxonomy. A taxonomy in which six learning tasks, varying in degrees of complexity, are identified for the cognitive domain: knowledge, comprehension, application, analysis, synthesis, and evaluation.

Branching program. A form of programmed instruction in which students responding incorrectly to a question proceed to one or more remedial frames for further clarification or practice before continuing on with new information.

Challenge. A situation in which a person believes that he or she can succeed with effort.

Checklist. An assessment mechanism that enables a teacher to evaluate students' performance in terms of specific qualities that their performance either does or does not have.

Classical conditioning. A form of learning whereby a new, involuntary response is acquired as a result of two stimuli being presented at the same time.

Classroom climate. The psychological atmosphere of the classroom.

Classroom management. Establishing and maintaining a classroom environment conducive to learning and achievement.

Cognitive apprenticeship. A mentorship in which a teacher and a student work together to accomplish a challenging task or solve a difficult problem; in the process, the teacher provides guidance about how to think about the task or problem.

Cognitive domain. The domain of learning tasks that includes knowledge of information, as well as ways of thinking about and using that information.

Cognitive processes. The ways in which one thinks about (processes) information.

Cognitive psychology. A theoretical perspective that focuses on the mental processes underlying human learning and behavior.

Community of learners. A classroom in which teacher and students actively and cooperatively work to help one another learn.

Comprehension monitoring. The process of checking oneself to make sure one understands the things being read or heard.

Computer-assisted instruction (CAI). Programmed instruction presented by means of a computer; it is one form of computer-based instruction.

Computer-based instruction (CBI). Instruction provided via computer technology.

Concept. A mental grouping of objects or events that have something in common.

Concept map. A diagram of concepts within an instructional unit and the interrelationships among them.

Conceptual change. Revising one's knowledge and understanding of a topic in response to new information about that topic.

Conceptual understanding. Knowledge acquired in an integrated and meaningful fashion.

Concrete operations stage. Piaget's third stage of cognitive development, in which adultlike logic appears but is limited to concrete reality.

Concrete reinforcer. A reinforcer that can be touched.

Conditioned response (CR). A response that, through classical conditioning, begins to be elicited by a particular stimulus.

Conditioned stimulus (CS). A stimulus that, through classical conditioning, begins to elicit a particular response.

Conditioning. Another word for learning; commonly used by behaviorists.

Confirmation bias. A tendency to look for evidence that confirms a hypothesis and to ignore evidence that contradicts the hypothesis.

Conservation. The realization that if nothing is added or taken away, amount stays the same regardless of any alterations in shape or arrangement.

Construction. The process of taking many separate pieces of information and using them to build an overall understanding or interpretation of an event.

Constructivism. A theoretical perspective that proposes that learners construct a body of knowledge from their experiences—knowledge that may or may not be an accurate representation of external reality. Adherents to this perspective are called **constructivists.**

Construct validity. The extent to which an assessment accurately measures an unobservable educational or psychological characteristic.

Content validity. The extent to which an assessment includes a representative sample of tasks within the content domain being assessed.

Contiguity. The occurrence of two or more events at the same time. **Contiguous** is the adjective used to refer to events having contiguity.

Contingency. A situation in which one event happens only after another event has already occurred. One event is **contingent** on another's prior occurrence.

Contingency contract. A formal agreement between a teacher and a student regarding behaviors the student will exhibit and reinforcers that will follow those behaviors.

Continuous reinforcement. Reinforcing a response every time it occurs.

Control group. A group of people in a research study who are given either no treatment or a presumably ineffective (placebo) treatment. The subsequent performance of this group is compared to the performance of one or more treatment groups.

Convergent thinking. Pulling several pieces of information together to draw a conclusion or solve a problem.

Cooperative learning. An approach to instruction whereby students work with their classmates to achieve group goals and help one another learn.

Cooperative teaching. A general education teacher and special education teacher collaborating to teach all students in a class, including students both with and without special educational needs, throughout the school day.

Correlation. The extent to which two variables are related to each other, such that when one variable increases, the other either increases or decreases in a somewhat predictable fashion.

Correlational feature. In concept learning, a characteristic present in many positive instances of a concept but not essential for concept membership.

Correlational study. A research study that explores relationships among variables. Such a study enables researchers to predict one variable on the basis of their knowledge of another but not to draw a conclusion about a cause-effect relationship.

Correlation coefficient. A statistic that indicates the nature of the relationship between two variables.

Creativity. New and original behavior that yields an appropriate and productive result.

Criterion-referenced score. A test score that specifically indicates what students know and can do.

Critical thinking. Evaluating information or arguments in terms of their accuracy and worth.

Cueing. A teacher's signal that a particular behavior is desired or that a particular behavior should stop.

Cultural bias. The extent to which the items or tasks of an assessment instrument either offend or unfairly penalize some students because of their ethnicity, gender, or socioeconomic status.

Cultural mismatch. A situation in which a child's home culture and the school culture hold conflicting expectations for the child's behavior.

Culture shock. A sense of confusion that occurs when students encounter a culture with very different expectations for behavior than the expectations with which the students have been raised.

Debilitating anxiety. Anxiety that interferes with performance. A high level of anxiety is likely to be debilitating.

Decay. A hypothesized weakening over time of information stored in long-term memory, especially if the information is used infrequently or not at all.

Declarative knowledge. Knowledge related to "what is," to the nature of how things are, were, or will be (as opposed to *procedural knowledge,* which relates to how to do something).

Deductive reasoning. Drawing a logical inference about something that must be true, given other information that has already been presented as true.

Deficiency need. In Maslow's hierarchy, a need that results from something a person lacks.

Defining feature. In concept learning, a characteristic that must be present in all positive instances of a concept.

Descriptive study. A research study that describes situations. Such a study enables researchers to draw conclusions about the current state of affairs but not about correlational or cause-effect relationships.

Developmental milestone. The appearance of a new, developmentally more advanced behavior.

Dialect. A form of English characteristic of a particular region or ethnic group.

Direct instruction. An approach to instruction that uses a variety of techniques (brief explanations, teacher questioning, rapid pacing, guided and independent practice) to promote learning of basic skills.

Discovery learning. An approach to instruction whereby students develop an understanding of a topic in a hands-on fashion through their interaction with the physical or social environment.

Discrimination. Phenomenon in operant conditioning whereby an individual learns that a response is reinforced in the presence of one stimulus but not in the presence of another, similar stimulus.

Disequilibrium. The state of being *un*able to explain new events in terms of existing schemes.

Distributed cognition. A process whereby people think about an issue or problem together, sharing ideas and working to draw conclusions or develop solutions.

Distributed intelligence. The idea that people are more likely to act "intelligently" when they have physical and/or social support systems to assist them.

Divergent thinking. Taking a single idea in many different directions.

Dynamic assessment. Examining how a student's knowledge or reasoning may change over the course of performing a specific task.

Egocentric speech. Speaking without taking the perspective and knowledge of the listener into account.

Elaboration. A cognitive process in which learners expand on new information based on what they already know.

Elaborative interrogation. A study strategy in which students develop and answer elaborative questions about the material they are trying to learn.

Emergent literacy. Knowledge and skills that lay a foundation for reading and writing; typically develops in the preschool years as a result of early experiences with oral and written language.

Emotional and behavioral disorders. A category of special needs characterized by behaviors or emotional states that have a substantial negative effect on students' classroom performance.

Empathy. Experiencing the same feelings as someone in unfortunate circumstances.

Encoding. Changing the format of new information as it is being stored in memory.

Epistemological beliefs. One's beliefs regarding the nature of knowledge and knowledge acquisition.

Equilibration. The movement from equilibrium to disequilibrium and back to equilibrium—a process that promotes the development of more complex forms of thought and knowledge.

Equilibrium. A state of being able to explain new events in terms of existing schemes.

Equity in instruction. Instruction without favoritism or bias toward particular individuals or groups of students.

Ethnic group. A group of people with a common set of values, beliefs, and behaviors. The group's roots either precede the creation of, or are external to, the country in which the group resides.

ETS score. A standard score with a mean of 500 and a standard deviation of 100.

Exemplar. A specific example that is an important part of a learner's general knowledge and understanding of a concept. Several exemplars taken together give the learner a sense of the variability that exists within any category of objects or events.

Experimental study (experiment). A research study that involves the manipulation of one variable to determine its possible effect on another variable. It enables researchers to draw conclusions about cause-effect relationships.

Expository instruction. An approach to instruction whereby information is presented in more or less the same form in which students are expected to learn it.

Expressive language. The ability to communicate effectively through speaking and writing.

Externalizing behavior. A symptom of an emotional or behavioral disorder that has direct or indirect effects on other people (e.g., aggression, disobedience, stealing).

Extinction. In classical conditioning, the eventual disappearance of a conditioned response as a result of the conditioned stimulus being repeatedly presented alone (i.e., in the absence of the unconditioned stimulus); in operant conditioning, the eventual disappearance of a response that is no longer being reinforced.

Extrinsic motivation. Motivation promoted by factors external to the individual and unrelated to the task being performed.

Extrinsic reinforcer. A reinforcer that comes from the outside environment, rather than from within the individual.

Facilitating anxiety. Anxiety that enhances performance. Relatively low levels of anxiety are usually facilitating.

Failure to store. One's failure to process information mentally in ways that promote its storage in long-term memory.

Formal assessment. A systematic attempt to ascertain what students have learned. It is typically planned in advance and used for a specific purpose.

Formal discipline. A view of transfer that postulates that the study of rigorous subjects enhances one's ability to learn other, unrelated things.

Formal operational egocentrism. The inability of individuals in Piaget's formal operations stage to separate abstract logical thinking from practical considerations and the unpredictability of human behavior.

Formal operations stage. Piaget's fourth and final stage of cognitive development, in which logical reasoning processes are applied to abstract ideas as well as to concrete objects.

Formative evaluation. Evaluation conducted during instruction to facilitate students' learning.

g. The theoretical notion that intelligence includes a *general factor* that influences people's ability to learn in a wide variety of content domains.

Generalization. A phenomenon in both classical conditioning and operant conditioning whereby an individual learns a response to a particular stimulus and then makes the same response in the presence of similar stimuli.

General transfer. An instance of transfer in which the original learning task and the transfer task do not overlap in content.

Giftedness. A category of special needs characterized by unusually high ability in one or more areas, to the point where students require special educational services to help them meet their full potential.

Grade-equivalent score. A test score that indicates the grade level of students to whom a student's test performance is most similar.

Group contingency. A situation in which an entire group must make a particular response before reinforcement occurs.

Group differences. Consistently observed differences, on average, among certain groups of individuals.

Growth need. In Maslow's hierarchy, a need that serves to enhance a person's growth and development and is never completely satisfied.

Guided participation. Giving a child the necessary guidance and support to perform an activity in the adult world.

Guilt. The feeling of discomfort that individuals experience when they know that they have caused someone else pain or distress.

Halo effect. A phenomenon whereby people are more likely to perceive positive behaviors in a person they like or admire.

Hearing loss. A category of special needs characterized by malfunctions of the ear or associated nerves that interfere with the perception of sounds within the frequency range of normal human speech.

Heuristic. A general problem-solving strategy that may or may not yield a problem solution.

Higher-level questions. Questions that require students to do something new with information they have learned—for example, to apply, analyze, synthesize, or evaluate it.

Higher-level thinking. Thought that involves going beyond information specifically learned (e.g., application, analysis, synthesis, evaluation).

Hot cognition. Learning or cognitive processing that is emotionally charged.

Hypermedia. A collection of computer-based instructional material, including both verbal text and such other media as pictures, sound, and animations. The material is interconnected in such a way that students can learn about one topic and then proceed to related topics of their own choosing.

Hypertext. A collection of computer-based verbal material that allows students to read about one topic and then proceed to related topics of their own choosing.

Identity. A self-constructed definition of who a person thinks he or she is and what things are important in life.

Ill-defined problem. A problem in which the desired goal is unclear, information needed to solve the problem is missing, and/or several possible solutions to the problem exist.

Illusion of knowing. Thinking one knows something that one actually does not know.

Imaginary audience. The belief that one is the center of attention in any social situation.

Immersion. An approach to second-language instruction in which students hear and speak that language almost exclusively within the classroom.

Inability to retrieve. Failing to locate information that currently exists in long-term memory.

Incentive. A hoped-for, but not certain, consequence of behavior.

Inclusion. The practice of educating all students, even those with severe and multiple disabilities, in neighborhood schools and general education classrooms.

Incompatible behaviors. Two or more behaviors that cannot be performed simultaneously.

Individual constructivism. A theoretical perspective that focuses on how people, as individuals, construct meaning from the events around them.

Individual differences. The ways in which people of the same age are different from one another.

Individualized education program (IEP). A written description of an appropriate instructional program for a student with special needs; mandated by the Individuals with Disabilities Education Act (IDEA) for all students with disabilities.

Individuals with Disabilities Education Act (IDEA). U.S. legislation granting educational rights to people with cognitive, emotional, or physical disabilities from birth until age 21; it guarantees a free and appropriate education, fair and nondiscriminatory evaluation, education in the least restrictive environment, an individualized education program, and due process.

Induction. Explaining why a certain behavior is unacceptable, often with a focus on the pain or distress that someone has caused another.

Informal assessment. Assessment that results from teachers' spontaneous, day-to-day observations of how students behave and perform in class.

Information processing theory. A theoretical perspective that focuses on the specific ways in which individuals mentally think about and "process" the information they receive.

Inner speech. "Talking" to oneself mentally rather than aloud.

In-school suspension. A form of punishment in which a student is placed in a quiet, boring room within the school building. It often lasts one or more school days and involves close adult supervision.

Instructional objective. A statement describing a final goal or outcome of instruction.

Intelligence. The ability to modify and adjust one's behaviors in order to accomplish new tasks successfully. It involves many different mental processes, and its nature may vary, depending on the culture in which one lives.

Intelligence test. A general measure of current cognitive functioning, used primarily to predict academic achievement over the short run.

Interference. A phenomenon whereby something stored in long-term memory inhibits one's ability to remember something else correctly.

Intermittent reinforcement. Reinforcing a response only occasionally, with some occurrences of the response going unreinforced.

Internalization. In Vygotsky's theory, the process through which social activities evolve into mental activities.

Internalizing behavior. A symptom of an emotional or behavioral disorder that primarily affects the student with the disorder, with little or no effect on others (e.g., anxiety, depression).

Intrinsic motivation. The internal desire to perform a particular task.

Intrinsic reinforcer. A reinforcer supplied by oneself or inherent in the task being performed.

IQ score. A score on an intelligence test. It is determined by comparing one's performance on the test with the performance of others in the same age-group; for most tests, it is a standard score with a mean of 100 and a standard deviation of 15.

Irreversibility. An inability to recognize that certain processes can be undone, or reversed.

Jigsaw technique. An instructional technique in which instructional materials are divided among members of a cooperative learning group, with individual students being responsible for learning different material and then teaching that material to other group members.

Keyword method. A mnemonic technique in which an association is made between two ideas by forming a visual image of one or more concrete objects (**keywords**) that either sound similar to, or symbolically represent, those ideas.

Knowledge base. One's knowledge about specific topics and the world in general.

Learned helplessness. A general belief that one is incapable of accomplishing tasks and has little or no control of the environment.

Learned industriousness. The recognition that one can succeed at some tasks only with effort, persistence, and well-chosen strategies.

Learning. A relatively permanent change, due to experience, in either behavior or mental associations.

Learning disabilities. A category of special needs characterized by lower academic achievement than would be predicted from students' IQ scores and a deficiency in one or more specific cognitive processes.

Learning goal. A desire to acquire additional knowledge or master new skills.

Learning strategy. One or more cognitive processes used intentionally for a particular learning task.

Least restrictive environment. The most typical and standard educational environment that can reasonably meet a student's needs.

Level of potential development. In Vygotsky's theory, the extent to which one can successfully execute a task with the assistance of a more competent individual.

Limited English proficiency (LEP). A limited ability to understand and communicate in oral or written English, usually because English is not one's native language.

Linear program. A form of programmed instruction in which all students proceed through the same sequence of instructional frames.

Live model. An individual whose behavior is observed "in the flesh."

Logical consequence. A consequence that follows logically from a student's misbehavior; in other words, the punishment fits the crime.

Long-term memory. The component of memory that holds knowledge and skills for a relatively long period of time.

Long-term objective. An objective that requires months or years of instruction and practice to be accomplished.

Lower-level questions. Questions that require students to express what they have learned in essentially the same way they learned it—for example, by reciting a textbook's definition of a concept or describing an application that their teacher presented in class.

Mainstreaming. The practice of having students with special needs join general education classrooms primarily when their abilities enable them to participate in normally scheduled activities as successfully as other students.

Maintenance rehearsal. *See rehearsal.*

Mastery learning. An approach to instruction whereby students learn one topic thoroughly before moving to a more difficult one.

Mastery orientation. A general belief that one is capable of accomplishing challenging tasks.

Maturation. The unfolding of genetically controlled changes as a child develops.

Mean. The arithmetic average of a set of scores. It is calculated by adding all the scores and then dividing by the total number of people who have obtained those scores.

Meaningful learning. A cognitive process in which learners relate new information to the things they already know.

Meaningful learning set. An attitude that one can make sense of the information one is studying.

Mediation training. Training that involves teaching students how to mediate conflicts among classmates by asking opposing sides to express their differing viewpoints and then working together to devise a reasonable resolution.

Memory. A learner's ability to save something (mentally) that he or she has previously learned, *or* the mental "location" where such information is saved.

Mental retardation. A category of special needs characterized by significantly below-average general intelligence and deficits in adaptive behavior.

Mental set. Encoding a problem in a way that excludes potential problem solutions.

Metacognition. One's knowledge and beliefs regarding one's own cognitive processes, and one's resulting attempts to regulate those cognitive processes to maximize learning and memory.

Metacognitive scaffolding. A supportive technique that guides students in their use of metacognitive strategies.

Metalinguistic awareness. The extent to which one is able to think about the nature of language.

Misbehavior. An action that has the potential to disrupt classroom learning and planned classroom activities.

Misconception. Previously learned but incorrect information.

Mnemonic. A special memory aid or trick designed to help students learn and remember information.

Model. In science, knowledge of the components of a particular scientific entity and the interrelationships among those components. In social cognitive theory, an individual (live or symbolic) who demonstrates a behavior for someone else.

Moral dilemma. A situation in which there is no clear-cut answer regarding the morally correct thing to do.

Motivation. A state that energizes, directs, and sustains behavior.

Motivation to learn. The tendency to find school-related activities meaningful and worthwhile and therefore to try to get the maximum benefit from them.

Multicultural education. Education that includes the perspectives and experiences of numerous cultural groups on a regular basis.

Multiple classification. The recognition that objects may belong to several categories simultaneously.

Need for affiliation. The tendency to seek out friendly relationships with others.

Need for approval. A desire to gain the approval and acceptance of others.

Negative instance. A nonexample of a concept.

Negative reinforcement. A consequence that brings about the increase of a behavior through the removal (rather than the presentation) of a stimulus.

Negative transfer. A phenomenon whereby something learned at one time interferes with learning or performance at a later time.

Negative wait time. The tendency to interrupt someone who has not yet finished speaking.

Neutral stimulus. A stimulus that does not elicit any particular response.

Normal distribution (normal curve). A theoretical pattern of educational and psychological characteristics in which most individuals lie somewhere in the middle range and only a few lie at either extreme.

Norm-referenced score. A score that indicates how a student's performance on an assessment compares with the average performance of other students (i.e., with the performance of a norm group).

Norms. As related to socialization, society's rules for acceptable and unacceptable behavior. As related to testing practice, data regarding the typical performance of various groups of students on a standardized test or other norm-referenced assessment.

Object permanence. The realization that objects continue to exist even after they are removed from view.

Operant conditioning. A form of learning whereby a response increases in frequency as a result of its being followed by reinforcement.

Operations. In Piaget's theory, organized and integrated systems of thought processes.

Organization. A cognitive process in which learners find connections (e.g., forming categories, identifying hierarchical relationships) among the various pieces of information they need to learn.

Outcomes-based education (OBE). An approach to instruction whereby objectives for students (**outcomes**) are specified before the school year begins and assessment is based on the extent to which such objectives have been achieved.

Overgeneralization. Having too broad a meaning for a word, applying the word in situations where it's not appropriate; identifying objects or events as examples of a concept when in fact they are not.

Overregularization. Applying syntactical rules in situations where those rules don't apply.

Paper-pencil assessment. Assessment in which students respond to written items in a written fashion.

Parenting style. The general pattern of behaviors that a parent uses to raise his or her children.

Pedagogical content knowledge. Knowledge about effective methods of teaching a specific content area.

Peer pressure. A phenomenon whereby a student's peers strongly encourage some behaviors and discourage others.

Peers. One's equals or age-mates.

Peer tutoring. An approach to instruction whereby students who have mastered a topic teach those who have not.

People-first language. Language in which a student's disability is identified *after* the student (e.g., "student with a learning disability" rather than "learning disabled student").

Percentile rank (percentile). A test score that indicates the percentage of people in the norm group getting a raw score less than or equal to a particular student's raw score.

Performance assessment. Assessment in which students demonstrate their knowledge and skills in a nonwritten fashion.

Performance goal. A desire either to look good and receive favorable judgments from others, or else *not* to look bad and receive unfavorable judgments.

Permissive parenting style. A parenting style characterized by emotional warmth but few expectations or standards for children's behavior.

Personal fable. The belief that one is completely unlike anyone else and so cannot be understood by other individuals.

Personality. Set of relatively enduring traits that characterize the way in which a person typically interacts with his or her physical and social environments.

Personal theory. A self-constructed explanation for one's observations about a particular aspect of the world; it may or may not be consistent with generally accepted explanations of scientific phenomena.

Phonological awareness. The ability to hear the distinct sounds (phonemes) within a word.

Physical and health impairments. A category of special needs characterized by general physical or medical conditions (usually long-term) that interfere with students' school performance to such an extent that special instruction, curricular materials, equipment, or facilities are necessary.

Portfolio. A systematic collection of a student's work over a lengthy period of time.

Positive behavioral support. A modification of traditional applied behavior analysis that includes identifying the purpose that an undesirable behavior serves for a student and providing an alternative way for the student to achieve the same purpose.

Positive feedback. A message that an answer is correct or a task has been well done.

Positive instance. A specific example of a concept.

Positive reinforcement. A consequence that brings about the increase of a behavior through the presentation (rather than removal) of a stimulus.

Positive transfer. A phenomenon whereby something learned at one time facilitates learning or performance at a later time.

Practicality. The extent to which an assessment instrument or procedure is relatively easy to use.

Pragmatics. Knowledge about the culture-specific social conventions guiding verbal interactions.

Predictive validity. The extent to which the results of an assessment predict future performance.

Premack principle. A phenomenon whereby individuals do less-preferred activities in order to engage in more-preferred activities.

Preoperational egocentrism. In Piaget's theory, the inability of children in the preoperational stage to view situations from another person's perspective.

Preoperational stage. Piaget's second stage of cognitive development, in which children can think about objects beyond their immediate view but do not yet reason in logical, adultlike ways.

Presentation punishment. A form of punishment involving the presentation of a new stimulus, presumably one that an individual finds unpleasant.

Primary reinforcer. A stimulus that satisfies a basic physiological need.

Principle. A description of how one variable influences another variable. It evolves when similar research studies yield similar results time after time.

Prior knowledge activation. Reminding students of information they have already learned relative to a new topic.

Private speech. See *self-talk.*

Procedural knowledge. Knowledge concerning how to do something (as opposed to *declarative knowledge,* which relates to how things are).

Programmed instruction (PI). An approach to instruction whereby students independently study a topic that has been broken into small, carefully sequenced segments.

Proportional thought. The ability to understand proportions (e.g., fractions, decimals, ratios) and use them effectively in mathematical problem solving.

Prosocial behavior. Behavior directed toward promoting the well-being of someone else.

Prototype. A mental representation of a "typical" positive instance of a concept.

Psychological punishment. Any consequence that seriously threatens a student's self-concept and self-esteem.

Psychomotor domain. The domain of learning tasks that includes simple and complex physical movements and actions.

Punishment. A consequence that decreases the frequency of the response it follows.

Rating scale. An assessment tool that enables one to evaluate students' performance in terms of one or more continua that reflect desired characteristics of the performance.

Raw score. A test score based solely on the number or point value of correctly answered items.

Recall task. A memory task in which one must retrieve information in its entirety from long-term memory.

Receptive language. The ability to understand the language that one hears or reads.

Reciprocal causation. The interdependence of environment, behavior, and personal variables as these three factors influence learning.

Reciprocal teaching. An approach to teaching reading and listening comprehension whereby students take turns asking teacherlike questions of their classmates.

Recognition task. A memory task in which one must recognize correct information among irrelevant information or incorrect statements.

Reconstruction error. Constructing a logical but incorrect "memory" by using information retrieved from long-term memory plus one's general knowledge of the world.

Rehearsal. A cognitive process in which information is repeated over and over as a possible way of learning and remembering it. When it is used to maintain information in working memory, it is called **maintenance rehearsal.**

Reinforcement. The act of following a particular response with a reinforcer and thereby increasing the frequency of that response.

Reinforcer. A consequence (stimulus) of a response that leads to an increased frequency of that response.

Reliability. The extent to which an assessment instrument yields consistent information about the knowledge, skills, or abilities one is trying to measure.

Removal punishment. A form of punishment involving the removal of an existing stimulus, presumably one that an individual views as desirable and doesn't want to lose.

Resilient self-efficacy. The belief that one can perform a task successfully even after experiencing setbacks; includes the belief that effort and perseverance are essential for success.

Resilient students. Students who succeed in school despite exceptional hardships in their home lives.

Response (R). A specific behavior that an individual exhibits.

Response cost. The loss either of a previously earned reinforcer or of an opportunity to obtain reinforcement.

Retrieval. The process of "finding" information previously stored in memory.

Retrieval cue. A hint about where to "look" for a piece of information in long-term memory.

Reversibility. The ability to recognize that certain processes can be undone, or reversed.

Roles. Patterns of behavior acceptable for individuals having different functions within a society.

Rote learning. Learning information primarily through verbatim repetition, without understanding it in a meaningful fashion.

Salience. In concept learning, the degree to which a particular feature or characteristic is obvious and easily noticeable.

Savant syndrome. A syndrome characterized by an extraordinary ability to perform a specific task despite difficulty in other aspects of mental functioning; occasionally observed in students with autism.

Scaffolding. A support mechanism, provided by a more competent individual, that helps a learner successfully perform a task within his or her zone of proximal development.

Schema. An organized body of knowledge about a specific topic.

Scheme. In Piaget's theory, an organized group of similar actions or thoughts.

Script. A schema that involves a predictable sequence of events related to a common activity.

Scripted cooperation. In cooperative learning, a technique in which cooperative groups follow a set of steps or "script" that guides members' verbal interactions.

Secondary reinforcer. A stimulus that becomes reinforcing over time through its association with another reinforcer; it is sometimes called a **conditioned reinforcer.**

Self-actualization. The tendency for human beings to enhance themselves and fulfill their potential—to strive toward becoming everything that they are capable of becoming.

Self-concept. One's beliefs about oneself.

Self-contained class. A class in which students with special needs are educated as a group apart from other students.

Self-determination. A sense that one has some choice and control regarding the future course of one's life.

Self-efficacy. The belief that one is capable of executing certain behaviors or reaching certain goals.

Self-esteem. The extent to which one believes oneself to be a capable and worthy individual.

Self-evaluation. The process of evaluating one's own performance or behavior.

Self-fulfilling prophecy. A situation in which one's expectations in and of themselves lead to the expected result.

Self-imposed contingencies. Contingencies that students impose on themselves; the self-reinforcements and self-punishments that follow various behaviors.

Self-instructions. Instructions that students give themselves as they perform a complex behavior.

Self-monitoring. The process of observing and recording one's own behavior.

Self-questioning. The process of asking oneself questions as a way of checking one's understanding of a topic.

Self-regulated learning. Regulating one's own cognitive processes to learn successfully; includes goal setting, planning, attention control, use of effective learning strategies, self-monitoring, and self-evaluation.

Self-regulated problem-solving strategy. A strategy that helps students solve their own interpersonal problems.

Self-regulation. The process of setting standards and goals for oneself and engaging in behaviors that lead to the accomplishment of those standards and goals.

Self-talk. Talking to oneself as a way of guiding oneself through a task; also known as *private speech.*

Semantics. The meanings of words and word combinations.

Sense of community. In the classroom, a widely shared feeling that teacher and students have common goals, are mutually respectful and supportive of one another's efforts, and believe that everyone makes an important contribution to classroom learning.

Sense of school community. The sense that all faculty and students within a school are working together to help every student learn.

Sensitive period. An age range during which a certain aspect of a child's development is especially susceptible to environmental conditions.

Sensorimotor stage. Piaget's first stage of cognitive development, in which schemes are based on behaviors and perceptions.

Sensory register. A component of memory that holds incoming information in an unanalyzed form for a very brief period of time (probably less than a second for visual input and two or three seconds for auditory input).

Separation and control of variables. The ability to test one variable at a time while holding all other variables constant.

Setting event. In behaviorism, a complex environmental condition in which a particular behavior is most likely to occur.

Severe and multiple disabilities. A category of special needs in which students have two or more disabilities, the combination of which requires significant adaptations and highly specialized services in their educational programs.

Shame. A feeling of embarrassment or humiliation that children feel after failing to meet the standards for moral behavior that adults have set.

Shaping. A process of reinforcing successively closer and closer approximations to a desired terminal behavior.

Short-term memory. See *working memory.*

Short-term objective. An objective that can typically be accomplished within the course of a single lesson or unit.

Signal. In expository instruction, a cue that lets students know that something is important to learn.

Single classification. The ability to classify objects in only one way at any given point in time.

Situated cognition. Knowledge and thinking skills that are acquired and used primarily within certain contexts, with limited if any transfer to other contexts.

Situated motivation. A phenomenon whereby aspects of one's immediate environment enhance one's motivation to learn particular things or behave in particular ways.

Social cognitive theory. A theoretical perspective in which learning by observing others is the focus of study.

Social constructivism. A theoretical perspective that focuses on people's collective efforts to impose meaning on the world.

Socialization. The process of shaping a child's behavior to fit the norms and roles of the child's society.

Social reinforcer. A gesture or sign that one person gives another to communicate positive regard.

Social skills. Behaviors that enable an individual to interact effectively with others.

Sociocultural perspective. A theoretical perspective that emphasizes the importance of society and culture for promoting cognitive development.

Socioeconomic status (SES). One's general social and economic standing in society, encompassing such variables as family income, occupation, and level of education.

Sociolinguistic conventions. Specific language-related behaviors that appear in some cultures or ethnic groups but not in others.

Specific transfer. An instance of transfer in which the original learning task and the transfer task overlap in content.

Speech and communication disorders. A category of special needs characterized by abnormalities in spoken language or language comprehension that significantly interfere with students' classroom performance.

Stage. A period in a child's development characterized by certain behaviors and/or reasoning skills. The nature and sequence of different stages of development are believed by stage theorists to be relatively consistent from one child to another.

Stage theory. A theory that depicts development as a series of stages, with relatively slow growth within each stage and more rapid growth during the transition from one stage to another.

Standard deviation (SD). A statistic that reflects how close together or far apart a set of scores are and thereby indicates the variability of the scores.

Standard English. The form of English generally considered acceptable at school, as reflected in textbooks, grammar instruction, and so on.

Standardization. The extent to which assessment instruments and procedures involve similar content and format and are administered and scored in the same way for everyone.

Standardized test. A test developed by test construction experts and published for use in many different schools and classrooms.

Standards. General statements regarding the knowledge and skills that students should achieve and the characteristics that their accomplishments should reflect.

Standard score. A test score that indicates how far a student's performance is from the mean in terms of standard deviation units.

Stanine. A standard score with a mean of 5 and a standard deviation of 2; it is always reported as a whole number.

State anxiety. A temporary feeling of anxiety elicited by a threatening situation.

Stereotype. A rigid, simplistic, and erroneous caricature of a particular group of people.

Stimulus (S) (pl. stimuli). A specific object or event that influences an individual's learning or behavior.

Storage. The process of "putting" new information into memory.

Students at risk. Students who have a high probability of failing to acquire the minimal academic skills necessary for success in the adult world.

Students with special needs. Students who are different enough from their peers that they require specially adapted instructional materials and practices.

Summative evaluation. An evaluation conducted after instruction is completed and used to assess students' final achievement.

Superimposed meaningful structure. A mnemonic technique in which a familiar shape, word, sentence, poem, or story is imposed on information and thereby used to remember it.

Symbolic model. A real or fictional character portrayed in the media that influences an observer's behavior.

Symbolic thinking. The ability to represent and think about external objects and events in one's head.

Syntax. The set of rules that one uses (often unconsciously) to put words together into sentences.

Table of specifications. A two-way grid that indicates both the topics to be covered in an assessment and the things that students should be able to do with each topic.

Task analysis. A process of identifying the specific knowledge and/or behaviors necessary to master a particular subject area or skill.

Teacher-developed assessment instrument. An assessment tool developed by an individual teacher for use in his or her own classroom.

Terminal behavior. The form and frequency of a response at the end of operant conditioning.

Test anxiety. Excessive anxiety about a particular test or about tests in general.

Testwiseness. Test-taking know-how that enhances test performance.

Theory. An organized body of concepts and principles developed to explain certain

phenomena; a description of possible underlying mechanisms to explain why certain principles are true.

Threat. A situation in which individuals believe that they have little or no chance of success.

Time-out. A procedure whereby a misbehaving student is placed in a dull, boring situation with no opportunity to interact with classmates and no opportunity to obtain reinforcement.

Token economy. A technique whereby desired behaviors are reinforced by tokens, reinforcers that students can use to "purchase" a variety of other reinforcers.

Traditional assessment. Assessment that focuses on measuring basic knowledge and skills in relative isolation from tasks more typical of the outside world.

Trait anxiety. A pattern of responding with anxiety even in nonthreatening situations.

Transductive reasoning. Making a mental leap from one specific thing to another, such as identifying one event as the cause of another simply because the two events occur close together in time.

Transfer. A phenomenon whereby something that an individual has learned at one time affects how the individual learns or performs in a later situation.

Translating. In writing, the process of converting one's ideas into written language.

Treatment group. A group of people in a research study who are given a particular experimental treatment (e.g., a particular method of instruction).

Unconditioned response (UCR). A response that, without prior learning, is elicited by a particular stimulus.

Unconditioned stimulus (UCS). A stimulus that, without prior learning, elicits a particular response.

Undergeneralization. An overly restricted meaning for a word that excludes some situations to which the word does, in fact, apply; an overly narrow view of what objects or events a concept includes.

Uninvolved parenting style. A parenting style characterized by a lack of emotional support and a lack of standards regarding appropriate behavior.

Universals (in development). The similar patterns we see in how children change over time regardless of the specific environment in which they are raised.

Validity. The extent to which an assessment instrument measures what it is supposed to measure.

Verbal mediator. A mnemonic technique in which a word or phrase is used to form a logical connection or "bridge" between two pieces of information.

Vicarious punishment. A phenomenon whereby a response decreases in frequency when another (observed) person is punished for that response.

Vicarious reinforcement. A phenomenon whereby a response increases in frequency when another (observed) person is reinforced for that response.

Visual imagery. The process of forming mental "pictures" of objects or ideas.

Visual impairments. A category of special needs characterized by malfunctions of the eyes or optic nerves that prevent students from seeing normally even with corrective lenses.

Visual-spatial thinking. The ability to imagine and mentally manipulate two- and three-dimensional figures in one's mind.

Wait time. The length of time a teacher pauses, either after asking a question or hearing a student's comment, before saying something else.

Well-defined problem. A problem in which the goal is clearly stated, all information needed to solve the problem is present, and only one correct answer exists.

Whole language instruction. An approach to teaching reading and writing in which basic skills are taught solely within the context of authentic reading and writing tasks.

Withitness. The appearance that a teacher knows what all students are doing at all times.

Word decoding. In reading, identifying the sounds associated with a word's letters and then determining what the word probably is.

Working memory. A component of memory that holds and processes a limited amount of information; also known as *short-term memory*. The duration of information stored in working memory is believed to be approximately five to twenty seconds.

Zone of proximal development (ZPD). In Vygotsky's theory, the range of tasks between one's actual developmental level and one's level of potential development—that is, the range of tasks that one cannot yet perform independently but *can* perform with the help and guidance of others.

z-score. A standard score with a mean of 0 and a standard deviation of 1.

References

Abdul-Jabbar, K., & Knobles, P. (1983). *Giant steps: The autobiography of Kareem Abdul-Jabbar.* New York: Bantam.

Abery, B., & Zajac, R. (1996). Self-determination as a goal of early childhood and elementary education. In D. J. Sands & M. L. Wehmeyer (Eds.), *Self-determination across the life span: Independence and choice for people with disabilities.* Baltimore: Paul H. Brookes.

Abi-Nader, J. (1993). Meeting the needs of multicultural classrooms: Family values and the motivation of minority students. In M. J. O'Hair & S. J. Odell (Eds.), *Diversity and teaching: Teacher education yearbook I.* Fort Worth, TX: Harcourt Brace Jovanovich.

Ablard, K. E., & Lipschultz, R. E. (1998). Self-regulated learning in high-achieving students: Relations to advanced reasoning, achievement goals, and gender. *Journal of Educational Psychology, 90,* 94–101.

Achenbach, T. M., & Edelbrock, C. S. (1981). Behavioral problems and competencies reported by parents of normal and disturbed children aged four through sixteen. *Monographs of the Society for Research in Child Development, 46*(1, Serial No. 188).

Adams, G. R., Gullotta, T. P., & Markstrom-Adams, C. (1994). *Adolescent life experiences* (3rd ed.). Pacific Grove, CA: Brooks/Cole.

Adams, M. J. (1990). *Beginning to read: Thinking and learning about print.* Cambridge, MA: MIT Press.

Adams, P. A., & Adams, J. K. (1960). Confidence in the recognition and reproduction of words difficult to spell. *American Journal of Psychology, 73,* 544–552.

Adelman, H. S. (1996). Appreciating the classification dilemma. In W. Stainback & S. Stainback (Eds.), *Controversial issues confronting special education: Diverse perspectives.* Boston: Allyn & Bacon.

Aiello, B. (1988). The Kids on the Block and attitude change: A 10-year perspective. In H. E. Yuker (Ed.), *Attitudes toward persons with disabilities.* New York: Springer.

Airasian, P. W. (1994). *Classroom assessment* (2nd ed.). New York: McGraw-Hill.

Alderman, M. K. (1990). Motivation for at-risk students. *Educational Leadership, 48*(1), 27–30.

Alexander, K. L., Entwisle, D. R., & Thompson, M. (1987). School performance, status relations, and the structure of sentiment: Bringing the teacher back in. *American Sociological Review, 52,* 665–682.

Alexander, P. A. (1996). The past, present, and future of knowledge research: A reexamination of the role of knowledge in learning and instruction. *Educational Psychologist, 31,* 89–92.

Alexander, P. A. (1997). Mapping the multidimensional nature of domain learning: The interplay of cognitive, motivational, and strategic forces. In P. R. Pintrich & M. L. Maehr (Eds.), *Advances in motivation and achievement* (Vol. 10). Greenwich, CT: JAI Press.

Alexander, P. A., Graham, S., & Harris, K. R. (1998). A perspective on strategy research: Progress and prospects. *Educational Psychology Review, 10,* 129–154.

Alexander, P. A., & Jetton, T. L. (1996). The role of importance and interest in the processing of text. *Educational Psychology Review, 8,* 89–121.

Alexander, P. A., & Judy, J. E. (1988). The interaction of domain-specific and strategic knowledge in academic performance. *Review of Educational Research, 58,* 375–404.

Alexander, P. A., Kulikowich, J. M., & Schulze, S. K. (1994). How subject-matter knowledge affects recall and interest. *American Educational Research Journal, 31,* 313–337.

Alfassi, M. (1998). Reading for meaning: The efficacy of reciprocal teaching in fostering reading comprehension in high school students in remedial reading classes. *American Educational Research Journal, 35,* 309–332.

Alleman, J., & Brophy, J. (1997). Elementary social studies: Instruments, activities, and standards. In G. D. Phye (Ed.), *Handbook of classroom assessment: Learning, achievement, and adjustment.* San Diego: Academic Press.

Alleman, J., & Brophy, J. (1998, April). *Strategic learning opportunities during out-of-school hours.* Paper presented at the annual meeting of the American Educational Research Association, San Diego.

Alley, G., & Deshler, D. (1979). *Teaching the learning disabled adolescent: Strategies and methods.* Denver, CO: Love.

Allington, R. L., & Weber, R. (1993). Questioning questions in teaching and learning from texts. In B. K. Britton, A. Woodward, & M. Binkley (Eds.), *Learning from textbooks: Theory and practice.* Hillsdale, NJ: Erlbaum.

Alvermann, D. E., & Moore, D. W. (1991). Secondary school reading. In R. Barr, M. L. Kamil, P. B. Mosenthal, & P. D. Pearson (Eds.), *Handbook of reading research: Vol. II.* New York: Longman.

Amabile, T. M., & Hennessey, B. A. (1992). The motivation for creativity in children. In A. K. Boggiano & T. S. Pittman (Eds.), *Achievement and motivation: A social-developmental perspective.* Cambridge, England: Cambridge University Press.

Ambrose, D., Allen, J., & Huntley, S. B. (1994). Mentorship of the highly creative. *Roeper Review, 17,* 131–133.

American Association on Mental Retardation. (1992). *Mental retardation: Definition, classification, and systems of supports* (9th ed.). Washington, DC: Author.

American Psychiatric Association. (1994). *Diagnostic and statistical manual of mental disorders* (4th ed.). Washington, DC: Author.

Ames, C. (1984). Competitive, cooperative, and individualistic goal structures: A cognitive-motivational analysis. In R. Ames & C. Ames (Eds.), *Research on motivation in education: Vol. 1. Student motivation.* San Diego: Academic Press.

Ames, C. (1992). Classrooms: Goals, structures, and student motivation. *Journal of Educational Psychology, 84,* 261–271.

Ames, C., & Archer, J. (1988). Achievement goals in the classroom: Students' learning strategies and motivation processes. *Journal of Educational Psychology, 80,* 260–267.

Ames, R. (1983). Help-seeking and achievement orientation: Perspectives from attribution theory. In A. Nadler, J. Fisher, & B. DePaulo (Eds.), *New directions in helping* (Vol. 2). New York: Academic Press.

Anderman, E. M., Griesinger, T., & Westerfield, G. (1998). Motivation and cheating during early adolescence. *Journal of Educational Psychology, 90,* 84–93.

Anderman, E. M., & Maehr, M. L. (1994). Motivation and schooling in the middle grades. *Review of Educational Research, 64,* 287–309.

Anderson, J. R. (1983). *The architecture of cognition.* Cambridge, MA: Harvard University Press.

Anderson, J. R. (1987). Skill acquisition: Compilation of weak-method problem solutions. *Psychological Review, 94,* 192–210.

Anderson, J. R. (1990). *Cognitive psychology and its implications* (3rd ed.). New York: W. H. Freeman.

Anderson, J. R. (1995). *Learning and memory: An integrated approach.* New York: Wiley.

Anderson, J. R., Reder, L. M., & Simon, H. A. (1996). Situated learning and education. *Educational Researcher, 25*(4), 5–11.

Anderson, L. M. (1993). Auxiliary materials that accompany textbook: Can they promote "higher-order" learning? In B. K. Britton, A. Woodward, & M. Binkley (Eds.), *Learning from textbooks: Theory and practice.* Hillsdale, NJ: Erlbaum.

Anderson, L. M., Brubaker, N. L., Alleman-Brooks, J., & Duffy, G. (1985). A qualitative study of seatwork in first-grade classrooms. *Elementary School Journal, 86,* 123–140.

Anderson, N. S. (1987). Cognition, learning, and memory. In M. A. Baker (Ed.), *Sex differences in human performance.* Chichester, England: Wiley.

Anderson, R. C., Reynolds, R. E., Schallert, D. L., & Goetz, E. T. (1977). Frameworks for comprehending discourse. *American Educational Research Journal, 14,* 367–381.

Anderson, R. C., Shirey, L., Wilson, P., & Fielding, L. (1987). Interestingness of children's reading materials. In R. Snow & M. Farr (Eds.), *Aptitude, learning, and instruction: III. Conative and affective process analyses.* Hillsdale, NJ: Erlbaum.

Anderson, R. C., Wilson, P. T., & Fielding, L. G. (1988). Growth in reading and how children spend their time outside of school. *Reading Research Quarterly, 23,* 285–303.

Anderson, R. G., & Freebody, P. (1981). Vocabulary knowledge. In J. T. Guthrie (Ed.), *Comprehension and teaching: Research reviews.* Newark, DE: International Reading Association.

Anderson, V., & Hidi, S. (1988/1989). Teaching students to summarize. *Educational Leadership, 46*(4), 26–28.

Andre, T. (1979). Does answering higher-level questions while reading facilitate productive learning? *Review of Educational Research, 49,* 280–318.

Andre, T. (1986). Problem solving and education. In G. D. Phye & T. Andre (Eds.), *Cognitive classroom learning: Understanding, thinking, and problem solving.* San Diego: Academic Press.

Anglin, J. M. (1977). *Word, object, and conceptual development.* New York: Norton.

Anzai, Y. (1991). Learning and use of representations for physics expertise. In K. A. Ericsson & J. Smith (Eds.), *Toward a general theory of expertise: Prospects and limits.* Cambridge, England: Cambridge University Press.

Archer, S. L. (1982). The lower age boundaries of identity development. *Child Development, 53,* 1551-1556.

Arenz, B. W., & Lee, M. J. (1990, April). *Gender differences in the attitude, interest and participation of secondary students in computer use.* Paper presented at the annual meeting of the American Educational Research Association, Boston.

Arlin, M. (1979). Teacher transitions can disrupt time flow in classrooms. *American Educational Research Journal, 16,* 42-56.

Arlin, M. (1984). Time, equality, and mastery learning. *Review of Educational Research, 54,* 65-86.

Armbruster, B. B. (1984). The problem of "inconsiderate text." In G. G. Duffy, L. R. Roehler, & J. Mason (Eds.), *Comprehension instruction: Perspectives and suggestions.* New York: Longman.

Armstrong, T. (1994). *Multiple intelligences in the classroom.* Alexandria, VA: Association for Supervision and Curriculum Development.

Arnett, J. (1995). The young and the reckless: Adolescent reckless behavior. *Current Directions in Psychological Science, 4,* 67-71.

Aronson, E., & Patnoe, S. (1997). *The jigsaw classroom: Building cooperation in the classroom* (2nd ed.). New York: Longman.

Arter, J. A., & Spandel, V. (1992). Using portfolios of student work in instruction and assessment. *Educational Measurement: Issues and Practice, 11*(1), 36-44.

Asai, S. (1993). In search of Asia through music: Guidelines and ideas for teaching Asian music. In T. Perry & J. W. Fraser (Eds.), *Freedom's plow: Teaching in the multicultural classroom.* New York: Routledge.

Asher, S. R., & Coie, J. D. (Eds.). (1990). *Peer rejection in childhood.* Cambridge, England: Cambridge University Press.

Asher, S. R., & Parker, J. G. (1989). Significance of peer relationship problems in childhood. In B. H. Schneider, G. Attili, J. Nadel, & R. P. Weissberg (Eds.), *Social competence in developmental perspective.* Dordrecht, The Netherlands: Kluwer.

Ashton, P. (1985). Motivation and the teacher's sense of efficacy. In C. Ames & R. Ames (Eds.), *Research on motivation in education: Vol. 2. The classroom milieu.* San Diego: Academic Press.

Assor, A., & Connell, J. P. (1992). The validity of students' self-reports as measures of performance affecting self-appraisals. In D. H. Schunk & J. L. Meece (Eds.), *Student perceptions in the classroom.* Hillsdale, NJ: Erlbaum.

Atkinson, R. C., & Shiffrin, R. M. (1968). Human memory: A proposed system and its control processes. In K. W. Spence & J. T. Spence (Eds.), *The psychology of learning and motivation: Advances in research and theory* (Vol. 2). San Diego: Academic Press.

Au, K. H. (1980). Participation structures in a reading lesson with Hawaiian children: Analysis of a culturally appropriate instructional event. *Anthropology and Education Quarterly, 11,* 91-115.

Aulls, M. W. (1998). Contributions of classroom discourse to what content students learn during curriculum enactment. *Journal of Educational Psychology, 90,* 56-69.

Ausubel, D. P. (1968). *Educational psychology: A cognitive view.* New York: Holt, Rinehart & Winston.

Ausubel, D. P., Novak, J. D., & Hanesian, H. (1978). *Educational psychology: A cognitive view* (2nd ed.). New York: Holt, Rinehart & Winston.

Babad, E. (1993). Teachers' differential behavior. *Educational Psychology Review, 5,* 347-376.

Baek, S. (1994). Implications of cognitive psychology for educational testing. *Educational Psychology Review, 6,* 373-389.

Bahrick, H. P., Bahrick, L. E., Bahrick, A. S., & Bahrick, P. E. (1993). Maintenance of foreign language vocabulary and the spacing effect. *Psychological Science, 4,* 316-321.

Baker, E. L. (1994). Learning-based assessments of history understanding. *Educational Psychologist, 29,* 97-106.

Baker, L. (1989). Metacognition, comprehension monitoring, and the adult reader. *Educational Psychology Review, 1,* 3-38.

Baker, L., & Brown, A. L. (1984). Metacognitive skills of reading. In D. Pearson (Ed.), *Handbook of reading research.* White Plains, NY: Longman.

Baker, L., Scher, D., & Mackler, K. (1997). Home and family influences on motivations for reading. *Educational Psychologist, 32,* 69-82.

Balla, D. A., & Zigler, E. (1979). Personality development in retarded persons. In N. R. Ellis (Ed.), *Handbook of mental deficiency: Psychological theory and research* (2nd ed.). Hillsdale, NJ: Erlbaum.

Bandura, A. (1965). Influence of models' reinforcement contingencies on the acquisition of imitative responses. *Journal of Personality and Social Psychology, 1,* 589-595.

Bandura, A. (1977). *Social learning theory.* Upper Saddle River, NJ: Prentice Hall.

Bandura, A. (1982). Self-efficacy mechanism in human agency. *American Psychologist, 37,* 122-147.

Bandura, A. (1986). *Social foundations of thought and action: A social cognitive theory.* Upper Saddle River, NJ: Prentice Hall.

Bandura, A. (1989). Human agency in social cognitive theory. *American Psychologist, 44,* 1175-1184.

Bandura, A., & McDonald, F. J. (1963). Influences of social reinforcement and the behavior of models in shaping children's moral judgments. *Journal of Abnormal and Social Psychology, 67,* 274-281.

Bandura, A., Ross, D., & Ross, S. A. (1961). Transmission of aggression through imitation of aggressive models. *Journal of Abnormal & Social Psychology, 63,* 575-582.

Bandura, A., Ross, D., & Ross, S. A. (1963). Imitation of film-mediated aggressive models. *Journal of Abnormal & Social Psychology, 66,* 3-11.

Bangert-Drowns, R. L., Kulik, C. C., Kulik, J. A., & Morgan, M. (1991). The instructional effect of feedback in test-like events. *Review of Educational Research, 61,* 213-238.

Banks, J. A. (1991). Multicultural literacy and curriculum reform. *Educational Horizons, 69*(3), 135-140.

Banks, J. A. (1994a). *An introduction to multicultural education.* Needham Heights, MA: Allyn & Bacon.

Banks, J. A. (1994b). Transforming the mainstream curriculum. *Educational Leadership, 51*(8), 4-8.

Banks, J. A. (1995). Multicultural education: Historical development, dimensions, and practice. In J. A. Banks & C. A. M. Banks (Eds.), *Handbook of research on multicultural education.* New York: Macmillan.

Barbetta, P. M. (1990). GOALS: A group-oriented adapted levels system for children with behavior disorders. *Academic Therapy, 25,* 645-656.

Barbetta, P. M., Heward, W. L., Bradley, D. M., & Miller, A. D. (1994). Effects of immediate and delayed error correction on the acquisition and maintenance of sight words by students with developmental disabilities. *Journal of Applied Behavior Analysis, 27,* 177-178.

Barga, N. K. (1996). Students with learning disabilities in education: Managing a disability. *Journal of Learning Disabilities, 29,* 413-421.

Barkley, R. A. (1990). *Attention-deficit hyperactivity disorder: A handbook for diagnosis and treatment.* New York: Guilford Press.

Barkley, R. A. (1994). Impaired delayed responding: A unified theory of attention-deficit hyperactivity disorder. In R. A. Barkley (Ed.), *Disruptive behavior disorders in childhood.* New York: Plenum Press.

Barkley, R. A. (1995a). ADHD and IQ. *ADHD Report, 3*(2), 1.

Barkley, R. A. (1995b). *Taking charge of ADHD: The complete, authoritative guide for parents.* New York: Guilford Press.

Barkley, R. A. (1996). Linkages between attention and executive functions. In G. R. Lyon & N. A. Krasnegor (Eds.), *Attention, memory, and executive function.* Baltimore: Paul H. Brookes.

Barnes, D. (1976). *From communication to curriculum.* London: Penguin.

Barnett, J. E., Di Vesta, F. J., & Rogozinski, J. T. (1981). What is learned in note taking? *Journal of Educational Psychology, 73,* 181-192.

Baron, J. B. (1987). Evaluating thinking skills in the classroom. In J. B. Baron & R. J. Sternberg (Eds.), *Teaching thinking skills: Theory and practice.* New York: W. H. Freeman.

Barrish, H. H., Saunders, M., & Wolf, M. M. (1969). Good behavior game: Effects of individual contingencies for group consequences on disruptive behavior in a classroom. *Journal of Applied Behavior Analysis, 2,* 119-124.

Bartlett, E. J. (1982). Learning to revise: Some component processes. In M. Nystrand (Ed.), *What writers know: The language, process, and structure of written discourse.* New York: Academic Press.

Bartlett, F. C. (1932). *Remembering: A study in experimental and social psychology.* Cambridge, England: Cambridge University Press.

Barton, K. C., & Levstik, L. S. (1996). "Back when God was around and everything": Elementary children's understanding of historical time. *American Educational Research Journal, 33,* 419-454.

Bassett, D. S., Jackson, L., Ferrell, K. A., Luckner, J., Hagerty, P. J., Bunsen, T. D., & MacIsaac, D. (1996). Multiple perspectives on inclusive education: Reflections of a university faculty. *Teacher Education and Special Education, 19,* 355-386.

Bassok, M. (1990). Transfer of domain-specific problem-solving procedures. *Journal of Experimental Psychology: Learning, Memory, and Cognition, 16,* 522-533.

Bassok, M. (1996). Using content to interpret structure: Effects on analogical transfer. *Current Directions in Psychological Science, 5,* 54-58.

Bates, E., & MacWhinney, B. (1987). Competition, variation, and language learning. In B. MacWhinney (Ed.), *Mechanisms of language acquisition.* Hillsdale, NJ: Erlbaum.

Batshaw, M. L., & Shapiro, B. K. (1997). Mental retardation. In M. L. Batshaw (Ed.), *Children with disabilities* (4th ed.). Baltimore: Paul H. Brookes.

Battistich, V., Solomon, D., Kim, D., Watson, M., & Schaps, E. (1995). Schools as communities, poverty levels of student populations, and students' attitudes, motives, and performance: A multilevel analysis. *American Educational Research Journal, 32,* 627-658.

Battistich, V., Solomon, D., Watson, M., & Schaps, E. (1997). Caring school communities. *Educational Psychologist, 32,* 137-151.

Baumeister, A. A. (1989). Mental retardation. In C. G. Lask & M. Hersen (Eds.), *Handbook of child psychiatric diagnosis.* New York: Wiley.

Baumrind, D. (1971). Current patterns of parental authority. *Developmental Psychology Monograph, 4*(No. 1, Part 2).

Baumrind, D. (1989). Rearing competent children. In W. Damon (Ed.), *Child development today and tomorrow.* San Francisco: Jossey-Bass.

Baxter, G. P., Elder, A. D., & Glaser, R. (1996). Knowledge-based cognition and performance assessment in the science classroom. *Educational Psychologist, 31,* 133-140.

Bay-Hinitz, A. K., Peterson, R. F., & Quilitch, H. R. (1994). Cooperative games: A way to modify aggressive and cooperative behaviors in young children. *Journal of Applied Behavior Analysis, 27,* 435-446.

Beal, C. R. (1996). The role of comprehension monitoring in children's revision. *Educational Psychology Review, 8,* 219-238.

Bean, T. W., & Steenwyk, F. L. (1984). The effect of three forms of summarization instruction on sixth graders' summary writing and comprehension. *Journal of Reading Behavior, 16,* 297-306.

Bear, G. G., & Richards, H. C. (1981). Moral reasoning and conduct problems in the classroom. *Journal of Educational Psychology, 73,* 644-670.

Beck, I. L., McKeown, M. G., & Gromoll, E. W. (1989). Learning from social studies texts. *Cognition and Instruction, 6,* 99-158.

Beck, I. L., McKeown, M. G., Sinatra, G. M., & Loxterman, J. A. (1991). Revising social studies text from a text-processing perspective: Evidence of improved comprehensibility. *Reading Research Quarterly, 26,* 251-276.

Beck, I. L., McKeown, M. G., Worthy, J., Sandora, C. A., & Kucan, L. (1996). Questioning the author: A yearlong classroom implementation to engage students with text. *The Elementary School Journal, 96,* 385-414.

Bédard, J., & Chi, M. T. H. (1992). Expertise. *Current Directions in Psychological Science, 1,* 135-139.

Begg, I., Anas, A., & Farinacci, S. (1992). Dissociation of processes in belief: Source recollection, statement familiarity, and the illusion of truth. *Journal of Experimental Psychology: General, 121,* 446-458.

Belfiore, P. J., Lee, D. L., Vargas, A. U., & Skinner, C. H. (1997). Effects of high-preference single-digit mathematics problem completion on multiple-digit mathematics problem performance. *Journal of Applied Behavior Analysis, 30,* 327-330.

Bellezza, F. S. (1986). Mental cues and verbal reports in learning. In G. H. Bower (Ed.), *The psychology of learning and motivation: Advances in research and theory* (Vol. 20). San Diego: Academic Press.

Bem, S. L. (1984). Androgyny and gender schema theory: A conceptual and empirical integration. In R. A. Dienstbier & T. B. Sonderegger (Eds.), *Nebraska symposium on motivation* (Vol. 34). Lincoln: University of Nebraska Press.

Bender, T. A. (1997). Assessment of subjective well-being during childhood and adolescence. In G. D. Phye (Ed.), *Handbook of classroom assessment: Learning, achievement, and adjustment.* San Diego: Academic Press.

Bennett, G. K., Seashore, H. G., & Wesman, A. G. (1982). *Differential Aptitude Tests.* San Antonio, TX: Psychological Corporation.

Benton, S. L. (1997). Psychological foundations of elementary writing instruction. In G. D. Phye (Ed.), *Handbook of academic learning: Construction of knowledge.* San Diego: Academic Press.

Benware, C., & Deci, E. L. (1984). Quality of learning with an active versus passive motivational set. *American Educational Research Journal, 21,* 755-765.

Bereiter, C. (1994). Implications of postmodernism for science, or, science as progressive discourse. *Educational Psychologist, 29*(1), 3-12.

Bereiter, C. (1995). A dispositional view of transfer. In A. McKeough, J. Lupart, & A. Marini (Eds.), *Teaching for transfer: Fostering generalization in learning.* Mahwah, NJ: Erlbaum.

Bereiter, C., & Scardamalia, M. (1987). *The psychology of written composition.* Hillsdale, NJ: Erlbaum.

Berk, L. E. (1994). Why children talk to themselves. *Scientific American, 271,* 78-83.

Berk, L. E. (1997). *Child development* (4th ed.). Boston: Allyn & Bacon.

Berkowitz, M. W., Guerra, N., & Nucci, L. (1991). Sociomoral development and drug and alcohol abuse. In W. M. Kurtines & J. L. Gewirtz (Eds.), *Moral behavior and development: Vol. 3. Application.* Hillsdale, NJ: Erlbaum.

Berliner, D. C. (1988, February). *The development of expertise in pedagogy.* Paper presented at the American Association of Colleges for Teacher Education, New Orleans, LA.

Berliner, D. C. (1997, March). Discussant's comments. In H. Borko (Chair), *Educational psychology and teacher education: Perennial issues.* Symposium conducted at the annual meeting of the American Educational Research Association, Chicago.

Berlyne, D. E. (1960). *Conflict, arousal, and curiosity.* New York: McGraw-Hill.

Bermejo, V. (1996). Cardinality development and counting. *Developmental Psychology, 32,* 263-268.

Berndt, T. J. (1992). Friendship and friends' influence in adolescence. *Current Directions in Psychological Science, 1,* 156-159.

Berndt, T. J., Laychak, A. E., & Park, K. (1990). Friends' influence on adolescents' academic achievement motivation: An experimental study. *Journal of Educational Psychology, 82,* 664-670.

Berninger, V. W., Fuller, F., & Whitaker, D. (1996). A process model of writing development across the life span. *Educational Psychology Review, 8,* 193-218.

Beyer, B. K. (1985). Critical thinking: What is it? *Social Education, 49,* 270-276.

Bialystok, E. (1994). Representation and ways of knowing: Three issues in second language acquisition. In N. C. Ellis (Ed.), *Implicit and explicit learning of languages.* London: Academic Press.

Bierman, K. L., Miller, C. L., & Stabb, S. D. (1987). Improving the social behavior and peer acceptance of rejected boys: Effect of social skill training with instructions and prohibitions. *Journal of Consulting and Clinical Psychology, 55,* 194-200.

Binns, K., Steinberg, A., Amorosi, S., & Cuevas, A. M. (1997). *The Metropolitan Life survey of the American teacher 1997: Examining gender issues in public schools.* New York: Louis Harris and Associates.

Bjorklund, D. F. (1987). How age changes in knowledge base contribute to the development of children's memory: An interpretive review. *Developmental Review, 7,* 93-130.

Bjorklund, D. F., & Coyle, T. R. (1995). Utilization deficiencies in the development of memory strategies. In F. E. Weinert & W. Schneider (Eds.), *Research on memory development: State of the art and future directions.* Hillsdale, NJ: Erlbaum.

Bjorklund, D. F., Schneider, W., Cassel, W. S., & Ashley, E. (1994). Training and extension of a memory strategy: Evidence for utilization deficiencies in high- and low-IQ children. *Child Development, 65,* 951-965.

Bjorkqvist, K., Osterman, K., & Kaukiainen, A. (1992). The development of direct and indirect aggressive strategies in males and females. In K. Bjorkqvist & P. Niemala (Eds.), *Of mice and women: Aspects of female aggression.* San Diego: Academic Press.

Blades, M., & Spencer, C. (1987). Young children's strategies when using maps with landmarks. *Journal of Environmental Psychology, 7,* 201-217.

Blake, S. B., & Clark, R. E. (1990, April). *The effects of metacognitive selection on far transfer in analogical problem solving tasks.* Paper presented at the annual meeting of the American Educational Research Association, Boston.

Blasi, A. (1980). Bridging moral cognition and moral action: A critical review of the literature. *Psychological Bulletin, 88,* 593-637.

Block, J. H. (1980). Promoting excellence through mastery learning. *Theory Into Practice, 19*(1), 66-74.

Block, J. H. (1983). Differential premises arising from differential socialization of the sexes: Some conjectures. *Child Development, 54,* 1335-1354.

Block, J. H., & Burns, R. B. (1976). Mastery learning. In L. Shulman (Ed.), *Review of research in education* (Vol. 4). Itasca, IL: Peacock.

Bloom, B. S. (1964). *Stability and change in human characteristics.* New York: Wiley.

Bloom, B. S. (1976). *Human characteristics and school learning.* New York: McGraw-Hill.

Bloom, B. S. (1981). *All our children learning.* New York: McGraw-Hill.

Bloom, B. S., Englehart, M. D., Furst, E. J., Hill, W. H., & Krathwohl, D. R. (1956). *Taxonomy of educational objectives. The classification of educational goals: Handbook I. Cognitive domain.* New York: David McKay.

Blumenfeld, P. C. (1992). The task and the teacher: Enhancing student thoughtfulness in science. In J. Brophy (Ed.), *Advances in research on teaching: Vol. 3. Planning and managing learning tasks and activities.* Greenwich, CT: JAI Press.

Blumenfeld, P. C., Marx, R. W., Soloway, E., & Krajcik, J. (1996). Learning with peers: From small group cooperation to collaborative communities. *Educational Researcher, 25*(8), 37-40.

Bochenhauer, M. H. (1990, April). *Connections: Geographic education and the National Geographic Society.* Paper presented at the annual meeting of the American Educational Research Association, Boston.

Boggiano, A. K., & Pittman, T. S. (Eds.). (1992). *Achievement and motivation: A social-developmental perspective.* Cambridge, England: Cambridge University Press.

Boiarsky, C. (1982). Prewriting is the essence of writing. *English Journal, 71,* 44-47.

Borko, H., & Putnam, R. T. (1996). Learning to teach. In D. C. Berliner & R. C. Calfee (Eds.), *Handbook of educational psychology.* New York: Macmillan.

Borkowski, J. G., Carr, M., Rellinger, E., & Pressley, M. (1990). Self-regulated cognition: Interdependence of metacognition, attributions, and self-esteem. In B. F. Jones & L. Idol (Eds.), *Dimensions of thinking and cognitive instruction.* Hillsdale, NJ: Erlbaum.

Born, D. G., & Davis, M. L. (1974). Amount and distribution of study in a personalized instruction course and in a lecture course. *Journal of Applied Behavior Analysis, 7,* 365-375.

Bornholt, L. J., Goodnow, J. J., & Cooney, G. H. (1994). Influences of gender stereotypes on adolescents' perceptions of their own achievement. *American Educational Research Journal, 31,* 675-692.

Boschee, F., & Baron, M. A. (1993). *Outcome-based education: Developing programs through strategic planning.* Lancaster, PA: Technomic.

Bouchard, T. J., Jr., Lykken, D. T., McGue, M., Segal, N. L., & Tellegen, A. (1990, October 12). Sources of human psychological differences: The Minnesota study of twins reared apart. *Science, 250,* 223-228.

Bousfield, W. A. (1953). The occurrence of clustering in the recall of randomly arranged associates. *Journal of General Psychology, 49,* 229-240.

Boutte, G. S., & McCormick, C. B. (1992). Authentic multicultural activities: Avoiding pseudomulticulturalism. *Childhood Education, 68*(3), 140-144.

Bower, G. H., Black, J. B., & Turner, T. J. (1979). Scripts in memory for text. *Cognitive Psychology, 11,* 177-220.

Bower, G. H., & Clark, M. C. (1969). Narrative stories as mediators for serial learning. *Psychonomic Science, 14,* 181-182.

Bower, G. H., Clark, M. C., Lesgold, A. M., & Winzenz, D. (1969). Hierarchical retrieval schemes in recall of categorized word lists. *Journal of Verbal Learning and Verbal Behavior, 8,* 323-343.

Bower, G. H., Karlin, M. B., & Dueck, A. (1975). Comprehension and memory for pictures. *Memory and Cognition, 3,* 216-220.

Bowey, J. (1986). Syntactic awareness and verbal performance from preschool to fifth grade. *Journal of Psycholinguistic Research, 15,* 285-308.

Bowie, R., & Bond, C. (1994). Influencing future teachers' attitudes toward Black English: Are we making a difference? *Journal of Teacher Education, 45*(2), 112-118.

Bowman, B. T. (1989). Educating language-minority children: Challenges and opportunities. *Phi Delta Kappan, 71,* 118-120.

Bowman, L. G., Piazza, C. C., Fisher, W. W., Hagopian, L. P., & Kogan, J. S. (1997). Assessment of preference for varied versus constant reinforcers. *Journal of Applied Behavior Analysis, 30,* 451-458.

Boyatzis, R. E. (1973). Affiliation motivation. In D. C. McClelland & R. S. Steele (Eds.), *Human motivation: A book of readings.* Morristown, NJ: General Learning Press.

Braden, J. P. (1992). Intellectual assessment of deaf and hard-of-hearing people: A quantitative and qualitative research synthesis. *School Psychology Review, 21,* 82-94.

Bradley, L., & Bryant, P. E. (1991). Phonological skills before and after learning to read. In S. A. Brady & D. P. Shankweiler (Eds.), *Phonological processes in literacy.* Hillsdale, NJ: Erlbaum.

Bradley, R. H., & Caldwell, B. M. (1984). The relation of infants' home environments to achievement test performance in first grade: A follow-up study. *Child Development, 55,* 803-809.

Brainerd, C. J., & Reyna, V. F. (1992). Explaining "memory free" reasoning. *Psychological Science, 3,* 332-339.

Brandes, A. A. (1996). Elementary school children's images of science. In Y. Kafai & M. Resnick (Eds.), *Constructionism in practice: Designing, thinking, and learning in a digital world.* Mahwah, NJ: Erlbaum.

Bransford, J. D., & Franks, J. J. (1971). The abstraction of linguistic ideas. *Cognitive Psychology, 2,* 331-350.

Bransford, J. D., Franks, J. J., Vye, N. J., & Sherwood, R. D. (1989). New approaches to instruction: Because wisdom can't be told. In S. Vosniadou & A. Ortony (Eds.), *Similarity and analogical reasoning.* Cambridge, England: Cambridge University Press.

Bransford, J. D., & Johnson, M. K. (1972). Contextual prerequisites for understanding: Some investigations of comprehension and recall. *Journal of Verbal Learning and Verbal Behavior, 11,* 717-726.

Brantlinger, E. (1997). Using ideology: Cases of nonrecognition of the politics of research and practice in special education. *Review of Educational Research, 67,* 425-459.

Braukmann, C. J., Kirigin, K. A., & Wolf, M. M. (1981). Behavioral treatment of juvenile delinquency. In S. W. Bijou & R. Ruiz (Eds.), *Behavior modification: Contributions to education.* Hillsdale, NJ: Erlbaum.

Brenner, M. E., Mayer, R. E., Moseley, B., Brar, T., Durán, R., Reed, B. S., & Webb, D. (1997). Learning by understanding: The role of multiple representations in learning algebra. *American Educational Research Journal, 34,* 663-689.

Brigham, F. J., & Scruggs, T. E. (1995). Elaborative maps for enhanced learning of historical information: Uniting spatial, verbal, and imaginal information. *Journal of Special Education, 28,* 440.

Britt, M. A., Rouet, J-F., Georgi, M. C., & Perfetti, C. A. (1994). Learning from history texts: From causal analysis to argument models. In G. Leinhardt, I. L. Beck, & C. Stainton (Eds.), *Teaching and learning in history.* Hillsdale, NJ: Erlbaum.

Broden, M., Hall, R. V., & Mitts, B. (1971). The effect of self-recording on the classroom behavior of two eighth grade students. *Journal of Applied Behavior Analysis, 4,* 191-199.

Brody, G. H., & Shaffer, D. R. (1982). Contributions of parents and peers to children's moral socialization. *Developmental Review, 2,* 31-75.

Brody, N. (1992). *Intelligence.* New York: Academic Press.

Brody, N. (1997). Intelligence, schooling, and society. *American Psychologist, 52,* 1046-1050.

Brodzinsky, D. M., Messer, S. M., & Tew, J. D. (1979). Sex differences in children's expression and control of fantasy and overt aggression. *Child Development, 50,* 372-379.

Brooke, R. R., & Ruthren, A. J. (1984). The effects of contingency contracting on student performance in a PSI class. *Teaching of Psychology, 11,* 87-89.

Brooks, L. W., & Dansereau, D. F. (1987). Transfer of information: An instructional perspective. In S. M. Cormier & J. D. Hagman (Eds.), *Transfer of learning: Contemporary research and applications.* San Diego: Academic Press.

Brooks-Gunn, J., Klebanov, P. K., & Duncan, G. J. (1996). Ethnic differences in children's intelligence test scores: Role of economic deprivation, home environment, and maternal characteristics. *Child Development, 67,* 396-408.

Brophy, J. E. (1985). Interactions of male and female students with male and female teachers. In L. C. Wilkinson & C. B. Marrett (Eds.), *Gender influences in classroom interaction.* San Diego: Academic Press.

Brophy, J. E. (1986). *On motivating students* (Occasional Paper No. 101). East Lansing: Michigan State University, Institute for Research on Teaching.

Brophy, J. E. (1987). Synthesis of research on strategies for motivating students to learn. *Educational Leadership, 45*(2), 40-48.

Brophy, J. E. (Ed.). (1991). *Advances in research on teaching: Vol. 2. Teacher's knowledge of subject matter as it relates to their teaching practice.* Greenwich, CT: JAI Press.

Brophy, J. E. (1992a). Conclusions: Comments on an emerging field. In J. Brophy (Ed.), *Advances in research on teaching: Vol. 3. Planning and managing learning tasks and activities.* Greenwich, CT: JAI Press.

Brophy, J. E. (1992b). Probing the subtleties of subject-matter teaching. *Educational Leadership, 49*(7), 4-8.

Brophy, J. E., & Alleman, J. (1991). Activities as instructional tools: A framework for analysis and evaluation. *Educational Researcher, 20*(4), 9-23.

Brophy, J. E., & Alleman, J. (1992). Planning and managing learning activities: Basic principles. In J. Brophy (Ed.), *Advances in research on teaching. Vol. 3. Planning and managing learning tasks and activities.* Greenwich, CT: JAI Press.

Brophy, J. E., & Evertson, C. (1976). *Learning from teaching: A developmental perspective.* Needham Heights, MA: Allyn & Bacon.

Brophy, J. E., & Good, T. L. (1970). Teachers' communication of differential expectations for children's classroom performance: Some behavioral data. *Journal of Educational Psychology, 61,* 365-374.

Brophy, J. E., & Good, T. L. (1986). Teacher effects. In M. C. Wittrock (Ed.), *Handbook of research on teaching* (3rd ed.). New York: Macmillan.

Brough, J. A. (1990). Changing conditions for young adolescents: Reminiscences and realities. *Educational Horizons, 68,* 78-81.

Brown, A. L., Ash, D., Rutherford, M., Nakagawa, K., Gordon, A., & Campione, J. C. (1993). Distributed expertise in the classroom. In G. Salomon (Ed.), *Distributed cognitions: Psychological and educational considerations.* Cambridge, England: Cambridge University Press.

Brown, A. L., & Campione, J. C. (1994). Guided discovery in a community of learners. In K. McGilly (Ed.), *Classroom lessons: Integrating cognitive theory and classroom practice*. Cambridge, MA: MIT Press.

Brown, A. L., & Campione, J. C. (1996). Psychological theory and the design of innovative learning environments: On procedures, principles, and systems. In L. Schauble & R. Glaser (Eds.), *Innovations in learning: New environments for education*. Mahwah, NJ: Erlbaum.

Brown, A. L., Campione, J., & Day, J. (1981). Learning to learn: On training students to learn from texts. *Educational Researcher, 10*(2), 14-21.

Brown, A. L., & Palincsar, A. S. (1987). Reciprocal teaching of comprehension strategies: A natural history of one program for enhancing learning. In J. Borkowski & J. D. Day (Eds.), *Cognition in special education: Comparative approaches to retardation, learning disabilities, and giftedness*. Norwood, NJ: Ablex.

Brown, A. L., & Palincsar, A. S. (1989). Guided, cooperative learning and individual knowledge acquisition. In L. B. Resnick (Ed.), *Knowing, learning, and instruction: Essays in honor of Robert Glaser*. Hillsdale, NJ: Erlbaum.

Brown, A. L., & Reeve, R. A. (1987). Bandwidths of competence: The role of supportive contexts in learning and development. In L. S. Liben (Ed.), *Development and learning: Conflict or congruence?* Hillsdale, NJ: Erlbaum.

Brown, A. L., Smiley, S. S., Day, J. D., Townsend, M. A. R., & Lawton, S. C. (1977). Intrusion of a thematic idea in children's comprehension and retention of stories. *Child Development, 48*, 1454-1466.

Brown, B. B. (1993). School culture, social politics, and the academic motivation of U.S. students. In T. M. Tomlinson (Ed.), *Motivating students to learn: Overcoming barriers to high achievement*. Berkeley, CA: McCutchan.

Brown, D. E. (1992). Using examples and analogies to remediate misconceptions in physics: Factors influencing conceptual change. *Journal of Research in Science Teaching, 29*, 17-34.

Brown, D. E., & Clement, J. (1989). Overcoming misconceptions via analogical reasoning: Abstract transfer versus explanatory model construction. *Instructional Science, 18*, 237-262.

Brown, J. S., Collins, A., & Duguid, P. (1989). Situated cognition and the culture of learning. *Educational Researcher, 18*(1), 32-42.

Brown, K. J., Sinatra, G. M., & Wagstaff, J. M. (1996). Exploring the potential of analogy instruction to support children's spelling development. *Elementary School Journal, 97*, 81-90.

Brown, R., & McNeill, D. (1966). The "tip of the tongue" phenomenon. *Journal of Verbal Learning and Verbal Behavior, 5*, 325-337.

Brown, R. D., & Bjorklund, D. F. (1998). The biologizing of cognition, development, and education: Approach with cautious enthusiasm. *Educational Psychology Review, 10*, 355-373.

Brown, R. T. (1989). Creativity: What are we to measure? In J. A. Glover, R. R. Ronning, & C. R. Reynolds (Eds.), *Handbook of creativity*. New York: Plenum Press.

Brown, W. H., Fox, J. J., & Brady, M. P. (1987). Effects of spatial density on 3- and 4-year-old children's socially directed behavior during freeplay: An investigation of a setting factor. *Education and Treatment of Children, 10*, 247-258.

Brownell, M. T., Mellard, D. F., & Deshler, D. D. (1993). Differences in the learning and transfer performance between students with learning disabilities and other low-achieving students on problem-solving tasks. *Learning Disabilities Quarterly, 16*, 138-156.

Brown-Mizuno, C. (1990). Success strategies for learners who are learning disabled as well as gifted. *Teaching Exceptional Children, 23*(1), 10-12.

Bruer, J. T. (1997). Education and the brain: A bridge too far. *Educational Researcher, 26*(8), 4-16.

Bruner, J. S. (1961). The act of discovery. *Harvard Educational Review, 31*, 21-32.

Bruner, J. S. (1966). *Toward a theory of instruction*. Cambridge, MA: Harvard University Press.

Bruner, J. S., Goodnow, J., & Austin, G. (1956). *A study of thinking*. New York: Wiley.

Bruning, R. H., Schraw, G. J., & Ronning, R. R. (1995). *Cognitive psychology and instruction* (2nd ed.). Upper Saddle River, NJ: Merrill/Prentice Hall.

Bryan, J. H. (1975). Children's cooperation and helping behaviors. In E. M. Hetherington (Ed.), *Review of child development research* (Vol. 5). Chicago: University of Chicago Press.

Bryan, T. (1991). Social problems and learning disabilities. In B. Y. L. Wong (Ed.), *Learning about learning disabilities*. San Diego: Academic Press.

Buchoff, T. (1990). Attention deficit disorder: Help for the classroom teacher. *Childhood Education, 67*(2), 86-90.

Budwig, N. (1995). *A developmental-functionalist approach to child language*. Mahwah, NJ: Erlbaum.

Bugelski, B. R., & Alampay, D. A. (1961). The role of frequency in developing perceptual sets. *Canadian Journal of Psychology, 15*, 205-211.

Buhrmester, D. (1992). The developmental courses of sibling and peer relationships. In F. Boer and J. Dunn (Eds.), *Children's sibling relationships: Developmental and clinical issues*. Hillsdale, NJ: Erlbaum.

Bulgren, J. A., Schumaker, J. B., & Deshler, D. D. (1994). The effects of a recall enhancement routine on the test performance of secondary students with and without learning disabilities. *Learning Disabilities Research and Practice, 9*, 2-11.

Burger, H. G. (1973). Cultural pluralism and the schools. In C. S. Brembeck & W. H. Hill (Eds.), *Cultural challenges to education: The influence of cultural factors in school learning*. Lexington, MA: Heath.

Burger, S., & Burger, D. (1994). Determining the validity of performance-based assessment. *Educational Measurement: Issues and Practices, 13*(1), 9-15.

Burkam, D. T., Lee, V. E., & Smerdon, B. A. (1997). Gender and science learning early in high school: Subject matter and laboratory experiences. *American Educational Research Journal, 34*, 297-331.

Burnett, R. E., & Kastman, L. M. (1997). Teaching composition: Current theories and practices. In G. D. Phye (Ed.), *Handbook of academic learning: Construction of knowledge*. San Diego: Academic Press.

Butler, D. L., & Winne, P. H. (1995). Feedback and self-regulated learning: A theoretical synthesis. *Review of Educational Research, 65*, 245-281.

Butterfield, E. C., & Ferretti, R. P. (1987). Toward a theoretical integration of cognitive hypotheses about intellectual differences among children. In J. G. Borkowski & J. D. Day (Eds.), *Cognition in special children: Approaches to retardation, learning disabilities, and giftedness*. Norwood, NJ: Ablex.

Byrne, B., Freebody, P., & Gates, A. (1992). Longitudinal data on the relations of word-reading strategies to comprehension, reading time, and phonemic awareness. *Reading Research Quarterly, 27*, 140-151.

Byrnes, J. P. (1996). *Cognitive development and learning in instructional contexts*. Boston: Allyn & Bacon.

Byrnes, J. P., & Fox, N. A. (1998). The educational relevance of research in cognitive neuroscience. *Educational Psychology Review, 10*, 297-342.

Cairns, H. S. (1996). *The acquisition of language* (2nd ed.). Austin, TX: Pro-Ed.

Calderhead, J. (1996). Teachers: Beliefs and knowledge. In D. C. Berliner & R. C. Calfee (Eds.), *Handbook of educational psychology*. New York: Macmillan.

Calfee, R. (1981). Cognitive psychology and educational practice. In D. C. Berliner (Ed.), *Review of research in education* (Vol. 9). Washington, DC: American Educational Research Association.

Calfee, R., & Chambliss, M. J. (1988, April). *The structure of social studies textbooks: Where is the design?* Paper presented at the annual meeting of the American Educational Research Association, New Orleans, LA.

Calfee, R., Dunlap, K., & Wat, A. (1994). Authentic discussion of texts in middle grade schooling: An analytic-narrative approach. *Journal of Reading, 37*, 546-556.

Calfee, R. C., & Masuda, W. V. (1997). Classroom assessment as inquiry. In G. D. Phye (Ed.), *Handbook of classroom assessment: Learning, achievement, and adjustment*. San Diego: Academic Press.

Cameron, C. A., Hunt, A. K., & Linton, M. J. (1996). Written expression as recontextualization: Children write in social time. *Educational Psychology Review, 8*, 125-150.

Cameron, J., & Pierce, W. D. (1994). Reinforcement, reward, and intrinsic motivation: A meta-analysis. *Review of Educational Research, 64*, 363-423.

Campbell, D. E. (1996). *Choosing democracy: A practical guide to multicultural education*. Upper Saddle River, NJ: Merrill/Prentice Hall.

Campbell, L., Campbell, B., & Dickinson, D. (1998). *Teaching and learning through multiple intelligences* (2nd ed.). Boston: Allyn & Bacon.

Campbell, P. A. (1986). What's a nice girl like you doing in a math class? *Phi Delta Kappan, 67*, 516-520.

Campione, J. C., Brown, A. L., & Bryant, N. R. (1985). Individual differences in learning and memory. In R. J. Sternberg (Ed.), *Human abilities: An information-processing approach*. New York: W. H. Freeman.

Campione, J. C., Shapiro, A. M., & Brown, A. L. (1995). Forms of transfer in a community of learners: Flexible learning and understanding. In A. McKeough, J. Lupart, & A. Marini (Eds.), *Teaching for transfer: Fostering generalization in learning*. Mahwah, NJ: Erlbaum.

Canady, R. L., & Hotchkiss, P. R. (1989). It's a good score! Just a bad grade. *Phi Delta Kappan, 71*, 68-71.

Candler-Lotven, A., Tallent-Runnels, M. K., Olivárez, A., & Hildreth, B. (1994, April). *A comparison of learning and study strategies of gifted, average-ability, and learning-disabled ninth grade students*. Paper presented at the annual meeting of the American Educational Research Association, New Orleans, LA.

Capron, C., & Duyme, M. (1989). Assessment of effects of socio-economic status on IQ in a full cross-fostering study. *Nature, 340,* 552-554.

Cardelle-Elawar, M. (1992). Effects of teaching metacognitive skills to students with low mathematics ability. *Teaching and Teacher Education, 8,* 109-121.

Carey, L. M. (1994). *Measuring and evaluating school learning* (2nd ed.). Needham Heights, MA: Allyn & Bacon.

Carey, S. (1978). The child as word learner. In M. Halle, J. Bresnan, & G. A. Miller (Eds.), *Linguistic theory and psychological reality.* Cambridge, MA: MIT Press.

Carey, S. (1985a). Are children fundamentally different kinds of thinkers and learners than adults? In S. F. Chipman, J. W. Segal, & R. Glaser (Eds.), *Learning and thinking skills: Vol. 2. Research and open questions.* Hillsdale, NJ: Erlbaum.

Carey, S. (1985b). *Conceptual change in childhood.* Cambridge, MA: MIT Press.

Carey, S. (1986). Cognitive science and science education. *American Psychologist, 41,* 1123-1130.

Carey, S., Evans, R., Honda, M., Jay, E., & Unger, C. (1989). "An experiment is when you try it and see if it works": A study of grade 7 students' understanding of the construction of scientific knowledge. *International Journal of Science Education, 11,* 514-529.

Carnine, D. (1989). Teaching complex content to learning disabled students: The role of technology. *Exceptional Children, 55,* 524-533.

Carpenter, P. A., & Just, M. A. (1986). Cognitive processes in reading. In J. Orasanu (Ed.), *Reading comprehension: From research to practice.* Hillsdale, NJ: Erlbaum.

Carr, A. A. (1997, March). *The participation "race": Kentucky's site based decision teams.* Paper presented at the annual meeting of the American Educational Research Association, Chicago.

Carr, E. G., Levin, L., McConnachie, G., Carlson, J. I., Kemp, D. C., & Smith, C. E. (1994). *Communication-based intervention for problem behavior: A user's guide for producing positive change.* Baltimore: Paul H. Brookes.

Carr, M., & Borkowski, J. G. (1989). Attributional training and the generalization of reading strategies with underachieving children. *Learning and Individual Differences, 1,* 327-341.

Carraher, T. N., Carraher, D. W., & Schliemann, A. D. (1985). Mathematics in the streets and in the schools. *British Journal of Developmental Psychology, 3,* 21-29.

Carrasco, R. L. (1981). Expanded awareness of student performance: A case study in applied ethnographic monitoring in a bilingual classroom. In H. T. Trueba, G. P. Guthrie, & K. H. Au (Eds.), *Culture and the bilingual classroom: Studies in classroom ethnography.* Rowley, MA: Newbury House.

Carter, K. R. (1991). Evaluation of gifted programs. In N. Buchanan & J. Feldhusen (Eds.), *Conducting research and evaluation in gifted education: A handbook of methods and applications.* New York: Teachers College Press.

Carter, K. R., & Ormrod, J. E. (1982). Acquisition of formal operations by intellectually gifted children. *Gifted Child Quarterly, 26,* 110-115.

Cartledge, G., & Milburn, J. F. (1995). *Teaching social skills to children and youth: Innovative approaches* (3rd ed.). Needham Heights, MA: Allyn & Bacon.

Carver, C. S., & Scheier, M. F. (1990). Origins and functions of positive and negative affect: A control-process view. *Psychological Review, 97,* 19-35.

Casanova, U. (1987). Ethnic and cultural differences. In V. Richardson-Koehler (Ed.), *Educator's handbook: A research perspective.* White Plains, NY: Longman.

Case, R. (Ed.). (1992). *The mind's staircase: Exploring the conceptual underpinnings of children's thought and knowledge.* Hillsdale, NJ: Erlbaum.

Caseau, D., Luckasson, R., & Kroth, R. L. (1994). Special education services for girls with serious emotional disturbance: A case of gender bias? *Behavioral Disorders, 20*(1), 51-60.

Casey, W. M., & Burton, R. V. (1982). Training children to be consistently honest through verbal self-instructions. *Child Development, 53,* 911-919.

Casserly, P. L. (1980). Factors affecting female participation in Advanced Placement programs in mathematics, chemistry, and physics. In L. H. Fox, L. Brody, & D. Tobin (Eds.), *Women and the mathematical mystique.* Baltimore: Johns Hopkins University Press.

Cazden, C. B. (1968). The acquisition of noun and verb inflections. *Child Development, 39,* 433-448.

Cazden, C. B. (1976). Play with language and metalinguistic awareness: One dimension of language experience. In J. Bruner, A. Jolly, & K. Sylva (Eds.), *Play: Its role in development and evolution.* New York: Basic Books.

Cazden, C. B. (1988). *Classroom discourse: The language of teaching and learning.* Portsmouth, NJ: Heinemann.

Cazden, C. B., & Leggett, E. L. (1981). Culturally responsive education: Recommendations for achieving *Lau* Remedies II. In H. T. Trueba, G. P. Guthrie, & K. H. Au (Eds.), *Culture and the bilingual classroom: Studies in classroom ethnography.* Rowley, MA: Newbury House.

Ceci, S. J., & Williams, W. M. (1997). Schooling, intelligence, and income. *American Psychologist, 52,* 1051-1058.

Chalfant, J. C. (1989). Learning disabilities: Policy issues and promising approaches. *American Psychologist, 44,* 392-398.

Chall, J. S. (1983). *Stages of reading development.* New York: McGraw-Hill.

Chalmers, J., & Townsend, M. (1990). The effects of training in social perspective taking on socially maladjusted girls. *Child Development, 61,* 178-190.

Chambliss, M. J. (1994). Why do readers fail to change their beliefs after reading persuasive text? In R. Garner & P. A. Alexander (Eds.), *Beliefs about text and instruction with text.* Hillsdale, NJ: Erlbaum.

Chambliss, M. J. (1998, April). *Children as thinkers composing scientific explanations.* Paper presented at the annual meeting of the American Educational Research Association, San Diego.

Chambliss, M. J., Calfee, R. C., & Wong, I. (1990, April). *Structure and content in science textbooks: Where is the design?* Paper presented at the annual meeting of the American Educational Research Association, Boston.

Chan, C., Burtis, J., & Bereiter, C. (1997). Knowledge building as a mediator of conflict in conceptual change. *Cognition and Instruction, 15,* 1-40.

Chapman, J. W. (1988). Learning disabled children's self-concepts. *Review of Educational Research, 58,* 347-371.

Cheatham, S. K., Smith, J. D., Rucker, H. N., Polloway, E. A., & Lewis, G. W. (1995, September). Savant syndrome: Case studies, hypotheses, and implications for special education. *Education and Training in Mental Retardation,* 243-253.

Chen, X., Rubin, K. H., & Sun, Y. (1992). Social reputation and peer relationships in Chinese and Canadian children: A cross-cultural study. *Child Development, 63,* 1336-1343.

Cheng, L. R. (1987). *Assessing Asian language performance.* Rockville, MD: Aspen.

Cheng, P. W. (1985). Restructuring versus automaticity: Alternative accounts of skill acquisition. *Psychological Review, 92,* 414-423.

Cherry, E. C. (1953). Some experiments on the recognition of speech, with one and with two ears. *Journal of the Acoustical Society of America, 25,* 975-979.

Chester, M. D., & Beaudin, B. Q. (1996). Efficacy beliefs of newly hired teachers in urban schools. *American Educational Research Journal, 33,* 233-257.

Cheyne, J. A., & Walters, R. H. (1970). Punishment and prohibition: Some origins of self-control. In T. M. Newcomb (Ed.), *New directions in psychology.* New York: Holt, Rinehart & Winston.

Chi, M. T. H. (1978). Knowledge structures and memory development. In R. S. Siegler (Ed.), *Children's thinking: What develops?* Hillsdale, NJ: Erlbaum.

Chi, M. T. H., de Leeuw, N., Chiu, M., & LaVancher, C. (1994). Eliciting self-explanations. *Cognitive Science, 18,* 439-477.

Chi, M. T. H., Feltovich, P., & Glaser, R. (1981). Categorization and representation of physics problems by experts and novices. *Cognitive Science, 5,* 121-152.

Chinn, C. A., & Brewer, W. F. (1993). The role of anomalous data in knowledge acquisition: A theoretical framework and implications for science instruction. *Review of Educational Research, 63,* 1-49.

Chipman, S. F., Brush, L. R., & Wilson, D. M. (Eds.). (1985). *Women and mathematics: Balancing the equation.* Hillsdale, NJ: Erlbaum.

Chomsky, C. S. (1969). *The acquisition of syntax in children from 5 to 10.* Cambridge, MA: MIT Press.

Chomsky, N. (1965). *Aspects of the theory of syntax.* Cambridge, MA: MIT Press.

Chomsky, N. (1972). *Language and mind* (enlarged ed.). San Diego: Harcourt Brace Jovanovich.

Christie, J. F., & Johnsen, E. P. (1983). The role of play in social-intellectual development. *Review of Educational Research, 53,* 93-115.

Clark, B. (1997). *Growing up gifted* (5th ed.). Upper Saddle River, NJ: Merrill/Prentice Hall.

Clark, C. C. (1992). Deviant adolescent subcultures: Assessment strategies and clinical interventions. *Adolescence, 27*(106), 283-293.

Clark, C. M., & Peterson, P. L. (1986). Teachers' thought processes. In M. C. Wittrock (Ed.), *Handbook on research on teaching* (3rd ed.). New York: Macmillan.

Clark, E. V. (1971). On the acquisition of the meaning of "before" and "after." *Journal of Verbal Learning and Verbal Behavior, 10,* 266-275.

Clark, J. M., & Paivio, A. (1991). Dual coding theory and education. *Educational Psychology Review, 3,* 149-210.

Clark, R. E. (1983). Reconsidering research on learning from media. *Review of Educational Research, 53,* 445-459.

Clarke, L. K. (1988). Invented versus traditional spelling in first graders' writings: Effects on learning to spell and read. *Research in the Teaching of English, 22,* 281-309.

Clarke, S., Dunlap, G., Foster-Johnson, L., Childs, K. E., Wilson, D., White, R., & Vera, A. (1995). Improving the conduct of students with behavioral disorders by incorporating student interests into curricular areas. *Behavioral Disorders, 20,* 221-237.

Clarke-Stewart, K. A. (1988). Parents' effects on children's development: A decade of progress? *Journal of Applied Developmental Psychology, 9,* 41-84.

Claude, D., & Firestone, P. (1995). The development of ADHD boys: A 12-year follow-up. *Canadian Journal of Behavioural Science, 27,* 226-249.

Clawson, D. L., & Fisher, J. S. (1998). *World regional geography: A development approach* (6th ed.). Upper Saddle River, NJ: Prentice Hall.

Clay, M. M. (1985). *The early detection of reading difficulties: A diagnostic survey with recovery procedure.* Portsmouth, NH: Heinemann.

Clement, J. (1982). Algebra word problem solutions: Thought processes underlying a common misconception. *Journal for Research in Mathematics Education, 13,* 16-30.

Clifford, M. M. (1990). Students need challenge, not easy success. *Educational Leadership, 48*(1), 22-26.

Cobb, P. (1994). Where is the mind? Constructivist and sociocultural perspectives on mathematical development. *Educational Researcher, 23*(7), 13-20.

Cobb, P., Wood, T., Yackel, E., Nicholls, J., Wheatley, G., Trigatti, B., & Perlwitz, M. (1991). Assessment of a problem centered second-grade mathematics project. *Journal for Research in Mathematics Education, 22,* 3-29.

Cobb, P., & Yackel, E. (1996). Constructivist, emergent, and sociocultural perspectives in the context of developmental research. *Educational Psychologist, 31,* 175-190.

Cochran, K. F., & Jones, L. L. (1998). The subject matter knowledge of preservice science teachers. In B. J. Fraser & K. G. Tobin (Eds.), *International Handbook of Science Education. Part II.* Dordrecht, The Netherlands: Kluwer.

Cochran-Smith, M. (1991). *The making of a reader.* Norwood, NJ: Ablex.

Coe, J., Salamon, L., & Molnar, J. (1991). *Homeless children and youth.* New Brunswick, NJ: Transaction.

Cognition and Technology Group at Vanderbilt. (1993). Anchored instruction and situated cognition revisited. *Educational Technology, 33*(3), 52-70.

Cohen, E. G. (1994). Restructuring the classroom: Conditions for productive small groups. *Review of Educational Research, 64,* 1-35.

Cohen, E. G., Lockheed, M. E., & Lohman, M. R. (1976). The center for interracial cooperation: A field experiment. *Sociology of Education, 59,* 47-58.

Cohen, E. G., & Lotan, R. A. (1995). Producing equal-status interaction in the heterogeneous classroom. *American Educational Research Journal, 32,* 99-120.

Cohen, R. L. (1989). Memory for action events: The power of enactment. *Educational Psychology Review, 1,* 57-80.

Coie, J. D., & Cillessen, A. H. N. (1993). Peer rejection: Origins and effects on children's development. *Current Directions in Psychological Science, 2,* 89-92.

Colby, A., & Kohlberg, L. (1984). Invariant sequence and internal consistency in moral judgment stages. In W. M. Kurtines & J. L. Gewirtz (Eds.), *Morality, moral behavior, and moral development.* New York: Wiley.

Colby, A., Kohlberg, L., Gibbs, J., & Lieberman, M. (1983). A longitudinal study of moral judgment. *Monographs of the Society for Research in Child Development, 48* (1-2, Serial No. 200).

Cole, N. S. (1990). Conceptions of educational achievement. *Educational Researcher, 19*(3), 2-7.

Coleman, J. M., & Minnett, A. M. (1992). Learning disabilities and social competence: A social ecological perspective. *Exceptional Children, 59,* 234-246.

Collier, V. P. (1992). The Canadian bilingual immersion debate: A synthesis of research findings. *Studies in Second Language Acquisition, 14,* 87-97.

Collins, A., Brown, J. S., & Newman, S. E. (1989). Cognitive apprenticeship: Teaching the crafts of reading, writing, and mathematics. In L. B. Resnick (Ed.), *Knowing, learning, and instruction: Essays in honor of Robert Glaser.* Hillsdale, NJ: Erlbaum.

Collins, A., Hawkins, J., & Carver, S. M. (1991). A cognitive apprenticeship for disadvantaged students. In B. Means, C. Chelemer, & M. S. Knapp (Eds.), *Teaching advanced skills to at-risk students.* San Francisco: Jossey-Bass.

Collins, A. M., & Loftus, E. F. (1975). A spreading-activation theory of semantic processing. *Psychological Review, 82,* 407-428.

Collins, J. L. (1982, March). *Self-efficacy and ability in achievement behavior.* Paper presented at the annual meeting of the American Educational Research Association, New York.

Combs, A. W., Richards, A. C., & Richards, F. (1976). *Perceptual psychology: A humanistic approach to the study of persons.* New York: Harper & Row.

Commins, N. L., & Miramontes, O. B. (1989). Perceived and actual linguistic competence: A descriptive study of four low-achieving Hispanic bilingual students. *American Educational Research Journal, 26,* 443-472.

Committee on High School Biology Education. (1990). *Fulfilling the promise: Biology education in the nation's schools.* Washington, DC: National Academy Press.

Cone, T. E., Wilson, L. R., Bradley, C. M., & Reese, J. H. (1985). Characteristics of LD students in Iowa: An empirical investigation. *Learning Disability Quarterly, 8,* 211-220.

Conlon, C. J. (1992). New threats to development: Alcohol, cocaine, and AIDS. In M. L. Batshaw & Y. M. Perret (Eds.), *Children with disabilities: A medical primer* (3rd ed.). Baltimore: Paul H. Brookes.

Connolly, F. W., & Eisenberg, T. E. (1990). The feedback classroom: Teaching's silent friend. *T.H.E. Journal, 17*(5), 75-77.

Conte, R. (1991). Attention disorders. In B. Y. L. Wong (Ed.), *Learning about learning disabilities.* San Diego: Academic Press.

Cooney, J. B. (1991). Reflections on the origin of mathematical intuition and some implications for instruction. *Learning and Individual Differences, 3,* 83-107.

Cooper, H. (1989). Synthesis of research on homework. *Educational Leadership, 47*(3), 85-91.

Cooper, H. M. (1979). Pygmalion grows up: A model for teacher expectation communication and performance influence. *Review of Educational Research, 49,* 389-410.

Cooper, H. M., & Good, T. (1983). *Pygmalion grows up: Studies in the expectation communication process.* White Plains, NY: Longman.

Cooper, H., Lindsay, J. J., Nye, B., & Greathouse, S. (1998). Relationships among attitudes about homework, amount of homework assigned and completed, and student achievement. *Journal of Educational Psychology, 90,* 70-83.

Corkill, A. J. (1992). Advance organizers: Facilitators of recall. *Educational Psychology Review, 4,* 33-67.

Cormier, S. M. (1987). The structural processes underlying transfer of training. In S. M. Cormier & J. D. Hagman (Eds.), *Transfer of learning: Contemporary research and applications.* San Diego: Academic Press.

Cornell, D. G., Pelton, G. M., Bassin, L. E., Landrum, M., Ramsay, S. G., Cooley, M. R., Lynch, K. A., & Hamrick, E. (1990). Self-concept and peer status among gifted program youth. *Journal of Educational Psychology, 82,* 456-463.

Corno, L. (1996). Homework is a complicated thing. *Educational Researcher, 25*(8), 27-30.

Corno, L., & Rohrkemper, M. M. (1985). The intrinsic motivation to learn in classrooms. In C. Ames & R. Ames (Eds.), *Research on motivation in education: Vol. 2. The classroom milieu.* San Diego: Academic Press.

Corno, L., & Snow, R. E. (1986). Adapting teaching to individual differences among learners. In M. C. Wittrock (Ed.), *Handbook of research on teaching* (3rd ed.). New York: Macmillan.

Correa, J., Nunes, T., & Bryant, P. (1998). Young children's understanding of division: The relationship between division terms in a noncomputational task. *Journal of Educational Psychology, 90,* 321-329.

Cothern, N. B., Konopak, B. C., & Willis, E. L. (1990). Using readers' imagery of literary characters to study text meaning construction. *Reading Research and Instruction, 30,* 15-29.

Cottrol, R. J. (1990). America the multicultural. *American Educator, 14*(4), 18-21.

Council for Exceptional Children. (1995). *Toward a common agenda: Linking gifted education and school reform.* Reston, VA: Author.

Courchesne, E., Townsend, J., Akshoomoff, N. A., Saitoh, O., Yeung-Courchesne, R., Lincoln, A. J., James, H. E., Haas, R. H., Schreibman, L., & Lau, L. (1994). Impairment of shifting attention in autistic and cerebellar patients. *Behavioral Neuroscience, 108,* 848-865.

Covill, A. E. (1997, March). *Students' revision practices and attitudes in response to surface-related feedback as compared to content-related feedback on their writing.* Paper presented at the annual meeting of the American Educational Research Association, Chicago.

Covington, M. V. (1987). Achievement motivation, self-attributions, and the exceptional learner. In J. D. Day & J. G. Borkowski (Eds.), *Intelligence and exceptionality.* Norwood, NJ: Ablex.

Covington, M. V. (1992). *Making the grade: A self-worth perspective on motivation and school reform.* Cambridge, England: Cambridge University Press.

Covington, M. V., & Beery, R. M. (1976). *Self-worth and school learning.* New York: Holt, Rinehart & Winston.

Cowan, N. (1995). *Attention and memory:An integrated framework*. New York: Oxford University Press.

Cox, B. D. (1997).The rediscovery of the active learner in adaptive contexts: A developmental-historical analysis of transfer of training. *Educational Psychologist, 32,* 41-55.

Craft, M. (1984). Education for diversity. In M. Craft (Ed.), *Educational and cultural pluralism.* London: Falmer Press.

Crago, M. B.,Annahatak, B., & Ningiuruvik, L. (1993). Changing patterns of language socialization in Inuit homes.*Anthropology and Education Quarterly, 24,* 205-223.

Craik, F. I. M., & Watkins, M. J. (1973). The role of rehearsal in short-term memory.*Journal of Verbal Learning and Verbal Behavior, 12,* 598-607.

Crain, S. (1993). Language acquisition in the absence of experience. In P.Bloom (Ed.), *Language acquisition: Core readings.* Cambridge, MA: MIT Press.

Crain-Thoreson, C., & Dale, P. S. (1992). Do early talkers become early readers? Linguistic precocity, preschool language, and emergent literacy. *Developmental Psychology, 28,* 421-429.

Cromer, R. F. (1993). Language growth with experience without feedback. In P.Bloom (Ed.), *Language acquisition: Core readings.* Cambridge, MA: MIT Press.

Crook, C. (1995). On resourcing a concern for collaboration within peer interactions. *Cognition and Instruction, 13,* 541-547.

Crooks,T. J. (1988).The impact of classroom evaluation practices on students. *Review of Educational Research, 58,* 438-481.

Cross, D. R., & Paris, S. G. (1988). Developmental and instructional analyses of children's metacognitive and reading comprehension.*Journal of Educational Psychology, 80,* 131-142.

Crowder, N.A., & Martin, G. (1961). *Trigonometry.* Garden City, NY: Doubleday.

Crowder, R. (1993). Short-term memory:Where do we stand? *Memory and Cognition, 21,* 142-145.

Crowne, D. P., & Marlowe, D. (1964). *The approval motive: Studies in evaluative dependence.* New York:Wiley.

Csikszentmihalyi, M. (1995). Education for the twenty-first century. *Daedalus, 124*(4), 107-114.

Csikszentmihalyi, M. (1996). *Creativity: Flow and the psychology of discovery and invention.* New York: HarperCollins.

Csikszentmihalyi, M., & Nakamura, J. (1989). The dynamics of intrinsic motivation: A study of adolescents. In C.Ames & R. Ames (Eds.), *Research on motivation in education:Vol. 3. Goals and cognitions.* San Diego:Academic Press.

Curtis, K.A., & Graham, S. (1991,April). *Altering beliefs about the importance of strategy:An attributional intervention.* Paper presented at the annual meeting of the American Educational Research Association, Chicago.

Cushing, L. S., & Kennedy, C. H. (1997).Academic effects of providing peer support in general education classrooms on students without disabilities. *Journal of Applied Behavior Analysis, 30,* 139-151.

Daiute, C. (1986). Do 1 and 1 make 2? *Written Communication, 3,* 382-408.

Daiute, C. (1989). Play as thought: Thinking strategies of young writers. *Harvard Educational Review, 59*(1), 1-23.

Daiute, C., & Dalton, B. (1993). Collaboration between children learning to write: Can novices be masters? *Cognition and Instruction, 10,* 281-333.

Dale, P. S. (1976). *Language development: Structure and function* (2nd ed.). New York: Holt, Rinehart & Winston.

Dalrymple, N. J. (1995). Environmental supports to develop flexibility and independence. In K.A. Quill (Ed.), *Teaching children with autism: Strategies to enhance communication and socialization.* New York: Delmar.

D'Amato, R. C., Chitooran, M. M., & Whitten, J. D. (1992). Neuropsychological consequences of malnutrition. In D. I.Templer, L. C. Hartlage, & W. G. Cannon (Eds.), *Preventable brain damage: Brain vulnerability and brain health.* New York: Springer.

Damon,W. (1977). *The social world of the child.* San Francisco: Jossey-Bass.

Damon,W. (1988). *The moral child: Nurturing children's natural moral growth.* New York: Free Press.

Damon,W. (1991). Putting substance into self-esteem: A focus on academic and moral values. *Educational Horizons, 70*(1), 12-18.

Danner, F.W., & Day, M. C. (1977). Eliciting formal operations. *Child Development, 48,* 1600-1606.

Dansereau, D. F. (1988). Cooperative learning strategies. In C. E.Weinstein, E.T. Goetz, & P.A.Alexander (Eds.), *Learning and study strategies: Issues in assessment, instruction, and evaluation.* San Diego:Academic Press.

Dansereau, D. F. (1995). Derived structural schemas and the transfer of knowledge. In A. McKeough, J. Lupart, & A. Marini (Eds.), *Teaching for transfer: Fostering generalization in learning.* Mahwah, NJ: Erlbaum.

Darley, J. M., & Gross, P. H. (1983).A hypothesis-confirming bias in labeling effects.*Journal of Personality and Social Psychology, 44,* 20-33.

Darling-Hammond, L. (1991).The implications of testing policy for quality and equality. *Phi Delta Kappan, 73,* 220-225.

Darling-Hammond, L. (1995). Inequality and access to knowledge. In J.A. Banks & C.A. M. Banks (Eds.), *Handbook of research on multicultural education.* New York: Macmillan.

Davis, G.A., & Rimm, S. B. (1998). *Education of the gifted and talented* (4th ed.). Boston:Allyn & Bacon.

Davis, G.A., & Thomas, M.A. (1989). *Effective schools and effective teachers.* Needham Heights, MA:Allyn & Bacon.

Deaux, K. (1984). From individual differences to social categories:Analysis of a decade's research on gender. *American Psychologist, 39,* 105-116.

deCharms, R. (1972). Personal causation training in the schools.*Journal of Applied Social Psychology, 2,* 95-113.

Deci, E. L. (1992).The relation of interest to the motivation of behavior:A self-determination theory perspective. In K.A. Renninger, S. Hidi, & A. Krapp (Eds.), *The role of interest in learning and development.* Hillsdale, NJ: Erlbaum.

Deci, E. L., & Ryan, R. M. (1985). *Intrinsic motivation and self-determination in human behavior.* New York: Plenum Press.

Deci, E. L., & Ryan, R. M. (1987).The support of autonomy and the control of behavior.*Journal of Personality and Social Psychology, 53,* 1024-1037.

Deci, E. L., & Ryan, R. M. (1992).The initiation and regulation of intrinsically motivated learning and achievement. In A. K. Boggiano & T. S. Pittman (Eds.), *Achievement and motivation:A social-developmental perspective.* Cambridge, England: Cambridge University Press.

De Corte, E., Greer, B., & Verschaffel, L. (1996). Mathematics teaching and learning. In D. C. Berliner & R. C. Calfee (Eds.), *Handbook of educational psychology.* New York: Macmillan.

Dee-Lucas, D., & Larkin, J. H. (1991). Equations in scientific proofs: Effects on comprehension. *American Educational Research Journal, 28,* 661-682.

DeGangi, G.A.,Wietlisbach, S., Poisson, S., Stein, E., & Royeen, C. (1994).The impact of culture and socioeconomic status on family-professional collaboration: Challenges and solutions. *Topics in Early Childhood Special Education, 14,* 503-520.

DeLain, M.T., Pearson, P. D., & Anderson, R. C. (1985). Reading comprehension and creativity in black language use: You stand to gain by playing the sounding game! *American Educational Research Journal, 22,* 155-173.

Delandshere, G., & Petrosky,A. R. (1998). Assessment of complex performances: Limitations of key measurement assumptions. *Educational Researcher, 27,* 14-24.

Delgado-Gaitan, C. (1992). School matters in the Mexican-American home: Socializing children to education. *American Educational Research Journal, 29,* 495-513.

Delgado-Gaitan, C. (1994). Socializing young children in Mexican-American families:An intergenerational perspective. In P. M. Greenfield & R. R. Cocking (Eds.), *Cross-cultural roots of minority child development.* Hillsdale, NJ: Erlbaum.

DeLisle, J. R. (1984). *Gifted children speak out.* New York:Walker.

DeLoache, J. S., & Todd, C. M. (1988). Young children's use of spatial categorization as a mnemonic strategy.*Journal of Experimental Child Psychology, 46,* 1-20.

Dempster, F. N. (1985). Proactive interference in sentence recall:Topic-similarity effects and individual differences. *Memory and Cognition, 13,* 81-89.

Dempster, F. N. (1991). Synthesis of research on reviews and tests. *Educational Leadership, 48*(7), 71-76.

Denis, M. (1984). Imagery and prose:A critical review of research on adults and children. *Text, 4,* 381-401.

Denkla, M. B. (1986). New diagnostic criteria for autism and related behavioral disorders: Guidelines for research protocols.*Journal of the American Academy of Child Psychiatry, 25,* 221-224.

DeRidder, L. M. (1993).Teenage pregnancy: Etiology and educational interventions. *Educational Psychology Review, 5,* 87-107.

Derry, S. J. (1996). Cognitive schema theory in the constructivist debate. *Educational Psychologist, 31,* 163-174.

Desberg, P., & Taylor, J. H. (1986). *Essentials of task analysis.* Lanham, MD: University Press of America.

Deshler, D. D., & Schumaker, J. B. (1988).An instructional model for teaching students how to learn. In J. L. Graden, J. E. Zins, & M. J. Curtis (Eds.), *Alternative educational delivery systems: Enhancing instructional options for all students.* Washington, DC: National Association of School Psychologists.

Deutsch, M. (1993). Educating for a peaceful world. *American Psychologist, 48,* 510-517.

DeVault, G., Krug, C., & Fake, S. (1996, September). Why does Samantha act that way: Positive behavioral support leads to successful inclusion. *Exceptional Parent,* 43-47.

DeVries, R., & Zan, B. (1996). A constructivist perspective on the role of the sociomoral atmosphere in promoting children's development. In C.T. Fosnot (Ed.), *Constructivism: Theory, perspectives, and practice.* New York: Teachers College Press.

Dewhurst, S.A., & Conway, M.A. (1994). Pictures, images, and recollective experience. *Journal of Experimental Psychology: Learning, Memory, and Cognition, 20,* 1088-1098.

Diamond, S. C. (1991). What to do when you can't do anything: Working with disturbed adolescents. *Clearing House, 64,* 232-234.

Diaz, R. M. (1983). Thought and two languages: The impact of bilingualism on cognitive development. In E.W. Gordon (Ed.), *Review of Research in Education* (Vol. 10). Washington, DC: American Educational Research Association.

Diaz, R. M., & Berk, L. E. (1995). A Vygotskian critique of self-instructional training. *Development and Psychopathology, 7,* 369-392.

Diaz, R. M., & Klingler, C. (1991). Toward an explanatory model of the interaction between bilingualism and cognitive development. In E. Bialystok (Ed.), *Language processing in bilingual children.* Cambridge, England: Cambridge University Press.

Diener, C. I., & Dweck, C. S. (1978). An analysis of learned helplessness: Continuous changes in performance, strategy, and achievement cognitions following failure. *Journal of Personality and Social Psychology, 36,* 451-462.

Dirks, J. (1982). The effect of a commercial game on children's Block Design scores on the WISC-R test. *Intelligence, 6,* 109-123.

diSessa, A.A. (1982). Unlearning Aristotelian physics: A study of knowledge-based learning. *Cognitive Science, 6,* 37-75.

diSessa, A.A. (1996). What do "just plain folk" know about physics? In D. R. Olson & N. Torrance (Eds.), *The handbook of education and human development: New models of learning, teaching, and schooling.* Cambridge, MA: Blackwell.

Di Vesta, F. J., & Gray, S. G. (1972). Listening and notetaking. *Journal of Educational Psychology, 63,* 8-14.

Di Vesta, F. J., & Peverly, S.T. (1984). The effects of encoding variability, processing activity and rule example sequences on the transfer of conceptual rules. *Journal of Educational Psychology, 76,* 108-119.

Di Vesta, F. J., & Smith, D.A. (1979). The pausing principle: Increasing the efficiency of memory for ongoing events. *Contemporary Educational Psychology, 4,* 288-296.

Doescher, S. M., & Sugawara, A. I. (1989). Encouraging prosocial behavior in young children. *Childhood Education, 65,* 213-216.

Dole, J.A., Duffy, G. G., Roehler, L. R., & Pearson, P. D. (1991). Moving from the old to the new: Research on reading comprehension instruction. *Review of Educational Research, 61,* 239-264.

Donaldson, M. (1978). *Children's minds.* New York: Norton.

Donnelly, C. M., & McDaniel, M.A. (1993). Use of analogy in learning scientific concepts. *Journal of Experimental Psychology: Learning, Memory, and Cognition, 19,* 975-987.

Doyle, A. (1982). Friends, acquaintances, and strangers: The influence of familiarity and ethnolinguistic backgrounds on social interaction. In K. Rubin & H. Ross (Eds.), *Peer relationships and social skills in childhood.* New York: Springer-Verlag.

Doyle, W. (1983). Academic work. *Review of Educational Research, 53,* 159-199.

Doyle, W. (1984). How order is achieved in classrooms: An interim report. *Journal of Curriculum Studies, 16,* 259-277.

Doyle, W. (1986a). Classroom organization and management. In M. C. Wittrock (Ed.), *Handbook of research on teaching* (3rd ed.). New York: Macmillan.

Doyle, W. (1986b). Content representation in teachers' definitions of academic work. *Journal of Curriculum Studies, 18,* 365-379.

Doyle, W. (1990). Classroom management techniques. In O. C. Moles (Ed.), *Student discipline strategies: Research and practice.* Albany: State University of New York Press.

Drake, D. D. (1993). Student diversity: Implications for classroom teachers. *The Clearing House, 66,* 264-266.

Dreikurs, R. (1998). *Maintaining sanity in the classroom: Classroom management techniques* (2nd ed.). Bristol, PA: Hemisphere.

Dreikurs, R., & Cassel, P. (1972). *Discipline without tears* (2nd ed.). New York: Dutton.

Drevno, G. E., Kimball, J.W., Possi, M. K., Heward, W. L., Gardner, R., III, & Barbetta, P. M. (1994). Effects of active student responding during error correction on the acquisition, maintenance, and generalization of science vocabulary by elementary students: A systematic replication. *Journal of Applied Behavior Analysis, 27,* 179-180.

Driver, B. L. (1996). Where do we go from here? Sustaining and maintaining co-teaching relationships. *Learning Disabilities Forum, 21*(2), 29-33.

Driver, R. (1995). Constructivist approaches to science teaching. In L. P. Steffe & J. Gale (Eds.), *Constructivism in education.* Hillsdale, NJ: Erlbaum.

Driver, R., Asoko, H., Leach, J., Mortimer, E., & Scott, P. (1994). Constructing scientific knowledge in the classroom. *Educational Researcher, 23*(7), 5-12.

Dryden, M.A., & Jefferson, P. (1994, April). *Use of background knowledge and reading achievement among elementary school students.* Paper presented at the annual meeting of the American Educational Research Association, New Orleans, LA.

DuBois, N. F., Kiewra, K.A., & Fraley, J. (1988, April). *Differential effects of a learning strategy course.* Paper presented at the annual meeting of the American Educational Research Association, New Orleans, LA.

Duchardt, B.A., Deshler, D. D., & Schumaker, J. B. (1995). A strategy intervention for enabling students with learning disabilities to identify and change their ineffective beliefs. *Learning Disability Quarterly, 18,* 186-201.

Duit, R. (1991). Students' conceptual frameworks: Consequences for learning science. In S. M. Glynn, R. H. Yeany, & B. K. Britton (Eds.), *The psychology of learning science.* Hillsdale, NJ: Erlbaum.

DuNann, D. G., & Weber, S. J. (1976). Short- and long-term effects of contingency managed instruction on low, medium, and high GPA students. *Journal of Applied Behavior Analysis, 9,* 375-376.

Duncker, K. (1945). On problem solving. *Psychological Monographs, 58,* Whole No. 270.

Dunlap, G., dePerczel, M., Clarke, S., Wilson, D., Wright, S., White, R., & Gomez, A. (1994). Choice making to promote adaptive behavior for students with emotional and behavioral challenges. *Journal of Applied Behavior Analysis, 27,* 505-518.

DuPaul, G. J., & Eckert, T. L. (1994). The effects of social skills curricula: Now you see them, now you don't. *School Psychology Quarterly, 9,* 113-132.

Duran, B. J., & Weffer, R. E. (1992). Immigrants' aspirations, high school process, and academic outcomes. *American Educational Research Journal, 29,* 163-181.

Durkin, K. (1987). Social cognition and social context in the construction of sex differences. In M.A. Baker (Ed.), *Sex differences in human performance.* Chichester, England: Wiley.

Durkin, K. (1995). *Developmental social psychology: From infancy to old age.* Cambridge, MA: Blackwell.

Dweck, C. S. (1975). The role of expectations and attributions in the alleviation of learned helplessness. *Journal of Personality and Social Psychology, 31,* 674-685.

Dweck, C. S. (1978). Achievement. In M. E. Lamb (Ed.), *Social and personality development.* New York: Holt, Rinehart & Winston.

Dweck, C. S. (1986). Motivational processes affecting learning. *American Psychologist, 41,* 1040-1048.

Dweck, C. S., & Elliott, E. S. (1983). Achievement motivation. In E. M. Hetherington (Ed.), *Handbook of child psychology: Vol. 4. Socialization, personality, and social development* (4th ed.). New York: Wiley.

Dweck, C. S., & Leggett, E. L. (1988). A social-cognitive approach to motivation and personality. *Psychological Review, 95,* 256-273.

Dweck, C. S., & Licht, B. (1980). Learned helplessness and intellectual achievement. In J. Garber & M. E. P. Seligman (Eds.), *Human helplessness: Theory and applications.* New York: Academic Press.

D'Ydewalle, G., Swerts, A., & De Corte, E. (1983). Study time and test performance as a function of test expectations. *Contemporary Educational Psychology, 8*(1), 55-67.

Dyer, H. S. (1967). The discovery and development of educational goals. *Proceedings of the 1966 Invitational Conference on Testing Problems.* Princeton, NJ: Educational Testing Service.

Eagly, A. H. (1987). *Sex differences in social behavior: A social-role interpretation.* Hillsdale, NJ: Erlbaum.

Eaton, J. F., Anderson, C.W., & Smith, E. L. (1984). Students' misconceptions interfere with science learning: Case studies of fifth-grade students. *Elementary School Journal, 84,* 365-379.

Eccles, J. S. (1989). Bringing young women to math and science. In M. Crawford & M. Gentry (Eds.), *Gender and thought: Psychological perspectives.* New York: Springer-Verlag.

Eccles, J. S., & Jacobs, J. E. (1986). Social forces shape math attitudes and performance. *Signs: Journal of Women in Culture and Society, 11,* 367-380.

Eccles, J. S., Jacobs, J., Harold-Goldsmith, R., Jayaratne, T., & Yee, D. (1989, April). *The relations between parents' category-based and target-based beliefs:*

Gender roles and biological influences. Paper presented at the Society for Research in Child Development, Kansas City, MO.

Eccles, J. S., & Midgley, C. (1989). Stage-environment fit: Developmentally appropriate classrooms for young adolescents. In C. Ames & R. Ames (Eds.), *Research on motivation in education: Vol. 3. Goals and cognition.* San Diego: Academic Press.

Eccles, J. S., & Wigfield, A. (1985). Teacher expectations and student motivation. In J. B. Dusek (Ed.), *Teacher expectancies.* Hillsdale, NJ: Erlbaum.

Eccles (Parsons), J. S. (1983). Expectancies, values, and academic behaviors. In J. T. Spence (Ed.), *Achievement and achievement motivation.* San Francisco: W. H. Freeman.

Eccles (Parsons), J. S. (1984). Sex differences in mathematics participation. In M. Steinkamp & M. Maehr (Eds.), *Women in science.* Greenwich, CT: JAI Press.

Eccles (Parsons), J. S., Adler, T. F., Futterman, R., Goff, S. B., Kaczala, C. M., Meece, J. L., & Midgley, C. (1983). Expectations, values, and academic behaviors. In J. T. Spence (Ed.), *Achievement and achievement motivation.* San Francisco: W. H. Freeman.

Eden, G. F., Stein, J. F., & Wood, F. B. (1995). Verbal and visual problems in reading disability. *Journal of Learning Disabilities, 28,* 272-290.

Eeds, M., & Wells, D. (1989). Grand conversations: An explanation of meaning construction in literature study groups. *Research in the Teaching of English, 23,* 4-29.

Ehri, L. C. (1992). Reconceptualizing the development of sight word reading and its relationship to recoding. In P. B. Gough, L. C. Ehri, & R. Treiman (Eds), *Reading acquisition.* Hillsdale, NJ: Erlbaum.

Ehri, L. C., & Wilce, L. S. (1987). Does learning to spell help beginners learn to read words? *Reading Research Quarterly, 22,* 47-65.

Eisenberg, N. (1982). The development of reasoning regarding prosocial behavior. In N. Eisenberg (Ed.), *The development of prosocial behavior.* San Diego: Academic Press.

Eisenberg, N., Lennon, R., & Pasternack, J. F. (1986). Altruistic values and moral judgment. In N. Eisenberg (Ed.), *Altruistic emotion, cognition, and behavior.* Hillsdale, NJ: Erlbaum.

Eisenberg, N., Lennon, R., & Roth, K. (1983). Prosocial development: A longitudinal study. *Developmental Psychology, 19,* 846-855.

Eisenberg, N., Martin, C. L., & Fabes, R. A. (1996). Gender development and gender effects. In D. C. Berliner & R. C. Calfee (Eds.), *Handbook of educational psychology.* New York: Macmillan.

Eisenberger, R. (1992). Learned industriousness. *Psychological Review, 99,* 248-267.

Elkind, D. (1981). *Children and adolescents: Interpretive essays on Jean Piaget* (3rd ed.). New York: Oxford University Press.

Elkind, D. (1984). *All grown up and no place to go.* Reading, MA: Addison-Wesley.

Ellenwood, S., & Ryan, K. (1991). Literature and morality: An experimental curriculum. In W. M. Kurtines & J. L. Gewirtz (Eds.), *Moral behavior and development: Vol. 3. Application.* Hillsdale, NJ: Erlbaum.

Elliott, D. J. (1995). *Music matters: A new philosophy of music education.* New York: Oxford University Press.

Elliott, R., & Vasta, R. (1970). The modeling of sharing: Effects associated with vicarious reinforcement, symbolization, age, and generalization. *Journal of Experimental Child Psychology, 10,* 8-15.

Elliott, S. N., & Busse, R. T. (1991). Social skills assessment and intervention with children and adolescents. *School Psychology International, 12,* 63-83.

Ellis, E. S., & Friend, P. (1991). Adolescents with learning disabilities. In B. Y. L. Wong (Ed.), *Learning about learning disabilities.* San Diego: Academic Press.

Ellis, H. C., & Hunt, R. R. (1983). *Fundamentals of human memory and cognition* (3rd ed.). Dubuque, IA: Wm. C. Brown.

Ellis, N. C. (Ed.). (1994). *Implicit and explicit learning of languages.* London: Academic Press.

Ellis, N. R. (Ed.). (1979). *Handbook of mental deficiency: Psychological theory and research.* Hillsdale, NJ: Erlbaum.

Elrich, M. (1994). The stereotype within. *Educational Leadership, 51*(8), 12-15.

Emmer, E. T. (1987). Classroom management and discipline. In V. Richardson-Koehler (Ed.), *Educators' handbook: A research perspective.* White Plains, NY: Longman.

Emmer, E. T. (1994, April). Teacher emotions and classroom management. Paper presented at the annual meeting of the American Educational Research Association, New Orleans, LA.

Emmer, E. T., & Evertson, C. M. (1981). Synthesis of research on classroom management. *Educational Leadership, 38,* 342-347.

Emmer, E. T., Evertson, C. M., Clements, B. S., & Worsham, M. E. (1994). *Classroom management for secondary teachers* (3rd ed.). Needham Heights, MA: Allyn & Bacon.

Englemann, S., & Carnine, D. (1982). *Theory of instruction: Principles and applications.* New York: Irvington.

Englert, C. S., Raphael, T. E., Anderson, L. M., Anthony, H. M., & Stevens, D. D. (1991). Making strategies and self-talk visible: Writing instruction in regular and special education classrooms. *American Educational Research Journal, 28,* 337-372.

Entwisle, N. J., & Ramsden, P. (1983). *Understanding student learning.* London: Croom Helm.

Epstein, H. (1978). Growth spurts during brain development: Implications for educational policy and practice. In J. Chall & A. Mirsky (Eds.), *Education and the brain: The 77th yearbook of the National Society for the Study of Education, Part II.* Chicago: University of Chicago Press.

Epstein, J. L. (1983). Longitudinal effects of family-school-person interactions on student outcomes. *Research in Sociology of Education and Socialization, 4,* 101-127.

Epstein, J. L. (1996). Perspectives and previews on research and policy for school, family, and community partnerships. In A. Booth & J. F. Dunn (Eds.), *Family-school links: How do they affect educational outcomes?* Mahwah, NJ: Erlbaum.

Ericsson, K. A., & Chalmers, N. (1994). Expert performance: Its structure and acquisition. *American Psychologist, 49,* 725-747.

Eriks-Brophy, A., & Crago, M. B. (1994). Transforming classroom discourse: An Inuit example. *Language and Education, 8*(3), 105-122.

Erikson, E. H. (1963). *Childhood and society* (2nd ed.). New York: Norton.

Erikson, E. H. (1972). *Eight ages of man.* In C. S. Lavatelli & F. Stendler (Eds.), *Readings in child behavior and child development.* San Diego: Harcourt Brace Jovanovich.

Erwin, P. (1993). *Friendship and peer relations in children.* Chichester, England: Wiley.

Esquivel, G. B. (1995). Teacher behaviors that foster creativity. *Educational Psychology Review, 7,* 185-202.

Etaugh, C. (1983). Introduction: The influence of environmental factors on sex differences in children's play. In M. B. Liss (Ed.), *Social and cognitive skills: Sex roles and children's play.* San Diego: Academic Press.

Evans, E. D., & Craig, D. (1990). Teacher and student perceptions of academic cheating in middle and senior high schools. *Journal of Educational Research, 84*(1), 44-52.

Evans, G. W., & Oswalt, G. L. (1968). Acceleration of academic progress through the manipulation of peer influence. *Behaviour Research and Therapy, 6,* 189-195.

Evertson, C. M., & Emmer, E. T. (1982). Effective management at the beginning of the year in junior high classes. *Journal of Educational Psychology, 74,* 485-498.

Evertson, C. M., & Harris, A. H. (1992). What we know about managing classrooms. *Educational Leadership, 49*(7), 74-78.

Eysenck, M. W. (1992). *Anxiety: The cognitive perspective.* Hove, England: Erlbaum.

Eysenck, M. W., & Keane, M. T. (1990). *Cognitive psychology: A student's handbook.* Hove, England: Erlbaum.

Fagot, B. I., Hagan, R., Leinbach, M. D., & Kronsberg, S. (1985). Differential reactions to assertive and communicative acts of toddler boys and girls. *Child Development, 56,* 1499-1505.

Fagot, B. I., & Leinbach, M. D. (1983). Play styles in early childhood: Social consequences for boys and girls. In M. B. Liss (Ed.), *Social and cognitive skills: Sex roles and children's play.* San Diego: Academic Press.

Fairbairn, D. M. (1987). The art of questioning your students. *Clearing House, 61,* 19-22.

Fairchild, H. H., & Edwards-Evans, S. (1990). African American dialects and schooling: A review. In A. M. Padilla, H. H. Fairchild, & C. M. Valadez (Eds.), *Bilingual education: Issues and strategies.* Newbury Park, CA: Sage.

Fantuzzo, J. W., King, J., & Heller, L. R. (1992). Effects of reciprocal peer tutoring on mathematics and school adjustment: A component analysis. *Journal of Educational Psychology, 84,* 331-339.

Faraone, S. V., Biederman, J., Chen, W. J., Milberger, S., Warburton, R., & Tsuang, M. T. (1995). Genetic heterogeneity in attention-deficit hyperactivity disorder (ADHD): Gender, psychiatric comorbidity, and maternal ADHD. *Journal of Abnormal Psychology, 104,* 334-345.

Feather, N. T. (1982). *Expectations and actions: Expectancy-value models in psychology.* Hillsdale, NJ: Erlbaum.

Feld, S., Ruhland, D., & Gold, M. (1979). Developmental changes in achievement motivation. *Merrill-Palmer Quarterly, 25,* 43-60.

Feldhusen, J. F. (1989). Synthesis of research on gifted youth. *Educational Leadership, 26*(1), 6-11.

Feldhusen, J. F., & Kroll, M. D. (1985). Parent perceptions of gifted children's educational needs. *Roeper Review, 7,* 249-252.

Feldhusen, J. F., & Treffinger, D. J. (1980). *Creative thinking and problem solving in gifted education.* Dubuque, IA: Kendall/Hunt.

Feldhusen, J. F., Treffinger, D. J., & Bahlke, S. J. (1970). Developing creative thinking: The Purdue Creativity Program. *Journal of Creative Behavior, 4,* 85-90.

Feldman, D. H., & Goldsmith, L. T. (1991). *Nature's gambit.* New York: Teachers College Press.

Fennema, E. (1987). Sex-related differences in education: Myths, realities, and interventions. In V. Richardson-Koehler (Ed.), *Educators' handbook: A research perspective.* White Plains, NY: Longman.

Fennema, E., Carpenter, T. P., Jacobs, V. R., Franke, M. L., & Levi, L. W. (1998). A longitudinal study of gender differences in young children's mathematical thinking. *Educational Researcher, 27*(5), 6-11.

Fennema, E., & Peterson, P. (1985). Autonomous learning behavior: A possible explanation of gender-related differences in mathematics. In L. C. Wilkinson & C. B. Marrett (Eds.), *Gender influences in classroom interaction.* San Diego: Academic Press.

Fennema, E., & Sherman, J. (1977). Sex related differences in mathematics achievement, spatial visualization and affective factors. *American Educational Research Journal, 14,* 51-71.

Ferguson, E. L., & Hegarty, M. (1995). Learning with real machines or diagrams: Application of knowledge to real-world problems. *Cognition and Instruction, 13,* 129-160.

Fessler, M. A., Rosenberg, M. S., & Rosenberg, L. A. (1991). Concomitant learning disabilities and learning problems among students with behavioral/emotional disorders. *Behavioral Disorders, 16,* 97-106.

Fey, M. E., Catts, H., & Larrivee, L. (1995). Preparing preschoolers for the academic and social challenges of school. In M. E. Fey, J. Windsor, & S. F. Warren (Eds.), *Language intervention: Preschool through elementary years.* Baltimore: Paul H. Brookes.

Fiedler, E. D., Lange, R. E., & Winebrenner, S. (1993). In search of reality: Unraveling the myths about tracking, ability grouping and the gifted. *Roeper Review, 16*(1), 4-7.

Field, D. (1987). A review of preschool conservation training: An analysis of analyses. *Developmental Review, 7,* 210-251.

Finders, M., & Lewis, C. (1994). Why some parents don't come to school. *Educational Leadership, 51*(8), 50-54.

Finn, J. D. (1989). Withdrawing from school. *Review of Educational Research, 59,* 117-142.

Finn, J. D. (1991). How to make the dropout problem go away. *Educational Researcher, 20*(1), 28-30.

Fischer, K. W., & Bidell, T. (1991). Constraining nativist inferences about cognitive capacities. In S. Carey & R. Gelman (Eds.), *The epigenesis of mind: Essays on biology and cognition.* Hillsdale, NJ: Erlbaum.

Fischer, K. W., & Farrar, M. J. (1987). Generalizations about generalizations: How a theory of skill development explains both generality and specificity. *International Journal of Psychology, 22,* 643-677.

Fischer, K. W., & Rose, S. P. (1996). Dynamic growth cycles of brain and cognitive development. In R.

Thatcher, G. R. Lyon, J. Rumsey, & N. Krasnegor (Eds.), *Developmental neuroimaging: Mapping the development of brain and behavior.* New York: Academic Press.

Fisher, W. W., & Mazur, J. E. (1997). Basic and applied research on choice responding. *Journal of Applied Behavior Analysis, 30,* 387-410.

Fitzgerald, J. (1987). Research on revision in writing. *Review of Educational Research, 57,* 481-506.

Fitzgerald, J. (1992). Variant views about good thinking during composing: Focus on revision. In M. Pressley, K. R. Harris, & J. T. Guthrie (Eds.), *Promoting academic competence and literacy in school.* San Diego: Academic Press.

Flavell, J. H. (1985). *Cognitive development* (2nd ed.). Upper Saddle River, NJ: Prentice Hall.

Flavell, J. H. (1996). Piaget's legacy. *Psychological Science, 7,* 200-203.

Flavell, J. H., Friedrichs, A. G., & Hoyt, J. D. (1970). Developmental changes in memorization processes. *Cognitive Psychology, 1,* 324-340.

Flavell, J. H., Miller, P. H., & Miller, S. A. (1993). *Cognitive development* (3rd ed.). Upper Saddle River, NJ: Prentice Hall.

Fletcher, K. L., & Bray, N. W. (1995). External and verbal strategies in children with and without mild mental retardation. *American Journal on Mental Retardation, 99,* 363-475.

Flower, L. S., & Hayes, J. R. (1981). A cognitive process theory of writing. *College Composition and Communication, 32,* 365-387.

Flynn, J. R. (1987). Massive IQ gains in 14 nations: What IQ tests really measure. *Psychological Bulletin, 101,* 171-191.

Foorman, B. R., Francis, D. J., Fletcher, J. M., Schatschneider, C., & Mehta, P. (1998). The role of instruction in learning to read: Preventing reading failure in at-risk children. *Journal of Educational Psychology, 90,* 37-55.

Foos, P. W., & Fisher, R. P. (1988). Using tests as learning opportunities. *Journal of Educational Psychology, 80,* 179-183.

Forbes, M. L., Ormrod, J. E., Bernardi, J. D., Taylor, S. L., & Jackson, D. L. (1999, April). *Children's conceptions of space, as reflected in maps of their hometown.* Paper presented at the annual meeting of the American Educational Research Association, Montreal.

Ford, D. Y. (1996). *Reversing underachievement among gifted black students.* New York: Teachers College Press.

Ford, D. Y., & Harris, J. J. (1992). The American achievement ideology and achievement differentials among preadolescent gifted and nongifted African American males and females. *Journal of Negro Education, 61*(1), 45-64.

Fosnot, C. T. (1996). Constructivism: A psychological theory of learning. In C. T. Fosnot (Ed.), *Constructivism: Theory, perspectives, and practice.* New York: Teachers College Press.

Foster-Johnson, L., Ferro, J., & Dunlap. G. (1994). Preferred curriculum activities and reduced problem behaviors in students with intellectual disabilities. *Journal of Applied Behavior Analysis, 27,* 493-504.

Fowler, S. A., & Baer, D. M. (1981). "Do I have to be good all day?" The timing of delayed reinforcement as a factor in generalization. *Journal of Applied Behavior Analysis, 14,* 13-24.

Fox, L. H. (1979). Programs for the gifted and talented: An overview. In A. H. Passow (Ed.), *The gifted and the talented: Their education and development. The seventy-eighth yearbook of the National Society for the Study of Education.* Chicago: University of Chicago Press.

Fox, L. H. (1981). *The problem of women and mathematics.* New York: Ford Foundation.

Fox, P. W., & LeCount, J. (1991, April). *When more is less: Faculty misestimation of student learning.* Paper presented at the annual meeting of the American Educational Research Association, Chicago.

Frasier, M. M. (1989). Identification of gifted black students: Developing new perspectives. In C. J. Maker & S. W. Schiever (Eds.), *Critical issues in gifted education: Vol. 2. Defensible programs for cultural and ethnic minorities.* Austin, TX: Pro-Ed.

Frazer, L. H., & Wilkinson, L. D. (1990, April). *At-risk students: Do we know which ones will drop out?* Paper presented at the annual meeting of the American Educational Research Association, Boston.

Frederiksen, J. R., & Collins, A. (1989). A systems approach to educational testing. *Educational Researcher, 18*(9), 27-32.

Frederiksen, N. (1984a). Implications of cognitive theory for instruction in problem-solving. *Review of Educational Research, 54,* 363-407.

Frederiksen, N. (1984b). The real test bias: Influences of testing on teaching and learning. *American Psychologist, 39,* 193-202.

Freedman, K. (1996). The social reconstruction of art education: Teaching visual culture. In C. A. Grant & M. L. Gomez (Eds.), *Making schooling multicultural: Campus and classroom.* Upper Saddle River, NJ: Merrill/Prentice Hall.

Freiberg, H. J. (1987). Teacher self-evaluation and principal supervision. *NASSP Bulletin* (National Association of Secondary School Principals), *71,* 85-92.

French, E. G. (1956). Motivation as a variable in work partner selection. *Journal of Abnormal and Social Psychology, 53,* 96-99.

Friedel, M. (1993). *Characteristics of gifted/creative children.* Warwick, RI: National Foundation for Gifted and Creative Children.

Friedman, L. (1995). The space factor in mathematics: Gender differences. *Review of Educational Research, 65,* 22-50.

Friedrich, L. K., & Stein, A. H. (1973). Aggressive and pro-social television programs and the natural behavior of preschool children. *Society for Research in Child Development Monographs, 38* (Whole No. 151).

Frisbie, D. A., & Waltman, K. K. (1992). Developing a personal grading plan. *Educational Measurement: Issues and Practices, 11,* 35-42. Reprinted in K. M. Cauley, F. Linder, & J. H. McMillan (Eds.), (1994), *Educational psychology 94/95.* Guilford, CT: Dushkin.

Fuchs, D., Fuchs, L. S., Mathes, P. G., & Simmons, D. C. (1997). Peer-assisted learning strategies: Making classrooms more responsive to diversity. *American Educational Research Journal, 34,* 174-206.

Fuchs, L. S., Fuchs, D., Hamlett, C. L., & Karns, K. (1998). High-achieving students' interactions and performance on complex mathematical tasks as a function of homogeneous and heterogeneous pairings. *American Educational Research Journal, 35,* 227-267.

Fuchs, L. S., Fuchs, D., & Karns, K. (1995). Acquisition and transfer effects of classwide peer-assisted learning strategies for students with varying learning histories. *School Psychology Review, 24,* 604–620.

Fuchs, L. S., Fuchs, D., Karns, K., Hamlett, C. L., Dutka, S., & Katzaroff, M. (1996). The relation between student ability and the quality and effectiveness of explanations. *American Educational Research Journal, 33,* 631–664.

Funder, D. C. (1991). Global traits: A neo-Allportian approach to personality. *Psychological Science, 2,* 31–39.

Fuson, K. C., & Briars, D. J. (1990). Using a base-ten blocks learning/teaching approach for first- and second-grade place-value and multidigit addition and subtraction. *Journal for Research in Mathematics Education, 21,* 180–206.

Fuson, K. C., & Hall, J. W. (1983). The acquisition of early word meanings: A conceptual analysis and review. In H. P. Ginsburg (Ed.), *Children's mathematical thinking.* New York: Academic Press.

Gage, N. L. (1991). The obviousness of social and educational research results. *Educational Researcher, 20*(1), 10–16.

Gagné, E. D. (1985). *The cognitive psychology of school learning.* Boston: Little, Brown.

Gagné, R. M. (1985). *The conditions of learning and theory of instruction* (4th ed.). New York: Holt, Rinehart & Winston.

Gagné, R. M., Briggs, L. J., & Wager, W. W. (1992). *Principles of instructional design* (4th ed.). Fort Worth, TX: Harcourt Brace Jovanovich.

Gaines, M. L., & Davis, M. (1990, April). *Accuracy of teacher prediction of elementary student achievement.* Paper presented at the annual meeting of the American Educational Research Association, Boston.

Gallagher, J. J. (1991). Personal patterns of underachievement. *Journal for the Education of the Gifted, 14,* 221–233.

Gallimore, R., & Tharp, R. (1990). Teaching mind in society: Teaching, schooling, and literate discourse. In L. C. Moll (Ed.), *Vygotsky and education: Instructional implications and applications of sociohistorical psychology.* Cambridge, England: Cambridge University Press.

Gallistel, C. R., & Gelman, R. (1992). Preverbal and verbal counting and computation. *Cognition, 44,* 43–74.

Gambrell, L. B., & Bales, R. J. (1986). Mental imagery and the comprehension-monitoring performance of fourth- and fifth-grade poor readers. *Reading Research Quarterly, 21,* 454–464.

Gambrell, L. B., & Chasen, S. P. (1991). Explicit story instruction and the narrative writing of fourth- and fifth-grade below-average readers. *Reading Research and Instruction, 31,* 54–62.

García, E. E. (1992). "Hispanic" children: Theoretical, empirical, and related policy issues. *Educational Psychology Review, 4,* 69–93.

García, E. E. (1994). *Understanding and meeting the challenge of student cultural diversity.* Boston: Houghton Mifflin.

García, E. E. (1995). Educating Mexican American students: Past treatment and recent developments in theory, research, policy, and practice. In J. A. Banks & C. A. M. Banks (Eds.), *Handbook of research on multicultural education.* New York: Macmillan.

Gardner, H. (1983). *Frames of mind: The theory of multiple intelligences.* New York: Basic Books.

Gardner, H. (1995). Reflections on multiple intelligences: Myths and messages. *Phi Delta Kappan, 77,* 200–209.

Gardner, H. (1998, April). *Where to draw the line: The perils of new paradigms.* Paper presented at the annual meeting of the American Educational Research Association, San Diego.

Gardner, H., & Hatch, T. (1990). Multiple intelligences go to school: Educational implications of the theory of multiple intelligences. *Educational Researcher, 18*(8), 4–10.

Gardner, H., Torff, B., & Hatch, T. (1996). The age of innocence reconsidered: Preserving the best of the progressive traditions in psychology and education. In D. R. Olson & N. Torrance (Eds.), *The handbook of education and human development: New models of learning, teaching, and schooling.* Cambridge, MA: Blackwell.

Gardner, R., III, Heward, W. L., & Grossi, T. A. (1994). Effects of response conditions on student participation and academic achievement: A systematic replication with inner-city students during whole-class science instruction. *Journal of Applied Behavior Analysis, 27,* 63–71.

Garhart, C., & Hannafin, M. J. (1986). The accuracy of cognitive monitoring during computer-based instruction. *Journal of Computer-Based Instruction, 13,* 88–93.

Garibaldi, A. M. (1992). Educating and motivating African American males to succeed. *The Journal of Negro Education, 61*(1), 4–11.

Garibaldi, A. M. (1993). Creating prescriptions for success in urban schools: Turning the corner on pathological explanations for academic failure. In T. M. Tomlinson (Ed.), *Motivating students to learn: Overcoming barriers to high achievement.* Berkeley, CA: McCutchan.

Garner, R. (1987). Strategies for reading and studying expository texts. *Educational Psychologist, 22,* 299–312.

Garner, R. (1998). Epilogue: Choosing to learn or not-learn in school. *Educational Psychology Review, 10,* 227–237.

Garner, R., Alexander, P. A., Gillingham, M. G., Kulikowich, J. M., & Brown, R. (1991). Interest and learning from text. *American Educational Research Journal, 28,* 643–659.

Garner, R., Brown, R., Sanders, S., & Menke, D. J. (1992). "Seductive details" and learning from text. In K. A. Renninger, S. Hidi, & A. Krapp (Eds.), *The role of interest in learning and development.* Hillsdale, NJ: Erlbaum.

Garnier, H. E., Stein, J. A., & Jacobs, J. K. (1997). The process of dropping out of high school: A 19-year perspective. *American Educational Research Journal, 34,* 395–419.

Garrison, L. (1989). Programming for the gifted American Indian student. In C. J. Maker & S. W. Schiever (Eds.), *Critical issues in gifted education: Vol. 2: Defensible programs for cultural and ethnic minorities.* Austin, TX: Pro-Ed.

Gathercole, S. E., & Hitch, G. J. (1993). Developmental changes in short-term memory: A revised working memory perspective. In A. F. Collins, S. E. Gathercole, M. A. Conway, & P. E. Morris (Eds.), *Theories of memory.* Hove, England: Erlbaum.

Gaudry, E., & Bradshaw, G. D. (1971). The differential effect of anxiety on performance in progressive and terminal school examinations. In E. Gaudry & C. D. Spielberger (Eds.), *Anxiety and educational achievement.* Sydney, Australia: Wiley.

Gauntt, H. L. (1991, April). *The roles of prior knowledge of text structure and prior knowledge of content in the comprehension and recall of expository text.* Paper presented at the annual meeting of the American Educational Research Association, Chicago.

Gay, J., & Cole, M. (1967). *The new mathematics and an old culture.* New York: Holt, Rinehart & Winston.

Gayford, C. (1992). Patterns of group behavior in open-ended problem solving in science classes of 15-year-old students in England. *Internal Journal of Science Education, 14,* 41–49.

Gearheart, B. R., Weishahn, M. W., & Gearheart, C. J. (1992). *The exceptional child in the regular classroom* (5th ed.). Upper Saddle River, NJ: Merrill/Prentice Hall.

Geary, D. C. (1994). *Children's mathematical development: Research and practical applications.* Washington, DC: American Psychological Association.

Geary, D. C. (1998). What is the function of mind and brain? *Educational Psychology Review, 10,* 377–387.

Gelman, R., & Baillargeon, R. (1983). A review of some Piagetian concepts. In J. H. Flavell & E. M. Markman (Eds.), *Handbook of child psychology: Vol. 3. Cognitive development.* New York: Wiley.

Gelman, R., & Gallistel, C. R. (1978). *The child's understanding of number.* Cambridge, MA: Harvard University Press.

Genesee, F. (1985). Second language learning through immersion: A review of U.S. programs. *Review of Educational Research, 55,* 541–561.

Genova, W. J., & Walberg, H. J. (1984). Enhancing integration in urban high schools. In D. E. Bartz & M. L. Maehr (Eds.), *Advances in motivation and achievement: Vol 1. The effects of school desegregation on motivation and achievement.* Greenwich, CT: JAI Press.

Genshaft, J. L., Greenbaum, S., & Borovosky, S. (1995). Stress and the gifted. In J. L. Genshaft, M. Bireley, & C. L. Hollinger (Eds.), *Serving gifted and talented students: A resource for school personnel.* Austin, TX: Pro-Ed.

Gernsbacher, M. A. (1994). *Handbook of psycholinguistics.* San Diego: Academic Press.

Gerst, M. S. (1971). Symbolic coding processes in observational learning. *Journal of Personality & Social Psychology, 19,* 7–17.

Gettinger, M. (1988). Methods of proactive classroom management. *School Psychology Review, 17,* 227–242.

Giaconia, R. M. (1988). Teacher questioning and wait-time (Doctoral dissertation, Stanford University, 1988). *Dissertation Abstracts International, 49,* 462A.

Giaconia, R. M., & Hedges, L. V. (1982). Identifying features of effective open education. *Review of Educational Research, 52,* 579–602.

Giangreco, M. F. (1997). Responses to Nietupski et al. *Journal of Special Education, 31,* 56–57.

Gick, M. L., & Holyoak, K. J. (1987). The cognitive basis of knowledge transfer. In S. M. Cormier & J. D. Hagman (Eds.), *Transfer of learning: Contemporary research and applications.* San Diego: Academic Press.

Gillberg, I. C., & Coleman, M. (1996). Autism and medical disorders: A review of the literature. *Developmental Medicine and Child Neurology, 38,* 191-202.

Gilligan, C. F. (1982). *In a different voice.* Cambridge, MA: Harvard University Press.

Gilligan, C. F. (1987). Moral orientation and moral development. In E. F. Kittay & D. T. Meyers (Eds.), *Women and moral theory.* Totowa, NJ: Rowman & Littlefield.

Gilligan, C. F., & Attanucci, J. (1988). Two moral orientations. In C. F. Gilligan, J. V. Ward, & J. M. Taylor (Eds.), *Mapping the moral domain: A contribution of women's thinking to psychological theory and education.* Cambridge, MA: Center for the Study of Gender, Education, and Human Development (distributed by Harvard University Press).

Gilliland, H. (1988). Discovering and emphasizing the positive aspects of the culture. In H. Gilliland & J. Reyhner (Eds.), *Teaching the Native American.* Dubuque, IA: Kendall/Hunt.

Gilpin, L. (1968). *The enduring Navaho.* Austin: University of Texas Press.

Ginsburg, H. P., Posner, J. K., & Russell, R. L. (1981). The development of mental addition as a function of schooling and culture. *Journal of Cross-Cultural Psychology, 12,* 163-178.

Girotto, V., & Light, P. (1993). The pragmatic bases of children's reasoning. In P. Light & G. Butterworth (Eds.), *Context and cognition: Ways of learning and knowing.* Hillsdale, NJ: Erlbaum.

Glanzer, M., & Nolan, S. D. (1986). Memory mechanisms in text comprehension. In G. H. Bower (Ed.), *The psychology of learning and motivation: Advances in research and theory* (Vol. 20). San Diego: Academic Press.

Glass, A. L., & Holyoak, K. J. (1975). Alternative conceptions of semantic memory. *Cognition, 3,* 313-339.

Glass, A. L., Holyoak, K. J., & Santa, J. L. (1979). *Cognition.* Reading, MA: Addison-Wesley.

Glasser, W. (1969). *Schools without failure.* New York: Harper & Row.

Glover, J. A., Ronning, R. R., & Reynolds, C. R. (Eds.) (1989). *Handbook of creativity.* New York: Plenum Press.

Glucksberg, S., & Krauss, R. M. (1967). What do people say after they have learned to talk? Studies of the development of referential communication. *Merrill-Palmer Quarterly, 13,* 309-316.

Glynn, S. M. (1991). Explaining science concepts: A teaching-with-analogies model. In S. M. Glynn, R. H. Yeany, & B. K. Britton (Eds.), *The psychology of learning science.* Hillsdale, NJ: Erlbaum.

Glynn, S. M., Yeany, R. H., & Britton, B. K. (1991). A constructive view of learning science. In S. M. Glynn, R. H. Yeany, & B. K. Britton (Eds.), *The psychology of learning science.* Hillsdale, NJ: Erlbaum.

Goldberg, R. A., Schwartz, S., & Stewart, M (1977). Individual differences in cognitive processes. *Journal of Educational Psychology, 69,* 9-14.

Goldenberg, C. (1992). The limits of expectations: A case for case knowledge about teacher expectancy effects. *American Educational Research Journal, 29,* 517-544.

Goldsmith-Phillips, J. (1989). Word and context in reading development: A test of the interactive-compensatory hypothesis. *Journal of Educational Psychology, 81,* 299-305.

Gollnick, D. M., & Chinn, P. C. (1994). *Multicultural education in a pluralistic society* (4th ed.). Upper Saddle River, NJ: Merrill/Prentice Hall.

Good, T. L., & Brophy, J. E. (1994). *Looking in classrooms* (6th ed.). New York: HarperCollins.

Good, T. L., McCaslin, M. M., & Reys, B. J. (1992). Investigating work groups to promote problem solving in mathematics. In J. Brophy (Ed.), *Advances in research on teaching: Vol. 3. Planning and managing learning tasks and activities.* Greenwich, CT: JAI Press.

Goodenow, C. (1991, April). *The sense of belonging and its relationship to academic motivation among pre- and early adolescent students.* Paper presented at the annual meeting of the American Educational Research Association, Chicago.

Goodman, K. S. (1989). Whole-language research: Foundations and development. *Elementary School Journal, 90,* 207-221.

Goodman, K. S., & Goodman, Y. M. (1979). Learning to read is natural. In L. B. Resnick & P. A. Weaver (Eds.), *Theory and practice of early reading* (Vol. 1). Hillsdale, NJ: Erlbaum.

Gootman, M. E. (1998). Effective in-house suspension. *Educational Leadership, 56*(1), 39-41.

Gorski, J. D., & Pilotto, L. (1993). Interpersonal violence among youth: A challenge for school personnel. *Educational Psychology Review, 5,* 35-61.

Gottfredson, D. C., Fink, C. M., & Graham, N. (1994). Grade retention and problem behavior. *American Educational Research Journal, 31,* 761-784.

Gottfredson, G. D., & Gottfredson, D. C. (1985). *Victimization in schools.* New York: Plenum Press.

Gottfried, A. E. (1990). Academic intrinsic motivation in young elementary school children. *Journal of Educational Psychology, 82,* 525-538.

Gottfried, A. E., Fleming, J. S., & Gottfried, A. W. (1994). Role of parental motivational practices in children's academic intrinsic motivation and achievement. *Journal of Educational Psychology, 86,* 104-113.

Grabe, M. (1986). Attentional processes in education. In G. D. Phye & T. Andre (Eds.), *Cognitive classroom learning: Understanding, thinking, and problem solving.* San Diego: Academic Press.

Graesser, A., Golding, J. M., & Long, D. L. (1991). Narrative representation and comprehension. In R. Barr, M. L. Kamil, P. Mosenthal, & P. D. Pearson (Eds.), *Handbook of reading research* (Vol. II). New York: Longman.

Graesser, A., & Person, N. K. (1994). Question asking during tutoring. *American Educational Research Journal, 31,* 104-137.

Graham, S. (1989). Motivation in Afro-Americans. In G. L. Berry & J. K. Asamen (Eds.), *Black students: Psychosocial issues and academic achievement.* Newbury Park, CA: Sage.

Graham, S. (1990). Communicating low ability in the classroom: Bad things good teachers sometimes do. In S. Graham & V. S. Folkes (Eds.), *Attribution theory: Applications to achievement, mental health, and interpersonal conflict.* Hillsdale, NJ: Erlbaum.

Graham, S. (1991). A review of attribution theory in achievement contexts. *Educational Psychology Review, 3,* 5-39.

Graham, S. (1994). Motivation in African Americans. *Review of Educational Research, 64,* 55-117.

Graham, S., & Barker, G. (1990). The downside of help: An attributional-developmental analysis of helping behavior as a low ability cue. *Journal of Educational Psychology, 82,* 7-14.

Graham, S., & Golen, S. (1991). Motivational influences on cognition: Task involvement, ego involvement, and depth of information processing. *Journal of Educational Psychology, 83,* 187-194.

Graham, S., & Harris, K. R. (1988). Instructional recommendations for teaching writing to exceptional children. *Exceptional Children, 54,* 506-512.

Graham, S., & Harris, K. R. (1992). Self-regulated strategy development: Programmatic research in writing. In B. Y. L. Wong (Ed.), *Contemporary intervention research in learning disabilities: An international perspective.* New York: Springer-Verlag.

Graham, S., MacArthur, C., & Schwartz, S. (1995). Effects of goal setting and procedural facilitation on the revising behavior and writing performance of students with writing and learning problems. *Journal of Educational Psychology, 87,* 230-240.

Graham, S., Schwartz, S. S., & MacArthur, C. A. (1993). Knowledge of writing and the composing process, attitude toward writing, and self-efficacy for students with and without learning disabilities. *Journal of Learning Disabilities, 26,* 237-249.

Graham, S., & Weiner, B. (1996). Theories and principles of motivation. In D. C. Berliner & R. C. Calfee (Eds.), *Handbook of educational psychology.* New York: Macmillan.

Grandin, T. (1995). *Thinking in pictures and other reports of my life with autism.* New York: Random House.

Granger, D. A., Whalen, C. K., Henker, B., & Cantwell, C. (1996). ADHD boys' behavior during structured classroom social activities: Effects of social demands, teacher proximity, and methylphenidate. *Journal of Attention Disorders, 1*(1), 16-30.

Grant, C. A., & Gomez, M. L. (Eds.). (1996). *Making schooling multicultural: Campus and classroom.* Upper Saddle River, NJ: Merrill/Prentice Hall.

Grant, L. (1985). Race-gender status, classroom interaction, and children's socialization in elementary school. In L. C. Wilkinson & C. B. Marrett (Eds.), *Gender influences in classroom interaction.* San Diego: Academic Press.

Graves, D. (1983). *Writing: Teachers and children at work.* Portsmouth, NH: Heinemann.

Gray, W. D., & Orasanu, J. M. (1987). Transfer of cognitive skills. In S. M. Cormier & J. D. Hagman (Eds.), *Transfer of learning: Contemporary research and applications.* San Diego: Academic Press.

Green, L., Fry, A. F., & Myerson, J. (1994). Discounting of delayed rewards: A life-span comparison. *Psychological Science, 5,* 33-36.

Greene, B. A. (1994, April). *Instruction to enhance comprehension of unfamiliar text: Should it focus on domain-specific or strategy knowledge?* Paper presented at the annual meeting of the American Educational Research Association, New Orleans, LA.

Greene, S., & Ackerman, J. M. (1995). Expanding the constructivist metaphor: A rhetorical perspective on literacy research and practice. *Review of Educational Research, 65,* 383-420.

Greenfield, P. M. (1994). Independence and interdependence as developmental scripts: Implications for theory, research, and practice. In P. M. Greenfield & R. R. Cocking (Eds.), *Cross-cultural roots of minority child development.* Hillsdale, NJ: Erlbaum.

Greeno, J. G. (1991). A view of mathematical problem solving in school. In M. U. Smith (Ed.), *Toward a unified theory of problem solving: Views from the content domains.* Hillsdale, NJ: Erlbaum.

Greeno, J. G. (1997). On claims that answer the wrong questions. *Educational Researcher, 26*(1), 5–17.

Greeno, J. G., Collins, A. M., & Resnick, L. B. (1996). Cognition and learning. In D. C. Berliner & R. C. Calfee (Eds.), *Handbook of educational psychology.* New York: Macmillan.

Greenspan, S., & Granfield, J. M. (1992). Reconsidering the construct of mental retardation: Implications of a model of social competence. *American Journal of Mental Retardation, 96*, 442–453.

Greenwood, C. R. (1991). Classwide peer tutoring: Longitudinal effects on the reading, language, and mathematics achievement of at-risk students. *Journal of Reading, Writing, and Learning Disabilities International, 7*(2), 105–123.

Greenwood, C. R., Carta, J. J., & Hall, R. V. (1988). The use of peer tutoring strategies in classroom management and educational instruction. *School Psychology Review, 17*, 258–275.

Gregg, M., & Leinhardt, G. (1994a, April). *Constructing geography.* Paper presented at the annual meeting of the American Educational Research Association, New Orleans, LA.

Gregg, M., & Leinhardt, G. (1994b). Mapping out geography: An example of epistemology and education. *Review of Educational Research, 64*, 311–361.

Gresham, F. M., & MacMillan, D. L. (1997). Social competence and affective characteristics of students with mild disabilities. *Review of Educational Research, 67*, 377–415.

Griffin, M. M., & Griffin, B. W. (1994, April). *Some can get there from here: Situated learning, cognitive style, and map skills.* Paper presented at the annual meeting of the American Educational Research Association, New Orleans, LA.

Griffin, S. A., & Case, R. (1996). Evaluating the breadth and depth of training effects when central conceptual structures are taught. In R. Case & Y. Okamoto (Eds.), The role of central structures in the development of children's thought. *Monographs of the Society for Research in Child Development, 61*, Serial No. 246, Nos. 1–2.

Griffin, S., Case, R., & Capodilupo, A. (1995). Teaching for understanding: The importance of the central conceptual structures in the elementary mathematics curriculum. In A. McKeough, J. Lupart, & A. Marini (Eds.), *Teaching for transfer: Fostering generalization in learning.* Mahwah, NJ: Erlbaum.

Griffin, S. A., Case, R., & Siegler, R. S. (1994). Rightstart: Providing the central conceptual prerequisites for first formal learning of arithmetic to students at risk for school failure. In K. McGilly (Ed.), *Classroom lessons: Integrating cognitive theory and classroom practice.* Cambridge, MA: MIT Press.

Griffore, R. J. (1981). *Child development: An educational perspective.* Springfield, IL: Charles C Thomas.

Grodzinsky, G. M., & Diamond, R. (1992). Frontal lobe functioning in boys with attention-deficit hyperactivity disorder. *Developmental Neuropsychology, 8*, 427–445.

Grolnick, W. S., & Ryan, R. M. (1987). Autonomy in children's learning: An experimental and individual difference investigation. *Journal of Personality and Social Psychology, 52*, 890–898.

Gronlund, N. E. (1993). *How to make achievement tests and assessments* (5th ed.). Needham Heights, MA: Allyn & Bacon.

Gronlund, N. E. (2000). *How to write and use instructional objectives* (6th ed.). Upper Saddle River, NJ: Merrill/Prentice Hall.

Gronlund, N. E., & Linn, R. L. (1990). *Measurement and evaluation in teaching* (6th ed.). New York: Macmillan.

Grusec, J. E., & Redler, E. (1980). Attribution, reinforcement, and altruism. *Developmental Psychology, 16*, 525–534.

Guess, D., Roberts, S., Siegel-Causey, E., & Rues, J. (1995). Replication and extended analysis of behavior state, environmental events, and related variables among individuals with profound disabilities. *American Journal on Mental Retardation, 100*, 36–51.

Gunstone, R. F. (1994). The importance of specific science content in the enhancement of metacognition. In P. J. Fensham, R. F. Gunstone, & R. T. White (Eds.), *The content of science: A constructivist approach to its teaching and learning.* London: Falmer Press.

Gunstone, R. F., & White, R. T. (1981). Understanding of gravity. *Science Education, 65*, 291–299.

Guskey, T. R. (1985). *Implementing mastery learning.* Belmont, CA: Wadsworth.

Guskey, T. R. (1994, April). *Outcome-based education and mastery learning: Clarifying the differences.* Paper presented at the annual meeting of the American Educational Research Association, New Orleans, LA.

Gustafsson, J., & Undheim, J. O. (1996). Individual differences in cognitive functions. In D. C. Berliner & R. C. Calfee (Eds.), *Handbook of educational psychology.* New York: Macmillan.

Guthrie, J. T., Cox, K. E., Anderson, E., Harris, K., Mazzoni, S., & Rach, L. (1998). Principles of integrated instruction for engagement in reading. *Educational Psychology Review, 10*, 177–199.

Hacker, D. J. (1995, April). *Comprehension monitoring of written discourse across early-to-middle adolescence.* Paper presented at the annual meeting of the American Educational Research Association, San Francisco.

Hadaway, N. L., Florez, V., Larke, P. J., & Wiseman, D. (1993). Teaching in the midst of diversity: How do we prepare? In M. J. O'Hair & S. J. Odell (Eds.), *Diversity and teaching: Teacher education yearbook I.* Fort Worth, TX: Harcourt Brace Jovanovich.

Hagen, J. W., & Stanovich, K. G. (1977). Memory: Strategies of acquisition. In R. V. Kail, Jr., & J. W. Hagen (Eds.), *Perspectives on the development of memory and cognition.* Hillsdale, NJ: Erlbaum.

Hahn, H. (1989). The politics of special education. In D. K. Lipsky & A. Gartner (Eds.), *Beyond separate education: Quality education for all.* Baltimore: Paul H. Brookes.

Hakuta, K., & McLaughlin, B. (1996). Bilingualism and second language learning: Seven tensions that define the research. In D. C. Berliner & R. C. Calfee (Eds.), *Handbook of educational psychology.* New York: Macmillan.

Hale, G. A. (1983). Students' predictions of prose forgetting and the effects of study strategies. *Journal of Educational Psychology, 75*, 708–715.

Hale-Benson, J. E. (1986). *Black children: Their roots, culture, and learning styles.* Baltimore: Johns Hopkins University Press.

Halford, G. S. (1989). Cognitive processing capacity and learning ability: An integration of two areas. *Learning and Individual Differences, 1*, 125–153.

Hall, R. H., & O'Donnell, A. (1994, April). *Alternative materials for learning: Cognitive and affective outcomes of learning from knowledge maps.* Paper presented at the annual meeting of the American Educational Research Association, New Orleans, LA.

Hall, W. S. (1989). Reading comprehension. *American Psychologist, 44*, 157–161.

Hallenbeck, M. J. (1996). The cognitive strategy in writing: Welcome relief for adolescents with learning disabilities. *Learning Disabilities Research and Practice, 11*, 107–119.

Haller, E. P., Child, D. A., & Walberg, H. J. (1988). Can comprehension be taught? A quantitative synthesis of "metacognitive" studies. *Educational Researcher, 17*(9), 5–8.

Hallowell, E. (1996). *When you worry about the child you love.* New York: Simon and Schuster.

Halpern, D. F. (1992). *Sex differences in cognitive abilities* (2nd ed.). Hillsdale, NJ: Erlbaum.

Halpern, D. F. (1997). Sex differences in intelligence: Implications for education. *American Psychologist, 52*, 1091–1102.

Halpern, D. F. (1998). Teaching critical thinking for transfer across domains. *American Psychologist, 53*, 449–455.

Hambleton, R. K. (1996). Advances in assessment models, methods, and practices. In D. C. Berliner & R. C. Calfee (Eds.), *Handbook of educational psychology.* New York: Macmillan.

Hamman, D., Shell, D. F., Droesch, D., Husman, J., Handwerk, M., Park, Y., & Oppenheim, N. (1995, April). *Middle school readers' on-line cognitive processes: Influence of subject-matter knowledge and interest during reading.* Paper presented at the annual meeting of the American Educational Research Association, San Francisco.

Hammer, D. (1997). Discovery learning and discovery teaching. *Cognition and Instruction, 15*, 485–529.

Hamp-Lyons, L. (1992). Holistic writing assessment for L.E.P. students. In *Focus on evaluation and measurement* (Vol. 2). Washington, DC: U.S. Department of Education.

Hampton, J. A. (1981). An investigation of the nature of abstract concepts. *Memory and Cognition, 9*, 149–156.

Hannah, M. E. (1988). Teacher attitudes toward children with disabilities: An ecological analysis. In H. E. Yuker (Ed.), *Attitudes toward persons with disabilities.* New York: Springer.

Hansen, J., & Pearson, P. D. (1983). An instructional study: Improving the inferential comprehension of good and poor fourth-grade readers. *Journal of Educational Psychology, 75*, 821–829.

Harlow, H. F., & Zimmerman, R. R. (1959). Affectional responses in the infant monkey. *Science, 130*, 421–432.

Harnishfeger, K. K. (1995). The development of cognitive inhibition: Theories, definitions, and research evidence. In F. N. Dempster & C. J. Brainerd (Eds.), *Interference and inhibition in cognition.* San Diego: Academic Press.

Harris, A. C. (1986). *Child development.* St. Paul, MN: West.

Harris, C. R. (1991). Identifying and serving the gifted new immigrant. *Teaching Exceptional Children, 23*(4), 26-30.

Harris, K. R. (1982). Cognitive-behavior modification: Application with exceptional students. *Focus on Exceptional Children, 15,* 1-16.

Harris, K. R. (1986). Self-monitoring of attentional behavior versus self-monitoring of productivity: Effects of on-task behavior and academic response rate among learning disabled children. *Journal of Applied Behavior Analysis, 19,* 417-423.

Harris, K. R., & Alexander, P. A. (1998). Integrated, constructivist education: Challenge and reality. *Educational Psychology Review, 10,* 115-127.

Harris, K. R., & Graham, S. (1992). Self-regulated strategy development: A part of the writing process. In M. Pressley, K. R. Harris, & J. T. Guthrie (Eds.), *Promoting academic competence and literacy in school.* San Diego: Academic Press.

Harris, M. J., & Rosenthal, R. (1985). Mediation of interpersonal expectancy effects: 31 meta-analyses. *Psychological Bulletin, 97,* 363-386.

Harris, R. J. (1977). Comprehension of pragmatic implications in advertising. *Journal of Applied Psychology, 62,* 603-608.

Harrow, A. J. (1972). *A taxonomy of the psychomotor domain: A guide for developing behavioral objectives.* New York: David McKay.

Harry, B., Allen, N., & McLaughlin, M. (1995). Communication versus compliance: African-American parents' involvement in special education. *Exceptional Children, 61,* 364-377.

Harter, S. (1975). Mastery motivation and the need for approval in older children and their relationship to social desirability response tendencies. *Developmental Psychology, 11,* 186-196.

Harter, S. (1982). The perceived competence scale for children. *Child Development, 53,* 87-97.

Harter, S. (1983). Developmental perspectives on the self-system. In E. M. Hetherington (Ed.), *Handbook of child psychology: Vol. 4: Socialization, personality, and social development* (4th ed.). New York: Wiley.

Harter, S. (1990). Causes, correlates, and the functional role of global self-worth: A life-span perspective. In R. J. Sternberg & J. Kolligian, Jr. (Eds.), *Competence considered.* New Haven, CT: Yale University Press.

Harter, S. (1992). The relationship between perceived competence, affect, and motivational orientation within the classroom: Processes and patterns of change. In A. K. Boggiano & T. S. Pittman (Eds.), *Achievement and motivation: A social-developmental perspective.* Cambridge, England: Cambridge University Press.

Harter, S., Whitesell, N. R., & Kowalski, P. (1992). Individual differences in the effects of educational transitions on young adolescents' perceptions of competence and motivational orientation. *American Educational Research Journal, 29,* 777-807.

Hartley, J., & Trueman, M. (1982). The effects of summaries on the recall of information from prose: Five experimental studies. *Human Learning, 1,* 63-82.

Hartmann, W. K., Miller, R., & Lee, P. (1984). *Out of the cradle: Exploring the frontiers beyond earth.* New York: Workman.

Hartup, W. W. (1983). Peer relations. In P. H. Mussen (Ed.), *Handbook of child psychology: Vol. IV. Socialization* (4th ed.). New York: Wiley.

Hartup, W. W. (1989). Social relationships and their developmental significance. *American Psychologist, 44,* 120-126.

Harway, M., & Moss, L. T. (1983). Sex differences: The evidence from biology. In M. B. Liss (Ed.), *Social and cognitive skills: Sex roles and children's play.* San Diego: Academic Press.

Hatano, G., & Inagaki, K. (1991). Sharing cognition through collective comprehension activity. In L. B. Resnick, J. M. Levine, & S. D. Teasley (Eds.), *Perspectives on socially shared cognition.* Washington, DC: American Psychological Association.

Hatano, G., & Inagaki, K. (1993). Desituating cognition through the construction of conceptual knowledge. In P. Light & G. Butterworth (Eds.), *Context and cognition: Ways of learning and knowing.* Hillsdale, NJ: Erlbaum.

Hatano, G., & Inagaki, K. (1996). Cognitive and cultural factors in the acquisition of intuitive biology. In D. R. Olson & N. Torrance (Eds.), *The handbook of education and human development: New models of learning, teaching, and schooling.* Cambridge, MA: Blackwell.

Hattie, J., Biggs, J., & Purdie, N. (1996). Effects of learning skills interventions on student learning: A meta-analysis. *Review of Educational Research, 66,* 99-136.

Hayes, C. B., Ryan, A. W., & Zseller, E. B. (1994, April). *African-American students' perceptions of caring teacher behaviors.* Paper presented at the annual meeting of the American Educational Research Association, New Orleans, LA.

Hayes, S. C., Rosenfarb, I., Wulfert, E., Munt, E. D., Korn, Z., & Zettle, R. D. (1985). Self-reinforcement effects: An artifact of social standard setting? *Journal of Applied Behavior Analysis, 18,* 201-214.

Hayes-Roth, B., & Thorndyke, P. W. (1979). Integration of knowledge from text. *Journal of Verbal Learning and Verbal Behavior, 18,* 91-108.

Hayslip, B., Jr. (1994). Stability of intelligence. In R. J. Sternberg (Ed.), *Encyclopedia of human intelligence* (Vol. 2). New York: Macmillan.

Healy, C. C. (1993). Discovery courses are great in theory, but . . . In J. L. Schwartz, M. Yerushalmy, & B. Wilson (Eds.), *The geometric supposer: What is it a case of?* Hillsdale, NJ: Erlbaum.

Heath, S. B. (1980). Questioning at home and at school: A comparative study. In G. Spindler (Ed.), *The ethnography of schooling: Educational anthropology in action.* New York: Holt, Rinehart & Winston.

Heath, S. B. (1989). Oral and literate traditions among black Americans living in poverty. *American Psychologist, 44,* 367-373.

Hedges, L. V., & Nowell, A. (1995). Sex differences in mental test scores, variability, and numbers of high-scoring individuals. *Science, 269,* 41-45.

Hegland, S., & Andre, T. (1992). Helping learners construct knowledge. *Educational Psychology Review, 4,* 223-240.

Heindel, P., & Kose, G. (1990). The effects of motoric action and organization on children's memory. *Journal of Experimental Child Psychology, 50,* 416-428.

Heller, J. I., & Hungate, H. N. (1985). Implications for mathematics instruction of research on scientific problem solving. In E. A. Silver (Ed.), *Teaching and learning mathematical problem solving: Multiple research perspectives.* Hillsdale, NJ: Erlbaum.

Helton, G. B., & Oakland, T. D. (1977). Teachers' attitudinal responses to differing characteristics of elementary school students. *Journal of Educational Psychology, 69,* 261-266.

Hembree, R. (1988). Correlates, causes, effects, and treatment of test anxiety. *Review of Educational Research, 58,* 47-77.

Hemphill, L., & Snow, C. (1996). Language and literacy development: Discontinuities and differences. In D. R. Olson & N. Torrance (Eds.), *The handbook of education and human development: New models of learning, teaching, and schooling.* Cambridge, MA: Blackwell.

Hennessey, B. A. (1995). Social, environmental, and developmental issues and creativity. *Educational Psychology Review, 7,* 163-183.

Hennessey, B. A., & Amabile, T. M. (1987). *Creativity and learning.* Washington, DC: National Education Association.

Herrnstein, R. J., & Murray, C. (1994). *The bell curve: Intelligence and class structure in American life.* New York: Free Press.

Hess, G. A., Jr., Lyons, A., & Corsino, L. (1990, April). *Against the odds: The early identification of dropouts.* Paper presented at the annual meeting of the American Educational Research Association, Boston.

Hess, R. D., & Holloway, S. D. (1984). Family and school as educational institutions. In R. D. Parke, R. N. Emde, H. P. McAdoo, & G. P. Sackett (Eds.), *Review of child development research* (Vol. 7). Chicago: University of Chicago Press.

Hess, R. D., & McDevitt, T. M. (1989). Family. In E. Barnouw (Ed.), *International encyclopedia of communications.* New York: Oxford University Press.

Heward, W. L. (1996). *Exceptional children: An introduction to special education* (5th ed.). Upper Saddle River, NJ: Merrill/Prentice Hall.

Hewitt, J., & Scardamalia, M. (1998). Design principles for distributed knowledge building processes. *Educational Psychology Review, 20,* 75-96.

Hickey, D. T. (1997). Motivation and contemporary socio-constructivist instructional perspectives. *Educational Psychologist, 32,* 175-193.

Hidalgo, N. M., Siu, S., Bright, J. A., Swap, S. M., & Epstein, J. L. (1995). Research on families, schools, and communities: A multicultural perspective. In J. A. Banks & C. A. M. Banks (Eds.), *Handbook of research on multicultural education.* New York: Macmillan.

Hidi, S., & Anderson, V. (1986). Producing written summaries: Task demands, cognitive operations, and implications for instruction. *Review of Educational Research, 86,* 473-493.

Hidi, S., & Anderson, V. (1992). Situational interest and its impact on reading and expository writing. In K. A. Renninger, S. Hidi, & A. Krapp (Eds.), *The role of interest in learning and development.* Hillsdale, NJ: Erlbaum.

Hiebert, E. H., & Fisher, C. W. (1992). The tasks of school literacy: Trends and issues. In J. Brophy (Ed.), *Advances in research on teaching: Vol. 3. Planning and managing learning tasks and activities.* Greenwich, CT: JAI Press.

Hiebert, E. H., & Raphael, T. E. (1996). Psychological perspectives on literacy and extensions to educational practice. In D. C. Berliner & R. C. Calfee (Eds.), *Handbook of educational psychology*. New York: Macmillan.

Hiebert, E. H., Valencia, S. W., & Afflerbach, P. P. (1994). Definitions and perspectives. In S. W. Valencia, E. H. Hiebert, & P. P. Afflerbach (Eds.), *Authentic reading assessment: Practices and possibilities*. Newark, DE: International Reading Association.

Hiebert, J., Carpenter, T. P., Fennema, E., Fuson, K., Human, P., Murray, H., Olivier, A., & Wearne, D. (1996). Problem solving as a basis for reform in curriculum and instruction: The case of mathematics. *Educational Researcher, 25*(4), 12–21.

Hiebert, J., & Lefevre, P. (1986). Conceptual and procedural knowledge in mathematics: An introductory analysis. In J. Hiebert (Ed.), *Conceptual and procedural knowledge: The case of mathematics*. Hillsdale, NJ: Erlbaum.

Hiebert, J., & Wearne, D. (1992). Links between teaching and learning place value with understanding in first grade. *Journal for Research in Mathematics Education, 23*, 98–122.

Hiebert, J., & Wearne, D. (1993). Instructional tasks, classroom discourse, and students' learning in second-grade arithmetic. *American Educational Research Journal, 30*, 393–425.

Hiebert, J., & Wearne, D. (1996). Instruction, understanding, and skill in multidigit addition and subtraction. *Cognition and Instruction, 14*, 251–283.

Higbee, K. L. (1977). *Your memory: How it works and how to improve it*. Upper Saddle River, NJ: Prentice Hall.

Higgins, A. T., & Turnure, J. E. (1984). Distractibility and concentration of attention in children's development. *Child Development, 55*, 1799–1810.

Hill, C. (1994). Testing and assessment: An applied linguistic perspective. *Educational Assessment, 2*(3), 179–212.

Hill, C., & Larsen, E. (1992). *Testing and assessment in secondary education: A critical review of emerging practices*. Berkeley: University of California, National Center for Research in Vocational Education.

Hill, K. T. (1984). Debilitating motivation and testing: A major educational problem, possible solutions, and policy applications. In R. Ames & C. Ames (Eds.), *Research on motivation in education: Vol. 1. Student motivation*. San Diego: Academic Press.

Hilliard, A., & Vaughn-Scott, M. (1982). The quest for the minority child. In S. G. Moore & C. R. Cooper (Eds.), *The young child: Reviews of research* (Vol. 3). Washington, DC: National Association for the Education of Young Children.

Hirsch, E. D., Jr. (1996). *The schools we need and why we don't have them*. New York: Doubleday.

Hirschfeld, L. A., & Gelman, S. A. (Eds.). (1994). *Mapping the mind: Domain specificity in cognition and culture*. Cambridge, England: Cambridge University Press.

Ho, D. Y. F. (1994). Cognitive socialization in Confucian heritage cultures. In P. M. Greenfield & R. R. Cocking (Eds.), *Cross-cultural roots of minority child development*. Hillsdale, NJ: Erlbaum.

Hobbs, N. (1980). An ecologically oriented service-based system for the classification of handicapped children. In E. Salzinger, J. Antrobus, & J. Glick (Eds.), *The ecosystem of the "risk" child*. New York: Academic Press.

Hocevar, D., & Bachelor, P. (1989). A taxonomy and critique of measurements used in the study of creativity. In J. A. Glover, R. R. Ronning, & C. R. Reynolds (Eds.), *Handbook of creativity*. New York: Plenum Press.

Hofer, B. K., & Pintrich, P. R. (1997). The development of epistemological theories: Beliefs about knowledge and knowing and their relation to learning. *Review of Educational Research, 67*, 88–140.

Hoffman, M. L. (1970). Moral development. In P. H. Mussen (Ed.), *Carmichael's manual of child psychology* (Vol. 2). New York: Wiley.

Hoffman, M. L. (1975). Altruistic behavior and the parent-child relationship. *Journal of Personality and Social Psychology, 31*, 937–943.

Hoffman, M. L. (1991). Empathy, social cognition, and moral action. In W. M. Kurtines & J. L. Gewirtz (Eds.), *Moral behavior and development. Vol. 1. Theory*. Hillsdale, NJ: Erlbaum.

Hogdon, L. A. (1995). *Visual strategies for improving communication. Vol. 1: Practical supports for school and home*. Troy, MI: Quirk Roberts.

Hoge, R. D., & Coladarci, T. (1989). Teacher-based judgments of academic achievement: A review of literature. *Review of Educational Research, 59*, 297–313.

Hoge, R. D., & Renzulli, J. S. (1993). Exploring the link between giftedness and self-concept. *Review of Educational Research, 63*, 449–465.

Holley, C. D., & Dansereau, D. F. (1984). *Spatial learning strategies: Techniques, applications, and related issues*. San Diego: Academic Press.

Holliday, B. G. (1985). Towards a model of teacher-child transactional processes affecting black children's academic achievement. In M. B. Spencer, G. K. Brookins, & W. R. Allen (Eds.), *Beginnings: The social and affective development of black children*. Hillsdale, NJ: Erlbaum.

Hollon, R. E., Roth, K. J., & Anderson, C. W. (1991). Science teachers' conceptions of teaching and learning. In J. Brophy (Ed.), *Advances in research on teaching: Vol. 2. Teacher's knowledge of subject matter as it relates to their teaching practice*. Greenwich, CT: JAI Press.

Holt-Reynolds, D. (1992). Personal history-based beliefs as relevant prior knowledge in course work. *American Educational Research Journal, 29*, 325–349.

Hom, A., & Battistich, V. (1995, April). *Students' sense of school community as a factor in reducing drug use and delinquency*. Paper presented at the annual meeting of the American Educational Research Association, San Francisco.

Hong, Y., Chiu, C., & Dweck, C. S. (1995). Implicit theories of intelligence: Reconsidering the role of confidence in achievement motivation. In M. H. Kernis (Ed.), *Efficacy, agency, and self-esteem*. New York: Plenum Press.

Hoover, Dempsey, K. V., & Sandler, H. M. (1997). Why do parents become involved in their children's education? *Review of Educational Research, 67*, 3–42.

Horgan, D. (1990, April). *Students' predictions of test grades: Calibration and metacognition*. Paper presented at the annual meeting of the American Educational Research Association, Boston.

Horgan, D. D. (1995). *Achieving gender equity: Strategies for the classroom*. Needham Heights, MA: Allyn & Bacon.

Horwitz, R. A. (1979). Psychological effects of the "open classroom." *Review of Educational Research, 49*, 71–85.

Hosmer, E. (1989). Paradise lost: The ravaged rainforest. In G. R. Pitzl (Ed.), *Geography 89/90* (4th ed.). Guilford, CT: Dushkin. (Reprinted from *Multinational Monitor*, 1987 [June], pp. 6–8, 13)

Hossler, D., & Stage, F. K. (1992). Family and high school experience influences on the postsecondary educational plans of ninth-grade students. *American Educational Research Journal, 29*, 425–451.

Houtz, J. C. (1990). Environments that support creative thinking. In C. Hedley, J. Houtz, & A. Baratta (Eds.), *Cognition, curriculum, and literacy*. Norwood, NJ: Ablex.

Howe, C. K. (1994). Improving the achievement of Hispanic students. *Educational Leadership, 51*(8), 42–44.

Howe, C., Tolmie, A., Greer, K., & Mackenzie, M. (1995). Peer collaboration and conceptual growth in physics: Task influences on children's understanding of heating and cooling. *Cognition and Instruction, 13*, 483–503.

Huff, J. A. (1988). Personalized behavior modification: An in-school suspension program that teaches students how to change. *School Counselor, 35*, 210–214.

Hughes, J. N. (1988). *Cognitive behavior therapy with children in schools*. New York: Pergamon.

Humphreys, L. G. (1992). What both critics and users of ability tests need to know. *Psychological Science, 3*, 271–274.

Hunt, P., & Goetz, L. (1997). Research on inclusive educational programs, practices, and outcomes for students with severe disabilities. *Journal of Special Education, 31*, 3–29.

Hunter, M. (1982). *Mastery teaching*. El Segundo, CA: TIP.

Huston, A. C. (1983). Sex-typing. In E. M. Hetherington (Ed.), *Handbook of child psychology: Vol. 4. Socialization, personality, and social development* (4th ed.). New York: Wiley.

Hutt, S. J., Tyler, S., Hutt, C., & Christopherson, H. (1989). *Play, exploration, and learning: A natural history of the pre-school*. London: Routledge.

Hyde, J. S., & Linn, M. C. (1988). Gender differences in verbal ability: A meta-analysis. *Psychological Bulletin, 104*, 53–69.

Hymel, S. (1986). Interpretations of peer behavior: Affective bias in childhood and adolescence. *Child Development, 57*, 431–445.

Hyona, J. (1994). Processing of topic shifts by adults and children. *Reading Research Quarterly, 29*, 76–90.

Igoe, A. R., & Sullivan, H. (1991, April). *Gender and grade-level differences in student attributes related to school learning and motivation*. Paper presented at the annual meeting of the American Educational Research Association, Chicago.

Inglehart, M., Brown, D. R., & Vida, M. (1994). Competition, achievement, and gender: A stress theoretical analysis. In P. R. Pintrich, D. R. Brown, & C. E. Weinstein (Eds.), *Student motivation, cognition, and learning: Essays in honor of Wilbert J. McKeachie*. Hillsdale, NJ: Erlbaum.

Inglis, A., & Biemiller, A. (1997, March). *Fostering self-direction in mathematics: A cross-age tutoring program that enhances math problem solving*. Paper presented at the annual meeting of the American Educational Research Association, Chicago.

Inhelder, B., & Piaget, J. (1958). *The growth of logical thinking from childhood to adolescence* (A. Parsons & S. Milgram, Trans.). New York: Basic Books.

Irujo, S. (1988). An introduction to intercultural differences and similarities in nonverbal communication. In J. S. Wurzel (Ed.), *Toward multiculturalism: A reader in multicultural education.* Yarmouth, ME: Intercultural Press.

Irvine, J. J., & York, D. E. (1995). Learning styles and culturally diverse students: A literature review. In J. A. Banks & C. A. M. Banks (Eds.), *Handbook of research on multicultural education.* New York: Macmillan.

Iwata, B. A., & Bailey, J. S. (1974). Reward versus cost token systems: An analysis of the effects on students and teacher. *Journal of Applied Behavior Analysis, 7,* 567-576.

Jacklin, C. N. (1989). Female and male: Issues of gender. *American Psychologist, 44,* 127-133.

Jackson, D. L., & Ormrod, J. E. (1998). *Case studies: Applying educational psychology.* Upper Saddle River, NJ: Merrill/Prentice Hall.

Jacobsen, B., Lowery, B., & DuCette, J. (1986). Attributions of learning disabled children. *Journal of Educational Psychology, 78,* 59-64.

Jacobson, J. L., & Wille, D. E. (1986). The influence of attachment pattern on developmental changes in peer interaction from the toddler to the preschool period. *Child Development, 57,* 338-347.

Jacoby, R., & Glauberman, N. (Eds.) (1995). *The bell curve debate: History, documents, opinions.* New York: Random House.

Jagacinski, C. M., & Nicholls, J. G. (1984). Conceptions of ability and related affects in task involvement and ego involvement. *Journal of Educational Psychology, 76,* 909-919.

Jagacinski, C. M., & Nicholls, J. G. (1987). Competence and affect in task involvement and ego involvement: The impact of social comparison information. *Journal of Educational Psychology, 79,* 107-114.

James, W. (1890). *Principles of psychology.* New York: Holt.

Janos, P. M., & Robinson, N. M. (1985). Psychosocial development in intellectually gifted children. In F. D. Horowitz & M. O'Brien (Eds.), *The gifted and talented: Developmental perspectives.* Washington, DC: American Psychological Association.

Jenlink, C. L. (1994, April). *Music: A lifeline for the self-esteem of at-risk students.* Paper presented at the annual meeting of the American Educational Research Association, New Orleans, LA.

Johnson, D. W., & Johnson, R. T. (1985). Classroom conflict: Controversy versus debate in learning groups. *American Educational Research Journal, 22,* 237-256.

Johnson, D. W., & Johnson, R. T. (1988). Critical thinking through structured controversy. *Educational Leadership, 45*(8), 58-64.

Johnson, D. W., & Johnson, R. T. (1991). *Learning together and alone: Cooperative, competitive, and individualistic learning* (3rd ed.). Upper Saddle River, NJ: Prentice Hall.

Johnson, D. W., & Johnson, R. T. (1996). Conflict resolution and peer mediation programs in elementary and secondary schools: A review of the research. *Review of Educational Research, 66,* 459-506.

Johnson, D. W., Johnson, R., Dudley, B., Ward, M., & Magnuson, D. (1995). The impact of peer mediation training on the management of school and home conflicts. *American Educational Research Journal, 32,* 829-844.

Johnson, H. C., & Friesen, B. (1993). Etiologies of mental and emotional disorders in children. In H. Johnson (Ed.), *Child mental health in the 1990s: Curricula for graduate and undergraduate.* Washington, DC: U.S. Department of Health and Human Services.

Johnson, R. T. (1989, October). Ways to change the way we teach. Workshop presented at the University of Northern Colorado, Greeley.

John-Steiner, V. (1997). *Notebooks of the mind: Explorations of thinking* (Rev. ed.). New York: Oxford University Press.

Johnston, P., & Afflerbach, P. (1985). The process of constructing main ideas from text. *Cognition and Instruction, 2,* 207-232.

Johnstone, A. H., & El-Banna, H. (1986). Capacities, demands and processes—a predictive model for science education. *Education in Chemistry, 23,* 80-84.

Jonassen, D. H. (1996). *Computers in the classroom: Mindtools for critical thinking.* Upper Saddle River, NJ: Merrill/Prentice Hall.

Jonassen, D. H., Hannum, W. H., & Tessmer, M. (1989). *Handbook of task analysis procedures.* New York: Praeger.

Jones, B. F., Pierce, J., & Hunter, B. (1988/1989). Teaching students to construct graphic representations. *Educational Leadership, 46*(4), 20-25.

Jones, G. P., & Dembo, M. H. (1989). Age and sex role differences in intimate friendships during childhood and adolescence. *Merrill-Palmer Quarterly, 35,* 445-462.

Jones, I., & Pellegrini, A. D. (1996). The effects of social relationships, writing media, and microgenetic development on first-grade students' written narratives. *American Educational Research Journal, 33,* 691-718.

Jones, L. P. (1990, April). *Black and white achievement gap: The role of teacher expectations.* Paper presented at the annual meeting of the American Educational Research Association, Boston.

Jones, M. C. (1924). The elimination of children's fears. *Journal of Experimental Psychology, 7,* 382-390.

Jozefowicz, D. M., Arbreton, A. J., Eccles, J. S., Barber, B. L., & Colarossi, L. (1994, April). *Seventh grade student, parent, and teacher factors associated with later school dropout or movement into alternative educational settings.* Paper presented at the annual meeting of the American Educational Research Association, New Orleans, LA.

Judd, C. H. (1932). Autobiography. In C. Murchison (Ed.), *History of psychology in autobiography* (Vol. 2). Worcester, MA: Clark University Press.

Juvonen, J. (1991). Deviance, perceived responsibility, and negative peer reactions. *Developmental Psychology, 27,* 672-681.

Juvonen, J., & Hiner, M. (1991, April). *Perceived responsibility and annoyance as mediators of negative peer reactions.* Paper presented at the annual meeting of the American Educational Research Association, Chicago.

Juvonen, J., & Weiner, B. (1993). An attributional analysis of students' interactions: The social consequences of perceived responsibility. *Educational Psychology Review, 5,* 325-345.

Kagan, J., Snidman, N., & Arcus, D. M. (1992). Initial reactions to unfamiliarity. *Current Directions in Psychological Science, 1,* 171-174.

Kahl, B., & Woloshyn, V. E. (1994). Using elaborative interrogation to facilitate acquisition of factual information in cooperative learning settings: One good strategy deserves another. *Applied Cognitive Psychology, 8,* 465-478.

Kahle, J. B. (1983). *The disadvantaged majority: Science education for women.* Burlington, NC: Carolina Biological Supply Co.

Kahle, J. B., & Lakes, M. K. (1983). The myth of equality in science classrooms. *Journal of Research in Science Teaching, 20,* 131-140.

Kail, R. (1990). *The development of memory in children* (3rd ed.). New York: W. H. Freeman.

Kane, R. J. (1983). In defense of grade inflation. *Today's Education, 67*(4), 41.

Karau, S. J., & Williams, K. D. (1995). Social loafing: Research findings, implications, and future directions. *Current Directions in Psychological Science, 4,* 134-140.

Kardash, C. M., & Amlund, J. T. (1991). Self-reported learning strategies and learning from expository text. *Contemporary Educational Psychology, 16,* 117-138.

Karmiloff-Smith, A. (1979). Language development after five. In P. Fletcher & M. Garman (Eds.), *Language acquisition: Studies in first language development.* Cambridge, England: Cambridge University Press.

Karmiloff-Smith, A. (1993). Innate constraints and developmental change. In P. Bloom (Ed.), *Language acquisition: Core readings.* Cambridge, MA: MIT Press.

Karplus, R., Pulos, S., & Stage, E. K. (1983). Proportional reasoning of early adolescents. In R. Lesh & M. Landau (Eds.), *Acquisition of mathematics concepts and processes.* San Diego: Academic Press.

Karpov, Y. V., & Haywood, H. C. (1998). Two ways to elaborate Vygotsky's concept of mediation: Implications for instruction. *American Psychologist, 53,* 27-36.

Katkovsky, W., Crandall, V. C., & Good, S. (1967). Parental antecedents of children's beliefs in internal-external control of reinforcements in intellectual achievement situations. *Child Development, 38,* 765-776.

Katz, E. W., & Brent, S. B. (1968). Understanding connectives. *Journal of Verbal Learning and Verbal Behavior, 7,* 501-509.

Katz, L. (1993). All about me: Are we developing our children's self-esteem or their narcissism? *American Educator, 17*(2), 18-23.

Katz, L., & Chard, S. (1989). *Engaging children's minds: The project approach.* Norwood, NJ: Ablex.

Kearins, J. M. (1981). Visual spatial memory in Australian aboriginal children of desert regions. *Cognitive Psychology, 13,* 434-460.

Kehle, T. J., Clark, E., & Jenson, W. R. (1996). Interventions for students with traumatic brain injury: Managing behavioral disturbances. *Journal of Learning Disabilities, 29,* 633-642.

Kehle, T., Clark, E., Jenson, W. R., & Wampold, B. (1986). Effectiveness of the self-modeling procedure with behaviorally disturbed elementary age children. *School Psychology Review, 15,* 289-295.

Keil, F. C. (1986). The acquisition of natural kind and artifact terms. In W. Demopolous & A. Marras (Eds.), *Language learning and concept acquisition.* Norwood, NJ: Ablex.

Keil, F. C. (1987). Conceptual development and category structure. In U. Neisser (Ed.), *Concepts and conceptual development: Ecological and intellectual factors in categorization.* Cambridge, England: Cambridge University Press.

Keil, F. C. (1989). *Concepts, kinds, and cognitive development.* Cambridge, MA: MIT Press.

Keil, F. C. (1991). Theories, concepts, and the acquisition of word meaning. In S.A. Gelman & J. P. Byrnes (Eds.), *Perspectives on language and thought: Interrelations in development.* Cambridge, England: Cambridge University Press.

Keil, F. C., & Silberstein, C. S. (1996). Schooling and the acquisition of theoretical knowledge. In D. R. Olson & N. Torrance (Eds.), *The handbook of education and human development: New models of learning, teaching, and schooling.* Cambridge, MA: Blackwell.

Kellogg, R. T. (1994). *The psychology of writing.* New York: Oxford University Press.

Kelly, A., & Smail, B. (1986). Sex stereotypes and attitudes to science among eleven-year-old children. *British Journal of Educational Psychology, 56,* 158-168.

Kennedy, R. (1992). What is performance assessment? *New Directions for Education Reform, 1*(2), 21-27.

Keogh, B. A., & Becker, L. D. (1973). Early detection of learning problems: Questions, cautions, and guidelines. *Exceptional Children, 39,* 5-11.

Keogh, B. K., & MacMillan, D. L. (1996). Exceptionality. In D. C. Berliner & R. C. Calfee (Eds.), *Handbook of educational psychology.* New York: Macmillan.

Kerkman, D. D., & Siegler, R. S. (1993). Individual differences and adaptive flexibility in lower-income children's strategy choices. *Learning and Individual Differences, 5,* 113-136.

Kermani, H., & Moallem, M. (1997, March). *Cross-age tutoring: Exploring features and processes of peer-mediated learning.* Paper presented at the annual meeting of the American Educational Research Association, Chicago.

Kern, L., Dunlap, G., Childs, K. E., & Clark, S. (1994). Use of a classwide self-management program to improve the behavior of students with emotional and behavioral disorders. *Education and Treatment of Children, 17,* 445-458.

Kernaghan, K., & Woloshyn, V. E. (1994, April). *Explicit versus implicit multiple strategy instruction: Monitoring grade one students' spelling performances.* Paper presented at the annual meeting of the American Educational Research Association, New Orleans, LA.

Kerns, L. L., & Lieberman, A. B. (1993). *Helping your depressed child.* Rocklin, CA: Prima.

Kerr, B. (1991). Educating gifted girls. In N. Coangelo & G. A. Davis (Eds.), *Handbook of gifted education.* Needham Heights, MA: Allyn & Bacon.

Kerr, M. M., & Nelson, C. M. (1989). *Strategies for managing behavior problems in the classroom* (2nd ed.). Upper Saddle River, NJ: Merrill/ Prentice Hall.

Kiewra, K. A. (1985). Investigating notetaking and review: A depth of processing alternative. *Educational Psychologist, 20,* 23-32.

Kiewra, K. A. (1989). A review of note-taking: The encoding-storage paradigm and beyond. *Educational Psychology Review, 1,* 147-172.

Kim, D., Solomon, D., & Roberts, W. (1995, April). *Classroom practices that enhance students' sense of community.* Paper presented at the annual meeting of the American Educational Research Association, San Francisco.

King, A. J. C. (1989). Changing sex roles, lifestyles and attitudes in an urban society. In K. Hurrelmann & U. Engel (Eds.), *The social world of adolescents: International perspectives.* New York: de Gruyter.

King, A. (1992). Comparison of self-questioning, summarizing, and notetaking-review as strategies for learning from lectures. *American Educational Research Journal, 29,* 303-323.

King, A. (1994). Guiding knowledge construction in the classroom: Effects of teaching children how to question and how to explain. *American Educational Research Journal, 31,* 338-368.

King, A. (1997). ASK to THINK—TEL WHY®©: A model of transactive peer tutoring for scaffolding higher level complex learning. *Educational Psychologist, 32,* 221-235.

King, A. (1998). Transactive peer tutoring: Distributing cognition and metacognition. *Educational Psychology Review, 10,* 57-74

King, A., Staffieri, A., & Adelgais, A. (1998). Mutual peer tutoring: Effects of structuring tutorial interaction to scaffold peer learning. *Journal of Educational Psychology, 90,* 134-152.

King, N. J., & Ollendick, T. H. (1989). Children's anxiety and phobic disorders in school settings: Classification, assessment, and intervention issues. *Review of Educational Research, 59,* 431-470.

Kirkland, M. C. (1971). The effect of tests on students and schools. *Review of Educational Research, 41,* 303-350.

Kirschenbaum, R. J. (1983). Let's cut out the cut-off score in the identification of the gifted. *Roeper Review, 5*(4), 6-10.

Kirschenbaum, R. J. (1989). Identification of the gifted and talented American Indian student. In C. J. Maker & S. W. Schiever (Eds.), *Critical issues in gifted education: Vol. 2. Defensible programs for cultural and ethnic minorities.* Austin, TX: Pro-Ed.

Kish, C. K., Zimmer, J. W., & Henning, M. J. (1994, April). *Using direct instruction to teach revision to novice writers: The role of metacognition.* Paper presented at the annual meeting of the American Educational Research Association, New Orleans, LA.

Klein, J. D. (1990, April). *The effect of interest, task performance, and reward contingencies on self-efficacy.* Paper presented at the annual meeting of the American Educational Research Association, Boston.

Kletzien, S. B. (1988, April). *Achieving and non-achieving high school readers' use of comprehension strategies for reading expository text.* Paper presented at the annual meeting of the American Educational Research Association, New Orleans, LA.

Knapp, M. S., Turnbull, B. J., & Shields, P. M. (1990). New directions for educating the children of poverty. *Educational Leadership, 48*(1), 4-9.

Knapp, M. S., & Woolverton, S. (1995). Social class and schooling. In J. A. Banks & C. A. M. Banks (Eds.), *Handbook of research on multicultural education.* New York: Macmillan.

Knight, S. L. (1988, April). *Examining the relationship between teacher behaviors and students' cognitive reading strategies.* Paper presented at the annual meeting of the American Educational Research Association, New Orleans, LA.

Knowlton, D. (1995). Managing children with oppositional behavior. *Beyond Behavior, 6*(3), 5-10.

Knudson, R. E. (1992). The development of written argumentation: An analysis and comparison of argumentative writing at four grade levels. *Child Study Journal, 22,* 167-181.

Koegel, L. K. (1995). Communication and language intervention. In R. L. Koegel & L. K. Koegel (Eds.), *Strategies for initiating positive interactions and improving learning opportunities.* Baltimore: Brookes.

Koegel, L. K., Koegel, R. L., & Dunlap, G. (Eds.). (1996). *Positive behavioral support: Including people with difficult behavior in the community.* Baltimore: Paul H. Brookes.

Koeppel, J., & Mulrooney, M. (1992). The Sister Schools Program: A way for children to learn about cultural diversity—when there isn't any in their school. *Young Children, 48*(1), 44-47.

Koestner, R., Ryan, R. M., Bernieri, F., & Holt, K. (1984). Setting limits in children's behavior: The differential effects of controlling versus informational styles on intrinsic motivation and creativity. *Journal of Personality, 52,* 233-248.

Kogan, N. (1983). Stylistic variation in childhood and adolescence: Creativity, metaphor, and cognitive style. In J. H. Flavell & E. M. Markman (Eds.), *Handbook of child psychology: Vol. 3. Cognitive development.* New York: Wiley.

Kohlberg, L. (1975). The cognitive-developmental approach to moral education. *Phi Delta Kappan, 57,* 670-677.

Kohlberg, L. (1976). Moral stages and moralization: The cognitive-developmental approach. In T. Lickona (Ed.), *Moral development and behavior: Theory, research, and social issues.* New York: Holt, Rinehart & Winston.

Kohlberg, L. (1981). *The philosophy of moral development: Moral stages and the idea of justice.* San Francisco: Harper & Row.

Kohlberg, L. (1984). *The psychology of moral development: The nature and validity of moral stages.* San Francisco: Harper & Row.

Kohlberg, L. (1986). A current statement on some theoretical issues. In S. Modgil & C. Modgil (Eds.), *Lawrence Kohlberg: Consensus and controversy.* Philadelphia: Falmer Press.

Kohlberg, L., & Candee, D. (1984). The relationship of moral judgment to moral action. In W. M. Kurtines & J. L. Gewirtz (Eds.), *Morality, moral behavior, and moral development.* New York: Wiley.

Kohn, A. (1993). Choices for children: Why and how to let students decide. *Phi Delta Kappan, 75*(1), 8-20.

Kolodner, J. (1985). Memory for experience. In G. H. Bower (Ed.), *The psychology of learning and motivation: Advances in research and theory* (Vol. 19). San Diego: Academic Press.

Konopak, B. C., Martin, S. H., & Martin, M. A. (1990). Using a writing strategy to enhance sixth-grade students' comprehension of content material. *Journal of Reading Behavior, 22,* 19-37.

Kontos, S. J., Carter, K. R., Ormrod, J. E., & Cooney, J. B. (1983). Reversing the revolving door: A strict interpretation of Renzulli's definition of giftedness. *Roeper Review, 6*(1), 35-39.

Koretz, D., Stecher, B., Klein, S., & McCaffrey, D. (1994). The Vermont portfolio assessment program: Findings and implications. *Educational Measurement: Issues and Practices, 13*(3), 5-16.

Kosslyn, S. M. (1985). Mental imagery ability. In R. J. Sternberg (Ed.), *Human abilities: An information-processing approach.* New York: W. H. Freeman.

Kounin, J. S. (1970). *Discipline and group management in classrooms.* New York: Holt, Rinehart & Winston.

Koyanagi, C., & Gaines, S. (1993). *All systems failure: An examination of the results of neglecting the needs of children with serious emotional disturbance.* Alexandria, VA: National Mental Health Association.

Koza, J. K. (1996). Multicultural approaches to music education. In C. A. Grant & M. L. Gomez (Eds.), *Making schooling multicultural: Campus and classroom.* Upper Saddle River, NJ: Merrill/Prentice Hall.

Kozulin, A., & Falik, L. (1995). Dynamic cognitive assessment of the child. *Current Directions in Psychological Science, 4,* 192-196.

Krajcik, J. S. (1991). Developing students' understanding of chemical concepts. In S. M. Glynn, R. H. Yeany, & B. K. Britton (Eds.), *The psychology of learning science.* Hillsdale, NJ: Erlbaum.

Krampen, G. (1987). Differential effects of teacher comments. *Journal of Educational Psychology, 79,* 137-146.

Krathwohl, D. R. (1994). Reflections on the taxonomy: Its past, present, and future. In L. W. Anderson & L. A. Sosniak (Eds.), *Bloom's taxonomy: A forty-year perspective. Ninety-third yearbook of the National Society for the Study of Education, Part II.* Chicago: National Society for the Study of Education.

Krathwohl, D. R., Bloom, B. S., & Masia, B. B. (1964). *Taxonomy of educational objectives: Handbook II. Affective domain.* New York: David McKay.

Krebs, D. L., Vermeulen, S. C. A., Carpendale, J. I., & Denton, K. (1991). Structural and situational influences on moral judgment: The interaction between stage and dilemma. In W. M. Kurtines & J. L. Gewirtz (Eds.), *Moral behavior and development: Vol. 2. Research.* Hillsdale, NJ: Erlbaum.

Kroll, B. M. (1984). Audience adaptation in children's persuasive letters. *Written Communication, 1,* 407-427.

Krueger, W. C. F. (1929). The effect of overlearning on retention. *Journal of Experimental Psychology, 12,* 71-78.

Krumboltz, J. D., & Krumboltz, H. B. (1972). *Changing children's behavior.* Upper Saddle River, NJ: Prentice Hall.

Kucan, L., & Beck, I. L. (1997). Thinking aloud and reading comprehension research: Inquiry, instruction, and social interaction. *Review of Educational Research, 67,* 271-299.

Kuhl, J. (1985). Volitional mediators of cognition-behavior consistency: Self-regulatory processes and actions versus state orientation. In J. Kuhl & J. Beckmann (Eds.), *Action control: From cognition to behavior.* Berlin: Springer-Verlag.

Kuhn, D. (1993). Connecting scientific and informal reasoning. *Merrill-Palmer Quarterly, 39,* 74-103.

Kuhn, D., Amsel, E., & O'Loughlin, M. (1988). *The development of scientific thinking skills.* San Diego: Academic Press.

Kuhn, D., Shaw, V., & Felton, M. (1997). Effects of dyadic interaction on argumentative reasoning. *Cognition and Instruction, 15,* 287-315.

Kulhavy, R. W., Lee, J. B., & Caterino, L. C. (1985). Conjoint retention of maps and related discourse. *Contemporary Educational Psychology, 10,* 28-37.

Kulik, C. C., Kulik, J. A., & Bangert-Drowns, R. L. (1990). Effectiveness of mastery learning programs: A meta-analysis. *Review of Educational Research, 60,* 265-299.

Kulik, J. A., & Kulik, C. C. (1988). Timing of feedback and verbal learning. *Review of Educational Research, 58,* 79-97.

Kulik, J. A., Kulik, C. C., & Cohen, P. A. (1979). A meta-analysis of outcome studies of Keller's Personalized System of Instruction. *American Psychologist, 34,* 307-318.

Kulik, J. A., Kulik, C. C., & Cohen, P. A. (1980). Effectiveness of computer-based college teaching: A meta-analysis of findings. *Review of Educational Research, 50,* 525-544.

Kunc, N. (1984). Integration: Being realistic isn't realistic. *Canadian Journal for Exceptional Children, 1*(1), 4-8.

Kuslan, L. I., & Stone, A. H. (1972). *Teaching children science: An inquiry approach* (2nd ed.). Belmont, CA: Wadsworth.

Kyle, W. C., & Shymansky, J. A. (1989, April). Enhancing learning through conceptual change teaching. *NARST News, 31,* 7-8.

LaBerge, D., & Samuels, S. J. (1974). Toward a theory of automatic information processing in reading. *Cognitive Psychology, 6,* 293-323.

LaBlance, G. R., Steckol, K. F., & Smith, V. L. (1994). Stuttering: The role of the classroom teacher. *Teaching Exceptional Children, 26*(2), 10-12.

Laboratory of Human Cognition. (1982). Culture and intelligence. In R. J. Sternberg (Ed.), *Handbook of human intelligence.* Cambridge, England: Cambridge University Press.

Labov, W. (1973). The boundaries of words and their meanings. In C.-J. N. Bailey & R. W. Shuy (Eds.), *New ways of analyzing variations in English.* Washington, DC: Georgetown University Press.

Ladson-Billings, G. (1994a). *The dreamkeepers: Successful teachers of African American children.* San Francisco: Jossey-Bass.

Ladson-Billings, G. (1994b). What we can learn from multicultural education research. *Educational Leadership, 51*(8), 22-26.

Ladson-Billings, G. (1995). Toward a theory of culturally relevant pedagogy. *American Educational Research Journal, 32,* 465-491.

Lahey, B. B., & Carlson, C. L. (1991). Validity of the diagnostic category of attention deficit disorder without hyperactivity: A review of the literature. *Journal of Learning Disabilities, 24,* 110-120.

Lam, T. C. M. (1992). Review of practices and problems in the evaluation of bilingual education. *Review of Educational Research, 62,* 181-203.

Lampe, J. R., & Rooze, G. E. (1994, April). *Enhancing social studies achievement among Hispanic students using cooperative learning work groups.* Paper presented at the annual meeting of the American Educational Research Association, New Orleans, LA.

Lampert, M. (1990). When the problem is not the question and the solution is not the answer: Mathematical knowing and teaching. *American Educational Research Journal, 27,* 29-63.

Lampert, M., Rittenhouse, P., & Crumbaugh, C. (1996). Agreeing to disagree: Developing sociable mathematical discourse. In D. R. Olson & N. Torrance (Eds.), *The handbook of education and human development: New models of learning, teaching, and schooling.* Cambridge, MA: Blackwell.

Lan, W. Y., Repman, J., Bradley, L., & Weller, H. (1994, April). *Immediate and lasting effects of criterion and payoff on academic risk taking.* Paper presented at the annual meeting of the American Educational Research Association, New Orleans, LA.

Landau, S., & McAninch, C. (1993). Young children with attention deficits. *Young Children, 48*(4), 49-58.

Landauer, T. K. (1962). Rate of implicit speech. *Perceptual and Motor Skills, 15,* 646.

Landesman, S., & Ramey, C. (1989). Developmental psychology and mental retardation: Integrating scientific principles with treatment practices. *American Psychologist, 44,* 409-415.

Lane, D. M., & Pearson, D. A. (1982). The development of selective attention. *Merrill-Palmer Quarterly, 28,* 317-337.

Langer, J. A., & Applebee, A. (1987). *How writing shapes thinking: A study of teaching and learning.* Champaign, IL: National Council of Teachers of English.

Lanthier, R. P., & Bates, J. E. (1997, March). *Does infant temperament predict adjustment in adolescence?* Paper presented at the annual meeting of the American Educational Research Association, Chicago.

Lanza, A., & Roselli, T. (1991). Effect of the hyper-textual approach versus the structured approach on students' achievement. *Journal of Computer-Based Instruction, 18*(2), 48-50.

Laosa, L. M. (1982). School, occupation, culture, and family: The impact of parental schooling on the parent-child relationship. *Journal of Educational Psychology, 74,* 791-827.

Lapsley, D. K., Jackson, S., Rice, K., & Shadid, G. (1988). Self-monitoring and the "new look" at the imaginary audience and personal fable: An ego-developmental analysis. *Journal of Adolescent Research, 3,* 17-31.

Lapsley, D. K., Milstead, M., Quintana, S., Flannery, D., & Buss, R. (1986). Adolescent egocentrism and formal operations: Tests of a theoretical assumption. *Developmental Psychology, 22,* 800-807.

Lave, J. (1988). *Cognition in practice: Mind, mathematics and culture in everyday life.* Cambridge, England: Cambridge University Press.

Lave, J. (1993). Word problems: A microcosm of theories of learning. In P. Light & G. Butterworth (Eds.), *Context and cognition: Ways of learning and knowing.* Hillsdale, NJ: Erlbaum.

Lave, J., & Wenger, E. (1991). *Situated learning: Legitimate peripheral participation.* Cambridge, England: Cambridge University Press.

Law, D. J., Pellegrino, J. W., & Hunt, E. B. (1993). Comparing the tortoise and the hare: Gender differences and experience in dynamic spatial reasoning tasks. *Psychological Science, 4,* 35-40.

Leary, M. R., & Hill, D. A. (1996). Moving on: Autism and movement disturbance. *Mental Retardation, 34,* 39-53.

Lee, C. D., & Slaughter-Defoe, D. T. (1995). Historical and sociocultural influences on African and American education. In J. A. Banks & C. A. M. Banks (Eds.), *Handbook of research on multicultural education.* New York: Macmillan.

Lee, J. F., Jr., & Pruitt, K. W. (1984). *Providing for individual differences in student learning: A mastery learning approach.* Springfield, IL: Charles C Thomas.

Lee, O., & Anderson, C.W. (1993). Task engagement and conceptual change in middle school science classrooms. *American Educational Research Journal, 30*, 585-610.

Lee, S. (1985). Children's acquisition of conditional logic structure: Teachable? *Contemporary Educational Psychology, 10*, 14-27.

Lein, L. (1975). Black American migrant children: Their speech at home and school. *Council on Anthropology and Education Quarterly, 6*, 1-11.

Leinhardt, G. (1993). Weaving instructional explanations in history. *British Journal of Educational Psychology, 63*, 46-74.

Leinhardt, G. (1994). History: A time to be mindful. In G. Leinhardt, I. L. Beck, & C. Stainton (Eds.), *Teaching and learning in history*. Hillsdale, NJ: Erlbaum.

Leinhardt, G., & Pallay, A. (1982). Restrictive educational settings: Exile or haven? *Review of Educational Research, 52*, 557-578.

Leinhardt, G., & Young, K. M. (1996). Two texts, three readers: Distance and expertise in reading history. *Cognition and Instruction, 14*, 441-486.

Leiter, J., & Johnsen, M. C. (1997). Child maltreatment and school performance declines: An event-history analysis. *American Educational Research Journal, 34*, 563-589.

Lenneberg, E. H. (1967). *Biological foundations of language*. New York: Wiley.

Lennon, R., Eisenberg, N., & Carroll, J. L. (1983). The assessment of empathy in early childhood. *Journal of Applied Developmental Psychology, 4*, 295-302.

Lennon, R., Ormrod, J. E., Burger, S. F., & Warren, E. (1990, October). *Belief systems of teacher education majors and their possible influences on future classroom performance*. Paper presented at the Northern Rocky Mountain Educational Research Association, Greeley, CO.

Lentz, F. E. (1988). Reductive procedures. In J. C. Witt, S. N. Elliott, & F. M. Gresham (Eds.), *Handbook of behavior therapy in education*. New York: Plenum Press.

Lepper, M. R. (1981). Intrinsic and extrinsic motivation in children: Detrimental effects of superfluous social controls. In W.A. Collins (Ed.), *Minnesota Symposia on Child Psychology* (Vol. 14). Hillsdale, NJ: Erlbaum.

Lepper, M. R., Aspinwall, L. G., Mumme, D. L., & Chabay, R.W. (1990). Self-perception and social perception processes in tutoring: Subtle social control strategies of expert tutors. In J. M. Olson & M. P. Zanna (Eds.), *Self-inference processes: The Ontario symposium*. Hillsdale, NJ: Erlbaum.

Lepper, M. R., & Gurtner, J. (1989). Children and computers: Approaching the twenty-first century. *American Psychologist, 44*, 170-178.

Lepper, M. R., & Hodell, M. (1989). Intrinsic motivation in the classroom. In C. Ames & R. Ames (Eds.), *Research on motivation in education, Vol. 3. Goals and cognitions*. San Diego: Academic Press.

Lerman, D. C., & Iwata, B.A. (1995). Prevalence of the extinction burst and its attenuation during treatment. *Journal of Applied Behavior Analysis, 28*, 93-94.

Lerner, J.W. (1985). *Learning disabilities: Theories, diagnosis, and teaching strategies* (4th ed.). Boston: Houghton Mifflin.

Lester, F. K. (1985). Methodological considerations in research on mathematical problem-solving instruction. In E.A. Silver (Ed.), *Teaching and learning mathematical problem solving: Multiple research perspectives*. Hillsdale, NJ: Erlbaum.

Lester, F. K., Jr., Lambdin, D.V., & Preston, R.V. (1997). A new vision of the nature and purposes of assessment in the mathematics classroom. In G. D. Phye (Ed.), *Handbook of classroom assessment: Learning, achievement, and adjustment*. San Diego: Academic Press.

Leu, D., & Kinzer, C. (1995). *Effective reading instruction* (3rd ed.). Upper Saddle River, NJ: Merrill/Prentice Hall.

Levin, G. R. (1983). *Child psychology*. Monterey, CA: Brooks/Cole.

Levin, J. R., & Berry, J. K. (1980). Children's learning of all the news that's fit to picture. *Educational Communications and Technology, 28*, 177-185.

Levin, J. R., & Mayer, R. E. (1993). Understanding illustrations in text. In B. K. Britton, A. Woodward, & M. Binkley (Eds.), *Learning from textbooks: Theory and practice*. Hillsdale, NJ: Erlbaum.

Levine, D. U., & Lezotte, L.W. (1995). Effective schools research. In J.A. Banks & C.A. M. Banks (Eds.), *Handbook of research on multicultural education*. New York: Macmillan.

Levine, M. (1966). Hypothesis behavior by humans during discrimination learning. *Journal of Experimental Psychology, 71*, 331-338.

Lewis, R. B., & Doorlag, D. H. (1991). *Teaching special students in the mainstream* (3rd ed.). Upper Saddle River, NJ: Merrill/Prentice Hall.

Liben, L. S., & Downs, R. M. (1989a). Educating with maps: Part I, the place of maps. *Teaching Thinking and Problem Solving, 11*(1), 6-9.

Liben, L. S., & Downs, R. M. (1989b). Understanding maps as symbols: The development of map concepts in children. In H.W. Reese (Ed.), *Advances in child development and behavior* (Vol. 22). San Diego: Harcourt Brace Jovanovich.

Licht, B. (1992). Achievement-related beliefs in children with learning disabilities. In L. J. Meltzer (Ed.), *Strategy assessment and instruction for students with learning disabilities: From theory to practice*. Austin, TX: Pro-Ed.

Lickona, T. (1991). Moral development in the elementary school classroom. In W. M. Kurtines & J. L. Gewirtz (Eds.), *Moral behavior and development: Vol. 3. Application*. Hillsdale, NJ: Erlbaum.

Lieberman, L. M. (1992). Preserving special education . . . for those who need it. In W. Stainback & S. Stainback (Eds.), *Controversial issues confronting special education: Divergent perspectives*. Boston: Allyn & Bacon.

Light, J. G., & Defries, J. C. (1995). Comorbidity of reading and mathematics disabilities: Genetic and environmental etiologies. *Journal of Learning Disabilities, 28*, 96-106.

Light, P., & Butterworth, G. (Eds.). (1993). *Context and cognition: Ways of learning and knowing*. Hillsdale, NJ: Erlbaum.

Lillard, A. S. (1997). Other folks' theories of mind and behavior. *Psychological Science, 8*, 268-274.

Lind, G. (1994, April). *Why do juvenile delinquents gain little from moral discussion programs?* Paper presented at the annual meeting of the American Educational Research Association, New Orleans, LA.

Linderholm, T., Gustafson, M., van den Broek, P., & Lorch, R. F., Jr. (1997, March). *Effects of reading goals on inference generation*. Paper presented at the annual meeting of the American Educational Research Association, Chicago.

Linn, M. C., Clement, C., Pulos, S., & Sullivan, P. (1989). Scientific reasoning during adolescence: The influence of instruction in science knowledge and reasoning strategies. *Journal of Research in Science Teaching, 26*, 171-187.

Linn, M. C., & Hyde, J. S. (1989). Gender, mathematics, and science. *Educational Researcher, 18*(8), 17-19, 22-27.

Linn, M. C., & Muilenburg, L. (1996). Creating lifelong science learners: What models form a firm foundation? *Educational Researcher, 25*(5), 18-24.

Linn, M. C., & Petersen, A. C. (1985). Emergence and characterization of sex differences in spatial ability: A meta-analysis. *Child Development, 56*, 1479-1498.

Linn, M. C., Songer, N. B., & Eylon, B. (1996). Shifts and convergences in science learning and instruction. In D. C. Berliner & R. C. Calfee (Eds.), *Handbook of educational psychology*. New York: Macmillan.

Linn, R. L. (1994). Performance assessment: Policy promises and technical measurement standards. *Educational Researcher, 23*(9), 4-14.

Lipson, M.Y. (1983). The influence of religious affiliation on children's memory for text information. *Reading Research Quarterly, 18*, 448-457.

Liss, M. B. (1983). Learning gender-related skills through play. In M. B. Liss (Ed.), *Social and cognitive skills: Sex roles and children's play*. San Diego: Academic Press.

Liu, L. G. (1990, April). *The use of causal questioning to promote narrative comprehension and memory*. Paper presented at the annual meeting of the American Educational Research Association, Boston.

Lloyd, D. N. (1978). Prediction of school failure from third-grade data. *Educational and Psychological Measurement, 38*, 1193-1200.

Locke, E.A., & Latham, G. P. (1990). *A theory of goal setting and task performance*. Upper Saddle River, NJ: Prentice Hall.

Loeber, R., & Stouthamer-Loeber, M. (1998). Development of juvenile aggression and violence. *American Psychologist, 53*, 242-259.

Loftus, E. F. (1991). Made in memory: Distortions in recollection after misleading information. In G. H. Bower (Ed.), *The psychology of learning and motivation: Advances in research and theory* (Vol. 27). San Diego: Academic Press.

Loftus, E. F., & Loftus, G. R. (1980). On the permanence of stored information in the human brain. *American Psychologist, 35*, 409-420.

Logan, K. R., Alberto, P.A., Kana, T. G., & Waylor-Bowen, T. (1994). Curriculum development and instructional design for students with profound disabilities. In L. Sternberg (Ed.), *Individuals with profound disabilities: Instructional and assistive strategies* (3rd ed.). Austin, TX: Pro-Ed.

Lomawaima, K.T. (1995). Educating Native Americans. In J.A. Banks & C.A. M. Banks (Eds.), *Handbook of research on multicultural education*. New York: Macmillan.

Long, M. (1995). The role of the linguistic environment in second language acquisition. In W. C. Ritchie & T. K. Bhatia (Eds.), *Handbook of language acquisition: Vol. 2. Second language acquisition*. San Diego: Academic Press.

Lonigan, C. J., Burgess, S. R., Anthony, J. L., & Barker, T. A. (1998). Development of phonological sensitivity in 2- to 5-year-old children. *Journal of Educational Psychology, 90,* 294-311.

Lorch, R. F., Jr., Lorch, E. P., & Inman, W. E. (1993). Effects of signaling topic structure on text recall. *Journal of Educational Psychology, 85,* 281-290.

Losey, K. M. (1995). Mexican American students and classroom interaction: An overview and critique. *Review of Educational Research, 65,* 283-318.

Lou, Y., Abrami, P. C., Spence, J. C., Poulsen, C., Chambers, B., & d'Apollonia, S. (1996). Within-class grouping: A meta-analysis. *Review of Educational Research, 66,* 423-458.

Lovell, K. (1979). Intellectual growth and the school curriculum. In F. B. Murray (Ed.), *The impact of Piagetian theory: On education, philosophy, psychiatry, and psychology.* Baltimore: University Park Press.

Lovett, S. B., & Flavell, J. H. (1990). Understanding and remembering: Children's knowledge about the differential effects of strategy and task variables on comprehension and memorization. *Child Development, 61,* 1842-1858.

Lovitt, T. C., Guppy, T. E., & Blattner, J. E. (1969). The use of free-time contingency with fourth graders to increase spelling accuracy. *Behaviour Research and Therapy, 7,* 151-156.

Lowry, R., Sleet, D., Duncan, C., Powell, K., & Kolbe, L. (1995). Adolescents at risk for violence. *Educational Psychology Review, 7,* 7-39.

Lubart, T. I. (1994). Creativity. In R. J. Sternberg (Ed.), *Thinking and problem solving.* San Diego: Academic Press.

Luchins, A. S., & Luchins, E. H. (1950). New experimental attempts at preventing mechanization in problem solving. *Journal of General Psychology, 42,* 279-297.

Lueptow, L. B. (1984). *Adolescent sex roles and social change.* New York: Columbia University Press.

Lundeberg, M. A., & Fox, P. W. (1991). Do laboratory findings on test expectancy generalize to classroom outcomes? *Review of Educational Research, 61,* 94-106.

Lupart, J. L. (1995). Exceptional learners and teaching for transfer. In A. McKeough, J. Lupart, & A. Marini (Eds.), *Teaching for transfer: Fostering generalization in learning.* Mahwah, NJ: Erlbaum.

Lyon, M. A. (1984). Positive reinforcement and logical consequences in the treatment of classroom encopresis. *School Psychology Review, 13,* 238-243.

Ma, X., & Kishor, N. (1997). Attitude toward self, social factors, and achievement in mathematics: A meta-analytic review. *Educational Psychology Review, 9,* 89-120.

MacArthur, C., & Ferretti, R. P. (1997, March). *The effects of elaborated goals on the argumentative writing of students with learning disabilities and their normally achieving peers.* Paper presented at the annual meeting of the American Educational Research Association, Chicago.

Maccoby, E. E., & Hagen, J. W. (1965). Effects of distraction upon central versus incidental recall: Developmental trends. *Journal of Experimental Child Psychology, 2,* 280-289.

Maccoby, E. E., & Jacklin, C. N. (1974). *The psychology of sex differences.* Stanford, CA: Stanford University Press.

Maccoby, E. E., & Martin, J. A. (1983). Socialization in the context of the family: Parent-child interaction. In E. M. Hetherington (Ed.), *Handbook of child psychology: Vol. 4. Socialization, personality, and social development* (4th ed.). New York: Wiley.

Mace, F. C., Belfiore, P. J., & Shea, M. C. (1989). Operant theory and research on self-regulation. In B. J. Zimmerman & D. H. Schunk (Eds.), *Self-regulated learning and academic achievement: Theory, research, and practice.* New York: Springer-Verlag.

Mace, F. C., Hock, M. L., Lalli, J. S., West, B. J., Belfiore, P., Pinter, E., & Brown, D. K. (1988). Behavioral momentum in the treatment of noncompliance. *Journal of Applied Behavior Analysis, 21,* 123-141.

Mace, F. C., & Kratochwill, T. R. (1988). Self-monitoring. In J. C. Witt, S. N. Elliott, & F. M. Gresham (Eds.), *Handbook of behavior therapy in education.* New York: Plenum Press.

Machiels-Bongaerts, M., Schmidt, H. G., & Boshuizen, H. P. A. (1991, April). *The effects of prior knowledge activation on free recall and study time allocation.* Paper presented at the annual meeting of the American Educational Research Association, Chicago.

MacLean, D. J., Sasse, D. K., Keating, D. P., Stewart, B. E., & Miller, F. K. (1995, April). *All-girls' mathematics and science instruction in early adolescence: Longitudinal effects.* Paper presented at the annual meeting of the American Educational Research Association, San Francisco.

MacMillan, D. L., & Meyers, C. E. (1979). Educational labeling of handicapped learners. In D. C. Berliner (Ed.), *Review of research in education, No. 7.* Washington, DC: American Educational Research Association.

Madden, N. A., & Slavin, R. E. (1983). Mainstreaming students with mild handicaps: Academic and social outcomes. *Review of Educational Research, 53,* 519-569.

Maehr, M. L. (1984). Meaning and motivation: Toward a theory of personal investment. In R. Ames & C. Ames (Eds.), *Research on motivation in education: Vol. 1. Student motivation.* San Diego: Academic Press.

Maehr, M. L., & Meyer, H. A. (1997). Understanding motivation and schooling: Where we've been, where we are, and where we need to go. *Educational Psychology Review, 9,* 371-409.

Magnusson, S. J., Boyle, R. A., & Templin, M. (1994, April). *Conceptual development: Re-examining knowledge construction in science.* Paper presented at the annual meeting of the American Educational Research Association, New Orleans, LA.

Maker, C. J. (1993). Creativity, intelligence, and problem solving: A definition and design for cross-cultural research and measurement related to giftedness. *Gifted Education International, 9*(2), 68-77.

Maker, C. J., & Schiever, S. W. (Eds.). (1989). *Critical issues in gifted education: Vol. 2. Defensible programs for cultural and ethnic minorities.* Austin, TX: Pro-Ed.

Mandler, G., & Pearlstone, Z. (1966). Free and constrained concept learning and subsequent recall. *Journal of Verbal Learning and Verbal Behavior, 5,* 126-131.

Mandler, J. M. (1987). On the psychological reality of story structure. *Discourse Processes, 10,* 1-29.

Manis, F. R. (1996). Current trends in dyslexia research. In B. J. Cratty & R. L. Goldman (Eds.), *Learning disabilities: Contemporary viewpoints.* Amsterdam: Harwood Academic.

Manset, G., & Semmel, M. I. (1997). Are inclusive programs for students with mild disabilities effective? A comparative review of model programs. *Journal of Special Education, 31,* 155-180.

Marcia, J. E. (1980). Identity in adolescence. In J. Adelson (Ed.), *Handbook of adolescent psychology.* New York: Wiley.

Marcus, G. F. (1996). Why do children say "breaked"? *Current Directions in Psychological Science, 5,* 81-85.

Markman, E. M. (1977). Realizing that you don't understand: A preliminary investigation. *Child Development, 48,* 986-992.

Markman, E. M. (1979). Realizing that you don't understand: Elementary school children's awareness of inconsistencies. *Child Development, 50,* 643-655.

Marks, J. (1995). *Human biodiversity: Genes, race, and history.* New York: Aldine de Gruyter.

Markus, H. R., & Kitayama, S. (1991). Culture and the self: Implications for cognition, emotion, and motivation. *Psychological Review, 98,* 224-253.

Marsh, H. W. (1989). Age and sex effect in multiple dimensions of self-concept: Preadolescence to early-adulthood. *Journal of Educational Psychology, 81,* 417-430.

Marsh, H. W. (1990a). Causal ordering of academic self-concept and academic achievement: A multiwave, longitudinal panel analysis. *Journal of Educational Psychology, 82,* 646-656.

Marsh, H. W. (1990b). A multidimensional, hierarchical model of self-concept: Theoretical and empirical justification. *Educational Psychology Review, 2,* 77-172.

Marsh, H. W., Chessor, D., Craven, R., & Roche, L. (1995). The effects of gifted and talented programs on academic self-concept: The big fish strikes again. *American Educational Research Journal, 32,* 285-319.

Marsh, H. W., & Craven, R. (1997). Academic self-concept: Beyond the dustbowl. In G. D. Phye (Ed.), *Handbook of classroom assessment: Learning, achievement, and adjustment.* San Diego: Academic Press.

Marsh, H. W., & Yeung, A. S. (1997). Coursework selection: Relations to academic self-concept and achievement. *American Educational Research Journal, 34,* 691-720.

Marsh, R. W. (1985). Phrenobylsis: Real or chimera? *Child Development, 56,* 1059-1061.

Marshall, H. H. (1981). Open classrooms: Has the term outlived its usefulness? *Review of Educational Research, 51,* 181-192.

Marshall, H. H. (1992). *Redefining student learning: Roots of educational change.* Norwood, NJ: Ablex.

Martin, S. S., Brady, M. P., & Williams, R. E. (1991). Effects of toys on the social behavior of preschool children in integrated and nonintegrated groups: Investigation of a setting event. *Journal of Early Intervention, 15,* 153-161.

Maslow, A. H. (1973). Theory of human motivation. In R. J. Lowry (Ed.), *Dominance, self-esteem, self-actualization: Germinal papers of A. H. Maslow.* Monterey, CA: Brooks/Cole.

Maslow, A. H. (1987). *Motivation and personality* (3rd ed.). New York: Harper & Row.

Massey, C. M., & Gelman, R. (1988). Preschoolers' ability to decide whether a photographed unfamiliar object can move itself. *Developmental Psychology, 24,* 307-317.

Massialas, B. G., & Zevin, J. (1983). *Teaching creatively: Learning through discovery.* Malabar, FL: Robert E. Krieger.

Masten, A. S., & Coatsworth, J. D. (1998). The development of competence in favorable and unfavorable environments. *American Psychologist, 53,* 205-220.

Mastropieri, M. A., & Scruggs, T. E. (1992). Science for students with disabilities. *Review of Educational Research, 62,* 377-411.

Masur, E. F., McIntyre, C. W., & Flavell, J. H. (1973). Developmental changes in apportionment of study time among items in a multitrial free recall task. *Journal of Experimental Child Psychology, 15,* 237-246.

Maxmell, D., Jarrett, O. S., & Dickerson, C. (1998, April). *Are we forgetting the children's needs? Recess through the children's eyes.* Paper presented at the annual meeting of the American Educational Research Association, San Diego.

Mayer, R. E. (1974). Acquisition processes and resilience under varying testing conditions for structurally different problem solving procedures. *Journal of Educational Psychology, 66,* 644-656.

Mayer, R. E. (1979a). Can advance organizers influence meaningful learning? *Review of Educational Research, 49,* 371-383.

Mayer, R. E. (1979b). Twenty years of research on advance organizers: Assimilation theory is still the best predictor of results. *Instructional Science, 8,* 133-167.

Mayer, R. E. (1982). Memory for algebra story problems. *Journal of Educational Psychology, 74,* 199-216.

Mayer, R. E. (1984). Aids to text comprehension. *Educational Psychologist, 19,* 30-42.

Mayer, R. E. (1985). Implications of cognitive psychology for instruction in mathematical problem solving. In E. A. Silver (Ed.), *Teaching and learning mathematical problem solving: Multiple research perspectives.* Hillsdale, NJ: Erlbaum.

Mayer, R. E. (1986). Mathematics. In R. F. Dillon & R. J. Sternberg (Eds.), *Cognition and instruction.* San Diego: Academic Press.

Mayer, R. E. (1987). *Educational psychology: A cognitive approach.* Boston: Little, Brown.

Mayer, R. E. (1989). Models for understanding. *Review of Educational Research, 59,* 43-64.

Mayer, R. E. (1992). *Thinking, problem solving, cognition* (2nd ed.). New York: W. H. Freeman.

Mayer, R. E. (1996). Learning strategies for making sense out of expository text: The SOI model for guiding three cognitive processes in knowledge construction. *Educational Psychology Review, 8,* 357-371.

Mayer, R. E. (1998). Does the brain have a place in educational psychology? *Educational Psychology Review, 10,* 389-396.

Mayer, R. E. (1999). *The promise of educational psychology: Learning in the content areas.* Upper Saddle River, NJ: Merrill/Prentice Hall.

Mayer, R. E., & Gallini, J. (1990). When is an illustration worth ten thousand words? *Journal of Educational Psychology, 82,* 715-726.

Mayer, R. E., & Greeno, J. G. (1972). Structural differences between learning outcomes produced by different instructional methods. *Journal of Educational Psychology, 63,* 165-173.

Mayer, R. E., & Wittrock, M. C. (1996). Problem-solving transfer. In D. C. Berliner & R. C. Calfee (Eds.), *Handbook of educational psychology.* New York: Macmillan.

McAdoo, H. P. (1985). Racial attitude and self-concept of young Black children over time. In H. P. McAdoo & J. L. McAdoo (Eds.), *Black children: Social, educational, and parental environments.* Newbury Park, CA: Sage.

McAlpine, L. (1992). Language, literacy and education: Case studies of Cree, Inuit and Mohawk communities. *Canadian Children, 17*(1), 17-30.

McAlpine, L., & Taylor, D. M. (1993). Instructional preferences of Cree, Inuit, and Mohawk teachers. *Journal of American Indian Education, 33*(1), 1-20.

McAshan, H. H. (1979). *Competency-based education and behavioral objectives.* Englewood Cliffs, NJ: Educational Technology.

McCall, R. B. (1993). Developmental functions for general mental performance. In D. K. Detterman (Ed.), *Current topics in human intelligence* (Vol. 3). Norwood, NJ: Ablex.

McCall, R. B. (1994). Academic underachievers. *Current Directions in Psychological Science, 3,* 15-19.

McCallum, R. S., & Bracken, B. A. (1993). Interpersonal relations between school children and their peers, parents, and teachers. *Educational Psychology Review, 5,* 155-176.

McCann, T. M. (1989). Student argumentative writing knowledge and ability at three grade levels. *Research in the Teaching of English, 23,* 62-72.

McCaslin, M., & Good, T. L. (1996). The informal curriculum. In D. C. Berliner & R. C. Calfee (Eds.), *Handbook of educational psychology.* New York: Macmillan.

McCloskey, M. (1983). Intuitive physics. *Scientific American, 248*(4), 122-130.

McCloskey, M. E., & Glucksberg, S. (1978). Natural categories: Well-defined or fuzzy sets? *Memory and Cognition, 6,* 462-472.

McCombs, B. L. (1988). Motivational skills training: Combining metacognitive, cognitive, and affective learning strategies. In C. E. Weinstein, E. T. Goetz, & P. A. Alexander (Eds.), *Learning and study strategies: Issues in assessment, instruction, and evaluation.* San Diego: Harcourt Brace Jovanovich.

McCormick, C. B., Busching, B. A., & Potter, E. F. (1992). Children's knowledge about writing: The development and use of evaluative criteria. In M. Pressley, K. R. Harris, & J. T. Guthrie (Eds.), *Promoting academic competence and literacy in school.* San Diego: Academic Press.

McCormick, M. E., & Wolf, J. S. (1993). Intervention programs for gifted girls. *Roeper Review, 16,* 85-88.

McCoy, K. (1994). *Understanding your teenager's depression.* New York: Perigee.

McCoy, L. P. (1990, April). *Correlates of mathematics anxiety.* Paper presented at the annual meeting of the American Educational Research Association, Boston.

McCutchen, D. (1996). A capacity theory of writing: Working memory in composition. *Educational Psychology Review, 8,* 299-325.

McCutchen, D., Kerr, S., & Francis, M. (1994, April). *Editing and revising: Effects of knowledge of topic and error location.* Paper presented at the annual meeting of the American Educational Research Association, New Orleans, LA.

McDaniel, M. A., & Einstein, G. O. (1989). Material-appropriate processing: A contextualist approach to reading and studying strategies. *Educational Psychology Review, 1,* 113-145.

McDaniel, M. A., & Masson, M. E. J. (1985). Altering memory representations through retrieval. *Journal of Experimental Psychology: Learning, Memory, and Cognition, 11,* 371-385.

McDaniel, M. A., & Schlager, M. S. (1990). Discovery learning and transfer of problem-solving skills. *Cognition and Instruction, 7,* 129-159.

McDaniel, M. A., Waddill, P. J., & Einstein, G. O. (1988). A contextual account of the generation effect: A three-factor theory. *Journal of Memory and Language, 27,* 521-536.

McDaniel, T. R. (1987). Practicing positive reinforcement. *The Clearing House, 60,* 389-392.

McDevitt, T. M. (1990). Encouraging young children's listening skills. *Academic Therapy, 25,* 569-577.

McDevitt, T. M., & Ford, M. E. (1987). Processes in young children's communicative functioning and development. In M. E. Ford & D. H. Ford (Eds.), *Humans as self-constructing living systems: Putting the framework to work.* Hillsdale, NJ: Erlbaum.

McDevitt, T. M., Spivey, N., Sheehan, E. P., Lennon, R., & Story, N. (1990). Children's beliefs about listening: Is it enough to be still and quiet? *Child Development, 61,* 713-721.

McGee, L. M. (1992). An exploration of meaning construction in first graders' grand conversations. In C. K. Kinzer & D. J. Leu (Eds.), *Literacy research, theory, and practice: Views from many perspectives.* Chicago: National Reading Conference.

McGinn, P. V., Viernstein, M. C., & Hogan, R. (1980). Fostering the intellectual development of verbally gifted adolescents. *Journal of Educational Psychology, 72,* 494-498.

McGowan, R. J., & Johnson, D. L. (1984). The mother-child relationship and other antecedents of childhood intelligence: A causal analysis. *Child Development, 55,* 810-820.

McGrew, K. S., Flanagan, D. P., Zeith, T. Z., & Vanderwood, M. (1997). Beyond *g*: The impact of *Gf-Gc* specific cognitive abilities research on the future use and interpretation of intelligence tests in the schools. *School Psychology Review, 26,* 189-210.

McGue, M., Bouchard, T. J., Jr., Iacono, W. G., & Lykken, D. T. (1993). Behavioral genetics of cognitive ability: A life-span perspective. In R. Plomin & G. E. McClearn (Eds.), *Nature, nurture, and psychology.* Washington, DC: American Psychological Association.

McKeachie, W. J., Lin, Y., Milholland, J., & Isaacson, R. (1966). Student affiliation motives, teacher warmth, and academic achievement. *Journal of Personality and Social Psychology, 4,* 457-461.

McKenna, M. C., Stratton, B. D., Grindler, M. C., & Jenkins, S. J. (1995). Differential effects of whole language and traditional instruction on reading attitudes. *Journal of Reading Behavior, 27,* 19-43.

McKeon, D. (1994). When meeting "common" standards is uncommonly difficult. *Educational Leadership, 51*(8), 45-49.

McKeown, M. G., & Beck, I. L. (1990). The assessment and characterization of young learners' knowledge of a topic in history. *American Educational Research Journal, 27*, 688-726.

McKeown, M. G., & Beck, I. L. (1994). Making sense of accounts of history: Why young students don't and how they might. In G. Leinhardt, I. L. Beck, & C. Stainton (Eds.), *Teaching and learning in history*. Hillsdale, NJ: Erlbaum.

McLeod, D. B., & Adams, V. M. (Eds.). (1989). *Affect and mathematical problem solving: A new perspective*. New York: Springer-Verlag.

McLoyd, V. C. (1998). Socioeconomic disadvantage and child development. *American Psychologist, 53*, 185-204.

McMahon, S. (1992). Book club: A case study of a group of fifth graders as they participate in a literature-based reading program. *Reading Research Quarterly, 27*(4), 292-294.

McMillan, J. H., & Reed, D. F. (1994). At-risk students and resiliency: Factors contributing to academic success. *Clearing House, 67*(3), 137-140.

McNamara, D. S., & Healy, A. F. (1995). A generation advantage for multiplication skill training and nonword vocabulary acquisition. In A. F. Healy & L. E. Bourne, Jr. (Eds.), *Learning and memory of knowledge and skills: Durability and specificity*. Thousand Oaks, CA: Sage.

McNamara, E. (1987). Behavioural approaches in the secondary school. In K. Wheldall (Ed.), *The behaviourist in the classroom*. London: Allen & Unwin.

McRobbie, C., & Tobin, K. (1995). Restraints to reform: The congruence of teacher and student actions in a chemistry classroom. *Journal of Research in Science Teaching, 32*, 373-385.

McWhiter, C. C., & Bloom, L. A. (1994). The effects of a student-operated business curriculum on the on-task behavior of students with behavioral disorders. *Behavioral Disorders, 19*(2), 136-141.

Meece, J. L. (1994). The role of motivation in self-regulated learning. In D. H. Schunk & B. J. Zimmerman (Eds.), *Self-regulation of learning and performance: Issues and educational applications*. Hillsdale, NJ: Erlbaum.

Mehan, H. (1979). *Social organization in the classroom*. Cambridge, MA: Harvard University Press.

Meichenbaum, D. (1977). *Cognitive-behavior modification: An integrative approach*. New York: Plenum Press.

Meichenbaum, D. (1985). Teaching thinking: A cognitive-behavioral perspective. In S. F. Chipman, J. W. Segal, & R. Glaser (Eds.), *Thinking and learning skills: Vol. 2. Research and open questions*. Hillsdale, NJ: Erlbaum.

Meichenbaum, D., & Goodman, J. (1971). Training impulsive children to talk to themselves: A means of developing self-control. *Journal of Abnormal Psychology, 77*, 115-126.

Meloth, M. S., & Deering, P. D. (1994). Task talk and task awareness under different cooperative learning conditions. *American Educational Research Journal, 31*, 138-165.

Menyuk, P., & Menyuk, D. (1988). Communicative competence: A historical and cultural perspective. In J. S. Wurzel (Ed.), *Toward multiculturalism: A reader in multicultural education*. Yarmouth, ME: Intercultural Press.

Mercer, C. D. (1991). *Students with learning disabilities* (4th ed.). Upper Saddle River, NJ: Merrill/Prentice Hall.

Mercer, C. D., Jordan, L., Allsopp, D. H., & Mercer, A. R. (1996). Learning disabilities definitions and criteria used by state education departments. *Learning Disabilities Quarterly, 19*, 217-231.

Merrill, M. D., & Tennyson, R. D. (1977). *Concept teaching: An instructional design guide*. Englewood Cliffs, NJ: Educational Technology.

Merrill, M. D., & Tennyson, R. D. (1978). Concept classification and classification errors as a function of relationships between examples and non-examples. *Improving Human Performance, 7*, 351-364.

Merrill, P. F., Hammons, K., Vincent, B. R., Reynolds, P. L., Christensen, L., & Tolman, M. N. (1996). *Computers in education* (3rd ed.). Needham Heights, MA: Allyn & Bacon.

Mervis, C. B. (1987). Child-basic object categories and early lexical development. In U. Neisser (Ed.), *Concepts and conceptual development: Ecological and intellectual factors in categorization*. Cambridge, England: Cambridge University Press.

Messick, S. (1994). The interplay of evidence and consequences in the validation of performance assessments. *Educational Researcher, 23*(2), 13-23.

Metz, K. E. (1995). Reassessment of developmental constraints on children's science instruction. *Review of Educational Research, 65*, 93-127.

Meyer, B. J. F., Brandt, D. H., & Bluth, G. J. (1980). Use of top-level structure in text: Key for reading comprehension of ninth-grade students. *Reading Research Quarterly, 16*, 72-103.

Meyer, D. K., Turner, J. C., & Spencer, C. A. (1994, April). *Academic risk taking and motivation in an elementary mathematics classroom*. Paper presented at the annual meeting of the American Educational Research Association, New Orleans, LA.

Meyers, D. T. (1987). The socialized individual and individual autonomy: An intersection between philosophy and psychology. In E. F. Kittay and D. T. Meyers (Eds.), *Women and moral theory*. Totowa, NJ: Rowman & Littlefield.

Miller, D. L., & Kelley, M. L. (1994). The use of goal setting and contingency contracting for improving children's homework performance. *Journal of Applied Behavior Analysis, 27*, 73-84.

Miller, G. A. (1956). The magical number seven, plus or minus two: Some limits on our capacity for processing information. *Psychological Review, 63*, 81-97.

Miller, L. S. (1995). *An American imperative: Accelerating minority educational advancement*. New Haven, CT: Yale University Press.

Miller, N. E., & Dollard, J. C. (1941). *Social learning and imitation*. New Haven, CT: Yale University Press.

Miller, P. H. (1993). Focus on the interface of cognition, social-emotional behavior and motivation. In P. H. Miller (Ed.), *Theories of developmental psychology* (3rd ed.). New York: W. H. Freeman.

Miller, R. R., & Barnet, R. C. (1993). The role of time in elementary associations. *Current Directions in Psychological Science, 2*, 106-111.

Millman, J., Bishop, C. H., & Ebel, R. (1965). An analysis of test-wiseness. *Educational and Psychological Measurement, 25*, 707-726.

Minami, M., & Ovando, C. J. (1995). Language issues in multicultural contexts. In J. A. Banks & C. A. M. Banks (Eds.), *Handbook of research on multicultural education*. New York: Macmillan.

Minstrell, J., & Stimpson, V. (1996). A classroom environment for learning: Guiding students' reconstruction of understanding and reasoning. In L. Schauble & R. Glaser (Eds.), *Innovations in learning: New environments for education*. Mahwah, NJ: Erlbaum.

Mintzes, J. J., Trowbridge, J. E., Arnaudin, M. W., & Wandersee, J. H. (1991). Children's biology: Studies on conceptual development in the life sciences. In S. M. Glynn, R. H. Yeany, & B. K. Britton (Eds.), *The psychology of learning science*. Hillsdale, NJ: Erlbaum.

Mintzes, J. J., Wandersee, J. H., & Novak, J. D. (1997). Meaningful learning in science: The human constructivist perspective. In G. D. Phye (Ed.), *Handbook of academic learning: Construction of knowledge*. San Diego: Academic Press.

Mischel, W. (1993). *Introduction to personality* (5th ed.). Fort Worth, TX: Harcourt Brace Jovanovich.

Mohatt, G., & Erickson, F. (1981). Cultural differences in teaching styles in an Odawa school: A sociolinguistic approach. In H. T. Trueba, G. P. Guthrie, and K. H. Au (Eds.), *Culture and the bilingual classroom: Studies in classroom ethnography*. Rowley, MA: Newbury House.

Moles, O. C. (Ed.). (1990). *Student discipline strategies: Research and practice*. Albany: State University of New York Press.

Moll, L. C., & Diaz, S. (1985). Ethnographic pedagogy: Promoting effective bilingual instruction. In E. E. Garcia & R. V. Padilla (Eds.), *Advances in bilingual education research*. Tucson: University of Arizona Press.

Montgomery, D. (1989). Identification of giftedness among American Indian people. In C. J. Maker & S. W. Schiever (Eds.), *Critical issues in gifted education: Vol. 2. Defensible programs for cultural and ethnic minorities*. Austin, TX: Pro-Ed.

Moon, S. M., Feldhusen, J. F., & Dillon, D. R. (1994). Long term effects of an enrichment program based on the Purdue three-stage model. *Gifted Child Quarterly, 38*, 38-47.

Mooney, C. M. (1957). Age in the development of closure ability in children. *Canadian Journal of Psychology, 11*, 219-226.

Moran, C. E., & Hakuta, K. (1995). Bilingual education: Broadening research perspectives. In J. A. Banks & C. A. M. Banks (Eds.), *Handbook of research on multicultural education*. New York: Macmillan.

Moran, S. (1991). Creative reading: Young adults and paperback books. *Horn Book Magazine, 67*, 437-441.

Morgan, D. P., & Jenson, W. R. (1988). *Teaching behaviorally disordered students: Preferred practices*. Upper Saddle River, NJ: Merrill/Prentice Hall.

Morrow, L. M. (1989). *Literacy development in the early years: Helping children read and write*. Boston: Allyn & Bacon.

Mueller, J. H. (1980). Test anxiety and the encoding and retrieval of information. In I. G. Sarason (Ed.), *Test anxiety: Theory, research, and applications*. Hillsdale, NJ: Erlbaum.

Munn, P., Johnstone, M., & Chalmers, V. (1990, April). *How do teachers talk about maintaining effective discipline in their classrooms?* Paper presented at the annual meeting of the American Educational Research Association, Boston.

Murphy, D. M. (1996). Implications of inclusion for general and special education. *Elementary School Journal, 96*, 469-492.

Murray, C. B., & Jackson, J. S. (1982/1983). The conditioned failure model of black educational underachievement. *Humboldt Journal of Social Relations, 10*, 276-300.

Musca, T. (Producer), & Menendez, R. (Director) (1988). *Stand and deliver* [videorecording]. Burbank, CA: Warner Home Video.

Mwangi, W., & Sweller, J. (1998). Learning to solve compare word problems: The effect of example format and generating self-explanations. *Cognition and Instruction, 16*, 173-199.

Narvaez, D. (1998). The influence of moral schemas on the reconstruction of moral narratives in eighth graders and college students. *Journal of Educational Psychology, 90*, 13-24.

National Assessment of Educational Progress. (1985). *The reading report card: Progress toward excellence in our schools; trends in reading over four national assessments, 1971-1984.* Princeton, NJ: NAEP.

National Association of Bilingual Education. (1993). Census reports sharp increase in number of non-English speaking Americans. *NABE News, 16*(6), 1, 25.

National Geographic Education Project. (1994). *Geography for life: National geography standards.* Washington, DC: National Geographic Research and Education, National Geographic Society.

National Joint Committee on Learning Disabilities. (1994). Learning disabilities: Issues on definition, a position paper of the National Joint Committee on Learning Disabilities. In *Collective perspectives on issues affecting learning disabilities: Position papers and statements.* Austin, TX: Pro-Ed.

National Science Education Standards. (1996). Washington, DC: National Academy Press.

Natriello, G., & Dornbusch, S. M. (1984). *Teacher evaluative standards and student effort.* White Plains, NY: Longman.

Navarro, R. A. (1985). The problems of language, education, and society: Who decides. In E. E. Garcia & R. V. Padilla (Eds.), *Advances in bilingual education research.* Tucson: University of Arizona Press.

NCSS Task Force on Ethnic Studies Curriculum Guidelines. (1992). Curriculum guidelines for multicultural education. *Social Education, 56*, 274-294.

Neel, R. S., Jenkins, Z. N., & Meadows, N. (1990). Social problem-solving behaviors and aggression in young children: A descriptive observational study. *Behavioral Disorders, 16*(1), 39-51.

Neisser, U. (1967). *Cognitive psychology.* New York: Appleton-Century-Crofts.

Neisser, U. (Ed.). (1987). *Concepts and conceptual development: Ecological and intellectual factors in categorization.* Cambridge, England: Cambridge University Press.

Neisser, U., Boodoo, G., Bouchard, T. J., Boykin, A. W., Brody, N., Ceci, S. J., Halpern, D. F., Loehlin, J. C., Perloff, R., Sternberg, R. J., & Urbina, S. (1996). Intelligence: Knowns and unknowns. *American Psychologist, 51*, 77-101.

Nelson, J. R., Smith, D. J., Young, R. K., & Dodd, J. M. (1991). A review of self-management outcome research conducted with students who exhibit behavioral disorders. *Behavioral Disorders, 16*, 169-179.

Nelson, T. O., & Dunlosky, J. (1991). When people's judgments of learning (JOLs) are extremely accurate at predicting subsequent recall: The "delayed-JOL effect." *Psychological Science, 2*, 267-270.

Nemerowicz, G. M. (1979). *Children's perceptions of gender and work roles.* New York: Praeger.

Nevin, J. A., Mandell, C., & Atak, J. R. (1983). The analysis of behavioral momentum. *Journal of the Experimental Analysis of Behavior, 39*, 49-59.

Newby, T. J., Ertmer, P. A., & Stepich, D. A. (1994, April). *Instructional analogies and the learning of concepts.* Paper presented at the annual meeting of the American Educational Research Association, New Orleans, LA.

Newcombe, N., & Huttenlocher, J. (1992). Children's early ability to solve perspective-taking problems. *Developmental Psychology, 28*, 635-643.

Newman, R. S., & Schwager, M. T. (1995). Students' help seeking during problem solving: Effects of grade, goal, and prior achievement. *American Educational Research Journal, 32*, 352-376.

Newmann, F. M. (1981). Reducing student alienation in high schools: Implications of theory. *Harvard Educational Review, 51*, 546-564.

Newmann, F. M. (1988). Can depth replace coverage in the high school curriculum? *Phi Delta Kappan, 70*, 345-348.

Newmann, F. M. (1997). Authentic assessment in social studies: Standards and examples. In G. D. Phye (Ed.), *Handbook of classroom assessment: Learning, achievement, and adjustment.* San Diego: Academic Press.

Newmann, F. M., & Wehlage, G. G. (1993). Five standards of authentic instruction. *Educational Leadership, 50*(7), 8-12.

Newport, E. L. (1993). Maturational constraints on language learning. In P. Bloom (Ed.), *Language acquisition: Core readings.* Cambridge, MA: MIT Press.

Nicholls, J. G. (1984). Conceptions of ability and achievement motivation. In R. Ames & C. Ames (Eds.), *Research on motivation in education: Vol 1. Student motivation.* San Diego: Academic Press.

Nicholls, J. G. (1990). What is ability and why are we mindful of it? A developmental perspective. In R. J. Sternberg & J. Kolligian (Eds.), *Competence considered.* New Haven, CT: Yale University Press.

Nichols, M. L., & Ganschow, L. (1992). Has there been a paradigm shift in gifted education? In N. Coangelo, S. G. Assouline, & D. L. Ambroson (Eds.), *Talent development: Proceedings from the 1991 Henry B. and Jocelyn Wallace National Research Symposium on Talent Development.* New York: Trillium.

Nickerson, R. S. (1989). New directions in educational assessment. *Educational Researcher, 18*(9), 3-7.

Nielsen, L. (1993). Students from divorced and blended families. *Educational Psychology Review, 5*, 177-199.

Nieto, S. (1995). A history of the education of Puerto Rican students in U.S. mainland schools: "Losers," "outsiders," or "leaders"? In J. A. Banks & C. A. M. Banks (Eds.), *Handbook of research on multicultural education.* New York: Macmillan.

Nippold, M. A. (1988). The literate lexicon. In M. A. Nippold (Ed.), *Later language development: Ages nine through nineteen.* Boston: Little, Brown.

Nist, S. L., Simpson, M. L., Olejnik, S., & Mealey, D. L. (1991). The relation between self-selected study processes and test performance. *American Educational Research Journal, 28*, 849-874.

Noddings, N. (1985). Small groups as a setting for research on mathematical problem solving. In E. A. Silver (Ed.), *Teaching and learning mathematical problem solving: Multiple research perspectives.* Hillsdale, NJ: Erlbaum.

Nolen, S. B. (1996). Why study? How reasons for learning influence strategy selection. *Educational Psychology Review, 8*, 335-355.

Norman, D. A. (1969). *Memory and attention: An introduction to human information processing.* New York: Wiley.

Northup, J., Broussard, C., Jones, K., George, T., Vollmer, T. R., & Herring, M. (1995). The differential effects of teachers and peer attention on the disruptive classroom behavior of three children with a diagnosis of attention deficit hyperactivity disorder. *Journal of Applied Behavior Analysis, 28*, 227-228.

Nottelmann, E. D. (1987). Competence and self-esteem during transition from childhood to adolescence. *Developmental Psychology, 23*, 441-450.

Novak, J. D., & Gowin, D. B. (1984). *Learning how to learn.* Cambridge, England: Cambridge University Press.

Novak, J. D., & Musonda, D. (1991). A twelve-year longitudinal study of science concept learning. *American Educational Research Journal, 28*, 117-153.

Nunner-Winkler, G. (1984). Two moralities? A critical discussion of an ethic of care and responsibility versus an ethic of rights and justice. In W. M. Kurtines & J. L. Gewirtz (Eds.), *Morality, moral behavior, and moral development.* New York: Wiley.

Nussbaum, J. (1985). The earth as a cosmic body. In R. Driver (Ed.), *Children's ideas of science.* Philadelphia: Open University Press.

Nussbaum, N., & Bigler, E. (1990). *Identification and treatment of attention deficit disorder.* Austin, TX: Pro-Ed.

Nuthall, G. (1996). Commentary: Of learning and language and understanding the complexity of the classroom. *Educational Psychologist, 31*, 207-214.

Oakhill, J., & Yuill, N. (1996). Higher order factors in comprehension disability: Processes and remediation. In C. Cesare & J. Oakhill (Eds.), *Reading comprehension difficulties.* Mahwah, NJ: Erlbaum.

O'Boyle, M. W., & Gill, H. S. (1998). On the relevance of research findings in cognitive neuroscience to educational practice. *Educational Psychology Review, 10*, 397-409.

O'Donnell, A. M., & O'Kelly, J. (1994). Learning from peers: Beyond the rhetoric of positive results. *Educational Psychology Review, 6*, 321-349.

Ogbu, J. U. (1992). Understanding cultural diversity and learning. *Educational Researcher, 21*(8), 5-14, 24.

Ogbu, J. U. (1994). From cultural differences to differences in cultural frame of reference. In P. M. Greenfield & R. R. Cocking (Eds.), *Cross-cultural roots of minority child development.* Hillsdale, NJ: Erlbaum.

Ogden, E. H., & Germinario, V. (1988). *The at-risk student: Answers for educators.* Lancaster, PA: Technomic.

O'Leary, K. D., Kaufman, K. F., Kass, R. E., & Drabman, R. S. (1970). The effects of loud and soft reprimands on the behavior of disruptive students. *Exceptional Children, 37,* 145-155.

O'Leary, K. D., & O'Leary, S. G. (Eds.). (1972). *Classroom management: The successful use of behavior modification.* New York: Pergamon Press.

Olneck, M. R. (1995). Immigrants and education. In J. A. Banks & C. A. M. Banks (Eds.), *Handbook of research on multicultural education.* New York: Macmillan.

Olsen, D. G. (1995, March). "Less" can be "more" in the promotion of thinking. *Social Education, 59*(3), 130-134.

O'Malley, P. M., & Bachman, J. G. (1983). Self-esteem: Change and stability between ages 13 and 23. *Developmental Psychology, 19,* 257-268.

Onosko, J. J. (1989). Comparing teachers' thinking about promoting students' thinking. *Theory and Research in Social Education, 17,* 174-195.

Onosko, J. J. (1996). Exploring issues with students despite the barriers. *Social Education, 60*(1), 22-27.

Onosko, J. J., & Newmann, F. M. (1994). Creating more thoughtful learning environments. In J. N. Mangieri & C. C. Block (Eds.), *Advanced educational psychology: Enhancing mindfulness.* Fort Worth, TX: Harcourt Brace Jovanovich.

Ormrod, J. E. (1999). *Human learning* (3rd ed.). Upper Saddle River, NJ: Merrill/Prentice Hall.

Ormrod, J. E., & Carter, K. R. (1985). Systematizing the Piagetian clinical interview for classroom use. *Teaching of Psychology, 12,* 216-219.

Ormrod, J. E., Jackson, D. L., Kirby, B., Davis, J., & Benson, C. (1999, April). *Cognitive development as reflected in children's conceptions of early American history.* Paper presented at the annual meeting of the American Educational Research Association, Montreal.

Ormrod, J. E., & Jenkins, L. (1989). Study strategies in spelling: Correlations with achievement and developmental changes. *Perceptual and Motor Skills, 68,* 643-650.

Ormrod, J. E., & Lewis, M. A. (1985). Comparison of memory skills in learning disabled, low-reading, and nondisabled adolescents. *Perceptual and Motor Skills, 61,* 191-195.

Ormrod, J. E., Ormrod, R. K., Wagner, E. D., & McCallin, R. C. (1988). Reconceptualizing map learning. *American Journal of Psychology, 101,* 425-433.

Ormrod, J. E., & Wagner, E. D. (1987, October). *Spelling conscience in undergraduate students: Ratings of spelling accuracy and dictionary use.* Paper presented at the annual meeting of the Northern Rocky Mountain Educational Research Association, Park City, UT.

O'Sullivan, J. T., & Joy, R. M. (1990, April). *Children's theories about reading difficulty: A developmental study.* Paper presented at the annual meeting of the American Educational Research Association, Boston.

Otero, J., & Kintsch, W. (1992). Failures to detect contradictions in a text: What readers believe versus what they read. *Psychological Science, 3,* 229-235.

Owens, R. E., Jr. (1996). *Language development* (4th ed.). Boston: Allyn & Bacon.

Packard, V. (1983). *Our endangered children: Growing up in a changing world.* Boston: Little, Brown.

Padilla, M. J. (1991). Science activities, process skills, and thinking. In S. M. Glynn, R. H. Yeany, & B. K. Britton (Eds.), *The psychology of learning science.* Hillsdale, NJ: Erlbaum.

Paige, J. M., & Simon, H. A. (1966). Cognitive processes in solving algebra word problems. In B. Kleinmuntz (Ed.), *Problem solving.* New York: Wiley.

Palardy, J. M., & Mudrey, J. E. (1973). Discipline: Four approaches. *Elementary School Journal, 73,* 297-305.

Palincsar, A. S., & Brown, A. L. (1984). Reciprocal teaching of comprehension-fostering and comprehension-monitoring activities. *Cognition and Instruction, 1,* 117-175.

Palincsar, A. S., & Brown, A. L. (1989). Classroom dialogues to promote self-regulated comprehension. In J. Brophy (Ed.), *Advances in research on teaching* (Vol. 1). Greenwich, CT: JAI Press.

Palmer, E. L. (1965). Accelerating the child's cognitive attainments through the inducement of cognitive conflict: An interpretation of the Piagetian position. *Journal of Research in Science Teaching, 3,* 324.

Pang, V. O. (1995). Asian Pacific American students: A diverse and complex population. In J. A. Banks & C. A. M. Banks (Eds.), *Handbook of research on multicultural education.* New York: Macmillan.

Paris, S. G. (1988). Models and metaphors of learning strategies. In C. E. Weinstein, E. T. Goetz, & P. A. Alexander (Eds.), *Learning and study strategies: Issues in assessment, instruction, and evaluation.* San Diego: Academic Press.

Paris, S. G., & Ayres, L. R. (1994). *Becoming reflective students and teachers with portfolios and authentic assessment.* Washington, DC: American Psychological Association.

Paris, S. G., & Byrnes, J. P. (1989). The constructivist approach to self-regulation and learning in the classroom. In B. J. Zimmerman & D. H. Schunk (Eds.), *Self-regulated learning and academic achievement: Theory, research, and practice.* New York: Springer-Verlag.

Paris, S. G., & Cunningham, A. E. (1996). Children becoming students. In D. C. Berliner & R. C. Calfee (Eds.), *Handbook of educational psychology.* New York: Macmillan.

Paris, S. G., Lawton, T. A., Turner, J. C., & Roth, J. L. (1991). A developmental perspective on standardized achievement testing. *Educational Researcher, 20*(5), 12-20, 40.

Paris, S. G., & Turner, J. C. (1994). Situated motivation. In P. R. Pintrich, D. R. Brown, & C. E. Weinstein (Eds.), *Student motivation, cognition, and learning: Essays in honor of Wilbert J. McKeachie.* Hillsdale, NJ: Erlbaum.

Paris, S. G., & Upton, L. R. (1976). Children's memory for inferential relationships in prose. *Child Development, 47,* 660-668.

Paris, S. G., & Winograd, P. (1990). How metacognition can promote academic learning and instruction. In B. F. Jones & L. Idol (Eds.), *Dimensions of thinking and cognitive instruction.* Hillsdale, NJ: Erlbaum.

Parke, R. D. (1974). Rules, roles, and resistance to deviation: Explorations in punishment, discipline, and self-control. In A. Pick (Ed.), *Minnesota Symposia on Child Psychology* (Vol. 8). Minneapolis: University of Minnesota Press.

Parker, W. D. (1997). An empirical typology of perfectionism in academically talented children. *American Educational Research Journal, 34,* 545-562.

Parks, C. P. (1995). Gang behavior in the schools: Reality or myth? *Educational Psychology Review, 7,* 41-68.

Parnes, S. J. (1967). *Creative behavior guidebook.* New York: Scribner's.

Parsons, J. E., Adler, T. F., & Kaczala, C. M. (1982). Socialization of achievement attitudes and beliefs: Parental influences. *Child Development, 53,* 310-321.

Parsons, J. E., Kaczala, C. M., & Meece, J. L. (1982). Socialization of achievement attitudes and beliefs: Classroom influences. *Child Development, 53,* 322-339.

Pascarella, E. T., & Terenzini, P. T. (1991). *How college affects students: Findings and insights from twenty years of research.* San Francisco: Jossey-Bass.

Patrick, H. (1997). Social self-regulation: Exploring the relations between children's social relationships, academic self-regulation, and school performance. *Educational Psychologist, 32,* 209-220.

Patterson, G. R., DeBaryshe, B. D., & Ramsey, E. (1989). A developmental perspective on antisocial behavior. *American Psychologist, 44,* 329-335.

Patton, J. R., Payne, J. S., & Beirne-Smith, M. (1990). *Mental retardation* (3rd ed.). Upper Saddle River, NJ: Merrill/Prentice Hall.

Patton, J. R., Payne, J. S., Kauffman, J. M., Brown, G. B., & Payne, R. A. (1987). *Exceptional children in focus* (4th ed.). Upper Saddle River, NJ: Merrill/Prentice Hall.

Paulson, F. L., Paulson, P. R., & Meyer, C. A. (1991). What makes a portfolio a portfolio? *Educational Leadership, 49*(5), 60-63.

Paulson, K., & Johnson, M. (1983). Sex-role attitudes and mathematical ability in 4th, 8th, and 11th grade students from a high socioeconomic area. *Developmental Psychology, 19,* 210-214.

Pavlov, I. P. (1927). *Conditioned reflexes* (G. V. Anrep, Trans.). London: Oxford University Press.

Pawlas, G. E. (1994). Homeless students at the school door. *Educational Leadership, 51*(8), 79-82.

Pea, R. D. (1992). Augmenting the discourse of learning with computer-based learning environments. In E. De Corte, M. C. Linn, H. Mandl, & L. Verschaffel (Eds.), *Computer-based learning environments and problem solving.* Berlin: Springer-Verlag.

Pea, R. D. (1993). Practices of distributed intelligence and designs for education. In G. Salomon (Ed.), *Distributed cognitions: Psychological and educational considerations.* Cambridge, England: Cambridge University Press.

Peak, L. (1993). Academic effort in international perspective. In T. M. Tomlinson (Ed.), *Motivating students to learn: Overcoming barriers to high achievement.* Berkeley, CA: McCutchan.

Pearson, P. D., Hansen, J., & Gordon, C. (1979). The effect of background knowledge on young children's comprehension of explicit and implicit information. *Journal of Reading Behavior, 11,* 201-209.

Pellegrini, A. D., & Bjorklund, D. F. (1997). The role of recess in children's cognitive performance. *Educational Psychologist, 32,* 35-40.

Pellegrini, A. D., & Horvat, M. (1995). A developmental contextualist critique of attention deficit hyperactivity disorder. *Educational Researcher, 24*(1), 13-19.

Pellegrini, A. D., Huberty, P. D., & Jones, I. (1995). The effects of recess timing on children's playground and classroom behaviors. *American Educational Research Journal, 32,* 845-864.

Pennington, B. F., Groisser, D., & Welsh, M. C. (1993). Contrasting cognitive deficits in attention deficit hyperactivity disorder versus reading disability. *Developmental Psychology, 29,* 511-523.

Perera, K. (1986). Language acquisition and writing. In P. Fletcher & M. Garman (Eds.), *Language acquisition: Studies in first language development* (2nd ed.). Cambridge, England: Cambridge University Press.

Perfetti, C. A., & McCutchen, D. (1987). Schooled language competence: Linguistic abilities in reading and writing. In S. Rosenberg (Ed.), *Advances in applied psycholinguistics.* Cambridge, England: Cambridge University Press.

Perkins, D. N. (1990). The nature and nurture of creativity. In B. F. Jones & L. Idol (Eds.), *Dimensions of thinking and cognitive instruction.* Hillsdale, NJ: Erlbaum.

Perkins, D. (1992). *Smart schools: From training memories to educating minds.* New York: Free Press/Macmillan.

Perkins, D. N. (1995). *Outsmarting IQ: The emerging science of learnable intelligence.* New York: Free Press.

Perkins, D. N., & Salomon, G. (1987). Transfer and teaching thinking. In D. N. Perkins, J. Lochhead, & J. Bishop (Eds.), *Thinking: The second international conference.* Hillsdale, NJ: Erlbaum.

Perkins, D. N., & Salomon, G. (1989). Are cognitive skills context-bound? *Educational Researcher, 18*(1), 16-25.

Perkins, D. N., & Simmons, R. (1988). Patterns of misunderstanding: An integrative model for science, math, and programming. *Review of Educational Research, 58,* 303-326.

Perry, D. G., & Perry, L. C. (1983). Social learning, causal attribution, and moral internalization. In J. Bisanz, G. L. Bisanz, & R. Kail (Eds.), *Learning in children: Progress in cognitive development research.* New York: Springer-Verlag.

Perry, M. (1991). Learning and transfer: Instructional conditions and conceptual change. *Cognitive Development, 6,* 449-468.

Petersen, G. A., Sudweeks, R. R., & Baird, J. H. (1990, April). *Test-wise responses of third-, fifth-, and sixth-grade students to clued and unclued multiple-choice science items.* Paper presented at the annual meeting of the American Educational Research Assocation, Boston.

Peterson, C. (1990). Explanatory style in the classroom and on the playing field. In S. Graham & V. S. Folkes (Eds.), *Attribution theory: Applications to achievement, mental health, and interpersonal conflict.* Hillsdale, NJ: Erlbaum.

Peterson, C., & Barrett, L. C. (1987). Explanatory style and academic performance among university freshmen. *Journal of Personality and Social Psychology, 53,* 603-607.

Peterson, L. R., & Peterson, M. J. (1959). Short-term retention of individual items. *Journal of Experimental Psychology, 58,* 193-198.

Peterson, P. L. (1979). Direct instruction reconsidered. In P. L. Peterson & H. L. Walberg (Eds.), *Research on teaching: Concepts, findings and implications.* Berkeley, CA: McCutchan.

Peterson, P. L. (1988). Teachers' and students' cognitional knowledge for classroom teaching and learning. *Educational Researcher, 17*(5), 5-14.

Peterson, P. L. (1992). Revising their thinking: Keisha Coleman and her third-grade mathematics class. In H. H. Marshall (Ed.), *Redefining student learning: Roots of educational change.* Norwood, NJ: Ablex.

Peterson, S. E. (1993). The effects of prior achievement and group outcome on attributions and affect in cooperative tasks. *Contemporary Educational Psychology, 18,* 479-485.

Pettigrew, T. F., & Pajonas, P. J. (1973). The social psychology of heterogeneous schools. In C. S. Brembeck & W. H. Hill (Eds.), *Cultural challenges to education: The influence of cultural factors in school learning.* Lexington, MA: Heath.

Pettito, A. L. (1985). Division of labor: Procedural learning in teacher-led small groups. *Cognition and Instruction, 2,* 233-270.

Pfiffner, L. J., & O'Leary, S. G. (1987). The efficacy of all-positive management as a function of the prior use of negative consequences. *Journal of Applied Behavior Analysis, 20,* 265-271.

Pfiffner, L. J., Rosen, L. A., & O'Leary, S. G. (1985). The efficacy of an all-positive approach to classroom management. *Journal of Applied Behavior Analysis, 18,* 257-261.

Phelan, P., Davidson, A. L., & Cao, H. T. (1991). Students' multiple worlds: Negotiating the boundaries of family, peer, and school cultures. *Anthropology and Education Quarterly, 22,* 224-250.

Phelan, P., Yu, H. C., & Davidson, A. L. (1994). Navigating the psychosocial pressures of adolescence: The voices and experiences of high school youth. *American Educational Research Journal, 31,* 415-447.

Phillip, R. A., Flores, A., Sowder, J. T., & Schappelle, B. P. (1994). Conceptions and practices of extraordinary mathematics teachers. *Journal of Mathematical Behavior, 13,* 155-180.

Phillips, B. N., Pitcher, G. D., Worsham, M. E., & Miller, S. C. (1980). Test anxiety and the school environment. In I. G. Sarason (Ed.), *Test anxiety: Theory, research, and applications.* Hillsdale, NJ: Erlbaum.

Phinney, J. (1989). Stages of ethnic identity development in minority group adolescents. *Journal of Early Adolescence, 9,* 34-39.

Phye, G. D. (1997). Classroom assessment: A multidimensional perspective. In G. D. Phye (Ed.), *Handbook of classroom assessment: Learning, achievement, and adjustment.* San Diego: Academic Press.

Piaget, J. (1928). *Judgment and reasoning in the child* (M. Warden, Trans.). New York: Harcourt, Brace.

Piaget, J. (1929). *The child's conception of the world.* New York: Harcourt, Brace.

Piaget, J. (1932). *The moral judgment of the child.* New York: Harcourt, Brace.

Piaget, J. (1952). *The origins of intelligence in children* (M. Cook, Trans.). New York: Norton.

Piaget, J. (1959). *The language and thought of the child* (3rd ed.; M. Gabain, Trans.). London: Routledge & Kegan Paul.

Piaget, J. (1970). Piaget's theory. In P. H. Mussen (Ed.), *Carmichael's manual of psychology.* New York: Wiley.

Piaget, J. (1980). *Adaptation and intelligence: Organic selection and phenocopy* (S. Eames, Trans.). Chicago: University of Chicago Press.

Piersel, W. C. (1987). Basic skills education. In C. A. Maher & S. G. Forman (Eds.), *A behavioral approach to education of children and youth.* Hillsdale, NJ: Erlbaum.

Pigott, H. E., Fantuzzo, J. W., & Clement, P. W. (1986). The effects of reciprocal peer tutoring and group contingencies on the academic performance of elementary school children. *Journal of Applied Behavior Analysis, 19,* 93-98.

Piirto, J. (1994). *Talented children and adults: Their development and education.* Upper Saddle River, NJ: Merrill/Prentice Hall.

Pinker, S. (1987). The bootstrapping problem in language acquisition. In B. MacWhinney (Ed.), *Mechanisms of language acquisition.* Hillsdale, NJ: Erlbaum.

Pintrich, P. R., & De Groot, E. V. (1990). Motivational and self-regulated learning components of classroom academic performance. *Journal of Educational Psychology, 82,* 33-40.

Pintrich, P. R., & Garcia, T. (1994). Regulating motivation and cognition in the classroom: The role of self-schemas and self-regulatory strategies. In D. Schunk & B. Zimmerman (Eds.), *Self-regulation of learning and performance: Issues and educational applications.* Hillsdale, NJ: Erlbaum.

Pintrich, P. R., Garcia, T., & De Groot, E. (1994, April). *Positive and negative self-schemas and self-regulated learning.* Paper presented at the annual meeting of the American Educational Research Association, New Orleans, LA.

Pintrich, P. R., Marx, R. W., & Boyle, R. A. (1993). Beyond cold conceptual change: The role of motivational beliefs and classroom contextual factors in the process of conceptual change. *Review of Educational Research, 63,* 167-199.

Pintrich, P. R., & Schunk, D. H. (1996). *Motivation in education: Theory, research, and applications.* Upper Saddle River, NJ: Merrill/Prentice Hall.

Piontkowski, D., & Calfee, R. (1979). Attention in the classroom. In G. A. Hale & M. Lewis (Eds.), *Attention and cognitive development.* New York: Plenum Press.

Pittman, K., & Beth-Halachmy, S. (1997, March). *The role of prior knowledge in analogy use.* Paper presented at the annual meeting of the American Educational Research Association, Chicago.

Plomin, R. (1989). Environment and genes: Determinants of behavior. *American Psychologist, 44,* 105-111.

Plomin, R. (1994). *Genetics and experience: The interplay between nature and nurture.* Thousand Oaks, CA: Sage.

Plomin, R., Fulker, D. W., Corley, R., & DeFries, J. C. (1997). Nature, nurture, and cognitive development from 1 to 16 years: A parent-offspring adoption study. *Psychological Science, 8,* 442-447.

Plumert, J. M. (1994). Flexibility in children's use of spatial and categorical organizational strategies in recall. *Developmental Psychology, 30,* 738-747.

Poche, C., Yoder, P., & Miltenberger, R. (1988). Teaching self-protection to children using television techniques. *Journal of Applied Behavior Analysis, 21,* 253-261.

Pogrow, S., & Londer, G. (1994). The effects of an intensive general thinking program on the motivation and cognitive development of at-risk students: Findings from the HOTS program. In H. F. O'Neil, Jr., & M. Drillings (Eds.), *Motivation: Theory and research*. Hillsdale, NJ: Erlbaum.

Pollard, S. R., Kurtines, W. M., Carlo, G., Dancs, M., & Mayock, E. (1991). Moral education from the perspective of psychosocial theory. In W. M. Kurtines & J. L. Gewirtz (Eds.), *Moral behavior and development: Vol. 3. Application*. Hillsdale, NJ: Erlbaum.

Polloway, E. A., & Patton, J. R. (1993). *Strategies for teaching learners with special needs* (5th ed.). Upper Saddle River, NJ: Merrill/Prentice Hall.

Poole, D. (1994). Routine testing practices and the linguistic construction of knowledge. *Cognition and Instruction, 12*, 125-150.

Popham, W. J. (1990). *Modern educational measurement: A practitioner's perspective* (2nd ed.). Upper Saddle River, NJ: Prentice Hall.

Popham, W. J. (1995). *Classroom assessment: What teachers need to know*. Needham Heights, MA: Allyn & Bacon.

Porath, M. (1988, April). *Cognitive development of gifted children: A neo-Piagetian perspective*. Paper presented at the annual meeting of the American Educational Research Association, New Orleans, LA.

Porter, A. C. (1989). A curriculum out of balance: The case of elementary school mathematics. *Educational Researcher, 18*(5), 9-15.

Portes, P. R. (1996). Ethnicity and culture in educational psychology. In D. C. Berliner & R. C. Calfee (Eds.), *Handbook of educational psychology*. New York: Macmillan.

Posner, G. J., Strike, K. A., Hewson, P. W., & Gertzog, W. A. (1982). Accommodation of a scientific conception: Toward a theory of conceptual change. *Science Education, 66*, 211-227.

Posner, M. I. (1973). *Cognition: An introduction*. Glenview, IL: Scott, Foresman.

Postman, L., & Underwood, B. J. (1973). Critical issues in interference theory. *Memory and Cognition, 1*, 19-40.

Powell, B. M. (1990, April). *Children's perceptions of classroom goal orientation: Relationship to learning strategies and intrinsic motivation*. Paper presented at the annual meeting of the American Educational Research Association, Boston.

Powell, S., & Nelson, B. (1997). Effects of choosing academic assignments on a study with attention deficit hyperactivity disorder. *Journal of Applied Behavior Analysis, 30*, 181-183.

Power, F. C., Higgins, A., & Kohlberg, L. (1989). *Lawrence Kohlberg's approach to moral education*. New York: Columbia University Press.

Power, F. C., & Power, M. R. (1992). A raft of hope: Democratic education and the challenge of pluralism. *Journal of Moral Education, 21*, 193-205.

Powers, L. E., Sowers, J. A., & Stevens, T. (1995). An exploratory, randomized study of the impact of mentoring on the self-efficacy and community-based knowledge of adolescents with severe physical challenges. *Journal of Rehabilitation, 61*(1), 33-41.

Powers, L. E., Wilson, R., Matuszewski, J., Phillips, A., Rein, C., Schumacher, D., & Gensert, J. (1996). Facilitating adolescent self-determination. In D. J. Sands & M. L. Wehmeyer (Eds.), *Self-determination across the life span: Independence and choice for people with disabilities*. Baltimore: Paul H. Brookes.

Powers, S. I., Hauser, S. T., & Kilner, L. A. (1989). Adolescent mental health. *American Psychologist, 44*, 200-208.

Prawat, R. S. (1989). Promoting access to knowledge, strategy, and disposition in students: A research synthesis. *Review of Educational Research, 59*, 1-41.

Prawat, R. S. (1992). From individual differences to learning communities: Our changing focus. *Educational Leadership, 49*(7), 9-13.

Prawat, R. S. (1993). The value of ideas: Problems versus possibilities in learning. *Educational Researcher, 22*(6), 5-16.

Premack, D. (1959). Toward empirical behavior laws: I. Positive reinforcement. *Psychological Review, 66*, 219-233.

Premack, D. (1963). Rate differential reinforcement in monkey manipulation. *Journal of Experimental Analysis of Behavior, 6*, 81-89.

Presseisen, B. Z., & Beyer, F. S. (1994, April). *Facing history and ourselves: An instructional tool for constructivist theory*. Paper presented at the annual meeting of the American Educational Research Association, New Orleans, LA.

Pressley, M. (1982). Elaboration and memory development. *Child Development, 53*, 296-309.

Pressley, M., Almasi, J., Schuder, T., Bergman, J., Hite, S., El-Dinary, P. B., & Brown, R. (1994). Transactional instruction of comprehension strategies: The Montgomery County, Maryland, SAIL program. *Reading and Writing Quarterly, 10*, 5-19.

Pressley, M., Borkowski, J. G., & Schneider, W. (1987). Cognitive strategies: Good strategy users coordinate metacognition and knowledge. In R. Vasta (Ed.), *Annals of child development* (Vol. 4). Greenwich, CT: JAI Press.

Pressley, M., El-Dinary, P. B., Marks, M. B., Brown, R., & Stein, S. (1992). Good strategy instruction is motivating and interesting. In K. A. Renninger, S. Hidi, & A. Krapp (Eds.), *The role of interest in learning and development*. Hillsdale, NJ: Erlbaum.

Pressley, M., Harris, K. R., & Marks, M. B. (1992). But good strategy instructors are constructivists! *Educational Psychology Review, 4*, 3-31.

Pressley, M., Levin, J. R., & Delaney, H. D. (1982). The mnemonic keyword method. *Review of Educational Research, 52*, 61-91.

Pressley, M. (with McCormick, C. B.) (1995). *Advanced educational psychology for educators, researchers, and policymakers*. New York: HarperCollins.

Pressley, M., Snyder, B. L., & Cariglia-Bull, T. (1987). How can good strategy use be taught to children? Evaluation of six alternative approaches. In S. M. Cormier & J. D. Hagman (Eds.), *Transfer of learning: Contemporary research and applications*. San Diego: Academic Press.

Pressley, M., Woloshyn, V., Lysynchuk, L. M., Martin, V., Wood, E., & Willoughby, T. (1990). A primer of research on cognitive strategy instruction: The important issues and how to address them. *Educational Psychology Review, 2*, 1-58.

Pressley, M., Yokoi, L., van Meter, P., Van Etten, S., & Freebern, G. (1997). Some of the reasons why preparing for exams is so hard: What can be done to make it easier? *Educational Psychology Review, 9*, 1-38.

Price-Williams, D. R., Gordon, W., & Ramirez, M. (1969). Skill and conservation. *Developmental Psychology, 1*, 769.

Pritchard, R. (1990). The effects of cultural schemata on reading processing strategies. *Reading Research Quarterly, 25*, 273-295.

Proctor, R. W., & Dutta, A. (1995). *Skill acquisition and human performance*. Thousand Oaks, CA: Sage.

Pruitt, R. P. (1989). Fostering creativity: The innovative classroom environment. *Educational Horizons, 68*(1), 51-54.

Pulos, S. (1997). Adolescents' implicit theories of physical phenomena: A matter of gravity. *International Journal of Behavioral Development, 20*, 493-507.

Pulos, S., & Linn, M. C. (1981). Generality of the controlling variables scheme in early adolescence. *Journal of Early Adolescence, 1*, 26-37.

Purcell-Gates, V., McIntyre, E., & Freppon, P. A. (1995). Learning written storybook language in school: A comparison of low-SES children in skills-based and whole language classrooms. *American Educational Research Journal, 32*, 659-685.

Purdie, N., & Hattie, J. (1996). Cultural differences in the use of strategies for self-regulated learning. *American Educational Research Journal, 33*, 845-871.

Purdie, N., Hattie, J., & Douglas, G. (1996). Student conceptions of learning and their use of self-regulated learning strategies: A cross-cultural comparison. *Journal of Educational Psychology, 88*, 87-100.

Putnam, R. T. (1992). Thinking and authority in elementary-school mathematics tasks. In J. Brophy (Ed.), *Advances in research on teaching: Vol. 3. Planning and managing learning tasks and activities*. Greenwich, CT: JAI Press.

Qin, Z., Johnson, D. W., & Johnson, R. T. (1995). Cooperative versus competitive efforts and problem solving. *Review of Educational Research, 65*, 129-143.

Quellmalz, E., & Hoskyn, J. (1997). Classroom assessment of reading strategies. In G. D. Phye (Ed.), *Handbook of classroom assessment: Learning, achievement, and adjustment*. San Diego: Academic Press.

Quill, K. A. (1995). Visually cued instruction for children with autism and pervasive developmental disorders. *Focus on Autistic Behavior, 10*(3), 10-20.

Raber, S. M. (1990, April). *A school system's look at its dropouts: Why they left school and what has happened to them*. Paper presented at the annual meeting of the American Educational Research Association, Boston.

Rabinowitz, M., & Glaser, R. (1985). Cognitive structure and process in highly competent performance. In F. D. Horowitz & M. O'Brien (Eds.), *The gifted and the talented: Developmental perspectives*. Washington, DC: American Psychological Association.

Rachlin, H. (1989). *Judgment, decision, and choice: A cognitive/behavioral synthesis*. New York: W. H. Freeman.

Rachlin, H. (1991). *Introduction to modern behaviorism* (3rd ed.). New York: W. H. Freeman.

Radke-Yarrow, M., Zahn-Waxler, C., & Chapman, M. (1983). Children's prosocial dispositions and behavior. In E. M. Hetherington (Ed.), *Handbook of* child psychology: Vol. 4. Socialization, personality, and social development. New York: Wiley.

Radziszewska, B., & Rogoff, B. (1991). Children's guided participation in planning imaginary errands with skilled adult or peer partners. *Developmental Psychology, 27,* 381-389.

Rakow, S. J. (1984). What's happening in elementary science: A national assessment. *Science and Children, 21*(4), 39-40.

Ramey, C. T. (1992). High-risk children and IQ: Altering intergenerational patterns. *Intelligence, 16,* 239-256.

Ramey, C. T., & Ramey, S. L. (1998). Early intervention and early experience. *American Psychologist, 53,* 109-120.

Ramsey, P. G. (1987). *Teaching and learning in a diverse world: Multicultural education for young children.* New York: Teachers College Press.

Rapport, M. D., Murphy, H. A., & Bailey, J. S. (1982). Ritalin vs. response cost in the control of hyperactive children: A within-subject comparison. *Journal of Applied Behavior Analysis, 15,* 205-216.

Raudenbush, S. W. (1984). Magnitude of teacher expectancy effects on pupil IQ as a function of credibility induction: A synthesis of findings from 18 experiments. *Journal of Educational Psychology, 76,* 85-97.

Redfield, D. L., & Rousseau, E. W. (1981). A meta-analysis of experimental research on teacher questioning behavior. *Review of Educational Research, 51,* 237-245.

Reeve, R. E. (1990). ADHD: Facts and fallacies. *Intervention in School and Clinic, 26*(2), 70-78.

Reich, P. A. (1986). *Language development.* Upper Saddle River, NJ: Prentice Hall.

Reid, N. (1989). Contemporary Polynesian conceptions of giftedness. *Gifted Education International, 6*(1), 30-38.

Reimann, P., & Schult, T. J. (1996). Turning examples into cases: Acquiring knowledge structures for analogical problem solving. *Educational Psychologist, 31,* 123-132.

Reimer, J., Paolitto, D. P., & Hersh, R. H. (1983). *Promoting moral growth: From Piaget to Kohlberg* (2nd ed.). White Plains, NY: Longman.

Reis, S. M. (1989). Reflections on policy affecting the education of gifted and talented students: Past and future perspectives. *American Psychologist, 44,* 399-408.

Reisberg, D. (1997). *Cognition: Exploring the science of the mind.* New York: W. W. Norton.

Reisberg, D., & Heuer, F. (1992). Remembering the details of emotional events. In E. Winograd & U. Neisser (Eds.), *Affect and accuracy in recall: Studies of "flashbulb" memories.* Cambridge, England: Cambridge University Press.

Reiter, S. N. (1994). Teaching dialogically: Its relationship to critical thinking in college students. In P. R. Pintrich, D. R. Brown, & C. E. Weinstein (Eds.), *Student motivation, cognition, and learning: Essays in honor of Wilbert J. McKeachie.* Hillsdale, NJ: Erlbaum.

Renkl, A., Mandl, H., & Gruber, H. (1996). Inert knowledge: Analyses and remedies. *Educational Psychologist, 31,* 115-121.

Renninger, K. A., Hidi, S., & Krapp, A. (Eds.). (1992). *The role of interest in learning and development.* Hillsdale, NJ: Erlbaum.

Renzulli, J. S. (1978). What makes giftedness? Reexamining a definition. *Phi Delta Kappan, 60,* 180-184.

Renzulli, J. S., & Reis, S. M. (1986). The enrichment triad/revolving door model: A school wide plan for the development of creative productivity. In J. Renzulli (Ed.), *Systems and models for developing programs for the gifted and talented.* Mansfield Center, CT: Creative Learning Press.

Rescorla, R. A. (1967). Pavlovian conditioning and its proper control procedures. *Psychological Review, 74,* 71-80.

Rescorla, R. A. (1988). Pavlovian conditioning: It's not what you think it is. *American Psychologist, 43,* 151-160.

Resnick, L. B. (1983). Mathematics and science learning: A new conception. *Science, 220,* 477-478.

Resnick, L. B. (1989). Developing mathematical knowledge. *American Psychologist, 44,* 162-169.

Resnick, L. B., Bill, V. L., Lesgold, S. B., & Leer, M. N. (1991). Thinking in arithmetic class. In B. Means, C. Chelemer, & M. S. Knapp (Eds.), *Teaching advanced skills to at-risk students.* San Francisco: Jossey-Bass.

Reusser, K. (1990, April). *Understanding word arithmetic problems: Linguistic and situational factors.* Paper presented at the annual meeting of the American Educational Research Association, Boston.

Reutzel, D. R., & Cooter, R. B., Jr. (1999). *Balanced reading strategies and practices.* Upper Saddle River, NJ: Merrill/Prentice Hall.

Reynolds, M. C. (1984). Classification of students with handicaps. In E. W. Gordon (Ed.), *Review of research in education, No. 11.* Washington, DC: American Educational Research Association.

Reynolds, M. C., & Birch, J. W. (1988). *Adaptive mainstreaming: A primer for teachers and principals* (3rd ed.). White Plains, NY: Longman.

Reynolds, R. E., & Shirey, L. L. (1988). The role of attention in studying and learning. In C. E. Weinstein, E. T. Goetz, & P. A. Alexander (Eds.), *Learning and study strategies: Issues in assessment, instruction, and evaluation.* San Diego: Academic Press.

Reynolds, R. E., Taylor, M. A., Steffensen, M. S., Shirey, L. L., & Anderson, R. C. (1982). Cultural schemata and reading comprehension. *Reading Research Quarterly, 17,* 353-366.

Ricciuti, H. N. (1993). Nutrition and mental development. *Current Directions in Psychological Science, 2,* 43-46.

Rice, M., Hadley, P. A., & Alexander, A. L. (1993). Social biases toward children with speech and language impairments: A correlative causal model of language limitations. *Applied Psycholinguistics, 14,* 445-471.

Richards, C. M., Symons, D. K., Greene, C. A., & Szuszkiewicz, T. A. (1995). The bidirectional relationship between achievement and externalizing behavior disorders. *Journal of Learning Disabilities, 28,* 8-17.

Riding, R. J., & Calvey, I. (1981). The assessment of verbal-imagery learning styles and their effect on the recall of concrete and abstract prose passages by 11-year-old children. *British Journal of Psychology, 72,* 59-64.

Rimm, D. C., & Masters, J. C. (1974). *Behavior therapy: Techniques and empirical findings.* San Diego: Academic Press.

Ripple, R. E. (1989). Ordinary creativity. *Contemporary Educational Psychology, 14,* 189-202.

Ritts, V., Patterson, M. L., & Tubbs, M. E. (1992). Expectations, impressions, and judgments of physically attractive students: A review. *Review of Educational Research, 62,* 413-426.

Ritvo, E. R., & Freeman, B. J. (1978). National Society for Autistic Children definition of the syndrome of autism. *Journal of Autism and Childhood Schizophrenia, 8,* 162-167.

Roberge, J. J. (1970). A study of children's abilities to reason with basic principles of deductive reasoning. *American Educational Research Journal, 7,* 583-596.

Robinson, A. (1991). Cooperation or exploitation? The argument against cooperative learning for talented students. *Journal for the Education of the Gifted, 14,* 9-27.

Roblyer, M. D., Castine, W. H., & King, F. J. (1988). *Assessing the impact of computer-based instruction: A review of recent research.* New York: Haworth.

Roderick, M. (1994). Grade retention and school dropout: Investigating the association. *American Educational Research Journal, 31,* 729-759.

Rogers, C. R. (1983). *Freedom to learn for the 80's.* Upper Saddle River, NJ: Merrill/Prentice Hall.

Rogoff, B. (1990). *Apprenticeship in thinking: Cognitive development in social context.* New York: Oxford University Press.

Rogoff, B. (1991). Social interaction as apprenticeship in thinking: Guidance and participation in spatial planning. In L. B. Resnick, J. M. Levine, & S. D. Teasley (Eds.), *Perspectives on socially shared cognition.* Washington, DC: American Psychological Association.

Rogoff, B. (1994, April). *Developing understanding of the idea of communities of learners.* Paper presented at the annual meeting of the American Educational Research Association, New Orleans, LA.

Rogoff, B., Matusov, E., & White, C. (1996). Models of teaching and learning: Participation in a community of learners. In D. R. Olson & N. Torrance (Eds.), *The handbook of education and human development: New models of learning, teaching, and schooling.* Cambridge, MA: Blackwell.

Rogoff, B., & Morelli, G. (1989). Perspectives on children's development from cultural psychology. *American Psychologist, 44,* 343-348.

Rogoff, B., & Waddell, K. J. (1982). Memory for information organized in a scene by children from two cultures. *Child Development, 53,* 1224-1228.

Rortvedt, A. K., & Miltenberger, R. G. (1994). Analysis of a high-probability instructional sequence and time-out in the treatment of child noncompliance. *Journal of Applied Behavior Analysis, 27,* 327-330.

Rosch, E. H. (1973a). Natural categories. *Cognitive Psychology, 4,* 328-350.

Rosch, E. H. (1973b). On the internal structure of perceptual and semantic categories. In T. E. Moore (Ed.), *Cognitive development and the acquisition of language.* San Diego: Academic Press.

Rosch, E. H. (1977). Human categorization. In N. Warren (Ed.), *Advances in cross-cultural psychology* (Vol. 1). San Diego: Academic Press.

Rosch, E. H., Mervis, C. B., Gray, W. D., Johnson, D. M., & Boyes-Braem, P. (1976). Basic objects in natural categories. *Cognitive Psychology, 8,* 382-439.

Rose, S. C., & Thornburg, K. R. (1984). Mastery motivation and need for approval in young children: Effects of age, sex, and reinforcement condition. *Educational Research Quarterly, 9*(1), 34-42.

Rosenshine, B., & Meister, C. (1992). The use of scaffolds for teaching higher-level cognitive strategies. *Educational Leadership, 49*(7), 26-33.

Rosenshine, B., & Meister, C. (1994). Reciprocal teaching: A review of the research. *Review of Educational Research, 64,* 479-530.

Rosenshine, B., Meister, C., & Chapman, S. (1996). Teaching students to generate questions: A review of the intervention studies. *Review of Educational Research, 66,* 181-221.

Rosenshine, B. V., & Stevens, R. (1986). Teaching functions. In M. C. Wittrock (Ed.), *Handbook of research on teaching* (3rd ed.). New York: Macmillan.

Rosenthal, R. (1994). Interpersonal expectancy effects: A 30-year perspective. *Current Directions in Psychological Science, 3,* 176-179.

Rosenthal, R., & Rubin, D. B. (1982). Further meta-analytic procedures for assessing cognitive gender differences. *Journal of Educational Psychology, 74,* 708-712.

Rosenthal, T. L., Alford, G. S., & Rasp, L. M. (1972). Concept attainment, generalization, and retention through observation and verbal coding. *Journal of Experimental Child Psychology, 13,* 183-194.

Rosenthal, T. L., & Bandura, A. (1978). Psychological modeling: Theory and practice. In S. L. Garfield & A. E. Begia (Eds.), *Handbook of psychotherapy and behavior change: An empirical analysis* (2nd ed.). New York: Wiley.

Rosenthal, T. L., & Zimmerman, B. J. (1978). *Social learning and cognition.* San Diego: Academic Press.

Ross, B. H., & Spalding, T. L. (1994). Concepts and categories. In R. J. Sternberg (Ed.), *Handbook of perception and cognition* (Vol. 12). New York: Academic Press.

Ross, J. A. (1988). Controlling variables: A meta-analysis of training studies. *Review of Educational Research, 58,* 405-437.

Rosser, R. (1994). *Cognitive development: Psychological and biological perspectives.* Needham Heights, MA: Allyn & Bacon.

Roth, K. J. (1990). Developing meaningful conceptual understanding in science. In B. F. Jones & L. Idol (Eds.), *Dimensions of thinking and cognitive instruction.* Hillsdale, NJ: Erlbaum.

Roth, K. J., & Anderson, C. (1988). Promoting conceptual change from science textbooks. In P. Ramsden (Ed.), *Improving learning: New perspectives.* London: Kogan Page.

Roth, W. (1996). Where is the context in contextual word problems? Mathematical practices and products in grade 8 students' answers to story problems. *Cognition and Instruction, 14,* 487-527.

Roughead, W. G., & Scandura, J. M. (1968). What is learned in mathematical discovery. *Journal of Educational Psychology, 59,* 283-289.

Rowe, M. B. (1974). Wait-time and rewards as instructional variables, their influence on language, logic, and fate control: Part one—wait time. *Journal of Research in Science Teaching, 11,* 81-94.

Rowe, M. B. (1978). *Teaching science as continuous inquiry.* New York: McGraw-Hill.

Rowe, M. B. (1987). Wait-time: Slowing down may be a way of speeding up. *American Educator, 11,* 38-43, 47.

Ruble, D. N. (1980). A developmental perspective on theories of achievement motivation. In L. J. Fyans, Jr. (Ed.), *Achievement motivation: Recent trends in theory and research.* New York: Plenum Press.

Ruble, D. N. (1988). Sex-role development. In M. H. Bornstein & M. E. Lamb (Eds.), *Developmental psychology: An advanced textbook* (2nd ed.). Hillsdale, NJ: Erlbaum.

Ruble, D. N., & Ruble, T. L. (1982). Sex stereotypes. In A. G. Miller (Ed.), *In the eye of the beholder.* New York: Praeger.

Rudman, M. K. (1993). Multicultural children's literature: The search for universals. In M. K. Rudman (Ed.), *Children's literature: Resource for the classroom* (2nd ed.). Norwood, MA: Christopher-Gordon.

Rueda, R., & Moll, L. C. (1994). A sociocultural perspective on motivation. In H. F. O'Neil, Jr., & M. Drillings (Eds.), *Motivation: Theory and research.* Hillsdale, NJ: Erlbaum.

Ruef, M. B., Higgins, C., Glaeser, B., & Patnode, M. (1998). Positive behavioral support: Strategies for teachers. *Intervention in School and Clinic, 34*(1), 21-32.

Rueger, D. B., & Liberman, R. P. (1984). Behavioral family therapy for delinquent substance-abusing adolescents. *Journal of Drug Abuse, 14,* 403-418.

Ruff, H. A., & Lawson, K. R. (1990). Development of sustained, focused attention in young children during free play. *Developmental Psychology, 26,* 85-93.

Ruffman, T., Perner, J., Olson, D. R., & Doherty, M. (1993). Reflecting on scientific thinking: Children's understanding of the hypothesis-evidence relation. *Child Development, 64,* 1617-1636.

Rumberger, R. W. (1995). Dropping out of middle school: A multilevel analysis of students and schools. *American Educational Research Journal, 32,* 583-625.

Rumelhart, D. E., & Ortony, A. (1977). The representation of knowledge in memory. In R. C. Anderson, R. J. Spiro & W. E. Montague (Eds.), *Schooling and the acquisition of knowledge.* Hillsdale, NJ: Erlbaum.

Runco, M. A., & Chand, I. (1995). Cognition and creativity. *Educational Psychology Review, 7,* 243-267.

Rushton, J. P. (1980). *Altruism, socialization, and society.* Upper Saddle River, NJ: Prentice Hall.

Russ, S. W. (1993). *Affect and creativity: The role of affect and play in the creative process.* Hillsdale, NJ: Erlbaum.

Rutter, M. L. (1997). Nature-nurture integration: The example of antisocial behavior. *American Psychologist, 52,* 390-398.

Ryan, R. M., Connell, J. P., & Grolnick, W. S. (1992). When achievement is *not* intrinsically motivated: A theory of internalization and self-regulation in school. In A. K. Boggiano & T. S. Pittman (Eds.), *Achievement and motivation: A social-developmental perspective.* Cambridge, England: Cambridge University Press.

Ryan, R. M., Mims, V., & Koestner, R. (1983). Relation of reward contingency and interpersonal context to intrinsic motivation: A review and test using cognitive evaluation theory. *Journal of Personality and Social Psychology, 45,* 736-750.

Sabers, D. S., Cushing, K. S., & Berliner, D. C. (1991). Differences among teachers in a task characterized by simultaneity, multidimensionality, and immediacy. *American Educational Research Journal, 28,* 63-88.

Sacks, C. H., & Mergendoller, J. R. (1997). The relationship between teachers' theoretical orientation toward reading and student outcomes in kindergarten children with different initial reading abilities. *American Educational Research Journal, 34,* 721-739.

Sadker, M. P., & Miller, D. (1982). *Sex equity handbook for schools.* White Plains, NY: Longman.

Sadker, M. P., & Sadker, D. (1985). Sexism in the schoolroom of the '80s. *Psychology Today, 19,* 54-57.

Sadker, M. P., & Sadker, D. (1994). *Failing at fairness: How our schools cheat girls.* New York: Touchstone.

Sadker, M. P., Sadker, D., & Klein, S. (1991). The issue of gender in elementary and secondary education. In G. Grant (Ed.), *Review of research in education.* Washington, DC: American Educational Research Association.

Sadoski, M., Goetz, E. T., & Fritz, J. B. (1993). Impact of concreteness on comprehensibility, interest, and memory for text: Implications for dual coding theory and text design. *Journal of Educational Psychology, 85,* 291-304.

Salend, S. J., & Hofstetter, E. (1996). Adapting a problem-solving approach to teaching mathematics to students with mild disabilities. *Intervention in School and Clinic, 31*(4), 209-217.

Salend, S. J., & Taylor, L. (1993). Working with families: A cross-cultural perspective. *Remedial and Special Education, 14*(5), 25-32, 39.

Salisbury, C. L., Evans, I. M., & Palombaro, M. M. (1997). Collaborative problem solving to promote the inclusion of young children with significant disabilities in primary grades. *Exceptional Children, 63,* 195-210.

Saljo, R., & Wyndhamn, J. (1992). Solving everyday problems in the formal setting: An empirical study of the school as context for thought. In S. Chaiklin & J. Lave (Eds.), *Understanding practice.* New York: Cambridge University Press.

Salomon, G. (Ed.). (1993). *Distributed cognitions: Psychological and educational considerations.* Cambridge, England: Cambridge University Press.

Saltz, E. (1971). *The cognitive bases of human learning.* Homewood, IL: Dorsey.

Sanborn, M. P. (1979). Counseling and guidance needs of the gifted and talented. In A. H. Passow (Ed.), *The gifted and the talented: Their education and development. The seventy-eighth yearbook of the National Society for the Study of Education.* Chicago: University of Chicago Press.

Sanchez, F., & Anderson, M. L. (1990). Gang mediation: A process that works. *Principal, 69*(4), 54-56.

Sanders, C. E. (1997). Assessment during the preschool years. In G. D. Phye (Ed.), *Handbook of classroom assessment: Learning, achievement, and adjustment.* San Diego: Academic Press.

Sanders, M. G. (1996). Action teams in action: Interviews and observations in three schools in the Baltimore School—Family—Community Partnership Program.

Journal of Education for Students Placed at Risk, 1, 249-262.

Sanders, S. (1987). Cultural conflicts: An important factor in academic failures of American Indian students. *Journal of Multicultural Counseling and Development, 15*(2), 81-90.

Sands, D. J., & Wehmeyer, M. L. (Eds.). (1996). *Self-determination across the life span: Independence and choice for people with disabilities.* Baltimore: Paul H. Brookes.

Santiago, I. S. (1986). The education of Hispanics in the United States: Inadequacies of the American melting-pot theory. In D. Rothermund & J. Simon (Eds.), *Education and the integration of ethnic minorities.* New York: St. Martin's Press.

Sapon-Shevin, M., Dobbelaere, A., Corrigan, C., Goodman, K, & Mastin, M. (1998). Everyone here can play. *Educational Leadership, 56*(1), 42-45.

Sarason, I. G. (Ed.). (1980). *Test anxiety: Theory, research, and applications.* Hillsdale, NJ: Erlbaum.

Sarason, S. B. (1972). What research says about test anxiety in elementary school children. In A. R. Binter & S. H. Frey (Eds.), *The psychology of the elementary school child.* Chicago: Rand McNally.

Savin-Williams, R. C., & Demo, D. H. (1984). Developmental change and stability in adolescent self-concept. *Developmental Psychology, 20,* 1100-1110.

Sax, G. (1989). *Principles of educational and psychological measurement and evaluation* (3rd ed.). Belmont, CA: Wadsworth.

Sayeki, Y., Ueno, N., & Nagasaka, T. (1991). Mediation as a generative model for obtaining an area. *Learning and Instruction, 1,* 229-242.

Scarcella, R. (1990). *Teaching language-minority students in the multicultural classroom.* Upper Saddle River, NJ: Prentice Hall.

Scardamalia, M., & Bereiter, C. (1985). Fostering the development of self-regulation in children's knowledge processing. In S. F. Chipman, J. W. Segal, & R. Glaser (Eds.), *Thinking and learning skills: Vol. 2. Research and open questions.* Hillsdale, NJ: Erlbaum.

Scardamalia, M., & Bereiter, C. (1986). Research on written composition. In M. C. Wittrock (Ed.), *Handbook of research on teaching* (3rd ed.). New York: Macmillan.

Scardamalia, M., & Bereiter, C. (1987). *The psychology of written composition.* Hillsdale, NJ: Erlbaum.

Scardamalia, M., Bereiter, C., & Goelman, H. (1982). The role of production factors in writing ability. In M. Nystrand (Ed.), *What writers know: The language, process, and structure of written discourse.* New York: Academic Press.

Scarr, S., & Weinberg, R. A. (1976). IQ test performance of black children adopted by white families. *American Psychologist, 31,* 726-739.

Scevak, J. J., Moore, P. J., & Kirby, J. R. (1993). Training students to use maps to increase text recall. *Contemporary Educational Psychology, 18,* 401-413.

Schank, R. C., & Abelson, R. P. (1995). Knowledge and memory: The real story. In R. S. Wyer, Jr. (Ed.), *Knowledge and memory: The real story. Vol. VIII. Advances in social cognition.* Hillsdale, NJ: Erlbaum.

Schauble, L. (1990). Belief revision in children: The role of prior knowledge and strategies for generating evidence. *Journal of Experimental Child Psychology, 49,* 31-57.

Schauble, L. (1996). The development of scientific reasoning in knowledge-rich contexts. *Developmental Psychology, 32,* 102-119.

Schell, T. L., Klein, S. B., & Babey, S. H. (1996). Testing a hierarchical model of self-knowledge. *Psychological Science, 7,* 170-173.

Schepis, M. M., Reid, D. H., & Fitzgerald, J. R. (1987). Group instruction with profoundly retarded persons: Acquisition, generalization, and maintenance of a remunerative work skill. *Journal of Applied Behavior Analysis, 20,* 97-105.

Schiefele, U. (1991a). Interest, learning, and motivation. *Educational Psychologist, 26,* 299-323.

Schiefele, U. (1991b). Topic interest and levels of text comprehension. In A. K. Renninger, S. Hidi, & A. Krapp (Eds.), *"Interest" in development and learning.* Hillsdale, NJ: Erlbaum.

Schiefele, U. (1992). Topic interest and levels of text comprehension. In K. A. Renninger, S. Hidi, & A. Krapp (Eds.), *The role of interest in learning and development.* Hillsdale, NJ: Erlbaum.

Schiefele, U., Krapp, A., & Winteler, A. (1992). Interest as a predictor of academic achievement: A meta-analysis of research. In K. A. Renninger, S. Hidi, & A. Krapp (Eds.), *The role of interest in learning and development.* Hillsdale, NJ: Erlbaum.

Schiffman, G., Tobin, D., & Buchanan, B. (1984). Microcomputer instruction for the learning disabled. *Annual Review of Learning Disabilities, 2,* 134-136.

Schimmoeller, M. A. (1998, April). *Influence of private speech on the writing behaviors of young children: Four case studies.* Paper presented at the annual meeting of the American Educational Research Association, San Diego.

Schirmer, B. R. (1994). *Language and literacy development in children who are deaf.* Needham Heights, MA: Allyn & Bacon.

Schlaefli, A., Rest, J. R., & Thoma, S. J. (1985). Does moral education improve moral judgment? A meta-analysis of intervention studies using the defining issues test. *Review of Educational Research, 55,* 319-352.

Schliemann, A. D., & Carraher, D. W. (1993). Proportional reasoning in and out of school. In P. Light & G. Butterworth (Eds.), *Context and cognition: Ways of learning and knowing.* Hillsdale, NJ: Erlbaum.

Schloss, P. J., & Smith, M. A. (1994). *Applied behavior analysis in the classroom.* Needham Heights, MA: Allyn & Bacon.

Schmidt, R. A., & Bjork, R. A. (1992). New conceptualizations of practice: Common principles in three paradigms suggest new concepts for training. *Psychological Science, 3,* 207-217.

Schneider, J. J. (1998, April). *Developing multiple perspectives and audience awareness in elementary writers.* Paper presented at the annual meeting of the American Educational Research Association, San Diego.

Schneider, W. (1993). Domain-specific knowledge and memory performance in children. *Educational Psychology Review, 5,* 257-273.

Schneider, W., & Pressley, M. (1989). *Memory development between 2 and 20.* New York: Springer-Verlag.

Schneider, W., & Shiffrin, R. M. (1977). Controlled and automatic human information processing: I. Detection, search, and attention. *Psychological Review, 84,* 1-66.

Schoenfeld, A. H. (1982). Measures of problem-solving performance and problem-solving instruction. *Journal for Research in Mathematics Education, 13,* 31-49.

Schoenfeld, A. H. (1985a). *Mathematical problem solving.* San Diego: Academic Press.

Schoenfeld, A. H. (1985b). Metacognitive and epistemological issues in mathematical understanding. In E. A. Silver (Ed.), *Teaching and learning mathematical problem solving: Multiple research perspectives.* Hillsdale, NJ: Erlbaum.

Schoenfeld, A. H. (1988). When good teaching leads to bad results: The disasters of "well-taught" mathematics courses. *Educational Psychologist, 23,* 145-166.

Schoenfeld, A. H. (1992). Learning to think mathematically: Problem solving, metacognition, and sense making in mathematics. In D. A. Grouws (Ed.), *Handbook of research on mathematics teaching and learning.* New York: Macmillan.

Schoenfeld, A. H., & Hermann, D. J. (1982). Problem perception and knowledge structure in expert and novice mathematical problem solvers. *Journal of Experimental Psychology: Learning, Memory, and Cognition, 8,* 484-494.

Schofield, J. W. (1995). Improving intergroup relations among students. In J. A. Banks & C. A. M. Banks (Eds.), *Handbook of research on multicultural education.* New York: Macmillan.

Schommer, M. (1994a). An emerging conceptualization of epistemological beliefs and their role in learning. In R. Garner & P. A. Alexander (Eds.), *Beliefs about text and instruction with text.* Hillsdale, NJ: Erlbaum.

Schommer, M. (1994b). Synthesizing epistemological belief research: Tentative understandings and provocative confusions. *Educational Psychology Review, 6,* 293-319.

Schommer, M. (1997). The development of epistemological beliefs among secondary students: A longitudinal study. *Journal of Educational Psychology 89,* 37-40.

Schonert-Reichl, K. A. (1993). Empathy and social relationships in adolescents with behavioral disorders. *Behavioral Disorders, 18,* 189-204.

Schraw, G., & Moshman, D. (1995). Metacognitive theories. *Educational Psychology Review, 7,* 351-371.

Schraw, G., Potenza, M. T., & Nebelsick-Gullet, L. (1993). Constraints on the calibration of performance. *Contemporary Educational Psychology, 18,* 455-463.

Schraw, G., & Wade, S. (1991, April). *Selective learning strategies for relevant and important text information.* Paper presented at the annual meeting of the American Educational Research Association, Chicago.

Schreibman, L. (1988). *Autism.* Newbury Park, CA: Sage.

Schubert, J. G. (1986). Gender equity in computer learning. *Theory into Practice, 25,* 267-275.

Schultz, G. F., & Switzky, H. N. (1990). The development of intrinsic motivation in students with learning problems: Suggestions for more effective instructional practice. *Preventing School Failure, 34*(2), 14-20.

Schultz, K., & Lochhead, J. (1991). A view from physics. In M. U. Smith (Ed.), *Toward a unified theory of problem solving: Views from the content domains.* Hillsdale, NJ: Erlbaum.

Schumaker, J. B., & Hazel, J. S. (1984). Social skill assessment and training for the learning disabled:

Who's on first and what's on second? (Part 1). *Journal of Learning Disabilities, 17,* 422-431.

Schunk, D. H. (1982). Effects of effort attributional feedback on children's perceived self-efficacy and achievement. *Journal of Educational Psychology, 74,* 548-556.

Schunk, D. H. (1983). Developing children's self-efficacy and skills: The roles of social comparative information and goal setting. *Contemporary Educational Psychology, 8,* 76-86.

Schunk, D. H. (1989a). Self-efficacy and achievement behaviors. *Educational Psychology Review, 1,* 173-208.

Schunk, D. H. (1989b). Self-efficacy and cognitive skill learning. In C. Ames & R. Ames (Eds.), *Research on motivation in education: Vol. 3. Goals and cognitions.* San Diego: Academic Press.

Schunk, D. H. (1989c). Social cognitive theory and self-regulated learning. In B. J. Zimmerman & D. H. Schunk (Eds.), *Self-regulated learning and academic achievement: Theory, research, and practice.* New York: Springer-Verlag.

Schunk, D. H. (1990, April). *Socialization and the development of self-regulated learning: The role of attributions.* Paper presented at the annual meeting of the American Educational Research Association, Boston.

Schunk, D. H. (1991). *Learning theories: An educational perspective.* Upper Saddle River, NJ: Merrill/Prentice Hall.

Schunk, D. H. (1996). *Learning theories* (2nd ed.). Upper Saddle River, NJ: Merrill/Prentice Hall.

Schunk, D. H., & Hanson, A. R. (1985). Peer models: Influence on children's self-efficacy and achievement. *Journal of Educational Psychology, 77,* 313-322.

Schunk, D. H., Hanson, A. R., & Cox, P. D. (1987). Peer-model attributes and children's achievement behaviors. *Journal of Educational Psychology, 79,* 54-61.

Schunk, D. H., & Swartz, C. W. (1993). Goals and progress feedback: Effects on self-efficacy and writing achievement. *Contemporary Educational Psychology, 18,* 337-354.

Schunk, D. H., & Zimmerman, B. J. (1997). Social origins of self-regulatory competence. *Educational Psychologist, 32,* 195-208.

Schwartz, B., & Reisberg, D. (1991). *Learning and memory.* New York: Norton.

Schwebel, A. I., & Cherlin, D. L. (1972). Physical and social distancing in teacher-pupil relationships. *Journal of Educational Psychology, 63,* 543-550.

Scott, J., & Bushell, D. (1974). The length of teacher contacts and students' off-task behavior. *Journal of Applied Behavior Analysis, 7,* 39-44.

Scott, R. C. (1989). *Physical geography.* St. Paul, MN: West.

Scott-Jones, D. (1984). Family influences on cognitive development and school achievement. In E. W. Gordon (Ed.), *Review of research in education* (Vol. 11). Washington, DC: American Educational Research Association.

Scruggs, T. E., & Mastropieri, M. A. (1989). Mnemonic instruction of learning disabled students: A field-based evaluation. *Learning Disabilities Quarterly, 12,* 119-125.

Scruggs, T. E., & Mastropieri, M. A. (1992). Classroom applications of mnemonic instruction: Acquisition, maintenance, and generalization. *Exceptional Children, 58,* 219-229.

Scruggs, T. E., & Mastropieri, M. A. (1994). Successful mainstreaming in elementary science classes: A qualitative study of three reputational cases. *American Educational Research Journal, 31,* 785-811.

Seeley, K. (1989). Facilitators for the gifted. In J. Feldhusen, J. VanTassel-Baska, & K. Seeley, *Excellence in educating the gifted.* Denver, CO: Love.

Seixas, P. (1996). Conceptualizing the growth of historical understanding. In D. R. Olson & N. Torrance (Eds.), *The handbook of education and human development: New models of learning, teaching, and schooling.* Cambridge, MA: Blackwell.

Seligman, M. E. P. (1975). *Helplessness: On depression, development, and death.* San Francisco: W. H. Freeman.

Seligman, M. E. P. (1991). *Learned optimism.* New York: Knopf.

Selman, R. L. (1980). *The growth of interpersonal understanding.* San Diego: Academic Press.

Selman, R. L., & Byrne, D. F. (1974). A structural-developmental analysis of levels of role taking in middle childhood. *Child Development, 45,* 803-806.

Selman, R. L., & Schultz, L. H. (1990). *Making a friend in youth.* Chicago: University of Chicago Press.

Seltzer, V. C. (1982). *Adolescent social development: Dynamic functional interaction.* Lexington, MA: Heath.

Semb, G. B., & Ellis, J. A. (1994). Knowledge taught in school: What is remembered? *Review of Educational Research, 64,* 253-286.

Semb, G. B., Ellis, J. A., & Araujo, J. (1993). Long-term memory for knowledge learned in school. *Journal of Educational Psychology, 85,* 305-316.

Semmel, M. I., Gottlieb, J., & Robinson, N. M. (1979). Mainstreaming: Perspectives on educating handicapped children in the public school. In D. C. Berliner (Ed.), *Review of research in education* (Vol. 7). Washington, DC: American Educational Research Association.

Sfard, A. (1998). On two metaphors for learning and the dangers of choosing just one. *Educational Researcher, 27*(2), 4-13.

Shachar, H., & Sharan, S. (1994). Talking, relating, and achieving: Effects of cooperative learning and whole-class instruction. *Cognition and Instruction, 12,* 313-353.

Shaffer, D. R. (1988). *Social and personality development* (2nd ed.). Pacific Grove, CA: Brooks/Cole.

Shanahan, T., & Tierney, R. J. (1990). Reading-writing connections: The relations among three perspectives. In J. Zutell & S. McCormick (Eds.), *Literacy theory and research: Analyses from multiple paradigms. Thirty-ninth yearbook of the National Reading Conference.* Chicago: National Reading Conference.

Shatz, M., & Gelman, R. (1973). The development of communication skills: Modifications in the speech of young children as a function of the listener. *Monographs of the Society for Research in Child Development, 38*(5, Serial No. 152).

Shavelson, R. J., & Baxter, G. P. (1992). What we've learned about assessing hands-on science. *Educational Leadership, 49*(8), 20-25.

Shavelson, R. J., Baxter, G. P., & Pine, J. (1992). Performance assessments: Political rhetoric and measurement reality. *Educational Researcher, 21*(4), 22-27.

Sheldon, A. (1974). The role of parallel function in the acquisition of relative clauses in English. *Journal of Verbal Learning and Verbal Behavior, 13,* 272-281.

Shepard, R. N., & Metzler, J. (1971). Mental rotation of three-dimensional objects. *Science, 171,* 701-703.

Sherrill, D., Horowitz, B., Friedman, S. T., & Salisbury, J. L. (1970). Seating aggregation as an index of contagion. *Educational and Psychological Measurement, 30,* 663-668.

Sheveland, D. E. (1994, April). *Motivational factors in the development of independent readers.* Paper presented at the annual meeting of the American Educational Research Association, New Orleans, LA.

Shipman, S., & Shipman, V. C. (1985). Cognitive styles: Some conceptual, methodological, and applied issues. In E. W. Gordon (Ed.), *Review of research in education* (Vol. 12). Washington, DC: American Educational Research Association.

Short, E. J., Schatschneider, C. W., & Friebert, S. E. (1993). Relationship between memory and metamemory performance: A comparison of specific and general strategy knowledge. *Journal of Educational Psychology, 85,* 412-423.

Shrager, L., & Mayer, R. E. (1989). Note-taking fosters generative learning strategies in novices. *Journal of Educational Psychology, 81,* 263-264.

Shrigley, R. L. (1979). Strategies in classroom management. *NASSP Bulletin, 63*(428), 1-9.

Shuell, T. J. (1996). Teaching and learning in a classroom context. In D. C. Berliner & R. C. Calfee (Eds.), *Handbook of educational psychology.* New York: Macmillan.

Shulman, L. S. (1986). Those who understand: Knowledge growth in teaching. *Educational Researcher, 15,* 4-14.

Shulman, L. S., & Quinlan, K. M. (1996). The comparative psychology of school subjects. In D. C. Berliner & R. C. Calfee (Eds.), *Handbook of educational psychology.* New York: Macmillan.

Shymansky, J. A., Hedges, L. V., & Woodworth, G. (1990). A reassessment of the effects of inquiry-based science curricula of the 60s on student performance. *Journal of Research in Science Teaching, 27,* 127-144.

Sieber, J. E., Kameya, L. I., & Paulson, F. L. (1970). Effect of memory support on the problem-solving ability of test-anxious children. *Journal of Educational Psychology, 61,* 159-168.

Siegel, L., & Hodkin, B. (1982). The garden path to the understanding of cognitive development: Has Piaget led us into the poison ivy? In S. Modgil & C. Modgil (Eds.), *Jean Piaget: Consensus and controversy.* New York: Praeger.

Siegler, R. S. (1989). Mechanisms of cognitive growth. *Annual Review of Psychology, 40,* 353-379.

Siegler, R. S. (1991). *Children's thinking* (2nd ed.). Upper Saddle River, NJ: Prentice Hall.

Siegler, R. S. (1994). Cognitive variability: A key to understanding cognitive development. *Current Directions in Psychological Science, 3,* 1-5.

Siegler, R. S., & Ellis, S. (1996). Piaget on childhood. *Psychological Science, 7,* 211-215.

Siegler, R. S., & Richards, D. D. (1982). The development of intelligence. In R. J. Sternberg (Ed.), *Handbook of human intelligence.* Cambridge, England: Cambridge University Press.

Silberman, M. L., & Wheelan, S.A. (1980). *How to discipline without feeling guilty: Assertive relationships with children.* Champaign, IL: Research Press.

Silver, E.A., & Kenney, P.A. (1995). Sources of assessment information for instructional guidance in mathematics. In T. Romberg (Ed.), *Reform in school mathematics and authentic assessment.* Albany, NY: State University of New York Press.

Silver, E.A., Shapiro, L. J., & Deutsch,A. (1991,April). *Sense-making and the solution of division problems involving remainders:An examination of students' solution processes and their interpretations of solutions.* Paper presented at the annual meeting of the American Educational Research Association, Chicago.

Simmons, R. G., & Blyth, D.A. (1987). *Moving into adolescence: The impact of pubertal change and school context.* New York: Aldine de Gruyter.

Simon, H.A. (1974). How big is a chunk? *Science, 183,* 482–488.

Simons, R. L., Whitbeck, L. B., Conger, R. D., & Conger, K. J. (1991). Parenting factors, social skills, and value commitments as precursors to school failure, involvement with deviant peers, and delinquent behavior. *Journal of Youth and Adolescence, 20,* 645–664.

Singley, M. K., & Anderson, J. R. (1989). *The transfer of cognitive skill.* Cambridge, MA: Harvard University Press.

Sisk, D.A. (1989). Identifying and nurturing talent among American Indians. In C. J. Maker & S.W. Schiever (Eds.), *Critical issues in gifted education: Vol. 2. Defensible programs for cultural and ethnic minorities.* Austin,TX: Pro-Ed.

Sizer,T. R. (1992). *Horace's school: Redesigning the American high school.* Boston: Houghton Mifflin.

Skeels, H. M. (1966).Adult status of children with contrasting early life experience:A follow-up study. *Monographs of the Society for Research in Child Development, 31*(Serial No. 105).

Skiba, R., & Raison, J. (1990). Relationship between the use of time-out and academic achievement. *Exceptional Children, 57,* 36–46.

Skinner, B. F. (1953). *Science and human behavior.* New York: Macmillan.

Skinner, B. F. (1954).The science of learning and the art of teaching. *Harvard Educational Review, 24,* 86–97.

Skinner, B. F. (1968). *The technology of teaching.* New York:Appleton-Century-Crofts.

Slavin, R. E. (1983).When does cooperative learning increase student achievement? *Psychological Bulletin, 94,* 429–445.

Slavin, R. E. (1987).Ability grouping and student achievement in elementary schools:A best-evidence synthesis. *Review of Educational Research, 57,* 293–336.

Slavin, R. E. (1989). Students at risk of school failure: The problem and its dimensions. In R. E. Slavin, N. L. Karweit, & N.A. Madden (Eds.), *Effective programs for students at risk.* Needham Heights, MA:Allyn & Bacon.

Slavin, R. E. (1990). *Cooperative learning: Theory, research, and practice.* Upper Saddle River, NJ: Prentice Hall.

Slavin, R. E., Karweit, N. L., & Madden, N.A. (Eds.). (1989). *Effective programs for students at risk.* Needham Heights, MA:Allyn & Bacon.

Slavin, R. E., Madden, N.A., & Karweit, N. L. (1989). Effective programs for students at risk: Conclusions for practice and policy. In R. E. Slavin, N. L. Karweit, & N.A. Madden (Eds.), *Effective programs for students at risk.* Boston, MA:Allyn & Bacon.

Sleeter, C. E., & Grant, C.A. (1994). *Making choices for multicultural education: Five approaches to race, class, and gender* (2nd ed.). Upper Saddle River, NJ: Merrill/Prentice Hall.

Slusher, M. P., & Anderson, C.A. (1996). Using causal persuasive arguments to change beliefs and teach new information: The mediating role of explanation availability and evaluation bias in the acceptance of knowledge. *Journal of Educational Psychology, 88,* 110–122.

Small, M.Y., Lovett, S. B., & Scher, M. S. (1993). Pictures facilitate children's recall of unillustrated expository prose. *Journal of Educational Psychology, 85,* 520–528.

Small, R.V., & Grabowski, B. L. (1992).An exploratory study of information-seeking behaviors and learning with hypermedia information systems. *Journal of Educational Multimedia and Hypermedia, 1,* 445–464.

Smetana, J. G. (1983). Social-cognitive development: Domain distinctions and coordinations. *Developmental Review, 3,* 131–147.

Smith, C., Maclin, D., Grosslight, L., & Davis, H. (1997). Teaching for understanding:A study of students' preinstruction theories of matter and a comparison of the effectiveness of two approaches to teaching about matter and density. *Cognition and Instruction, 15,* 317–393.

Smith, D. C., & Neale, D. C. (1991).The construction of subject-matter knowledge in primary science teaching. In J. Brophy (Ed.), *Advances in research on teaching: Vol. 2. Teacher's knowledge of subject matter as it relates to their teaching practice.* Greenwich, CT: JAI Press.

Smith, D. J., Young, K. R., West, R. P., Morgan, R. P., & Rhode, G. (1988). Reducing the disruptive behavior of junior high school students:A classroom self-management procedure. *Behavioral Disorders, 13,* 231–239.

Smith, F. (1988). *Understanding reading* (4th ed.). Hillsdale, NJ: Erlbaum.

Smith, J., & Russell, G. (1984).Why do males and females differ? Children's beliefs about sex differences. *Sex Roles, 11,* 1111–1120.

Smith, K., Johnson, D.W., & Johnson, R.T. (1981). Can conflict be constructive? Controversy versus concurrence seeking in learning groups. *Journal of Educational Psychology, 73,* 651–663.

Smith, M. U. (1991).A view from biology. In M. U. Smith (Ed.), *Toward a unified theory of problem solving: Views from the content domains.* Hillsdale, NJ: Erlbaum.

Smith, P. B., & Bond, M. H. (1994). *Social psychology across cultures:Analysis and perspectives.* Needham Heights, MA:Allyn & Bacon.

Smith, R. E., & Smoll, F. L. (1997). Coaching the coaches: Youth sports as a scientific and applied behavioral setting. *Current Directions in Psychological Science, 6*(1), 16–21.

Sneider, C., & Pulos, S. (1983). Children's cosmographies: Understanding the earth's shape and gravity. *Science Education, 67,* 205–221.

Snow, C. E (1990). Rationales for native language instruction: Evidence from research. In A. M. Padilla, H. H. Fairchild, & C. M.Valadez (Eds.), *Bilingual education: Issues and strategies.* Newbury Park, CA: Sage.

Snow, R. E., Corno, L., & Jackson, D., III (1996). Individual differences in affective and conative functions. In D. C. Berliner & R. C. Calfee (Eds.), *Handbook of educational psychology.* New York: Macmillan.

Solnick, J.V., Rincover,A., & Peterson, C. R. (1977). Some determinants of the reinforcing and punishing effects of timeout. *Journal of Applied Behavior Analysis, 10,* 415–424.

Sosniak, L.A., & Stodolsky, S. S. (1994). Making connections: Social studies education in an urban fourth-grade classroom. In J. Brophy (Ed.), *Advances in research on teaching: Vol. 4. Case studies of teaching and learning in social studies.* Greenwich, CT: JAI Press.

Spandel,V. (1997). Reflections on portfolios. In G. D. Phye (Ed.), *Handbook of academic learning: Construction of knowledge.* San Diego:Academic Press.

Spaulding, C. L. (1992). *Motivation in the classroom.* New York: McGraw-Hill.

Spearman, C. (1904). General intelligence, objectively determined and measured. *American Journal of Psychology, 15,* 201–293.

Spearman, C. (1927). *The abilities of man: Their nature and measurement.* New York: Macmillan.

Spencer, M. B., & Markstrom-Adams, C. (1990). Identity processes among racial and ethnic minority children in America. *Child Development, 61,* 290–310.

Sperling, G. (1967). Successive approximations to a model for short-term memory. *Acta Psychologia, 27,* 285–292.

Sperling, M. (1996). Revisiting the writing-speaking connection: Challenges for research on writing and writing instruction. *Review of Educational Research, 66,* 53–86.

Spicker, H. H. (1992). Identifying and enriching: Rural gifted children. *Educational Horizons, 70*(2), 60–65.

Spires, H.A. (1990,April). *Learning from a lecture: Effects of comprehension monitoring.* Paper presented at the annual meeting of the American Educational Research Association, Boston.

Spires, H.A., & Donley, J. (1998). Prior knowledge activation: Inducing engagement with informational texts. *Journal of Educational Psychology, 90,* 249–260.

Spires, H.A., Donley, J., & Penrose,A. M. (1990,April). *Prior knowledge activation: Inducing text engagement in reading to learn.* Paper presented at the annual meeting of the American Educational Research Association, Boston.

Spivey, N. N. (1997). *The constructivist metaphor: Reading, writing, and the making of meaning.* San Diego:Academic Press.

Sprafkin, C., Serbin, L.A., Denier, C., & Connor, J. M. (1983). Sex-differentiated play: Cognitive consequences and early interventions. In M. B. Liss (Ed.), *Social and cognitive skills: Sex roles and children's play.* San Diego:Academic Press.

Sroufe, L.A. (1983). Infant-caregiver attachment and patterns of adaptation in preschool: The roots of maladaptation. In M. Perlmutter (Ed.), *Minnesota Symposium on Child Psychology* (Vol. 16). Hillsdale, NJ: Erlbaum.

Stacey, K. (1992). Mathematical problem solving in groups:Are two heads better than one? *Journal of Mathematical Behavior, 11,* 261–275.

Stahl, S. A., McKenna, M. C., & Pagnucco, J. R. (1994). The effects of whole-language instruction: An update and reappraisal. *Educational Psychologist, 29,* 175-185.

Stahl, S. A., & Miller, P. D. (1989). Whole language and language experience approaches for beginning reading: A quantitative research synthesis. *Review of Educational Research, 59,* 87-116.

Stainback, S., & Stainback, W. (Eds.). (1985). *Integrating students with severe handicaps into regular schools.* Reston, VA: Council for Exceptional Children.

Stainback, S., & Stainback, W. (1990). Inclusive schooling. In W. Stainback & S. Stainback (Eds.), *Support networks for inclusive schooling: Interdependent integrated education.* Baltimore: Paul H. Brookes.

Stainback, S., & Stainback, W. (1992). Schools as inclusive communities. In W. Stainback & S. Stainback (Eds.), *Controversial issues confronting special education: Divergent perspectives.* Needham Heights, MA: Allyn & Bacon.

Stainback, W., & Stainback, S. (1992). *Controversial issues confronting special education: Divergent perspectives.* Boston: Allyn & Bacon.

Stanley, J. C. (1980). On educating the gifted. *Educational Researcher, 9*(3), 8-12.

Stanovich, K. E. (1998). Cognitive neuroscience and educational psychology: What season is it? *Educational Psychology Review, 10,* 419-426.

Steffensen, M. S., Joag-Dev, C., & Anderson, R. C. (1979). A cross-cultural perspective on reading comprehension. *Reading Research Quarterly, 15,* 10-29.

Steinberg, E. R. (1989). Cognition and learner control: A literature review, 1977-1988. *Journal of Computer-Based Instruction, 16*(4), 117-121.

Steinberg, L. (1993). *Adolescence* (3rd ed.). New York: McGraw-Hill.

Steinberg, L., Blinde, P. L., & Chan, K. S. (1984). Dropping out among language minority youth. *Review of Educational Research, 54,* 113-132.

Steinberg, L., Elmen, J., & Mounts, N. (1989). Authoritative parenting, psychosocial maturity, and academic success among adolescents. *Child Development, 60,* 1424-1436.

Stepans, J. (1991). Developmental patterns in students' understanding of physics concepts. In S. M. Glynn, R. H. Yeany, & B. K. Britton (Eds.), *The psychology of learning science.* Hillsdale, NJ: Erlbaum.

Stephens, T. M., Blackhurst, A. E., & Magliocca, L. A. (1988). *Teaching mainstreamed students* (2nd ed.). Oxford, England: Pergamon.

Sternberg, R. J. (1984). Toward a triarchic theory of human intelligence. *Behavioral and Brain Sciences, 7,* 269-287.

Sternberg, R. J. (1985). *Beyond IQ: A triarchic theory of human intelligence.* Cambridge, England: Cambridge University Press.

Sternberg, R. J. (1996a). Educational psychology has fallen, but it can get up. *Educational Psychology Review, 8,* 175-185.

Sternberg, R. J. (1996b). Myths, countermyths, and truths about intelligence. *Educational Researcher, 25*(2), 11-16.

Sternberg, R. J. (1997). The concept of intelligence and its role in lifelong learning and success. *American Psychologist, 52,* 1030-1037.

Sternberg, R. J., & Detterman, D. K. (Eds.). (1986). *What is intelligence? Contemporary views on its nature and definition.* Norwood, NJ: Ablex.

Sternberg, R. J., & Frensch, P. A. (1993). Mechanisms of transfer. In D. K. Detterman & R. J. Sternberg (Eds.), *Transfer on trial: Intelligence, cognition, and instruction.* Norwood, NJ: Ablex.

Sternberg, R. J., & Horvath, J. A. (1995). A prototype view of expert teaching. *Educational Researcher, 24*(6), 9-17.

Sternberg, R. J., & Wagner, R. K. (Eds.). (1994). *Mind in context: Interactionist perspectives on human intelligence.* Cambridge, England: Cambridge University Press.

Sternberg, R. J., & Zhang, L. (1995). What do we mean by giftedness? A pentagonal implicit theory. *Gifted Child Quarterly, 39,* 88-94.

Steuer, F. B., Applefield, J. M., & Smith, R. (1971). Televised aggression and the interpersonal aggression of preschool children. *Journal of Experimental Child Psychology, 11,* 442-447.

Stevahn, L., Johnson, D. W., Johnson, R. T., & Real, D. (1996). The impact of a cooperative or individualistic context on the effectiveness of conflict resolution training. *American Educational Research Journal, 33,* 801-823.

Stevens, R. J., & Slavin, R. E. (1995). The cooperative elementary school: Effects of students' achievement, attitudes, and social relations. *American Educational Research Journal, 32,* 321-351.

Stevenson, H. C., & Fantuzzo, J. W. (1986). The generality and social validity of a competency-based self-control training intervention for underachieving students. *Journal of Applied Behavior Analysis, 19,* 269-272.

Stevenson, H. W., Chen, C., & Uttal, D. H. (1990). Beliefs and achievement: A study of black, white, and Hispanic children. *Child Development, 61,* 508-523.

Stiggins, R. J. (1997). *Student-centered classroom assessment* (2nd ed.). Upper Saddle River, NJ: Merrill/Prentice Hall.

Stiggins, R. J., & Conklin, N. F. (1992). *In teachers' hands: Investigating the practices of classroom assessment.* Albany: State University of New York Press.

Stipek, D. J. (1981). Children's perceptions of their own and their classmates' ability. *Journal of Educational Psychology, 73,* 404-410.

Stipek, D. J. (1984). Sex differences in children's attributions for success and failure on math and spelling tests. *Sex Roles, 11,* 969-981.

Stipek, D. J. (1993). *Motivation to learn: From theory to practice* (2nd ed.). Needham Heights, MA: Allyn & Bacon.

Stipek, D. J. (1996). Motivation and instruction. In D. C. Berliner & R. C. Calfee (Eds.), *Handbook of educational psychology.* New York: Macmillan.

Stipek, D. J., & Gralinski, H. (1990, April). *Gender differences in children's achievement-related beliefs and emotional responses to success and failure in math.* Paper presented at the annual meeting of the American Educational Research Association, Boston.

Stodolsky, S. S., Salk, S., & Glaessner, B. (1991). Student views about learning math and social studies. *American Educational Research Journal, 28,* 89-116.

Strike, K. A., & Posner, G. J. (1992). A revisionist theory of conceptual change. In R. A. Duschl & R. J. Hamilton (Eds.), *Philosophy of science, cognitive psychology, and educational theory and practice.* Albany: State University of New York Press.

Sue, S., & Chin, R. (1983). The mental health of Chinese-American children: Stressors and resources. In G. J. Powell (Ed.), *The psychosocial development of minority children.* New York: Brunner/Mazel.

Sugar, W. A., & Bonk, C. J. (1998). Student role play in the World Forum: Analyses of an Arctic learning apprenticeship. In C. J. Bonk & K. S. King (Eds.), *Electronic collaborators: Learner-centered technologies for literacy, apprenticeship, and discourse.* Mahwah, NJ: Erlbaum.

Suina, J. H., & Smolkin, L. B. (1994). From natal culture to school culture to dominant society culture: Supporting transitions for Pueblo Indian students. In P. M. Greenfield & R. R. Cocking (Eds.), *Cross-cultural roots of minority child development.* Hillsdale, NJ: Erlbaum.

Sullivan, J. S. (1989). Planning, implementing, and maintaining an effective in-school suspension program. *Clearing House, 62,* 409-410.

Sullivan, R. C. (1994). Autism: Definitions past and present. *Journal of Vocational Rehabilitation, 4,* 4-9.

Sullivan-DeCarlo, C., DeFalco, K., & Roberts, V. (1998). Helping students avoid risky behavior. *Educational Leadership, 56*(1), 80-82.

Sulzby, E., & Teale, W. (1991). Emergent literacy. In R. Barr, M. L. Kamil, P. B. Mosenthal, & P. D. Pearson (Eds.), *Handbook of reading research* (Vol. II). New York: Longman.

Sund, R. B. (1976). *Piaget for educators.* Upper Saddle River, NJ: Merrill/Prentice Hall.

Swan, K., Mitrani, M., Guerrero, F., Cheung, M., & Schoener, J. (1990, April). *Perceived locus of control and computer-based instruction.* Paper presented at the annual meeting of the American Educational Research Association, Boston.

Swann, W. B., Jr. (1997). The trouble with change: Self-verification and allegiance to the self. *Psychological Science, 8,* 177-180.

Swanson, D. B., Norman, G. R., & Linn, R. L. (1995). Performance-based assessment: Lessons from the health professions. *Educational Researcher, 24*(5), 5-11, 35.

Swanson, H. L. (1992). Generality and modifiability of working memory among skilled and less skilled readers. *Journal of Educational Psychology, 84,* 473-488.

Swanson, H. L. (1993). An information processing analysis of learning disabled children's problem solving. *American Educational Research Journal, 30,* 861-893.

Swanson, H. L., & Cooney, J. B. (1991). Learning disabilities and memory. In B. Y. L. Wong (Ed.), *Learning about learning disabilities.* San Diego: Academic Press.

Tamburrini, J. (1982). Some educational implications of Piaget's theory. In S. Modgil & C. Modgil (Eds.), *Jean Piaget: Consensus and controversy.* New York: Praeger.

Tarver, S. G. (1992). Direct Instruction. In W. Stainback & S. Stainback (Eds.), *Controversial issues confronting special education.* Boston: Allyn & Bacon.

Taylor, B. M. (1982). Text structure and children's comprehension and memory for expository material. *Journal of Educational Psychology, 74,* 323-340.

Taylor, I. A. (1976). A retrospective view of creativity investigation. In I. A. Taylor & J. W. Getzels (Eds.), *Perspectives in creativity.* Chicago: Aldine.

Taylor, J. (1983). Influence of speech variety on teachers' evaluation of reading comprehension. *Journal of Educational Psychology, 75*, 662-667.

Taylor, J. C., & Romanczyk, R. G. (1994). Generating hypotheses about the function of student problem behavior by observing teacher behavior. *Journal of Applied Behavior Analysis, 27*, 251-265.

Taylor, S. M. (1994, April). *Staying in school against the odds: Voices of minority adolescent girls.* Paper presented at the annual meeting of the American Educational Research Association, New Orleans, LA.

Tennyson, R. D., & Cocchiarella, M. J. (1986). An empirically based instructional design theory for teaching concepts. *Review of Educational Research, 56*, 40-71.

Terrell, S. L., & Terrell, F. (1993). African-American cultures. In D. E. Battles (Ed.), *Communication disorders in multicultural populations.* Stoneham, MA: Butterworth-Heineman.

Terwilliger, J. S. (1989). Classroom standard setting and grading practices. *Educational Measurement: Issues and Practices, 8*(2), 15-19.

Tessler, M., & Nelson, K. (1994). Making memories: The influence of joint encoding on later recall by young children. *Consciousness and Cognition, 3*, 307-326.

Tharp, R. G. (1989). Psychocultural variables and constants: Effects on teaching and learning in schools. *American Psychologist, 44*, 349-359.

Tharp, R. G. (1994). Intergroup differences among Native Americans in socialization and child cognition: An ethnogenetic analysis. In P. M. Greenfield & R. R. Cocking (Eds.), *Cross-cultural roots of minority child development.* Hillsdale, NJ: Erlbaum.

Théberge, C. L. (1994, April). *Small-group vs. whole-class discussion: Gaining the floor in science lessons.* Paper presented at the annual meeting of the American Educational Research Association, New Orleans, LA.

Thomas, J. R., & French, K. E. (1985). Gender differences across age in motor performance: A meta-analysis. *Psychological Bulletin, 98*, 260-282.

Thomas, J. W. (1993a). Expectations and effort: Course demands, students' study practices, and academic achievement. In T. M. Tomlinson (Ed.), *Motivating students to learn: Overcoming barriers to high achievement.* Berkeley, CA: McCutchan.

Thomas, J. W. (1993b). Promoting independent learning in the middle grades: The role of instructional support practices. *Elementary School Journal, 93*, 575-591.

Thomas, M. H., & Dieter, J. N. (1987). The positive effect of writing practice on integration of foreign words in memory. *Journal of Educational Psychology, 79*, 249-253.

Thomas, S., & Oldfather, P. (1997). Intrinsic motivations, literacy, and assessment practices: "That's my grade. That's me." *Educational Psychologist, 32*, 107-123.

Thomas, S. P., Groër, M., & Droppleman, P. (1993). Physical health of today's school children. *Educational Psychology Review, 5*, 5-33.

Thomas, W. P., Collier, V. P., & Abbott, M. (1993). Academic achievement through Japanese, Spanish, or French: The first two years of partial immersion. *Modern Language Journal, 77*, 170-179.

Thompson, A. G., & Thompson, P. W. (1989). Affect and problem solving in an elementary school mathematics classroom. In D. B. McLeod & V. M. Adams (Eds.), *Affect and mathematical problem solving: A new perspective.* New York: Springer-Verlag.

Thompson, H., & Carr, M. (1995, April). *Brief metacognitive intervention and interest as predictors of memory for text.* Paper presented at the annual meeting of the American Educational Research Association, San Francisco.

Thorndike, E. L. (1924). Mental discipline in high school studies. *Journal of Educational Psychology, 15*, 1-22, 83-98.

Thorndike, R. M. (1997). *Measurement and evaluation in psychology and education* (6th ed.). Upper Saddle River, NJ: Merrill/Prentice Hall.

Thousand, J. S., Villa, R. A., & Nevin, A. I. (1994). *Creativity and collaborative learning: A practical guide for empowering students and teachers.* Baltimore: Paul H. Brookes.

Threadgill-Sowder, J. (1985). Individual differences and mathematical problem solving. In E. A. Silver (Ed.), *Teaching and learning mathematical problem solving: Multiple research perspectives.* Hillsdale, NJ: Erlbaum.

Thurstone, L. L. (1938). *Primary mental abilities.* Chicago: University of Chicago Press.

Thurstone, L. L., & Jeffrey, T. E. (1956). *FLAGS: A test of space thinking.* Chicago: Industrial Relations Center.

Tirosh, D., & Graeber, A. O. (1990). Evoking cognitive conflict to explore preservice teachers' thinking about division. *Journal for Research in Mathematics Education, 21*, 98-108.

Tobias, S. (1977). A model for research on the effect of anxiety on instruction. In J. E. Sieber, H. F. O'Neil, Jr., & S. Tobias (Eds.), *Anxiety, learning, and instruction.* Hillsdale, NJ: Erlbaum.

Tobias, S. (1980). Anxiety and instruction. In I. G. Sarason (Ed.), *Test anxiety: Theory, research, and applications.* Hillsdale, NJ: Erlbaum.

Tobias, S. (1985). Test anxiety: Interference, defective skills, and cognitive capacity. *Educational Psychologist, 20*, 135-142.

Tobias, S. (1994). Interest, prior knowledge, and learning. *Review of Educational Research, 64*, 37-54.

Tobin, K. (1987). The role of wait time in higher cognitive level learning. *Review of Educational Research, 57*, 69-95.

Torrance, E. P. (1970). *Encouraging creativity in the classroom.* Dubuque, IA: Wm. C. Brown.

Torrance, E. P. (1976). Creativity research in education: Still alive. In I. A. Taylor & J. W. Getzels (Eds.), *Perspectives in creativity.* Chicago: Aldine.

Torrance, E. P. (1989). A reaction to "Gifted black students: Curriculum and teaching strategies." In C. J. Maker & S. W. Schiever (Eds.), *Critical issues in gifted education: Vol. 2. Defensible programs for cultural and ethnic minorities.* Austin, TX: Pro-Ed.

Torrance, E. P. (1995). Insights about creativity: Questioned, rejected, ridiculed, ignored. *Educational Psychology Review, 7*, 313-322.

Torrance, E. P., & Myers, R. E. (1970). *Creative learning and teaching.* New York: Dodd, Mead.

Tourniaire, F., & Pulos, S. (1985). Proportional reasoning: A review of the literature. *Educational Studies in Mathematics, 16*, 181-204.

Trawick-Smith, J. (1997). *Early childhood development: A multicultural perspective.* Upper Saddle River, NJ: Merrill/Prentice Hall.

Treiman, R. (1993). *Beginning to spell: A study of first-grade children.* New York: Oxford University Press.

Triandis, H. C. (1995). *Individualism and collectivism.* Boulder, CO: Westview Press.

Trueba, H. T. (1988). Peer socialization among minority students: A high school dropout prevention program. In H. T. Trueba & C. Delgado-Gaitan (Eds.), *School and society: Learning content through culture.* New York: Praeger.

Tryon, G. S. (1980). The measurement and treatment of anxiety. *Review of Educational Research, 50*, 343-372.

Tudge, J. (1990). Vygotsky, the zone of proximal development, and peer collaboration: Implications for classroom practice. In L. C. Moll (Ed.), *Vygotsky and education: Instructional implications and applications of sociohistorical psychology.* Cambridge, England: Cambridge University Press.

Tudor, R. M. (1995). Isolating the effects of active responding in computer-based instruction. *Journal of Applied Behavior Analysis, 28*, 343-344.

Tulving, E. (1962). Subjective organization in free recall of "unrelated" words. *Psychological Review, 69*, 344-354.

Tulving, E. (1983). *Elements of episodic memory.* Oxford, England: Oxford University Press.

Tulving, E., & Thomson, D. M. (1973). Encoding specificity and retrieval processes in episodic memory. *Psychological Review, 80*, 352-373.

Turiel, E. (1983). *The development of social knowledge: Morality and convention.* Cambridge, England: Cambridge University Press.

Turiel, E., Smetana, J. G., & Killen, M. (1991). Social contexts in social cognitive development. In W. M. Kurtines & J. L. Gewirtz (Eds.), *Moral behavior and development: Vol. 2. Research.* Hillsdale, NJ: Erlbaum.

Turnbull, A. P. (1974). Teaching retarded persons to rehearse through cumulative overt labeling. *American Journal of Mental Deficiency, 79*, 331-337.

Turnbull, A. P., Pereira, L., & Blue-Banning, M. (in press). Teachers as friendship facilitators. *Teaching Exceptional Children.*

Turnbull, A., Turnbull, R., Shank, M., & Leal, D. (1999). *Exceptional lives: Special education in today's schools* (2nd ed.). Upper Saddle River, NJ: Merrill/Prentice Hall.

Turner, J. C. (1995). The influence of classroom contexts on young children's motivation for literacy. *Reading Research Quarterly, 30*, 410-441.

Tuttle, D. W., & Tuttle, N. R. (1996). *Self-esteem and adjusting with blindness: The process of responding to life's demands* (2nd ed.). Springfield, IL: Charles C Thomas.

Tyler, B. (1958). Expectancy for eventual success as a factor in problem solving behavior. *Journal of Educational Psychology, 49*, 166-172.

Udall, A. J. (1989). Curriculum for gifted Hispanic students. In C. J. Maker & S. W. Schiever (Eds.), *Critical issues in gifted education: Vol. 2. Defensible programs for cultural and ethnic minorities.* Austin, TX: Pro-Ed.

Ulichny, P. (1994, April). *Cultures in conflict.* Paper presented at the annual meeting of the American Educational Research Association, New Orleans, LA.

Underwood, B. J. (1948). "Spontaneous recovery" of verbal associations. *Journal of Experimental Psychology, 38*, 429-439.

Underwood, B. J. (1954). Studies of distributed practice: XII. Retention following varying degrees of original learning. *Journal of Experimental Psychology, 47*, 294-300.

Underwood, B. J. (1957). Interference and forgetting. *Psychological Review, 64,* 49-60.

Urdan, T. C., & Maehr, M. L. (1995). Beyond a two-goal theory of motivation and achievement: A case for social goals. *Review of Educational Research, 65,* 213-243.

Urdan, T. C., Midgley, C., & Anderman, E. M. (1998). The role of classroom goal structure in students' use of self-handicapping strategies. *American Educational Research Journal, 35,* 101-122.

U.S. Department of Education. (1992). *To assure the free appropriate public education of all children with disabilities: Fourteenth annual report to Congress on the implementation of the Individuals with Disabilities Education Act.* Washington, DC: Author.

U.S. Department of Education. (1993a). *National excellence: A case for developing America's talent.* Washington, DC: Office of Educational Research and Improvement.

U.S. Department of Education. (1993b). *To assure the free appropriate public education of all children with disabilities: Fifteenth annual report to Congress on the implementation of the Individuals with Disabilities Education Act.* Washington, DC: Author.

U.S. Department of Education. (1995). *To assure the free appropriate public education of all children with disabilities: Seventeenth annual report to Congress on the implementation of the Individuals with Disabilities Education Act.* Washington, DC: Author.

U.S. Department of Education. (1996). *To assure the free appropriate public education of all children with disabilities: Eighteenth annual report to Congress on the implementation of the Individuals with Disabilities Education Act.* Washington, DC: Author.

U.S. Department of Education. (1997). *To assure the free appropriate public education of all children with disabilities: Nineteenth annual report to Congress on the implementation of the Individuals with Disabilities Education Act.* Washington, DC: Author.

U.S. Department of Education, Office of Civil Rights. (1993). *Annual report to Congress.* Washington, DC: Author.

Valencia, S. W., Hiebert, E. H., & Afflerbach, P. P. (1994). Realizing the possibilities of authentic assessment: Current trends and future issues. In S. W. Valencia, E. H. Hiebert, & P. P. Afflerbach (Eds.), *Authentic reading assessment: Practices and possibilities.* Newark, DE: International Reading Association.

Van Houten, R., Nau, P., MacKenzie-Keating, S., Sameoto, D., & Colavecchia, B. (1982). An analysis of some variables influencing the effectiveness of reprimands. *Journal of Applied Behavior Analysis, 15,* 65-83.

Van Rossum, E. J., & Schenk, S. M. (1984). The relationship between learning conception, study strategy, and learning outcome. *British Journal of Educational Psychology, 54,* 73-83.

VanSledright, B., & Brophy, J. (1992). Storytelling, imagination, and fanciful elaboration in children's historical reconstructions. *American Educational Research Journal, 29,* 837-859.

Vasquez, J. A. (1988). Contexts of learning for minority students. *Educational Forum, 6,* 243-253.

Vasquez, J. A. (1990). Teaching to the distinctive traits of minority students. *Clearing House, 63,* 299-304.

Vaughn, B. J., & Horner, R. H. (1997). Identifying instructional tasks that occasion problem behaviors and assessing the effects of student versus teacher choice among these tasks. *Journal of Applied Behavior Analysis, 30,* 299-312.

Vaughn, S. (1991). Social skills enhancement in students with learning disabilities. In B. Y. L. Wong (Ed.), *Learning about learning disabilities.* San Diego: Academic Press.

Veenman, S. (1984). Perceived problems of beginning teachers. *Review of Educational Research, 54,* 143-178.

Vernon, P. A. (1993). Intelligence and neural efficiency. In D. K. Detterman (Ed.), *Current topics in human intelligence* (Vol. 3). Norwood, NJ: Ablex.

Villegas, A. (1991). *Culturally responsive pedagogy for the 1990s and beyond.* Princeton, NJ: Educational Testing Service.

Vorrath, H. (1985). *Positive peer culture.* New York: Aldine.

Vosniadou, S. (1991). Conceptual development in astronomy. In S. M. Glynn, R. H. Yeany, & B. K. Britton (Eds.), *The psychology of learning science.* Hillsdale, NJ: Erlbaum.

Vosniadou, S. (1994). Universal and culture-specific properties of children's mental models of the earth. In L. A. Hirschfeld & S. A. Gelman (Eds.), *Mapping the mind: Domain specificity in cognition and culture.* Cambridge, England: Cambridge University Press.

Vosniadou, S., & Brewer, W. F. (1987). Theories of knowledge restructuring in development. *Review of Educational Research, 57,* 51-67.

Voss, J. F. (1987). Learning and transfer in subject-matter learning: A problem-solving model. *International Journal of Educational Research, 11,* 607-622.

Voss, J. F., Greene, T. R., Post, T. A., & Penner, B. D. (1983). Problem-solving skill in the social sciences. In G. H. Bower (Ed.), *The psychology of learning and motivation* (Vol. 17). San Diego: Academic Press.

Voss, J. F., & Schauble, L. (1992). Is interest educationally interesting? An interest-related model of learning. In K. A. Renninger, S. Hidi, & A. Krapp (Eds.), *The role of interest in learning and development.* Hillsdale, NJ: Erlbaum.

Vygotsky, L. S. (1962). *Thought and language* (E. Haufmann & G. Vakar, Eds. and Trans.). Cambridge, MA: MIT Press.

Vygotsky, L. S. (1978). *Mind in society: The development of higher psychological processes.* Cambridge, MA: Harvard University Press.

Vygotsky, L. S. (1987). *The collected works of L. S. Vygotsky, Vol 3.* (R. W. Rieber & A. S. Carton, Eds.). New York: Plenum Press.

Vygotsky, L. S. (1997). *Educational psychology.* Boca Raton, FL: St. Lucie Press.

Wade, S. E. (1992). How interest affects learning from text. In K. A. Renninger, S. Hidi, & A. Krapp (Eds.), *The role of interest in learning and development.* Hillsdale, NJ: Erlbaum.

Wagner, A. R. (1981). SOP: A model of automatic memory processing in animal behavior. In N. E. Spear & R. R. Miller (Eds.), *Information processing in animals: Memory mechanisms.* Hillsdale, NJ: Erlbaum.

Wagner, M. (1995). *The contributions of poverty and ethnic background to the participation of secondary school students in special education.* Washington, DC: U.S. Department of Education.

Walberg, H. J., & Uguroglu, M. (1980). Motivation and educational productivity: Theories, results, and implications. In L. J. Fyans, Jr. (Ed.), *Achievement motivation: Recent trends in theory and research.* New York: Plenum Press.

Walker, L. J. (1991). Sex differences in moral reasoning. In W. M. Kurtines & J. L. Gewirtz (Eds.), *Moral behavior and development: Vol. 2. Research.* Hillsdale, NJ: Erlbaum.

Walters, G. C., & Grusec, J. E. (1977). *Punishment.* San Francisco: W. H. Freeman.

Wang, P. P., & Baron, M. A. (1997). Language and communication: Development and disorders. In M. L. Batshaw (Ed.), *Children with disabilities* (4th ed.). Baltimore: Paul H. Brookes.

Ward, T. J., Jr. (1991, April). The effects of field articulation and interestingness on text processing. In G. Schraw (Chair), *Cognitive processing and text comprehension in specific knowledge domains.* Symposium presented at the annual meeting of the American Educational Research Association, Chicago.

Warren, G. (1979). Essay versus multiple-choice tests. *Journal of Research in Science Teaching, 16*(6), 563-567.

Warren, R. L. (1988). Cooperation and conflict between parents and teachers: A comparative study of three elementary schools. In H. T. Trueba & C. Delgado-Gaitan (Eds.), *School and society: Learning content through culture.* New York: Praeger.

Wasik, B., Karweit, N., Burns, L., & Brodsky, E. (1998, April). *Once upon a time: The role of rereading and retelling in storybook reading.* Paper presented at the annual meeting of the American Educational Research Association, San Diego.

Wason, P. (1968). Reasoning about a rule. *Quarterly Journal of Experimental Psychology, 20,* 273-281.

Waters, H. S. (1982). Memory development in adolescence: Relationships between metamemory, strategy use, and performance. *Journal of Experimental Child Psychology, 33,* 183-195.

Way, N. (1998). *Everyday courage: The lives and stories of urban teenagers.* New York: New York University Press.

Weaver, C. (1990). *Understanding whole language: From principles to practice.* Portsmouth, NH: Heinemann.

Weaver, C. A., III, & Kelemen, W. L. (1997). Judgments of learning at delays: Shifts in response patterns or increased metamemory accuracy? *Psychological Science, 8,* 318-321.

Weaver, C. A., III, & Kintsch, W. (1991). Expository text. In R. Barr, M. L. Kamil, P. B. Mosenthal, & P. D. Pearson (Eds.), *Handbook of reading research* (Vol. 2). New York: Longman.

Webb, J. T., Meckstroth, E. A., & Tolan, S. S. (1982). *Guiding the gifted child: A practical source for parents and teachers.* Dayton, OH: Ohio Psychology Press.

Webb, N. M. (1989). Peer interaction and learning in small groups. *International Journal of Educational Research, 13,* 21-39.

Webb, N. M., & Farivar, S. (1994). Promoting helping behavior in cooperative small groups in middle school mathematics. *American Educational Research Journal, 31,* 369-395.

Webb, N. M., & Palincsar, A. S. (1996). Group processes in the classroom. In D. C. Berliner & R. C. Calfee (Eds.), *Handbook of educational psychology.* New York: Macmillan.

Webber, J., Scheuermann, B., McCall, C., & Coleman, M. (1993). Research on self-monitoring as a behavior management technique in special education classrooms: A descriptive review. *Remedial and Special Education, 14*(2), 38–56.

Webster's Ninth New Collegiate Dictionary. (1991). Springfield, MA: Merriam-Webster.

Wehmeyer, M. L. (1996). Self-determination as an educational outcome. In D. J. Sands & M. L. Wehmeyer (Eds.), *Self-determination across the life span: Independence and choice for people with disabilities.* Baltimore: Paul H. Brookes.

Weiner, B. (1984). Principles for a theory of student motivation and their application within an attributional framework. In R. Ames & C. Ames (Eds.), *Research on motivation in education: Vol. 1. Student motivation.* San Diego: Academic Press.

Weiner, B. (1986). *An attributional theory of motivation and emotion.* New York: Springer-Verlag.

Weiner, B. (1994). Ability versus effort revisited: The moral determinants of achievement evaluation and achievement as a moral system. *Educational Psychologist, 29,* 163–172.

Weiner, B., Russell, D., & Lerman, D. (1978). Affective consequences of causal ascriptions. In J. Harvey, W. Ickes, & R. Kidd (Eds.), *New directions in attribution research* (Vol. 2). Hillsdale, NJ: Erlbaum.

Weiner, B., Russell, D., & Lerman, D. (1979). The cognition-emotion process in achievement-related contexts. *Journal of Personality and Social Psychology, 37,* 1211–1220.

Weinert, F. E., & Helmke, A. (1995). Learning from wise Mother Nature or Big Brother Instructor: The wrong choice as seen from an educational perspective. *Educational Psychologist, 30,* 135–142.

Weinstein, C. E. (1978). Elaboration skills as a learning strategy. In H. F. O'Neil, Jr. (Ed.), *Learning strategies.* San Diego: Academic Press.

Weinstein, C. E., Goetz, E. T., & Alexander, P. A. (Eds.). (1988). *Learning and study strategies: Issues in assessment, instruction, and evaluation.* San Diego: Academic Press.

Weinstein, C. E., Hagen, A. S., & Meyer, D. K. (1991, April). *Work smart ... not hard: The effects of combining instruction in using strategies, goal using, and executive control on attributions and academic performance.* Paper presented at the annual meeting of the American Educational Research Association, Chicago.

Weinstein, C. S. (1979). The physical environment of the school: A review of the research. *Review of Educational Research, 49,* 577–610.

Weinstein, R. S. (1993). Children's knowledge of differential treatment in school: Implications for motivation. In T. M. Tomlinson (Ed.), *Motivating students to learn: Overcoming barriers to high achievement.* Berkeley, CA: McCutchan.

Weinstein, R. S., Madison, S. M., & Kuklinski, M. R. (1995). Raising expectations in schooling: Obstacles and opportunities for change. *American Educational Research Journal, 32,* 121–159.

Weisberg, R. W. (1993). *Creativity: Beyond the myth of genius.* New York: W. H. Freeman.

Weiss, M. R., & Klint, K. A. (1987). "Show and tell" in the gymnasium: An investigation of developmental differences in modeling and verbal rehearsal of motor skills. *Research Quarterly for Exercise and Sport, 58,* 234–241.

Weissberg, R. P. (1985). Designing effective social problem-solving programs for the classroom. In B. H. Schneider, K. H. Rubin, & J. E. Ledingham (Eds.), *Children's peer relations: Issues in assessment and intervention.* New York: Springer-Verlag.

Welch, G. J. (1985). Contingency contracting with a delinquent and his family. *Journal of Behavior Therapy and Experimental Psychiatry, 16,* 253–259.

Wellman, H. M. (1985). The child's theory of mind: The development of conceptions of cognition. In S. R. Yussen (Ed.), *The growth of reflection in children.* San Diego: Academic Press.

Wellman, H. M. (1988). The early development of memory strategies. In F. Weinert & M. Perlmutter (Eds.), *Memory development: Universal changes and individual differences.* Hillsdale, NJ: Erlbaum.

Wellman, H. M., & Gelman, S. A. (1992). Cognitive development: Foundational theories of core domains. In M. R. Rosenzweig & L. W. Porter (Eds.), *Annual review of psychology* (Vol. 43). Palo Alto, CA: Annual Reviews.

Wentzel, K. R., & Wigfield, A. (1998). Academic and social motivational influences on students' academic performance. *Educational Psychology Review, 10,* 155–175.

Werner, E. E. (1995). Resilience in development. *Current Directions in Psychological Science, 4,* 81–85.

West, C. K., Farmer, J. A., & Wolff, P. M. (1991). *Instructional design: Implications from cognitive science.* Upper Saddle River, NJ: Prentice Hall.

West, R. F., & Stanovich, K. E. (1978). Automatic contextual facilitation in readers of three ages. *Child Development, 49,* 717–727.

White, A. G., & Bailey, J. S. (1990). Reducing disruptive behaviors of elementary physical education students with sit and watch. *Journal of Applied Behavior Analysis, 23,* 353–359.

White, B. Y., & Frederiksen, J. R. (1998). Inquiry, modeling, and metacognition: Making science accessible to all students. *Cognition and Instruction, 16,* 3–118.

White, J. J., & Rumsey, S. (1994). Teaching for understanding in a third-grade geography lesson. In J. Brophy (Ed.), *Advances in research on teaching: Vol. 4. Case studies of teaching and learning in social studies.* Greenwich, CT: JAI Press.

White, R., & Cunningham, A. M. (1992). *Ryan White: My own story.* New York: Signet.

Whitehurst, G. J., Arnold, D. S., Epstein, J. N., Angell, A. L., Smith, M., & Fischel, J. E. (1994). A picture book reading intervention in day care and home for children from low-income families. *Developmental Psychology, 30,* 679–689.

Whitley, B. E., Jr., & Frieze, I. H. (1985). Children's causal attributions for success and failure in achievement settings: A meta-analysis. *Journal of Educational Psychology, 77,* 68–616.

Wigfield, A. (1994). Expectancy-value theory of achievement motivation: A developmental perspective. *Educational Psychology Review, 6,* 49–78.

Wigfield, A., Eccles, J. S., & Pintrich, P. R. (1996). Development between the ages of 11 and 25. In D. C. Berliner & R. C. Calfee (Eds.), *Handbook of educational psychology.* New York: Macmillan.

Wigfield, A., & Meece, J. L. (1988). Math anxiety in elementary and secondary school students. *Journal of Educational Psychology, 80,* 210–216.

Wiggins, G. (1992). Creating tests worth taking. *Educational Leadership, 49*(8), 26–33.

Wilkinson, L. C., & Marrett, C. B. (Eds.). (1985). *Gender influences in classroom interaction.* San Diego: Academic Press.

Wilkinson, L. D., & Frazer, L. H. (1990, April). *Fine-tuning dropout prediction through discriminant analysis: The ethnic factor.* Paper presented at the annual meeting of the American Educational Research Association, Boston.

Will, M. C. (1986). Educating children with learning problems: A shared responsibility. *Exceptional Children, 52,* 411–415.

Williams, B., & Newcombe, E. (1994). Building on the strengths of urban learners. *Educational Leadership, 51*(8), 75–78.

Williams, D. (1996). *Autism: An inside-outside approach.* London: Jessica Kingsley.

Williams, J. P. (1991, November). *Comprehension of learning disabled and nondisabled students: Identification of narrative themes and idiosyncratic text representation.* Paper presented at the annual meeting of the National Reading Conference, Austin, TX.

Willig, A. C. (1985). A meta-analysis of selected studies on the effectiveness of bilingual education. *Review of Educational Research, 55,* 269–317.

Wilson, J. E. (1988). Implications of learning strategy research and training: What it has to say to the practitioner. In C. E. Weinstein, E. T. Goetz, & P. A. Alexander (Eds.), *Learning and study strategies: Issues in assessment, instruction, and evaluation.* San Diego: Academic Press.

Wilson, P. S. (1988, April). The relationship of students' definitions and example choices in geometry. In D. Tirosh (Chair), *The role of inconsistent ideas in learning mathematics.* Symposium conducted at the annual meeting of the American Educational Research Association, New Orleans, LA.

Wilson, P. T., & Anderson, R. C. (1986). What they don't know will hurt them: The role of prior knowledge in comprehension. In J. Orasanu (Ed.), *Reading comprehension: From research to practice.* Hillsdale, NJ: Erlbaum.

Wine, J. D. (1980). Cognitive-attentional theory of test anxiety. In I. G. Sarason (Ed.), *Test anxiety: Theory, research, and applications.* Hillsdale, NJ: Erlbaum.

Wineburg, S. S. (1994). The cognitive representation of historical texts. In G. Leinhardt, I. L. Beck, & C. Stainton (Eds.), *Teaching and learning in history.* Hillsdale, NJ: Erlbaum.

Winer, G. A., & Cottrell, J. E. (1996). Does anything leave the eye when we see? Extramission beliefs of children and adults. *Current Directions in Psychological Science, 5,* 137–142.

Wingfield, A., & Byrnes, D. L. (1981). *The psychology of human memory.* San Diego: Academic Press.

Winn, W. (1991). Learning from maps and diagrams. *Educational Psychology Review, 3,* 211–247.

Winne, P. H. (1995). Inherent details in self-regulated learning. *Educational Psychologist, 30,* 173–187.

Winner, E. (1997). Exceptionally high intelligence and schooling. *American Psychologist, 52,* 1070–1081.

Winograd, P., & Jones, D. L. (1992). The use of portfolios in performance assessment. *New Directions for Education Reform, 1*(2), 37–50.

Wittmer, D. S., & Honig, A. S. (1994). Encouraging positive social development in young children. *Young Children, 49*(5), 4–12.

Wittrock, M. C. (1994). Generative science teaching. In P. J. Fensham, R. F. Gunstone, & R. T. White (Eds.), *The content of science: A constructivist approach to its teaching and learning.* London: Falmer Press.

Wixson, K. K. (1984). Level of importance of post-questions and children's learning from text. *American Educational Research Journal, 21,* 419-433.

Wlodkowski, R. J. (1978). *Motivation and teaching: A practical guide.* Washington, DC: National Education Association.

Wlodkowski, R. J., & Ginsberg, M. B. (1995). *Diversity and motivation: Culturally responsive teaching.* San Francisco: Jossey-Bass.

Wolfe, P., & Brandt, R. (1998). What do we know from brain research? *Educational Leadership, 56*(3), 8-13.

Wolpe, J. (1969). *The practice of behavior therapy.* Oxford: Pergamon Press.

Wolters, C. A. (1997, March). *Self-regulated learning and college students' regulation of motivation.* Paper presented at the annual meeting of the American Educational Research Association, Chicago.

Wong, B. Y. L. (1985). Self-questioning instructional research: A review. *Review of Educational Research, 55,* 227-268.

Wong, B. Y. L. (Ed.). (1991a). *Learning about learning disabilities.* San Diego: Academic Press.

Wong, B. Y. L. (1991b). The relevance of metacognition to learning disabilities. In B. Y. L. Wong (Ed.), *Learning about learning disabilities.* San Diego: Academic Press.

Wood, C. J., Schau, C., & Fiedler, M. L. (1990, April). *Attribution, motivation, and self-perception: A comparative study—elementary, middle, and high school students.* Paper presented at the annual meeting of the American Educational Research Association, Boston.

Wood, D., Bruner, J. S., & Ross, G. (1976). The role of tutoring in problem-solving. *Journal of Child Psychology and Psychiatry, 17,* 89-100.

Wood, D., Wood, H., Ainsworth, S., & O'Malley, C. (1995). On becoming a tutor: Toward an ontogenetic model. *Cognition and Instruction, 13,* 565-581.

Wood, E., Willoughby, T., Reilley, S., Elliott, S., & DuCharme, M. (1994, April). *Evaluating students' acquisition of factual material when studying independently or with a partner.* Paper presented at the annual meeting of the American Educational Research Association, New Orleans, LA.

Wood, J. W. (1989). *Mainstreaming: A practical approach for teachers.* Upper Saddle River, NJ: Merrill/Prentice Hall.

Wood, J. W., & Rosbe, M. (1985). Adapting the classroom lectures for the mainstreamed student in the secondary schools. *Clearing House, 58,* 354-358.

Woolfolk, A. E., & Brooks, D. M. (1985). The influence of teachers' nonverbal behaviors on students' perceptions and performances. *Elementary School Journal, 85,* 513-528.

Worthen, B. R., & Leopold, G. D. (1992). Impediments to implementing alternative assessment: Some emerging issues. *New Directions for Education Reform, 1*(2), 1-20.

Wright, L. S. (1982). The use of logical consequences in counseling children. *School Counselor, 30,* 37-49.

Wright, S., & Taylor, D. (1995). Identity and the language of the classroom: Investigating the impact of heritage versus second-language instruction on personal and collective self-esteem. *Journal of Educational Psychology, 87,* 241-252.

Wynne, E. A. (1990). Improving pupil discipline and character. In O. C. Moles (Ed.), *Student discipline strategies: Research and practice.* Albany: State University of New York Press.

Yarmey, A. D. (1973). I recognize your face but I can't remember your name: Further evidence on the tip-of-the-tongue phenomenon. *Memory and Cognition, 1,* 287-290.

Yeager, E. A., Foster, S. J., Maley, S. D., Anderson, T., Morris, J. W., III, & Davis, O. L., Jr. (1997, March). *The role of empathy in the development of historical understanding.* Paper presented at the annual meeting of the American Educational Research Association, Chicago.

Yee, A. H. (1992). Asians as stereotypes and students: Misperceptions that persist. *Educational Psychology Review, 4,* 95-132.

Yee, A. H. (1995). Evolution of the nature-nurture controversy: Response to J. Philippe Rushton. *Educational Psychology Review, 7,* 381-390.

Yee, D. K., & Eccles, J. S. (1988). Parent perceptions and attributions for children's math achievement. *Sex Roles, 19,* 317-333.

Yell, M. L. (1993). Cognitive behavior therapy. In T. J. Zirpoli & K. J. Melloy, *Behavior management: Applications for teachers and parents.* Upper Saddle River, NJ: Merrill/Prentice Hall.

Yerkes, R. M., & Dodson, J. D. (1908). The relation of strength of stimulus to rapidity of habit-formation. *Journal of Comparative Neurology of Psychology, 18,* 459-482.

Yokoi, L. (1997, March). *The developmental context of notetaking: A qualitative examination of notetaking at the secondary level.* Paper presented at the annual meeting of the American Educational Research Association, Chicago.

Ysseldyke, J. E., & Algozzine, B. (1984). *Introduction to special education.* Boston: Houghton Mifflin.

Yu, S. L., Elder, A. D., & Urdan, T. C. (1995, April). *Motivation and cognitive strategies in students with a "good student" or "poor student" self-schema.* Paper presented at the annual meeting of the American Educational Research Association, San Francisco.

Yuker, H. E. (Ed.) (1988). *Attitudes toward persons with disabilities.* New York: Springer.

Zahorik, J. A. (1994, April). *Making things interesting.* Paper presented at the annual meeting of the American Educational Research Association, New Orleans, LA.

Zeaman, D., & House, B. J. (1979). A review of attention theory. In N. R. Ellis (Ed.), *Handbook of mental deficiency: Psychological theory and research* (2nd ed.). Hillsdale, NJ: Erlbaum.

Zhu, X., & Simon, H. A. (1987). Learning mathematics from examples and by doing. *Cognition and Instruction, 4,* 137-166.

Ziegler, S. G. (1987). Effects of stimulus cueing on the acquisition of groundstrokes by beginning tennis players. *Journal of Applied Behavior Analysis, 20,* 405-411.

Zigler, E. F., & Finn-Stevenson, M. (1987). *Children: Development and social issues.* Lexington, MA: Heath.

Zigler, E. F., & Finn-Stevenson, M. (1992). Applied developmental psychology. In M. H. Bornstein & M. E. Lamb (Eds.), *Developmental psychology: An advanced textbook.* Hillsdale, NJ: Erlbaum.

Zigler, E. F., & Seitz, V. (1982). Social policy and intelligence. In R. J. Sternberg (Ed.), *Handbook of human intelligence* (pp. 586-641). Cambridge, England: Cambridge University Press.

Zigmond, N., Jenkins, J., Fuchs, L. S., Deno, S., Fuchs, D., Baker, J. N., Jenkins, L., & Couthino, M. (1995, March). Special education in restructured schools: Findings from three multi-year studies. *Phi Delta Kappan,* 531-540.

Zimmerman, B. J., & Bandura, A. (1994). Impact of self-regulatory influences on writing course attainment. *American Educational Research Journal, 31,* 845-862.

Zimmerman, B. J., Bandura, A., & Martinez-Pons, M. (1992). Self-motivation for academic attainment: The role of self-efficacy beliefs and personal goal setting. *American Educational Research Journal, 29,* 663-676.

Zimmerman, B. J., & Bonner, S. (in press). A social cognitive view of strategic learning. In C. E. Weinstein & B. L. McCombs (Eds.), *Strategic learning: Skill, will, and self-regulation.* Hillsdale, NJ: Erlbaum.

Zimmerman, B. J., & Risemberg, R. (1997). Self-regulatory dimensions of academic learning and motivation. In G. D. Phye (Ed.), *Handbook of academic learning: Construction of knowledge.* San Diego: Academic Press.

Zirin, G. (1974). How to make a boring thing more boring. *Child Development, 45,* 232-236.

Zirpoli, T. J., & Melloy, K. J. (1993). *Behavior management: Applications for teachers and parents.* Upper Saddle River, NJ: Merrill/Prentice Hall.

Zook, K. B. (1991). Effects of analogical processes on learning and misrepresentation. *Educational Psychology Review, 3,* 41-72.

Zook, K. B., & Di Vesta, F. J. (1991). Instructional analogies and conceptual misrepresentations. *Journal of Educational Psychology, 83,* 246-252.

Zuckerman, G. A. (1994). A pilot study of a ten-day course in cooperative learning for beginning Russian first graders. *Elementary School Journal, 94,* 405-420.

Name Index

Subject Index